Teacher's Edition

PRENTICE HALL
WORLD STUDIES
WESTERN HEMISPHERE

Geography • History • Culture

SCHOOL OF EDUCATION
CURRICULUM LABORATORY
UM-DEARBORN

In association with

PEARSON

Prentice
Hall

Boston, Massachusetts
Upper Saddle River, New Jersey

Program Consultants

Heidi Hayes Jacobs

Heidi Hayes Jacobs, Ed.D., has served as an education consultant to more than 1,000 schools across the nation and abroad. Dr. Jacobs serves as an adjunct professor in the Department of Curriculum on Teaching at Teachers College, Columbia University. She has written two best-selling books and numerous articles on curriculum reform. She received an M.A. from the University of Massachusetts, Amherst, and completed her doctoral work at Columbia University's Teachers College in 1981. The core of Dr. Jacobs's experience comes from her years teaching high school, middle school, and elementary school students. As an educational consultant, she works with K–12 schools and districts on curriculum reform and strategic planning.

Michal L. LeVasseur

Michal LeVasseur is the Executive Director of the National Council for Geographic Education. She is an instructor in the College of Education at Jacksonville State University and works with the Alabama Geographic Alliance. Her undergraduate and graduate work were in the fields of anthropology (B.A.), geography (M.A.), and science education (Ph.D.). Dr. LeVasseur's specialization has moved increasingly into the area of geography education. Since 1996 she has served as the Director of the National Geographic Society's Summer Geography Workshops. As an educational consultant, she has worked with the National Geographic Society as well as with schools and organizations to develop programs and curricula for geography.

Senior Reading Consultants

Kate Kinsella

Kate Kinsella, Ed.D., is a faculty member in the Department of Secondary Education at San Francisco State University. A specialist in second-language acquisition and content area literacy, she consults nationally on school-wide practices that support adolescent English learners and striving readers to make academic gains. Dr. Kinsella earned her M.A. in TESOL from San Francisco State University, and her Ed.D. in Second Language Acquisition from the University of San Francisco.

Kevin Feldman

Kevin Feldman, Ed.D., is the Director of Reading and Early Intervention with the Sonoma County Office of Education (SCOE) and an independent educational consultant. At the SCOE, he develops, organizes, and monitors programs related to K–12 literacy. Dr. Feldman has an M.A. from the University of California, Riverside in Special Education, Learning Disabilities and Instructional Design. He earned his Ed.D. in Curriculum and Instruction from the University of San Francisco.

Acknowledgments appear on page 605, which constitutes an extension of this copyright page.

Copyright © 2008 by Pearson Education, Inc., publishing as Pearson Prentice Hall, Boston, Massachusetts 02116.

MapMaster™ is a trademark of Pearson Education, Inc.
Pearson Prentice Hall™ is a trademark of Pearson Education, Inc.
Pearson® is a registered trademark of Pearson plc.
Prentice Hall® is a registered trademark of Pearson Education, Inc.
ExamView® is a registered trademark of FSCreations, Inc.

DK is a registered trademark of Dorling Kindersley Limited. Prentice Hall World Studies is published in collaboration with DK Designs, Dorling Kindersley Limited, 80 Strand, London WC2R 0RL. A Penguin Company.

PEARSON
Prentice Hall

ISBN 0-13-204161-8
5 6 7 8 9 10 V092 15 14 13

Cartography Consultant

 **Andrew Heritage**

Andrew Heritage has been publishing atlases and maps for more than 25 years. In 1991, he joined the leading illustrated nonfiction publisher Dorling Kindersley (DK) with the task of building an international atlas list from scratch. The DK atlas list now includes some 10 titles, which are constantly updated and appear in new editions either annually or every other year.

Academic Reviewers

Africa
Barbara B. Brown, Ph.D.
African Studies Center
Boston University
Boston, Massachusetts

Ancient World
Evelyn DeLong Mangie, Ph.D.
Department of History
University of South Florida
Tampa, Florida

Central Asia and the Middle East
Pamela G. Sayre
History Department,
    Social Sciences Division
Henry Ford Community College
Dearborn, Michigan

East Asia
Huping Ling, Ph.D.
History Department
Truman State University
Kirksville, Missouri

Eastern Europe
Robert M. Jenkins, Ph.D.
Center for Slavic, Eurasian and
    East European Studies
University of North Carolina
Chapel Hill, North Carolina

Latin America
Dan La Botz
Professor, History Department
Miami University
Oxford, Ohio

Medieval Times
James M. Murray
History Department
University of Cincinnati
Cincinnati, Ohio

North Africa
Barbara E. Petzen
Center for Middle Eastern Studies
Harvard University
Cambridge, Massachusetts

Religion
Charles H. Lippy, Ph.D.
Department of Philosophy
    and Religion
University of Tennessee
    at Chattanooga
Chattanooga, Tennessee

Russia
Janet Vaillant
Davis Center for Russian
    and Eurasian Studies
Harvard University
Cambridge, Massachusetts

United States and Canada
Victoria Randlett
Geography Department
University of Nevada, Reno
Reno, Nevada

Western Europe
Ruth Mitchell-Pitts
Center for European Studies
University of North Carolina
    at Chapel Hill
Chapel Hill, North Carolina

Reviewers

Sean Brennan
Brecksville-Broadview Heights
    City School District
Broadview Heights, Ohio

Stephen Bullick
Mt. Lebanon School District
Pittsburgh, Pennsylvania

Louis P. De Angelo, Ed.D.
Archdiocese of Philadelphia
Philadelphia, Pennsylvania

Paul Francis Durietz
Social Studies
    Curriculum Coordinator
Woodland District #50
Gurnee, Illinois

Gail Dwyer
Dickerson Middle School,
    Cobb County
Marietta, Georgia

Michal Howden
Social Studies Consultant
Zionsville, Indiana

Rosemary Kalloch
Springfield Public Schools
Springfield, Massachusetts

Deborah J. Miller
Office of Social Studies,
    Detroit Public Schools
Detroit, Michigan

Steven P. Missal
Plainfield Public Schools
Plainfield, New Jersey

Catherine Fish Petersen
Social Studies Consultant
Saint James, Long Island,
    New York

Joe Wieczorek
Social Studies Consultant
Baltimore, Maryland

WESTERN HEMISPHERE

Professional Development: NCLB and Social Studies T20
Reading Support. T22
Differentiated Instruction T26
Geographic Literacy T28
Assessment T30
Instructional Strategies T32
Skills Scope and Sequence. T38
Pacing Options T39
Correlation to the National Geography Standards T40
Correlation to the NCSS Curriculum Standards. T42

Develop Skills

Use these pages to develop students' reading, writing,
and geography skills.

Reading and Writing Handbook RW1

MAP◆MASTER™ Skills Handbook M1

How to Read Social Studies:
 Target Reading Skills. M18, 138, 328

Focus on Geography

Introduce students to the basic tools and concepts of geography.

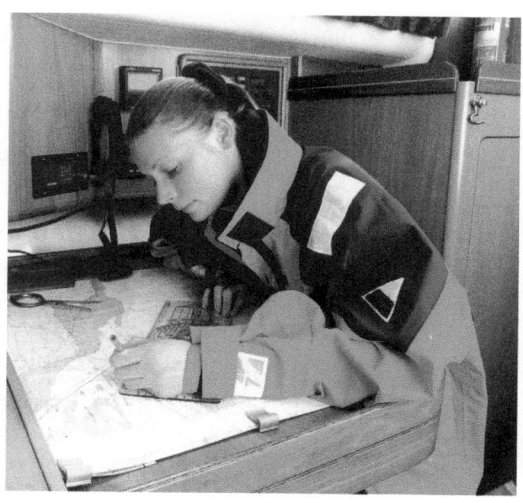

Introduction to Foundations of Geography **1**

 **World Overview** **2**

CHAPTER 1 The World of Geography **8**
   1 The Five Themes of Geography 10
   2 The Geographer's Tools 16
      Chapter 1 Review and Assessment 23

CHAPTER 2 Earth's Physical Geography **26**
   1 Our Planet, Earth 28
   2 Forces Shaping Earth 33
   3 Climate and Weather 40
   4 How Climate Affects Vegetation 50
      Chapter 2 Review and Assessment 55

CHAPTER 3 Earth's Human Geography **58**
   1 Population 60
   2 Migration 67
   3 Economic Systems 74
   4 Political Systems 80
      Chapter 3 Review and Assessment 85

CHAPTER 4 **Cultures of the World** **90**

    1 Understanding Culture. 92

    2 Culture and Society. 96

    3 Cultural Change 104

    Chapter 4 Review and Assessment. 109

CHAPTER 5 **Interacting With Our Environment** . . **112**

    1 Natural Resources. 114

    2 Land Use 120

    3 People's Effect on the Environment 128

    Chapter 5 Review and Assessment. 133

Projects **136**

Build a Regional Background

Introduce students to the geography, history, and culture of the United States and Canada.

Introduction to the United States and Canada . .139

 **Regional Overview 140**

CHAPTER 6 **The United States and Canada:
Physical Geography 146**
   1 Land and Water. 148
   2 Climate and Vegetation 156
   3 Resources and Land Use. 163
      Chapter 6 Review and Assessment 169

CHAPTER 7 **The United States and Canada:
Shaped by History 172**
   1 The Arrival of the Europeans 174
   2 Growth and Conflict in the United States 180
   3 The U.S. on the Brink of Change 187
   4 The History of Canada. 193
   5 The United States and Canada Today 202
      Chapter 7 Review and Assessment 209

CHAPTER 8 **Cultures of the United States
and Canada 212**
   1 A Heritage of Diversity and Exchange 214
   2 The United States: A Nation of Immigrants. 222
   3 The Canadian Mosaic. 227
      Chapter 8 Review and Assessment 231

Focus on Countries

Create an understanding of the United States and Canada by focusing on specific regions.

CHAPTER 9 The United States 234
Country Databank 236

1 The Northeast: An Urban Center 248
2 The South: The Growth of Industry 255
3 The Midwest: Leaving the Farm 264
4 The West: Using and Preserving Resources 271
Chapter 9 Review and Assessment 277

CHAPTER 10 Canada 284
Country Databank 286

1 Ontario and Quebec: Bridging Two Cultures 290
2 The Prairie Provinces: Canada's Breadbasket 298
3 British Columbia: Economic and Cultural Changes . . 304
4 The Atlantic Provinces: Relying on the Sea 311
5 The Northern Territories: New Frontiers 318
Chapter 10 Review and Assessment 323

Projects 326

Build a Regional Background

Introduce students to the geography, history, and culture of Latin America.

Introduction to Latin America **329**

📖 **Regional Overview** **330**

CHAPTER 11 Latin America: Physical Geography. .336
  1 Land and Water. 338
  2 Climate and Vegetation 343
  3 Resources and Land Use. 352
    Chapter 11 Review and Assessment 359

CHAPTER 12 Latin America:
           Shaped by Its History **366**
  1 Early Civilizations of Middle America 368
  2 The Incas: People of the Sun 373
  3 European Conquest 378
  4 Independence 385
  5 From Past to Present. 392
    Chapter 12 Review and Assessment 397

CHAPTER 13 Cultures of Latin America **400**
  1 Cultures of Mexico and Central America. 402
  2 The Cultures of the Caribbean 410
  3 The Cultures of South America. 415
    Chapter 13 Review and Assessment 421

Focus on Countries

Create an understanding of Latin America by focusing on specific countries.

CHAPTER 14 Mexico and Central America 424

Country Databank 426

1 Mexico: Moving to the City 430

2 Guatemala: Descendants of an Ancient People 437

3 Panama: An Important Crossroads 444

Chapter 14 Review and Assessment 451

CHAPTER 15 The Caribbean 454

Country Databank 456

1 Cuba: Clinging to Communism 462

2 Haiti: A Struggle for Democracy 470

3 Puerto Rico: An American Commonwealth 476

Chapter 15 Review and Assessment 483

CHAPTER 16 **South America** **486**

    Country Databank 488

    1 Brazil: Geography Shapes a Nation 494

    2 Peru: An Ancient Land Looks to the Future 501

    3 Chile: Land of Contrasts 507

    4 Venezuela: Oil Powers the Economy 516

    Chapter 16 Review and Assessment 523

Projects **526**

Reference Section **528**

     Atlas 530

    Country Databank 546

    Glossary of Geographic Terms 554

    Gazetteer 556

    Glossary 562

    Index 576

    Acknowledgments 605

MAP✦MASTER™	DK	Interactive Textbook
• **Learn map skills with the MapMaster Skills Handbook.** • **Practice your skills with every map in this book.** • **Interact with every map online and on CD-ROM.**	**Maps and illustrations created by DK help build your understanding of the world. The DK World Desk Reference Online keeps you up to date.**	**The** *World Studies* **Interactive Textbook online and on CD-ROM uses interactive maps and other activities to help you learn.**

COUNTRY DATABANK

Read about the states that make up the United States.

Alabama 236
Alaska 236
Arizona 237
Arkansas 237
California 237
Colorado 237
Connecticut 238
Delaware 238
Florida 238
Georgia 238
Hawaii 239
Idaho 239
Illinois 239
Indiana 239
Iowa 239
Kansas 240
Kentucky 240
Louisiana 240
Maine 240
Maryland 240
Massachusetts 240
Michigan 241
Minnesota 241
Mississippi 241
Missouri 241
Montana 242
Nebraska 242
Nevada 242
New Hampshire 242
New Jersey 243
New Mexico 243
New York 243
North Carolina 243
North Dakota 244
Ohio 244
Oklahoma 244
Oregon 244
Pennsylvania 244
Rhode Island 244
South Carolina 245
South Dakota 245
Tennessee 245
Texas 245
Utah 246
Vermont 246
Virginia 246
Washington 246
West Virginia 247
Wisconsin 247
Wyoming 247

Read about the provinces and territories that make up Canada.

Alberta 286
British Columbia 286
Manitoba 287
New Brunswick 287
Newfoundland
  and Labrador 287
Northwest Territories . . .287
Nova Scotia 287
Nunavut 288
Ontario 288
Prince Edward Island . .288
Quebec 289
Saskatchewan 289
Yukon Territory 289

COUNTRY DATABANK

Read about the countries that make up Latin America.

Belize 426
Costa Rica 427
El Salvador 427
Guatemala 427
Honduras 428
Mexico 428
Nicaragua 429
Panama 429
Antigua and Barbuda 456
Bahamas 457
Barbados 457
Cuba 457
Dominica 458
Dominican Republic 458
Grenada 458
Haiti 459
Jamaica 459
Puerto Rico 459
Saint Kitts and Nevis 460
Saint Lucia 460
Saint Vincent and the Grenadines 460
Trinidad and Tobago 461
Argentina 488
Bolivia 489
Brazil 489
Chile 489
Colombia 490
Ecuador 490
Guyana 491
Paraguay 491
Peru 491
Suriname 492
Uruguay 492
Venezuela 493

COUNTRY PROFILES

Theme-based maps and charts provide a closer look at countries, regions, and provinces.

The Northeast (Economics) 250
The South (Culture) 256
The Midwest (Economics) 265
The West (Geography) 272
Ontario (Government) 292
Quebec (History) 296
Prairie Provinces (Economics) 300
British Columbia (Geography) 306
The Atlantic Provinces (Economics) 313
The Northern Territories (Government) 320
Mexico (Economics) 432
Guatemala (Culture) 439
Panama (Geography) 446
Cuba (Government) 465
Haiti (History) 472
Puerto Rico (Government) 479
Brazil (Culture) 498
Peru (Geography) 502
Chile (Economics) 508
Venezuela (Economics) 518

Skills for Life

Teach skills that students will use all of their lives.

Using Reliable Information 14
Using Climate Graphs 48
Analyzing and Interpreting Population Density Maps . . 72
Making Valid Generalizations 102
Making Predictions 126
Identifying Frame of Reference 154
Interpreting Diagrams 200
Using Graphic Organizers 220
Understanding Circle Graphs 262
Writing a Summary 316
Analyzing and Interpreting Climate Maps 350
Making a Timeline 390
Distinguishing Fact and Opinion 408
Drawing Inferences and Conclusions 442
Comparing and Contrasting 468
Synthesizing Information 514

Citizen Heroes

Introduce people who have made a difference in their country.

Clara Barton 186
Louis Riel 195
José Martí 388
Mothers of the "Disappeared" 418
Justina Tzoc 440
Loune Viaud 473

Links

See the fascinating links between social studies and other disciplines.

Links Across Time

The Silk Road 78

Living Underground 191

Why "Latin" America? .340

Links Across the World

Higher and Higher. 268

The Baseball Connection. 466

Links to Language Arts

V. S. Naipaul: Trinidad and Beyond 412

The "Real" Robinson Crusoe. 511

Links to Math

Time Zones and Longitude 29

Acres and Timber Yields 129

Using Your Fingers and Toes 216

The Concept of Zero 369

Links to Science

Plant Fossils 51

The Next Hawaiian Island 150

Sanctuary 301

High Tide. 314

What Is a Hurricane? 345

Earthquake-Proof Buildings. 376

The Photosynthesis "Factory" 495

Links to Technology

Digital Tunes 107

Target Reading Skills

Chapter-by-chapter reading skills help students read and understand social studies concepts.

Clarifying Meaning 8, 172, 366

Comparing and Contrasting. 58, 234, 486

Identifying the Main Idea 112, 212, 454

Using Cause and Effect 400

Using Context 26, 284, 424

Using the Reading Process. 146, 336

Using Sequence 90

Eyewitness Technology

Detailed drawings show how technology shapes places and societies.

Weather Forecasting 46

The Hybrid Car 130

Pueblo Village 176

The Skyscraper 252

Aztec Farming 371

The Panama Canal 449

DIAGRAPHICS

Investigate geographic concepts using diagrams, maps, and photographs.

The Hemispheres 11

The Global Grid 12

Maps of Different Scale 22

The Revolution of Earth 30

Earth's Layers. 34

How Continents Move 36

Plate Movements 38

The Water Cycle 41

Air Circulation and Wind 42

The World: Climate Regions 44

The World: Natural Vegetation 53

The World: Population Density 62

Migration in South Asia 69

How Does World Trade Work? 78

The Development of Agricultural Technology 94

The World: Major Language Groups. 98

The World: Major Religions 100

Stages of Economic Activity 122

Boston: A Changing Landscape 124

Literature

Selections by noted authors bring social studies to life.

My Side of the Mountain
   by Jean Craighead George 88
Childtimes by Eloise Greenfield, *et. al.* 280
The Surveyor by Alma Flor Ada 362

Maps and Charts

MAP✳MASTER™

Same-Shape Maps M6
Equal-Area Maps M7
Robinson Maps M7
Western Europe M8
London M9
Political Africa M10
Physical Africa M11
India: Climate Regions M12
India: Official Languages M13
Migration to Latin America, 1500–1800 . . . . M14
World Land Use M16
The World: Political 2
The World: Physical 4
The World: Population Density 6
The Hemispheres 11
The Global Grid 12
Making a Mercator Map 18
Making an Equal-Area Map 19
The World: Robinson Projection 19
China: Physical 20
Georgia Highways 21
Greater London 22
Central London 22
The Globe: Place Location .24
The World: Time Zones 29
Zones of Latitude 32
Plates 250 Million Years Ago 38
Plates 150 Million Years Ago 38
Plates 75 Million Years Ago 38
Present-Day Plates 38
The World: Precipitation 43
The World: Climate Regions 44
The World: Natural Vegetation 53
Oceans and Seas: Place Location 56
The World: Early Farming and Modern Industry 61
The World: Population Density 62
Migration in South Asia 69
The World: Levels of Development 77
Continents: Place Location .86
The World: Major Language Groups 98
The World: Major Religions 100

The World: Natural Resources 115
Boston: A Changing Landscape 124
Natural Resources: Place Location 134
The United States and Canada: Relative Location 140
The United States and Canada: Relative Size 140
Political United States and Canada 141
Physical United States and Canada 142
Climates of the United States and Canada 143
Focus on Regions of the United States and Canada . . . 144
United States and Canada: Physical 147
Tornadoes in the United States 158
United States and Canada: Vegetation 160
United States and Canada: Natural Resources 164
The United States and Canada: Place Location 170
North America in 1753 173
North America in 1783 177
Growth of the United States From 1783 181
Indian Removal During the 1830s 182
A Nation Divided, 1861 184
Canada's Provinces and Territories 196
Wind Patterns and Air Pollution 204
Canada: Place Location 210
Migration to North America 213
Native Americans and Europeans, 1753 215
Native American Groups: Place Location 232
Regions of the United States 235
An Urban Megalopolis 249
The Northeast: Population Density 250
The South: Land Use 256
The Sun Belt States 260
The Midwest: Major Highways 265
Major Rail Routes of the Late 1800s 269
The West: Precipitation 272
The United States: Place Location 278
Canada: Political 285
Ontario: Population Density 292
Quebec: Population Density 296
Prairie Provinces: Land Use 300
British Columbia: Natural Resources 306
Major Trade Routes Across the Pacific 309
Atlantic Provinces: Natural Resources 313

European Land Claims, 1682 and 1763 314

The Northern Territories:
    Native North American Groups. 320

Canada: Place Location 324

Latin America: Relative Location 330

Latin America: Relative Size. 330

Political Latin America. 331

Physical Latin America. 332

Latin America: Major Hydroelectric Plants. 333

Focus on Countries in Latin America 334

Latin America: Physical 337

Regions of Latin America. 339

Latin America: Climate Regions. 344

Latin America: Vegetation Regions 348

Latin America: Natural Resources 353

Latin America: Place Location 360

Latin America: Early Civilizations. 367

European Conquest of Latin America 382

South American Independence 387

Latin America: Place Location 398

Latin America: Languages 401

Latin America: Place Location 422

Mexico and Central America: Political 425

Mexico: Resources and Manufacturing 432

The Growth of Mexico City 434

Guatemala: Languages 439

Shipping Routes and the Panama Canal 445

Panama: Vegetation 446

Mexico and Central America: Place Location 452

The Caribbean: Political 455

Cuba: Political 465

Haiti: Political. 472

Puerto Rico: Population Density. 479

The Caribbean: Place Location 484

South America: Political 487

Brazil: Population Density 498

Peru: Three Regions 502

Chile: Products and Resources 508

Venezuela: Products and Resources. 518

South America: Place Location 524

MAP✴MASTER™

Atlas 530
  The World: Political 530
  The World: Physical 532
  United States: Political. 534
  North and South America: Political 536
  North and South America: Physical 537
  Europe: Political. 538
  Europe: Physical 539
  Africa: Political 540
  Africa: Physical 541
  Asia: Political. 542
  Asia: Physical. 543
  Oceania. 544
  The Arctic. 545
  Antarctica 545

Charts, Graphs, and Tables

World Population. 6
Climate Graph: São Paulo, Brazil 48
Charleston, South Carolina 49
Climate Graph: Helsinki. 56
Birth and Death Rates in Selected Countries, 2006 64
World Population Growth, 1200–2000 65
World Urban and Rural Populations, 1800–2000. 70
World Internet Users, 1996–2005 107
The World's Top Petroleum Producers and Consumers . 118
Average Temperatures for Miami and Toronto 157
Electric Power 167
Timeline: Post-Civil War to the Present 190
The Great Lakes and the St. Lawrence Seaway 206
Origin of Immigrants to the United States, 2003 224
Canada: Ethnic Groups and Immigrants. 228
The Northeast: Types of Services 250
Northeast Population Density, 2000. 250
Economy of the Northeast 250
African American Migration by Region, 1990–2000 . . 256
Hispanic Population of the South, 2002. 256
The United States: Ethnic Groups. 263
Major Religions 263
Midwest Economy 265
Chicago, Major Transportation Hub 265

MAP✴MASTER™ Interactive

Go online to find an interactive version of every MapMaster™ map in this book. Use the Web Code provided to gain direct access to these maps.

How to Use Web Codes:

1. Go to **www.PHSchool.com**.

2. Enter the Web Code.

3. Click Go!

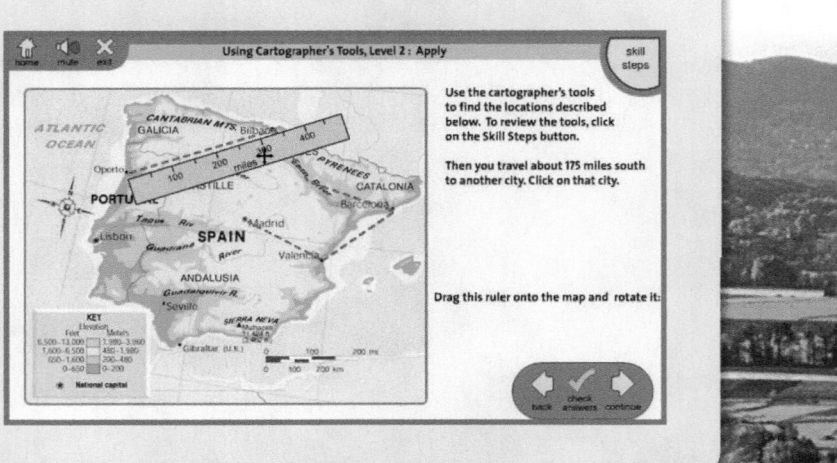

Number of United States Farm Workers, 1910–2000 . . .266
California Cropland 272
Leading Hydroelectric Power-Producing States, 2006 . .272
Internet Company Shutdowns 275
The Canadian Government 291
The House of Commons 292
The Structure of Government 292
Languages Spoken in Montreal 296
Timeline: Early Canadian History 296
Timeline: Recent Quebec History 296
Number of Farms in Prairie Provinces 300
Average Size of Farms in Prairie Provinces 300
Percent of Canadian Grains Grown in
    Prairie Provinces 300
Income From Mining in British Columbia, 2005 306
Canadian Wood and Paper Products Production 306
Cod Fishing in Newfoundland 313
Aquaculture in Newfoundland and Labrador 313
Economic Activities in the Atlantic Provinces 313
Population and Area of Northern Canada 320
Nunavut Legislature 320
Latin America: Sources of Energy 333
Vertical Climate Zones 346
World Coffee Prices, 1965–2005 356
Timeline: Mayan, Aztec, and Incan Civilizations,
    A.D. 300–1600 374
The Columbian Exchange 383

Foreign Debt of Latin American Nations, 2005 394
The World's Five Largest Urban Areas, 2003 405
Mexico's Exports 432
Mexico's Trading Partners 432
Guatemala: Ethnic Groups 439
Mayan Towns 439
Panama Canal Facts 446
Land Use 446
Cuba: Control of Productive Land, 1980 and 2002 465
Party Representation in Cuba and the
    United States, 2004 465
Timeline: Foreign Influence in Haiti Since
    Independence 472
About One in Seven Haitians Has Emigrated 472
Haiti Today 472
Puerto Ricans in the Mainland United States, 2000 . . .477
Citizen Status in Iowa versus Puerto Rico 479
2004 Puerto Rico Election Results 479
Two Cities, Two Climates 496
Cultural Regions of Brazil 498
Brazil's Ethnic Groups 498
Peru: Characteristics of Three Regions 502
Peru's Population 502
Chile: Average Annual Income per Citizen 508
Chile's Exports 508
U.S. Petroleum Imports From Venezuela, 1980–2005 . .517
World Crude Oil Prices, 1970–2005 518
Leading World Oil Exporters, 2004 518
Venezuela: Earnings From Exports, 2005 518

NCLB Implications for Social Studies

The No Child Left Behind (NCLB) legislation was a landmark in educational reform designed to improve student achievement and create a fundamental shift in American education. In the essay that follows, we will explore the implications of NCLB on social studies curriculum, instruction, assessment, and instructional programs.

Facts about NCLB

The No Child Left Behind Act of 2001 (NCLB) calls for sweeping educational reform, requiring all students to perform proficiently on standardized tests in reading, mathematics, and (soon to be added) science by the year 2014. Under NCLB, schools will be held accountable for students' academic progress. In exchange for this accountability, the law offers more flexibility to individual states and school districts to decide how best to use federal education funds. NCLB places an emphasis on implementing scientifically proven methods in teaching reading and mathematics, and promotes teacher quality. It also offers parental choice for students in failing schools.

Effects on Curriculum, Instruction, and Assessment

Since the primary focus of NCLB is on raising the achievement of students in reading and mathematics, some educators have wondered how it relates to social studies. Some teachers have expressed concerns that since NCLB does not require yearly testing of social studies, state and school districts may decide to shift resources and class time away from teaching social studies. However, NCLB considers the social studies areas of history, geography, economics, and government and civics to be core academic subjects. Many states are requiring middle grades social studies teachers to be highly qualified in history and geography in order to comply with the principle of improving teacher quality in NCLB.

NCLB sets the goal of having every child meet state-defined education standards. Since social studies educators have been leaders in the development of standards-based education and accountability through student testing over the past decade, many state and local districts have their own standards and assessments for social studies already in place. Assessment, including screening, diagnostic, progress-monitoring—including end-of-year, end-of-schooling, grade level, district, and state testing—and large-scale assessments, will continue to play a significant role in shaping social studies curriculum and instruction in the near future.

Integrating Reading into Social Studies Instruction

Due to the increased emphasis on reading and mathematics required by NCLB, social studies teachers may be called on to help improve their students' reading and math skills. For example, a teacher might use a graph about exports and imports to reinforce math skills, or a primary source about a historical event to improve reading skills. The connection between reading and social studies is especially important. Since many state and local assessments of reading require students to read and interpret informational texts, social studies passages are often used in the exams. Therefore, social studies teachers may assist in raising reading scores by integrating reading instruction into their teaching of social studies content.

Implications for Instructional Programs

The environment created by the NCLB legislation has implications for instructional programs. In keeping with the spirit of NCLB, social studies programs should clearly tie their content to state and local standards. Programs should also provide support so that all students can master these standards, ensuring that no child is left behind. An ideal instructional program is rooted in research, embeds reading instruction into the instructional design, and provides assessment tools that inform instruction—helping teachers focus on improving student performance.

Prentice Hall Response

We realize that raising the achievement level of all students is the number one challenge facing teachers today. To assist you in meeting this challenge, Prentice Hall enlisted a team of respected consultants who specialize in middle grades issues, reading in the content areas, and geographic education. This team created a middle grades world studies program that breaks new ground and meets the changing needs of you and your students.

With Prentice Hall, you can be confident that your students will not only be motivated, inspired, and excited to learn world studies, but they will also achieve the success needed in today's environment of the No Child Left Behind (NCLB) legislation and testing reform.

In the following pages, you will find the key elements woven throughout this World Studies program that truly set it apart and assure success for you and your students.

Teacher's Edition Contents in Brief

Reading
Support T22

Differentiated
Instruction T26

Geographic
Literacy T28

Assessment T30

Instructional Strategies
for Improving Student
Comprehension T32

Skills Scope
and Sequence T38

Pacing Options T39

National Geography
Standards Correlation T40

NCSS Curriculum
Standards Correlation T42

Research on Effective Reading Instruction

Why do many students have difficulty reading textbooks? How can we help students read to learn social studies? In the pages that follow, we examine the research on the challenge of reading textbooks; explain the direct, systematic, and explicit instruction needed to help students; and then show how Prentice Hall has responded to this research.

What is skilled reading?

Recent research (Snow et al., 2002) suggests that skillful and strategic reading is a long-term developmental process in which "readers learn how to simultaneously extract and construct meaning through interaction with written language." In other words, successful readers know how to decode all kinds of words, read with fluency and expression, have well-developed vocabularies, and possess various comprehension strategies such as note-taking and summarizing to employ as the academic reading task demands.

Many students lack reading skills

Sadly, many secondary students do not have solid reading skills. In the early years, students read mainly engaging and accessible narratives, such as stories, poems, and junior biographies. But in the upper elementary years, they shift toward conceptually dense and challenging nonfiction, or expository texts. It is no accident that the infamous "Fourth-Grade Slump" (Chall and Jacobs, 2003; Hirsch 2003)— a well-documented national trend of declining literacy after grade four—occurs during this time. The recent National Assessment of Educational Progress (NAEP, 2002) found that only 33 percent of eighth-grade students scored at or above the proficient level in reading.

Even students quite skilled in reading novels, short stories, and adolescent magazines typically come to middle school ill-equipped for the rigors of informational texts or reading to learn. They tend to dive right into a social studies chapter as if reading a recreational story. They don't first preview the material to create a mental outline and establish a reading purpose. They have not yet learned other basic strategies, including reading a section more than once, taking notes as they read, and reading to answer specific questions.

Dr. Kate Kinsella
Reading Consultant for *World Studies*
Department of Secondary Education
San Francisco State University, CA

Dr. Kevin Feldman
Reading Consultant for *World Studies*
Director of Reading and Early Intervention
Sonoma County, CA

"Even students quite skilled in reading novels, short stories, and adolescent magazines typically come to middle school ill-equipped for the rigors of informational texts or reading to learn."

The unique demands of textbooks

The differences between textbooks and the narratives students are used to reading are dramatic. The most distinctive challenges include dense conceptual content, heavy vocabulary load, unfamiliar paragraph and organizational patterns, and complex sentence structures. Academic texts present such a significant challenge to most students that linguists and language researchers liken them to learning a foreign language (Schleppegrell, 2002). In other words, most secondary students are second language learners: they are learning the academic language of informational texts!

Effective reading instruction

Research illustrates that virtually all students benefit from direct, systematic, and explicit instruction in reading informational texts (Baker & Gersten, 2000). There are three stages to the instructional process for content-area reading:

(1) **before reading:** instructional frontloading;

(2) **during reading:** guided instruction;

(3) **after reading:** reflection and study.

Before reading

Placing a major emphasis on preteaching, or "front-loading" your instruction—building vocabulary, setting a purpose for reading, and explicitly teaching students strategies for actively engaging with the text—helps you structure learning to ensure student success (see Strategies 1 and 2 on pages T32-T33). Frontloading strategies are especially critical in mixed-ability classrooms with English language learners, students with special needs, and other students performing below grade level in terms of literacy.

During reading

In guided instruction, the teacher models approaches for actively engaging with text to gain meaning. The teacher guides students through the first reading of the text using passage reading strategies (see Strategies 3-7 on pages T33-35), and then guides discussion about the content using participation strategies (see Strategies 8-11 on pages T35-T37). Finally, students record key information in a graphic organizer.

After reading

During the reflection and study phase, the teacher formally checks for student understanding, offers remediation if necessary, and provides activities that challenge students to apply content in a new way. To review the chapter, students recall content, analyze the reading as a whole, and study key vocabulary and information likely to be tested.

References

Baker, Scott and Russell Gersten. "What We Know About Effective Instructional Practices for English Language Learners." *Exceptional Children*, 66 (2000):454–470.

Chall, Jeanne S. and Vicki A. Jacobs. "Poor Children's Fourth-Grade Slump." *American Educator* (Spring 2003):14.

Donahue, P.L., et al. *The 1998 NAEP Reading Report Card for the Nation and the States* (NCES 1999-500). Washington, D.C.: U.S. Department of Education, Office of Education Research and Improvement, National Center for Education Statistics, 1999.

Grigg, W.S. et al. *The Nation's Report Card: Reading 2002* (NCES 2003-521). Washington, D.C.: U.S. Department of Education, Institute of Education Sciences, National Center for Education Statistics, 2003.

Hirsch, E.D., Jr. "Reading Comprehension Requires Knowledge—of Words and the World." *American Educator* (Spring 2003):10-29.

Kinsella, Kate, et al. *Teaching Guidebook for Universal Access.* Upper Saddle River, NJ: Prentice Hall, 2002.

Schleppegrell, M. "Linguistic Features of the Language of Schooling." *Linguistics and Education*, 12, no. 4 (2002): 431–459.

Snow, C., et al. *Reading for Understanding: Toward an R&D Program in Reading Comprehension.* Santa Monica, California: The Rand Corporation, 2002.

Reading Support

Putting Research Into Practice

Prentice Hall enlisted the assistance of Dr. Kate Kinsella and Dr. Kevin Feldman to ensure that the new middle grades world studies program would provide the direct, systematic, and explicit instruction needed to foster student success in reading informational texts. To help students rise to the challenge of reading an informational text, *World Studies* embedded reading support right into the student text.

Embedded Reading Support in the Student Text

Before students read
- **Objectives** set the purpose for what students will read.
- **Target Reading Skill** for the section is explained.
- **Key Terms** are defined up front with pronunciation and part of speech.

During the section
- **Target Reading Skill** is applied to help students read and understand the narrative.
- **Key Terms** are defined in context, with terms and definitions called out in blue type.
- **Reading Checks** reinforce students' understanding by slowing them down to review after every concept is discussed.
- **Caption Questions** draw students into the art and photos, helping them to connect the content to the images.

After students read
- **Section Assessment** revisits the **Key Terms**, provides an opportunity to master the **Target Reading Skill**, allows student to rehearse their understanding of the text through the **Writing Activity**.

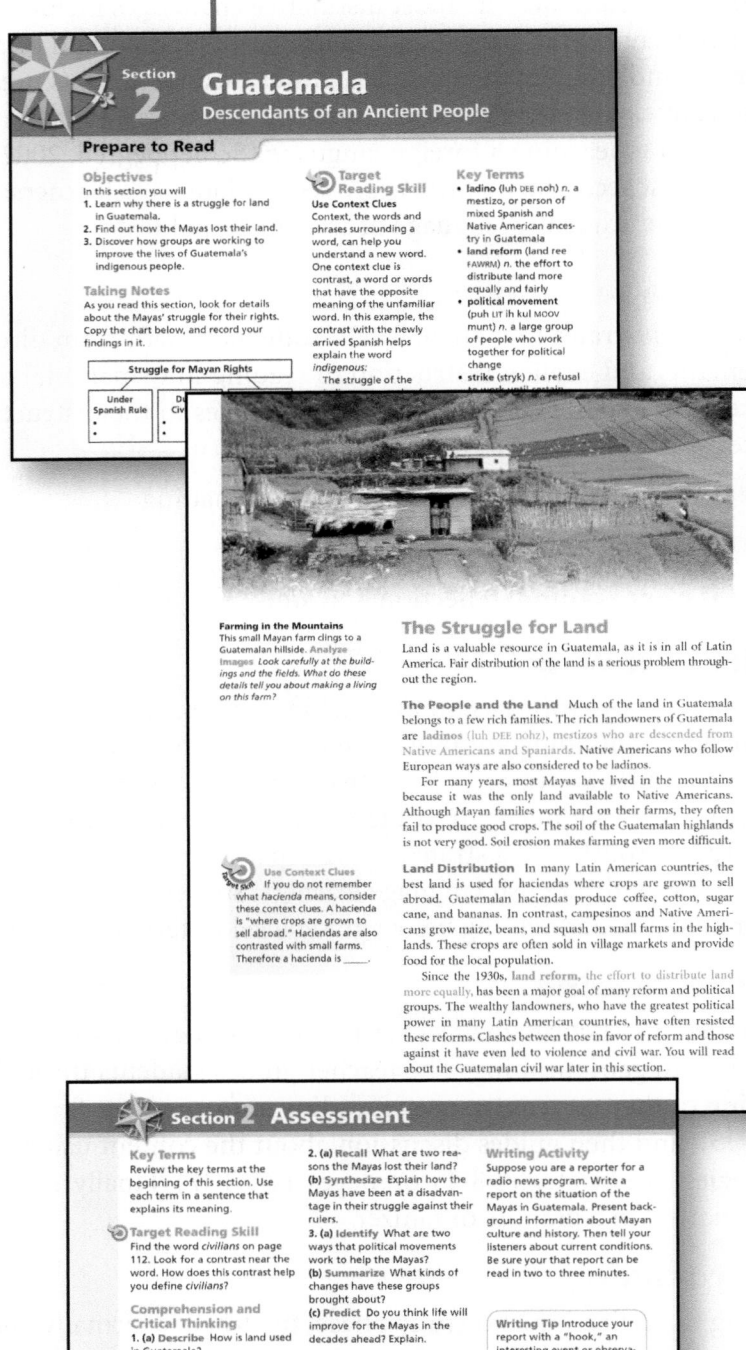

T24

Putting Research Into Practice

World Studies offers teachers guidance in direct, systematic, and explicit reading instruction. The instructional sequence in the Teacher's Edition explicitly guides you in the use of effective strategies at each stage of the instructional process.

Reading Instruction in *World Studies* Teacher's Edition

Before Reading

Every lesson plan begins with suggestions that help you integrate frontloading strategies into your teaching. Build Background Knowledge activates and builds prior knowledge. Set a Purpose for Reading prompts students to predict and anticipate content and motivates students to engage with the text. Preview Key Terms helps students learn Key Terms to understand the text. Target Reading Skill models a reading strategy to help students gain meaning from the text. Vocabulary Builder gives teachers definitions and sample sentences to help teach high-use words.

During Reading

In the Instruct part of the lesson plan, you can use suggestions for getting students actively engaged in the text. Guided Instruction clarifies high-use words, applies a passage-reading strategy to promote text comprehension, and guides discussion to construct meaning. Independent Practice prompts students to reread and take notes in the graphic organizer provided to rehearse understanding.

After Reading

The lesson plan closes with specific strategies for the reflection and study phase after reading is completed. Monitor Progress checks students' note taking, and verifies students' prereading predictions. Assess and Reteach measures students' recall of content and provides additional instruction if needed. Review Chapter Content promotes retention of key concepts and vocabulary.

Integrated Reading Resources

The *World Studies* program provides instructional materials to support the reading instruction in the Teacher's Edition.

The **All-in-One Teaching Resources** provides reading instruction support worksheets, such as a Reading Readiness Guide, Word Knowledge, and Vocabulary Development.

Students can use the **Reading and Vocabulary Study Guide** (English and Spanish) to reinforce reading instruction and vocabulary development, and to review section summaries of every section of the student text.

Research on Differentiated Instruction

It's basic, but it's true—not all our students learn in the same manner and not all our students have the same academic background or abilities. As educators, we need to respond to this challenge through the development and utilization of instructional strategies that address the needs of diverse learners, or the number of children who "fall through the cracks" will continue to rise (Kame'enui & Carnine, 1998).

Providing universal access

Universal access happens when curriculum and instruction are provided in ways that allow all learners to participate and to achieve (Kinsella, et al., 2002). Teachers who teach in heterogeneous, inclusive classrooms can provide universal access by modifying their teaching to respond to the needs of typical learners, gifted learners, less proficient readers, English language learners, and special needs students. Many of these learner populations benefit from extensive reading support (see pages T14-T17).

It is also critical to properly match the difficulty level of tasks with the ability level of students. Giving students tasks that they perceive as too hard lowers their expectations of success. However, giving students assignments that they think are too easy, undermines their feelings of competence (Stipek, 1996). Therefore, it is important for a program to give teachers leveled activities that allow them to match tasks with the abilities of their individual students.

When students connect to and are engaged with the content, comprehension and understanding increase. Technology, such as online activities, can provide an ideal opportunity for such engagement. It also can be used to provide additional opportunities to access content. For example, a less proficient reader may reinforce understanding of a key concept through watching a video. A complete social studies program makes content available in a variety of formats, including text, audio, visuals, and interactivities.

> "Universal access happens when curriculum and instruction are provided in ways that allow all learners to participate and to achieve (Kinsella, et al., 2002)."

Kame'enui, Edward and Douglas Carnine. *Effective Teaching Strategies that Accommodate Diverse Learners.* Upper Saddle River, NJ: Prentice Hall, 1998.

Kinsella, Kate, et al. *Teaching Guidebook for Universal Access.* Upper Saddle River, NJ: Prentice Hall, 2002.

Stipek, D.J. "Motivation and Instruction," in R.C. Clafee and D.C. Berlinger (Eds.), *Handbook of Educational Psychology.* New York: Macmillan, 1996.

Putting Research Into Practice

Prentice Hall recognizes that today's classrooms include students with diverse backgrounds and ability levels. Accordingly, the *World Studies* program was designed to provide access to the content for all students. The program provides both the instructional materials to meet the learning needs of all students and the guidance you need to accommodate these needs.

Differentiated Instruction in the Teacher's Edition

The Teacher's Edition was designed to make it easy for teachers to modify instruction for diverse learners. Teaching strategies, provided by Dr. Kate Kinsella and Dr. Kevin Feldman, to help you modify your teaching are incorporated into every lesson plan. Specific activities help you differentiate instruction for individual students in five categories—less proficient readers, advanced readers, special needs students, gifted and talented, and English language learners. Resources are identified as being appropriate for use by each of these categories. All resources are also assigned a level—basic, average, and above average—so you know exactly how to assign tasks of appropriate difficulty level.

All-in-One Teaching Resources

Everything you need to provide differentiated instruction for each lesson, including reading support, activities and projects, enrichment, and assessment—in one convenient location.

Student Edition on Audio CD

The complete narrative is read aloud, section by section, providing extra support for auditory learners, English language learners, and reluctant readers. Also available is the Guided Reading Audio CD (English/Spanish), containing section summaries read aloud.

Interactive Textbook—The Student Edition Online and on CD-ROM

The Interactive Textbook allows students to interact with the content, including reading aids, visual and interactive learning tools, and instant feedback assessments.

Differentiated Instruction

For Less Proficient Readers L1
Have students read the section in the Reading and Vocabulary Study Guide. This version provides basic-level instruction in an interactive format with questions and write-on lines.

Chapter 4, Section 1, Latin America **Reading and Vocabulary Study Guide,** pp. 42–44

For Special Needs Students L1
Have students read the section as they listen to the recorded version on the Student Edition on Audio CD. Check for comprehension by pausing the CD and asking students to share their answers to the Reading Checks.

Chapter 4, Section 1, **Student Edition on Audio CD**

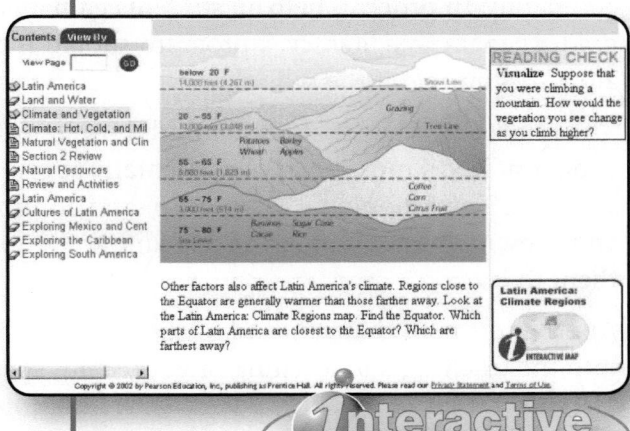

Research on Geographic Literacy

As the *Geography for Life: National Geography Standards* (1994) state, "There is now a widespread acceptance among the people of the United States that being literate in geography is essential if students are to leave school equipped to earn a decent living, enjoy the richness of life, and participate responsibly in local, national, and international affairs." A middle grades social studies program needs to help teachers produce students who are literate in geography.

Geographic literacy defined

Results for the 2001 National Assessment of Educational Progress (NAEP) Geography assessment show that the average scores of fourth- and eighth-grade students have improved since 1994. The average score of twelfth-grade students, however, has not changed significantly. In order to make the critical leap from basic geography skills to the kind of geographic literacy needed by the twelfth grade and beyond, a program must teach both geography content and geography skills, and then help students think critically. Geography content is made up of the essential knowledge that students need to know about the world. Geography skills are the ability to ask geographic questions, acquire and analyze geographic information, and answer these questions. To be truly literate in geography, students must be able to apply their knowledge and skills to understand the world.

Elements for success in middle grades

Students in the elementary grades don't always get enough training in geography. In order to help all students gain a base upon which to build middle grades geographic literacy, a program should introduce basic geography skills at the beginning of the school year.

The quality of maps is also vital to the success of a middle grades world studies program. Maps must be developmentally appropriate for middle grades students. They should be clean, clear, and accurate. Maps should be attractive and present subject matter in appealing ways, so that students *want* to use them to learn.

Another element that can lead to success is the incorporation of technology into the teaching and learning of geography, specifically the Internet. Research has shown that 8th grade students with high Internet usage scored higher in geography (NAEP, 2001).

U.S. Department of Education, Office of Educational Research and Improvement, National Center for Education Statistics, National Assessment of Educational Progress (NAEP), 2001 Geography Assessment.

Andrew Heritage
Head of Cartography
Dorling Kindersley (DK)

"Maps should be attractive and present subject matter in appealing ways, so that students *want* to use them to learn."

Putting Research Into Practice

Prentice Hall partnered with DK—internationally known for their dynamic atlases—to develop the *World Studies* program. DK's Andrew Heritage and his world-renowned cartography team designed all maps, resulting in stunning, high quality maps that are middle grades appropriate.

The MapMaster™ System

World Studies offers the first interactive geography instruction system available with a world studies textbook.

Introduce Basic Map Skills

The MapMaster™ Skills Handbook, a DK-designed introduction to the basics, brings students up to speed with a complete overview at the beginning of every book.

Build Geographic Literacy with Every Map

Scaffolded questions start with questions that require basic geography content and skills, and then ask students to demonstrate geographic literacy by thinking critically about the map.

Activate Learning Online

MapMaster™ Interactive—online and on CD-ROM—allows students to put their knowledge of geography skills and content into practice through interactivities.

Extend Learning with DK

- **DK World Desk Reference Online** is filled with up-to-date data, maps, and visuals that connect students to a wealth of information about the world's countries.

- **DK Compact Atlas of the World** with Map Master™ Teacher's Companion provides activities to introduce, develop, and master geography and map skills.

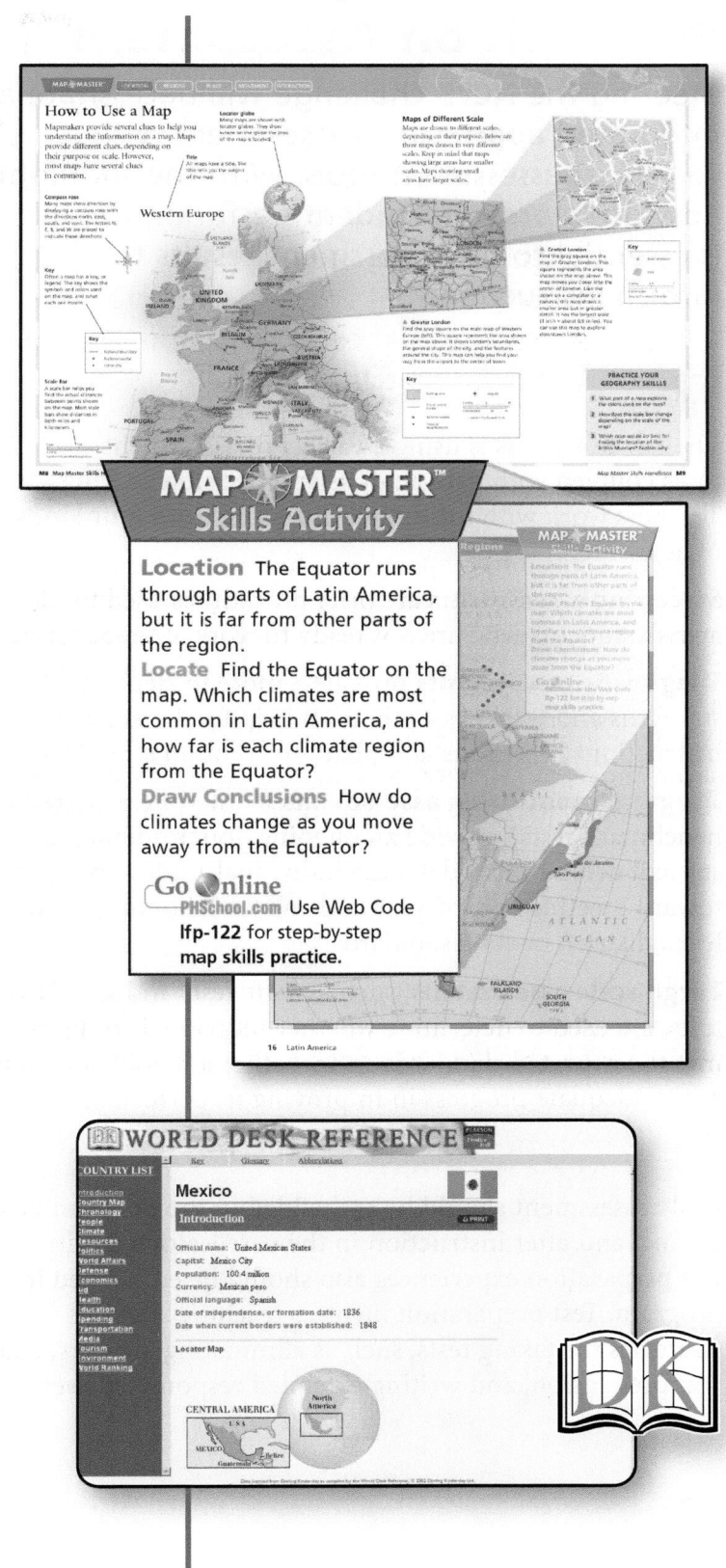

Research on Assessment

Meeting the NCLB challenge will necessitate an integrated approach to assessment with a variety of assessment tools. With the spotlight now on *improving* student performance, it is essential to use assessment results to inform instruction.

Assessments Tools for Informing Instruction

The key to success is using a variety of assessment tools coupled with data analysis and decision making. Teachers work with information coming from four kinds of assessment.

Screening assessments are brief procedures used to identify at-risk students who are not ready to work at grade level.

Diagnostic assessments provide a more in-depth analysis of strengths and weaknesses that can help teachers make instructional decisions and plan intervention strategies.

Progress-monitoring assessments (sometimes referred to as benchmark tests) provide an ongoing, longitudinal record of student achievement detailing individual student progress toward meeting end-of-year and end-of-schooling, grade level, district, or state standards.

Large-scale assessments, such as state tests and standardized tests, are used to determine whether individual students have met the expected standards and whether a school system has made adequate progress in improving its performance.

Ongoing Assessment

Daily assessment should be embedded in the program before, during, and after instruction in the core lessons. Legitimate test preparation experiences also should be embedded in the program. Test preparation involves teaching students strategies for taking tests, such as eliminating answers, reading comprehension, and writing extended response answers.

Eileen Depka
Supervisor of Standards and Assessment
Waukesha, WI

"Meeting the NCLB challenge will necessitate an integrated approach to assessment with a variety of assessment tools."

Putting Research Into Practice

Prentice Hall developed the *World Studies* program with a variety of assessment tools, including ongoing assessment in the student text.

Assessments for Informing Instruction

World Studies was designed to provide you with all four kinds of assessment.

- **Screening test** identifies students who are reading 2-3 years below grade level.

- **Diagnostic tests** focus on skills needed for success in social studies, including subtests in geographic literacy, visual analysis, critical thinking and reading, and communications skills, as well as vocabulary and writing.

- **Benchmark tests**, to be given six times throughout the year, monitor student progress in the course.

- **Outcome test**, to be administered at the end of the year, evaluates student mastery of social studies content standards.

Ongoing Assessment

- **Student Edition** offers section and chapter assessments with questions building from basic comprehension to critical thinking and writing.

- **Test Prep Workbook** and **Test-taking Strategies with Transparencies** develop students' test-taking skills and improve their scores on standardized tests.

- ***ExamView® Test Bank CD-ROM*** allows you to quickly and easily develop customized tests from a bank of thousands of questions.

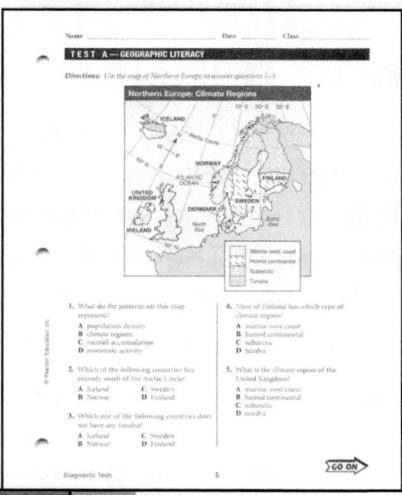

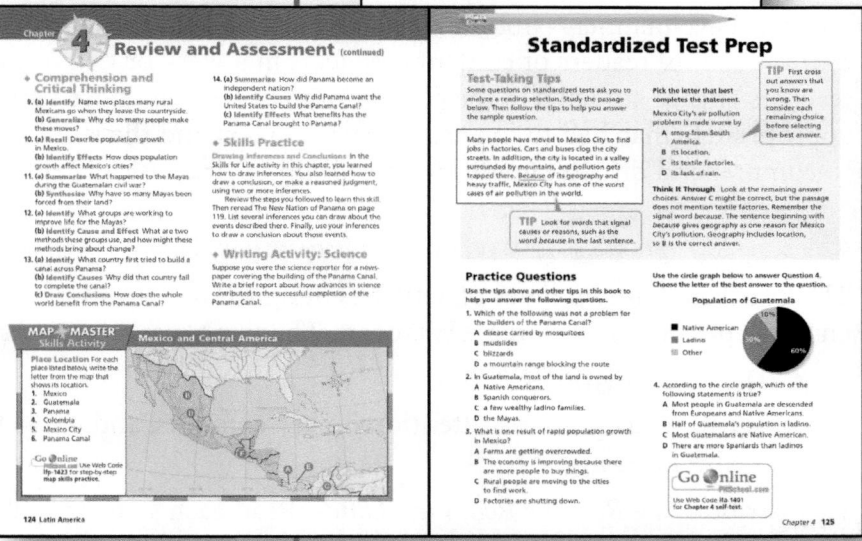

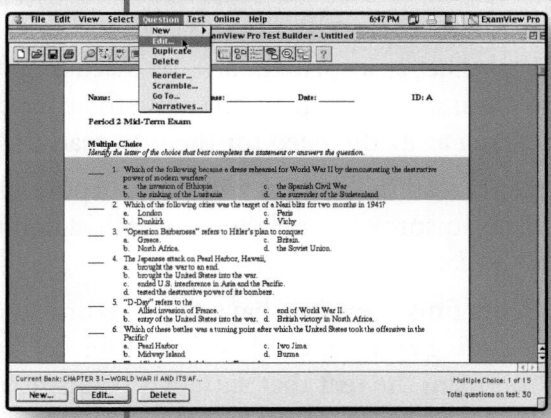

Instructional Strategies for Improving Student Comprehension

In response to today's environment of the NCLB legislation and testing reform, Prentice Hall asked Dr. Kate Kinsella and Dr. Kevin Feldman to provide specific instructional strategies you can use to improve student comprehension. Their guidance informed the development of the *World Studies* Teacher's Edition. The lesson plans in this Teacher's Edition incorporate the following instructional strategies to enhance students' comprehension.

There is no single magical strategy that will solve all of the difficulties students encounter in reading challenging content area texts. Secondary students in mixed-ability classrooms depend on teachers to use a consistent set of research-informed and classroom-tested strategies in a patient and recursive manner—not the occasional or random use of different strategies. Students will not become skillful readers of content area texts in a week or two of instruction. However, when teachers engage students in the consistent use of a well-chosen set of content reading strategies appropriately matched to the demands of the text and the students' level of knowledge, their ability to comprehend difficult grade level texts will be dramatically enhanced.

Strategy 1: Set a Purpose for Reading

This program has two types of activities designed to help students set a purpose for reading: an Anticipation Guide and a KWL chart. The two types rotate by section.

A. Anticipation Guide

Purpose: To focus students' attention on key concepts, and guide them to interact with ideas in the text

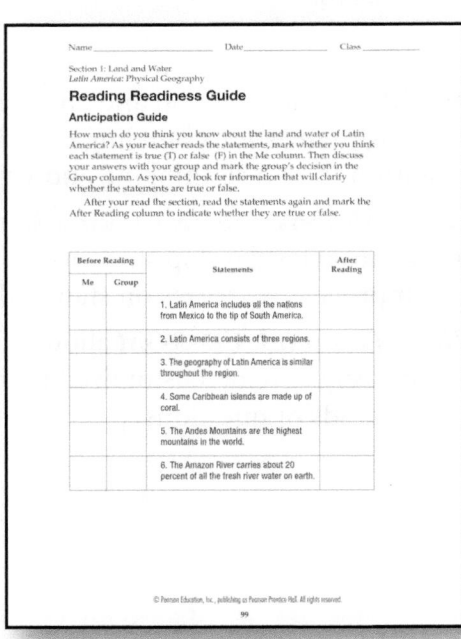

1. Distribute the *Reading Readiness Guide*. Read each statement aloud, and then ask students to react to the statements individually and in groups, marking their responses in the Before Reading column.

2. Use the worksheet as a springboard for discussing the section's key concepts as a unified class. Refrain from revealing the correct responses at this time, to avoid taking away the need for them to read the text.

3. Have students read the section with the purpose of finding evidence that confirms, disproves, or elaborates each statement in the *Reading Readiness Guide*.

4. After students finish reading, have them return to the statements and mark the After Reading column on their worksheets. Have them locate information from the text that supports or disproves each statement.

5. Discuss what the class has learned and probe for any lingering confusion about key concepts.

B. KWL

Purpose: To engage students before, during, and after reading

The KWL worksheet guides students to recall what they **K**now, determine what they **W**ant to learn, and identify what they **L**earn as they read.

1. Distribute the *Reading Readiness Guide*. Brainstorm with the group about what they already know about the topic. List students' ideas on the board. Encourage students to generate questions at points of ambiguity.

2. Students then list pieces of information they already know and questions they want to answer in the first two columns of their worksheets.

3. As students read the section, ask them to note information that answers their questions or adds to what they know.

4. After reading, facilitate a class discussion about what the students have learned. Clarify any lingering confusion about key concepts.

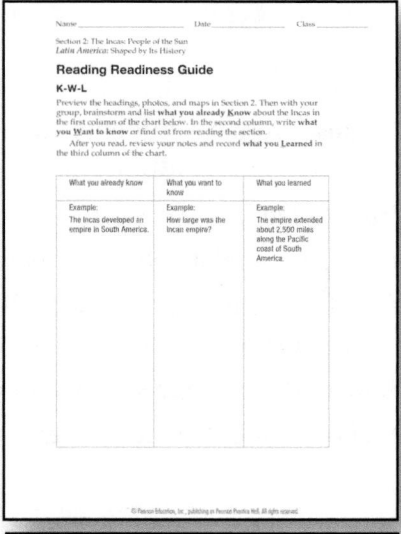

Strategy 2: Teach High-Use Academic Words

Purpose: To teach students words used often in academic texts, beyond the content-specific Key Terms

How to Do It

1. Have students rate how well they know each word on their *Word Knowledge* worksheets. Tell them there is no penalty for a low rating.

2. Survey students' ratings to decide which words need the most instruction.

3. Provide a brief definition or sample sentence for each word. (See Vocabulary Builder at the beginning of each section for definitions and sample sentences.) Rephrase your explanation, leaving out the word and asking students to substitute it aloud.

4. Work with students as they fill in the "Definition or Example" column of their *Word Knowledge* worksheets.

5. Point out each word in context as you read the chapters. Consider allowing students to earn extra credit if they use a word correctly in class discussion or assignments.

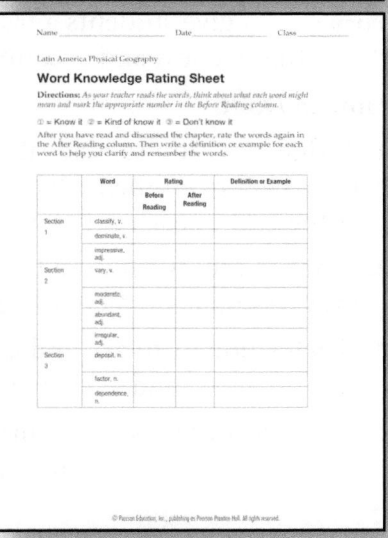

Strategy 3: Oral Cloze

Purpose: To help students read actively while the teacher reads aloud

How to Do It

1. Choose a passage and direct students to "read aloud silently using their inner voices." Be sure students understand reading is an active process, not simply a listening activity, and their job is to follow along—eyes riveted to each word, saying the words to themselves as you read aloud.

2. Tell students to be on their "reading toes," for you will be leaving out an occasional word and their task is to chorally supply the word.

3. The first few times you use the Oral Cloze, demonstrate by telling the students in advance what word you will be leaving out, directing them to read the word at the right time. Practice this a few times until they have the feel for the procedure. Leave out fewer words as students become more familiar with the Oral Cloze and require less direction to remain focused during teacher read alouds.

Strategies for Improving Student Comprehension *(continued)*

Strategy 4: Choral Reading

Purpose: To have students attend to the text in a non-threatening atmosphere

How to Do It

1. Choose a relatively short passage.

2. Tell students that you will all read the text aloud at once. Direct students to "keep your voice with mine" as they read.

3. Read the passage slowly and clearly.

4. Have students read the text again silently.

Strategy 5: Structured Silent Reading

Purpose: To give students a task as they read silently to increase their attentiveness and accountability

How to Do It

1. Assign a section to read silently. Pose a question for the whole class to answer from their silent reading, such as the Reading Check question at the end of each subsection. Model how one thinks while reading to find answers to a question.

2. When students get used to reading to answer the Reading Check question, pose more in-depth questions, progressing from factual recall to questions that stimulate interpretive or applied thinking.

3. Teach students to ask and answer their own questions as they read. Model this process by reading a section aloud and asking and answering your own questions as you read.

4. After the students have finished reading, engage the class in a brief discussion to clarify questions, vocabulary, and key concepts.

Strategy 6: Paragraph Shrinking

Purpose: To increase comprehension during reading

How to Do It

1. Partner struggling students with more proficient students and assign a manageable portion of the text.

2. Ask one member of each pair to identify the "who or what" the paragraph is about and tell the other.

3. Have the other member of the pair identify important details about the "who or what" and tell the other.

4. Ask the first member to summarize the paragraph in fifteen to twenty words or less using the most important details. The second member of the pair monitors the number of words and says "Shrink it!" if the summary goes over twenty words.

5. Have the partners reverse roles and continue reading.

6. Discuss the reading as a class to make sure students' paragraphs have correctly hit upon the main ideas of the passage.

Strategy 7: ReQuest (Reciprocal Questioning)

Purpose: To ask and answer questions during reading to establish a purpose for reading and monitor one's own comprehension

How to Do It

1. Prepare students to read by doing the section's Build Background Knowledge, Set a Purpose for Reading, and Preview Key Terms activities.

2. Begin reading a brief portion of the text aloud. Ask and answer your own questions about the text, progressing from recall to critical thinking questions.

3. After modeling this question and response pattern with a brief passage, ask students to read the next section of the text. Tell students that they will be taking turns asking you questions about what they read, and you will answer their questions, just like you modeled for them.

4. Ask students to read the next section. Inform them that you will be asking them questions about the section and they will be answering your questions.

5. Continue to alternate between student-generated questions and teacher-generated questions until the entire designated passage has been read. As students become used to the strategy, they gradually assume more responsibility in the process.

6. When the students have read enough information to make predictions about the remainder of the assignment, stop the exchange of comprehension questions. Instead, ask prediction questions, such as, "What do you think will be discussed in the next section? Why do you think so?"

7. Assign the remaining portion for students to read silently. Then lead a wrap-up discussion of the material.

Strategy 8: Idea Wave

Purpose: To engage students in active class discussions

How to Do It

1. Pose a question or task.

2. Give students quiet time to consider what they know about the topic and record a number of responses.

3. Whip around the class in a fast-paced and structured manner (e.g. down rows, around tables), allowing as many students as possible to share an idea in 15 seconds or less.

4. After several contributions, if there tends to be repetition, ask students to point out similarities in responses rather than simply stating that their idea has already been mentioned.

Strategies for Improving Student Comprehension *(continued)*

Strategy 9: Numbered Heads

Purpose: To engage students in active class discussions

How to Do It

1. Seat students in groups of four and number off one through four (if possible, combine established partners to form groups of four).

2. After giving the discussion prompt, allow students to discuss possible responses for an established amount of time.

3. Remind students to pay close attention to the comments of each group member because you will be randomly selecting one student to represent the best thinking of the entire group.

4. Call a number (one through four), and ask all students with that number to raise their hands, ready to respond to the topic at hand in a teacher-directed, whole-class discussion.

5. Add comments, extend key ideas, ask follow-up questions, and make connections between individual student's comments to create a lively whole-class discussion.

6. Provide any summary comments required to ensure that all students understand critical points.

Strategy 10: Think-Write-Pair–Share

Purpose: To engage students in responding to instruction

How to Do It

1. **Think**—Students listen while the teacher poses a question or a task related to the reading or classroom discussion. The level of questions should vary from lower level literal to higher order inferential or analytical.

2. **Write**—Provide quiet thinking or writing time for students to deal with the question, and go back to the text or review notes. Have students record their ideas in their notebooks.

3. **Pair/Share**—Cue students to find a partner and discuss their responses, noting similarities and differences. Teach students to encourage one another to clarify and justify responses.

4. Randomly call on students to share during a unified class discussion after they have all rehearsed answers with their partners.

5. Invite any volunteers to contribute additional ideas and points of view to the discussion after calling on a reasonable number of students randomly.

6. Direct students to go back to notes and add any important information garnered during the partner and class discussions.

Strategy 11: Give One, Get One

Purpose: To foster independent reflection and peer interaction prior to a unified class discussion

How to Do It

1. Pose a thought-provoking question or a concrete task to the class.

2. Allow three to five minutes of quiet time for students to consider what they may already know about the topic and jot down a number of potential responses.

3. Ask students to place a check mark next to the two or three ideas that they perceive as their strongest and then draw a line after their final idea to separate their ideas from those that they will gather from classmates.

4. Give students a set amount of time (about eight to ten minutes) to get up from their seats and share ideas with classmates. After finding a partner, the two students exchange papers and first quietly read each other's ideas. They discuss the ideas briefly, then select one idea from their partner's list and add it to their own, making sure to accurately copy the idea alongside the partner's name.

5. When one exchange is completed, students move on to interact with a new partner.

6. At the end of the exchange period, facilitate a unified class discussion. Call on a volunteer to share one new idea acquired from a conversation partner. The student whose idea has just been reported then shares the next idea, gleaned from a different conversation partner.

Professional Development

For more information about these strategies, see the end of each chapter's Interleaf.

Western Hemisphere Skills Scope and Sequence

Prentice Hall *World Studies* contains a comprehensive program of core skills. Each skill is taught in every book of the series. A Target Reading Skill is located at the beginning of each chapter and expanded upon in each section within the chapter. Core skills are also taught either in the "Skills for Life Activity" in the Student Edition, or in a "Skills Mini Lesson" in the Teacher's Edition. In addition, worksheets for the students' use in completing each skill are located in the All-in-One Teaching Resources. The chart below lists the skills covered in *Prentice Hall World Studies: Western Hemisphere* and the chapter where each skill is taught.

Western Hemisphere Analysis Skills	SE	TE
Analyzing Graphic Data	Chs. 2, 7, 8, 9	Chs. 2, 3, 7, 8, 9, 12
Analyzing Images		Chs. 2, 6, 11
Analyzing Primary Sources		Chs. 5, 7, 12
Clarifying Meaning	Chs. 1, 7, 12	Chs. 1, 7, 12
Comparing and Contrasting	Chs. 3, 9, 15, 16	Chs. 2, 3, 9, 11, 15, 16
Decision Making		Chs. 3, 8, 15
Distinguishing Fact and Opinion	Ch. 13	Chs. 4, 9, 13
Drawing Inferences and Conclusions	Ch. 14	Chs. 1, 8, 14
Identifying Cause and Effect/Making Predictions	Chs. 5, 11, 13	Chs. 2, 5, 6, 7, 13
Identifying Frame of Reference and Point of View	Chs. 3, 6	Chs. 3, 6, 16
Identifying Main Ideas/Summarizing	Chs. 5, 7, 8, 12, 15	Chs. 3, 5, 7, 8, 12, 13, 15
Making Valid Generalizations	Ch. 4	Chs. 4, 6, 11
Problem Solving		Chs. 5, 7, 14
Recognizing Bias and Propaganda		Chs. 4, 10, 12
Sequencing	Chs. 4, 12	Chs. 1, 4, 10, 12
Supporting a Position		Chs. 5, 10, 15
Synthesizing Information	Ch. 16	Chs. 4, 9, 16
Transferring Information From One Medium to Another		Chs. 2, 7, 16
Using the Cartographer's Tools		Chs. 2, 9, 14
Using Context	Chs. 2, 10, 14	Chs. 2, 10, 14
Using the Reading Process	Chs. 6, 11	Chs. 6, 11
Using Reliable Information	Ch. 1	Chs. 1, 8, 14
Using Special-Purpose Maps	Chs. 3, 11	Chs. 3, 9, 11

Pacing Options

World Studies offers many aids to help you plan your instruction time, whether regular class periods or block scheduling. Section-by-section lesson plans for each chapter include suggested times, based on the a year-long course configuration below. Teacher Express CD-ROM will help you manage your time electronically.

Pacing Options		Year-long unit	Block Schedule
Chapter 1	Section 1	6	3
	Section 2	5	2.5
Chapter 2	Section 1	2	1
	Section 2	2.5	1.25
	Section 3	4	2
	Section 4	4.5	2.25
Chapter 3	Section 1	2	1
	Section 2	4	2
	Section 3	2	1
	Section 4	6.5	3.25
Chapter 4	Section 1	2	1
	Section 2	4.5	2.25
	Section 3	4.5	2.25
Chapter 5	Section 1	2	1
	Section 2	4	2
	Section 3	4.5	2.25
Chapter 6	Section 1	7	3.5
	Section 2	2	1
	Section 3	3.5	1.75
Chapter 7	Section 1	2	1
	Section 2	2	1
	Section 3	2	1
	Section 4	3.5	1.75
	Section 5	4	2
Chapter 8	Section 1	3.5	1.75
	Section 2	2	1
	Section 3	4	2
Chapter 9	Section 1	3	1.5
	Section 2	3.5	1.75
	Section 3	2	1
	Section 4	4	2
Chapter 10	Section 1	2.5	1.25
	Section 2	1.5	.75
	Section 3	1.5	.75
	Section 4	3	1.5
	Section 5	3.5	1.75

Pacing Options		Year-long unit	Block Schedule
Chapter 11	Section 1	5.5	2.75
	Section 2	2.5	1.25
	Section 3	4	2
Chapter 12	Section 1	1.5	.75
	Section 2	1.5	.75
	Section 3	1.5	.75
	Section 4	3	1.5
	Section 5	3.5	1.75
Chapter 13	Section 1	3	1.5
	Section 2	1.5	.75
	Section 3	3.5	1.75
Chapter 14	Section 1	2.5	1.25
	Section 2	3	1.5
	Section 3	3.5	1.75
Chapter 15	Section 1	3.5	1.75
	Section 2	1.5	.75
	Section 3	4	2
Chapter 16	Section 1	3	1.5
	Section 2	1.5	.75
	Section 3	3	1.5
	Section 4	3.5	1.75
Total Number of Days		**180 days**	**90 blocks**

Correlation to *Geography for Life,* the National Geography Standards

On the following pages, *Prentice Hall World Studies: Western Hemisphere* is correlated with *Geography for Life,* the National Geography Standards. These standards were prepared in response to the Goals 2000, Educate America Act, by the Geography Education Standards Project. Participating in the project were the American Geographical Society, the Association of American Geographers, the National Council for Geographic Education, and the National Geographic Society. Concepts and skills contained in the Geography Standards are incorporated throughout the program. This correlation displays places where the standards are directly addressed.

Standard	Western Hemisphere
The World in Spatial Terms	
Standard 1 Use maps and other geographic representations, tools, and technologies to acquire, process, and report information from a spatial perspective.	MapMaster Skills Handbook, 1:1–2, 2:1–4, 3:1, 3:2, 4:2, 5:1–3, 6:1–3, 7:1, 7:2, 7:4, 7:5, 8:1, 9:1–4, 10:1–5, 11:1–3, 12:1, 12:2, 12:3, 12:4, 14:1–3, 15:1–3, 16:1–4, Review and Assessment: Chs. 1–10
Standard 2 Use mental maps to organize information about people, places, and environments in a spatial context.	MapMaster Skills Handbook, 2:4, 3:1, 6:1, 6:3, 11:3, 14:1, Skills for Life: Ch. 3, Review and Assessment: Ch. 1
Standard 3 Analyze the spatial organization of people, places, and environments on Earth's surface.	MapMaster Skills Handbook, 1:1–2, 2:2, 2:3, 2:4, 3:1, 3:2, 3:3, 4:2, 5:2, 6:1–3, 7:1–5, 8:1, 9:1–4, 10:1–5, 11:1–3, 14:1, 14:2, 15:3, 16:1, Skills for Life: Ch. 3, Review and Assessment: Chs. 1, 2, 4, 6–10
Places and Regions	
Standard 4 Understand the physical and human characteristics of places.	MapMaster Skills Handbook, 1:1, 2:1–4, 3:1–4, 4:1, 4:2, 5:2, 5:3, 6:1–3, 7:1–5, 8:1–3, 9:1–4, 10:1–5, 11:1, 11:2, 14:1, 14:2, 16:1–4, Country Databanks: Chs. 9, 10, 14, 15, 16, Skills for Life: Ch. 2, Review and Assessment: Chs. 2–10
Standard 5 Understand that people create regions to interpret Earth's complexity.	MapMaster Skills Handbook, 1:1–2, 2:1, 2:4, 3:1, 3:3, 3:4, 6:1, 6:2, 9:1–4, 10:1–5, 11:1, 11:2, 14:1, 15:3, 16:2, Review and Assessment: Chs. 1, 3, 6–10
Standard 6 Understand how culture and experience influence people's perception of places and regions.	MapMaster Skills Handbook, 2:1, 3:1–4, 4:1–3, 5:2, 5:3, 7:1–5, 8:1–3, 9:1–4, 10:1–5, 13:1–3, 14:1–3, 15:1–3, 16:1–4, Review and Assessment: Chs. 3, 4, 5, 7, 8, 10
Physical Systems	
Standard 7 Understand the physical processes that shape the patterns of Earth's surface.	2:1–4, 3:1, 6:1–3, 7:1, 8:2, 9:3, 9:4, 10:1–5, 11:1–3. 12:5, 16:1, 16:2, Review and Assessment: Chs. 2, 9
Standard 8 Understand the characteristics and spatial distribution of ecosystems on Earth's surface.	MapMaster Skills Handbook, 2:2, 2:3, 2:4, 3:1, 5:1–3, 6:1–3, 7:5, 9:2, 10:1–5, 11:1–3, 4:3, 6:1, 6:2, 6:3 Review and Assessment: Chs. 2, 5, 6

Correlation to *Geography for Life*, the National Geography Standards *(continued)*

Standard	Western Hemisphere
Human Systems	
Standard 9 Understand the characteristics, distribution, and migration of human populations on Earth's surface.	MapMaster Skills Handbook, 3:1–4, 4:1–3, 5:1–3, 7:1, 7:2, 7:3, 7:4, 8:1–3, 9:1, 9:2, 9:4, 10:1–5, 12:1, 12:2, 12:3, 12:5, 13:1–3, 14:1, 15:1–3, 16:1–4, Review and Assessment: Chs. 3, 4, 8, 9, 10
Standard 10 Understand the characteristics, distribution, and complexity of Earth's cultural mosaics.	MapMaster Skills Handbook, 3:1, 3:2, 3:3, 4:1–3, 5:2, 7:1, 7:4, 8:1–3, 9:1, 10:1–5, 12:1, 12:2, 12:3, 13: 1–3, 14:1, 14:2, 15:1–3, 16:1–4, Review and Assessment: Chs. 3, 4, 5, 8, 10
Standard 11 Understand the patterns and networks of economic interdependence on Earth's surface.	MapMaster Skills Handbook, 3:1, 3:2, 3:3, 4:3, 5:1–3, 6:3, 7:3, 7:4, 7:5, 8:1, 9:1–4, 10:2, 10:3, 10:4, 11:3, 12:5, 13:1, 13:3, 14:1, 14:3, 15:1, 15:3, 16:1, 16:3, 16:4, Review and Assessment: Chs. 3, 5, 7, 8, 9, 10
Standard 12 Understand the processes, patterns, and functions of human settlement.	MapMaster Skills Handbook, 3:1, 3:2, 4:1, 4:2, 5:2, 7:1, 7:2, 7:3, 7:4, 8:1–3, 9:1–4, 10:1–5, 12:1, 12:2, 12:3, 12:5, 13:1–3, 14:1, 15:3, 16:1–4, Review and Assessment: Chs. 3, 4, 5, 7, 8, 9, 10
Standard 13 Understand how the forces of cooperation and conflict among people influence division and control of Earth's surface.	3:1, 3:2, 3:3, 4:1–3, 5:1–3, 6:1, 7:1, 7:2, 7:3, 7:4, 8:1–3, 9:4, 10:1, 10:2, 10:3, 10:4, 12:1–5, 14:2, 14:3, 15:1–3, 16:1, Review and Assessment: Chs. 3, 4, 5, 7, 8, 9, 10
Environment and Society	
Standard 14 Understand how human actions modify the physical environment.	3:1, 3:2, 3:3, 4:1, 5:1–3, 6:1, 7:5, 8:3, 9:4, 10:2, 10:3, 10:4, 12:5, 14:1, 14:3, 16:1, 16:3, Review and Assessment: Chs. 3, 5, 7
Standard 15 Understand how physical systems affect human systems.	2:2, 2:3, 2:4, 3:1, 4:1, 5:1–3, 6:1–3, 7:5, 8:1, 9:2, 9:4, 10:2, 10:3, 10:4, 10:5, 11:1–3, 13:3, 16:2, 16:3, Review and Assessment: Chs. 2, 3, 4, 5, 6, 7, 9, 10
Standard 16 Understand the changes that occur in the meaning, use, distribution, and importance of resources.	2:2, 3:1, 3:2, 3:3, 4:1, 4:3, 5:1–3, 6:1–3. 7:2, 7:4, 7:5, 8:1, 8:2, 9:1–4, 10:1–5, 11:1, 11:3, 12:5, 16:3, 16:4, Review and Assessment: Chs. 3, 4, 5, 6, 7, 9
The Uses of Geography	
Standard 17 Understand how to apply geography to interpret the past.	MapMaster Skills Handbook, 1:1, 2:2, 3:1, 3:2, 3:3, 4:1–3, 5:1–3, 6:1, 7:1, 7:2, 7:3, 7:1, 8:1, 8:3, 8:4, 10:1, 10:2, 10:3, 10:4, 12:1, 12:2, 12:3, 13:2, 15:3, 16:2, 16:3, 16:4, Review and Assessment: Chs. 3, 4, 5, 7, 9
Standard 18 Understand how to apply geography to interpret the present and plan for the future.	MapMaster Skills Handbook, 3:1, 3:2, 3:3, 4:2, 4:3, 5:1–3, 6:2, 6:3, 7:5, 9:1–4, 10:1–5, 11:3, 13:1, 14:1, 15:1–3, 16:1, 16:3, 16:4, Review and Assessment: Chs. 3, 4, 5, 6, 9, 10

Correlation to the NCSS Curriculum Standards

On the following pages *Prentice Hall World Studies: Western Hemisphere* is correlated with *Expectations of Excellence*, the Curriculum Standards for Social Studies. These standards were developed by the National Council for the Social Studies to address overall curriculum design and comprehensive student performance expectations.

Standard	Western Hemisphere
Performance Expectations 1: Culture	
• compare similarities and differences in the ways groups, societies, and cultures meet human needs and concerns • explain how information and experiences may be interpreted by people from diverse cultural perspectives and frames of reference • explain and give examples of how language, literature, the arts, architecture, other artifacts, traditions, beliefs, values, and behaviors contribute to the development and transmission of culture • explain why individuals and groups respond differently to their physical and social environments and/or changes to them on the basis of shared assumptions, values, and beliefs • articulate the implications of cultural diversity, as well as cohesion, within and across groups	MapMaster Skills Handbook, 4:1–3, 5:2, 7:1–5, 8:1–3, 9:1–4, 10:1–5, 12:1, 12:2, 12:3, 13:1–3, 14:2, 15:1, 15:3, 16:2, Review and Assessment: Chs. 4, 5, 7, 8, 10
Performance Expectations 2: Time, Continuity, and Change	
• demonstrate an understanding that different scholars may describe the same event or situation in different ways but must provide reasons or evidence for their view • identify and use key concepts such as chronology, causality, change, conflict, and complexity to explain, analyze, and show connections among patterns of historical change and continuity • identify and describe selected historical periods and patterns of change within and across cultures • identify and use processes important to reconstructing and reinterpreting the past • develop critical sensitivities regarding attitudes, values, and behaviors of people in different historical contexts • use knowledge of facts and concepts drawn from history, along with methods of historical inquiry, to inform decision-making about and action-taking on public issues	2:2, 3:1, 3:2, 3:3, 4:1, 4:3, 5:2, 7:1–5, 8:3, 8:4, 9:2, 10:1–5, 12:1–5. 14:2, Review and Assessment: Chs. 3, 4, 7, 8, 9, 10
Performance Expectations 3: People, Places, and Environment	
• elaborate mental maps of locales, regions, and the world that demonstrate understanding of relative location, direction, size, and shape • create, interpret, use, and distinguish various representations of the earth • use appropriate resources, data sources, and geographic tools to generate, manipulate, and interpret information • estimate distance, calculate scale, and distinguish geographic relationships • locate and describe varying landforms and geographic features and explain their relationship with the ecosystem • describe physical system changes and identify geographic patterns associated with them • describe how people create places that reflect cultural values and ideals • examine, interpret, and analyze physical and cultural patterns and their interactions • describe ways that historical events have been influenced by, and have influenced, physical and human geographic factors in local, regional, national, and global settings • observe and speculate about social and economic effects of environmental changes and crises resulting from natural phenomena • propose, compare, and evaluate alternative uses of land and resources in communities, regions, nations, and the world	MapMaster Skills Handbook, 1:1–2, 2:1–4, 3:1, 3:2, 3:3, 4:1–3, 5:1–3, 6:1–3, 7:1, 7:2, 7:4, 7:5, 8:1–3, 9:1–4, 10:1–5, 11:1–3, 12:5, 13:1, 13:3, 14:1, 14:3, 15:1–3, 16:1, 16:2, 16:3, Skills for Life: Chs. 2, 3, 6, Review and Assessment: Chs. 1– 10

Correlation to the NCSS Curriculum Standards *(continued)*

Standard	Western Hemisphere
Performance Expectations 4: Individual Development and Identity	
• relate personal changes to social, cultural, and historical contexts • describe personal connections to place—as associated with community, nation, and world • describe the ways family, gender, ethnicity, nationality, and institutional affiliations contribute to personal identity • relate such factors as physical endowment and capabilities, learning, motivation, personality, perception, and behavior to individual development • identify and describe ways regional, ethnic, and national cultures influence individuals' daily lives • identify and describe the influence of perception, attitudes, values, and beliefs on personal identity • identify and interpret examples of stereotyping, conformity, and altruism • work independently and cooperatively to accomplish goals	3:1, 3:2, 3:3, 4:1–3, 5:2, 5:3, 7:1, 7:2, 7:4, 8:1–3, 9:1–4, 10:1, 12:1, 12:2, 13:1–3, 14:1, 15:1–3, 16:2, Skills for Life: Ch. 6, Review and Assessment: Chs. 3, 4, 5, 6, 7, 8, 9
Performance Expectations 5: Individuals, Groups, & Institutions	
• demonstrate an understanding of concepts such as role, status, and social class in describing interactions of individuals and social groups • analyze group and institutional influences on people, events, and elements of culture • describe the various forms institutions take and the interactions of people with institutions • identify and analyze examples of tensions between expressions of individuality and group or institutional efforts to promote social conformity • identify and describe examples of tensions between belief systems and government policies and laws • describe the role of institutions in furthering both continuity and change • apply knowledge of how groups and institutions work to meet individual needs and promote the common good	3:3, 3:4, 4:1, 4:2, 7:1–5, 8:1–3, 10:1–5, 12:3, 12:5, 14:2, 14:3, 15:1, 15:2, 16:1, Review and Assessment: Chs. 3, 4, 7, 8, 10
Performance Expectations 6: Power, Authority, and Governance	
• examine persistent issues involving the rights, roles, and status of the individual in relation to general welfare • describe the purpose of government and how its powers are acquired, used, and justified • analyze and explain ideas and governmental mechanisms to meet needs and wants of citizens, regulate territory, manage conflict, and establish order and security • describe the ways nations and organizations respond to forces of unity and diversity affecting order and security • identify and describe the basic features of the political system in the United States, and identify representative leaders from various levels and branches of government • explain conditions, actions, and motivations that contribute to conflict and cooperation within and among nations • describe and analyze the role of technology as it contributes to or helps resolve conflicts • explain how power, role, status, and justice influence the examination of persistent issues and social problems • give examples and explain how governments attempt to achieve their stated ideals at home and abroad	3:3, 3:4, 4:1, 7:1–5, 8:1–3, 9:1, 9:2, 9:4, 10:1–5, 12:1–5, 14:1, 14:2, 14:3, 15:1–3, 16:1–4, Review and Assessment: Chs. 3, 7, 8, 10

Correlation to the NCSS Curriculum Standards *(continued)*

Standard	Western Hemisphere
Performance Expectation 7: Production, Distribution, and Consumption	
• give examples of ways that economic systems structure choices about how goods and services are to be produced and distributed • describe the role that supply and demand, prices, incentives, and profits play in determining what is produced and distributed in a competitive market system • explain differences between private and public goods and services • describe a range of examples of the various institutions that make up economic systems • describe the role of specialization and exchange in the economic process • explain and illustrate how values and beliefs influence different economic decisions • differentiate among various forms of exchange and money • compare basic economic systems according to who determines what is produced, distributed, and consumed • use economic concepts to help explain historical and current events in local, national, or global concepts • use economic reasoning to compare different proposals for dealing with contemporary social issues	3:3, 4:3, 5:1–3, 6:3, 7:1–5, 8:1, 9:1–4, 10:2, 10:3, 10:4, 11:3, 12:5, 16:1–4, Review and Assessment: Chs. 3, 5, 7, 8, 9, 10
Performance Expectation 8: Science, Technology, and Society	
• examine and describe the influence of culture on scientific and technological choices and advancement • show through specific examples how science and technology have changed peoples' perceptions of their social and natural world • describe examples in which values, beliefs, and attitudes have been influenced by new scientific and technological knowledge • explain the need for laws and policies to govern scientific and technological applications • seek reasonable and ethical solutions to problems that arise when scientific advancements and social norms or values come into conflict	1:2, 2:1–4, 3:1, 3:3, 4:1, 4:3, 5:1–3, 6:1, 6:3, 7:2, 7:3, 7:4, 7:5, 9:2, 9:3, 8:4, 10:2, 10:3, 10:4, 12:5, 13:1–3, 14:1, 14:3, 16:1, 16:4, Review and Assessment: Chs. 2, 3, 4, 5, 9, 10
Performance Expectation 9: Global Connections	
• describe instances in which language, art, music, and belief systems, and other cultural elements can facilitate global understanding or cause misunderstanding • analyze examples of conflict, cooperation, and interdependence among groups, societies, and nations • describe and analyze the effects of changing technologies on the global community • explore the causes, consequences, and possible solutions to persistent contemporary and emerging global interests • describe and explain the relationships and tensions between national sovereignty and global interests • demonstrate understanding of concerns, standards, issues, and conflicts related to universal human rights • identify and describe the roles of international and multinational organizations	3:1, 3:2, 3:3, 4:1–3, 5:1–3, 6:3, 7:1–5, 8:1–3, 10:1–5, 12:3, 12:5, 13:1–3, 14:1–3, 15:1–3, 16:1, 16:3, 16:4, Review and Assessment: Chs. 3, 4, 5, 7, 8, 10

Correlation to the NCSS Curriculum Standards *(continued)*

Standard	Western Hemisphere
Performance Expectation 10: Civic Ideals and Practices	
• examine the origins and continuing influence of key ideals of the democratic republican form of government, such as individual human dignity, liberty, justice, equality, and rule of law • identify and interpret sources and examples of the rights and responsibilities of citizens • locate, access, analyze, organize, and apply information about selected public issues—recognizing and explaining multiple points of view • practice forms of civic discussion and participation consistent with the ideals of citizens in a democratic republic • explain and analyze various forms of citizen action that influence public policy decisions • identify and explain the roles of formal and informal political actors in influencing and shaping public policy and decision-making • analyze the influence of diverse forms of public opinion on the development of public policy and decision-making • analyze the effectiveness of selected public policies and citizen behaviors in realizing the stated ideals of a democratic republican form of government • explain the relationship between policy statements and action plans used to address issues of public concern • examine strategies designed to strengthen the "common good," which consider a range of options for citizen action	4:1–3, 5:1, 5:3, 7:1–5, 9:4, 10:1, 10:5, 12:3, 12:4, 12:5, 14:2, 14:3, 15:1–3, Review and Assessment: Chs. 4, 7

Objective

■ Learn how to read nonfiction critically by analyzing an author's purpose, distinguishing between facts and opinions, identifying evidence, and evaluating credibility.

Prepare to Read

Build Background Knowledge L2

Write the phrase "Don't believe everything you read" on the board. Ask students to brainstorm examples that illustrate the saying. Provide a few simple examples to get them started (*tall tales, advertisements.*)

Instruct

Reading Informational Texts L2

Guided Instruction

■ Tell students that they must actively evaluate the information in most of the nonfiction they read.

■ Read the sample editorial on this page aloud. Tell students that an editorial usually expresses a person's opinion. Ask students to consider why the author wrote this editorial. (*The author expresses the opinion that the proposal to build the new shopping center should have been approved.*) Ask **How might this purpose affect what the editorial says?** (*The author may present information in the best possible light to prove his or her belief.*)

■ Another important step in evaluating nonfiction is distinguishing between facts and opinions. Ask each student to write one fact and one opinion, on any subject, in their notebooks. Use the Idea Wave strategy (TE, p. T35) to get students to share their facts and opinions. If students have incorrectly categorized examples, help them to see why.

Reading Informational Texts

Reading a magazine, an Internet page, or a textbook is not the same as reading a novel. The purpose of reading nonfiction texts is to acquire new information. On page M18 you'll read about some 🔄 **Target Reading Skills** that you'll have a chance to practice as you read this textbook. Here we'll focus on a few skills that will help you read nonfiction with a more critical eye.

Analyze the Author's Purpose

Different types of materials are written with different purposes in mind. For example, a textbook is written to teach students information about a subject. The purpose of a technical manual is to teach someone how to use something, such as a computer. A newspaper editorial might be written to persuade the reader to accept a particular point of view. A writer's purpose influences how the material is presented. Sometimes an author states his or her purpose directly. More often, the purpose is only suggested, and you must use clues to identify the author's purpose.

Distinguish Between Facts and Opinions

It's important when reading informational texts to read actively and to distinguish between fact and opinion. A fact can be proven or disproven. An opinion cannot—it is someone's personal viewpoint or evaluation.

For example, the editorial pages in a newspaper offer opinions on topics that are currently in the news. You need to read newspaper editorials with an eye for bias and faulty logic. For example, the newspaper editorial at the right shows factual statements in blue and opinion statements in red. The underlined words are examples of highly charged words. They reveal bias on the part of the writer.

> More than 5,000 people voted last week in favor of building a new shopping center, but the opposition won out. The margin of victory is irrelevant. Those radical voters who opposed the center are obviously self-serving elitists who do not care about anyone but themselves.
>
> This month's unemployment figure for our area is 10 percent, which represents an increase of about 5 percent over the figure for this time last year. These figures mean unemployment is getting worse. But the people who voted against the mall probably do not care about creating new jobs.

■ Tell students that identifying evidence is another way to read nonfiction critically. Ask students to look again at the facts highlighted in the sample editorial. **Does the evidence presented in these facts convince you that building a new shopping center is a good idea?** (*The evidence is incomplete—the author has not shown that the new shopping center would solve the unemployment problem.*)

■ Tell students that analyzing an author's purpose, distinguishing between facts and opinions, and identifying evidence are all ways to evaluate the credibility of the author. Tell students to look at the checklist for evaluating Web sites. Ask students to think about Web sites they have visited. Do those Web sites pass the checklist's test? Why or why not?

Identify Evidence

Before you accept an author's conclusion, you need to make sure that the author has based the conclusion on enough evidence and on the right kind of evidence. An author may present a series of facts to support a claim, but the facts may not tell the whole story. For example, what evidence does the author of the newspaper editorial on the previous page provide to support his claim that the new shopping center would create more jobs? Is it possible that the shopping center might have put many small local businesses out of business, thus increasing unemployment rather than decreasing it?

Evaluate Credibility

Whenever you read informational texts, you need to assess the credibility of the author. This is especially true of sites you may visit on the Internet. All Internet sources are not equally reliable. Here are some questions to ask yourself when evaluating the credibility of a Web site.

- ☐ Is the Web site created by a respected organization, a discussion group, or an individual?
- ☐ Does the Web site creator include his or her name as well as credentials and the sources he or she used to write the material?
- ☐ Is the information on the site balanced or biased?
- ☐ Can you verify the information using two other sources?
- ☐ Is there a date telling when the Web site was created or last updated?

Independent Practice

Ask students to bring in an editorial from the local newspaper, or distribute copies of an appropriate editorial. Ask students to critically assess their editorial by analyzing the author's purpose; underlining facts and circling opinions in the text of the editorial; summarizing the evidence presented in the editorial; and finally drawing a conclusion about the credibility of the editorial.

Monitor Progress

Pair students and have them share their editorial assessments. Ask them to explain the reasoning behind the conclusions they drew about the editorial's credibility. Circulate and offer assistance as needed.

Assess and Reteach

Assess Progress   L2
Collect students' papers and review their assessments.

Reteach   L1
If students are struggling, tell them to approach the task by asking themselves the following questions as they read a piece of nonfiction: **Why** did the author write this? **How** has the author made his or her points, using facts or opinions? **What** evidence has the author used to support the main idea? **Who** is the author, and what sources has he or she used?

Extend   L3
To extend this lesson, tell students to turn to the Table of Contents in the Student Edition and pick a chapter name that intrigues them. Then, ask them to search the Internet and find two Web sites about the chapter's topic. Finally, ask them to use the checklist on this page to evaluate each Web site and compare the two in terms of credibility.

Differentiated Instruction

For Advanced Readers   L3
Draw students' attention to the checklist under the heading "Evaluate Credibility." Ask students to create a similar checklist for analyzing an author's purpose, distinguishing between fact and opinion, and identifying evidence.

For Special Needs Students   L1
If special needs students are having trouble making the distinction between facts and opinions, partner them with more proficient students to do the *Distinguishing Fact and Opinion* lesson on the Social Studies Skill Tutor CD-ROM.

⊙ *Distinguishing Fact and Opinion,* **Social Studies Skill Tutor CD-ROM**

Objective

- Use a systematic approach to write narrative, persuasive, expository, and research essays.

Prepare to Read

Build Background Knowledge L2

As a group, brainstorm all the ways that people use writing to communicate. Start with these examples: labeling a folder, writing an email. Conduct an Idea Wave (TE, p. T35) and write students' responses on the board. Tell them that people often write to express ideas or information. Give them *Four Purposes for Writing* and tell them to keep it in their notebooks for future reference.

All in One United States and Canada Teaching Resources, *Four Purposes for Writing,* p. 5

Instruct

Narrative Essays L2

Guided Instruction

- Tell students that narrative essays tell a story about their own experiences. Discuss the steps listed in the Student Edition.

- Choose an event in your own life (or invent one) such as visiting friends in another city. Write your topic on the board and model how to list details. *(what the trip was like, what you did while you were there, what your friends are like)* Cross out the least interesting details.

- Think aloud as you form your topic into a sentence that conveys the main idea of your essay.

- Tell students that you will go on to flesh out the details into a colorful story.

Independent Practice

- Tell students to write a narrative essay about a recent positive experience. Have student pairs brainstorm topics.

Writing for Social Studies

Writing is one of the most powerful communication tools you will ever use. You will use it to share your thoughts and ideas with others. Research shows that writing about what you read actually helps you learn new information and ideas. A systematic approach to writing—including prewriting, drafting, revising, and proofing—can help you write better, whether you're writing an essay or a research report.

Narrative Essays

Writing that tells a story about a personal experience

1 Select and Narrow Your Topic

A narrative is a story. In social studies, it might be a narrative essay about how an event affected you or your family.

2 Gather Details

Brainstorm a list of details you'd like to include in your narrative.

3 Write a First Draft

Start by writing a simple opening sentence that conveys the main idea of your essay. Continue by writing a colorful story that has interesting details. Write a conclusion that sums up the significance of the event or situation described in your essay.

4 Revise and Proofread

Check to make sure you have not begun too many sentences with the word *I*. Replace general words with more colorful ones.

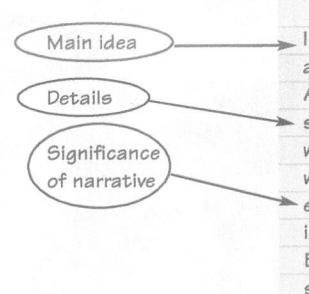

Main idea
Details
Significance of narrative

In my last year of college, I volunteered for an organization called Amigos De Las Americas (Friends of the Americas). I was sent to a remote village in Brazil and worked with villagers to improve the community's water supply and sanitation systems. The experience made me realize I wanted to work in the field of public health. When I went to Brazil, I never imagined what an incredible sense of purpose it would add to my life.

- Give students *Writing to Describe* to help them write their essays. After they have written the body of their essay, give them *Writing the Conclusion* to help them complete it.

  All in One United States and Canada Teaching Resources, *Writing to Describe,* p. 6; *Writing the Conclusion,* p. 7

Monitor Progress

Have students share their drafts with their partners. Give them *Using the Revision Checklist* and ask them to review their partners' papers. Urge them to provide constructive criticism and suggestions for improvement.

All in One United States and Canada Teaching Resources, *Using the Revision Checklist,* p. 8

Persuasive Essays

Writing that supports an opinion or position

1 **Select and Narrow Your Topic**
Choose a topic that provokes an argument and has at least two sides. Choose a side. Decide which argument will appeal most to your audience and persuade them to understand your point of view.

2 **Gather Evidence**
Create a chart that states your position at the top and then lists the pros and cons for your position below, in two columns. Predict and address the strongest arguments against your stand.

3 **Write a First Draft**
Write a strong thesis statement that clearly states your position. Continue by presenting the strongest arguments in favor of your position and acknowledging and refuting opposing arguments.

4 **Revise and Proofread**
Check to make sure you have made a logical argument and that you have not oversimplified the argument.

Main Idea → It is vital to vote in elections. When people vote, they tell public officials how to run the government. Not every proposal is carried
Supporting (pro) argument → out; however, **politicians do their best to listen to what the majority of people want.**
Opposing (con) argument →
Transition words → Therefore, **every vote is important.**

Persuasive Essays L2

Guided Instruction
- Tell students that the purpose of writing a persuasive essay is to convince other people to believe your point of view. However, you must use solid, reliable evidence and arguments to make your points.
- Model the thought process by pointing out how the writer presents his or her argument in the paragraph on this page.

Independent Practice
- Tell students to write a persuasive essay about a topic that is important to them. Have students form pairs. One student in each pair should state his or her position. The other student then shares opposing arguments, which the first student should refute in his or her essay. Then the pairs switch roles.
- Give students *Writing to Persuade* to help them write their essays.

   All in One **United States and Canada Teaching Resources,** *Writing to Persuade,* p. 9

Monitor Progress
If students are having trouble structuring their paragraphs, give them *Structuring Paragraphs* and *Creating Paragraph Outlines* to provide a framework.

   All in One **United States and Canada Teaching Resources,** *Structuring Paragraphs,* p. 10; *Creating Paragraph Outlines,* p. 11

Differentiated Instruction

For Less Proficient Readers L1

Tell students to use looping to help them focus on a topic. Have them follow these steps: Write freely on your topic for about five minutes. Read what you have written and circle the most important idea. Write for five minutes on the circled idea. Repeat the process until you isolate a topic narrow enough to cover well in a short essay.

Expository Essays L2

Guided Instruction
- Read the steps for writing expository essays with students.
- Tell students that the graphic organizer example given on the Student Edition page is for a cause-and-effect expository essay. They might use a Venn diagram for a compare-and-contrast essay and a flow-chart for a problem-and-solution essay.
- Model how to create a topic sentence from the information in the cause-and-effect graphic organizer. *(Sample topic sentence: In Mexico, several factors are causing rural families to move from the countryside to the city.)*
- Create a brief outline showing how you will organize the paragraphs in your essay.

Independent Practice
Tell students to write an expository essay based on a recent current event. Have them brainstorm ideas with a partner, then choose which type of essay best suits their topic (cause and effect, compare and contrast, or problem and solution.) Give them *Writing to Inform and Explain* and *Gathering Details* to help them start drafting their essays.

All in One **United States and Canada Teaching Resources,** *Writing to Inform and Explain,* p. 12; *Gathering Details,* p. 13

Monitor Progress
If students are struggling with their essays, give them *Writing a Cause-and-Effect Essay* or *Writing a Problem-and-Solution Essay.*

All in One **United States and Canada Teaching Resources,** *Writing a Cause-and-Effect Essay,* p. 14; *Writing a Problem-and-Solution Essay,* p. 15

Research Papers L2

Guided Instruction
Go over the steps for writing a research paper carefully. Ask students to share questions about the process, using the Idea Wave strategy (TE, p. T35). Answer any questions they might have.

Reading and Writing Handbook

Expository Essays

Writing that explains a process, compares and contrasts, explains causes and effects, or explores solutions to a problem

1 Identify and Narrow Your Topic
Expository writing is writing that explains something in detail. It might explain the similarities and differences between two or more subjects (compare and contrast). It might explain how one event causes another (cause and effect). Or it might explain a problem and describe a solution.

2 Gather Evidence
Create a graphic organizer that identifies details to include in your essay.

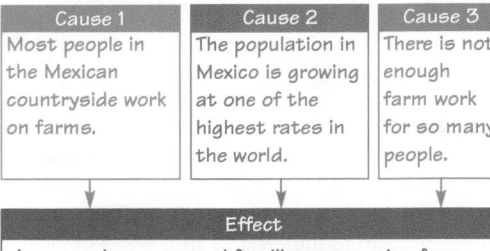

Cause 1	Cause 2	Cause 3
Most people in the Mexican countryside work on farms.	The population in Mexico is growing at one of the highest rates in the world.	There is not enough farm work for so many people.

Effect
As a result, many rural families are moving from the countryside to live in Mexico City.

3 Write Your First Draft
Write a topic sentence and then organize the essay around your similarities and differences, causes and effects, or problem and solutions. Be sure to include convincing details, facts, and examples.

4 Revise and Proofread

Research Papers

Writing that presents research about a topic

1 Narrow Your Topic
Choose a topic you're interested in and make sure that it is not too broad. For example, instead of writing a report on Panama, write about the construction of the Panama Canal.

2 Acquire Information
Locate several sources of information about the topic from the library or the Internet. For each resource, create a source index card like the one at the right. Then take notes using an index card for each detail or subtopic. On the card, note which source the information was taken from. Use quotation marks when you copy the exact words from a source.

Source #1
McCullough, David. *The Path Between the Seas: The Creation of the Panama Canal, 1870-1914.* N.Y., Simon and Schuster, 1977.

3 Make an Outline
Use an outline to decide how to organize your report. Sort your index cards into the same order.

Outline
I. Introduction
II. Why the canal was built
III. How the canal was built
   A. Physical challenges
   B. Medical challenges
IV. Conclusion

Differentiated Instruction

For Gifted and Talented L3
Tell students that a verb is in active voice when the subject performs the action named by the verb. A verb is in passive voice when the subject undergoes the action named by the verb.

Give these examples:

Passive voice: The house is being painted by my sister and me.

Active voice: My sister and I are painting the house.

Tell students that using the active voice whenever possible will make their writing more dynamic and concise.

Introduction

Building the Panama Canal

Ever since Christopher Columbus first explored the Isthmus of Panama, the Spanish had been looking for a water route through it. They wanted to be able to sail west from Spain to Asia without sailing around South America. However, it was not until 1914 that the dream became a reality.

Conclusion

It took eight years and more than 70,000 workers to build the Panama Canal. It remains one of the greatest engineering feats of modern times.

④ Write a First Draft

Write an introduction, a body, and a conclusion. Leave plenty of space between lines so you can go back and add details that you may have left out.

⑤ Revise and Proofread

Be sure to include transition words between sentences and paragraphs. Here are some examples:

To show a contrast—*however, although, despite*.

To point out a reason—*since, because, if*.

To signal a conclusion—*therefore, consequently, so, then*.

Evaluating Your Writing

Use this table to help you evaluate your writing.

	Excellent	Good	Acceptable	Unacceptable
Purpose	Achieves purpose—to inform, persuade, or provide historical interpretation—very well	Informs, persuades, or provides historical interpretation reasonably well	Reader cannot easily tell if the purpose is to inform, persuade, or provide historical interpretation	Purpose is not clear
Organization	Develops ideas in a very clear and logical way	Presents ideas in a reasonably well-organized way	Reader has difficulty following the organization	Lacks organization
Elaboration	Explains all ideas with facts and details	Explains most ideas with facts and details	Includes some supporting facts and details	Lacks supporting details
Use of Language	Uses excellent vocabulary and sentence structure with no errors in spelling, grammar, or punctuation	Uses good vocabulary and sentence structure with very few errors in spelling, grammar, or punctuation	Includes some errors in grammar, punctuation, and spelling	Includes many errors in grammar, punctuation, and spelling

Reading and Writing Handbook **RW5**

Independent Practice

- Have students consider topics for a research paper. Give them *Choosing a Topic* to help them learn how to evaluate potential topics.

  All in One **United States and Canada Teaching Resources,** *Choosing a Topic,* p. 16

- Once students have selected a topic, tell them they will need facts to support their ideas. Give them *Using the Library, Summarizing and Taking Notes,* and *Preparing Note Cards* to help them start their research.

  All in One **United States and Canada Teaching Resources,** *Using the Library,* p. 17; *Summarizing and Taking Notes,* p. 18; *Preparing Note Cards,* p. 19

Monitor Progress

Give students *Writing an Introduction* and *Writing the Body of an Essay* to help them write their essays.

  All in One **United States and Canada Teaching Resources,** *Writing an Introduction,* p. 20; *Writing the Body of an Essay,* p. 21

Assess and Reteach

Assess Progress **L2**

Ask students to pick the best essay they have written so far and evaluate it using the rubric on this page.

Reteach **L1**

Collect students' essays and self-evaluations. Meet with students to go over good points and areas for improvement. Revisit each type of essay as needed with the whole class.

Extend **L3**

To extend this lesson, tell students there are many other different types of writing. Have them complete *Writing for Assessment* and *Writing a Letter* to learn about two more types of writing.

  All in One **United States and Canada Teaching Resources,** *Writing for Assessment,* p. 22; *Writing a Letter,* p. 23

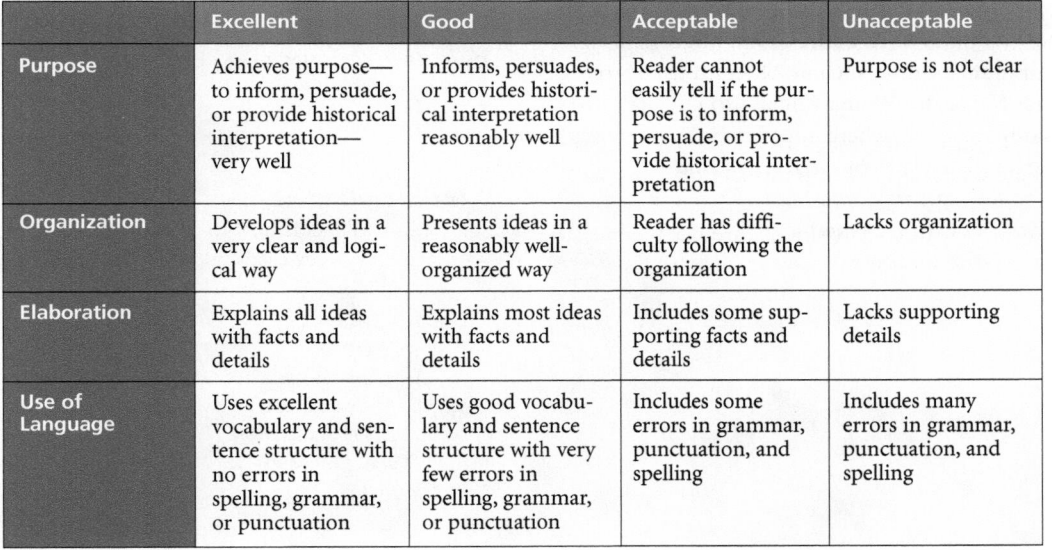

Differentiated Instruction

For English Language Learners **L2**

To help students understand the tasks you have given them, provide them with an example of a well-executed essay from a different class or a previous year. The example essay should be well written and organized but not above grade level. You could look for and save good examples each year you teach.

Objective

- Identify and define the five themes of geography.

Prepare to Read

Build Background Knowledge `L2`

Assign students to small groups and give them five minutes to write a definition of geography. Then write the five themes of geography on the board. Remind students that a theme is an important underlying idea. As a class, decide which parts of their definitions go under each of the geography themes. For example, "landforms" would fall under the theme of place.

Instruct

Five Themes of Geography `L2`

Guided Instruction

- Divide the text using the headings and ask students to read the pages using the Structured Silent Reading technique (TE, p. T34). Clarify the meanings of any unfamiliar words.

- Ask students to give the relative locations of their homes.

- Mention the popularity of different kinds of ethnic foods in the United States. Ask **What theme of geography are these foods a good example of?** *(movement)* Encourage students to name other examples of the movement of cultural traditions from one region to another.

- Discuss the climate in your area. Ask **How does the environment affect how we live?** *(affects dress, travel, sports and other recreational activities, the way homes are built)*

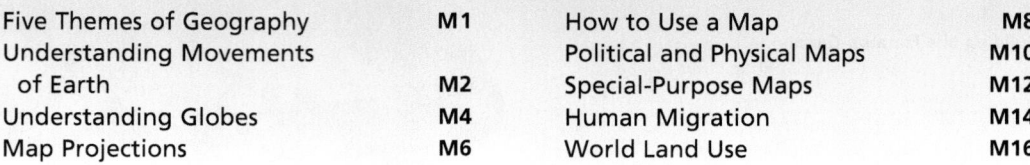

MAP MASTER   SKILLS HANDBOOK

CONTENTS

Five Themes of Geography	M1	How to Use a Map	M8
Understanding Movements of Earth	M2	Political and Physical Maps	M10
		Special-Purpose Maps	M12
Understanding Globes	M4	Human Migration	M14
Map Projections	M6	World Land Use	M16

Go Online PHSchool.com Use Web Code **lap-0000** for all of the maps in this handbook.

Five Themes of Geography

Studying the geography of the entire world is a huge task. You can make that task easier by using the five themes of geography: location, regions, place, movement, and human-environment interaction. The themes are tools you can use to organize information and to answer the where, why, and how of geography.

▲ **Location**
This museum in England has a line running through it. The line marks its location at 0° longitude.

`LOCATION`

1 Location answers the question, "Where is it?" You can think of the location of a continent or a country as its address. You might give an absolute location such as 22 South Lake Street or 40° N and 80° W. You might also use a relative address, telling where one place is by referring to another place. *Between school and the mall* and *eight miles east of Pleasant City* are examples of relative locations.

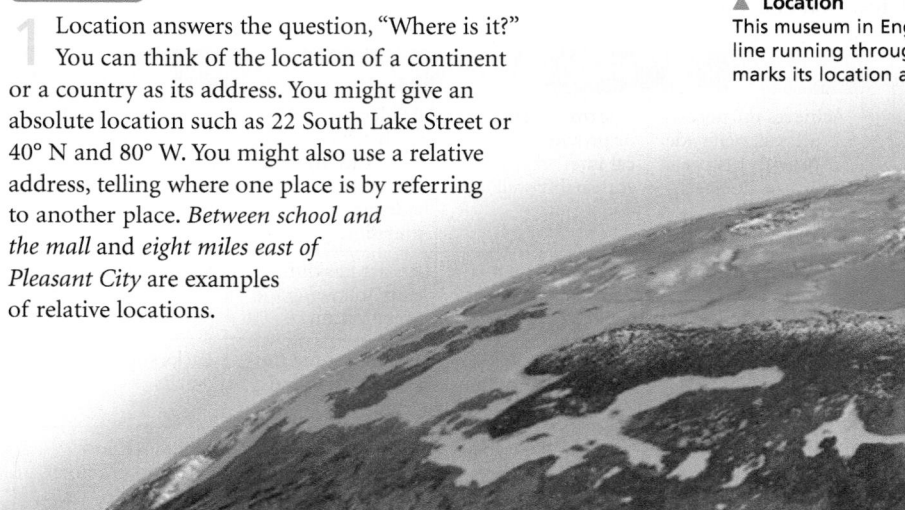

MapMaster Skills Handbook

Differentiated Instruction

For English Language Learners `L1`

Students may find it difficult to pronounce some of the multisyllable words in this section such as *relative, environment, interaction, government, signature,* and *communicate.* Show students how to break down these words into smaller parts to help them sound out the pronunciation.

For Advanced Readers `L3`

Have students find articles in newspapers or magazines that illustrate the five themes of geography. Have students underline the relevant sections and identify the theme or themes they illustrate. Suggest that students create a bulletin board to share their examples with the class.

REGIONS

2 Regions are areas that share at least one common feature. Geographers divide the world into many types of regions. For example, countries, states, and cities are political regions. The people in any one of these places live under the same government. Other features, such as climate and culture, can be used to define regions. Therefore the same place can be found in more than one region. For example, the state of Hawaii is in the political region of the United States. Because it has a tropical climate, Hawaii is also part of a tropical climate region.

MOVEMENT

4 Movement answers the question, "How do people, goods, and ideas move from place to place?" Remember that what happens in one place often affects what happens in another. Use the theme of movement to help you trace the spread of goods, people, and ideas from one location to another.

PLACE

3 Place identifies the natural and human features that make one place different from every other place. You can identify a specific place by its landforms, climate, plants, animals, people, language, or culture. You might even think of place as a geographic signature. Use the signature to help you understand the natural and human features that make one place different from every other place.

INTERACTION

5 Human-environment interaction focuses on the relationship between people and the environment. As people live in an area, they often begin to make changes to it, usually to make their lives easier. For example, they might build a dam to control flooding during rainy seasons. Also, the environment can affect how people live, work, dress, travel, and communicate.

◄ **Interaction**
These Congolese women interact with their environment by gathering wood for cooking.

PRACTICE YOUR GEOGRAPHY SKILLS

1 Describe your town or city, using each of the five themes of geography.

2 Name at least one thing that comes into your town or city and one that goes out. How is each moved? Where does it come from? Where does it go?

MapMaster Skills Handbook **M1**

MapMaster Skills Handbook **M1**

Objective

■ Explain how the movements of the Earth cause night and day, as well as the seasons.

Prepare to Read

Build Background Knowledge L2

Remind students that while the Earth revolves around the sun, it also rotates on its own axis. Review the meanings of "revolve" and "rotate" in this context. Ask students to brainstorm ways that the Earth's revolving and rotating might affect their lives. Conduct an Idea Wave (TE, p. T35) to generate a list of ideas.

Instruct

Understanding Movements of Earth L2

Guided Instruction

■ Read the text as a class using the Oral Cloze technique (TE, p. T33). Explain the illustrations on pages M2 and M3 show the information in the text visually. Clarify the meanings of any unfamiliar words.

■ Ask students **How does Earth rotating on its axis cause day and night?** (*It is daytime on the side of Earth facing the sun, while the side facing away from the sun is dark.*)

■ Ask **How does the tilt of Earth affect the seasons?** (*The farther away a part of Earth is from the sun's rays, the colder it is.*)

Independent Practice

Partner students and have them complete *Understanding the Movements of the Earth*.

All in One United States and Canada Teaching Resources, *Understanding Movements of the Earth,* p. 28

Understanding Movements of Earth

The planet Earth is part of our solar system. Earth revolves around the sun in a nearly circular path called an orbit. A revolution, or one complete orbit around the sun, takes 365¼ days, or one year. As Earth orbits the sun, it also spins on its axis, an invisible line through the center of Earth from the North Pole to the South Pole. This movement is called a rotation.

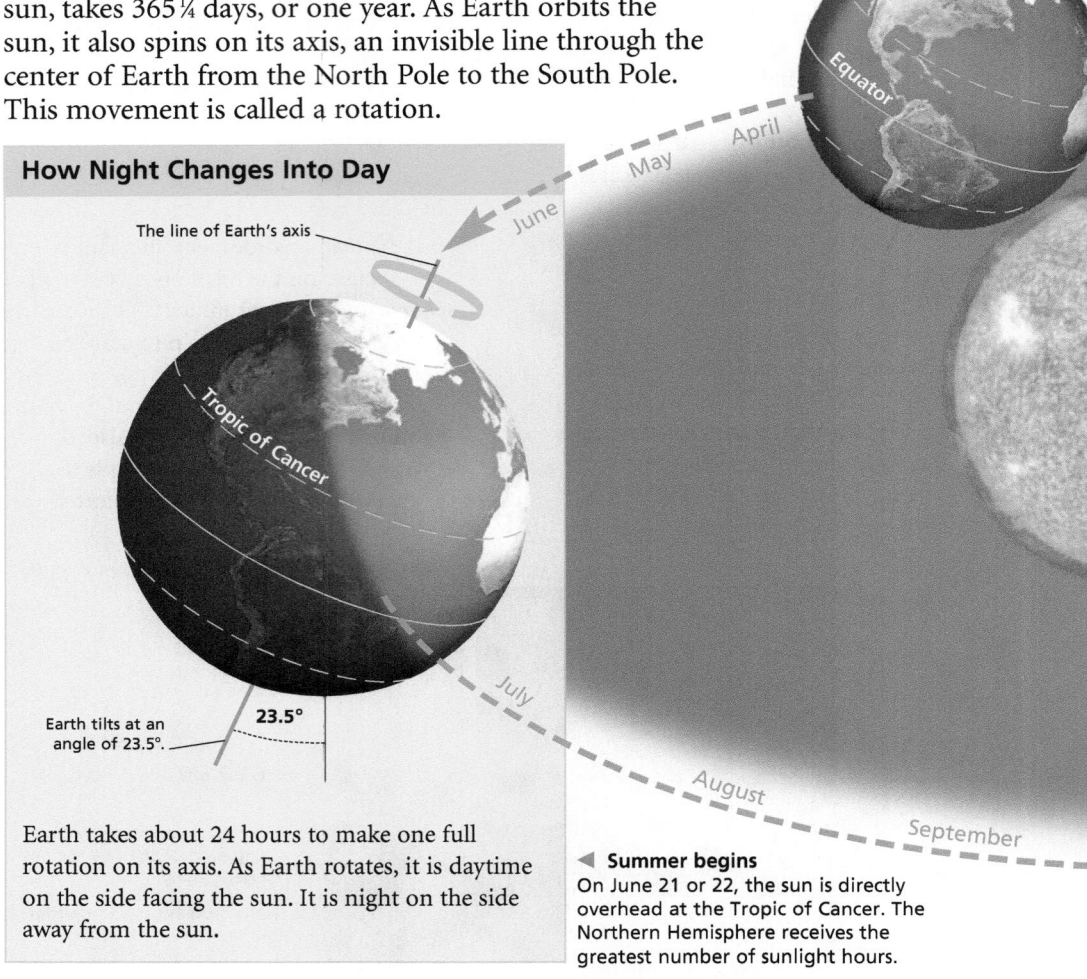

How Night Changes Into Day

The line of Earth's axis

Tropic of Cancer

Earth tilts at an angle of 23.5°. 23.5°

Earth takes about 24 hours to make one full rotation on its axis. As Earth rotates, it is daytime on the side facing the sun. It is night on the side away from the sun.

▼ **Spring begins**
On March 20 or 21, the sun is directly overhead at the Equator. The Northern and Southern Hemispheres receive almost equal hours of sunlight and darkness.

Equator

May April

June

July

August

September

◄ **Summer begins**
On June 21 or 22, the sun is directly overhead at the Tropic of Cancer. The Northern Hemisphere receives the greatest number of sunlight hours.

M2 MapMaster Skills Handbook

Background: Links Across Place

Sunrise and Sunset Most people have heard the saying "The sun rises in the east and sets in the west." However, the sun does not ever actually change position. Every day, Earth rotates on its axis so that as each region faces the sun, it experiences day. The rotation continues so that as a region turns away from the sun, it experiences night. The sun stays in the same place. A person viewing sunrise or sunset is really seeing Earth's slow turn on its axis, not the sun rising or setting.

The Seasons

Earth's axis is tilted at an angle. Because of this tilt, sunlight strikes different parts of Earth at different times in the year, creating seasons. The illustration below shows how the seasons are created in the Northern Hemisphere. In the Southern Hemisphere, the seasons are reversed.

PRACTICE YOUR GEOGRAPHY SKILLS

1 What causes the seasons in the Northern Hemisphere to be the opposite of those in the Southern Hemisphere?

2 During which two days of the year do the Northern Hemisphere and Southern Hemisphere have equal hours of daylight and darkness?

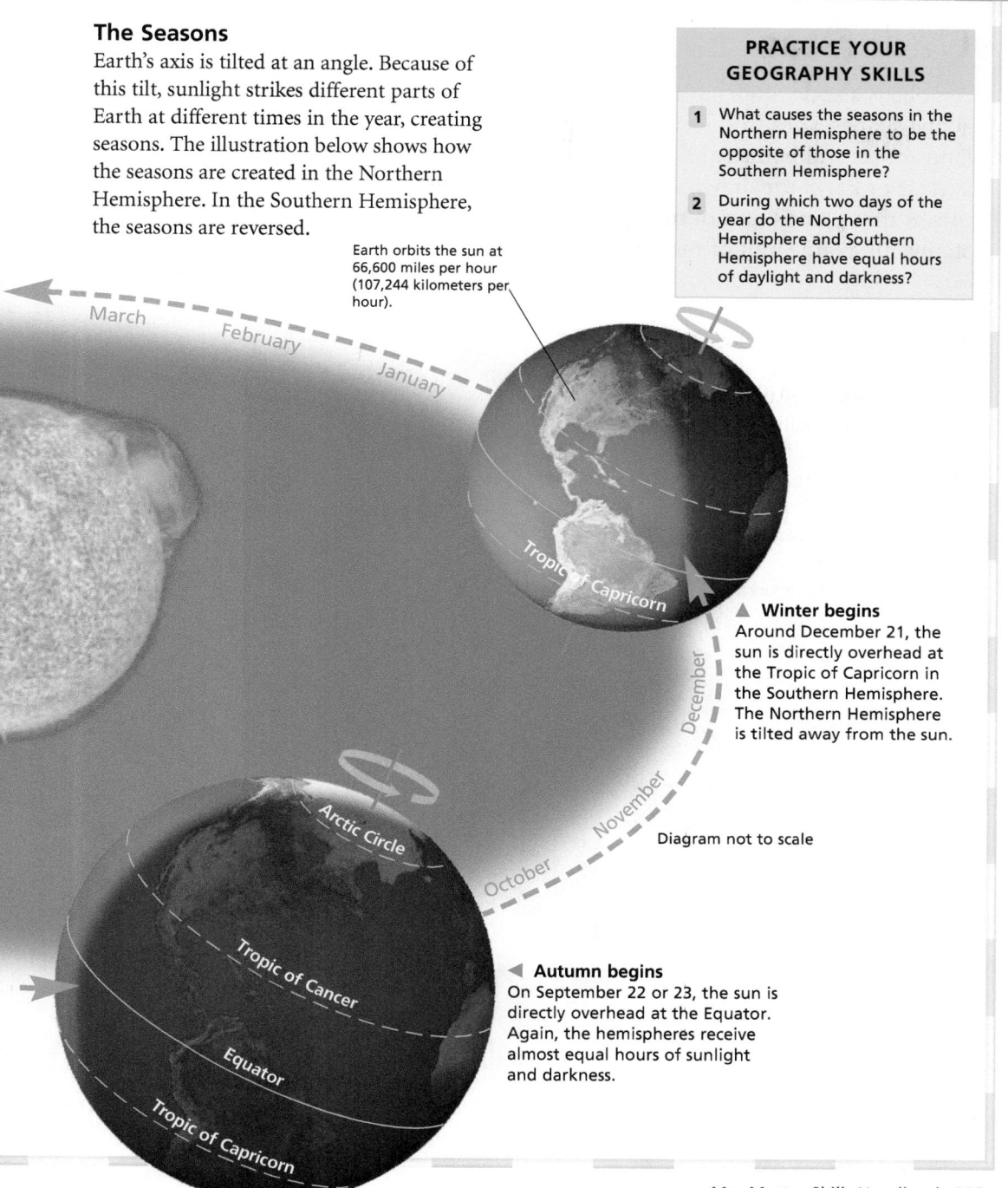

Earth orbits the sun at 66,600 miles per hour (107,244 kilometers per hour).

March
February
January

Tropic of Capricorn

December

▲ **Winter begins**
Around December 21, the sun is directly overhead at the Tropic of Capricorn in the Southern Hemisphere. The Northern Hemisphere is tilted away from the sun.

November

Diagram not to scale

October

Arctic Circle

Tropic of Cancer

◀ **Autumn begins**
On September 22 or 23, the sun is directly overhead at the Equator. Again, the hemispheres receive almost equal hours of sunlight and darkness.

Equator

Tropic of Capricorn

MapMaster Skills Handbook **M3**

Objectives

- Understand how a globe is marked with a grid to measure features on Earth.

- Learn how to use longitude and latitude to locate a place.

Prepare to Read

Build Background Knowledge

Tell students that in this lesson, they will learn how to use globes. Ask students what it would be like to see Earth from a spacecraft. Discuss the shape that students would see. Then discuss why a globe is a more accurate rendering of Earth than a flat map. Point out that a globe is like a model car in that it is a small version of something larger. If a globe is available, have students examine it.

Instruct

Understanding Globes

Guided Instruction

- Read the text as a class using the Oral Cloze strategy (TE, p. T33). Have students study the illustrations carefully.

- Ask **What line of latitude divides the Northern and Southern Hemispheres?** *(the Equator)* **At what degrees latitude is this line?** *(0º)*

- Ask **Where do the lines of longitude come together?** *(at the North and South Poles)* **What is the name of the meridian at 0 degrees?** *(Prime Meridian)*

- Have students look at the global grid on *Color Transparency USC 3: The Global Grid.* Ask **What is the global grid?** *(a pattern of lines formed where the parallels of latitude and meridians of longitude cross)* **What continent in the Eastern Hemisphere does the 100° E meridian pass through?** *(Asia)*

  📖 **United States and Canada Transparencies,** *Color Transparency USC 3: The Global Grid*

Understanding Globes

A globe is a scale model of Earth. It shows the actual shapes, sizes, and locations of all Earth's landmasses and bodies of water. Features on the surface of Earth are drawn to scale on a globe. This means that a small unit of measure on the globe stands for a large unit of measure on Earth.

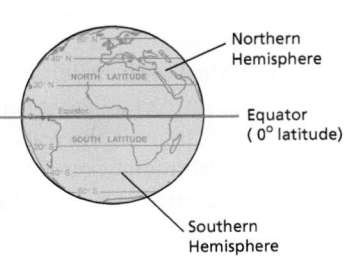

Northern Hemisphere

Equator (0° latitude)

Southern Hemisphere

Parallels of Latitude

Geographers divide the globe along imaginary horizontal lines called parallels of latitude. One of these latitude lines is the Equator, located halfway between the North and South poles. Parallels of latitude are measured in degrees (°). One degree of latitude represents a distance of about 69 miles (111 kilometers).

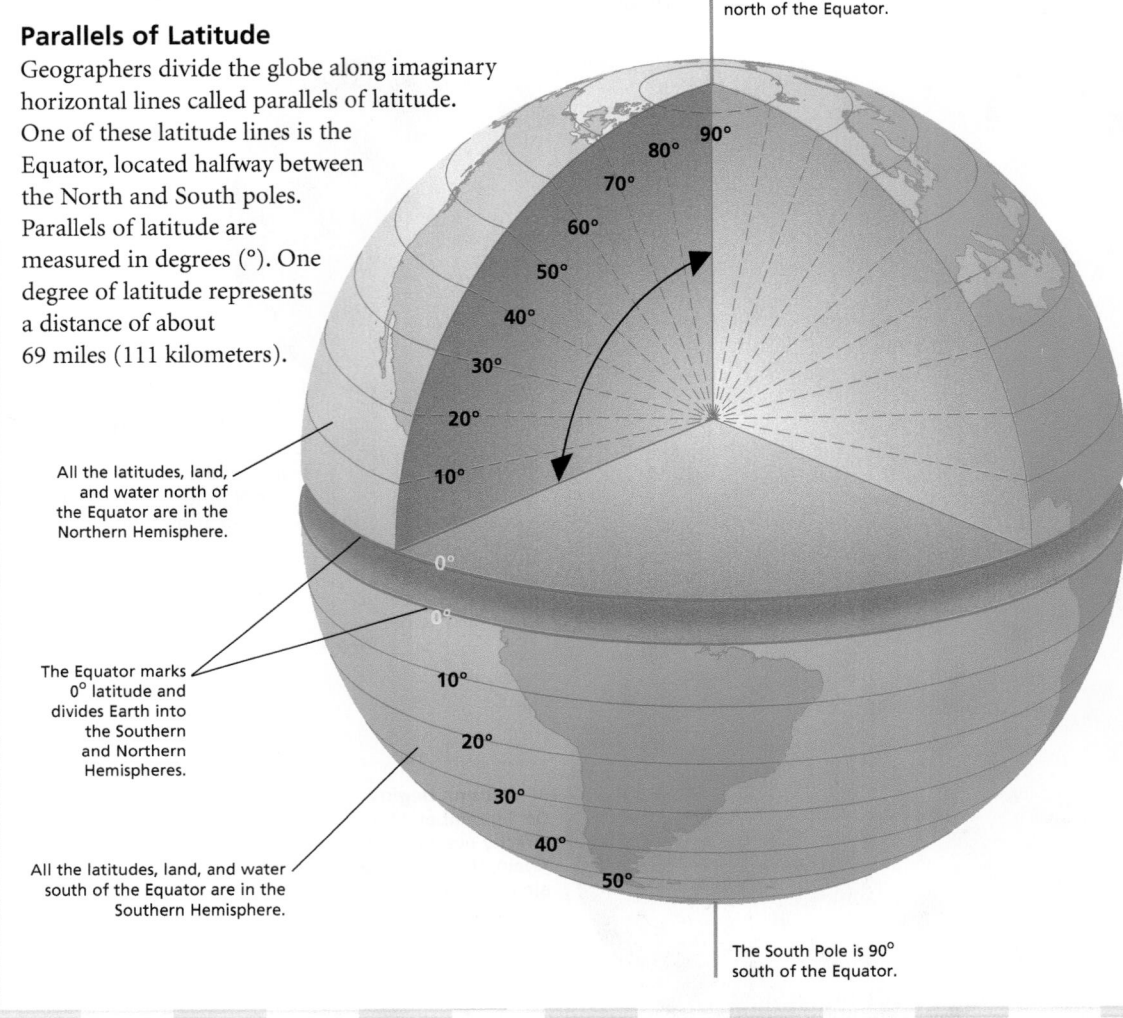

The North Pole is 90° north of the Equator.

90°
80°
70°
60°
50°
40°
30°
20°
10°

All the latitudes, land, and water north of the Equator are in the Northern Hemisphere.

0°
0°

The Equator marks 0° latitude and divides Earth into the Southern and Northern Hemispheres.

10°
20°
30°
40°
50°

All the latitudes, land, and water south of the Equator are in the Southern Hemisphere.

The South Pole is 90° south of the Equator.

Background: Links Across Time

The First Globes Historians believe that the first globe may have been made in the second century B.C. by a Greek geographer known as Crates of Mallus. The mathematician Ptolemy represented Earth as a globe in his written works in the second century A.D. In late 1492 Martin Behaim made a terrestrial globe that, although inaccurate by today's knowledge, reflected the best geographical knowledge of the time. This globe still exists and is on display in Behaim's hometown of Nuremberg, Germany.

Meridians of Longitude

Geographers also divide the globe along imaginary vertical lines called meridians of longitude, which are measured in degrees (°). The longitude line called the Prime Meridian runs from pole to pole through Greenwich, England. All meridians of longitude come together at the North and South Poles.

PRACTICE YOUR GEOGRAPHY MAP SKILLS

1 Which continents lie completely in the Northern Hemisphere? In the Western Hemisphere?

2 Is there land or water at 20° S latitude and the Prime Meridian? At the Equator and 60° W longitude?

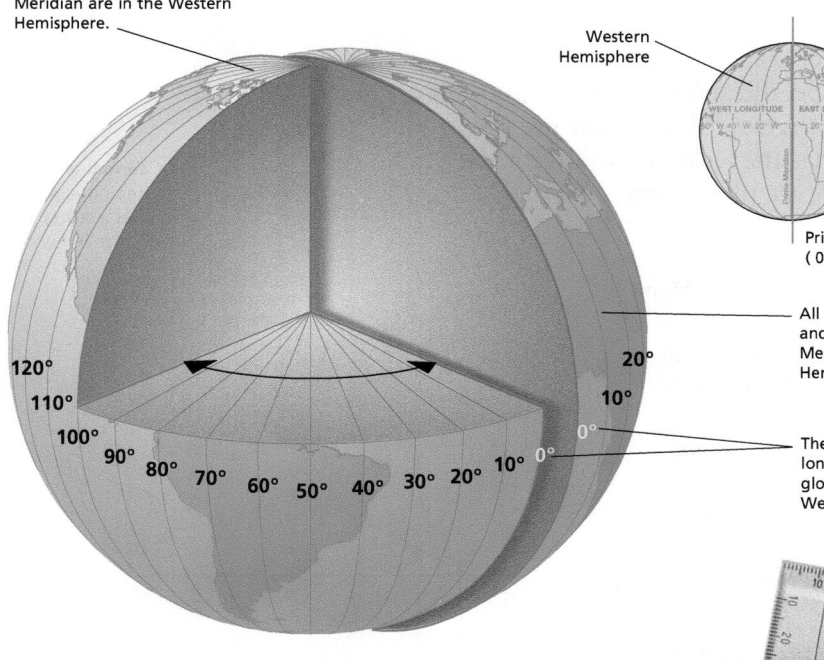

All the longitudes, land, and water west of the Prime Meridian are in the Western Hemisphere.

Western Hemisphere

Eastern Hemisphere

Prime Meridian (0° longitude)

All the longitudes, land, and water east of the Prime Meridian are in the Eastern Hemisphere.

The Prime Meridian marks 0° longitude and divides the globe into the Eastern and Western Hemispheres.

120° 110° 100° 90° 80° 70° 60° 50° 40° 30° 20° 10° 0° 10° 20°

The Global Grid

Together, the pattern of parallels of latitude and meridians of longitude is called the global grid. Using the lines of latitude and longitude, you can locate any place on Earth. For example, the location of 30° north latitude and 90° west longitude is usually written as 30° N, 90° W. Only one place on Earth has these coordinates—the city of New Orleans, in the state of Louisiana.

▲ **Compass**
Wherever you are on Earth, a compass can be used to show direction.

Independent Practice

Have students work in pairs to complete *Understanding Hemispheres* and *Understanding Latitude and Longitude.*

All in One United States and Canada Teaching Resources, *Understanding Hemispheres,* p. 30; *Understanding Latitude and Longitude,* p. 31

Monitor Progress

As students do the worksheets, circulate to make sure pairs understand the key concepts. Show *Color Transparency USC 2: The Hemispheres* to help students.

United States and Canada Transparencies, *Color Transparency USC 2: The Hemispheres*

Assess and Reteach

Assess Progress   L2

Have students answer the questions under Practice Your Geography Map Skills.

Reteach   L1

Use the DK Atlas activity *Understanding Latitude and Longitude* to review these skills with students. Have students complete the activity in pairs.

All in One United States and Canada Teaching Resources, *DK Compact Atlas of the World Activity: Understanding Latitude and Longitude,* p. 32

Extend   L3

To extend the lesson, have students complete *Using Latitude and Longitude.* Then have students use the map and with a partner, play a game of Can You Find …? Each partner takes a turn giving the coordinates for a place on the map and the other partner must name the place.

All in One United States and Canada Teaching Resources, *Using Latitude and Longitude,* p. 33

Differentiated Instruction

For Less Proficient Readers   L1
For students having difficulty understanding the concept of a global grid, give them *Understanding Grids* and help them complete it. Then follow up with *Using a Grid.*

All in One United States and Canada Teaching Resources, *Understanding Grids,* p. 34; *Using a Grid,* p. 35

For Advanced Readers   L3
Have students complete *Comparing Globes and Maps.* Then ask them to make a chart showing the pros and cons of these two ways of representing Earth.

All in One United States and Canada Teaching Resources, *Comparing Globes and Maps,* p. 36

Answers

PRACTICE YOUR GEOGRAPHY SKILLS

1. Northern Hemisphere: North America; Europe; Western Hemisphere: North America; South America

2. water; land

Objectives

- Compare maps of different projections.
- Describe distortions in map projections.

Prepare to Read

Build Background Knowledge   L1

In this lesson, students will learn how cartographers depict Earth on a two-dimensional map. Remind students that if they were traveling in a spaceship, they would see Earth as a globe. Ask if they could ever see the entire Earth at one time from space. Help students recognize that a flat map is the only way to see all of Earth at once.

Instruct

Map Projections   L2

Guided Instruction

- Read the text as a class using the Choral Reading technique (TE, p. T34). Direct students to look at the relevant maps after you read each section together. Follow up by having students do a second silent reading.

- Help students locate Greenland on the Mercator and Robinson maps. Ask **What difference do you notice in the way Greenland is shown?** *(It appears much larger on the Mercator Map.)* **How would you explain this?** *(The Mercator is a same-shape map and the shapes toward the poles are enlarged.)*

- Ask **Where does the distortion usually occur on an equal-area map?** *(at the edges of the map)*

- Have students compare Antarctica on the three projections. *(It is largest and most distorted on the Mercator map; smallest on the equal-area map; covers the entire bottom edge of the Robinson map.)*

Map Projections

Maps are drawings that show regions on flat surfaces. Maps are easier to use and carry than globes, but they cannot show the correct size and shape of every feature on Earth's curved surface. They must shrink some places and stretch others. To make up for this distortion, mapmakers use different map projections. No one projection can accurately show the correct area, shape, distance, and direction for all of Earth's surface. Mapmakers use the projection that has the least distortion for the information they are presenting.

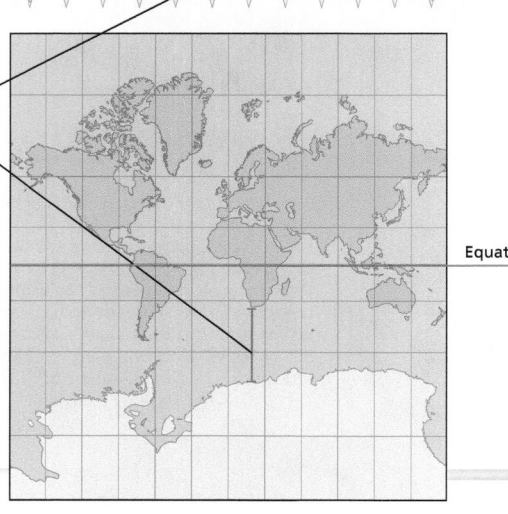

▲ **Global gores**
Flattening a globe creates a string of shapes called gores.

Same-Shape Maps

Map projections that accurately show the shapes of landmasses are called same-shape maps. However, these projections often greatly distort, or make less accurate, the size of landmasses as well as the distance between them. In the projection below, the northern and southern areas of the globe appear more stretched than the areas near the Equator.

To turn Earth into a same-shape map, mapmakers must stretch the gores into rectangles.

Equator

Stretching the gores makes parts of Earth larger. This enlargement becomes greater toward the North and South Poles.

Equator

Mercator projection ▶
One of the most common same-shape maps is the Mercator projection, named for the mapmaker who invented it. The Mercator projection accurately shows shape and direction, but it distorts distance and size. Because the projection shows true directions, ships' navigators use it to chart a straight-line course between two ports.

M6 MapMaster Skills Handbook

Differentiated Instruction

For Special Needs Students   L1

If students have difficulty understanding why distortion occurs, draw a simple picture on an orange. Then have students try to peel the orange in one piece. Challenge students to place the peel flat on a piece of paper without any tears and spaces. Talk about what happens to the drawing. Explain that mapmakers face this same challenge when drawing Earth on a flat paper.

For Gifted and Talented   L3

Have students complete *Great Circles and Straight Lines*. Then ask them to use their completed page and a globe to explain the concept of great circles to the class.

All in One **United States and Canada Teaching Resources,** *Great Circles and Straight Lines*, p. 38

Equal-Area Maps

Map projections that show the correct size of landmasses are called equal-area maps. In order to show the correct size of landmasses, these maps usually distort shapes. The distortion is usually greater at the edges of the map and less at the center.

PRACTICE YOUR GEOGRAPHY SKILLS

1 What feature is distorted on an equal-area map?

2 Would you use a Mercator projection to find the exact distance between two locations? Tell why or why not.

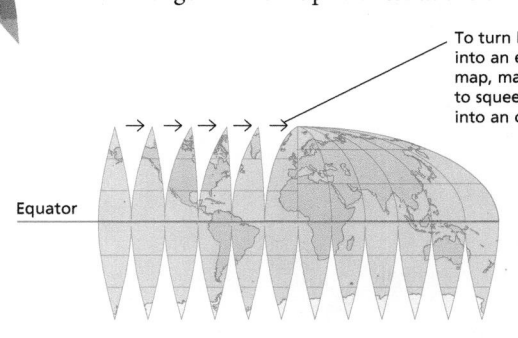

To turn Earth's surface into an equal-area map, mapmakers have to squeeze each gore into an oval.

Equator

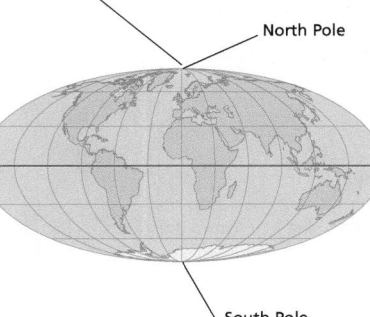

The tips of all the gores are then joined together. The points at which they join form the North and South Poles. The line of the Equator stays the same.

North Pole

Equator

South Pole

Robinson Maps

Many of the maps in this book use the Robinson projection, which is a compromise between the Mercator and equal-area projections. The Robinson projection gives a useful overall picture of the world. It keeps the size and shape relationships of most continents and oceans, but distorts the size of the polar regions.

The entire top edge of the map is the North Pole.

The map is least distorted at the Equator.

Equator

The entire bottom edge of the map is the South Pole.

MapMaster Skills Handbook **M7**

Independent Practice

Have students work with partners to complete *Understanding Projection*.

All in One **United States and Canada Teaching Resources,** *Understanding Projection,* p. 37

Monitor Progress

As students do the worksheet, circulate to make sure individuals comprehend the key concepts. Provide assistance as needed.

Assess and Reteach

Assess Progress L2

Have students complete the Practice Your Geography Skills questions.

Reteach L1

Use *Maps with Accurate Shapes: Conformal Maps* and *Maps with Accurate Areas: Equal-Area Maps* to help students go over the information in the lesson. Model thinking for each question and partner students to complete each page together. Circulate to provide explanations and help as students work.

All in One **United States and Canada Teaching Resources,** *Maps with Accurate Shapes: Conformal Maps,* p. 39; *Maps with Accurate Areas: Equal-Area Maps,* p. 40

Extend L3

To extend the lesson, ask students to complete *Maps with Accurate Direction: Azimuthal Maps.* Then have students write a sentence or two describing the different projections they have learned about.

All in One **United States and Canada Teaching Resources,** *Maps with Accurate Directions: Azimuthal Maps,* p. 41

Background: Biography

Gerardus Mercator (1512–1594) The Mercator projection takes its name from a Flemish geographer, Gerhard Kremer. Kremer, who used the Latin form of his name, Gerardus Mercator, wrote books on ancient geography and cartography. He made his first world map in 1538. In 1554 he made a map of Europe. In 1568, the first map using the Mercator projection bearing his name appeared. Mercator also began an atlas of his maps which was finished by his son and published in 1594.

Answers

PRACTICE YOUR GEOGRAPHY SKILLS

1. shapes
2. No; the Mercator projection distorts distances.

Objective

- Identify and use the parts of a map.

Prepare to Read

Build Background Knowledge L1

In this lesson, students will learn about the practical aspects of maps. Ask students to name reasons that they might use a map; for example, to find directions, boundaries, distances. Conduct an Idea Wave (TE, p. T35) to generate a list of ideas. List the ideas on the board.

Instruct

How to Use a Map L2

Guided Instruction

- Divide the text and captions in the lesson using the headings and ask students to read the pages using the Structured Silent Reading strategy (TE, p. T34). Remind students to use the illustrations to acquire additional understanding. Refer to the list on the board, then ask students which map part (key, compass rose, scale, symbol, title) would be helpful in using a map for a specific purpose.
- Ask **What is the purpose of a compass rose?** *(to show directions)*
- Talk about how the three maps show different amounts of Earth's surface. Ask **Which map shows the largest area?** *(Western Europe)* **Which map shows the smallest area?** *(Central London)*
- Ask **What are some symbols that you might find on a map key?** *(border, national capital, city, airport, park, point of interest)*

Independent Practice

Partner students and have them complete *Using the Map Key* and *Using the Compass Rose.*

All in One **United States and Canada Teaching Resources,** *Using the Map Key,* p. 42; *Using the Compass Rose,* p. 43

MAP MASTER™ | LOCATION | REGIONS | PLACE | MOVEMENT | INTERACTION

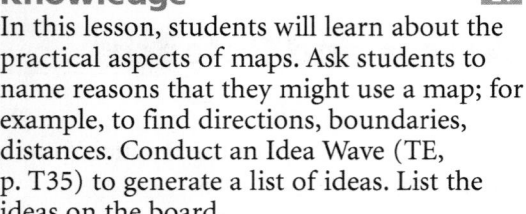

How to Use a Map

Mapmakers provide several clues to help you understand the information on a map. Maps provide different clues, depending on their purpose or scale. However, most maps have several clues in common.

Locator globe
Many maps are shown with locator globes. They show where on the globe the area of the map is located.

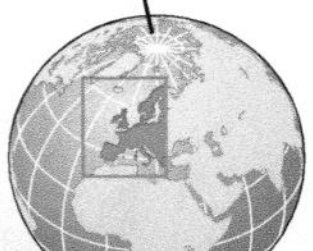

Title
All maps have a title. The title tells you the subject of the map.

Compass rose
Many maps show direction by displaying a compass rose with the directions north, east, south, and west. The letters N, E, S, and W are placed to indicate these directions.

Key
Often a map has a key, or legend. The key shows the symbols and colors used on the map, and what each one means.

Scale bar
A scale bar helps you find the actual distances between points shown on the map. Most scale bars show distances in both miles and kilometers.

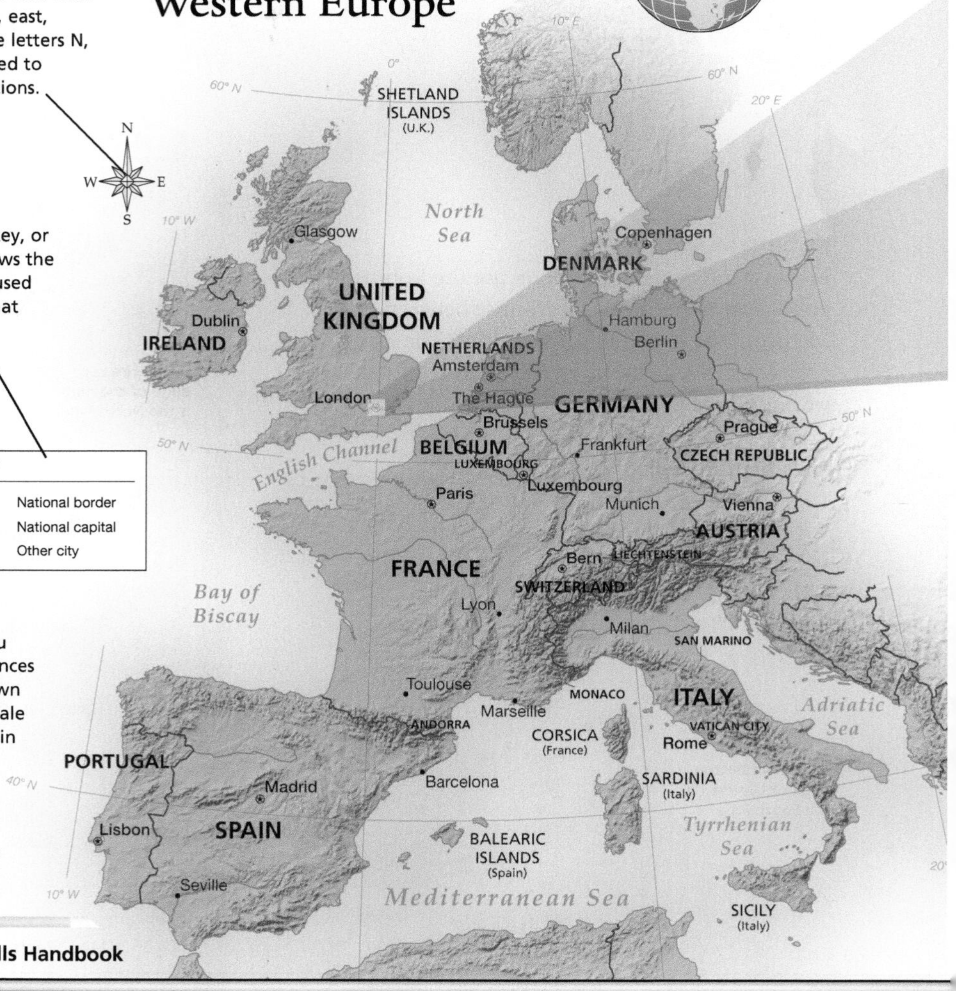

Western Europe
N
E
S
W
Key
National border
National capital
Other city
0 miles 300
0 kilometers 300
Lambert Azimuthal Equal Area
SHETLAND ISLANDS (U.K.)
North Sea
Glasgow
Copenhagen
DENMARK
UNITED KINGDOM
Dublin
IRELAND
Hamburg
Berlin
NETHERLANDS
Amsterdam
London
The Hague
GERMANY
Brussels
Prague
English Channel
BELGIUM
LUXEMBOURG
Frankfurt
CZECH REPUBLIC
Paris
Luxembourg
Munich
Vienna
AUSTRIA
FRANCE
Bern
LIECHTENSTEIN
SWITZERLAND
Bay of Biscay
Lyon
Milan
SAN MARINO
Toulouse
MONACO
ITALY
Adriatic Sea
Marseille
ANDORRA
CORSICA (France)
VATICAN CITY
Rome
PORTUGAL
Madrid
Barcelona
SARDINIA (Italy)
Lisbon
SPAIN
BALEARIC ISLANDS (Spain)
Tyrrhenian Sea
Seville
Mediterranean Sea
SICILY (Italy)

M8 MapMaster Skills Handbook

Differentiated Instruction

For Less Proficient Readers L2

If students have difficulty recalling the purposes of different parts of a map, have them make a table using each map part as a heading. Under each heading, help students list the important function or functions of that map part. Suggest that students refer to their table when they are working with maps.

For English Language Learners L1

Some of the words in the lesson, such as *symbol* and *scale,* may be unfamiliar to students acquiring English. Have students identify difficult words, look them up in the dictionary, and write sentences explaining what the terms mean.

Maps of Different Scales

Maps are drawn to different scales, depending on their purpose. Here are three maps drawn to very different scales. Keep in mind that maps showing large areas have smaller scales. Maps showing small areas have larger scales.

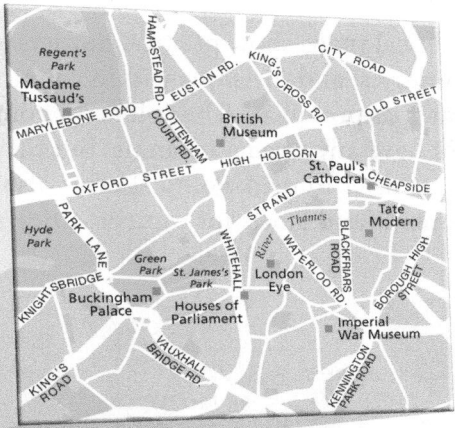

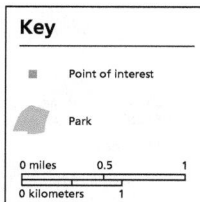

▲ **Central London**
Find the gray square on the map of Greater London. This square represents the area shown on the map above. This map moves you closer into the center of London. Like the zoom on a computer or a camera, this map shows a smaller area but in greater detail. It has the largest scale (1 inch represents about 0.9 mile). You can use this map to explore downtown London.

Key

■ Point of interest

▱ Park

```
0 miles        0.5        1
0 kilometers         1
```

▲ **Greater London**
Find the gray square on the main map of Western Europe (left). This square represents the area shown on the map above. It shows London's boundaries, the general shape of the city, and the features around the city. This map can help you find your way from the airport to the center of town.

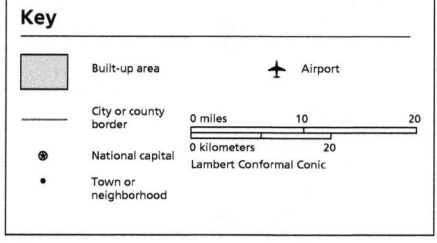

Key

▱ Built-up area   ✈ Airport

— City or county border

```
0 miles        10        20
0 kilometers        20
Lambert Conformal Conic
```

⊙ National capital

• Town or neighborhood

PRACTICE YOUR GEOGRAPHY SKILLS

1 What part of a map explains the colors used on the map?

2 How does the scale bar change depending on the scale of the map?

3 Which map would be best for finding the location of the British Museum? Explain why.

Monitor Progress

Circulate around the room as students complete the worksheets. Make sure that individuals comprehend the material. Provide assistance as needed.

Assess and Reteach

Assess Progress   L2

Have students complete the questions under Practice Your Geography Skills.

Reteach   L1

Some DK Atlas Activities will be helpful in reteaching the lesson. Give students more practice using these concepts by doing the activities for *Using the Map Key; Using the Compass Rose;* and *Using the Map Scale.*

All in One **United States and Canada Teaching Resources,** *DK Compact Atlas of the World Activity: Using the Map Key,* p. 44; *DK Compact Atlas of the World Activity: Using the Compass Rose,* p. 45; *DK Compact Atlas of the World Activity: Using the Map Scale,* p. 46

Extend   L3

To extend the lesson, have students complete *Comparing Maps of Different Scale* and *Maps with Accurate Distances: Equidistant Maps.*

All in One **United States and Canada Teaching Resources,** *Comparing Maps of Different Scale,* p. 47; *Maps with Accurate Distances: Equidistant Maps,* p. 48

Answers

PRACTICE YOUR GEOGRAPHY SKILLS

1. key

2. The larger the scale of the map, the smaller the distance shown on the scale bar.

3. the map of Central London; it shows the streets in more detail and includes the British Museum as a point of interest

Objectives
- Understand and use political maps.
- Understand and use physical maps.

Prepare to Read

Build Background Knowledge   L1
Tell students that they will learn about political maps and physical maps in this lesson. Explain that a political map is one that shows the boundaries and cities of an area as established by its people. Physical maps show information about the physical features of the area. These physical features would exist whether people lived in a place or not.

Instruct

Political Maps   L2
Physical Maps   L2

Guided Instruction
- Read the text as a class using the Choral Reading technique (TE, p. T34) and ask students to study the map.

- Ask students to identify what river forms the boundary between Zimbabwe and South Africa. *(Limpopo River)* Then ask them to name at least two capitals on the Mediterranean Sea. *(Tripoli, Algiers, Tunis)*

- Read the text with the class and draw students' attention to the map and its key.

- Explain that sea level is the average height of the ocean's surface; sea level is at zero elevation. Ask students what color represents sea level on the map key. *(dark green)*

- Have students find the Qattara Depression. Ask **What is its elevation?** *(from 0 to 650 feet)*

- Ask **What is the difference between elevation and relief?** *(Elevation is the height of land above sea level while relief shows how quickly the land rises or falls.)*

Answers

PRACTICE YOUR GEOGRAPHY SKILLS
1. solid line, star in a circle, dot
2. Luanda

Political Maps

Political maps show political borders: continents, countries, and divisions within countries, such as states or provinces. The colors on political maps do not have any special meaning, but they make the map easier to read. Political maps also include symbols and labels for capitals, cities, and towns.

PRACTICE YOUR GEOGRAPHY SKILLS

1 What symbols show a national border, a national capital, and a city?

2 What is Angola's capital city?

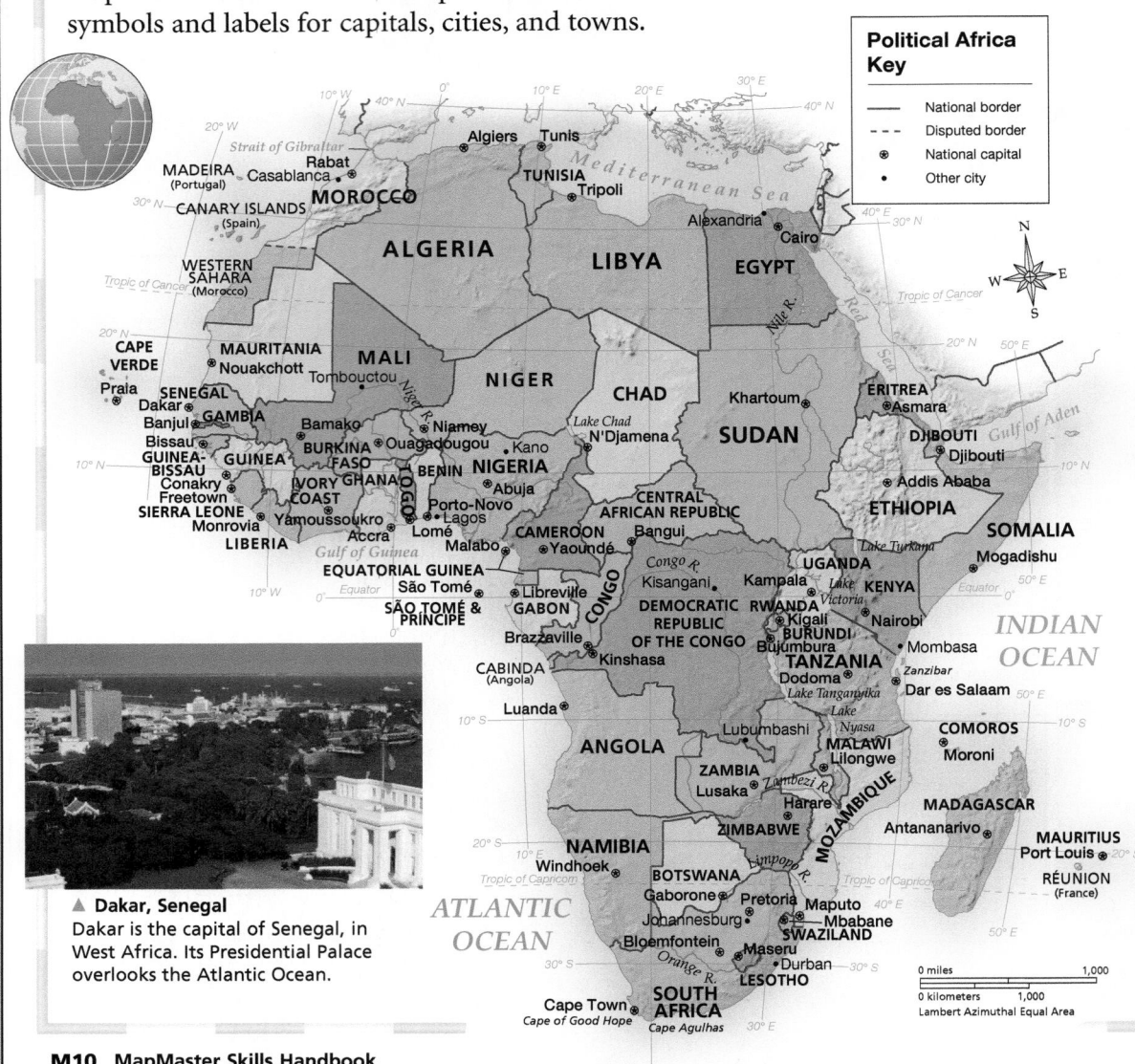

Political Africa Key

——————	National border
- - - - - -	Disputed border
⊛	National capital
•	Other city

▲ Dakar, Senegal
Dakar is the capital of Senegal, in West Africa. Its Presidential Palace overlooks the Atlantic Ocean.

M10 MapMaster Skills Handbook

Background: Global Perspectives

Africa's Highest Peaks Africa's two highest mountains are both extinct volcanoes that rise near the equator on the eastern part of the continent. The tallest mountain, Kilimanjaro in Tanzania, reaches 19,340 feet (5,895 meters) at its highest point. Although snow covers its peaks, farmers raise coffee and plantains on the lower southern slopes of Kilimanjaro. Africa's second highest mountain is Mt. Kenya at 17,058 feet (5,199 meters) located in central Kenya. Like Kilimanjaro, it is snowcapped in its highest regions. Both Kilimanjaro and Mt. Kenya are attractions for mountain climbers from all over the world.

Physical Maps

Physical maps represent what a region looks like by showing its major physical features, such as hills and plains. Physical maps also often show elevation and relief. Elevation, indicated by colors, is the height of the land above sea level. Relief, indicated by shading, shows how quickly the land rises or falls.

PRACTICE YOUR GEOGRAPHY SKILLS

1 Which areas of Africa have the highest elevation?

2 How can you use relief to plan a hiking trip?

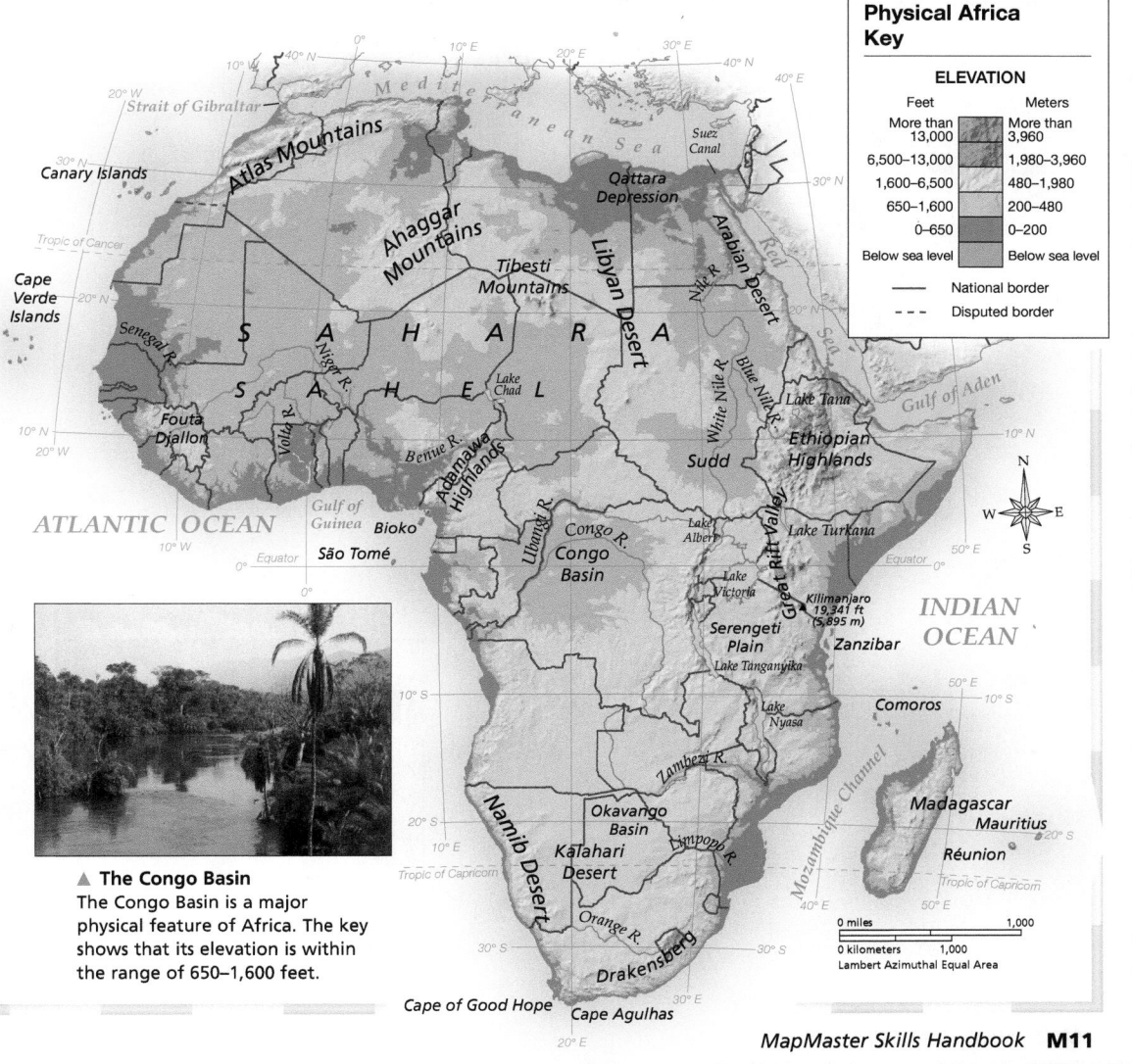

Physical Africa Key

ELEVATION

Feet		Meters
More than 13,000		More than 3,960
6,500–13,000		1,980–3,960
1,600–6,500		480–1,980
650–1,600		200–480
0–650		0–200
Below sea level		Below sea level

—— National border
--- Disputed border

▲ **The Congo Basin**
The Congo Basin is a major physical feature of Africa. The key shows that its elevation is within the range of 650–1,600 feet.

MapMaster Skills Handbook **M11**

Independent Practice

Have students complete *Reading a Political Map*, *Reading a Physical Map* and *Elevation on a Map* working with partners.

All in One **United States and Canada Teaching Resources**, *Reading a Political Map*, p. 49; *Reading a Physical Map*, p. 54; *Elevation on a Map*, p. 55

Monitor Progress

As students complete the worksheets, circulate around the room to make sure individuals understand the key concepts. Provide assistance as needed.

Assess and Reteach

Assess Progress   L2

Have students answer the questions under Practice Your Geography Skills on pages M10 and M11.

Reteach   L1

Use the DK Atlas Activities *Reading a Political Map* and *Reading a Physical Map* to review the concepts in this lesson.

All in One **United States and Canada Teaching Resources**, *DK Compact Atlas of the World Activity: Reading a Political Map*, p. 50; *DK Compact Atlas of the World Activity: Reading a Physical Map*, p. 56

Extend   L3

To extend the lesson, have students fill in the name of each country and its capital on the outline maps *North Africa*, *West and Central Africa*, and *East and Southern Africa*. Also, ask them to use colors and shading to indicate the Atlas Mountains, the Ethiopian Highlands, the Congo Basin, and the Namib Desert.

All in One **United States and Canada Teaching Resources**, *Outline Map 22: North Africa*, p. 51; *Outline Map 23: West and Central Africa*, p. 52; *Outline Map 24: East and Southern Africa*, p. 53

Differentiated Instruction

For Special Needs Students   L1

Reuse *Reading a Political Map* to help students understand political maps. Point to the symbol for a national border in the key, then trace the borders of several countries. Invite students to trace others.

All in One **United States and Canada Teaching Resources**, *Reading a Political Map*, p. 49

For Advanced Readers   L3

Challenge students to explore the concepts of relief and elevation further by completing *Relief on a Map* and *Maps of the Ocean Floor*.

All in One **United States and Canada Teaching Resources**, *Relief on a Map*, p. 57; *Maps of the Ocean Floor*, p. 58

Answers

PRACTICE YOUR GEOGRAPHY SKILLS

1. Ethiopian Highlands and Great Rift Valley

2. It can help you find out where the land rises and falls.

Objectives

- Understand and use climate maps.
- Understand and use language maps.

Prepare to Read

Build Background Knowledge   L1

Ask students to think of as many meanings for the word *special* as they can. Tell them that maps can be special too. Ask **What do you think a special-purpose map might show?** List suggestions on the board.

Instruct

Special-Purpose Maps: Climate   L1

Guided Instruction

- Ask students to read the text using the Structured Silent Reading strategy (TE, p. T34). Point out that the map shows Bangladesh, Bhutan, Nepal, and parts of Myanmar and Pakistan as well as India.

- Point out the map and key. Ask **What areas have a tropical wet climate?** *(area along the southern western coast; eastern part of Bangladesh)*

- Ask **What color represents an arid climate?** *(brown)*

Independent Practice

Partner students and have them complete *Reading a Climate Map*.

All In One United States and Canada Teaching Resources, *Reading a Climate Map,* p. 59

Monitor Progress

As students complete the worksheet, circulate around the room to make sure individuals comprehend the key concepts. Provide assistance as needed.

Answers

PRACTICE YOUR GEOGRAPHY SKILLS

1. the key
2. the northwestern part; No major cities are in the arid region.

Special-Purpose Maps: Climate

Unlike the boundary lines on a political map, the boundary lines on climate maps do not separate the land into exact divisions. For example, in this climate map of India, a tropical wet climate gradually changes to a tropical wet and dry climate.

> ### PRACTICE YOUR GEOGRAPHY SKILLS
>
> 1 What part of a special-purpose map tells you what the colors on the map mean?
>
> 2 Where are arid regions located in India? Are there major cities in those regions?

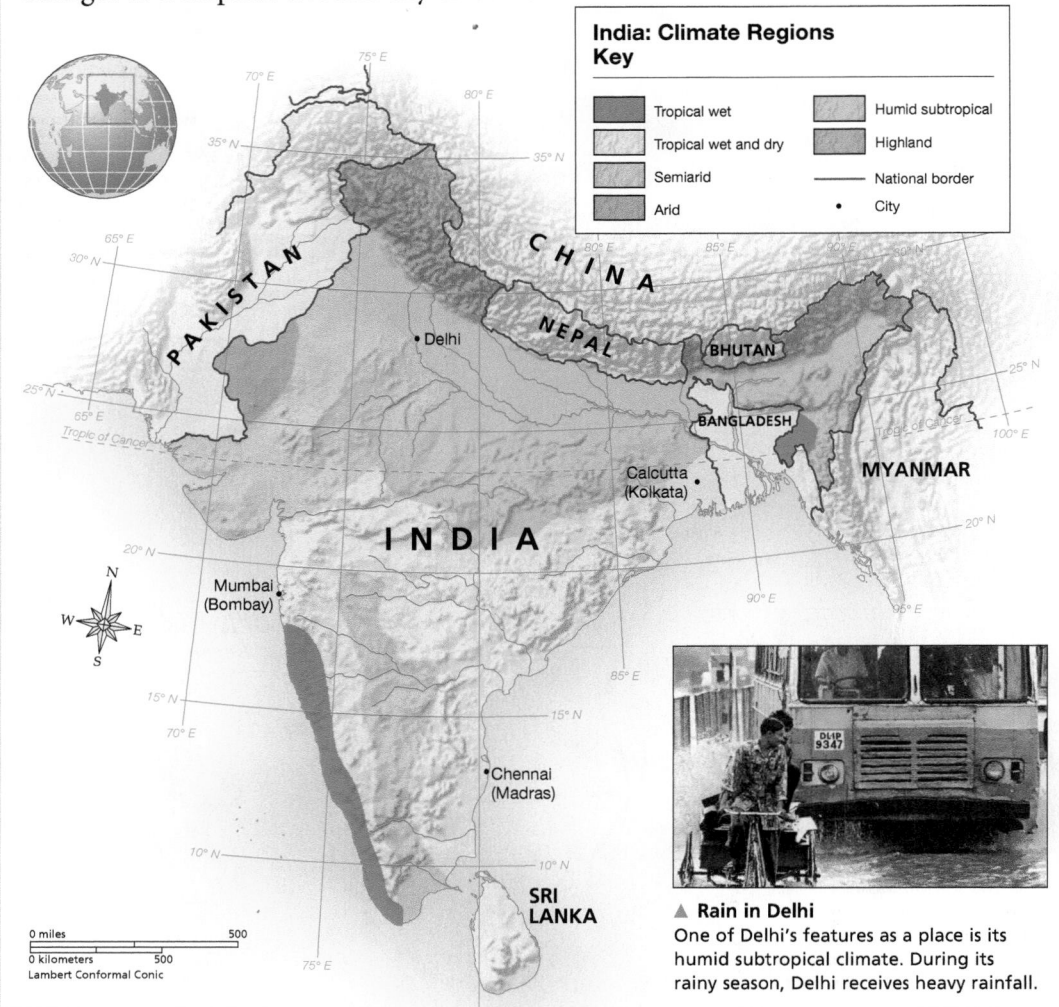

India: Climate Regions Key

- Tropical wet
- Tropical wet and dry
- Semiarid
- Arid
- Humid subtropical
- Highland
- —— National border
- • City

▲ Rain in Delhi
One of Delhi's features as a place is its humid subtropical climate. During its rainy season, Delhi receives heavy rainfall.

0 miles 500
0 kilometers 500
Lambert Conformal Conic

Differentiated Instruction

For English Language Learners   L1

If students are unfamiliar with words in the lesson, help them identify and look up those words in the dictionary. For example: *arid*—adj. having little or no rainfall; dry *humid*—adj. having a lot of water; damp *semi*—adj. part or partially

Follow up by having students determine the meaning of *semiarid*.

For Gifted and Talented   L3

Give students *Reading a Climate Graph*. Ask students to compare the information in the graph with the information on the map above. Ask them to write a sentence synthesizing about the climate of Mumbai.

All In One United States and Canada Teaching Resources, *Reading A Climate Graph,* p. 60

Special-Purpose Maps: Language

This map shows the official languages of India. An official language is the language used by the government. Even though a region has an official language, the people there may speak other languages as well. As in other special-purpose maps, the key explains how the different languages appear on the map.

PRACTICE YOUR GEOGRAPHY SKILLS

1 What color represents the Malayalam language on this map?

2 Where in India is Tamil the official language?

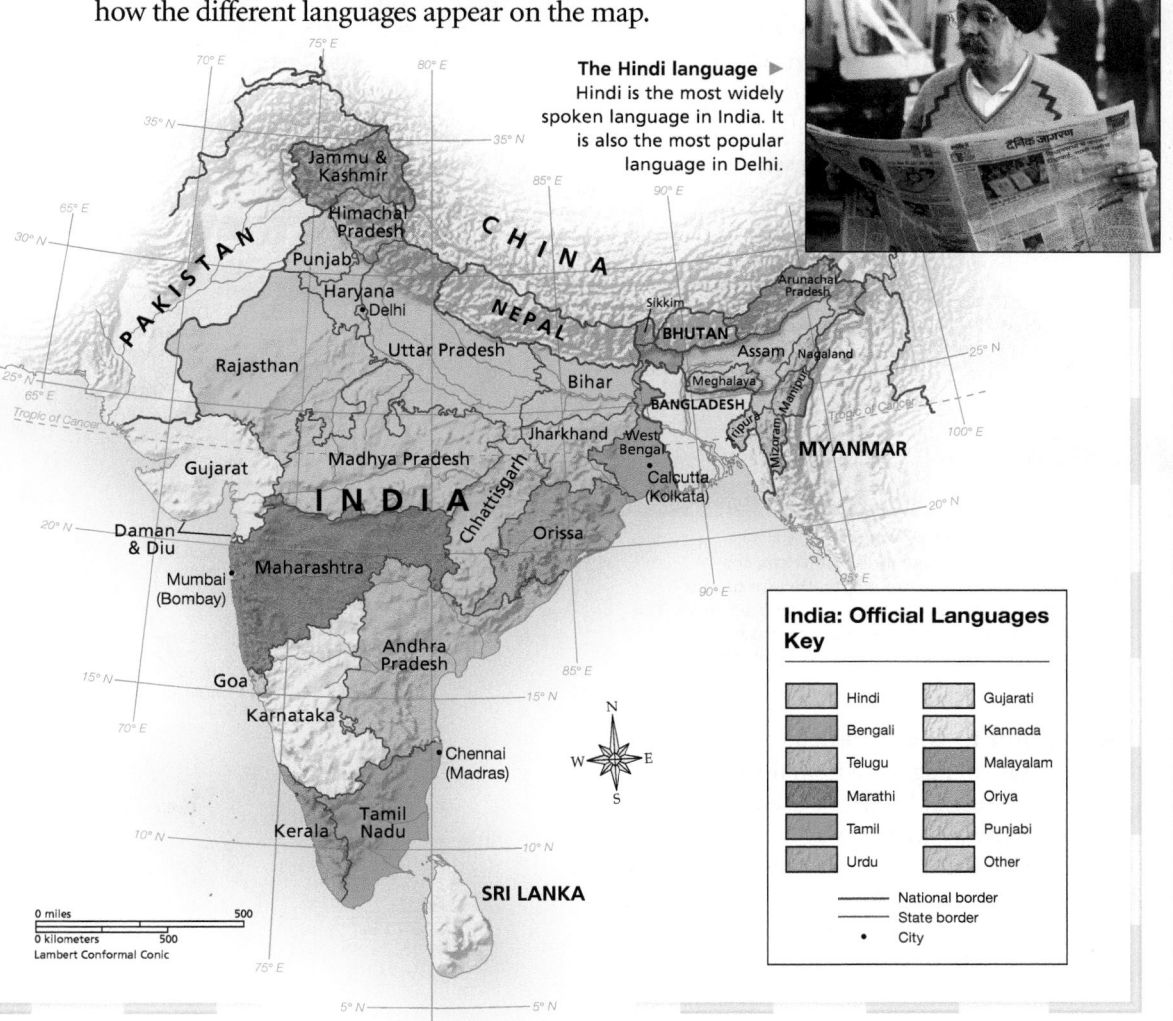

The Hindi language ▶
Hindi is the most widely spoken language in India. It is also the most popular language in Delhi.

India: Official Languages Key

Hindi	Gujarati
Bengali	Kannada
Telugu	Malayalam
Marathi	Oriya
Tamil	Punjabi
Urdu	Other

—— National border
—— State border
• City

0 miles 500
0 kilometers 500
Lambert Conformal Conic

MapMaster Skills Handbook **M13**

Background: Daily Life

The Hindi Language Hindi is the official language of India and is the primary language for about 300 million people. English is also spoken by many Indians and is considered the language of politics and commerce. However, the diversity of the country is reflected in the enormous number of languages spoken there, more than 1,500 in all. Ten of India's major states are organized along linguistic lines, and the Indian constitution recognizes 15 regional languages.

Special-Purpose Maps: Language   L2

Guided Instruction
- Read the text as a class. Draw students' attention to the map and its key.

- Have students consider the diversity of official languages. Ask **Why might it be important for a state to have a common language in addition to local ones?** (*Communication is easier with a common language.*)

Independent Practice

Have students work with partners to read another special purpose map, *Reading a Natural Vegetation Map.*

All in One United States and Canada Teaching Resources, *Reading a Natural Vegetation Map,* p. 61

Monitor Progress

As students complete the worksheet, circulate around the room and make sure individuals understand key concepts. Provide assistance as needed.

Assess and Reteach

Assess Progress   L2
Have students answer the questions under Practice Your Geography Skills on pp. M12–M13.

Reteach   L1
Have students practice using a special purpose map by completing *Analyzing and Interpreting Special Purpose Maps.*

⊙ *Analyzing and Interpreting Special-Purpose Maps,* **Social Studies Skills Tutor CD-ROM**

Extend   L3
Have students learn about another type of special-purpose map by completing *Reading a Time Zone Map.* Then ask students to find out the time zones in India and create their own time zone map, using *Outline Map 26: South Asia: Political.*

All in One United States and Canada Teaching Resources, *Reading a Time Zone Map.* p. 63; *Outline Map 26: South Asia,* p. 62

Answers

PRACTICE YOUR GEOGRAPHY SKILLS

1. dark purple
2. southeast India

Objectives
- Learn why people migrate.
- Understand how migration affects environments.

Prepare to Read

Build Background Knowledge　L1
Remind students that they studied the theme of movement earlier in this unit. Brainstorm with students why people move from place to place, particularly those who move from one country to another. Use the Numbered Heads participation strategy (TE, p. T36) to generate ideas.

Instruct

Human Migration　L2

Guided Instruction
- Divide the text using the headings and ask students to read the pages using the Paragraph Shrinking strategy (TE, p. T34). Clarify the meanings of any unfamiliar words.

- Have students look at the map. Ask **From what European countries did people migrate to the Americas in the years between 1500 and 1800?** *(Portugal, Spain, France, Netherlands, England)*

- Ask **Where did the French settle in the Americas?** *(French Guiana and Haiti)* **Which European country had the most possessions in the Americas?** *(Spain)*

- Ask **Why were some Africans forced to migrate?** *(They were imported as slaves from their homeland. Europeans wanted them to work on the land they claimed in the Americas.)*

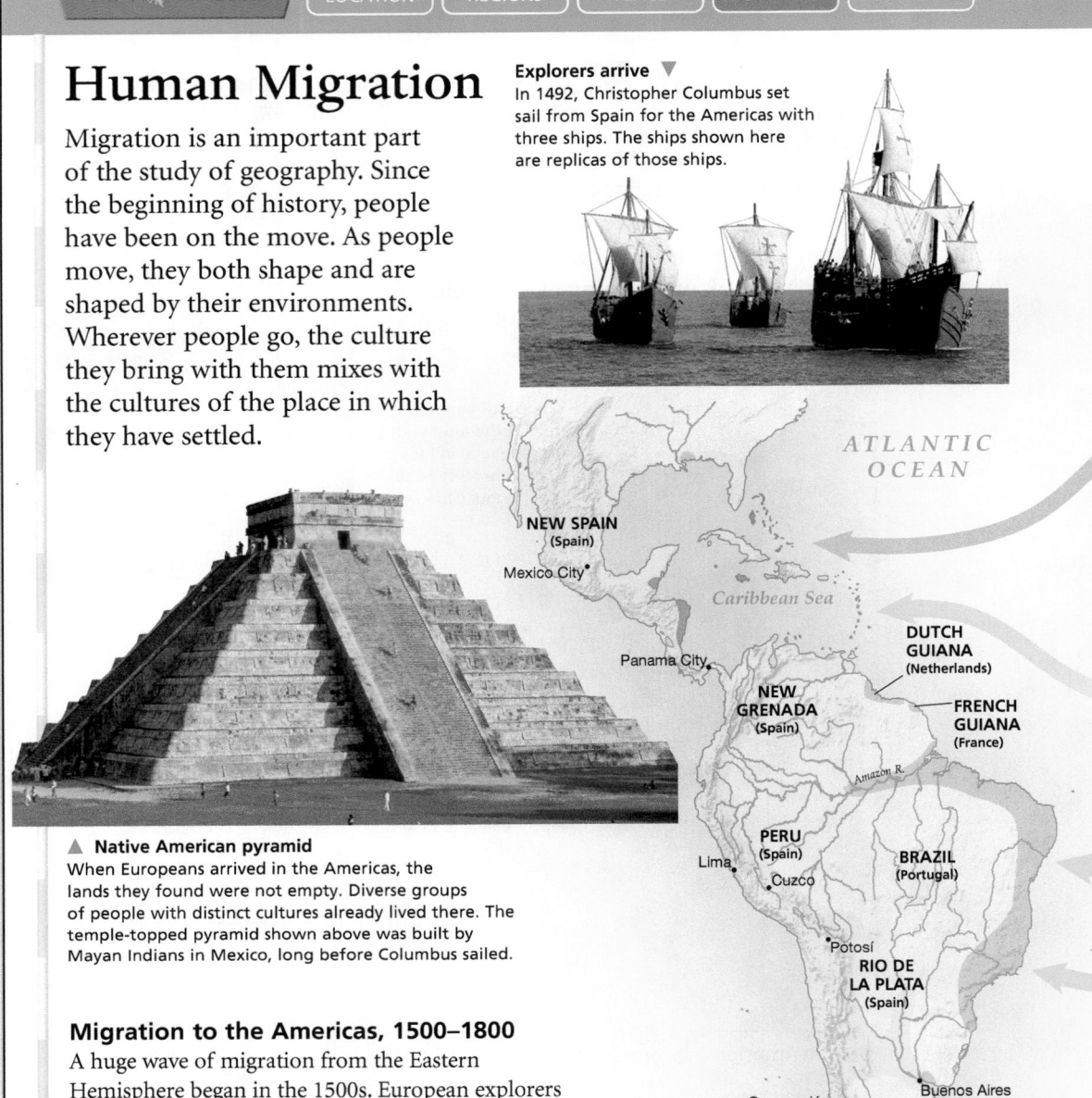

MAP MASTER   LOCATION   REGIONS   PLACE   MOVEMENT   INTERACTION

Human Migration

Migration is an important part of the study of geography. Since the beginning of history, people have been on the move. As people move, they both shape and are shaped by their environments. Wherever people go, the culture they bring with them mixes with the cultures of the place in which they have settled.

Explorers arrive ▼
In 1492, Christopher Columbus set sail from Spain for the Americas with three ships. The ships shown here are replicas of those ships.

▲ **Native American pyramid**
When Europeans arrived in the Americas, the lands they found were not empty. Diverse groups of people with distinct cultures already lived there. The temple-topped pyramid shown above was built by Mayan Indians in Mexico, long before Columbus sailed.

Migration to the Americas, 1500–1800
A huge wave of migration from the Eastern Hemisphere began in the 1500s. European explorers in the Americas paved the way for hundreds of years of European settlement there. Forced migration from Africa started soon afterward, as Europeans began to import African slaves to work in the Americas. The map to the right shows these migrations.

M14 MapMaster Skills Handbook

Differentiated Instruction

For Less Proficient Readers　L1
Review with students the meaning of "push" and "pull" factors in terms of human migration. Model for students how to make a table with the headings Push and Pull. Then work with students to list as many factors as they can under each heading.

For Advanced Readers　L3
Have students complete *Analyzing Statistics*. When they have finished, have them write a paragraph explaining how economic and social statistics are related to "push" and "pull" factors.

All in One United States and Canada Teaching Resources, *Analyzing Statistics*, p. 65

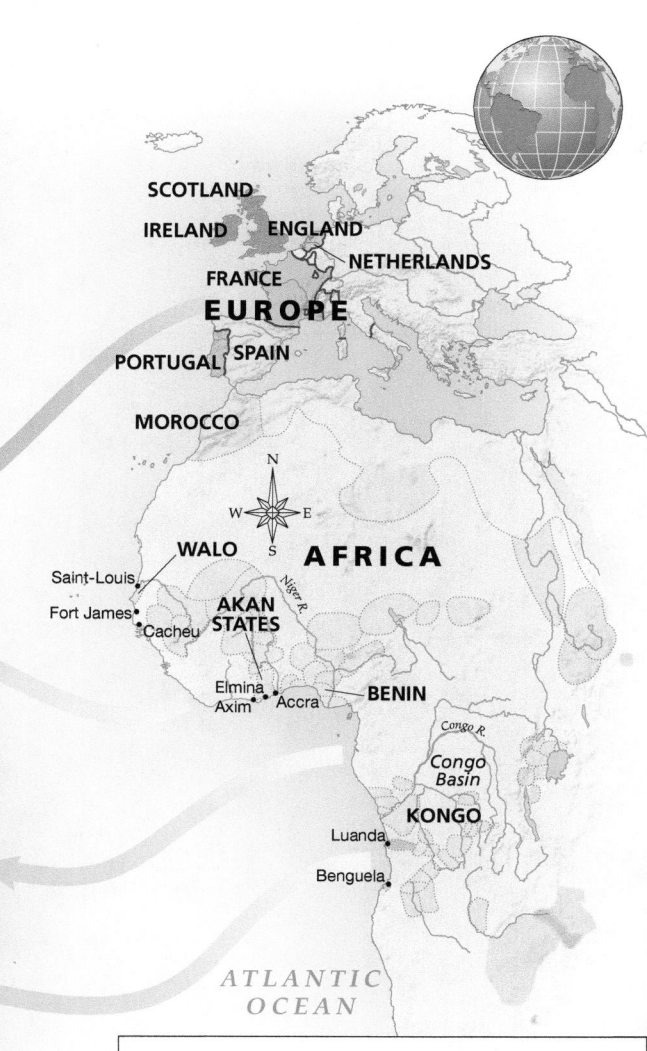

SCOTLAND
IRELAND ENGLAND
FRANCE NETHERLANDS
EUROPE
PORTUGAL SPAIN
MOROCCO

WALO AFRICA
Saint-Louis
Fort James Cacheu
AKAN STATES
Elmina Accra
Axim BENIN
Congo R.
Congo Basin
KONGO
Luanda
Benguela

Niger R.

ATLANTIC OCEAN

N
W E
S

Migration to Latin America, 1500–1800
Key

- ← European migration
- ← African migration
- —— National or colonial border
- ········· Traditional African border
- African State

- Spain and possessions
- Portugal and possessions
- Netherlands and possessions
- France and possessions
- England and possessions

1 Where did the Portuguese settle in the Americas?

2 Would you describe African migration at this time as a result of both push factors and pull factors? Explain why or why not.

"Push" and "Pull" Factors

Geographers describe a people's choice to migrate in terms of "push" factors and "pull" factors. Push factors are things in people's lives that push them to leave, such as poverty and political unrest. Pull factors are things in another country that pull people to move there, including better living conditions and hopes of better jobs.

▲ **Elmina, Ghana**
Elmina, in Ghana, is one of the many ports from which slaves were transported from Africa. Because slaves and gold were traded here, stretches of the western African coast were known as the Slave Coast and the Gold Coast.

Independent Practice

Have students work with partners to complete *Reading a Historical Map*. Have students be ready to explain how the movement of European groups changed the map of Africa. (*Much of Africa was colonized by Europeans.*)

All in One **United States and Canada Teaching Resources,** *Reading a Historical Map,* p. 64

Monitor Progress

As students complete the worksheet, circulate around the room to make sure individuals comprehend the key concepts. Provide assistance as needed.

Assess and Reteach

Assess Progress   L2

Have students complete the questions under Practice Your Geography Skills.

Reteach   L1

Help students make an outline of the lesson. Show *Transparency B15: Outline* as a model. Then work with students to identify the main points. Encourage students to refer to their outlines to review the material.

📖 **United States and Canada Transparencies,** *Transparency B15: Outline*

Extend   L3

To extend the lesson, have students complete *The Global Refugee Crisis*. Then ask them to choose a specific region on the graph and find out more about refugees from one country in that region.

Go Online
PHSchool.com **For:** Environmental and Global Issues: *The Global Refugee Crisis*
Visit: PHSchool.com
Web Code: lhd-4001

Answers

PRACTICE YOUR GEOGRAPHY SKILLS

1. Brazil

2. most likely push factors because people were forced to leave; the need for workers in the Americas was a pull factor although it was the Europeans who responded to it by importing Africans as slaves

Objectives

- Understand and use a land use map.
- Learn how land use and economic structures are linked.

Prepare to Read

Build Background Knowledge L1

Discuss with the class the ways that people in your community are using land. For example, is all the land used for homes? How much is used for commercial purposes? What kinds? Are there farms or manufacturing facilities? Point out that communities in all parts of the world use land in different ways.

Instruct

World Land Use L2

Guided Instruction

- Read the text as a class using the Oral Cloze strategy (TE, p. T33). Follow up by having students do a second silent reading. Encourage students to study the map and photographs.

- Talk about the difference between commercial and subsistence farming. Have them look closely at the photographs on pages M16 and M17. Ask **How do the tools and equipment people use differ in these types of farming?** (*Large power machines are used in commercial farming; hand tools are used in subsistence farming.*) **Why might people use more land in commercial farming?** (*Machines make it possible to cultivate more land. The more land cultivated, the more sales possible.*)

- Ask **What color represents nomadic herding on this map?** (*light purple*) **In what parts of the world is this an economic activity?** (*Africa, Asia, Europe*)

- Ask **Why might some parts of the world have little or no land use activity?** (*Land and/or climate might not be suitable for farming or other activity.*)

World Land Use

People around the world have many different economic structures, or ways of making a living. Land-use maps are one way to learn about these structures. The ways that people use the land in each region tell us about the main ways that people in that region make a living.

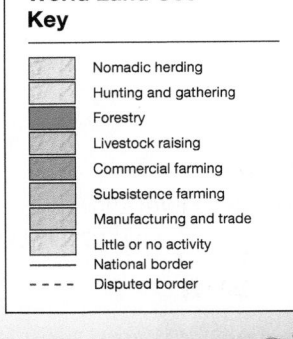

World Land Use Key

- Nomadic herding
- Hunting and gathering
- Forestry
- Livestock raising
- Commercial farming
- Subsistence farming
- Manufacturing and trade
- Little or no activity
- —— National border
- - - - - Disputed border

▲ **Wheat farming in the United States**
Developed countries practice commercial farming rather than subsistence farming. Commercial farming is the production of food mainly for sale, either within the country or for export to other countries. Commercial farmers like these in Oregon often use heavy equipment to farm.

Levels of Development

Notice on the map key the term *subsistence farming*. This term means the production of food mainly for use by the farmer's own family. In less-developed countries, subsistence farming is often one of the main economic activities. In contrast, in developed countries there is little subsistence farming.

▲ **Growing barley in Ecuador**
These farmers in Ecuador use hand tools to harvest barley. They will use most of the crop they grow to feed themselves or their farm animals.

NORTH AMERICA

SOUTH AMERICA

0 miles 2,000
0 kilometers 2,000
Robinson

M16 MapMaster Skills Handbook

Background: Global Perspectives

Agriculture Almost 50 percent of the world's population is occupied in agriculture. A much higher proportion of this is in developing countries where dense populations, small land holdings, and traditional techniques predominate. In areas where there is intense cultivation using people and animals but few machines, the yield is low in relation to the output of energy. In leading food producing countries such as the United States, industrial farms make use of new technology and crop specialization to increase output.

▲ **Growing rice in Vietnam**
Women in Vietnam plant rice in wet rice paddies, using the same planting methods their ancestors did.

PRACTICE YOUR GEOGRAPHY SKILLS

1 In what parts of the world is subsistence farming the main land use?

2 Locate where manufacturing and trade are the main land use. Are they found more often near areas of subsistence farming or areas of commercial farming? Why might this be so?

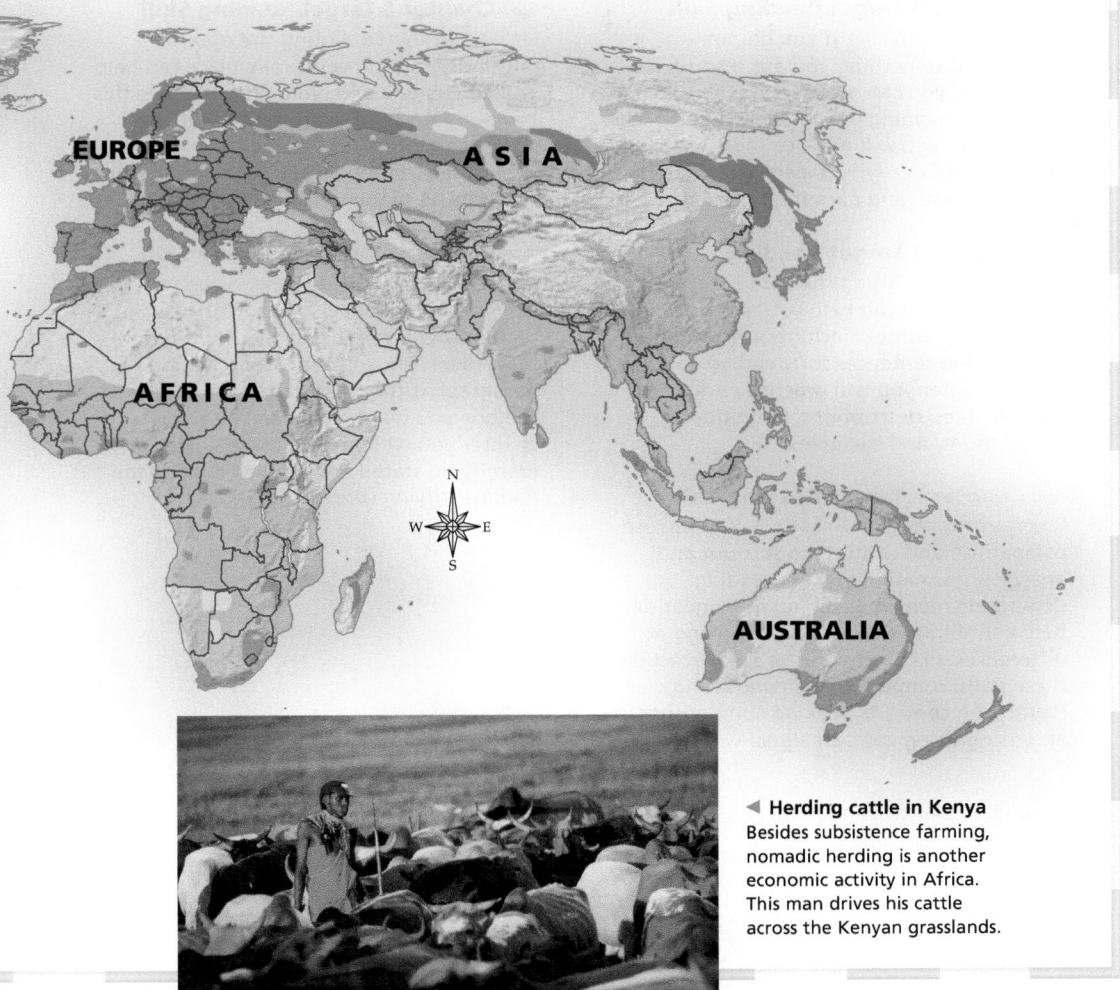

EUROPE

ASIA

AFRICA

AUSTRALIA

◄ **Herding cattle in Kenya**
Besides subsistence farming, nomadic herding is another economic activity in Africa. This man drives his cattle across the Kenyan grasslands.

MapMaster Skills Handbook **M17**

Independent Practice

Partner students and have them complete *Reading an Economic Activity Map.* Have students be ready to offer explanations for how the economic activity in Somalia might affect the lives of people there.

All in One **United States and Canada Teaching Resources,** *Reading an Economic Activity Map,* p. 66

Monitor Progress

Circulate around the room as students complete the worksheet to make sure individuals comprehend the key concepts. Provide assistance as needed.

Assess and Reteach

Assess Progress [L2]

Have students complete the questions under Practice Your Geography Skills.

Reteach [L1]

Help students make a table to identify the main kinds of land use. Draw a model on the board for students to follow. Use these headings: Nomadic Herding, Forestry, Livestock Raising, Commercial Farming, Subsistence Farming, Manufacturing and Trade. Under each heading, help students write a short explanation. Then have students find one or two places on the map in their books where that activity takes place.

Extend [L3]

To extend the lesson, have students complete *Reading a Natural Resources Map.* Point out that this map shows mineral resources. Then ask students to write a paragraph relating mineral resources to land use.

All in One **United States and Canada Teaching Resources,** *Reading a Natural Resources Map,* p. 67

Answers

PRACTICE YOUR GEOGRAPHY SKILLS

1. Africa, Asia, South America, North America

2. areas of commercial farming; both manufacturing and trade and commercial farming require technology that subsistence farmers do not have

Teaching the Target Reading Skills

The Prentice Hall *World Studies* program has interwoven essential reading skills instruction throughout the Student Edition, Teacher's Edition, and ancillary resources. In the Foundations of Geography section, students will learn five reading skills.

Student Edition The *World Studies* Student Edition provides students with reading skills instruction, practice, and application opportunities in each chapter within the program.

Teacher's Edition The *World Studies* Teacher Edition supports your teaching of each skill by providing full modeling in each chapter's interleaf and modeling of the specific sub-skills in each section lesson.

All in One Teaching Resources The *World Studies* All-in-One Teaching Resources provides a worksheet explaining and supporting the elements of each Target Reading Skill. Use these to help struggling students master skills, or as more practice for every student.

Target Reading Skills

The Target Reading Skills introduced on this page will help you understand the words and ideas in this section on geography and in other social studies reading you do. Each chapter focuses on one of these reading skills. Good readers develop a bank of reading strategies, or skills. Then they draw on the particular strategies that will help them understand the text they are reading.

Chapter 1 Target Reading Skill

Clarifying Meaning If you do not understand something you are reading right away, you can use several skills to help clarify the meaning of the word or idea. In this chapter you will practice these strategies for clarifying meaning: rereading, reading ahead, and paraphrasing.

Chapter 2 Target Reading Skill

Using Context Using the context of an unfamiliar word can help you understand its meaning. Context includes the words, phrases, and sentences surrounding a word. In this chapter you will practice using these context clues: descriptions, definitions, comparisons, and examples.

Chapter 3 Target Reading Skill

Comparing and Contrasting You can use comparison and contrast to sort out and analyze information you are reading. Comparing means examining the similarities between things. Contrasting is looking at differences. In this chapter you will practice these skills: comparing and contrasting, identifying contrasts, making comparisons, and recognizing contrast signal words.

Chapter 4 Target Reading Skill

Using Sequence Noting the order in which significant events take place can help you understand and remember them. In this chapter you will practice these sequence skills: sequencing, or finding the order of events, sequencing important changes, and recognizing sequence signal words.

Chapter 5 Target Reading Skill

Identifying the Main Idea Since you cannot remember every detail of what you read, it is important that you identify the main ideas. The main idea of a section or paragraph is the most important point and the one you want to remember. In this chapter you will practice these skills: identifying stated and implied main ideas and identifying supporting details.

M18 Foundations of Geography

Assessment Resources

Use the diagnosing readiness tests from **AYP Monitoring Assessments** to help you identify problems before students begin to study geography.

Determine students' reading level and identify challenges:

📄 *Screening Tests,* pp. 1–10

Evaluate students' verbal skills:

📄 *Critical Thinking and Reading Tests,* pp. 25–34

📄 *Vocabulary Tests,* pp. 45–52

📄 *Writing Tests,* pp. 53–60

FOUNDATIONS of GEOGRAPHY

Are you curious about our world? Do you want to know why winters are cold and summers are hot? Have you wondered why some people live and work in cities and others work on farms in the countryside? If you answered yes to any of these questions, you want to know more about geography.

Guiding Questions

The text, photographs, maps, and charts in this book will help you discover answers to these Guiding Questions.

1. **Geography** What are Earth's major physical features?

2. **History** How have people's ways of life changed over time?

3. **Culture** What is a culture?

4. **Government** What types of government exist in the world today?

5. **Economics** How do people use the world's natural resources?

Project Preview

You can also discover answers to the Guiding Questions by working on projects. Project possibilities are listed on page 136 of this book.

Foundations of Geography **1**

Assess students' social studies skills:

- 📄 *Geographic Literacy Tests,* pp. 13–20
- 📄 *Visual Analysis Tests,* pp. 21–24
- 📄 *Communications Tests,* pp. 35–44

The World Studies program provides instruction and practice for all of these skills. Use students' test results to pinpoint the skills your students have mastered and the skills they need to practice. Then use *Correlation to Program Resources* to prescribe skills practice and reinforcement.

📄 *Correlation to Program Resources,* pp. 64–77

Guiding Questions

- This section was developed around five Guiding Questions about the foundations of geography. They appear on the reduced Student Edition page to the left. The Guiding Questions are intended as an organizational focus for the book. The Guiding Questions act as a kind of umbrella under which all of the material falls.

- You may wish to add your own Guiding Questions to the list in order to tailor them to your particular course.

- Draw students' attention to the Guiding Questions. Ask them to write the questions in their notebooks for future reference.

- In the Teacher's Edition, each section's themes are linked to a specific Guiding Question at the beginning of each chapter. Then, an activity at the end of the chapter returns to the Guiding Questions to review key concepts.

Project Preview

- The projects for this section are designed to provide students with hands-on involvement in the content area. Students are introduced to some projects on page 136.

- *Book Projects* give students directions on how to complete these projects, and more.

  All in One Foundations of Geography Teaching Resources, *Book Project: Focus on Part of the Whole,* pp. 27–29; *Book Project: The Geography Game,* pp. 30–32; *Book Project: Desktop Countries,* pp. 33–35; *Book Project: World News Today,* pp. 36–38

- Assign projects as small group activities, whole-class projects, or individual projects. Consider assigning a project at the beginning of the course.

Objectives

- Examine country borders that are shaped by geography, politics, and culture.

- Locate and name the seven continents.

- Analyze a physical map of the world to learn about elevation.

- Examine landforms and bodies of water that act as barriers to movement across countries and continents.

- Analyze the population density of the world and investigate the world's urban and rural populations.

Prepare to Read

Build Background Knowledge L2

Have students brainstorm similarities and differences among the world's continents. Encourage them to think about physical and cultural similarities and differences. Tell students that they will either confirm or revise these comparisons during their study of Earth's geography.

Instruct

Investigate the Political World L2

Guided Instruction

- Read the introductory and Location paragraphs as a class. Direct students' attention to the border between the country of Canada and state of Alaska. Ask **Do you think the border is shaped by politics or geography? Explain.** (*politics, because the border is straight*)

- Hand out the *World Overview* worksheet. Direct students to fill in the answers to the questions as they read.

  All In One Foundations of Geography Teaching Resources, *World Overview,* pp. 43–45

Answers

LOCATION Rivers and lakes may form the crooked portion of the border in the east. The straight portion of the border was probably shaped by politics.

Investigate the Political World

There are more than 190 independent countries in the world. Some of those countries have dependencies, or areas outside of those countries that belong to them. Every land area where people live belongs to some country. The blue areas on maps in this book show the world's oceans, seas, and lakes. The other colors on this map show the areas of the world's countries and dependencies.

Go Online PHSchool.com   Use Web Code **nfp-3020** for the **interactive maps** on these pages.

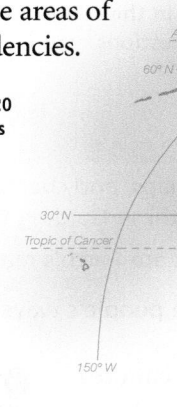

▲ **Denmark**
Denmark is one of the oldest continuously existing states. Christiansborg Palace is the seat of the Danish Parliament.

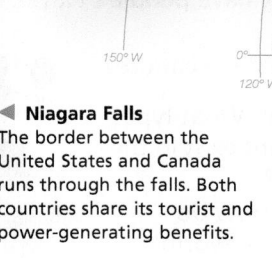

◄ **Niagara Falls**
The border between the United States and Canada runs through the falls. Both countries share its tourist and power-generating benefits.

LOCATION

1 Examine Country Borders

Governments have drawn the borders between countries. Some borders follow mountains or rivers. Others are straight lines. On the map, look at the United States and Canada. These are the large yellow and pink countries in North America. Parts of their borders are straight, but others are crooked. Why might this be? What might explain the location of other borders on this map?

The World: Political Key

—— National border
- - - Disputed border

Mental Mapping

The Shape of the World Have students close their textbooks. Take down or cover any maps of the world that may be hanging in your classroom. Then give each student a blank piece of paper. Ask them to draw a map of the seven continents.

Encourage them to draw the shapes of the continents as accurately as possible. Have them draw in any continent borders that appear on land. Remind them to label the continents.

PLACE

2 Analyze the Continents

Notice the six black labels on the world map. These labels name continents. Which continent's name is also the name of a country? You can see that some continents have more countries than others. Which continent is made up mostly of small countries?

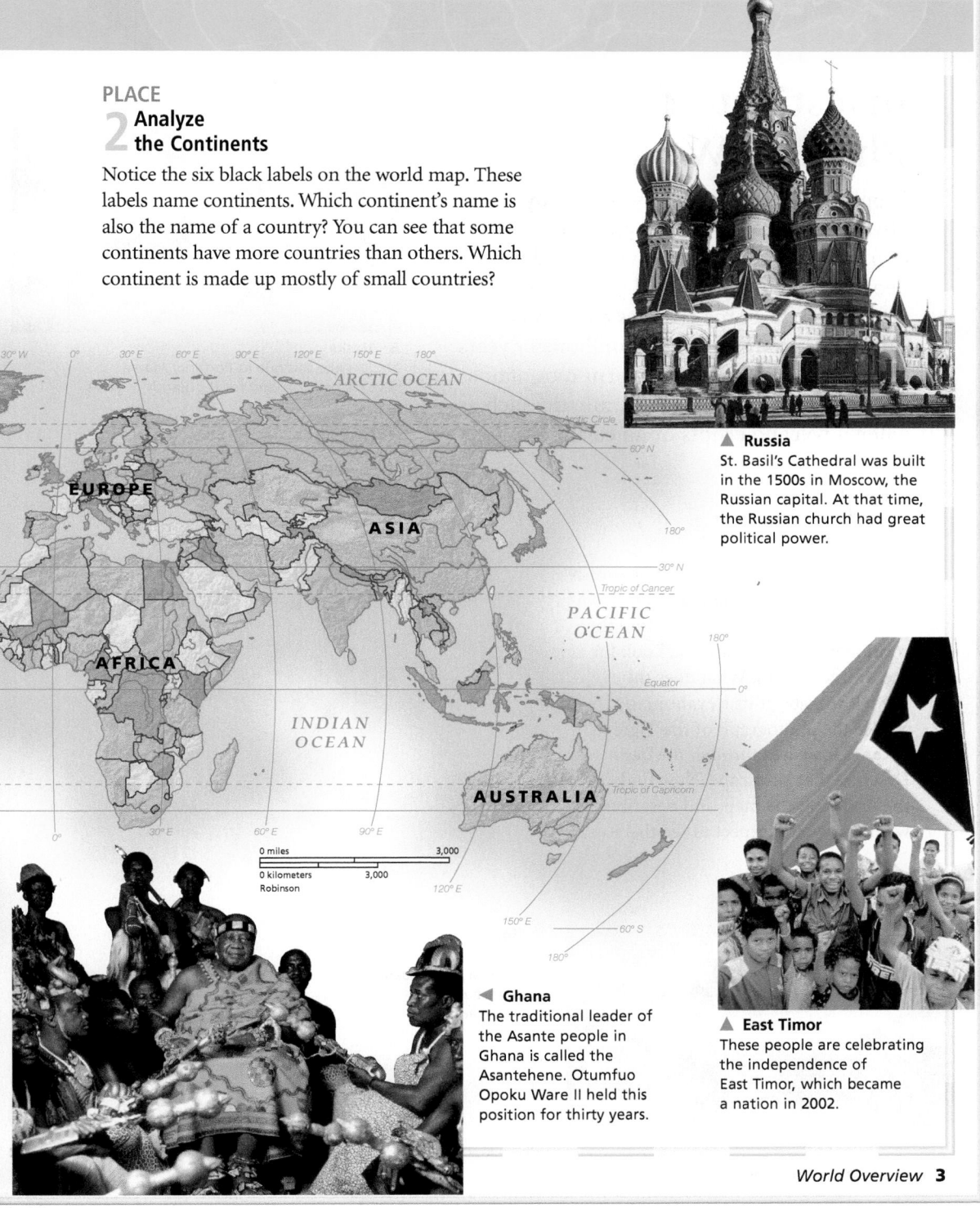

ARCTIC OCEAN

EUROPE

ASIA

AFRICA

PACIFIC OCEAN

INDIAN OCEAN

AUSTRALIA

0 miles 3,000
0 kilometers 3,000
Robinson

▲ Russia
St. Basil's Cathedral was built in the 1500s in Moscow, the Russian capital. At that time, the Russian church had great political power.

◄ Ghana
The traditional leader of the Asante people in Ghana is called the Asantehene. Otumfuo Opoku Ware II held this position for thirty years.

▲ East Timor
These people are celebrating the independence of East Timor, which became a nation in 2002.

Background: Links Across Time

Historical Borders Geographic features such as rivers and mountains have played an important role in history. By 1803, the United States stretched from the Atlantic Ocean to the Mississippi River. France controlled the territory—called Louisiana—that extended from the Mississippi River west to the Rocky Mountains. In 1803, the United States purchased Louisiana, extending the United States to the Rocky Mountains. Today, the Mississippi River still serves as a border—but between neighboring states rather than neighboring country territories.

Investigate the Physical World

L2

Guided Instruction

- Read the introduction and the Place paragraphs. Have students study the physical map of the world. Ask them to use the map key to determine the highest range of elevations in Asia and Australia. *(Asia—more than 13,000 feet [3,960 meters]; Australia—1,600–6,500 feet [480–1,980 meters])*

- Ask students to identify the elevation range of Scandinavia's northern and western coasts. *(0–650 feet [0–200 meters])*

- Read the Human-Environment Interaction paragraph. Direct students' attention to Europe and Asia. Have them again locate the border between these two continents. Ask **What physical feature serves as a physical barrier between these two continents?** *(Ural Mountains)*

- After students have read the caption about Mount Fuji, ask them to trace their finger over the islands along the rim of the Pacific Ocean. Be sure they locate the islands on both pages of the map. Point out that some of these islands are considered to be part of Asia and others are part of a region that is sometimes called Oceania. The islands off the east coast of Asia from Japan south to Sumatra and Java and east to New Guinea are part of Asia while the islands of Micronesia, Melanesia, and Polynesia are part of Oceania.

- Have students continue to complete the *World Overview* worksheet.

   All in One Foundations of Geography Teaching Resources, *World Overview,* pp. 43–45

Answer

PLACE The elevation of the Amazon Basin is 0 to 650 feet or 0 to 200 meters above sea level. The landscape around the Tigre River appears very flat. You would expect to see tall peaks in the Andes.

Investigate the Physical World

People's lives are constantly shaped by their physical environment. The physical features of a place often determine where and how people live. Yet the physical world is always changing, too. Some changes come very slowly. For example, it took millions of years for Earth's crust to lift and form mountains. Other changes are fast and dramatic, such as when a volcano erupts or an earthquake hits.

▲ **Alaska**
Glaciers like this one at Portage, Alaska, have shaped the land for thousands of years.

PLACE

3 **Infer From a Map**

Notice the bumpy texture and brownish colors on the map. These indicate a mountainous landscape. Now find the continent of South America. Look for the Amazon Basin. What does the key tell you about its elevation? Notice the photograph of the Tigre River as it weaves through the basin. Describe that landscape. Now find the Andes on the map, and describe what you would expect to see there.

◄ **Tigre River**
The Tigre River, a tributary of the Amazon, winds through the Peruvian rain forest.

4 Foundations of Geography

Differentiated Instruction

For Less Proficient Readers   L1

For students having trouble reading the physical map of the world, distribute *Reading a Physical Map* and *Elevation on a Map*. Have students complete the activities in pairs.

All in One Foundations of Geography Teaching Resources, *Reading a Physical Map,* p. 47; *Elevation on a Map,* p. 48

For Advanced Readers   L3

Tell students that another way mapmakers can show elevation on a map is by using isolines. Assign *Understanding Isolines* and *Reading a Contour Map* to help students explore this concept.

All in One Foundations of Geography Teaching Resources, *Understanding Isolines,* p. 49; *Reading a Contour Map,* p. 50

HUMAN-ENVIRONMENT INTERACTION

4 Examine Landforms as Barriers

Physical barriers can make movement between areas difficult. For example, take a look at the continents in the map below. Some of them are separated from one another by vast areas of water. Examine the elevation key. Look closely at the map's labels. What other physical landforms might have acted as barriers to movement?

▲ **Mount Fuji, Japan**
Volcanoes such as this one have created islands along the rim of the Pacific Ocean.

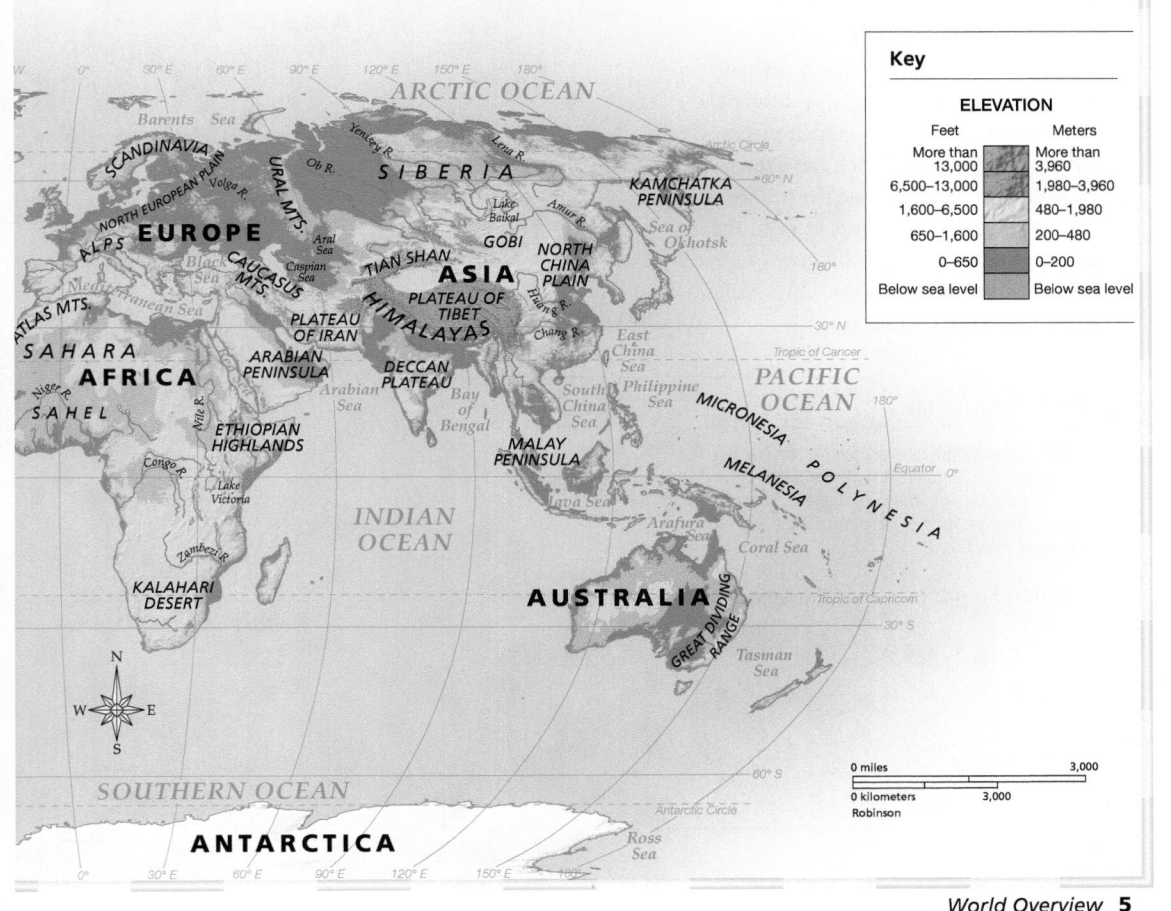

Key

ELEVATION

Feet		Meters
More than 13,000		More than 3,960
6,500–13,000		1,980–3,960
1,600–6,500		480–1,980
650–1,600		200–480
0–650		0–200
Below sea level		Below sea level

0 miles 3,000
0 kilometers 3,000
Robinson

Independent Practice

■ Have students explore the location of the world's highest peaks by placing them on an outline map.

■ Give them the following statistics:

Continent	Highest Point	Elevation
Africa	Kilimanjaro	19,340 feet
Antarctica	Vinson Massif	16,864 feet
Asia	Mount Everest	29,035 feet
Australia	Mount Kosciusko	7,310 feet
North America	Mount McKinley	20,320 feet
South America	Mount Aconcagua	22,834 feet

■ Have them research the location of the highest point on each continent. Then distribute *Outline Map 1: The World: Physical.* Ask students to create a symbol to represent the highest point and show it in a map key. Then have them label the points on each continent. Ask them to write in the height of each point near each label.

All in One Foundations of Geography Teaching Resources, *Outline Map 1: The World: Physical,* p. 51

Monitor Progress

Make sure students are creating maps correctly. Check student maps for map keys and appropriate labels.

Answer

HUMAN-ENVIRONMENT INTERACTION
Possible answer: Mountain ranges and deserts also might have acted as barriers to movement.

Investigate Population

Guided Instruction

- Use the Choral Reading technique (TE, p. 34) to read the text.

- Ask students **Which color on the map represents the most densely populated areas?** *(purple)* **Which color represents the most sparsely populated areas?** *(yellow)*

- Direct students' attention to Africa on the map. Tell them to use what they know about Africa's physical geography to explain why much of North Africa is sparsely populated. *(Much of North Africa is covered by the Sahara.)*

- Have students study the circle graphs at the bottom of p. 6. Ask **In which of these countries does the greatest percentage of people live in urban areas?** *(the United Kingdom)*

Independent Practice

Display *Color Transparency FG 5: The World: Continents and Oceans* and *Color Transparency FG 6: Some Major Cities of the World.* Have students compare them with the population density map on pp. 6–7 in the Student Edition. Ask students to list one densely populated city on each continent. Then have them compare the transparencies with the physical map on pp. 4–5 of the Student Edition. Have them locate the cities they listed on the physical map and their nearby landforms. Finally, ask them to synthesize the information by writing a sentence about each city.

📖 **Foundations of Geography Transparencies,** *Color Transparency FG 5: The World: Continents and Oceans; Color Transparency FG 6: Some Major Cities of the World*

Monitor Progress

Circulate to make sure students are able to locate the most populated cities on the maps. Check students' sentences for appropriate details.

Answer

REGIONS Much of Europe, eastern North America, and southeastern and southern Asia have many people, while Northern North America, Australia, and northern Asia have few people. Possible answer: People choose where to live based on climate and geography.

Investigate Population

For thousands of years, the world's population grew slowly. In the past 200 years, however, health care, living conditions, and food production have greatly improved. This has led to a huge population burst. In 1800, the world's population numbered less than 1 billion people. Today, it is more than 6 billion, and growing quickly.

▲ **China**
A crowd of people walk through a park in the capital city of Beijing. China has the largest population of any country in the world.

REGIONS

5 Analyze Population Density

A population density map shows you where the world's people live. Study the world population map. Which places have many people? Which have few? Why do you think people live where they do? As you study the map, refer to the world physical map on the previous page. It may give you some clues to help you answer these questions.

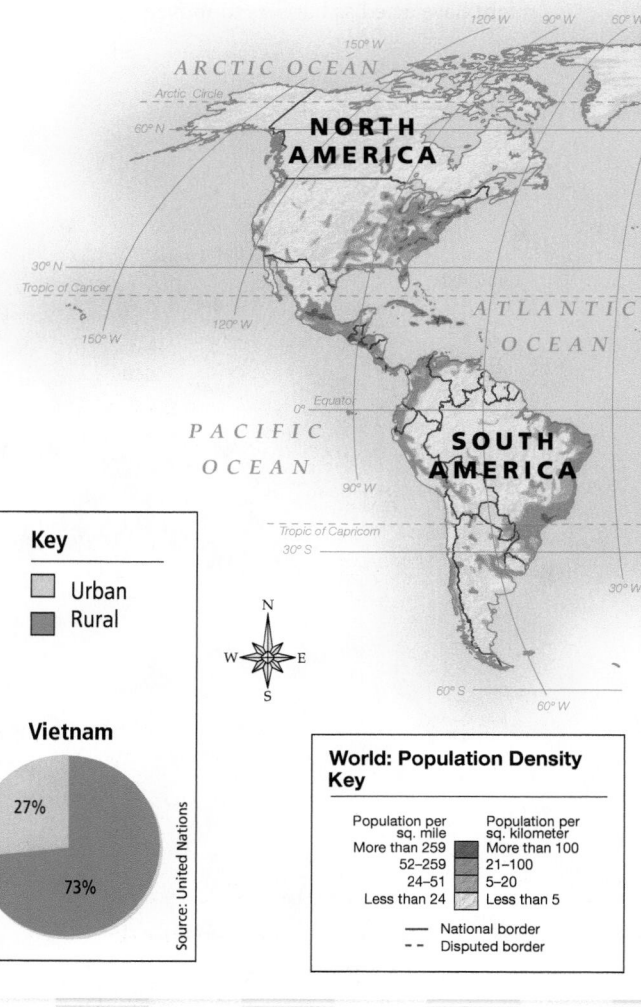

World Population

In the United Kingdom, most people live in cities. In Panama, the population is almost equally divided between urban and rural areas. In some Asian countries, such as Vietnam, people live mainly in rural areas.

Key
- Urban
- Rural

United Kingdom — 11%, 89%
Panama — 58%, 42%
Vietnam — 27%, 73%

Source: United Nations

World: Population Density Key

Population per sq. mile	Population per sq. kilometer
More than 259	More than 100
52–259	21–100
24–51	5–20
Less than 24	Less than 5

— National border
-- Disputed border

Differentiated Instruction

For English Language Learners L1
Spend extra time reviewing the meaning of important terms that may be difficult for English language learners such as *population density, urban,* and *rural.* Point out the map key and review what a square mile is. Have students find at least one area on the map that corresponds to each density range and have them say aloud the number of people it represents as they point to the area on the map.

MOVEMENT

6 Compare Continents

When high population densities cover large areas, those areas have large populations. Look at the continents on the map. Which continent do you think has the largest population, based on the size of its areas of high population density? Which continent do you think has the lowest population? Compare North America and South America on the map. Which continent do you think has the larger population?

▲ **New Zealand**
The Whanganui River flows through a New Zealand national park. New Zealand has a low population density.

PRACTICE YOUR GEOGRAPHY SKILLS

1. In Asia there is a ring of dense population next to an area with low population. Look at the physical map of the world on pages 4 and 5. What landform may explain this difference?

2. Look at Northern Africa. Find the area of heavy population that forms a curving line on the map. How does the physical map on pages 4 and 5 explain this?

Monaco is the most densely populated European nation. ▶

Differentiated Instruction

For Advanced Readers L3
Have students complete the *Urban Population, Past and Projected* activity individually so they can learn more about the world's urban population.

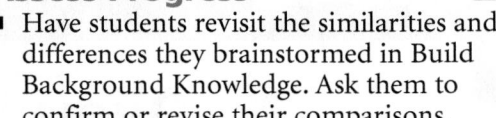

Go Online PHSchool.com **For:** Environmental and Global Issues: *Urban Population, Past and Projected*
Visit: PHSchool.com
Web Code: led-3307

Assess and Reteach

Assess Progress L2

- Have students revisit the similarities and differences they brainstormed in Build Background Knowledge. Ask them to confirm or revise their comparisons.

- Ask students to complete Practice Your Geography Skills on page 7.

Reteach L1

Have students review key concepts in the World Overview by completing *DK Compact Atlas of the World Activity: Reading a Political Map, DK Compact Atlas of the World Activity: Reading a Physical Map,* and *Reading a Population Density Map* in partners or small groups.

All in One Foundations of Geography Teaching Resources, *DK Compact Atlas of the World Activity: Reading a Political Map,* p. 52; *DK Compact Atlas of the World Activity: Reading a Physical Map,* p. 53; *Reading a Population Density Map,* p. 54

Extend L3

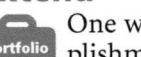 One way of assessing student accomplishments is by having them build a portfolio of their best work. To begin their portfolios for Foundations of Geography, have students choose one of the continents. Then, assign a project on this continent. Students can choose what type of project they would like to do. Options include collages, maps, stories, paragraphs, dioramas, and more.

- Give students *Writing an Outline for Research* to help them get started.

All in One Foundations of Geography Teaching Resources, *Writing an Outline for Research,* p. 55

Answers

MOVEMENT Possible answer: Asia, because it seems to have the largest areas of high population density. Australia, because most of it has low population density and there is very little area with a high population density. North America, because it seems to have larger areas of high population density.

PRACTICE YOUR GEOGRAPHY SKILLS

1. Possible answer: the Plateau of Tibet, the Gobi desert

2. The Nile River is located along the curving line of dense population.

Overview

Section 1

The Five Themes of Geography
1. Learn about the study of Earth.
2. Discover five ways to look at Earth.

Section 2

The Geographer's Tools
1. Find out how maps and globes show information about Earth's surface.
2. See how mapmakers show Earth's round surface on flat maps.
3. Learn how to read maps.

Technology Resources

Go Online
PHSchool.com

Students use embedded Web codes to access Internet activities, chapter self-tests, and additional map practice. They may also access Dorling Kindersley's Online Desk Reference to learn more about each country they study.

Interactive Textbook

Use the Interactive Textbook to make content and concepts come alive through animations, videos, and activities that accompany the complete basal text—online and on CD-ROM.

PRENTICE HALL

TeacherEXPRESS
Plan • Teach • Assess

Use this complete suite of powerful teaching tools to make planning lessons and administering tests quicker and easier.

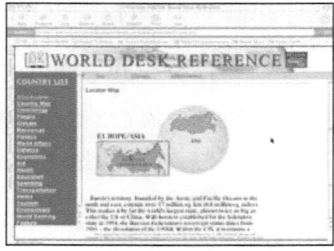

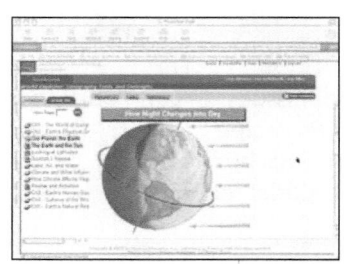

Reading and Assessment

Reading and Vocabulary Instruction

🔊 Model the Target Reading Skill

Clarifying Meaning Explain to students that they can use several strategies to clarify the meaning of unfamiliar words and concepts in the text. They can reread a difficult passage and try to make connections between familiar and unfamiliar words or ideas. They can read ahead to see if the author provides definitions or examples later in the passage. After reading, students can solidify their knowledge of a passage by paraphrasing, or putting what they have read into their own words.

Model clarifying meaning by thinking aloud as you read the paragraph below, from page 17, to the class.

A geographic information system, or GIS, is a computer-based system that links information to locations. Think aloud: What does *link information to locations* mean? I'll keep reading, maybe the author will give me a definition or example. *A GIS is useful not only to geographers but also to governments and businesses. A GIS connects information with places. For example, if a business needs to decide where to open an office, it can use a GIS to choose a location where it will reach the most customers.* Think aloud: This is an example of linking information (number of possible customers) to locations (possible site of new office). To paraphrase, a GIS is used by geographers, governments, and businesses to determine information about specific locations.

Use the following worksheets from All-in-One Foundations of Geography Teaching Resources (pp. 68–69) to support this chapter's Target Reading Skill.

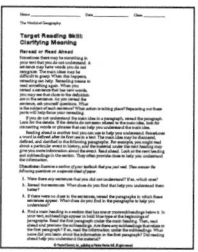 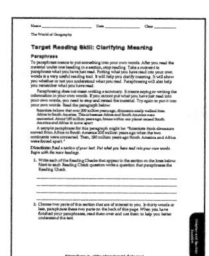

Vocabulary Builder
High-Use Academic Words

Use these steps to teach this chapter's high-use words:

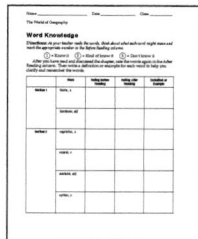

1. Have students rate how well they know each word on their Word Knowledge worksheets (All-in-One Foundations of Geography Teaching Resources, p. 70).
2. Pronounce each word and ask students to repeat it.
3. Provide a brief definition and sample sentence (provided on TE pp. 11 and 17).
4. Work with students as they fill in the "Definition or Example" column of their Word Knowledge worksheets.

Assessment

Formal Assessment

Test students' understanding of core knowledge and skills.

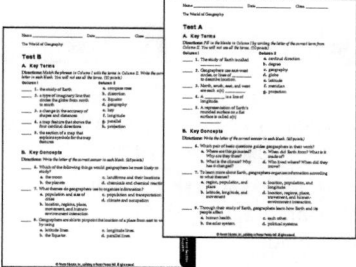

Chapter Tests A and B, All-in-One Foundations of Geography Teaching Resources, pp. 96–101

Customize the Chapter Tests to suit your needs.

ExamView® Test Bank CD-ROM

Skills Assessment

Assess geographic literacy.

MapMaster Skills, Student Edition, pp. 22, 24

Assess reading and comprehension.

Target Reading Skills, Student Edition, pp. 12, 17, and in Section Assessments

Chapter 1 Assessment, Reading and Vocabulary Study Guide, p. 8

Performance Assessment

Assess students' performance on this chapter's Writing Activities using the rubric from All-in-One Foundations of Geography Teaching Resources.

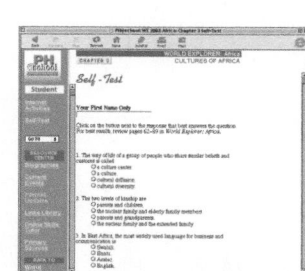

Rubric for Assessing a Writing Assignment, p. 95

Assess students' work through performance tasks.

Small Group Activity: Plotting a Route Around the World, All-in-One Foundations of Geography Teaching Resources pp. 73–76

Online Assessment

Have students check their own understanding.

Chapter Self-Test

Test Preparation

Assess students' skills and diagnose problems as students begin their study of this region.

Screening Tests and Diagnosing Readiness Tests, AYP Monitoring Assessments, pp. 1–11, 13–63

Section 1 The Five Themes of Geography

 4 periods, 2 blocks (includes Skills for Life)

Social Studies Objectives
1. Learn about the study of Earth.
2. Discover five ways to look at Earth.

Reading/Language Arts Objective
Reread or read ahead to clarify the meaning of unfamiliar words and ideas.

Prepare to Read	Instructional Resources	Differentiated Instruction
Build Background Knowledge Show students a video, and then ask them to think about the five themes of geography. **Set a Purpose for Reading** Have students evaluate statements on the *Reading Readiness Guide*. **Preview Key Terms** Teach the section's Key Terms using a "See It—Remember It" chart. **Target Reading Skill** Introduce the section's Target Reading Skill of **rereading or reading ahead**.	**All in One Foundations of Geography Teaching Resources** L2 Reading Readiness Guide, p. 61 L2 Reread or Read Ahead, p. 68	**Spanish Reading and Vocabulary Study Guide** L1 Chapter 1, Section 1, pp. 3–4 ELL

Instruct	Instructional Resources	Differentiated Instruction
The Study of Earth **Five Ways to Look at Earth** Discuss the ways people study Earth and its people. **Target Reading Skill** Review **reading ahead**.	**All in One Foundations of Geography Teaching Resources** L2 Guided Reading and Review, p. 62 L2 Reading Readiness Guide, p. 61 **Foundations of Geography Transparencies** L2 Section Reading Support Transparency FG 43	**All in One Foundations of Geography Teaching Resources** L2 Skills for Life, p. 72 AR, GT, LPR, SN **Spanish Support** L2 Guided Reading and Review (Spanish), p. 4 ELL

Assess and Reteach	Instructional Resources	Differentiated Instruction
Assess Progress Evaluate student comprehension with the section assessment and section quiz. **Reteach** Assign the Reading and Vocabulary Study Guide to help struggling students. **Extend** Extend the lesson by having students do a map activity.	**All in One Foundations of Geography Teaching Resources** L2 Section Quiz, p. 63 L3 Understanding Hemispheres, p. 79 L3 Understanding Grids, p. 80 L3 Using a Grid, p. 81 L3 Understanding Latitude and Longitude, p. 82 L3 Using Latitude and Longitude, p. 83 Rubric for Assessing a Writing Assignment, p. 95 **Reading and Vocabulary Study Guide** L1 Chapter 1, Section 1, pp. 2–4	**Spanish Support** L2 Section Quiz (Spanish), p. 3 ELL **Teacher's Edition** L1 For Less Proficient Readers, TE p. 15 L1 For Special Needs Students, TE p. 15 **Social Studies Skills Tutor CD-ROM** L1 Using Reliable Information ELL, LPR, SN

Key
L1 Basic to Average   L3 Average to Advanced
L2 For All Students

LPR Less Proficient Readers
AR Advanced Readers
SN Special Needs Students

GT Gifted and Talented
ELL English Language Learners

Section 2 The Geographer's Tools

 5 periods, 2.5 blocks (includes Chapter Review and Assessment)

Social Studies Objectives
1. Find out how maps and globes show information about Earth's surface.
2. See how mapmakers show Earth's round surface on flat maps.
3. Learn how to read maps.

Reading/Language Arts Objective
Paraphrase to clarify the meaning of unfamiliar words and ideas.

Section Lesson Planner

Prepare to Read	**Instructional Resources**	**Differentiated Instruction**
Build Background Knowledge Ask students to preview the section and predict what they will learn about maps and globes. **Set a Purpose for Reading** Have students begin to fill out the *Reading Readiness Guide.* **Preview Key Terms** Teach the section's Key Terms. **Target Reading Skill** Introduce the section's Target Reading Skill of **paraphrasing**.	**All in One Foundations of Geography Teaching Resources** L2 Reading Readiness Guide, p. 65 L2 Paraphrase, p. 69	**Spanish Reading and Vocabulary Study Guide** L1 Chapter 1, Section 2, pp. 5–6 ELL

Instruct	**Instructional Resources**	**Differentiated Instruction**
Target Reading Skill Review **paraphrasing**. **Globes and Maps** Ask about the creation and uses of maps and globes. **Getting It All on the Map** Ask about the different kinds of map projections. **Reading Maps** Discuss the parts of a map.	**All in One Foundations of Geography Teaching Resources** L2 Guided Reading and Review, p. 66 L2 Reading Readiness Guide, p. 65 **Foundations of Geography Transparencies** L2 Section Reading Support Transparency FG 44	**All in One Foundations of Geography Teaching Resources** L3 Understanding Projection, Maps with Accurate Shapes, Maps with Accurate Areas, Maps with Accurate Directions, pp. 84–87 AR GT L3 Enrichment, p. 71 ELL, LPR, SN L1 Outline Map 1, p. 91 ELL, LPR, SN L3 Captain Scott's Letter to the British Public, pp. 92–93 AR, GT L2 Using the Map Key, Using the Compass Rose, Using the Map Scale, pp. 88–90 ELL L3 Small Group Activity, pp. 73–76 AR, GT **Teacher's Edition** L3 For Gifted and Talented, TE pp. 19, 21 L1 For Special Needs Students, TE p. 20 L3 For Advanced Readers, TE p. 20 L2 For English Language Learners, TE p. 21

Assess and Reteach	**Instructional Resources**	**Differentiated Instruction**
Assess Progress Evaluate student comprehension with the section assessment and section quiz. **Reteach** Assign the Reading and Vocabulary Study Guide to help struggling students. **Extend** Extend the lesson by having students create their own maps.	**All in One Foundations of Geography Teaching Resources** L2 Section Quiz, p. 67 Rubric for Assessing a Writing Assignment, p. 95 L2 Vocabulary Development, p. 94 L2 Word Knowledge, p. 70 L2 Chapter Tests A and B, pp. 96–101	**Spanish Support** L2 Section Quiz (Spanish), p. 5 ELL L2 Chapter Summary (Spanish), p. 6 ELL L2 Vocabulary Development (Spanish), p. 7 ELL **Reading and Vocabulary Study Guide** L1 Chapter 1, Section 2, pp. 5–7

Key
L1 Basic to Average L3 Average to Advanced

L2 For All Students

LPR Less Proficient Readers
AR Advanced Readers
SN Special Needs Students

GT Gifted and Talented
ELL English Language Learners

Reading Background

Previewing and Prereading

Students who do a brief, preliminary reading of complex material are in a strategic position to take control of their learning and comprehension. Previewing also helps students identify the text structure and develop a mental framework for ideas to be encountered in the text. Follow the steps below to teach students how to preview and preread, using Section 1 of this chapter as an example:

1. Tell students that previewing will help them identify the text structure and develop a mental outline of ideas they will encounter in the text.
2. Skim the section, getting clues from such features as titles, bold-faced headings, captions, and discussion questions. Take notes as you go along. (*Notes could include: the study of Earth; five ways to look at Earth; location; latitude and longitude; regions; place; movement; human-environment interaction.*)
3. Use these notes to make predictions about what you will learn from the selection. (*Think aloud: "This section will probably be about how people study Earth. They use five different methods to study it. Some of these might include location, regions, place, movement, and human-environment interaction."*)

4. Reflect on what you've previewed. Write down any questions you may have. (*Questions may include: I am not sure what latitude and longitude are. What kind of movement are they referring to? How do humans interact with their environments and how does this relate to geography?*)
5. Return to the notes and questions after reading part of the selection. Revise your predictions as needed, and answer your questions.

Pre-Teaching Vocabulary

Research literature on academic vocabulary instruction indicates that effective strategies require students to go beyond simply looking up dictionary definitions or examining the context. Vocabulary learning must be based on the learner's dynamic engagement in constructing understanding.

If students are not retaining the meaning of the Key Terms or high-use words, use this extended vocabulary sequence to engage them in learning new words.

World Studies Background

The Longitude Problem

Due to the absence of landmarks at sea, sailors must determine their location by measuring latitude and longitude. In the late 1600s, sailors could measure latitude but had no tool for measuring longitude. After several disasters caused by navigation errors, the British government announced it would give an award to the person who could discover a way to measure longitude at sea.

British carpenter John Harrison solved the problem. He developed a timekeeper that looked like a large pocket watch. This watch kept the time of Greenwich, England. Everywhere the sailors went, they could find the local time by the position of the sun, and compare it to the time in Greenwich, determining longitude.

Fields of Geography

The study of geography is divided into the three professional subcategories of study: physical, human, and regional geography. Although distinct fields, they are interrelated in many ways. Physical geography is the study of the surface of Earth, including the examination of human impact on the environment. Human geography is the analysis of the attributes and populations of different societies. Regional geography is a narrower study of a particular region. It combines elements of physical and human geography because regional geographers look at the physical boundaries, climates, and cultural features of regions.

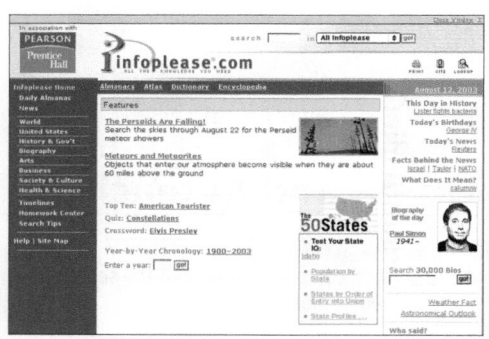

Infoplease® provides a wealth of useful information for the classroom. You can use this resource to strengthen your background on the subjects covered in this chapter. Have students visit this advertising-free site as a starting point for projects requiring research.

Use Web code **led-3100** for **Infoplease.**

1. Present the word in writing and point out the part of speech.
2. Pronounce the word and have students pronounce the word.
3. Provide a range of familiar synonyms (or "it's like" words) before offering definitions.
4. Provide an accessible definition and concrete examples, or "showing sentences."
5. Rephrase the simple definition or example sentence, asking students to complete the statement by substituting the word aloud.
6. Check for understanding by providing an application task/ question requiring critical thinking.

Sample instructional sequence:

1. Our first word is *geography*. It is a noun, a word that names a person, place, or thing.
2. Say the word *geography* after me. (Students repeat.)
3. *Geography* is similar to *geology* because both involve studying something on Earth.
4. The word *geography* means *the study of Earth*. By taking *geography*, we learned a lot more about our world.
5. We learned more about our world by taking _____ . (Students substitute missing word.)
6. Would studying the stars in the sky be part of *geography*? Yes-No-Why? (Students answer the question.)

Scaffolding Tips

Scaffolding is a technique used to help students transition from seeing and hearing the teacher demonstrate and model a particular skill to performing the skill independently. A teacher may begin with a recall question about a topic and lead students toward forming their own interpretive question. Scaffolding is especially effective for less proficient readers, English language learners, and some special needs students. When the teacher uses scaffolding, students should eventually be able to perform the skill completely on their own. To test the effectiveness of scaffolding, ask yourself each time students do an activity how much you had to help them. The answer should decrease with every attempt.

The Trimetrogon Method

Before World War II, many countries lacked detailed maps of their national areas. In fact, by 1940 only about 10 percent of the world was mapped out in any detail. Because airplane pilots needed more comprehensive maps during the war, the United States Air Force developed the trimetrogon method of mapping to create the World Aeronautical Charts.

The trimetrogon mapping technique is a system in which land is photographed, and then plotted for data such as elevation. Remote areas of Earth are now charted in a large enough scale to be significant, using the trimetrogon method. Today, about 62 percent of the world is mapped adequately.

Maps of the Moon

The only celestial body that has been mapped in any detail besides Earth is the moon. Two German astronomers, Wilhelm Beer and Johann Heinrich von Mädler, published the first comprehensive map of the moon in 1836. The map included a detailed study of the moon's surface. A year later, the pair supplemented the map with a book that gave the measurements of 148 of the moon's craters and 830 of its mountains.

Chapter 1

Guiding Questions

Remind students about the Guiding Questions introduced at the beginning of this section.

Section 1 relates to **Guiding Question** ❶
What are Earth's major physical features?
(The five central themes of geography are location, regions, place, movement, and human-environment interaction.)

Section 2 relates to **Guiding Question** ❶
What are Earth's major physical features?
(Tools such as globes and maps communicate important information about Earth's physical features.)

⟲ Target Reading Skill

In this chapter, students will learn and apply the reading skill of clarifying meaning. Use the following worksheets to help students practice this skill:

> All in One **Foundations of Geography Teaching Resources,** *Reread or Read Ahead,* p. 68; *Paraphrase,* p. 69

Chapter 1

The World of Geography

Chapter Preview

This chapter will introduce you to the study of Earth, the planet where we live.

Section 1
The Five Themes of Geography

Section 2
The Geographer's Tools

⟲ Target Reading Skill

Clarifying Meaning In this chapter you will focus on clarifying meaning by learning how to read ahead and how to paraphrase.

▶ A satellite launched from the space shuttle *Discovery* orbits Earth.

8 Foundations of Geography

Differentiated Instruction

The following Teacher's Edition strategies are suitable for students of varying abilities.

Advanced Readers, p. 20
English Language Learners, p. 21
Gifted and Talented, pp. 19, 21
Less Proficient Readers, p. 15
Special Needs Students, pp. 15, 20

Bibliography

For the Teacher
Dorling Kindersley. *Geography of the World.* DK Publishing, 2003.
Rhatigan, Joe and Smith, Heather. *Geography Crafts for Kids: 50 Cool Projects and Activities for Exploring the World.* Lark Books, NC, 2002.
Five Themes of Geography. 100 Percent Education, 2002. Videocassette.

For the Student
L1 American Education. *The Complete Book of Maps & Geography.* American Education Publishing, 1998.
L1 Johnson, Sylvia. *Mapping the World.* Atheneum, 1999.
L2 National Geographic Society. *National Geographic Student Atlas of the World.* National Geographic Society, 2001.
L3 Young, Karen Romano. *Maps and Map Making.* Scholastic Paperbacks, 2002.

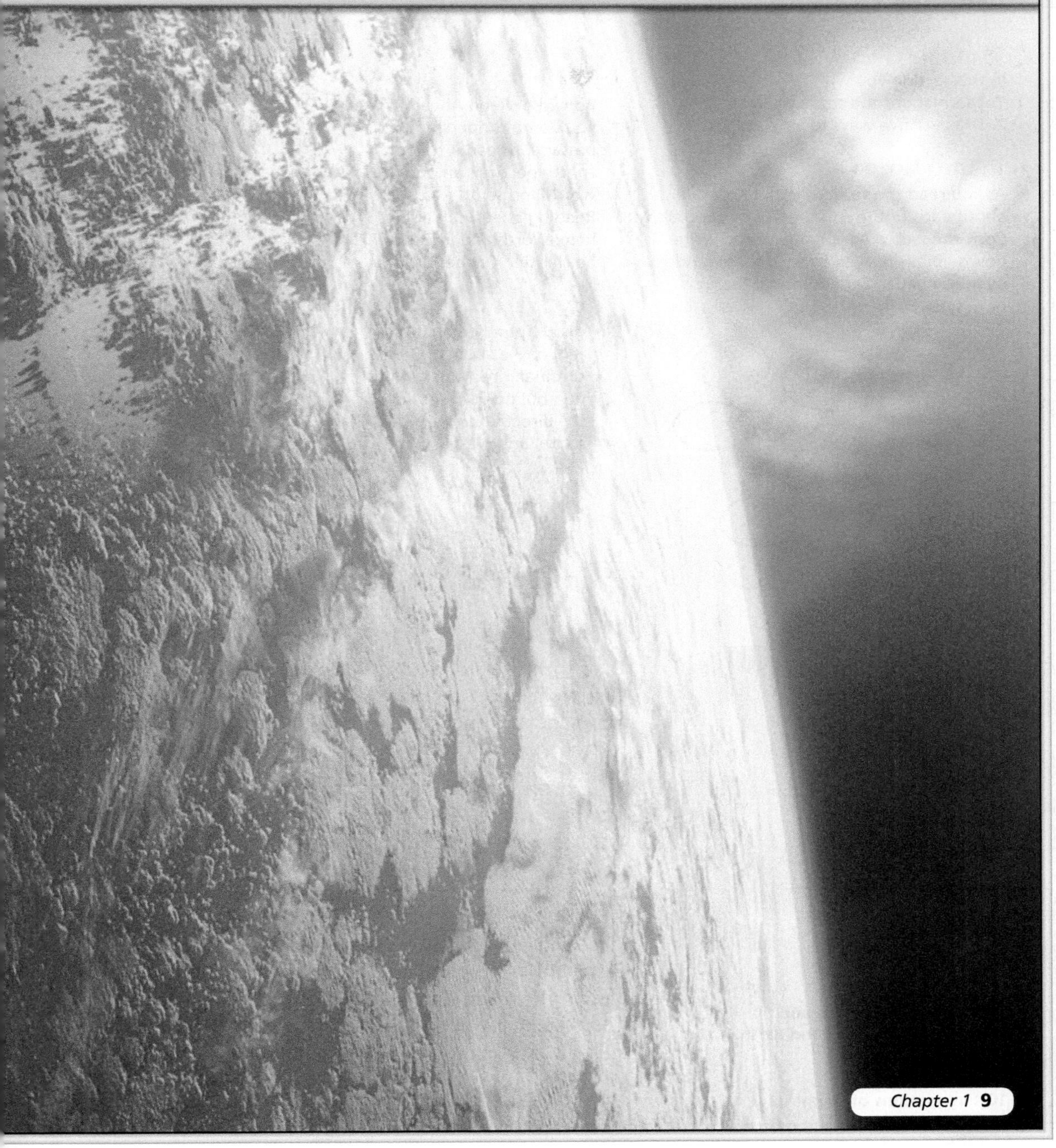

Using the Visual L2

Reach Into Your Background Draw students' attention to the picture and caption on pages 8–9. Remind them that satellites travel hundreds of miles above Earth's surface.

Discuss the idea that mapmakers can use satellite pictures of Earth to make maps of our planet. There are even detailed satellite maps of cities. Have students discuss ways people might take pictures to make a map of their neighborhood. Have students share their ideas. *(Possible answer: take pictures from a helicopter or airplane)*

Chapter Resources

Teaching Resources

Letter Home, p. 59
L2 Vocabulary Development, p. 94
L2 Skills for Life, p. 72
L2 Chapter Tests A and B, pp. 96–101

Spanish Support

Spanish Letter Home, p. 1
Spanish Vocabulary Development, p. 7
Spanish Chapter Summary, p. 6

Media and Technology

L1 Student Edition on Audio CD
L1 Guided Reading Audiotapes, English and Spanish
L2 Social Studies Skills Tutor CD-ROM
ExamView® Test Bank CD-ROM

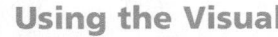

PRENTICE HALL
Presentation EXPRESS™
Teach · Connect · Inspire

Teach this chapter's content using the PresentationExpress™ CD-ROM including:

- slide shows
- transparencies
- interactive maps and media
- ***ExamView®*** QuickTake Presenter

Objectives

Social Studies
1. Learn about the study of Earth.
2. Discover five ways to look at Earth.

Reading/Language Arts
Reread or read ahead to clarify the meaning of unfamiliar words and ideas.

Prepare to Read

Build Background Knowledge
L2

Tell students that they will begin their study of geography by learning five important ideas of geography. Show the video *What is Geography?*, then ask students to list the five themes of geography. Ask students what topics they think they will learn about within each theme, and have them use the Think-Write-Pair-Share strategy (TE, p. T36) to share their ideas.

What Is Geography?, **World Studies Video Program**

Set a Purpose for Reading
L2

- Preview the Objectives.

- Read each statement in the *Reading Readiness Guide* aloud. Ask students to mark the statements true or false.

  All in One Foundations of Geography Teaching Resources, *Reading Readiness Guide,* p. 61

- Have students discuss the statements in pairs or groups of four, then mark their worksheets again. Use the Numbered Heads participation strategy (TE, p. T36) to call on students to share their group's perspectives.

Vocabulary Builder
Preview Key Terms
L2

Create a three column "See It—Remember It" chart of the Key Terms on the board. Write a term in the first column, a short definition in the second column, and a sketch in the third column. Guide students as they copy and complete the chart.

Answer

✓**Reading Check** Where are things located? Why are they there?

The Five Themes of Geography

Prepare to Read

Objectives

In this section you will
1. Learn about the study of Earth.
2. Discover five ways to look at Earth.

Taking Notes

As you read the section, look for details about each of the five themes of geography. Copy the web diagram below and write down details related to each theme. Add ovals as needed for additional themes or details.

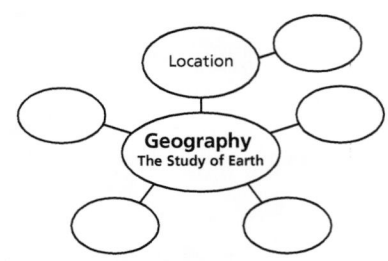

Target Reading Skill

Reread or Read Ahead If you do not understand a passage, reread it to look for connections among the words and sentences. Reading ahead can also help. Words and ideas may be clarified further on.

Key Terms

- **geography** (jee AHG ru fee) *n.* the study of Earth
- **cardinal directions** (KAHR duh nul duh REK shunz) *n.* the directions north, east, south, and west
- **latitude** (LAT uh tood) *n.* the distance north or south of Earth's Equator, in degrees
- **longitude** (LAHN juh tood) *n.* the distance east or west of the Prime Meridian, in degrees
- **hemisphere** (HEM ih sfeer) *n.* a half of Earth
- **parallel** (PA ruh lel) *n.* a line of latitude
- **meridian** (muh RID ee un) *n.* a line of longitude

Geographers use maps and other tools to understand Earth.

The Study of Earth

Geography is the study of Earth, our home planet. Geographers try to answer two basic questions: Where are things located? and, Why are they there? To find answers to these questions, geographers consider Earth from many points of view.

✓ **Reading Check** What questions do geographers try to answer?

Five Ways to Look at Earth

Five themes can help you organize information about Earth and its people. These themes are location, regions, place, movement, and human-environment interaction. They can help you understand where things are located, and why they are there.

Target Reading Skill
L2

Reread or Read Ahead Point out the Target Reading Skill. Tell students that rereading a difficult passage or reading ahead in the text can help them clarify meaning.

Model rereading using the first paragraph on this page to find the meaning of the word *geographer*. By rereading, students will see that geographers are people who study Earth. Model reading ahead using this sentence from p. 11: "Longitude is the distance east or west of the Prime Meridian, measured in degrees." Students can read ahead to find an explanation of the Prime Meridian.

Give students *Reread or Read Ahead*. Have them complete the activity in groups.

All in One Foundations of Geography Teaching Resources, *Reread or Read Ahead,* p. 68

Location Geographers begin to study a place by finding where it is, or its location. Geographers use both cardinal and intermediate directions to describe location. The **cardinal directions** are north, east, south, and west. Intermediate directions lie between the cardinal directions. For example, northwest is halfway between north and west.

Geographers also use two special measurements of Earth to describe location. **Latitude** is the distance north or south of the Equator, measured in units called degrees. Degrees are units that measure angles. **Longitude** is the distance east or west of the Prime Meridian, measured in degrees.

Lines of latitude are east-west circles around the globe. All points on the circle have the same latitude. The line of latitude around the middle of the globe, at 0 degrees (0°) of latitude, is the Equator. Lines of longitude run north and south. The Prime Meridian is the line of longitude that marks 0° of longitude.

The Hemispheres

The Equator and the Prime Meridian both divide Earth in two. Each half of Earth is called a **hemisphere.** The Equator divides Earth into Northern and Southern hemispheres. The Prime Meridian divides Earth into Eastern and Western hemispheres.

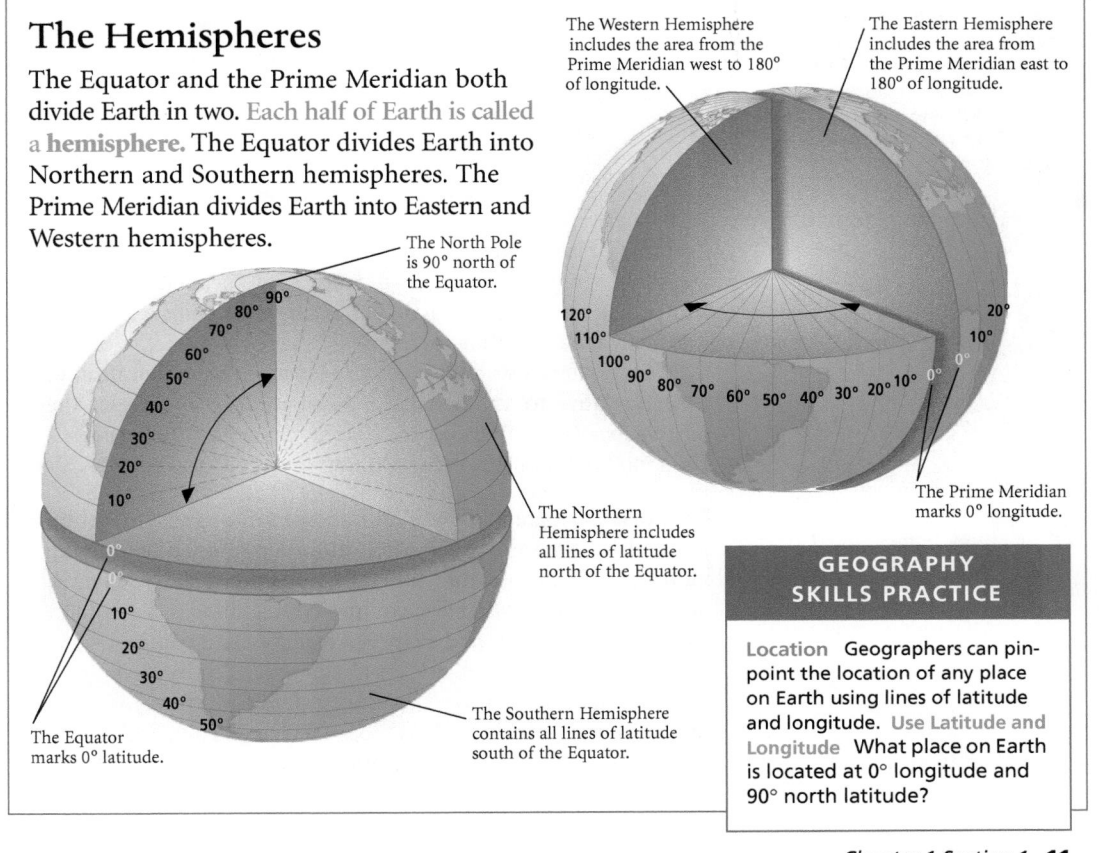

The Western Hemisphere includes the area from the Prime Meridian west to 180° of longitude.

The Eastern Hemisphere includes the area from the Prime Meridian east to 180° of longitude.

The North Pole is 90° north of the Equator.

The Northern Hemisphere includes all lines of latitude north of the Equator.

The Prime Meridian marks 0° longitude.

The Equator marks 0° latitude.

The Southern Hemisphere contains all lines of latitude south of the Equator.

GEOGRAPHY SKILLS PRACTICE

Location Geographers can pinpoint the location of any place on Earth using lines of latitude and longitude. Use Latitude and Longitude What place on Earth is located at 0° longitude and 90° north latitude?

Vocabulary Builder

Use the information below to teach students this section's high-use words.

High-Use Word	Definition and Sample Sentence
theme, p. 10	*n.* the main subject or idea of something The students identified the **theme** of the paragraph.
traditional, p. 13	*adj.* something handed down from generation to generation Her mother taught her to make a **traditional** Italian meal.

Instruct

The Study of Earth [L2]

Five Ways to Look at Earth [L2]

Guided Instruction

- **Vocabulary Builder** Clarify the high-use words **theme** and **traditional** before reading.

- Read The Study of Earth and Five Ways to Look at Earth, using the Paragraph Shrinking strategy (TE, p. T34). Have students study the diagrams on this page and page 12.

- Have students name the five themes that geographers use to organize information about Earth and its people, then brainstorm examples of each. *(The five themes and an example of each are: location—the United States is in the Western Hemisphere; regions—a physical region of the United States is the Mojave Desert; place—the climate of the Mojave Desert is hot and dry; movement—radios have helped spread music from the United States to many parts of the world; human-environment interaction— people have cut trails into a mountainside. Other examples will vary, but should illustrate an understanding of each theme.)*

- Ask students **How are latitude and longitude similar? How are they different?** *(Similar: both are measurements of Earth to describe location; both are measured in degrees. Different: latitude is distance north or south of the Equator; longitude is distance east or west of the Prime Meridian.)*

Answer

Geography Skills Practice Use Latitude and Longtitude the North Pole

Chapter 1 Section 1 **11**

- Ask students to link their area to the theme of regions. Have them name a region that their location could fall into. Next, ask them to think of an example of the themes of movement and human-environment interaction in their area. (*Responses will vary.*)

Independent Practice

Ask students to create the Taking Notes graphic organizer on a blank piece of paper. Then have them complete the organizer with the information they have just learned. Briefly model how to identify which details to record.

Monitor Progress

- Show *Section Reading Support Transparency FG 43* and ask students to check their graphic organizers individually. Go over key concepts and clarify key vocabulary as needed.

  📖 **Foundations of Geography Transparencies,** *Section Reading Support Transparency FG 43*

- Tell students to fill in the last column of the *Reading Readiness Guide.* Probe for what they learned that confirms or invalidates each statement.

  All in One **Foundations of Geography Teaching Resources,** *Reading Readiness Guide,* p. 61

🎯 Target Reading Skill   L2

Read Ahead As a follow up, ask students to answer the Target Reading Skill question in the Student Edition. (*Areas that share physical features, such as landforms or a particular climate, are often defined as regions, such as the Rocky Mountains or the Mojave Desert.*)

Answers

Geography Skills Practice Compare and Contrast the Equator; the Prime Meridian

The Global Grid

Lines of longitude and latitude form a global grid. Geographers can identify the absolute location of any point on Earth by finding the latitude and longitude lines that intersect at that point. Lines of latitude are also called **parallels,** because they run east and west and are parallel to one another. This means that they never cross. Lines of longitude are also called **meridians.** Meridians run north and south, from the North Pole to the South Pole.

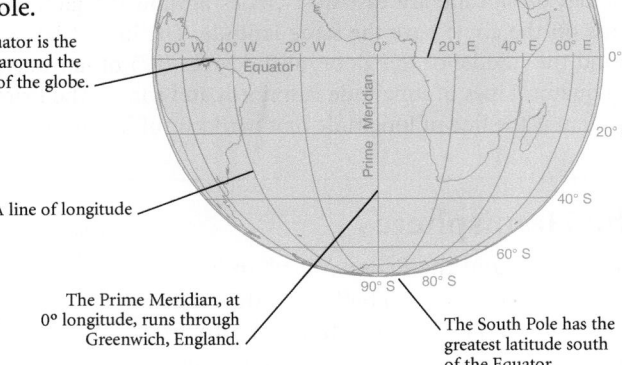

The North Pole has the greatest latitude north of the Equator.

The Equator, at 0° latitude, circles Earth midway between the North and South poles.

The Equator is the parallel around the middle of the globe.

A line of longitude

The Prime Meridian, at 0° longitude, runs through Greenwich, England.

The South Pole has the greatest latitude south of the Equator.

GEOGRAPHY SKILLS PRACTICE

Location Latitude and longitude are measured in degrees from imaginary lines on Earth's surface. Compare and Contrast From which line is latitude measured? Where do degrees of longitude start?

Read Ahead Read ahead to see how physical features may define regions.

Lines of longitude and latitude form a global grid. This grid allows geographers to state the absolute location, or exact address, of any place on Earth. For example, Savannah, Georgia, is located at 32° north latitude and 81° west longitude.

Geographers also discuss relative location, or the location of a place relative to another place. A geographer might give the relative location of Tallahassee, Florida, by saying, "Tallahassee is about 400 miles northwest of Miami."

Regions Geographers use the theme of regions to group places that have something in common. A region has a unifying human or physical feature such as population, history, climate, or landforms. For example, a country is a region with a common national government, and a city is a region with a common local government. A school district is a region defined by a common school system. Land areas can also be divided into regions that share physical features, such as mountains or a dry climate. Physical regions of the western United States include the Rocky Mountains and the Mojave (mo HAH vee) Desert.

Skills Mini Lesson

Drawing Inferences and Conclusions   L2

1. Explain that inferences are based on facts and that conclusions are based on inferences.

2. Students can practice the skill using the photograph on p. 10. Have them identify what the photograph shows (*Fact: The geographer is using a map.*), connect it to the themes of geography (*Inference: She is locating a place on the map.*), and then draw a conclusion about which theme the geographer is focusing on (*She is focusing on location.*)

3. Have students compare the photographs on pp. 10 and 13, to draw conclusions about where the weather is warmer. (*The farmers' weather is warmer.*)

Place Geographers also study place. Place includes the human and physical features at a specific location. To describe physical features, you might say the climate is hot or cold. Or you might say that the land is hilly. To discuss human features, you might talk about how many people live in a place and the kinds of work they do. You might also describe their religions or the languages they speak.

Movement The theme of movement helps explain how people, goods, and ideas get from one place to another. For example, when people from other countries came to the United States, they brought traditional foods that enriched the American way of life. The theme of movement helps you understand such cultural changes. Movement helps you understand many other facts about the world. For example, radios and computers have helped music from the United States to spread and become popular around the world.

Human-Environment Interaction This theme explores how people affect their environment, or their natural surroundings, and how their environment affects them. Perhaps they have cut trails into the mountainside. Or they may have learned how to survive with little water.

Farmers in India
These women are using the wind to separate grain for flour from chaff, or husks. Farming is an example of human-environment interaction. **Infer** *Do you think that these farmers use much modern machinery?*

✓ Reading Check **What is the purpose of the five themes of geography?**

Section 1 Assessment

Key Terms
Review the key terms at the beginning of this section. Use each term in a sentence that explains its meaning.

⟳ **Target Reading Skill**
What did you learn about physical features and regions by reading ahead?

Comprehension and Critical Thinking
1. (a) **Recall** What do geographers study?

(b) **Explain** What basic questions guide geographers?
2. (a) **Explain** How can the five themes help geographers?
(b) **Predict** How might a geographer use the theme of movement to describe the area where you live?
3. (a) **Define** What does the theme of location cover?
(b) **Contrast** How would a description of your home town as a place be different from a description of your home town's location?

Writing Activity
Read the passage above on human-environment interaction. Then write a paragraph describing ways that people in your area interact with their natural environment.

For: An activity on the five themes of geography
Visit: PHSchool.com
Web Code: led-3101

Writing Activity
Use the *Rubric for Assessing a Writing Assignment* to evaluate students' paragraphs.

ALL in One **Foundations of Geography Teaching Resources,** *Rubric for Assessing a Writing Assignment,* p. 95

Go Online PHSchool.com Typing in the Web code when prompted will bring students directly to detailed instructions for this activity.

Assess and Reteach

Assess Progress L2
Have students complete the Section Assessment. Administer the *Section Quiz.*

ALL in One **Foundations of Geography Teaching Resources,** *Section Quiz,* p. 63

Reteach L1
If students need more instruction, have them read this section in the Reading and Vocabulary Study Guide.

📖 Chapter 1, Section 1, **Western Hemisphere Reading and Vocabulary Study Guide,** pp. 2–4

Extend L3
Organize students into five groups. Ask each group to complete one of the worksheets listed below to help them fully understand latitude and longitude. Have each group give a brief presentation of its work.

ALL in One **Foundations of Geography Teaching Resources,** *Understanding Hemispheres, Understanding Grids, Using a Grid, Understanding Latitude and Longitude, Using Latitude and Longitude,* pp. 79–83

Answers

Infer Probably not, because they are separating grain from straw by hand.
✓ Reading Check They are ways to organize information about Earth and its people

Section 1 Assessment

Key Terms
Students' sentences should reflect knowledge of each Key Term.

⟳ **Target Reading Skill**
Physical features refer to climate and landforms, and can be used to form regions.

Comprehension and Critical Thinking
1. (a) Earth (b) Where are things located? Why are they there?

2. (a) They help geographers organize information about Earth and its people. (b) The geographer could explain how people, goods, and ideas came to the area.

3. (a) finding a particular place (b) For place, you might use human and physical features to describe the town; for location, you might use longitude and latitude to describe where the town is.

Objective

Learn to determine the reliability of information.

Prepare to Read

Build Background Knowledge L2

Ask students to suppose that they are going to a movie. Have them list the information that they will need. *(start time, location of theater, cost of ticket)* Discuss possible sources of information *(newspaper, friend, Web site)* and what may happen if they use unreliable sources. *(may arrive late, may not be able to find the theater, may not have enough money to cover the cost of a ticket)*

Instruct

Using Reliable Information L2

Guided Instruction

- Read the steps for judging the reliability of information as a class and write them on the board.

- Practice the skill by following the steps on p. 14 as a class. Model each step of the activity by selecting a topic, such as the location of the capital of a country or state, and researching it. Students should identify the source of the information they have found *(examples: an atlas, an encyclopedia, or other source)*, determine whether the information is current *(by checking the publication date)*, consult multiple sources to be sure that they agree *(by comparing information in two or more sources)*, and investigate the author to check for his or her qualifications and possible biases.

Independent Practice

Assign *Skills for Life* and have students complete it individually.

All in One Foundations of Geography Teaching Resources, *Skills for Life,* p. 72

Skills for Life — Using Reliable Information

Would you seek medical advice from a plumber? Would you go to an encyclopedia to keep track of this season's basketball scores? Of course you wouldn't. Information is only as good as its source. To get reliable information, you have to go to an appropriate, trustworthy, and knowledgeable source.

Learn the Skill

Follow these steps to determine whether information is reliable.

1. **Find out the source of the information.** If it comes from a printed source, find out the name of the source, the author, and the date of publication. If it appeared on television, find out the name, date, and type of program (news, drama, or documentary). Do not accept information from Internet sites that do not give a date and an author.

2. **Find out if the information is recent enough for your purpose.** If you need current information, search for recent newspaper articles and up-to-date Web sites. Even if your topic is historic, researchers may have discovered new information about it. Seek the most current information.

3. **Find out if the information is accurate.** On certain topics, nearly all sources agree. For other topics, try to find information on which several respected sources agree. To be clear, you might say, "Several sources agree that" or "According to." If reliable sources disagree, you might note that disagreement in your writing.

4. **Look up the author's qualifications and methods.** When you check out an author's qualifications, always ask yourself whether he or she has a bias, or a one-sided view.

Is it Reliable?

To see if a source is reliable, ask
- What is the source?
- Is it recent enough?
- Is it accurate?
- Is the author qualified or biased?

---

14 Foundations of Geography

Monitor Progress

Monitor students doing the *Skills for Life* worksheet, checking to make sure they understand the skill steps.

Practice the Skill

Now use steps 1–4 to answer some questions about reliable information.

1. Where might you go to find information on the location of the capital of Japan? On the population of North Carolina? On the major industries of Cuba? On presidential election results in Russia?

2. Would a 20-year-old encyclopedia be a reliable source of information on active volcanoes in Hawaii? On the type of money used in Europe? On the longest river in the world? Explain your answers.

3. If you heard in a television documentary that most of the world's diamonds are mined in southern Africa, how could you check the accuracy of that statement?

4. Suppose you do an Internet search for information on the amount of beef produced in the United States last year. The search leads you to articles by three authors. Who would be the best source of information: an economist for the U.S. Department of Agriculture, the largest cattle rancher in Texas, or a leading university expert on beef production? Explain your answer.

Apply the Skill

If you had to research a report on the health of children in India, what kinds of sources would you search for reliable information? Name at least two sources, and explain why they would be reliable.

These boys are playing ball in front of the famed Taj Mahal, in India.

Assess and Reteach

Assess Progress L2

Ask students to do the Apply the Skill activity.

Reteach L1

If students are having trouble applying the skill steps, have them review the skill using Level 1 of the interactive Social Studies Skills Tutor CD-ROM.

⊙ *Using Reliable Information,* **Social Studies Skills Tutor CD-ROM**

Extend L3

Have students create a bibliography for Chapter 1, Section 1 that contains at least three sources. Students should explain why they consider each source to be reliable.

Answers
Apply the Skill

Possible answers: A Web site containing government data or a recent book by a well-regarded expert would be good sources because the information would be recent, and the authors would be reliable. Student answers will vary, but should reflect that students understand the skill steps for determining if a source is reliable.

Objectives

Social Studies

1. Find out how maps and globes show information about Earth's surface.

2. See how mapmakers show Earth's round surface on flat maps.

3. Learn how to read maps.

Reading/Language Arts

Paraphrase to clarify the meaning of unfamiliar words and ideas.

Prepare to Read

Build Background Knowledge L2

Tell students that in this section they will learn about maps and globes. Have them glance through the section, paying attention to the visuals and headings. Then write the headings Maps and Globes on the board. Under each heading, make a list of what students already know and what they think they will learn. Use the Idea Wave participation strategy (TE, p. T35) to help generate a list of suggestions. Students can refer to these lists when they are filling in the first two columns of their *Reading Readiness Guides*.

Set a Purpose for Reading L2

■ Preview the Objectives.

■ Organize students into pairs or groups of four. Distribute the *Reading Readiness Guide*. Ask the students to fill in the first two columns of the chart. Use the Numbered Heads participation strategy (TE, p. T36) to call on students to share one piece of information they already know and one piece of information they want to know.

All in One Foundations of Geography Teaching Resources, *Reading Readiness Guide,* p. 65

Vocabulary Builder
Preview Key Terms L2

Pronounce each Key Term, then ask students to say the word with you. Provide a simple explanation such as, "A compass rose is a diagram showing north, south, east, and west on a map."

Prepare to Read

Objectives

In this section you will

1. Find out how maps and globes show information about Earth's surface.

2. See how mapmakers show Earth's round surface on flat maps.

3. Learn how to read maps.

Taking Notes

As you read this section, look for details about each of the following map topics: comparing maps with globes, map projections, and parts of a map. Copy the outline below and write each detail under the correct topic.

> I. Maps and globes
>   A. Globes
>   B.
>   1.
>   2.
> II. Projections
>   A.

A map can help you find directions.

 Target Reading Skill

Paraphrase When you paraphrase, you restate what you have read in your own words. For example, you could paraphrase the first paragraph after the heading Globes and Their Weaknesses this way:

"Mapmakers found that globes are the best way to show the shapes of continents, but at a different size."

As you read this section, paraphrase or restate the information after each red or blue heading.

Key Terms

- **scale** (skayl) *n.* relative size
- **distortion** (dih STAWR shun) *n.* loss of accuracy
- **geographic information systems** (jee uh GRAF ik in fur MAY shun SIS tumz) *n.* computer-based systems that provide information about locations
- **projection** (proh JEK shun) *n.* a way to map Earth on a flat surface
- **compass rose** (KUM pus rohz) *n.* a diagram of a compass showing direction
- **key** (kee) *n.* the section of a map that explains the symbols and colors on the map

Globes and Maps

As people explored Earth, they collected information about the shapes and sizes of islands, continents, and bodies of water. Map makers wanted to present this information accurately.

Globes and Their Weaknesses The best way was to put the information on a globe, or a model with the same round shape as Earth itself. By using an accurate shape for Earth, mapmakers could show the continents and oceans of Earth much as they really are. The only difference would be the **scale,** or relative size.

But there is a problem with globes. Try making a globe large enough to show the streets in your town. The globe might have to be larger than your school building. Imagine putting a globe that big in your pocket every morning! A globe just cannot be complete enough to be useful for finding directions and at the same time small enough to be convenient for everyday use.

 Target Reading Skill L2

Paraphrase Point out the Target Reading Skill. Tell students that saying or writing a difficult passage in their own words can help them clarify meaning.

Model paraphrasing using the paragraph under the heading Aerial Photographs and Satellite Images on p. 17. (*Aerial photographs and satellite images provide information about Earth's surface in great detail. However, they cannot show objects that are hidden from the air, and they show a distorted view of Earth's surface.*)

Give students *Paraphrase*. Have them complete the activity in their groups.

All in One Foundations of Geography Teaching Resources, *Paraphrase,* p. 69

Maps and Mapping People, therefore, use flat maps. Flat maps, however, present another problem. Earth is round. A map is flat. Can you flatten an orange peel without stretching or tearing it? There will be sections that are stretched or bent out of shape. The same thing happens when mapmakers create flat maps. It is impossible to show Earth on a flat surface without some **distortion,** or loss of accuracy. Something will look too large, too small, or out of place. Mapmakers have found ways to limit distortion of shape, size, distance, and direction.

Mapmakers rely on ground surveys, or measurements made on the ground, to make maps. They also use aerial photographs and satellite images.

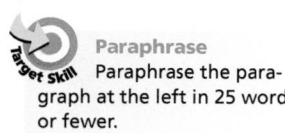

Paraphrase
Paraphrase the paragraph at the left in 25 words or fewer.

Aerial Photographs and Satellite Images

Aerial photographs are photographs of Earth's surface taken from the air. Satellite images are pictures of Earth's surface taken from a satellite in orbit. Both types of image are valuable sources of information for mapmakers because they provide current information about Earth's surface in great detail. But they are not useful for finding objects that are hidden, such as underground transit lines, or features such as streams that may be covered by vegetation. Also, like any map, flat aerial photographs and satellite images give a distorted view of Earth's surface.

Geographic Information Systems A **geographic information system,** or GIS, is a computer-based system that links information to locations. A GIS is useful not only to geographers but also to governments and businesses. A GIS connects information with places. For example, if a business needs to decide where to open an office, it can use a GIS to choose a location where it will reach the most customers. Military planners may use a GIS to improve their knowledge of the places where troops will operate. A GIS also may be used to produce maps.

✓ **Reading Check** What are the advantages and disadvantages of each way of showing Earth's surface?

Satellite Image of North and South America
This satellite view shows parts of North and South America. A storm system covers part of the southeastern United States. **Analyze Images** *How might this image pose problems as a source for making maps?*

Vocabulary Builder

Use the information below to teach this section's high-use words.

High-Use Word	Definition and Sample Sentence
transit, p. 17	*adj.* movement from one place to another Many large cities have public **transit** systems.
vegetation, p. 17	*n.* plant life Rainforests have a wide variety of **vegetation**.
available, p. 19	*adj.* that can be gotten, used, or reached She sat in the last **available** seat on the crowded bus.
symbol, p. 21	*n.* a mark or sign that represents another object or an idea A key lists the **symbols** that a map uses.

Paraphrase As a follow up, ask students to complete the Target Reading Skill activity on this page of the Student Edition. *(Answers will vary, but should include an explanation of why flat maps have distortion.)*

Instruct

Globes and Maps L2

Guided Instruction

- **Vocabulary Builder** Clarify the high-use words **transit** and **vegetation** before reading.

- Read Globes and Maps using the Oral Cloze reading strategy (TE, p. T33).

- Have students discuss one use for a globe and one use for a map. *(globe: to see an accurate view of Earth; map: to show roads in your state or streets in your town)*

- Ask students **How does technology help geographers understand Earth better?** *(Aerial photographs and satellite images provide current information about Earth's surface, while a GIS links geographical information to places.)*

Independent Practice

Ask students to create the Taking Notes graphic organizer on a blank piece of paper. Have them fill in details about maps and globes.

Monitor Progress

As students fill in the graphic organizer, circulate and make sure individuals are choosing the correct details.

Answers

✓ **Reading Check** globes—show accurate shape, distance, and direction; not convenient for everyday use; maps—easy to use; some distortion of shape, distance, and/or direction; aerial photographs and satellite images—provide current information, but do not show features that are hidden; GIS—links information to location, but is probably not useful for navigating

Analyze Images Clouds and vegetation block the view of parts of Earth's surface.

Getting It All on the Map

Guided Instruction

- **Vocabulary Builder** Clarify the high-use word **available.**

- Read Getting It All on the Map with students. As students read, circulate and make sure individuals can answer the Reading Check question.

- Have students describe a Mercator projection. *(Mercator maps expand the area between the longitudes near the poles.)*

- Ask students who these maps were useful to, and why. *(to sailors, because they showed directions accurately)*

- Have students study Making a Mercator Map diagram and discuss the problem with Mercator projections. *(Distances and size become distorted the farther the area is from the Equator.)*

Getting It All on the Map

In 1569, a mapmaker named Gerardus Mercator (juh RAHR dus mur KAY tur) created a flat map to help sailors navigate, or plan journeys, around the globe. To make his map flat and to keep his grid rectangular, Mercator expanded the area between lines of longitude near the poles. Mercator's map was very useful to sailors because it showed directions accurately, even though sizes and distances were distorted. More than 400 years later, nearly all seagoing navigators still use the Mercator **projection,** or method of mapping Earth on a flat surface.

The Mercator Projection Mercator maps make areas near the poles look bigger than they are. This is because on a globe, the lines of longitude meet at the poles. To keep lines of longitude straight up and down, Mercator had to stretch the spaces between them north and south of the Equator. Land near the Equator was about the right size, but land areas near the poles became much larger. For example, on Mercator's map, Greenland looks bigger than South America. Greenland is actually only about one eighth as big as South America. Geographers call a Mercator projection a conformal map. It shows correct shapes but not true distances or sizes. What other areas, besides Greenland, do you think might look larger than they should?

Making a Mercator Map

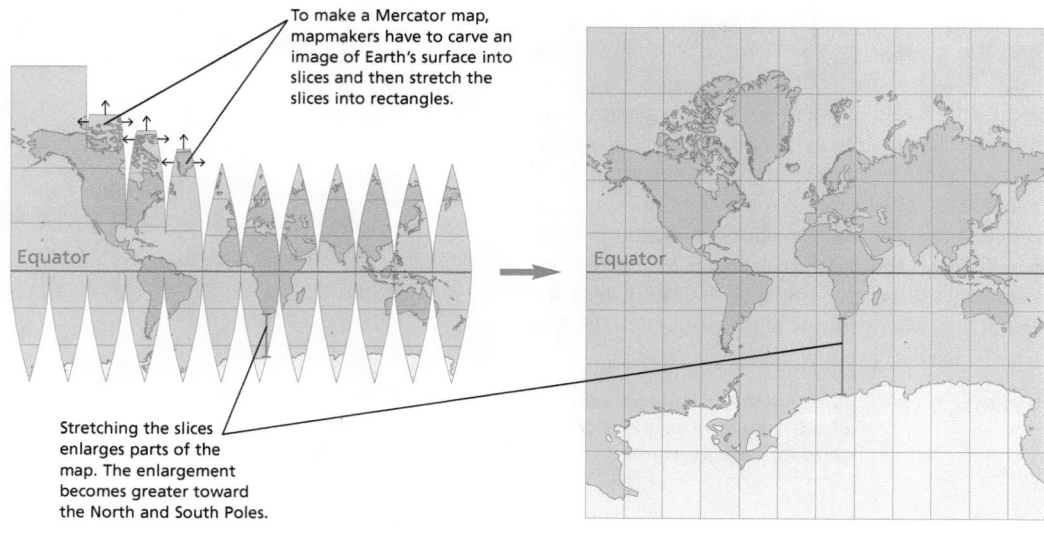

To make a Mercator map, mapmakers have to carve an image of Earth's surface into slices and then stretch the slices into rectangles.

Stretching the slices enlarges parts of the map. The enlargement becomes greater toward the North and South Poles.

Skills Mini Lesson

Sequencing

1. Teach the skill by explaining that sequencing means putting pieces of information in a logical order, using a diagram if necessary.

2. Help students practice the skill by looking at the visuals on p. 18. As a class, first identify the topic, then the steps in the process, and then the order. Then draw a flowchart of the process on the board. *(flowchart will have three boxes: get image of Earth's surface, cut image into gores, stretch gores to form rectangle)*

3. Have students apply the skill by creating a similar flowchart about equal-area maps. *(flowchart will have three boxes: get image of Earth's surface, cut image into gores, squeeze gores into oval)*

Equal-Area Projections An equal-area map shows the correct size of landmasses, but their shapes are altered. Lines that would be straight on Earth may be forced into curves to fit on the map's flat surface.

The Robinson Projection This projection is named for its designer, Arthur Robinson. Today, many geographers believe that the Robinson projection is the best world map available. It is used for most of the world maps in this book. This projection shows most distances, sizes, and shapes quite accurately. However, even a Robinson projection has distortions, especially in areas around the edges of the map.

Other Projections There are many other types of projections besides the ones shown here. Some are useful for showing small areas but not for showing the whole world. Others are good for specific purposes, such as planning a plane's flight route.

✓ Reading Check **What are the strengths and weaknesses of the Mercator, equal-area, and Robinson projections?**

Making an Equal-Area Map

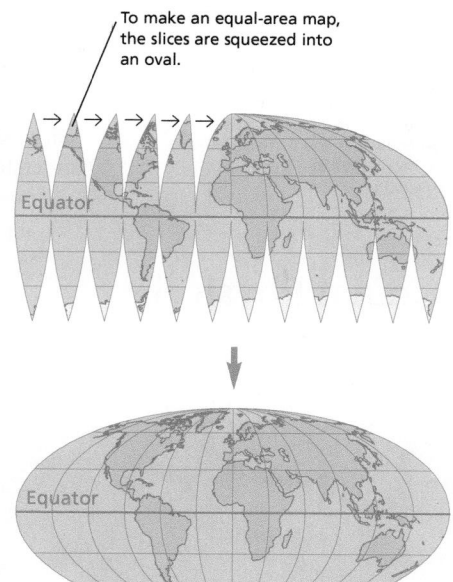

To make an equal-area map, the slices are squeezed into an oval.

Equator

Equator

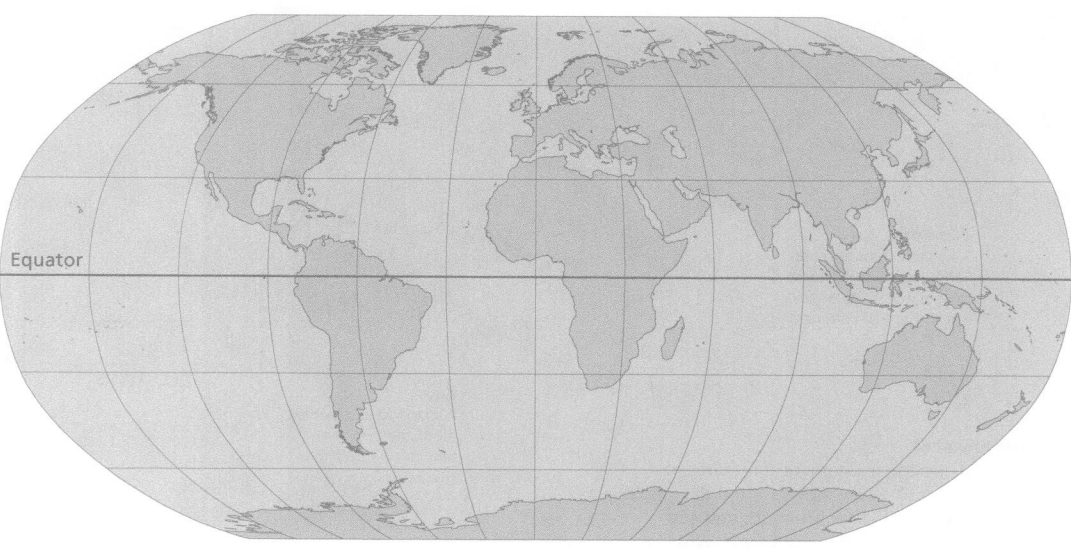

The World: Robinson Projection

Differentiated Instruction

For Gifted and Talented [L3]
Challenge students to learn more about map projections. Assign *Understanding Projection, Maps with Accurate Shapes: Conformal Maps, Maps with Accurate Areas: Equal-Area Maps,* and *Maps with Accurate Directions: Azimuthal Maps.*

Then, have students identify one instance in which each type of map would be used.

All in One Foundations of Geography Teaching Resources, *Understanding Projection, Maps with Accurate Shapes: Conformal Maps, Maps with Accurate Areas: Equal-Area Maps,* and *Maps with Accurate Directions: Azimuthal Maps,* pp. 84–87

Guided Instruction (continued)

■ Have students describe an equal-area projection. *(shows the correct size of landmasses, but alters their shapes)*

■ Ask students **Why do geographers believe that the Robinson projection is the best world map available?** *(It shows most distances, sizes, and shapes accurately.)*

■ Ask students **If you were planning to travel by ship from Los Angeles to Hong Kong, which map projection would you use? Why?** *(Mercator—its accurate directions are useful for navigation at sea.)*

Independent Practice
Have students continue filling in the graphic organizer with details from the information they have just learned.

Monitor Progress
As students fill in the graphic organizer, circulate and make sure individuals are choosing appropriate details. Provide assistance as needed.

Answer

✓ Reading Check Mercator—shows shapes and directions accurately, but distances and sizes are distorted; equal-area—shows correct size of landmasses, but shapes are distorted; Robinson—most distances, sizes, and shapes are accurate, but some distortions around edges of map

Reading Maps L2

Guided Instruction

- **Vocabulary Builder** Clarify the high-use word **symbol** before reading.

- Ask students to read Reading Maps and to review the maps on pp. 20–22.

- Have students list the parts of the map shown on the China: Physical and Georgia Highways maps. Then ask students **How does each part help you read a map?** (*title tells you what type of information the map contains and what area it is focusing on; locator globe shows the area's location on a globe; compass rose shows direction; scale bar shows how distances on the map compare to distances on land; a key identifies symbols and coloring*)

- Have students discuss what the colors show on the physical map of China. (*The colors show ranges of elevation.*)

- Ask students **What is the distance between Atlanta and Augusta? Which highway connects the two cities?** (*about 130 miles or 200 kilometers; Interstate 20*)

Reading Maps

Look at the maps shown on these two pages. One is a physical map of the country of China. The other is a highway map of the state of Georgia. These maps cover completely different areas and show different kinds of information. Despite their differences, both maps have all of the basic parts that you will find on most maps. Knowing how to use these parts will help you to read and understand any kind of map.

Title
Most maps have a title near the top of the map. The title generally tells you the type of information and the area covered on the map.

Locator Globe
Maps may include a locator globe that shows on a globe the location of the area covered by the map.

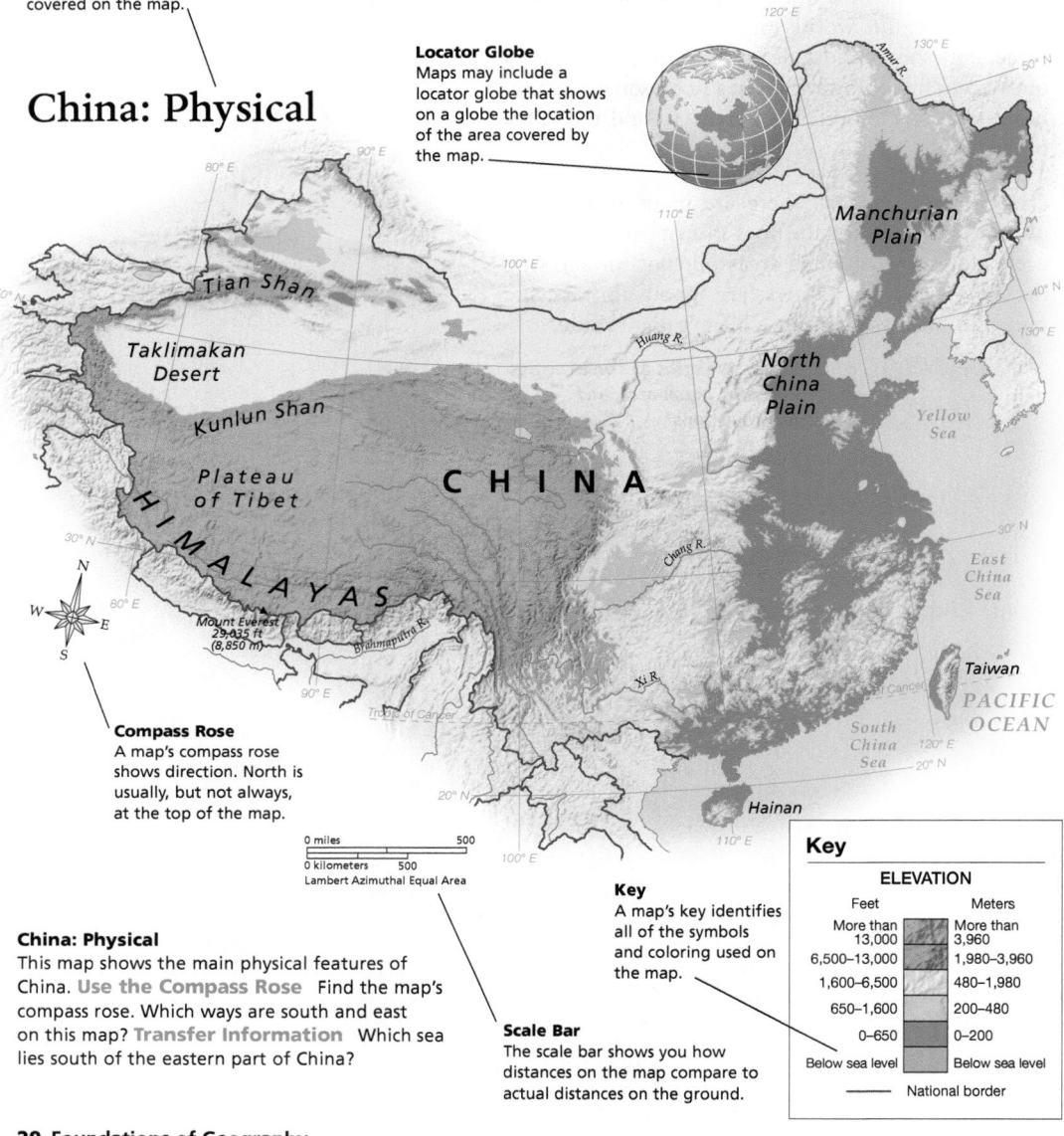

Compass Rose
A map's compass rose shows direction. North is usually, but not always, at the top of the map.

China: Physical
This map shows the main physical features of China. **Use the Compass Rose** Find the map's compass rose. Which ways are south and east on this map? **Transfer Information** Which sea lies south of the eastern part of China?

Key
A map's key identifies all of the symbols and coloring used on the map.

Scale Bar
The scale bar shows you how distances on the map compare to actual distances on the ground.

Key

ELEVATION

Feet	Meters
More than 13,000	More than 3,960
6,500–13,000	1,980–3,960
1,600–6,500	480–1,980
650–1,600	200–480
0–650	0–200
Below sea level	Below sea level

——— National border

20 Foundations of Geography

Differentiated Instruction

For Special Needs Students L1
Have students work with more advanced students to complete *Enrichment*. Then hand out *Outline Map 1* and have them color and label the continents and oceans.

All in One **Foundations of Geography Teaching Resources,** *Enrichment*, p. 71; *Outline Map 1: The World: Physical*, p. 91

For Advanced Readers L3
Have students read *Captain Scott's Letter to the British Public* to learn about his expedition to the South Pole. Have students research and chart the journey on a map.

All in One **Foundations of Geography Teaching Resources,** *Captain Scott's Letter to the British Public*, pp. 92–93

Answers

Use the Compass Rose south is down and east is to the right **Transfer Information** South China Sea

Georgia Highways

The Parts of a Map Both maps on these pages have what geographers call a **compass rose,** a diagram of a compass showing direction. If you want to find directions such as north, south, east, or west, just look for the map's compass rose.

Both maps also have a scale bar. The scale bar shows how distances on the map compare to actual distances on the land. Scales vary, depending on the map. If you compare the scale bar on the map of China to the bar on the map of Georgia, you will see that the map of China covers much greater distances on the ground even though the map is not much bigger.

On any map, the **key,** or legend, is the part of the map that explains the symbols and shading on the map. For example, the key on the highway map of Georgia shows the colored lines that stand for different kinds of highways. While some maps use symbols, other maps, like the physical map of China, use coloring to present information. The key shows which colors stand for which elevations.

√ Reading Check **How do the different parts of a map help you to find information?**

Georgia Highways
Notice that this map of Georgia has the same basic parts as the physical map of China: a title, a key, a locator globe, a compass rose, and a scale bar.
Use Scale *Using a ruler, measure the distance on the map between Atlanta and Macon. Then hold the ruler against the scale bar. How many miles is Atlanta from Macon?*

Differentiated Instruction

For English Language Learners L2
To sharpen students' map skills, have them complete *Using the Map Key, Using the Compass Rose,* and *Comparing Maps of Different Scale.*

All in One **Foundations of Geography Teaching Resources,** *Using the Map Key, Using the Compass Rose, Using the Map Scale,* pp. 88–90

For Gifted and Talented L3
Form students into groups. Have each group plot a trip around the world by completing *Small Group Activity: Plotting a Route Around the World.*

All in One **Foundations of Geography Teaching Resources,** *Small Group Activity: Plotting a Route Around the World,* pp. 73–76

Guided Instruction (continued)
■ Ask students **What are the scales used in the two maps of London on page 22?** (*Greater London: 0 to 10 miles or 0 to 15 km; Central London: 0 to 1 mile or 0 to 1 km*) **Which map provides the most detail?** (*Central London*) **Why would the smaller scale not be used for the map of Greater London?** (*If the map of Greater London showed the same area using a smaller scale, it would make the map quite large and too detailed for its use.*)

Independent Practice
Have students complete their graphic organizers by adding a head labeled "Parts of a Map" and filling in the details they have just learned.

Monitor Progress
■ Show *Section Reading Support Transparency FG 44* and ask students to check their graphic organizers individually. Go over key concepts and clarify key vocabulary as needed.

📖 **Foundations of Geography Transparencies,** *Section Reading Support Transparency FG 44*

■ Tell students to fill in the last column of the *Reading Readiness Guide.* Ask them to evaluate if what they learned was what they had expected to learn.

All in One **Foundations of Geography Teaching Resources,** *Reading Readiness Guide,* p. 65

Answers
Use Scale about 80 miles

√ Reading Check compass rose—shows directions; scale bar—shows how map distances compare to actual distances; key—explains map's symbols and shading; title—tells subject of map; grid—helps find locations

Assess and Reteach

Assess Progress [L2]

Have students complete the Section Assessment. Administer the *Section Quiz*.

All in One Foundations of Geography Teaching Resources, *Section Quiz,* p. 67

Reteach [L1]

If students need more instruction, have them read this section in the Reading and Vocabulary Study Guide.

Chapter 1, Section 2, **Western Hemisphere Reading and Vocabulary Study Guide,** pp. 5–7

Extend [L3]

Have students invent their own country and create a map including a title, a key, a scale bar, a grid, and a compass rose. Students should include their country's major cities, physical features, and major sites such as airports or tourist attractions.

Answers

MAP MASTER Skills Activity Analyze the map titled Greater London; the map titled Central London

Go Online PHSchool.com Students may practice their map skills using the interactive online version of this map.

Section 2 Assessment

Key Terms

Students' sentences should reflect knowledge of each Key Term.

Target Reading Skill

Answers will vary, but should include the strengths and weaknesses of the Mercator projection.

Comprehension and Critical Thinking

1. (a) ground surveys, aerial photographs, and satellite images **(b)** ground surveys—record details at ground level, but can be out of date; aerial photographs and satellite images—provide current, detailed information, but some features can be hidden from the air and flat photographs and images can distort Earth's curved surface **(c)** ground survey

2. (a) Mercator projection—shows directions and shapes accurately, but distances and sizes are distorted; equal-area projection—shows correct size of landmasses, but shapes are distorted **(b)** Mercator

---

Maps of Different Scale

Maps with different scales have different uses. Maps with a large scale, such as the map of Greater London, give a general picture of a large area. Maps with a smaller scale, such as the map of Central London, show more detail and are useful for finding landmarks.

Greater London

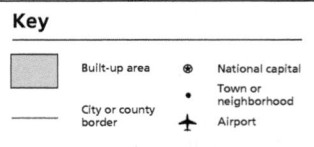

0 miles 5 10
0 kilometers 10
Lambert Conformal Conic

Central London

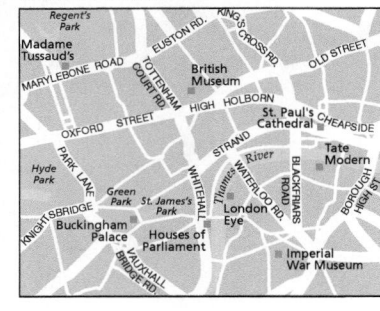
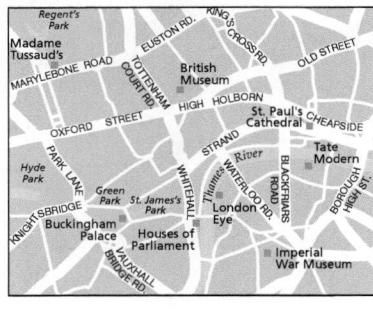
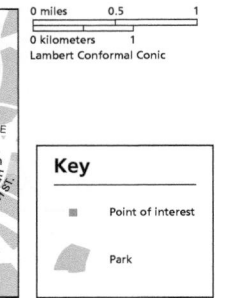

0 miles 0.5 1
0 kilometers 1
Lambert Conformal Conic

Key

Built-up area
City or county border
National capital
Town or neighborhood
Airport

Key

Point of interest
Park

MAP MASTER Skills Activity

Two Maps of London
The map of Central London zooms in on the area inside the red box on the map of Greater London. **Analyze** Which map shows the city's size? Which shows tourist attractions?

Go Online PHSchool.com Use Web Code **lep-3112** for step-by-step **map skills practice.**

Section 2 Assessment

Key Terms
Review the key terms at the beginning of this section. Use each term in a sentence that explains its meaning.

Target Reading Skill
Go back and find the paragraph under the heading The Mercator Projection. Paraphrase this paragraph, or rewrite it in your own words.

Comprehension and Critical Thinking
1. (a) Identify What information sources do mapmakers use?
(b) Evaluate What are the advantages and disadvantages of each information source?

(c) Predict To make a map of small streams in an area of thick vegetation, what source would a mapmaker most likely use?
2. (a) Recall What are the advantages and disadvantages of a Mercator projection and of an equal-area projection?
(b) Apply Information Which projection would you use to plan a voyage by ship in a straight line across an ocean?
3. (a) Define On a map, what are the key, title, compass rose, and scale bar?
(b) Synthesize Information If you made a map of places to shop in your area, what might you put in the map's key?

Writing Activity
Look at the physical map of China. Plan a route for a trip from its east coast to its western border. Using information from the map, describe the landscape that you will see along the way.

Go Online PHSchool.com

For: An activity on maps
Visit: PHSchool.com
Web Code: led-3102

---

3. (a) key—explains map's symbols and shading; title—tells subject of map; compass rose—shows directions; scale bar—shows how map distances compare to actual distances **(b)** Answers will vary, but should show an understanding of a key's purpose.

Writing Activity
Use the *Rubric for Assessing a Writing Assignment* to evaluate students' descriptions.

All in One Foundations of Geography Teaching Resources, *Rubric for Assessing a Writing Assignment,* p. 95

Go Online PHSchool.com Typing in the Web code when prompted will bring students directly to detailed instructions for this activity.

Review and Assessment

◆ Chapter Summary

Section 1: The Five Themes of Geography

- Geography is the study of Earth.
- Geographers can pinpoint any location on the surface of Earth using lines of latitude and longitude, which form an imaginary grid.
- There are five themes of geography—location, regions, place, movement, and human-environment interaction. They offer five ways to gather and understand information about places on Earth.

Section 2: The Geographer's Tools

- Maps can show more details of Earth's surface than globes, but showing Earth's round surface on flat maps causes distortion.
- Projections are different ways of showing Earth's round surface on a flat map.
- Parts of the map such as the key, compass rose, and scale bar can help you to find and understand information on any map.

Earth viewed from space

◆ Key Terms

Each of the statements below contains a key term from the chapter. If the statement is true, write *true*. If it is false, rewrite the statement to make it true.

1. The cardinal directions are north, east, south, and west.
2. Latitude is a measure of the distance north or south of Earth's Equator.
3. Longitude is a measure of the distance north or south of the Equator.
4. A hemisphere is a half of Earth.
5. A meridian is a line of latitude.
6. The scale is the part of the map that shows cardinal directions.
7. A projection is a way of mapping the flat surface of Earth onto a round globe.
8. The compass rose is the part of a map that shows symbols and their meanings.
9. The key is the part of the map that shows relative distances.

Chapter 1 **23**

┌ Vocabulary Builder ─────────

Revisit this chapter's high-use academic words:

available   transit   vegetation
symbol   theme   traditional

Ask students to review the definitions they recorded on their *Word Knowledge* worksheets.

Consider allowing students to earn extra credit if they use the words in their answers to the questions in the Chapter Review and Assessment. The words must be used correctly and in a natural context to earn the extra points.

Review Chapter Content

- Tell students that each statement in the Chapter Summary is an answer to one of the chapter's Guiding Questions. Have students determine the number of the Guiding Question that relates to each statement and then pair students to discuss their classifications. Refer to p. 1 of the Student Edition for text of Guiding Questions.

- Assign *Vocabulary Development* for students to review Key Terms.

Answers

Key Terms

1. True
2. True
3. False. Longitude is a measure of the distance east or west of the Prime Meridian.
4. True
5. False. A meridian is a line of longitude.
6. False. The scale is the part of the map that shows how distances on the map compare to actual distances on the land.
7. False. A projection is a way of mapping the round surface of Earth onto a flat surface.
8. False. A compass rose shows direction on a map.
9. False. The key is the part of the map that explains the map's symbols and shading.

Review and Assessment

Comprehension and Critical Thinking

10. (a) location, regions, place, movement, human-environment interaction **(b)** human-environment interaction

11. (a) by giving its longitude and latitude **(b)** Knowing the exact location of a place could enable you to measure its distance from your current location, or find out how to travel there.

12. (a) human or physical features **(b)** Yes; a single place might fit into one political region, but another region based on the physical features of the area.

13. (a) A globe with enough detail for daily use would be enormous. Maps have some degree of distortion of size, distance, shape, and/or direction. **(b)** globe

14. (a) shows directions and shapes accurately, but distances and sizes are distorted **(b)** Navigators are most interested in plotting routes in the correct direction. **(c)** when you were most interested in accurate distances or sizes

15. (a) compass rose, scale bar, key, title, grid **(b)** compass rose—shows directions; scale bar—shows how distances on a map compare to actual distances; key—explains map's symbols and shading; title—tells subject of map; grid—helps find locations

Skills Practice

Students' answers will vary. Some may say that the first three sentences are reliable because the writer makes firsthand observations, while the last sentence is not reliable because the writer is making an assumption.

Writing Activity: Geography

Students' answers will vary, but should show an understanding of each of the five themes of geography.

Use *Rubric for Assessing a Writing Assignment* to evaluate students' descriptions.

All in One Foundations of Geography Teaching Resources, *Rubric for Assessing a Writing Assignment,* p. 95

◆ Comprehension and Critical Thinking

10. (a) List What five themes can help you organize information about Earth? **(b) Categorize** Under which theme would you discuss building a dam on a river in a desert?

11. (a) Recall How do geographers pinpoint the exact location of any place on Earth? **(b) Infer** Why might it be useful to know the exact location of a place?

12. (a) Identify What unifying characteristics might be used to describe a region? **(b) Draw Conclusions** Might a single place be part of more than one region? Explain.

13. (a) Recall What are the disadvantages of globes? What are the disadvantages of maps? **(b) Apply Information** Which would be more helpful for studying the exact shapes of continents, a globe or a map?

14. (a) Describe What are the main features of the Mercator projection? **(b) Infer** Why is the Mercator projection still used by navigators today? **(c) Generalize** When might you want to use a projection other than the Mercator projection?

15. (a) List What are the basic parts that most maps have? **(b) Synthesize Information** How can you use the parts of a new map to understand it?

◆ Skills Practice

Using Reliable Information In the Skills for Life activity in this chapter, you learned how to use reliable information. Review the steps for this skill. Then apply them to the text below. Suppose you found this text in a teen magazine. Decide whether you think the information is reliable. Write a sentence that explains why or why not.

"Japan is a very clean country. I spent a whole week in Japan. The buses and trains were very clean. I didn't go inside a Japanese home, but I bet they are very clean, too."

◆ Writing Activity: Geography

Write down the name of the place where you live. Below that name, list the five themes of geography. Next to each theme, describe how it applies to your city, town, or state.

MAP MASTER™
Skills Activity

The Globe

Place Location For each place listed below, write the letter from the map that shows its location.
1. Prime Meridian
2. Equator
3. North Pole
4. South Pole
5. Europe
6. Africa
7. South America
8. North America

Go Online
PHSchool.com Use Web Code lep-3113 for an interactive map.

MAP MASTER™
Skills Activity

1. A	**2.** F
3. B	**4.** H
5. C	**6.** E
7. G	**8.** D

Go Online
PHSchool.com Students may practice their map skills using the interactive online version of this map.

Standardized Test Prep

Test-Taking Tips

Some questions on standardized tests ask you to make mental maps. Do the exercise in the box below. Then follow the tips to answer the sample question.

Draw a simple map of the world based on maps you have seen. Draw a rough shape for each landmass. Draw the Prime Meridian and the Equator across the map.

TIP Find the continents on your map. How is the world divided into hemispheres?

Pick the letter that best answers the question.

Which continent lies completely in both the Northern Hemisphere and the Western Hemisphere?

A Europe
B Greenland
C North America
D Australia

TIP Beware of careless errors. Read the question twice and think carefully about each answer choice.

Think It Through Australia is located completely in both the Southern Hemisphere and the Eastern Hemisphere. Europe is in the Northern Hemisphere but also mostly in the Eastern Hemisphere. Greenland is completely in both the Northern Hemisphere and the Western Hemisphere—as the question asks. But be careful! Greenland is not a continent. The answer is C.

Practice Questions

Use the tips above and other tips in this book to help you answer the following questions.

1. Which of the following is NOT a tool a geographer would use to study absolute location?
   A cardinal directions
   B climate
   C lines of latitude
   D degrees

2. What disadvantage do all flat maps share?
   A They have some sort of distortion.
   B They are hard to carry.
   C There are few sources to create them.
   D They can only show areas at a small scale.

3. A map with cities and colored lines marked with numbers is probably a type of
   A climate map.
   B road map.
   C physical map.
   D vegetation map.

Read the passage below and answer the question that follows.

This area is located in the United States, west of the Mississippi River. It is mainly hot and dry, with little rainfall, so people have built many dams there. Its landforms include rivers, canyons, and deserts.

4. Which of the five themes are used to describe this area?
   A location, movement, regions
   B movement, place, regions, human-environment interaction
   C regions, location, movement
   D location, place, human-environment interaction

Use Web Code **lea-3103**
for a **Chapter 1 self-test.**

Standardized Test Prep

Answers

1. B
2. A
3. B
4. D

Go Online
PHSchool.com Students may use the Chapter 1 self-test on PHSchool.com to prepare for the Chapter Test.

Assessment Resources

Use Chapter Tests A and B to assess students' mastery of chapter content.

All in One Foundations of Geography Teaching Resources, *Chapter Tests A and B,* pp. 96–101

Tests are also available on the *ExamView® Test Bank CD-ROM.*

⊙ *ExamView® Test Bank CD-ROM*

Earth's Physical Geography

Overview

Our Planet, Earth

Section 1

1. Learn about Earth's movement in relation to the sun.
2. Explore seasons and latitude.

Forces Shaping Earth

Section 2

1. Learn about the planet Earth.
2. Explore the forces inside Earth.
3. Explore the forces on Earth's surface.

Climate and Weather

Section 3

1. Learn about weather and climate.
2. Explore latitude, landforms, and precipitation.
3. Discover how oceans affect climate.

How Climate Affects Vegetation

Section 4

1. Investigate the relationship between climate and vegetation.
2. Explore Earth's vegetation regions.
3. Study vertical climate zones.

Technology Resources

Students use embedded Web codes to access Internet activities, chapter self-tests, and additional map practice. They may also access Dorling Kindersley's Online Desk Reference to learn more about each country they study.

Use the Interactive Textbook to make content and concepts come alive through animations, videos, and activities that accompany the complete basal text—online and on CD-ROM.

Use this complete suite of powerful teaching tools to make planning lessons and administering tests quicker and easier.

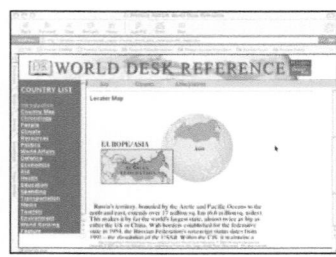

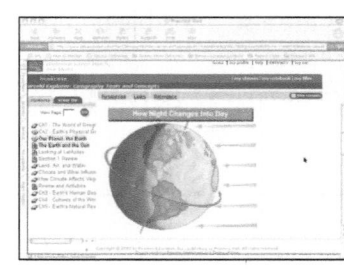

Reading and Assessment

Reading and Vocabulary Instruction

🎯 Model the Target Reading Skill

Using Context Clues Using context clues involves reading the words and sentences that surround an unfamiliar word or idea to clarify its meaning. The context can describe, define, or restate the term, or provide a comparison that allows you to figure out the term's meaning. Model using context clues by writing the following sentences on the board:

1. An archipelago is a series of island chains.

2. A tsunami is like a wall of water 15 to 30 feet above the usual level of the sea.

3. The river carved out an enormous gorge, or deep, narrow valley with steep, rocky walls.

Ask students to circle the unfamiliar word in each sentence, and then underline the context clues that help to define it. Explain that in the first sentence, the context clue is a definition—*is a series of island chains* defines *archipelago*. In the second sentence, *like a wall of water 15 to 30 feet above the usual level of the sea* provides a comparison. In the third sentence, *or deep narrow valley with steep, rocky walls* restates the word *gorge*. Challenge students to find unfamiliar words in the chapter and write down how they used context clues to gain an understanding of these words.

Use the following worksheets from All-in-One Foundations of Geography Teaching Resources (pp. 121–124) to support this chapter's Target Reading Skill.

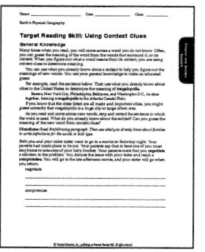 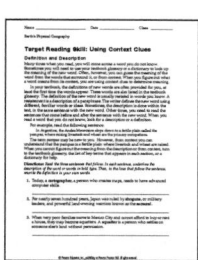 

Vocabulary Builder
High-Use Academic Words

Use these steps to teach this chapter's high-use words:

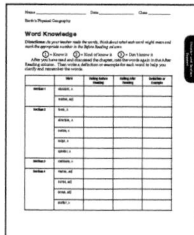

1. Have students rate how well they know each word on their Word Knowledge worksheets (All-in-One Foundations of Geography Teaching Resources, p. 125).

2. Pronounce each word and ask students to repeat it.

3. Give students a brief definition and sample sentence (provided on TE pp. 29, 34, 41, and 51).

4. Work with students as they fill in the "Definition or Example" column of their Word Knowledge worksheets.

Assessment

Formal Assessment

Test students' understanding of core knowledge and skills.

Chapter Tests A and B, All-in-One Foundations of Geography Teaching Resources, pp. 151–156

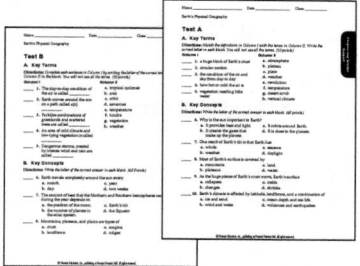

Customize the Chapter Tests to suit your needs.

ExamView Test Bank CD-ROM

Skills Assessment

Assess geographic literacy.

MapMaster Skills, Student Edition, pp. 29, 43, 44, 45, 53, 56

Assess reading and comprehension.

Target Reading Skills, Student Edition, pp. 30, 35, 43, 52, and in Section Assessments

Chapter 2 Assessment, Western Hemisphere Reading and Vocabulary Study Guide, p. 21

Performance Assessment

Assess students' performance using the following rubrics from All-in-One Foundations of Geography Teaching Resources.

Rubric for Assessing a Student Poem, p. 146

Rubric for Assessing a Role-Playing Activity, p. 147

Rubric for Assessing a Bar Graph, p. 148

Rubric for Assessing a Line Graph, p. 149

Rubric for Assessing a Poster, p. 150

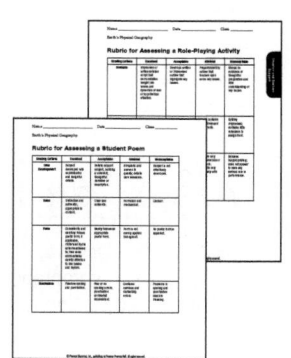

Assess students' work through performance tasks.

Small Group Activity, All-in-One Foundations of Geography Teaching Resources, pp. 128–131

Online Assessment

Have students check their own understanding.

Chapter Self-Test

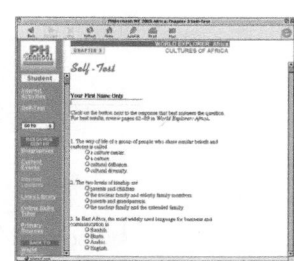

Test Preparation

Foundations of Geography Benchmark Test 1, AYP Monitoring Assessments, pp. 81–84

Section 1 Our Planet, Earth

 2 periods, 1 block

Social Studies Objectives

1. Learn about Earth's movement in relation to the sun.
2. Explore seasons and latitude.

Reading/Language Arts Objective

Use context clues from surrounding phrases to determine the meaning of unfamiliar words.

Prepare to Read	Instructional Resources	Differentiated Instruction
Build Background Knowledge Ask students to predict the effect of Earth's movements. **Set a Purpose for Reading** Have students begin to fill out the *Reading Readiness Guide.* **Preview Key Terms** Teach the section's Key Terms. **Target Reading Skill** Introduce the section's Target Reading Skill of **using context clues.**	**All in One Foundations of Geography Teaching Resources** L2 Reading Readiness Guide, p. 106 L2 Use Context Clues: General Knowledge, p. 121	**Spanish Reading and Vocabulary Study Guide** L1 Chapter 2, Section 1, pp. 8–9 ELL

Instruct	Instructional Resources	Differentiated Instruction
Earth and the Sun Discuss how the Earth's rotation affects the way we keep track of time. **Seasons and Latitude** Ask questions about the Earth's tilt and how it relates to the seasons. **Target Reading Skill** Review **using context clues.**	**All in One Foundations of Geography Teaching Resources** L2 Guided Reading and Review, p. 107 L2 Reading Readiness Guide, p. 106 **Foundations of Geography Transparencies** L2 Section Reading Support Transparency FG 45	**All in One Foundations of Geography Teaching Resources** L3 Enrichment, p. 126 AR, GT L1 Understanding Movements of the Earth, p. 134 ELL, LPR, SN **Teacher's Edition** L3 For Gifted and Talented, TE p. 31 L1 For Less Proficient Readers, TE p. 31 **Spanish Support** L2 Guided Reading and Review (Spanish), p. 8 ELL

Assess and Reteach	Instructional Resources	Differentiated Instruction
Assess Progress Evaluate student comprehension with the section assessment and section quiz. **Reteach** Assign the Reading and Vocabulary Study Guide to help struggling students. **Extend** Extend the lesson by assigning an Activity Shop Lab.	**All in One Foundations of Geography Teaching Resources** L2 Section Quiz, p. 108 L3 Activity Shop Lab: The Earth's Seasons, pp. 132–133 Rubric for Assessing a Writing Assignment, p. 145 **Reading and Vocabulary Study Guide** L1 Chapter 2, Section 1, pp. 9–11	**Spanish Support** L2 Section Quiz (Spanish), p. 9 ELL

Key

L1 Basic to Average   L3 Average to Advanced   LPR Less Proficient Readers   GT Gifted and Talented

L2 For All Students   AR Advanced Readers   ELL English Language Learners

     SN Special Needs Students

Section 2 Forces Shaping Earth

 *2.5 periods, 1.25 block*

Social Studies Objectives
1. Learn about the planet Earth.
2. Explore the forces inside Earth.
3. Explore the forces on Earth's surface.

Reading/Language Arts Objective
Use context clues, such as restatement, to determine the meaning of an unfamiliar word or phrase.

Prepare to Read

Build Background Knowledge
Show a video to start a discussion about how forces shape Earth.

Set a Purpose for Reading
Have students begin to fill out the *Reading Readiness Guide*.

Preview Key Terms
Teach the section's Key Terms.

Target Reading Skill
Introduce the section's Target Reading Skill of **using context clues**.

Instructional Resources

All in One Foundations of Geography Teaching Resources
- L2 Reading Readiness Guide, p. 110
- L2 Use Context Clues: Definition/Description, p. 122

Differentiated Instruction

Spanish Reading and Vocabulary Study Guide
- L1 Chapter 2, Section 2, pp. 10–11 ELL

Instruct

Understanding Earth
Discuss the properties of Earth, from its core to its atmosphere.

Target Reading Skill
Review **using context clues**.

Forces Inside Earth
Discuss the different forces beneath Earth's surface.

Forces on Earth's Surface
Discuss how the surface of Earth is changing.

Instructional Resources

All in One Foundations of Geography Teaching Resources
- L2 Guided Reading and Review, p. 111
- L2 Reading Readiness Guide, p. 110

Foundations of Geography Transparencies
- L2 Section Reading Support Transparency FG 46

Differentiated Instruction

All in One Foundations of Geography Teaching Resources
- L3 A Huge Black Umbrella, pp. 138–140 AR, GT

Teacher's Edition
- L1 For English Language Learners, TE p. 36
- L3 For Gifted and Talented, TE p. 36

Spanish Support
- L2 Guided Reading and Review (Spanish), p. 10 ELL

Assess and Reteach

Assess Progress
Evaluate student comprehension with the section assessment and section quiz.

Reteach
Assign the Reading and Vocabulary Study Guide to help struggling students.

Extend
Extend the lesson by assigning a Small Group Activity.

Instructional Resources

All in One Foundations of Geography Teaching Resources
- L2 Section Quiz, p. 112
- L3 Small Group Activity: Simulation: Making a Poster for the Whitney Classic, pp. 128–131 Rubric for Assessing a Writing Assignment, p. 145

Reading and Vocabulary Study Guide
- L1 Chapter 2, Section 2, pp. 12–14

Differentiated Instruction

Spanish Support
- L2 Section Quiz (Spanish), p. 11 ELL

Key
- L1 Basic to Average
- L3 Average to Advanced
- L2 For All Students

- LPR Less Proficient Readers
- AR Advanced Readers
- SN Special Needs Students

- GT Gifted and Talented
- ELL English Language Learners

Section 3 Climate and Weather

 4 periods, 2 blocks (includes Skills for Life)

Social Studies Objectives

1. Learn about weather and climate.
2. Explore latitude, landforms, and precipitation.
3. Discover how oceans affect climate.

Reading/Language Arts Objective

Use context clues that give a comparison to determine the meaning of a word or phrase.

Prepare to Read

Build Background Knowledge
Have students share ideas about weather and climate.

Set a Purpose for Reading
Have students begin to fill out the *Reading Readiness Guide*.

Preview Key Terms
Teach the section's Key Terms.

Target Reading Skill
Introduce the section's Target Reading Skill of **using context clues.**

Instructional Resources

All in One Foundations of Geography Teaching Resources
- L2 Reading Readiness Guide, p. 114
- L2 Use Context Clues: Compare and Contrast, p. 123

Differentiated Instruction

Spanish Reading and Vocabulary Study Guide
- L1 Chapter 2, Section 3, pp. 12–13 ELL

Instruct

Weather or Climate?
Why Climates Vary
Discuss climate and weather.

Oceans and Climates
Discuss how the ocean affects climate.

Target Reading Skill
Review **using context clues.**

Eyewitness Technology
Have students read about weather forecasting, and then create an outline of the information they learned.

Raging Storms
Ask a question about the characteristics that different storms have in common.

Instructional Resources

All in One Foundations of Geography Teaching Resources
- L2 Guided Reading and Review, p. 115
- L2 Reading Readiness Guide, p. 114

Foundations of Geography Transparencies
- L2 Section Reading Support Transparency FG 47
- L3 Color Transparency FG 41: Climate Graphs

Differentiated Instruction

All in One Foundations of Geography Teaching Resources
- L1 Reading a Climate Map, p. 135 ELL, LPR, SN
  Rubric for Assessing a Student Poem, p. 146 AR, GT
- L3 Writing a Letter, p. 143 AR, GT
- L2 Skills for Life, p. 127 AR, GT, LPR, SN
- L1 Reading a Climate Graph, p. 136 ELL, LPR, SN

Teacher's Edition
- L1 For Special Needs Students, TE p. 42
- L1 For Less Proficient Readers, TE p. 45
- L3 For Gifted and Talented, TE p. 45
- L1 For English Language Learners, TE p. 46
- L3 For Advanced Readers, TE p. 46

Student Edition on Audio CD
- L1 Chapter 2, Section 3 ELL, LPR, SN

Assess and Reteach

Assess Progress
Evaluate student comprehension with the section assessment and section quiz.

Reteach
Assign the Reading and Vocabulary Study Guide to help struggling students.

Extend
Extend the lesson by assigning a role-playing activity.

Instructional Resources

All in One Foundations of Geography Teaching Resources
- L2 Section Quiz, p. 116
  Rubric for Assessing a Role-Playing Activity, p. 147
  Rubric for Assessing a Writing Assignment, p. 145
  Rubric for Assessing a Bar Graph, p. 148
  Rubric for Assessing a Line Graph, p. 149

Reading and Vocabulary Study Guide
- L1 Chapter 2, Section 3, pp. 15–17

Differentiated Instruction

Spanish Support
- L2 Section Quiz (Spanish), p. 15 ELL

Teacher's Edition
- L1 For Special Needs Students, TE p. 49

Social Studies Skills Tutor CD-ROM
- L1 Analyzing Graphic Data ELL, LPR, SN

Key

L1 Basic to Average	L3 Average to Advanced	
L2 For All Students		

LPR Less Proficient Readers
AR Advanced Readers
SN Special Needs Students

GT Gifted and Talented
ELL English Language Learners

Section 4 How Climate Affects Vegetation

 4.5 periods, 2.25 blocks (includes Chapter Review and Assessment)

Social Studies Objectives
1. Investigate the relationship between climate and vegetation.
2. Explore Earth's vegetation regions.
3. Study vertical climate zones.

Reading/Language Arts Objective
Use context to determine the meaning of a word or phrase when examples are provided.

Section Lesson Planner

Prepare to Read

Build Background Knowledge
Have students brainstorm how climate zones affect daily life.

Set a Purpose for Reading
Have students evaluate statements on the *Reading Readiness Guide*.

Preview Key Terms
Teach the section's Key Terms.

Target Reading Skill
Introduce the section's Target Reading Skill of **using context clues**.

Instructional Resources

All in One Foundations of Geography Teaching Resources
- L2 Reading Readiness Guide, p. 118
- L2 Use Context Clues: Examples, p. 124

Differentiated Instruction

Spanish Reading and Vocabulary Study Guide
- L1 Chapter 2, Section 4, pp. 14–15 ELL

Instruct

Climate and Vegetation
Discuss the five broad types of climate.

Earth's Vegetation Regions
Ask a question about the locations of various vegetation regions.

Target Reading Skill
Review **using context clues**.

Vertical Climate Zones
Discuss climates in higher elevations.

Instructional Resources

All in One Foundations of Geography Teaching Resources
- L2 Guided Reading and Review, p. 119
- L2 Reading Readiness Guide, p. 118

Foundations of Geography Transparencies
- L2 Section Reading Support Transparency FG 48
- L2 Color Transparency FG 10: The World: Annual Precipitation (Base)
- L2 Color Transparency FG 12: The World: Desert and Desert Scrub Vegetation Regions (Overlay)

Differentiated Instruction

All in One Foundations of Geography Teaching Resources
- L3 The Endless Steppe, pp. 141–142 AR, GT
- L1 Reading a Natural Vegetation Map, p. 137 ELL, LPR, SN

Teacher's Edition
- L3 For Advanced Readers, TE p. 52
- L1 For Less Proficient Readers, TE p. 52

Spanish Support
- L2 Guided Reading and Review (Spanish), p. 14 ELL

Assess and Reteach

Assess Progress
Evaluate student comprehension with the section assessment and section quiz.

Reteach
Assign the Reading and Vocabulary Study Guide to help struggling students.

Extend
Extend the lesson by having students create posters.

Instructional Resources

All in One Foundations of Geography Teaching Resources
- L2 Section Quiz, p. 120
       Rubric for Assessing a Poster, p. 150
       Rubric for Assessing a Writing Assignment, p. 145
- L2 Vocabulary Development, p. 144
- L2 Word Knowledge, p. 125
- L2 Chapter Tests A and B, pp. 151–156

Reading and Vocabulary Study Guide
- L1 Chapter 2, Section 4, pp. 18–20

Differentiated Instruction

Spanish Support
- L2 Section Quiz (Spanish), p. 15 ELL
- L2 Chapter Summary (Spanish), p. 16 ELL
- L2 Vocabulary Development (Spanish), p. 17 ELL

Key
- L1 Basic to Average
- L2 For All Students
- L3 Average to Advanced
- LPR Less Proficient Readers
- AR Advanced Readers
- SN Special Needs Students
- GT Gifted and Talented
- ELL English Language Learners

Reading Background

Paragraph Puzzles

In this activity, students are asked to put a paragraph's sentences in the correct order. Explain to students that this activity will help them understand paragraph structure. The activity teaches students to distinguish a topic sentence that contains the main idea from the supporting details. Doing a paragraph puzzle activity also helps students practice sequencing steps and ideas.

Begin by writing a paragraph on a piece of paper with each sentence on its own line. Cut the sentences into narrow strips, and place the strips in an envelope. Divide students into pairs and distribute one envelope to each pair. Ask students to arrange the sentences into a logical paragraph.

Extend this strategy by challenging students to recall the plot of a short story, the sequence of events necessary to solve a math problem, or the steps involved in a scientific experiment. Ask students to write down the sentences, cut them into individual sentences, and place them in an envelope. Have students exchange envelopes with a partner and put the sentences in the correct order. Students should then explain their rationale.

Power Notes

This strategy can help students clarify the difference between main ideas and details. The Power Notes strategy is similar to creating an outline, but simpler because main ideas and details are assigned different numbers. Main ideas are power 1 ideas. Details are either power 2s or 3s. Students can use this technique to organize information for reading, writing, and studying.

Write the following on the board:

Power 1: Main Idea

Power 2: Detail or support for power 1

Power 3: Detail or support for power 2

Model this approach by using information from the chapter:

Power 1: The effect of Earth's tilt on its axis

Power 2: Toward the sun creates Summer

Power 3: Longer daylight and more direct sunlight

Power 2: Away from the sun creates Winter

Power 3: Shorter daylight and sunlight is less direct

Another way to practice this skill is to write power 1s from the chapter on the board and have students take turns filling in the supporting details.

World Studies Background

Our Solar System

The nine planets of our solar system orbit around the sun in a counterclockwise direction. The innermost planets—Mercury, Venus, Earth, and Mars—are relatively small and have solid surfaces. They have few or no moons and no ring systems. The outermost planets—Jupiter, Saturn, Uranus, and Neptune—are larger and are made up of gases. They have many moons, ranging in number from eight for Neptune to at least 18 for Saturn. Each of the outer planets has a ring system. Pluto is in a category by itself because it resembles the icy moons of the outer planets. It has only one moon and does not have any rings.

Volcanoes

More than 80 percent of Earth's surface—above and below sea level—is of volcanic origin. Most volcanoes are located on the edges of continents, along island chains, or beneath the sea in long mountain ranges. About 500 volcanoes have erupted above sea level throughout history. More than half of them encircle the Pacific Ocean to form the Ring of Fire. After Indonesia and Japan, the United States has the highest number of historically active volcanoes.

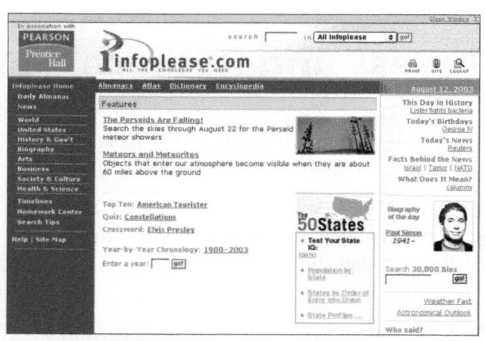

Infoplease® provides a wealth of useful information for the classroom. You can use this resource to strengthen your background on the subjects covered in this chapter. Have students visit this advertising-free site as a starting point for projects requiring research.

Use Web code **led-3200** for **Infoplease.**

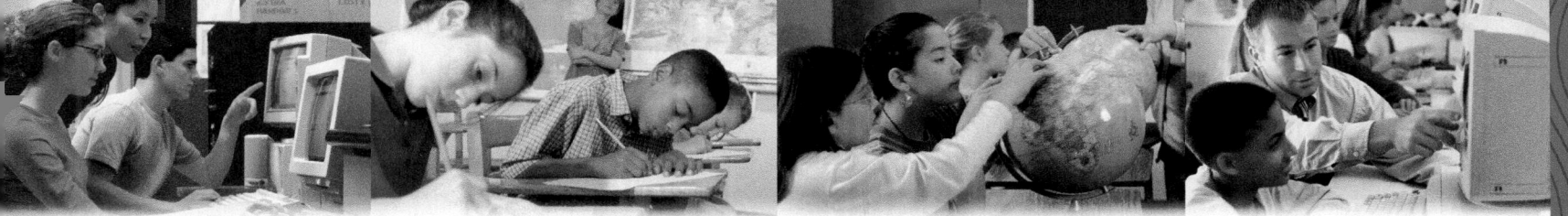

Using the Choral Reading Technique Effectively

The Choral Reading strategy encourages participation by all students because it provides a non-threatening reading environment. To maximize success with this strategy, choose shorter passages (fewer than 500 words) and encourage students to stay with your voice, so that everyone reads at the same rate. When students have finished reading in unison, allow time for students to reread the passage silently, focusing on new or unfamiliar words.

Read-Cover-Recite-Check

Read-Cover-Recite-Check is a useful strategy for helping students to retain the information they read. It can be especially effective when students are studying for a test. Model the steps for using Read-Cover-Recite-Check to read the first paragraph on page 28 of the Student Edition.

1. Read the paragraph quickly to grasp the main ideas. *(Think aloud about the main idea: this paragraph is about a galaxy.)*
2. Reread the paragraph, looking for details and key information. *(Think aloud, noting the details: the Milky Way is a galaxy. It is made up of Earth, the sun, other planets, and stars. Our sun is a star in the Milky Way.)*
3. Cover the paragraph with your hand or a piece of paper. Recall and repeat the information from the paragraph, including the topic and important details. *(Think aloud: repeat the main idea and details from steps 1 and 2, using different phrasing.)*
4. Rephrase the paragraph in your own words. *(The Milky Way is a galaxy that includes planets and stars. It looks like a white streak across the sky. The sun is not the center of the Milky Way, but it is the center of Earth's orbit.)*
5. Check to make sure you remembered correctly.

Weather Conditions

Weather takes place in the lowest region of the atmosphere known as the troposphere. Geographic features such as mountains and large bodies of water significantly impact the weather. The temperature of the ocean can be responsible for a drought in one area and heavy rains in another. Because weather has such a great effect on human settlement patterns, food production, and personal comfort, people are often reliant on forecasts. The National Meteorological Center (NMC) collects data from devices such as weather satellites, barometers, and radar. This information is used to create weather maps for geographic regions throughout the world.

The Amazon Rainforest

The Amazon Rainforest in northern South America exists because of the high rainfall, high humidity, and high temperatures of the region. About half of the Amazon's rainfall is evaporated moisture from the Atlantic. The rest is moisture evaporated from the rainforest itself. Blanketing an area of 2,300,000 square miles (6,000,000 sq km), this rainforest is the world's richest and most biologically diverse, with millions of species of animals and plants.

Chapter 2 Earth's Physical Geography

Guiding Questions

Remind students about the Guiding Questions introduced at the beginning of this section.

Section 1 relates to **Guiding Question** ①
What are Earth's major physical features?
(Earth's movement in relation to the sun causes day and night. The tilt of Earth combined with Earth's rotation around the sun causes seasons.)

Section 2 relates to **Guiding Question** ①
What are Earth's major physical features?
(More than 70 percent of Earth's surface is made up of water. Landforms such as mountains, plains, hills, volcanoes, and plateaus cover the other 30 percent of Earth's surface.)

Section 3 relates to **Guiding Question** ①
What are Earth's major physical features?
(Earth's oceans and landforms can affect climates. Places located on coasts have more moderate temperatures due to the slow cooling and heating of the ocean. Mountains can also affect climates.)

Section 4 relates to **Guiding Question** ①
What are Earth's major physical features?
(Vegetation varies widely across Earth according to climate and type of soil.)

⤴ Target Reading Skill

In this chapter, students will learn and apply the reading skill of using context clues. Use the following worksheets to help students practice this skill:

 **Foundations of Geography Teaching Resources,** *Use Context Clues: General Knowledge,* p. 121; *Use Context Clues: Definition/Description,* p. 122; *Use Context Clues: Compare and Contrast,* p. 123; *Use Context Clues: Examples,* p. 124

Differentiated Instruction

The following Teacher's Edition strategies are suitable for students of varying abilities.

Advanced Readers, pp. 46, 52
English Language Learners, pp. 36, 46
Gifted and Talented, pp. 31, 36, 45
Less Proficient Readers, pp. 31, 45, 52
Special Needs Students, pp. 42, 49

Chapter Preview

This chapter will introduce you to the physical geography of Earth, including the planet's structure, climate, and vegetation.

Section 1
Our Planet, Earth

Section 2
Forces Shaping Earth

Section 3
Climate and Weather

Section 4
How Climate Affects Vegetation

⟳ **Target Reading Skill**

Context In this chapter you will focus on using context to help you understand unfamiliar words. Context includes the words, phrases, and sentences surrounding a word.

▶ Delicate Arch in Arches National Park, Utah

26 Foundations of Geography

Bibliography

For the Teacher
Erickson, Jon and Ernest H. Muller. *Plate Tectonics: Unraveling the Mysteries of the Earth.* Checkmark Books, 2001.
Zeilinga De Boer, Jelle and Donald Theodore Sanders. *Volcanoes in Human History: The Far-Reaching Effects of Major Eruptions.* Princeton University Press, 2001.

For the Student
L1 Arthus-Bertrand, Yann. *Earth from Above for Young Readers.* Abrams, 2002.
L2 Berger, Melvin. *Why Do Volcanoes Blow Their Tops?* Scholastic Reference, 2000.
L3 Oldershaw, Cally, *Atlas of Geology and Landforms.* Scholastic Library, 2001.

Using the Visual ᴸ²

Reach Into Your Background Draw students' attention to the caption accompanying the picture on page 26.

Discuss the visual with your students. What strikes them about the image in this photo? Encourage students to share their ideas about how these rock formations may have formed. Ask students to share any experiences they have had traveling to state and national parks to see unusual landforms.

Chapter Resources

Teaching Resources
- ᴸ² Vocabulary Development, p. 144
- ᴸ² Skills for Life, p. 127
- ᴸ² Chapter Tests A and B, pp. 151–156

Spanish Support
- ᴸ² Spanish Chapter Summary, p. 16
- ᴸ² Spanish Vocabulary Development, p. 17

Media and Technology
- ᴸ¹ Student Edition on Audio CD
- ᴸ¹ Guided Reading Audiotapes, English and Spanish
- ᴸ² Social Studies Skills Tutor CD-ROM

ExamView Test Bank CD-ROM

PRENTICE HALL
Presentation EXPRESS™
Teach · Connect · Inspire

Teach this chapter's content using the PresentationExpress™ CD-ROM including:
- slide shows
- transparencies
- interactive maps and media
- *ExamView*® QuickTake Presenter

Objectives

Social Studies

1. Learn about Earth's movement in relation to the sun.
2. Explore seasons and latitude.

Reading/Language Arts

Use context clues from surrounding phrases to determine the meaning of unfamiliar words.

Prepare to Read

Build Background Knowledge L2

Tell students that they will learn about Earth's movements and how they affect the seasons and latitude in this section. Ask students to look through the section and predict the effects of Earth's movements. Provide a few simple examples to get students started. Conduct an Idea Wave (TE, p. T35) to generate a list.

Set a Purpose for Reading L2

■ Preview the Objectives.

■ Form students into pairs or groups of four. Distribute the *Reading Readiness Guide.* Ask students to fill in the first two columns of the chart. Use the Numbered Heads participation strategy (TE, p. T36) to call on students to share one piece of information they already know and one piece of information they want to know.

All in One **Foundations of Geography Teaching Resources,** *Reading Readiness Guide*, p. 106

Vocabulary Builder
Preview Key Terms L2

Create a three-column "See It—Remember It" chart of the Key Terms on the board. Write a term in the first column, a short definition in the second column, and a sketch in the third column. Guide students as they copy and complete the chart.

Prepare to Read

Objectives

In this section you will
1. Learn about Earth's movement in relation to the sun.
2. Explore seasons and latitude.

Taking Notes

Copy the table below. As you read this section, fill in the table with information about the movements of Earth relative to the sun, days and nights, seasons, and latitude. Add more lines as you need them.

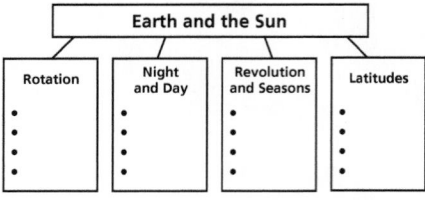

Earth and the Sun

Rotation	Night and Day	Revolution and Seasons	Latitudes
•	•	•	•
•	•	•	•
•	•	•	•

Target Reading Skill

Use Context Clues You can sometimes find the meaning of a word by using context—the words and sentences around that word. In some cases the context will describe the word. In this example, the phrase in italics describes a planet:

A planet is a *large object that circles a star.*

As you read, look at the context for the word *galaxy* in the paragraph below. What do you think *galaxy* means?

Key Terms

- **orbit** (AWR bit) *n.* the path one body makes as it circles around another
- **revolution** (rev uh LOO shun) *n.* circular motion
- **axis** (AK sis) *n.* an imaginary line through Earth between the North and South poles, around which Earth turns
- **rotation** (roh TAY shun) *n.* a complete turn

Earth and the Sun

The Milky Way Galaxy

Earth, the sun, the planets, and the stars in the sky are all part of a galaxy, or family of stars. Our galaxy is just one of the billions of galaxies in the universe. We call our galaxy the Milky Way because, in a dark night sky, away from city lights, its billions of stars look like a trail of spilled milk. Our sun is one of those stars. The sun is just a tiny speck compared to the rest of the Milky Way, but it is the center of everything for Earth and the other planets in the solar system. The solar system includes Earth, the other planets, and other objects that orbit the sun.

Even though the sun is about 93 million miles (150 million kilometers) away, it provides Earth with heat and light. Earth travels around the sun in a nearly circular **orbit,** which is the path one body makes as it circles around another. Earth takes 365¼ days, or one year, to complete one **revolution,** or circular motion, in its orbit around the sun.

Target Reading Skill L2

Use Context Clues Point out the Target Reading Skill. Tell students that information surrounding an unknown word can provide clues to the word's meaning.

Model context clues to find the meaning of *polar zones* in this sentence from page 32: "The areas above the Arctic Circle and below the Antarctic Circle are the high latitudes, or the polar zones." *(The* polar zones *are defined*

in context as the areas of high latitude above the Arctic Circle and below the Antarctic Circle.)

Give students *Use Context Clues: General Knowledge.* Have them complete the activity in groups.

All in One **Foundations of Geography Teaching Resources,** *Use Context Clues: General Knowledge*, p. 121

Understanding Days and Nights As Earth circles the sun, it also spins in space. Earth turns around its **axis**—an imaginary line running through Earth between the North and South poles. Each complete turn, or **rotation,** takes about 24 hours. As Earth rotates, it is night on the side away from the sun. As Earth turns toward the sun, the sun appears to rise. When a side of Earth faces the sun, it is daytime. Then, as that side of Earth turns away from the sun, the sun appears to set.

Time Zones Earth rotates toward the east, so the day starts earlier in the east. The time difference is just a few seconds per mile. If every town had its own local time, it would be very confusing. So, governments have divided the world into standard time zones. Times in neighboring zones are one hour apart. There are also a few nonstandard time zones with times less than a full hour away from their neighbors.

✓ Reading Check **What is the connection between Earth's rotation and the change from day to night?**

Links to
Math

Time Zones and Longitude
Earth's surface is divided into 360 degrees of longitude: 180 degrees east and west of the Prime Meridian. Since Earth rotates at a steady rate in about 24 hours, its 24 standard time zones are centered the same number of degrees of longitude apart. Can you find this number? (*Hint:* The number is 360° ÷ 24.)

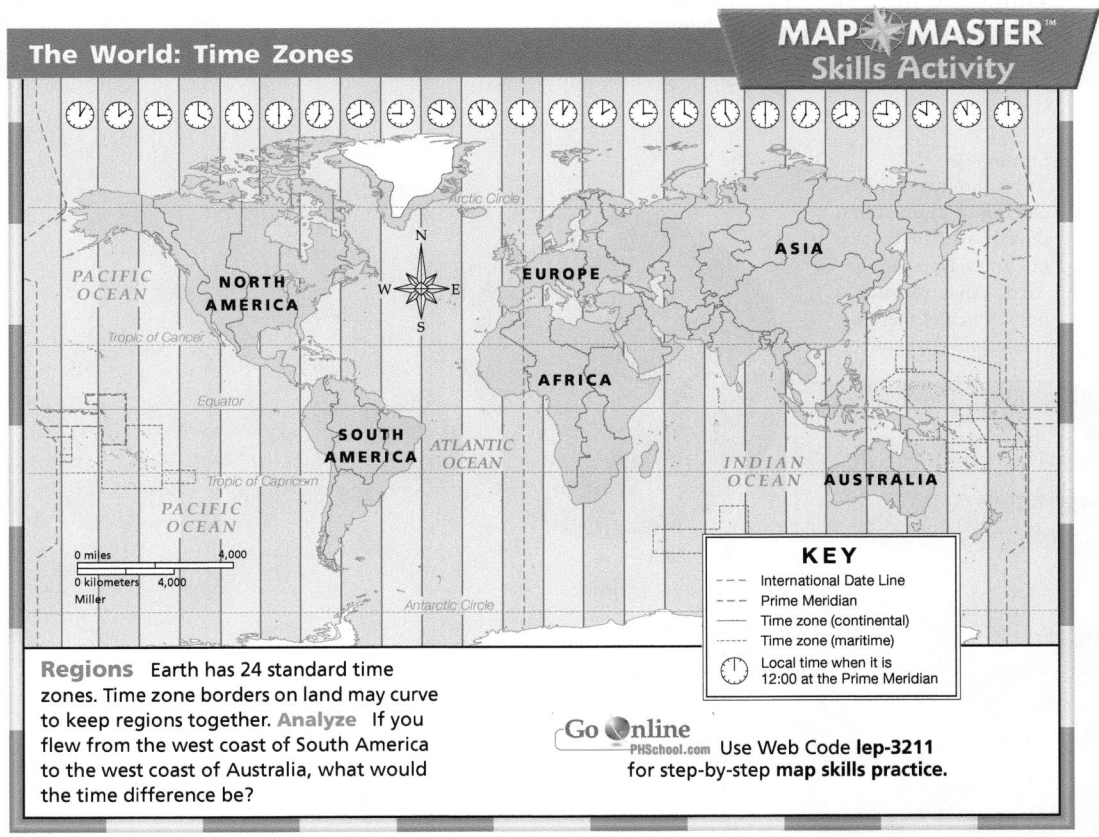

The World: Time Zones

MAP✦MASTER™
Skills Activity

KEY
- – – International Date Line
- – – – Prime Meridian
- ——— Time zone (continental)
- ········· Time zone (maritime)
- 🕐 Local time when it is 12:00 at the Prime Meridian

Regions Earth has 24 standard time zones. Time zone borders on land may curve to keep regions together. **Analyze** If you flew from the west coast of South America to the west coast of Australia, what would the time difference be?

Go Online
PHSchool.com Use Web Code **lep-3211** for step-by-step **map skills practice.**

Chapter 2 Section 1 **29**

Vocabulary Builder

Use the information below to teach students this section's high-use words.

High-Use Word	Definition and Sample Sentence
standard, p. 29	*n.* something set up as a rule or model with which others are compared Juan's excellent presentation set the **standard** for the rest of the class.
relative, p. 30	*adj.* as compared with someone or something else My teacher is very short **relative** to the principal.

Instruct

Earth and the Sun L2

Guided Instruction
- **Vocabulary Builder** Clarify the high-use word **standard** before reading.

- Read Earth and the Sun using the Paragraph Shrinking strategy (TE, p. T34). Ask students to study The World: Time Zones map and the caption on this page.

- Ask students **What is the relationship between Earth's rotation and time zones?** *(It takes 24 hours for Earth to rotate through each of its 24 time zones.)*

- Ask students to predict how the cycle of day and night would be affected if Earth's rotation were slower. *(If Earth's rotation were slower, the day would be longer than 24 hours.)*

- Tell students that every four years is a leap year of 366 days. Have them draw a conclusion as to why. *(If there are 365 1/4 days every year, then every four years there is one extra day, so leap year has 366 days.)*

Independent Practice
Ask students to create the Taking Notes graphic organizer on a blank piece of paper. Then have them fill in the "Rotation" and "Night and Day" boxes with information they have just learned. Briefly model how to identify which details to record.

Monitor Progress
As students fill in the graphic organizer, circulate and make sure individuals are selecting the correct details. Provide assistance as needed.

⬛ Links

Read the **Links to Math** box on this page with students. Guide them as they calculate that 360 divided by 24 is 15.

Answers

✓ Reading Check As Earth rotates, it is night on the side facing away from the sun. When the side away from the sun faces the sun, it is daytime.

MAP✦MASTER™ Skills Activity **Analyze** 11 hours

Seasons and Latitude L2

Guided Instruction

■ **Vocabulary Builder** Clarify the high-use word **relative** before reading.

■ Read how Earth's movement and latitude affect the seasons in Seasons and Latitude. Ask students to study the diagram titled The Revolution of Earth. As a class, answer the Geography Skills Practice question.

■ Ask students **What happens in the Northern Hemisphere during the summer solstice?** *(The Northern Hemisphere is tilted farthest toward the sun.)* **How does this tilt affect the region?** *(The days are longer and the temperature is higher.)*

■ Ask students **What is the season in Australia when it is winter in the United States?** *(summer)*

◑ Target Reading Skill L2

Using Context Clues As a follow up, ask students to perform the Target Reading Skill activity in the Student Edition. Then ask **What words in the text describe the summer solstice?** *(the Northern Hemisphere is tilted farthest toward the sun)*

Seasons and Latitude

Target Skill **Use Context Clues** If you do not know what the summer solstice is, look at the words that follow this term in the text. They describe the summer solstice.

The axis of Earth is tilted relative to its orbit. At different points in Earth's orbit, the Northern Hemisphere may tilt toward or away from the sun. At other points in the orbit, neither hemisphere tilts toward or away from the sun. The revolution of the tilted planet Earth causes seasons.

At the summer solstice, the Northern Hemisphere is tilted farthest toward the sun. Places in this hemisphere have longer daylight and more direct sunlight at the solstice than at other times of the year. This direct sunlight causes the heat of summer.

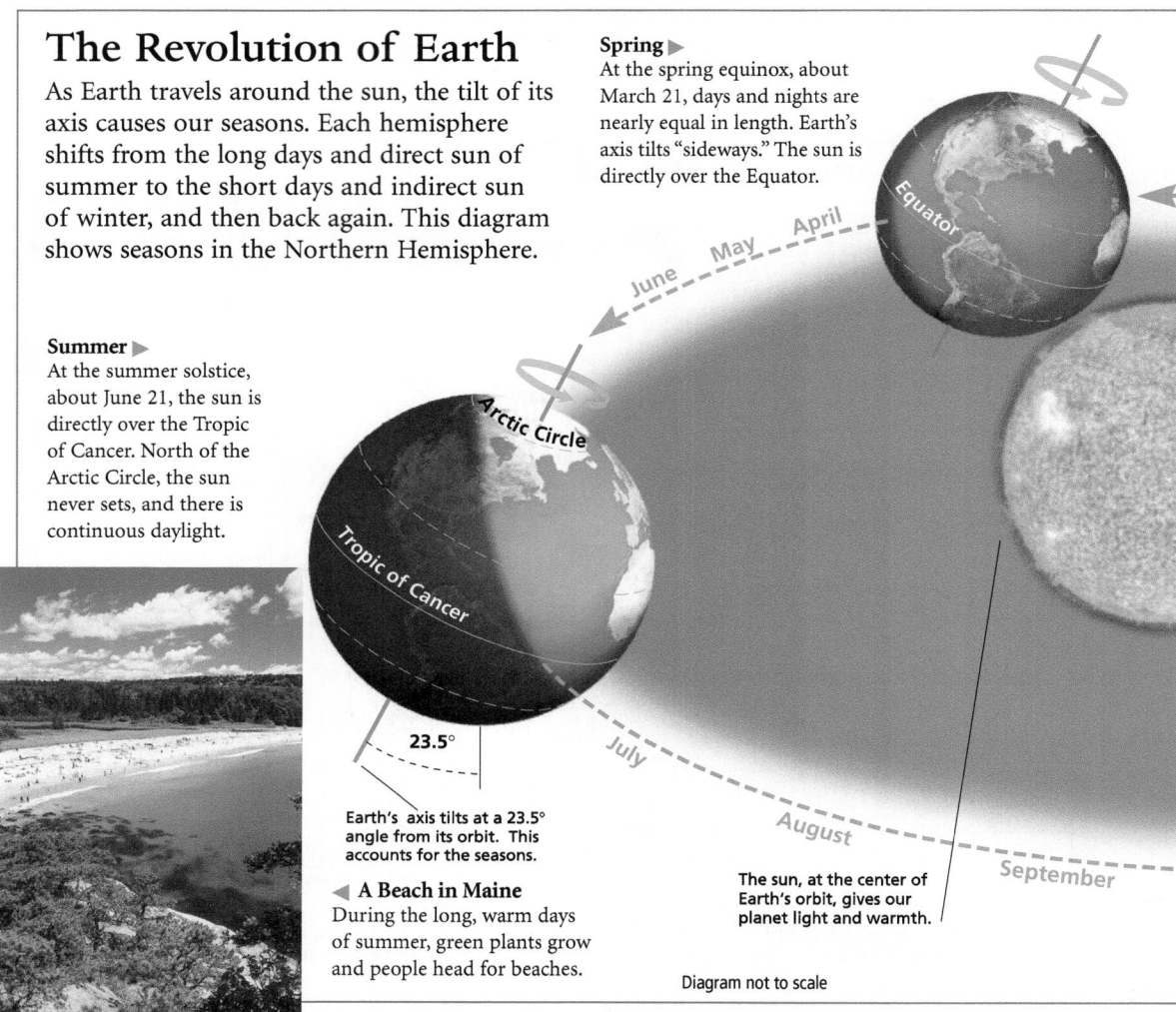

The Revolution of Earth

As Earth travels around the sun, the tilt of its axis causes our seasons. Each hemisphere shifts from the long days and direct sun of summer to the short days and indirect sun of winter, and then back again. This diagram shows seasons in the Northern Hemisphere.

Spring ▶
At the spring equinox, about March 21, days and nights are nearly equal in length. Earth's axis tilts "sideways." The sun is directly over the Equator.

Summer ▶
At the summer solstice, about June 21, the sun is directly over the Tropic of Cancer. North of the Arctic Circle, the sun never sets, and there is continuous daylight.

23.5°
Earth's axis tilts at a 23.5° angle from its orbit. This accounts for the seasons.

◀ A Beach in Maine
During the long, warm days of summer, green plants grow and people head for beaches.

The sun, at the center of Earth's orbit, gives our planet light and warmth.

Diagram not to scale

30 Foundations of Geography

Skills for Life — Skills Mini Lesson

Identifying Cause and Effect

1. Teach identifying cause and effect by pointing out that students can choose a specific event as a starting point and look at earlier events to determine possible causes. They can look at later events to help them identify effects.

2. Help students practice the skill by looking at the diagram on pp. 30–31. Have students determine an effect of Earth's movement.

3. Have students apply the skill by determining the effect of the following cause: the sun is directly over the Tropic of Cancer north of the Arctic Circle at summer solstice.

As Earth moves through its orbit, the Northern Hemisphere is tilted farther from the sun. Sunlight is less direct, and we have the chill of fall. When the Northern Hemisphere is tilted farthest from the sun at the winter solstice, days are short, the sun's rays reach us at a steep angle, and we have cold weather. Finally, Earth's revolution moves the Northern Hemisphere back toward the sun, and we have the warming trend of spring.

When the Northern Hemisphere is tilted toward the sun, the Southern Hemisphere is tilted away, and vice versa, so the seasons are reversed in the Southern Hemisphere.

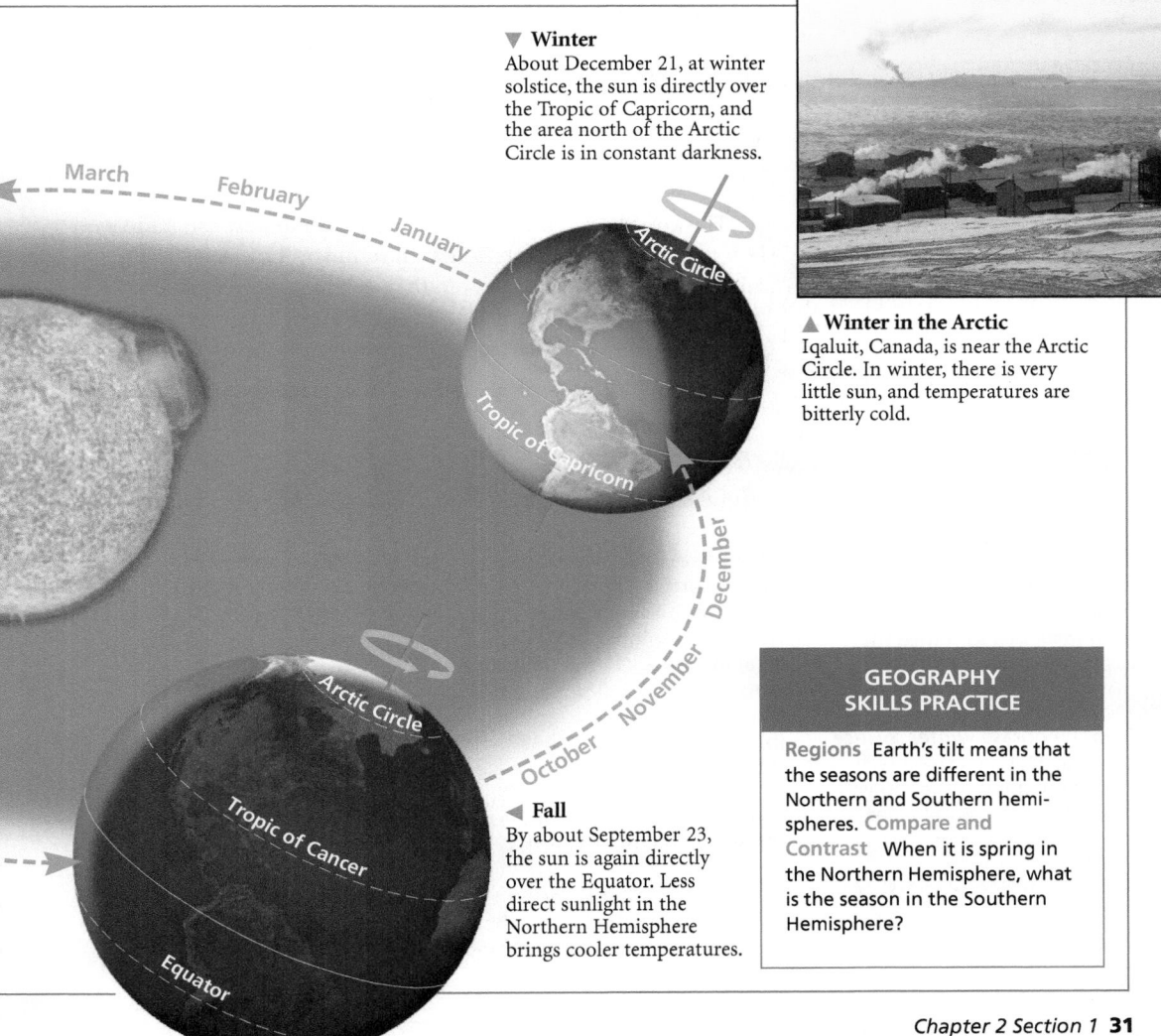

▼ **Winter**
About December 21, at winter solstice, the sun is directly over the Tropic of Capricorn, and the area north of the Arctic Circle is in constant darkness.

▲ **Winter in the Arctic**
Iqaluit, Canada, is near the Arctic Circle. In winter, there is very little sun, and temperatures are bitterly cold.

◄ **Fall**
By about September 23, the sun is again directly over the Equator. Less direct sunlight in the Northern Hemisphere brings cooler temperatures.

GEOGRAPHY SKILLS PRACTICE

Regions Earth's tilt means that the seasons are different in the Northern and Southern hemispheres. **Compare and Contrast** When it is spring in the Northern Hemisphere, what is the season in the Southern Hemisphere?

Chapter 2 Section 1 **31**

Guided Instruction (continued)

■ Ask students **Where are the high latitudes located?** (*above the Arctic and below the Antarctic circles*) **If this area receives very long hours of sunlight, why do you think it is so cold?** (*The sun is not directly overhead and therefore doesn't cause the temperature to rise.*)

Independent Practice
Have students complete the graphic organizer by filling in the "Revolution and Seasons" and "Latitudes" boxes.

Monitor Progress
■ Show *Section Reading Support Transparency FG 45* and ask students to check their graphic organizers individually. Go over key concepts and clarify key vocabulary as needed.

📖 **Foundations of Geography Transparencies,** *Section Reading Support Transparency FG 45*

■ Tell students to fill in the last column of their *Reading Readiness Guides.* Ask them to evaluate if what they learned was what they had expected to learn.

All in One Foundations of Geography Teaching Resources, *Reading Readiness Guide,* p. 110

Differentiated Instruction

For Gifted and Talented L3
Have students learn more about the Tropics of Cancer and Capricorn by completing the *Enrichment* activity. Then, have them write a brief summary of their research to attach to their map and diagrams.

All in One Foundations of Geography Teaching Resources, *Enrichment,* p. 126

For Less Proficient Readers L1
To help students who are having difficulty understanding the concepts described in this section, have students complete *Understanding Movements of the Earth.*

All in One Foundations of Geography Teaching Resources, *Understanding Movements of the Earth,* p. 134

Answer
Geography Skills Practice Compare and Contrast Fall

Assess and Reteach

Assess Progress [L2]

Have students complete the Section Assessment. Administer the *Section Quiz*.

[All in One] **Foundations of Geography Teaching Resources,** Section Quiz, p. 108

Reteach [L1]

If students need more instruction, have them read this section in the Reading and Vocabulary Study Guide.

Chapter 2, Section 1, **Western Hemisphere Reading and Vocabulary Study Guide,** pp. 9–11

Extend [L3]

To extend the lesson, pair students and distribute the *Activity Shop Lab: The Earth's Seasons.* Have students make a model of Earth's path around the sun. Then, have them describe their observations as they follow the activity's steps as well as answer the questions provided.

[All in One] **Foundations of Geography Teaching Resources,** *Activity Shop Lab: The Earth's Seasons,* pp. 132–133

Answer

✓ Reading Check   The higher the latitude the longer the winter, and the lower the latitude the longer the summer. For the middle latitude, the four seasons are more distinct.

Section 1 Assessment

Key Terms
Students' sentences should reflect knowledge of each Key Term.

Target Reading Skill
The winter solstice occurs when the Northern Hemisphere is tilted farthest from the sun. The clue is given in the phrase before the term in the sentence.

Comprehension and Critical Thinking
1. (a) A rotation is one complete turn of Earth around its axis, which takes 24 hours.
(b) As Earth rotates, it is night on the side facing away from the sun. As that side of Earth turns toward the sun, it becomes day.
2. (a) Answers will vary, but students should be able to identify the correct time zone.
(b) Answers will vary, but students should correctly calculate the time difference between the Prime Meridian and where they live.

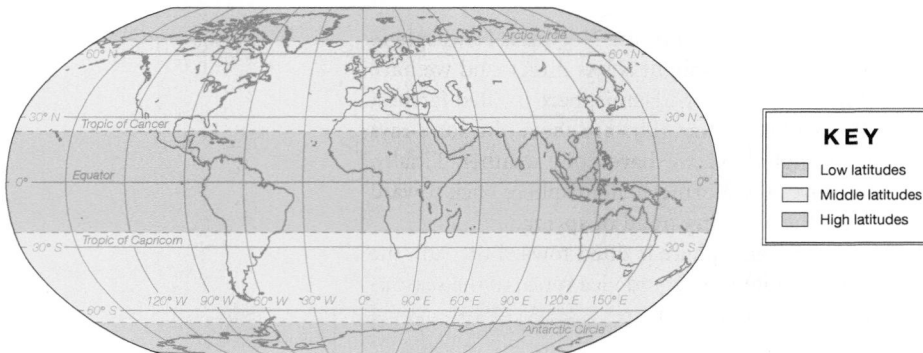

Zones of Latitude
The low latitudes, or tropics, are the single orange band around the Equator. The middle latitudes are the two yellow bands just to the north and south. The two green zones in the far north and south are the high latitudes, or polar zones.

Latitudes The areas between the Tropic of Cancer and the Tropic of Capricorn are called the low latitudes, or the tropics. The tropics have fairly direct sunlight and hot weather all year.

The areas above the Arctic Circle and below the Antarctic Circle are the high latitudes, or the polar zones. Though the polar zones may receive long hours of sunlight during the summer, the sun is never directly overhead. They are cool or very cold all year.

The areas between the high and low latitudes are the middle latitudes, or the temperate zones. In summer, these areas receive fairly direct sunlight. In winter, they get very indirect sunlight. So, the middle latitudes have marked seasons: a hot summer, a cold winter, and a moderate spring and fall.

✓ Reading Check **What is the relation between seasons and latitude?**

Section 1 Assessment

Key Terms
Review the key terms at the beginning of this section. Use each term in a sentence that explains its meaning.

Target Reading Skill
Find the phrase *winter solstice* on page 31. Use context to figure out its meaning. What do you think it means? What clues helped you find a meaning?

Comprehension and Critical Thinking
1. (a) Define What is the rotation of Earth?

(b) Synthesize Information How is Earth's rotation connected to the change from day to night?
2. (a) Identify On the time zone map on page 29, find the time zone where you live.
(b) Evaluate What is the time difference between your home and Greenwich, England?
(c) Analyze How is this time difference related to Earth's rotation?
3. (a) Recall What is Earth's tilt?
(b) Describe How does Earth's orbit affect its tilted hemispheres?

(c) Identify Cause and Effect How do Earth's tilt and orbit cause the seasons?

Writing Activity
Write a short passage for a younger child, explaining the movements of Earth.

For: An activity on our planet, Earth
Visit: PHSchool.com
Web Code: led-3201

32 Foundations of Geography

(c) Earth is divided into 24 standard time zones because Earth takes about 24 hours to rotate. The time at a location differs depending on how far from the Prime Meridian its time zone is located.

3. (a) Earth's tilt is the degree to which Earth leans toward or away from the sun. **(b)** At different points in Earth's orbit, the hemispheres tilt at varying degrees toward or away from the sun. **(c)** The shift in Earth's tilt causes the seasons by changing the distance and angle of different parts of the Earth from the sun.

Writing Activity
Use the *Rubric for Assessing a Writing Assignment* to evaluate students' passages.

[All in One] **Foundations of Geography Teaching Resources,** *Rubric for Assessing a Writing Assignment,* p. 145

Go Online PHSchool.com Typing in the Web code when prompted will bring students directly to detailed instructions for this activity.

Prepare to Read

Objectives

In this section you will
1. Learn about the planet Earth.
2. Explore the forces inside Earth.
3. Explore the forces on Earth's surface.

Taking Notes

As you read this section, look for details about Earth's structure, Earth's landforms, forces inside Earth, how continents move, and forces on Earth's surface. Copy the web diagram below, add more branches and ovals as needed, and write each detail in the correct oval.

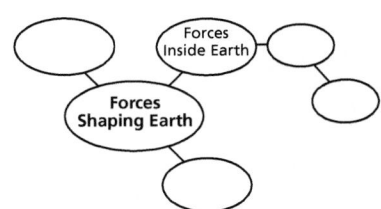

🎯 Target Reading Skill

Use Context Clues You can sometimes find the meaning of a word or phrase by using context. Sometimes the context will define or restate the word. In this example, the phrase in italics defines *continent*:

A continent, or *one of Earth's large land areas* . . .

As you read, look at the context for the phrase *Ring of Fire* in the paragraph below. What do you think the phrase *Ring of Fire* means?

Key Terms

- **core** (kawr) *n.* the sphere of very hot metal at the center of Earth
- **mantle** (MAN tul) *n.* the thick layer around Earth's core
- **crust** (krust) *n.* the thin, rocky layer on Earth's surface
- **magma** (MAG muh) *n.* soft, nearly molten rock
- **plate** (playt) *n.* a huge block of Earth's crust
- **weathering** (WETH ur ing) *n.* a process that breaks rocks down into small pieces
- **erosion** (ee ROH zhun) *n.* the removal of small pieces of rock by water, ice, or wind

Understanding Earth

Around the rim of the Pacific Ocean is a string of volcanoes and earthquake belts called the "Ring of Fire." About 80 percent of the world's earthquakes and many of the world's active volcanoes occur in that ring. Earthquakes and volcanoes are two forces that shape and reshape Earth. They are one reason why Earth's surface constantly changes. They also provide clues about Earth's structure.

Hot rock from inside Earth flows into the Pacific Ocean to form new land in Hawaii.

🎯 Target Reading Skill L2

Use Context Clues Point out the Target Reading Skill. Tell students that using context clues, such as definition and restatement, is one way to find the meaning of an unfamiliar word or phrase.

Model using context clues to find the meaning of fresh water in this sentence from page 35: "Very little of Earth's water is fresh water, or water without salt." *(The phrase fresh water means water without salt.)*

Give students *Use Context Clues: Definition/Description.* Have them complete the activity in groups.

All in One **Foundations of Geography Teaching Resources,** *Use Context Clues: Definition/Description,* p. 122

Objectives

Social Studies
1. Learn about the planet Earth.
2. Explore the forces inside Earth.
3. Explore the forces on Earth's surface.

Reading/Language Arts
Use context clues, such as restatement, to determine the meaning of an unfamiliar word or phrase.

Prepare to Read

Build Background Knowledge L2

Tell students that in this section they will learn about the forces that shape Earth, both inside and out. Show students the *The Ever-Changing Earth.* Then ask students how moving plates cause volcanic eruptions. Use the Give One, Get One participation strategy (TE, p. T37) to generate answers.

📼 *The Ever-Changing Earth,* **World Studies Video Program**

Set a Purpose for Reading L2

- Preview the Objectives.

- Read each statement in the *Reading Readiness Guide* aloud. Ask students to mark the statements true or false.

- Have students discuss the statements in pairs or groups of four, then mark their worksheets again. Use the Numbered Heads participation strategy (TE, p. T36) to call on students to share their group's perspectives.

All in One **Foundations of Geography Teaching Resources,** *Reading Readiness Guide,* p. 110

Vocabulary Builder
Preview Key Terms

Pronounce each Key Term, then ask the students to say the word with you. Provide a simple explanation such as, "The shifting of Earth's plates can sometimes be felt as an earthquake."

Instruct

Understanding Earth L2

Guided Instruction

- **Vocabulary Builder** Clarify the high-use word **force** before reading.

- Read Understanding Earth using the Oral Cloze strategy (TE, p. T33). Ask students to review the diagram of Earth's Layers on this page. As a class, answer the Analyze Images question. Allow students to discuss their answers with a partner before sharing them with the class.

- Ask students to name the sources of heat that help shape Earth's crust. *(the core: a ball of very hot metal at the center of the earth; the mantle: the hot, rocky layer around the core)*

Answers

Analyze Images Possible answers: A person could not withstand the extremely high temperatures; the disturbance might cause a volcano to erupt or an earthquake; the escaping gases might affect the atmosphere that surrounds Earth.

What Is Earth Made Of? To understand the forces that shape Earth, you must study Earth's structure. A sphere of very hot metal at the center of Earth is called the **core**. The **mantle** is a thick, hot, rocky layer around the core. The thin layer of rocks and minerals that surrounds the mantle is called the **crust**. In effect, the crust floats on top of the mantle. The heat of the core and mantle helps shape Earth's crust. The surface of the crust includes Earth's land areas as well as the ocean floors.

Earth's Layers

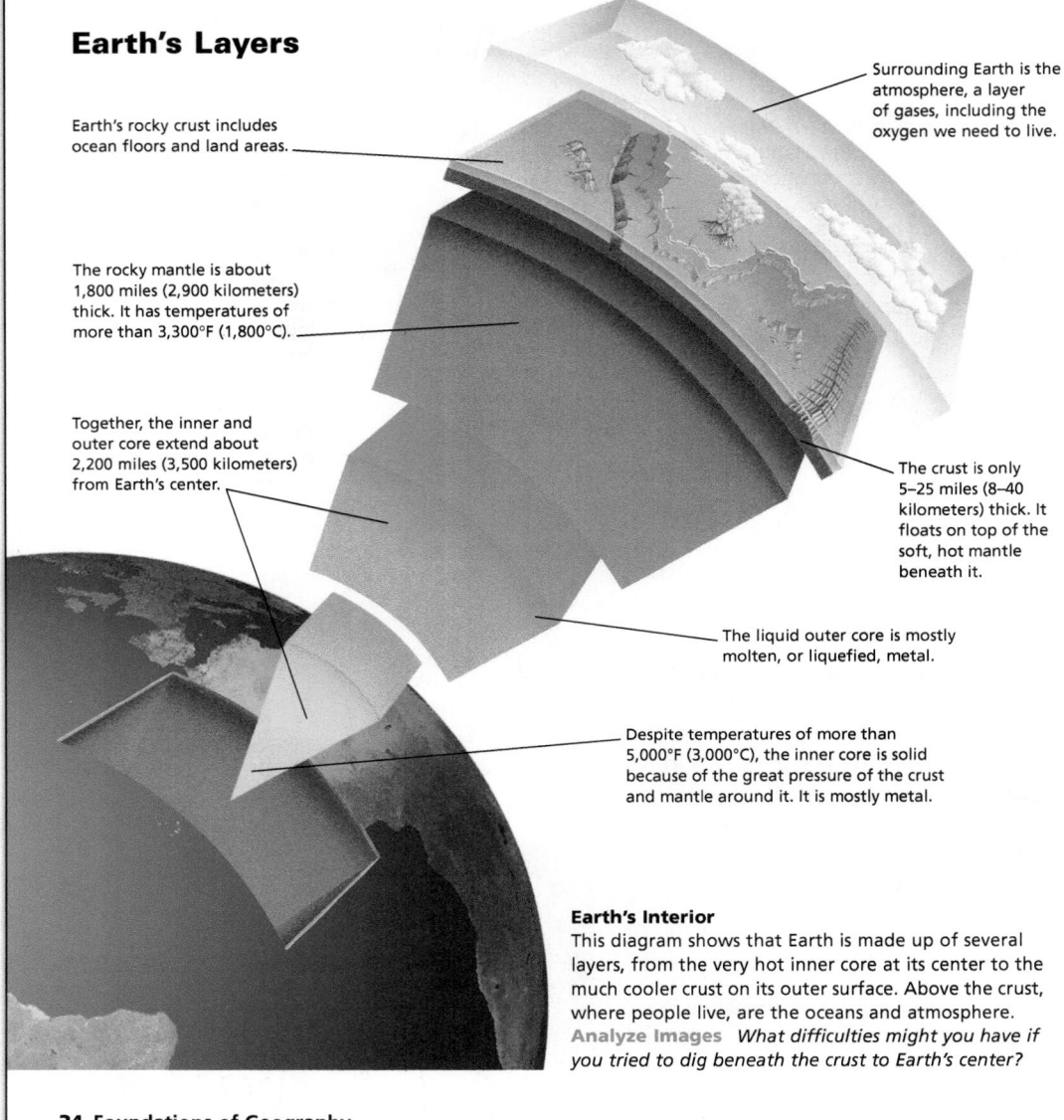

Earth's rocky crust includes ocean floors and land areas.

The rocky mantle is about 1,800 miles (2,900 kilometers) thick. It has temperatures of more than 3,300°F (1,800°C).

Together, the inner and outer core extend about 2,200 miles (3,500 kilometers) from Earth's center.

Surrounding Earth is the atmosphere, a layer of gases, including the oxygen we need to live.

The crust is only 5–25 miles (8–40 kilometers) thick. It floats on top of the soft, hot mantle beneath it.

The liquid outer core is mostly molten, or liquefied, metal.

Despite temperatures of more than 5,000°F (3,000°C), the inner core is solid because of the great pressure of the crust and mantle around it. It is mostly metal.

Earth's Interior
This diagram shows that Earth is made up of several layers, from the very hot inner core at its center to the much cooler crust on its outer surface. Above the crust, where people live, are the oceans and atmosphere.
Analyze Images *What difficulties might you have if you tried to dig beneath the crust to Earth's center?*

34 Foundations of Geography

Vocabulary Builder

Use the information below to teach students this section's high-use words.

High-Use Word	Definition and Sample Sentence
force, p. 33	*n.* strength, power, energy The pitcher threw the baseball with great **force**.
collide, p. 37	*v.* to crash against each other The icy road conditions caused the two cars to **collide**.
surge, p. 37	*v.* to swell and move with force She felt her energy **surge** after her third cup of coffee.
splinter, p. 37	*v.* to split into fragments or parts If the wind blows hard enough, the dead tree may **splinter** and fall.

Water and Air Less than 30 percent of Earth's surface is land. Water covers more than 70 percent of Earth's surface in lakes, rivers, seas, and oceans. The oceans hold about 97 percent of Earth's water. This water is salty. Very little of Earth's water is fresh water, or water without salt. Most fresh water is frozen in ice sheets near the North and South poles. People can use only a small part of Earth's fresh water. This fresh water comes from lakes, rivers, and ground water, which are fed by rain.

Above Earth's surface is the atmosphere, a layer of gases a few miles thick. It provides life-giving oxygen to people and animals, and carbon dioxide to plants.

Landforms Many different landforms, or shapes and types of land, cover Earth's land surfaces. Mountains are landforms that rise more than 2,000 feet (610 meters) above sea level or the sur-rounding flatlands. They are wide at the bottom and rise steeply to a narrow peak or ridge. A volcano is a kind of mountain. Hills are landforms with rounded tops, which rise above the sur-rounding land but are lower and less steep than mountains. A plateau is a large, mostly flat area that rises above the surround-ing land. At least one side of a plateau has a steep slope. Plains are large areas of flat or gently rolling land.

✓ **Reading Check** Which layer of Earth contains all of its landforms?

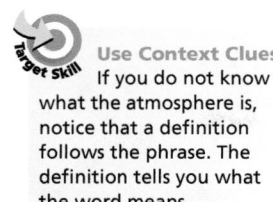

Use Context Clues
If you do not know what the atmosphere is, notice that a definition follows the phrase. The definition tells you what the word means.

Land and Water
Ice floes float near Alexander Island, off the coast of Antarctica. Salt water covers most of Earth's surface. Most fresh water is ice, frozen in polar regions such as Antarctica. **Analyze Images** *What landforms can you see in this photograph?*

Chapter 2 Section 2 **35**

Chapter 2 Section 2 **35**

Guided Instruction (continued)

- Ask students **What is the atmosphere and why is it important to our survival on Earth?** *(The atmosphere is a thick layer of gases, including the air we breathe.)*

- Ask students to draw a conclusion about how much of the world's water is fresh water if 97 percent of the world's water is in oceans. *(about 3 percent)*

- Ask students to name four types of land-forms that cover Earth's surface. *(mountains, hills, plateaus, and plains)* Then have students list landforms in your county or state that are one of these four types. *(An-swers will vary, but should show an under-standing of these landforms.)*

Independent Practice

Ask students to create the Taking Notes graphic organizer on a blank piece of paper. Then have them add more branches and circles in order to fill in the information about Earth's structure and landforms.

Monitor Progress

As students fill in the graphic organizer, circulate and make sure individuals are selecting the correct details. Provide assis-tance as needed.

Target Reading Skill   L2

Using Context Clues As a follow up, ask students to review the Target Reading Skill in the Student Edition. *(a thick layer of gases)*

Skills Mini Lesson

Analyzing Images

1. Teach the skill by pointing out to stu-dents that to analyze an image, they can ask these questions: Who or what is the image is showing? When or where does the scene take place? What general feel-ing do you get from the image? Who created the image and why?

2. Help students practice the skill by look-ing at the image of the volcano on page 37. Ask students What evidence besides the caption indicates that the molten rock is very hot? *(The color of the liquid pouring out from the top of the volcano shows it is hot.)*

3. Have students apply the skill by answer-ing this question: What might have been the photographer's reason for taking the photo on page 37? *(to show how erupting volcanoes change the surface of Earth)*

Answers

✓ **Reading Check** Earth's crust

Analyze Images mountains

Chapter 2 Section 2 **35**

Forces Inside Earth

Guided Instruction

- **Vocabulary Builder** Clarify the high-use words **collide, surge,** and **splinter** before reading.

- Read how the movement underneath Earth's surface affects our planet in Forces Inside Earth. As a class, study the diagram and captions under How Continents Move and partner students to answer the Geography Skills Practice question on page 37.

- Ask students **What forces inside Earth cause mountains to form?** (*The pressure exerted where two plates push against each other causes Earth's crust to bend and buckle, forming mountains.*)

- Ask students **Which different forces inside Earth cause volcanoes in Hawaii and earthquakes in California?** (*Volcanoes form when ocean crust plunges beneath continental crust and streams of magma to rise to the surface. Earthquakes occur when blocks of crust rub against each other along faults, releasing huge amounts of energy.*)

Forces Inside Earth

Heat deep inside Earth is constantly reshaping the planet's surface. The intense heat causes rock to rise toward the surface. Where streams of this soft, nearly molten rock called **magma** reach Earth's crust, they push up the crust to form volcanoes. Volcanoes spew molten rock, or lava, from inside Earth. Streams of magma may also push the crust apart along seams. Huge blocks of Earth's crust called **plates** are separated by these seams. Plates may include continents or parts of continents. Each plate also includes part of the ocean floor. Along seams, mainly beneath oceans, streams of magma rise from inside Earth. As the magma cools, it forms new crust and pushes the old crust away from the seams.

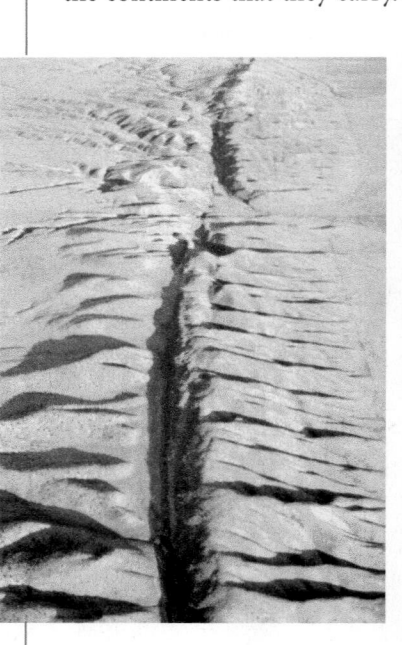

How Continents Move

Rising magma forms new crust along seams between Earth's plates. Beneath the surface, some scientists believe, magma moves like a conveyor belt. The belt drags the growing plates and the continents that they carry.

Where two plates push against each other, the pressure makes the crust bend and buckle to form steep mountains.

Plates move only an inch or two (a few centimeters) a year.

Crust

Mantle

Earthquakes occur when blocks of crust slide sideways against each other.

Some scientists think that sheets of mantle act like conveyor belts that move the plates of crust above them.

Sheets of magma rise to the surface from Earth's interior along a seam between plates of crust.

◄ **Two plates rub together along the San Andreas Fault in California.**

36 Foundations of Geography

Differentiated Instruction

For English Language Learners   L1
Students may have difficulty pronouncing some of the longer words in this section, such as *reshaping, continental, boundaries, earthquakes,* and *geographers*. Encourage students to break down these words into smaller parts to help them sound out the pronunciations.

For Gifted and Talented   L3
The forces of nature can affect people both directly and indirectly. Ask students to read the selection *A Huge Black Umbrella* to experience how an event altered the lives of several individuals.

All in One **Foundations of Geography Teaching Resources,** *A Huge Black Umbrella,* pp. 138–140

Volcanoes and Earthquakes Where a plate of ocean crust collides with a plate of continental crust, the ocean crust plunges underneath the continental plate and melts. Molten rock surges upward, exploding onto the surface through a volcano. The Ring of Fire surrounds the plates that make up the Pacific Ocean. Streams of magma also form volcanoes at places other than plate boundaries. Such volcanoes have shaped the Hawaiian Islands, which are far from a plate boundary.

When two plates push together, the crust cracks and splinters from the pressure. The cracks in Earth's crust are called faults. When blocks of crust rub against each other along faults, they release huge amounts of energy in the form of earthquakes.

▲ **Molten rock pours from a volcano in Hawaii.**

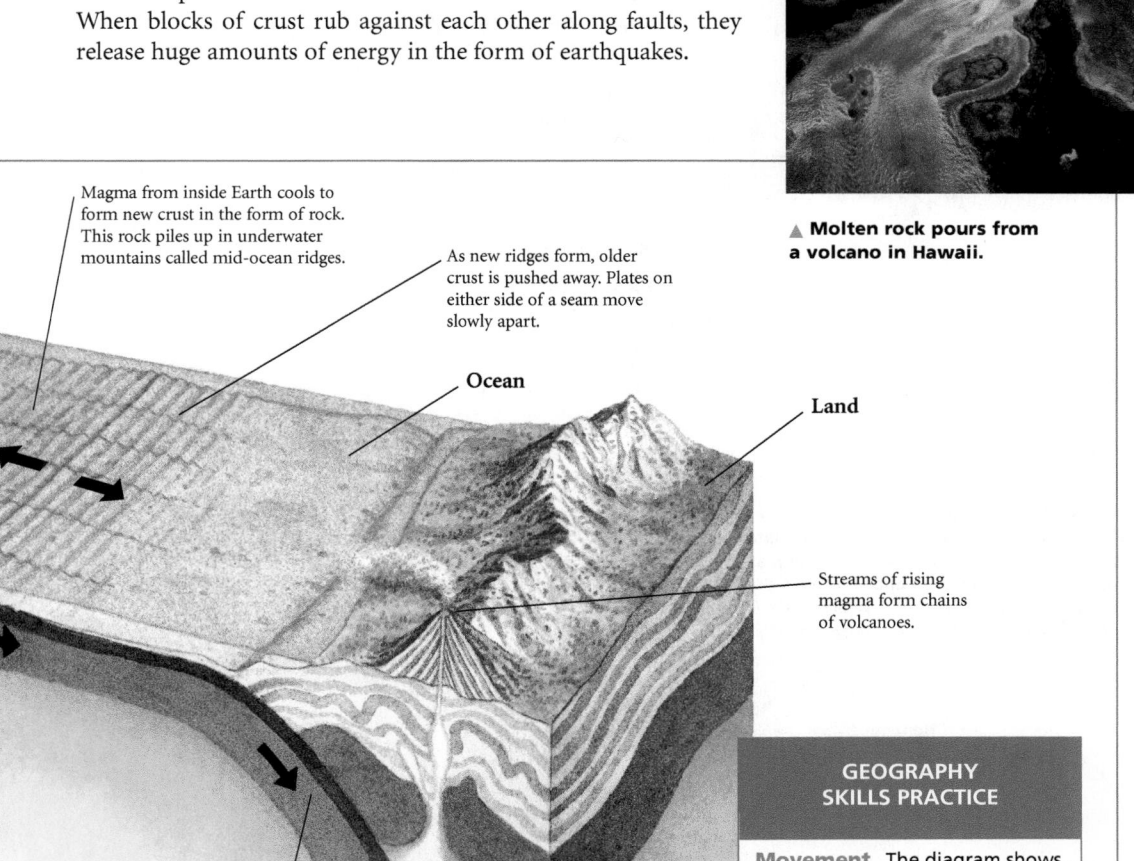

Magma from inside Earth cools to form new crust in the form of rock. This rock piles up in underwater mountains called mid-ocean ridges.

As new ridges form, older crust is pushed away. Plates on either side of a seam move slowly apart.

Ocean

Land

Streams of rising magma form chains of volcanoes.

When ocean crust plunges beneath land, it melts into streams of magma that rise to the surface.

GEOGRAPHY SKILLS PRACTICE

Movement The diagram shows how moving plates behave. **Predict** If a plate of ocean crust plunged underneath a continental plate, what landforms would you expect to develop?

Chapter 2 Section 2 **37**

Guided Instruction (continued)

■ Have students review the maps on page 38 and ask **How do some scientists believe that continents move?** *(Magma beneath Earth's crust may act like a slow-moving conveyor belt, dragging the plates that carry the continents a few centimeters a year.)* Then, using The World: Physical map in the Atlas on pp. 140–141, have students discuss ways of how the continents could have once been one land mass.

■ Ask students **How can magma cause the plates that carry the continents to move apart?** *(Sheets of magma rise to the surface along a seam between the plates to form ridges in the crust. As new ridges form, older crust is pushed away, forcing the plates on either side of a seam to move slowly apart.)*

Independent Practice

Have students continue to fill in the graphic organizer web by including details from the information they have just learned. Remind them to add more branches and circles if necessary.

Monitor Progress

Survey the class and determine if individuals are absorbing the content. Provide assistance as needed.

Background: Links Across Time

A New Island For thousands of years, magma from underwater volcanoes built up until it rose above sea level to create the Hawaiian Islands. Today, a new island, named Loihi (low EE hee), is forming just southeast of the big island of Hawaii.

Already more than two miles (about 3.7 kilometers) high, it has 3,180 feet (969 meters) to go before it breaks the ocean's surface. Loihi erupts often, causing earthquakes and tidal waves.

Answer

Geography Skills Practice Predict volcanoes and islands

Forces on Earth's Surface

Guided Instruction

- Read Forces on Earth's Surface. Circulate to make sure individuals can answer the Reading Check question.

- Ask students **What is weathering?** *(a process that breaks down rocks into tiny pieces)* **How does it differ from erosion?** *(Weathering is the breaking down of rocks into tiny pieces while erosion is the removal of these pieces.)*

- Ask students to predict what the area where they live might look like 10,000 years from now. *(Answers will vary but students should note that forces such as weathering and erosion will change a region over time.)*

Independent Practice

Have students complete their graphic organizers.

Monitor Progress

- Show *Section Reading Support Transparency FG 46* and ask students to check their graphic organizers individually. Go over key concepts and clarify key vocabulary as needed.

  📖 **Foundations of Geography Transparencies,** *Section Reading Support Transparency FG 46*

- Tell students to fill in the last column of their *Reading Readiness Guides*. Probe for what they learned that confirms or invalidates each statement.

  All In One **Foundations of Geography Teaching Resources,** *Reading Readiness Guide,* p. 110

Answers

✓ **Reading Check** Parts of Earth's crust called plates shift in response to movements of magma beneath the crust.

Analyze According to the first map, all of the present-day continents were once joined together. **Identify** the Cocos Plate

---

A World of Moving Plates For hundreds of years, geographers wondered how Earth's landmasses took their present shapes and positions. When they looked at the globe, they thought they saw matching shapes in continents that are very far apart. Now that they know how forces inside Earth move continents, they know that those continents were once close together.

✓ **Reading Check** How do continents move apart?

Plate Movements

Plates 250 million years ago

Plates Shifting Through Time
Most geographers believe that long ago Earth had only one huge continent. They call it Pangaea (pan JEE uh). About 200 million years ago, they conclude, plate movement began to split Pangaea apart. They think that these pieces came to form the continents that we know today. **Analyze** *According to these maps, which present-day continents were once joined together?*

Plates 150 million years ago

Plates 75 million years ago

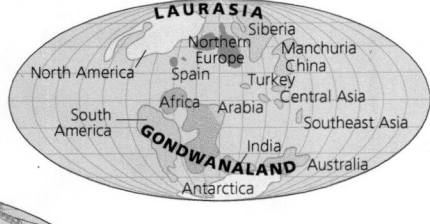

Present-Day Plates
The map below shows Earth's modern plates and plate edges. It also shows how the plates are moving. Earthquakes and volcanoes cluster along plate edges. **Identify** *Which plate is colliding with the North American Plate?*

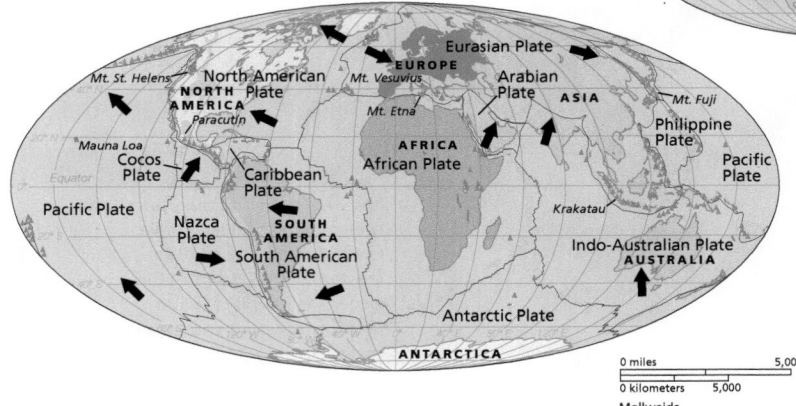

KEY
- Plate boundary
- ➡ Plate movement
- Earthquake zone
- ▲ Volcano

0 miles 5,000
0 kilometers 5,000
Mollweide

38 Foundations of Geography

Background: Biography

One Big Landmass Alfred Lothar Wegener (1880–1930) studied astronomy and taught meteorology. Even though his education focused on the sky, Wegener was interested in the shapes of continental landmasses. In 1912, Wegener proposed that a single large landmass broke apart to form the continents we see today. As evidence, he pointed to closely related fossil organisms and similar rock strata that occur on the continents. Geologists rejected his ideas. More than forty years later, precise dating of rocks on the opposite sides of the Atlantic Ocean indicated that Wegener's ideas were not only plausible, but likely.

Forces on Earth's Surface

Forces inside Earth move plates apart, produce volcanoes, and slowly build up Earth's crust. Other forces slowly wear it down and reshape it. The forces that wear Earth down are not as dramatic as volcanoes, but over time they are just as effective.

Weathering is a process that breaks rocks down into tiny pieces. Water, ice, and living things like lichens on rocks all cause weathering. Weathering helps create soil, too. Tiny pieces of rock combine with decayed animal and plant material to form soil.

Once this breaking down has taken place, landforms are reshaped by **erosion,** or the removal of small pieces of rock by water, ice, or wind. Hundreds of millions of years ago, the Appalachian Mountains in the eastern United States were as high as the Rocky Mountains of the western United States now are. Rain, snow, and wind slowly wore them down into much lower peaks.

When water, ice, and wind remove material, they deposit it downstream or downwind to create new landforms. Plains are often made of material carried from upstream by rivers.

Weathering and erosion formed this natural sandstone bridge in Jordan.

✓ **Reading Check** What landforms are products of weathering and erosion?

Section 2 Assessment

Key Terms
Review the key terms at the beginning of this section. Use each term in a sentence that explains its meaning.

⟳ **Target Reading Skill**
Find the word *landforms* in the last paragraph of page 35. Use the context to find its meaning. What does it mean? What clues did you use to find its meaning?

Comprehension and Critical Thinking

1. (a) List What are Earth's three main layers?

(b) Synthesize Information How do those layers interact?
2. (a) Recall What forces inside Earth shape Earth's surface?
(b) Explain How do these forces explain the movement of the continents?
(c) Predict How might a continent split in two?
3. (a) Identify What forces cause weathering and erosion?
(b) Compare and Contrast How is erosion different from weathering?

Writing Activity
Think about the region where you live. Does it have steep mountains or volcanoes, rounded hills, or plains? Write a paragraph describing some of the natural forces that are slowly reshaping your region.

For: An activity on Pangaea
Visit: PHSchool.com
Web Code: led-3202

Chapter 2 Section 2 **39**

Section 2 Assessment

Key Terms
Students' sentences should reflect knowledge of each Key Term.

⟳ **Target Reading Skill**
Landforms are shapes and types of land. Clue: The meaning of landforms was restated after the word.

Comprehension and Critical Thinking
1. (a) the crust, the mantle, and the core **(b)** The crust floats on top of the mantle and the heat of the mantle and the core help shape Earth's crust.

2. (a) magma and moving plates **(b)** Some scientists think that sheets of mantle form conveyor belts that move the plates of crust above them, causing the continents to move. **(c)** A continent that sits on two or more of Earth's plates can split apart when those plates move in opposite directions.

3. (a) water, ice, living things, and wind **(b)** Weathering is a process that breaks down rocks into small pieces. Erosion is the removal of small pieces of rock by water, ice, or wind.

Assess and Reteach

Assess Progress ⬛L2
Have Students complete the Section Assessment. Administer the *Section Quiz*.

All in One **Foundations of Geography Teaching Resources,** *Section Quiz,* p. 112

Reteach ⬛L1
If students need more instruction, have them read this section in the Reading and Vocabulary Study Guide.

📖 Chapter 2, Section 2, **Western Hemisphere Reading and Vocabulary Study Guide,** pp. 12–14

Extend ⬛L3
Have students learn more about varying landforms and elevations from Death Valley to Mt. Whitney by completing the *Small Group Activity: Simulation: Making a Poster for the Whitney Classic.*

All in One **Foundations of Geography Teaching Resources,** *Small Group Activity: Simulation: Making a Poster for the Whitney Classic,* p. 128–131

Answer

✓ **Reading Check** hills, some mountains, deserts, and plains

Writing Activity
Use the *Rubric for Assessing a Writing Assignment* to evaluate students' paragraphs.

All in One **Foundations of Geography Teaching Resources,** *Rubric for Assessing a Writing Assignment,* p. 145

Go Online PHSchool.com Typing in the Web code when prompted will bring students directly to detailed instructions for this activity.

Objectives

Social Studies

1. Learn about weather and climate.
2. Explore latitude, landforms, and precipitation.
3. Discover how oceans affect climate.

Reading/Language Arts

Use context clues that give a comparison to determine the meaning of a word or phrase.

Prepare to Read

Build Background Knowledge   **L2**

Tell students that in this section they will explore climate and weather. Ask students to think about what they know about weather, and then look at the two photographs and related captions on pp. 40 and 41. Then ask what they think the difference between weather and climate is. Conduct an Idea Wave (TE, p. T35) to share ideas as a class.

Set a Purpose for Reading   **L2**

■ Preview the Objectives.

■ Form students into pairs or groups of four. Distribute the *Reading Readiness Guide.* Ask students to fill in the first two columns of the chart. Use the Numbered Heads participation strategy (TE, p. T36) to call on students to share one piece of information they already know and one piece of information they want to know.

All in One Foundations of Geography Teaching Resources, *Reading Readiness Guide,* p. 114

Vocabulary Builder
Preview Key Terms

Pronounce each Key Term, then ask the students to say the word with you. Provide a simple explanation such as, "The tropical cyclone arrived on shore with such force that roads were flooded, trees and power lines were torn down, and many homes were damaged."

Answer

✓ **Reading Check** Weather is the condition of the air and sky from day to day. Climate is the average weather of a place over many years.

Prepare to Read

Objectives

In this section you will
1. Learn about weather and climate.
2. Explore latitude, landforms, and precipitation.
3. Discover how oceans affect climate.

Taking Notes

As you read this section, look for topics related to climate and weather, such as landforms, precipitation, oceans, and storms. Copy the outline below and add headings as needed to show the relationships among these topics.

```
I.  Weather
II. Climate
    A. Latitudes
    B.
        1.
        2.
III. Storms
```

Target Reading Skill

Use Context Clues You can sometimes learn the meaning of a word or phrase when the context gives a comparison. In this example, the word *cyclone* is compared to the phrase in italics.

> A cyclone is like *a huge spiral escalator moving air upward.*

Key Terms

- **weather** (WETH ur) *n.* the condition of the air and sky from day to day
- **precipitation** (pree sip uh TAY shun) *n.* water that falls to the ground as rain, sleet, hail, or snow
- **temperature** (TEM pur uh chur) *n.* how hot or cold the air is
- **climate** (KLY mut) *n.* the average weather over many years
- **tropical cyclone** (TRAHP ih kul SY klohn) *n.* an intense wind and rain storm that forms over oceans in the tropics.

This Inuit woman and child are dressed for their cold climate.

Weather or Climate?

Every morning, most people check the weather before they get dressed. But in some parts of India, people have very serious reasons for watching the **weather,** or the condition of the air and sky from day to day. In parts of India, it rains only during one time of year. No one living there wants the rainy days to end too soon. That rain must fill the wells with enough fresh water to last for the entire year.

In India, people are concerned about **precipitation,** or water that falls to the ground as rain, sleet, hail, or snow. When you get dressed in the morning, you may want to know the **temperature,** or how hot or cold the air is. Weather is mainly measured by temperature and precipitation.

The **climate** of a place is the average weather over many years. Climate is not the same as weather. Weather is what people see from day to day. Climate is what usually happens from year to year.

✓ **Reading Check** What is the difference between weather and climate?

 Target Reading Skill   **L2**

Use Context Clues Point out the Target Reading Skill. Tell students that one way to find the meaning of a word or phrase is to look for comparisons between the unfamiliar word and a familiar word or phrase within the context.

Model using comparison context clues by finding the meaning of *tsunami.* Write the following sentence on the board: "The tsunami approached the southern coast of Japan like an enormous tower of water and crashed upon the shore flooding everything it its path." (enormous tower of water *and* crashed upon the shore *implies a large wave*) Point out to students that words such as *like* and *as* signal that a comparison is being made.

Give students *Use Context Clues: Compare and Contrast.* Have them complete the activity in groups.

All in One Foundations of Geography Teaching Resources, *Use Context Clues: Compare and Contrast,* p. 123

Why Climates Vary

Earth has many climates. Some climates are so hot that people rarely need to wear a sweater. In some cold climates, snow stays on the ground most of the year. And there are places on Earth where more than 30 feet (9 meters) of rain falls in a single year.

Climate depends on location. Places in the low latitudes, or tropics, have hot climates, because they get direct sunlight. Places in the high latitudes, or polar regions, have cold climates, because their sunlight is indirect.

Air and water spread heat around the globe as they move. Without wind and water, places in the tropics would overheat. Oceans gain and lose heat slowly, so they keep temperatures mild near coasts. Mountains can also affect climates.

✓ Reading Check **How does latitude affect temperature?**

Cherrapunji, India, averages 37 feet (11 meters) of rain a year. The rain then flows into lakes, streams, and waterfalls.

The Water Cycle

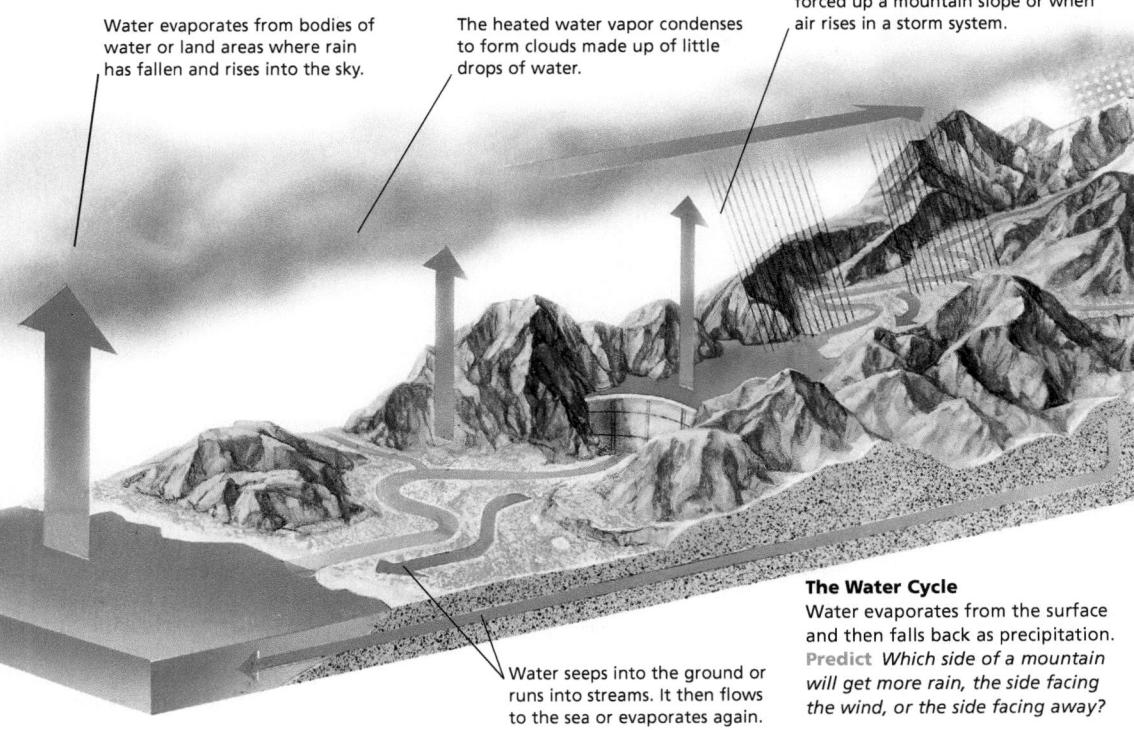

Water evaporates from bodies of water or land areas where rain has fallen and rises into the sky.

The heated water vapor condenses to form clouds made up of little drops of water.

As moist air rises, it cools and drops its moisture. This can happen when air is forced up a mountain slope or when air rises in a storm system.

Water seeps into the ground or runs into streams. It then flows to the sea or evaporates again.

The Water Cycle
Water evaporates from the surface and then falls back as precipitation.
Predict *Which side of a mountain will get more rain, the side facing the wind, or the side facing away?*

Chapter 2 Section 3 **41**

Oceans and Climates L2

Guided Instruction

- **Vocabulary Builder** Clarify the high-use word **distribute** before reading.

- Review the diagram and map on pages 42 and 43 with students. Read how global wind patterns and bodies of water affect the regions of the world in Oceans and Climates.

- Ask students **What do wind and air currents move?** (*heat and moisture between different parts of Earth*) **How are they affected by latitude?** (*The currents flow in regular circular patterns depending on the latitude through which they are moving.*)

- Ask students **What happens when air rises?** (*The moisture it contains condenses and falls as rain or snow.*) **What happens when air sinks?** (*The air becomes drier creating dry climates such as those at the poles or in the desert.*)

A strong onshore wind blows in Miami Beach, Florida.

Air Circulation and Wind

Winds and air currents move heat and moisture between different parts of Earth. These currents follow regular patterns related to latitude. The diagram below shows these circular patterns of air movement, which form a series of belts, or cells, that circle Earth.

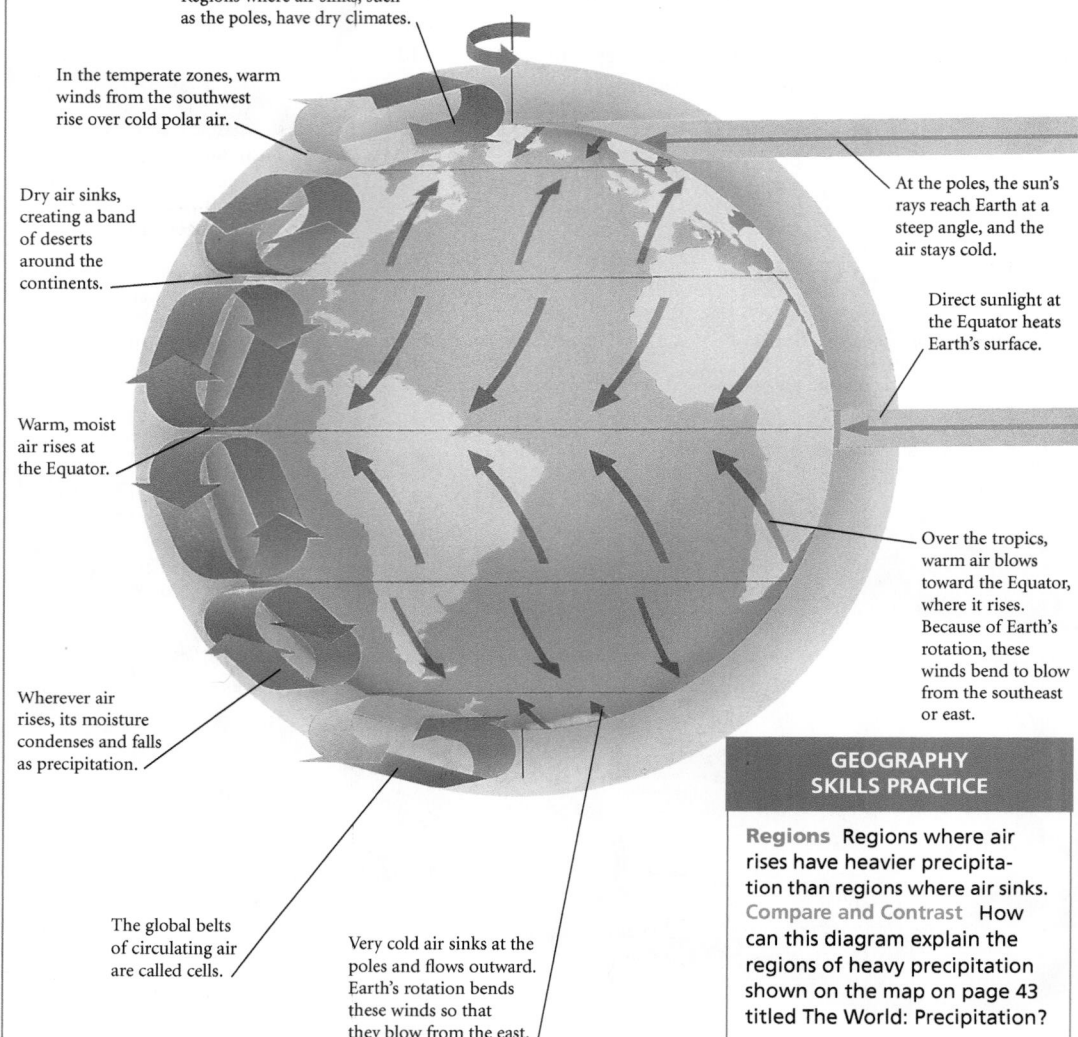

Regions where air sinks, such as the poles, have dry climates.

In the temperate zones, warm winds from the southwest rise over cold polar air.

Dry air sinks, creating a band of deserts around the continents.

Warm, moist air rises at the Equator.

Wherever air rises, its moisture condenses and falls as precipitation.

The global belts of circulating air are called cells.

Very cold air sinks at the poles and flows outward. Earth's rotation bends these winds so that they blow from the east.

At the poles, the sun's rays reach Earth at a steep angle, and the air stays cold.

Direct sunlight at the Equator heats Earth's surface.

Over the tropics, warm air blows toward the Equator, where it rises. Because of Earth's rotation, these winds bend to blow from the southeast or east.

GEOGRAPHY SKILLS PRACTICE

Regions Regions where air rises have heavier precipitation than regions where air sinks. **Compare and Contrast** How can this diagram explain the regions of heavy precipitation shown on the map on page 43 titled The World: Precipitation?

42 Foundations of Geography

Differentiated Instruction

For Special Needs Students L1

Have students read the section as they listen to the recorded version on the Student Edition on Audio CD. Check for comprehension by pausing the CD and asking students to share their answers to the Reading Check.

⊙ Chapter 2, Section 3, **Student Edition on Audio CD**

Answer

Geography Skills Practice Compare and Contrast The regions of heavy precipitation on the map have belts of warm, moist air that rises, causing heavy precipitation.

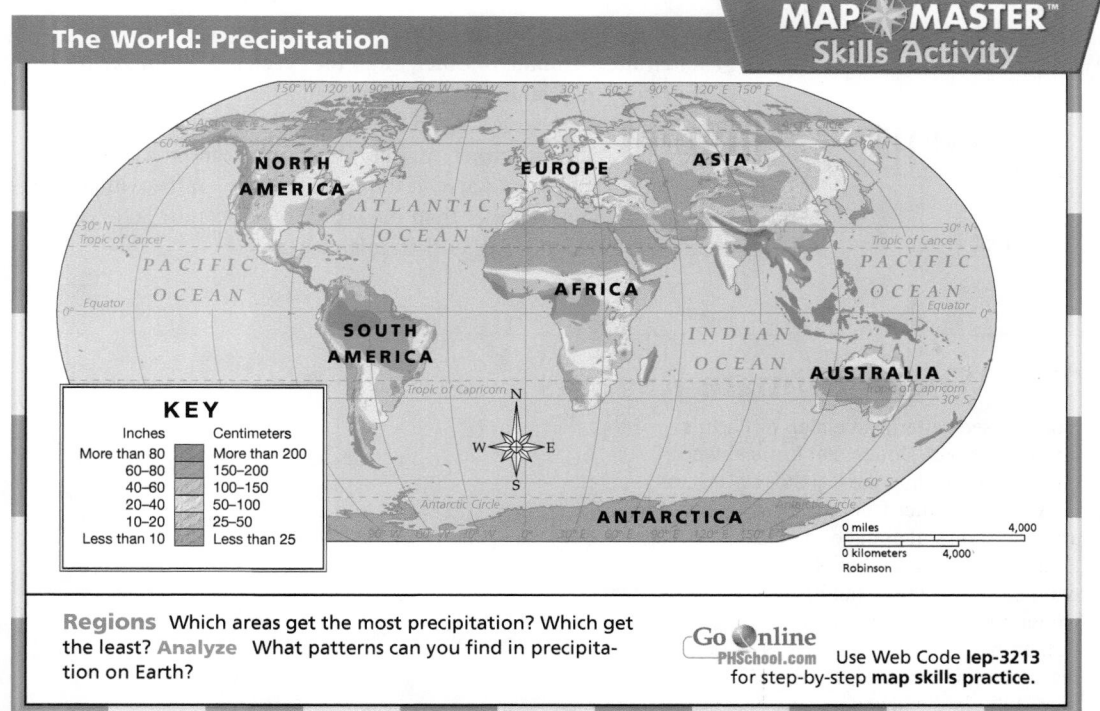

MAP MASTER™
Skills Activity

KEY

Inches	Centimeters
More than 80	More than 200
60–80	150–200
40–60	100–150
20–40	50–100
10–20	25–50
Less than 10	Less than 25

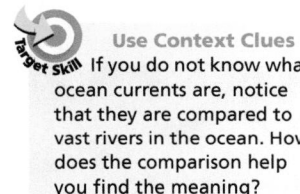

0 miles 4,000
0 kilometers 4,000
Robinson

Regions Which areas get the most precipitation? Which get the least? **Analyze** What patterns can you find in precipitation on Earth?

Go Online
PHSchool.com Use Web Code **lep-3213** for step-by-step **map skills practice**.

Oceans and Climates

The oceans help distribute Earth's heat and shape climates. Global wind patterns help create ocean currents, which are like vast rivers in the oceans. Ocean currents move across great distances. Generally, warm water flows away from the Equator, while cold water moves toward the Equator.

Oceans and Currents In the Atlantic Ocean, the Gulf Stream, a warm current, travels northeast from the tropics. The Gulf Stream and the North Atlantic Current carry warm water all the way to western Europe. That warm water gives western Europe a milder climate than other regions at the same latitude.

The cold Peru Current moves north from Antarctica along the coast of South America. The city of Antofagasta (ahn toh fah GAHS tah) lies along that coast, in Chile. Even though Antofagasta is closer than Miami, Florida, is to the Equator, the average temperature in Antofagasta during the hottest month of summer is just 68°F (20°C).

Target Skill **Use Context Clues** If you do not know what ocean currents are, notice that they are compared to vast rivers in the ocean. How does the comparison help you find the meaning?

Chapter 2 Section 3 **43**

Guided Instruction (continued)

■ Ask students **Why does western Europe have a milder climate than other regions at the same latitude?** *(The Gulf Stream and the North Atlantic Current carry warm water to western Europe.)*

■ Ask students to draw a conclusion about why the temperature in Antofagasta, Chile, is not as warm as Florida, even though it is closer to the Equator. *(The cold-water current from the South Pole called the Peru Current moves north past Chile, giving Antofagasta a cooler climate than Florida.)*

Target Reading Skill
L2

Use Context Clues As a follow up, ask students to answer the Target Reading Skill question in the Student Edition. *(Possible answer: Since river is a familiar concept, it can help one understand a more unfamiliar concept like ocean current.)*

Answers

MAP MASTER Skills Activity **Regions** central region of northern South America; portions of Africa's west coast; parts of Southeast Asia; island countries located in the Pacific Ocean **Analyze** Generally, areas around the Equator get the most precipitation. As you move north or south of the Equator, the amount of precipitation decreases.

Go Online
PHSchool.com Students may practice their map skills using the interactive online version of this map.

Skills for Life ✓ Skills Mini Lesson

Using Cartographer's Tools

1. Teach the skill by pointing out that a map key explains symbols and special colors used on a map. Explain that it helps students interpret the information being shown on the map.

2. Help students practice the skill by looking at the map on this page. Read the key with students and have them identify what each color represents on the map.

3. Have students apply the skill by choosing a continent and describing its pattern of precipitation.

Guided Instruction (continued)

- Have students discuss the cooling and warming affects of the ocean and other bodies of water.

- Have students compare and contrast the climates of San Francisco and St. Louis. *(Because San Francisco borders the Pacific Ocean, it is warmer than St. Louis in the winter and cooler than St. Louis in the summer.)* Ask students if there are any bodies of water nearby that may affect the region in which they live.

- As a class, study The World: Climate Regions on these pages. Answer the Map-Master Skills Activity questions as a class. Then, ask the class to compare the climate regions of North America and Europe. *(North America and Europe have similar types of climate regions, but the southern portion of North America has tropical regions while Europe does not.)*

The Ocean's Cooling and Warming Effects Bodies of water affect climate in other ways, too. Water takes longer to heat or cool than land. As the air and land heat up in summer, the water remains cooler. Wind blowing over the water cools the nearby land. So in summer, a region near an ocean or lake will be cooler than an inland area at the same latitude. In the winter, the water remains warmer than the land. So places near lakes or oceans are warmer in winter than inland areas.

The World: Climate Regions

You can see patterns in a map of Earth's climate regions. Notice that tropical wet climate regions hug the Equator on several continents. Farther from the Equator are arid and semiarid climate regions. Elsewhere, regions where the wind blows off the ocean have wetter climates than regions farther inland. Each climate region on this map is described more fully in the next section.

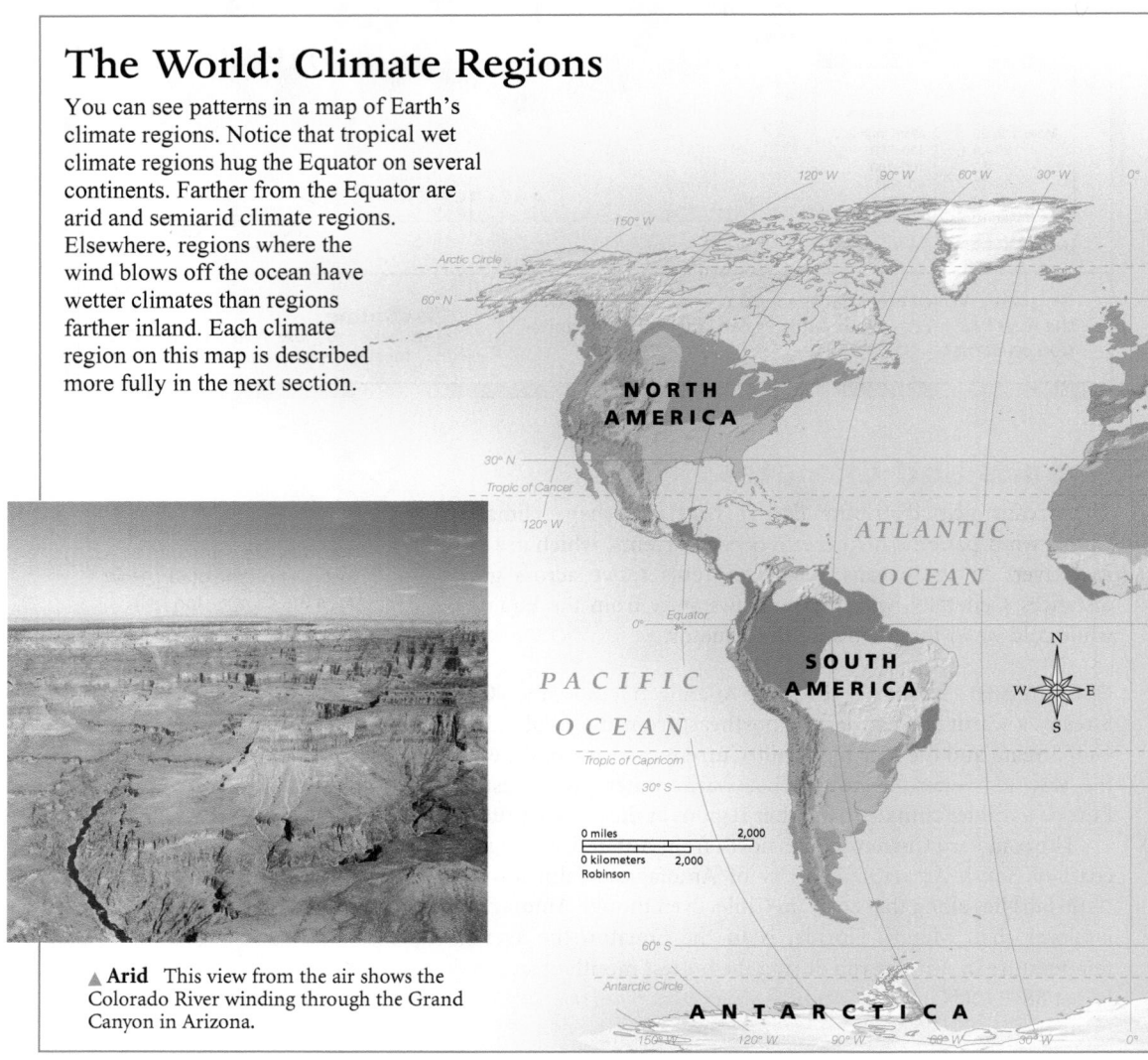

 **Arid** This view from the air shows the Colorado River winding through the Grand Canyon in Arizona.

Skills Mini Lesson

Comparing and Contrasting

1. Teach the skill by pointing out to students that comparison involves similarities, and contrast involves differences. It is important to first identify the topic and purpose in their comparison and contrast. Similarities and differences will then be easier to determine.

2. Help students practice the skill by looking at The World: Climate Regions map on these pages and comparing and contrasting North and South America.

3. Have students apply the skill by comparing and contrasting the climate regions of Australia and Greenland.

Consider San Francisco, California, and St. Louis, Missouri. Both cities are near 38° north latitude. However, San Francisco borders the Pacific Ocean. In winter, the ocean is warmer than the air. The ocean keeps San Francisco much warmer than St. Louis in winter. In summer, the ocean is cooler than the air, so it keeps San Francisco cool.

✓ **Reading Check** During the summer, are places near the ocean warmer or cooler than places inland?

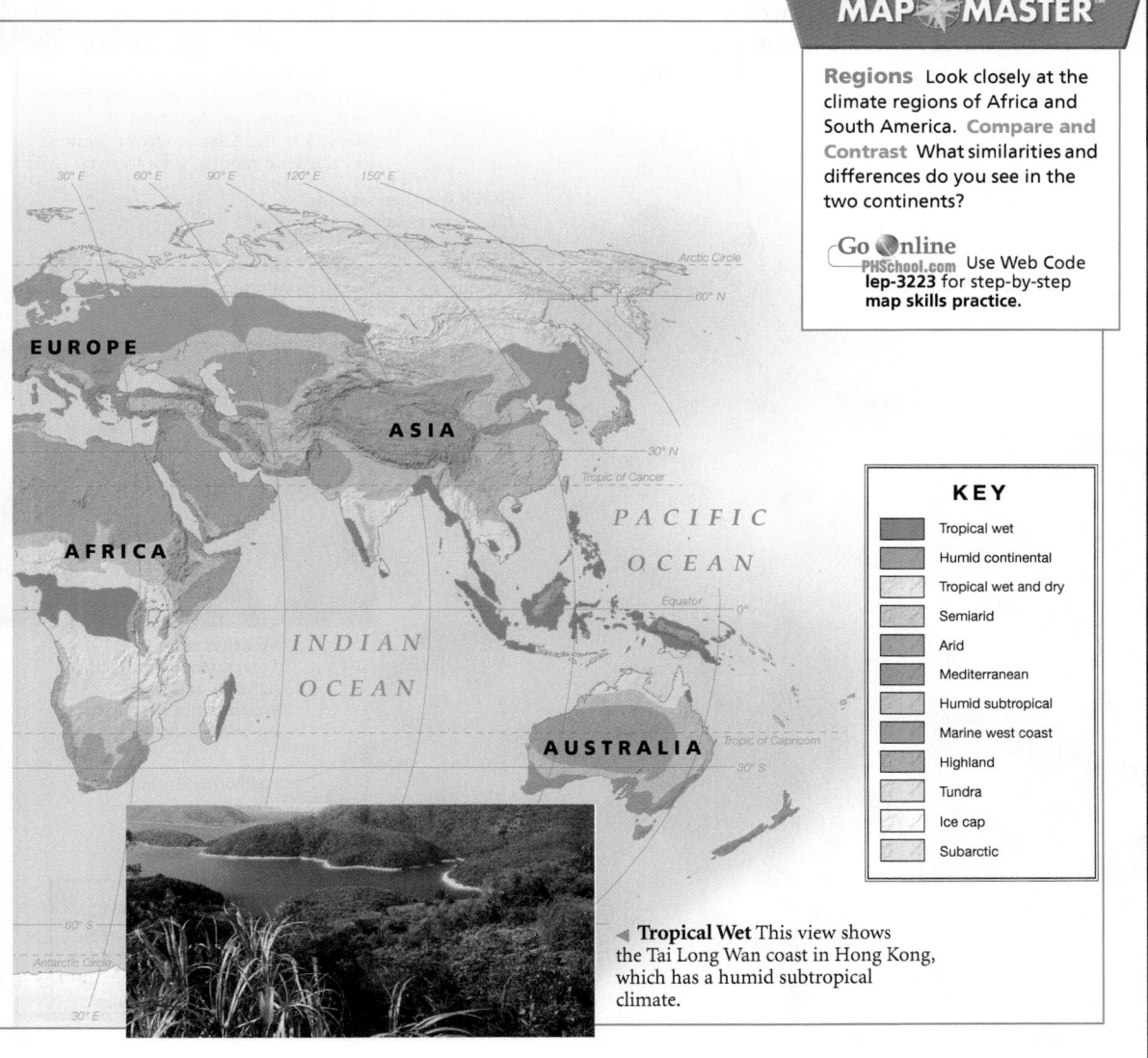

MAP MASTER™

Regions Look closely at the climate regions of Africa and South America. **Compare and Contrast** What similarities and differences do you see in the two continents?

Go Online
PHSchool.com Use Web Code **lep-3223** for step-by-step **map skills practice.**

KEY

- Tropical wet
- Humid continental
- Tropical wet and dry
- Semiarid
- Arid
- Mediterranean
- Humid subtropical
- Marine west coast
- Highland
- Tundra
- Ice cap
- Subarctic

◀ **Tropical Wet** This view shows the Tai Long Wan coast in Hong Kong, which has a humid subtropical climate.

Chapter 2 Section 3 **45**

Guided Instruction (continued)
■ Partner students to analyze the images on pages 44 and 45. Coach students to think about what each image shows and what general feeling each image inspires. Then ask them **If there were no captions, what climate regions would they assign each image based on its content?** (*The image on page 44 shows a dry, arid landscape; the image on page 45 shows a lush, tropical area with heavy vegetation.*)

Independent Practice
Have students continue to fill in their graphic organizer with details from the information they have just learned.

Monitor Progress
As students fill in the graphic organizer, circulate and make sure individuals are selecting the correct details. Provide assistance as needed.

Answers

✓ Reading Check cooler

MAP MASTER™ Skills Activity **Compare and Contrast**
The two continents share many of the same types of climate regions, but Africa has a much larger arid region.

Go Online PHSchool.com Students may practice their map skills using the interactive online version of this map.

Weather Forecasting `L2`

Guided Instruction
Ask students to read the feature and review the images and captions. Then have students discuss why it might be important to be forewarned about weather conditions. As a class, answer the Analyzing Images question.

Independent Practice
Have students create an outline of the information on this page.

Raging Storms `L2`

Guided Instruction
■ Read Raging Storms as a class. Make sure that individuals are able to answer the Reading Check question.

■ Have students list the storms mentioned in the reading. (*tropical cyclones, hurricanes, tornadoes, blizzards, severe rainstorms, and thunderstorms*) Ask **What elements are common to these storms?** (*high winds and heavy precipitation*)

Independent Practice
Tell students to complete their graphic organizers.

Monitor Progress
■ Show *Section Reading Support Transparency FG 47.* Go over key concepts and clarify key vocabulary as needed.

📖 **Foundations of Geography Transparencies,** *Section Reading Support Transparency FG 47*

■ Tell students to fill in the last column of their *Reading Readiness Guides.* Ask them to evaluate if what they learned was what they had expected to learn.

All in One Foundations of Geography Teaching Resources, *Reading Readiness Guide,* p. 114

Answer
ANALYZING IMAGES Satellites gather information about locations all over the world. Forecasters might use the weather patterns in other parts of the world to predict what the weather might be like in their area.

 EYEWITNESS TECHNOLOGY

Weather Forecasting

Television weather forecasters rely on scientists and equipment from all over the world. Weather stations record local conditions. Satellites orbit overhead to photograph large weather systems. Weather balloons and radar provide still more data. The results, displayed on weather maps or presented in forecasts, can warn citizens of an approaching hurricane or simply remind people to carry an umbrella.

Weather station
This ranger is measuring rainfall at a weather station on the island of Madeira in the Atlantic Ocean. Stations like this send reports to forecasters.

Weather satellites
Scientists use satellites in space to record everything from wind patterns to the height of waves.

Solar cell panels power the spacecraft.

GOES weather satellite
U.S. weather satellites are called GOES (Geostationary Operational Environmental Satellites). They circle Earth in time with Earth's rotation, so they always stay above the same spot.

A hurricane

Weather map
Forecasters track weather patterns and storm systems, and display data on weather maps.

A gathering storm

ANALYZING IMAGES
How might a satellite help forecasters predict the weather?

46 Foundations of Geography

Differentiated Instruction

For English Language Learners `L1`
Partner students with English speakers to reread the information on this page. Have them summarize, in their own words, the information they have read. Make sure they clarify words they find difficult to pronounce or understand.

For Advanced Readers `L3`
Have students write a letter to a local television weather forecaster asking three questions that would help them learn more about predicting weather. Give them *Writing a Letter* to help them get started.

All in One Foundations of Geography Teaching Resources, *Writing a Letter,* p. 143

Raging Storms

Wind and water can make climates milder, but they also can create large and dangerous storms. **Tropical cyclones** are intense wind and rain storms that form over oceans in the tropics. Tropical cyclones that form over the Atlantic Ocean are called hurricanes. The winds near the center of a hurricane can reach speeds of more than 100 miles (160 kilometers) per hour. Hurricanes produce huge swells of water called storm surges, which flood over shorelines and can destroy buildings.

Tornadoes are like funnels of wind that can reach 200 miles (320 kilometers) per hour. The winds and the low air pressure they create in their centers can wreck almost anything in their path. They can be just as dangerous as hurricanes, but they affect much smaller areas.

Other storms are less dangerous. In winter, blizzards dump huge amounts of snow on parts of North America. And severe rainstorms and thunderstorms strike the continent most often in spring and summer.

Hurricane Katrina
In 2005 Hurricane Katrina caused massive destruction along the southeastern coast of the United States.
Synthesizing Information
Is a hurricane more likely on a tropical coast or in a polar region far from the ocean?

✓ **Reading Check** Which storms cover larger areas, hurrricanes or tornadoes?

Section 3 Assessment

Key Terms
Review the key terms at the beginning of this section. Use each term in a sentence that explains its meaning.

Target Reading Skill
Find the word *tornadoes* in the second paragraph on this page. Using the context, find out its meaning. What clues did you use to find its meaning?

Comprehension and Critical Thinking
1. (a) Identify What is climate?
(b) Explain How is climate different from weather?

(c) Analyze Are hurricanes an example of climate or of weather?
2. (a) Recall What kind of climate occurs in most places near the Equator?
(b) Contrast Why are climates near the poles different from climates near the Equator?
3. (a) Recall How do bodies of water affect temperatures?
(b) Predict A city in the interior of a continent has very cold winters. How would you expect winter temperatures to differ in a coastal city at the same latitude as the interior city?

Writing Activity
Write a paragraph describing your region's climate, or average weather. Are winters usually warm or cold? What can you say about summers? Do oceans affect your climate? How much precipitation does your region get? Is it mostly rain, or snow, or a mix?

> **Writing Tip** Remember that every paragraph needs a main idea. Make a general statement about your climate in a topic sentence. Then add sentences with supporting details about your climate.

Chapter 2 Section 3 **47**

Objective

Use and interpret climate graphs.

Prepare to Read

Build Background Knowledge L2

Invite students to brainstorm a list of all the kinds of graphs they know, such as circle, line, and bar. Then ask them what they usually want or need to know about the weather (*temperature and precipitation*). Tell students that climate graphs answer the questions most people have about weather.

Instruct

Using Climate Graphs L2

Guided Instruction

- Read the steps to using climate graphs as a class and write them on the board.

- Practice the skill by following the steps on page 49 as a class. Model each step in the activity by first reading the labels on the graph (*Fahrenheit degrees; inches; months of the year*); identifying what the bar and line graphs show (*bar: rainfall in inches; line: temperature in Fahrenheit degrees*); describing the shape of the line graph and look of the bar graph (*line: relatively flat indicating little temperature change; bar graph: varying heights indicating higher precipitation during the spring and summer than the fall and winter*). Remind students that seasons in the Southern Hemisphere are the reverse of seasons in the Northern Hemisphere. Then draw conclusions. (*Possible conclusions: São Paulo's temperatures remain in the same small range year round; therefore the city has a moderate climate. São Paulo has a wet and dry season. The wet season runs from October through March and the dry season runs from April through September.*)

Independent Practice

Assign *Skills for Life* and have students complete it individually.

All in One **Foundations of Geography Teaching Resources**, *Skills for Life*, p. 127

Menghai, China, receives about 40 to 60 inches (100 to 150 centimeters) of rainfall each year.

"Everybody talks about the weather, but nobody does anything about it," goes an old joke attributed to the humorist Mark Twain. It's still true, although today we track the weather so that we can predict and prepare for it. One way geographers track weather patterns is by making a climate graph. A climate graph usually presents information about average precipitation and average temperature. Often it shows a whole year of information, so you can see how conditions change with the seasons.

Learn the Skill

To read a climate graph, follow the steps below.

1. **Identify the elements of the graph.** A climate graph is actually two graphs in one: a line graph that shows temperature and a bar graph that shows rainfall. The scale on the left side goes with the line graph, and the scale on the right side goes with the bar graph. The scale along the bottom shows a time period.

2. **Study the line graph.** Notice changes in temperature from month to month and from season to season. Draw a conclusion about the temperature of the place.

3. **Study the bar graph.** Again, notice changes for months and for seasons. Draw a conclusion about rainfall.

4. **Use your conclusions about both graphs to draw an overall conclusion about the climate of the location.** Does the location appear to have hot seasons and cold seasons? Or does it have a rainy season and a dry season? State your conclusion.

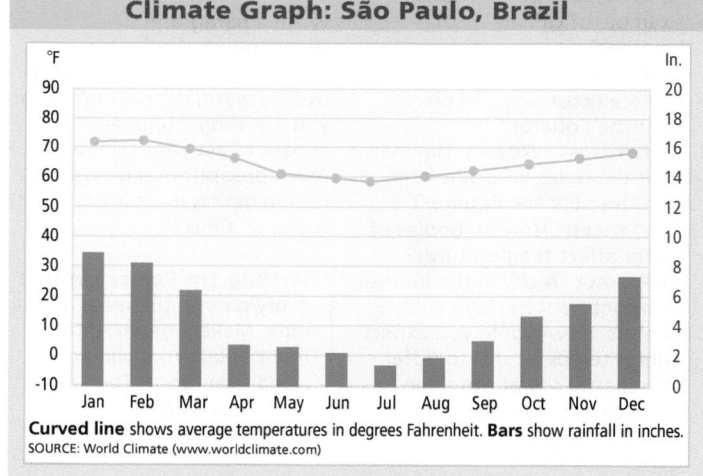

Climate Graph: São Paulo, Brazil

Curved line shows average temperatures in degrees Fahrenheit. **Bars** show rainfall in inches.
SOURCE: World Climate (www.worldclimate.com)

Monitor Progress

As students are completing *Skills for Life*, circulate to make sure individuals are applying the skill steps effectively. Provide assistance as needed.

Practice the Skill

Look at the graph of São Paulo, Brazil, on page 48.

1 Read the labels on the sides and bottom of the graph. What do the numbers on the left side measure? What do the numbers on the right side measure? Look at the green bars. Which do they measure, temperature or rainfall? How do you know? Look at the line graph. What does it show? Now, look at the scale along the bottom of the graph. What period of time does it show?

2 Describe the shape of the line graph—is it generally flat, or does it go up and down? What and when is São Paulo's highest average temperature? Its lowest temperature? Do you think São Paulo has a hot season and a cold season? Write a conclusion about temperatures in the city.

3 What do the bars in the bar graph show? Are they generally the same height, or do they differ from month to month? What and when are São Paulo's highest and lowest average rainfall? Do you think São Paulo has a wet season and a dry season? Write a conclusion about rainfall in the city.

4 Using your conclusions about São Paulo's climate, write a summary that includes answers to these questions: What kind of seasons does the city have? Does the weather change much during the year?

Apply the Skill

To make your own climate graph, draw a large square on graph paper. Divide the square into 10 horizontal rows and 12 vertical columns. Title your graph "Climate Graph of Charleston, South Carolina." Then label the left side of your graph using one colored pencil and the right side with a different colored pencil. Write the months of the year along the bottom. Using the temperature and precipitation information in the table above, plot your line graph. Draw the lines with the same colored pencils you used to make the labels for temperature and precipitation.

Charleston, South Carolina

Month	Temperature (°Fahrenheit)	Precipitation (inches)
Jan	48.4	2.9
Feb	50.9	3.0
Mar	57.7	3.6
Apr	65.3	2.4
May	72.7	3.2
Jun	78.8	4.7
Jul	81.7	6.8
Aug	81.0	6.4
Sept	76.6	5.1
Oct	67.8	2.9
Nov	59.5	2.1
Dec	52.2	2.7

Assess and Reteach

Assess Progress L2
Ask students to do the Apply the Skill activity.

Reteach L1
If students are having trouble applying the skill steps, pair students and ask them to complete *Reading a Climate Graph.*

All in One **Foundations of Geography Teaching Resources,** *Reading a Climate Graph,* p. 136

Extend L3
To extend the skill, show students *Color Transparency FG 41: Climate Graphs.* Have students follow the steps outlined in the skill feature to draw conclusions on the climates of Karachi, Pakistan, and Chennai, India. Then have students write a brief summary of their findings.

Foundations of Geography Transparencies, *Color Transparency FG 41: Climate Graphs*

Answer
Apply the Skill

Student's climate graphs should have the same format as the São Paulo climate graph but reflect the data in the table for Charleston, South Carolina.

All in One **Foundations of Geography Teaching Resources,** *Rubric for Assessing a Bar Graph,* p. 148; *Rubric for Assessing a Line Graph,* p. 149

Section 4
Step-by-Step Instruction

Objectives

Social Studies
1. Investigate the relationship between climate and vegetation.
2. Explore Earth's vegetation regions.
3. Study vertical climate zones.

Reading/Language Arts
Use context to determine the meaning of a word or phrase when examples are provided.

Prepare to Read

Build Background Knowledge 〔L2〕

Tell students that in this section they will learn about different climates, and the relationship between climate and vegetation. Ask students to think of ways in which their environments would be different if they lived in a different climate zone. Model the thought process by encouraging them to think about how plants and trees would be different, how buildings might be constructed differently, and how their clothing might be different. Use the Numbered Heads participation strategy (TE, p. T36) to have students generate a list.

Set a Purpose for Reading 〔L2〕

■ Preview the Objectives.

■ Read each statement in the *Reading Readiness Guide* aloud. Ask students to mark the statements true or false.

■ Have students discuss the statements in pairs or groups of four, then mark their worksheets again. Use the Numbered Heads participation strategy (TE, p. T36) to call on students to share their group's perspectives.

〔All in One〕 **Foundations of Geography Teaching Resources,** *Reading Readiness Guide,* p. 118

Vocabulary Builder
Preview Key Terms

Pronounce each Key Term, then ask the students to say the word with you. Provide a simple explanation such as, "The tree canopy was so thick that very little sunlight reached the floor of the rain forest."

Section 4
How Climate Affects Vegetation

Prepare to Read

Objectives

In this section you will
1. Investigate the relationship between climate and vegetation.
2. Explore Earth's vegetation regions.
3. Study vertical climate zones.

Taking Notes

As you read, look for details about Earth's natural vegetation regions. Copy the chart below and list each type of climate in the first row of boxes. Add boxes as needed. In the box underneath each type of climate, list facts about each vegetation region that occurs in that type of climate.

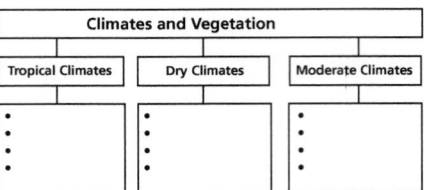

Climates and Vegetation		
Tropical Climates	Dry Climates	Moderate Climates
•	•	•
•	•	•
•	•	•

〔Target Reading Skill〕

Use Context Clues
You can sometimes learn the meaning of a word or phrase when the context gives examples. In the passage below, the meaning of the word *scrub* is given by the examples in italics.

> Scrub includes *bushes, small trees, and low, woody undergrowth.*

Key Terms

• **vegetation** (vej uh TAY shun) *n.* plants that grow in a region

• **tundra** (TUN druh) *n.* an area of cold climate and low-lying vegetation
• **canopy** (KAN uh pea) *n.* the layer formed by the uppermost branches of a rain forest
• **savanna** (suh VAN uh) *n.* a parklike combination of grasslands and scattered trees
• **desert scrub** (DEZ urt skrub) *n.* desert vegetation that needs little water
• **deciduous trees** (dee SIJ oo us treez) *n.* trees that lose their leaves seasonally
• **coniferous trees** (koh NIF ur us treez) *n.* trees that produce cones to carry seeds

Jackfruit, an Asian fruit, grows huge in the tropical wet climate of Hainan Island, China.

50 Foundations of Geography

Climate and Vegetation

There are five broad types of climate: tropical, dry, temperate marine, temperate continental, and polar. Each climate has its own types of natural **vegetation,** or plants that grow in a region. This is because different plants require different amounts of water and sunlight and different temperatures to survive. The map titled The World: Natural Vegetation, on page 53, shows the location of Earth's vegetation regions. If you compare this map with the map on pages 44 and 45 titled The World: Climate Regions, you will see that climate regions and vegetation regions often cover similar areas.

Tropical Climates In the tropics, there are two main climates. Both are hot. A tropical wet climate has year-round rainfall. Its typical vegetation is tropical rain forest. A tropical wet and dry climate has two seasons: a rainy season and a dry season. This climate supports grasslands and scattered trees.

〔Target Reading Skill〕 〔L2〕

Use Context Clues Point out the Target Reading Skill. Tell students that when the context of a sentence provides examples, they can help determine the meaning of an unfamiliar word or phrase.

Model the skill by finding out what vegetation makes up a tropical savanna in this sentence from page 52: "In tropical areas with winter dry seasons or more limited rainfall, there is a parklike landscape of grass-lands with scattered trees known as savanna." *(Tropical savannas are made up of grasslands and scattered trees.)*

Give students *Use Context Clues: Examples.* Have them complete the activity in their groups.

〔All in One〕 **Foundations of Geography Teaching Resources,** *Use Context Clues: Examples,* p. 124

---

50 *Foundations of Geography*

Dry Climates Arid and semiarid climates have very hot summers and generally mild winters. They get very little rain. The driest arid climate regions have little or no vegetation. Others have plants that need little water. Semiarid climates get a little more rain. They support shrubs and grasses.

Temperate Marine Climates Temperate marine climates are found in the middle latitudes, usually near coastlines. There are three types: Mediterranean, marine west coast, and humid subtropical. The marine west coast and humid subtropical climates get plenty of rain. In the humid subtropical climate, the rain falls mainly in summer. Mediterranean climates get less rain, and it falls mainly in winter. All of the climates have mild winters. Mediterranean and humid subtropical climates generally have hot summers. With their heavy rainfall, marine west coast and humid subtropical climates support a variety of forests. The drier Mediterranean climates have their own vegetation, known as Mediterranean vegetation.

Temperate Continental Climates In a humid continental climate, summer temperatures are moderate to hot, but winters can be very cold. This climate supports grasslands and forests. Regions with subarctic climates are drier, with cool summers and cold winters. Most subarctic climate regions are forested.

Polar Climates The polar climates are cold all year-round. The tundra is an area, near the Arctic Circle, of cold climate and low-lying vegetation. The word *tundra* refers both to the vegetation and the climate, which has short, cool summers and long, very cold winters. Ice cap climates are bitterly cold all year. These areas are covered with ice. No vegetation can grow there.

✓ Reading Check **Why are climate and vegetation related?**

Earth's Vegetation Regions

Geographers divide Earth into regions that share similar vegetation. A place's vegetation depends mainly on its climate, but also on other things, such as soil quality.

Polar bears crossing the tundra in Churchill, Manitoba, Canada

Plant Fossils In ancient rocks in Wyoming, scientists have found fossils of palm trees. Millions of years ago, sediments such as sand or ash buried the plants quickly. Over thousands of years, the sediment and plants within turned to rock. Scientists study fossils to learn about ancient climate and vegetation.

Vocabulary Builder

Use the information below to teach students this section's high-use words.

High-Use Word	Definition and Sample Sentence
marine, p. 50	*adj.* of or relating to the sea A **marine** biologist studies ocean plants and animals.
humid, p. 51	*adj.* full of water vapor; moist The weather was hot and **humid.**
dense, p. 52	*adj.* packed in, crowded together We struggled to get through the **dense** bushes.
scatter, p. 52	*v.* to throw loosely about in no specific direction A gust of strong wind made the leaves **scatter.**

Instruct

Climate and Vegetation L2

Guided Instruction
- **Vocabulary Builder** Clarify the high-use words **marine** and **humid** before reading.

- Read Climate and Vegetation using the Structured Silent Reading strategy (TE, p. T34). Ask students to study the photos and captions on pp. 50–51.

- Ask students **What are the five broad types of climate?** *(tropical, dry, temperate marine, temperate continental, and polar)* **What factors are used to distinguish climates?** *(the amount or lack of rainfall and the amount or lack of heat)*

- Ask students **What kinds of climates have forests?** *(Tropical wet climates, marine west coast, humid subtropical, and temperate continental climates all support forests.)* **Which do not and why?** *(Dry climates, tropical wet and dry climates, and Mediterranean climates do not support forests because there is not enough rainfall. Polar climates do not support forests because the temperatures are too cold.)*

Independent Practice
Ask students to create the Taking Notes graphic organizer on a blank piece of paper. Remind them to add extra boxes to include all of the broad types of climates. Then have them fill in each box with facts about vegetation for each of the five different types of climates.

Monitor Progress
As students fill in the graphic organizer, circulate and make sure individuals are selecting the correct details. Provide assistance as needed.

Links

Read the **Links to Science** box on this page. Ask students **What information do plant fossils give scientists?** *(Plant fossils help scientists learn about ancient climate and vegetation.)*

Answer

✓ Reading Check Different plants require different amounts of water and sunlight and different temperatures to survive.

Earth's Vegetation Regions L2

Guided Instruction

- **Vocabulary Builder** Clarify the high-use words **dense** and **scatter** before reading.

- As a class, show students *The World: Annual Precipitation* and *The World: Desert and Desert Scrub Vegetation Regions* for a more detailed view of desert and desert scrub vegetation regions.

  📖 **Foundations of Geography Transparencies,** *Color Transparency FG 10: The World: Annual Precipitation (Base); Color Transparency FG 12: The World: Desert and Desert Scrub Vegetation Regions (Overlay)*

- Write the different types of vegetation on the board. Ask students to brainstorm locations where they think the types of vegetation would be found. Have students refer to the map on page 53 to get ideas.

Independent Practice

Have students complete their graphic organizers with the information they just learned.

Monitor Progress

- Show *Section Reading Support Transparency FG 48* and ask students to check their graphic organizers individually. Go over key concepts and clarify key vocabulary as needed.

  📖 **Foundations of Geography Transparencies,** *Section Reading Support Transparency FG 48*

⊙ Target Reading Skill L2

Use Context Clues As a follow up, ask students to answer the Target Reading Skill question in the Student Edition. *(It includes grasses, shrubs, and low trees.)*

Answer

✓ Reading Check desert scrub and vegetation that has roots which can absorb water before it evaporates

---

This tropical rain forest in Brazil supports dense vegetation.

Use Context Clues
If you do not know what Mediterranean vegetation is, consider the examples and other information given by the context. What does the context tell you about this vegetation?

- **Tropical Rain Forest** Because there is so much sunlight, heat, and rain, thousands of kinds of plants grow in a rain forest. Some trees rise 130 feet (40 meters) into the air. The dense, leafy layer formed by the uppermost branches of the rainforest is called the **canopy.** Other plants grow to lower heights in the shade beneath the canopy.
- **Tropical Savanna** In tropical areas with winter dry seasons or more limited rainfall, there is a parklike landscape of grasslands with scattered trees known as **savanna.**
- **Desert** In the driest parts of deserts, there may be no vegetation at all. Elsewhere, plants grow far apart. Their roots absorb scarce water before it evaporates in the heat.
- **Desert Scrub** Semiarid areas and deserts with a little more rain support **desert scrub,** or low desert vegetation that needs little water. Some plants flower only when it rains, so that seeds have a better chance to survive.
- **Mediterranean Vegetation** Mediterranean vegetation includes grasses, shrubs, and low trees. These plants must hold water from the winter rains to survive warm, dry summers.
- **Temperate Grassland** Vast grasslands straddle regions with semiarid and humid continental climates. The wetter grasslands, in humid continental climates, have a mix of tall grasses and other plants that is sometimes called prairie.
- **Deciduous Forest** Marine west coast, humid subtropical, and humid continental climates all support forests of **deciduous trees,** or trees that lose their leaves in the fall.
- **Coniferous and Mixed Forest** These same climates also support areas of coniferous and mixed forest. **Coniferous trees** are trees that produce cones to carry seeds. They generally have needles, not leaves. These features protect trees in drier climates. Mixed forests combine both coniferous and deciduous trees.
- **Tundra** The tundra is an area of cold climate and low-lying vegetation. Tundra vegetation includes mosses, grasses, and low shrubs that bloom during the brief, cool summers.
- **Highland** In highland regions, vegetation depends on elevation, since temperatures drop as elevation rises. Tropical forests may grow at low elevations, with grasslands and coniferous forests farther up. Still higher, tundra vegetation may grow.
- **Ice Cap and Pack Ice** Around the poles, thick ice caps form on land. Masses of ice called pack ice cover the sea. No vegetation can grow there.

✓ **Reading Check** **What types of vegetation grow in deserts?**

Differentiated Instruction

For Advanced Readers L3
Have students read *The Endless Steppe.* Using its location and description in the selection, have students identify its climate and vegetation regions. Then have students check their conclusions by locating Rubtsovsk in an atlas, encyclopedia, or on the Internet.

All in One **Foundations of Geography Teaching Resources,** *The Endless Steppe,* pp. 141–142

For Less Proficient Readers L1
To ensure students know how to read the natural vegetation map on page 53, have students complete *Reading a Natural Vegetation Map* in pairs.

All in One **Foundations of Geography Teaching Resources,** *Reading a Natural Vegetation Map,* p. 137

The World: Natural Vegetation

This map shows the natural vegetation regions of the world. The locations of these regions depend mainly on climate. Like the climates that support them, vegetation regions vary according to their distance from the Equator and the amount of precipitation they receive.

The Sahara ▶
The world's largest desert has vast sand dunes with little or no vegetation. This picture also shows an oasis, or a place in the desert where underground water allows trees or crops to grow.

◀ Mixed Forest
The mixed forests of California support trees such as pines, redwoods, and tan oaks.

◀ Lichen, Northern Russia

0 miles 3,000
0 kilometers 3,000
Robinson

KEY

Tropical rain forest	Desert scrub
Deciduous forest	Desert (no vegetation)
Mixed forest	Highland
Coniferous forest	Tundra
Mediterranean forest	Ice cap
Tropical savanna	Pack ice
Temperate grassland	—— National border
	----- Disputed border

Vertical Climate Zones L2

Guided Instruction

- Read Vertical Climate Zones as a class. As you read, circulate to make sure students are able to answer the Reading Check question.

- Ask students **Why do mountains have a vertical climate?** (*Climate depends on elevation. Elevation changes the farther you go up a mountain causing the climate to change significantly.*)

- Ask students to predict how their clothing might change as they climb a mountain in a temperate climate. (*They might need shorts or light clothing at the base of the mountain; a jacket or coat in the coniferous forest; and polar gear as they climb toward the peak.*)

Independent Practice
Assign *Guided Reading and Review*.

All in One Foundations of Geography Teaching Resources, *Guided Reading and Review*, p. 119

Monitor Progress
Tell students to fill in the last column of their *Reading Readiness Guides*. Probe for what they learned that confirms or invalidates each statement.

All in One Foundations of Geography Teaching Resources, *Reading Readiness Guide*, p. 118

Skills Mini Lesson

Transferring Information from One Medium to Another

1. Teach the skill using these skill steps: first, state the main idea you want to communicate; next, choose a visual aid such as a map, diagram, or graph that would communicate the information clearly; finally, transfer each piece of data into the visual aid.

2. Help students practice the skill by summarizing the information in Vertical Climate Zones on page 54.

3. Have students apply the skill by transferring the main idea to a visual aid.

Answers

MAP MASTER Skills Activity **Location** near the Equator **Compare and Contrast** areas with tropical forests are similar to areas of tropical climates

Go Online PHSchool.com Students may practice their map skills using the interactive online version of this map.

Assess and Reteach

Assess Progress L2
Have students complete the Section Assessment. Administer the *Section Quiz*.

All in One Foundations of Geography Teaching Resources, *Section Quiz*, p. 120

Reteach L1
If students need more instruction, have them read this section in the Reading and Vocabulary Study Guide.

Western Hemisphere Reading and Vocabulary Study Guide, pp. 18–20

Extend L3
To extend the lesson, have students create a natural vegetation poster identifying at least five plants that are native to the climate region in which they live. The poster should include information about the climate region, the names of the plants and why they are suited to this particular region, and, if possible, illustrations.

All in One Foundations of Geography Teaching Resources, *Rubric for Assessing a Student Poster*, p. 150

Answer

✓ **Reading Check** The amount and types of vegetation decrease as the elevation increases until the cold temperature prevents any vegetation.

Section 4 Assessment

Key Terms
Students' sentences should reflect knowledge of each Key Term.

Target Reading Skill
Tundra vegetation includes mosses, grasses, and low shrubs that bloom during brief, cool summers. The examples of mosses and grasses provide clues to the meaning of the phrase.

Comprehension and Critical Thinking
1. (a) tropical, dry, temperate marine, temperate continental, and polar **(b)** Because different plants require different amounts of water, sun, and different temperatures, each climate region has its own types of vegetation. **(c)** Low-lying plants and scrub grow in climates with little precipitation and forests grow in climates with heavier precipitation.

Forested valley at the foot of Machapuchare, a mountain in Nepal

Vertical Climate Zones

The climate at the top of Mount Everest, in southern Asia, is like Antarctica's. But Mount Everest is near the Tropic of Cancer, far from the South Pole. It is so cold at the top of the mountain because the air becomes cooler as elevation increases. Mountains have vertical climate zones, where the climate and vegetation depend on elevation.

In a tropical region, vegetation that needs a tropical climate will grow only near the bottom of a mountain. Farther up is vegetation that can grow in a temperate climate. Near the top is vegetation that can grow in a polar climate.

Picture yourself on a hike up a mountain in a temperate climate. Grassland surrounds the base of the mountain, and temperatures are warm. You begin to climb and soon enter an area with more precipitation and lower temperatures than below. The grassland gives way to a coniferous forest.

As you continue to climb, you find only scattered, short trees. Finally, it is too cold even for them. There are only the low shrubs, short grasses, and mosses of a tundra. At the mountain's peak, you find permanent ice, where no vegetation grows.

✓ **Reading Check** How does vegetation change with elevation?

Section 4 Assessment

Key Terms
Review the key terms at the beginning of this section. Use each term in a sentence that explains its meaning.

Target Reading Skill
Find the phrase *tundra vegetation* on page 52. Use context to figure out its meaning. What do you think it means? What clues helped you find the meaning?

Comprehension and Critical Thinking
1. (a) List What are the five main types of climate?
(b) Evaluate How do differences in climate affect plant life?

(c) Analyze Why do low-lying plants, such as scrub or tundra, grow in some climates, while rich forests grow in others?
2. (a) Recall How do desert plants survive in dry climates?
(b) Transfer Information What features of the plants in your region allow them to grow in your region's climate?
3. (a) Define What is a vertical climate zone?
(b) Explain How do vertical climate zones affect vegetation on a mountain?
(c) Compare and Contrast Why is vegetation at the top of a tall mountain different from vegetation at the bottom?

Writing Activity
Look at the map titled The World: Natural Vegetation on page 53 in this section. Choose three places on the map that are in different natural vegetation regions. Then write a description of the types of plants you would expect to see if you visited each place you have chosen.

Writing Tip Since you are writing about three different types of natural vegetation, you may want to compare and contrast them. When you compare, you point out similarities. When you contrast, you focus on differences.

2. (a) Desert plants have roots that absorb scarce water before it evaporates; some desert plants flower only when it rains so that as many seeds survive as possible. **(b)** Students' answers will vary by region.

3. (a) A vertical climate zone is one where the climate and vegetation depend on elevation. **(b)** The climate region at the bottom of a mountain can usually support a wide variety of vegetation because it is relatively warm. The climate region at the peak of a mountain

is usually much colder and supports less vegetation. **(c)** The climate at the top of a mountain is colder than the climate at the bottom.

Writing Activity
Use the *Rubric for Assessing a Writing Assignment* to evaluate students' essays.

All in One Foundations of Geography Teaching Resources, *Rubric for Assessing a Writing Assignment*, p. 145

Review and Assessment

◆ Chapter Summary

Section 1: Our Planet, Earth
- Earth's rotation on its axis changes day to night and night to day.
- The tilt of Earth's axis causes our seasons.

Section 2: Forces Shaping Earth
- Earth's three main layers are the crust, the mantle, and the core.
- Forces inside Earth move plates of crust to form mountains and volcanoes.
- Wind, water, and ice wear down and reshape Earth's surface.

Section 3: Climate and Weather
- Climate is the average weather in a region over a long period of time.
- Climate depends on latitude, landforms, and nearness to an ocean.
- Winds and ocean currents help spread Earth's warmth. They can also cause dangerous storms.

Section 4: How Climate Affects Vegetation
- Vegetation depends mainly on climate.
- Earth can be divided into several natural vegetation regions.
- Climate and vegetation change with elevation.

Delicate Arch, Utah

◆ Key Terms

Each of the statements below contains a key term from the chapter. If the statement is true, write *true*. If it is false, rewrite the statement to make it true.

1. Earth's movement around the sun is called rotation.
2. The mantle is a thick, rocky layer around Earth's core.
3. Earth's crust is at the center of the planet.
4. Magma is hot, flowing rock beneath Earth's surface.

5. The Appalachian Mountains have been worn down over time by erosion.
6. If you want to know how hot it will be tomorrow, you can look at a climate report.
7. Temperature measures how hot or how cold something is.
8. Vegetation is a term for the plants that grow in a region.
9. Deciduous forests grow in polar climates.

┌ Vocabulary Builder

Revisit this chapter's high-use words:

standard	surge	marine
relative	splinter	humid
force	indirect	dense
collide	distribute	scatter

Ask students to review the definitions they recorded on their *Word Knowledge* worksheets.

All in One Foundations of Geography Teaching Resources, *Word Knowledge,* p. 125

Consider allowing students to earn extra credit if they use the words in their answers to the questions in the Chapter Review and Assessment. The words must be used correctly and in a natural context to win the extra points.

Chapter 2

Review and Assessment
Review Chapter Content

- Review and revisit the major themes of this chapter by asking students to classify what Guiding Question each bulleted statement in the Chapter Summary answers. Have students write the Chapter Summary on a separate piece of paper. Then with a partner have them determine which Guiding Question applies to each statement and number the statements accordingly. Refer to page 1 in the Student Edition for the text of the Guiding Questions.

- Assign *Vocabulary Development* for students to review Key Terms.

  All in One Foundations of Geography Teaching Resources, *Vocabulary Development,* p. 144

Answers
Key Terms

1. False. Earth travels around the sun in an oval-shaped orbit.
2. True
3. False. Earth's core is at the center of the planet.
4. True
5. True
6. False. If you want to know how hot it will be tomorrow, you could look at a weather report.
7. True
8. True
9. False. Deciduous forests grow in marine west coast, humid subtropical, and humid continental climates.

Review and Assessment

Comprehension and Critical Thinking

10. (a) 24 (b) Earth is divided into 24 time zones because it takes 24 hours for Earth to complete one rotation.

11. (a) the summer solstice, or the longest day of the year (b) When a hemisphere tilts toward the sun, it receives direct sunlight, making summers hot. When a hemisphere tilts away from the sun, it receives indirect sunlight, making winters cold. (c) The sun is never directly overhead in Antarctica because it is in a high latitude, or polar zone, that is cold year round.

12. (a) three percent (b) Possible answer: Lakes, rivers, and ground water might freeze decreasing the fresh water supply.

13. (a) Wind is caused by air currents that follow regular patterns related to latitude. (b) Negative—tropical cyclones; hurricanes; tornadoes; Positive—wind and water can make climates milder.

14. (a) Ocean currents help distribute Earth's heat. Warm water flows away from the Equator and cold water moves away from the poles. (b) Water remains cooler as the air and land heats up in summer; so wind blowing over the water cools coastal land nearby.

15. (a) Different kinds of vegetation grow in each of the five broad types of climate areas because different plants require different amounts of water and sunlight and different temperatures. (b) Tropical climates with year-round rainfall will support a tropical rainforest, because such vegetation requires high rainfall.

Skills Practice

Paragraphs should include information about the average daily temperature changes from month to month and how the amount of precipitation stays about the same.

Writing Activity

Students' plant descriptions will vary but should include information about dry climates and desert vegetation regions.

All in One **Foundations of Geography Teaching Resources,** *Rubric for Assessing a Writing Assignment,* p. 145

Review and Assessment (continued)

◆ Comprehension and Critical Thinking

10. (a) **Recall** How many standard time zones is Earth divided into?
(b) **Analyze** How are time differences related to the rotation of Earth?

11. (a) **Identify** As Earth moves around the sun, what event happens about June 21?
(b) **Explain** How does Earth's movement make summers hot and winters cold?
(c) **Apply Information** Why is Antarctica cold even in summer?

12. (a) **Recall** How much of Earth's water is fresh?
(b) **Predict** If Earth's climate became colder, how might the fresh water supply be affected?

13. (a) **Recall** What causes winds?
(b) **Contrast** What are some negative and positive effects of wind and water in the tropics?

14. (a) **Describe** How do oceans shape climate?
(b) **Synthesize Information** Why do some coastal cities in the tropics stay cool?

15. (a) **Describe** How does climate affect vegetation?
(b) **Evaluate** A tropical climate has year-round rainfall. Can forests grow there? Explain why or why not.

◆ Skills Practice

Using Special Geography Graphs Review the steps you learned in the Skills For Life activity in this chapter. Then look at the climate graph for Helsinki, Finland, below. After you have analyzed the graph, write a paragraph that summarizes Helsinki's climate.

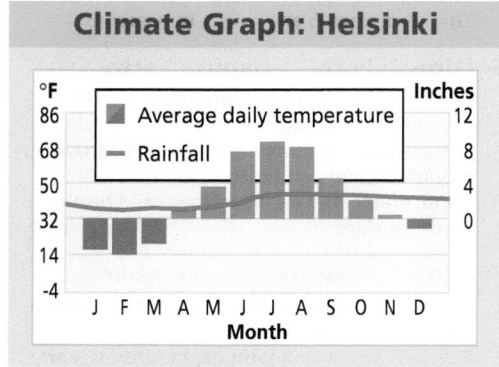

Climate Graph: Helsinki

◆ Writing Activity: Science

Reread the descriptions of dry climates and of desert vegetation regions. Then design a plant that could live in these regions. Describe how it would get light, water, and nutrients.

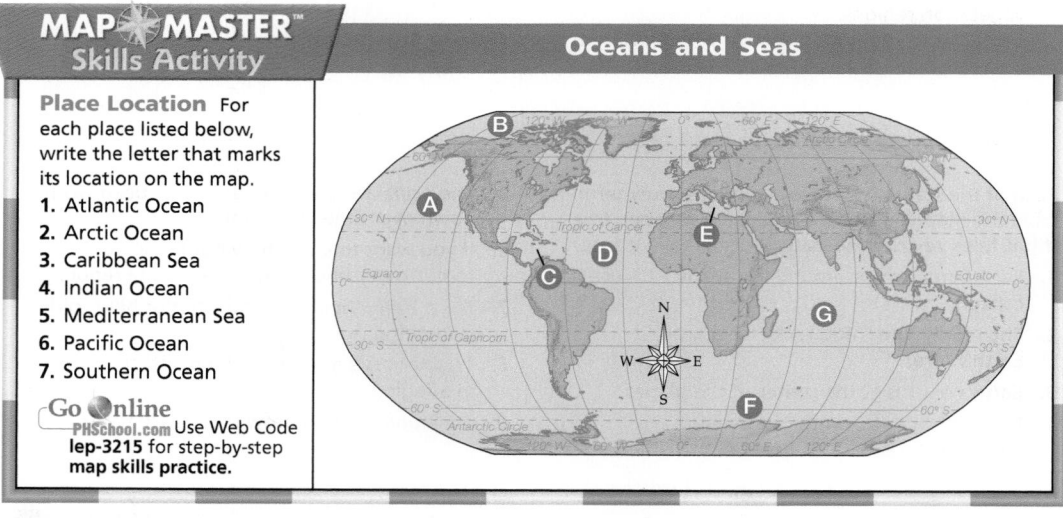

MAP MASTER™ Skills Activity

Oceans and Seas

Place Location For each place listed below, write the letter that marks its location on the map.
1. Atlantic Ocean
2. Arctic Ocean
3. Caribbean Sea
4. Indian Ocean
5. Mediterranean Sea
6. Pacific Ocean
7. Southern Ocean

Go Online
PHSchool.com Use Web Code **lep-3215** for step-by-step map skills practice.

56 Foundations of Geography

MAP MASTER™
Skills Activity

1. D	**2.** B
3. C	**4.** G
5. E	**6.** A
7. F	

Go Online
PHSchool.com Students may practice their map skills using the interactive online version of this map.

Standardized Test Prep

Test-Taking Tips

Some questions on standardized tests ask you to use map keys. Read the precipitation map key below. Then follow the tips to answer the sample question.

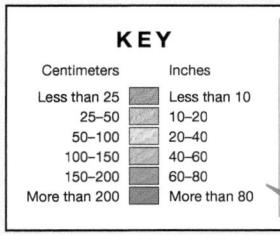

KEY

Centimeters		Inches
Less than 25		Less than 10
25–50		10–20
50–100		20–40
100–150		40–60
150–200		60–80
More than 200		More than 80

TIP On a map key, the colors line up with the data. To find information, read the numbers to the left or right of a given color.

Pick the letter that best answers the question.
On a precipitation map, the southern coastal states are colored dark green. According to the key at the left, how many inches of rain does this region get each year?

A 20–40
B 60–80
C 50–100
D 150–200

TIP To be sure you understand what the question is asking, restate it in your own words: *The color DARK GREEN on the map key stands for how many inches of rain each year?*

Think It Through The question asks about inches of rain, but the answers C and D show numbers from the centimeter column. The numbers 20–40 (answer A) are next to yellow, not dark green. The numbers 60–80 are next to dark green in the inches column. The answer is B.

Practice Questions

Use the tips above and other tips in this book to help you answer the following questions:

1. When the Northern Hemisphere has days and nights of equal length, it is
A summer solstice.
B spring equinox.
C New Year's Day.
D winter solstice.

2. Which of the following is NOT an example of a landform?
A a mountain
B a plateau
C a plain
D an atmosphere

3. In which vegetation region would you find a plant with shallow roots, meant to absorb water before it evaporates?
A desert
B deciduous forest
C coniferous forest
D tropical savanna

Study the following map key and answer the question that follows.

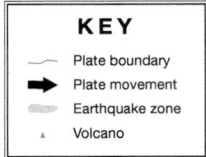

KEY

〜 Plate boundary
➡ Plate movement
▬ Earthquake zone
▲ Volcano

4. On a map with this key, you would find places where earthquakes happen by looking for
A a brown area.
B a red triangle.
C a black arrow.
D a black line.

Use Web Code lea-3201 for a **Chapter 2 self-test.**

Standardized Test Prep

Answers

1. B
2. D
3. A
4. A

Go Online **PHSchool.com** Students may use the Chapter 2 self-test on PHSchool.com to prepare for the Chapter Test.

Assessment Resources

Use *Chapter Tests A and B* to assess students' mastery of the chapter content.

All in One **Foundations of Geography Teaching Resources,** *Chapter Tests A and B,* pp. 151–156

Tests also available on the *ExamView Test Bank CD-ROM.*

⊙ *ExamView Test Bank CD-ROM*

Use a benchmark test to evaluate students' cumulative understanding of what they have learned in Chapters 1 and 2.

📄 Foundations of Geography Benchmark Test 1, **AYP Monitoring Assessments,** pp. 81–84

Earth's Human Geography

Overview

Section 1
Population
1. Learn about population distribution.
2. Explore population density.
3. Investigate population growth.

Section 2
Migration
1. Learn about migration, or people's movement from one region to another.
2. Investigate urbanization, or people's movement to cities.

Section 3
Economic Systems
1. Examine different kinds of economies.
2. Investigate levels of economic development.
3. Study global trade patterns.

Section 4
Political Systems
1. Examine different types of states.
2. Investigate types of government.
3. Learn about alliances and international organizations.

Technology Resources

Students use embedded Web codes to access Internet activities, chapter self-tests, and additional map practice. They may also access Dorling Kindersley's Online Desk Reference to learn more about each country they study.

Use the Interactive Textbook to make content and concepts come alive through animations, videos, and activities that accompany the complete basal text—online and on CD-ROM.

Use this complete suite of powerful teaching tools to make planning lessons and administering tests quicker and easier.

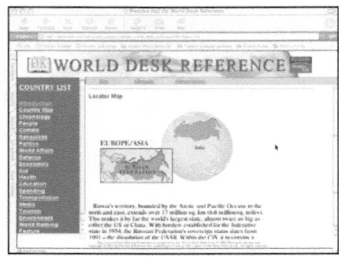

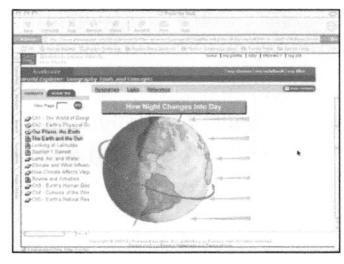

Reading and Assessment

Reading and Vocabulary Instruction

⤹ Model the Target Reading Skill

Compare and Contrast Remind students that when they compare and contrast, they analyze two objects or situations to find their similarities and differences. Model comparing and contrasting using information from page 75 of the Student Edition. Draw a Venn diagram on the board. Label the left-hand section "capitalism," the middle section "both," and the right-hand section "communism." Tell students that they make comparisons when they find similarities and contrasts when they find differences.

Ask yourself the following questions aloud, as you fill in the diagram. "What is the same about capitalism and communism? *(they are types of economic systems.)* What are the differences between capitalism and communism? *(capitalism: businesses are privately owned; communism: the government has control of the economy)* How can I summarize these comparisons and contrasts? *(Capitalism and communism are both types of economic systems, but in communism the government controls the entire economy, and capitalism has a free-market economy.)*"

Use the following worksheets from All-in-One Foundations of Geography Teaching Resources (pp. 177–179) to support this chapter's Target Reading Skill.

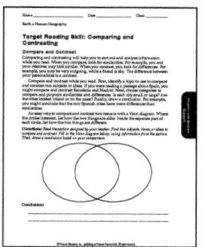 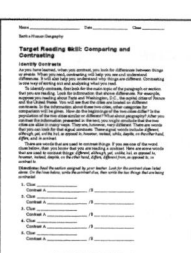

Vocabulary Builder

High-Use Academic Words

Use these steps to teach this chapter's high-use words:

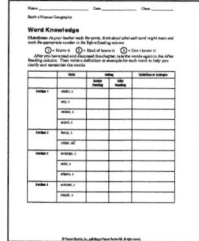

1. Have students rate how well they know each word on their Word Knowledge worksheets (All-in-One Foundations of Geography Teaching Resources, p. 180).
2. Pronounce each word and ask students to repeat it.
3. Give students a brief definition or sample sentence (provided on TE pp. 61, 68, 75, and 81).
4. Work with students as they fill in the "Definition or Example" column of their Word Knowledge worksheets.

Assessment

Formal Assessment

Test students' understanding of core knowledge and skills.

Chapter Tests A and B, Foundations of Geography Teaching Resources, pp. 199–204

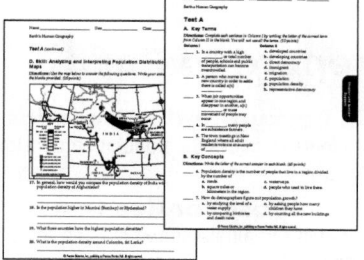

Customize the Chapter Tests to suit your needs.
ExamView Test Bank CD-ROM

Skills Assessment

Assess geographic literacy.

MapMaster Skills, Student Edition pp. 61, 62, 63, 69, 77, 86

Assess reading skills.

Target Reading Skills, Student Edition, pp. 62, 68, 76, 81, and in Section Assessments

Chapter 3 Assessment, Western Hemisphere Reading and Vocabulary Study Guide, p. 34

Performance Assessment

Assess students' performance on this chapter's Writing Activities using rubrics from All-in-One Foundations of Geography Teaching Resources.

Rubric for Assessing a Writing Assignment, p. 197

Rubric for Assessing a Bar Graph, p. 198

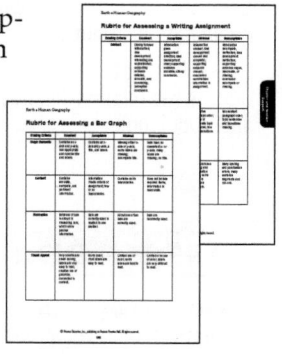

Assess students' work through performance tasks.

Small Group Activity: Making an Immigration Map, All-in-One Foundations of Geography Teaching Resources, pp. 183–186

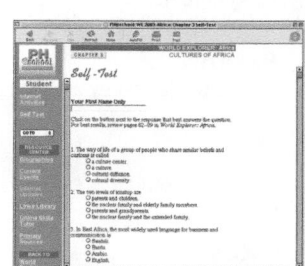

Online Assessment

Have students check their own understanding.

Chapter Self-Test

Section 1 Population

 2 periods, 1 block

Social Studies Objectives

1. Learn about population distribution.
2. Explore population density.
3. Investigate population growth.

Reading/Language Arts Objective

Compare and contrast to analyze information.

Prepare to Read

Build Background Knowledge
Ask students to guess the population densities of local cities.

Set a Purpose for Reading
Have students evaluate statements on the *Reading Readiness Guide*.

Preview Key Terms
Teach the section's Key Terms.

Target Reading Skill
Introduce the section's Target Reading Skill of **comparing and contrasting.**

Instructional Resources

All in One Foundations of Geography Teaching Resources
- L2 Reading Readiness Guide, p. 162
- L2 Compare and Contrast, p. 177

Differentiated Instruction

Spanish Reading and Vocabulary Study Guide
- L1 Chapter 3, Section 1, pp. 17–18 ELL

Instruct

Population Distribution
Ask questions about factors that affect population size and distribution.

Target Reading Skill
Review **comparing and contrasting.**

Population Density
Compare and contrast population density and population distribution.

Population Growth
Discuss the relationship between birthrate, death rate, and population.

Instructional Resources

All in One Foundations of Geography Teaching Resources
- L2 Guided Reading and Review, p. 163
- L2 Reading Readiness Guide, p. 162

Foundations of Geography Transparencies
- L2 Section Reading Support Transparency FG 49

Differentiated Instruction

All in One Foundations of Geography Teaching Resources
- L3 Analyzing Statistics, p. 187 AR, GT
- L3 Enrichment, p. 181 AR, GT

Teacher's Edition
- L1 For Less Proficient Readers, TE pp. 62, 63
- L1 For Special Needs Students, TE p. 62
- L3 For Gifted and Talented, TE pp. 63, 64
- L3 For Advanced Readers, TE p. 64

Student Edition on Audio CD
- L1 Chapter 3, Section 1 ELL, LPR, SN

Assess and Reteach

Assess Progress
Evaluate student comprehension with the section assessment and section quiz.

Reteach
Assign the Reading and Vocabulary Study Guide to help struggling students.

Extend
Extend the lesson by assigning an Internet activity.

Instructional Resources

All in One Foundations of Geography Teaching Resources
- L2 Section Quiz, p. 164
  Rubric for Assessing a Writing Assignment, p. 197

Reading and Vocabulary Study Guide
- L1 Chapter 3, Section 1, pp. 22–24

PHSchool.com
- L3 **For:** Environmental and Global Issues: Evaluating Solutions
  Web Code: led-3300

Differentiated Instruction

Spanish Support
- L2 Section Quiz (Spanish), p. 23 ELL

Key

L1 Basic to Average	L3 Average to Advanced	LPR Less Proficient Readers	GT Gifted and Talented
L2 For All Students		AR Advanced Readers	ELL English Language Learners
		SN Special Needs Students	

Section 2 Migration

 4 periods, 2 blocks (includes Skills for Life)

Social Studies Objectives
1. Learn about migration, or people's movement from one region to another.
2. Investigate urbanization, or people's movement to cities.

Reading/Language Arts Objective
Identify contrasts to understand how situations differ.

Prepare to Read

Build Background Knowledge
Have students brainstorm why people move to different places.

Set a Purpose for Reading
Have students evaluate statements on the *Reading Readiness Guide.*

Preview Key Terms
Teach the section's Key Terms.

Target Reading Skill
Introduce the section's Target Reading Skill of **identifying contrasts.**

Instructional Resources

All in One Foundations of Geography Teaching Resources
- L2 Reading Readiness Guide, p. 166
- L2 Identify Contrasts, p. 178

Differentiated Instruction

Spanish Reading and Vocabulary Study Guide
- L1 Chapter 3, Section 2, pp. 19–20 ELL

Instruct

Why People Migrate
Ask questions about migration and discuss the push-pull theory.

Target Reading Skill
Review **identifying contrasts.**

Urbanization
Ask about urbanization and discuss some problems it can cause.

Instructional Resources

All in One Foundations of Geography Teaching Resources
- L2 Guided Reading and Review, p. 167
- L2 Reading Readiness Guide, p. 166
- L2 Message from the Rain Forest Amerindians, p. 188

Foundations of Geography Transparencies
- L2 Section Reading Support Transparency FG 50
- L2 Transparency B2: Flow Chart

Differentiated Instruction

All in One Foundations of Geography Teaching Resources
- L3 Small Group Activity: Making an Immigration Map, pp. 183–186 AR, GT
- L2 Skills for Life, p. 182 AR, GT, LPR, SN

Teacher's Edition
- L3 For Advanced Readers, TE p. 70
- L1 For English Language Learners, TE p. 70

Spanish Support
- L2 Guided Reading and Review (Spanish), p. 22 ELL

Assess and Reteach

Assess Progress
Evaluate student comprehension with the section assessment and section quiz.

Reteach
Assign the Reading and Vocabulary Study Guide to help struggling students.

Extend
Extend the lesson by having students research an American who immigrated to the United States.

Instructional Resources

All in One Foundations of Geography Teaching Resources
- L2 Section Quiz, p. 168
  Rubric for Assessing a Writing Assignment, p. 197

Reading and Vocabulary Study Guide
- L1 Chapter 3, Section 2, pp. 25–27

Differentiated Instruction

Spanish Support
- L2 Section Quiz (Spanish), p. 23 ELL

Foundations of Geography Transparencies
- L3 Color Transparency FG 5: The World: Continents and Oceans (Base) AR, GT
- L3 Color Transparency FG 16: The World: Population Density (Overlay) AR, GT

Teacher's Edition
- L1 For Special Needs Students, TE p. 73

Social Studies Skills Tutor CD-ROM
- L1 Analyzing and Interpreting Special Purpose Maps ELL, LPR, SN

Key
L1 Basic to Average	L3 Average to Advanced	
L2 For All Students		
	LPR Less Proficient Readers	GT Gifted and Talented
	AR Advanced Readers	ELL English Language Learners
	SN Special Needs Students	

Section 3 Economic Systems

 *2 periods, 1 block*

Social Studies Objectives

1. Examine different kinds of economies.
2. Investigate levels of economic development.
3. Study global trade patterns.

Reading/Language Arts Objective

Make comparisons to understand what things have in common.

Prepare to Read	Instructional Resources	Differentiated Instruction
Build Background Knowledge Ask students to brainstorm the meaning of *economy*. **Set a Purpose for Reading** Have students evaluate statements on the *Reading Readiness Guide*. **Preview Key Terms** Teach the section's Key Terms. **Target Reading Skill** Introduce the section's Target Reading Skill of **making comparisons.**	**All in One Foundations of Geography Teaching Resources** L2 Reading Readiness Guide, p. 170 L2 Make Comparisons, p. 179	**Spanish Reading and Vocabulary Study Guide** L1 Chapter 3, Section 3, pp. 21–22 ELL

Instruct	Instructional Resources	Differentiated Instruction
Different Kinds of Economies Discuss various types of economies. **Levels of Economic Development** Discuss the differences between developed and developing countries' economies. **Target Reading Skill** Review **making comparisons.** **World Trade Patterns** Ask questions about and discuss world trade.	**All in One Foundations of Geography Teaching Resources** L2 Guided Reading and Review, p. 171 L2 Reading Readiness Guide, p. 170 **Foundations of Geography Transparencies** L2 Section Reading Support Transparency FG 51	**Teacher's Edition** L1 For Less Proficient Readers, TE p. 77 L3 For Gifted and Talented, TE p. 77 **Spanish Support** L2 Guided Reading and Review (Spanish), p. 22 ELL

Assess and Reteach	Instructional Resources	Differentiated Instruction
Assess Progress Evaluate student comprehension with the section assessment and section quiz. **Reteach** Assign the Reading and Vocabulary Study Guide to help struggling students. **Extend** Extend the lesson by assigning an Internet activity.	**All in One Foundations of Geography Teaching Resources** L2 Section Quiz, p. 172 Rubric for Assessing a Writing Assignment, p. 197 **Reading and Vocabulary Study Guide** L1 Chapter 3, Section 3, pp. 28–30 **PHSchool.com** L3 **For:** Environmental and Global Issues: Trade in a Global Economy **Web Code:** led-3306	**Spanish Support** L2 Section Quiz (Spanish), p. 23 ELL

Key

L1 Basic to Average   L3 Average to Advanced
L2 For All Students

LPR Less Proficient Readers
AR Advanced Readers
SN Special Needs Students

GT Gifted and Talented
ELL English Language Learners

Section 4 Political Systems

 4.5 periods, 2.25 blocks (includes Chapter Review and Assessment, and Literature)

Social Studies Objectives
1. Examine different types of states.
2. Investigate types of government.
3. Learn about alliances and international organizations.

Reading/Language Arts Objective
Recognize contrast signal words to understand how things are different.

Prepare to Read

Build Background Knowledge
Discuss different types of leaders.

Set a Purpose for Reading
Have students evaluate statements on the *Reading Readiness Guide*.

Preview Key Terms
Teach the section's Key Terms.

Target Reading Skill
Introduce the section's Target Reading Skill of **recognizing contrast signal words.**

Instructional Resources

All in One Foundations of Geography Teaching Resources
- **L2** Reading Readiness Guide, p. 174
- **L2** Identify Contrasts, p. 178

Differentiated Instruction

Spanish Reading and Vocabulary Study Guide
- **L1** Chapter 3 Section 4, pp. 23–24 ELL

Instruct

Target Reading Skill
Review **using contrast signal words.**

Types of States
Discuss characteristics of different kinds of states.

Types of Government
Compare and contrast different types of government.

International Organizations
Discuss the purpose of alliances and international organizations.

Instructional Resources

All in One Foundations of Geography Teaching Resources
- **L2** Guided Reading and Review, p. 175
- **L2** Reading Readiness Guide, p. 174

Foundations of Geography Transparencies
- **L2** Section Reading Support Transparency FG 52
- **L2** Transparency B3: Tree Map/Flow Chart

Differentiated Instruction

All in One Foundations of Geography Teaching Resources
- **L3** Your Government Has Returned to You! pp. 189–190 AR, GT
- **L2** Creating Paragraph Outlines, p. 195 AR, GT, LPR, SN

Teacher's Edition
- **L3** For Advanced Readers, TE p. 82

Spanish Support
- **L2** Guided Reading and Review (Spanish), p. 24 ELL

Assess and Reteach

Assess Progress
Evaluate student comprehension with the section assessment and section quiz.

Reteach
Assign the Reading and Vocabulary Study Guide to help struggling students.

Extend
Extend the lesson by having students research alliances or international organizations from the section.

Instructional Resources

All in One Foundations of Geography Teaching Resources
- **L2** Section Quiz, p. 176
  Rubric for Assessing a Writing Assignment, p. 197
- **L2** Vocabulary Development, p. 196
- **L2** Word Knowledge, p. 180
  Rubric for Assessing a Bar Graph, p. 198
- **L2** Chapter Tests A and B, pp. 199–204

Reading and Vocabulary Study Guide
- **L3** Chapter 3 Section 4 pp. 31–33

Differentiated Instruction

All in One Foundations of Geography Teaching Resources
- **L3** Hatchet, pp. 191–194 AR, GT

Spanish Support
- **L2** Section Quiz (Spanish), p. 25 ELL
- **L2** Chapter Summary (Spanish), p. 26 ELL
- **L2** Vocabulary Development (Spanish), p. 27 ELL

Key
- **L1** Basic to Average
- **L3** Average to Advanced
- **L2** For All Students

- LPR Less Proficient Readers
- AR Advanced Readers
- SN Special Needs Students

- GT Gifted and Talented
- ELL English Language Learners

Professional Development

Reading Background

Structured Silent Reading

In this chapter, students will use the Structured Silent Reading technique. To achieve success, always pose a question for students to answer when they finish reading. If students have trouble reading large sections, break the text into chunks of one to four paragraphs, and give students a question to answer for each one. You may ask students to preview the Reading Check question for a selection and then read to find the answer. Students may also preview the headings to develop their own questions before they read.

Model this approach using the paragraph under the heading *New Population Clusters* on page 61 of the Student Edition. Point out that headings in the text are a good place to start when thinking of a question. Think aloud: *The heading for this paragraph is "New Population Clusters." Population means people, and clusters means groups. It must be about how groups of people came to be. So I am going to read to answer this question: "How did new groups of population form?"*

Have students use this method for other selections. Suggest to students that they write down their questions before reading.

Key Terms

Tell students that the Key Terms in Chapter 3 often appear in the news. Challenge them to find at least three of these Key Terms from the chapter used in their daily lives:

population, immigrants, urbanization, capitalism, developing nations

Encourage students to look at newspapers and magazines, listen to the radio, and watch television to find uses of these words. As "evidence," have them bring in a newspaper clipping with the word or write down the sentence in which the word was used during a radio or television broadcast, and note the time and date of the broadcast.

World Studies Background

People Counting People

Demography can trace its beginnings to the work of an English scholar named John Graunt. In 1662, Graunt published his then unique analysis of over fifty years of death and baptism records. During the next century, nations began conducting basic censuses. In 1790, the United States government conducted the first nation-wide census for a political purpose; the Constitution mandates that a census of the United States be taken every ten years because population determines representation in the House of Representatives. The idea caught on, and Britain took its first census in 1801. In 1953, China became the last major area to release its census data. Today, demographers have access to vital statistics such as births, deaths, and marriages, and to census data from virtually the entire world.

Worldwide Urbanization

Urbanization is a worldwide trend, although high levels of urbanization are becoming more common in developing countries. The top ten largest urban centers in 1975 were all in developed countries, including New York, Paris, France, and Beijing, China. In 2000, four of the top ten urban centers were in the developing nations of India and Bangladesh.

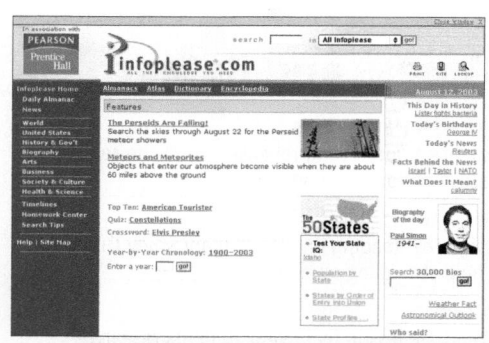

Infoplease® provides a wealth of useful information for the classroom. You can use this resource to strengthen your background on the subjects covered in this chapter. Have students visit this advertising-free site as a starting point for projects requiring research.

Use Web code **led-3304** for **Infoplease**.

Discussion Ideas

Discussing what students have read is important for them to absorb information. Empower students by having them provide topics for discussion. Explain that they must begin with a strong idea, or seed, to spark a good discussion. The following questions will motivate students to come up with strong seeds for discussion:

What don't I understand?
What have I learned that I did not know before?
What is interesting or surprising?
What words are confusing?
What reminds me of other things I know?

Write the questions on the board, and have students read *Population Growth* on pages 64–66 of the Student Edition. Ask students to answer one of the questions above on an index card. *(For example: I am surprised that large increases in population could drain Earth of its resources. I wonder what we can do to prevent that from happening?)* When students have finished, put the index cards into a bowl. Have students take turns pulling one out and reading it to the class, and discuss each one for five minutes.

Making Choices

Help students to build their understanding of Key Terms and high-use words from the chapter by asking them to make choices between correct and incorrect examples of the words.

Word: *vary*
Example 1: I eat something different for lunch every day. *(correct)*
Example 2: I always eat chicken for dinner.

Word: *immigrants*
Example 1: People move from the country to the city looking for jobs.
Example 2: Many people move from Mexico to the United States each year. *(correct)*

Word: *consumer*
Example 1: Nancy sells her food at the grocery store.
Example 2: Nancy buys her food at the grocery store. *(correct)*

Word: *dispute*
Example 1: Frank argued with his brother over who would play with the toy. *(correct)*
Example 2: Frank and his brother shared the toy.

UNICEF

One of the best-known organizations in the world is UNICEF, the United Nations Children's Fund. Originally created in 1946 to feed the starving children of postwar Europe and China, it was so successful that it was made a permanent organization in 1953. The organization has grown into a powerful and compassionate group of over 7,000 people working in 158 countries "to overcome the obstacles that poverty, violence, disease and discrimination place in a child's path." UNICEF provides food, vaccinations, and education to children around the world, but focuses its efforts on improving the lives of children in developing nations.

Thomas Malthus

In 1798, English writer Thomas Malthus published a book on population. Malthus expressed concern that the world's population was growing too quickly. He believed that future generations would not be able to raise enough food to keep up with population growth. He predicted widespread misery and starvation unless population growth slowed. Although some of Malthus's ideas have been substantiated, others have proven incorrect.

Guiding Questions

Remind students about the Guiding Questions introduced at the beginning of this section.

Section 1 relates to **Guiding Question** ⑤

How do people use the world's natural resources? *(Many forests are disappearing as the growing world population uses trees for wood and fuel.)*

Section 2 relates to **Guiding Question** ②

How have people's ways of life changed over time? *(Since the 1800s, more people have moved from the countryside to cities.)*

Section 3 relates to **Guiding Question** ⑤

How do people use the world's natural resources? *(Some developing nations sell natural resources, such as oil, to developed nations.)*

Section 4 relates to **Guiding Question** ④

What types of government exist in the world today? *(States are controlled by different types of governments. These include absolute monarchies, dicatorships, oligarchies, constitutional monarchies, and representative democracies.)*

⦿ Target Reading Skill

In this chapter, students will learn and apply the reading skill of comparing and contrasting. Use the following worksheets to help students practice this skill:

▷ **All in One Foundations of Geography Teaching Resources,** *Compare and Contrast,* p. 177; *Identify Contrasts,* p. 178; *Make Comparisons,* p. 179

Chapter Preview

This chapter will introduce you to Earth's human geography, or the patterns of human activity on Earth.

Section 1
Population

Section 2
Migration

Section 3
Economic Systems

Section 4
Political Systems

 Target Reading Skill

Comparison and Contrast In this chapter you will focus on the text structure by learning how to compare and contrast. Comparing and contrasting can help you to sort out and analyze information.

▶ **Woman harvesting rice on a terrace built by people in southern China**

Bibliography

For the Teacher

Gilbert, Geoffrey. *World Population: A Reference Handbook.* ABC-CLIO, 2001.

Pinder, John. *The European Union: A Very Short Introduction.* Oxford University Press, 2001.

Spellman, William M. *The Global Community: Migration and the Making of the Modern World.* Sutton Publishing, 2002.

For the Student

L1 Giesecke, Ernestine. *Governments Around the World (Kid's Guide).* Heinemean Library, 2000.

L2 Press, Petra. *European Union.* World Almanac, 2003.

L3 Tarsitano, Frank. *United Nations.* World Almanac, 2003.

Chapter 3 59

Using the Visual

Reach Into Your Background Ask students to study the photograph on pp. 58–59. Direct their attention to the caption. Tell students that in this chapter they will learn about the world's urban and rural populations, or populations in cities and the countryside. Ask them if they live in an urban or rural community. Ask students if they think the woman in the picture lives in an urban or rural area. How do they know? (*The woman probably lives in a rural area because she is working on a farm.*)

Chapter Resources

Teaching Resources
- L2 Vocabulary Development, p. 196
- L2 Skills for Life, p. 182
- L2 Chapter Tests A and B, pp. 199–204

Spanish Support
- L2 Spanish Chapter Summary, p. 26
- L2 Spanish Vocabulary Development, p. 27

Media and Technology
- L1 Student Edition on Audio CD
- L1 Guided Reading Audiotapes, English and Spanish
- L2 Social Studies Skills Tutor CD-ROM
- *ExamView Test Bank CD-ROM*

PRENTICE HALL
Presentation EXPRESS™
Teach · Connect · Inspire

Teach this chapter's content using the PresentationExpress™ CD-ROM including:
- slide shows
- transparencies
- interactive maps and media
- *ExamView*® QuickTake Presenter

Objectives

Social Studies

1. Learn about population distribution.
2. Explore population density.
3. Investigate population growth.

Reading/Language Arts

Compare and contrast to analyze information.

Prepare to Read

Build Background Knowledge L2

Tell students that in this section they will learn about where on Earth people live, and why they might choose to live there. To introduce the topic, write the names of two locations in your state with which students will be familiar. One should have a high population density and one should have a low population density. Ask students to predict in which location more people live and in which location less people live and why, then conduct an Idea Wave (TE, p.T35) to get students to share their ideas. After they read the section, ask them if their predictions were correct.

Set a Purpose for Reading L2

- Preview the Objectives.

- Read each statement in the *Reading Readiness Guide* aloud. Ask students to mark the statements true or false.

    All in One Foundations of Geography Teaching Resources, *Reading Readiness Guide,* p. 162

- Have students discuss the statements in pairs or groups of four, then mark their worksheets again. Use the Numbered Heads participation strategy (TE, p. T36) to call on students to share their group's perspectives.

Vocabulary Builder
Preview Key Terms L2

Pronounce each Key Term, and then ask students to say the word with you. Provide a simple explanation such as, "Demography is the study of where people live and why."

Prepare to Read

Objectives

In this section you will

1. Learn about population distribution.
2. Explore population density.
3. Investigate population growth.

Taking Notes

Copy the concept web below. As you read this section, fill in the web with information about the causes and effects of population density and of population growth. Add more ovals as needed.

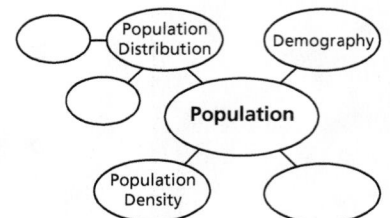

 **Target Reading Skill**

Comparison and Contrast Comparing and contrasting can help you sort out information. When you compare, you examine the similarities between things. When you contrast, you look at the differences. As you read this section, compare and contrast population distribution and population density. Look for the similarities and differences between these two concepts.

Key Terms

- **population** (pahp yuh LAY shun) *n.* total number of people in an area

- **population distribution** (pahp yuh LAY shun dis trih BYOO shun) *n.* the way the population is spread out over an area
- **demography** (dih MAH gruh fee) *n.* the science that studies population distribution and change
- **population density** (pahp yuh LAY shun DEN suh tee) *n.* the average number of people per square mile or square kilometer
- **birthrate** (BURTH rayt) *n.* the number of live births each year per 1,000 people
- **death rate** (deth rayt) *n.* the number of deaths each year per 1,000 people

A crowded village on the Nile River near Aswan, Egypt

60 Foundations of Geography

Population Distribution

The world's **population,** or total number of people, lives in uneven clusters on Earth's surface. Some places have many people. Other places are almost empty. **Population distribution** is the way the population is spread out over an area.

Demography is the science that tries to explain how populations change and why population distribution is uneven. Demographers study rates of birth, marriage, and death. And they ask why people move from one place to another.

Population and Places People usually don't move without a good reason. People may move because they can live better in a new place. Other times, people are forced to move, or they move because they cannot feed their families. However, as long as people can make a living where they are, they usually stay in that area. So, regions with large populations tend to keep them.

 **Target Reading Skill** L2

Compare and Contrast Point out the Target Reading Skill. Tell students that when they compare and contrast information, they identify similarities and differences.

Provide an example of comparing and contrasting by reading the paragraph on p. 63, and then identifying the similarities and differences between Japan and Canada. (*Similarities: Both countries have populations in the millions. Differences: Canada is huge in land area, yet has a population of 32 million people, and a population density of about 9 people per square mile; Japan is small in land area and has a population of 127 million people.*)

Give students *Compare and Contrast.* Have them complete the activity in groups.

All in One Foundations of Geography Teaching Resources, *Compare and Contrast,* p. 177

Population and History In the past, most people lived on farms where they grew their own food. They lived where the climate provided enough water and warm weather to support crops. Regions with a long history of farming, good soil, and plenty of water became crowded. These regions still have large populations. Most places too cold or too dry for farming still have small populations.

New Population Clusters However, after about 1800, improved transportation and new ways of making a living changed things. Railroads and steamships made it easier for people to move long distances, even across oceans. New jobs in factories and offices meant that more people were living in cities, where they could make a living without farming the land. Crowded cities grew in regions that once had few people, such as the United States, Australia, and northern Europe.

Villages in France have grown through centuries of farming.

✓ Reading Check **Why are some parts of the world more crowded than others?**

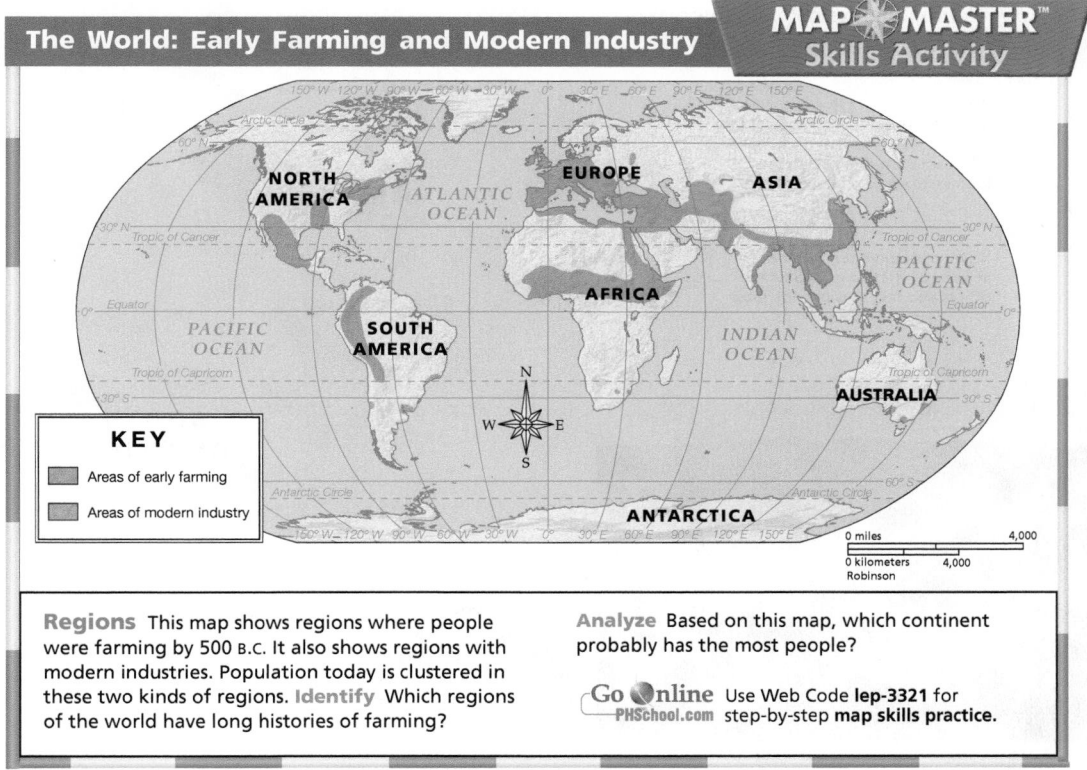

The World: Early Farming and Modern Industry

MAP MASTER™ Skills Activity

KEY
- Areas of early farming
- Areas of modern industry

Regions This map shows regions where people were farming by 500 B.C. It also shows regions with modern industries. Population today is clustered in these two kinds of regions. **Identify** Which regions of the world have long histories of farming?

Analyze Based on this map, which continent probably has the most people?

Go Online PHSchool.com Use Web Code **lep-3321** for step-by-step **map skills practice.**

Chapter 3 Section 1 **61**

Instruct

Population Distribution
L2

Guided Instruction

- **Vocabulary Builder** Clarify the high-use word **cluster** before reading.

- Read Population Distribution using the Structured Silent Reading strategy (TE, p. T34).

- Discuss with students why some regions of the world have larger populations than others. Ask **What do regions with larger populations have in common?** *(Generally, they are regions with good soil and plenty of water.)*

- Ask **How did changes in technology affect the distribution of population?** *(The inventions of railroads and steamships made it easier for people to move long distances; the development of factories meant that people did not need to live on land where they could farm to make a living; cities began to develop as people moved to obtain jobs in the new industries.)*

Independent Practice

Have students create the Taking Notes concept web on a blank piece of paper. Then have them begin to fill in the ovals with the information they have just learned. Briefly model how to fill in the graphic organizer by adding one detail about population distribution or demography.

Monitor Progress

As students fill in the graphic organizer, circulate and make sure that individuals are choosing the correct details. Provide assistance as needed.

Answers

✓ Reading Check Some parts of the world are more crowded because they have good soil and plenty of water for farming or cities have grown up there.

MAP MASTER Skills Activity **Identify** parts of North America, South America, Europe, Asia, Africa **Analyze** Asia

Go Online PHSchool.com Students may practice their map skills using the interactive online version of this map.

Compare and Contrast As a follow up, ask students to answer the Target Reading Skill question in the Student Edition. *(Population density is the average number of people who live in a square mile or square kilometer. Population distribution is the number of people who actually live in an area.)*

Population Density `L2`

Guided Instruction

- **Vocabulary Builder** Clarify the high-use word **vary** before reading.

- With students, read about the differences between population density and distribution in Population Density.

- Ask **What is population density?** *(the average number of people living in one square mile or square kilometer)* **How does this differ from population distribution?** *(Population distribution gives actual numbers of people for an area.)*

- Have students find the region where their community is located on the map on pages 62 and 63. Discuss whether your area has a high or low population density. Then have students speculate why. *(Answers will vary, but student answers should give the general population density for their community and why.)*

Compare and Contrast How is population density different from population distribution?

Population Density

How many people live in your neighborhood? How big is that neighborhood? If you take the population of an area and divide it by the size of that area in square miles or square kilometers, you can get a sense of how crowded or empty that area is. The average number of people per square mile or square kilometer is called **population density.**

Population distribution and population density both describe where people live. Population density differs from population distribution, however, because it gives an average number of people for an area. Population distribution gives actual numbers of people for an area.

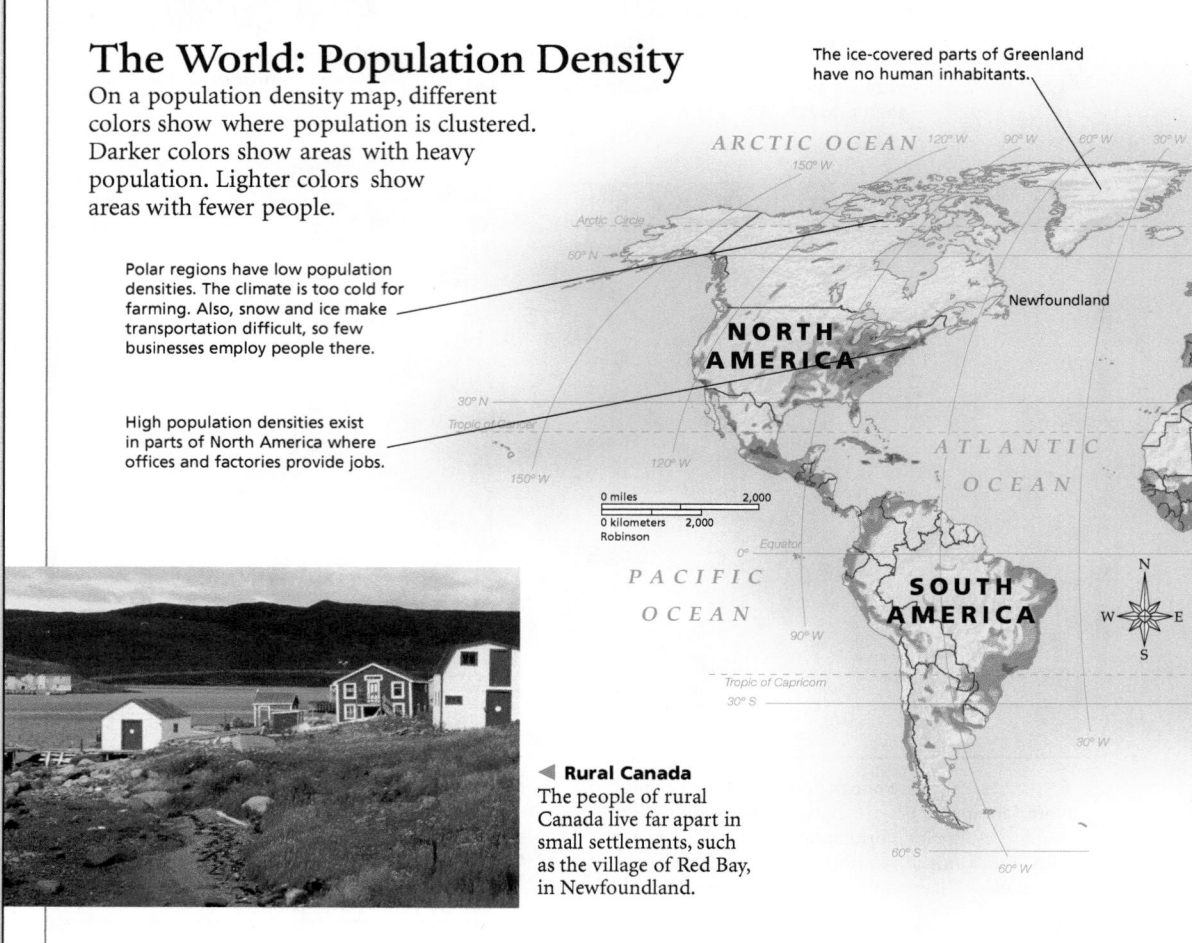

The World: Population Density

On a population density map, different colors show where population is clustered. Darker colors show areas with heavy population. Lighter colors show areas with fewer people.

The ice-covered parts of Greenland have no human inhabitants.

Polar regions have low population densities. The climate is too cold for farming. Also, snow and ice make transportation difficult, so few businesses employ people there.

High population densities exist in parts of North America where offices and factories provide jobs.

ARCTIC OCEAN

NORTH AMERICA

Newfoundland

ATLANTIC OCEAN

PACIFIC OCEAN

SOUTH AMERICA

0 miles 2,000
0 kilometers 2,000
Robinson

Tropic of Capricorn

◄ **Rural Canada**
The people of rural Canada live far apart in small settlements, such as the village of Red Bay, in Newfoundland.

62 Foundations of Geography

Differentiated Instruction

For Less Proficient Readers `L1`

Have students read this section in the Reading and Vocabulary Study Guide. This version provides basic-level instruction in an interactive format with questions and write-on lines.

📖 Chapter 3, Section 1, **Western Hemisphere Reading and Vocabulary Study Guide,** pp. 22–24

For Special Needs Students `L1`

Have students read the section as they listen to the recording on the Student Edition on Audio CD. Check for comprehension by pausing the CD and asking students to share their answers to the Reading Check questions.

⊙ Chapter 3, Section 1, **Student Edition on Audio CD**

Population density varies from one area to another. In a country with a high density, such as Japan, people are crowded together. Almost half of Japan's 127 million people live on only 17 percent of the land, or an area the size of West Virginia. In Tokyo, there is a population density of more than 25,000 people per square mile (9,664 per square kilometer). In contrast, Canada has a low overall population density. It has about 9 people per square mile (3 per square kilometer). Canada is bigger than the United States, but has only about one ninth as many people.

√ Reading Check **Which has a higher population density, a city or an area in the countryside?**

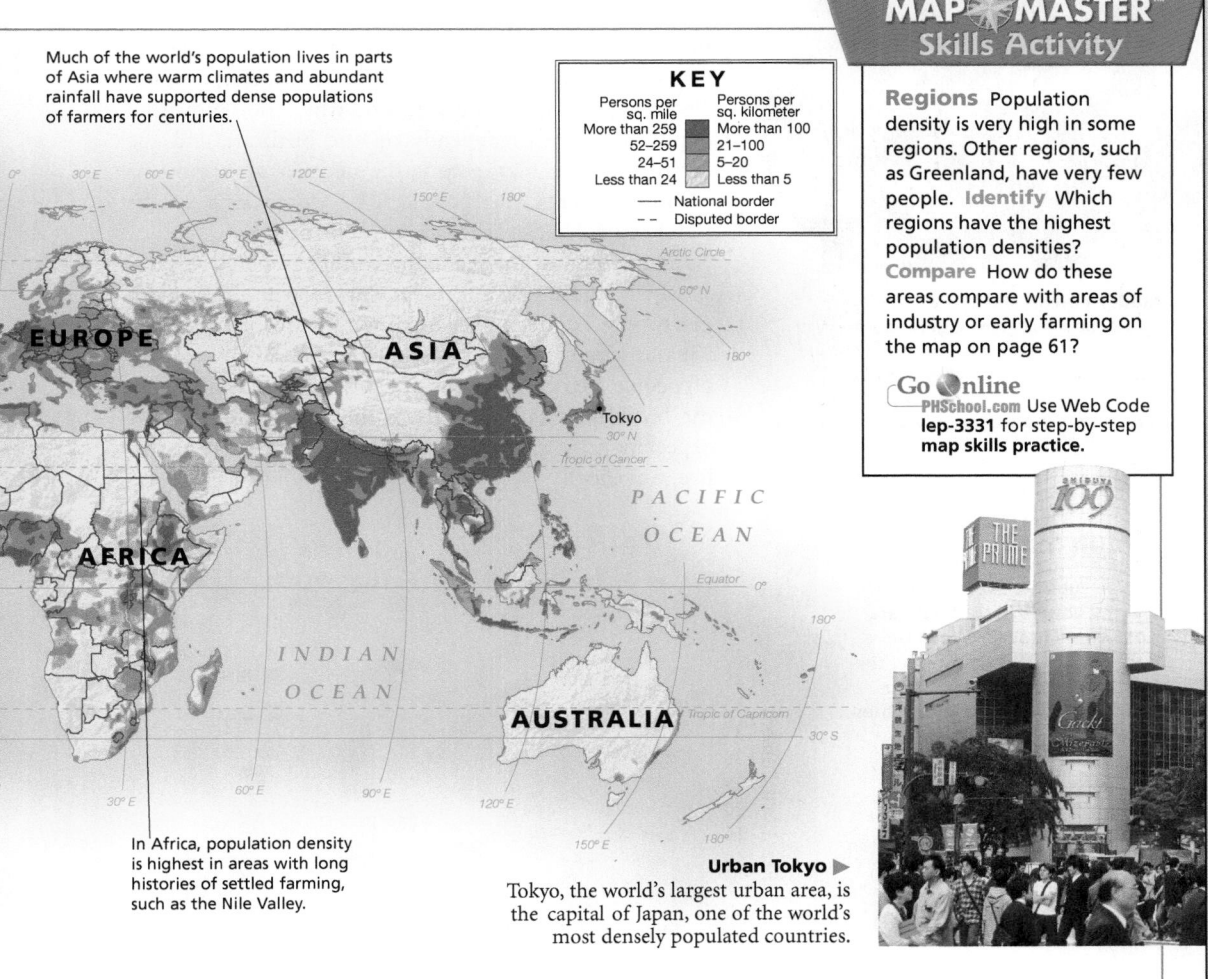

Much of the world's population lives in parts of Asia where warm climates and abundant rainfall have supported dense populations of farmers for centuries.

KEY

Persons per sq. mile	Persons per sq. kilometer
More than 259	More than 100
52–259	21–100
24–51	5–20
Less than 24	Less than 5

— National border
-- Disputed border

EUROPE
ASIA
AFRICA
• Tokyo
PACIFIC OCEAN
INDIAN OCEAN
AUSTRALIA

In Africa, population density is highest in areas with long histories of settled farming, such as the Nile Valley.

Urban Tokyo ▶
Tokyo, the world's largest urban area, is the capital of Japan, one of the world's most densely populated countries.

MAP MASTER™ Skills Activity

Regions Population density is very high in some regions. Other regions, such as Greenland, have very few people. **Identify** Which regions have the highest population densities? **Compare** How do these areas compare with areas of industry or early farming on the map on page 61?

Go Online
PHSchool.com Use Web Code **lep-3331** for step-by-step **map skills practice.**

Chapter 3 Section 1 **63**

Differentiated Instruction

For Gifted and Talented   L3
Have students do research to gather information about population densities for their community, state, and the United States. Then have them create a table showing this information.

For Less Proficient Readers   L1
Remind students that it is important to

read the captions that appear with pictures or photographs. Direct students' attention to the captions on pages 62 and 63. Have students reread them to find one noun to describe what is shown, and one adjective that describes the climate or vegetation.

When students are finished, ask them to describe one of the photographs without referring to its caption.

Population Growth

Guided Instruction

- **Vocabulary Builder** Clarify the high-use words **method** and **aspect** before reading.

- Read how the world's human population has grown and changed over time in Population Growth.

- Ask **What does population growth depend on?** *(birthrate and death rate)* Then ask **What are birthrate and death rate?** *(Birthrate is the number of live births each year per 1,000 people; death rate is the number of deaths each year per 1,000 people.)*

- Have students study the Birth and Death Rates in Selected Countries, 2006 bar graph on page 64. Then have them predict what kinds of challenges a country like Yemen might face with such a high birthrate and a low death rate. *(Answers will vary, but students should mention that it might become difficult to provide enough food, water, housing, public services, and education for so many people; the environment might also suffer.)*

- Have students look at the line graph of World Population Growth A.D. 1200–2000 on page 65. Ask **About how much has the population increased in the last 100 years?** *(about 4.5 billion)* Ask **How has the development of modern science affected the recent population growth?** *(New farming methods have increased the world's food supply; scientific advances in health and medicine have allowed people to live longer.)*

Modern Medicine
This Rwandan refugee is getting a measles vaccination in Tanzania. Modern medicine has lengthened lifespans worldwide.
Analyze *Does vaccination raise birth rates or lower death rates? Explain why.*

■ Graph Skills

If you subtract deaths from births, you get a country's rate of natural growth. When there are more deaths than births, the native-born population drops. **Identify** Which of the countries shown here has the highest birthrate? **Compare** Where is the population growing, Russia or the United States?

Population Growth

Suppose that all the years from A.D. 1 to A.D. 2000 took place in a single day. As the day began at midnight, there would be 300 million people in the world. Twelve hours later, at noon, there would be just 310 million people. By 8:24 P.M., the population would double to 600 million. It would double again by 10:05 P.M. to 1.2 billion. By 11:20, it would double again to 2.4 billion, and then double yet again by 11:48 to 4.8 billion, before reaching 6 billion as the day ended at midnight. As you can see, the world's population has grown very quickly in recent times. There are several reasons for this rapid growth.

Birthrates and Death Rates At different times in history, populations have grown at different rates. Demographers want to understand why. They know that population growth depends on the birthrate and the death rate. The **birthrate** is the number of live births each year per 1,000 people. The **death rate** is the number of deaths each year per 1,000 people.

For thousands of years, the world's population grew slowly. In those years, farmers worked without modern machinery. Food supplies often were scarce. People lived without clean water or waste removal. Many millions of people died of infectious diseases. As a result, although the birthrate was high, so was the death rate. The life expectancy, or the average number of years that people live, was short.

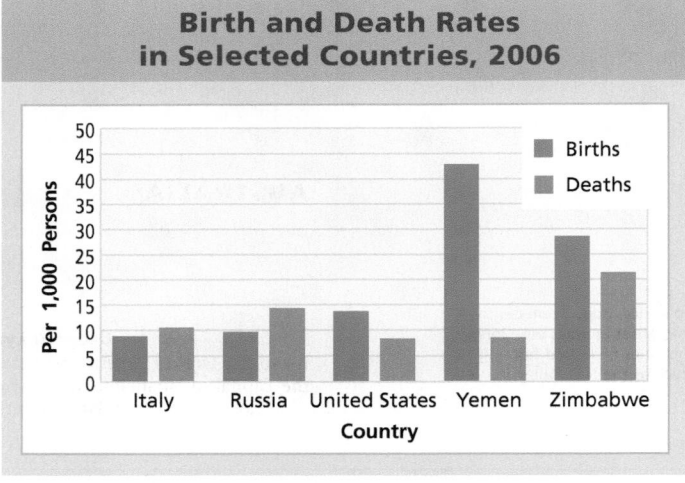

Birth and Death Rates in Selected Countries, 2006

(Bar graph: Per 1,000 Persons (y-axis, 0–50) vs. Country (x-axis). Legend: Births, Deaths.)

Italy, Russia, United States, Yemen, Zimbabwe

Differentiated Instruction

For Gifted and Talented L3

Have students explore the concepts of demographics and statistics further by completing *Analyzing Statistics*.

All in One Foundations of Geography Teaching Resources, *Analyzing Statistics,* p. 187

For Advanced Readers L3

To gain a better understanding of how population growth can affect the environment, assign students the *Enrichment* activity. Have students complete the activity in pairs.

All in One Foundations of Geography Teaching Resources, *Enrichment,* p. 181

Answers

Analyze Vaccinations lower death rates by improving people's immunity to disease, and therefore their life expectancy.
Graph Skills Identify Yemen
Compare the United States

Reasons for Population Growth Today This all changed after the 1700s. Death rates dropped sharply. In some countries, birthrates increased. As a result, populations have grown very fast. In some countries, the population has doubled in less than 20 years. Meanwhile, people live longer than ever. In the United States, people born in 1900 could expect to live for 47 years. Today, they can expect to live for 77 years.

Scientific progress explains much of this change. First, new farming methods have increased the world's food supply. Scientists have improved important food crops and found new ways to protect crops against insects. Scientists have also found ways to raise crops with less water. These recent scientific improvements in agriculture are called the Green Revolution.

The second set of scientific advances has come in health and medicine. Scientists have convinced local governments to provide clean drinking water and sanitary waste removal. These measures sharply reduce disease. Researchers have also developed vaccines to prevent disease and antibiotics to fight infections. As a result, people live many more years.

Due to a high birthrate and a low death rate, Yemen's population is skyrocketing.

Graph Skills

In recent centuries, population growth has soared. There are now 18 times as many people as there were 600 years ago. **Identify** Around what year did the world's population begin to rise rapidly? **Analyze a Graph** Looking at this graph, how can you tell that the world's population rose more quickly in recent years than in earlier centuries?

World Population Growth, 1200–2000

SOURCE: United States Census Bureau

Chapter 3 Section 1 **65**

Independent Practice
Have students complete their concept webs using the information in this section.

Monitor Progress
- When students are finished with their concept webs, show *Section Reading Support Transparency FG 49* and ask students to check their work individually. Go over key concepts and clarify key vocabulary as needed.

  📖 **Foundations of Geography Transparencies,** *Section Reading Support Transparency FG 49*

- Tell students to fill in the last column of their *Reading Readiness Guides*. Probe for what they learned that confirms or invalidates each statement.

  All in One **Foundations of Geography Teaching Resources,** *Reading Readiness Guide,* p. 162

Assess and Reteach

Assess Progress   L2
Have students complete the Section Assessment. Then administer the *Section Quiz.*

  All in One **Foundations of Geography Teaching Resources,** *Section Quiz,* p. 164

Reteach   L1
If students need more instruction, have them read this section in the Reading and Vocabulary Study Guide.

  📖 Chapter 3, Section 1, **Western Hemisphere Reading and Vocabulary Study Guide,** pp. 22–24

Skills Mini Lesson

Analyzing Graphic Data

1. Point out that information is often given in the form of charts and graphs. Tell students that charts and graphs can help them see information quickly, and can also help them draw conclusions.

2. Refer students to the bar graph on page 64. Have them practice the skill by identifying the title of the graph, the labels, and any similarities or differences they notice in the information being presented in the graph. Then have them draw a conclusion about the populations of the countries shown on the graph.

3. Have students apply the skill by identifying the parts of the graph on this page and drawing conclusions from the information illustrated on the graph.

Answers

Graph Skills **Identify** 1800 **Analyze a Graph** because of the steep upward movement of the line between 1900 and 2000

Extend

To extend the lesson, have students complete the *Evaluating Solutions* Internet activity to learn about possible solutions to the problem of overpopulation. Then have them answer the questions and partner with another student to create a chart of the options discussed.

Go Online PHSchool.com **For:** Environmental and Global Issues: *Evaluating Solutions*
Visit: PHSchool.com
Web Code: led-3300

Answers

Infer Jobs, schools, and adequate housing may also be scarce.

✓ **Reading Check** Developments such as better farming methods and advances in health and medicine have led to a population increase.

Section 1 Assessment

Key Terms

Students' sentences should reflect an understanding of each Key Term.

Target Reading Skill

Similar: Both are used to measure and study demographics. Different: Population density is the average number of people who live in a given space; population distribution is the actual number of people who live in an area.

Comprehension and Critical Thinking

1. (a) areas with good soil and plenty of water **(b)** With advances in methods of transportation, people were able to move to other places; as industry developed, people did not need to farm to provide food and could move to work in places with factories. **(c)** Today more people live in cities than in the countryside.

2. (a) the average number of people living in a square mile or square kilometer **(b)** total population and land area.

Overcrowding in Bangladesh
These Bangladeshis are returning from a festival. Bangladesh's population has grown faster than its public services. This results in overcrowding, as seen on this train. **Infer** *What other aspects of life in Bangladesh might be affected by rapid population growth?*

The Challenges of Population Growth Today, food supplies have increased and people live longer. Even so, people in many countries still face serious problems. Some nations, such as those in Southwest Asia, do not have enough fresh water. In parts of Asia and Africa, the population is growing faster than the food supply. Often, these countries do not have enough money to buy food elsewhere.

Population growth puts pressure on all aspects of life. The populations of many countries are increasing so fast that not everyone can find jobs. There are not enough schools to educate the growing number of children. Decent housing is scarce. Public services such as transportation and sanitation are inadequate.

Rapid population growth also affects the environment. For instance, forests in many countries are disappearing. People in poorer countries cut down the trees for wood and fuel. Clearing forests causes other problems. In a forest, tree roots hold soil in place, and forest soils soak up rain. With the forest gone, heavy rainfall may wash away the soil and cause dangerous floods. Demand for wood and fuel in wealthier countries also uses up the world's scarce resources. All of Earth's people must work to meet this challenge.

✓ **Reading Check** **Why have populations risen rapidly in recent times?**

Section 1 Assessment

Key Terms

Review the key terms at the beginning of this section. Use each term in a sentence that explains its meaning.

Target Reading Skill

How are population density and population distribution similar? How are they different?

Comprehension and Critical Thinking

1. (a) Recall In what parts of the world did most people live before modern times?
(b) Explain How does history help explain population distribution today?

(c) Contrast How is population distribution today different from the days before modern science was developed?
2. (a) Define What is population density?
(b) Transfer Information To figure out the population density of an area, what two pieces of information do you need?
3. (a) Recall How has population growth changed in 100 years?
(b) Explain What accounts for this change?
(c) Identify Cause and Effect What are the effects of this change in population growth?

Writing Activity

Suppose that you are a demographer studying the area where you live. How does population density vary across your area? Where is population growth taking place? Write a short description of your area's demography.

Go Online PHSchool.com
For: An activity on population
Visit: PHSchool.com
Web Code: led-3301

66 *Foundations of Geography*

3. (a) Population growth has been huge in the last 100 years. **(b)** advances in health and medicine and improved farming methods **(c)** Effects can include lack of jobs, schools, and public services and dangers to the environment.

Writing Activity

Use the *Rubric for Assessing a Writing Assignment* to evaluate students' descriptions of local demography.

All in One Foundations of Geography Teaching Resources, *Rubric for Assessing a Writing Assignment*, p. 197

Go Online PHSchool.com Typing in the Web code when prompted will bring students directly to detailed instructions for this activity.

2 Migration

Prepare to Read

Objectives
In this section you will
1. Learn about migration, or people's movement from one region to another.
2. Investigate urbanization, or people's movement to cities.

Taking Notes
Copy the chart below. As you read this section, fill in the chart with information about voluntary and involuntary migration and about urbanization.

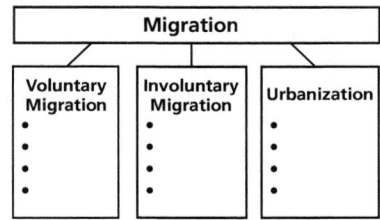

Migration
- Voluntary Migration
  - •
  - •
  - •
  - •
- Involuntary Migration
  - •
  - •
  - •
  - •
- Urbanization
  - •
  - •
  - •
  - •

Target Reading Skill

Identify Contrasts
When you contrast two situations, you examine how they differ. Although both voluntary and involuntary migration involve the movement of people, the reasons for that movement differ. As you read, list the differences between voluntary and involuntary migration.

Key Terms
- **migration** (my GRAY shun) *n.* the movement of people from one place or region to another
- **immigrants** (IM uh grunts) *n.* people who move into one country from another
- **urbanization** (ur bun ih ZAY shun) *n.* the movement of people to cities, and the growth of cities
- **rural** (ROOR ul) *adj.* located in the countryside
- **urban** (UR bun) *adj.* located in cities and towns

Why People Migrate

For thousands of years, people have moved to new places. People's movement from one place or region to another is called **migration**. **Immigrants** are people who move into one country from another.

In the years from 1850 to 1930, more than 30 million Europeans moved to the United States. Since 1971, more than 4.5 million people have migrated here from Mexico, and more than 2.5 million have migrated from the Caribbean islands. Since 1971, Central America, the Philippines, China, and Vietnam have all lost more than 1 million immigrants to the United States. More than 800,000 immigrants have come from both South Korea and India.

During the late 1800s and early 1900s, millions of immigrants to the United States stopped at Ellis Island in New York Harbor.

Chapter 3 Section 2 **67**

Target Reading Skill

Identify Contrasts Point out the Target Reading Skill. Tell students that identifying contrasts between two situations will help them understand how they are different.

Read the first paragraph on page 71 to students. Model identifying contrasts by pointing out that in the past most Indonesians lived in rural areas, but today the population is increasingly urban; and, in 1970 about 3.9 million people lived in Jakarta, but in 2000, 11 million people lived there.

Give students *Identify Contrasts*. Have them complete the activity in groups.

All in One Foundations of Geography Teaching Resources, *Identify Contrasts,* p. 178

Objectives
Social Studies
1. Learn about migration, or people's movement from one region to another.
2. Investigate urbanization, or people's movement to cities.

Reading/Language Arts
Identify contrasts to understand how situations differ.

Prepare to Read

Build Background Knowledge   L2
Tell students that this section is about the movement of people. Have students brainstorm a list of reasons why people might move from the countryside to the city, from one town to another, or from one country to another. Conduct an Idea Wave (TE p. T35) to elicit student responses, and then record them on the board.

Set a Purpose for Reading   L2
■ Preview the Objectives.

■ Read each statement in the *Reading Readiness Guide* aloud. Ask students to mark the statements true or false.

All in One Foundations of Geography Teaching Resources, *Reading Readiness Guide,* p. 166

■ Have students discuss the statements in pairs or groups of four, then mark their worksheets again. Use the Numbered Heads participation strategy (TE, p. T36) to call on students to share their group's perspectives.

Vocabulary Builder
Preview Key Terms   L2
Pronounce each Key Term, and then ask students to say the word with you. Provide a simple explanation such as, "New York City is urban because large numbers of people live close together there."

Instruct

Why People Migrate L2

Guided Instruction

- **Vocabulary Builder** Clarify the high-use word **theory** before reading.

- Read Why People Migrate using the Oral Cloze strategy (TE, p. T33).

- Discuss with students the push-pull theory. Ask **What is it and how does it work?** (*The theory helps explain why people migrate. It says that bad conditions "push" people to leave their countries, and good conditions in another country "pull" the people to migrate there.*)

- Ask **What kinds of things make people migrate voluntarily?** (*hunger or other difficulties, the search for a better quality of life, better jobs, and political freedom*)
What kinds of things force people to migrate involuntarily? (*punishment, enslavement, war*)

 Target Reading Skill L2

Identify Contrasts As a follow up, ask students to answer the Target Reading Skill question in the Student Edition (*Involuntary migration is when people are forced to move against their will. Voluntary migration is when people move because they want to.*)

Cubans in Little Havana
These men ordering food at a cafe are part of a large community of Cuban immigrants in Miami, Florida.
Analyze Images *What aspects of their life in Cuba have these immigrants preserved in their new home?*

Identify Contrasts
How is involuntary migration different from voluntary migration?

Voluntary Migration in the Past Voluntary migration is the movement of people by their own choice. Today, most people move by their own choice. The push-pull theory says that people migrate because difficulties "push" them to leave. At the same time, the hope for a better life "pulls" people to a new country.

The push-pull theory helps to explain the great Irish migration in the 1840s and 1850s. In those years, 1.5 million people left Ireland for the United States. What pushed so many Irish people to come to America? In the 1840s, disease destroyed Ireland's main crop—potatoes. Hunger pushed people to migrate. Job opportunities pulled Irish families to the United States.

Voluntary Migration Today The same theory explains most migration today. The main sources of migration are countries where many people are poor and jobs are few. In some countries, such as Vietnam and Central American countries, wars have made life dangerous and difficult.

In China, Vietnam, and Cuba, governments limit people's freedom. These problems push people to leave. Meanwhile, the possibility of good jobs and political freedom pulls people to the United States and other well-off, democratic countries.

Involuntary Migration Sometimes people are forced to move. Because these people do not choose to move, their movement is known as involuntary migration. During the early 1800s, the British sent prisoners to Australia to serve their sentences. When their sentences were done, many stayed. War also forces people to migrate to escape death or serious danger.

The Transatlantic Slave Trade Perhaps the biggest involuntary migration in history was the transatlantic slave trade. From the 1500s to the 1800s, millions of Africans were enslaved and taken against their will to European colonies in North and South America. These Africans traveled under inhumane conditions across the Atlantic Ocean, chained inside ships for more than a month.

At first, their descendants in the United States lived mainly on the east coast. As cotton farming spread west, many enslaved African Americans were forced to migrate again, this time to new plantations in the Mississippi Valley and Texas.

✓ **Reading Check** **Why do people migrate?**

Answers

Analyze Images They have preserved their Spanish language and possibly some types of food that might be sold at this cafe.

✓**Reading Check** Some people migrate for a better quality of life, better jobs, religious or political freedom, or safety from war or violence. Other people are forced to move through enslavement or imprisonment.

Vocabulary Builder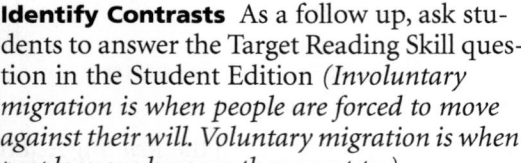

Use the information below to teach students this section's high-use words.

High-Use Word	Definition and Sample Sentence
theory, p. 68	*n.* an idea or belief about how something is done Laura's **theory** was that she would pass the test if she studied.
unique, p. 71	*adj.* being the only one; having no equal Many rain forest plants are **unique** because they are found nowhere else in the world.

Migration in South Asia

At the end of British colonial rule in 1947, most of South Asia was divided along religious lines into two countries. India had a Hindu majority. Pakistan was mainly Muslim. Fearing religious discrimination or violence, Muslims from India and Hindus from Pakistan fled across the new borders. Many died when violence broke out during these massive migrations.

MAP MASTER™
Skills Activity

Movement This map shows migrations by South Asians. **Identify** Which countries did South Asia's largest migrations involve? **Contrast** How do the reasons for movement out of South Asia differ from the reasons for migration within the region?

Go Online
PHSchool.com Use Web Code **lep-3312** for step-by-step map skills practice.

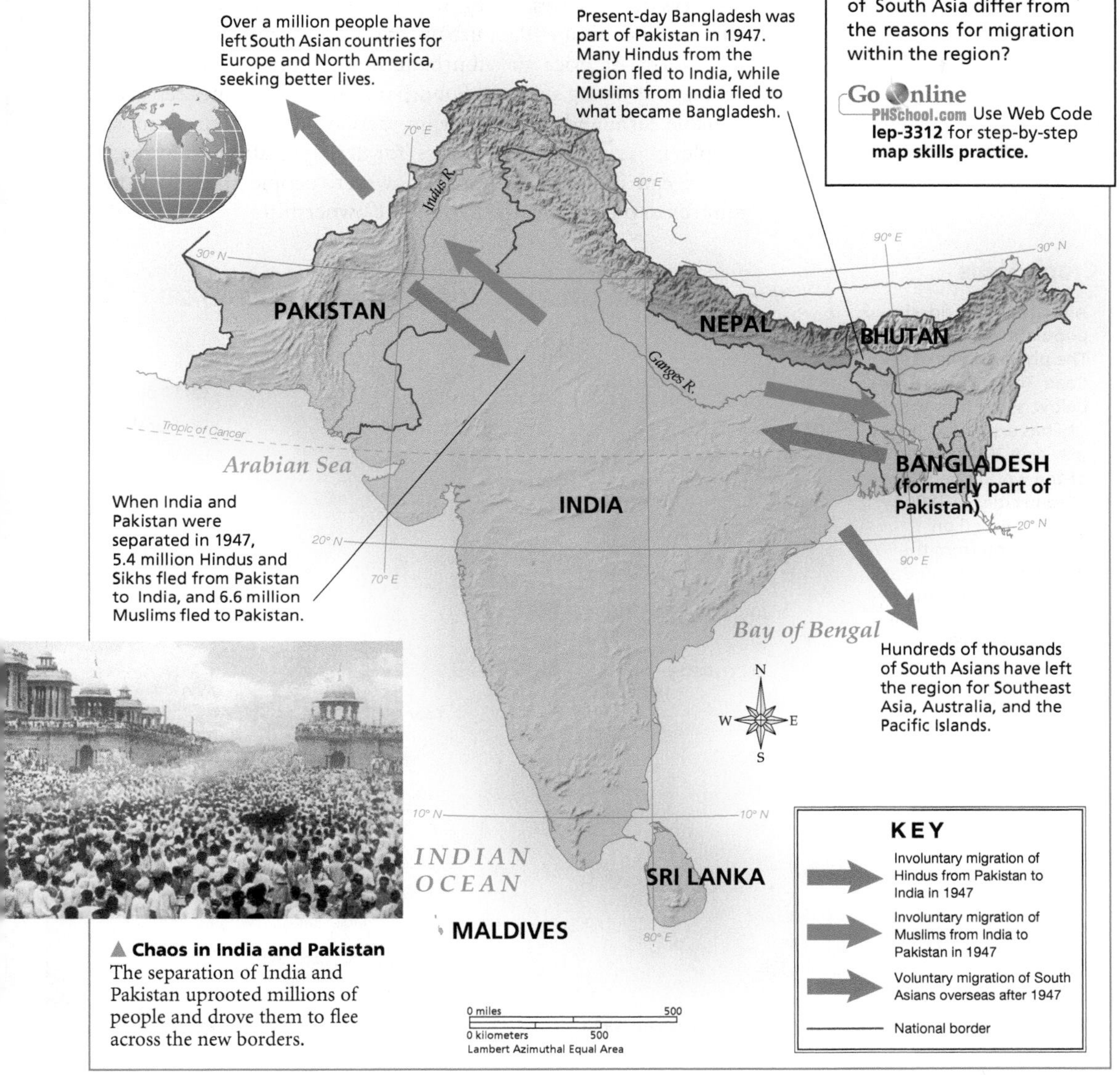

Over a million people have left South Asian countries for Europe and North America, seeking better lives.

Present-day Bangladesh was part of Pakistan in 1947. Many Hindus from the region fled to India, while Muslims from India fled to what became Bangladesh.

When India and Pakistan were separated in 1947, 5.4 million Hindus and Sikhs fled from Pakistan to India, and 6.6 million Muslims fled to Pakistan.

Indus R.

PAKISTAN

70° E

30° N

80° E

30° N

90° E

NEPAL

BHUTAN

Ganges R.

Tropic of Cancer

Arabian Sea

INDIA

20° N

70° E

BANGLADESH (formerly part of Pakistan)

20° N

90° E

Bay of Bengal

Hundreds of thousands of South Asians have left the region for Southeast Asia, Australia, and the Pacific Islands.

N W E S

10° N

10° N

INDIAN OCEAN

SRI LANKA

MALDIVES

80° E

0 miles 500
0 kilometers 500
Lambert Azimuthal Equal Area

KEY

→ Involuntary migration of Hindus from Pakistan to India in 1947

→ Involuntary migration of Muslims from India to Pakistan in 1947

→ Voluntary migration of South Asians overseas after 1947

— National border

▲ **Chaos in India and Pakistan**
The separation of India and Pakistan uprooted millions of people and drove them to flee across the new borders.

Chapter 3 Section 2 **69**

Skills for Life — Skills Mini Lesson

Identifying Frame of Reference and Point of View

1. Explain that point of view is a person's opinion about an issue. Frame of reference is a person's background and often influences a person's point of view.

2. Have students practice the skill by reviewing the information about the division of India and Pakistan. Discuss how these people's frame of reference or point of view affected their decision to migrate.

3. Have students apply the skill by identifying Krenak's frame of reference and point of view in the following selection:

All in One Foundations of Geography Teaching Resources, *Message from the Rain Forest Amerindians,* p. 188

Guided Instruction (continued)

■ Direct students' attention to the map on this page. Ask **What caused the migration of Muslims and Hindus in Southeast Asia in 1947?** *(Following the end of British colonial rule in India, most of South Asia was divided along religious lines into the countries of India and Pakistan; fearing religious discrimination or violence, Hindus and Muslims in the minority fled across the new borders.)* **Do you think this migration was voluntary or involuntary? Why?** *(Possible answer: involuntary, since people migrated to avoid possible religious persecution and violence)*

Independent Practice

Have students create the Taking Notes graphic organizer on a blank piece of paper. Model how to fill in the graphic organizer using the *Flow Chart* transparency. Students should then fill in the chart with information they have just learned.

Foundations of Geography Transparencies, *Transparency B2: Flow Chart*

Monitor Progress

As students fill in the graphic organizer, circulate and make sure that individuals are choosing the correct details. Provide assistance as needed.

Answers

MAP MASTER Skills Activity Identify India and Pakistan **Contrast** Within the region, people migrated to avoid violence and religious persecution; they migrated outside the region to seek better lives.

Go Online PHSchool.com Students may practice their map skills using the interactive online version of this map.

Urbanization L2

Guided Instruction

- **Vocabulary Builder** Clarify the high-use word **unique** before reading.

- Have students read Urbanization and study the bar graph and photos.

- Ask **What is the general trend in population movement since 1800?** *(More people are moving from rural to urban areas.)* **Why?** *(People are pulled to the city by the promise of better-paying jobs.)*

- Have students discuss some of the problems caused by rapid urbanization. *(Cities often cannot provide enough housing, jobs, schools, hospitals, and other services people need; traffic jams and crowds make it difficult for people to get around.)*

Independent Practice

Have students finish filling in their charts with details about urbanization.

Monitor Progress

- When students are finished with their charts, show *Section Reading Support Transparency FG 50* and ask students to check their work individually.

  📖 **Foundations of Geography Transparencies,** *Section Reading Support Transparency FG 50*

- Tell students to fill in the last column of their *Reading Readiness Guides.* Probe for what they learned that confirms or invalidates each statement.

  All In One Foundations of Geography Teaching Resources, *Reading Readiness Guide,* p. 166

Answers

Graph Skills Identify about 3–4 percent
Predict The urban population will probably be greater than the rural population.

Urbanization

Millions of people in many countries have migrated to cities from farms and small villages. In recent years, the population of some cities has grown tremendously. The movement of people to cities and the growth of cities is called **urbanization.**

Cities and Suburbs In Europe and North America, the growth of industry during the 1800s pulled people from the countryside to cities. They hoped for jobs in factories and offices. Since about 1950, urbanization has given way in Europe and North America to suburbanization, or the movement of people to growing suburbs. Suburbanization sometimes replaces valuable farmland with sprawling development. Because most people in suburbs rely on cars for transportation, suburban sprawl can increase pollution. However, people still move to suburbs to pursue the dream of home ownership.

▢ Graph Skills

All over the world, city populations have soared. The photographs of Cape Town, South Africa, below, show how that city has expanded.
Identify What percent of the world's people lived in cities in 1800?
Predict Based on information from the graph, how do you think the world's rural and urban populations will compare in 2050?

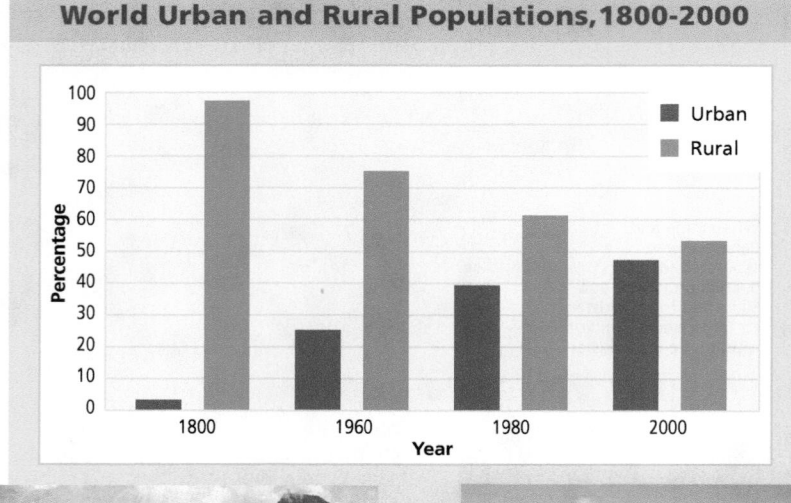

World Urban and Rural Populations, 1800-2000

Cape Town, 1938

Modern Cape Town

70 Foundations of Geography

Differentiated Instruction

For Advanced Readers L3

To help students gain better understanding about immigrants and their migrations, divide them into groups to complete the *Small Group Activity: Making an Immigration Map.*

All In One Foundations of Geography Teaching Resources, *Small Group Activity: Making an Immigration Map,* pp. 183–186

For English Language Learners L1

Students may have difficulty pronouncing some of the longer words in this section, such as *tremendously, urbanization,* and *opportunities.* Encourage students to break down these words into smaller parts to help them sound out the pronunciations.

Urbanization on Other Continents In Asia, Africa, and Latin America, people are still streaming from the countryside to growing cities. Indonesia is an example. In the past, most Indonesians lived in **rural** areas, or areas in the countryside. Recently, more and more Indonesians have moved to **urban** areas, or areas in cities and nearby towns. For example, in 1970, about 3.9 million people lived in Greater Jakarta, Indonesia's capital. By 2000, its population was about 11 million. Jakarta is not unique. Greater São Paulo, Brazil, grew from 8 million residents in 1970 to nearly 18 million residents in 2000.

The problem in cities like Jakarta and São Paulo is that too many people are moving to the city too fast. Cities cannot keep up. They cannot provide the housing, jobs, schools, hospitals, and other services that people need. Traffic jams and crowds often make getting around a struggle.

With so many daily problems, why do people flock to São Paulo and other big cities? As hard as life is in the cities, it can be even harder in the countryside, where there are few jobs and a shortage of land to farm. Most migrants to the city are seeking a better life for their families. They are looking for jobs, modern houses, and good schools. Above all, most want better lives for their children.

√ **Reading Check** How is the population of urban areas changing in Africa, Asia, and Latin America?

São Paulo, Brazil
São Paulo is Brazil's largest city.
Analyze Images *Do you think that this city has a high or a low population density?*

Section 2 Assessment

Key Terms
Review the key terms at the beginning of this section. Use each term in a sentence that explains its meaning.

Target Reading Skill
Contrast involuntary migration and voluntary migration. How are these two forms of migration different? List at least two differences between the two kinds of migration.

Comprehension and Critical Thinking
1. (a) Identify What are push factors and what are pull factors?
(b) Explain How do push factors and pull factors explain people's decision to migrate?
(c) Compare and Contrast Do push and pull factors account for involuntary migration? Explain why or why not.
2. (a) Recall What is urbanization?
(b) Identify Cause and Effect What are the causes and some of the effects of urbanization?

Writing Activity
Suppose that you are moving to the United States from one of the countries listed in the second paragraph on page 67. Write a paragraph describing your reasons for leaving that country and what attracts you to the United States.

For: An activity on migration
Visit: PHSchool.com
Web Code: led-3302

Objective
Read and interpret population density maps.

Prepare to Read

Build Background Knowledge   L2
Briefly review with students the information they learned about population density in Section 1. Ask students why it might be useful to know the population density of a particular area, and who might need to know this information. On the board, begin a concept web with *Population Density* in the center oval and two sub-ovals labeled *Why?* and *Who?* Conduct an Idea Wave (TE p. T35) to elicit student responses.

Instruct

Analyzing and Interpreting Population Density Maps   L2

Guided Instruction
■ Read the steps to read and interpret a population density map as a class and write them on the board.

■ Practice the skill by following the steps on p. 73 with the class. Model each step by taking note of the map's topic and features *(South Asia's population density; relief and labels)*, studying the map key carefully to note what the colors show *(population density)*, using the key to identify the areas of lowest and highest population density *(lowest: parts of Afghanistan and Nepal; highest: parts of Pakistan, India, Bangladesh, and Sri Lanka)*, and writing a conclusion about South Asia's population density and possible reasons for its patterns *(Areas with lower population densities are generally mountainous and farther from coasts. This is probably because they are difficult to reach and hard to make a living in. Areas with higher population densities are near the coasts and in non-mountainous areas. This is probably because they are easier to reach and people can make a living there).*

Skills for Life
Analyzing and Interpreting Population Density Maps

Crowds gather in Amsterdam on Queen's Day, a national holiday in the Netherlands.

72 Foundations of Geography

How dense is the population where you live? If you drew an imaginary five-mile square around your house and counted the number of people who lived within the square, would there be many residents, or few?

Population density is the average number of persons living within a certain area. You can find out how densely populated a place is by reading a population density map.

Learn the Skill
To read and interpret a population density map, follow these steps.

1. **Read the title and look at the map to get a general idea of what it shows.** The title and map key will show you that the topic of the map is population density.

2. **Read the key to understand how the map uses symbols and colors.** Each color represents a different population density range, as explained in the map key.

3. **Use the key to interpret the map.** Identify areas of various densities on the map. Some places average less than one person per square mile. In other places, thousands of people might be crammed into one square mile.

4. **Draw conclusions about what the map shows.** The history, geography, and cultural traditions of a place affect its population density. Draw on this information, plus what you read on the map, to make conclusions about why particular areas have a higher or a lower population density.

Independent Practice
Assign *Skills for Life* and have students complete it individually.

All in One Foundations of Geography Teaching Resources, *Skills for Life,* p. 182

Monitor Progress
As students are completing *Skills for Life*, circulate to make sure individuals are applying the skill steps effectively. Provide assistance as needed.

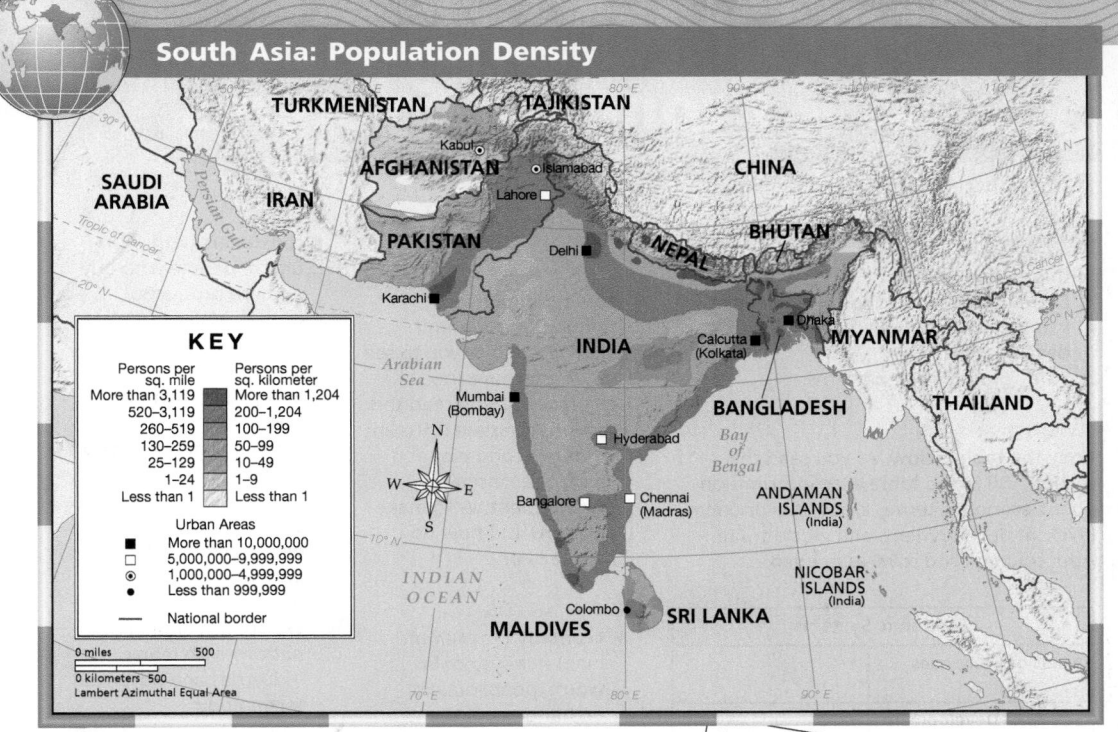

South Asia: Population Density

KEY

Persons per sq. mile	Persons per sq. kilometer
More than 3,119	More than 1,204
520–3,119	200–1,204
260–519	100–199
130–259	50–99
25–129	10–49
1–24	1–9
Less than 1	Less than 1

Urban Areas
■ More than 10,000,000
□ 5,000,000–9,999,999
◉ 1,000,000–4,999,999
• Less than 999,999

— National border

0 miles 500
0 kilometers 500
Lambert Azimuthal Equal-Area

Practice the Skill

Use steps 1–4 to read and interpret the population density map above.

1. What is the topic of this map? Notice that the map has relief—that is, markings that indicate hills and mountains. It also has labels for cities and nations of South Asia.

2. Study the map key carefully. How many different colors are in the key? What color is used for the lowest population density? What color is used for the highest density?

3. Using the key, identify the areas of highest and lowest population densities in South Asia. Write a sentence or two that describes where the most and the fewest people are located.

4. Write a conclusion that makes a general statement about South Asia's population density and suggests possible reasons for the patterns shown on the map.

Apply the Skill

Now take a closer look at the map titled The World: Population Density on pages 62 and 63. Find the areas of greatest density. From what you already know and what you see on the map, what features do you think influence where people choose to live? Think about rivers and mountains as well as nearness to a coast or to the Equator.

Chapter 3 **73**

Assess and Reteach

Assess Progress L2

Ask students to complete the Apply the Skill activity.

Reteach L1

If students are having trouble applying the skill steps, have them review the skill using the interactive Social Studies Skills Tutor CD-ROM.

◉ *Analyzing and Interpreting Special Purpose Maps,* **Social Studies Skills Tutor CD-ROM**

Extend L3

■ To extend the lesson, ask students to apply the skill steps to the population density map on the transparency *The World: Population Density*.

📖 **Foundations of Geography Transparencies,** *Color Transparency FG 5: The World: Continents and Oceans (Base); Color Transparency FG 16: The World: Population Density (Overlay)*

■ Ask students to identify what the shaded areas indicate. *(population density)* Then have them identify the areas of highest population density in the world. *(parts of North America, Latin America, Asia, Europe, Africa)* Ask **Which continent has the most areas of lowest population density?** *(Antarctica)* Then discuss with students what about certain areas might cause them to have the lowest population densities. *(extremely cold areas, such as the North and South poles, and extremely hot areas, such as deserts, where harsh climates make it difficult for people to live)*

Answer

Apply the Skill

The areas of the highest population density probably have good farmland, adequate water, and climates that are warm enough to allow many plants to grow.

Section 3
Step-by-Step Instruction

Objectives

Social Studies

1. Examine different kinds of economies.
2. Investigate levels of economic development.
3. Study global trade patterns.

Reading/Language Arts

Make comparisons to understand what things have in common.

Prepare to Read

Build Background Knowledge L2

Ask students to quickly preview the headings and visuals in the section. Then, write the word *economy* on the board, and have students use the Think-Write-Pair-Share strategy (TE p. T36) to make a list of five words that they think of when they hear the word *economy (examples: money, goods, services)*. Tell students to predict what *economy* might mean, and then read the section to find out if their predictions were correct.

Set a Purpose for Reading L2

- Preview the Objectives.

- Read each statement in the *Reading Readiness Guide* aloud. Ask students to mark the statements true or false.

  All in One **Foundations of Geography Teaching Resources,** *Reading Readiness Guide,* p. 170

- Have students discuss the statements in pairs or groups of four, then mark their worksheets again. Use the Numbered Heads participation strategy (TE, p. T36) to call on students to share their group's perspectives.

Vocabulary Builder
Preview Key Terms L2

Pronounce each Key Term, and then ask students to say the word with you. Provide a simple explanation such as, "The carpenter who builds a table is a producer. The person who buys the table is a consumer."

Section 3
Economic Systems

Prepare to Read

Key Questions

In this section you will
1. Examine different kinds of economies.
2. Investigate levels of economic development.
3. Study global trade patterns.

Taking Notes

Copy the table below. As you read this section, fill in the table with information about economic terms, kinds of economies, levels of development, and world trade. Add columns and rows as needed.

Economic Systems	
Kinds of Economies	• •
Levels of Development	• •

Consumers choose produce at a market in Honolulu, Hawaii.

74 Foundations of Geography

Target Reading Skill

Make Comparisons
Comparing economic systems enables you to see what they have in common. As you read this section, compare different kinds of economies and levels of economic development. Who makes decisions and how do people live?

Key Terms

- **economy** (ih KAHN uh mee) *n.* a system in which people make, exchange, and use things that have value
- **producers** (pruh DOOS urz) *n.* owners and workers

- **consumers** (kun SOOM urz) *n.* people who buy and use products
- **capitalism** (KAP ut ul iz um) *n.* an economic system in which individuals own most businesses
- **communism** (KAHM yoo niz um) *n.* an economic system in which the central government owns factories, farms, and offices
- **developed nations** (dih VEL upt NAY shunz) *n.* nations with many industries and advanced technology
- **developing nations** (dih VEL up ing NAY shunz) *n.* nations with few industries and simple technology

Different Kinds of Economies

An **economy** is a system in which people make, exchange, and use things that have value and that meet their wants or needs. Economies differ from one country to another. In any economy, owners and workers are **producers.** The things they sell are called products **Consumers** are people who buy and use products.

There are three basic economic questions: What will be produced? How will it be produced? And, for whom will it be produced? The answers to these questions depend on the economy.

Modern economies differ in who owns workplaces. The owners generally decide how products are produced. In some countries, most workplaces are privately owned. In others, the government owns most workplaces.

Target Reading Skill L2

Make Comparisons Point out the Target Reading Skill. Tell students that making comparisons will help them see what things have in common.

Model the skill by reading the last paragraph on p. 79 and comparing NAFTA and the European Union. *(Both groups are trade*

alliances and are made up of several countries in the same region.)

Give students *Make Comparisons.* Have them complete the activity in groups.

All in One **Foundations of Geography Teaching Resources,** *Make Comparisons,* p. 179

Private Ownership Capitalism is an economic system in which private individuals own most businesses. Capitalism is also called a free-market economy because producers compete freely for consumers' business.

In capitalism, people may save money in banks. Banks lend money to people and businesses in return for interest, or a percentage fee for the use of money. Banks also pay interest to savers. Under capitalism, people may directly invest in, or commit money to, a business. Owners of a business are also investors in that business.

Government Ownership Communism is an economic system in which the central government owns farms, factories, and offices. It controls the prices of goods and services, how much is produced, and how much workers are paid. The government decides where to invest resources. Today, only a few of the world's nations practice communism.

Mixed Ownership Hardly any nation has a "pure" economic system. For example, the United States has a capitalist economy. However, governments build and maintain roads and provide other services. In communist countries, you may find a few small private businesses.

In some countries, the government may own some industries, while others belong to private owners. This system of mixed ownership is sometimes called a mixed economy.

√ Reading Check **What are the differences between capitalism and communism?**

New York Stock Exchange
Stocks are bought and sold on the busy trading floor of the New York Stock Exchange. **Draw Conclusions** *Would you expect to find a busy stock exchange in a communist economy? Explain why or why not.*

Vocabulary Builder

Use the information below to teach students this section's high-use words.

High-Use Word	Definition and Sample Sentence
exchange, p. 74	*v.* to give and receive Sarah had to **exchange** the large sweater for a smaller one.
value, p. 74	*n.* worth Because it was damaged, the car had little **value**.
alliance, p. 79	*n.* a union The two schools formed an **alliance** to help raise money for their music programs.

Instruct

Different Kinds of Economies L2

Guided Instruction

■ **Vocabulary Builder** Clarify the high-use words **exchange** and **value** before reading.

■ Read Different Kinds of Economies using the ReQuest Procedure (TE, p. T35).

■ Discuss with students the three different types of economies and the differences among them. *(In capitalism, private individuals own most businesses. In communism, the central government controls the economy. In a mixed economy, the government has partial control of the economy.)*

■ Ask **What kind of economy does the United States have?** *(capitalist economy, but the government runs schools, builds and maintains roads, and provides other services)*

Independent Practice
Have students create the Taking Notes graphic organizer on a blank piece of paper. Then have them begin to fill in the organizer with information they have just learned.

Monitor Progress
As students fill in the graphic organizer, circulate and make sure that individuals are choosing the correct details. Provide assistance as needed.

Answers

Draw Conclusions No; in a communist country there probably would be no need for a stock market, because the government controls the prices of goods, and goods and shares are not open to free buying and selling.

√ Reading Check Capitalism is an economic system in which producers compete freely for consumers' business. Communism is an economic system in which the government controls the prices of goods and services.

Levels of Economic Development L2

Guided Instruction

- Read about the differences between developed and developing countries in Levels of Economic Development.

- Have students describe the ways in which people in developed countries and in developing countries produce food. *(In developed countries, most of the food is grown by commercial farmers; in developing countries, most of the people are subsistence farmers.)*

- Ask **What challenges might commercial and subsistence farmers have in common?** *(Bad weather, pollution, and lack of water might be challenges that affect both types of farmers.)*

🔁 Target Reading Skill L2

Make Comparisons As a follow up, ask students to answer the Target Reading Skill question in the Student Edition. *(Both kinds of countries have farms.)*

Levels of Economic Development

Three hundred years ago, most people made their own clothes. Then came a great change. People invented machines to make goods. They found new sources of power to run the machines. Power-driven machines were a new technology, or way of putting knowledge to practical use. This change in the way people made goods was called the Industrial Revolution.

The Industrial Revolution created a new economic pattern. Nations with more industries and more advanced technology are considered **developed nations.** Because they are still developing economically, nations with fewer industries and simpler technology are considered **developing nations.** People live differently in developed and developing nations.

Make Comparisons
What do developed nations have in common with developing nations?

Developed Nations Only about one fifth of the world's people live in developed nations. These nations include the United States, Canada, Japan, and most European nations. People in these nations use goods made in factories. Businesses use advanced technologies to produce goods and services.

In developed nations, most people live in towns and cities. They work in offices and factories. Machines do most of the work. Most people have enough food and water. Most citizens can get an education and healthcare.

In developed nations, most food is grown by commercial farmers. These are farmers who grow crops mainly for sale rather than for their own needs. Commercial farms use modern technologies, so they need fewer workers than traditional farms.

Developed nations can have some problems. Unemployment is a challenge. Not everyone can find a job. Industry and cars can cause air, land, and water pollution. Developed nations are working to solve these problems.

Most of Thailand's subsistence farmers grow rice.

Skills for Life — Skills Mini Lesson

Identifying Main Ideas

1. Tell students that to identify main ideas, they should identify the subject, identify details about the subject, and decide what their overall impression is of the details. Then they should draw a conclusion about what the details tell them.

2. Help students practice the skill by reading the first paragraph on this page with them. Have them note the details and use them to identify the main idea in that paragraph. *(Main idea: The Industrial Revolution changed the way people made goods.)*

3. Have students apply the skill by identifying the details and main idea in the third paragraph on page 77.

The World: Levels of Development

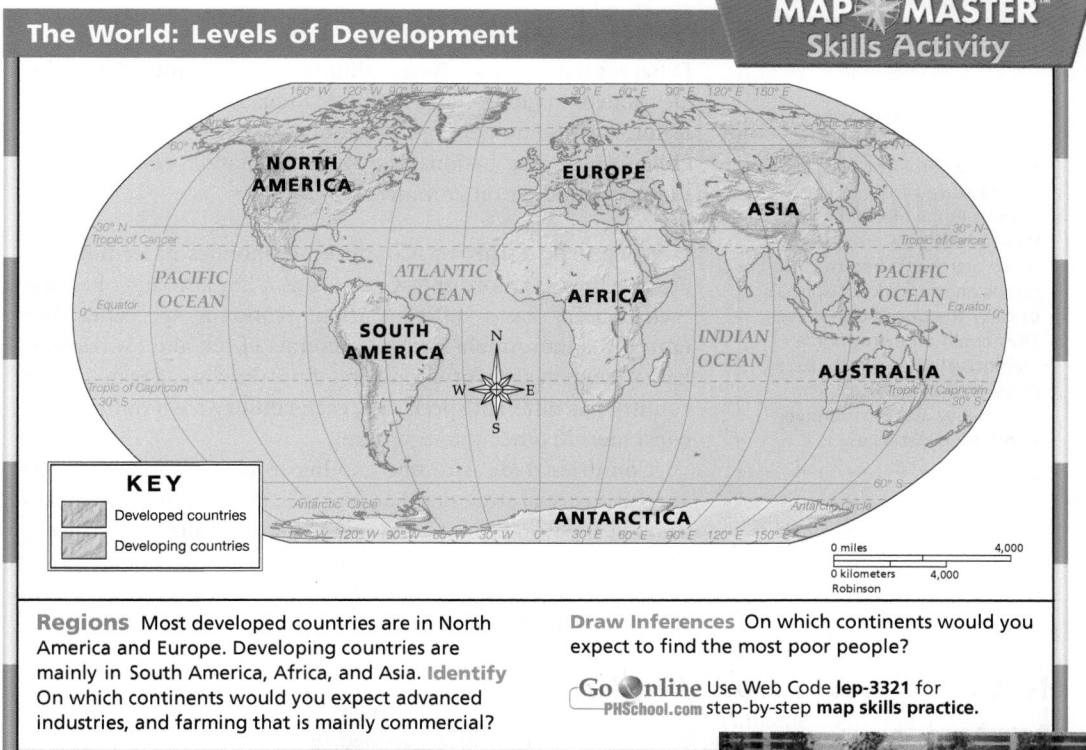

MAP MASTER™ Skills Activity

KEY
- Developed countries
- Developing countries

0 miles 4,000
0 kilometers 4,000
Robinson

Regions Most developed countries are in North America and Europe. Developing countries are mainly in South America, Africa, and Asia. **Identify** On which continents would you expect advanced industries, and farming that is mainly commercial?

Draw Inferences On which continents would you expect to find the most poor people?

Go Online Use Web Code lep-3321 for PHSchool.com step-by-step **map skills practice**.

Monitor Progress
As students continue to fill in the graphic organizer, circulate and make sure they are filling in the correct details. Provide assistance as needed.

Developing Nations Not every economy is like that of the United States. Most of the people in the world live in developing nations, which are mainly in Africa, Asia, and Latin America.

Developing nations do not have great wealth. Many people are subsistence farmers, or farmers who raise food and animals mainly to feed their own families. Their farms have little or no machinery. People and animals do most of the work.

Many developing nations face great challenges. These include disease, food shortages, unsafe water, poor education and healthcare, and political unrest.

People in developing nations are confronting these challenges. Some nations, such as Saudi Arabia and South Africa, have grown richer by selling natural resources. Others, such as Thailand and China, have built successful industries. The more industrial developing nations are gradually becoming developed countries themselves.

✓ **Reading Check** How do developed nations differ from developing nations?

Many people in developed nations work in offices.

Chapter 3 Section 3 **77**

Differentiated Instruction

For Less Proficient Readers   L1
To help students better understand the differences and similarities among developed and developing countries have them create a Venn diagram. Have students label one circle "Developing Countries," and the other "Developed Countries." As they read, have students record information in the appropriate circles.

For Gifted and Talented   L3
Divide students into groups and assign each group one world region: United States and Canada, Latin America, Asia and the Pacific, Africa, or Europe and Russia. Have each group do research to find out what economic systems the countries in their region have, and then create a table with this information.

Answers

MAP MASTER Skills Activity **Identify** North America, Europe, the northern half of Asia, Australia **Draw Inferences** Africa, the southern half of Asia, the southern half of North America and South America

✓ **Reading Check** In developed nations food is grown by commercial farmers; in developing nations many people are subsistence farmers. Most people in developed countries live in towns and cities, and can get food, healthcare, good housing, and a good education; in developing countries many face a lack of food, clean water, education, healthcare, and land.

Go Online PHSchool.com Students may practice their map skills using the interactive online version of this map.

World Trade Patterns L2

Guided Instruction

- **Vocabulary Builder** Clarify the high-use word **alliance** before reading.

- Have students read World Trade Patterns and study the flow chart.

- Have students summarize the world trade diagram in their own words. *(Country A sells oil to Countries B and C so it can buy wheat and computers; Country B sells wheat to Countries A and C so it can buy computers and oil; Country C sells computers to countries A and B so it can buy wheat and oil.)*

- **What might be some benefits of belonging to a trade alliance? What might be some drawbacks?** *(Benefits: able to trade goods easily with other member countries. Drawbacks: cannot make decisions about trade alone; member countries might make better, cheaper goods than your country and take business away from your country's producers.)*

Independent Practice

Have students complete the graphic organizer by adding a row entitled "World Trade Patterns" and filling it in with information from this section.

Monitor Progress

- Show *Section Reading Support Transparency FG 51* and ask students to check their work.

   📖 **Foundations of Geography Transparencies,** *Section Reading Support Transparency FG 51*

- Tell students to fill in the last column of their *Reading Readiness Guides.*

   All in One Foundations of Geography Teaching Resources, *Reading Readiness Guide,* p. 170

Answer

Predict Country A

World Trade Patterns

Different countries have different economic strengths. Developed nations have strong industries with advanced technology. Some developing nations have low-cost industries. Other developing nations may grow plantation cash crops, or they may produce oil or minerals.

Different Specialties Countries' economies differ not only because they are more or less developed. They also differ because each country has a different set of economic specialties. For example, Saudi Arabia has vast amounts of oil, and Switzerland has a long history of producing fine watches. Because each country has different specialties, each country has products that consumers in other countries want.

Countries trade with one another to take advantage of one another's special strengths. For example, the United States makes some of the world's best computers. But the United States needs oil. Saudi Arabia has plenty of oil, but it needs computers. So Saudi Arabia sells oil to the United States, and the United States sells computers to Saudi Arabia.

How Does World Trade Work?

Country A produces more oil than it needs. It sells this oil so that it can buy computers and wheat.

Country B produces more wheat than it needs. It sells this wheat so that it can buy oil and computers.

Country C makes more computers than it needs. It sells computers so that it can buy wheat and oil.

How Trade Works
Countries sell what they have and what other countries want so that they can buy what they lack. **Predict** *Which country from the diagram would you expect to sell oil so that it can buy tea?*

78 Foundations of Geography

Interdependence As world trade has grown, countries have grown interdependent, or dependent on one another. The United States depends on other countries for oil and inexpensive industrial goods. Meanwhile, other countries depend on the United States for computers and other products.

Developed nations tend to sell products made using advanced technologies. Developing nations tend to sell foods, natural resources such as oil, and simple industrial products. In return, they buy high-technology goods from developed countries.

Some countries have formed trade alliances to reduce the costs of trade. For example, the United States, Canada, and Mexico belong to the North American Free Trade Agreement, or NAFTA. Most European countries belong to the European Union. Businesses may face increased competition from foreign competitors within these alliances, and workers may lose their jobs. However, businesses may benefit from increased sales in other countries. Consumers benefit from these alliances because they pay less for products from other countries.

✓ **Reading Check** Why do countries trade with one another?

Moving Goods
Much of the world's trade travels on container ships, like this one in Dubai, United Arab Emirates. These ships can carry huge loads across oceans. **Draw Conclusions** *How does technology make world trade easier?*

Section 3 Assessment

Key Terms
Review the key terms at the beginning of this section. Use each term in a sentence that explains its meaning.

Target Reading Skill
What are two ways developed and developing countries are similar?

Comprehension and Critical Thinking
1. (a) **Identify** Who owns farms, factories, and offices in a communist economy?
(b) **Compare and Contrast** How is ownership different in a capitalist economy?

2. (a) **Identify** What is a country's level of development?
(b) **Describe** What are the main differences in level of development between countries?
(c) **Predict** What can we predict about a country's economy if we know its level of development?
3. (a) **List** What are two major trade alliances?
(b) **Explain** What is the main purpose of these alliances?
(c) **Analyze** What are some reasons why a country might want to join a trade alliance?

Writing Activity
Suppose you run a company, and you want to expand to another nation. Would you choose a capitalist or communist nation? A developed or developing nation? Would you choose a nation that belongs to a trade alliance? Write a letter to investors explaining your choice.

For: An activity on economic systems
Visit: PHSchool.com
Web Code: led-3303

Section 3 Assessment

Key Terms
Students' sentences should reflect an understanding of each Key Term.

Target Reading Skill
Both developed countries and developing countries have farms and trade with other nations.

Comprehension and Critical Thinking
1. (a) the government (b) Individuals own
farms, factories, and offices.
2. (a) It is based on the numbers of industries and level of advanced technology it has.
(b) its level and type of food production; type of trade goods; the availability of healthcare, education, and housing; the kinds of work most people do (c) We can predict that the higher the level of development, the stronger the economy will be.

Assess and Reteach

Assess Progress [L2]
Have students complete the Section Assessment. Then administer the *Section Quiz.*

All in One **Foundations of Geography Teaching Resources,** *Section Quiz,* p. 172

Reteach [L1]
If students need more instruction, have them read this section in the Reading and Vocabulary Study Guide.

Chapter 3, Section 3, **Western Hemisphere Reading and Vocabulary Study Guide,** pp. 28–30

Extend [L3]
To extend the lesson, have students access the online activity *Trade in a Global Economy.*

Go Online PHSchool.com **For:** Environmental and Global Issues: *Trade in a Global Economy*
Visit: PHSchool.com
Web Code: led-3306

Answers

Draw Conclusions Technology allows more goods to be traded in a shorter amount of time and over long distances.

✓ **Reading Check** to take advantage of each other's special strengths

Writing Activity
Use the *Rubric for Assessing a Writing Assignment* to evaluate students' letters.

All in One **Foundations of Geography Teaching Resources,** *Rubric for Assessing a Writing Assignment,* p. 197

Go Online PHSchool.com Typing in the Web code when prompted will bring students directly to detailed instructions for this activity.

3. (a) NAFTA and the European Union (b) to reduce costs of trade (c) to gain new places to sell its goods and to be able to get goods from its partners more cheaply.

Objectives

Social Studies

1. Examine different types of states.
2. Investigate types of government.
3. Learn about alliances and international organizations.

Reading/Language Arts

Recognize contrast signal words to understand how things are different.

Prepare to Read

Build Background Knowledge L2

Tell students that in this section they will learn about different kinds of rulers and types of governments. To introduce the topic, remind students that the United States is a representative democracy, headed by a President. Ask them to think of other titles they may know for leaders of a country (*prime minister, queen, king*). Conduct an Idea Wave (TE, p. T35) to elicit responses and make a list on the board.

Set a Purpose for Reading L2

■ Preview the Objectives.

■ Read each statement in *the Reading Readiness Guide* aloud. Ask students to mark the statements true or false.

  All in One **Foundations of Geography Teaching Resources,** *Reading Readiness Guide,* p. 174

■ Have students discuss the statements in pairs or groups of four, then mark their worksheets again. Use the Numbered Heads participation strategy (TE, p. T36) to call on students to share their group's perspectives.

Vocabulary Builder L2
Preview Key Terms

Pronounce each Key Term, and then ask students to say the word with you. Provide a simple explanation such as, "The constitution of the United States set the framework for our government."

Prepare to Read

Objectives

In this section you will

1. Examine different types of states.
2. Investigate types of government.
3. Learn about alliances and international organizations.

Taking Notes

Copy the table below. As you read, fill the table with information about types of states, types of governments, and international organizations.

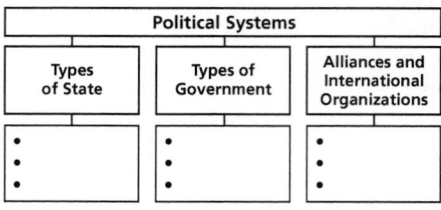

Political Systems		
Types of State	Types of Government	Alliances and International Organizations
• • •	• • •	• • •

🎯 Target Reading Skill

Use Contrast Signal Words
Signal words point out relationships among ideas or events. Certain words, such as *like* or *unlike,* can signal a comparison or contrast. As you read this section, notice the comparisons and contrasts among different types of states and governments. What signal words indicate the comparisons and contrasts?

Key Terms

• **government** (GUV urn munt) *n.* a body that makes and enforces laws
• **state** (stayt) *n.* a region that shares a government
• **dependency** (dee PEN dun see) *n.* a region that belongs to another state
• **nation-state** (NAY shun stayt) *n.* a state that is independent of other states
• **city-state** (SIH tee stayt) *n.* a small city-centered state
• **empire** (EM pyr) *n.* a state containing several countries
• **constitution** (kahn stuh TOO shun) *n.* a set of laws that define and often limit a government's power

In 1994, Eritreans celebrated the first anniversary of their country's independence.

80 Foundations of Geography

Types of States

Long ago, most people lived in small, traditional communities. All adults took part in group decisions. Some small communities still make decisions this way, but they are now part of larger units called nations. Nations are too large for everyone to take part in every decision. Still, nations have to protect people and resolve conflicts between individuals and social groups. In modern nations, these needs are met by governments, or organizations that set up and enforce laws.

You may remember that a region is an area united by a common feature. A state is a region that shares a government. You probably live in a state that is part of the United States. But the political units that we call "states" in the United States are just one kind of state. The entire United States can also be called a state. It is a region that shares a common government—the federal government.

🎯 Target Reading Skill L2

Use Contrast Signal Words Point out the Target Reading Skill. Tell students that being able to recognize words that signal a contrast will let them know when a writer is showing how things are different.

Model recognizing contrast signal words using this passage on p. 80: "You probably live in a state that is part of the United States. But the political units that we call 'states' are just one kind of state. The entire country can also be called a state." (*The word* but *signals a contrast. It alerts the reader that the word* "state" *can have two meanings.*)

Give students *Identify Contrasts.* Have them complete the activity in groups.

  All in One **Foundations of Geography Teaching Resources,** *Identify Contrasts,* p. 178

Dependencies and Nation-States Some regions are **dependencies,** or regions that belong to another state. Others, like the United States, are **nation-states,** or states that are independent of other states. Each has a common body of laws. Nation-states are often simply called nations. Every place in the world where people live is part of a nation-state or dependency.

Most nation-states are large, but some are tiny. The smallest is Vatican City, which is surrounded by the city of Rome in Italy. Vatican City covers only about 109 acres (44 hectares)!

How States Developed The first real states formed in Southwest Asia more than 5,000 years ago when early cities set up governments. Small city-centered states are called **city-states.** Later, military leaders conquered large areas and ruled them as **empires,** or states containing several countries.

After about 1500, European rulers founded the first true nation-states. European nations established dependencies all over the world. When those dependencies became independent, they formed new nation-states.

✓ Reading Check **What is the difference between a government and a state?**

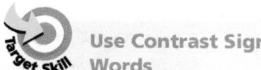
Use Contrast Signal Words
The first sentence in the paragraph at the left begins with the word *some*. The second sentence begins with *others*. These words signal that a contrast will be made. What contrast is being made?

Vatican City
St. Peter's Basilica, shown below, is the seat of the pope. He leads the Roman Catholic Church and rules Vatican City. **Infer** *What must be true about Vatican City for it to be a nation-state?*

Vocabulary Builder

Use the information below to teach students this section's high-use words.

High-Use Word	Definition and Sample Sentence
surround, p. 81	*v.* to shut in on all sides The farmer decided to **surround** the field with a fence to keep his animals from wandering away.
dispute, p. 84	*n.* an argument or disagreement The neighbors settled the **dispute** by agreeing to build a fence between their properties.

Use Contrast Signal Words As a follow up, ask students to answer the Target Reading Skill question in the Student Edition. *(Two types of states—dependencies and nation-states—are being contrasted.)*

Instruct

Types of States [L2]

Guided Instruction

■ **Vocabulary Builder** Clarify the high-use word **surround** before reading.

■ Read Types of States using the Paragraph Shrinking technique (TE, p. T34).

■ Discuss with students the kinds of states that exist today or have in the past, and the characteristics of each type. *(A state is a region that shares the same government. Some regions like the United States are nation-states, which are states that are independent of other states. Some states have dependencies, or regions that belong to them. Empires are states that contain several countries, while many ancient states were small, contained city-states.)*

Independent Practice

Have students create the Taking Notes graphic organizer on a blank piece of paper. Then have them begin to fill in the chart with information they have just learned. Briefly model how to record details by using the *Tree Map/Flow Chart* transparency.

📖 **Foundations of Geography Transparencies,** *Transparency B3: Tree Map/Flow Chart*

Monitor Progress

As students fill in the graphic organizer, circulate and make sure that individuals are choosing the correct details. Provide assistance as needed.

Answers

Infer Vatican City must be independent of any other states.

✓ Reading Check Government is a system that sets up and enforces rules; a state is a region that shares a government.

Types of Government L2

Guided Instruction

- Have students read about the different kinds of governments in Types of Government.

- Have students name the different types of government and who makes the decisions in each. *(direct democracy, all adult residents; tribal rule, the chief or elders; absolute monarchy, the king or queen; dictatorship, the dictator; oligarchy, a small group of people; constitutional monarchy, representatives selected by the people; representative democracy, representatives selected by the people.)*

- Ask **What is the difference between a direct democracy and a representative democracy?** *(In a direct democracy, all adult residents take part in decisions; in a representative democracy, governments are run by representatives that the people choose.)*

Independent Practice

Have students continue to fill in the graphic organizer with details from this section.

Monitor Progress

Circulate to make sure that individuals are choosing relevant details and recording them in the appropriate box on their charts. Provide assistance as needed.

Kim Jong Il
Kim Jong Il, the dictator of North Korea, making a rare public appearance.
Analyze Images *What group in North Korea might be a source of power for Kim Jong II?*

Types of Government

Each state has a government. There are many different kinds of government. Some governments are controlled by a single person or a small group of people. Others are controlled by all of the people.

Direct Democracy The earliest governments were simple. People lived in small groups. They practiced direct democracy, a form of government in which all adults take part in decisions. Many towns in New England today practice direct democracy. Decisions are made at town meetings where all adult residents can speak and vote.

Tribal Rule In time, communities banded together into larger tribal groups. Members of the tribe had a say in group decisions. But chiefs or elders usually made the final decision about what to do. Decisions were based upon the culture's customs and beliefs.

Absolute Monarchy Until about 200 years ago, one of the most common forms of government was absolute monarchy. In that system, a king or queen who inherits the throne by birth has complete control. Few absolute monarchies still exist today. Saudi Arabia is an example of a surviving absolute monarchy.

Dictatorship There are other countries today, however, where just one person rules. A leader who is not a king or queen but who has almost total power over an entire country is called a dictator. Dictatorship is rule by such a leader. Nations ruled by dictators include Cuba, Libya, and North Korea. Dictatorships differ from absolute monarchies because most dictators don't inherit power. Instead, they seize power. Dictators usually remain in power by using violence against their opponents. Dictators deny their people the right to make their own decisions.

Oligarchy Oligarchies are governments controlled by a small group of people. The group may be the leadership of a ruling political party. For example, China is an oligarchy controlled by the leadership of the Communist Party. There are other types of oligarchy. Myanmar, also called Burma, is run by a group of military officers. A group of religious leaders controls Iran. As in a dictatorship, ordinary people have little say in decisions.

Differentiated Instruction

For Advanced Readers L3

Tell students that sometimes the form of government may change within a country as a result of a revolution or change in leadership. Have students read *Your Government Has Returned to You!* to see an example of this event in the former European country of Czechoslovakia.

 **Foundations of Geography Teaching Resources,** *Your Government Has Returned to You!,* pp. 189–190

Answer

Analyze Images Kim Jong Il appears before the military, which may be a source of power for him.

Constitutional Monarchy Most monarchies today are constitutional monarchies, or governments in which the power of the king or queen is limited by law. The United Kingdom, the Netherlands, and Kuwait are examples. These nations have **constitutions,** or sets of laws that define and often limit the government's power. In a constitutional monarchy, the king or queen is often only a symbol of the country.

Representative Democracy Representative democracies are governments run by representatives that the people choose. Many constitutional monarchies are also representative democracies. In a representative democracy, the people indirectly hold power to govern and rule. They elect representatives who create laws. If the people do not like what a representative does, they can refuse to reelect that person. Citizens can also work to change laws they do not like. A constitution sets rules for elections, defines the rights of citizens, and limits the powers of the government. This system ensures that power is shared. The United States, Canada, and India are examples of representative democracies.

✓ Reading Check **What do absolute monarchies, dictatorships, and oligarchies have in common?**

Queen Beatrix of the Netherlands heads a constitutional monarchy.

Representative Democracy
Members of the United States House of Representatives, shown below, are elected by the people of their districts. **Contrast** *How does a representative democracy differ from a direct democracy?*

International Organizations L2

Guided Instruction
- **Vocabulary Builder** Clarify the high-use word **dispute** before reading.

- Read about the different ways in which countries work together in International Organizations.

- Have students name three purposes of alliances or international organizations. *(Possible answers: to promote trade, to keep peace, for defense, to work for health and welfare of children.)*

- Ask **What is NATO, and what do its members agree to do?** *(the North Atlantic Treaty Organization; its members have agreed to defend any fellow member that is attacked)*

Independent Practice
As they read about alliances and international organizations, have students complete their charts by recording details in the third box.

Monitor Progress
- When students are finished with their flow charts, show *Section Reading Support Transparency FG 52* and ask students to check their work individually. Go over key concepts and clarify key vocabulary as needed.

  📖 **Foundations of Geography Transparencies,** *Section Reading Support Transparency FG 52*

- Tell students to fill in the last column of their *Reading Readiness Guides*. Probe for what they learned that confirms or invalidates each statement.

  All in One **Foundations of Geography Teaching Resources,** *Reading Readiness Guide*, p. 174

Chapter 3 Section 4 **83**

Skills Mini Lesson

Decision Making

1. Tell students that when they make decisions, they should identify the problem, list the options, evaluate each option, and then choose the best one.

2. Help students practice the skill by reading the following scenario and then identifying how Tom made his decision: Tom had two choices for an activity on Saturday. He could baby-sit, which would be work, but he would get paid. He could play soccer with his friends which would be fun, but would depend on good weather. Tom decided to baby-sit because he wanted to get paid.

3. Have students apply the skill by writing a short description of a decision they made and how they arrived at that decision.

Answers

✓ Reading Check In all three types of government, one group or individual has all the power.

Contrast While all adults take part in decisions in a direct democracy, in a representative democracy, people choose representatives to make decisions on their behalf.

Assess and Reteach

Assess Progress L2

Have students complete the Section Assessment. Then administer the *Section Quiz.*

All in One **Foundations of Geography Teaching Resources,** *Section Quiz,* p. 176

Reteach L1

If students need more instruction, have them read this section in the Reading and Vocabulary Study Guide.

Chapter 3, Section 4, **Western Hemisphere Reading and Vocabulary Study Guide,** pp. 31–33

Extend L3

To extend the lesson, have students do research to learn more about any of the alliances or international organizations mentioned in this section. Students should work in groups to create a display with information about their organization. Then allow students to share their displays with the class.

Answer

✓ Reading Check Its purpose is to resolve disputes and promote peace among nations.

Section 4 Assessment

Key Terms

Students' sentences should reflect an understanding of each Key Term.

Target Reading Skill

Governments controlled by a single person are contrasted with governments controlled by all of the people. The words *some* and *others* signal the contrast.

Comprehension and Critical Thinking

1. (a) city-states **(b)** City-states were small and usually controlled only the lands around the city. Modern nation-states are larger.

International Organizations

Nations may make agreements to work together in an alliance. Members of an alliance are called allies. Alliances provide for nations to assist each other with defense. For example, members of the North Atlantic Treaty Organization (NATO) have agreed to defend any fellow member who is attacked.

Military bodies such as NATO are just one type of organization that is international, or involving more than one nation. Some international bodies are mainly economic in purpose. The European Union, for example, promotes economic unity among member nations in Europe.

The United Nations is an international organization meant to resolve disputes and promote peace. Almost all nations of the world belong to the United Nations. Every member has a vote in the General Assembly of the United Nations. But only the United Nations Security Council can make decisions over the use of force. The United States and four other permanent members have the power to prevent action in the Security Council.

The United Nations sponsors other international organizations with special purposes. For example, the Food and Agriculture Organization combats hunger worldwide. The United Nations Children's Fund (UNICEF) promotes the rights and well-being of children.

The United Nations headquarters in New York, New York

✓ Reading Check **What is the purpose of the United Nations?**

Section 4 Assessment

Key Terms

Review the key terms at the beginning of this section. Use each term in a sentence that explains its meaning.

Target Reading Skill

Reread the first paragraph on page 82. Which two main types of government are contrasted? Look for contrast signal words.

Comprehension and Critical Thinking

1. (a) Identify What were the earliest types of states?

(b) Compare and Contrast How did those early states differ from modern nation-states?

2. (a) List What are the main types of government?

(b) Categorize In which types of government do ordinary citizens take part in decisions?

3. (a) Define What is an alliance?

(b) Compare and Contrast What are the differences and similarities between alliances and other international organizations?

Writing Activity

Which type of government described in this section appeals most to you? Write a paragraph explaining your preference, and why it appeals to you.

Writing Tip When you write a paragraph, state the main idea in a topic sentence. In this case, the topic sentence will tell the type of government that you prefer. Other sentences should support the main idea with arguments.

84 Foundations of Geography

---

2. (a) direct democracy, absolute monarchy, dictatorship, oligarchy, constitutional monarchy, representative democracy **(b)** direct democracy, constitutional monarchy, representative democracy

3. (a) a group of nations that has agreed to work together **(b)** An alliance is often created to assist members in the event of a military attack, while an international organization may mainly be economic in purpose.

Writing Activity

Use the *Rubric for Assessing a Writing Assignment* to evaluate students' paragraphs.

All in One **Foundations of Geography Teaching Resources,** *Rubric for Assessing a Writing Assignment,* p. 197

◆ Chapter Summary

Section 1: Population

- Where people live depends on factors such as climate, soil, and history.
- Population density measures the average number of people living in an area.
- Scientific progress has spurred population growth, which is straining Earth's resources.

Section 2: Migration

- People migrate to seek a better life, or, in some cases, because they have no other choice.
- Cities are growing rapidly in some regions.

Section 3: Economic Systems

- Economic systems may have private ownership of businesses, government ownership, or a mixture of both.
- Developed countries have more industry and technology than developing countries.
- Trade connects countries as buyers and sellers.

Section 4: Political Systems

- The world is divided into nation-states.
- States have governments that differ in the amount of power that citizens have.
- Nation-states may join together in alliances and international organizations.

Harvesting rice in China

◆ Key Terms

Each of the statements below contains a key term from the chapter. If the statement is true, write *true*. If it is false, rewrite the statement to make it true.

1. A country's population is the number of people who live there.
2. Population density measures the size of cities.
3. The movement of people from one region to another is migration.
4. Urbanization is the movement of people to cities.

5. An economy is a system of government.
6. Consumers are people who sell products.
7. Developing nations have few industries and simple technologies.
8. A government is a body that makes and enforces laws and resolves conflicts among its people.
9. A state is a system of government.

⌐ Vocabulary Builder

Revisit this chapter's high-use words:

cluster	theory	rely
vary	unique	alliance
method	exchange	surround
aspect	value	dispute

Ask students to review the definitions they recorded on their *Word Knowledge* worksheets.

Alⅼ In One Foundations of Geography Teaching Resources, *Word Knowledge,* p. 180

Consider allowing students to earn extra credit if they use the words in their answers to the questions in the Chapter Review and Assessment. The words must be used correctly and in a natural context to win the extra points.

Review Chapter Content

- Review and revisit the major themes of this chapter by asking students to classify what Guiding Question each bulleted statement in the Chapter Summary answers. Have students write each statement down and work in pairs to determine which statement applies to which Guiding Question. Refer to page 1 in the Student Edition for text of Guiding Questions.

- Assign *Vocabulary Development* for students to review Key Terms.

Alⅼ In One Foundations of Geography Teaching Resources, *Vocabulary Development,* p. 196

Answers

Key Terms

1. True

2. False. Population density measures the average number of people living in an area.

3. True

4. True

5. False. An economy is a system in which people make, exchange, and use things that have value.

6. False. Consumers are people who buy products.

7. True

8. True

9. False. A state is a region that shares a government.

Comprehension and Critical Thinking

10. (a) the way a population is spread out over an area **(b)** climate, natural resources, availability of water, availability of soil for farming **(c)** Because of advancements in food production and transportation, not everyone needs to farm for a living and can therefore live away from rural areas, in cities.

11. (a) It has grown enormously. **(b)** Difficulties include: overcrowding, hunger, unemployment, lack of housing, fresh water, and schools, and inadequate public services

12. (a) when people move by their own choice **(b)** Some people are pulled to a new country by better opportunities, more jobs, or a better climate. Others are pushed to escape hunger, or war, or because they want political freedom.

13. (a) an economic system in which private individuals own most businesses **(b)** Capitalism is an economic system that is controlled by the producers and consumers while communism is an economic system controlled by the government.

14. (a) inadequate healthcare, housing, education, and public services, such as water and electricity **(b)** Developing countries do not have much wealth or industry and have shortages of land and water, which makes it difficult to overcome the challenges.

15. (a) direct democracy and representative democracy **(b)** In democracies a greater number of the citizens get to have a say in government actions than in other forms.

Skills Practice
Purple: more than 260 persons per sq. mile, more than 100 persons per sq. kilometer; pink: 52–259 persons per sq. mile, 21–100 per sq. kilometer; orange: 24–51 persons per sq. mile, 5–20 per sq. kilometer; yellow: less than 24 persons per sq. mile, less than 5 per sq. kilometer; most sparsely populated areas include parts of North and South America, Asia, Africa, and most of Australia; students' conclusions will vary, but may mention that areas that have small populations usually have difficult living conditions, such as climate or terrain, or are not easily accessible.

◆ Comprehension and Critical Thinking

10. (a) Define What is population distribution?
(b) Explain What factors affect population distribution in a region?
(c) Compare and Contrast How are those factors different today than they were when most people were farmers?

11. (a) Identify How has the size of world populations changed in recent years?
(b) Identify Cause and Effect What difficulties have resulted from the change in the size of world populations?

12. (a) Define What is voluntary migration?
(b) Make Generalizations Why do people choose to migrate?

13. (a) Define What is capitalism?
(b) Contrast How does capitalism differ from communism?

14. (a) List What are some challenges faced by developing countries?
(b) Infer Why do developing countries face these challenges?

15. (a) Identify What are two types of democracy?
(b) Contrast How do democracies differ from other forms of government?

◆ Skills Practice

Using Population Density Maps In the Skills for Life activity in this chapter, you learned how to read a population density map using the map key.

Review the steps you followed to learn this skill. Then review the map on pages 62 and 63, titled The World: Population Density. Using the map key, describe what each color on the map represents and then list the most sparsely populated areas shown. Finally, draw conclusions about why these areas have such small populations.

◆ Writing Activity: Math

Suppose you are a demographer projecting population growth for three countries. Use the following information to create a population bar graph for each country:

	Birthrate	Death Rate
Country A	14.2	8.7
Country B	9.8	9.7
Country C	9.4	13.9

Then, write a brief paragraph explaining your graph. For each country, is the population increasing, decreasing, or stable? Explain why.

MAP MASTER™
Skills Activity

Continents

Place Location For each place listed below, write the letter from the map that shows its location.
1. Asia
2. Antarctica
3. Africa
4. South America
5. North America
6. Europe
7. Australia

Go Online
PHSchool.com Use Web Code **lep-3215** for an **interactive map.**

Writing Activity: Math
Students' bar graphs should show that Country A has a growing population, Country B's population is staying about the same, and Country C's population is declining. Their paragraphs should explain these findings.

Use *Rubric for Assessing a Bar Graph* to evaluate students' graphs.

All in One **Foundations of Geography Teaching Resources,** *Rubric for Assessing a Bar Graph,* p. 198

Standardized Test Prep

Test-Taking Tips

Some questions on standardized tests ask you to analyze a reading selection for a main idea. Read the passage in the box below. Then follow the tips to answer the sample question.

> This region has one of the highest population densities in the world. As many as 5,000 people per square mile live in parts of the region. There are good reasons for this heavy population density. The land is fertile. Though the desert is not far away, the river contains plenty of water for the people who live there.

TIP As you read each sentence, think about what main idea it supports.

Pick the letter that best answers the question.

Which sentence states this passage's main idea?
- A ~~Demographers study human populations.~~
- B Egypt's Nile River valley supports a large population.
- C ~~People find ways to adapt to their environment.~~
- D Many people live near the Mississippi River.

TIP Cross out answer choices that don't make sense. Then pick from the remaining choices the one that BEST answers the question.

Think It Through The passage does not mention demographers. So you can cross out answer A. You can also rule out C, because the passage does not discuss people adapting to their environment. Answers B and D both mention specific regions. Which region does the paragraph describe? The paragraph mentions a desert. There is no desert near the Mississippi River. So the answer is B.

Practice Questions

Use the tips above and other tips in this book to help you answer the following questions.

1. The number of people per square mile is a region's
   - A population distribution.
   - B population.
   - C elevation.
   - D population density.

2. People moving to a different region to seek better farming opportunities is an example of
   - A trade.
   - B voluntary migration.
   - C involuntary migration.
   - D urbanization.

3. In which of the following does the government own most workplaces?
   - A capitalism
   - B developing country
   - C communism
   - D developed country

Read the following passage, and answer the question that follows.

A constitutional monarch has little power. Under some constitutions, elected representatives have the law-making power instead of the monarch. In such cases, the government works much like other representative democracies.

4. What is the main idea of this passage?
   - A An absolute monarch has great power.
   - B Constitutions are always democratic.
   - C A constitutional monarchy may also be a representative democracy.
   - D A constitutional monarch cannot interfere with representative democracy.

Use Web Code lea-3301 for a **Chapter 3 self-test.**

Standardized Test Prep
Answers

1. D
2. B
3. C
4. C

Objectives

1. Identify the skills Sam needs to survive alone in the wilderness.

2. Discover how Sam came to understand the natural world.

3. Identify devices used by the author to create effects.

4. Analyze the effectiveness of elements of plot, such as setting and character.

Prepare to Read

Build Background Knowledge L2

Have students read the Background Information in the Student Edition. Then ask them to brainstorm a list of items they would want to have with them if they were going to live in the woods. Use the Think-Write-Pair-Share strategy (TE, p. T36) to elicit student responses. Then list them on the board.

Instruct

My Side of the Mountain L2

Guided Instruction

- Point out that some potentially unfamiliar words are defined in the margin. Clarify the meanings of the words before reading.

- Have students read the selection using the Silent Structured Reading strategy (TE p. T34).

- Tell students that the author of this story uses a literary technique called figurative language to convey Sam's ability to read the weather and animal behavior. One type of figurative language is personification, or describing an object, animal, or idea as if it had human characteristics. Ask students to look through the text to find examples of personification. (*"the moods of storms;" "the air said snow," "trees cry out," and "wind gets caught in a ravine and screams until it dies."*)

- Similes, or phrases that compare things using the words *like* or *as*, are another form of figurative language. Ask students to look through the story and identify similes.

My Side of the Mountain
By Jean Craighead George

Prepare to Read

Background Information
Have you ever camped out overnight? Have you ever built a fire in order to keep warm? Suppose you had no electricity or your home had no heating system. How would you cope with the natural world without modern technology? Do you think that living closer to the natural world would change you in any significant way?

Sam Gribley is the fictional hero of the novel *My Side of the Mountain.* When he decided to live close to nature, he built a tree house in the Catskill Mountains of New York and then moved in with his only companion, Frightful, a falcon. This excerpt describes their first winter in the mountains.

Objectives
As you read this selection, you will
- Identify the skills Sam needed to survive alone in the wilderness.
- Discover how Sam came to understand the natural world.

I lived close to the weather. It is surprising how you watch it when you live in it. Not a cloud passed unnoticed, not a wind blew untested. I knew the moods of the storms, where they came from, their shapes and colors. When the sun shone, I took Frightful to the meadow and we slid down the mountain on my snapping-turtle-shell sled. She really didn't care much for this.

When the winds changed and the air smelled like snow, I would stay in my tree, because I had gotten lost in a blizzard one afternoon and had to hole up in a rock ledge until I could see where I was going. That day the winds were so strong I could not push against them, so I crawled under the ledge; for hours I wondered if I would be able to dig out when the storm blew on. Fortunately I only had to push through a foot of snow. However, that taught me to stay home when the air said "snow." Not that I

Fog-shrouded woodland in the Catskill Mountains, New York

Read Fluently

Form the class into partners. Choose a paragraph from the selection. Have students take turns reading the paragraph aloud. Ask them to underline words that give them trouble as they read. Then, have them decode the problem words with their partner. Provide assistance as needed. Have them reread the paragraph two more times to improve their reading speed. Remind them to stop at the commas and periods and to read with expression. Guide students to see that using figurative language allows the author to make her points about Sam's life among nature more vividly.

was afraid of being caught far from home in a storm, for I could find food and shelter and make a fire anywhere, but I had become as attached to my <u>hemlock</u> house as a brooding bird to her nest. Caught out in the storms and weather, I had an urgent desire to return to my tree, even as The Baron Weasel returned to his den, and the deer to their <u>copse</u>. We all had our little "patch" in the wilderness. We all fought to return there.

I usually came home at night with the nuthatch that roosted in a nearby sapling. I knew I was late if I tapped the tree and he came out. Sometimes when the weather was icy and miserable, I would hear him high in the trees near the edge of the meadow, <u>yanking</u> and yanking and flicking his tail, and then I would see him wing to bed early. I considered him a pretty good <u>barometer</u>, and if he went to his tree early, I went to mine early too. When you don't have a newspaper or radio to give you weather bulletins, watch the birds and animals. They can tell when a storm is coming. I called the nuthatch "Barometer," and when he holed up, I holed up, lit my light, and sat by my fire <u>whittling</u> or learning new tunes on my reed whistle. I was now really into the <u>teeth of winter</u>, and quite fascinated by its activity. There is no such thing as a "still winter night." Not only are many animals running around in the breaking cold, but the trees cry out and limbs snap and fall, and the wind gets caught in a ravine and screams until it dies.

✓ Reading Check   **What did Sam name the nuthatch? Explain why.**

Review and Assessment

Comprehension and Critical Thinking

1. (a) Identify When the weather is bad, what is Sam's "urgent desire"?
(b) Compare To what does Sam compare this desire?
(c) Interpret What does Sam tell us about himself when he makes a comparison?
2. (a) Recall What are some of the clues Sam has about what the weather will be like?
(b) Describe What parts of the natural world does Sam seem to notice most?
(c) Evaluate Sometimes Sam talks about the wind and trees

as if they were alive. Think about your relationship with nature. How is it like Sam's? How is it different?

Writing Activity

Make a list of sounds you hear only in winter. What are the tastes and smells that make you think of winter? List them. What are the sights of winter? Add them to your list. Then write an essay describing the place you most like to be in winter and explain why.

---

hemlock (HEM lahk) *n.* an evergreen tree with drooping branches and short needles
copse (kahps) *n.* a thicket of small trees or shrubs
yank (yangk) *v.* to give the call made by a nuthatch
barometer (buh RAHM uh tur) *n.* an instrument for forecasting changes in the weather; anything that indicates a change
whittle (WHIT ul) *v.* to cut or pare thin shavings from wood with a knife
teeth of winter (teeth uv WIN tur) *n.* the coldest, harshest time of winter

About the Selection

My Side of the Mountain, by Jean Craighead George (New York: E. P. Dutton, 1959), includes sketches of Sam Gribley's adventures.

About the Author

Jean Craighead George (b. 1919) often went camping, climbed trees, and studied living things as she grew up. Ms. George has been writing about nature and its lessons since she was eight years old, and has written more than 80 books for young readers.

Literature **89**

Review and Assessment

Comprehension and Critical Thinking

1. (a) to return to his tree **(b)** to the desire of animals to go to their shelters **(c)** that he relates to the animals because he thinks of himself as one of them

2. (a) the air smells like snow; the winds change; the nuthatch goes to bed early **(b)** the behavior of animals **(c)** Answers

will vary, but students should indicate how their relationship with nature is similar to or different than Sam's.

Writing Activity
Students should create lists of the sights, sounds, tastes, and smells of winter.

All in One **Foundations of Geography Teaching Resources,** *Rubric for Assessing a Writing Assignment,* p. 197

Guided Instruction (continued)

■ *Hint:* Have them look at how Sam describes the animals he lives near. *(Examples of similes are: on page 89, "I had become as attached to my hemlock house as a brooding bird to her nest." "...even as The Baron Weasel returned to his den."* Guide students to see that using figurative language allows the author to make her points about Sam's life among nature more vividly.

Independent Practice
Have students write a response to the following statement: "I would/would not want to live like Sam does because…" Make sure that students include at least three reasons why they would or would not like to live like Sam, and that they support each reason with details. Give students *Creating Paragraph Outlines* to help them prepare for writing.

All in One **Foundations of Geography Teaching Resources,** *Creating Paragraph Outlines,* p. 195

Monitor Progress
As students work on their paragraphs, circulate around the room and provide assistance as needed.

Assess and Reteach

Assess Progress   L2
Have students answer the assessment questions.

Reteach   L1
If students are having difficulty understanding the story, write the words *Plot, Character,* and *Setting* on the board. Help students identify these elements in the story and list them under the correct heading on the board.

Extend   L3
To extend the lesson, have students read the selected excerpt from *Hatchet* and answer the questions that follow. Ask students to make a chart in which they compare and contrast the experiences of the boy in each selection.

All in One **Foundations of Geography Teaching Resources,** *Hatchet,* pp. 191–194

Answer

✓ Reading Check   Barometer; because its actions told Sam when a storm might be coming.

Overview

Section 1 Understanding Culture
1. Learn about culture.
2. Explore how culture has developed.

Section 2 Culture and Society
1. Learn how people are organized into groups.
2. Investigate language.
3. Explore the role of religion.

Section 3 Cultural Change
1. Explore how cultures change.
2. Learn how ideas spread from one culture to another.

Technology Resources

Students use embedded Web codes to access Internet activities, chapter self-tests, and additional map practice. They may also access Dorling Kindersley's Online Desk Reference to learn more about each country they study.

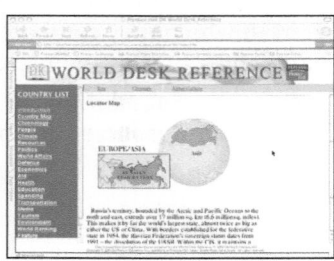

Use the Interactive Textbook to make content and concepts come alive through animations, videos, and activities that accompany the complete basal text—online and on CD-ROM.

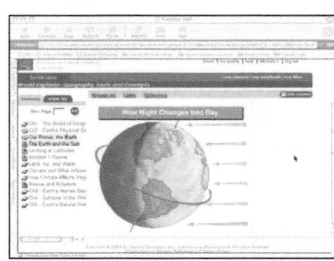

Use this complete suite of powerful teaching tools to make planning lessons and administering tests quicker and easier.

Reading and Assessment

Reading and Vocabulary Instruction

⤷ Model the Target Reading Skill

Sequence Explain to students that recognizing the sequence, or order, of events in written material can help them organize ideas and analyze patterns. Becoming familiar with words that signal sequence is one way for students to strengthen and apply this skill. Have students practice identifying sequence and recognizing sequence signal words by putting the following statements in order:

1. *Then I remembered that there was a shopping list in my pocket.*
2. *Before I left my house, I wrote out a grocery list.*
3. *Later, when I start cooking, I will have all the ingredients I need.*
4. *When I first entered the store, I could not remember what items I needed.*
5. *Soon, my cart was filled up with groceries.*

Model the approach by thinking out loud: "I am going to look for signal words to put these sentences in order. I see the following signal words: *then, before, later, first, soon*. I think sentence two should be first in the sequence, because it happens *before* the person goes to the store. The first sentence that takes place in the store is four, when she *first entered*, so that comes next. I think sentence one comes after that because she needed the shopping list before she could fill her cart with groceries. She finishes her shopping in sentence five. Finally, she uses the future tense and the word *Later* in sentence three. The correct sequence should be: sentences 2, 4, 1, 5, 3."

Use the following worksheets from All-in-One Foundations of Geography Teaching Resources (pp. 221–222) to support this chapter's Target Reading Skill.

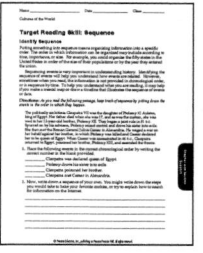 

Vocabulary Builder

High-Use Academic Words

Use these steps to teach this chapter's high-use words:

1. Have students rate how well they know each word on their Word Knowledge worksheets (All-in-One Foundations of Geography Teaching Resources, p. 223).
2. Pronounce each word and ask students to repeat it.
3. Give students a brief definition or sample sentence (provided on TE pp. 93, 97, and 105).
4. Work with students as they fill in the "Definition or Example" column of their Word Knowledge worksheets.

Assessment

Formal Assessment

Test students' understanding of core knowledge and skills.

Chapter Tests A and B, All-in-One Foundations of Geography Teaching Resources, pp. 235–240

Customize the Chapter Tests to suit your needs.

ExamView Test Bank CD-ROM

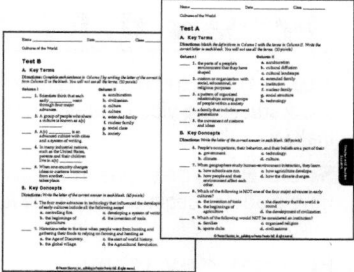

Skills Assessment

Assess geographic literacy.

MapMaster Skills, Student Edition, pp. 99, 100, 110

Assess reading and comprehension.

Target Reading Skills, Student Edition, pp. 95, 97, 106, and in Section Assessments

Chapter 4 Assessment, Western Hemisphere Reading and Vocabulary Study Guide, p. 44

Performance Assessment

Assess students' performance on this chapter's Writing Activities using the following rubrics from All-in-One Foundations of Geography Teaching Resources.

Rubric for Assessing a Writing Assignment, p. 233

Rubric for Assessing a Journal Entry, p. 234

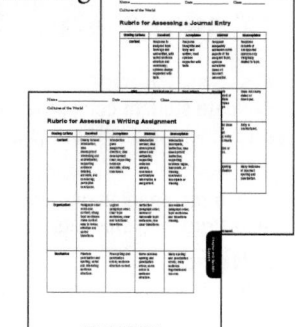

Assess students' work through performance tasks.

Small Group Activity: Creating a Report on World Music, All-in-One Foundations of Geography Teaching Resources, pp. 226–229

Online Assessment

Have students check their own understanding.

Chapter Self-Test

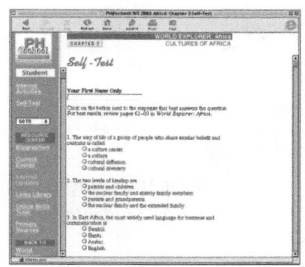

Section 1 Understanding Culture

🕐 *2 periods, 1 block*

Social Studies Objectives
1. Learn about culture.
2. Explore how culture has developed.

Reading/Language Arts Objective
Identify the sequence of events to help you understand and remember them.

Prepare to Read	Instructional Resources	Differentiated Instruction
Build Background Knowledge Show students a video and discuss the elements that make up culture. **Set a Purpose for Reading** Have students begin to fill out the *Reading Readiness Guide.* **Preview Key Terms** Teach the section's Key Terms. **Target Reading Skill** Introduce the section's Target Reading Skill of **understanding sequence.**	**All in One Foundations of Geography Teaching Resources** L2 Reading Readiness Guide, p. 210 L2 Identify Sequence, p. 221	**Spanish Reading and Vocabulary Study Guide** L1 Chapter 4, Section 1, pp. 26–27 ELL

Instruct	Instructional Resources	Differentiated Instruction
What Is Culture? Discuss how elements of culture differ throughout the world. **The Development of Culture** Ask about the four major advances of early cultures. **Target Reading Skill** Review **understanding sequence.**	**All in One Foundations of Geography Teaching Resources** L2 Guided Reading and Review, p. 211 L2 Reading Readiness Guide, p. 210 **Foundations of Geography Transparencies** L2 Section Reading Support Transparency FG 53	**Spanish Support** L2 Guided Reading and Review (Spanish), p. 28 ELL

Assess and Reteach	Instructional Resources	Differentiated Instruction
Assess Progress Evaluate student comprehension with the section assessment and section quiz. **Reteach** Assign the Reading and Vocabulary Study Guide to help struggling students. **Extend** Extend the lesson by assigning a Book Project.	**All in One Foundations of Geography Teaching Resources** L2 Section Quiz, p. 212 L3 Book Project: Desktop Countries, pp. 33–35 Rubric for Assessing a Writing Assignment, p. 233 **Reading and Vocabulary Study Guide** L1 Chapter 4, Section 1, pp. 35–37	**Spanish Support** L2 Section Quiz (Spanish), p. 29 ELL

Key

L1 Basic to Average	L3 Average to Advanced	LPR Less Proficient Readers	GT Gifted and Talented
L2 For All Students		AR Advanced Readers	ELL English Language Learners
		SN Special Needs Students	

Section 2 Culture and Society

 4.5 periods, 2.25 blocks (includes Skills for Life)

Social Studies Objectives

1. Learn how people are organized into groups.
2. Investigate language.
3. Explore the role of religion.

Reading/Language Arts Objective

Learning to notice the sequence of important changes can help you understand, remember, and interpret these changes.

Prepare to Read

Build Background Knowledge
Discuss three elements of culture: social structure, language, and religion.

Set a Purpose for Reading
Have students evaluate statements on the *Reading Readiness Guide*.

Preview Key Terms
Teach the section's Key Terms.

Target Reading Skill
Introduce the section's Target Reading Skill of **understanding sequence**.

Instructional Resources

All in One Foundations of Geography Teaching Resources
- L2 Reading Readiness Guide, p. 214
- L2 Identify Sequence, p. 221

Differentiated Instruction

Spanish Reading and Vocabulary Study Guide
- L1 Chapter 4, Section 2, pp. 28–29 ELL

Instruct

How Society Is Organized
Ask about extended and nuclear families.

Target Reading Skill
Review **understanding sequence**.

Language
Discuss language and how it can uphold or reflect particular customs.

Religion
Discuss features of different religions.

Instructional Resources

All in One Foundations of Geography Teaching Resources
- L2 Guided Reading and Review, p. 215
- L2 Reading Readiness Guide, p. 214

Foundations of Geography Transparencies
- L2 Section Reading Support Transparency FG 54
- L2 Transparency B15: Outline

Differentiated Instruction

All in One Foundations of Geography Teaching Resources
- L3 City Kids in China, pp. 230–231 AR, GT
- L2 Skills for Life, p. 225 AR, GT, LPR, SN

Teacher's Edition
- L3 For Advanced Readers, TE p. 99
- L3 For Gifted and Talented, TE p. 99

Spanish Support
- L2 Guided Reading and Review (Spanish), p. 20 ELL

Assess and Reteach

Assess Progress
Evaluate student comprehension with the section assessment and section quiz.

Reteach
Assign the Reading and Vocabulary Study Guide to help struggling students.

Extend
Have students work in groups to learn about rituals of world religions.

Instructional Resources

All in One Foundations of Geography Teaching Resources
- L2 Section Quiz, p. 216
  Rubric for Assessing a Journal Entry, p. 234

Reading and Vocabulary Study Guide
- L1 Chapter 4, Section 2, pp. 38–40

Differentiated Instruction

All in One Foundations of Geography Teaching Resources
  Rubric for Assessing a Writing Assignment, p. 233

Teacher's Edition
- L1 For Less Proficient Readers, TE p. 103
- L1 For Special Needs Students, TE p. 103

Social Studies Skills Tutor CD-ROM
- L1 Making Valid Generalizations ELL, LPR, SN

Spanish Support
- L2 Section Quiz (Spanish), p. 19 ELL

Key
- L1 Basic to Average
- L3 Average to Advanced
- L2 For All Students
- LPR Less Proficient Readers
- AR Advanced Readers
- SN Special Needs Students
- GT Gifted and Talented
- ELL English Language Learners

Section 3 Cultural Change

 4.5 periods, 2.25 blocks (includes Chapter Review and Assessment)

Social Studies Objectives
1. Explore how cultures change.
2. Learn how ideas spread from one culture to another.

Reading/Language Arts Objective
Identify signal words to help keep the order of events clear.

Prepare to Read	**Instructional Resources**	**Differentiated Instruction**
Build Background Knowledge Ask students to identify elements of their cultures that have been borrowed from others. **Set a Purpose for Reading** Have students evaluate statements on the *Reading Readiness Guide.* **Preview Key Terms** Teach the section's Key Terms. **Target Reading Skill** Introduce the section's Target Reading Skill of **recognizing words that signal sequence.**	**All in One Foundations of Geography Teaching Resources** L2 Reading Readiness Guide, p. 218 L2 Recognize Sequence Signal Words, p. 222	**Spanish Reading and Vocabulary Study Guide** L1 Chapter 4, Section 3, pp. 30–31 ELL

Instruct	**Instructional Resources**	**Differentiated Instruction**
How Cultures Change Discuss cultural change and have students predict future changes in their own cultures. **How Ideas Spread** Discuss cultural diffusion. **Target Reading Skill** Review **recognizing words that signal sequence.**	**All in One Foundations of Geography Teaching Resources** L2 Guided Reading and Review, p. 219 L2 Reading Readiness Guide, p. 218 **Foundations of Geography Transparencies** L2 Section Reading Support Transparency FG 55 L2 Transparency B18: Concept Web	**All in One Foundations of Geography Teaching Resources** L3 Enrichment, p. 224 AR, GT **Teacher's Edition** L3 For Advanced Readers, TE p. 106 L1 For English Language Learners, TE p. 106 **Spanish Support** L2 Guided Reading and Review (Spanish), p. 32 ELL

Assess and Reteach	**Instructional Resources**	**Differentiated Instruction**
Assess Progress Evaluate student comprehension with the section assessment and section quiz. **Reteach** Assign the Reading and Vocabulary Study Guide to help struggling students. **Extend** Extend the lesson by assigning a Small Group Activity.	**All in One Foundations of Geography Teaching Resources** L2 Section Quiz, p. 220 L3 Small Group Activity: Creating a Report on World Music, pp. 226–229 Rubric for Assessing a Writing Assignment, p. 233 L2 Vocabulary Development, p. 232 L2 Word Knowledge, p. 223 L2 Chapter Tests A and B, pp. 235–240 **Reading and Vocabulary Study Guide** L1 Chapter 4, Section 3, pp. 41–43	**Spanish Support** L2 Section Quiz (Spanish), p. 33 ELL L2 Chapter Summary (Spanish), p. 34 ELL L2 Vocabulary Development (Spanish), p. 35 ELL

Key

L1 Basic to Average	L3 Average to Advanced	LPR Less Proficient Readers	GT Gifted and Talented
L2 For All Students		AR Advanced Readers	ELL English Language Learners
		SN Special Needs Students	

Reading Background

Oral Cloze Reading

In Section 1 of this chapter, students may use the Oral Cloze Reading strategy to explore the section called Understanding Culture. Help students get the most out of this reading strategy by choosing meaningful words to leave out, such as nouns and verbs, rather than prepositions or conjunctions, and by choosing words that are not particularly long or difficult. For example, in the following paragraph from page 92 of the Student Edition, you might leave out the words indicated in bold.

What Is Culture?

*Culture is the way of life of a **people**, including their beliefs, customs, and practices. The **language** people speak and the way they **dress** are both parts of their **culture**. So are the work people do, what they do after **work** or school, and the **ideas** that influence them.*

Processing Information

Because students will be studying sequence in this chapter's Target Reading Skill, use this opportunity to talk to them about different plans or structures authors may use to organize, or craft, their ideas. Sequence, or chronological order, is one type of author's craft, and others may include comparison and contrast, or cause and effect. Ask students to read the two paragraphs on page 99 of the Student Edition and determine what kind of structure the author is using. Ask: *Is the information in sequence? Is there a clear cause and effect? Is the author highlighting similarities and differences?* Students should see that the author is comparing and contrasting the languages of different groups and countries.

World Studies Background

Folk Art

Folk art can tell us a great deal about a society. Folk artists do not follow the trends of popular art. They develop their own art that reflects the local culture. Folk art includes clothing, toys, and religious figurines that express the typical costumes, forms of entertainment, and beliefs of a society. Because the art is both decorative and functional, it reveals the aesthetic style and everyday routines of a people.

Languages Spread and Shrink

In the 1990s, scholars counted about 6,000 languages spoken across the world. However, scholars predict that within the next 100 years, as societies become more interconnected through improved communication, distinct languages will blend together and unique local languages will die out, leaving only 3000 languages in use. This equals a loss of one language every 12 days.

Computers Finding Cures

As technology advances, computer users can help scientists further their research toward curing diseases. In similar programs launched in 2001 and 2003, volunteers downloaded a screensaver that allowed their computers to perform complicated calculations related to disease research. The power of so many computers working on a project is immensely more powerful than the largest supercomputer and can yield faster results.

Chapter 4

Guiding Questions

Remind students about the Guiding Questions introduced at the beginning of each section.

Section 1 relates to **Guiding Question ③**
What is a culture? *(A culture is the way of life of a people, including their beliefs, customs, and practices.)*

Section 2 relates to **Guiding Question ③**
What is a culture? *(Social organization, language, and religion are all parts of a culture.)*

Section 3 relates to **Guiding Question ③**
What is a culture? *(A culture changes through the spread of new technologies and new ideas.)*

⟲ Target Reading Skill

In this chapter, students will learn and apply the reading skill of sequence. Use the following worksheets to help students practice this skill:

All in One Foundations of Geography Teaching Resources, *Identify Sequence,* p. 221, *Recognize Sequence Signal Words,* p. 222

Chapter 4 Cultures of the World

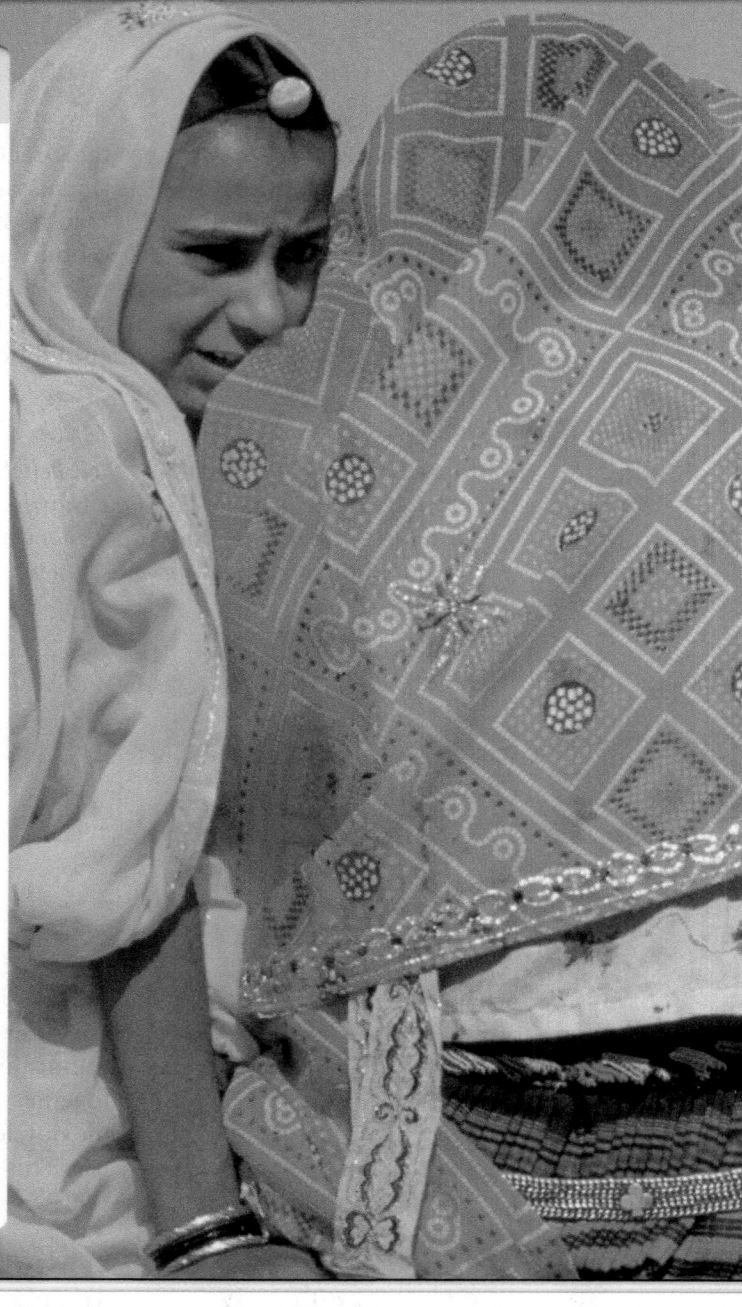

Chapter Preview

This chapter will introduce you to the concept of culture, the things that make up culture, and the ways in which cultures change.

Section 1
Understanding Culture

Section 2
Culture and Society

Section 3
Cultural Change

⟲ Target Reading Skill

Sequence In this chapter, you will focus on the text structure by identifying the order, or sequence, of events. Noting the sequence of events can help you understand and remember the events.

▶ Young women in traditional dress at a festival in Pushkar, India

90 Foundations of Geography

Differentiated Instruction

The following Teacher Edition strategies are suitable for students of varying abilities.

Advanced Readers, pp. 99, 106
English Language Learners, p. 106
Gifted and Talented, p. 99
Less Proficient Readers, p. 103
Special Needs Students, p. 103

Bibliography

For the Teacher
Kohl, MaryAnn F., and Jean Potter. *Global Art: Activities, Projects and Inventions from Around the World.* Gryphon House, 1998.
Knight, Margy Burns. *Talking Walls: The Stories Continue.* Tillbury House Publishers, 2003.
Perry, Phyllis Jean. *Keeping the Traditions: A Multicultural Resource.* Fulcrum Publishers, 2000.

For the Student
L1 Wroble, Lisa A. *Kids During the Industrial Revolution* (Kids Throughout History). Rosen Publishing Group, 2003.
L2 Macdonald, Fiona. *Clothing and Jewelry* (Discovering World Cultures). Bt Bound, 2001.
L3 Na, An. *A Step From Heaven.* Front Street Press, 2001.

Reach Into Your Background Have students read the caption and study the photograph on pp. 90–91. Ask them if they have seen or participated in ceremonies where traditional dress is worn. Ask them why wearing traditional dress during special occasions might be important to Indian culture. Have students share their ideas.

Chapter 4 **91**

Chapter Resources

Teaching Resources
L2 Vocabulary Development, p. 232
L2 Skills for Life, p. 225
L2 Chapter Tests A and B, pp. 235–240

Spanish Support
L2 Spanish Chapter Summary, p. 34
L2 Spanish Vocabulary Development, p. 35

Media and Technology
L1 Student Edition on Audio CD
L1 Guided Reading Audiotapes, English and Spanish
L2 Social Studies Skills Tutor CD-ROM
ExamView Test Bank CD-ROM

PRENTICE HALL
Presentation EXPRESS™
Teach · Connect · Inspire

Teach this chapter's content using the PresentationExpress™ CD-ROM including:

- slide shows
- transparencies
- interactive maps and media
- *ExamView*® QuickTake Presenter

Section 1
Step-by-Step Instruction

Objectives

Social Studies
1. Learn about culture.
2. Explore how culture has developed.

Reading/Language Arts
Identify the sequence of events to help you understand and remember them.

Prepare to Read

Build Background Knowledge L2
Tell students that in this chapter they will be learning about the elements that make up culture. Show the video *What is Culture?* and as they watch, ask students to write down a definition of culture and some of its parts. Point out the definition in the text to help students sharpen their answers. Conduct an Idea Wave (TE, p. T35) to generate a list of definitions on the board.

📼 *What Is Culture?*, **World Studies Video Program**

Set a Purpose for Reading L2
- Preview the objectives.
- Form students into pairs or groups of four. Distribute the *Reading Readiness Guide*. Ask the students to fill in the first two columns of the chart. Use the Numbered Heads participation strategy (TE, p. T36) to call on students to share one piece of information they already know and one piece of information they want to know.

  All in One Foundations of Geography Teaching Resources, *Reading Readiness Guide,* p. 210

Vocabulary Builder
Preview Key Terms L2
Pronounce each Key Term, then ask the students to say the word with you. Provide a simple explanation such as, "A civilization is a society advanced in art, science, and government."

Section 1
Understanding Culture

Prepare to Read

Objectives
In this section you will
1. Learn about culture.
2. Explore how culture has developed.

Taking Notes
Copy the concept web below. As you read this section, fill in the web with information about culture, its relation to the environment, and how it has developed. Add ovals as needed for concepts in the section.

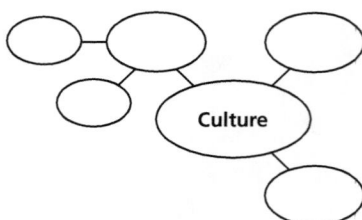

🎯 Target Reading Skill
Understand Sequence
A sequence is the order in which a series of events occurs. Noting the sequence of important events can help you understand and remember the events. You can show the order of events by making a sequence chart. Write the first event, or thing that sets the other events in motion, in the first box. Then write each additional event in a box. Use arrows to show how one event leads to the next.

Key Terms
- **culture** (KUL chur) *n.* the way of life of a people, including their beliefs and practices
- **cultural landscape** (KUL chur ul LAND skayp) *n.* the parts of a people's environment that they have shaped and the technology they have used to shape it
- **civilization** (sih vuh luh ZAY shun) *n.* an advanced culture with cities and a system of writing
- **institution** (in stuh TOO shun) *n.* a custom or organization with social, educational, or religious purposes

A grandfather in Japan teaching his grandson to use chopsticks

92 Foundations of Geography

What Is Culture?

Culture is the way of life of a people, including their beliefs, customs, and practices. The language people speak and the way they dress are both parts of their culture. So are the work people do, what they do after work or school, and the ideas that influence them.

Elements of Culture Parents pass culture on to their children, generation after generation. Ideas and ways of doing things are called cultural traits. Over time, cultural traits may change.

Some elements of a culture are easy to see. They include material things, such as houses, television sets, food, and clothing. Sports and literature are visible elements of culture as well. Things you cannot see or touch are also part of culture. They include spiritual beliefs, government, and ideas about right and wrong. Finally, language is a very important part of culture.

🎯 Target Reading Skill L2

Understand Sequence Explain that one way to organize ideas is by sequence, or time order. Explain sequence by asking students to consider the order of events in their day. Tell students that events in history also can be organized in a logical sequence.

Model understanding sequence using the first two paragraphs under the head "Technology and Civilization" on p. 94 of the Student Edition. Make a sequence chart on the board using the events leading to the Agricultural Revolution.

Give students *Identify Sequence.* Have them complete the activity in groups.

All in One Foundations of Geography Teaching Resources, *Identify Sequence,* p. 221

People and Their Land Geographers study themes of culture, especially human activities related to the environment. The theme of human-environment interaction deals with these activities. Geographers want to know how the environment affects culture. For example, Japan is a nation of mountainous islands, with limited farmland. So the Japanese have turned to the sea. Fish and seaweed are popular foods in Japan.

However, environment does not dictate culture. Like Japan, Greece is a nation of mountainous islands and peninsulas surrounded by the sea. The Greeks eat some fish, but they have cleared mountainsides as well for use as pasture. Goats and sheep graze on the mountainsides and provide food for the Greeks.

Geographers are also interested in the effect people have on their environment. Often the effect is tied to a culture's technology, even if that technology is simple. For example, the Greeks have cleared their rugged land for pasture. The Japanese harvest seaweed.

A **cultural landscape** is the parts of a people's environment that they have shaped and the technology they have used to shape it. This varies from place to place. On hilly Bali (BAH lee), in Indonesia, farmers have carved terraces into hillsides. On the plains of northern India, farmers have laid out broad, flat fields.

✔ **Reading Check** How are culture and environment related?

Balinese Terraces
A farmer on the island of Bali, in Indonesia, crosses terraced rice fields. **Analyze** *How has Bali's environment affected its culture? How has Bali's culture affected its environment?*

Instruct

What Is Culture?   L2

Guided Instruction

- **Vocabulary Builder** Clarify the high-use words **trait** and **dictate** before reading.

- Read What Is Culture? using the Oral Cloze strategy (TE, p. T33).

- Ask students **What are some elements of culture?** *(houses, television sets, food, clothing, sports, entertainment, literature, spiritual beliefs, government, ideas about right and wrong, and language)*

- Point out to students that people in Japan and Greece share similar physical geography but have chosen to utilize their resources in different ways. Ask students **How do people in Greece interact with their environment differently than people in Japan?** *(The Greeks have cleared their rugged land for pasture; the Japanese fish and harvest seaweed.)*

Independent Practice
Ask students to create the Taking Notes graphic organizer on a blank piece of paper. Have students fill in some of the ovals with information from the passage. Model choosing appropriate details.

Monitor Progress
As students read the passage and expand the Taking Notes concept web, circulate through the classroom to answer questions and provide assistance as needed.

Answers

✔ Reading Check Physical environment may influence the types of food, housing, and work that are most common in a culture. The development of technology in a culture can influence environment by allowing people to change the landscape.

Analyze Bali's environment provides a climate suitable for raising rice. The technology of the Balinese culture allows farmers to modify the environment by terracing the land.

Vocabulary Builder

Use the information below to teach students this section's high-use words.

High-Use Word	Definition and Sample Sentence
trait, p. 92	*n.* distinguishing feature or characteristic One of Adam's **traits** is his unusual sense of humor.
dictate, p. 93	*v.* to control or command Culture often **dictates** the kinds of food people eat.
advance, p. 94	*n.* development Doctors made an important **advance** in fighting the disease.
complex, p. 95	*adj.* complicated, made up of several parts It took him almost an hour to solve the **complex** math problem.

The Development of Culture

L2

Guided Instruction

- **Vocabulary Builder** Clarify the high-use words **advance** and **complex** before reading.

- Ask students to read The Development of Culture. As students read, circulate to make sure individuals can answer the Reading Check question.

- Ask **What are the four major advances of early cultures? Why do you think each is important?** *(Possible answers: Tools could be used for hunting and building shelters; fire allowed people to live in colder climates and cook food; farming provided a steady food supply; civilizations helped people live better through new technologies.)*

- Ask students why they think the development of cities created a need for institutions such as armies and governments. *(People living together in large groups need more organization, such as laws to ensure safety, as well as means to protect themselves.)*

Independent Practice

Have students complete the Taking Notes graphic organizer by asking them to add more information from the section. Students may add ovals as needed.

Monitor Progress

- Show *Section Reading Support Transparency FG 53* and ask students to check their graphic organizers individually. Go over key concepts and clarify key vocabulary as needed.

  📖 **Foundations of Geography Transparencies,** *Section Reading Support Transparency FG 53*

- Tell students to fill in the last column of the *Reading Readiness Guide.* Ask them to evaluate if what they learned was what they had expected to learn.

  All In One Foundations of Geography Teaching Resources, *Reading Readiness Guide,* p. 210

Answer

Draw Conclusions Farmers were able to harvest more with more powerful tools.

The Development of Agricultural Technology

Sickle
The first farmers used hand-held sickles to harvest grain. The first sickles had stone blades. Later sickles, like the one shown here, had metal blades.

Horse-drawn reaper
By the late 1800s, farmers were using animal-powered machinery, such as this sail reaper, to harvest grain.

Combine harvester
Today, farmers harvest grain with large-scale, motorized machinery, such as this combine.

The Development of Culture

Scientists think that early cultures had four major advances in technology. First was the invention of tools millions of years ago. Second and third were the control of fire and the beginnings of agriculture. Fourth was the development of **civilizations,** or advanced cultures with cities and the use of writing.

Technology and Civilization For most of human existence, people were hunters and gatherers. While traveling from place to place, they collected wild plants, hunted game, and fished.

Later, people discovered how to grow crops. They tamed wild animals to help them with work or to raise for food. Over time, more and more people relied on farming for most of their food. Historians call this great change the Agricultural Revolution.

Agriculture provided a steady food supply. Agriculture let farmers grow more food than they needed. In parts of Asia and Africa, some people worked full time on crafts such as metalworking. They traded their products for food. People began to develop laws and government. To store information, they developed writing. These advances in culture produced the first true civilizations about 5,000 years ago.

Early civilizations developed new technologies, such as irrigation, that let people grow more crops. Over time, farming and civilization spread throughout the world.

Tools for Harvesting When the Agricultural Revolution began, people used simple hand-powered tools. The Industrial Revolution later brought industrial tools to the fields. **Draw Conclusions** *How do you think the development of tools for harvesting affected the amount that each farmer could harvest?*

Skills Mini Lesson

Recognizing Bias L2

1. Define *bias* as a one-sided view. Explain that to detect bias students should look for false or missing information, words that express emotion, and how the writer's purpose affects the information.

2. Practice the skill using this statement from a school newspaper: *Our team will win the big game because we have better players.* Ask: What words express emotion rather than fact? *(better players)* Why might the paper show a bias? *(The writer wants his or her own team to win.)*

3. Discuss what could make the article less biased.

Then, about 200 years ago, people began to invent new technologies that used power-driven machinery. This change marked the beginning of the Industrial Revolution. It led to the growth of cities, science, and even more advanced technologies, such as computers and space flight.

Development of Institutions Before the Agricultural Revolution, people had simple **institutions,** customs and organizations with social, educational, or religious purposes. These included extended families and simple political institutions, such as councils of elders.

As people gathered in larger groups and formed cities, they needed more complex institutions. People developed organized religions, with priests, ceremonies, and temples. Armies and governments appeared with states. Teachers started schools.

In the modern world, we have many different kinds of institutions, including museums, sports clubs, corporations, political parties, and universities. These institutions are important parts of our culture.

✓ **Reading Check** What allowed civilizations to develop?

Oxford University, in Oxford, England, is more than 800 years old.

Understand Sequence What important events led to the Industrial Revolution?

Section 1 Assessment

Key Terms
Review the key terms at the beginning of this section. Use each term in a sentence that explains its meaning.

 Target Reading Skill
Place the following events in the order in which they occurred: the development of civilization; the invention of tools; the development of industry; and the beginnings of agriculture.

Comprehension and Critical Thinking
1. (a) Define What is a cultural landscape?
(b) Explain What are the most important cultural traits that shape a people's cultural landscape?
(c) Identify Cause and Effect If two cultures occupy similar environments, why might their cultural landscapes still differ?
2. (a) Identify What was the Agricultural Revolution?
(b) Sequence What cultural advances followed the Agricultural Revolution?

Writing Activity
Think of all the ways that the culture of your region has shaped its landscape. Write a short paragraph describing your cultural landscape and the cultural traits that shaped it.

For: An activity on culture
Visit: PHSchool.com
Web Code: led-3401

Section 1 Assessment

Key Terms
Students' sentences should reflect knowledge of each Key Term.

Target Reading Skill
the invention of tools; the beginnings of agriculture; the development of civilization; the development of industry

Comprehension and Critical Thinking
1. (a) the parts of a people's environment that they have shaped and the technology they have used to shape it **(b)** a group's customs, ideas, and ways of doing things **(c)** because of the way they have developed and applied technology, or because of their customs
2. (a) The Agricultural Revolution was a change in which people began growing crops and taming wild animals. They began to depend more on farming for food than hunting and gathering. **(b)** the rise of birthrates and population, the ability to grow excess crops, the development of crafts, the institution of laws and government, and the development of writing

Assess and Reteach

Assess Progress L2
Have students complete the Section Assessment. Administer the *Section Quiz.*

All in One Foundations of Geography Teaching Resources, *Section Quiz,* p. 212

Reteach L1
If students need more instruction, have them read this section in the Reading and Vocabulary Study Guide.

Chapter 4, Section 1, **Western Hemisphere Reading and Vocabulary Study Guide,** pp. 35–37

Extend L3
Have students complete *Book Project: Desktop Countries.*

All in One Foundations of Geography Teaching Resources, *Book Project: Desktop Countries,* pp. 33–35

Answer

✓ **Reading Check** advances in culture such as agriculture and writing

Writing Activity
Use the *Rubric for Assessing a Writing Assignment* to evaluate students' paragraphs.

All in One Foundations of Geography Teaching Resources, *Rubric for Assessing a Writing Assignment,* p. 233

Objectives

Social Studies

1. Learn how people are organized into groups.
2. Investigate language.
3. Explore the role of religion.

Reading/Language Arts

Learning to notice the sequence of important changes can help you understand and remember and interpret these changes.

Prepare to Read

Build Background Knowledge L2

In this section, students will learn about three elements of culture: social structure, language, and religion. Have students look at the section's headings and photographs with this question in mind: **Why are these ideas important to a society's culture?** Conduct an Idea Wave (TE, p. T35) to generate a list.

Set a Purpose for Reading L2

- Preview the Objectives.

- Read each statement in the *Reading Readiness Guide* aloud. Ask students to mark the statements true or false.

- Have students discuss the statements in pairs or groups of four, then mark their worksheets again. Use the Numbered Heads participation strategy (TE, p. T36) to call on students to share their group's perspectives.

  All in One Foundations of Geography Teaching Resources, *Reading Readiness Guide,* p. 214

Vocabulary Builder
Preview Key Terms L2

Pronounce each Key Term, then ask the students to say the word with you. Provide a simple explanation such as, "An extended family can include grandparents, aunts, uncles, and cousins."

Prepare to Read

Objectives

In this section you will

1. Learn how people are organized into groups.
2. Investigate language.
3. Explore the role of religion.

Taking Notes

Copy the outline below. As you read this section, fill in the outline with information about how society is organized, about language, and about religion. Add letters and numbers as needed.

> I. How society is organized
>   A. Social classes
>   B.
>   1.
>   2.
> II. Language
>   A.

Target Reading Skill

Understand Sequence
Noting the sequence of important changes can help you understand and remember the changes. You can show a sequence of changes by simply listing the changes in the order in which they occurred. As you read this section, list the sequence of the changes in people's ability to improve their status.

Key Terms

- **society** (suh SY uh tee) *n.* a group of people sharing a culture
- **social structure** (SOH shul STRUK chur) *n.* a pattern of organized relationships among groups of people within a society
- **social class** (SOH shul klas) *n.* a grouping of people based on rank or status
- **nuclear family** (NOO klee ur FAM uh lee) *n.* a mother, a father, and their children
- **extended family** (ek STEN did FAM uh lee) *n.* a family that includes several generations

How Society Is Organized

Think about the people you see every day. Do you spend each day meeting random strangers? Or do you see the same family members, classmates, and teachers every day? Chances are, there is a pattern to your interactions.

A group of people sharing a culture is known as a **society.** Every society has a **social structure,** or a pattern of organized relationships among groups of people within the society. A society may be as small as a single community or as large as a nation or even a group of similar nations. Smaller groups within a society work together on particular tasks. Some groups work together to get food. Others protect the community. Still others educate children. Social structure helps people work together to meet one another's basic needs.

The family is the basic, most important social unit of any society. Families teach the customs and traditions of the culture to their children. Through their families, children learn how to dress, to be polite, to eat, and to play.

A nuclear family in the United Kingdom

96 Foundations of Geography

Target Reading Skill L2

Understand Sequence Explain to students that they can show a sequence of changes by listing the changes in the order in which they occurred.

Model understanding sequence using the text on p. 100 of the Student Edition. Ask **In what order did the religions of Christianity, Islam, and Judaism start?** Then write on the board, *1. Judaism; 2. Christianity; 3. Islam.* Point out the sentence in the passage in which the answer can be found, emphasizing the clue words "first," "then," and "finally."

Give students *Identify Sequence.* Have them complete the activity in groups.

All in One Foundations of Geography Teaching Resources, *Identify Sequence,* p. 221

Social Classes Cultures also have another kind of social organization—**social classes,** or groupings of people based on rank or status. A person's status or position may come from his or her wealth, land, ancestors, or education. In some cultures in the past, it was often hard—or impossible—for people to move from one social class to another. Today, people in many societies can improve their status. They can obtain a good education, make more money, or marry someone of a higher class.

Kinds of Families Not all cultures define family in the same way. In some cultures, the basic unit is a **nuclear family,** or a mother, a father, and their children. This pattern is common in developed nations such as the United States, Australia, and Germany. The nuclear family gets its name from the word *nucleus,* which means "center."

Other cultures have **extended families,** or families that include several generations. In addition to a central nuclear family of parents and their sons or daughters, there are the wives or husbands of those sons or daughters. The family also includes grandchildren, or the children of those sons or daughters. In extended families, older people often help care for the children. They are respected for their knowledge and experience. Older family members pass on traditions. Extended families are less common than they used to be. As rural people move to cities, nuclear families are becoming more common.

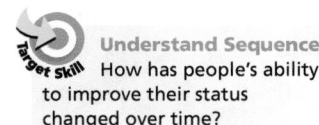

Understand Sequence
How has people's ability to improve their status changed over time?

✓ Reading Check **What is the basic social unit of societies?**

A Salvadoran-American Family
This family includes grandparents and more than one set of parents.
Infer *Is this a nuclear family or an extended family?*

Chapter 4 Section 2 **97**

─ Vocabulary Builder ─

Use information below to teach students this section's high-use words.

High-Use Word	Definition and Sample Sentence
status, p. 97	*n.* rank or position Going to college is one way to improve your **status** in life.
concept, p. 98	*n.* idea The **concept** behind the invention was very simple.
ritual, p. 101	*n.* ceremony or custom Many religions have a marriage **ritual.**

Language

L2

Guided Instruction

■ **Vocabulary Builder** Clarify the high-use word **concept** before reading.

■ Read Language and examine The World: Major Language Groups. Encourage students to ask questions about using the map.

■ Ask students if they can think of examples of a word having different meanings in two different cultures. *(Possible answer: "Football" in the United States is not the same as "football" in England. There, "football" refers to soccer.)*

■ Ask students to examine the photograph at the top of p. 98. Ask **What other forms of cultural communication might depend on senses other than hearing?** *(Answers will vary, but might include a green light that means "go," or a handshake that means "nice to meet you.")*

■ Ask **Why might the customs of a French-speaking Canadian differ from those of an English-speaking Canadian?** *(because people who speak different languages may have different ideas and traditions)*

■ Have students list the language groups found in Australia *(Indo-European, other)*. Ask **Why might Australia share a language group with Europe?** *(Most Australians are descended from British settlers.)*

A teacher using sign language with hearing-impaired students

Language

All cultures have language. In fact, language provides a basis for culture. People learn their cultures mainly through language. Most communication with others depends on language. Think how hard it would be if you had no way to say, "Meet me by the gate after school." How could you learn if you could not ask questions?

A culture's language reflects the things that are important in that culture. For example, English has words for Christian and Jewish concepts, such as *baptism* and *sabbath*. Some languages lack words for these concepts because their speakers are not Jewish or Christian. But those languages have words for concepts in their people's religions that have no English translation.

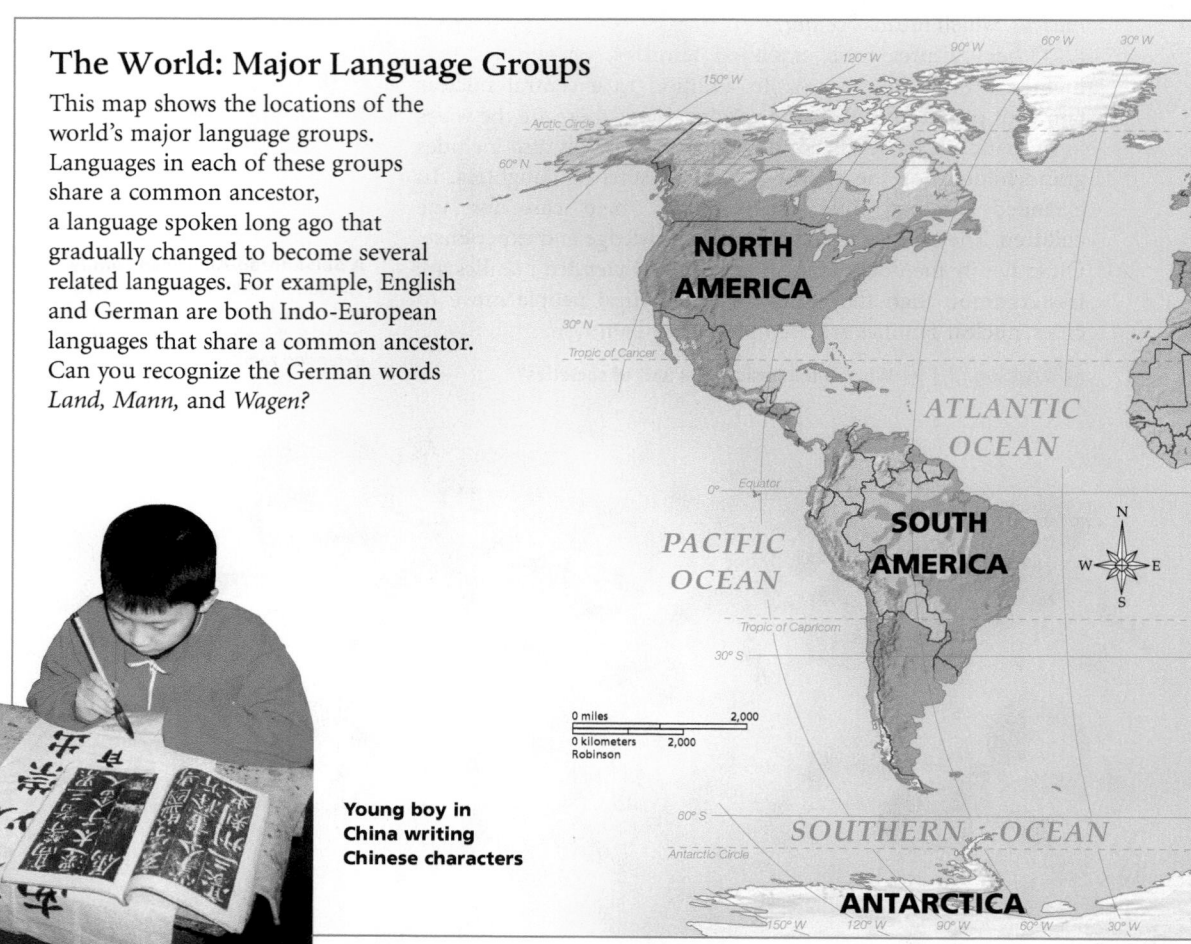

The World: Major Language Groups

This map shows the locations of the world's major language groups. Languages in each of these groups share a common ancestor, a language spoken long ago that gradually changed to become several related languages. For example, English and German are both Indo-European languages that share a common ancestor. Can you recognize the German words *Land*, *Mann*, and *Wagen*?

Young boy in China writing Chinese characters

Background: Daily Life

Religion Affects Daily Life Many religions require daily activities, such as prayers and rituals, to be performed by believers. In a Jewish group called Hasidim, or "pious ones," religion governs how believers dress, what they eat, and how they wear their hair. Men wear beards and have a long side lock of hair hanging on each side of their faces. Married women cover their hair with wigs or scarves in public. Like other Orthodox Jews, Hasidim observe special laws about food, called *kashrus*, which are outlined in the Jewish Torah. Shellfish and pork are forbidden. Meat and dairy foods may not be eaten at the same meal or cooked in the same pot.

In some countries, people speak more than one language. For example, Canada has two official languages, French and English. In the United States, you may usually hear English, but you can also hear Spanish, Chinese, Haitian Creole, and many other languages. India has 16 official languages, but people there speak more than 800 languages!

People who speak each language are culturally different in some ways from other people in their country who speak other languages. They may celebrate different festivals or have different customs for such things as dating or education. That is because each language preserves shared ideas and traditions.

✓ Reading Check **What is the relation between language and culture?**

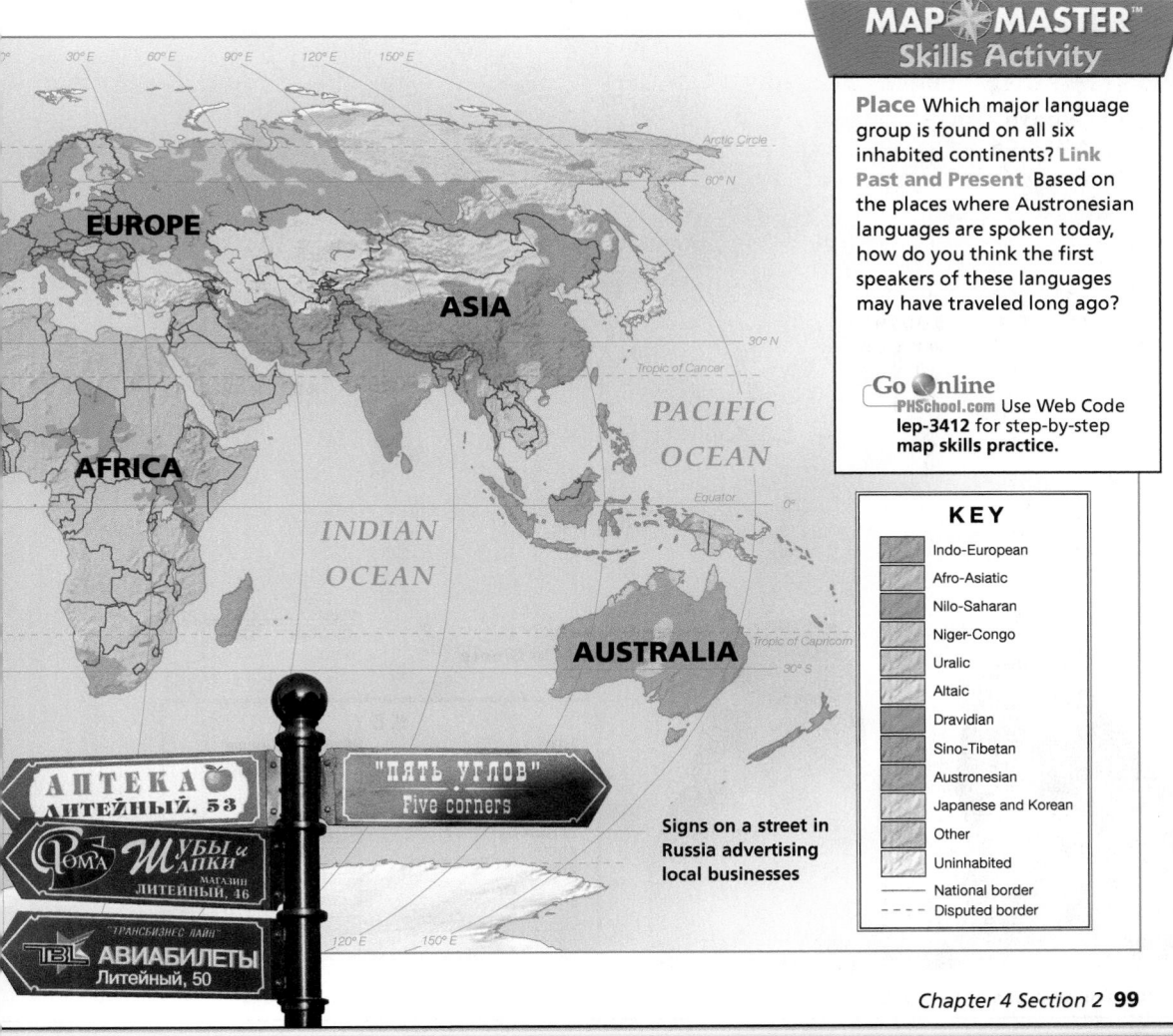

MAP MASTER™ Skills Activity

Place Which major language group is found on all six inhabited continents? **Link Past and Present** Based on the places where Austronesian languages are spoken today, how do you think the first speakers of these languages may have traveled long ago?

Go Online
PHSchool.com Use Web Code **lep-3412** for step-by-step map skills practice.

KEY

- Indo-European
- Afro-Asiatic
- Nilo-Saharan
- Niger-Congo
- Uralic
- Altaic
- Dravidian
- Sino-Tibetan
- Austronesian
- Japanese and Korean
- Other
- Uninhabited
- —— National border
- - - - Disputed border

Signs on a street in Russia advertising local businesses

Chapter 4 Section 2 **99**

Differentiated Instruction

For Advanced Readers L3
Have students read the primary source *City Kids in China* and look for elements of social structure. Have them compare the Chinese students' experiences to their own and write a paragraph that describes an element of social structure in the United States.

All in One Foundations of Geography Teaching Resources, *City Kids in China,* pp. 230–231

For Gifted and Talented L3
Have students go on a "language hunt." By using the library or Internet and talking to their families, have each student learn ten words in another language. Each student should make a chart with the word, the English translation, and the name of the language. Have students share their new words with the class.

Independent Practice

Have students continue working with the Taking Notes graphic organizer by asking them to expand and complete the section of the outline on Language. If students need assistance, show the blank *Outline Transparency* as a model.

Foundations of Geography Transparencies, *Transparency B15: Outline*

Monitor Progress

As students continue to fill in the graphic organizer, make sure individuals are adding appropriate details about language. Provide assistance as needed.

Answers

✓ Reading Check Language provides a basis for culture, because people learn their cultures mainly through language.

MAP MASTER™ Skills Activity **Place** Indo-European **Link Past and Present** Austronesian languages are spoken on many islands in the Pacific and Indian oceans. The first speakers of Austronesian probably traveled by boat to new areas.

Go Online
PHSchool.com Students may practice their map skills using the interactive online version of this map.

Religion

L2

Guided Instruction

- **Vocabulary Builder** Clarify the high-use word **ritual** before reading.

- Have students read Religion and examine The World: Major Religions map and its accompanying text. As students read, circulate to make sure individuals can answer the Reading Check question.

- Direct students' attention to the map and ask **What religions are practiced in South America?** *(Roman Catholic, Protestant, and traditional)*

- Ask students to look at the map key and consider what "Sunni" and "Shi'a" might designate. *(Sunni and Shi'a are branches of Islam, just as Roman Catholic, Protestant, and Eastern Churches are branches of Christianity.)*

- Ask students to list some of the common features among the world's religions. *(All have prayers and rituals, celebrate important places and times, and have standards of proper behavior.)*

Independent Practice

Have students complete the Taking Notes outline by adding a heading on Religion and filling in the appropriate details.

Monitor Progress

- Show *Section Reading Support Transparency FG 54* and ask students to check their graphic organizers individually.

  All In One Foundations of Geography Teaching Resources, *Section Reading Support Transparency FG 54*

- Tell students to fill in the last column of the *Reading Readiness Guide.*

  All In One Foundations of Geography Teaching Resources, *Reading Readiness Guide,* p. 214

Answers

The World: Major Religions

The major religions of the world all began in Asia. India was the birthplace of Sikhism, Hinduism, and Buddhism, all of which later spread to other countries. The other great world religions had their start in Southwest Asia: first Judaism, then Christianity, and finally Islam. These religions also later spread to other parts of the world.

Young Buddhist monks in Thailand

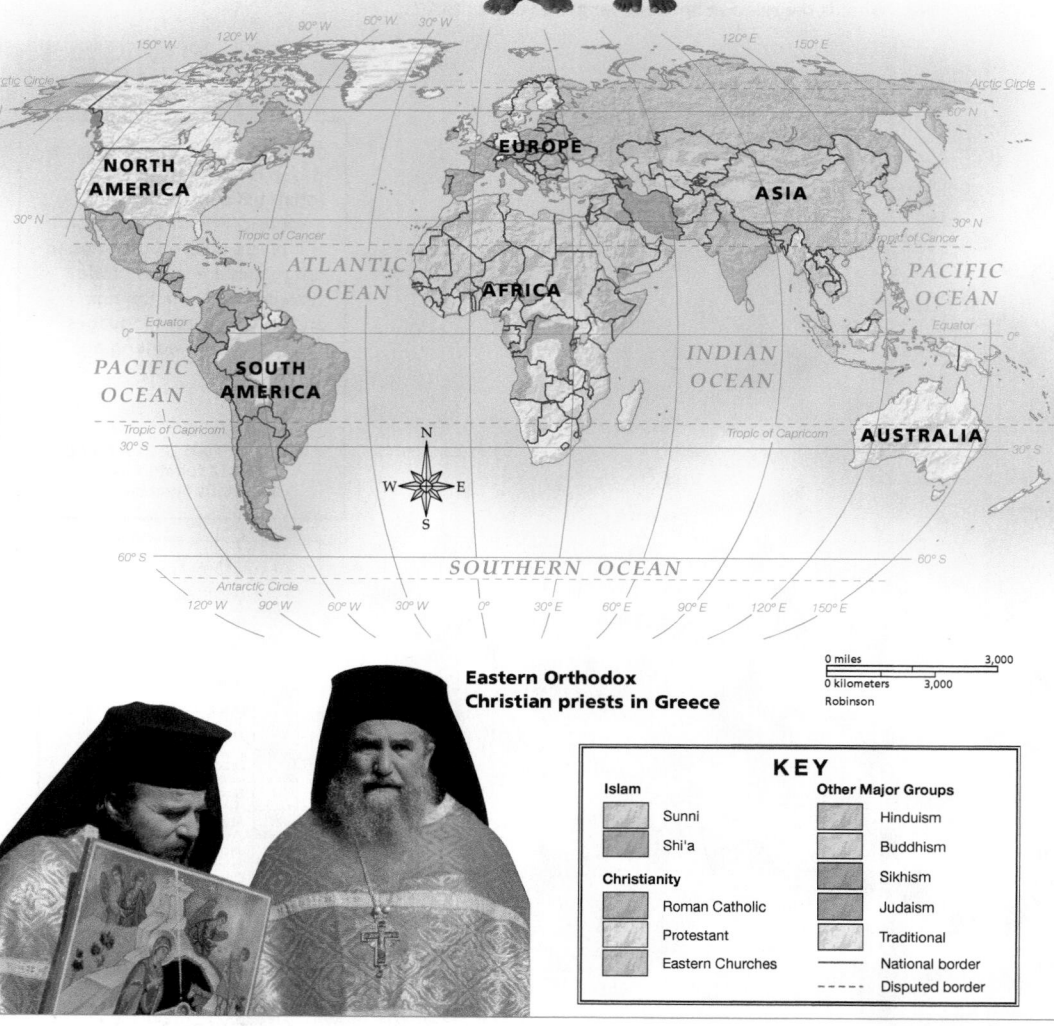

Eastern Orthodox Christian priests in Greece

0 miles 3,000
0 kilometers 3,000
Robinson

KEY

Islam
- Sunni
- Shi'a

Christianity
- Roman Catholic
- Protestant
- Eastern Churches

Other Major Groups
- Hinduism
- Buddhism
- Sikhism
- Judaism
- Traditional
- ——— National border
- - - - - Disputed border

100 Foundations of Geography

Skills for Life — Skills Mini Lesson

Synthesizing Information

1. Explain that to synthesize information, students should find the main idea of each fact, then find supporting details, and look for connections.

2. State the idea from the text on p. 101, "Most of the people of Saudi Arabia are Muslim." The map and text on p. 100 confirm the fact that Islam started in Southwest Asia. You can conclude: *Many people living near where Islam began are Muslims.*

3. Read the text on p. 101 that says that members of Islam, Judaism, and Christianity believe in one God. The map on p. 100 shows that people of these religions live in the same area. Ask: What conclusion can you draw from this information?

Religion

Religion is an important part of every culture. For example, most of the people of Saudi Arabia are Muslim. In some countries, such as the United States, people follow more than one religion. Beliefs and practices may differ among religions. However, religion remains important to many people.

Religion can help people make sense of the world. Religion can provide comfort and hope for people facing difficult times. And religion can help answer questions about the meaning and purpose of life. Religion also guides people in ethics, or standards of accepted behavior.

Religious beliefs vary. Members of some religions, such as Islam, Judaism, and Christianity, believe in one God. Members of other religions, such as Hinduism and traditional religions, believe in more than one god. But all religions have prayers and rituals. Every religion celebrates important places and times. And all religions expect people to treat one another well and to behave properly.

✓ Reading Check **Why is religion important to people?**

This temple, in Amritsar, India, is a holy place of Sikhism.

Section 2 Assessment

Key Terms
Review the key terms at the beginning of this section. Use each term in a sentence that explains its meaning.

Target Reading Skill
Place the following events in young people's lives in the correct sequence: learning their culture's language and learning their culture's beliefs.

Comprehension and Critical Thinking
1. (a) Identify What is the role of social structure in society?

(b) Explain What is the place of families in a social structure?
(c) Predict Would you expect the members of one family to fall within one social class or more than one?
2. (a) Recall How is language related to culture?
(b) Identify Cause and Effect Why do you think people who speak different languages tend to have different cultures?
3. (a) Identify What values do all religions share?
(b) Draw Conclusions How might those values help people of different religions overcome conflicts?

Writing Activity
In a journal entry, explore the ways in which family and language connect you to other people in your society.

> **Writing Tip** When you write a journal entry, write about experiences from your own life. You may also express your own opinions and perspectives. For this exercise, think about which of your activities and interests involve family or the use of language.

Assess Progress
Have students complete the Section Assessment. Administer the *Section Quiz*.

All in One **Foundations of Geography Teaching Resources,** *Section Quiz,* p. 216

Reteach
If students need more instruction, have them read this section in the Reading and Vocabulary Study Guide.

Chapter 4, Section 2, **Western Hemisphere Reading and Vocabulary Study Guide,** pp. 38–40

Extend
Have students work in small groups to investigate the rituals of world religions. Assign each group a different religion, and ask the groups to use the library or Internet to find out about one major holiday celebrated as part of the religion, including the name of the holiday, what it celebrates, when it is celebrated, and how it is celebrated. Have students create posters using the information they have gathered, and present their posters to the class.

Answer

✓ Reading Check Religion is important to people because it helps them make sense of the world, answers questions about the meaning of life, and guides their behavior.

Writing Activity
Use the *Rubric for Assessing a Journal Entry* to evaluate students' journal entries.

All in One **Foundations of Geography Teaching Resources,** *Rubric for Assessing a Journal Entry,* p. 234

Section 2 Assessment

Key Terms
Students' sentences should reflect knowledge of each Key Term.

Target Reading Skill
Learning their culture's language; learning their culture's beliefs.

Comprehension and Critical Thinking
1. (a) Social structure organizes a society through a pattern of relationships, and helps people work together to meet the basic needs of individuals, families, and communities. **(b)** Families are the most basic and important unit in a social structure. **(c)** Members of one nuclear family would likely fall within one social class, but the members of an extended family might fall within more than one social class.

2. (a) People learn culture mainly through language. **(b)** Each language preserves shared ideas and traditions.

3. (a) All have prayers and rituals, celebrate important places and times, and have standards of behavior. **(b)** People may be able to focus on their similarities rather than their differences.

Objective
Learn how to make valid generalizations.

Prepare to Read

Build Background Knowledge L2
Ask students to think of words or terms they already know that may help them to determine the meaning of the word *generalization*. Suggest terms such as "generally," "general store," "in general," and "general idea" to get them started. Conduct an Idea Wave (TE, p. T35) to create a list, then point out that the word *general* usually means "for all" or "for the whole." Have students refer to a dictionary to sharpen their definitions.

Instruct

Making Valid Generalizations L2

Guided Instruction
■ Read the steps to make valid generalizations as a class and write them on the board.

■ Practice the skill by following the steps on p. 103 as a class. Identify the topic of the text and three facts that support it *(corn in the Americas before the 1200s; corn was the principle crop of the Mayas of present-day Mexico and Central America, the Hohokam grew corn in Arizona and the Anasazi grew corn in the northeastern United States.)* Identify what the facts have in common *(all are about Native American groups who grew corn)*. Work with students to create a generalization. *(Possible generalization: Corn was an important and versatile crop in the Americas before the 1200s.)* Ask students to test the generalization using the bulleted questions on p. 102.

Testing for Validity
To find whether a generalization is valid, ask
• Are there enough facts—at least three in a short passage—to support the generalization?
• Do I know any other facts that support the generalization?
• Does the statement overgeneralize or stereotype a group of people? Words such as *all*, *always*, or *every* signal overgeneralization. Words such as *some*, *many*, *most*, and *often* help prevent a statement from being overgeneralized.

A generalization is a broad conclusion. Some generalizations are valid—that is, they have value or worth—because they can be drawn reasonably from specific facts. Other generalizations are not valid, because they draw unreasonably broad conclusions and are not based on fact.

Many statements have clues that tell you they should be evaluated for validity. For example, statements with words such as *everybody* or *everyone* are very broad. They should always be evaluated. Is the statement "Everybody needs salt" a valid generalization? It is, because it is based on the scientifically proven fact that humans cannot survive without salt in our diet. However, generalizations such as "Everybody loves chocolate" are not valid. They draw unreasonably broad conclusions and cannot be proved.

You need to know how to evaluate a generalization to see if it is valid. You also have to know how to make a valid generalization yourself.

Learn the Skill
To make a valid generalization, follow these steps:

1 **Identify specific facts contained within a source of information.** Make sure you understand the topic that the facts support.

2 **State what the facts have in common, and look for patterns.** Do any of the facts fit together in a way that makes a point about a broad subject? Do data in a table or graph point toward a general statement?

3 **Make a generalization, or broad conclusion, about the facts.** Write your generalization as a complete sentence or a paragraph.

4 **Test the generalization and revise it if necessary.** You can test the validity of a generalization by using the guidelines in the box at the left.

Practice the Skill

Read the passage at the right describing three cultures, and then make a generalization about these cultures.

1 What is the topic of the text? List at least three specific facts that relate to that topic.

2 What do the facts you listed have in common? Do they suggest a general idea about the topic?

3 Make a generalization about the topic. Write it in a complete sentence. List three facts that support it.

4 Test your generalization to see if it is valid. If it is not valid, try rewriting it so that it is more limited. Be careful of exaggerated wording.

Apply the Skill

Turn to page 97 and read the paragraph under the heading Kinds of Families. Make as many generalizations as you can, and test them for their validity. Explain why each generalization is or is not valid.

The Maya thrived in present-day Mexico and Central America from about A.D. 300 to 900. Corn was their principal crop. They developed a sophisticated civilization, but they had abandoned their great cities by about A.D. 900. At about that time, the Hohokam people were growing corn and beans in what is now Arizona. The Hohokam left their settlements during the 1400s, possibly because of drought. Meanwhile, between about A.D. 900 and 1300, the Anasazi people lived to the northeast. They also grew corn. The Anasazi built multistory dwellings up against high cliff walls. Many families lived in these homes. During a drought in the late 1200s, the Anasazi abandoned some of their villages.

An extended Islamic family, spanning three generations, from the rural east coast of Malaysia

Independent Practice

Assign *Skills for Life* and have students complete it individually.

All in One **Foundations of Geography Teaching Resources,** *Skills for Life*, p. 225

Monitor Progress

As students are completing the *Skills for Life* worksheet, circulate and check to make sure they understand the skill steps.

Assess and Reteach

Assess Progress [L2]

Ask students to do the Apply the Skill activity.

Reteach [L1]

If students are having trouble applying the skill steps, have them review the skill using the interactive Social Studies Skills Tutor CD-ROM.

⊙ *Making Valid Generalizations,* **Social Studies Skills Tutor CD-ROM**

Extend [L3]

Ask students to read the last paragraph on p. 107 of the Student Edition. Point out that the first sentence, "Technology has brought many benefits," is a generalization. Ask them if the paragraph contains enough facts to support this generalization, and have them brainstorm other facts that support it. Students should then write a paragraph explaining whether or not the generalization is valid. Use *Rubric for Assessing a Writing Assignment* to evaluate students' paragraphs.

All in One **Foundations of Geography Teaching Resources,** *Rubric for Assessing a Writing Assignment*, p. 233

Differentiated Instruction

For Less Proficient Readers [L1]

Partner these students with more proficient readers to do Level 1 of the *Making Valid Generalizations* lesson on the interactive Social Studies Skills Tutor CD-ROM. When they have successfully completed Level 1, they can move on to Level 2 alone.

⊙ *Making Valid Generalizations,* **Social Studies Skills Tutor CD-ROM**

For Special Needs Students [L1]

Help students make valid generalizations about items or people in the classroom. Students should look for patterns, and then write sentences expressing their generalizations, such as, "Most of the chairs in this room are green." Help students discuss whether or not their generalizations are valid.

Answers

Apply the Skill

Answers will vary, but students should show that they made generalizations and tested them for their validity.

Objectives

Social Studies

1. Explore how cultures change.
2. Learn how ideas spread from one culture to another.

Reading/Language Arts

Identify signal words to help keep the order of events clear.

Prepare to Read

Build Background Knowledge   L2

Tell students that in this section they will learn about how cultures change over time. Point out to students that some sports, foods, and words in American culture may have been borrowed or adapted from other cultures. Ask if they are familiar with the sport of karate or have ever eaten shish kebab. Point out that these both originated in different cultures. Have students engage in a Give One, Get One activity (TE, pp. T37) to identify other aspects of American culture that have been borrowed or adapted from different cultures.

Set a Purpose for Reading   L2

■ Preview the Objectives.

■ Read each statement in the *Reading Readiness Guide* aloud. Ask students to mark the statements true or false.

■ Have students discuss the statements in pairs or groups of four, then mark their worksheets again. Use the Numbered Heads participation strategy (TE, p. T36) to call on students to share their group's perspectives.

All in One Foundations of Geography Teaching Resources, *Reading Readiness Guide,* p. 218

Vocabulary Builder
Preview Key Terms   L2

Pronounce each Key Term, then ask the students to say the word with you. Provide a simple explanation such as "Playing the American sport of baseball in Japan is an example of cultural diffusion."

Prepare to Read

Objectives

In this section you will
1. Explore how cultures change.
2. Learn how ideas spread from one culture to another.

Taking Notes

Copy the concept web below. As you read this section, fill in the web with information about cultural change. Add ovals as needed for the concepts in the section.

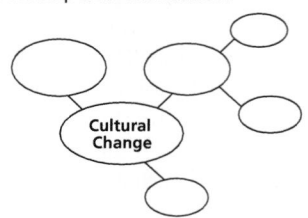

Target Reading Skill

Recognize Words That Signal Sequence

Signal words point out relationships among ideas or events. To help keep the order of events clear, look for words such as *first, later,* or *at that time* that signal the order in which the events took place.

Key Terms

● **cultural diffusion** (KUL chur ul dih FYOO zhun) *n.* the movement of customs and ideas

● **acculturation** (uh kul chur AY shun) *n.* the process of accepting new ideas and fitting them into a culture

Blue jeans and denim shirts have changed with the times.

How Cultures Change

All cultures change over time. The history of blue jeans is an example of cultural change. Some people think that blue jeans are typical American clothes. But many cultures contributed to them. Blue jeans were invented in the United States in the 1800s. They were marketed by Levi Strauss. Strauss was a German-born merchant who moved to California. He made the jeans with a cloth called denim. This may be a shortened form of *serge de Nîmes,* the name of a similar cloth from France.

At first, only Americans wore blue jeans, but they later became popular in other countries. In the 1980s, the Japanese and the French developed stonewashing. It made brand-new denim jeans look worn. Since then, designers from Asia, Europe, and America have promoted new styles, such as ripped and "dirty" denim. Today, jeans are popular all over the world. And the word *jeans* comes from an old French name for Genoa, an Italian city where a cloth similar to denim was first made. What could be more American than jeans?

Target Reading Skill   L2

Recognize Words That Signal Sequence Point out the Target Reading Skill. Explain that by identifying words that signal time order, readers can better understand the sequence of events being presented.

Model recognizing words that signal sequence by reading the second paragraph on p. 104 aloud. Then ask students to make a list of words and terms in the paragraph that signal sequence. On the board, list: "At first," "later," "In the 1980s," "Since then," and "Today." Have students brainstorm other sequence signal words and terms to add to the list *(before, after, then, soon, in the future.)*

Give students *Recognize Sequence Signal Words.* Have them complete the activity in groups.

All in One Foundations of Geography Teaching Resources, *Recognize Sequence Signal Words,* p. 222

Why Cultures Change Just as jeans have changed over time, so, too, has American culture. Cultures change all the time. Because culture is an entire way of life, a change in one part changes other parts. Changes in the natural environment, technology, and ideas all affect culture.

New Technologies New technologies also change a culture. During the 1800s and early 1900s, the growth of industry and the spread of factories drew large numbers of Americans from the countryside to the nation's cities. Factories offered jobs to thousands of men, women, and children. Limited transportation meant that people had to live close to the factories. Cities grew larger as a result.

This all changed after the invention of the car in the late 1800s. Within a few years, advances in technology made cars more affordable. By 1920, many Americans had cars. People could live farther from their jobs and drive to work. Soon after, the idea of owning a house with a yard became more popular. The result has been the growth of sprawling suburbs since the mid-1900s and a new culture based on car travel.

A teenager using a cell phone

A "bullet train" in Japan
Japanese engineers have developed new technologies that allow these trains to travel at speeds of more than 180 miles (300 kilometers) per hour. **Infer** *How might such high speeds affect how far away people can live from their work?*

Chapter 4 Section 3   **105**

Vocabulary Builder

Use the information below to teach students this section's high-use words.

High-Use Word	Definition and Sample Sentence
contribute, p. 104	*v.* to give Kim **contributed** cans of food to the food bank.
promote, p. 104	*v.* to help bring about Eating a healthy diet will **promote** a long life.
obtain, p. 106	*v.* to gain possession of You must **obtain** a passport before traveling out of the country.
focus, p. 106	*v.* to concentrate Jenny couldn't **focus** on her book in the noisy airport.

How Ideas Spread

Guided Instruction

- **Vocabulary Builder** Clarify the high-use words **obtain** and **focus** before reading.

- Read How Ideas Spread and direct students' attention to the photographs, Links to Technology, and line graph on these pages.

- Ask students **What is cultural diffusion?** *(the movement of customs and ideas from one culture to another)*

- Ask **How does cultural diffusion occur?** *(As people move they bring customs and ideas with them, and also obtain new customs and ideas.)*

- Discuss with students how the use of computers and the Internet affects their daily lives. *(Libraries, schools, and many homes now have computers and access to the Internet. Students may suggest that this technology helps them with their homework, helps them communicate with their friends or family, or provides entertainment.)*

🔁 Target Reading Skill

L2

Recognize Words That Signal Sequence
As a follow-up, ask students to answer the Target Reading Skill question in the Student Edition. (*The words* before that *signal what comes first in sequence. The events after those words happened before the events in the preceding sentence.*)

Answer

✓ Reading Check The invention of cars allowed people to live farther away from their jobs, which led to the growth of suburbs.

🔁 **Recognize Words That Signal Sequence**

What do the words *before that,* in the paragraph at the right, tell you about the sequence of events? Which happened first — the events after those words or the events in the preceding sentence?

A woman practicing yoga, a form of meditation that spread from Asia to Europe and North America

---

How One Change Can Lead to Others Think of other ways technology has changed the culture of the United States. Radio and television brought entertainment and news into homes. Today instant information is part of our culture. Computers change how and where people work. Computers even help people live longer since doctors use computers to diagnose and treat patients. Radio, television, and computers add new words to our language, such as *broadcast, channel surfing,* and *hacker.* What other new words can you think of?

Cultural Change Over Time Cultural change has been going on for a long time. Controlling fire helped early people survive in colder climates. When people started raising animals and growing crops, ways of life also changed. People began to work in the same fields year after year. Before that, they had roamed over a wider area looking for wild plant and animal foods.

✓ Reading Check **How did the invention of cars change culture?**

How Ideas Spread

Advances in transportation technology, such as the airplane, make it easier for people to move all over the world. When they move, people bring new kinds of clothing and tools with them. They also bring ideas about such things as ways to prepare food, teach children, practice their religion, or govern themselves.

Ideas can travel to new places in other ways. People may obtain goods from another culture by trade and then learn to make those goods themselves. People may also learn from other cultures through written material. The movement of customs and ideas is called **cultural diffusion.**

How Cultures Adopt New Ideas One example of cultural diffusion is the game of baseball. Baseball began as an American sport, but today it is played in countries all around the world. That is an example of cultural diffusion. The Japanese love baseball. However, they have changed the game to fit their culture. These changes are an example of **acculturation**, or the process of accepting new ideas and fitting them into a culture. Americans value competition. They focus on winning. A game of baseball does not end until one team wins. But in Japan, a game can end in a tie. The Japanese do not mind a tie game. In Japan, how well you play is more important than winning.

Differentiated Instruction

For Advanced Readers L3

Have students complete the *Enrichment* activity, which centers on the spread of wheat-growing. After they have answered the questions, ask if they can think of other examples of ideas and customs that have spread around the world.

All in One Foundations of Geography Teaching Resources, *Enrichment*, p. 224

For English Language Learners L1

As students read, ask them to list unfamiliar words and record any questions they may have about the section on a blank sheet of paper. Label a box "Questions" and tell students that they may place their papers in the box anonymously at a specific time. Go over all of the words and questions with the class.

Communication Technology and the Speed of Change

What's the fastest way to get from your house to Japan? Would you use a jet plane? A phone call? The Internet? A fax? All these answers can be correct. The answer depends on whether you want to transport your body, your voice, a picture, or just words on a sheet of paper.

For thousands of years, cultures changed slowly. People and goods moved by foot or wagon or sailing ship, so ideas and technology also moved slowly. Recently, communication technology has increased the speed of change. Faxes and computers transport information almost instantly. Magazines and television shows can bring ideas and information from all over the world to any home. This rapid exchange of ideas speeds up cultural change.

Technology has brought many benefits. Computers let scientists share information about how to cure diseases. Telephones let us instantly talk to relatives thousands of miles away. In the Australian Outback, students your age use closed-circuit television and two-way radios to take part in class from their own homes.

Links to Technology

Digital Tunes Until recent years, music lovers had to lug around tapes or CDs. The invention of MP3s and MP3 players changed that. Fans can now download and store thousands of songs in MP3 format from the Internet. They no longer need bulky tapes and CDs.

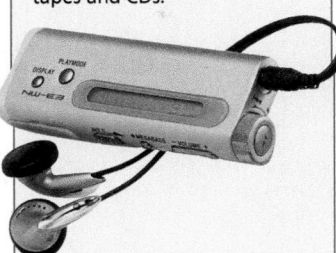

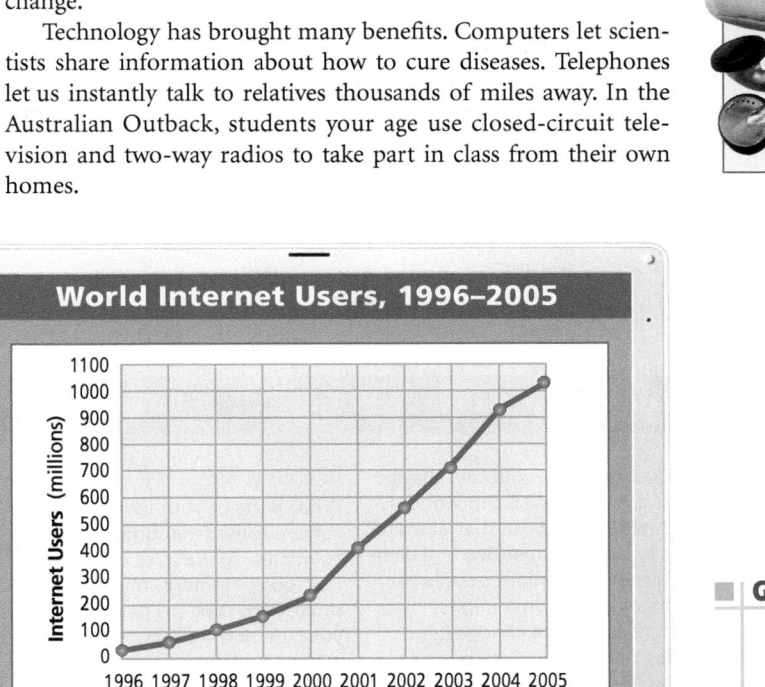

World Internet Users, 1996–2005

Graph Skills

Internet use grew rapidly after 1996. **Identify** What was the number of Internet users in 2005?

Predict Based on the trend shown in the graph, how do you think the number of Internet users has changed since 2005?

Links

Read the **Links to Technology** on this page of the Student Edition. Ask **Why are MP3s more convenient than CDs or tapes?** *(Because MP3s are digital files, they are easier to transport and obtain than CDs or tapes.)*

Guided Instruction (continued)

- Direct students' attention to the graph at the bottom of the page. Ask **According to the graph, which year had the greatest increase of Internet users?** *(2003)*

- Ask students to name one benefit of technology and one challenge of technology. *(Students may say that technology helps people to communicate more quickly or assists people with research, but that the customs of traditional societies may be lost as technology spreads.)*

Independent Practice

Have students complete the Taking Notes graphic organizer by asking them to add more information from the section.

Monitor Progress

- Show *Section Reading Support Transparency FG 55* and ask students to check their graphic organizers individually. Go over key concepts and clarify key vocabulary as needed.

    All in One Foundations of Geography Teaching Resources, *Section Reading Support Transparency FG 55*

- Tell students to fill in the last column of the *Reading Readiness Guide.* Ask them to evaluate if what they learned was what they had expected to learn.

    All in One Foundations of Geography Teaching Resources, *Reading Readiness Guide,* p. 218

Skills Mini Lesson

Distinguishing Fact and Opinion

1. Explain that a fact can be proved to be true or false and an opinion is a personal belief. Tell students that facts answer the question *Who? What? When? Where?* or *Why?* Opinions often use words like *good, bad, think,* or *feel.*

2. Help students practice the skill by writing these statements on the board:

A. *"Dirty" denim jeans are the best jeans.*
B. *Blue jeans were invented in the 1800s.* Then explain, "I can prove B is true or false using an encyclopedia. I can't prove A. A is an opinion, B is a fact."

3. Have students apply the skill to the following statements: A. *The first telephone was built in 1876. B. I think cell phones should be banned.*

Answers

Graph Skills **Identify** more than one billion

Predict Because the graph shows a steady increase, it is likely that the number of Internet users has grown since 2005.

Assess and Reteach

Assess Progress `L2`

Have students complete the Section Assessment. Then administer the *Section Quiz*.

All in One **Foundations of Geography Teaching Resources,** *Section Quiz*, p. 220

Reteach `L1`

If students need more instruction, have them read this section in the Reading and Vocabulary Study Guide.

 Chapter 4, Section 3, **Western Hemisphere Reading and Vocabulary Study Guide,** pp. 41–43

Extend `L3`

To learn more about aspects of cultural diffusion, assign the small group activity *Creating a Report on World Music*. Students may work in pairs to complete the activity.

All in One **Foundations of Geography Teaching Resources,** *Small Group Activity: Creating a Report on World Music*, pp. 226–229

Answers

Analyze Images The aborigines in the photo are wearing modern-day clothing.

✓ **Reading Check** New technology allows information to travel more quickly, speeding up cultural change.

Section 3 Assessment

Key Terms

Students' sentences should reflect knowledge of each Key Term.

Target Reading Skill

the words "For thousands of years" and "Recently"

Comprehension and Critical Thinking

1. (a) the ability of many people to live farther away from their jobs, and the rapid growth of suburbs **(b)** Cars allowed people to travel longer distances between their homes and workplaces, which meant they could live outside cities. **(c)** More Americans might choose to work from their homes, communicating electronically, rather than driving to work. Americans could live even farther away from their workplaces.

Defending Their Heritage
In 1988 Aborigines, descendants of Australia's original inhabitants, protested the 200th anniversary of the arrival of Europeans. **Analyze Images** *What evidence do you see that the Aborigines' culture has changed over the past 200 years?*

Defending Traditions Change can help, but it can also hurt. If things change too fast, people may feel that their culture is threatened. Valuable traditions can disappear. Once traditional knowledge has been lost, it can never be regained. In many parts of the world, people are working to preserve, or save, their own cultures before it is too late. They do not want to lose what is valuable in their culture. They want to save the artistic traditions, the religious beliefs, and the wisdom that enriched the lives of past generations for the sake of future generations.

✓ **Reading Check** **How has technology affected the speed of cultural change?**

 ## Section 3 Assessment

Key Terms
Review the key terms at the beginning of this section. Use each term in a sentence that explains its meaning.

Target Reading Skill
Review the second paragraph on page 107. Find the words that signal a sequence of events related to communication technologies.

Comprehension and Critical Thinking
1. (a) Describe What cultural changes in America followed the invention of cars?

(b) Explain How did cars change where people lived and worked?
(c) Predict Suppose that gasoline became more expensive and computers allowed more people to work at home. How might American culture change?
2. (a) List What are two main ways in which ideas travel from one culture to another?
(b) Describe Give an example of an idea that has passed from one culture to another.
(c) Compare and Contrast How has the spread of ideas changed with modern communication technologies?

Writing Activity
What parts of your own culture come from other countries? Make a list detailing the foods, fashions, music, or customs that are part of your life and that come from other countries.

For: An activity on cultural change
Visit: PHSchool.com
Web Code: led-3403

---

2. (a) trade and written materials **(b)** the people of the culture accepting the idea usually adapt it to fit in with their ideas, customs, and traditions through the process of acculturation. **(c)** The spread of ideas has become much faster due to modern communication technologies.

Writing Activity
Use *Rubric for Assessing a Writing Assignment* to evaluate students' lists.

All in One **Foundations of Geography Teaching Resources,** *Rubric for Assessing a Writing Assignment*, p. 233

Go Online **PHSchool.com** Typing in the Web code when prompted will bring students directly to detailed instructions for this activity.

Review and Assessment

◆ Chapter Summary

Section 1: Understanding Culture
- Culture is an entire way of life that is shaped by people's environment and that also shapes people's environment.
- Culture developed over time from simple technologies and institutions to more advanced technologies and institutions.

Section 2: Culture and Society
- A society is a group of people sharing a culture and held together by a social structure.
- Language expresses the basic concepts of a culture and transmits those concepts to young people.
- Religions help people make sense of the world. They are an important source of values for cultures and teach people to treat one another fairly.

Section 3: Cultural Change
- Changes in the environment or in technology lead to changes in culture.
- Ideas move among cultures through the movement of people, through trade, and through communication technologies.

Traditional dress in India

◆ Key Terms

Each of the statements below contains a key term from the chapter. If the statement is true, write *true*. If it is false, rewrite the statement to make it true.

1. The culture of a people is their way of life, including their beliefs and customs.

2. A civilization is an organization with social, educational, or religious purposes.

3. An institution is an advanced culture with cities and the use of writing.

4. A society is a group of people sharing a culture.

5. A pattern of organized relationships among groups of people is a social structure.

6. An extended family consists of two parents and their children.

7. A nuclear family includes two grandparents, their children, and their grandchildren.

8. Cultural diffusion is the movement of customs or ideas from one culture to another.

9. Acculturation is an accumulation of several cultures in a single place.

Chapter 4 **109**

Review Chapter Content

- Review and revisit the major themes of this chapter by asking students to classify what Guiding Questions each bulleted statement in the Chapter Summary answers. Have students work in groups to match the statements with the appropriate questions. Conduct an Idea Wave (TE, p. T35) with the class to share their answers. Refer to page 1 of the Student Edition for the text of the Guiding Questions.

- Assign *Vocabulary Development* for students to review Key Terms.

  All In One Foundations of Geography Teaching Resources, *Vocabulary Development,* p. 232

Answers

Key Terms

1. True

2. False. A civilization is an advanced culture with cities and the use of writing.

3. False. An institution is an organization with social, educational, or religious purposes.

4. True

5. True

6. False. An extended family includes several generations.

7. False. A nuclear family consists of two parents and their children.

8. True

9. Acculturation is the process of accepting new ideas and fitting them into a culture.

Review and Assessment

Comprehension and Critical Thinking

10. (a) material things, sports, entertainment, literature, spiritual beliefs, ideals, government, morals, language, and technology **(b)** Technology, because through even simple technology, people can change their land.

11. (a) the change from hunting and gathering food to raising crops and animals **(b)** Population increased. **(c)** because people could stay in one area year round, trade extra food for other goods, learn crafts, develop writing systems, and create technologies that gave rise to cities

12. (a) The social class to which a person belongs often comes from his or her wealth, education, or family connections, which affects his or her status in society. **(b)** People's ability to change their status has improved over time, as access to education, the ability to get a high-paying job, or the chance of marrying into a family of high status has increased.

13. (a) Sikhism, Hinduism, and Buddhism in India; and Judaism, Christianity, and Islam in Southwest Asia **(b)** The spread of these religions might be explained by cultural diffusion; as people of various religions traveled to new areas of the world, they brought their beliefs with them and taught them to others, and written materials of different religions could be read by people in other countries.

14. (a) The development of industry and factories led to the advancement of science, the development of even newer technologies, and the growth of cities and institutions, such as governments, schools, and armies. **(b)** Both caused the world to seem smaller by allowing people to work and communicate faster. One difference is that the Internet has changed the way that people find and handle information, while the Industrial Revolution changed the way physical goods were manufactured.

15. (a) forms of communication such as the Internet, scientific advancements in medicine, advances in transportation technology, and other areas **(b)** They have greatly increased the rate of cultural change.

Skills Practice

Students' answers will vary, but should include several facts from the paragraphs and a valid generalization about the information.

◆ Comprehension and Critical Thinking

10. (a) Describe What elements make up a culture? **(b) Apply Information** Which of these elements might influence a people's environment, and how?

11. (a) Describe What was the Agricultural Revolution? **(b) Explain** How did it affect population? **(c) Draw Conclusions** How did it allow the growth of cities?

12. (a) Describe How does social class affect a person's status in society? **(b) Link Past and Present** How has people's ability to improve their status changed?

13. (a) Recall Which major religions started in Asia? **(b) Infer** What might explain their spread?

14. (a) Describe How did the development of industry and factories change culture? **(b) Compare and Contrast** How do those changes compare with the ways technology has changed culture in your lifetime?

15. (a) List What technologies contribute to cultural change today? **(b) Draw Conclusions** How have new technologies affected the rate of cultural change?

◆ Skills Practice

Making Valid Generalizations In the Skills for Life activity in this chapter, you learned to make generalizations. You also learned how to make sure that generalizations are valid, or justified, based on facts. You learned not to overgeneralize, or make claims that go beyond the facts.

Review the steps that you followed to learn this skill. Then reread the paragraphs on pages 94 and 95 under the heading Development of Culture. List several facts about the changes described there. Finally, use these facts to make a valid generalization about those changes.

◆ Writing Activity: Math

Look at the graph titled World Internet Users 1996–2005 on page 107. Find the number of Internet users in 1996 and the number of Internet users nine years later in 2005. How many more users were there in 2005 than in 1996? Based on this information, predict how many Internet users there will be in 2014, nine years after the latest date shown on this graph. Write a short paragraph describing your results and your prediction.

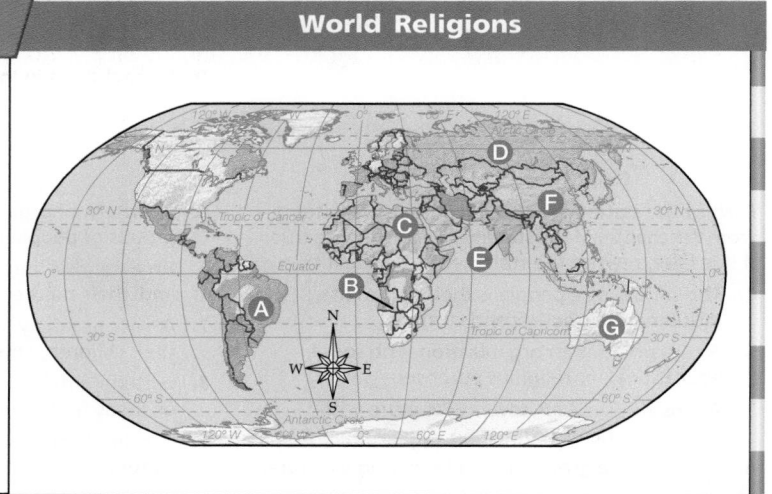

MAP MASTER™ Skills Activity

Place Location For each religion listed below, write the letter that marks its location on the map.
1. Buddhism
2. Eastern Christianity
3. Hinduism
4. Islam
5. Protestant Christianity
6. Roman Catholic Christianity
7. Traditional religions

Go Online
PHSchool.com Use Web Code **lep-3414** for an **interactive map.**

World Religions

Writing Activity: Math
There were about 990 million more Internet users in 2005 than in 1996. Students' paragraphs should indicate that there is likely to be a similar dramatic increase in Internet users between 2005 and 2014. Students may express that as computer technology becomes more affordable and accessible, the number of Internet users should continue to rise.

Use *Rubric for Assessing a Writing Assignment* to evaluate students' paragraphs.

All in One Foundations of Geography Teaching Resources, *Rubric for Assessing a Writing Assignment,* p. 233

Standardized Test Prep

MAP MASTER
Skills Activity

1. F	**2.** D
3. E	**4.** C
5. G	**6.** A
7. B	

Test-Taking Tips

Some questions on standardized tests ask you to supply information using prior knowledge. Analyze the web diagram below. Then follow the tips to answer the sample question.

TIP The title in the center circle describes all of the languages. Think about the word *Indo-European* and how it describes languages.

Pick the letter that best answers the question.

Another language that belongs on this web is

- **A** Mandarin Chinese.
- **B** Swahili.
- **C** Japanese.
- **D** Greek.

TIP Use your prior knowledge—what you know about history, geography, or government—to help you rule out choices.

Think It Through The word *Indo-European* describes languages of India and Europe. Therefore, you can rule out answers A and C because these languages do not come from India or Europe. That leaves Swahili and Greek. You may not be sure about where Swahili is spoken, but you probably know from prior reading that Greece (where people speak Greek) is in Europe. The correct answer is D.

Practice Questions

Use the tips above and other tips in this book to help you answer the following questions:

1. The Agricultural Revolution led
   - **A** to a rebellion by farmers against taxes.
   - **B** to widespread hunger.
   - **C** to an increase in population.
   - **D** people to begin using tools.

2. How does family structure change when countries become more developed?
   - **A** People lose interest in their families.
   - **B** Nuclear families become more common.
   - **C** People move in with their grandparents, aunts, and uncles.
   - **D** Extended families become more common.

3. Which of the following does NOT contribute to cultural change?
   - **A** technological change
   - **B** migration
   - **C** tradition
   - **D** television

Read the following passage, and answer the question that follows.

This country is the birthplace of three major religions. It is located on Earth's largest continent. Its neighbors include Bangladesh and Sri Lanka. The country has more than a billion inhabitants. Its people speak hundreds of different languages. Many people from this country have migrated overseas.

4. What country does the passage describe?
   - **A** Israel
   - **B** Mexico
   - **C** India
   - **D** China

Go Online
PHSchool.com
Use Web Code **lea-3401** for a **Chapter 4 self-test.**

Chapter 4 **111**

Go Online PHSchool.com Students may practice their map skills using the interactive online version of this map.

Standardized Test Prep

Answers

1. C
2. B
3. C
4. C

Go Online PHSchool.com Students may use the Chapter 4 self-test on PHSchool.com to prepare for the Chapter Test.

Assessment Resources

Use *Chapter Tests A and B* to assess students' mastery of the chapter content.

All in One **Foundations of Geography Teaching Resources,** *Chapter Tests A and B,* pp. 235–240

Tests also available on the *ExamView Test Bank CD-ROM.*

◉ *ExamView Test Bank CD-ROM*

Overview

Natural Resources
Section 1
1. Learn about natural resources.
2. Investigate energy.

Land Use
Section 2
1. Study the relation between land use and culture.
2. Investigate the relation between land use and economic activity.
3. Explore changes in land use.

People's Effect on the Environment
Section 3
1. Investigate how first-level activities affect the environment.
2. Explore how second- and third-level activities affect the environment.

Technology Resources

Students use embedded Web codes to access Internet activities, chapter self-tests, and additional map practice. They may also access Dorling Kindersley's Online Desk Reference to learn more about each country they study.

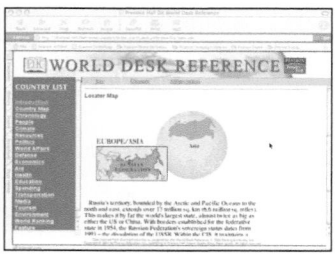

Use the Interactive Textbook to make content and concepts come alive through animations, videos, and activities that accompany the complete basal text—online and on CD-ROM.

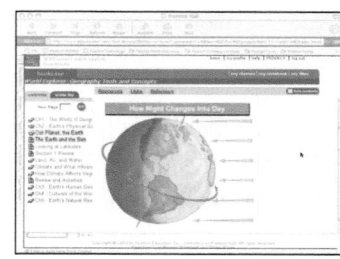

PRENTICE HALL

Use this complete suite of powerful teaching tools to make planning lessons and administering tests quicker and easier.

Reading and Assessment

Reading and Vocabulary Instruction

Model the Target Reading Skill

Main Idea The main idea is the most important point in a written passage. All of the details in a well-written paragraph or section should add up to the main idea. Write the paragraph below, from page 131, on the board. Explain that the main idea is usually stated in the first or last sentence. Model identifying the main idea by thinking aloud: "I will read the first and last sentences to see if either may be the main idea. I think the first sentence is the main idea because it is more general. Let me read the entire paragraph to see if I can find details that support the first sentence."

Point out the supporting details by underlining each one: *Other industrial and service activities have side effects on the environment. For example, <u>shopping malls require large areas to be paved for parking. Industries use large amounts of resources and release industrial wastes</u> into the environment. <u>Service activities require the construction of roads, telephone lines, and power lines.</u>*

Think aloud: "What do these details have in common? They are all examples of how service activities and industries negatively influence the environment. They support the main idea, that *other industrial and service activities have side effects on the environment.*"

Use the following worksheets from All-in-One Foundations of Geography Teaching Resources (pp. 256–258) to support this chapter's Target Reading Skill.

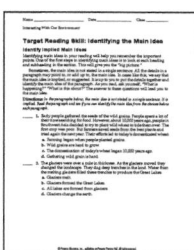

Vocabulary Builder
High-Use Academic Words

Use these steps to teach this chapter's high-use words:

1. Have students rate how well they know each word on their Word Knowledge worksheets (All-in-One Foundations of Geography Teaching Resources, p. 259).
2. Pronounce each word and ask students to repeat it.
3. Give students a brief definition or sample sentence (provided on TE pp. 115, 121, and 129).
4. Work with students as they fill in the "Definition or Example" column of their Word Knowledge worksheets.

Assessment

Formal Assessment

Test students' understanding of core knowledge and skills.

Chapter Tests A and B, Final Exams A and B, All-in-One Foundations of Geography Teaching Resources, pp. 278–283, 287–292

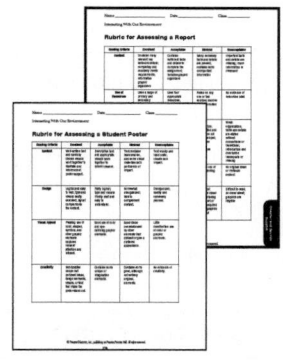

Customize the Chapter Tests to suit your needs. *ExamView Test Bank CD-ROM*

Skills Assessment

Assess geographic literacy.

MapMaster Skills, Student Edition, pp. 115, 124, 134

Assess reading and comprehension.

Target Reading Skills, Student Edition, pp. 115, 122, 131 and in Section Assessments

Chapter 5 Assessment, Western Hemisphere Reading and Vocabulary Study Guide, p. 54

Performance Assessment

Assess students' performance on this chapter's Writing Activities using the following rubrics from All-in-One Foundations of Geography Teaching Resources.

Rubric for Assessing a Student Poster, p. 274

Rubric for Assessing a Report, p. 275

Assess students' work through performance tasks.

Small Group Activity, All-in-One Foundations of Geography Teaching Resources, pp. 262–265

Online Assessment

Have students check their own understanding.

Chapter Self-Test

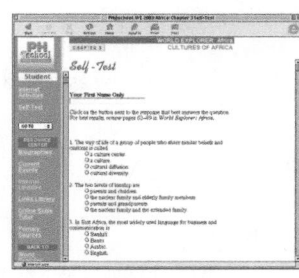

Test Preparation

Foundations of Geography Practice Tests A, B and C, Test Prep Workbook, pp. 49–60

Foundations of Geography Benchmark Test and Outcome Test, AYP Monitoring Assessments, pp. 80–85, 128–131

Section 1 Natural Resources

 1.5 periods, .75 block

Social Studies Objectives

1. Learn about natural resources.
2. Investigate energy.

Reading/Language Arts Objective

Learn how to identify the main idea of a paragraph.

Prepare to Read

Build Background Knowledge
Discuss raw materials.

Set a Purpose for Reading
Have students evaluate statements on the *Reading Readiness Guide.*

Preview Key Terms
Teach the section's Key Terms.

Target Reading Skill
Introduce the section's Target Reading Skill of **identifying main ideas.**

Instructional Resources

All in One Foundations of Geography Teaching Resources
- **L2** Reading Readiness Guide, p. 245
- **L2** Identify Main Ideas, p. 256

Differentiated Instruction

Spanish Reading and Vocabulary Study Guide
- **L1** Chapter 5, Section 1, pp. 33–34 ELL

Instruct

What are Natural Resources?
Ask for examples of natural resources and discuss some of them.

Target Reading Skill
Review **identifying main ideas.**

A Special Resource: Energy
Discuss different sources of energy and how they are consumed and protected.

Instructional Resources

All in One Foundations of Geography Teaching Resources
- **L2** Guided Reading and Review, p. 246
- **L2** Reading Readiness Guide, p. 245

Foundations of Geography Transparencies
- **L2** Section Reading Support Transparency FG 56
- **L2** Transparency B15: Outline

Differentiated Instruction

All in One Foundations of Geography Teaching Resources
- Rubric for Assessing a Student Poster, p. 274 GT, AR
- **L1** Reading a Natural Resources Map, p. 267 ELL, LPR, SN
- **L3** Reading an Economic Activity Map, p. 266 AR, GT

Teacher's Edition
- **L3** For Gifted and Talented, TE p. 116
- **L1** For Less Proficient Readers, TE p. 116
- **L3** For English Language Learners, TE p. 117
- **L3** For Advanced Readers, TE p. 117

Assess and Reteach

Assess Progress
Evaluate student comprehension with the section assessment and section quiz.

Reteach
Assign the Reading and Vocabulary Study Guide to help struggling students.

Extend
Extend the lesson by assigning an online activity.

Instructional Resources

All in One Foundations of Geography Teaching Resources
- **L2** Section Quiz, p. 247
  Rubric for Assessing a Journal Entry, p. 276

Reading and Vocabulary Study Guide
- **L1** Chapter 5, Section 1, pp. 45–47

PHSchool.com
- **L3** **For:** Environmental and Global Issues: Alternative Sources of Energy
  Web Code: led-3504

Differentiated Instruction

Spanish Support
- **L2** Section Quiz (Spanish), p. 37 ELL

Key

L1 Basic to Average	**L3** Average to Advanced
L2 For All Students	

LPR Less Proficient Readers
AR Advanced Readers
SN Special Needs Students

GT Gifted and Talented
ELL English Language Learners

Section 2 Land Use

 2 periods, 1 block (includes Skills for Life)

Social Studies Objectives
1. Study the relation between land use and culture.
2. Investigate the relation between land use and economic activity.
3. Explore changes in land use.

Reading/Language Arts Objective
Learn how to identify sentences that include details that support the main idea of a paragraph.

Prepare to Read	Instructional Resources	Differentiated Instruction
Build Background Knowledge Discuss how land is used to extract raw materials. **Set a Purpose for Reading** Have students begin to fill out the *Reading Readiness Guide.* **Preview Key Terms** Teach the section's Key Terms. **Target Reading Skill** Introduce the section's Target Reading Skill of **identifying supporting details.**	**All in One Foundations of Geography Teaching Resources** L2 Reading Readiness Guide, p. 249 L2 Identify Supporting Details, p. 257	**Spanish Reading and Vocabulary Study Guide** L1 Chapter 5, Section 2, pp. 35–36 ELL

Instruct	Instructional Resources	Differentiated Instruction
Land Use and Culture Discuss how different cultures use the materials in their environments. **Land Use and Economic Activity** Discuss first-, second-, and third-level activities related to land use. **Target Reading Skill** Review **identifying supporting details.** **Changes in Land Use** Discuss how human actions can affect land use.	**All in One Foundations of Geography Teaching Resources** L2 Guided Reading and Review, p. 250 L2 Reading Readiness Guide, p. 249 **Foundations of Geography Transparencies** L2 Section Reading Support Transparency FG 57	**All in One Foundations of Geography Teaching Resources** L2 Celia's Island Journal, pp. 270–271 AR, GT, LPR, SN L3 The Road From Coorain, pp. 268–269 AR, GT L2 Skills for Life, p. 261 AR, GT, LPR, SN **Teacher's Edition** L3 For Advanced Readers, TE p. 123 L1 For English Language Learners, TE p. 123 **Reading and Vocabulary Study Guide** L1 Chapter 5, Section 2, pp. 48–50 ELL, LPR, SN

Assess and Reteach	Instructional Resources	Differentiated Instruction
Assess Progress Evaluate student comprehension with the section assessment and section quiz. **Reteach** Assign the Reading and Vocabulary Study Guide to help struggling students. **Extend** Extend the lesson by assigning a Book Project.	**All in One Foundations of Geography Teaching Resources** L2 Section Quiz, p. 251 L3 Book Project: World News Today, pp. 36–38 Rubric for Assessing a Report, p. 275 **Reading and Vocabulary Study Guide** L1 Chapter 5, Section 2, pp. 48–50	**Spanish Support** L2 Section Quiz (Spanish), p. 39 ELL **Teacher's Edition** L1 For Special Needs Students, TE p. 127 **Social Studies Skills Tutor CD-ROM** L1 Identifying Cause and Effect ELL, LPR, SN

Key

L1 Basic to Average	L3 Average to Advanced	
L2 For All Students		
	LPR Less Proficient Readers	GT Gifted and Talented
	AR Advanced Readers	ELL English Language Learners
	SN Special Needs Students	

Section 3 People's Effect on the Environment

 4.5 periods, 2.25 blocks (includes Chapter Review and Assessment)

Social Studies Objectives
1. Investigate how first-level activities affect the environment.
2. Explore how second- and third-level activities affect the environment.

Reading/Language Arts Objective
Learn how to identify implied main ideas.

Prepare to Read	Instructional Resources	Differentiated Instruction
Build Background Knowledge Discuss the natural resources of soil, water and air. **Set a Purpose for Reading** Have students evaluate statements on the *Reading Readiness Guide*. **Preview Key Terms** Teach the section's Key Terms. **Target Reading Skill** Introduce the section's Target Reading Skill of **identifying implied main ideas.**	**All in One Foundations of Geography Teaching Resources** L2 Reading Readiness Guide, p. 253 L2 Identify Implied Main Ideas, p. 258	**Spanish Reading and Vocabulary Study Guide** L1 Chapter 5, Section 3, pp. 37–38 ELL

Instruct	Instructional Resources	Differentiated Instruction
First-Level Activities Discuss the negative effects of first-level activities on the environment. **Eyewitness Technology** Discuss the hybrid car. **Target Reading Skill** Review **identifying implied main ideas.** **Second- and Third-Level Activities** Discuss the effects of industrial and service activities on the environment.	**All in One Foundations of Geography Teaching Resources** L2 Guided Reading and Review, p. 254 L2 Reading Readiness Guide, p. 253 L2 Small Group Activity: Community Service Project: Protect the Environment, pp. 262–265 **Foundations of Geography Transparencies** L2 Section Reading Support Transparency FG 58	**Spanish Support** L2 Guided Reading and Review (Spanish), p. 40 ELL

Assess and Reteach	Instructional Resources	Differentiated Instruction

Assess Progress
Evaluate student comprehension with the section assessment and section quiz.
 	
Reteach
Assign the Reading and Vocabulary Study Guide to help struggling students.
 	
Extend
Extend the lesson by assigning an Enrichment Activity.
	All in One Foundations of Geography Teaching Resources
	L2 Section Quiz, p. 255
	L3 Enrichment, p. 260
	   Rubric for Assessing a Journal Entry, p. 276
	L2 Vocabulary Development, p. 273
	   Rubric for Assessing a Writing Assignment, p. 277
	L2 Word Knowledge, p. 259
	L2 Chapter Tests A and B, pp. 278–283
	L2 Final Exams A and B, pp. 287–292
	
	Reading and Vocabulary Study Guide
	L1 Chapter 5, Section 3, pp. 51–53
		Spanish Support
		L2 Section Quiz (Spanish), p. 41 ELL
		L2 Chapter Summary (Spanish), p. 42 ELL
		L2 Vocabulary Development (Spanish), p. 43 ELL

Key

L1 Basic to Average	L3 Average to Advanced	LPR Less Proficient Readers	GT Gifted and Talented
L2 For All Students		AR Advanced Readers	ELL English Language Learners
		SN Special Needs Students	

Reading Background

Summarizing

Research has shown that summarizing helps students understand and recall what they have read. Explain to students that good summarizers begin by taking notes while reading. They identify main ideas and list important supporting details. Describe the following steps for writing good summaries:

1. After reading the selection aloud, ask students to recall information from the text. List their responses on the board.
2. Have students reread the selection to verify the accuracy of the recalled information.
3. Have students eliminate any information that is not important enough to include in their summaries.
4. Write the summary together as a class.

Use scaffolding to teach the skill by starting small; ask students to summarize a paragraph from their texts. Then have them extend their summarizing skills by gradually applying the skill to groups of paragraphs, entire sections, and complete chapters.

Using Paragraph Shrinking Effectively

The Paragraph Shrinking strategy can help students extract key ideas from each paragraph they read. To maximize success with this strategy, have students read the paragraph twice. The first time, students should scan the text to understand the general idea of the paragraph. The second time, students should read the paragraph more carefully to identify key ideas.

Demonstrate Paragraph Shrinking by modeling the following steps based on the last paragraph on page 115:

1. Identify the subject of the paragraph. *(types of energy that are renewable resources)*
2. Identify two to three important supporting details. *(The way the sun heats Earth causes wind, which can be used as energy. Solar power and geothermal energy, or the heat within Earth, are types of energy. These resources will never run out.)*
3. Help the student to "shrink" the paragraph by stating the main idea of the paragraph in a complete sentence. The sentence should use approximately ten words or less. *(Wind, solar, and geothermal energy are renewable resources used as energy.)*

World Studies Background

Solar Energy

Solar energy is free, but collecting and converting it to electricity is not. Solar cells can convert only about 10 percent of the sun's energy into electricity. Consequently, several cells must be connected to create power for large areas. This is costly and takes up a great deal of space. Smaller systems used to heat individual homes are more cost-effective.

Raw Materials in the United States

The demand for raw materials in the United States results in substantial internal trade. Forest products from the West are traded particularly to the Northeast and the Midwest. Oil from Texas is essential throughout the United States. Metals from the Midwest are a necessity in the Northeast and the West. These raw materials often travel through manufacturing centers in major cities before the final products are sent to their ultimate destinations.

The Amazon Rainforest and Medicine

Concerns about deforestation in the Amazon rainforest often focus on the threat posed to its unique gene pool. Many organisms found exclusively in the rainforest are essential to the development of pharmaceutical products. About twenty-five percent of the pharmaceuticals used in the Western world are created from rainforest ingredients.

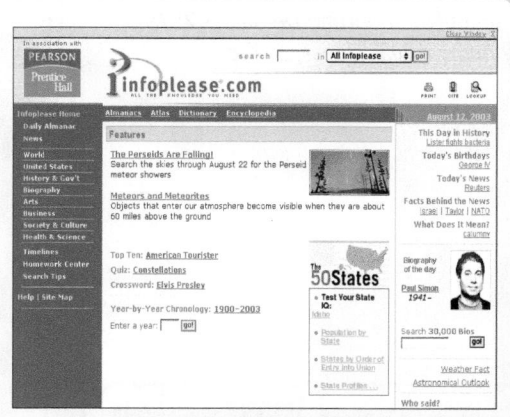

Infoplease® provides a wealth of useful information for the classroom. You can use this resource to strengthen your background on the subjects covered in this chapter. Have students visit this advertising-free site as a starting point for projects requiring research.

Use Web Code **led-3500** for **Infoplease®**.

Chapter 5

Guiding Questions

Remind students about the Guiding Questions introduced at the beginning of this section.

Section 1 refers to **Guiding Question** ❸
How do people use the world's natural resources? (*Everything that people use or consume is made with natural resources, which can be divided into renewable resources, living resources, and nonrenewable resources.*)

Section 2 refers to **Guiding Question** ❸
How do people use the world's natural resources? (*People use land in a variety of ways, depending on culture, environment, history, and industrialization.*)

Section 3 refers to **Guiding Question** ❸
How do people use the world's natural resources? (*People change Earth's landscape through farming and industrialization, and struggle to find a balance between industry and protecting the environment.*)

 Target Reading Skill L2

In this chapter, students will learn and apply the reading skill of identifying main ideas. Use the following worksheets to help students practice this skill.

All In One Foundations of Geography Teaching Resources, *Identify Main Ideas,* p. 256; *Identify Supporting Details,* p. 257; *Identify Implied Main Ideas,* p. 258

Differentiated Instruction

The following Teacher's Edition strategies are suitable for students of varying abilities.
Advanced Readers, pp. 117, 123
English Language Learners, pp. 117, 123
Gifted and Talented, p. 116
Less Proficient Readers, p. 116
Special Needs Students, p. 127

Chapter 5 Interacting With Our Environment

Chapter Preview

This chapter will introduce you to the ways in which people interact with their natural surroundings.

Section 1
Natural Resources

Section 2
Land Use

Section 3
People's Effect on the Environment

Target Reading Skill

Main Idea In this chapter you will construct meaning by identifying the main idea in a paragraph and the details that support it. Identifying a paragraph's main idea can help you remember what you have read.

▶ Windmills capturing the wind's energy in Tehachapi Pass, California

112 Foundations of Geography

Bibliography

For the Teacher
Nadakavukaren, Anne. *Our Global Environment: A Health Perspective.* Waveland Press, 5th Edition, 2000.
Smith, Dan & Anne Braein. *The Penguin State of the World Atlas.* Penguin USA, 7th Edition, 2003.
The Worldwatch Institute. *State of the World 2003 (annual).* W.W. Norton & Company, 2003.

For the Student
L1 Ditchfield, Christian. *Oil (True Books: Natural Resources).* Children's Book Press, 2003.
L2 Allaby, Michael. *The Environment (How It Works).* Award Publications, 2002.
L3 Morgan, Sally. *Alternative Energy Sources (Science at the Edge).* Heinemann Library, 2002.

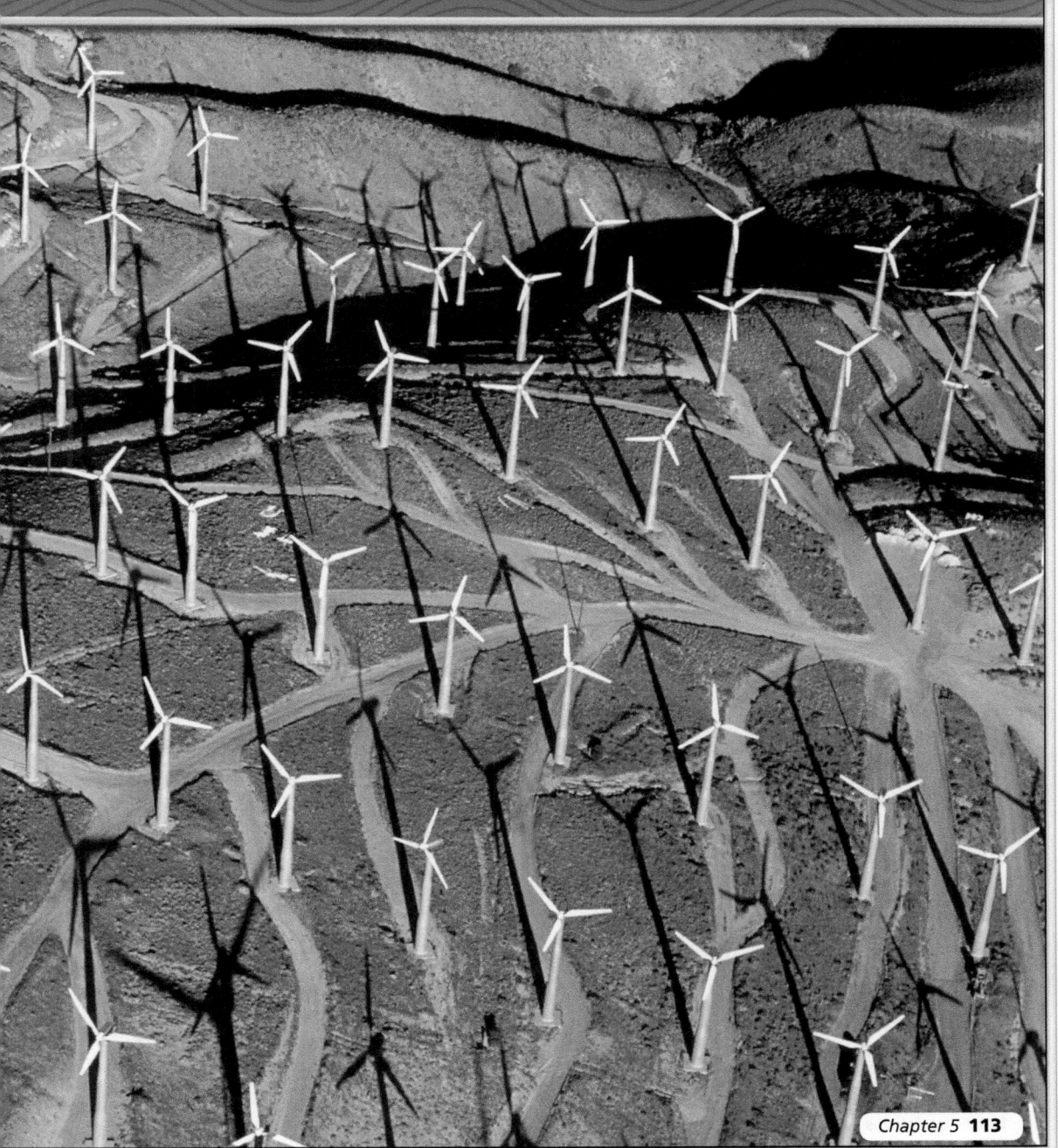

Chapter 5 **113**

Using the Visual L2

Reach Into Your Background Have students study the photo on pp. 112–113 and read the accompanying caption. Draw their attention to the title of the chapter. Ask students to think about how the photograph illustrates interaction between humans and their environment. *(People are using wind to create energy.)* Then ask them to think of some other examples of people interacting with their environment. *(Possible answers: damming rivers to create electricity and regulate water supply; farming; harnessing natural materials to make things used in everyday life, such as clothing)*

Chapter Resources

Teaching Resources
- L2 Vocabulary Development, p. 273
- L2 Skills for Life, p. 261
- L2 Chapter Tests A and B, pp. 278–283

Spanish Support
- L2 Spanish Chapter Summary, p. 42
- L2 Spanish Vocabulary Development, p. 43

Media and Technology
- L1 Student Edition on Audio CD
- L1 Guided Reading Audiotapes, English and Spanish
- L2 Social Studies Skills Tutor CD-ROM

ExamView Test Bank CD-ROM

PRENTICE HALL
Presentation EXPRESS™
Teach · Connect · Inspire

Teach this chapter's content using the PresentationExpress™ CD-ROM including:
- slide shows
- transparencies
- interactive maps and media
- *ExamView*® QuickTake Presenter

Objectives

Social Studies

1. Learn about natural resources.
2. Investigate energy.

Reading/Language Arts

Learn how to identify the main idea of a paragraph.

Prepare to Read

Build Background Knowledge `L2`

Tell students that in this section they will learn about natural resources and how people use them. Ask students to identify things in the classroom that are in their natural forms, such as a glass of water or a plant. Then have the students name several objects in the room made of raw materials, such as a desk or an item of clothing. Ask them to identify what raw material each was made from and how the raw materials were changed for human use. Conduct an Idea Wave (TE, p. T35) to help students share their ideas.

Set a Purpose for Reading `L2`

- Preview the Objectives.

- Read each statement in the *Reading Readiness Guide* aloud. Ask students to mark the statements true or false.

  All in One Foundations of Geography Teaching Resources, *Reading Readiness Guide,* p. 245

- Have students discuss the statements in pairs or groups of four, then mark their worksheets again. Use the Numbered Heads participation strategy (TE, p. T36) to call on students to share their group's perspectives.

Vocabulary Builder

Preview Key Terms `L2`

Pronounce each Key Term, then ask the students to say the word with you. Provide a simple explanation such as, "Natural resources are things found in nature that people use."

Natural Resources

Prepare to Read

Objectives

In this section you will

1. Learn about natural resources.
2. Investigate energy.

Taking Notes

Copy the outline below. Add letters, numbers, and headings as needed. As you read this section, fill in the outline with information about natural resources and energy.

> I. Natural resources
>   A. Renewable resources
>   B.
>   1.
>   2.
> II. Energy
>   A.

Target Reading Skill

Identify Main Ideas
Good readers identify the main idea in every written paragraph. The main idea is the most important point—the one that includes all of the other points. Sometimes this idea is stated directly. For example, in the first paragraph below, the first sentence states the paragraph's main idea. As you read, note the main idea of each paragraph.

Key Terms

- **natural resources** (NACH ur ul REE sawr siz) *n.* useful materials found in the environment
- **raw materials** (raw muh TIHR ee ulz) *n.* natural resources that must be worked to be useful
- **renewable resources** (rih NOO uh bul REE sawr siz) *n.* natural resources that can be replaced
- **nonrenewable resources** (nahn rih NOO uh bul REE sawr siz) *n.* natural resources that cannot be replaced

Men constructing a wooden hut in Kenya

114 Foundations of Geography

What Are Natural Resources?

Everything that people use or consume is made with **natural resources,** or useful materials found in the environment. When people talk about natural resources, they usually mean such things as water, minerals, and vegetation.

All people need water, food, clothing, and shelter to survive. People drink water. People eat food that the soil produces. So do the animals that provide eggs, cheese, meat, and wool. Homes are made from wood, clay, and steel.

People can use some resources just as they are found in nature. Fresh water is one of these. But most resources must be changed before people can use them. Natural resources that must be worked to be useful are called **raw materials.** For example, people cannot just go out and cut down a tree if they want paper. Trees are the raw materials for paper and wood. To make paper, the wood must be soaked and broken up to create pulp. (Pulp is a kind of soup of wood fibers.) Machines collect the wet fibers on screens to form sheets of paper.

Target Reading Skill `L2`

Identify Main Ideas Direct students' attention to the Target Reading Skill. Tell them that identifying the main idea will help them to focus on the most important points of a paragraph.

Model identifying main ideas by having students read the third paragraph on this page. Students should make a list of the three ideas presented in the paragraph.

Then ask students **Which of these three points is the most important and includes all the other points?** (*Most resources must be changed before people use them.*)

Give students *Identify Main Ideas.* Have them complete the activity in groups.

All in One Foundations of Geography Teaching Resources, *Identify Main Ideas,* p. 256

Renewable Resources The environment is filled with natural resources, but not all resources are alike. Geographers divide them into two main groups.

The first group is **renewable resources,** or resources that can be replaced. Some resources are replaced naturally because of the way Earth works. In the water cycle, water evaporates into the air and falls as rain, snow, hail, or sleet. This happens over and over again. Therefore, Earth has an unchanging amount of water. Other materials that go through natural cycles include nitrogen and carbon.

Some types of energy are also renewable resources. Using wind to make electricity will not use the wind up. Wind results from differences in the way the sun heats Earth. As long as the sun shines, there will always be more wind. Solar energy, or energy from the sun, is a renewable resource. No matter how much people use, there will always be more. Geothermal energy uses differences in heat between Earth's surface and its interior. This heat difference will not disappear in the foreseeable future.

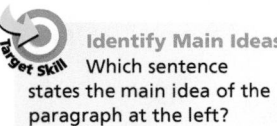

Identify Main Ideas
Which sentence states the main idea of the paragraph at the left?

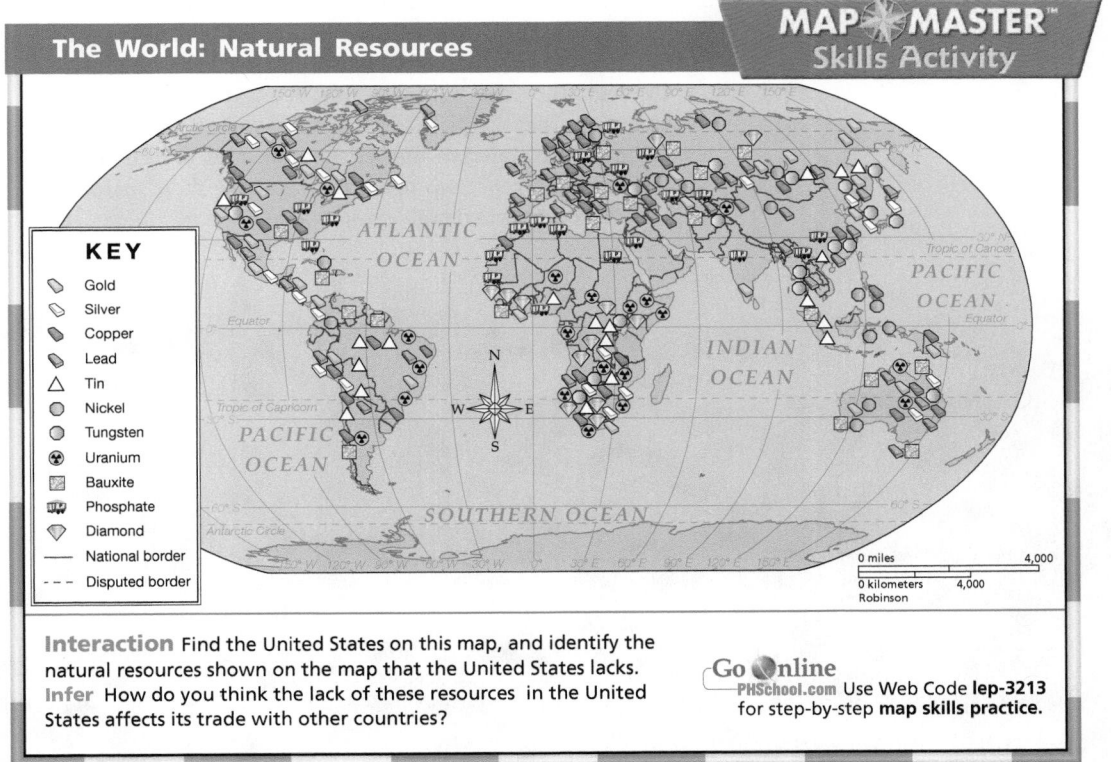

The World: Natural Resources

MAP MASTER
Skills Activity

KEY
- Gold
- Silver
- Copper
- Lead
- Tin
- Nickel
- Tungsten
- Uranium
- Bauxite
- Phosphate
- Diamond
- —— National border
- – – – Disputed border

ATLANTIC OCEAN
PACIFIC OCEAN
INDIAN OCEAN
PACIFIC OCEAN
SOUTHERN OCEAN

0 miles 4,000
0 kilometers 4,000
Robinson

Interaction Find the United States on this map, and identify the natural resources shown on the map that the United States lacks.
Infer How do you think the lack of these resources in the United States affects its trade with other countries?

Go Online
PHSchool.com Use Web Code **lep-3213**
for step-by-step **map skills practice.**

Vocabulary Builder

Use the information below to teach students this section's high-use words.

High-Use Word	Definition and Sample Sentence
consume, p. 114	*v.* to use something Larger cars **consume** more gasoline than smaller ones.
evaporate, p. 115	*v.* to change from a liquid into a vapor Puddles **evaporate** quickly on a sunny day.
harness, p. 117	*v.* to bring under control and direct the force of something Windmills **harness** the energy of the wind.
hybrid, p. 119	*n.* something made up of two different elements A **hybrid** car runs on gasoline and electric power.

Instruct

What Are Natural Resources? L2

Guided Instruction

- **Vocabulary Builder** Clarify the high-use words **consume** and **evaporate** before reading.

- Read What Are Natural Resources? using the ReQuest reading strategy (TE, p. T35). Ask students to study the map on p. 115.

- Ask students **What are natural resources?** *(useful materials found in the environment)*

- Ask students **What are renewable resources?** *(natural resources that can be replaced)* **What are some examples of renewable resources?** *(water, wind, solar energy, geothermal energy)*

- Have students examine the map and brainstorm what some of the natural resources shown might be used for. *(Possible answers: gold, silver, diamonds—jewelry; copper—coins, wire; tin—cans; lead— pipes)*

Target Reading Skill L2

Identify Main Ideas As a follow up, ask students to answer the Target Reading Skill question in the Student Edition. *(Some types of energy are also renewable resources.)*

Answers

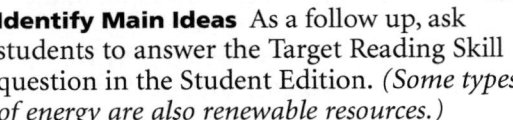

Interaction nickel and diamonds **Infer** Since the United States does not have these resources, it probably has to purchase them from other countries.

Go Online
PHSchool.com Students may practice their map skills using the interactive online version of this map.

- Ask students **What are living resources?** *(living things that provide natural resources, such as plants and animals)*

- Ask students to define nonrenewable resources and list examples. *(resources that cannot be replaced; metal ores, most minerals, natural gas, petroleum)*

- Ask students **How does recycling help conserve nonrenewable resources?** *(Recycling recovers and processes used materials so they can be used again.)*

- Ask students **What are examples of fossil fuels?** *(coal, natural gas, and petroleum)* Have students discuss how they are created and if they are renewable. *(They were created over millions of years from remains of prehistoric living things. They are renewable, but if used up they would take millions of years to form again. So for the purposes of people living today, fossil fuels are non-renewable resources.)*

Independent Practice

Show students the *Outline Transparency*. Then ask students to create the Taking Notes graphic organizer on a blank piece of paper. Have them begin to fill in the outline by adding information about natural resources. Briefly model how to create and fill in the outline.

Foundations of Geography Transparencies, *Transparency B15: Outline*

Monitor Progress

As students fill in the graphic organizer, circulate and make sure students are choosing appropriate headings and details. Provide assistance as needed.

Solar cells on the roof of a house in Felsberg, Germany

Living Resources Living things that provide natural resources, such as plants and animals, are also renewable resources. Like other resources, they must be properly managed so that people do not overuse them.

For example, a timber company may cut down all the trees in an area for use as wood. But the company may then plant new trees to replace the ones they cut. Even if they do not, seeds left in the ground will probably produce new trees. Every day, the people of the world eat many chickens and ears of corn. But farmers always make sure to grow more corn and chickens to replace what people eat. If people are careful, they can have a steady supply of these renewable living resources.

Nonrenewable Resources The second major group of resources is called **nonrenewable resources**, or resources that cannot be replaced. Most nonliving things, such as metal ores, most minerals, natural gas, and petroleum—or crude oil—are nonrenewable resources. If people keep mining minerals and burning fuels such as coal and oil, they will eventually run out. Therefore, people need to use these resources carefully. If they do run out, people will need to find substitutes for them.

Although they are nonrenewable, many metals, minerals, and materials such as plastics can be recycled. Recycling does not return these materials to their natural state. Still, they can be recovered and processed for reuse. Recycling these materials helps to conserve nonrenewable resources.

116 Foundations of Geography

Differentiated Instruction

For Gifted and Talented [L3]

Have students do library or Internet research to identify their region's resources. Then have them design posters to attract businesses to their region based upon the types of natural resources available.

All in One Foundations of Geography Teaching Resources, *Rubric for Assessing a Student Poster,* p. 274

For Less Proficient Readers [L1]

Reinforce students' ability to read and interpret a natural resources map by giving them *Reading a Natural Resource Map* and having them answer the questions.

All in One Foundations of Geography Teaching Resources, *Reading a Natural Resources Map,* p. 267

Fossil Fuels Most scientists think that coal, natural gas, and petroleum are fossil fuels, or fuels created over millions of years from the remains of prehistoric living things. If people continue using coal at today's rate, known supplies may run out in several hundred years. At current rates of use, known supplies of oil and natural gas may run out in less than 100 years.

If oil and natural gas are fossil fuels, they are renewable, since living things today will become fossil fuels in millions of years. But if these fuels take so long to develop, they are nonrenewable for our purposes.

✓ Reading Check **What is the difference between renewable and nonrenewable resources?**

A Special Resource: Energy

Many natural resources are sources of energy. People use energy not only from fossil fuels, but also from the wind and the sun. Dams produce hydroelectric power by harnessing the power of falling water.

Energy is itself a resource that is needed to make use of other natural resources. Consider cotton. It takes energy to harvest cotton from a field, to spin the cotton into thread, and to weave it into fabric. Workers use energy to travel to a garment factory. It takes energy to sew a shirt with a sewing machine. It also takes energy to transport the shirt by ship and truck to a retail store. Finally, the consumer uses energy to bring the shirt home.

Located on the border between Oregon and Washington, the Bonneville Dam produces hydroelectric power.

Strip Mining Coal
The machine below extracts coal from this exposed deposit in Banwen Pyrddin, Wales, United Kingdom. **Apply Information** *Do you think that coal is a recyclable, renewable, or nonrenewable resource?*

Guided Instruction

■ **Vocabulary Builder** Clarify the high-use words **harness** and **hybrid** before reading.

■ Read A Special Resource: Energy with students and have them examine the graph on p. 118. Circulate to make sure individuals can answer the Graph Skills questions.

■ Ask students to name some different sources of energy. (*Possible answers: fossil fuels, wind, water, sun*) Ask students **How is energy needed to make use of other natural resources?** (*It takes energy to convert the natural resource into a usable form, to make it into a product, to transport the product, and to consume the product.*)

Differentiated Instruction

For English Language Learners   L1
Tell students that natural resources maps often use symbols to represent different resources. The map key shows what each symbol stands for. Tell students the natural resources of their state. Students can then create a map key to show the symbols and the natural resources they stand for.

For Advanced Readers   L3
Pair students and have them complete *Reading an Economic Activity Map*. Ask each pair to use the map on page 115 and the map on the worksheet to compare Somalia's resources and economic activities.

All in One **Foundations of Geography Teaching Resources,** *Reading an Economic Activity Map,* p. 266

Answers

✓ Reading Check Renewable resources are natural resources that can be replaced, whereas nonrenewable resources are natural resources that cannot be replaced.

Apply Information Coal is a renewable resource; over millions of years more coal will be created from the remains of living things. Practically, coal is generally considered to be a nonrenewable resource because its supplies are limited.

Guided Instruction (continued)

- Have students name two countries that can sell oil and two countries that have to buy energy. *(Mexico and Saudi Arabia sell oil; Japan and the United States have to buy energy.)*

- Ask students to list energy alternatives to fossil fuels. *(wind energy, solar energy, tidal energy, geothermal energy, biomass, atomic energy)*

- Direct students' attention to the graph on this page to help them answer the following question: **What are the names of at least three countries that consume more petroleum than they produce?** *(Possible answers: India, China, Germany, Japan, and the United States)*

- Have students list some ways of conserving energy discussed in the text. Then have them brainstorm other ways they could save energy at home or at school. *(In text: hybrid cars, new technologies that conserve energy used for heat and light; other possible answers: turning off lights when not in use at home or in school, turning down heat or air conditioning at night or when not at home)*

Independent Practice

Have students complete the graphic organizer by adding details about energy usage.

Monitor Progress

- Show *Section Reading Support Transparency FG 56* and ask students to check their graphic organizers individually. Go over key concepts and clarify key vocabulary as needed.

    Foundations of Geography Transparencies, *Section Reading Support Transparency FG 56*

- Tell students to fill in the last column of their *Reading Readiness Guides.* Probe for what they learned that confirms or invalidates each statement.

    All in One **Foundations of Geography Teaching Resources,** *Reading Readiness Guide,* p. 245

Answers

Graph Skills Identify Germany and Japan Compare and Contrast the United States

Pipes running across an oil field in Meyal, Pakistan

Energy "Have's" and "Have Not's" People in every country need energy. But energy resources are not evenly spread around the world. Certain areas are rich in energy resources. Others have very few.

Countries with many rivers, such as Canada and Norway, can use water energy to create electricity. Countries like Saudi Arabia and Mexico have huge amounts of oil that they sell to other countries. Countries like Japan and the United States do not produce as much energy as they use. These countries have to buy energy from other countries.

Meeting Energy Needs in the Future Over time, energy use worldwide has grown rapidly. Yet our supplies of fossil fuels may be limited. It seems likely that the world's people will need to find other sources of energy. Many possibilities exist.

Already, some countries, such as Denmark and Germany, are developing renewable energy sources such as wind and solar energy. Other sources of energy that will not run out are tidal energy, from the rise and fall of Earth's oceans, and geothermal energy, or energy from the heat of Earth's interior. Biomass, or plant material, is a renewable source of energy. These energy sources can reduce a country's need for imported oil.

Atomic energy uses radioactive materials, which are nonrenewable but plentiful. Some people oppose atomic energy because radioactive materials can be dangerous. Others support it as a plentiful energy source that does not pollute the air.

Graph Skills

Some countries produce more oil than they use. These countries can sell their extra oil to other countries. Others consume more oil than they produce and have to buy it from other countries. **Identify** Which of the countries on this graph have to buy almost all of their oil? **Compare and Contrast** Which country buys the most oil?

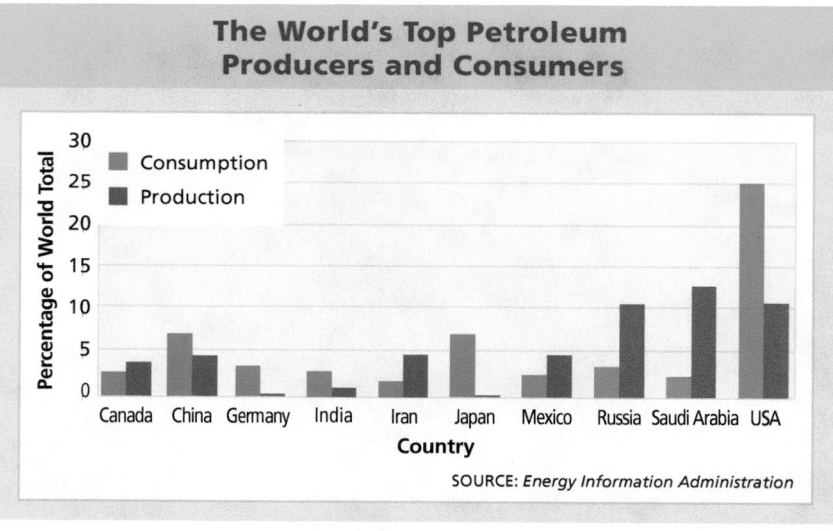

The World's Top Petroleum Producers and Consumers

SOURCE: *Energy Information Administration*

Skills Mini Lesson

Skills for Life

Problem-Solving

1. To solve a problem, students should identify the problem, evaluate its effect, identify possible solutions, choose a solution, and determine its effectiveness.

2. Have students read the second paragraph on this page to identify some problem-solving steps used to meet countries' energy needs.

3. Have students apply the skill by asking them to reread the text under Meeting Energy Needs in the Future on pp. 118–119. Have students suppose they live in a cloudy, windless place with a limited oil supply, no large bodies of water, and no biomass available. Ask them how problem-solving can be used to help them meet their energy needs. *(Possible solutions: geothermal or atomic energy)*

Geothermal power
In addition to producing energy, the geothermal power plant at Svartsengi, Iceland, heats the mineral-rich water of the Blue Lagoon. **Infer** *Are fossil fuels used to heat this pool?*

Fossil fuels will last longer if people use less energy. New technologies, such as hybrid cars, can reduce a country's need for imported oil by burning less gas per mile. Other technologies offer energy savings in heating and lighting buildings and in making new products. If people manage to use less energy, they will not need to buy as much from foreign countries. They will also have an easier time meeting their energy needs in the future.

 Reading Check **Why do some countries have to import energy?**

Section 1 Assessment

Key Terms
Review the key terms at the beginning of this section. Use each term in a sentence that explains its meaning.

Target Reading Skill
State the main idea of the paragraph on this page.

Comprehension and Critical Thinking
1. (a) **Identify** Why is wood considered a renewable resource?

(b) **Apply Information** What needs to happen after trees are cut in order for wood to remain a renewable resource?
2. (a) **List** Name some sources of energy other than fossil fuels.
(b) **Categorize** What do these energy sources have in common, and how do they differ from fossil fuels?
(c) **Draw Conclusions** Why might we need to use more of these energy sources in the future?

Writing Activity
Think about what you did this morning before you came to school. Write a journal entry describing the natural resources that you used and all of the ways that you used energy at home and on your way to school.

For: An activity on natural resources
Visit: PHSchool.com
Web Code: led-3501

Chapter 5 Section 1 **119**

Section 1 Assessment

Key Terms
Students' sentences should reflect knowledge of each Key Term.

Target Reading Skill
Fossil fuels will last longer if people use less energy.

Comprehension and Critical Thinking
1. (a) It can be replaced by the growth of new trees. (b) New trees need to be planted.
2. (a) wind energy, solar energy, geothermal energy, hydroelectric power, tidal energy, biomass, atomic energy (b) All of the types of energy listed above except atomic energy are renewable resources, and fossil fuels are not. (c) Reserves of important fossil fuels will eventually run out.

Assess and Reteach

Assess Progress L2
Have students complete the Section Assessment. Administer the *Section Quiz.*

 **Foundations of Geography Teaching Resources,** *Section Quiz,* p. 247

Reteach L1
If students need more instruction, have them read this section in the Reading and Vocabulary Study Guide.

📖 Chapter 5, Section 1, **Western Hemisphere Reading and Vocabulary Study Guide,** pp. 45-47

Extend L3
Have students explore alternative energy by completing *Alternative Sources of Energy*. Use the activity as a springboard for a discussion about the use of renewable sources of energy.

Go Online PHSchool.com

For: Environmental and Global Issues: *Alternative Sources of Energy*
Visit: PHSchool.com
Web Code: led-3504

Answers

Infer Fossil fuels are not used; geothermal energy is used.

√ Reading Check Some countries need to import energy because the energy they consume is greater than the energy they produce.

Go Online PHSchool.com Typing in the Web code when prompted will bring students to detailed instructions for this activity.

Writing Activity
Use the *Rubric for Assessing a Journal Entry* to evaluate students' journals.

Foundations of Geography Teaching Resources, *Rubric for Assessing a Journal Entry,* p. 276

Section 2
Step-by-Step Instruction

Objectives

Social Studies
1. Study the relation between land use and culture.
2. Investigate the relation between land use and economic activity.
3. Explore changes in land use.

Reading/Language Arts
Learn how to identify sentences that include details that support the main idea of a paragraph.

Prepare to Read

Build Background Knowledge L2
Tell students they will learn about how people use land resources in this section. Ask students to choose a familiar product (such as a box of cereal) that they use in their everyday lives. Then have them think about what raw materials were used to make the product. Finally, ask them to describe how the products are made and relate this process to land use (For example, farm land is needed to grow the ingredients of cereal.) Use the Think-Write-Pair-Share participation strategy (TE, p. T36) to structure the activity.

Set a Purpose for Reading L2
■ Preview the Objectives.

■ Form students into pairs or groups of four. Distribute the *Reading Readiness Guide.* Ask students to fill in the first two columns of the chart. Use the Numbered Heads participation strategy (TE, p. T36) to call on students to share one piece of information they already know and one piece of information they want to know.

  All in One **Foundations of Geography Teaching Resources,** *Reading Readiness Guide,* p. 249

Vocabulary Builder
Preview Key Terms L2
Pronounce each Key Term, then ask the students to say the words with you. Provide a simple explanation such as, "Manufacturing refers to making many things by hand or using machines."

Section 2 — Land Use

Prepare to Read

Objectives
In this section you will
1. Study the relation between land use and culture.
2. Investigate the relation between land use and economic activity.
3. Explore changes in land use.

Taking Notes
Copy the concept web below. As you read the section, fill in the ovals with information about land use. Add ovals as needed.

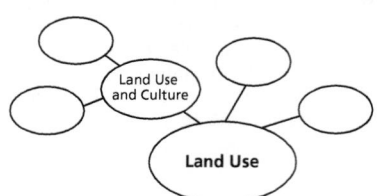

Target Reading Skill

Identify Supporting Details Sentences in a paragraph may provide details that support the main idea. These details may give examples or explanations. In the second paragraph on this page, this sentence states the main idea: "Even in similar environments, people may use land differently because they have different cultural traits." Note three details in the paragraph that explain this main idea.

Key Terms
- **environment** (en VY run munt) *n.* natural surroundings
- **manufacturing** (man yoo FAK chur ing) *n.* the large-scale production of goods by hand or by machine
- **colonization** (kayl uh nih ZAY shun) *n.* the movement of settlers and their culture to a new country
- **industrialization** (in dus tree ul ih ZAY shun) *n.* the growth of machine-powered production in an economy

A peanut farmer in Georgia inspecting his crop

120 Foundations of Geography

Land Use and Culture

How people use the land depends on their culture. People may use their land differently because their cultures have developed in different **environments, or natural surroundings.** For example, the Inuit live in a cold, arctic climate. It is too cold to grow crops, so the Inuit use their land mainly for hunting wild animals, and they rely heavily on fishing. The Japanese live in a warmer, moister climate. Although much of Japan is too steep to farm, the Japanese use much of the remaining land for crops. Their main crop is rice, which grows well in the warm, moist climate of Japan.

Even in similar environments, however, people may use land differently because they have different cultural traits. For example, Georgia has a warm, moist climate like that of southern Japan. But Georgia does not produce much rice. Instead, Georgians raise chickens and grow crops such as peanuts. While the Japanese eat rice at nearly every meal, Americans eat more meat and peanut butter.

Target Reading Skill L2

Identify Supporting Details Point out the Target Reading Skill. Tell students that sentences in a paragraph may provide additional details that support the main idea.

Model identifying supporting details by reading the first paragraph on p. 121 aloud. Ask students to identify the main idea. (*People's cultures help shape the landscapes where they live.*) Then ask them to identify one detail that supports the main idea. (*Possible*

supporting details: In some parts of the Philippines, a culture of rice farming and a shortage of level land has led people to carve terraces into hillsides; people cleared forests in Western Europe for farm land.)

Give students *Identify Supporting Details.* Have them complete the activity in groups.

  All in One **Foundations of Geography Teaching Resources,** *Identify Supporting Details,* p. 257

Cultures and Landscapes The examples of the Inuit and the Japanese show how people's environments help to shape their cultures. People's cultures, in turn, help shape the landscapes where they live. For example, in some parts of the Philippines, a culture of rice farming and a shortage of level land has led people to carve terraces into hillsides. Thousands of years ago, Western Europe was covered with forests. As farming cultures spread across that region, people cleared forests to use the land for farming. Today, most of Western Europe is open fields and pastures. Few forests remain.

Land Use and Cultural Differences As the examples of Japan and Georgia show, however, similar environments do not necessarily produce similar cultures. People may respond differently to those environments, depending on their culture. For example, much of the western United States has a dry climate. Many crops need irrigation, or an artificial water supply. The Middle East also has climates too dry for most crops to grow without irrigation. However, the two regions have different cultures and different responses to this challenge. In the western United States, farmers use modern irrigation systems. For example, drip irrigation provides water to each plant through little pipes or tubes. Some Middle Eastern farmers use qanats, or brick irrigation channels, to bring water to their crops. Both cultures face similar environments, but they interact with those environments differently.

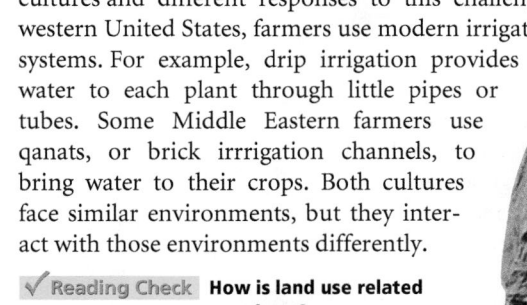

Drip irrigation of grape vines in eastern Washington State

Irrigation in Yemen
This man is walking along a qanat, or brick irrigation channel, in Jiblah, Yemen.
Analyze Images *What clues do you see in this landscape that suggest a need for irrigation?*

✓ Reading Check **How is land use related to culture?**

Chapter 5 Section 2 **121**

Vocabulary Builder

Use the information below to teach students this section's high-use words.

High-Use Word	Sample Sentence and Definition
respond, p. 121	*v.* to do something in reaction to something else Firefighters must **respond** to alarms quickly.
channel, p. 121	*n.* path through which water flows A new bridge was built over the **channel.**
distribute, p. 122	*v.* to pass out or deliver The group decided to **distribute** flyers in support of their cause.
correspond, p. 122	*v.* to match or agree with The number of chairs in the theater should **correspond** to the number of tickets sold.

Guided Instruction

■ **Vocabulary Builder** Clarify the high-use words **respond** and **channel** before reading.

■ Have students use the Paragraph Shrinking strategy (TE, p. T34) to read Land Use and Culture.

■ Ask students **What is the relationship between the environment and land use?** *(The environment affects how people use the land. People may use the land differently because their cultures developed in different environments.)*

■ Ask students to compare and contrast land use in the western United States with land use in the Middle East. *(Both cultures have responded to their dry environment by devising systems of irrigation, but each culture has a different method. People in the western United States use modern irrigation systems that rely on the latest technologies, whereas Middle Eastern farmers use more traditional means of irrigation. These different responses are the result of cultural differences.)*

Independent Practice

Ask students to create the Taking Notes graphic organizer on a blank piece of paper. Have them begin filling in the concept web with details about land use and culture. Briefly model which details to record.

Monitor Progress

As students begin to fill in the graphic organizer, circulate and help individuals understand which details to include. Provide assistance as needed.

Answers

Analyze Images Possible answer: vegetation is sparse and the land looks dry.

✓ Reading Check Land use is determined in part by the environment in which a culture lives. Therefore, the environment will often contribute to the development of a culture. However, different cultures may respond differently to similar environments.

Land Use and Economic Activity

Guided Instruction

- **Vocabulary Builder** Clarify the high-use words **distribute** and **correspond** before reading.

- Have students read Land Use and Economic Activity. Review the photographs and captions on pp. 122 and 123 with students. Circulate to make sure individuals can answer the Reading Check question.

- Ask students **What are first-level activities?** *(economic activities in which people use land and resources directly to make products)*

- Ask students **How much of the world's land is used for first-level activities?** *(Most of the world's land is used for first-level activities.)* **How much land is used for these activities in developed countries like the United States?** *(In developed countries only a small percentage of the land is used for first-level activities.)*

⊙ Target Reading Skill

Identify Supporting Details As a follow up, ask students to answer the Target Reading Skill question in the Student Edition. *(Possible answers: hunting, cutting wood, mining, fishing, herding animals, and raising crops)*

Land Use and Economic Activity

In some places, people use the land and its resources to make a living by farming, fishing, or mining. In other places, people work in factories, where they turn natural resources into finished products. In still other places, people sell or distribute products and make a living by providing services. These three ways of making a living correspond to three stages of economic activity. Geographers use stages of economic activity as a way to understand land use.

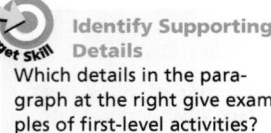
Identify Supporting Details
Which details in the paragraph at the right give examples of first-level activities?

First-Level Activities In the first stage, people use land and resources directly to make products. They may hunt, cut wood, mine, or fish. They also may herd animals or raise crops. This is the first stage of activities. At this stage, people interact directly with the land or the sea. Most of the world's land is used for first-level activities. However, in developed countries such as the United States, only a small percentage of the people make a living at first-level activities.

Stages of Economic Activity

A series of economic activities connect a flock of sheep in a pasture to a wool sweater in a store. Sheep-raising, a first-level activity, makes it possible to manufacture woolen goods such as sweaters, a second-level activity. Manufacturing makes it possible to deliver sweaters to stores. Stores can then sell the sweaters. Delivery and sales are both third-level activities.

▲ **Farming, a first-level activity**
This farmer is shearing a sheep, or trimming away its wool. Raising and shearing sheep are first-level activities, or direct uses of natural resources.

A flock of sheep being driven to a pasture in New Zealand

Skills Mini Lesson

Analyzing Primary Sources

1. Help students define primary and secondary sources. To analyze these sources, students should identify who created the source, when, and why. They should then identify the main idea, separate facts from opinions, look for evidence of bias, and evaluate how reliable the source is.

2. In groups, have students use the steps above to analyze an encyclopedia article, a secondary source, about islands.

3. Have students analyze the primary source *Celia's Island Journal.*

All in One Foundations of Geography Teaching Resources, *Celia's Island Journal,* pp. 270–271

Second-Level Activities At the second stage, people process the products of first-level activities. Most second-level activity is **manufacturing**, or the large-scale production of goods by hand or by machine. Manufacturing may turn a farmer's corn crop into cornflakes for your breakfast. Manufacturing, especially in urban areas, is an important land use in developed countries.

Third-Level Activities At the third stage, a person delivers boxes of cornflakes to your local grocery store. Third-level activities are also known as services. These activities do not produce goods. They may help sell goods. They often involve working directly for customers or for businesses. Many businesses offering services—doctors' offices, banks, automobile repair shops, shopping malls, and fast-food restaurants—are part of everyday living. Services are also clustered in urban areas, especially in developed countries.

✓ Reading Check **How is most of the world's land used?**

▲ **Manufacturing, a second-level activity** Second-level activities process natural resources to make goods, such as the wool this worker is processing at a New Zealand mill.

Retail sales, a third-level activity ▶ Selling manufactured goods, such as this sweater, in a store is a third-level activity. This woolen-goods store is in New Zealand.

> ### GEOGRAPHY SKILLS PRACTICE
>
> **Human-Environment Interaction** Each activity shown here occurs in a different part of New Zealand.
> **Apply Information** Which activities occur in rural areas, and which activities are likely to occur in urban areas?

Differentiated Instruction

For Advanced Readers   L3
Ask students to read the primary source *The Road from Coorain*. Have them describe how the natural resources listed in the selection are used for various economic activities.

   All in One **Foundations of Geography Teaching Resources**, *The Road from Coorain*, pp. 268–269

For English Language Learners   L1
Read the summary of this chapter in the Reading and Vocabulary Study Guide aloud to students. This will provide an oral synopsis of key content before students read the selection on land use and culture.

   Chapter 5, Section 2, **Western Hemisphere Reading and Vocabulary Study Guide,** pp. 48–50

Guided Instruction (continued)

■ Ask students **What type of economic activity is performed during second-level activities?** *(For the most part, second-level activities consist of manufacturing.)*

■ Ask students **What are third-level activities?** *(Third-level activities consist of providing services, do not produce goods, and often involve working directly for customers or businesses.)*

■ Ask students to examine the graphic Stages of Economic Activity on pp. 122 and 123. Then have them name and describe other products that use all three levels of economic activity. *(Possible answer: Jewelry is made of raw materials extracted from Earth, such as gold and silver. The raw materials are processed to manufacture things such as necklaces and watches. Finally, the jewelry is sold in stores or online.)*

Independent Practice
Have students continue to fill in their graphic organizers by adding details about land use and economic activity.

Monitor Progress
Circulate among students to provide assistance as needed to individuals as they develop their concept webs.

Answers

✓ Reading Check Most of the world's land is used for first-level activities.

Geography Skills Practice Apply Information First-level activities, such as farming, occur in rural areas. Second-level activities, such as manufacturing, and third-level activities, such as retail sales, would probably take place in urban areas.

Changes in Land Use L2

Guided Instruction

- Have students examine the text and visuals on p. 124 and read Changes in Land Use on p. 125.

- Ask students **How has human-environment interaction shaped the city of Boston?** *(Colonists cleared forests and built structures along the waterfront; marshes were drained and filled in to create new land.)*

- Ask **How can colonization affect land use?** *(It may change a landscape to fit colonists' cultural practices.)*

- Ask students **How has industrialization changed land use in developed countries?** *(Since 1900, suburbs have increased around cities in developed countries.)*

Independent Practice

Have students complete the graphic organizer by filling in details about changes in land use.

Monitor Progress

- Show *Section Reading Support Transparency FG 57* and ask students to check their graphic organizers individually. Go over key concepts and clarify key vocabulary as needed.

  Foundations of Geography Transparencies, *Section Reading Support Transparency FG 57*

- Tell students to fill in the last column of their *Reading Readiness Guides*. Ask them if what they learned was what they had expected to learn.

  All in One Foundations of Geography Teaching Resources, *Reading Readiness Guide, p. 249*

Answers

MAP MASTER Skills Activity **Identify** Only a small area to the west of South Boston remained forested after colonization. **Compare and Contrast** The city has grown because people created new land.

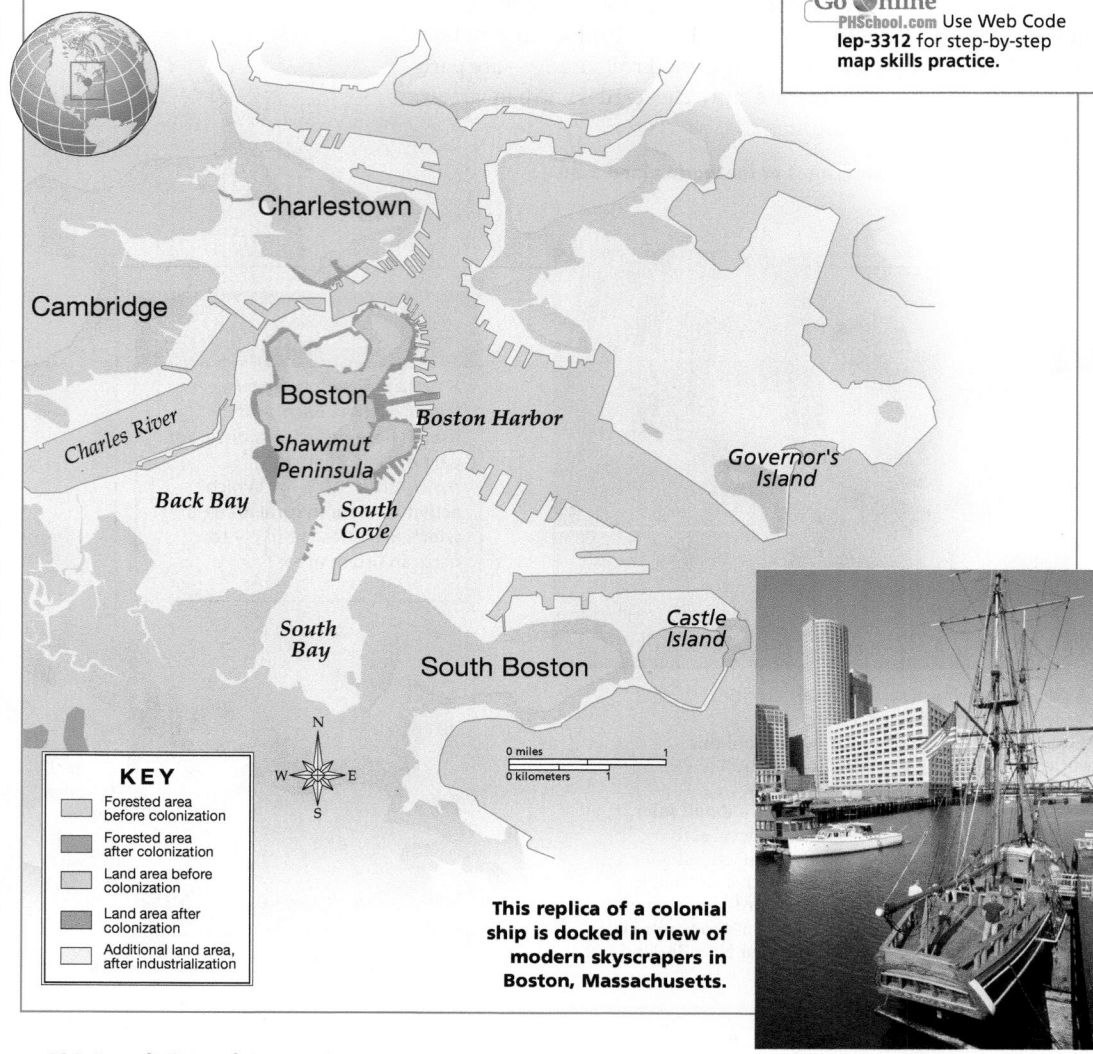

Boston: A Changing Landscape

English colonists founded Boston, Massachusetts, on a narrow peninsula surrounded by water, marshes, and forest. The colonists cleared most of the forest for farmland. The colonists also built dams, piers, and retaining walls along the waterfront. By the 1800s, Boston's growing industries and growing population of workers faced a land shortage. Boston's solution was to drain marshes and to create new land by filling in areas of water. At first, Boston's people filled in around existing piers. Then, they filled in tidal ponds behind dams. Finally, they filled in whole bodies of open water.

Human-Environment Interaction Colonization and industrialization transformed Boston's landscape. **Identify** How much of the forest around Boston remained after colonization? **Compare and Contrast** How did Boston's land area change between colonial times and today?

Go Online PHSchool.com Use Web Code **lep-3312** for step-by-step map skills practice.

Charlestown

Cambridge

Boston

Charles River

Shawmut Peninsula

Boston Harbor

Governor's Island

Back Bay

South Cove

Castle Island

South Bay

South Boston

KEY

- Forested area before colonization
- Forested area after colonization
- Land area before colonization
- Land area after colonization
- Additional land area, after industrialization

0 miles
0 kilometers

N W E S

This replica of a colonial ship is docked in view of modern skyscrapers in Boston, Massachusetts.

124 Foundations of Geography

Background: Links Across Place

The Netherlands Large portions of the Netherlands, a country in northwestern Europe, have been reclaimed from the sea much like the city of Boston. The country is mostly flat, low-lying land. Over one-quarter is located below sea level, and much of the land is naturally lakes or marshes and unusable for farming. However, ingenious civil engineering projects dating as far back as medieval times have managed to make the land more habitable. Lakes and marshes have been drained, and a series of dunes and dikes protect the land from the sea.

Changes in Land Use

When a region undergoes **colonization**, or a movement of new settlers and their culture to a country, the newcomers may change that region's landscape to fit their cultural practices. For example, if farmers move to a region without farms, they will create farms. Similarly, as people find new ways of making a living, they start using the land in new ways, too.

Colonization Before European colonists came to Australia, there was no farming and no livestock raising. In North and South America before colonization, European crops such as wheat and grapes were unknown. So were livestock such as cows and chickens. When Europeans settled these continents, they cleared large areas for use as farmland and livestock pasture.

Industrialization and Sprawl Since the 1800s, the growth of machine-powered production, or **industrialization,** has changed landscapes in many countries. Cities have grown around industrial facilities worldwide. Since 1900, suburbs have spread out from cities in the United States and other developed countries to cover more and more land. The spread of cities and suburbs is known as sprawl.

√ **Reading Check** How did European colonization change landscapes in North and South America?

Vineyards in Australia
Grapes did not grow in Australia before European colonists arrived. Now grapes thrive in Australia's Hunter Valley. **Infer** *What would have been different about this landscape before European colonization?*

Section 2 Assessment

Key Terms
Review the key terms at the beginning of this section. Use each term in a sentence that explains its meaning.

🌀 **Target Reading Skill**
State three details that explain the main idea of the second paragraph on page 120.

Comprehension and Critical Thinking
1. (a) Describe How have rice farmers in the Philippines transformed the landscape?
(b) Infer Why is the Philippines' farm landscape different from Western Europe's?
2. (a) Recall What are second-level activities?
(b) Categorize Name some examples of second-level activities.
(c) Compare and Contrast How do second-level activities differ from third-level activities?
3. (a) Recall What is industrialization?
(b) Identify Causes How is industrialization related to sprawl?

Writing Activity
Write a short encyclopedia article on land use around your hometown. Describe how culture has affected land use. Mention the different levels of economic activity around your town. Finally, give an example of a change in land use in or near your hometown.

Writing Tip Encyclopedia articles contain descriptions and statements of facts. Be careful not to express personal thoughts or opinions.

Chapter 5 Section 2 **125**

Assess and Reteach

Assess Progress L2
Have students complete the Section Assessment. Administer the *Section Quiz.*

📖 **All in One** **Foundations of Geography Teaching Resources,** *Section Quiz,* p. 251

Reteach L1
If students need more instruction, have them read this section in the Reading and Vocabulary Study Guide.

📖 Chapter 5, Section 2, **Western Hemisphere Reading and Vocabulary Study Guide,** pp. 48–50

Extend L3
Extend students' understanding of the relationship between natural resources and economic activity by having them complete the *Book Project: World News Today.* Have students work in pairs to complete the project.

📖 **All in One** **Foundations of Geography Teaching Resources,** *Book Project: World News Today,* pp. 36–38

Answers

Infer Possible answer: Before European colonization, grapes were not grown in Australia. The land might have been a forest.

√ **Reading Check** Large areas of land were cleared and transformed for use as farmland and livestock pasture. However, different cultures may respond differently to similar environments.

Writing Activity
Use the *Rubric for Assessing a Report* to evaluate students' encyclopedia articles.

📖 **All in One** **Foundations of Geography Teaching Resources,** *Rubric for Assessing a Report,* p. 275

Section 2 Assessment

Key Terms
Students' sentences should reflect knowledge of each Key Term.

🌀 **Target Reading Skill**
Possible answers: Georgia and southern Japan both have moist, warm climates; rice is a major crop in Japan; people in Georgia raise chickens and grow crops such as peanuts.

Comprehension and Critical Thinking
1. (a) Due to a shortage of land, Philippine farmers have carved terraces into hillsides in order to grow rice. **(b)** There is a shortage of level land in the Philippines.
2. (a) Second-level activities are economic activities in which people process the products of first-level activities. **(b)** Possible answers include: processing food and making sweaters from wool. **(c)** Second-level activities are based upon the manufacture of goods, whereas third-level activities produce services rather than goods.
3. (a) the growth of machine-powered production in an economy **(b)** Cities tend to grow around industrial facilities. As cities grow, suburbs grow as well. As cities and suburbs spread out, sprawl is increased.

Objective

Learn how to make predictions.

Prepare to Read

Build Background Knowledge L2

Tell students that in this skill lesson they will learn how to make an educated prediction. Explain to students that they make predictions every day when they decide whether to take a certain action. For example, students who walk to school may have to choose among several routes they can take. They choose routes based on which they predict is the safest and will get them to school the fastest. Have students brainstorm other common examples of making predictions.

Instruct

Making Predictions L2

Guided Instruction

■ Read the steps on p. 126 as a class and have student volunteers write them on the board.

■ Practice the skill by following the steps on p. 127 as a class. First, identify the issue in the passage. *(Some countries control water supplies of downstream nations.)* Then have students explain how the issue in the passage is similar to oil issues they already learned about. *(Possible similarity: Both oil and water are important natural resources that are in short supply in some countries.)* Next, have students read aloud the possible effects shown in the graphic organizer. Finally, ask them to predict which effect seems most likely. *(Accept any of the three effects, but be sure students supply a valid reason for their choice.)*

Independent Practice

Assign *Skills for Life* and have students complete it individually.

All in One **Foundations of Geography Teaching Resources,** *Skills for Life,* p. 261

 **Making Predictions**

The Oval Office, where leaders make predictions, is at the center of this photo of the White House.

When you watch an adventure movie, half the fun is in predicting what happens next. Decision makers, such as American presidents, make predictions, too, and their predictions guide their decisions. Good decision makers take actions that they predict will have good results. When you predict, you make an educated guess about the effects of a certain cause. The key word here is *educated*. Without knowledge, you can't predict—you just guess.

Learn the Skill

Follow these steps to make a good prediction.

1 **Identify a situation that has not been resolved.** As you read information, ask yourself questions, such as, "What will happen next? What effects will this situation produce?"

2 **Make a list of probable outcomes, or effects.** If possible, analyze examples of similar causes that have known effects.

3 **Make an educated guess about which outcome is most likely.** In order to make an *educated* guess, use information that you know or that you research.

4 **State your prediction.** In your prediction, explain why you think the cause will produce a particular effect, or outcome.

126 Foundations of Geography

Monitor Progress

As students are completing the *Skills for Life* worksheet, circulate to make sure students are applying the skill steps effectively. Provide assistance as needed.

Practice the Skill

Read the text in the box at the right. Then predict the consequences of global struggles for water.

1. From what you have read about water supplies in Southwest Asia, identify a major issue that has not been resolved. State the problem as a question.

2. This chapter discusses problems in global oil supply. How are oil and water issues similar? What effects have resulted from world oil shortages? Study the graphic organizer below. It shows results that might occur when one country controls other countries' water.

3. Of the possible outcomes in the graphic organizer, which seems the most likely? Make an educated guess, using what you know about the oil issue.

4. Here's how your prediction might begin: "As the world's need for water grows, water-rich countries will probably _____."

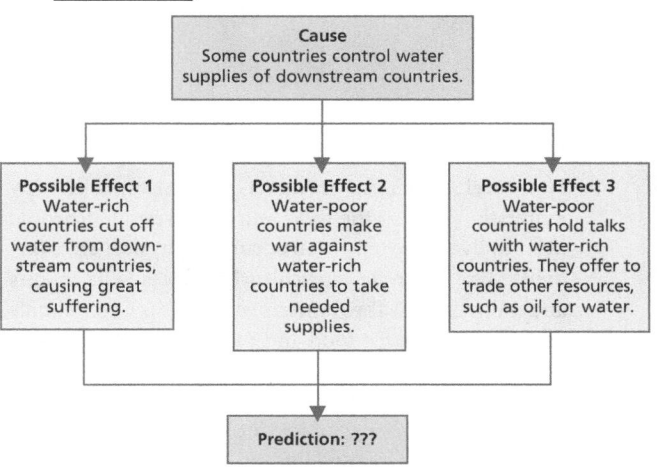

During the 1900s, oil-rich nations became wealthy and powerful by controlling world oil supplies. In the present century, water supplies may determine who is rich or poor. Much of the world's usable fresh water comes from rivers that flow through many countries. Nearly half the people in the world live in international river basins. Yet many of the countries that share rivers have no water treaties. Countries along these rivers build dams to store water for themselves. Nations downstream worry that they might run out of water. In Southwest Asia, Turkey controls sources of water flowing south into Syria and Iraq. A proposed system of 22 dams could allow Turkey to withhold water from its neighbors. Syria and Iraq have plentiful oil but not enough water.

Apply the Skill

Study the graph on page 118. Note how much oil the United States consumes and produces. What do you learn from these facts? Make a prediction about what America might do when world oil supplies run low. Create a graphic organizer like the one on this page to help you make a prediction.

Assess and Reteach

Assess Progress L2
Ask students to do the Apply the Skill activity.

Reteach L1
Identifying cause and effect is a vital part of making predictions. If students are having trouble with this skill, have them review it using the Social Studies Skills Tutor CD-ROM.

⊙ *Identifying Cause and Effect,* **Social Studies Skills Tutor CD-ROM**

Extend L3
- Have students reread p. 124. Ask them to identify the effect of Boston's growing population and industrialization. *(Boston's people filled in some bodies of water to create more land.)* Explain that this effect can also be a cause.

- Tell students to make a graphic organizer like the one on p. 127. Have them identify two to three possible effects of Boston's people filling in bodies of water to create more land. *(Possible effects: Industries that rely on bodies of water and their resources, such as fishing, may no longer exist; goods may no longer be able to be shipped to and from Boston via waterways.)* Then tell them to predict which effect is most likely. *(Accept any of the effects, but be sure students supply a valid reason for their choice.)*

Answers
Apply the Skill
Students should note from the graph that the United States consumes more oil than any other country in the world.

Students' graphic organizers should look like the graphic organizer on p. 127. Cause: The United States is highly dependent on oil, but world oil supplies are running low. Possible effects: The United States looks for other sources of energy. The United States taps into any oil resources it has not yet used. The United States conserves energy and uses less oil.

Students should choose one of the effects they listed as their prediction and supply a valid reason for their choice.

Section 3
Step-by-Step Instruction

Objectives

Social Studies

1. Investigate how first-level activities affect the environment.
2. Explore how second- and third-level activities affect the environment.

Reading/Language Arts

Learn how to identify implied main ideas.

Prepare to Read

Build Background Knowledge [L2]

In this section, students will learn about people's effect on the environment. Write the following words on the board: *soil, water, air.* Ask students to list some ways that these natural resources are important. *(Possible answers: soil for growing food, water to irrigate crops and drink, air to breathe)* Then have students describe human activities that could threaten these natural resources. Use the Give One, Get One participation strategy (TE, p. T37) to generate student responses. *(Driving cars can lead to air pollution; cutting down trees can lead to soil erosion and deforestation; dumping trash can cause water pollution.)*

Set a Purpose for Reading [L2]

■ Preview the Objectives.

■ Read each statement in the *Reading Readiness Guide* aloud. Ask students to mark the statements true or false.

> **All in One Foundations of Geography Teaching Resources,** *Reading Readiness Guide,* p. 253

■ Have students discuss the statements in pairs or groups of four, then mark their worksheets again. Use the Numbered Heads participation strategy (TE, p. T36) to call on students to share their group's perspectives.

Vocabulary Builder
Preview Key Terms [L2]

Pronounce each Key Term, then ask the students to say the word with you. Provide a simple explanation such as, "Pollution is waste, such as the exhaust that comes out of cars when we drive, that makes our air, water, or soil less clean."

Prepare to Read

Objectives

In this section you will

1. Investigate how first-level activities affect the environment.
2. Explore how second- and third-level activities affect the environment.

Taking Notes

Copy the table below. As you read this section, fill in the table with information about people's effect on the environment. Add rows to the table as needed.

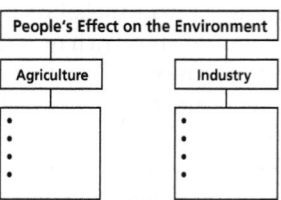

Target Reading Skill

Identify Implied Main Ideas Identifying main ideas can help you remember what you read. The details in a paragraph can add up to the main idea, even if it is not stated directly. For example, the details in the first paragraph below add up to this main idea: "While first-level activities are necessary for human survival, they also reshape the environment."

Key Terms

• **deforestation** (dee fawr uh STAY shun) *n.* a loss of forest cover in a region
• **biodiversity** (by oh duh VUR suh tee) *n.* a richness of different kinds of living things in a region
• **civil engineering** (SIV ul en juh NIHR ing) *n.* technology for building structures that alter the landscape, such as dams, roads, and bridges
• **pollution** (puh LOO shun) *n.* waste, usually man-made, that makes the air, water, or soil less clean

128 Foundations of Geography

First-Level Activities

First-level activities, or direct interaction with raw materials, provide the food and resources that people need to live. They also transform the physical environment. For example, agriculture replaces wild plants and animals with the domesticated plants and animals that people need for food and other products.

Creating Farmland As countries have grown, they have met the challenge of feeding their people in different ways. The Great Plains of North America once supported wild grasses and buffalo. Today, farmers in that region grow corn and wheat and raise cattle. In the Netherlands, the people have drained lakes, bays, and marshes to create dry farmland. While creating new farmland destroyed wild grasslands and wetlands, the new land has fed millions.

A rancher driving cattle in Manitoba, Canada

Target Reading Skill [L2]

Identify Implied Main Ideas Point out the Target Reading Skill. Tell students that identifying implied main ideas can help them to remember what they read.

Model identifying implied main ideas by reading the first paragraph on p. 132. Think aloud as you read to show how you arrived at the main idea. (*There are many different sources of pollution.*)

Give students *Identify Implied Main Ideas.* Have them complete the activity in groups.

> **All in One Foundations of Geography Teaching Resources,** *Identify Implied Main Ideas,* p. 258

Environmental Challenges Agriculture, forestry, and fishing provide food and resources that people need to live. At the same time, they sometimes have harmful effects on the environment. For example, wood is needed to build houses. But cutting down too many trees can result in deforestation, or the loss of forest cover in a region. Cutting forests may result in the loss of more than trees and other plants. Animals that depend on the forest for survival may also suffer. Deforestation can lead to a loss of biodiversity, which is a richness of different kinds of living things. So timber companies face the challenge of harvesting needed wood while limiting damage to the environment.

Farmers often use fertilizers and other chemicals to grow more crops. This makes it possible to feed more people. But when rain washes these chemicals into streams, they sometimes harm fish and other water-dwelling creatures. Fish are a tasty and healthy food source. But if fishers catch too many, they may threaten the fishes' survival. Farmers and fishers face the challenge of feeding the world's people without harming important resources.

Finding a Balance The key is to find a balance. Around the world, governments, scientists, and business people are working to find ways of meeting our need for food and resources without harming the environment. One solution is planting tree farms for timber. When the trees are mature, they can be cut and new trees can be replanted without harming ancient forests. Farmers can grow crops using natural methods or use chemicals that will not damage waterways. Fishers can limit their catch of endangered fish and harvest fish that are more plentiful.

✓ **Reading Check** How do people benefit when new farmland is created?

Deforestation
Timber companies and farmers have cut down rain forests in Indonesia. **Apply Information** *What are some of the advantages and disadvantages of cutting down forests?*

Links to Math

Acres and Timber Yields
Tree farms, like the one below, in Newbury, England, are one way to fight deforestation. If these oak trees grow to yield 80,000 board feet of timber per acre (466 cubic meters per hectare), and the farm covers 300 acres (121 hectares), how much timber will the farm produce?

Vocabulary Builder

Use the information below to teach students this section's high-use words.

High-Use Words	Definition and Sample Sentence
interaction, p. 128	*n.* the process of acting together Jake's new job calls for **interaction** with customers.
transform, p. 128	*v.* to change the form or look of Dusting **transformed** the room's appearance.
domesticated, p. 128	*adj.* tamed to be used by humans Our cat is **domesticated.**
prosperity, p. 131	*n.* the condition of being successful or wealthy Good times brought **prosperity** to the town.

First-Level Activities [L2]

Guided Instruction
- **Vocabulary Builder** Clarify the high-use words **interaction, transform,** and **domesticated** before reading.

- Read First-Level Activities using the Paragraph Shrinking technique (TE, p. T34).

- Ask students **What can people do to limit the negative effects of first-level activities?** (*Tree farms can be planted to help preserve ancient forests. Crops can be grown without fertilizers or with chemicals that do not harm the environment. Fishers can avoid catching endangered fish.*)

- Ask students **Why do you think it is important to limit the negative impact of first-level activities on the environment?** (*Possible answer: so that resources such as fish and trees are available to future generations*)

Independent Practice
Ask students to create the Taking Notes graphic organizer on a blank piece of paper. As students read, have them fill in the table with information about people's effect on the environment. Briefly model how to identify which information to record.

Monitor Progress
Circulate throughout the classroom to ensure that individuals are filling in their tables correctly. Provide assistance as needed.

Links

Read the **Links to Math** on this page and have them answer the question. (*Help students calculate that the farm will produce 24 million feet, or 56,386 cubic meters of timber.*)

Answers

Apply Information Advantages: wood can be used to make products; clears land for farming. Disadvantages: threatens the survival of animals and plants; a loss of biodiversity.

✓ **Reading Check** New farmland allows more people to be fed.

The Hybrid Car

Guided Instruction

Ask students to study the Eyewitness Technology feature on this page. Have them silently read the introduction. Then read each caption together with students. Pause after each caption is read aloud to solicit comments and questions from students. Then answer the Analyzing Images question as a class.

Independent Practice

Distribute *Small Group Activity: Community Service Project: Protect the Environment.* Have students work in small groups to propose community education and project proposals that focus on transportation and improving the environment. Possible projects include: an educational campaign about the benefits of using hybrid-car technology; a proposal to establish bike paths for commuters; an education program that encourages carpooling for commuters.

All In One **Foundations of Geography Teaching Resources,** *Small Group Activity: Community Service Project: Protect the Environment,* pp. 262–265

Answer

ANALYZING IMAGES by drawing energy from the battery; being lighter in weight reduces the amount of fuel used; higher tire pressure helps reduce energy loss and conserve fuel

The Hybrid Car

Cars with gasoline engines are fast and can go long distances, but they pollute. Electric cars don't emit dangerous chemicals, but they can be driven only for a short distance before their batteries need to be recharged. The hybrid car combines the best features of gasoline and electric cars. It is fast and can go long distances, but it uses less gasoline and pollutes less. The hybrid car gets about 46 miles per gallon, while the conventional car of the same size gets about 33.

Traffic Jam
Today, traffic jams are common as drivers commute daily in and out of cities. Waiting in traffic jams wastes a lot of fuel and adds to air pollution.

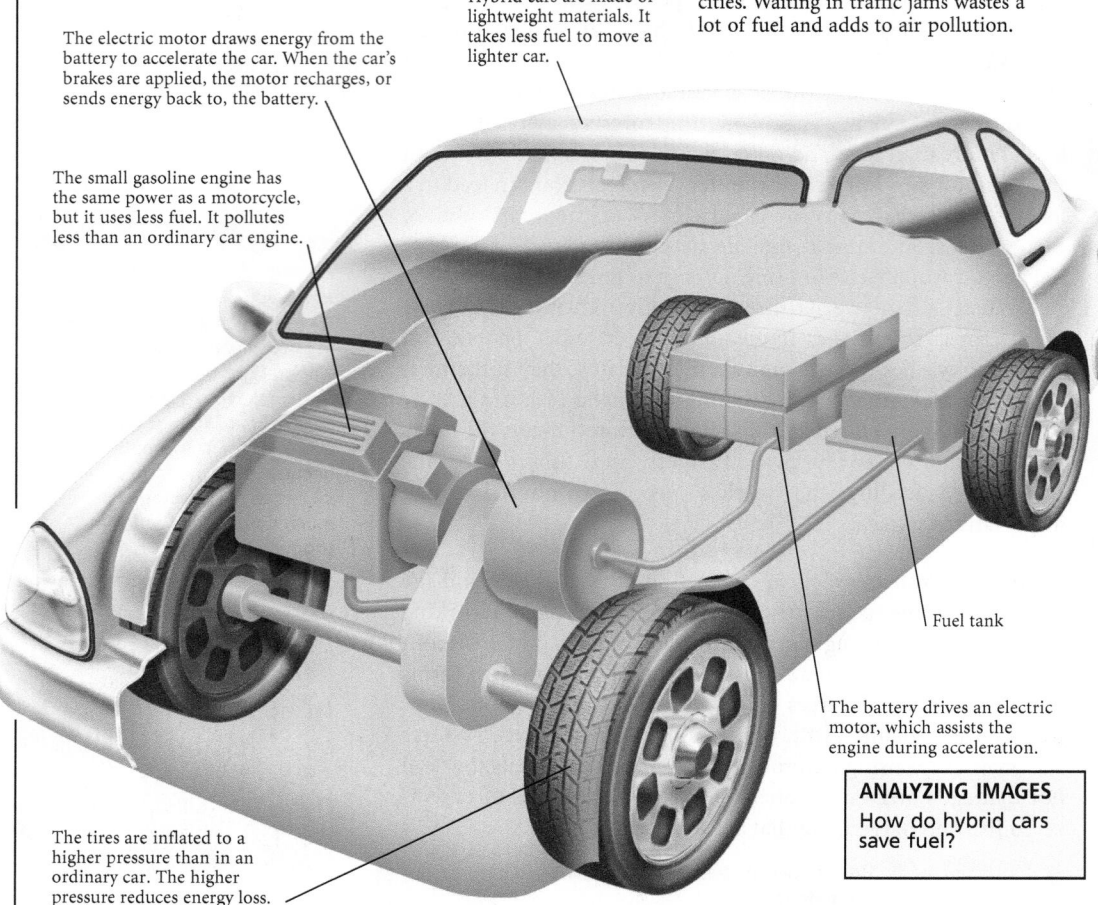

Hybrid cars are made of lightweight materials. It takes less fuel to move a lighter car.

The electric motor draws energy from the battery to accelerate the car. When the car's brakes are applied, the motor recharges, or sends energy back to, the battery.

The small gasoline engine has the same power as a motorcycle, but it uses less fuel. It pollutes less than an ordinary car engine.

Fuel tank

The battery drives an electric motor, which assists the engine during acceleration.

The tires are inflated to a higher pressure than in an ordinary car. The higher pressure reduces energy loss.

ANALYZING IMAGES
How do hybrid cars save fuel?

Background: Global Perspectives

The Kyoto Protocol In 1997, representatives from 160 nations met in Kyoto, Japan, to discuss concerns about increasing global gas emissions. Many scientists believe that these gases cause global warming, a gradual increase in the average temperature on Earth that could lead to melting of polar ice caps and flooding of coastal areas.

At Kyoto, the nations reached an agreement, called the Kyoto Protocol, to reduce the amount of certain gases released into the atmosphere. The agreement called for global emissions to be reduced by approximately 5 percent by 2012. The United States has not ratified the agreement.

Second- and Third-Level Activities

Over the years, industry, or second-level activities, and services, or third-level activities, have transformed deserts, prairies, woodlands, and marshes. They have created our familiar urban landscapes of housing developments, offices, factories, railroads, and highways.

Providing Jobs, Reshaping the Environment Industrial and service activities provide most of the jobs in developed countries such as the United States. Those activities are the basis for the developed countries' prosperity. They are also the main land use in urban areas.

The main purpose of some of these activities is to change the environment. **Civil engineering** is technology for building structures that alter the landscape, such as dams, canals, roads, and bridges. Dams create reservoirs that cover large areas with water. They also provide water for farms and cities and protect areas downstream from flooding.

Other industrial and service activities have side effects on the environment. For example, shopping malls require large areas to be paved for parking. Industries use large amounts of resources and release industrial wastes into the environment. Service activities require the construction of roads, telephone lines, and power lines.

Identify Implied Main Ideas
In one sentence, state what all the details in the paragraph at the left are about.

A Landscape Shaped by Industry
The waterfront in Rotterdam, Netherlands, has been shaped to meet the needs of industry. **Analyze Images** How might this landscape have been different before it was shaped by industry?

Chapter 5 Section 3 **131**

Skills Mini Lesson

Supporting a Position

1. To support a position, tell students they should state their position clearly in a sentence; identify at least three reasons to support their position; support each reason with accurate evidence; put their reasons and supporting evidence in an effective order; and add a conclusion.

2. Have students practice the skill using information from the section to support this position: All communities should have a recycling program.

3. Have students apply the skill by asking them to follow the steps to state and support their position on reducing car emissions.

Target Reading Skill　L2

Identify Implied Main Ideas As a follow up, ask students to answer the Target Reading Skill question in the Student Edition. (*Second- and third-level activities have reshaped the environment we live in.*)

Second- and Third-Level Activities　L2

Guided Instruction

- **Vocabulary Builder** Clarify the high-use word **prosperity** before reading.

- Ask students to read Second- and Third-Level Activities. As students read, circulate and make sure individuals can answer the Reading Check question.

- Ask **How is most land used in urban areas?** (*for industrial and service activities*) **Why are these activities important to developed countries?** (*They provide most of the jobs and are the basis of developed countries' prosperity.*)

- Ask students **How are people trying to reduce pollution?** (*by using fuel-efficient vehicles, developing renewable energy resources, and recycling*)

Independent Practice

Have students complete the table by filling in details about people's effect on the environment.

Monitor Progress

- Show *Section Reading Support Transparency FG 58* and ask students to check their graphic organizers individually.

  Foundations of Geography Transparencies, *Section Reading Support Transparency FG 58*

- Tell students to fill in the last column of their *Reading Readiness Guides.* Probe for what they learned that confirms or invalidates each statement.

  All In One Foundations of Geography Teaching Resources, *Reading Readiness Guide,* p. 253

Answer

Analyze Images Possible answer: The land along the water may have been covered by vegetation.

Assess and Reteach

Assess Progress `L2`

Have students complete the Section Assessment. Administer the *Section Quiz*.

All in One **Foundations of Geography Teaching Resources,** *Section Quiz,* p. 255

Reteach `L1`

If students need more instruction, have them read this section in the Reading and Vocabulary Study Guide.

📖 Chapter 5, Section 3, **Western Hemisphere Reading and Vocabulary Study Guide,** pp. 51–53

Extend `L3`

Have students complete the *Enrichment* activity so that they may study an instance in which environmental concerns and providing jobs had to be balanced.

All in One **Foundations of Geography Teaching Resources,** *Enrichment,* p. 260

Answers

Apply Information Recycling reduces the amount of waste that local governments must burn or dump and saves natural resources.

✓ Reading Check Some industrial activities, such as building dams and bridges, change the environment. Others use large amounts of resources and can harm the environment with the release of industrial wastes.

Section 3 Assessment

Key Terms
Students' sentences should reflect knowledge of each Key Term.

⊘ Target Reading Skill
(1) There are many sources of pollution that affect our air, water, and soil. (2) People are working together to find ways to reduce pollution. (3) Recycling is being used in the United States to reduce waste and save natural resources. (4) By working together, we can find solutions to environmental problems.

Comprehension and Critical Thinking
1. (a) cutting trees to clear land for farms and to use for timber **(b)** Deforestation threatens the survival of animals and plants and can lead to a loss of biodiversity.

2. (a) Industrial and service activities have transformed deserts, prairies, woodlands, and marshes into urban landscapes that include housing developments, offices,

---

Recycling
These seventh-grade students in Syracuse, New York, are sorting materials for recycling. **Apply Information** *What environmental problems does recycling help to solve?*

Environmental Challenges Industry is not the only source of **pollution**, waste that makes the air, soil, or water less clean. The trash that we throw away may pollute the soil, water, or air. Exhaust from cars and trucks is another source of air pollution. Many scientists believe that air pollution may cause higher temperatures or other changes in our climate.

Finding Solutions Working together, scientists, governments, businesses, and ordinary people can find solutions to these problems. One solution is to use more fuel-efficient vehicles, such as hybrid cars. Vehicles that burn less fuel create less air pollution. Renewable energy sources, such as solar power and wind power, can also reduce the need to burn fuels that pollute the air. In addition, reducing pollution may reduce the risk of harmful climate changes.

Many cities and counties in the United States have introduced waste recycling. Recycling reduces the amount of waste that local governments must burn or dump. It also saves natural resources. For example, when paper is recycled, fewer trees must be cut down to make new paper.

Finding solutions to environmental problems is one of the greatest challenges of our time. If we all work together, we can meet this challenge.

✓ Reading Check **How do industrial activities affect the environment?**

 Section 3 Assessment

Key Terms
Review the key terms at the beginning of this section. Use each term in a sentence that explains its meaning.

⊘ Target Reading Skill
State the main idea of each paragraph on this page.

Comprehension and Critical Thinking
1. (a) Recall What are the causes of deforestation?

(b) Identify Cause and Effect How does deforestation threaten the environment?
2. (a) List List ways in which industrial and service activities transform landscapes.
(b) Categorize Which of these ways are common to both industrial and service activities?
(c) Analyze How are industrial activities different from service activities in their impact on the environment?

Writing Activity
Write a journal entry in which you discuss how your own activities today may have affected the environment.

For: An activity on the environment
Visit: PHSchool.com
Web Code: led-3503

132 Foundations of Geography

---

factories, roads, railroads, highways, dams, canals, bridges, reservoirs, shopping malls, and telephone and power lines. **(b)** Service and industrial activities both often require railroads, roads, and telephone and power lines. **(c)** Possible answer: Industrial activities seem to harm the environment more than service activities.

Writing Activity
Use the *Rubric for Assessing a Journal Entry* to evaluate students' entries.

All in One **Foundations of Geography Teaching Resources,** *Rubric for Assessing a Journal Entry,* p. 276

Go Online
PHSchool.com Typing in the Web code when prompted will bring students to detailed instructions for this activity.

Review and Assessment

Review Chapter Content

- Review and revisit the major themes of the chapter by asking students to classify what Guiding Question each bulleted statement in the Chapter Summary answers. Form students into groups and ask them to complete the activity together. Use the Numbered Heads participation strategy (TE, p. T36) to have the groups share their answers in the group discussion. Refer to page 1 of the Student Edition for the text of the Guided Questions.

- Assign *Vocabulary Development* for students to review Key Terms.

  All in One **Foundations of Geography Teaching Resources,** *Vocabulary Development,* p. 273

◆ Chapter Summary

Section 1: Natural Resources
- Almost everything that people use or consume is made with natural resources, which are either renewable or nonrenewable.
- Energy is a special resource needed for most economic activities, but some sources of energy are in limited supply, and some nations need to buy energy resources from others.

Section 2: Land Use
- How people use the land depends on their culture.
- Three levels of economic activity account for most land use.
- Land use changes when newcomers settle a region and as cultures change over time.

Section 3: People's Effect on the Environment
- First-level activities provide needed food and resources, but they reduce the land available for wild plants and animals.
- Second- and third-level activities provide jobs, but they can also pollute the environment.

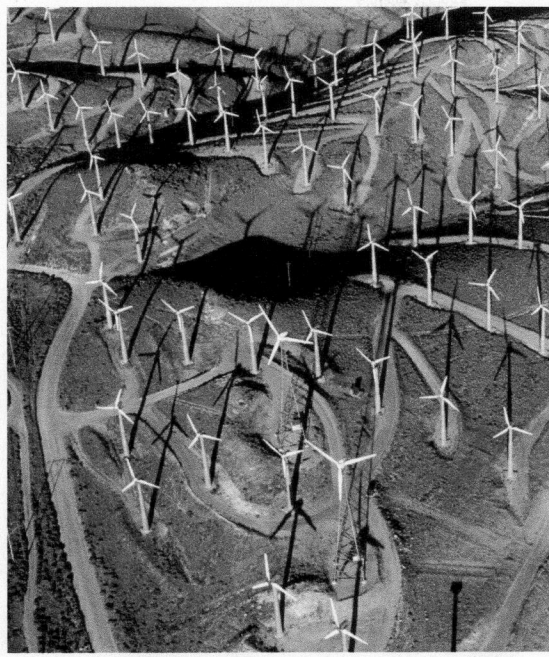

Windmills in California

◆ Key Terms

Each of the statements below contains a key term from the chapter. If the statement is true, write *true*. If it is false, rewrite the statement to make it true.

1. Raw materials are natural resources that can be used without reworking.
2. Renewable resources are natural resources that can be replaced.
3. Natural resources that cannot be replaced are called nonrenewable resources.
4. Our environment is our natural surroundings.

5. Manufacturing does not produce goods but involves working directly for customers.
6. Industrialization is the growth of manufacturing in an economy.
7. Deforestation is the planting of trees to replace forests cut down for timber.
8. Biodiversity is the loss of plant and animal life due to deforestation.
9. Pollution is waste, usually made by people, that makes air, soil, or water less clean.

Chapter 5 **133**

Answers

Key Terms
1. False. Raw materials are natural resources that must be reworked to be useful.
2. True
3. True
4. True
5. False. Manufacturing is the large-scale production of goods by hand or by machine.
6. False. Industrialization is the growth of machine-powered production in an economy.
7. False. Deforestation is a loss of forest cover in a region.
8. False. Biodiversity is a richness of different kinds of living things in a region.
9. True

─ Vocabulary Builder ─

Revisit this chapter's high-use words:

consume	respond	interaction
evaporate	channel	transform
harness	distribute	domesticated
hybrid	correspond	prosperity

Ask students to review the definitions they recorded on their *Word Knowledge* worksheets.

All in One **Foundations of Geography Teaching Resources,** *Word Knowledge,* p. 259

Consider allowing students to earn extra credit if they use the words in their answers to the questions in the Chapter Review and Assessment. The words must be used correctly and in a natural context to win the extra points.

Review and Assessment

Comprehension and Critical Thinking

10. (a) Possible answers: water; wind, geothermal energy, solar energy; living things **(b)** because they can be replaced **(c)** Renewable resources can be replaced, while nonrenewable resources cannot be replaced.

11. (a) no **(b)** solar and wind energy and biomass

12. (a) yes **(b)** Possible answer: The land might be used differently, based on how the colonial culture traditionally uses the type of land available in the region.

13. (a) Possible answers: fishing, hunting, cutting wood, mining, herding, raising crops **(b)** Workers engaging in first-level activities use the land and its resources directly to make products. Second-level activities process the products of first-level activities. Third-level activities do not involve the process of creating goods at all; they may involve working directly for customers or for businesses.

14. (a) Tree farms can be planted and used to produce wood. **(b)** Biodiversity would be preserved.

15. (a) industrial and service activities, trash disposal, and car exhaust **(b)** Possible answers: by using more fuel-efficient vehicles such as hybrids, using renewable energy sources such as solar and wind power, and waste recycling

Skills Practice

Students' answers will vary, but should show an understanding of the skill steps.

Possible facts Worldwide energy usage has grown rapidly; fossil fuel supplies may be limited; some countries are using alternative energy resources; alternative energy resources include wind, solar, tidal, atomic, and geothermal energy, as well as biomass; atomic energy uses radioactive materials, which are plentiful; some people oppose atomic energy because radioactive materials can be dangerous; new technologies that help people to use less energy, such as hybrid cars and those that offer energy savings in heating and lighting, can be used to help fossil fuels last longer.

Possible prediction Advancements in energy technology will help us meet the energy needs of the future.

Review and Assessment (continued)

◆ Comprehension and Critical Thinking

10. (a) List List at least three renewable resources.
(b) Explain Why is each of these resources renewable?
(c) Compare and Contrast How do renewable resources differ from nonrenewable resources?

11. (a) Recall Do all countries have adequate energy supplies?
(b) Analyze What energy sources are available to all countries?

12. (a) Recall Does culture affect land use?
(b) Predict What might happen to land use in a region if people with a different culture colonized it?

13. (a) List List three first-level activities.
(b) Compare and Contrast How do those activities differ from second- and third-level activities?

14. (a) Describe How can people obtain wood without cutting down wild forests?
(b) Predict How would leaving forests in place affect biodiversity?

15. (a) Describe What causes pollution?
(b) Infer How might companies and individuals reduce pollution?

◆ Skills Practice

Making Predictions In the Skills for Life activity on pages 126 and 127, you learned to make predictions. You also learned how to make sure that a prediction is an educated guess. That is, predictions should be based on information about the situation or about similar situations.

Review the steps that you followed to learn this skill. Then reread the paragraphs on pages 118 and 119 under the heading Meeting Energy Needs in the Future. List several facts about the issues described there. Finally, use these facts to make a prediction about how those issues might be resolved in the future.

◆ Writing Activity: Language Arts

Identify an environmental problem that interests you. Write a story about people solving the environmental problem. For your story, create characters with different roles in creating or solving the environmental problem. You should also create a plot for your story that describes how people come up with a solution to the problem and carry out that solution.

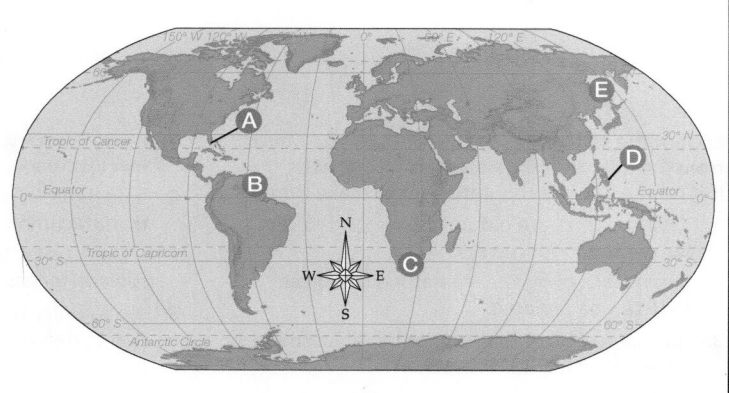

MAP MASTER™
Skills Activity

Natural Resources

Place Location Refer to the map titled The World: Natural Resources on page 115. For each natural resource listed below, write the letter from the map at the right that shows its location.
1. Bauxite
2. Diamond
3. Nickel
4. Phosphate
5. Tungsten

Go Online
PHSchool.com Use Web Code **lep-3514** for an **interactive map.**

134 Foundations of Geography

Writing Activity: Language Arts
Students' stories will vary, but should include a problem, a solution, characters with various roles, and a plot.
Use *Rubric for Assessing a Writing Assignment* to evaluate students' stories.

**All in One Foundations of Geography
Teaching Resources,** *Rubric for Assessing a Writing Assignment,* p. 277

Standardized Test Prep

Test-Taking Tips

Some questions on standardized tests ask you to find a main idea by analyzing a reading selection. Read the passage below. Then follow the tips to answer the sample question.

> Saudi Arabia, Mexico, Iraq, Venezuela, and Russia have large oil reserves. The United States and China are rich in coal and natural gas. Many Northern European countries have rivers with water energy to create electricity. By contrast, Japan has few energy sources.

TIP As you read the paragraph, try to identify its main idea, or most important point. Every sentence in a paragraph supports this main idea.

Pick the letter that best answers the question.
This paragraph describes which kind of resources?
  A capital resources
  B human resources
  C natural resources
  D entrepreneurial resources

TIP Look for key words in the question and in the answer choices that connect to the paragraph. In this case, the key word is *resources*.

Think It Through Start with the main idea of the paragraph: Different countries have different energy sources. What kind of resources are these energy sources: oil, coal, gas, and water? Energy is not a human resource. You may not know the words *entrepreneurial* or *capital*. But you probably recognize *natural resources* as useful materials found in the environment—such as oil, coal, gas, and water. The correct answer is C.

Practice Questions

Use the tips above and other tips in this book to help you answer the following questions:

1. Wind energy is a
   A fossil fuel.
   B raw material.
   C renewable resource.
   D nonrenewable resource.

2. When colonists settle in a new environment,
   A they will use land just as they did in their old environment.
   B the environment will not change.
   C they will adjust their previous land uses to the new environment.
   D they will give up all familiar land uses.

3. Which of the following environmental problems does paper recycling help solve?
   A deforestation
   B pollution
   C deforestation and pollution
   D neither deforestation nor pollution

Read the following passage and answer the question that follows.

Sierra Leone's economy produces raw materials and cash crops. The country's people mine diamonds, iron ore, and aluminum ore. People on the coast catch fish. Its farmers produce coffee, cocoa, rice, and palm oil. They also raise poultry and other livestock.

4. The passage's main idea refers to which type of activities?
   A first-level activities
   B second-level activities
   C third-level activities
   D financial activities

Use Web Code **lea-3501** for a **Chapter 5 self-test.**

Chapter 5 **135**

Standardized Test Prep

Answers

1. C
2. C
3. C
4. A

Go Online
PHSchool.com Students may use the Chapter 5 self-test on PHSchool.com to prepare for the Chapter Test.

Assessment Resources

Teaching Resources
Chapter Tests A and B, pp. 190–195
Final Exams A and B, pp. 196–201

Test Prep Workbook
Foundations of Geography Study Sheet, pp. 113–115
Foundations of Geography Practice Tests A, B, and C, pp. 49–60

AYP Monitoring Assessments
Foundations of Geography Benchmark Test 2 and Report Sheet, pp. 85–88
Foundations of Geography Outcome Test, pp. 170–175

Technology
⊙ *ExamView Test Bank CD-ROM*

Chapter 5 **135**

Projects

- Students can further explore the Guiding Questions by completing hands-on projects.

- Three pages of structured guidance in All-in-One Foundations of Geography Teaching Resources support each of the projects described on this page.

  All In One Foundations of Geography Teaching Resources, *Book Project: Focus on Part of the Whole, pp. 27–29; Book Project: Desktop Countries, pp. 33–35*

- There are also two additional projects introduced, explained, and supported in the All-in-One Foundations of Geography Teaching Resources.

  All In One Foundations of Geography Teaching Resources, *Book Project: The Geography Game, pp. 30–32; Book Project: World News Today, pp. 36–38*

- Go over the four project suggestions with students.

- Ask each student to select one of the projects, or design his or her own. Work with students to create a project description and a schedule.

Projects

Create your own projects to learn more about geography. At the beginning of this book, you were introduced to the Guiding Questions for studying the chapters and the special features. But you can also find answers to these questions by doing projects on your own or with a group. Use the questions to find topics you want to explore further. Then try the projects described on this page or create your own.

1. **Geography** What are Earth's major physical features?

2. **History** How have people's ways of life changed over time?

3. **Culture** What is a culture?

4. **Government** What types of government exist in the world today?

5. **Economics** How do people use the world's natural resources?

Project

CREATE A PHYSICAL MAP

Focus on Part of the Whole
The world and its population are extremely varied. Choose a particular region or country. If you are working with a group, have each person choose a different country on a continent. Learn everything you can about the country's physical geography, the population, and the lifestyles of the people there. Use encyclopedias, almanacs, or other books.

Set up a display based on your research. Prepare a large map that includes important physical features of the land. Add captions that explain how the land's physical geography affects people's lives.

Project

RESEARCH A COUNTRY'S CULTURE

Desktop Countries
What countries did your ancestors come from? Select one country and do some research on it. Interview someone, perhaps a relative from that country, or read about it. Find a recipe you can prepare to share with the class. Then make a desktop display about the country you have chosen. Write the name of the country on a card and put it on your desk. Add a drawing of the country's flag or map, or display a souvenir. On place cards, write several sentences about each object. Take turns visiting everyone's "desktop countries."

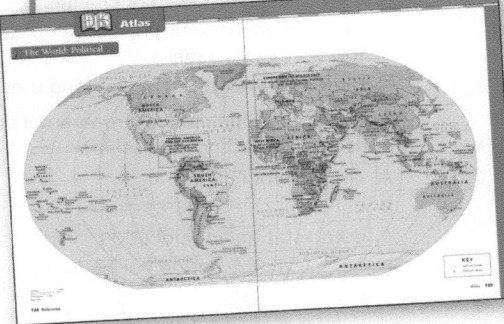

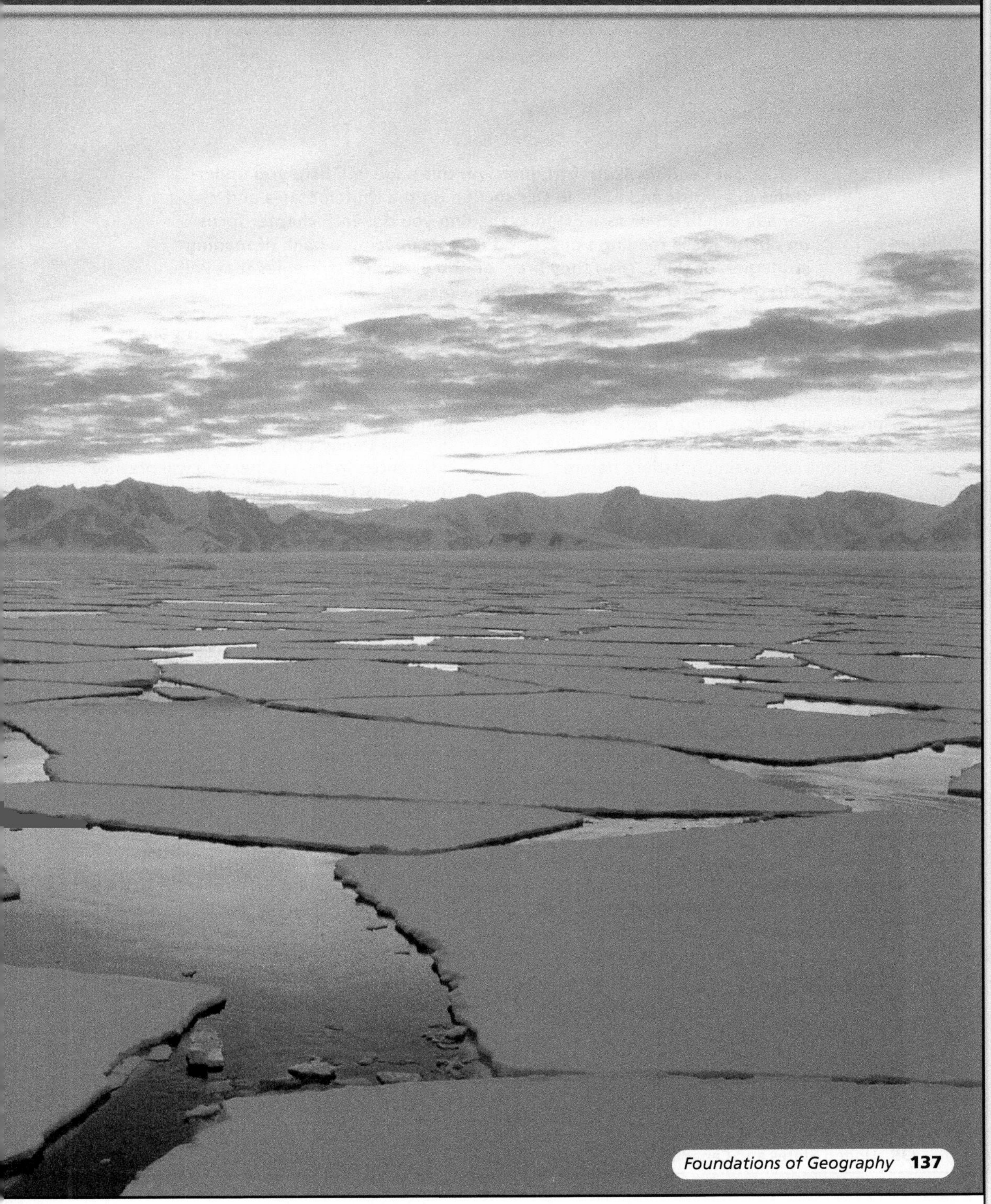

- Post project schedules and monitor student progress by asking for progress reports.
- Assess student projects using rubrics from the All-in-One Foundations of Geography Teaching Resources.

All in One **Foundations of Geography Teaching Resources,** *Rubric for Assessing a Student Performance on a Project,* p. 39; *Rubric for Assessing Performance of an Entire Group,* p. 40; *Rubric for Assessing Individual Performance in a Group,* p. 41

Portfolio Activity Tell students they can add their completed Book Project as the final item in their portfolios. Assess student portfolios with *Rubric for Assessing a Student Portfolio.*

All in One **Foundations of Geography Teaching Resources,** *Rubric for Assessing a Student Portfolio,* p. 42

Teaching the Target Reading Skills

The Prentice Hall *World Studies* program has interwoven essential reading skills instruction throughout the Student Edition, Teacher's Edition, and ancillary resources. In the United States and Canada section, students will learn five reading skills.

Student Edition The *World Studies* Student Edition provides students with reading skills instruction, practice, and application opportunities in each chapter within the program.

Teacher's Edition The *World Studies* Teacher Edition supports your teaching of each skill by providing full modeling in each chapter's interleaf and modeling of the specific sub-skills in each section lesson.

All in One Teaching Resources The *World Studies* All-in-One Teaching Resources provides a worksheet explaining and supporting the elements of each Target Reading Skill. Use these to help struggling students master skills, or as more practice for every student.

Target Reading Skills

The Target Reading Skills introduced on this page will help you understand the words and ideas in this section on the United States and Canada and in other social studies reading you do. Each chapter focuses on one of these reading skills. Good readers develop a bank of reading strategies, or skills. Then they draw on the particular strategies that will help them understand the text they are reading.

Chapter 6 Target Reading Skills

Reading Process Previewing can help you understand and remember what you read. In this chapter you will practice using these previewing skills: setting a purpose for reading, predicting what the text will be about, and asking questions before you read.

Chapter 7 Target Reading Skills

Clarifying Meaning If you do not understand something you are reading right away, you can use several skills to clarify the meaning of the word or idea. In this chapter you will practice these strategies for clarifying meaning: rereading, reading ahead, paraphrasing, and summarizing.

Chapter 8 Target Reading Skills

Main Idea Since you cannot remember every detail of what you read, it is important to identify the main ideas. The main idea of a section or paragraph is the most important point and the one you want to remember. In this chapter you will practice these skills: identifying both stated and implied main ideas and identifying supporting details.

Chapter 9 Target Reading Skills

Comparison and Contrast You can use comparison and contrast to sort out and analyze information you are reading. Comparing means examining the similarities between things. Contrasting is looking at differences. In this chapter you will practice these skills: comparing and contrasting, using signal words, identifying contrasts, and making comparisons.

Chapter 10 Target Reading Skills

Using Context Using the context of an unfamiliar word can help you understand its meaning. Context includes the words, phrases, and sentences surrounding a word. In this chapter you will practice using these context clues: definitions, interpreting nonliteral meanings, your own general knowledge, and cause and effect.

138 United States and Canada

Assessment Resources

Use the diagnosing readiness tests from **AYP Monitoring Assessments** to help you identify problems before students begin to study the United States and Canada.

Determine students' reading level and identify challenges:

📄 *Screening Tests,* pp. 1–10

Evaluate students' verbal skills:

📄 *Critical Thinking and Reading Tests,* pp. 25–34

📄 *Vocabulary Tests,* pp. 45–52

📄 *Writing Tests,* pp. 53–60

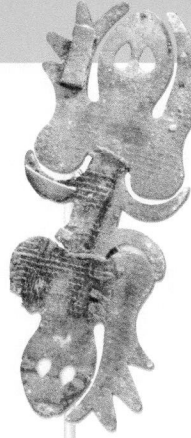

The UNITED STATES and CANADA

Spreading "from sea to shining sea," the United States and Canada take up nearly seven eighths of North America. In this book, you'll see how the United States and Canada are working to create a good life for every citizen in these vast countries.

Guiding Questions

The text, photographs, maps, and charts in this book will help you discover answers to these Guiding Questions.

1 **Geography** How has physical geography affected the cultures of the United States and Canada?

2 **History** How have historical events affected the cultures of the United States and Canada?

3 **Culture** How has the variety of people in the United States and Canada benefited and challenged the two nations?

4 **Government** How do the governments of the United States and Canada differ? How are they alike?

5 **Economics** How did the United States and Canada become two of the wealthiest nations in the world?

Project Preview

You can also discover answers to the Guiding Questions by working on projects. Several project possibilities are listed on page 326 of this book.

Assess students' social studies skills:

- *Geographic Literacy Tests*, pp. 13–20
- *Visual Analysis Tests*, pp. 21–24
- *Communications Tests*, pp. 35–44

The World Studies program provides instruction and practice for all of these skills. Use students' test results to pinpoint the skills your students have mastered and the skills they need to practice. Then use *Correlation to Program Resources* to prescribe skills practice and reinforcement.

- *Correlation to Program Resources*, pp. 64–77

Guiding Questions

- This section was developed around five Guiding Questions about the United States and Canada. They appear on the reduced Student Edition page to the left. The Guiding Questions are intended as an organizational focus for the section. The Guiding Questions act as a kind of umbrella under which all of the material falls.

- You may wish to add your own Guiding Questions to the list in order to tailor them to your particular course.

- Draw students' attention to the Guiding Questions. Ask them to write the questions in their notebooks for future reference.

- In the Teacher's Edition, each section's themes are linked to a specific Guiding Question at the beginning of each chapter. Then, an activity at the end of the chapter returns to the Guiding Questions to review key concepts.

Project Preview

- The projects for this book are designed to provide students with hands-on involvement in the content area. Students are introduced to some projects on pages 326–327.

- *Book Projects* give students directions on how to complete these projects, and more.

  All in One **United States and Canada Teaching Resources**, *Book Project: Set Up a Weather Station*, pp. 73–75; *Book Project: Write a Children's Book*, pp. 76–78; *Book Project: Make a Timeline of Local History*, pp. 79–81; *Book Project: Create a Diorama*, pp. 82–84

- Assign projects as small group activities, whole-class projects, or individual projects. Consider assigning a project at the beginning of the course.

Objectives

- Describe the size and relative location of the United States and Canada.

- Locate and name the major bodies of water surrounding the United States and Canada.

- Analyze the range of climates in the United States and Canada.

- Examine the different regions of the United States and Canada.

Prepare to Read

Build Background Knowledge `L2`

Have students describe the location of their community. Tell students that they will compare their home to other parts of the United States and Canada as they study this region.

Instruct

Investigate the United States and Canada `L2`

Guided Instruction

- Read the introductory, Location, and Regions paragraphs as a class. Divide the class into small groups of three or four.

- Hand out the *Regional Overview* worksheet. Direct students to fill in the worksheet as they study the Regional Overview.

  All in One **United States and Canada Teaching Resources,** *Regional Overview,* pp. 89–91

Independent Practice

Ask groups to write a statement comparing the location and size of the United States and Canada.

Monitor Progress

Circulate and make sure the groups are communicating effectively.

Answers

LOCATION Canada; the U.S.; Canada; Canada must have a colder climate.
REGIONS Canada is longer and wider.

Investigate the United States and Canada

Stretching from the Pacific Ocean to the Atlantic Ocean, the United States is the world's fourth largest country. Canada is slightly larger and stretches across five time zones. Though roughly the same size, the United States has far more people—nearly 10 times the population of Canada.

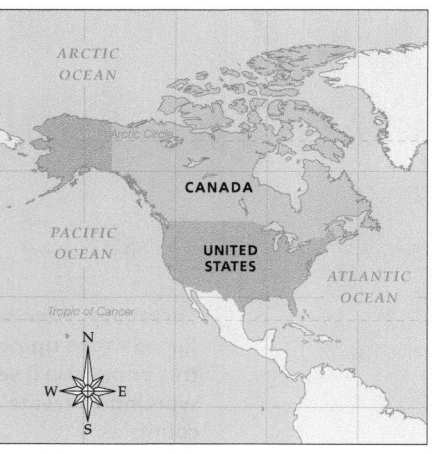

▲ **The Northern Territories, Canada**
Snowmobiles and dogsleds make travel possible in the far north.

CANADA

UNITED STATES

LOCATION

1 Locate the United States and Canada

How would you describe Canada's location? One way would be to compare its location to that of the United States. Which country extends farther north? Which country is closer to Russia? Which country has more of its land touching the Arctic Ocean? Based on the relative locations of these two countries, estimate which has a colder climate.

REGIONS

2 Estimate the Length of the United States and Canada

How does Canada's length from north to south compare to the length of the continental United States? With a ruler, measure the United States from its southernmost border to its border with Canada. Now measure the length of Canada. Which is longer? Now measure both countries from east to west. Which is wider?

140 United States and Canada

Mental Mapping

Everything in Its Place Distribute *Outline Map 11: The United States: Political.* Ask students to locate and label as many of the states as they can from memory, without looking in their textbooks. Tell them to name some of the states they cannot locate and write these state names on the board. Ask students to keep this outline map so they can update it as they study the region.

All in One **United States and Canada Teaching Resources,** *Outline Map 11: The United States: Political,* p. 92

Political United States and Canada

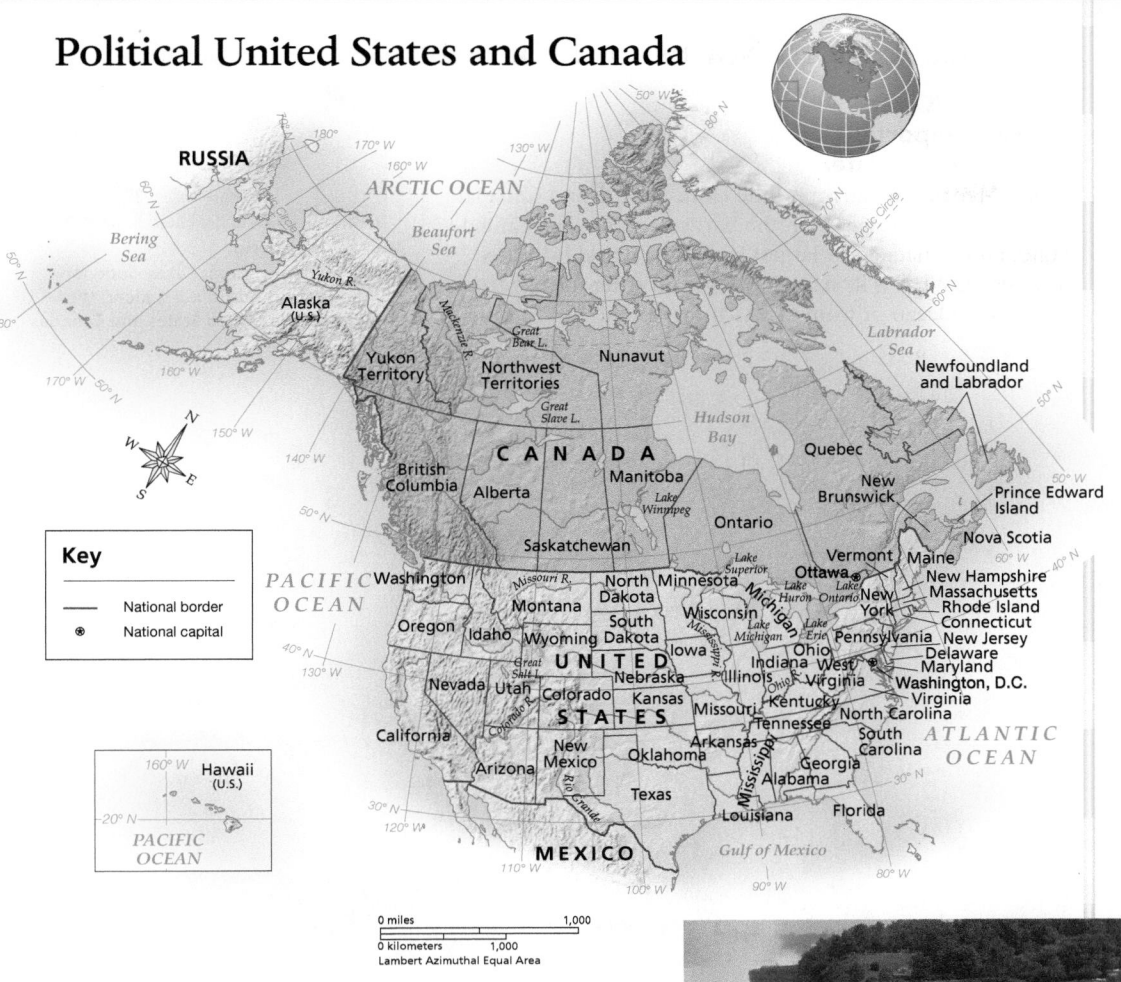

RUSSIA

ARCTIC OCEAN

Bering Sea

Beaufort Sea

Yukon R.

Alaska (U.S.)

Mackenzie R.

Great Bear L.

Yukon Territory

Northwest Territories

Nunavut

Labrador Sea

Newfoundland and Labrador

Great Slave L.

Hudson Bay

C A N A D A

British Columbia

Alberta

Manitoba

Lake Winnipeg

Saskatchewan

Quebec

New Brunswick

Prince Edward Island

Ontario

Nova Scotia

Key
— National border
⊛ National capital

PACIFIC OCEAN

Washington

Montana

Missouri R.

North Dakota

Minnesota

Lake Superior

Lake Huron

Ottawa

Vermont

Maine

New Hampshire

Massachusetts

Rhode Island

Michigan

Lake Ontario

New York

Oregon

Idaho

Wyoming

South Dakota

Wisconsin

Lake Michigan

Lake Erie

Pennsylvania

Connecticut

New Jersey

Nevada

Utah

Great Salt L.

U N I T E D

Nebraska

Iowa

Illinois

Indiana

Ohio

Ohio R.

Virginia

West Virginia

Maryland

Delaware

Washington, D.C.

California

Colorado

Colorado R.

Kansas

Missouri

Kentucky

Tennessee

North Carolina

S T A T E S

Arizona

New Mexico

Oklahoma

Arkansas

Mississippi R.

Georgia

South Carolina

ATLANTIC OCEAN

Texas

Alabama

Louisiana

Rio Grande

Florida

MEXICO

Gulf of Mexico

Hawaii (U.S.)

PACIFIC OCEAN

0 miles 1,000
0 kilometers 1,000
Lambert Azimuthal Equal Area

PLACE
3 Find States, Provinces, and Territories

Which two of the 50 United States do not share a border with any other state? Which Canadian territory reaches the farthest north? Which states border Canada? Which provinces border the United States? Name the cities that are the national capitals of the United States and Canada. Notice that the United States and Canada together make up most of the continent of North America. What other country is on the same continent?

▲ **Niagara Falls**
The Niagara Falls lie on the border between Canada and the United States.

Background: Global Perspectives

The Longest Borders The United States and Canada share 5,526 miles (8,893 kilometers) of border. This is often called "the world's longest undefended border," since most of the long border is not fenced or guarded by armies. Some of the other long international borders are: Russia and Kazakhstan, 4,254 miles (6,846 kilometers); Argentina and Chile, 3,200 miles (5,150 kilometers); Mongolia and China, 2,906 miles (4,677 kilometers); Brazil and Bolivia, 2,113 miles (3,400 kilometers); United States and Mexico, 1,951 miles (3,141 kilometers); India and Pakistan, 1,809 miles (2,912 kilometers).

Guided Instruction

- Read the Place paragraph. Direct students' attention to the political map of the United States and Canada. Ask students to try to locate the three biggest states in the United States and write their answers on the board. Direct students to the Country Databank on pages 236–247 to check their answers. *(Alaska, Texas, California)*

- Ask students **Which Canadian province borders the Pacific Ocean?** *(British Columbia)* **Which states in the United States border Mexico?** *(Texas, New Mexico, Arizona, California)*

- Ask students to continue completing the *Regional Overview* worksheet.

  All in One **United States and Canada Teaching Resources,** *Regional Overview,* pp. 89–91

Independent Practice

Provide students with *Outline Map 10: The United States and Canada: Political.* Have students label the United States and Canada, and the oceans surrounding these countries. Ask them to label Alaska and Hawaii, indicating which country each is a part of. Have students label the capital of each country. Encourage students to include other details on their maps.

  All in One **United States and Canada Teaching Resources,** *Outline Map 10: The United States and Canada: Political,* p. 93

Monitor Progress

Circulate while students complete their maps and provide assistance where needed.

Answers

PLACE Alaska and Hawaii do not border any other states; Nunavut is the farthest north; Alaska, Washington, Idaho, Montana, North Dakota, Minnesota, Michigan, New York, Vermont, New Hampshire, and Maine border Canada; British Columbia, Alberta, Saskatchewan, Manitoba, Ontario, Quebec, and New Brunswick border the United States; Washington, D.C., is the capital of the United States, Ottawa is the capital of Canada; Mexico is also in North America.

Physical United States and Canada

Guided Instruction

- Read the Interaction paragraph. Have students study the physical map of the United States and Canada, noting the location of major bodies of water.

- Ask students to identify the major mountain chains in the United States and Canada. *(Rocky Mountains, Appalachian Mountains.)* Ask students **Which of these ranges has higher mountains?** *(the Rocky Mountains)*

- Tell students that the highest peak in the United States and Canada is located in Alaska. Ask them to name this peak and give its height *(Mt. McKinley, 20,320 feet [6,194 meters]).*

- Ask **Where is most of the land in the 0–650 feet elevation range located?** *(along the coasts)*

- Ask students to continue completing the Regional Overview worksheet.
  All in One United States and Canada Teaching Resources, *Regional Overview,* pp. 89–91

Independent Practice

To give students practice working with physical maps, provide them with the *Elevation on a Map* worksheet. Ask students to study the map and map key, and then answer the questions at the bottom of the worksheet.
All in One United States and Canada Teaching Resources, *Elevation on a Map,* p. 94

Monitor Progress

Circulate while students complete their worksheets. Make sure individuals understand how to use the map key.

Answers

INTERACTION The Atlantic, Pacific, and Arctic oceans surround the United States and Canada; lakes Superior, Michigan, Huron, Erie, and Ontario, which are known as the Great Lakes, lie between the countries; Hudson Bay; the Atlantic Ocean.

Physical United States and Canada

INTERACTION
4 Find Important Bodies of Water

What three oceans surround the United States and Canada? What bodies of water lie on the border between the United States and Canada? The largest bay in the world is located in Canada. What is its name? Would you enter the bay from the Pacific Ocean or from the Atlantic Ocean?

▲ **Lake Superior**
One of the five Great Lakes, Superior is the farthest north. It lies along the border of the United States and Canada.

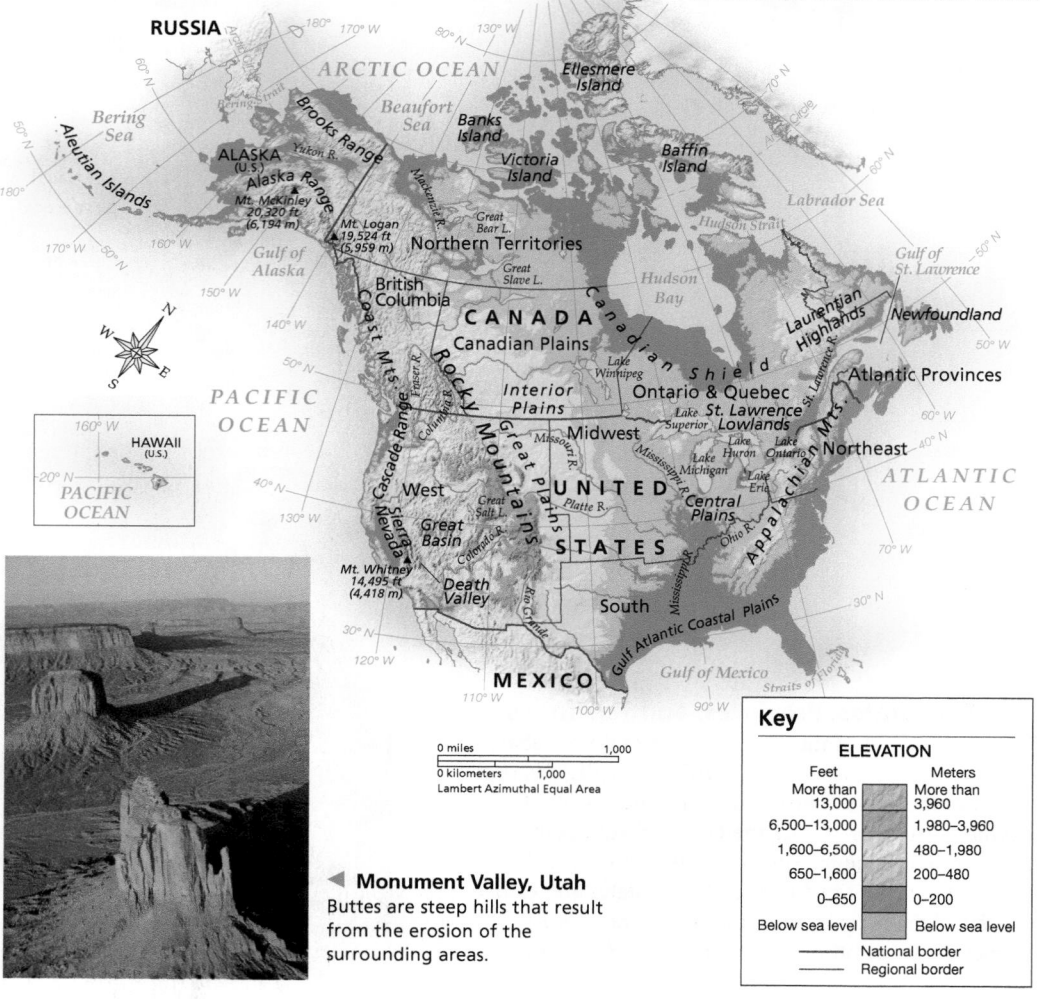

0 miles 1,000
0 kilometers 1,000
Lambert Azimuthal Equal Area

◄ **Monument Valley, Utah**
Buttes are steep hills that result from the erosion of the surrounding areas.

Key

ELEVATION

Feet	Meters
More than 13,000	More than 3,960
6,500–13,000	1,980–3,960
1,600–6,500	480–1,980
650–1,600	200–480
0–650	0–200
Below sea level	Below sea level

National border
Regional border

Differentiated Instruction

For Special Needs Students L1
If possible, show students the United States and Canada flyover segment on the Passport to the World CD-ROM. Ask students to list several of the region's major landforms on the board after viewing the segment.

⊙ *Flyover segment,* **Passport to the World CD-ROM**

Climates of the United States and Canada

The climates of the United States and Canada range widely. Average annual temperatures vary from 71° F in Florida to 27° F in Alaska. Because of its greater distance from the Equator, Canada has much cooler temperatures than the United States. In both countries it is hotter in the interior in the summer and colder and windier in the winter.

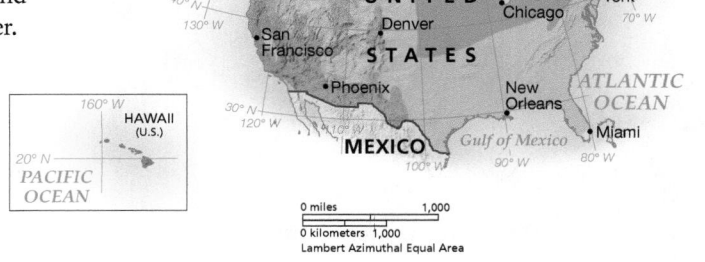

Key

———	National border
▧	Tropical wet
▫	Tropical wet and dry
▨	Semiarid
▨	Arid
▨	Mediterranean
▨	Humid continental
▨	Marine west coast
▨	Humid subtropical
▫	Subarctic
▫	Tundra
▨	Highland

0 miles 1,000
0 kilometers 1,000
Lambert Azimuthal Equal Area

REGIONS

5 Explore Influences on Climate

Compare the physical map of the United States and Canada on the previous page with the climate map above. How might landforms affect weather and rainfall? Notice that from Miami, Florida to Yellowknife, Canada the climate changes from tropical wet and dry to subarctic. Give reasons for this great shift in climates.

PRACTICE YOUR GEOGRAPHY SKILLS

1 On your hike in the western mountains you camped at the foot of Mount Rainier. Then you crossed an international border. What country are you in now?

2 You just flew over the mouth of the Mackenzie River and are headed for Victoria Island in Canada. Are you north or south of the Arctic Circle?

3 You are traveling through the Gulf of St. Lawrence toward the Great Lakes. What river will you take?

▲ Mount Rainier National Park, Washington

Regional Overview **143**

Guided Instruction

- Read the introductory paragraph and the Regions paragraph. Have students study the climate map, referring to the map key to locate the warmest and coldest regions of these two countries.

- Ask students **In what climate region is the city of Toronto?** *(humid continental)* **In what climate region is Seattle located?** *(marine west coast)*

- Ask students **Where are the coldest climates shown on this map located?** *(northern Canada)* **Does Hawaii get a lot of rain? How can you tell?** *(Yes; the state is located in a tropical wet region.)*

- Direct students to finish the Regional Overview worksheet.

  All in One United States and Canada Teaching Resources, *Regional Overview,* pp. 89–91

Independent Practice

Ask students to write a brief statement describing the climate of their own community. Then ask them to find the location of their community on the climate map. Have them compare their descriptions to the information on the map.

Monitor Progress

If students are having trouble with their statements, have them focus on typical summer and winter weather in their area. You may want to help students find the location of their community on the climate map.

Answers

REGIONS The Rocky Mountains are shaped like the highlands climate region; mountains effect weather in that temperatures are usually lower at higher elevations and there is usually less rainfall on one side of a mountain range; Reasons for the shift in climate from Florida to Nunavut are: their respective distances from the Equator; the bodies of water each area borders.

PRACTICE YOUR GEOGRAPHY SKILLS

1. Canada

2. north of the Arctic Circle

3. St. Lawrence River

Focus on Regions of the United States and Canada

L2

Guided Instruction

- Read the introduction and photo captions as a class. Students will notice that not every region of the United States and Canada is discussed in a photo caption.

- Point out that Alaska and Hawaii are part of the West. Ask **Which region of the United States is the largest?** (*the West*) Ask students to identify the smallest region. (*the Northeast*)

- Ask students to name Canada's two most populous provinces. (*Ontario and Quebec*) Ask them to give two reasons why Vancouver is a busy trading center. (*Its harbor never freezes and it handles almost all Canadian trade with Pacific Rim countries.*)

Independent Practice

Ask students to take out their copy of *Outline Map 11: The United States: Political.* Have students draw in the borders of the four regions of the United States. Ask them to label each region and put a star in the region that they live in.

All In One **United States and Canada Teaching Resources,** *Outline Map 11: The United States: Political,* p. 92

Monitor Progress

Circulate while students complete their maps and provide assistance where needed.

Focus on Regions of the United States and Canada

Now that you've investigated the geography of the United States and Canada, take a closer look at some of the regions that make up these two countries.

Go Online PHSchool.com **Use Web Code lhp-4000 for the interactive maps on these pages.**

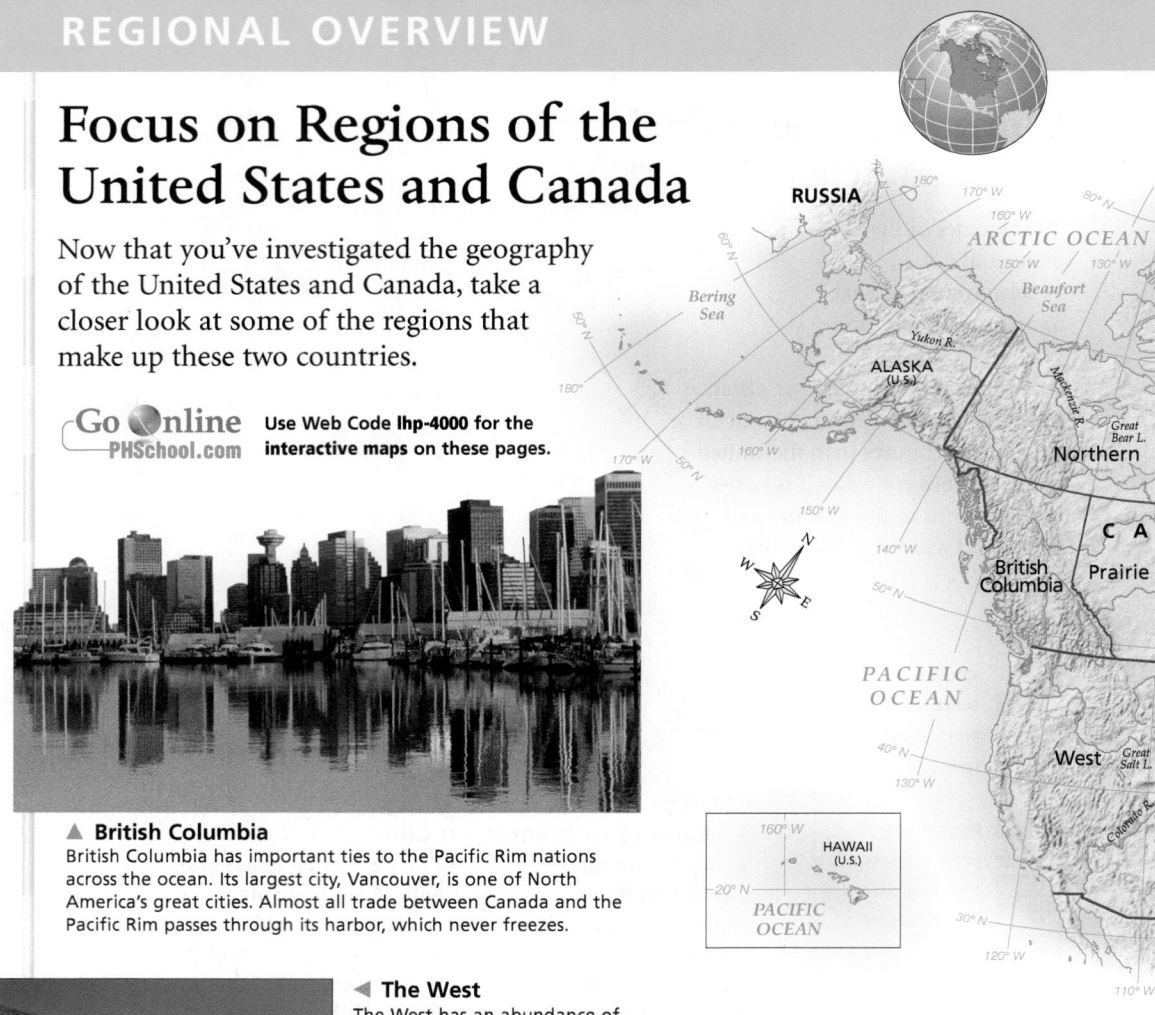

▲ **British Columbia**
British Columbia has important ties to the Pacific Rim nations across the ocean. Its largest city, Vancouver, is one of North America's great cities. Almost all trade between Canada and the Pacific Rim passes through its harbor, which never freezes.

◄ **The West**
The West has an abundance of natural and human resources. Although the West produces 85 percent of America's gold, water is one of the most precious natural resources in the region.

The South ►
The South is a warm region with a climate perfect for growing crops. Its booming industries have drawn many people from within the country and overseas. The Mardi Gras festival is one example of the region's cultural diversity.

144 United States and Canada

Background: Links Across Place

Pollution Crosses Borders Activities in one region can contribute to environmental problems in another region. For example, air pollution generated by power plants in the Midwestern United States rises into the atmosphere and is blown east by the wind. These pollutants combine with moisture in the air and fall as acid rain in the Northeastern United States and eastern Canada. The governments of the United States and Canada have recognized that they need to work together to solve problems that affect both countries.

Atlantic Provinces ▶
The four Canadian provinces that make up the Atlantic Provinces all border the Atlantic Ocean. Fishing and other maritime industries have always supported the economy and way of life of this region.

▲ Ontario and Quebec
These two provinces are Canada's most populous provinces. Ontario contains Ottawa, the national capital, shown above. French speakers make up a majority of the population of Quebec.

Key

——	National border
——	Regional border
⊛	Capital city

◀ The Midwest
Though the Midwest is still "America's Breadbasket," most family farms there have given way to larger corporate farms. The region is also an important transportation center.

Regional Overview **145**

Assess Progress [L2]

- Have students revisit the ideas they brainstormed in Build Background Knowledge. Using the information they have learned so far, ask them to expand on their description of their region of the United States. How does it differ from other regions of the United States and Canada?

- Ask students to complete Practice Your Geography Skills on page 143.

Reteach [L1]

For more exploration of the region, have students view the United States and Canada portion of the Passport to the World CD-ROM and complete the Customs Quiz.

⊙ *The United States and Canada,* **Passport to the World CD-ROM**

Extend [L3]

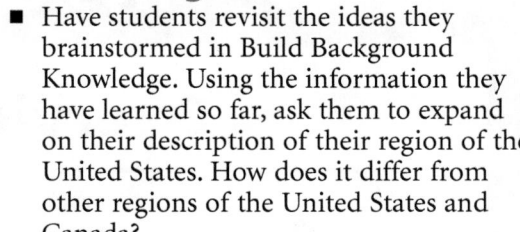

Portfolio Activity One way of assessing student accomplishments is by having them build a portfolio of their best work. To begin their portfolios for the United States and Canada, have students choose a region of the United States or a Canadian province from the map on pages 144–145. Then have them complete a project on this region or province. Students can choose what type of project they would like to do. Options include physical maps, resource maps, travel brochures, brief history reports, and more.

- Give students *Choosing a Topic* to help them get started on their project.

All In One **United States and Canada Teaching Resources,** *Choosing a Topic,* p. 95

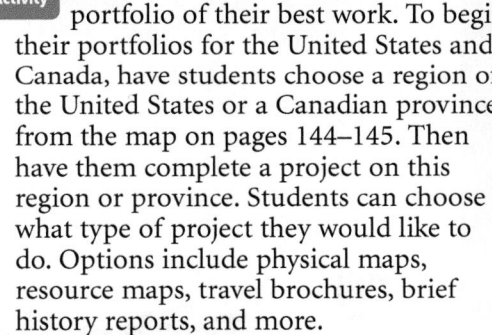

Differentiated Instruction

For English Language Learners [L2]
Pair English learners with native speakers and have each pair write three questions based on the information on pages 144–145.

Have pairs discuss any words or ideas in the text that are unfamiliar. Ask each pair to share its questions with the class.

Overview

Section 1 — Land and Water
1. Learn where the United States and Canada are located.
2. Find out about the major landforms of the United States and Canada.
3. Explore major bodies of water that are important to the United States and Canada.

Section 2 — Climate and Vegetation
1. Learn what climate zones the United States and Canada have.
2. Identify the natural vegetation zones of the United States and Canada.

Section 3 — Resources and Land Use
1. Learn about the major resources of the United States.
2. Find out about the major resources of Canada.

Technology Resources

Go Online
PHSchool.com

Students use embedded Web codes to access Internet activities, chapter self-tests, and additional map practice. They may also access Dorling Kindersley's Online Desk Reference to learn more about each country they study.

Interactive Textbook

Use the Interactive Textbook to make content and concepts come alive through animations, videos, and activities that accompany the complete basal text—online and on CD-ROM.

PRENTICE HALL
TeacherEXPRESS™
Plan · Teach · Assess

Use this complete suite of powerful teaching tools to make planning lessons and administering tests quicker and easier.

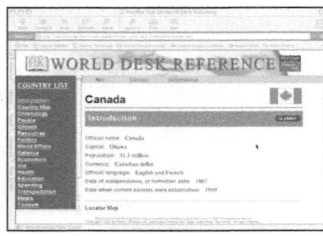

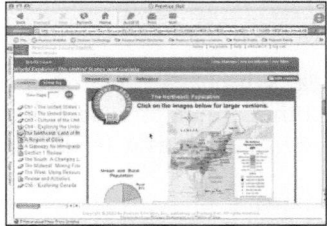

Reading and Assessment

Reading and Vocabulary Instruction

🔄 Model the Target Reading Skill

Reading Process Ask students to consider the difference between passive and active reading. Passive readers simply look at the words. Active readers think about what they are reading, how it relates to previous knowledge, and what might come next. Setting a purpose before reading is one way to remain active and engaged with the text. As students read, they can continually return to their stated purpose to make sure it is being fulfilled. Model setting a purpose for reading by thinking aloud about the chapter:

> I want to set a purpose for reading this chapter to help me focus. The chapter's title is *The U.S. and Canada: Physical Geography,* and the titles of the three sections are *Land and Water, Climate and Vegetation,* and *Resources and Land Use.* For the chapter as a whole, my purpose for reading will be to learn about the major landforms and bodies of water, the major climate and vegetation zones, and different kinds of natural resources in the United States and Canada. If I take notes as I read, it will be easier for me to keep track of the information I have learned and how it relates to my purpose.

Use the following worksheets from All-in-One United States and Canada Teaching Resources (pp. 110–112) to support this chapter's Target Reading Skill.

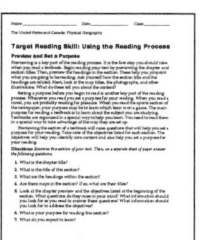 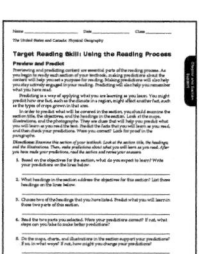

Vocabulary Builder
High-Use Academic Words

Use these steps to teach this chapter's high-use words:

1. Have students rate how well they know each word on their Word Knowledge worksheets (All-in-One United States and Canada Teaching Resources, p. 113).
2. Pronounce each word and ask students to repeat it.
3. Give students a brief definition and sample sentence (provided on TE pp. 149, 157, and 164).
4. Work with students as they fill in the "Definition or Example" column of their Word Knowledge worksheets.

Assessment

Formal Assessment

Test students' understanding of core knowledge and skills.

Chapter Tests A and B, All-in-One United States and Canada Teaching Resources, pp. 129–134

Customize the Chapter Tests to suit your needs.
Exam*View*®
Test Bank CD-ROM

Skills Assessment

Assess geographic literacy.
MapMaster Skills, Student Edition, pp. 151, 158, 160, 164, 170

Assess reading and comprehension.
Target Reading Skills, Student Edition, pp. 151, 159, 166, and in Section Assessments

Chapter 6 Assessment, Western Hemisphere Reading and Vocabulary Study Guide, p. 65

Performance Assessment

Assess students' performance on this chapter's Writing Activities using the following rubrics from All-in-One United States and Canada Teaching Resources.

Rubric for Assessing a Writing Assignment, p. 127

Rubric for Assessing a Map Produced by a Student, p. 128

Assess students' work through performance tasks.

Small Group Activity: Creating Travel Posters for National Parks, United States and Canada Teaching Resources, pp. 116–119

Online Assessment

Have students check their own understanding.
Chapter Self-Test

Test Preparation

Assess students' skills and diagnose problems as students begin their study of this region.

Screening Tests and Diagnosing Readiness Tests, AYP Monitoring Assessments, pp. 1–11, 13–63

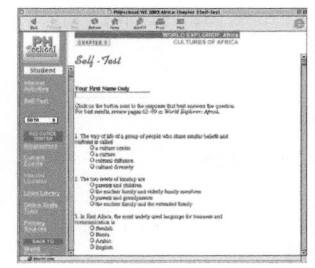

Section 1 Land and Water

 3 periods, 1.5 block (includes Skills for Life)

Social Studies Objectives

1. Learn where the United States and Canada are located.
2. Find out about the major landforms of the United States and Canada.
3. Explore major bodies of water that are important to the United States and Canada.

Reading/Language Arts Objective

Learn how to set a purpose for reading.

Prepare to Read	**Instructional Resources**	**Differentiated Instruction**
Build Background Knowledge Use a video to prompt discussion about the physical geography of the United States and Canada. **Set a Purpose for Reading** Have students evaluate statements on the *Reading Readiness Guide*. **Preview Key Terms** Teach the section's Key Terms. **Target Reading Skill** Introduce the section's Target Reading Skill of **setting a purpose for reading.**	**All in One United States and Canada Teaching Resources** ▫ L2 Reading Readiness Guide, p. 99 ▫ L2 Preview and Set a Purpose, p. 110	**Spanish Reading and Vocabulary Study Guide** ▫ L1 Chapter 6, Section 1, pp. 43–44 ELL

Instruct	**Instructional Resources**	**Differentiated Instruction**
A Global Perspective Discuss the locations of the United States and Canada. **Landforms** Discuss physical features of the United States and Canada. **Target Reading Skill** Review **setting a purpose for reading.** **Major Bodies of Water** Discuss the key bodies of water in the United States and Canada.	**All in One United States and Canada Teaching Resources** ▫ L2 Guided Reading and Review, p. 100 ▫ L2 Reading Readiness Guide, p. 99 **United States and Canada Transparencies** ▫ L2 Section Reading Support Transparency USC 43	**All in One United States and Canada Teaching Resources** ▫ L1 Outline Map 9: The United States and Canada: Physical, p. 120 ELL, LPR, SN ▫ L2 Skills for Life, p. 115 AR, GT, LPR, SN **Teacher's Edition** ▫ L1 For English Language Learners, TE p. 150 ▫ L1 For Less Proficient Readers, TE p. 150 ▫ L3 For Gifted and Talented, TE p. 152 **United States and Canada Transparencies** ▫ L1 Color Transparency USC 22: United States and Canada: Physical and Political ELL, LPR, SN

Assess and Reteach	**Instructional Resources**	**Differentiated Instruction**
Assess Progress Evaluate student comprehension with the section assessment and section quiz. **Reteach** Assign the Reading and Vocabulary Study Guide to help struggling students. **Extend** Extend the lesson by assigning a Book Project.	**All in One United States and Canada Teaching Resources** ▫ L2 Section Quiz, p. 101 Rubric for Assessing a Writing Assignment, p. 127 ▫ L3 Book Project: Create a Diorama, pp. 82–84 **Reading and Vocabulary Study Guide** ▫ L1 Chapter 6, Section 1, pp. 56–58	**Teacher's Edition** ▫ L1 For Special Needs Students, TE p. 155 **Spanish Support** ▫ L2 Section Quiz (Spanish), p. 58 ELL **Social Studies Skills Tutor CD-ROM** ▫ L1 Identifying Frame of Reference and Point of View ELL, LPR, SN

Key

▫ L1 Basic to Average   ▫ L3 Average to Advanced   LPR Less Proficient Readers   GT Gifted and Talented
▫ L2 For All Students   AR Advanced Readers   ELL English Language Learners
                                                      SN Special Needs Students

Section 2 Climate and Vegetation

 *2 periods, 1 block*

Social Studies Objectives
1. Learn what climate zones the United States and Canada have.
2. Identify the natural vegetation zones of the United States and Canada.

Reading/Language Arts Objective
Learn how to make predictions about what you read.

Prepare to Read	Instructional Resources	Differentiated Instruction
Build Background Knowledge Discuss the local climate with students. **Set a Purpose for Reading** Have students evaluate statements on the *Reading Readiness Guide.* **Preview Key Terms** Teach the section's Key Terms. **Target Reading Skill** Introduce the section's Target Reading Skill of **predicting**.	**All in One United States and Canada Teaching Resources** L2 Reading Readiness Guide, p. 103 L2 Preview and Predict, p. 111	**Spanish Reading and Vocabulary Study Guide** L1 Chapter 6, Section 2, pp. 45–46 ELL

Instruct	Instructional Resources	Differentiated Instruction
Climate Zones Describe how Canada's climate differs by region. **Target Reading Skill** Review **predicting**. **Natural Vegetation Zones** Study a map and review vegetation zones.	**All in One United States and Canada Teaching Resources** L2 Guided Reading and Review, p. 104 L2 Reading Readiness Guide, p. 103 **United States and Canada Transparencies** L2 Transparency B3: Tree Map/Flow Chart L2 Section Reading Support Transparency USC 44	**All in One United States and Canada Teaching Resources** L3 Enrichment, p. 114 AR, GT L3 Hatchet, pp. 122–125 AR, ELL, GT **Teacher's Edition** L1 For Special Needs Students, TE p. 159 L3 For Gifted and Talented, TE pp. 158, 159 L3 For Advanced Readers, TE p. 161 L2 For English Language Learners, TE p. 161 **United States and Canada Transparencies** L3 Color Transparency USC 22: The United States and Canada: Physical-Political (Base) AR, GT L3 Color Transparency USC 24: The United States and Canada: Population Distribution (Overlay) AR, GT

Assess and Reteach	Instructional Resources	Differentiated Instruction
Assess Progress Evaluate student comprehension with the section assessment and section quiz. **Reteach** Assign the Reading and Vocabulary Study Guide to help struggling students. **Extend** Extend the lesson by assigning a Book Project.	**All in One United States and Canada Teaching Resources** L2 Section Quiz, p. 105 L3 Book Project: Set Up a Weather Station, pp. 73–75 Rubric for Assessing a Writing Assignment, p. 127 **Reading and Vocabulary Study Guide** L1 Chapter 6, Section 2, pp. 59–61	**Spanish Support** L2 Section Quiz (Spanish), p. 61 ELL

Key
L1 Basic to Average
L2 For All Students
L3 Average to Advanced

LPR Less Proficient Readers
AR Advanced Readers
SN Special Needs Students

GT Gifted and Talented
ELL English Language Learners

Section 3 Resources and Land Use

 3.5 periods, 1.75 blocks (includes Chapter Review and Assessment)

Social Studies Objectives
1. Learn about the major resources of the United States.
2. Find out about the major resources of Canada.

Reading/Language Arts Objective
Learn how to preview and ask questions to see what a reading selection is about.

Prepare to Read	Instructional Resources	Differentiated Instruction
Build Background Knowledge Brainstorm about resources in the United States and Canada. **Set a Purpose for Reading** Have students evaluate statements on the *Reading Readiness Guide*. **Preview Key Terms** Teach the section's Key Terms. **Target Reading Skill** Introduce the section's Target Reading Skill of **previewing and asking questions**.	**All in One United States and Canada Teaching Resources** L2 Reading Readiness Guide, p. 107 L2 Preview and Ask Questions, p. 112	**Spanish Reading and Vocabulary Study Guide** L1 Chapter 6, Section 3, pp. 47–48 ELL

Instruct	Instructional Resources	Differentiated Instruction
Resources of the United States Derive information from a map and discuss the United States' natural resources. **Target Reading Skill** Review **previewing and asking questions**. **Resources of Canada** Ask questions about and discuss the resources of Canada.	**All in One United States and Canada Teaching Resources** L2 Guided Reading and Review, p. 108 L2 Reading Readiness Guide, p. 107 **United States and Canada Transparencies** L2 Section Reading Support Transparency USC 45	**All in One United States and Canada Teaching Resources** L1 Reading a Natural Resources Map, p. 121 ELL, LPR, SN **Teacher's Edition** L3 For Gifted and Talented, TE p. 166 L1 For Less Proficient Readers, TE p. 166 **Spanish Support** L2 Guided Reading and Review (Spanish), p. 62 ELL

Assess and Reteach	Instructional Resources	Differentiated Instruction
Assess Progress Evaluate student comprehension with the section assessment and section quiz. **Reteach** Assign the Reading and Vocabulary Study Guide to help struggling students. **Extend** Extend the lesson by assigning a Small Group Activity.	**All in One United States and Canada Teaching Resources** L2 Section Quiz, p. 109 L3 Small Group Activity: Creating Travel Posters for National Parks, pp. 116–119 Rubric for Assessing a Writing Assignment, p. 127 L2 Vocabulary Development, p. 126 L2 Word Knowledge, p. 113 Rubric for Assessing a Map Produced by a Student, p. 128 L2 Chapter Tests A and B, pp. 129–134 **Reading and Vocabulary Study Guide** L1 Chapter 6, Section 3, pp. 62–64	**Spanish Support** L2 Section Quiz (Spanish), p. 63 ELL L2 Chapter Summary (Spanish), p. 64 ELL L2 Vocabulary Development (Spanish), p. 65 ELL

Key
L1 Basic to Average	L3 Average to Advanced	LPR Less Proficient Readers	GT Gifted and Talented
L2 For All Students		AR Advanced Readers	ELL English Language Learners
		SN Special Needs Students	

Reading Background

Previewing and Prereading

This chapter's Target Reading Skill asks students to preview each section and set a purpose for reading. Students who do a brief, preliminary reading of complex material are in a strategic position to take control of their learning and comprehension. Previewing helps students consider what they already know about a topic they will be studying and gives some idea of what a text selection is about before they read it. Previewing also helps students identify the text structure and develop a mental framework for ideas to be encountered in the text. This can help them in formulating a more realistic reading and study plan.

Follow the steps below to teach students how to preview and preread.

1. Tell students that previewing will help them identify the text structure and develop a mental outline of ideas they will encounter in the text.

2. List the various text features you will be previewing in the order in which you would like students to examine them: section title, text headings, introduction, list of key terms, questions or tasks in the reading selection, photographs, drawings, maps, charts and other visuals in the text. Focus students' attention on some of these items, or ask them to look at all of them.

3. Prompt students to reflect after examining various text features. They may ask themselves questions such as: What is this reading selection about? What are some key words I will learn? How should I tackle this reading and divide up the task?

Using Paragraph Shrinking Effectively

In this chapter, students will use the Paragraph Shrinking technique to help them learn the important ideas in the text. Students will first read the paragraph independently. Because everyone reads at a different pace, minimize anxiety by telling students that you will not have them move on to the next step until everyone has finished reading. If they finish the paragraph before the time is up, they can read it again more slowly. Then monitor the class for signs that all students have finished reading silently before asking students to continue.

When the partner work begins, remind students of polite ways to express disagreement, such as, "I have a different idea. Can I share it with you?" or, "I hadn't thought of that. I was going to say …."

World Studies Background

Mississippi River

The Mississippi, the largest river in the United States, provides a home to more than 240 kinds of fish, about 50 kinds of mammals, and 40 percent of the migratory birds in the United States—not to mention the 12 million people who live along its banks. The Mississippi River rises in Lake Itasca in Minnesota and flows south to empty into the Gulf of Mexico. With its tributaries, the Mississippi drains all or part of 31 states and two Canadian provinces.

The Canadian Shield

The Canadian Shield is a layer of ancient rock that covers more than half of Canada, most of Greenland, and stretches into the northern United States. This makes it one of the largest continental shields. More than 540 million years old, the rock that makes up the shield is constantly being eroded by atmospheric factors, making it relatively flat. During the ice age, glaciers scraped across the shield, carving out lakes and creating smooth hills. Although the area is mostly undeveloped, it is a good source of natural resources.

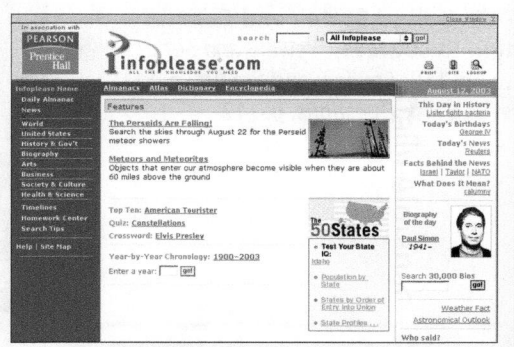

Infoplease® provides a wealth of useful information for the classroom. You can use this resource to strengthen your background on the subjects covered in this chapter. Have students visit this advertising-free site as a starting point for projects requiring research.

 Use Web Code **lhd-4100** for **Infoplease®**.

Chapter 6

Guiding Questions

Remind students about the Guiding Questions introduced at the beginning of this section.

Section 1 relates to Guiding Question ⑤ **How has physical geography affected the cultures of the United States and Canada?** *(The physical geography of the United States and Canada varies greatly, ranging from tall mountain ranges to rolling plains. People work different types of jobs and engage in different types of recreational activities based on the physical geography in their region.)*

Section 2 relates to Guiding Question ② **How has physical geography affected the cultures of the United States and Canada?** *(The various climates and vegetation zones across the two countries affect the way people live and work.)*

Section 3 relates to Guiding Question ⑤ **How did the United States and Canada become two of the wealthiest nations in the world?** *(The abundant natural resources found in these countries helped them to build two of the world's leading economies.)*

⟳ Target Reading Skill

In this chapter, students will learn and apply the reading skill of reading process. Use the following worksheets to help students practice this skill:

> **All in One United States and Canada Teaching Resources,** *Preview and Set a Purpose,* p. 110; *Preview and Predict,* p. 111; *Preview and Ask Questions,* p. 112

Differentiated Instruction

The following Teacher's Edition strategies are suitable for students of varying abilities.

Advanced Readers, p. 161
English Language Learners, pp. 150, 161
Gifted and Talented, pp. 152, 158, 159, 166
Less Proficient Readers, pp. 150, 158, 166
Special Needs Students, pp. 155, 159

Chapter 6

The U.S. and Canada: Physical Geography

Chapter Preview

This chapter will introduce you to the geography of the United States and Canada and show how geography affects the people who live in the region.

Section 1
Land and Water

Section 2
Climate and Vegetation

Section 3
Resources and Land Use

 Target Reading Skill

Reading Process In this chapter you will use previewing to help you understand and remember what you read.

▶ Talbot Lake, Canada

Bibliography

For the Teacher
Dennis, Jerry. *The Living Great Lakes: Searching for the Heart of the Inland Seas.* St. Martin's Press, 2003.
Hudson, John C. *Across This Land: A Regional Geography of the United States and Canada.* Johns Hopkins University Press, 2002.

For the Student
L1 Ylvisaker, Anne and Rosanne W. Fortner. *Lake Erie.* Capstone Press, 2003.
L1 Rau, Dana Meachen. *North America.* The Child's World Incorporated, 2003.
L2 Beckett, Harry. *Manitoba.* Weigl Educational Associates, 2003.
L3 Currie, Stephen. *Mississippi.* Lucent Books, 2003.

MAP★MASTER™
Skills Activity

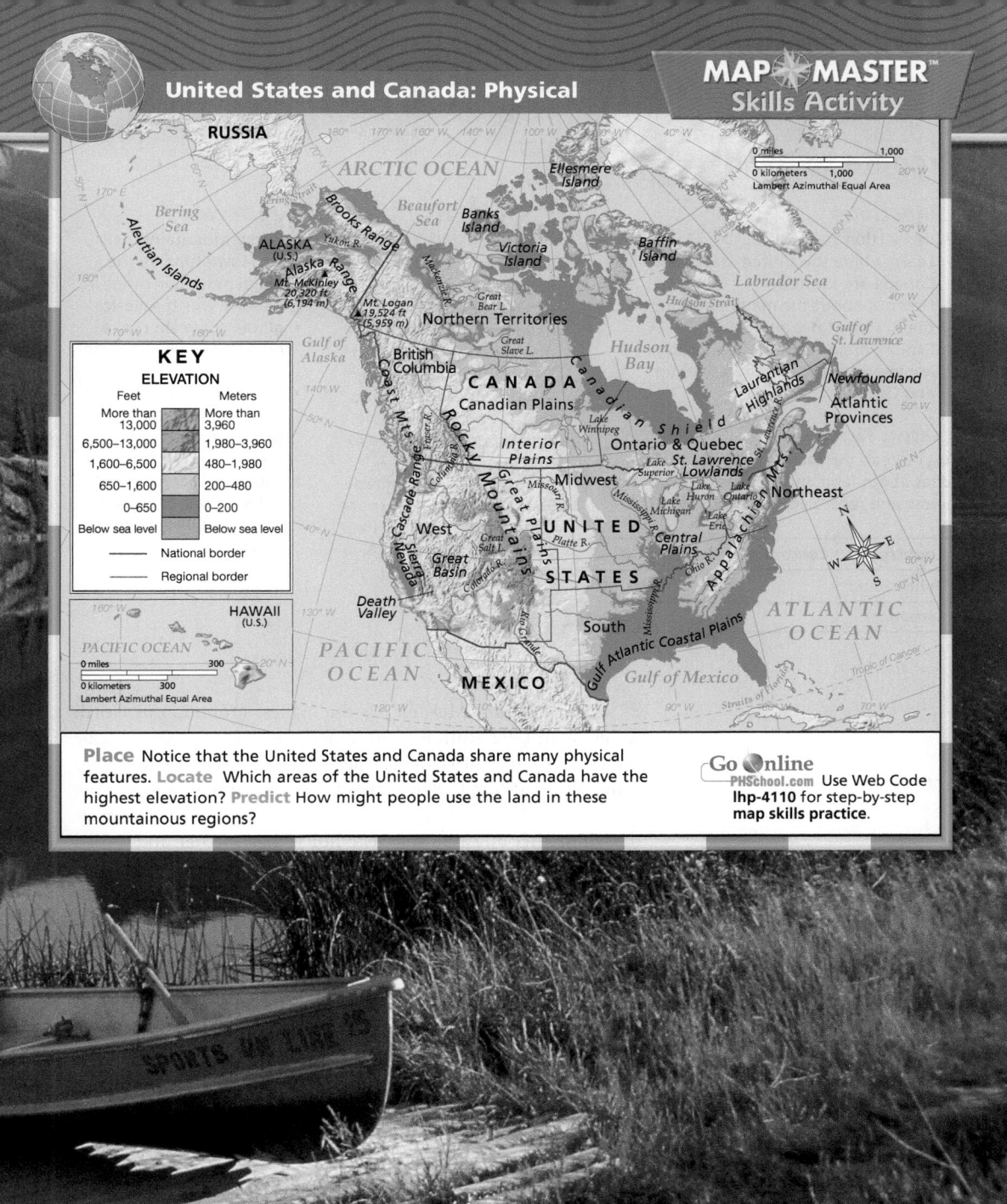

KEY
ELEVATION

Feet	Meters
More than 13,000	More than 3,960
6,500–13,000	1,980–3,960
1,600–6,500	480–1,980
650–1,600	200–480
0–650	0–200
Below sea level	Below sea level

— National border
— Regional border

Place Notice that the United States and Canada share many physical features. **Locate** Which areas of the United States and Canada have the highest elevation? **Predict** How might people use the land in these mountainous regions?

Go Online
PHSchool.com Use Web Code **lhp-4110** for step-by-step **map skills practice**.

Chapter 6 **147**

MAP★MASTER™
Skills Activity

- Have students create a table listing the regions of the United States and the physical features and elevations found in each region, as shown on the map. Remind them to label the columns and rows and give the table a title. Then have them create a similar table for Canada.

Go Online
PHSchool.com Students may practice their map skills using the interactive online version of this map.

Using the Visual L2

Reach Into Your Background Draw students' attention to the photograph on this spread. Ask them if a photograph containing similar physical features could be taken in their town. Tell them to explain what would be the same and what would be different about the photograph. What physical features might a scenic photograph taken in their town or city include?

Answers

MAP★MASTER
Skills Activity   **Locate** areas in the Rocky Mountains, Sierra Nevada, and Alaska Range **Predict** Possible answer: for ski resorts and other recreational businesses.

Chapter Resources

Teaching Resources
Letter Home, p. 97
L2 Vocabulary Development, p. 126
L2 Skills for Life, p. 115
L2 Chapter Tests A and B, pp. 129–134

Spanish Support
Spanish Letter Home, p. 57
L2 Spanish Chapter Summary, p. 64
L2 Spanish Vocabulary Development, p. 65

Media and Technology
L1 Student Edition on Audio CD
L1 Guided Reading Audiotapes, English and Spanish
L2 Social Studies Skills Tutor CD-ROM
ExamView® Test Bank CD-ROM

PRENTICE HALL
Presentation EXPRESS™
Teach · Connect · Inspire

Teach this chapter's content using the PresentationExpress™ CD-ROM including:
- slide shows
- transparencies
- interactive maps and media
- *ExamView®* QuickTake Presenter

Objectives

Social Studies

1. Learn where the United States and Canada are located.

2. Find out about the major landforms of the United States and Canada.

3. Explore major bodies of water that are important in the United States and Canada.

Reading/Language Arts

Learn how to set a purpose for reading.

Prepare to Read

Build Background Knowledge L2

Tell students that they will start their study of the United States and Canada by learning about their land and water. Show the video *The Geography of the United States and Canada.* Ask students to note three to five facts about the land and water of United States and Canada as they watch. Have students engage in a Give One, Get One activity (TE, p. T37) to share the information they gathered.

The Geography of the United States and Canada, **World Studies Video Program**

Set a Purpose for Reading L2

■ Preview the Objectives.

■ Read each statement in the *Reading Readiness Guide* aloud. Ask students to mark the statements true or false.

■ Have students discuss the statements in pairs or groups of four, then mark their worksheets again. Use the Numbered Heads participation strategy (TE, p. T36) to call on students to share their group's perspectives.

All in One **United States and Canada Teaching Resources,** *Reading Readiness Guide,* p. 99

Vocabulary Builder

Preview Key Terms L2

Create a three-column "See It—Remember It" chart of the Key Terms on the board. Write a term in the first column, a short definition in the second column, and a sketch in the third column. Guide students as they copy and complete the chart.

Prepare to Read

Objectives

In this section you will

1. Learn where the United States and Canada are located.

2. Find out about the major landforms of the United States and Canada.

3. Explore major bodies of water that are important to the United States and Canada.

Taking Notes

As you read the section, look for the main ideas about land and water. Copy the table below and record your findings in it.

Country	Landforms	Bodies of Water
United States		
Canada		

Target Reading Skill

Set a Purpose for Reading
Before you read this section, look at the headings, maps, and photographs to see what the section is about. Then set a purpose for reading this section. For example, your purpose might be to find out about the geography of the United States and Canada. Use the Taking Notes table to help you meet your purpose.

Key Terms

• **Rocky Mountains** (RAHK ee MOWN tunz) *n.* the major mountain range in western North America

• **glacier** (GLAY shur) *n.* a huge, slow-moving mass of snow and ice

• **Great Lakes** (grayt layks) *n.* the world's largest group of freshwater lakes

• **tributary** (TRIB yoo tehr ee) *n.* a river or stream that flows into a larger river

Alaska's Mount McKinley is the highest mountain in North America. In 1992, Ruth Kocour joined a team of climbers to scale the 20,320-foot (6,194-meter) peak. After the team had set up camp at 9,500 feet (2,896 meters), the first storm arrived. The team quickly built walls of packed snow to shield their tents from the wind. They dug a snow cave to house their kitchen and waited for the storm to end. Kocour recalls, "Someone on another team went outside for a few minutes, came back, and had a hot drink. His teeth cracked."

Maybe camping in the mountains is not for you. Perhaps you would prefer the sunny beaches of Florida, the giant forests of the Northwest, or the rugged coastline of Nova Scotia. Maybe you would like to see the Arizona desert or the plains of central Canada. The landscape of the United States and Canada varies greatly.

Climbers on Mount McKinley

148 United States and Canada

Target Reading Skill L2

Set a Purpose for Reading Draw students' attention to the Target Reading Skill. Tell students that setting a purpose for reading means choosing a focus for reading before they begin. Encourage students to preview photographs, maps, diagrams, captions, and headings before they begin reading. Explain that these items can be clues to what their purpose for reading might be.

Model the skill using the photographs on pages 148 and 149 of the Student Edition.

Tell students that because the photographs show mountains, a river, a field and trees, a reasonable purpose for reading these pages would be to learn about the geographic features of the United States and Canada.

Give students *Preview and Set a Purpose.* Have them complete the activity in groups.

All in One **United States and Canada Teaching Resources,** *Preview and Set a Purpose,* p. 110

A Global Perspective

The United States and Canada are located in North America. To the east is the Atlantic Ocean, and to the west is the Pacific Ocean. To the north, Canada borders the Arctic Ocean, while to the south, the United States borders Mexico and the Gulf of Mexico. The United States also includes Alaska, a huge state bordering northwest Canada, and Hawaii, a group of Pacific islands more than 2,000 miles (3,220 kilometers) west of California.

√ Reading Check **Which bodies of water border the United States and Canada?**

Landforms

From outer space, the United States and Canada appear as one landmass, with mountain ranges or systems, and vast plains running from north to south. Locate these mountains and plains on the United States and Canada: Physical map on page 9.

Extending about 3,000 miles (4,830 kilometers) along the western section of the continent, the Rocky Mountains are the largest mountain system in North America. In the east, the Appalachian (ap uh LAY chun) Mountains are the United States' second-largest mountain system. They stretch about 1,500 miles (2,415 kilometers). In Canada, the Appalachian Mountains meet the Laurentian (law REN shun) Highlands.

Between the Rockies and the Appalachians lies a huge plains area. In Canada, these lowlands are called the Interior Plains. In the United States, they are called the Great Plains and the Central Plains. Much of this region has rich soil. In the wetter, eastern area, farmers grow crops like corn and soybeans. In the drier, western area, farmers grow wheat and ranchers raise livestock.

A Scenic Landscape
This view of the Pioneer Valley along the Connecticut River in Massachusetts was taken from Mount Sugarloaf. *Draw Conclusions* *What can you conclude about the northeastern region of the United States from this photo?*

Vocabulary Builder

Use the information below to teach students this section's high-use words.

High-Use Word	Definition and Sample Sentence
border, p. 149	*v.* to touch at the edge or boundary Rose bushes **border** the garden path.
unique, p. 150	*adj.* unusual The tennis player has a **unique** style of serving the ball.
notable, p. 150	*adj.* remarkable; worth noting His research paper was a **notable** addition to the field of science.
navigate, p. 153	*v.* to steer a course Using the road map, he was able to

Instruct

A Global Perspective   L2

Guided Instruction

■ **Vocabulary Builder** Clarify the high-use word **border** before reading.

■ Read A Global Perspective using the Choral Reading technique (TE, p. T34).

■ Have students describe the location of the United States and Canada. *(They are located in North America with the Pacific Ocean bordering the west and the Atlantic Ocean bordering the east. The Arctic Ocean borders Canada to the north, and Canada borders the United States to the north. Mexico and the Gulf of Mexico border the United States to the south.)*

■ Ask students to consider the advantages of having ocean boundaries to the east and west. *(Possible answers: Access to ocean resources, such as fish, the ability to set up ports for trade with other countries, fewer neighbors to have potential conflicts with.)*

Independent Practice

Assign *Guided Reading and Review.*

All in One **United States and Canada Teaching Resources,** *Guided Reading and Review,* p. 100

Monitor Progress

Circulate to make sure students can answer the questions in the *Guided Reading and Review.*

Answers

Draw Conclusions Possible responses: the northeastern region of the United States has rivers, gentle hills, and forests. The region has a climate where trees and grass can grow.

√ Reading Check The Atlantic, Pacific, and Arctic oceans and the Gulf of Mexico border the United States and Canada.

Landforms

L2

Guided Instruction

- **Vocabulary Builder** Clarify the high-use words **unique** and **notable** before reading.

- Ask students to read Landforms of the United States and Canada. Circulate to make sure that students can answer the Reading Check question.

- Have students contrast the Gulf-Atlantic Coastal Plain with the Great Basin. *(Students should note that the Gulf-Atlantic Coastal Plain is flat, fertile, and close to water, while the Great Basin is bowl-shaped, very hot, and dry.)*

- Ask students to discuss ways in which the physical geography of the United States and Canada affects the people who live there. Ask students to provide specific examples of the geography's effects. *(Answers will vary, but may include that areas with rich soil, such as the Great Plains, encourage farming; places with access to the sea, such as the Gulf-Atlantic Coastal Plain, promote shipping and fishing; people cannot easily live in areas with glaciers, such as the valleys of Alaska, or very rugged areas, such as the Canadian Shield; more than half of Canada's population lives in the small St. Lawrence Lowlands because of good conditions for manufacturing and farming.)*

Independent Practice

Ask students to create the Taking Notes graphic organizer on a blank piece of paper. Then have them fill in the "Landforms" column with the information they have just learned. Model one example of choosing a detail to record in the Landforms column.

Monitor Progress

Circulate among the students as they work on the first column of the organizer, and offer help to individuals as needed.

Links
Read the **Links to Science** on this page. Ask students **How do scientists know that Loihi erupts?** *(Scientists know that the volcano is erupting because it is growing in height as layers of lava from the eruptions pile on top of one another.)*

Links to Science

The Next Hawaiian Island Volcanic eruptions in the Pacific Ocean, like the one shown above in Volcano National Park, created the islands of Hawaii. Loihi (loh EE hee), off the southern tip of Hawaii, is the world's most active volcano. But no one has seen it erupt. Its peak is 3,000 feet (914 meters) below the ocean's surface. Years of continuous eruption have produced layer after layer of molten lava. Scientists predict that in 100,000 years or less, Loihi will rise above the surface of the ocean and become the next Hawaiian island.

Special Features of the United States The United States has several unique features. The Gulf-Atlantic Coastal Plain runs along its eastern and southern coasts. In the Northeast, this plain is narrow; it broadens as it spreads south and west. Flat, fertile land and access to the sea attracted many settlers to this area.

A region of plateaus and basins lies west of the Rockies. Perhaps the most notable feature of this area is the Great Basin. In the northeast section of this bowl-shaped region is the Great Salt Lake. Death Valley is in the southwest section. Much of Death Valley lies below sea level. It is also the hottest place in North America. Summer temperatures there exceed 125°F (52°C).

Volcanoes To the west of this region lie three more mountain ranges. They are the Coast Ranges along the Pacific, the Sierra Nevada in California, and the Cascades in Washington and Oregon. Volcanoes produced the Cascades. Volcanoes form when magma, or molten rock, breaks through Earth's crust. Once it comes up to the surface, the molten rock is called lava. One of the volcanoes in the Cascades—Mount St. Helens— erupted in 1980. The eruption was so powerful that people as far away as Montana had to sweep volcanic ash off of their cars.

Glaciers Far to the north, snow and ice cover Alaska's many mountains. **Glaciers,** huge, slow-moving sheets of ice, fill many of the valleys among these mountains. Glaciers form over many years when layers of snow press together, thaw a little, and then turn to ice. Valley glaciers are found in high mountain valleys where the climate is too cold for the ice to melt. In North America, these valley glaciers move through the Rocky and Cascade mountains, the Sierra Nevada, and the Alaskan ranges.

150 United States and Canada

Differentiated Instruction

For English Language Learners L1
Show *Color Transparency USC 22: United States and Canada: Physical and Political.* Ask individual students to take turns coming up to trace the geographical features mentioned in the text on the transparency's map.

📖 **United States and Canada Transparencies,** *Color Transparency USC 22: United States and Canada: Physical and Political*

For Less Proficient Readers L1
Distribute *Outline Map 9: The United States and Canada: Physical.* As students read A Global Perspective, have them label The United States, Canada, and Mexico and fill in the names of the bodies of water described in the text. Provide assistance as needed.

 United States and Canada Teaching Resources, *Outline Map 9: The United States and Canada: Physical,* p. 120

Special Features of Canada Canada, too, has a number of unique features. East of Alaska lies the Yukon (YOO kahn) Territory. Mount Logan, Canada's highest peak, is located there. It is also part of the Coast Mountains, which stretch south along the Pacific Ocean.

Farther east, beyond the Interior Plains, lies the Canadian Shield. This huge region of ancient rock covers about half of Canada. The land on the shield is rugged, so few people live there.

Southeast of the shield along the St. Lawrence River are the St. Lawrence Lowlands. These lowlands are Canada's smallest land region. However, they are home to more than half of the country's population. The region is also Canada's manufacturing center. And because the lowlands have fertile soil, farmers in this region produce about one third of the country's crops.

✓ Reading Check **Describe two physical features of the United States and Canada.**

Major Bodies of Water

Both the United States and Canada have important lakes and rivers. People use these bodies of water for transportation, recreation, and industry. Many American and Canadian cities developed near these bodies of water. Find these waterways on the United States and Canada: Physical map on page 147.

The Great Lakes Lakes Superior, Michigan, Huron, Erie, and Ontario make up the **Great Lakes,** the world's largest group of freshwater lakes. Lake Superior is the deepest lake, with a mean depth of 487 feet (148 meters). Lake Erie is the shallowest lake at only 62 feet (19 meters) deep. Only Lake Michigan lies entirely in the United States. The other four lakes lie on the border between the United States and Canada.

Glaciers formed the Great Lakes during an ice age long ago. As the glaciers moved, they dug deep trenches in the land. Water from the melting glaciers filled these trenches to produce the Great Lakes. Today, the Great Lakes are important waterways in both the United States and Canada. Shipping on the Great Lakes has helped to develop the industries of both countries.

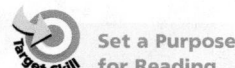

Set a Purpose for Reading
If your purpose is to learn about the geography of Canada, how do the three paragraphs at the left help you meet your goal?

A satellite image of the Great Lakes, which create a natural border between the United States and Canada

---

Background: Links Across Place

The Mother of Rivers Canada's Columbia Icefield, which overlaps part of the British Columbia–Alberta border, is the largest accumulation of permanent ice and snow in the Rocky Mountains. Because the icefield's main accumulation of ice lies on the Continental Divide, its glacial melt waters feed major rivers on either side of the divide—hence its nickname, "the mother of rivers." Meltwater from one glacier follows a river-and-lake network eastward through Alberta, Saskatchewan, and Manitoba and finally drains into Hudson Bay. Water from the northwestern part of the icefield flows into the Fraser and Columbia rivers, eventually emptying into the Pacific Ocean.

⌾ Target Reading Skill L2

Set a Purpose for Reading As a follow up, ask students to answer the Target Reading Skill question in the Student Edition. *(These paragraphs provide information about the Yukon Territory, Canadian Shield, and St. Lawrence Lowlands, which are all geographical features of Canada.)*

Major Bodies of Water L2

Guided Instruction
- **Vocabulary Builder** Clarify the high-use word **navigate** before reading.

- Have students read about the Great Lakes and major rivers of the United States and Canada in Major Bodies of Water.

- Have students identify the longest river in the United States and the longest river in Canada. *(the Mississippi River in the United States and the Mackenzie River in Canada)*

- Ask students why major bodies of water are important to people of the United States and Canada. *(Waterways can be used for transportation, shipping goods, recreation, and industry.)*

Answer

✓ Reading Check Students should describe any two of the following: the Gulf-Atlantic Coastal Plain, the Great Basin, the Great Salt Lake, Death Valley, the Coast Ranges, the Sierra Nevada, the Cascades, the glaciers of Alaska, Mount Logan, the Interior Plains, the Canadian Shield, or the St. Lawrence Lowlands.

Independent Practice

Have students complete the Taking Notes graphic organizer by filling in the "Bodies of Water" column.

Monitor Progress

■ Show *Section Reading Support Transparency USC 43* and ask students to check their graphic organizers individually. Go over key concepts and clarify key vocabulary as needed.

📖 **United States and Canada Transparencies,** *Section Reading Support Transparency USC 43*

■ Tell students to fill in the last column of the *Reading Readiness Guide.* Probe for what they learned that confirms or invalidates each statement.

📄 **All in One United States and Canada Teaching Resources,** *Reading Readiness Guide,* p. 99

Assess and Reteach

Assess Progress L2

Have students complete the Section Assessment. Administer the *Section Quiz.*

📄 **All in One United States and Canada Teaching Resources,** *Section Quiz,* p. 101

Reteach L1

If students need more instruction, have them read this section in the Reading and Vocabulary Study Guide.

📖 Chapter 6, Section 1, **Western Hemisphere Reading and Vocabulary Study Guide,** pp. 56–58

Extend L3

To learn more about the geographic features of the United States and Canada, have students complete the *Book Project: Create a Diorama.*

📄 **All in One United States and Canada Teaching Resources,** *Book Project: Create a Diorama,* pp. 82–84

The Continental Divide
The Rocky Mountains form the continental divide and are the site of several national parks, including Grand Teton National Park in Wyoming (large photo). White-water rafters paddle along Flathead River in Montana, west of the Rockies (small photo).
Explain *In what direction does the Flathead River flow?*

Major Rivers of the United States The largest river in the United States is the Mississippi River. Its source, or starting point, is in Minnesota. From there, the river flows through the Central Plains to the Gulf of Mexico. Two other major rivers, the Ohio and the Missouri, are tributaries of the Mississippi. A **tributary** (TRIB yoo tehr ee) is a stream or river that flows into a larger river. The Mississippi River system includes hundreds of tributaries and branches. Together they form about 12,000 miles (19,000 kilometers) of navigable water.

The Mighty Mississippi Water levels tend to rise in the spring when heavy rain combines with melting snow from the mountains. If the soil cannot soak up the excess water, flooding can occur. In 1993, the Upper Mississippi Valley experienced a disastrous flood. It caused nearly 50 deaths and damages totaling more than 15 billion dollars.

People have used the Mississippi River as an important transportation route for hundreds of years. Today, it is one of the busiest waterways in the world. Cargo ships transport many products, including iron, steel, chemicals, and even space rockets.

Look at the United States and Canada: Physical map on page 147 and find the Rocky Mountains. Notice that the Fraser, Columbia, and Colorado rivers form in the Rockies and flow west. Now find the Platte and Missouri rivers. They flow east from the Rockies. This is because the Rockies form the Continental Divide, the boundary that separates rivers flowing to the Pacific Ocean from those flowing to the Atlantic Ocean.

Major Rivers of Canada The Mackenzie River, Canada's longest, forms in the Rocky Mountains and flows north to the Arctic Ocean. It runs for more than 2,600 miles (4,197 kilometers). Although for most of its course the Mackenzie winds through sparsely populated, dense forest area, it is an important transportation route.

152 United States and Canada

Differentiated Instruction

For Gifted and Talented L3
Have students conduct research on locks and canals, individually or in groups. Ask them to find out why locks and canals are needed to help larger ships navigate the St. Lawrence River. If possible, ask students to find or create a visual representation of a lock system. Have students share their findings with the class.

Answer

Explain The Flathead River flows west because it is west of the Continental Divide.

In the 1880s, steamboats on the Mackenzie took supplies to local trading posts. Today, ships carry energy and mineral resources from the oil and natural gas fields in the region.

Canada's second major river is the St. Lawrence River. It is one of North America's most important transportation routes, flowing from the Great Lakes to the Atlantic Ocean. A system of locks and canals enables large ships to navigate it. From the St. Lawrence, ships can reach the Great Lakes ports that serve the farmland and industries of the region. Thus, the St. Lawrence is an important trade route between the United States and Canada. Millions of tons of cargo move along the St. Lawrence River each year.

✓ Reading Check **Name the five Great Lakes.**

Section **1** Assessment

Key Terms
Review the key terms at the beginning of this section. Use each term in a sentence that explains its meaning.

Target Reading Skill
How did having a purpose for reading help you to understand important ideas in this section?

Comprehension and Critical Thinking
1. (a) Recall Describe the borders of the United States and Canada.
(b) Predict How do you think the climates of Hawaii and Alaska differ?

2. (a) Describe What is the largest mountain system in North America?
(b) Identify Effects How have the physical features of the United States and Canada affected the lives of the people there?
3. (a) Locate Which bodies of water lie on the border between the United States and Canada?
(b) Explain Why are these bodies of water important?
(c) Draw Conclusions Why did many people coming to the United States and Canada hundreds of years ago settle along coastal plains and rivers?

Writing Activity
Suppose that you are on vacation in the United States or Canada. Write a postcard to a friend describing the physical features that you have seen. Before you begin, review the information you recorded in your Taking Notes table.

For: An activity on Mt. McKinley
Visit: PHSchool.com
Web Code: lhd-4101

Answers

✓ Reading Check Lakes Superior, Michigan, Huron, Erie, and Ontario

Section 1 Assessment

Key Terms
Students' sentences should reflect knowledge of each Key Term.

⟲ **Target Reading Skill**
Students should explain that having a purpose for reading helped them to find the main focus of the section.

Comprehension and Critical Thinking
1. (a) The United States and Canada are bordered to the east by the Atlantic Ocean, to the west by the Pacific Ocean, to the north by the Arctic Ocean, and to the south by Mexico and the Gulf of Mexico. Alaska borders northwest Canada, and the Hawaiian islands are located in the Pacific Ocean, west of California. **(b)** Students should be able to predict that Alaska's climate is colder than Hawaii's because Alaska is located farther north.

2. (a) the Rocky Mountains **(b)** They affect where people decide to live, and what kind of work they do. For example, the Interior Plains and the Great Plains have rich soil making them good places to farm.

3. (a) the Great Lakes **(b)** These bodies of water provide important shipping routes that have benefited industries in both countries. **(c)** Coastal plains provided flat, fertile land, and rivers provided transportation for people who came to the United States and Canada many years ago.

Writing Activity
Use the *Rubric for Assessing a Writing Assignment* to evaluate students' postcards.

All In One **United States and Canada Teaching Resources,** *Rubric for Assessing a Writing Assignment,* p. 127

Go Online
PHSchool.com Typing in the Web code when prompted will bring students directly to detailed instructions for this activity.

Objective

Learn how to identify and understand frame of reference.

Prepare to Read

Build Background Knowledge `L2`

Ask students what it might be like if they had to attend school in another country for one week. Have students brainstorm what kinds of things they might experience that they would find unusual or surprising such as the language the classes are taught in, the food served in the cafeteria, and what time school starts and ends. Then explain that these judgments would be based on their frame of reference, or background.

Instruct

Identifying Frame of Reference `L2`

Guided Instruction

- Read the steps to identify frame of reference as a class and write them on the board.

- Practice the skill by following the steps on p. 155 as a class. First choose an appropriate title for the boxed text. *(Possible answer: "An Inuit Homeland")* Then identify descriptive parts of the text *(the first two paragraphs)*, and opinions *(the last paragraph)*. Next, list facts about the authors. *(They are tenth-grade students at a high school in Nunavut.)* Finally, suggest how your own frame of reference might make you have a different opinion about Nunavut. *(Possible answer: Because you are not Canadian or Inuit, the creation of Nunavut might not seem as important to you as it does to the authors.)*

- Ask students to return to the Build Background Knowledge activity, to identify their own frame of reference, and to explain how that frame of reference would affect their opinions about attending school overseas.

Identifying Frame of Reference

> "It's a freak storm," Ian e-mailed excitedly to his friends. "Four inches of snow already, and we might get six inches total. It's awful!"
>
> "Awful?" Janet replied. "It's just a few inches. What's the big deal?"
>
> "JUST a few inches?" Ian typed. "This city is paralyzed. Cars are stuck everywhere. Our camping trip this weekend is cancelled. It's a disaster."
>
> Luann responded to both of her friends. "Of course it's a disaster to Ian. He lives in Georgia. No way is the South prepared to deal with a snowstorm in April."
>
> "Well, up here in Quebec, we're not afraid of a little snow!" Janet wrote back.
>
> "Okay, calm down," wrote Luann. "Your opinion depends on what you're used to."
>
> In other words, your opinion depends on your frame of reference.

154 United States and Canada

Learn the Skill

Follow the steps below to understand frame of reference.

1. **Identify the topic being discussed.** Look for evidence that an opinion is being expressed. When people state their opinions, they often reveal information about their frame of reference.

2. **Identify the author's opinion on the issue.** An opinion is what someone believes. It is not a fact, which is something that can be proved.

3. **Identify what you know about the author's background.** Some background factors are age, personality, family, culture, nationality, concerns, and historical era.

4. **Ask how the author's background might have influenced his or her beliefs.** Think about whether the person's opinions would be different if he or she came from a different place, culture, family, or time in history.

Independent Practice

Assign *Skills for Life* and have students complete it individually.

All in One **United States and Canada Teaching Resources,** *Skills for Life*, p. 115

Monitor Progress

Monitor the students doing the *Skills for Life* worksheet, checking to make sure they understand the skills steps.

Practice the Skill

The text in the box on the right comes from Inuit students in Nunavut. The Inuit, a Native American culture group, persuaded the Canadian government to create the territory of Nunavut in 1999. Read what the students wrote just before the creation of their new homeland.

1 This text has no title, but you can give it a title that reflects the main topic. What title would you give it?

2 The students give both description and opinion. Which parts of the text are description, and which are opinion?

3 You already know some facts about the students' background: They are Canadian, and they are Inuit. What else can you discover about the students' background?

4 The students' opinions are shaped by their frame of reference. Explain how your own frame of reference might make you feel differently about Nunavut.

"There are not very many people, but all of us are friends. We share the same culture and language, Inuktitut. You can learn from elders. We help each other. . . .

"[W]e go to school, church, cadets, the hall, and the gym. We play [games], watch T.V., listen to music, play and watch sports (especially hockey), . . . dance, and sleep. We also stay home, visit with our parents, clean, look after children, and try to finish our homework. . . . We eat seal meat, caribou, arctic char, walrus, . . . and also we eat various types of birds. . . .

"Nunavut is independence. The creation of Nunavut means that we, the Inuit, are going to have our own land. . . . It means a lot to us, the Inuit youth. It means making choices for ourselves. We are proud of Nunavut."
—*Grade 10 students at Ataguttaaluk High in Igloolik, a town in central Nunavut, above the Arctic Circle*

Inuit sculptor

Apply the Skill

Think of an issue that you feel strongly about. Describe your own frame of reference, and show how it has influenced your opinion.

Differentiated Instruction

For Special Needs Students L1

Partner special needs students with more proficient students to do Level 1 of the *Identifying Frame of Reference and Point of View* lesson on the Social Studies Skills Tutor CD-ROM together.

When the students feel more confident, they can move on to Level 2 alone.

⊙ *Identifying Frame of Reference and Point of View,* **Social Studies Skills Tutor CD-ROM**

Assess and Reteach

Assess Progress L2

Ask students to do the Apply the Skill activity.

Reteach L1

If students are having trouble applying the skill steps, have them review the skill using the interactive Social Studies Skills Tutor CD-ROM.

⊙ *Identifying Frame of Reference and Point of View,* **Social Studies Skills Tutor CD-ROM**

Extend L3

Ask students to bring in an editorial or a letter to the editor from a recent newspaper. Working individually or in pairs, have students follow the four steps they have learned in the skills lesson in order to identify the possible frame of reference of the editorial or letter.

Answers
Apply the Skill

Answers will vary, but should reflect an accurate frame of reference (age, nationality, culture, etc.) and show a reasonable influence on the stated opinion.

Section 2
Step-by-Step Instruction

Section 2 Climate and Vegetation

Objectives

Social Studies

1. Learn what climate zones the United States and Canada have.

2. Identify the natural vegetation zones of the United States and Canada.

Reading/Language Arts

Learn how to make predictions about what you read.

Prepare to Read

Build Background Knowledge L2

In this section students will learn about the climate and vegetation of the United States and Canada. Have students preview the headings and visuals of this section with the following question in mind: **What would best describe the climate and vegetation of the region I live in?** Use the Think-Write-Pair-Share participation strategy (TE, p. T36) to share students responses.

Set a Purpose for Reading L2

■ Preview the Objectives.

■ Read each statement in the *Reading Readiness Guide* aloud. Ask students to mark the statements true or false.

■ Have students discuss the statements in pairs or groups of four, then mark their worksheets again. Use the Numbered Heads participation strategy (TE, p. T36) to call on students to share their group's perspectives.

All in One United States and Canada Teaching Resources, *Reading Readiness Guide,* p. 103

Vocabulary Builder
Preview Key Terms L2

Pronounce each Key Term, then ask the students to say the word with you. Provide a simple explanation such as, "Just as Montana is a state in the United States, Alberta is a province in Canada."

Prepare to Read

Objectives

In this section you will

1. Learn what climate zones the United States and Canada have.

2. Identify the natural vegetation zones of the United States and Canada.

Taking Notes

As you read the section, look for details about climate and vegetation. Copy the chart below and write each detail under the correct heading.

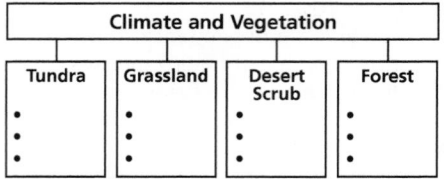

Climate and Vegetation			
Tundra	Grassland	Desert Scrub	Forest
•	•	•	•
•	•	•	•
•	•	•	•

Target Reading Skill

Predict Making predictions about your text helps you set a purpose for reading and remember what you read. Before you begin, preview the section by looking at the headings, photographs, and maps. Then predict what the text might discuss about climate and vegetation. As you read the section, connect what you read to your prediction. If what you learn doesn't support your prediction, change it.

Key Terms

• **tundra** (TUN druh) *n.* a cold, dry region covered with snow for more than half the year

• **permafrost** (PUR muh frawst) *n.* a permanently frozen layer of ground below the top layer of soil

• **prairie** (PREHR ee) *n.* a region of flat or rolling land covered with grasses

• **province** (PRAH vins) *n.* a political division of land in Canada

On a hot and sunny February morning, a reporter left his home in Miami Beach, Florida, and headed for the airport. Wearing lightweight pants and a short-sleeved shirt, he boarded a plane to snowy Toronto. Was he forgetting something? Surely he knew that the temperature would be below freezing in Canada.

He did, indeed, know all about the bitter cold that would greet him when he got off the plane. But he was going to research an article on Toronto's tunnels and underground malls. He wanted to find out whether people could really visit hotels, restaurants, and shops without having to go outside and brave the harsh Canadian winter.

A climate-controlled shopping center in Toronto, Ontario

156 United States and Canada

Target Reading Skill L2

Predict Point out the Target Reading Skill. Tell students that predicting is making an educated guess. Remind students that a prediction can be revised at any time if they discover it is not accurate.

Model the skill by pointing out the title of the map on page 158 of the Student Edition. Make a prediction about what students will learn from the map. (*I predict that students*

will learn about the patterns of tornadoes in the United States.)

Give students *Preview and Predict*. Have them complete the activity in groups.

All in One United States and Canada Teaching Resources, *Preview and Predict,* p. 111

Climate Zones

Climate is weather patterns that an area experiences over a long period of time. Climate zones in the United States and Canada range from a desert climate to a polar climate. Factors such as latitude, or a location's distance north or south of the Equator, mountains, and oceans all affect the climates found in different regions.

Climates of Canada Generally, the farther a location is from the Equator, the colder its climate. Look at the climate regions map on page 143 of the Regional Overview. Notice that much of Canada lies well north of the 40° N line of latitude, a long way from the Equator. Therefore, much of Canada is very cold!

Ocean Effects The ocean affects Canada's climates, too. Water heats up and cools down more slowly than land. Winds blowing across water on to land tend to warm the land in winter and cool the land in summer. Therefore, areas that are near an ocean generally have milder climates. Also, winds blowing across the ocean pick up moisture. When these winds blow over land, they drop the moisture in the form of rain or snow.

Being a great distance from the ocean also affects climate. Inland areas often have climate extremes. Find Winnipeg, in Canada's Interior Plains, on the climate map. Winter temperatures here are very cold, averaging around 0°F (–18°C). Yet summer temperatures run between 70°F and 90°F (20°C and 32°C).

Mountain Effects Mountains are another factor that influence climate. Winds blowing from the Pacific Ocean rise as they meet mountain ranges in the west. As they rise, the winds cool and drop their moisture. The air is dry by the time it reaches the other side of the mountains, and it warms up as it returns to lower altitudes. This is called the Chinook effect. The area on the side of the mountains away from the wind is in a rain shadow. A rain shadow is an area on the dry, sheltered side of a mountain, which receives little rainfall.

Graph Skills

Located in different climate regions, Miami, Florida, and Toronto, Canada, experience very different average temperatures. **Identify** In which month does Miami experience the coolest temperatures? Which month is the coolest in Toronto? **Compare** Which month has the least difference between the average temperature in Miami and Toronto?

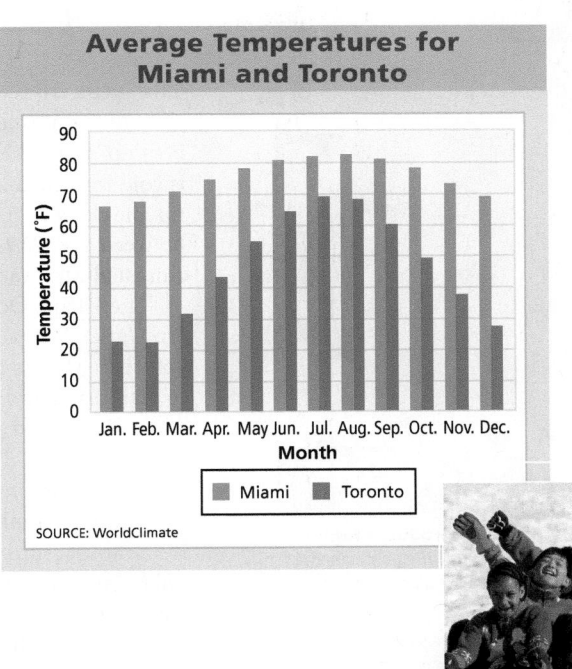

Average Temperatures for Miami and Toronto

SOURCE: WorldClimate

Chapter 6 Section 2 **157**

Instruct

Climate Zones [L2]

Guided Instruction

■ Read Climate Zones using the Structured Silent Reading strategy (TE, p. T34).

■ Ask students to explain how oceans affect Canada's climate. (*Because water heats and cools more slowly than land, areas near oceans have milder temperatures; winds blowing across the oceans drop more rain and snow over coastal areas*).

■ Have students imagine that they are traveling from the northwest coast of Canada to Winnipeg during winter. **How would the weather change as they traveled? Why?** (*In winter, the northwest coast would be rainy, but mild. Inland, in Winnipeg, the temperatures would be significantly lower, and precipitation could fall as snow. The mild, rainy climate of the northwestern coast is influenced by proximity to the Pacific Ocean. Winnipeg is far from the ocean, and experiences much more extreme temperatures.*)

─ Vocabulary Builder ─

Use the information below to teach students this section's high-use words.

High-Use Word	Definition and Sample Sentence
ideal, p. 160	*adj.* perfect The amount of snow on the hill made it **ideal** for skiing.
support, p. 161	*v.* to promote or provide for The income from the bake sale helped **support** the chess club.

Answers

Graph Skills Identify January; February
Compare July

Guided Instruction (continued)

- Have students describe the climate of the United States east of the Great Plains. (*This part of the country has a continental climate with cold winters and warm summers in the north, and mild winters and long, hot summers in the south.*)

- Ask students to use the map on this page to determine the line of latitude closest to your area. Then ask students to think about the words they used to describe the area's climate in the Build Background Knowledge activity at the beginning of this section. How might those climate characteristics be related to the distance of the area from the Equator? (*Answers will vary according to region, but students should be able to make the correlation that areas closer to the Equator are generally hotter than those farther away from it*).

Independent Practice

Assign *Guided Reading and Review.*

All in One **United States and Canada Teaching Resources,** *Guided Reading and Review,* p. 104

Monitor Progress

As students work on the *Guided Reading and Review,* circulate to check their answers and comprehension of the section.

Answers

✓ Reading Check oceans, mountains, and proximity to the Equator

MAP MASTER Skills Activity **Explain** The area has more tornadoes each year than other parts of the United States. **Draw Conclusions** The Plains areas do not have many hills or mountains to stall or impede the tornadoes.

Go Online PHSchool.com Students may practice their map skills by using the interactive online version of this map.

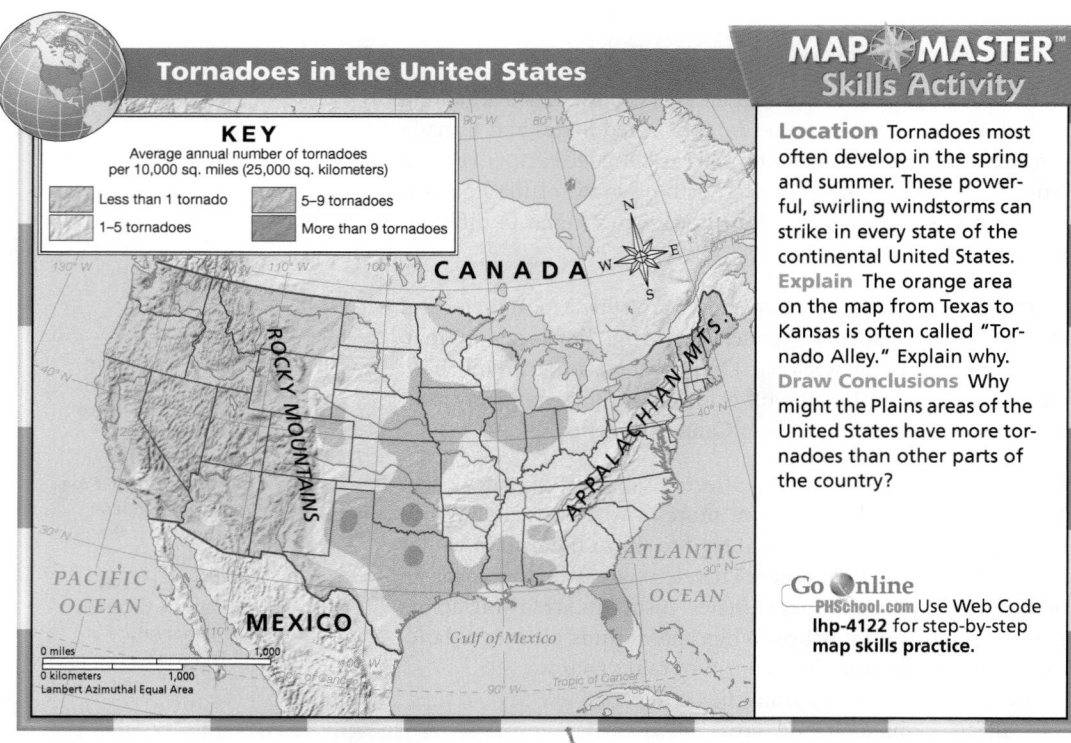

Tornadoes in the United States

MAP MASTER™ Skills Activity

KEY
Average annual number of tornadoes per 10,000 sq. miles (25,000 sq. kilometers)

- Less than 1 tornado
- 1–5 tornadoes
- 5–9 tornadoes
- More than 9 tornadoes

CANADA

ROCKY MOUNTAINS

APPALACHIAN MTS.

PACIFIC OCEAN

MEXICO

Gulf of Mexico

ATLANTIC OCEAN

Tropic of Cancer

0 miles   1,000
0 kilometers   1,000
Lambert Azimuthal Equal Area

Location Tornadoes most often develop in the spring and summer. These powerful, swirling windstorms can strike in every state of the continental United States. **Explain** The orange area on the map from Texas to Kansas is often called "Tornado Alley." Explain why. **Draw Conclusions** Why might the Plains areas of the United States have more tornadoes than other parts of the country?

Go Online PHSchool.com Use Web Code lhp-4122 for step-by-step map skills practice.

A tornado produces high winds and flying debris that can cause heavy damage to structures in its path.

Climates of the United States Location also influences climate. On the climate map on page 143, notice that Alaska lies north of the 60° N line of latitude. Far from the Equator, Alaska is cold for much of the year. Now find Hawaii and the southern tip of Florida. They lie near or within the tropics, the area between the $23\frac{1}{2}°$ N and $23\frac{1}{2}°$ S lines of latitude. There, it is almost always warm.

The Pacific Ocean and mountains affect climate in the western United States. Wet winds from the ocean drop their moisture before they cross the mountains. As a result, the eastern sections of California and Arizona are semiarid or desert. Death Valley, which is located there, has the lowest average rainfall in the country—about 2 inches (5 centimeters) a year.

East of the Great Plains, the country has continental climates. In the north, summers are warm and winters are cold and snowy. In the south, summers tend to be long and hot, while winters are mild. The coastal regions of these areas sometimes experience violent weather. In summer and fall, hurricanes and tropical storms develop in the Atlantic Ocean.

✓ Reading Check **What factors affect climate?**

158 United States and Canada

Differentiated Instruction

For Gifted and Talented Students **L3**
Display *Color Transparency USC 24: United States and Canada: Population Distribution.* Briefly review how to read the map. Then have students compare it with the climate map on p. 143 and identify what climate zones are the most densely populated.

📖 **United States and Canada Transparencies,** *Color Transparency USC 22: United States and Canada: Physical and Political (Base); Color Transparency USC 24: Population Distribution (Overlay)*

Natural Vegetation Zones

Climate in the United States and Canada helps produce four major kinds of natural vegetation, or plant life. As you can see on the United States and Canada: Vegetation map on page 160, these are tundra, grassland, desert scrub, and forest.

Northern Tundras The **tundra,** found in the far north, is a cold, dry region that is covered with snow for more than half the year. The Arctic tundra contains **permafrost,** a layer of permanently frozen soil. During the short, cool summer, the soil above the permafrost thaws. Mosses, grasses, and bright wildflowers grow there. Life is hard in the tundra. However, some Inuits (IN oo its), a native people of Canada and Alaska, once called Eskimos, live there. They make a living by fishing and hunting.

Grasslands Grasslands are regions of flat or rolling land covered with grasses. They are located in areas where there is enough rain to support grasses but not enough to support forests. In North America, grasslands are called **prairies.** The world's largest prairie lies in the Central and Great Plains of North America. It stretches from the American central states into the Canadian provinces of Alberta, Saskatchewan (sas KACH uh wahn), and Manitoba. These three provinces are sometimes called the Prairie Provinces. A **province** is a political division of Canada, much like one of our states. Look at the temperate grasslands region of the United States and Canada: Vegetation map on page 160 to locate the prairies, or plains areas, of the United States and Canada.

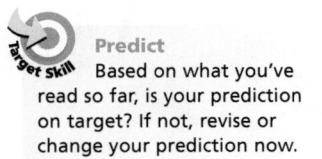

Predict
Based on what you've read so far, is your prediction on target? If not, revise or change your prediction now.

Two Vegetation Zones
The natural vegetation of the northern tundra (large photo) differs greatly from the natural vegetation of the grasslands (smaller photo). *Draw Conclusions How does climate affect the vegetation that grows in the tundra and grasslands?*

Predict As a follow up, ask students to answer the Target Reading skill question in the Student Edition. (*Answers will vary. Students should be able to recognize whether their original prediction is accurate or needs to be revised.*)

Natural Vegetation Zones L2

Guided Instruction

- **Vocabulary Builder** Clarify the high-use words **ideal** and **support** before reading.

- Read about tundras, grasslands, desert scrub, and forests in Natural Vegetation Zones. Circulate to make sure that students can answer the Reading Check question.

- Have students study the map. Then ask them to list all of the vegetation zones of the United States and Canada. (*tropical rain forest, mixed forest, deciduous forest, coniferous forest, Mediterranean forest, tropical savanna, temperate grassland, desert scrub, desert, tundra, ice cap*)

- Ask students **Why do you think few plants grow in the tundra?** (*Possible answer: Snow covers the ground for more than half the year, and permafrost, or permanently frozen soil, does not support growth.*)

- Ask students **Why do you think few people live in the tundra?** (*Possible answer: The region is very cold and crops cannot be grown in the frozen soil.*)

Differentiated Instruction

For Special Needs Students L1
Have students listen to the recorded version of the section on the Student Edition on Audio CD. Pause the CD several times to discuss correlations between the audio text and the photos and maps on these pages.

◉ Chapter 6, Section 2, **Western Hemisphere Student Edition on Audio CD**

For Gifted and Talented L3
Have students learn more about Canada's national parks by completing the *Enrichment* activity. Students should read the passage and then select a project to complete from the list provided. Students should present their projects to the class.

All In One **United States and Canada Teaching Resources,** *Enrichment,* p. 114

Answers

Draw Conclusions Few types of vegetation grow in the harsh climate of the tundra, and the climate of the grasslands can support grasses but not forests.

- Have students describe the location of the Great Basin, and identify one kind of animal that can thrive in the Great Basin. (*The Great Basin is located between the Rocky Mountains and the Sierras. Sheep graze on the area's vegetation.*)

- Ask students to name Canada's Prairie Provinces. (*Alberta, Manitoba, and Saskatchewan*) Then have them explain why they are called the Prairie Provinces. (*The world's largest prairie stretches into the provinces.*)

- Tell students that forests are an important type of vegetation. Ask students whether coniferous or deciduous forests are more prevalent in your area. Have the class brainstorm names of different kinds of deciduous trees. (*Answers will vary. Students may know the names of some deciduous trees, such as oak, birch, ash, willow, or others.*)

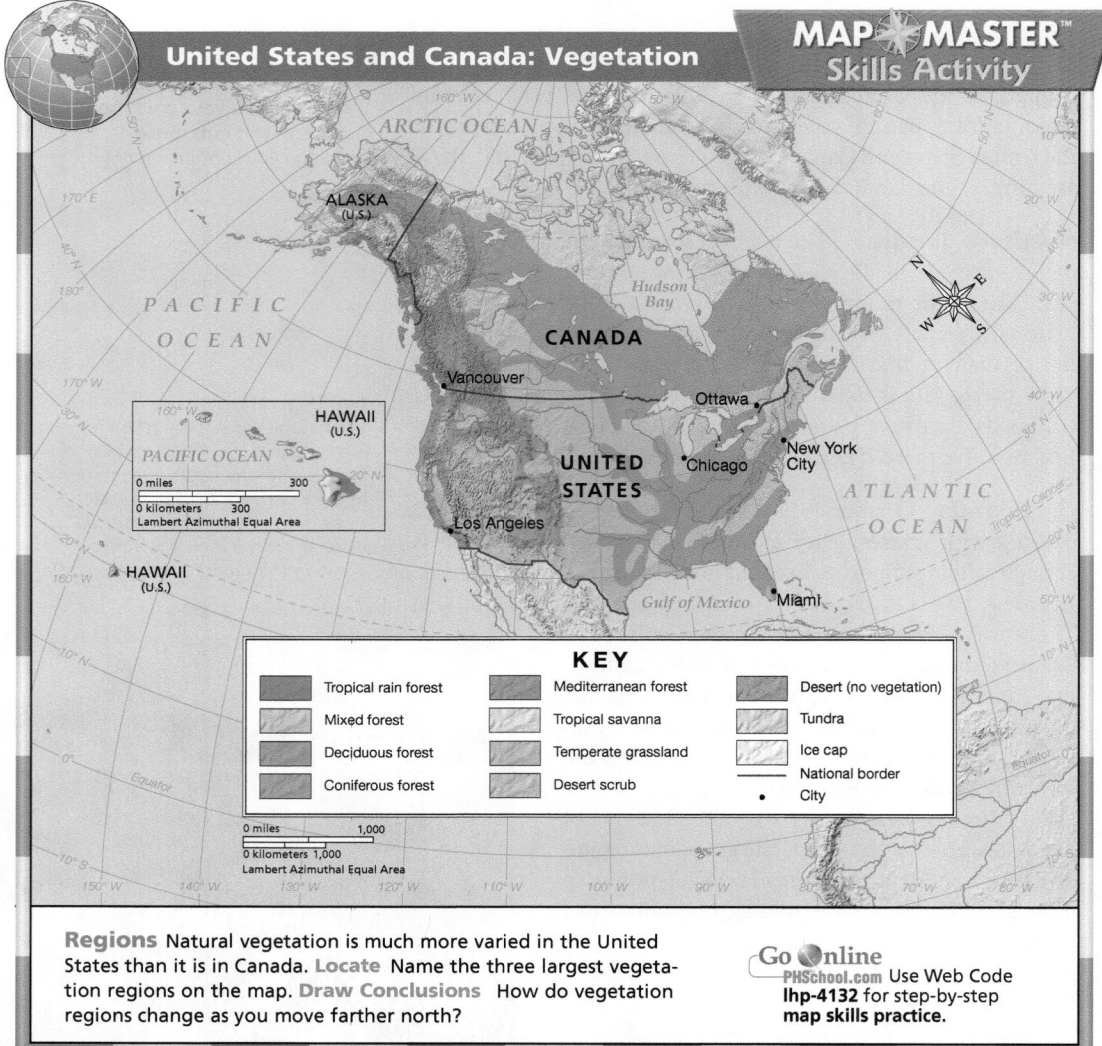

MAP MASTER™ Skills Activity

United States and Canada: Vegetation

KEY

- Tropical rain forest
- Mixed forest
- Deciduous forest
- Coniferous forest
- Mediterranean forest
- Tropical savanna
- Temperate grassland
- Desert scrub
- Desert (no vegetation)
- Tundra
- Ice cap
- National border
- City

Regions Natural vegetation is much more varied in the United States than it is in Canada. **Locate** Name the three largest vegetation regions on the map. **Draw Conclusions** How do vegetation regions change as you move farther north?

Go Online
PHSchool.com Use Web Code
lhp-4132 for step-by-step **map skills practice.**

When pioneers first encountered the prairies in what is now the Midwest, they described it as "a sea of grass." Today, farmers grow fields of corn and soybeans there. Farther west, the Great Plains receive less rainfall. Therefore, only short grasses will grow. These grasses are ideal for grazing cattle. The land is also suitable for growing wheat. The Prairie Provinces, too, have many wheat farms and cattle ranches.

160 United States and Canada

Answers

MAP MASTER™ Skills Activity **Locate** coniferous forest, temperate grassland, and tundra **Draw Conclusions** There are primarily tundra, mixed forest, and coniferous forest regions as you move farther north.

Go Online
PHSchool.com Students may practice their map skills by using the interactive online version of this map.

Skills Mini Lesson

Skills for Life

Analyzing Images   L2

1. Teach the skill by telling students that images supply important information. Tell them to study images carefully and read their captions. While studying images students should ask themselves the following questions: Who or what is the image showing? Where and when does the scene take place? What feeling do I get from it? Why do I think this image was created?

2. Help students practice the skill by helping them answer these questions as they look at the larger photo on page 159. (*The image shows a polar bear in the northern tundra; student answers will vary as to how the image makes them feel and why they think it was created.*)

3. Have students apply the skill by answering the questions as they study the smaller image on page 159.

Desert Scrub With little rainfall, desert and semiarid regions have limited vegetation. What plants there are have adapted to drought conditions or survive through their deep root systems. The Great Basin, a large, dry region between the Rocky Mountains and the Sierra Nevada in the United States, is one example of a desert region. It covers about 190,000 square miles (492,000 square kilometers) of the West and includes Death Valley. The majority of Nevada and western Utah lie within the Great Basin.

The Sierras block the Great Basin from moisture-bearing winds that come off the Pacific Ocean. Thus, the entire region is in a rain shadow. With annual rainfall of only six to twelve inches (15 to 30 centimeters), the basin cannot support large numbers of people. But, many sheep graze on the area's shrubs.

For many years, the Great Basin was an obstacle that delayed the development of the West, because conditions made it difficult for explorers to cross it. Many people sought alternate routes around the Great Basin as they headed west during the California Gold Rush in 1849.

Life in the Desert
Despite little rain and scorching heat, hundreds of plants and animals, such as the scorpion below, live in the desert. **Draw Conclusions** *How might these plants and animals have adapted to the harsh desert environment?*

Have students create the Taking Notes graphic organizer on a blank piece of paper. Ask them to fill in the climate and vegetation information for "Tundra" and "Grassland." Display the *Tree Map/Flow Chart* transparency and model how to fill in a few details to get them started. Then have students complete the graphic organizer by filling in the "Desert Scrub" and "Forest" sections.

📖 **United States and Canada Transparencies,** *Transparency B3: Tree Map/Flow Chart*

Monitor Progress
- Show *Section Reading Support Transparency USC 44* and ask students to check their graphic organizers individually. Go over key concepts and clarify key vocabulary as needed.

📖 **United States and Canada Transparencies,** *Section Reading Support Transparency USC 44*

- Tell students to fill in the last column of the *Reading Readiness Guide*. Probe for what they learned that confirms or invalidates each statement.

All in One **United States and Canada Teaching Resources,** *Reading Readiness Guide*, p. 103

Differentiated Instruction

For Advanced Readers L3
To get a sense of what it might be like to experience a forest in Canada, have students read *Hatchet* and discuss what resources the forest offered to Brian when he was stranded there.

All in One **United States and Canada Teaching Resources,** *Hatchet*, pp. 122–125

For English Language Learners L2
Pair native English-speaking students with English learners and have them read *Hatchet* together. Encourage students to answer each other's questions about the material. Circulate and ask students questions about the material to be sure they understand what they have read.

All in One **United States and Canada Teaching Resources,** *Hatchet*, pp. 122–125

Answer

Draw Conclusions Possible answer: They might have adapted by finding ways to store water and protect themselves from the heat of the sun.

Assess and Reteach

Assess Progress   L2
Have students complete the Section Assessment Administer the *Section Quiz.*

All in One **United States and Canada Teaching Resources,** *Section Quiz,* p. 105

Reteach   L1
If students need more instruction, have them read this section in the Reading and Vocabulary Study Guide.

Chapter 6, Section 2, **Western Hemisphere Reading and Vocabulary Study Guide,** pp. 59–61

Extend   L3
Students can extend their knowledge of climate and its effects on your local environment by working in teams to complete the *Book Project: Set Up a Weather Station.*

All in One **United States and Canada Teaching Resources,** *Book Project: Set Up a Weather Station,* pp. 73–75

Answers

✓Reading Check   tundra, grassland, desert scrub, forest

Section 2 Assessment

Key Terms
Students' sentences should reflect knowledge of each Key Term.

Target Reading Skill
Answers will vary, but students' predictions should involve learning about the climate and vegetation of the United States and Canada.

Comprehension and Critical Thinking
1. (a) The climate on the Pacific coast is generally mild and rainy. The climate just east of the Rocky Mountains is dryer and warmer. Much of the east coast has a continental climate with warm summers and cold winters. Northern Canada has a colder climate than much of the United States.
(b) Water heats up and cools down more slowly than land, making coastal climates more moderate. Winds pick up moisture as they move across the water, bringing more rain to some coastal areas. **(c)** Vancouver, close to the Pacific coast, has mild temperatures all year long. Winnipeg, which is

---

An autumn landscape in the Charlevoix region of Quebec, Canada

Forests   Forests cover nearly one third of the United States and almost one half of Canada. The mild climate of the northern Pacific Coast encourages great forests of coniferous (koh NIF ur us) trees, such as pine, fir, and spruce. Coniferous trees have cones that carry and protect their seeds. The Rockies are blanketed with coniferous forests. From the Great Lakes across southeastern Canada and New England, and down to the southeastern United States, you will find mixed forests. These are forests of coniferous trees mixed with deciduous (dee SIJ oo us) trees. Deciduous trees shed their leaves in the fall.

One of Canada's best-known symbols is the deciduous sugar maple tree. The sugar maple leaf appears on Canada's flag. In addition, sugar maples produce a sweet sap that can be made into maple syrup and maple sugar—two Canadian specialties.

✓ Reading Check   **Name the four major kinds of natural vegetation in the United States and Canada.**

Section 2 Assessment

Key Terms
Review the key terms at the beginning of this section. Use each term in a sentence that explains its meaning.

Target Reading Skill
What did you predict about this section? How did your prediction guide your reading?

Comprehension and Critical Thinking
1. (a) Recall Describe the major climate zones of the United States and Canada.

(b) Summarize How do oceans influence climate?
(c) Generalize What geographic features might lead someone to settle in Vancouver rather than in Winnipeg?
2. (a) Locate Where is the largest prairie in the world?
(b) Infer Why do more people live in the prairies than in the tundra?
(c) Identify Effects How does the vegetation of the prairies affect economic activity there?

Writing Activity
Describe the climate zones you would pass through if you traveled from northwestern Canada to the southeastern United States.

For: An activity on Florida's Everglades
Visit: PHSchool.com
Web Code: lhd-4102

---

inland, has more extreme temperatures and winters get very cold.

2. (a) It stretches from the American central states into the Canadian provinces of Alberta, Saskatchewan, and Manitoba. **(b)** The tundra is extremely cold, so very little can grow there. The prairies have a much warmer climate, more rainfall, and a great deal of natural vegetation. **(c)** The prairies support numerous crops, so many people there make their living as farmers. The natural grasses of the prairies are ideal for cattle ranching.

Writing Activity
Use the *Rubric for Assessing a Writing Assignment* to evaluate students' descriptions.

All in One **United States and Canada Teaching Resources,** *Rubric for Assessing a Writing Assignment,* p. 127

Go Online PHSchool.com   Typing in the Web code when prompted will bring students directly to detailed instructions for this activity.

Resources and Land Use

Prepare to Read

Objectives
In this section you will
1. Learn about the major resources of the United States.
2. Find out about the major resources of Canada.

Taking Notes
As you read the section, look for details about the resources of the United States and Canada. Copy the table below and write each detail under the correct subject heading.

Resource	United States	Canada
Farmland		
Water		
Energy and minerals		
Forests		

 **Target Reading Skill**

Preview and Ask Questions Before you read this section, preview the headings and photographs to see what the section is about. Write one or two questions that will help you understand or remember something important in the section. Then read to answer your questions.

Key Terms
- **alluvial soil** (uh LOO vee ul soyl) *n.* fertile topsoil left by a river, especially after a flood
- **agribusiness** (AG ruh biz niz) *n.* a large company that runs huge farms
- **hydroelectricity** (hy droh ee lek TRIH suh tee) *n.* electric power produced by moving water
- **fossil fuel** (FAHS ul FYOO ul) *n.* a fuel formed over millions of years from animal and plant remains

Surrounded by majestic redwood forests, Carlotta, California, has little more than a gas station and a general store. Yet on one day in September 1996, police arrested more than 1,000 people there. Was Carlotta filled with outlaws like some old Wild West town? No, but it was the scene of a showdown. A logging company wanted to cut down some of the oldest redwood trees in the world. Protesters wanted to preserve the forest and the animals that live there. Both sides believed in the importance of natural resources. But they disagreed strongly about how to use them. As in Carlotta, people all over North America use their natural resources for recreation, industry, and energy.

Redwood National Park, California

Objectives
Social Studies
1. Learn about the major resources of the United States.
2. Find out about the major resources of Canada.

Reading/Language Arts
Learn how to preview and ask questions to see what a reading selection is about.

Prepare to Read

Build Background Knowledge [L2]
Tell students that in this section they will learn about the natural resources that are available in the United States and Canada. Have students preview the headings and visuals in the section with the following question in mind: **How are the resources of the United States and Canada similar?** Use the Idea Wave participation strategy (TE, p. T35) to solicit answers.

Set a Purpose for Reading [L2]
- Preview the Objectives.
- Read each statement in the *Reading Readiness Guide* aloud. Ask students to mark the statements true or false.
- Have students discuss the statements in pairs or groups of four, then mark their worksheets again. Use the Numbered Heads participation strategy (TE, p. T36) to call on students to share their group's perspectives.

All in One United States and Canada Teaching Resources, *Reading Readiness Guide,* p. 107

Vocabulary Builder
Preview Key Terms [L2]
Pronounce each Key Term, then ask the students to say the word with you. Provide a simple explanation such as, "Hydroelectricity comes from dams built on rivers. Hoover Dam in the Colorado River supplies much of the electric power for portions of the United States and Canada."

Target Reading Skill [L2]

Preview and Ask Questions Ask students to focus on the Target Reading Skill. Tell them that they can preview a section to see what they will learn about and create questions that will help them remember important information.

Model previewing and asking questions using page 164. Have students read the page heading and identify what the map shows to preview the page. Tell them they can use this information to write a question such as, "What are the major resources of the United States?" Have students read the subsection, and then reinforce the skill by modeling the answer to the questions.

Give students *Preview and Ask Questions.* Have them complete the activity in groups.

All in One United States and Canada Teaching Resources, *Preview and Ask Questions,* p. 112

Instruct

Resources of the United States [L2]

Guided Instruction

- **Vocabulary Builder** Clarify the high-use words **abundant** and **generate** before reading.

- Read Resources of the United States using the Paragraph Shrinking strategy (TE, p. T34).

- Ask students to explain why they think soil is considered an important natural resource of the United States. *(Possible answer: Without fertile soil, Americans would not be able to grow the crops needed to feed the people of the United States and to sell to other countries to help our economy.)*

- Lead a discussion about what life would be like if the United States did not have access to so much water. *(An absence of water would affect how much Americans were able to drink, make it difficult for farmers to raise crops, make it hard for factories to operate, decrease routes of transportation, and eliminate hydroelectricity as an available energy source.)*

Answers

MAP MASTER Skills Activity **List** The two countries share all of the resources mentioned in the key except for bauxite and phosphates, which only the United States has.

Draw Conclusions Canada's location between the Pacific and Atlantic oceans allows the country to export goods by sea, and its long border with the United States allows for easy trade between the two countries.

Go Online PHSchool.com **Students may practice their map skills by using the interactive online version of this map.**

Resources of the United States

Native Americans, pioneers, and explorers in North America knew centuries ago that it was a land of plenty. Abundant resources helped to build two of the world's leading economies.

Farmland Both the Midwest and the South have rich, dark soils that are suitable for farming. Along the Mississippi and other river valleys are **alluvial** (uh LOO vee ul) **soils**, the fertile topsoil left by a river after a flood. Until the 1900s, most American farms were owned by families. Since then, large companies have bought many family farms. Southern California's Imperial Valley has vast vegetable fields operated by agribusinesses. An **agribusiness** is a large company that runs huge farms.

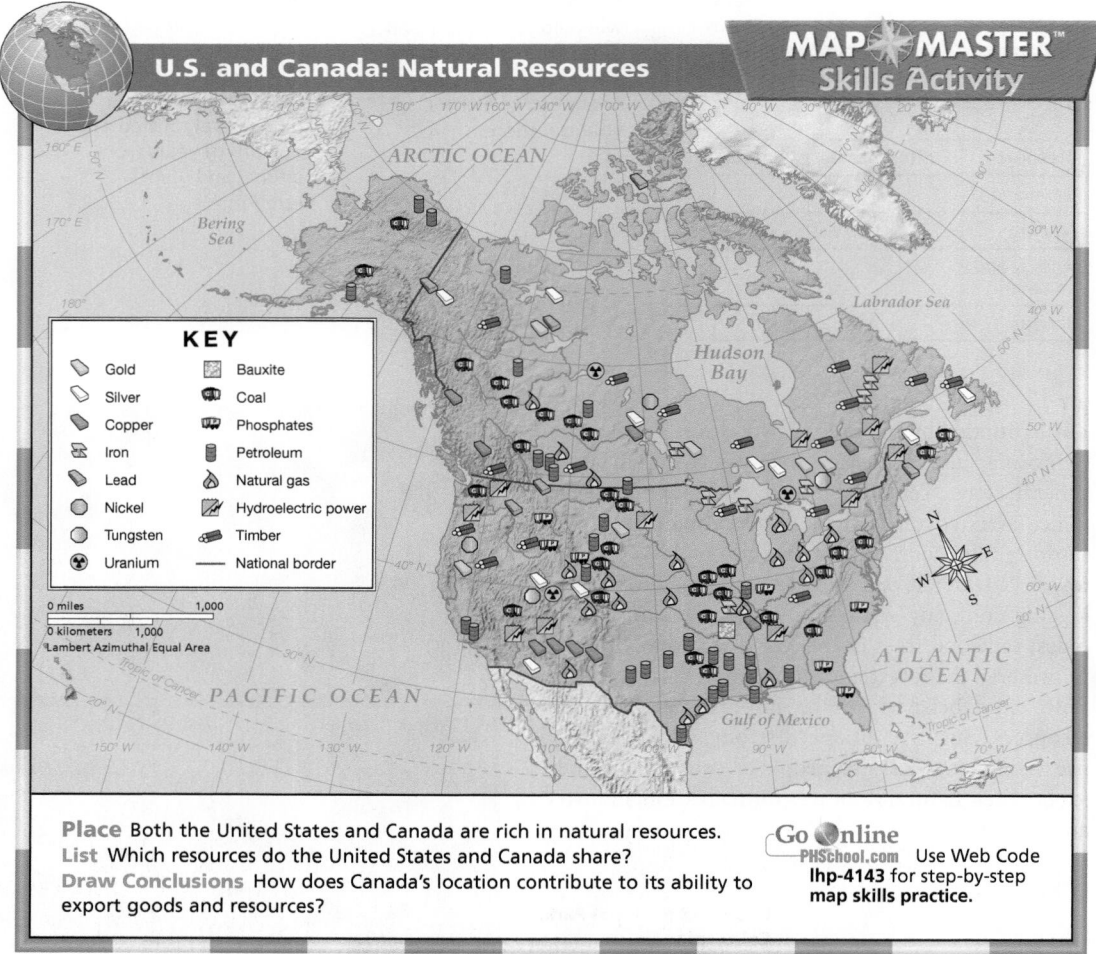

MAP MASTER™ Skills Activity

U.S. and Canada: Natural Resources

KEY

Gold	Bauxite
Silver	Coal
Copper	Phosphates
Iron	Petroleum
Lead	Natural gas
Nickel	Hydroelectric power
Tungsten	Timber
Uranium	National border

0 miles 1,000
0 kilometers 1,000
Lambert Azimuthal Equal Area

Place Both the United States and Canada are rich in natural resources.
List Which resources do the United States and Canada share?
Draw Conclusions How does Canada's location contribute to its ability to export goods and resources?

Go Online PHSchool.com Use Web Code lhp-4143 for step-by-step map skills practice.

164 United States and Canada

Vocabulary Builder

Use the information below to teach students this section's high-use words.

High-Use Word	Definition and Sample Sentence
abundant, p. 164	*adj.* plentiful The perfect weather allowed the farmer to grow an **abundant** crop of corn.
generate, p. 165	*v.* produce The energy **generated** by the battery powered the flashlight.
suitable, p. 167	*adj.* appropriate, fitting The gym was a **suitable** place to hold the dance.
harness, p. 167	*v.* to use or control The dam **harnessed** the power of the waterfall.

Water Water is a vital resource. People need water to drink and to grow crops. Factories rely on water for many industrial processes, including cooling machinery. Both industry and farmers use rivers to transport goods. The Mississippi, Ohio, and Missouri rivers are important shipping routes.

Water is used for other purposes, too. Dams along many rivers produce **hydroelectricity** (hy droh ee lek TRIH suh tee), or electric power generated by moving water. The Grand Coulee (KOO lee) Dam on the Columbia River in the state of Washington produces more hydroelectricity than any other dam in the United States.

An irrigation system watering several fields on a California farm

Forests People have claimed that before Europeans arrived, a squirrel could leap from one tree to another all the way from the Atlantic Coast to the Mississippi River. That is no longer true, but America's forests are still an important resource. Large forests extend across the Pacific Northwest, the South, the Appalachians, and areas around the Great Lakes. They produce lumber, wood pulp for paper, and fine wood for furniture.

Energy and Mineral Resources The United States produces and consumes more fossil fuels than any other country. **Fossil fuels** are sources of energy that formed from animal and plant remains. Petroleum, natural gas, and coal are all fossil fuels. Although the United States imports most of its oil from other countries, the biggest oil reserves in North America are along the northern coast of Alaska. A pipeline carries oil from the wells in Prudhoe Bay to the port of Valdez in the south. From here, giant tankers carry the oil away to be refined.

The Trans-Alaska Pipeline
Workers prepare a section of the 800-mile (1,280-kilometer) pipeline for welding.
Identify Effects *How did the construction of the Trans-Alaska Pipeline produce growth for both the population and the economy of Alaska?*

Chapter 6 Section 3 **165**

Guided Instruction (continued)

- Direct students' attention to the map on page 164, and ask them to identify the major products and resources of Alaska. *(petroleum and coal)*

- Ask students to list the United States' energy and mineral resources. *(Energy resources—petroleum, natural gas, coal, oil; mineral resources—copper, gold, iron ore, lead)*

✔ Skills for Life **Skills Mini Lesson**

Making Generalizations   L2

1. Teach the skill by explaining to students that a generalization is a conclusion drawn from specific facts and applied to a broader situation.

2. Have students practice the skill by reading the text under the heading Water on this page. Point out that the first sentence is a generalization. Then point out that the facts in the rest of the paragraph and in the next paragraph support this generalization.

3. Have students apply the skill by reading the text under the heading Energy and Mineral Resources. Have them make a generalization based on what they read. Then have them write down the sentences from the reading that support their generalizations.

Answer

Identify Effects Workers needed to build and maintain the pipeline may have increased the population of Alaska. The pipeline brings both income and jobs to Alaska, which aids the economy.

Independent Practice

Have students create the Taking Notes graphic organizer on a blank piece of paper and ask them to record details about the resources of the United States. Model how to choose details by selecting one detail and recording it in the correct column.

Monitor Progress

As students fill in the graphic organizer, circulate and make sure students are choosing the correct details. Help students as needed.

◎ Target Reading Skill   L2

Preview and Ask Questions As a follow up, ask students to perform the Target Reading Skill activity in the student edition. (*Students should ask a question that reflects important information from the paragraph, such as "Why is coal a useful natural resource?"*)

Natural Gas Natural gas is a mixture of gases found beneath Earth's surface. To be usable, natural gas must be processed after it is removed from the ground. Its major use is as a fuel. Natural gas heats many homes in the United States. Large gas fields can be found in the Texas Panhandle, Louisiana, and Alaska. Natural gas can be transported by pipeline or in specially designed tanker ships.

Target Skill

Preview and Ask Questions
Ask yourself a question about the paragraph at the right.

Coal Coal is another important fossil fuel. Many power plants burn coal to produce electricity. It is also used to produce steel, as well as to heat and power industrial facilities. The United States has about 2,500 coal mines, totaling nearly 25 percent of the world's coal reserves. Over the past 30 years, modern mining equipment has nearly tripled the productivity of these mines. Wyoming, Kentucky, West Virginia, and Pennsylvania are the main coal-producing states in the country.

Mining In addition, the United States has valuable deposits of copper, gold, iron ore, and lead. Mining accounts for a small percentage of the country's economy and employs less than one percent of its workers. But these minerals are very important to other industries and have fueled industrial expansion.

✓ Reading Check **Why is water an important natural resource?**

Mining Machinery
A coal miner uses a mining machine to dig into the face of a coal deposit. **Analyze** *Why is coal such an important resource in the United States?*

166 United States and Canada

Differentiated Instruction

For Gifted and Talented   L3
Have students conduct Internet or library research to find out the major exports of the United States. Then have them look at the map on page 26 to find out which states produce these products or resources related to the products. Have them create a table showing their findings.

For Less Proficient Readers   L1
Have students complete the *Reading a Natural Resources Map* activity to help them read the map on page 26.

All in One **United States and Canada Teaching Resources,** *Reading a Natural Resources Map,* p. 121

Answers

✓ Reading Check Water is an important natural resource because it is needed to drink, grow crops, cool moving parts in industrial processes, and transport goods by ship.

Analyze Energy gained from coal supports industry in the United States.

Resources of Canada

Canada's first European settlers earned their living as fur trappers, loggers, fishers, and farmers. Today, the economic picture has changed. Less than five percent of Canada's workers earn their living in these ways.

Farmland Less than 10 percent of Canada's land is suitable for farming. Most is located in the Prairie Provinces. This region produces most of Canada's wheat and beef. The St. Lawrence Lowlands are another major agricultural region. This area produces grains, milk, vegetables, and fruits.

Water Canada has more lakes than any other country in the world. About nine percent of the world's fresh water is in Canada. Before the first railroads were built in the 1800s, the only way to reach some parts of the country was by water. Today, the St. Lawrence and Mackenzie rivers serve as important shipping routes.

Minerals and Energy Resources The Canadian Shield contains much of Canada's mineral wealth. Most of the nation's iron ore comes from mines near the Quebec-Newfoundland border. The region also has large deposits of gold, silver, zinc, copper, and uranium. The Prairie Provinces, particularly Alberta, have large oil and natural gas deposits.

Canada harnesses the rivers of Quebec Province to make hydroelectricity. These rivers generate enough hydroelectric power that some of it can be sold to the northeastern United States.

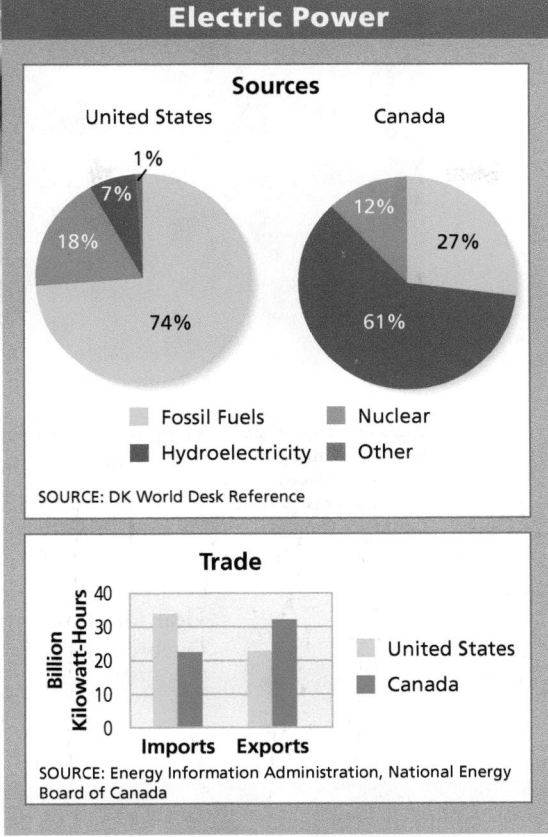

Electric Power

Sources

United States

1%
7%
18%
74%

Canada

12%
27%
61%

Fossil Fuels — Nuclear
Hydroelectricity — Other

SOURCE: DK World Desk Reference

Trade

Billion Kilowatt-Hours
40
30
20
10
0

Imports   Exports

United States
Canada

SOURCE: Energy Information Administration, National Energy Board of Canada

▤ Chart Skills

Both the United States and Canada use fossil fuels to produce electricity. Fossil fuels are nonrenewable resources, meaning that once used they are not easily replaced. The United States and Canada also make use of renewable resources such as the hydroelectricity produced by the dam above. **Name** What energy source produces the largest percentage of Canada's electricity? **Analyze** Which nation is more dependent on the other for its energy? Explain.

Chapter 6 Section 3 **167**

Background: Global Perspectives

Canadian Inventions If necessity is the mother of invention, the world can thank Canada's northerly climate and abundant natural resources for many practical and familiar innovations. For example, kerosene, snowmobiles, and snow blowers all appeared first in Canada. Canada also lays claim to the McIntosh variety of apple.

Assess and Reteach

Assess Progress `L2`

Have students complete the Section Assessment. Administer the *Section Quiz*.

All in One **United States and Canada Teaching Resources,** *Section Quiz,* p. 109

Reteach `L1`

If students need more instruction, have them read this section in the Reading and Vocabulary Study Guide.

Chapter 6, Section 3, **Western Hemisphere Reading and Vocabulary Study Guide,** pp. 62–64

Extend `L3`

Have students work in groups to complete the *Small Group Activity: Creating Travel Posters for National Parks*.

All in One **United States and Canada Teaching Resources,** *Small Group Activity: Creating Travel Posters for National Parks,* pp. 116–119

Answers

 Reading Check The Canadian Shield contains many mineral resources, including iron ore, gold, silver, zinc, copper, and uranium.

Section 3 Assessment

Key Terms
Students' sentences should reflect knowledge of each Key Term.

Target Reading Skill
Students' questions should reflect that they previewed the section and identified important information.

Comprehension and Critical Thinking
1. (a) The major natural resources of the United States include fertile soil, water, energy and mineral resources, and forests.
(b) Because the United States is rich in many energy resources, the country is able to both provide them to its residents and sell them to other countries at a profit. **(c)** Possible answer: A country with few natural resources would have to find a way to buy the resources it needed from other countries.

2. (a) Less than 10 percent of Canada's land can be used for farming. **(b)** Canada uses its water resources as major shipping routes and to generate hydroelectricity. **(c)** The United States and Canada are located on the same continent, and share many physical features,

Tugboats tow huge booms, or lines of connected floating logs, harvested from Canada's forests.

Forests With almost half its land covered in forests, Canada is a leading producer and exporter of timber products. These products include lumber, paper, plywood, and wood pulp. The climate in British Columbia produces Canada's densest tall-timber forests. Large amounts of rain and a long growing season contribute to the growth of large evergreens with hard wood ideal for construction lumber. The provinces of Ontario and Quebec also produce large amounts of timber.

√ **Reading Check** What resources are found in the Canadian Shield?

 ## Section 3 Assessment

Key Terms
Review the key terms at the beginning of this section. Use each term in a sentence that explains its meaning.

Target Reading Skill
What questions did you ask that helped you to learn and remember something from this section?

Comprehension and Critical Thinking
1. (a) List Describe the major natural resources of the United States.

(b) Explain How have energy resources shaped the economy and the standard of living of the United States?
(c) Infer What economic challenges might a country with few natural resources face?
2. (a) Note How much of Canada's land can be used for farming?
(b) Summarize How is water used as a resource in Canada?
(c) Compare Based on what you know about the physical geography of the two countries, in what ways do you think the resources are similar?

Writing Activity
What do you think is the most important resource in the United States and Canada? Write a paragraph explaining your choice.

Writing Tip Be sure to include examples, details, facts, and reasons that support the main idea of your paragraph.

including the Great Lakes, the Interior and Great Plains, and the Rocky Mountains. Thus, the two countries have many similar resources.

Writing Activity
Use *Rubric for Assessing a Writing Assignment* to evaluate students' paragraphs.

All in One **United States and Canada Teaching Resources,** *Rubric for Assessing a Writing Assignment,* p. 127

Chapter 6 Review and Assessment

◆ Chapter Summary

Section 1: Land and Water

- Both the United States and Canada are located in North America.
- The United States and Canada have many mountain ranges and plains areas.
- Bodies of water such as the Great Lakes provide transportation and support industry.

Section 2: Climate and Vegetation

- Climate zones in the United States and Canada range from a desert climate to a polar climate.
- Varied climates in the United States and Canada help to produce varied vegetation.

Section 3: Resources and Land Use

- Farmland, forests, water, and minerals are all important resources for the United States and Canada.
- Natural resources affect the economies of the United States and Canada.

Montana

Scorpion in a desert in California

◆ Key Terms

Use each key term below in a sentence that shows the meaning of the term.

1. agribusiness
2. alluvial soil
3. glacier
4. Great Lakes
5. hydroelectricity
6. Rocky Mountains
7. tributary
8. tundra
9. permafrost
10. prairie
11. province
12. fossil fuel

⌐ Vocabulary Builder

Revisit this chapter's high-use words:

border	ideal	generate
unique	support	suitable
notable	abundant	harness
navigate		

Ask students to review the definitions they recorded on their *Word Knowledge* worksheets.

All in One **United States and Canada Teaching Resources,** *Word Knowledge,* p. 113

Consider allowing students to earn extra credit if they use the words in their answers to the questions in the Chapter Review and Assessment. The words must be used correctly and in a natural context to win the extra points.

Chapter 6 Review and Assessment

Review Chapter Content

- Review the major themes of this chapter by asking students to match the correct Guiding Question to each bulleted statement in the Chapter Summary. Have students determine the number of the Guiding Question that relates to each statement individually, then pair students and have them discuss their classifications with their partner. Refer to page 139 in the Student Edition for text of Guiding Questions.

- Assign *Vocabulary Development* for students to review Key Terms.

  All in One **United States and Canada Teaching Resources,** *Vocabulary Development,* p. 126

Answers

Key Terms

1–12. Students' sentences should reflect knowledge of each Key Term.

Review and Assessment

Comprehension and Critical Thinking

13. (a) a huge plains area, called the Interior Plains in Canada and the Great Plains and the Central Plains in the United States **(b)** In the wetter eastern part of the plains, farmers grow corn and soybeans, while in the drier west, farmers grow wheat.

14. (a) The Canadian Shield is a huge rugged region of ancient rock. **(b)** More people live in the St. Lawrence Lowlands because the Shield has rugged terrain on which nothing can grow, while the Lowlands has fertile soil.

15. (a) The Pacific Ocean heats up and cools down more slowly than land, and winds blowing across the water warm Canada's west coast in the winter and cool it in the summer. **(b)** The weather there is much more extreme, with very cold winters and very hot summers, because the winds that blow across the ocean affect the coast but never reach the country's interior.

16. (a) Regions close to the Equator are much warmer than regions far from the Equator. **(b)** Nunavut is far from the Equator, making its climate very cold. Permafrost prevents a lot of vegetation growth. People who live there must rely on hunting and fishing for food, and adapt their lifestyles to the cold temperatures.

17. (a) natural vegetation **(b)** The climate and vegetation of the tundra affects Inuit life in that they must hunt and fish for food, rather than grow crops, and their clothing, methods of transportation, and homes have been created to withstand snow and cold.

18. (a) families **(b)** Today, agribusinesses run most American farms. **(c)** This change has made it difficult for individual and family farmers to compete in the marketplace, as they cannot grow as many crops or keep their costs as low as agribusinesses can.

Skills Practice

Topic: whether or not to cut down old redwood trees in Carlotta, California
Possible reasons for differing opinions: The people who work for the logging company might feel that they need the forest to make a profit and make a living. The protesters might feel that it is more important to preserve the forest because redwood trees of that age cannot be easily replaced.

Review and Assessment (continued)

◆ Comprehension and Critical Thinking

13. (a) Identify What landform lies between the Rocky and Appalachian mountains?
(b) Draw Conclusions How does climate affect the crops grown there?

14. (a) Define What is the Canadian Shield?
(b) Compare and Contrast Why do more people live in the St. Lawrence Lowlands than on the Canadian Shield?

15. (a) Explain How does the Pacific Ocean help to keep Canada's west coast climate mild?
(b) Contrast How does the west coast climate differ from the climate that Canada's Interior Plains experiences? Explain.

16. (a) Explain How does latitude affect climate?
(b) Apply Information How might geography and climate affect the way people live in the Canadian territory of Nunavut?

17. (a) Recall Tundra, grassland, desert scrub, and forests are major types of what?
(b) Identify Cause and Effect How do the climate and vegetation of the tundra affect how Inuits live?

18. (a) Identify Until the 1900s, who owned and ran most American farms?
(b) Explore the Main Idea How are most American farms run today?
(c) Draw Conclusions How has this change in ownership affected American farmers?

◆ Skills Practice

Identifying Frame of Reference Review the steps you followed in the Skills for Life activity in this chapter. Then reread the first two paragraphs of Section 3. First, identify the topic being discussed. Then, list some reasons why the logging company and the protesters might have different opinions on how to use natural resources. Finally, identify the frames of reference for people on both sides of the issue.

◆ Writing Activity: Science

Suppose that you are a meteorologist, or a scientist who studies Earth's weather patterns. Create two possible weather maps for the United States and Canada. One map should show a typical winter day and the other a typical summer day. The weather maps should show changes in the weather across the two countries.

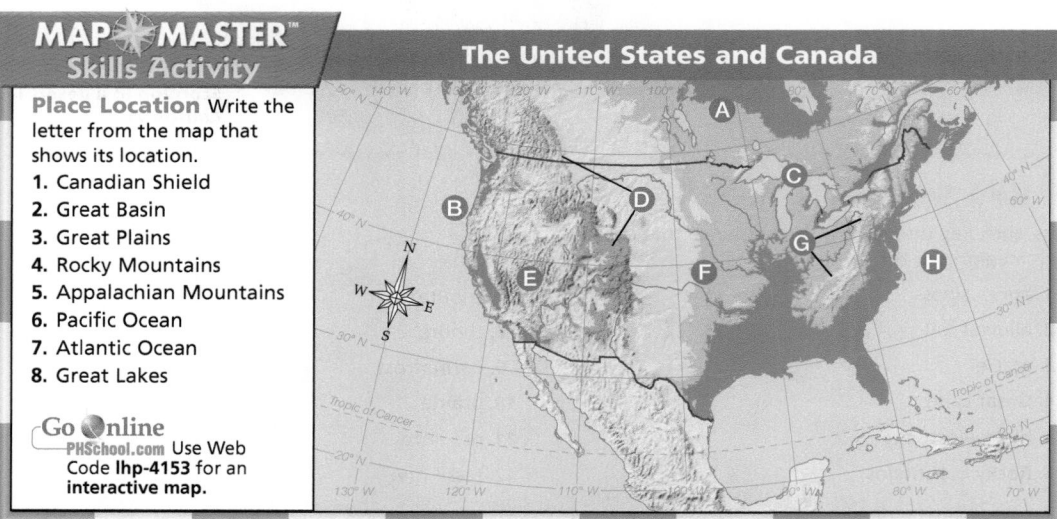

MAP MASTER™
Skills Activity

The United States and Canada

Place Location Write the letter from the map that shows its location.
1. Canadian Shield
2. Great Basin
3. Great Plains
4. Rocky Mountains
5. Appalachian Mountains
6. Pacific Ocean
7. Atlantic Ocean
8. Great Lakes

Go Online
PHSchool.com Use Web Code **lhp-4153** for an **interactive map**.

170 United States and Canada

Possible frames of reference: The frame of reference for the logging company would be that of a company who wants to expand their business, provide jobs for many people, and make a profit. The frame of reference for the protesters would be that of environmentalists who want to preserve unique natural resources.

Writing Activity: Science
Students' weather maps should reflect an understanding in the general summer and winter climates for the United States and Canada. Use *Rubric for Assessing a Map Produced by a Student* to evaluate students' weather maps.

All in One United States and Canada Teaching Resources, *Rubric for Assessing a Map Produced by a Student,* p. 128

Standardized Test Prep

Test-Taking Tips

Some questions on standardized tests ask you to make mental maps. Read the paragraph below. Then follow the tips to answer the sample question about Canada.

> Jessie is working on a crossword puzzle. She studies the following clue and knows the correct answer: Which large Canadian city is located on one of the Great Lakes?
>
> What is her answer?

TIP Try to picture a map of the United States and Canada. Then try to place each of the cities on this mental map—from east to west.

Make a mental map of the United States and Canada. Then pick the letter that best answers the question.

A Ottawa
B Toronto
C ~~Chicago~~
D ~~Vancouver~~

TIP Rule out choices that do not make sense. Then choose the best answer from the remaining choices.

Think It Through You can rule out Vancouver because it is on the west coast of Canada. Chicago is on Lake Michigan, but it is in the United States. That leaves Ottawa and Toronto. Ottawa is farther north than Toronto. It is on a waterway, the Ottawa River, but not on one of the Great Lakes. The answer is B, Toronto, which is on Lake Ontario.

Practice Questions

Use the tips above and other tips in this book to help you answer the following questions.

1. Because of its location near the Pacific Ocean and the Coast Mountains, Canada's northwestern coast is
   A hot and dry.
   B bitterly cold.
   C wet and snowy.
   D wet and mild.

2. Which vegetation region shared by the United States and Canada is the largest in the world of its kind?
   A prairie
   B tundra
   C desert
   D savanna

3. The United States is the world's second-largest producer of
   A coal, petroleum, and natural gas.
   B iron ore.
   C hydroelectricity.
   D wood and wood products.

Make a mental map of Canada. Then answer the question below.

4. This region of Canada lies east of the Interior Plains. It covers about half of Canada. Few people live in this region.
   A the St. Lawrence Lowlands
   B the Canadian Shield
   C the Laurentian Highlands
   D the St. Lawrence Seaway

Use Web Code lha-4103 for a **Chapter 6 self-test.**

Chapter 6 **171**

Standardized Test Prep

Answers

1. D
2. A
3. A
4. B

Assessment Resources

Use *Chapter Tests A and B* to assess students' mastery of chapter content.

All in One **United States and Canada Teaching Resources,** *Chapter Tests A and B*, pp. 129–134

Tests are also available on the **Exam***View*® **Test Bank CD-ROM.**

⊙ **Exam***View*® **Test Bank CD-ROM**

The United States and Canada: Shaped by History

Chapter Overview

Overview

Section 1

The Arrival of the Europeans
1. Learn who the first Americans were.
2. Discover the effects the arrival of Europeans had on Native Americans.
3. Find out how the United States won its independence from Great Britain.

Section 2

Growth and Conflict in the United States
1. Explore the effects of westward expansion in the United States.
2. Discover the causes and effects of the Civil War.

Section 3

The United States on the Brink of Change
1. Explore what happened in the United States from 1865 to 1914.
2. Find out what happened during the World Wars.
3. Explore the challenges the United States faces at home and abroad.

Section 4

The History of Canada
1. Learn about why France and Britain were rivals in Canada.
2. Discover how Canada became an independent nation.
3. Explore how Canada became a world power in the 1900s.

Section 5

The United States and Canada Today
1. Identify the environmental concerns the United States and Canada share today.
2. Find out about the economic ties the United States and Canada have to each other and to the world.

Technology Resources

Students use embedded Web codes to access Internet activities, chapter self-tests, and additional map practice. They may also access Dorling Kindersley's Online Desk Reference to learn more about each country they study.

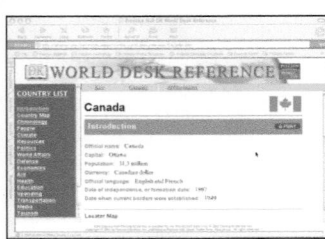

Use the Interactive Textbook to make content and concepts come alive through animations, videos, and activities that accompany the complete basal text—online and on CD-ROM.

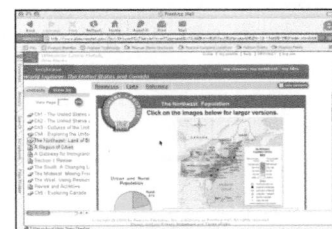

PRENTICE HALL
TeacherEXPRESS™
Plan • Teach • Assess

Use this complete suite of powerful teaching tools to make planning lessons and administering tests quicker and easier.

Reading and Assessment

Reading and Vocabulary Instruction

🔊 Model the Target Reading Skill

Clarifying Meaning There are several strategies readers can use to help clarify the meanings of words in passages. First, they can reread or read ahead, looking for connections among words. Next, they can paraphrase, or restate what they have read in their own words. Finally, readers can summarize, or state the main points. Write this selection from Chapter 7 on the board:

Many Americans believed that the United States had a right to own all the land from the Atlantic to the Pacific. This belief, called Manifest Destiny, was used to justify further westward expansion. In the 1840s, American wagon trains began to cross the continent heading for the West.

Ask students to read the passage, stopping at the words *Manifest Destiny.* Have them reread the sentence to find words to clarify the meaning of this term. Have a volunteer come to the board and draw a line under the words that help to explain *Manifest Destiny (the United States had a right to own all the land from the Atlantic to the Pacific).* Ask students to read ahead. Draw a double line under the words and phrases that help students further clarify the meaning *(justify further westward expansion).* Challenge students to restate the passage in their own words and state the most important points of the passage in a sentence or two.

Use the following worksheets from All-in-One United States and Canada Teaching Resources (pp. 159–161) to support this chapter's Target Reading Skill.

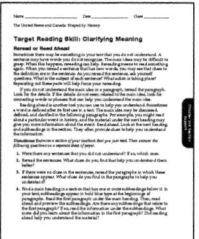 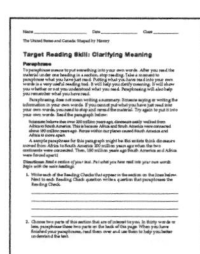 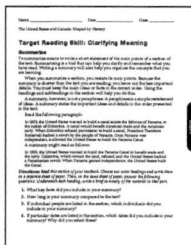

Vocabulary Builder

High-Use Academic Words

Use these steps to teach this chapter's high-use words:

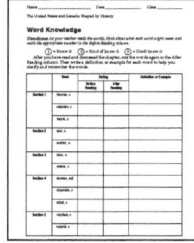

1. Have students rate how well they know each word on their Word Knowledge worksheets (All-in-One United States and Canada Teaching Resources, p. 162).
2. Pronounce each word and ask students to repeat it.
3. Give students a brief definition and sample sentence (provided on TE pp. 175, 181, 188, 194 and 203).
4. Work with students as they fill in the "Definition or Example" column of their Word Knowledge worksheets.

Assessment

Formal Assessment

Test students' understanding of core knowledge and skills.

Chapter Tests A and B, All-in-One United States and Canada Teaching Resources, pp. 185–190

Customize the Chapter Tests to suit your needs.

Exam*View*® Test Bank CD-ROM

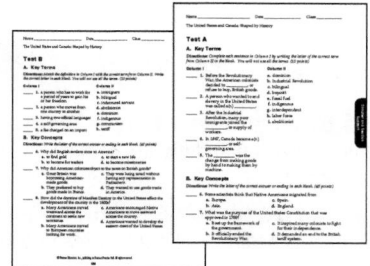

Skills Assessment

Assess geographic literacy.

MapMaster Skills, Student Edition, pp. 173, 177, 181, 182, 184, 196, 204, 210

Assess reading and comprehension.

Target Reading Skills, Student Edition, pp. 178, 184, 188, 196, 206, and in Section Assessments

Chapter 7 Assessment, Western Hemisphere Reading and Vocabulary Study Guide, p. 81

Performance Assessment

Assess students' performance on this chapter's Writing Activities using the following rubrics from All-in-One United States and Canada Teaching Resources.

Rubric for Assessing a Writing Assignment, p. 183

Rubric for Assessing a Journal Entry, p. 184

Assess students' work through performance tasks.

Small Group Activity: Presenting an Oral Biography, United States and Canada Teaching Resources, pp. 165–168

Online Assessment

Have students check their own understanding.

Chapter Self-Test

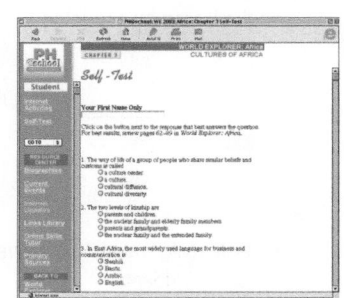

Section 1 The Arrival of the Europeans

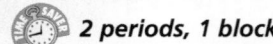 *2 periods, 1 block*

Social Studies Objectives

1. Learn who the first Americans were.
2. Discover the effects the arrival of Europeans had on Native Americans.
3. Find out how the United States won its independence from Great Britain.

Reading/Language Arts Objective

Learn how to clarify and understand new words and ideas in a text by rereading.

Prepare to Read	Instructional Resources	Differentiated Instruction
Build Background Knowledge Preview the section and discuss settlement in North America. **Set a Purpose for Reading** Have students begin to fill out the *Reading Readiness Guide.* **Preview Key Terms** Teach the section's Key Terms. **Target Reading Skill** Introduce the section's Target Reading Skill of **rereading**.	**All in One United States and Canada Teaching Resources** L2 Reading Readiness Guide, p. 140 L2 Reread or Read Ahead, p. 159	**Spanish Reading and Vocabulary Study Guide** L1 Chapter 7, Section 1, pp. 50–51 ELL

Instruct	Instructional Resources	Differentiated Instruction
The First Americans **The Europeans Arrive** Discuss the first people who came to America, and colonization of the Americas and its effects. **Eyewitness Technology** Have students read about and discuss life in a Pueblo village. **The Break With Britain** Discuss how the Revolutionary War began. **Target Reading Skill** Review **rereading**.	**All in One United States and Canada Teaching Resources** L2 Guided Reading and Review, p. 141 L2 Reading Readiness Guide, p. 140 Rubric for Assessing a Writing Assignment, p. 183 **United States and Canada Transparencies** L2 Section Reading Support Transparency USC 46	**Spanish Support** L2 Guided Reading and Review (Spanish), p. 66 ELL

Assess and Reteach	Instructional Resources	Differentiated Instruction
Assess Progress Evaluate student comprehension with the section assessment and section quiz. **Reteach** Assign the Reading and Vocabulary Study Guide to help struggling students. **Extend** Extend the lesson by assigning a primary source reading.	**All in One United States and Canada Teaching Resources** L2 Section Quiz, p. 142 L3 Closing Speech to the Constitutional Convention, September 17, 1787, pp. 172–173 Rubric for Assessing a Writing Assignment, p. 183 **Reading and Vocabulary Study Guide** L1 Chapter 7, Section 1, pp. 66–68	**Spanish Support** L2 Section Quiz (Spanish), p. 67 ELL

Key

L1 Basic to Average   L3 Average to Advanced
L2 For All Students

LPR Less Proficient Readers
AR Advanced Readers
SN Special Needs Students

GT Gifted and Talented
ELL English Language Learners

Section 2 Growth and Conflict in the United States

 *2 periods, 1 block*

Social Studies Objectives
1. Explore the effects of westward expansion in the United States.
2. Discover the causes and effects of the Civil War.

Reading/Language Arts Objective
Learn how to clarify words or ideas in a text by reading ahead.

Prepare to Read

Build Background Knowledge
Discuss what students already know about American history.

Set a Purpose for Reading
Have students begin to fill out the *Reading Readiness Guide.*

Preview Key Terms
Teach the section's Key Terms.

Target Reading Skill
Introduce the section's Target Reading Skill of **reading ahead.**

Instructional Resources

All in One United States and Canada Teaching Resources
- L2 Reading Readiness Guide, p. 144
- L2 Reread or Read Ahead, p. 159

Differentiated Instruction

Spanish Reading and Vocabulary Study Guide
- L1 Chapter 7, Section 2, pp. 52–53 ELL

Instruct

A Nation Grows
Discuss the major events that occurred in the United States during the early to middle 1800s.

The Civil War and Reconstruction
Ask questions about abolition and the Civil War.

Target Reading Skill
Review **reading ahead.**

Instructional Resources

All in One United States and Canada Teaching Resources
- L2 Guided Reading and Review, p. 145
- L2 Reading Readiness Guide, p. 144

United States and Canada Transparencies
- L2 Section Reading Support Transparency USC 47

Differentiated Instruction

All in One United States and Canada Teaching Resources
- L3 Morning Girl, pp. 174–176 AR, GT
- L3 Journal Entry, p. 177 AR, GT
- L3 Chief Joseph Surrenders, p. 178 AR, GT

Teacher's Edition
- L3 For Advanced Readers, TE p. 182

Spanish Support
- L2 Guided Reading and Review (Spanish), p. 68 ELL

Assess and Reteach

Assess Progress
Evaluate student comprehension with the section assessment and section quiz.

Reteach
Assign the Reading and Vocabulary Study Guide to help struggling students.

Extend
Extend the lesson by assigning a Small Group Activity.

Instructional Resources

All in One United States and Canada Teaching Resources
- L2 Section Quiz, p. 146
- L3 Small Group Activity: Presenting an Oral Biography, pp. 165–168
  Rubric for Assessing a Journal Entry, p. 184

Reading and Vocabulary Study Guide
- L1 Chapter 7, Section 2, pp. 69–71

Differentiated Instruction

Spanish Support
- L2 Section Quiz (Spanish), p. 69 ELL

Key
- L1 Basic to Average
- L2 For All Students
- L3 Average to Advanced
- LPR Less Proficient Readers
- AR Advanced Readers
- SN Special Needs Students
- GT Gifted and Talented
- ELL English Language Learners

Section 3 The United States on the Brink of Change

2 periods, 1 block

Social Studies Objectives

1. Explore what happened in the United States from 1865 to 1914.
2. Find out what happened during the World Wars.
3. Explore the challenges the United States faces at home and abroad.

Reading/Language Arts Objective

Use paraphrasing to help you understand what you read.

Prepare to Read	Instructional Resources	Differentiated Instruction
Build Background Knowledge Ask students to complete an idea web with details about the United States as a world power. **Set a Purpose for Reading** Have students evaluate statements on the *Reading Readiness Guide*. **Preview Key Terms** Teach the section's Key Terms. **Target Reading Skill** Introduce the section's Target Reading Skill of **paraphrasing**.	**All in One United States and Canada Teaching Resources** L2 Reading Readiness Guide, p. 148 L2 Paraphrase, p. 160	**Spanish Reading and Vocabulary Study Guide** L1 Chapter 7, Section 3, pp. 54–55 ELL

Instruct	Instructional Resources	Differentiated Instruction
From 1865 to 1914 Discuss different attempts to fight poverty. **Target Reading Skill** Review **paraphrasing**. **The World at War** Discuss the Great Depression and World War II. **The U.S. at Home and Abroad** Discuss the tension between the United States and the Soviet Union, and ask about the civil rights movement in the United States.	**All in One United States and Canada Teaching Resources** L2 Guided Reading and Review, p. 149 L2 Reading Readiness Guide, p. 148 **United States and Canada Transparencies** L2 Section Reading Support Transparency USC 48	**All in One United States and Canada Teaching Resources** L1 Book Project: Make a Timeline of Local History, pp. 79–81 ELL, LPR, SN **Teacher's Edition** L1 For English Language Learners, TE p. 190 L3 For Gifted and Talented, TE p. 190 L3 For Advanced Readers, TE p. 191 L1 For Special Needs Students, TE p. 191 **Spanish Support** L1 Guided Reading and Review (Spanish), p. 70 ELL

Assess and Reteach	Instructional Resources	Differentiated Instruction
Assess Progress Evaluate student comprehension with the section assessment and section quiz. **Reteach** Assign the Reading and Vocabulary Study Guide to help struggling students. **Extend** Extend the lesson by assigning a primary source reading.	**All in One United States and Canada Teaching Resources** L2 Section Quiz, p. 150 L3 A Child in Prison Camp, pp. 179–181 Rubric for Assessing a Writing Assignment, p. 183 **Reading and Vocabulary Study Guide** L1 Chapter 7, Section 3, pp. 72–74	**Spanish Support** L2 Section Quiz (Spanish), p. 71 ELL

Key

L1 Basic to Average   L3 Average to Advanced

L2 For All Students

LPR Less Proficient Readers
AR Advanced Readers
SN Special Needs Students

GT Gifted and Talented
ELL English Language Learners

Section 4 The History of Canada

3.5 periods, 1.75 blocks (includes Skills for Life)

Social Studies Objectives
1. Learn about why France and Britain were rivals in Canada.
2. Discover how Canada became an independent nation.
3. Explore how Canada became a world power in the 1900s.

Reading/Language Arts Objective
Use summarizing to help comprehend the main points you have read.

Prepare to Read	Instructional Resources	Differentiated Instruction
Build Background Knowledge As a class, compare the histories of Canada and the United States. **Set a Purpose for Reading** Have students evaluate statements on the *Reading Readiness Guide*. **Preview Key Terms** Teach the section's Key Terms. **Target Reading Skill** Introduce the section's Target Reading Skill of **summarizing**.	**All in One United States and Canada Teaching Resources** L2 Reading Readiness Guide, p. 152 L2 Summarize, p. 161	**Spanish Reading and Vocabulary Study Guide** L1 Chapter 7, Section 4, pp. 56–57 ELL

Instruct	Instructional Resources	Differentiated Instruction
The French and the British Discuss the conflicts between the French and the British in Canada. **Canada Seeks Independence** Ask questions about and discuss Canada's independence. **Target Reading Skill** Review **summarizing**. **Canada: Postwar to the Present** Discuss how Canada changed after World War II.	**All in One United States and Canada Teaching Resources** L2 Guided Reading and Review, p. 153 L2 Reading Readiness Guide, p. 152 **United States and Canada Transparencies** L2 Section Reading Support Transparency USC 49	**All in One United States and Canada Teaching Resources** L2 Activity Shop Interdisciplinary: Transportation, pp. 169–170 ELL, LPR, SN L2 Skills for Life, p. 164 AR, GT, LPR, SN **Teacher's Edition** L1 For English Language Learners, TE p. 196 L1 For Special Needs Students, TE p. 196 L1 For Less Proficient Readers, TE p. 198 L3 For Gifted and Talented, TE p. 198 **Student Edition on Audio CD** L1 Chapter 7, Section 4 ELL, LPR, SN

Assess and Reteach	Instructional Resources	Differentiated Instruction
Assess Progress Evaluate student comprehension with the section assessment and section quiz. **Reteach** Assign the Reading and Vocabulary Study Guide to help struggling students. **Extend** Extend the lesson by assigning an Enrichment activity.	**All in One United States and Canada Teaching Resources** L2 Section Quiz, p. 154 L3 Enrichment, p. 163 Rubric for Assessing a Writing Assignment, p. 183 **Reading and Vocabulary Study Guide** L1 Chapter 7, Section 4, pp. 75–77	**All in One United States and Canada Teaching Resources** L3 Reading a Diagram, p. 171 AR, GT **Teacher's Edition** L1 For Special Needs Students, TE p. 201 L3 For Gifted and Talented, TE p. 201 **Spanish Support** L2 Section Quiz (Spanish), p. 73 ELL

Key
L1 Basic to Average   L3 Average to Advanced
L2 For All Students

LPR Less Proficient Readers
AR Advanced Readers
SN Special Needs Students

GT Gifted and Talented
ELL English Language Learners

Section 5 The United States and Canada Today

 4 periods, 2 blocks (includes Chapter Review and Assessment)

Social Studies Objectives
1. Identify the environmental concerns the United States and Canada share today.
2. Find out about the economic ties the United States and Canada have to each other and to the world.

Reading/Language Arts Objective
Use the rereading or reading ahead strategies to better understand the words and ideas in a text.

Prepare to Read	Instructional Resources	Differentiated Instruction
Build Background Knowledge Have students brainstorm different ways to protect the environment. **Set a Purpose for Reading** Have students evaluate statements on the *Reading Readiness Guide.* **Preview Key Terms** Teach the section's Key Terms. **Target Reading Skill** Introduce the section's Target Reading Skill of **rereading or reading ahead.**	**All in One United States and Canada Teaching Resources** L2 Reading Readiness Guide, p. 156 L2 Reread or Read Ahead, p. 159	**Spanish Reading and Vocabulary Study Guide** L1 Chapter 7, Section 5, pp. 58–59 ELL

Instruct	Instructional Resources	Differentiated Instruction
Environmental Issues Ask about the effects of pollution and discuss ways to combat it. **Target Reading Skill** Review **rereading.** **"Economics Has Made Us Partners"** Ask questions about and discuss the economic partnership between the United States and Canada.	**All in One United States and Canada Teaching Resources** L2 Guided Reading and Review, p. 157 L2 Reading Readiness Guide, p. 156 **United States and Canada Transparencies** L2 Section Reading Support Transparency USC 50	**All in One United States and Canada Teaching Resources** L3 Book Project: Write A Children's Book, pp. 76–78 AR, GT **Teacher's Edition** L1 For Special Needs Students, TE p. 204 L3 For Advanced Readers, TE p. 206 L1 For English Language Learners, TE p. 207 L3 For Gifted and Talented, TE p. 207 **United States and Canada Transparencies** L1 Transparency B10: Effects Chart ELL, LPR, SN **PHSchool.com** L3 **For:** Long-Term Integrated Projects: Mapping World Trade **Web Code:** lhd-4206 AR, GT

Assess and Reteach	Instructional Resources	Differentiated Instruction
Assess Progress Evaluate student comprehension with the section assessment and section quiz. **Reteach** Assign the Reading and Vocabulary Study Guide to help struggling students. **Extend** Extend the lesson by assigning an online activity.	**All in One United States and Canada Teaching Resources** L2 Section Quiz, p. 158 Rubric for Assessing a Writing Assignment, p. 183 L2 Vocabulary Development, p. 182 L2 Word Knowledge, p. 162 L2 Chapter Tests A and B, pp. 185–190 **Reading and Vocabulary Study Guide** L1 Chapter 7, Section 5, pp. 78–80	**Spanish Support** L2 Section Quiz (Spanish), p. 75 ELL L2 Chapter Summary (Spanish), p. 76 ELL L2 Vocabulary Development (Spanish), p. 77 ELL **PHSchool.com** L3 **For:** Environmental and Global Issues: The Imbalance of Energy Consumption **Web code:** lhd-4207

Key
L1 Basic to Average   L3 Average to Advanced   LPR Less Proficient Readers   GT Gifted and Talented
L2 For All Students   AR Advanced Readers   ELL English Language Learners
SN Special Needs Students

Reading Background

Pre-Teaching Vocabulary

Research literature on academic vocabulary instruction indicates that effective strategies require students to go beyond simply looking up dictionary definitions or examining the context. Vocabulary learning must be based on the learner's dynamic engagement in constructing understanding.

If students are not retaining the meaning of the Key Terms or high-use words, use this extended vocabulary sequence to engage them in learning new words.

1. Present the word in writing and point out the part of speech.
2. Pronounce the word and have students pronounce the word.
3. Provide a range of familiar synonyms (or "it's like" words) before offering definitions.
4. Provide an accessible definition and concrete examples, or "showing sentences."
5. Rephrase the simple definition or example sentence, asking students to complete the statement by substituting the word aloud.
6. Check for understanding by providing an application task/question requiring critical thinking.

Sample instructional sequence:

1. Our first word is *abolitionist*. It is a noun, a word that names a person, place, or thing. In this case, it is a person.
2. Say the word *abolitionist* after me. (Students repeat.)
3. An *abolitionist* is like a *reformer* or an *activist*.
4. The word *abolitionist* means *a person who believed that enslaving people was wrong, and wanted to end the practice.* The *abolitionist* hid runaway slaves in her home.
5. An _____ would not return a runaway slave to his or her master. (Students substitute missing word.)
6. Was Harriet Beecher Stowe an abolitionist? Yes-No-Why? (Refer students to page 185 to help them answer the question.)

Word Wizard: Going Beyond the Classroom

Challenge students to take their word knowledge beyond the classroom to find or use Key Terms in their everyday lives. Work with students to set up a system in which students earn points for bringing in evidence of having heard, seen, or used the Key Terms outside the classroom. *Boycott, free trade,* and *civil rights* are terms that are likely to appear in newspapers, or on radio or television news shows. *Bilingual* is a term that students might hear at school. And *abolitionist,* a more obscure term for everyday use, is likely to appear in books or movies about the Civil War.

World Studies Background

The Great Compromise

Written in 1787, the United States Constitution was an exercise in political compromise. Delegates argued whether the number of representatives in the legislature should be the same for each state, or different depending upon a state's population. The framers eventually adopted a proposal for a legislature that included both a *Senate*, in which all states were equally represented, and a *House of Representatives*, in which representation would be based on the state's free population, plus three fifths of its slave population. This came to be called "The Great Compromise."

Canada's Role in World War II

In 1939, Canada's Parliament voted in a virtually unanimous decision to declare war on Germany, assuming that Canadians would primarily contribute supplies to the war effort. In the summer of 1940, as Canada's allies in Europe began falling to the Germans, Canada realized it would have to take a more active part in the war.

The first step was to sign an agreement with the United States for the defense of North America. More than one million Canadians served in the armed forces. Canadian troops fought in Italy and were part of the Normandy Invasion in June 1944. In addition to soldiers, Canada provided food, money, and weapons to the war effort.

Guiding Questions

Remind students about the Guiding Questions introduced at the beginning of this section.

Section 1 relates to **Guiding Question** ②
How have historical events affected the cultures of the United States and Canada? *(The United States became independent from Britain.)*

Section 2 relates to **Guiding Question** ②
How have historical events affected the cultures of the United States and Canada? *(The Industrial Revolution brought new technology, and the Civil War ended slavery.)*

Section 3 relates to **Guiding Question** ②
How have historical events affected the cultures of the United States and Canada? *(Reformers fought for civil rights and the United States took on greater responsibility in world affairs.)*

Section 4 relates to **Guiding Question** ②
How have historical events affected the cultures of the United States and Canada? *(Canada gained its independence, grew industrially, and adopted a constitution.)*

Section 5 relates to **Guiding Question** ⑤
How did the United States and Canada become two of the wealthiest nations in the world? *(The St. Lawrence Seaway and trade agreements have helped them become economic powers.)*

⦿ Target Reading Skill

In this chapter, students will learn and apply the reading skill of clarifying meaning. Use the following worksheets to help students practice this skill:

All in One United States and Canada Teaching Resources, *Reread or Read Ahead,* p. 159; *Paraphrase,* p. 160; *Summarize,* p. 161

Differentiated Instruction

The following Teacher Edition strategies are suitable for students of varying abilities.

Advanced Readers pp. 182, 191, 204
English Language Learners pp. 190, 196, 207
Gifted and Talented pp. 190, 198, 201, 204, 207
Less Proficient Readers p. 198
Special Needs Students pp. 191, 196, 201, 204

The U.S. and Canada: Shaped by History

Chapter Preview

This chapter presents the history of the United States and Canada and shows how that history affects the region to this day.

Section 1
The Arrival of the Europeans

Section 2
Growth and Conflict in the United States

Section 3
The United States on the Brink of Change

Section 4
The History of Canada

Section 5
The United States and Canada Today

Target Reading Skill

Clarifying Meaning In this chapter you will focus on skills you can use to clarify meaning as you read.

▶ The Washington Monument as seen from the Lincoln Memorial in Washington, D.C.

172 United States and Canada

Bibliography

For the Teacher

Berkin, Carol. *Making America: A History of the United States.* Houghton Mifflin Co., 2002.

Brown, Craig. *The Illustrated History of Canada.* Key Porter Books, 2003.

Josephy, Alvin M. *500 Nations: An Illustrated History of North American Indians.* Knopf, 1998.

Zinn, Howard. *A People's History of the United States, Abridged and Updated Teaching Edition.* New Press, 2003.

For the Student

L1 Bowers, Vivian. *Only in Canada: From the Colossal to the Kooky (Wow Canada).* Owl Books, 2002.

L2 Hakim, Joy. *A History of Us: From Colonies to Country (A History of Us, Vol. 4.)* Oxford Univ Pr Children's Books, 2002.

L3 McPherson, James M. *Fields of Fury: The American Civil War.* Atheneum, 2002.

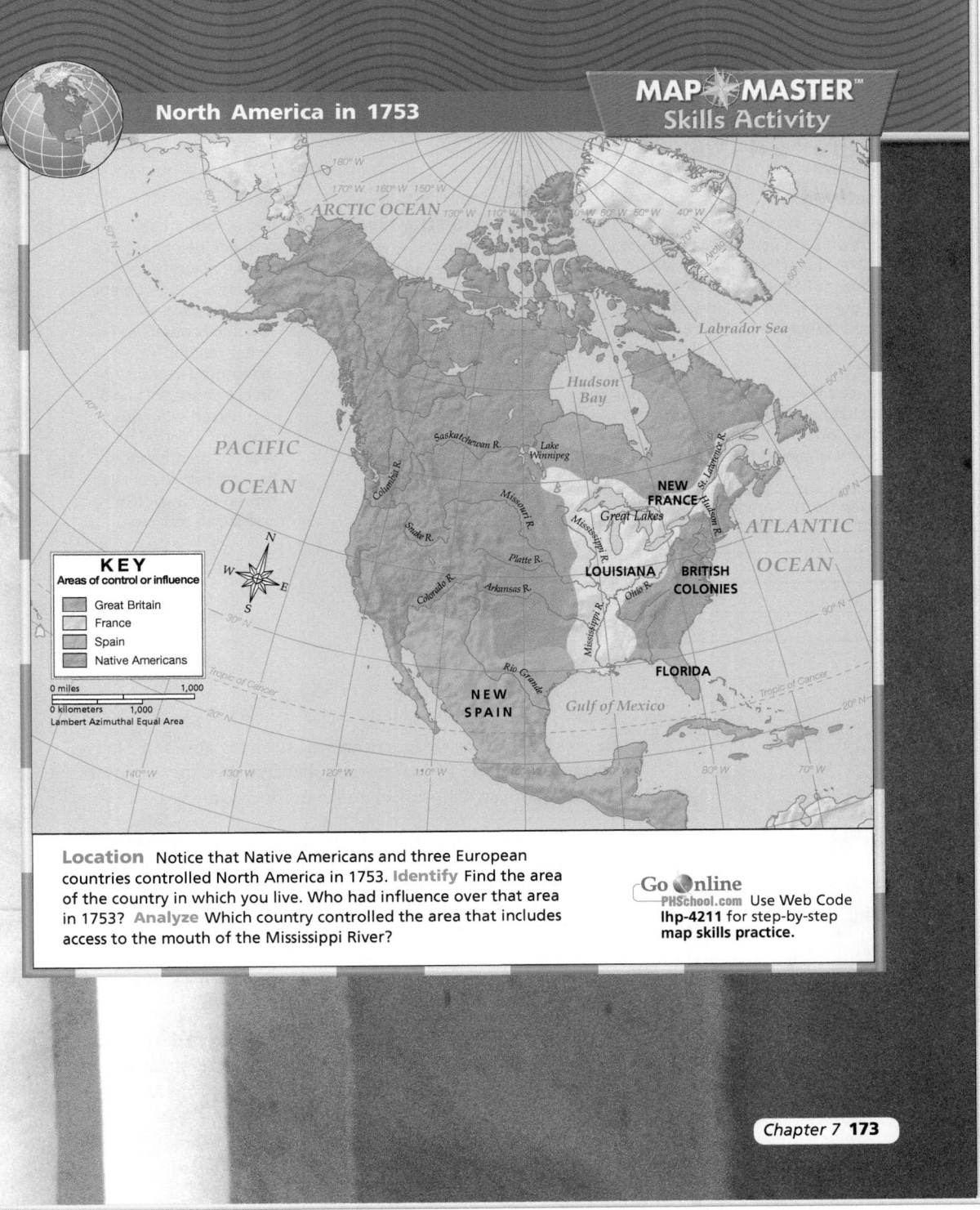

North America in 1753

KEY
Areas of control or influence

- Great Britain
- France
- Spain
- Native Americans

0 miles 1,000
0 kilometers 1,000
Lambert Azimuthal Equal Area

Location Notice that Native Americans and three European countries controlled North America in 1753. **Identify** Find the area of the country in which you live. Who had influence over that area in 1753? **Analyze** Which country controlled the area that includes access to the mouth of the Mississippi River?

Go Online
PHSchool.com Use Web Code
lhp-4211 for step-by-step
map skills practice.

Chapter 7 **173**

MAP MASTER™ Skills Activity

Have students study the map of North America in 1753, directing their attention to the title and the key. Then have them write a short paragraph describing what region of North America each group controlled.

- Pair students and ask them to compare the map from the text with a current map of North America. Assign each pair a few states, provinces, territories, or cities from the current map, and ask them to identify which group or groups controlled that region in 1753.

Go Online Students may practice their map skills using the interactive online version of this map.

Using the Visual   L2

Reach Into Your Background Draw students' attention to the photograph and its caption. Ask students to name any monuments or memorials they know of or have visited. Ask them to think about how monuments keep history alive, and conduct an Idea Wave (TE, p. T35) to help them share their answers.

Answers

MAP MASTER Skills Activity **Identify** Answers will vary according to where students live. **Analyze** France

---

Chapter Resources

Teaching Resources
- L2 Vocabulary Development, p. 182
- L2 Skills for Life, p. 164
- L2 Chapter Tests A and B, pp. 185–190

Spanish Support
- L2 Spanish Chapter Summary, p. 76
- L2 Spanish Vocabulary Development, p. 77

Media and Technology
- L1 Student Edition on Audio CD
- L1 Guided Reading Audiotapes, English and Spanish
- L2 Social Studies Skills Tutor CD-ROM
  ExamView Test Bank CD-ROM

PRENTICE HALL
Presentation EXPRESS
Teach · Connect · Inspire

Teach this chapter's content using the PresentationExpress™ CD-ROM including:
- slide shows
- transparencies
- interactive maps and media
- *ExamView®* QuickTake Presenter

The Arrival of the Europeans

Objectives

Social Studies

1. Learn who the first Americans were.
2. Discover the effects the arrival of Europeans had on Native Americans.
3. Find out how the United States won its independence from Great Britain.

Reading/Language Arts

Learn how to clarify and understand new words and ideas in a text by rereading.

Prepare to Read

Build Background Knowledge L2

Tell students that in this section they will learn about the history of settlement in North America. Have students preview the headings and visuals in this section with the following question in mind: **From where did the people who settled North America come?** Use the Idea Wave participation strategy (TE, p. T35) to solicit answers.

Set a Purpose for Reading L2

■ Preview the Objectives.

■ Form students into pairs or groups of four. Distribute the *Reading Readiness Guide.* Ask students to fill in the first two columns of the chart. Use the Numbered Heads participation strategy (TE, p. T36) to call on students to share one piece of information they already know and one piece of information they want to know.

 **United States and Canada Teaching Resources,** *Reading Readiness Guide,* p. 140

Vocabulary Builder

Preview Key Terms L2

Pronounce each Key Term, then ask the students to say the word with you. Provide a simple explanation such as, "Indentured servants were permitted to work for their freedom, while slaves were forced to work for life."

Prepare to Read

Objectives

In this section you will
1. Learn who the first Americans were.
2. Discover the effects the arrival of Europeans had on Native Americans.
3. Find out how the United States won its independence from Great Britain.

Taking Notes

As you read the section, look for important events that have taken place in North America. Copy the table below and write each event in the correct time period.

Events in North American History	
1400s	
1500s	
1600s	
1700s	

Target Reading Skill

Reread Rereading is a strategy that can help you understand words and ideas in the text. If you do not understand a certain passage, reread it to look for connections among the words and sentences.

Key Terms

• **indigenous** (in DIJ uh nus) *adj.* belonging to a certain place
• **missionary** (MISH un ehr ee) *n.* a person who tries to convert others to his or her religion
• **indentured servant** (in DEN churd SUR vunt) *n.* a person who must work for a period of years to gain freedom
• **boycott** (BOY kaht) *n.* a refusal to buy or use goods and services

Native American artifacts

Louise Erdrich is an American writer. She is also part Native American. In one of her novels, she describes the variety of Native American cultures before the Europeans arrived:

❝[They] had hundreds of societies . . . whose experience had told them that the world was a pretty diverse place. Walk for a day in any direction and what do you find: A tribe with a whole new set of gods, a language as distinct from your own as Tibetan is from Dutch. . . .❞

—*Louise Erdrich*, The Crown of Columbus

The First Americans

Many scientists think that Native Americans migrated from Asia. Perhaps as early as 30,000 years ago, they theorize, small groups of hunters and gatherers reached North America from Asia.

Target Reading Skill L2

Reread Point out the Target Reading Skill. Tell students that going back into the text will allow them to make connections among words and sentences. In this way, rereading can help clarify or explain a new word or an idea in a passage.

Model the strategy by using rereading to determine what theory is being referenced in this sentence from The First Americans: "Many Native Americans disagree with this theory, believing they have always lived in the Americas." *(the theory that people migrated to North America from Asia during the last ice age using an exposed land bridge)*

Give students *Reread or Read Ahead.* Have them complete the activity in their groups.

 **United States and Canada Teaching Resources,** *Reread or Read Ahead,* p. 159

This migration from Asia to North America took place during the last ice age. At that time, so much water froze into thick ice sheets that the sea level dropped. As a result, a land bridge was exposed between Siberia and Alaska. Hunters followed herds of bison and mammoths across this land bridge. Other migrating people may have paddled small boats and fished along the coasts.

Over time, the first Americans spread throughout North and South America. They developed different ways of life to suit the environment of the places where they settled.

Many Native Americans disagree with this theory, believing they have always lived in the Americas. In any case, all people consider Native Americans **indigenous** (in DIJ uh nus) people, meaning they belong to and are native to this place.

✓ Reading Check **How did migrating people reach North America?**

The Europeans Arrive

Life for the millions of indigenous people in the Americas began to change after 1492. That year, Christopher Columbus, a sea captain sailing from Spain, explored islands in the Caribbean Sea. His voyage opened the way for European colonization.

Spanish Claims to the Americas   The Spanish settlers who followed Columbus spread out across the Americas. Some went to the present-day southwestern United States and Mexico. Others went to Florida, the Caribbean islands, and South America. Spain gained great wealth from its American colonies.

Taos, New Mexico
Although Native Americans had inhabited the area for centuries, Spanish explorers arrived in present-day Taos (TAH ohs), New Mexico in 1540. They built the church below in 1617. **Predict** *How might life have changed for Native Americans after Spanish explorers arrived?*

Chapter 7 Section 1 **175**

Vocabulary Builder

Use the information below to teach students this section's high-use words.

High-Use Word	Definition and Sample Sentence
theorize, p. 174	*v.* to make a statement or give an opinion based on facts The professor wrote a paper **theorizing** how dinosaurs lived.
establish, p. 178	*v.* to set up, to bring about Our club was **established** after getting permission from the school board.
inspire, p. 179	*v.* to cause or influence to do something Reading the author's first novel **inspired** me to read all of his work.

Pueblo Village

L2

Guided Instruction

Have students read the introductory paragraph on this page. Then read the captions aloud as students study the diagram and photos. Pair students and have them discuss the Analyzing Images question.

Independent Practice

Using the information on this page, have students write a paragraph about what life might have been like in a Pueblo village. Use the *Rubric for Assessing a Writing Assignment* to evaluate students' paragraphs.

All in One United States and Canada Teaching Resources, *Rubric for Assessing a Writing Assignment,* p. 183

Pueblo Village

When the Pueblo Indians of the Southwest learned how to grow corn and other crops, they no longer had to move about to hunt and gather food. As they became more settled and grew larger harvests, they built stone corn cribs. Over time, these storerooms became larger, and the Pueblos began to build their houses and villages around them.

Acoma Pueblo, New Mexico
The Acoma Pueblo sits high on a 357-foot (109-meter) sandstone rock. It is also known as "Sky City."

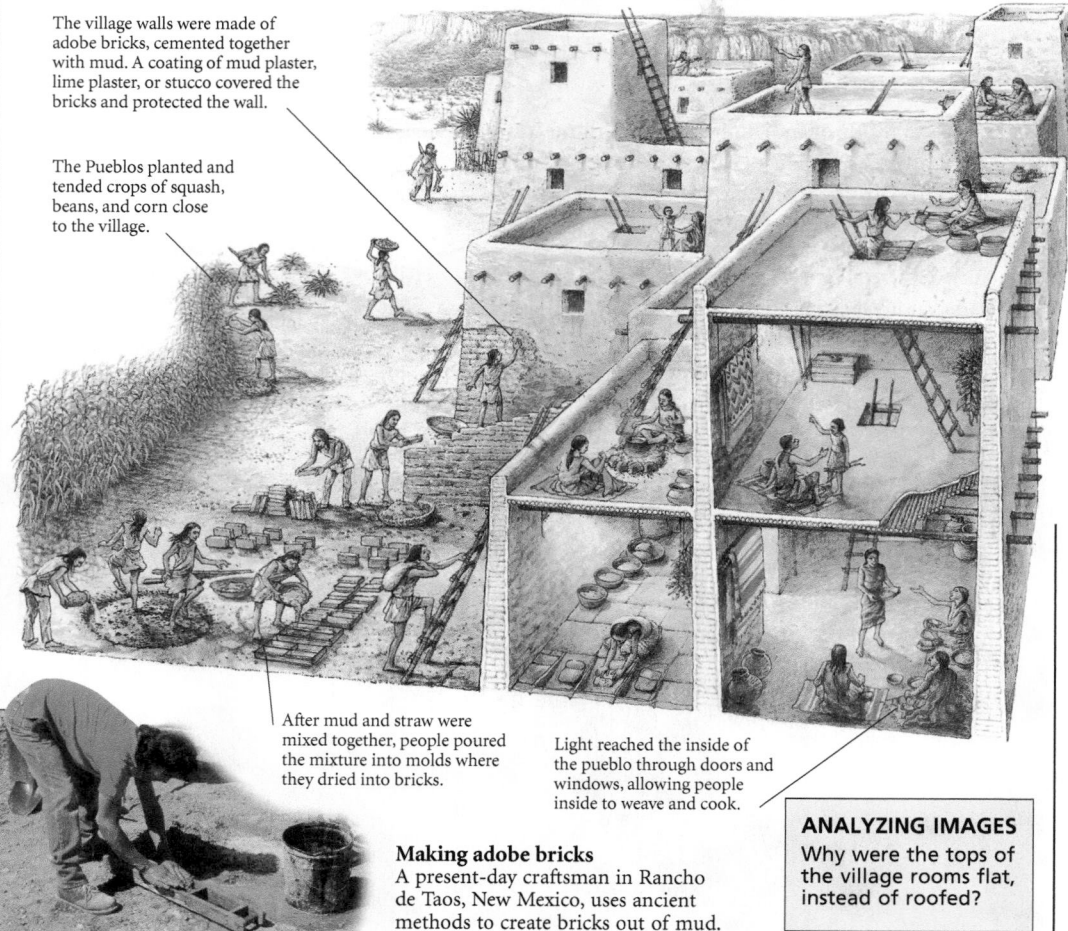

The village walls were made of adobe bricks, cemented together with mud. A coating of mud plaster, lime plaster, or stucco covered the bricks and protected the wall.

The Pueblos planted and tended crops of squash, beans, and corn close to the village.

After mud and straw were mixed together, people poured the mixture into molds where they dried into bricks.

Light reached the inside of the pueblo through doors and windows, allowing people inside to weave and cook.

Making adobe bricks
A present-day craftsman in Rancho de Taos, New Mexico, uses ancient methods to create bricks out of mud.

ANALYZING IMAGES
Why were the tops of the village rooms flat, instead of roofed?

176 United States and Canada

Answers

ANALYZING IMAGES Possible answer: The flat roofs were probably used as a safe place to work and to watch for and escape from enemies.

The colonists often enslaved Native Americans. They forced Native Americans to work in mines or on farms. Working conditions were so harsh that thousands died. Spanish missionaries tried to make Native Americans more like Europeans, often by force. **Missionaries** (MISH un ehr ees) are religious people who want to convert others to their religion.

French Claims to the Americas Seeing Spain's success, other countries also wanted colonies in the Americas. French explorers claimed land along the St. Lawrence and Mississippi rivers. Unlike the Spanish, who were interested in gold, the French were interested in fur. French traders and missionaries often lived among the Native Americans and learned their ways. However, both the French and the Spanish brought disease along with them. Millions of Native Americans died from diseases that they had never been exposed to before, such as smallpox and measles.

Independent Practice
Have students create the Taking Notes graphic organizer on a blank piece of paper. Then have them fill in the first three lines with what the have learned from the text. Briefly model how to identify which details to record.

Monitor Progress
As students fill in the graphic organizer, circulate and make sure individuals are choosing the correct details. Provide assistance as needed.

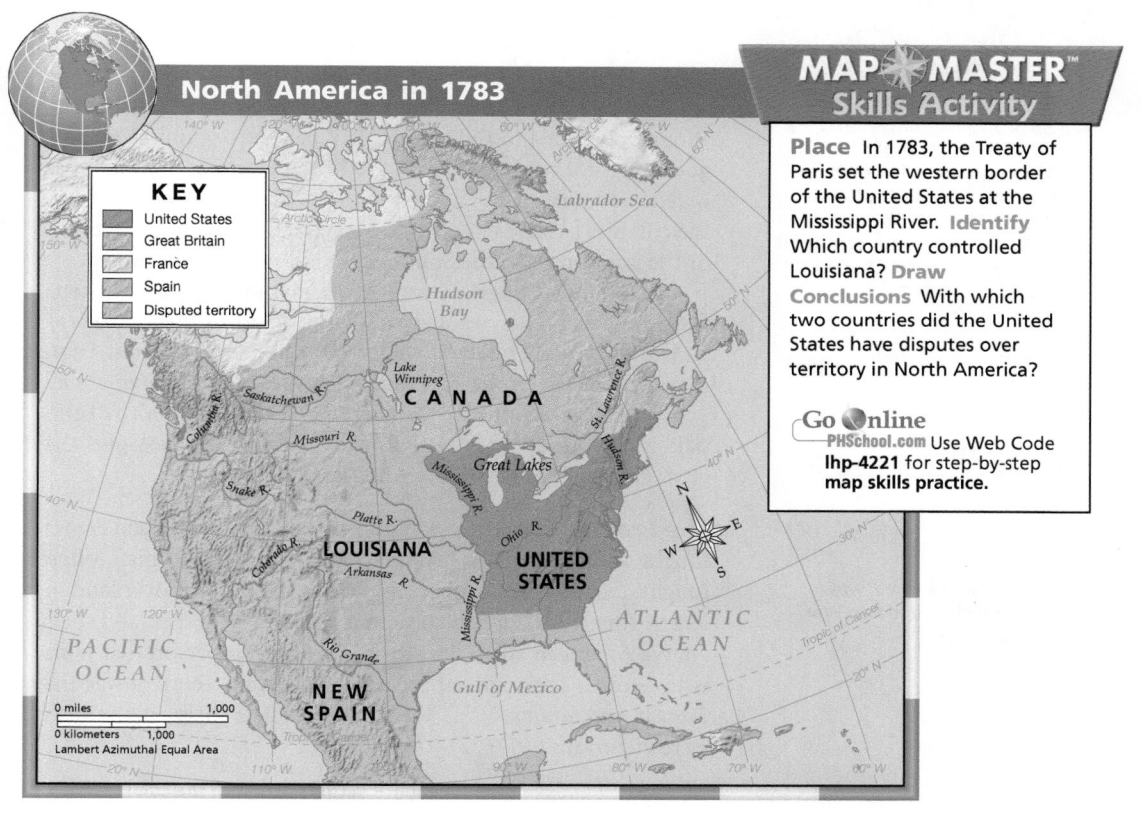

North America in 1783

MAP MASTER™
Skills Activity

KEY
- United States
- Great Britain
- France
- Spain
- Disputed territory

Place In 1783, the Treaty of Paris set the western border of the United States at the Mississippi River. **Identify** Which country controlled Louisiana? **Draw Conclusions** With which two countries did the United States have disputes over territory in North America?

Go Online
PHSchool.com Use Web Code **lhp-4221** for step-by-step **map skills practice.**

Chapter 7 Section 1 **177**

Background: Biography

Pocahontas (c. 1595–1617) According to a story told by John Smith, a leading Jamestown settler, a young Native American woman named Pocahontas interceded to stop her people from executing him. She later married Englishman John Rolfe, and their marriage helped smooth uneasy relations between the English settlers and the native peoples of Virginia.

Answers

MAP MASTER Skills Activity **Identify** Spain **Draw Conclusions** Great Britain and Spain

Go Online
PHSchool.com Students may practice their map skills using the interactive online version of this map.

The Break with Britain [L2]

Guided Instruction

- **Vocabulary Builder** Clarify the high-use word **inspire** before reading.

- Read The Break With Britain. As students read, circulate and make sure individuals can answer the Reading Check question.

- Discuss the chain of events between Britain and the colonies that led to the Revolutionary War. *(The British taxed the colonies to help pay for the French and Indian War. Colonists thought this was unfair since they had no representation in the British government. The colonists boycotted British goods in order to avoid paying taxes. A war began and colonists delivered the Declaration of Independence to Great Britain.)*

Independent Practice

Ask students to complete their graphic organizer with the information they have just learned about the 1700s.

Monitor Progress

- Show *Section Reading Support Transparency USC 46* and ask students to check their graphic organizers individually. Go over key concepts and clarify key vocabulary as needed.

  📖 **United States and Canada Transparencies,** *Section Reading Support Transparency USC 46*

- Tell students to fill in the last column of the *Reading Readiness Guide.* Ask them to evaluate if what they learned was what they had expected to learn.

  All in One United States and Canada Teaching Resources, *Reading Readiness Guide,* p. 140

⊙ Target Reading Skill

Reread As a follow up, ask students to answer the Target Reading Skill question in the Student Edition. *(Britain and France went to war over land in North America. The British and their colonists fought against the French and their Native American allies.)*

Answer

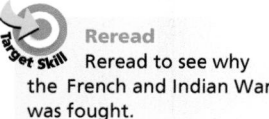 **Reading Check** The English settled the colonies in order to establish a new way of life. Some wanted to own land or practice their religion freely. Others wanted to escape debt.

178 *United States and Canada*

THE LANDING OF THE PILGRIMS.
ON PLYMOUTH ROCK, DEC. 11TH 1620.

In 1620, a group of about 100 Pilgrims sailed to New England on the *Mayflower* (right). In 1682, William Penn (left) arrived in the colony of Pennsylvania, which means "Penn's woods."

Reread
Reread to see why the French and Indian War was fought.

The English Colonists English settlers also arrived, establishing a strip of colonies along the Atlantic Coast. These settlers came to start a new life. Some wanted to be free from debt. Others wanted to own land or practice their religions freely. Some came as **indentured servants,** or people who had to work for a period of years to gain freedom.

The first permanent English settlement was Jamestown, Virginia, founded in 1607. By 1619, it had the beginnings of self-government. In the same year, the first Africans arrived there as indentured servants. Later, about 1640, Africans were brought to the colonies as slaves. Many were forced to work on plantations, or the large farms in the South where cash crops were grown.

In 1620, the Pilgrims arrived in Plymouth, Massachusetts from England. They wanted to worship God in their own way and to govern themselves. About 60 years later, William Penn founded the Pennsylvania Colony. He wanted a place where all people, regardless of race or religion, were treated fairly. Penn paid Native Americans for their land. Later, settlers took over the land, and then fought Native Americans to control it.

The French and Indian War In the 1700s, Britain and France fought several wars. When they fought, their colonists often fought, too. In 1754, Britain and France went to war over land in North America. The British fought against the French and their Native American allies. An ally is a country or person that joins with another for a special purpose. Americans call this war the French and Indian War. With the colonists' help, the British were victorious in 1763.

✓ **Reading Check** Why did English settlers establish the colonies?

178 United States and Canada

🎯 Skills Mini Lesson

Recognizing Cause and Effect

1. Teach the skill by surrounding a marble with an outer circle of marbles. Have a volunteer roll the center marble at the outer circle. Point out that the *cause* is the moving marble, the *effect* is the disruption of the circle. The *cause* is what makes something happen; the *effect* is what happens.

2. Help students practice the skill by rereading the first paragraph under The Break With Britain and determine what caused Britain to start taxing the colonists. *(the expense of an army to protect the colonies)*

3. Have students apply the skill by answering this question: What was the effect of the taxation? *(The colonists became angry and boycotted British goods.)*

The Break With Britain

Despite their victory, the British wanted an army in North America to protect the colonists. The British thought the colonists should help pay for the war and for their defense. They put taxes on many British goods the colonists bought. Because no one represented the colonists in the British Parliament, they could not protest these taxes. Many of them began to demand "no taxation without representation." They also **boycotted**, or refused to buy, British goods.

Resentment grew against British rule, causing the Revolutionary War to break out in 1775. Thomas Jefferson summarized the colonists' views in the Declaration of Independence. His words inspired many colonists to fight. In 1781, George Washington led the American forces to victory. The Treaty of Paris, signed in 1783, made American independence official.

Before they won independence, the 13 colonies worked on a plan of government called the Articles of Confederation. But Congress was not given the power to tax. After the war, the 13 new states agreed to form a stronger central government. They wrote the Constitution, which set up the framework for our federal government. Approved in 1788, it is still the highest law of the United States.

✓ **Reading Check** What was the problem with the Articles of Confederation?

This statue commemorates the Minutemen of the American Revolution who stood their ground against British troops on April 19, 1775.

Section 1 Assessment

Key Terms
Review the key terms at the beginning of this section. Use each term in a sentence that explains its meaning.

Target Reading Skill
What word or idea were you able to clarify by rereading?

Comprehension and Critical Thinking
1. (a) Recall Where do many scientists think the first Americans came from?

(b) Identify Point of View Why might Native Americans today disagree with the theory of migration?
2. (a) Explain Describe how different European groups settled in the Americas.
(b) Summarize How did Europeans affect Native American life?
3. (a) Name What document is the framework for the United States government?
(b) Identify Cause and Effect Why did the colonists object to the taxes placed on them by the British?

Writing Activity
Write a paragraph discussing how life in the Americas might have been different if Columbus's voyage had not taken place.

> **Writing Tip** Begin your paragraph with a topic sentence that states your main idea. Give at least two examples of how life might have been different.

Chapter 7 Section 1 **179**

Assess Progress   L2
Have students complete the Section Assessment. Administer the *Section Quiz*.

  All in One **United States and Canada Teaching Resources,** *Section Quiz*, p. 142

Reteach   L1
If students need more instruction, have them read this section in the Reading and Vocabulary Study Guide.

  Chapter 7, Section 1, **Western Hemisphere Reading and Vocabulary Study Guide**, pp. 66–68

Extend   L3
Have students read *Closing Speech to the Constitutional Convention, September 17, 1787*. Assign students to work in groups to answer the questions provided.

  All in One **United States and Canada Teaching Resources,** *Closing Speech to the Constitutional Convention, September 17, 1787,* pp. 172–173

Answers

✓ **Reading Check** The Articles of Confederation did not provide for a strong central government that had the power to tax.

Writing Activity
Use the *Rubric for Assessing a Writing Assignment* to evaluate students' paragraphs.

  All in One **United States and Canada Teaching Resources,** *Rubric for Assessing a Writing Assignment*, p. 183

Section 1 Assessment

Key Terms
Students' sentences should reflect knowledge of each Key Term.

Target Reading Skill
Answers will vary, but student responses should show an understanding of the reading strategy.

Comprehension and Critical Thinking
1. (a) from Asia **(b)** Some Native Americans claim they are indigenous and that they have always lived on this land.

2. (a) Spanish settlers spread out across the Americas after the arrival of Columbus. The French, who were interested in fur trade, settled along the St. Lawrence and Mississippi Rivers. The English, who came for a new way of life, settled along the Atlantic coast.

(b) Most Europeans took the land from the Native Americans then fought them to control it. Also, many Europeans tried to convert the Native Americans to their religion.

3. (a) the Constitution **(b)** They felt that they should not be forced to pay taxes to a government in which they had no representatives.

Section 2
Step-by-Step Instruction

Objectives
Social Studies
1. Explore the effects of westward expansion in the United States.
2. Discover the causes and effects of the Civil War.

Reading/Language Arts
Learn how to clarify words or ideas in a text by reading ahead.

Prepare to Read

Build Background Knowledge L2
In this section students will learn more about the growth of the United States and the challenges the country faced during the 1800s. Have students preview the headings and visuals in the section. Each student should select a heading and write two or three facts that they already know about the event they selected. Have students engage in the Think-Write-Pair-Share activity (TE, p. T36) to share their answers.

Set a Purpose for Reading L2
■ Preview the Objectives.

■ Form students into pairs or groups of four. Distribute the *Reading Readiness Guide*. Ask the students to fill in the first two columns of the chart. Use the Numbered Heads participation strategy (TE, p. T36) to call on students to share one piece of information they already know and one piece of information they want to know.

All in One United States and Canada Teaching Resources, *Reading Readiness Guide,* p. 144

Vocabulary Builder
Preview Key Terms L2
Pronounce each Key Term, then ask the students to say the word with you. Provide a simple explanation such as, "Immigrants have come to the United States from all parts of the world."

Section 2
Growth and Conflict in the United States

Prepare to Read

Objectives
In this section you will
1. Explore the effects of westward expansion in the United States.
2. Discover the causes and effects of the Civil War.

Taking Notes
As you read the section, look for details about the causes and effects of westward expansion and the Civil War. Copy the flow-chart below and write each detail under the correct heading.

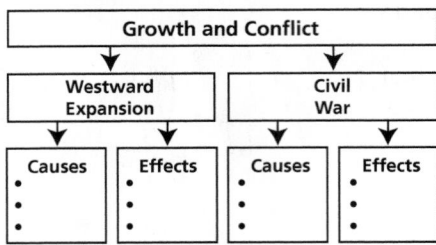

Target Reading Skill
Read Ahead Reading ahead is a strategy that can help you understand words and ideas in the text. If you do not understand a certain passage, it might help to read ahead. A word or an idea may be clarified further on.

Key Terms
• **Louisiana Purchase** (loo ee zee AN uh PUR chus) *n.* the sale of land in North America in 1803 by France to the United States

• **immigrant** (IM uh grunt) *n.* a person who moves to a new country in order to settle there
• **Industrial Revolution** (in DUS tree ul rev uh LOO shun) *n.* the change from making goods by hand to making them by machine
• **abolitionist** (ab uh LISH un ist) *n.* a person who believed that enslaving people was wrong and who wanted to end the practice
• **segregate** (SEG ruh gayt) *v.* to set apart, typically because of race or religion

Meriwether Lewis and William Clark with their Native American translator Sacajawea

180 United States and Canada

In 1804, President Thomas Jefferson sent Meriwether Lewis and William Clark with a company of men to explore the land west of the Mississippi River. They would eventually travel all the way to the Pacific Coast and back—about 8,000 miles (13,000 kilometers).

As they journeyed up the Missouri River, Lewis and Clark found plants and animals completely new to them. They also created accurate, highly valuable maps of the region. As they traveled with their Native American translator, a Shoshone (shoh SHOH nee) woman named Sacajawea, Lewis and Clark met many Native American groups. Sacajawea helped Lewis and Clark communicate with the various groups. During these meetings, the two men tried to learn about the region and set up trading alliances. Few of the Native Americans they met had any idea how the visit would change their way of life.

Target Reading Skill L2

Read Ahead Point out the Target Reading Skill. Tell students that reading ahead can help to clarify words and ideas if the words are further explained, or concepts are further developed.

Model the strategy using these sentences from p. 181: "First France, and then Spain, owned the Louisiana Territory. In 1800, war in Europe forced Spain to give it back to France." To understand exactly what land is referenced by the term "Louisiana Territory," students can read ahead to the next sentence to learn it is "all the land between the Mississippi River and the eastern slopes of the Rocky Mountains."

Give students *Reread or Read Ahead*. Have them complete the activity in their groups.

All in One United States and Canada Teaching Resources, *Reread or Read Ahead,* p. 159

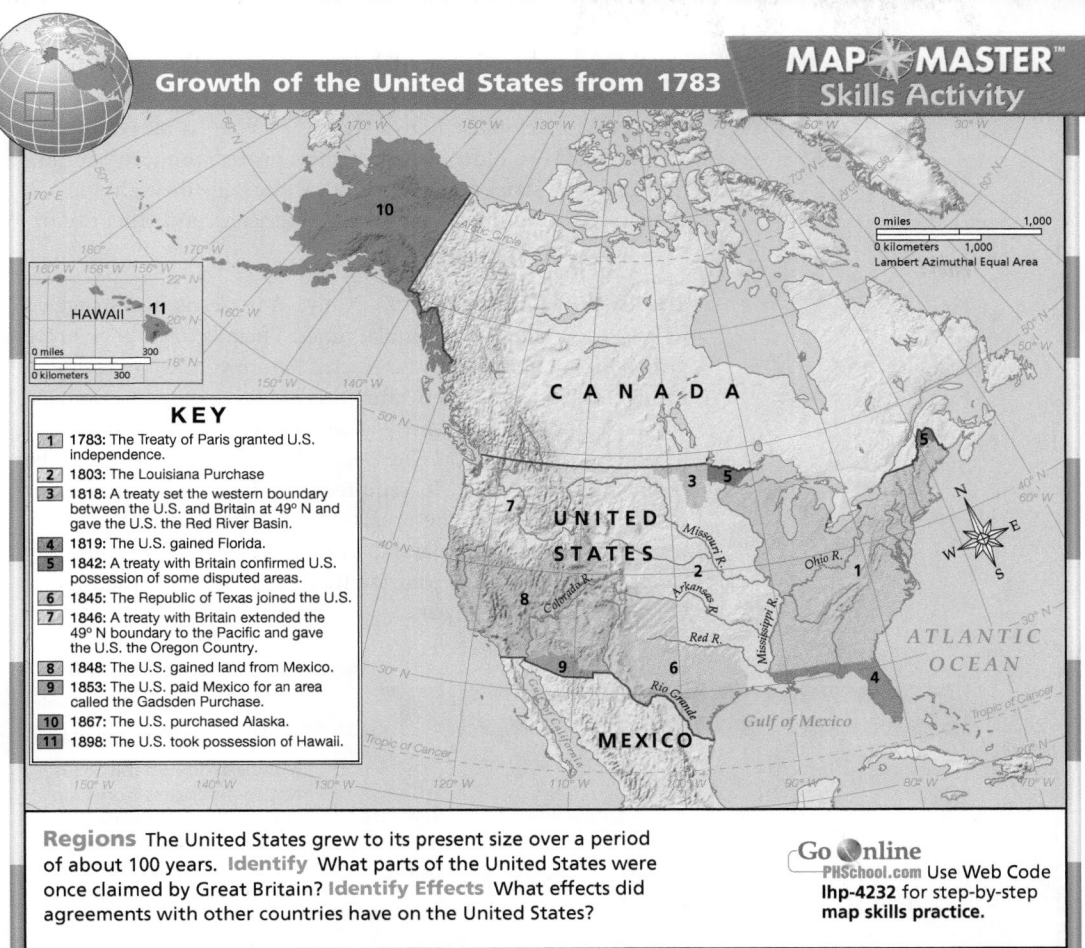

Growth of the United States from 1783

MAP MASTER™
Skills Activity

10

0 miles 1,000
0 kilometers 1,000
Lambert Azimuthal Equal Area

HAWAII **11**

0 miles 300
0 kilometers 300

KEY

1 1783: The Treaty of Paris granted U.S. independence.
2 1803: The Louisiana Purchase
3 1818: A treaty set the western boundary between the U.S. and Britain at 49° N and gave the U.S. the Red River Basin.
4 1819: The U.S. gained Florida.
5 1842: A treaty with Britain confirmed U.S. possession of some disputed areas.
6 1845: The Republic of Texas joined the U.S.
7 1846: A treaty with Britain extended the 49° N boundary to the Pacific and gave the U.S. the Oregon Country.
8 1848: The U.S. gained land from Mexico.
9 1853: The U.S. paid Mexico for an area called the Gadsden Purchase.
10 1867: The U.S. purchased Alaska.
11 1898: The U.S. took possession of Hawaii.

CANADA

UNITED STATES

ATLANTIC OCEAN

MEXICO

Gulf of Mexico

Regions The United States grew to its present size over a period of about 100 years. **Identify** What parts of the United States were once claimed by Great Britain? **Identify Effects** What effects did agreements with other countries have on the United States?

Go Online
PHSchool.com Use Web Code
lhp-4232 for step-by-step
map skills practice.

A Nation Grows

The United States had not always owned the land that Lewis and Clark explored, called the Louisiana Territory. But, the purchase of this land set the country on a new course of westward expansion.

The Louisiana Purchase   First France, and then Spain, owned the Louisiana Territory. In 1800, war in Europe forced Spain to give it back to France. In 1803, France offered to sell all the land between the Mississippi River and the eastern slopes of the Rocky Mountains to the United States—for only $15 million. This sale of land, called the **Louisiana Purchase,** doubled the size of the United States. The land would later be split into more than a dozen states.

Vocabulary Builder

Use the information below to teach students this section's high-use words.

High-Use Word	Definition and Sample Sentence
spur, p. 183	*v.* to encourage or motivate Losing the game **spurred** the team to practice harder.
conflict, p. 184	*n.* a disagreement A **conflict** arose between the two friends when they couldn't agree on which film to see.

Instruct

A Nation Grows   **L2**

Guided Instruction

■ **Vocabulary Builder** Clarify the high-use word **spur** before reading.

■ Read A Growing Nation using the ReQuest Procedure (TE, p. T35).

■ Ask **How much did the Louisiana Purchase cost?** *($15 million)* Tell students that the Louisiana Purchase was the sale of 828,000 square miles of land, and ask them to calculate the price per square mile. *($18.11 per square mile)* Explain that this works out to less than 3 cents per acre.

Answers

MAP MASTER™ *Skills Activity*   **Identify** The Red River Basin, the area between the Red River Basin and the Great Lakes, the northern tip of Maine, and the Oregon Country were all disputed between the United States and Great Britain. **Identify Effects** Agreements with other countries caused the land claimed by the United States to grow.

Go Online
PHSchool.com Students may practice their map skills using the interactive online version of this map.

Guided Instruction (continued)

■ Ask students to identify three major events that occurred between 1830 and 1860. *(In 1830, Congress passed the Indian Removal Act, requiring Native Americans in the Southeast to leave their homelands to make way for poor farmers, laborers, and settlers. In 1836, settlers in the territory of Texas rebelled against Mexican rule. In 1845, Texas became part of the United States.)*

■ Ask **What were the positive and negative effects of the westward expansion?** *(Positive effects: Increased land for settlers gave them an opportunity to make better lives for themselves; new states broadened voting privileges to include white men who did not own property. Negative effects: the relocation of Native Americans, and the death of many Native Americans in their forced migrations)*

As the country grew, so did the meaning of democracy. In the 13 original states, only white males who owned property could vote. New states passed laws giving the vote to all white men 21 years old or older, whether they owned property or not. Eventually, all states gave every adult white male the right to vote. Women, African Americans, Native Americans, and other minorities, however, could not vote.

The Indian Removal Act   Native Americans had struggled to keep their land since colonial times. Their struggle grew more difficult in 1828, when voters elected Andrew Jackson President. President Jackson looked after the interests of poor farmers, laborers, and settlers who wanted Native American lands in the Southeast. In 1830, he persuaded Congress to pass the Indian Removal Act. It required the Cherokees and other Native Americans in the area to leave their homelands. They were sent to live on new land in present-day Oklahoma. So many Cherokees died on the journey that the route they followed is known as the Trail of Tears.

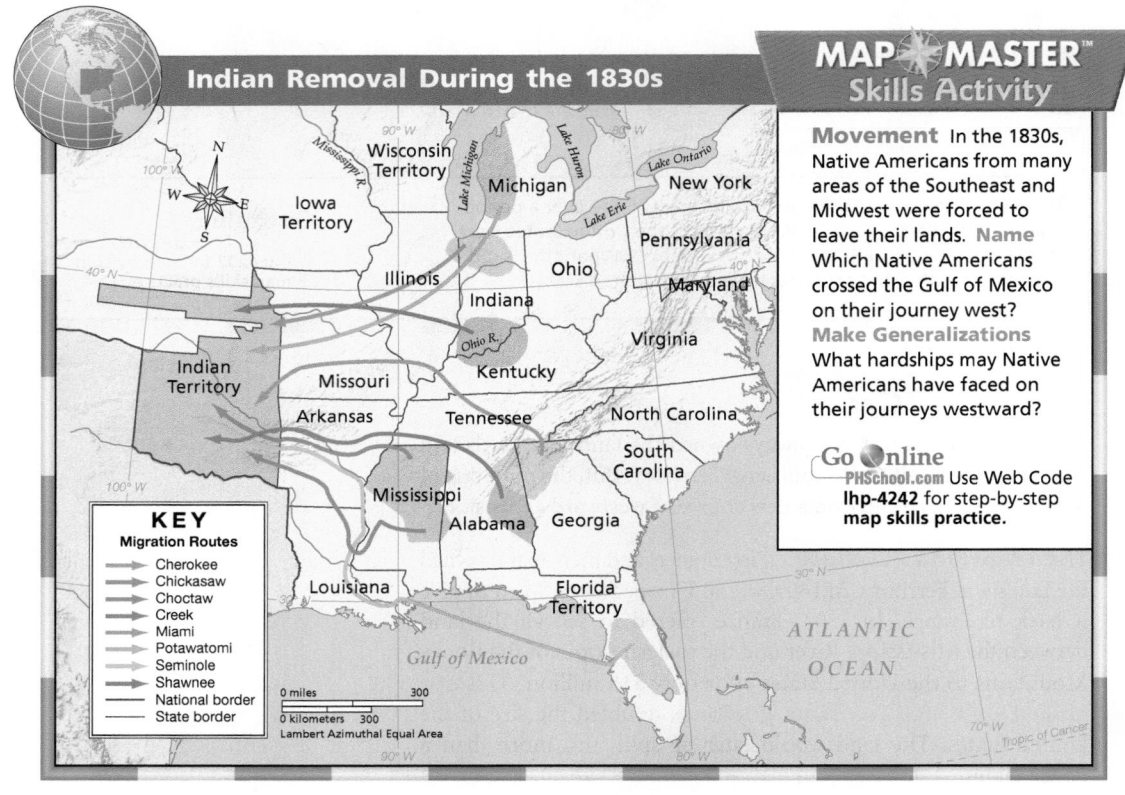

MAP MASTER™ Skills Activity

Movement In the 1830s, Native Americans from many areas of the Southeast and Midwest were forced to leave their lands. **Name** Which Native Americans crossed the Gulf of Mexico on their journey west? **Make Generalizations** What hardships may Native Americans have faced on their journeys westward?

Go Online PHSchool.com Use Web Code **lhp-4242** for step-by-step map skills practice.

182 United States and Canada

Answers

MAP MASTER™ Skills Activity **Name** The Seminole
Make Generalizations Native Americans probably had to face exhaustion and disease during their journeys westward, especially during winter or bad weather. It was also probably difficult for them to leave their homelands.

Go Online PHSchool.com Students may practice their map skills using the interactive online version of this map.

Differentiated Instruction

For Advanced Readers   L3
Have students read *Morning Girl, Journal Entry* and *Chief Joseph Surrenders*. In pairs, have students discuss how the relationship between Native Americans and Europeans changed over time.

All In One **United States and Canada Teaching Resources,** *Morning Girl,* pp. 174–176; *Journal Entry,* p. 177; *Chief Joseph Surrenders,* p. 178

Manifest Destiny Many Americans believed that the United States had a right to own all the land from the Atlantic to the Pacific. This belief, called Manifest Destiny, was used to justify further westward expansion. In the 1840s, American wagon trains began to cross the continent heading for the West.

The United States also looked to the Southwest. In 1836, American settlers in the Mexican territory of Texas had rebelled against Mexican rule. The Texans had then set up the Lone Star Republic. In 1845, Texas became part of the United States. Only a year later, the United States went to war with Mexico. The United States won the war and gained from Mexico much of what is now the Southwest region.

The Industrial Revolution At the same time, thousands of people were pouring into cities in the Northeast. Some had left farms to work in factories. Others were **immigrants**, or people who move to one country from another. These people came from Europe in search of jobs in the United States. They were spurred by the **Industrial Revolution**, or the change from making goods by hand to making them by machine.

The first industry to change was textiles, or cloth-making. New spinning machines and power looms enabled people to make cloth more quickly than they could by hand. Other inventions, such as the steam engine, made travel easier and faster. Steamboats and steam locomotives moved people and goods rapidly. By 1860, railroads linked most major northeastern and southeastern cities.

√ Reading Check **What did the Indian Removal Act do?**

The Clermont, 1807
Robert Fulton demonstrates his steam-powered paddle-wheel boat, the *Clermont,* which used a steam engine improved by James Watt.
Draw Conclusions *How did the inventions of the Industrial Revolution change people's lives?*

 **Skills Mini Lesson**

Transferring Information from One Medium to Another

1. Teach the skill by explaining to students that information from the written text on a page is often transferred to maps, charts, and photos. By looking closely at the visuals, students can learn more about the text.

2. Help students practice the skill by rereading A Nation Grows and studying the map on page 182 in the Student Edition for additional information.

3. Have students apply the skill by transferring the additional information from the map into a brief paragraph.

Independent Practice
Ask students to create the Taking Notes graphic organizer on a blank piece of paper. Then have them fill it in with information about westward expansion. Briefly model how to identify which details to record.

Monitor Progress
As students fill in the graphic organizer, circulate and make sure individuals are choosing the correct details. Provide assistance as needed.

Answers

√ Reading Check The Indian Removal Act forced Native American nations, such as the present-day Cherokee, to relocate from their homes to the Indian Territory in present-day Oklahoma. Their journey was harsh and many people died along the way.

Draw Conclusions Inventions of the Industrial Revolution allowed people to make products more quickly than they could by hand, and made travel easier and faster. Many people left farms or immigrated from other countries to work in factories.

The Civil War and Reconstruction
L2

Guided Instruction

- **Vocabulary Builder** Clarify the high-use word **conflict** before reading.

- Read about The Civil War and Reconstruction with students. As students read, circulate and make sure individuals can answer the Reading Check question.

- Ask students to identify at least one important event that led to the Civil War. *(Possible answers: publication of* Uncle Tom's Cabin *led more Northerners to become abolitionists; California entered the nation as a free state; the Fugitive Slave Act was passed; Lincoln was elected President, causing the South to secede from the Union.)*

- Ask students to debate the following question: **Do you think the Civil War and Reconstruction achieved all of the abolitionists' goals?** *(Some students may argue that they did, because slavery was abolished. Others may say that they did not, because the Southern states passed segregation laws.)*

🎯 Target Reading Skill

Read Ahead As a follow up, ask students to perform the Target Reading Skill activity in the Student Edition. *(When Eli Whitney invented the cotton gin, cotton farming boomed. To keep up production, farmers expanded into western lands and wanted to bring slavery with them.)*

Answers

MAP MASTER Skills Activity **List** Florida, Alabama, Georgia, Mississippi, Texas, Louisiana, Arkansas, Tennessee, South Carolina, North Carolina, and Virginia **Draw Conclusions** States that grew cotton depended on the labor of enslaved people; the cotton belt states joined the Confederacy.

Go **O**nline
PHSchool.com **Students may practice their map skills using the interactive online version of this map.**

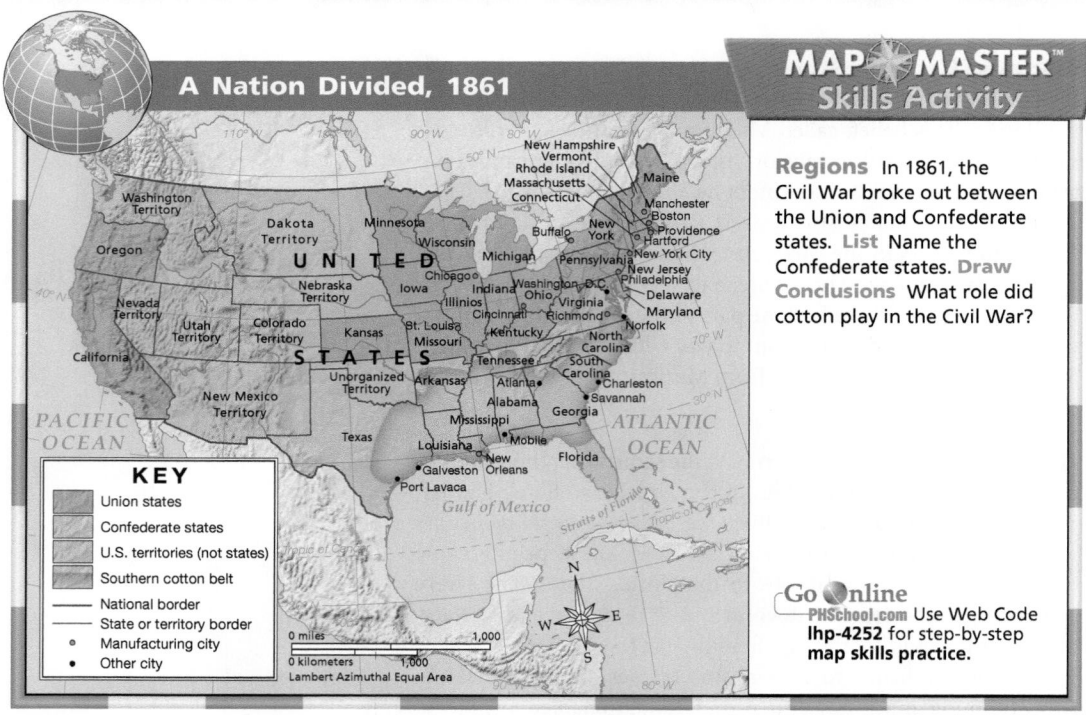

A Nation Divided, 1861

MAP MASTER™ Skills Activity

Regions In 1861, the Civil War broke out between the Union and Confederate states. **List** Name the Confederate states. **Draw Conclusions** What role did cotton play in the Civil War?

KEY
- Union states
- Confederate states
- U.S. territories (not states)
- Southern cotton belt
- National border
- State or territory border
- ○ Manufacturing city
- • Other city

0 miles 1,000
0 kilometers 1,000
Lambert Azimuthal Equal Area

Go **O**nline
PHSchool.com Use Web Code **lhp-4252** for step-by-step **map skills practice.**

Read Ahead
Keep reading to see how harvesting cotton affected the nation's history.

The Civil War and Reconstruction

With the textile industry growing as a result of the Industrial Revolution, the demand for cotton grew as well. Cotton required many laborers for planting and harvesting. This is one reason why slaves were an important part of plantation life.

In 1793, Eli Whitney invented the cotton gin, which quickly removed seeds from cotton. The cotton gin made cotton easier to process after it was picked. Cotton farming boomed. However, growing cotton quickly wore out the soil. To keep up production, farmers wanted to expand into western lands. But that meant that slavery would spread into the new territories. Some people did not want this. The debate began. Should the states or the federal government decide about the issue of slavery in the new territories?

Causes of Conflict Before California asked to be admitted to the union as a free state in 1850, there were equal numbers of slave and free states. After a heated debate, Congress granted California's request. The Southern states were not pleased. To gain their support, Congress also passed the Fugitive Slave Act. It required that runaway slaves must be returned to their owners. This action only intensified the argument over slavery.

184 United States and Canada

Background: Biography

Harriet Tubman (c. 1820–1913) Harriet Tubman spent the first 29 years of her life in slavery. In 1849 she escaped to the North but returned to guide other slaves to freedom. Tubman soon became one of the most tireless "conductors" on the Underground Railroad. The secret flights were very dangerous for all involved, and Tubman did not tolerate any risky behavior. She kept people in line by making sure they knew she carried a gun. Such no-nonsense behavior led abolitionist John Brown to admiringly dub her "General Tubman."

The South Breaks Away In 1852, Harriet Beecher Stowe published *Uncle Tom's Cabin,* a novel about the evils of slavery. After reading this book, thousands of Northerners became abolitionists (ab uh LISH un ists). **Abolitionists** were people who believed that slavery was wrong and wanted to end, or abolish, its practice. Many helped enslaved people escape to Canada. There, slavery was illegal. Most Southerners, however, felt that abolitionists were robbing them of their property.

The debate over slavery raged. When Abraham Lincoln, a Northerner, was elected President in 1860, many Southerners feared they would have little say in the government. As a result, some Southern states seceded, or withdrew, from the United States. They founded a new country—the Confederate States of America, or the Confederacy.

The Civil War In 1861, the Civil War between the Northern states and the Confederacy erupted. It lasted four years. The North, known as the Union, had more industry, wealth, and soldiers. The Confederacy had experienced military officers. It also had cotton. Many foreign countries bought southern cotton. Southerners hoped that these countries would help support the Confederacy in its struggle.

Despite the North's advantages, the war dragged on. In 1863, Lincoln issued the Emancipation Proclamation. This declared that enslaved people in areas loyal to the Confederacy were free, and it gave the North a new battle cry—freedom! Thousands of African Americans joined the fight against the South.

Fighting for Their Cause
These African American soldiers are outside of their barracks at Fort Lincoln, Washington, D.C. Twenty-three African Americans received the Congressional Medal of Honor (below right), the country's highest military honor. **Draw Conclusions** *Why do you think African Americans were willing to fight for the Union?*

Background: Daily Life

Segregation Laws The South's segregation laws were known as Jim Crow laws. These laws attempted to prevent any meeting of blacks and whites on an equal footing. For example, blacks and whites could not attend the same schools, eat in the same restaurants, or even be buried in the same cemeteries. The laws began to be outlawed in 1954, when the Supreme Court ruled that segregation in public schools was unconstitutional.

Independent Practice
Have students complete the graphic organizer by filling in details about the causes and effects of the Civil War.

Monitor Progress
- Show *Section Reading Support Transparency USC 47* and ask students to check their graphic organizers individually. Go over key concepts and clarify key vocabulary as needed.

    United States and Canada Transparencies, *Section Reading Support Transparency USC 47*

- Tell students to fill in the last column of the *Reading Readiness Guide.* Ask them to evaluate if what they learned was what they had expected to learn.

    All in One United States and Canada Teaching Resources, *Reading Readiness Guide,* p. 144

Assess and Reteach

Assess Progress   L2
Have students complete the Section Assessment. Administer the *Section Quiz.*

    All in One United States and Canada Teaching Resources, *Section Quiz,* p. 146

Reteach   L1
If students need more instruction, have them read this section in the Reading and Vocabulary Study Guide.

    Chapter 7, Section 2, **Western Hemisphere Reading and Vocabulary Study Guide,** pp. 69–71

Extend   L3
Assign the *Small Group Activity: Presenting an Oral Biography.* Have students work in groups to create an oral presentation about a historical figure of the Civil War.

    All in One United States and Canada Teaching Resources, *Small Group Activity: Presenting an Oral Biography,* pp. 165–168

Answer

Draw Conclusions Possible answer: African Americans wanted to fight to support the end of slavery in the United States.

Citizen Heroes

Read the **Citizens Heroes** on this page. Ask students **What sort of dangers do you think Barton and other nurses faced during the Civil War?** *(Civil War nurses may have faced dangers such as battlefield injury and disease spread in makeshift hospitals.)*

Answers

✓ **Reading Check** Some Southern states seceded after a Northerner, Abraham Lincoln, was elected President because they believed they would no longer have a voice in the government.

Section 2 Assessment

Key Terms

Students' sentences should reflect knowledge of each Key Term.

Target Reading Skill

Answers will vary, but should indicate that students understand the concept of clarifying a word or an idea by reading ahead.

Comprehension and Critical Thinking

1. (a) The United States increased its size by purchasing the Louisiana Territory, moving Native Americans off their land, and winning land in wars. **(b)** Settlers took the land of Native Americans, often fighting them to control it. Also, government actions, such as the Indian Removal Act, forced Native Americans to give up their land and relocate to Indian Territory in Oklahoma. **(c)** The Industrial Revolution spurred farmers to come to the cities to work in factories. It also encouraged immigrants to come to the United States in search of jobs. The invention of the railroad and steam engines also made transportation to big cities more efficient.

2. (a) The Southern states, which supported slavery, seceded after a Northerner, Abraham Lincoln, was elected President. They believed they would no longer have a voice in the government. **(b)** Many Northerners opposed slavery, while white Southerners felt slavery was necessary to the South's economy. The debate raged on until the Southern states, seeing the balance of power tipping toward the North, finally seceded. **(c)** African Americans were separated from whites in most public places, including schools, restaurants, and trains.

Writing Activity

Use the *Rubric for Assessing a Journal Entry* to evaluate students' diary entries.

All in One United States and Canada Teaching Resources, *Rubric for Assessing a Journal Entry,* p. 184

Go Online PHSchool.com Typing in the Web code when prompted will bring students directly to detailed instructions for this activity.

Citizen Heroes

Clara Barton

When the Civil War began, Clara Barton learned that many soldiers were suffering because of the lack of supplies on the front lines. She decided to help by setting up an organization to deliver supplies to men wounded in battle. She also worked as a nurse in hospitals located near battlefields. Because of her gentle and helpful ways, Barton earned the name Angel of the Battlefield. Years later, she founded the American branch of the Red Cross.

Reconstruction The Civil War ended in 1865 when the Confederates surrendered. Lincoln wanted the Southern states to return willingly to the Union. This was the first step in his plan for the Reconstruction, or rebuilding, of the nation. Less than a week after the end of the war, Lincoln was assassinated, or murdered. Vice President Andrew Johnson tried to carry out Lincoln's plan. But Congress resisted his efforts. Finally, Congress took complete control of Reconstruction. The Union Army governed the South until new state officials were elected.

In 1877, the Union Army withdrew. But Southern lawmakers soon voted to **segregate**, or separate, black people from white people. Segregation affected all aspects of life. Southern states passed laws, called Jim Crow laws, that separated blacks and whites in schools, restaurants, theaters, trains, streetcars, playgrounds, hospitals, and even cemeteries. Some African Americans brought lawsuits to challenge segregation. The laws passed during Reconstruction would become the basis of the civil rights movement in later years. The difficult struggle to preserve the United States had succeeded. But the long struggle to guarantee equality to all Americans still lay ahead.

✓ **Reading Check** **Why did some Southern states secede from the United States?**

Section 2 Assessment

Key Terms

Review the key terms at the beginning of this section. Use each term in a sentence that explains its meaning.

Target Reading Skill

What word or idea were you able to clarify by reading ahead?

Comprehension and Critical Thinking

1. (a) List In what ways did the United States increase the area of its land?
(b) Identify Effects How did the growing nation affect Native Americans?
(c) Identify Causes What factors led to a population boom in northeastern cities?

2. (a) Identify Why did the Southern states withdraw from the Union?
(b) Explore the Main Idea How did the issue of slavery become a cause of the Civil War?
(c) Analyze How did segregation affect African Americans?

Writing Activity

Write an entry on a plan for Reconstruction that President Lincoln might have made in his diary.

Go Online PHSchool.com

For: An activity on the Civil War
Visit: PHSchool.com
Web Code: lhd-4202

The U.S. on the Brink of Change

Prepare to Read

Objectives

In this section you will
1. Explore what happened in the United States from 1865 to 1914.
2. Find out what happened during the World Wars.
3. Explore the challenges the United States faces at home and abroad.

Taking Notes

As you read the section, look for details about the United States becoming a world power. Copy the outline below and fill in each main idea and detail.

```
I. The United States from 1865 to 1914
   A. Moving to the Midwest
      1.
      2.
   B.
II.
```

Target Reading Skill

Paraphrase Paraphrasing can help you understand what you read. When you paraphrase, you restate in your own words what you have read. As you read this section, paraphrase, or "say back," the information following each red or blue heading.

Key Terms

- **labor force** (LAY bur fawrs) *n.* the supply of workers

- **Holocaust** (HAHL uh kawst) *n.* the murder of six million Jews during World War II
- **Cold War** (kohld wawr) *n.* a period of great tension between the United States and the Soviet Union
- **civil rights** (SIV ul ryts) *n.* the basic rights due to all citizens
- **terrorist** (TEHR ur ist) *n.* a person who uses violence and fear to achieve goals

Objectives

Social Studies

1. Explore what happened in the United States from 1865 to 1914.
2. Find out what happened during the World Wars.
3. Explore the challenges the United States faces at home and abroad.

Reading/Language Arts

Use paraphrasing to help you understand what you read.

Prepare to Read

Build Background Knowledge L2

Draw the beginning of an idea web, placing the words "The United State Becomes a World Power" in the center. Ask students to glance through the section's headings, photographs, and captions. They can also recall any prior knowledge about the Industrial Revolution, World War I, World War II, or the civil rights movement. Ask students what kinds of events they think led to the United States becoming a world power, using an Idea Wave (TE, p. T35) to add students' ideas to the web.

Set a Purpose for Reading L2

- Preview the Objectives.

- Read each statement in the *Reading Readiness Guide* aloud. Ask students to mark the statements true or false.

  All in One **United States and Canada Teaching Resources,** *Reading Readiness Guide,* p. 148

- Have students discuss the statements in pairs or groups of four, then mark their worksheets again. Use the Numbered Heads participation strategy (TE, p. T36) to call on students to share their group's perspectives.

Vocabulary Builder

Preview Key Terms L2

Pronounce each Key Term, then ask the students to say the word with you. Provide a simple explanation such as, "The Cold War refers to the political tension and military rivalry between the United States and the Soviet Union following World War II."

Jacob Riis was an angry man. In one of his books, he introduced his readers to slum life in the late 1800s. He wanted other people to be angry, too—angry enough to change things.

> **Come over here. Step carefully over this baby—it is a baby, in spite of its rags and dirt—under these iron bridges called fire escapes, but loaded down . . . with broken household goods, with washtubs and barrels, over which no man could climb from a fire. . . . That baby's parents live in the rear tenement [apartment] here. . . . There are plenty of houses with half a hundred such in [them].**
>
> —*Jacob Riis,* How the Other Half Lives

An 1886 photo of a slum by Jacob Riis

Target Reading Skill L2

Paraphrase Point out the Target Reading Skill. Explain to students that paraphrasing, or restating the information you have just read in your own words, helps you understand what you read.

Model paraphrasing by reading aloud the first paragraph on page 188 and working with the class to paraphrase the information (*The Industrial Revolution improved*

life for the rich and middle class, but did little for the poor. Many of these people were workers who could barely speak English. They earned so little that even children had to work to help their families survive.)

Give students *Paraphrase*. Have them complete the activity in their groups.

All in One **United States and Canada Teaching Resources,** *Paraphrase* p. 160

Instruct

From 1865 to 1914 `L2`

Guided Instruction

- **Vocabulary Builder** Clarify the high-use word **slum** before reading.

- Read From 1865 to 1914, using the Paragraph Shrinking technique, (TE, p. T34).

- Discuss what reformers did to help fight poverty. *(Jacob Riis wrote a book exposing the hardships of the poor, Jane Addams set up a community center in Chicago, and Mary Harris Jones helped miners fight for better wages, earning the nickname Mother Jones.)*

- Ask **How did the Homestead Act help people living in cities?** *(The Homestead Act gave poor people in the cities the opportunity to own land that they could not otherwise afford.)*

Independent Practice

Ask students to create the Taking Notes graphic organizer on a blank piece of paper. Then have them fill in the outline with the information they have just learned. Briefly model how to identify which details to record.

Monitor Progress

As students fill in the graphic organizer, circulate and make sure individuals are choosing the correct details. Provide assistance as needed.

Target Reading Skill `L2`

Paraphrase As a follow up, ask students to perform the Target Reading Skill activity in the Student Edition. *(By the 1900s, the United States expanded and grew stronger by taking control of Alaska, Hawaii, Puerto Rico, Guam, and the Philippines.)*

Answers

Draw Conclusions The Homestead Act gave people incentive to settle in the Midwest, and the railroad got them there faster and easier than previous methods.

✓ Reading Check The United States bought Alaska from Russia.

Settling the Plains
A wagon train travels in the Oklahoma Territory around 1900 (above). Railroads such as the Hannibal and St. Joseph recruited farmers to buy and settle land, as advertised in the poster above. **Draw Conclusions** *How did the Homestead Act and the railroads help to speed up settlement of the Midwest?*

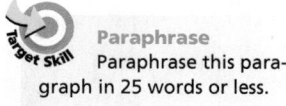
Paraphrase
Paraphrase this paragraph in 25 words or less.

From 1865 to 1914

By the late 1800s, a handful of rich people had made millions of dollars in industry. The Industrial Revolution had also made life easier for the middle class—the group of people that included skilled workers and successful farmers. But life did not improve for the poor. City slums were crowded with immigrants. These newcomers were a huge labor force, or supply of workers. Many couldn't speak English. Employers paid them little. Even small children worked so that families could make ends meet.

Reformers like Jacob Riis began to protest such poverty. In Chicago, Jane Addams set up a settlement house, or community center, for poor immigrants. Mary Harris Jones helped miners organize for better wages. Because of her work to end child labor, people called her Mother Jones.

Moving to the Midwest To leave poverty behind, many people moved to the open plains and prairies of the Midwest. The United States government attracted settlers to this region with the Homestead Act of 1862. This act gave free land to settlers. Settlers faced a difficult life on the plains. Still, thousands came west, helped by the development of railroads that connected the East Coast with the West.

New Territories The United States also expanded beyond its continental borders. In 1867, the United States bought the territory of Alaska from Russia. In 1898, the United States took control of Hawaii. In that same year, the United States fought and won the Spanish-American War. The victory gave the United States control of the Spanish lands of Puerto Rico, Guam, and the Philippines. By the 1900s, America had a strong economy, military might, and overseas territory.

✓ Reading Check **How did the United States get Alaska?**

Vocabulary Builder

Use the information below to teach students this section's high-use words.

High-Use Word	Definition and Sample Sentence
slum, p. 187	*n.* overcrowded and poor area of housing in a city or town Many city governments are improving living conditions so there are no more **slums**.
restore, p. 189	*v.* to bring back or establish again The damaged car was **restored** and looked brand new.

Guided Instruction

- **Vocabulary Builder** Clarify the high-use word **restore** before reading.

- Read about The World at War with students. As students read, circulate and make sure individuals can answer the Reading Check question.

- Discuss with students how Roosevelt tried to lift America out of the Great Depression. *(Roosevelt created a plan called the New Deal, a series of government programs to help people get jobs and restore the economy.)*

- Ask students **What role did the United States play in World War II?** *(After the Japanese attacked Pearl Harbor, the United States declared war and helped the Allies win important battles in Europe and the Pacific.)*

Independent Practice

Tell students to continue to fill in their outlines with the information they have just learned.

Monitor Progress

Circulate and make sure students are choosing the correct details as they fill in their graphic organizers. Provide assistance as needed.

The World at War

Now the United States had a major role in world affairs. As a result, the country was drawn into international conflicts. In 1914, World War I broke out in Europe. President Woodrow Wilson did not want America to take part, but when Germany began sinking American ships, Wilson had no choice. He declared war. The United States joined the Allied Powers of Great Britain and France. In 1917, thousands of American soldiers sailed to Europe. They fought against the Central Powers, which included Germany, Austria-Hungary, and Turkey. With this added strength, the Allies won the war in 1918. The terms of peace in the Treaty of Versailles punished Germany severely. Its harshness led to another worldwide conflict 20 years later.

The Economy Collapses Following World War I, the United States' economy boomed. Women enjoyed new freedoms and the hard-won right to vote. More and more people bought cars, refrigerators, radios, and other modern conveniences.

In 1929, however, the world was overcome by an economic disaster called the Great Depression. In America, factories closed, people lost their jobs, and farmers lost their farms. Many banks closed, and people lost their life's savings. In 1933, President Franklin D. Roosevelt took office. He created a plan called the New Deal. This was a series of government programs to help people get jobs and to restore the economy. Some of these programs, like Social Security, are still in place today. Social Security provides income to people who are retired or disabled.

Americans at War
Nurses place a wounded soldier on a stretcher during World War I (below). Recruitment posters such as the one below called on Americans to join the military. **Draw Inferences** *Why do you think this poster was effective in getting Americans to volunteer for military duty?*

Skills for Life Skills Mini Lesson

Analyze Primary Sources

1. Tell students that a *primary source* is written by someone who actually experienced what is being described. To analyze a primary source, identify who created the source and when, look for bias, then evaluate the source.

2. Help students practice by reading the primary source on page 187.

3. Have students apply the skill by answering the following questions: Who created the primary source? Does the writer have any bias? *(Jacob Riis, a writer angry about slums)* How reliable is the source? *(His statements are facts and provide a first-hand account of the conditions.)*

Answer

Draw Inferences This poster was probably very effective because the slogan and image directly address the viewer.

The U.S. At Home and Abroad

Guided Instruction

- Read about the United States after World War II in The U.S. At Home and Abroad.

- Discuss with students the postwar events that created tension between the United States and the Soviet Union. (*As the Soviet Union began to take control of many eastern European nations, the U.S. feared that it planned to spread communism throughout the world. Two wars stemmed from this tension: in Korea and Vietnam.*)

- Point out that Martin Luther King, Jr., was much admired for his nonviolent approach to social change. Ask students to think of other examples of nonviolent approaches to social change. (*Possible answers: writing to legislators; striking; demonstrating; writing letters to editors; helping candidates for public office; running for office. If not mentioned, suggest that one of the most important methods is voting.*)

- Ask students **What challenges does the United States face today?** (*the fight against terrorism; having a stable economy*)

This Rosie the Riveter poster from World War II encouraged women to join the workforce.

A Second World War The Great Depression affected people around the world. In Germany, Adolf Hitler rose to power, promising to restore Germany's wealth and power. He began World War II. In 1941, Germany's ally, Japan, attacked the United States naval base at Pearl Harbor, Hawaii. The United States declared war on Japan. Germany then declared war on the United States.

The United States sent armed forces to fight in Europe and in the Pacific. President Roosevelt, who led the nation in war, did not live to see peace. He died in April 1945, and Vice President Harry S Truman became President.

In May of 1945, the Allies defeated the Germans. During the summer of 1945, President Truman decided to drop two atomic bombs on Japan. That convinced Japan to surrender. Finally, World War II was over.

By the end of the war in 1945, Europe was in ruins. People around the world learned that Hitler had forced Jews, Gypsies, Slavs, and others into brutal prison camps. Millions of people, including some six million Jews, were murdered. This horrible mass murder is called the **Holocaust** (HAHL uh kawst).

✓ Reading Check **What led the United States to take part in World War II?**

Timeline Skills

The United States has been involved in both domestic and international conflicts since the Civil War ended. **Identify** Which of the wars shown did not involve open warfare? **Compare** How long was this war, compared to the others shown on the timeline?

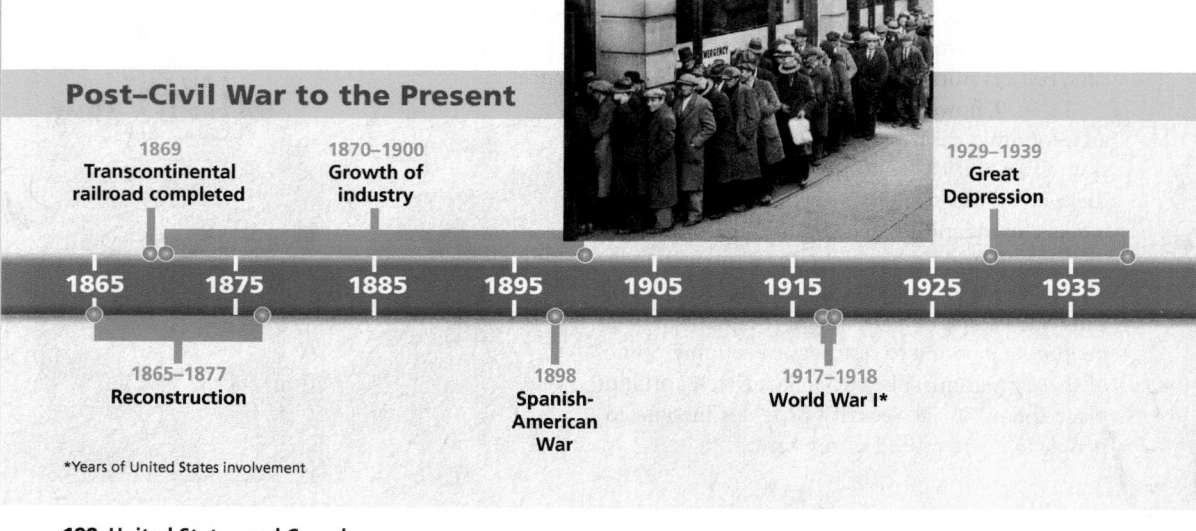

Post–Civil War to the Present

| 1865 | 1875 | 1885 | 1895 | 1905 | 1915 | 1925 | 1935 |

1869 Transcontinental railroad completed

1870–1900 Growth of industry

1929–1939 Great Depression

1865–1877 Reconstruction

1898 Spanish-American War

1917–1918 World War I*

*Years of United States involvement

190 United States and Canada

Answers

✓ Reading Check When Japan attacked the U.S. naval base at Pearl Harbor, the United States declared war on Japan. Germany then declared war on the United States.

Timeline Skills Identify the Cold War Compare It was the longest war, lasting 46 years. The next-longest war, the Vietnam War, lasted 20 years.

Differentiated Instruction

For English Language Learners   L1
If appropriate assign *Guided Reading and Review (Spanish)* to help facilitate understanding of how the United States became a world power.

📄 *Guided Reading and Review (Spanish)*, **Spanish Support,** p. 70

For Gifted and Talented   L3
Ask students to research the art, music, literature, or drama that emerged from the Great Depression. Ask students to present their research to the class.

The U.S. at Home and Abroad

Following World War II, the United States was a world super-power. It faced new challenges and responsibilities both at home and abroad.

Tension with the Soviets   In 1922, the Soviet Union had been created. It adopted a form of government called commu-nism. Under this system, the state owns all property, such as farms and factories, on behalf of its citizens.

After World War II, the Soviet Union took control of many Eastern European countries. The United States feared the Soviets were trying to spread communism throughout the world. As a result, the United States and the Soviet Union entered the Cold War, a period of great tension. The Cold War lasted about four decades. Although the two countries never faced each other in an actual war, two wars grew out of this tension—the Korean War and the Vietnam War.

The Fight for Civil Rights   The economy boomed in the post-war years, but not all citizens shared in the benefits. In the South, racial segregation was a way of life. Many African Ameri-cans began to unite to win their civil rights, or the rights belong-ing to all citizens. The movement had many leaders, including Martin Luther King, Jr. He led peaceful marches and organized boycotts against companies that practiced discrimination, or unfair treatment of a group or person. The movement's success inspired others who felt they were treated unfairly, including women and Mexican Americans.

Links Across Time

Living Underground During the Cold War, many Americans became concerned about the possibility of a nuclear war with the Soviet Union. The United States government encouraged families to build fallout, or bomb, shelters as shown below. A fallout shelter is a concrete and steel structure designed to protect people from nuclear radiation. Many of these shelters were under-ground. A typical bomb shelter would have canned food, bottled water, first-aid supplies, and other necessities.

Links

Read the **Links Across Time** on this page. Ask students **What was the pur-pose of fallout shelters?** (*The purpose was to protect people from nuclear radia-tion in the event of nuclear war with the Soviet Union.*)

Independent Practice
Ask students to complete their outlines with the information they have just learned.

Monitor Progress
- Show *Section Reading Support Transpar-ency USC 48* and ask students to check their graphic organizers individually. Go over key concepts and clarify key vocabu-lary as needed.

   United States and Canada Transpar-encies, *Section Reading Support Transparency USC 48*

- Tell students to fill in the last column of the *Reading Readiness Guide.* Probe for what they learned that confirms or invalidates each statement.

   All in One **United States and Canada Teaching Resources,** *Reading Readiness Guide,* p. 148

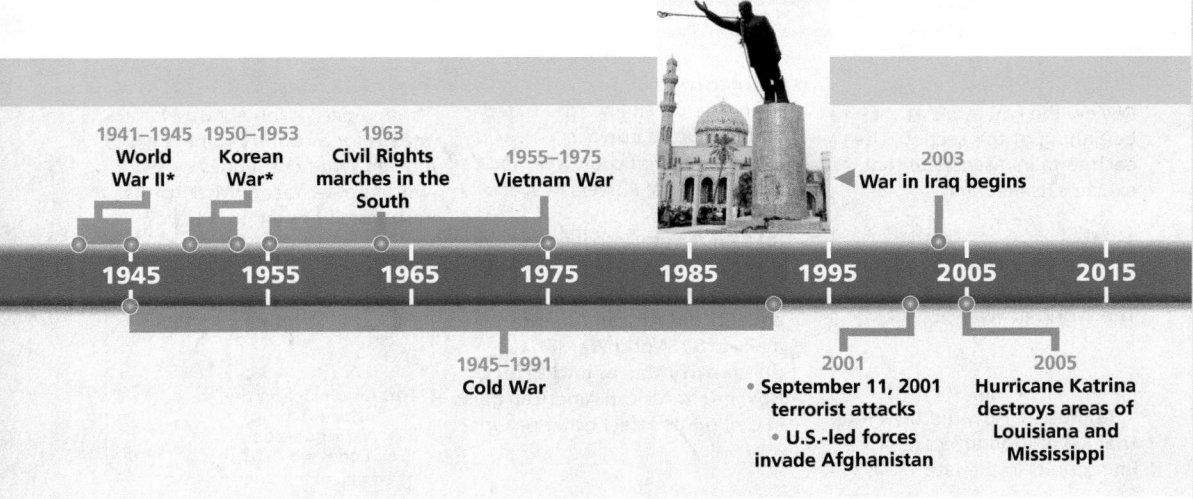

1941–1945 World War II*	**1950–1953** Korean War*	**1963** Civil Rights marches in the South

1955–1975 Vietnam War

2003 War in Iraq begins

1945   1955   1965   1975   1985   1995   2005   2015

1945–1991 Cold War

2001
• September 11, 2001 terrorist attacks
• U.S.-led forces invade Afghanistan

2005 Hurricane Katrina destroys areas of Louisiana and Mississippi

Chapter 7 Section 3 **191**

Differentiated Instruction

For Advanced Readers L3
Have students research the Civil Rights Movement, starting with the Montgomery Bus Boycott and ending with the signing of the Civil Rights Act by President Lyndon B. Johnson. Ask students to work in pairs to create a time line of the Civil Rights Movement.

For Special Needs Students L1
Pair students with more proficient students to learn more about the history of their city or town by completing the *Book Project: Make a Timeline of Local History.*

   All in One **United States and Canada Teaching Resources,** *Book Project: Make a Timeline of Local History,* pp. 79–81

Assess and Reteach

Assess Progress L2
Have students complete the Section Assessment. Administer the *Section Quiz*.

All In One **United States and Canada Teaching Resources**, *Section Quiz*, p. 150

Reteach L1
If students need more instruction, have them read this section in the Reading and Vocabulary Study Guide.

📖 Chapter 7, Section 3, **Western Hemisphere Reading and Vocabulary Study Guide**, pp. 72–74

Extend L3
Have students learn more about the lives of the people in the United States and Canada during World War II by reading *A Child in Prison Camp*. Assign students to work in groups to discuss the questions at the end of the selection.

All In One **United States and Canada Teaching Resources**, *A Child in Prison Camp*, pp. 179–181

Answers

✓ **Reading Check** The two principal countries in the Cold War were the United States and the Soviet Union.

Section 3 Assessment

Key Terms
Students' sentences should reflect knowledge of each Key Term.

🔖 Target Reading Skill
Answers will vary, but should include important information such as the United States' involvement in international affairs, the United States entering the war, and the peace agreement that later caused conflict.

Comprehension and Critical Thinking
1. (a) Because poor immigrants worked for low wages, they lived in poverty in tenement slums. Even children had to work to help their families. **(b)** The United States acquired Alaska from the Russians, took control of Hawaii, won the Spanish-American War, and acquired Puerto Rico, Guam, and the Philippines.

2. (a) Germany, Austria-Hungary, and Turkey **(b)** The war began when Germany invaded Poland in 1939. The United States entered in 1941 when Japan attacked Pearl Harbor.

Firefighters walk away from the rubble of the World Trade Center towers in New York City.

America in the World Today   At the beginning of the twenty-first century, Americans continued to look for solutions to long-term problems, such as homelessness, low wages, and pollution.

The economy reached new heights in the 1990s, powered by the Internet business revolution. The Internet is a network of interconnected computers that allows users to access computerized information. After a downturn in the early 2000s, the economy continued to grow. At the same time, it faced challenges such as high oil prices and rising federal debt.

The United States also faced a new challenge at home and abroad—on September 11, 2001, terrorists attacked the World Trade Center in New York City and the Pentagon in Washington, D.C. **Terrorists** use violence to frighten people or governments or to express their views. In response to these and possible future attacks, the United States took military action in both Afghanistan and Iraq. Saddam Hussein (sah DAHM hoo SAYN), Iraq's brutal dictator, was captured by coalition troops in December 2003. However, the United States continues to maintain a military presence in Iraq. The United States works with its allies around the world, especially Great Britain, to fight terrorism.

✓ **Reading Check** **What countries were involved in the Cold War?**

Section 3 Assessment

Key Terms
Review the key terms at the beginning of this section. Use each term in a sentence that explains its meaning.

🔖 Target Reading Skill
Paraphrase the paragraph on page 189 under the red heading The World at War.

Comprehension and Critical Thinking
1. (a) Recall How did the Industrial Revolution affect poor immigrants in the late 1800s?

(b) Identify Causes What three events helped make the United States a world power?
2. (a) List What countries made up the Central Powers in World War I?
(b) Sequence Describe the events that led to World War II.
3. (a) Explain What gains in equality did African Americans make after World War II?
(b) Identify Cause and Effect How might African American gains in civil rights affect other groups?

Writing Activity
Write a paragraph about what it means for a country to be a world power. What challenges would a world power face? What special responsibilities might it have?

Go Online
PHSchool.com

For: An activity on the Homestead Act
Visit: PHSchool.com
Web Code: lhp-4203

3. (a) African Americans began winning civil rights. **4. (b)** By winning their civil rights, African Americans inspired other groups, such as women, the disabled, and Mexican Americans, to fight for their rights.

Writing Activity
Use the *Rubric for Assessing a Writing Assignment* to evaluate students' paragraphs.

All In One **United States and Canada Teaching Resources**, *Rubric for Assessing a Writing Assignment*, p. 183

Go Online
PHSchool.com Typing in the Web code when prompted will bring students directly to detailed instructions for this activity.

The History of Canada

Prepare to Read

Objectives

In this section you will

1. Learn about why France and Britain were rivals in Canada.
2. Discover how Canada became an independent nation.
3. Explore how Canada became a world power in the 1900s.

Taking Notes

As you read the section, look for events that happened before and after the British North America Act in 1867. Copy the table below and write each event in the correct column.

British North America Act (1867)	
Before	**After**
•	•
•	•
•	•

Target Reading Skill

Summarize When you summarize, you review and state, in the correct order, the main points you have read. Summarizing what you read is a good technique to help you comprehend and study. As you read, pause occasionally to summarize what you have read.

Key Terms

- **dominion** (duh MIN yun) *n.* a self-governing area subject to Great Britain
- **bilingual** (by LIN gwul) *adj.* able to speak two languages

The Haida people of British Columbia tell this tale. As in many Native American tales, nature plays an important role.

> **While he was crying and singing his dirge [sad song], a figure emerged from the lake. It was a strange animal, in its mouth a stick that it was gnawing. On each side of the animal were two smaller ones also gnawing sticks. Then the largest figure . . . spoke, 'Don't be so sad! It is I, your wife, and your two children. We have returned to our home in the water. . . . Call me the Beaver woman.'**
>
> —*Haida tale*

To the Haida and other native peoples in Canada, beavers were especially important. Imagine how they felt when European trappers killed almost all of the beavers to make fur hats.

Haida portrait mask

Target Reading Skill L2

Summarize Point out the Target Reading Skill. Tell students that a summary reviews and states what the paragraph or passage is about. To summarize, you must determine what the most important idea is and leave out the less important details.

Model the strategy by working with students to summarize the first paragraph on page 194. (*Fur trade in Canada was a source of conflict between France and Great Britain. A peace treaty in 1713 gave Great Britain what is now the southeastern corner of Canada.*)

Give students *Summarize*. Have them complete the activity in their groups.

All in One United States and Canada Teaching Resources, *Summarize,* p. 161

Objectives

Social Studies

1. Learn about why France and Britain were rivals in Canada.
2. Discover how Canada became an independent nation.
3. Explore how Canada became a world power in the 1900s.

Reading/Language Arts

Use summarizing to help comprehend the main points you have read.

Prepare to Read

Build Background Knowledge L2

Tell students that in this section they will learn about the history of Canada. Have students preview the headers and visuals in the section with the following question in mind: **How are the histories of Canada and the United States similar and how are they different?** Conduct an Idea Wave (TE, p. T35) to generate a class list of similarities and differences on the board.

Set a Purpose for Reading L2

- Preview the Objectives.

- Read each statement in the *Reading Readiness Guide* aloud. Ask students to mark the statements true or false.

  All in One United States and Canada Teaching Resources, *Reading Readiness Guide,* p. 152

- Have students discuss the statements in pairs or groups of four, then mark their worksheets again. Use the Numbered Heads participation strategy (TE, p. T36) to get students to share their group's perspective.

Vocabulary Builder
Preview Key Terms L2

Pronounce each Key Term, then ask the students to say the word with you. Provide a simple explanation such as, "A person who is bilingual speaks more than one language fluently."

Instruct

The French and the British L2

Guided Instruction

- **Vocabulary Builder** Clarify the high-use word **decisive** before reading.

- Read The French and the British, using the Oral Cloze strategy (TE, p. T33).

- Discuss how the first two British governors of Canada tried to keep peace with the French settlers. (*They passed the Quebec Act, giving the French people in Quebec the right to speak their own language, practice their own religion, and follow their own customs.*)

- Ask students **What do you think was the greatest source of conflict between the French and British—control of land or cultural differences? Explain.** (*In the late 1700s, the French wanted land for trading and the British wanted land for settlements. By the 1800s, cultural differences became the greater problem and Great Britain had to divide the land into two colonies: one for the British and the other for the French.*)

Independent Practice

Ask students to create the Taking Notes graphic organizer on a blank piece of paper. Tell students that the British North America Act was accepted in 1867. Then have them fill in the table with the information they have just learned.

Monitor Progress

As students fill in the graphic organizer, circulate and make sure individuals are choosing the correct details. Provide assistance as needed.

Answers

Analyze Images Probably not, because the British would not have been able to attack Quebec.

√ **Reading Check** After the American Revolution, many Loyalists moved to Canada. Most did not want to live in a French culture, so Great Britain divided the land into two colonies: Upper and Lower Canada.

The Battle of Quebec, 1759
The Battle of Quebec was a turning point in the Seven Years' War. This painting illustrates how British troops found a passage through the cliffs that protected Quebec. **Analyze Images** *Do you think that Quebec would have fallen to the British if troops had not found a passage in? Explain why or why not.*

The French and the British

The profitable fur trade in Canada was a source of conflict for France and Great Britain. They had fought wars all over the world, but had signed a peace treaty in 1713. The treaty gave Great Britain the Hudson Bay region, Newfoundland, and part of Acadia, which later became the southeastern corner of Canada.

The peace was uneasy. Against their will, French Catholics in Acadia came under the rule of British Protestants. The French controlled the lowlands south of Hudson Bay and lands around the St. Lawrence River. Both countries wanted to control the Ohio River valley, farther to the south. The French wanted the beavers for furs. The British wanted the land for settlement.

Great Britain Gains Control The contest for this region erupted into the Seven Years' War in 1756. The British won the decisive Battle of Quebec in 1759. The Treaty of Paris, signed in 1763, gave Great Britain complete control over Canada. Some French settlers returned to France. Those who stayed resisted English culture. The first two British governors of Canada were sympathetic to the French and passed the Quebec Act. It gave the French people in Quebec the right to speak their own language, practice their own religion, and follow their own customs.

Two Colonies Emerge During the American Revolution, some Americans did not want independence from Britain. They were called Loyalists. After the war, many Loyalists moved to Canada. But most did not want to live in a French culture. To avoid problems, Great Britain divided the land into two colonies, Upper Canada and Lower Canada. Most Loyalists moved into Upper Canada, which is now called Ontario. French Canadians remained in Lower Canada, which is now Quebec.

√ Reading Check **Why was Canada divided into two colonies?**

194 United States and Canada

Vocabulary Builder

Use the information below to teach students this section's high-use words.

High-Use Word	Definition and Sample Sentence
decisive, p. 194	*adj.* affecting what comes next, most important That championship match was a **decisive** moment in her career.
cooperate, p. 195	*v.* to work together for a common purpose For the team to be successful, it is important that they **cooperate**.
adopt, p. 198	*v.* to accept an idea or way of doing things The employees **adopted** the work ethic of their new supervisor.

Canada Seeks Independence

The people of Upper and Lower Canada worked together during the War of 1812. They fought to protect Canada from invasion by the United States. Once the War of 1812 ended, however, Canadians with different backgrounds stopped cooperating with one another. Both French Canadians and British Canadians hated British rule. Many felt Britain was too far away to understand their needs. But the two groups did not join in rebellion. In 1837, a French Canadian named Louis Papineau (LOO ee pah pea NOH) organized a revolt in Lower Canada. His goal was to establish the region as a separate country. The British easily defeated the rebels. The same thing happened in Upper Canada. William Mackenzie led the people against British rule. Again, the British put down the separatist rebellion.

A Peaceful Revolution Still, British leaders were afraid more trouble was coming. They sent the Earl of Durham to learn what was wrong. When Durham returned, he had many suggestions. First, he suggested that the Canadians be given more control of their government. He also thought all of the colonies should be united. But the British government united only Upper and Lower Canada to form the Province of Canada. Nova Scotia, Newfoundland, Prince Edward Island, and New Brunswick were not included in this union. If Canada were completely united, the British feared the Canadians might make a successful rebellion.

Citizen Heroes

Louis Riel

A Voice of Protest
In 1869, the Canadian government wanted to finish the cross-country railroad across the flat plains region. Louis Riel, leader of the Métis (may TEEZ)—mixed European and Native American people—objected to the plan. The Métis said that the railroad would bring new settlers, who would take away their land. The government refused to stop, so Riel led an armed revolt. It failed, and Riel was later executed for treason, but the government did set aside land for the Métis. Today, the Métis consider Riel a hero.

The Canadian Pacific Railway
On November 7, 1885, Canada's far-flung provinces were tied together as the last spike was driven in, completing the Canadian Pacific Railway. **Draw Conclusions** *Why was a railroad connecting all of Canada important to Canadians?*

Chapter 7 Section 4 **195**

Citizen Heroes

Read the **Citizens Heroes** on this page. Ask students **Why do the Métis think Riel was heroic?** (*The efforts of Riel led to land being set aside for the Métis.*)

Canada Seeks Independence L2

Guided Instruction

■ **Vocabulary Builder** Clarify the high-use word **cooperate** before reading.

■ Read Canada Seeks Independence. As students read, circulate and make sure individuals can answer the Reading Check question.

■ Discuss the role the Earl of Durham played in helping to move Canadians toward self-rule. (*The Earl of Durham suggested that Canadians be given more control over their government and that all the colonies be united.*)

■ Ask students to compare and contrast the United States and Canada's break from Great Britain. (*The United States fought a war to break from Great Britain, while Canada's break was peaceful. After the Revolutionary War, the United States became completely separate from Great Britain. Under the British North American Act, Canada was not completely independent, but had a central government to run the country.*)

Skills Mini Lesson

Problem-Solving

1. Tell students that identifying problems and their solutions in a passage can help them understand what they read.

2. Have students practice the skill by determining the problem that existed between the British and their Canadian subjects. (*Both French and British Canadians hated British rule.*)

3. Have students list attempts to solve the problem and the successful solution. (*Attempts: rebellions by French and British Canadians; uniting Upper and Lower Canada. Solution: uniting all the provinces under the British North America Act.*)

Answer

Draw Conclusions The railroad made traveling across the vast spaces of Canada much easier.

Guided Instruction (continued)

- Discuss the effects of the British North America Act. *(It made Canada more independent, but not completely self-governing. Canada could now elect their own leaders and control their own government.)*

- Ask students **Why did Canada enter World War I?** *(Because Britain entered the war, and Canada was a British subject at the time.)*

Independent Practice

Ask students to continue to fill in their graphic organizer with the information the have just learned.

Monitor Progress

Circulate and make sure students are choosing the correct details as they fill in the graphic organizer. Provide assistance as needed.

Target Reading Skill

Summarize As a follow up, ask students to answer the Target Reading Skill question in the Student Edition. *(Canada became a dominion of Great Britain in 1867. After this "peaceful revolution," Canada saw years of growth and change. When World War I broke out, Canada sent soldiers and resources overseas and contributed greatly to the Allied victory.)*

Answers

MAP MASTER Skills Activity **Name** Alberta, Saskatchewan, Newfoundland and Labrador, and Nunavut
Analyze eastern Canada, because Britain gained control of this area in the 1700s

Go Online PHSchool.com Students may practice their map skills using the interactive online version of this map.

✓ Reading Check The British feared that if Canada was completely united, it might have the strength for a successful rebellion.

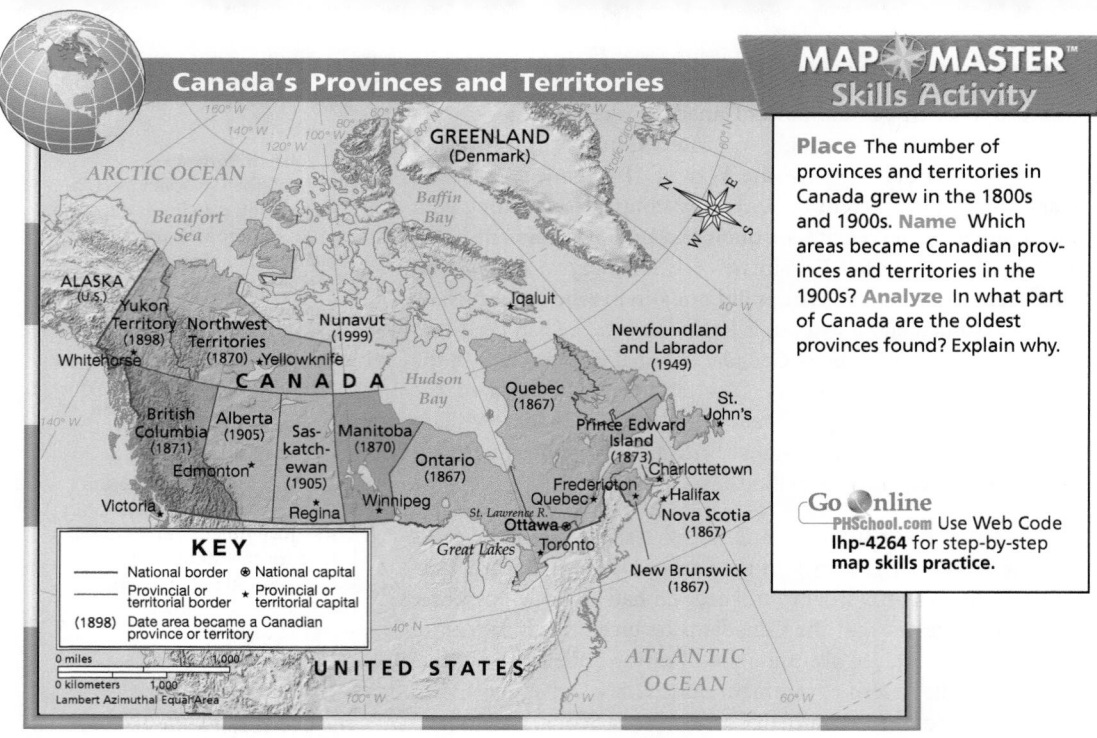

Summarize
Summarize this page. Be sure to include two factors that led Canada to become a world power.

Canadians believed that all provinces should be represented in their government. In 1864, leaders met to work out a plan to form a union. On July 1, 1867, the British Parliament accepted the British North America Act. This made Canada "one Dominion under the name of Canada." A **dominion** is a self-governing area. Canada was not completely independent from Great Britain, but now a central government would run the country. Canadians would elect their own leaders. Without a war, Canadians had won the right to control their own government.

After its "peaceful revolution," Canada saw years of growth and change. Skilled European farmers settled in Canada's western plains. Gold and other valuable minerals were discovered in the Yukon Territory in the 1890s. That brought miners to the far northwest. Canada was becoming rich and important.

Canada Becomes a World Power When Britain entered World War I, Canadians were still British subjects. Canada, therefore, entered the war, too. Canada willingly sent soldiers and resources overseas. Canada contributed so much to the Allied victory that the young country became a world power.

✓ Reading Check Why didn't the British want Canada to be united?

Differentiated Instruction

For English Language Learners [L1]
Have students listen to the recorded version of the section on the Student Edition on Audio CD. Check for understanding by pausing the CD and asking students to share their answers to the Reading Checks.

- Chapter 7, Section 4, **Student Edition on Audio CD**

For Special Needs Students [L1]
Pair students with more proficient partners to complete the *Activity Shop Interdisciplinary: Transportation* activity.

All in One United States and Canada Teaching Resources, *Activity Shop Interdisciplinary: Transportation,* pp. 169–170

Canada: Postwar to the Present

During World War II, Canadians built factories. They made war supplies and goods such as clothes and shoes. Because of the war, people could not get such products from Europe. After the war, Canadian goods found a ready market in the United States and Europe.

Also, during the postwar years, immigrants poured into Canada. They came from Asia, Europe, Africa, and the Caribbean. The newcomers filled jobs in factories and businesses. Soon, Canada became one of the world's most important industrial nations.

The Growth of Industry Industrialization strengthened the economy but brought back old arguments. British Canadians built new factories in Quebec. That alarmed French Canadians. In 1969, the government passed new laws that made Canada a **bilingual** country. That is, Canada had two official languages—English and French. However, by 1976 some French Canadians did not want to be part of Canada. Quebec, they argued, should be independent. Many people in Quebec still feel that way today.

Canadian Industry
Canadians, such as this factory worker tending to spools of nylon (above), made important supplies during World War II. One year after the war, plans for the first Canadian-designed and built jet fighter (left) began. Nearly 700 planes were built to defend North America in case of a future attack and to participate in overseas operations. **Draw Conclusions** *What were the effects of WWII on Canadian industries?*

Guided Instruction

■ **Vocabulary Builder** Clarify the high-use word **adopt** before reading.

■ Read Canada: Postwar to the Present with students.

■ Discuss with students the good and bad aspects of postwar industrialization in Canada. *(Good: Canadians found ready markets in the United States and Europe for their goods. This strengthened the Canadian economy and created jobs. Bad: Industrialization brought back old arguments between French and British Canadians as British Canadians built factories in French Canadian Quebec.)*

■ Ask students **How did adopting a new constitution change the relationship between Canada and Great Britain?** *(The new constitution gave Canadians the power to change their constitution without British permission. This meant that Canada was now completely independent.)*

Answer

Draw Conclusions Canadian industries grew stronger as a result of World War II. Canada became an important industrial nation.

Independent Practice
Ask students to complete the table with the information they have just learned.

Monitor Progress
- Show *Section Reading Support Transparency USC 49* and ask students to check their graphic organizers individually. Go over key concepts and clarify key vocabulary as needed.

  United States and Canada Transparencies, *Section Reading Support Transparency USC 49*

- Tell students to fill in the last column of the *Reading Readiness Guide*. Probe for what they learned that confirms or invalidates each statement.

  All in One United States and Canada Teaching Resources, *Reading Readiness Guide,* p. 152

Assess and Reteach

Assess Progress　L2
Have students complete the Section Assessment. Administer the *Section Quiz.*

All in One United States and Canada Teaching Resources, *Section Quiz,* p. 154

Reteach　L1
If students need more instruction, have them read this section in the Reading and Vocabulary Study Guide.

Chapter 7, Section 4, **Western Hemisphere Reading and Vocabulary Study Guide,** pp. 75–77

Extend　L3
Have students learn more about French traders by completing the *Enrichment* worksheet. Assign students to work in pairs to check each other's responses.

All in One United States and Canada Teaching Resources, *Enrichment,* p. 163

Answer
Draw Conclusions The Parliament Buildings are in a style of architecture that developed in Western Europe between the 1100s and 1500s.

Canada's Parliament Buildings
The Parliament Buildings are an example of the Gothic style of architecture, which is from medieval times. This type of architecture developed in Western Europe between the 1100s and 1500s. **Draw Conclusions** *How do the Parliament Buildings reflect Canada's heritage?*

198 United States and Canada

A New Constitution Although the British North America Act in 1867 gave Canadians the right to control their own government, it was still necessary for Great Britain to approve amendments to the Canadian constitution. That changed in 1982 when the Canadians adopted a new constitution. It gave Canadians the power to change their constitution without Great Britain's permission. Canada was now completely independent.

A Parliamentary System Canada's government is modeled on the British parliamentary system. Canada has a constitutional monarchy. A set of laws states what the monarch—the king or queen—can or cannot do. Because the monarch lives in Great Britain, he or she must appoint someone in Canada to act as a representative. This position is called the governor-general. Since World War II, the governor-general has been a Canadian citizen. Although the monarch is the head of state, he or she does not make any political decisions. That is the job of the prime minister, who is the head of government.

Canada is also called a parliamentary democracy. The group of representatives that makes its laws is modeled on the British parliament. Canada's Parliament, like Great Britain's, has two chambers: the House of Commons and the Senate. The House of Commons is made up of elected representatives. The governor-general appoints the members of the Senate. Senators are allowed to hold office until they are 75 years old.

Differentiated Instruction

For Less Proficient Readers　L1
Have students work with more advanced readers to make a diagram that shows how the Canadian government works. Encourage students to use the steps for interpreting diagrams laid out in the Skills for Life lesson, on pages 200 and 201 of the Student Edition.

For Gifted and Talented　L3
Have students research the Commonwealth of Nations in the twenty-first century, and report to the class on the following: Who are the member nations? Where and when do they meet? What has Great Britain provided to the member nations? Do you think it is important for these nations to maintain this alliance? Why or why not?

The Commonwealth of Nations Another tie between Canada and Great Britain is its membership in the Commonwealth of Nations. It is a voluntary organization, whose member countries are former British colonies. The purpose of the Commonwealth of Nations is to consult and cooperate with one another, particularly in matters of trade and economics. In addition, Great Britain gives members financial aid and advice. At one time, the Commonwealth of Nations was the only worldwide political organization besides the United Nations.

Although Great Britain's Queen Elizabeth II is the head of the Commonwealth of Nations, her role is symbolic. In 2002, for the celebration of her fiftieth year as monarch, she traveled from one end of the Commonwealth to the other, from Nunavut to Australia.

Canada in the World Today Today, Canada works both on its own and closely with international agencies to carry out foreign policy. It provides humanitarian aid to nations struck by natural disasters, such as Indonesia after a 2006 earthquake. Canada is involved in diplomatic and humanitarian missions to troubled countries from Haiti to Sudan. It has contributed to rebuilding both Afghanistan and Iraq. In addition, Canada maintains close trade and diplomatic ties with the United States.

✓ **Reading Check** Why did Canadians write a new constitution?

Supporters greet Queen Elizabeth in Iqaluit, Nunavut, at the start of her twelve-day tour of Canada.

Section 4 Assessment

Key Terms
Review the key terms at the beginning of this section. Use each term in a sentence that explains its meaning.

↻ **Target Reading Skill**
Write a summary of the paragraph on page 196 called Canada Becomes a World Power.

Comprehension and Critical Thinking
1. (a) **List** What two countries came into conflict in Canada in the 1700s?

(b) **Sequence** How did the fur trade lead to war in Canada?
2. (a) **Explain** Why did Canadians object to British rule?
(b) **Summarize** How did Canadians win control of their government without going to war?
3. (a) **Recall** How did Canada become an industrial power after World War II?
(b) **Link Past and Present** How is Canada still tied to Britain today?

Writing Activity
Compare and contrast the ways in which Canada and the United States became independent nations.

> **Writing Tip** One way to organize your comparison is subject by subject, or by first explaining how the United States became independent and then how Canada did.

Answers

✓ Reading Check to give Canadians the power to change their constitution without Great Britain's permission and, therefore, make them independent

Section 4 Assessment

Key Terms
Students' sentences should reflect knowledge of each Key Term.

↻ **Target Reading Skill**
Answers will vary, but should include that Canada entered World War I when Britain did, and was granted more independence from Britain for its contributions.

Comprehension and Critical Thinking
1. (a) France and Great Britain (b) The French wanted land for its beaver furs; the British wanted land for settlements.
2. (a) Canadians believed the British were too far away to understand their needs. (b) Although Britain united a portion of Canada, Canadians believed that all the provinces should be represented in their government. Leaders met and worked out a plan to form a union. The British Parliament accepted the plan and passed the British North America Act.
3. (a) Canada built factories during the war to supply goods that European nations desperately needed. This fueled their economy and encouraged immigrants to come to Canada for jobs. With a strong economy, a strong work force, and factories in place to make goods, Canada became a world leader in industry. (b) Canada's government is modeled after the British Parliament; Canada is a constitutional monarchy, meaning the British monarch is head of state; Canada is part of the Commonwealth of Nations.

Writing Activity
Use the *Rubric for Assessing a Writing Assignment* to evaluate students' comparisons.

All in One **United States and Canada Teaching Resources,** *Rubric for Assessing a Writing Assignment,* p. 183

Objective
Interpret information in a diagram.

Prepare to Read

Build Background Knowledge [L2]
Ask students if they can think of examples of things that use both text and pictures to present information. *(Examples: catalogs, cookbooks, encyclopedia articles, instruction manuals, Web sites, newspapers)* Ask students why they think these use both pictures and words.

Instruct

Interpreting Diagrams [L2]

Guided Practice
- Read the steps to interpreting diagrams as a class and write them on the board.

- Practice the skill by following the steps on p. 200 as a class. Model each step in the activity by choosing a well-known item, such as a pocket calculator, and using it to draw a simple diagram. Be sure to think aloud as you create the diagram so students can follow your thought process.

- Ask students to then write a summary describing what the diagram shows.

Independent Practice
Assign *Skills for Life* and have students complete it individually.

 United States and Canada Teaching Resources, *Skills for Life,* p. 164

Monitor Progress
As students are completing *Skills for Life,* circulate to make sure individuals are applying the skill steps effectively. Provide assistance as needed.

 # Interpreting Diagrams

Suppose that your pen pal in Canada wants to know what your school looks like. Which should you do: write her a letter describing your school or send her a photograph?

A photo would show her in an instant what your school looks like. But a letter could describe details a photograph might not show. Perhaps you would send both.

There is another way to show what something looks like *and* describe it in words: You could draw a diagram. A diagram is a picture that shows how something works or is made. It usually includes labels that tell about certain parts of the picture. It is a combination of the letter and the photograph you would send to your pen pal.

A diagram is like a game of show-and-tell—the picture shows and the labels tell.

Learn the Skill
To understand how to interpret information in a diagram, follow the steps below.

1 **Study the picture.** Notice the various parts of the picture. Get visual information from it.

2 **Read the labels.** Sometimes the labels will be numbered or will appear in a certain order to explain a step-by-step process.

3 **Summarize the information in the diagram.** From the information you gather by studying the picture and the labels, write a summary describing what the diagram shows you.

200 United States and Canada

Practice the Skill

Look at How a Locomotive Works, below, as you practice interpreting a diagram.

1 From the title, you can tell what the diagram shows. As you look at the picture, what information can you learn—even before you read the labels?

2 The labels in this diagram are meant to be read in a particular order. Do you know why? Notice that this diagram has both labels and arrows. What do the arrows show?

3 Write a paragraph describing how a locomotive works. Write as if the reader did not have the picture to look at. Don't simply repeat the text in the labels, but summarize the information in the labels and picture.

How a Locomotive Works

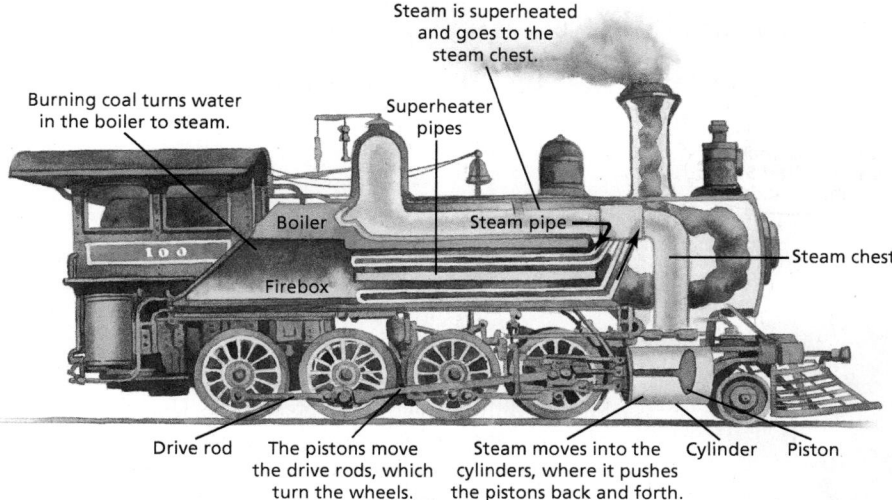

Steam is superheated and goes to the steam chest.

Burning coal turns water in the boiler to steam.

Superheater pipes

Boiler

Steam pipe

Steam chest

Firebox

Drive rod

The pistons move the drive rods, which turn the wheels.

Steam moves into the cylinders, where it pushes the pistons back and forth.

Cylinder

Piston

Apply the Skill

Find a photograph of a bicycle in a catalog or a magazine. Then, write a paragraph describing what the bicycle looks like, what parts it has, and how the parts work.

Now draw a diagram of a bicycle. Make labels showing how it works.

Compare the picture, the paragraph, and the diagram. Which one does the best job of showing and explaining how a bicycle works?

Assess Progress L2
Ask students to do the Apply the Skill activity.

Reteach L1
Have students look at the diagram of the locomotive on this page of the Student Edition. Using the skill steps, have them summarize the information that the diagram shows.

Extend L3
To extend the lesson, ask students to apply the skill steps to interpret a diagram on the *Reading a Diagram* worksheet. Here they will interpret visual representations of a strait, an inlet, a peninsula, an archipelago, and an isthmus.

All in One **United States and Canada Teaching Resources,** *Reading a Diagram,* p. 171

Differentiated Instruction

For Special Needs Students L1
To make the activity more concrete, group students with one or two more proficient readers and have them use the skill steps to create a diagram of an object in the classroom, such as a backpack. Encourage students to study the object they have chosen to help them make the diagram.

For Gifted and Talented L3
Ask students to draw a diagram, showing how a household item such as a clock, washing machine or television works. Ask them to omit the title, but include all pictures, labels, and a brief summary of the information on the diagram. Have volunteers then present their diagrams so classmates can guess which household item they are describing.

Answers
Apply the Skill
Answers will vary, but should reflect an understanding of the different methods of presenting information.

Section 5 The United States and Canada Today

Objectives

Social Studies

1. Identify the environmental concerns the United States and Canada share today.

2. Find out about the economic ties the United States and Canada have to each other and to the world.

Reading/Language Arts

Use the rereading or reading ahead strategies to better understand the words and ideas in a text.

Prepare to Read

Build Background Knowledge   L2

In this section students will learn about environmental and economic issues in the United States and Canada today. Have students preview the headings and visuals in this section. Then have students make a list of two or three ways that their communities help protect their environment. Provide a few examples (*recycling, conserving water, collecting litter*) to get them started. Use the Give One, Get One strategy (TE, p. T37) to generate ideas.

Set a Purpose for Reading   L2

■ Preview the Objectives.

■ Read each statement in the *Reading Readiness Guide*. Ask students to mark the statements true or false.

■ **All in One United States and Canada Teaching Resources,** *Reading Readiness Guide,* p. 156

■ Have students discuss the statements in pairs or groups of four, then mark their guides again. Use the Numbered Heads participation strategy (TE, p. T36) to call on students to share their group's perspectives.

Vocabulary Builder

Preview Key Terms   L2

Pronounce each Key Term, then ask the students to say the word with you. Provide a simple explanation such as, "Imported cars often cost more than cars made in the United States because of the tariff placed on them."

Prepare to Read

Objectives

In this section you will

1. Identify the environmental concerns the United States and Canada share today.

2. Find out about the economic ties the United States and Canada have to each other and to the world.

Taking Notes

As you read the section, look for details about the environmental concerns and economic ties that the United States and Canada share. Copy the concept web below and fill in the details.

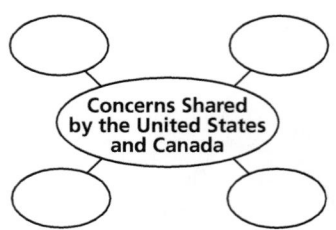

Target Reading Skill

Reread or Read Ahead Rereading and reading ahead are strategies that can help you understand words and ideas in the text. If you do not understand a certain passage, reread it to look for connections among the words and sentences. It might also help to read ahead, because a word or an idea may be clarified further on.

Key Terms

• **acid rain** (as id rayn) *n.* rain containing acids that are harmful to plants and trees

• **tariff** (tar if) *n.* a fee charged on imported goods

• **free trade** (free trayd) *n.* trade without taxes on imported goods

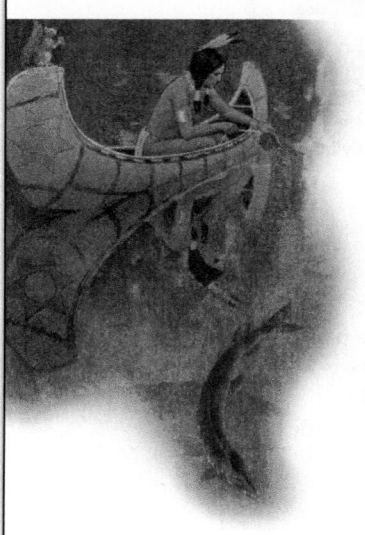

A painting of an Iroquois fishing from a canoe

202 United States and Canada

The birch-bark canoes paddled into the village of Sault Sainte Marie, on the border of the present-day United States and Canada. The canoes carried fishing nets made from strands of willow bark and baskets full of lake trout. The Native American fishermen unloaded their baskets at the shore. Any fish they did not eat that day would be dried on racks and saved for later or ground up and used as fertilizer for crops.

For centuries, the lake trout of the Great Lakes provided food for both Native Americans and European settlers. By the mid-1950s, lake trout were the most valuable fish in the Upper Great Lakes. Lake trout were soon overharvested. In some of the Great Lakes, the lake trout almost disappeared.

In 1955, Canada and the United States joined to create the Great Lakes Fishery Commission. Members of the commission worked together to find ways of protecting lake trout and many other species of fish in the Great Lakes. This is just one of the ways the United States and Canada have become cooperative neighbors.

Target Reading Skill

Reread or Read Ahead Point out the Target Reading Skill. Tell students that rereading and reading ahead often clarify words or ideas that are unfamiliar or hard to understand.

Model using these strategies using the term "cooperative neighbors" at the end of the last paragraph on page 202. By rereading the preceding sentence students learn that "members of the commission *work together*."

By reading ahead they learn that environmental issues "concern *both* the United States and Canada." "Cooperative neighbors" work together to benefit all.

Give students *Reread or Read Ahead.* Have them complete the activity in their groups.

All in One United States and Canada Teaching Resources, *Reread or Read Ahead,* p. 159

Environmental Issues

The United States and Canada share many geographic features—the coasts of the Atlantic and Pacific oceans, the Great Lakes, and the Rocky Mountains, for example. Both countries use natural resources in similar ways. And both have used technology to meet their needs. But technology has left its mark on their water, air, forests, and futures.

Solving Water Problems Can you picture a river on fire? Impossible, you say? In 1969, a fire started on the Cuyahoga River (ky uh HOH guh RIV er). That river flows past Cleveland, Ohio, and then empties into Lake Erie. For many years, Cleveland had poured waste, garbage, and oil into the river. The layer of pollutants was so thick that it caught on fire.

The Cuyahoga was typical of the rivers that empty into Lake Erie. So much pollution had been dumped into the lake that most of the fish had died. Swimming in the river was unthinkable. The fire on the Cuyahoga was a wake-up call. The United States and Canada signed an agreement promising to cooperate in cleaning up the lake. Agreements such as this have greatly reduced freshwater pollution in the United States. Today, people again enjoy fishing and boating on the Cuyahoga.

The Cuyahoga River
In June 1969, firefighters hosed down flames from the Cuyahoga River fire (below). **Analyze Images** *Looking at the river today (inset), what positive effects came out of the cleanup effort?*

Vocabulary Builder

Use the information below to teach students this section's high-use words.

High-Use Word	Definition and Sample Sentence
maintain, p. 205	*v.* to keep in good repair; protect To keep the fountain in working order, the plumber has to **maintain** the pipes.
expand, p. 208	*v.* to grow in size Adding water to the sponge caused it to **expand** to twice its normal size.

Instruct

Environmental Issues [L2]

Guided Instruction

- **Vocabulary Builder** Clarify the high-use word **maintain** before reading.

- Read Environmental Issues, using the Paragraph Shrinking strategy (TE, p. T34)

- Write the following causes of pollution on the board, and discuss with students the long-term effects of each: dumping garbage and waste in rivers; burning fossil fuels; excessive logging of trees. (*Garbage and waste pollute water and kill fish. Burning fossil fuels pollutes the air and creates acid rain. Without trees, soil washes away so that plants die and animals lose their homes.*)

Answer

Analyze Images The river is no longer dangerous and can even be used for pleasure cruising.

- Ask **What is being done to solve water problems?** (*The United States and Canada have signed agreements to clean up polluted areas.*) **How has air quality been improved?** (*by reducing pollutants released into the air*) **What steps have been taken to preserve forests?** (*Laws were passed to protect forests and create new regulations for loggers.*)

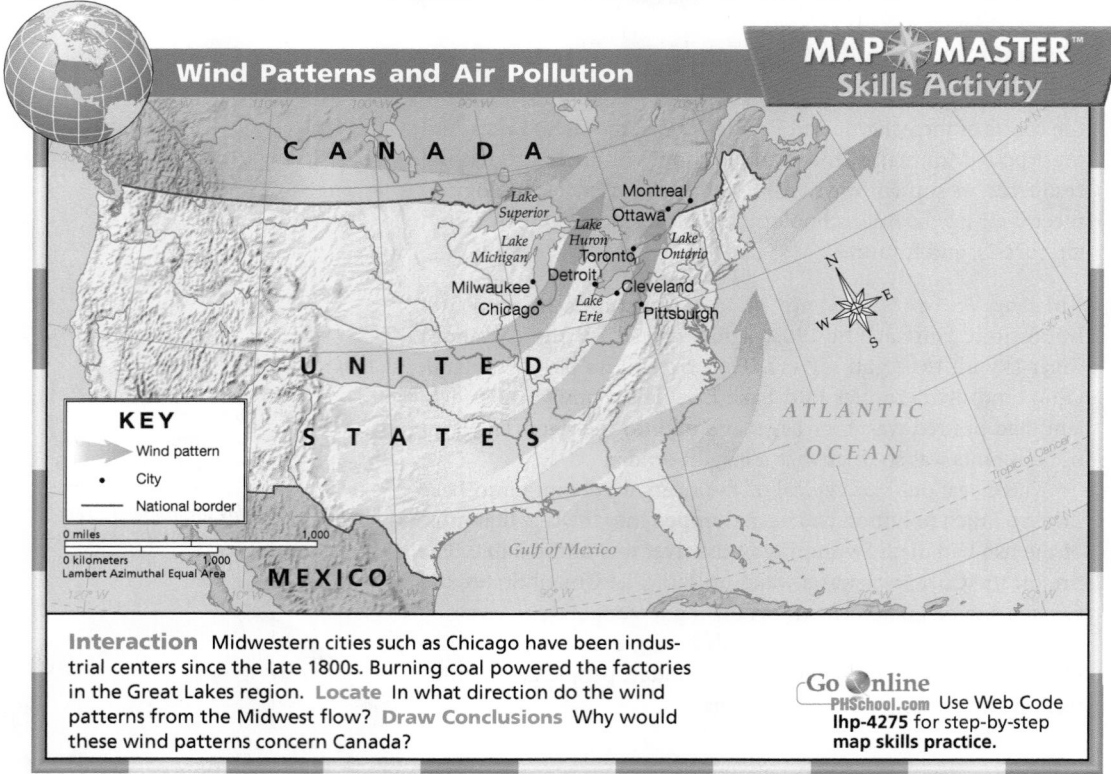

MAP MASTER™
Skills Activity

Wind Patterns and Air Pollution

KEY
→ Wind pattern
• City
— National border

0 miles   1,000
0 kilometers   1,000
Lambert Azimuthal Equal Area

Interaction Midwestern cities such as Chicago have been industrial centers since the late 1800s. Burning coal powered the factories in the Great Lakes region. **Locate** In what direction do the wind patterns from the Midwest flow? **Draw Conclusions** Why would these wind patterns concern Canada?

Go Online
PHSchool.com Use Web Code
lhp-4275 for step-by-step map skills practice.

Improving Air Quality On many days, you can look around most big cities and see that the air is filled with a brown haze. This pollution is caused by cars and factories burning fossil fuels. Not only is this air unhealthy to breathe, but it can also create other serious problems hundreds of miles away. Pollutants in the air combine with moisture to form acid. **Acid rain** is rain that dissolves these acids and carries them to Earth. This acid kills plants, trees, and fish. Coal-burning power plants in the West and Midwest United States create acid rain problems in the Northeast and in the Great Lakes area. Winds carry these acids long distances.

Acid rain caused by United States power plants has affected forests and lakes in Canada. The two countries signed agreements to control air quality in the 1980s. A 2002 government progress report showed that rain acidity was reduced in Canada by 45 percent and in the United States by 35 percent.

Aerial view of Toronto's hazy skyline and harbor, Ontario, Canada

204 United States and Canada

Answers

MAP MASTER™
Skills Activity
Locate The wind patterns from the Midwest flow in a northeastern direction. **Draw Conclusions** Wind patterns bring air pollution from the United States to Canada, where it falls in acid rain.

Go Online
PHSchool.com Students may practice their map skills using the interactive online version of this map.

Differentiated Instruction

For Special Needs Students   L1
Pair students with more proficient partners to create a cause-and-effect chart that shows the causes and effects of the following environmental problems: water pollution, acid rain, and soil erosion in forests. Have students then create a third column to show a possible solution for each one. Use the *Effects Chart* graphic organizer

transparency to help students get started. Label the four columns "Environmental Problems," "Causes," "Effects," and "Possible Solutions."

📖 **United States and Canada Transparencies,** *Transparency B10: Effects Chart*

Renewing Forests "I'm like a tree—you'll have to cut me down," cried Kim McElroy in 1993. The other demonstrators with her agreed. They were blocking the path of logging trucks trying to enter the forest of Clayoquot Sound on Vancouver Island, British Columbia. The protesters believed that cutting down the trees would damage the environment. In similar forests throughout the United States and Canada, logging companies practiced clear-cutting, or cutting down all the trees in an area. Without trees, soil washes away, other plants die, and animals lose their homes.

On the other hand, people need lumber for building. Paper companies need wood pulp to make their products. People who work for logging companies need their jobs.

The Canadian and American governments want to maintain both the forests and the timber industry. They are working to develop ways of doing that. For example, British Columbia passed a law that sets aside parts of the Clayoquot Sound's forests for logging. The law also imposes new rules on loggers to prevent damage in the areas where cutting is allowed.

✓ Reading Check **Why is there disagreement about logging in some forests?**

The Old and the New
A hill in the Queen Charlotte Islands of British Columbia, Canada (below), shows clear-cut forest growth. The man in the inset photo plants new trees. Draw Conclusions *How does planting new trees help to keep soil from washing away? Why is that important?*

Background: Links Across Place

Acid Rain in Europe Emissions from cars, trucks, power plants, and industrial facilities in Great Britain, Germany, and Poland and other countries have been causing severe acid rain problems on the continent. In fact, so many forests in Europe contain trees that have been stunted or killed by acid rain that a new word, *waldsterben* ("forest death"), has come into use. But the damage does not stop with trees. Contaminated winds blow northward from industrial facilities in nearby countries and reach Scandinavia. Rain that falls over parts of Scandinavia is, as a result, considerably more acidic than normal. Currently, about one-fifth of Swedish lakes have been damaged by acidification.

Independent Practice
Ask students to fill in the concept web with information they have just learned. Briefly model how to identify which details to record.

Monitor Progress
As students fill in the graphic organizer, circulate and make sure individuals are choosing the correct details. Provide assistance as needed.

Answers

Draw Conclusions Trees keep soil from washing away. Soil erosion can cause plants to die and animals to lose their food and homes.

✓ Reading Check People want to preserve the trees in order to maintain the forests that are home to plants and animals. However, people also want timber for building. Loggers also want the industry to survive in order for them to maintain their jobs.

Chapter 7 Section 5 **205**

Target Reading Skill

Reread As a follow up, ask students to perform the Target Reading Skill activity in the Student Edition. *(Reread: The U.S. and Canada maintain economic ties through lumber and fishing industries. Read ahead: The U.S. and Canada maintain economic ties through trade.)*

"Economics Has Made Us Partners"

L2

Guided Instruction

- **Vocabulary Builder** Clarify the high-use word **expand** before reading.

- Read "Economics Has Made Us Partners" with students. As students read, circulate and make sure individuals can answer the Reading Check question.

- Have students provide examples of the economic partnership between the the United States and Canada. *(Possible answers: the United States and Canada built the St. Lawrence Seaway; each country is the other's largest trading partner; both have signed trade agreements.)*

- Ask students **What might be two benefits to the United States of importing goods from Canada rather than Europe?** *(cheaper transportation costs; no tariff on imported products from Canada)*

- Ask students **What is the St. Lawrence Seaway?** *(a system of locks, canals, and dams that allows ships to move from one water level to another)*

- Have students discuss how the Seaway benefits both the United States and Canada. *(It makes trade between the two countries and with Europe easier.)*

- Ask students **Where can ships leaving from Duluth, Minnesota, travel as a result of the St. Lawrence Seaway?** *(the Atlantic Ocean)*

Answers

Diagram Skills **Describe** The St. Lawrence Seaway's locks allow ships to be raised and lowered from one water level to another. **Identify Effects** The Seaway makes it easier for the United States and Canada to trade with each other and with Europe.

"Economics Has Made Us Partners"

Not all next-door neighbors get along as well as the United States and Canada. President John F. Kennedy once described the relationship this way: "Geography has made us neighbors. History has made us friends. Economics has made us partners." With 5,527 miles (8,895 kilometers) of border between the two countries, economic cooperation has benefited both. Part of this cooperation has been in transportation between the countries, particularly around the Great Lakes.

The St. Lawrence Seaway Have you ever heard of someone going over Niagara Falls in a barrel? The barrel would drop about 190 feet (58 meters)—a crazy stunt! Suppose you have a cargo of manufactured goods in Cleveland to send to Montreal. You would like to ship by water, because it is the cheapest and most direct means of transportation. But Niagara Falls lies between Cleveland and Montreal. And after passing the falls, your cargo would have to travel down another 250 feet (76 meters) in the St. Lawrence River before it reached Montreal. What do you do?

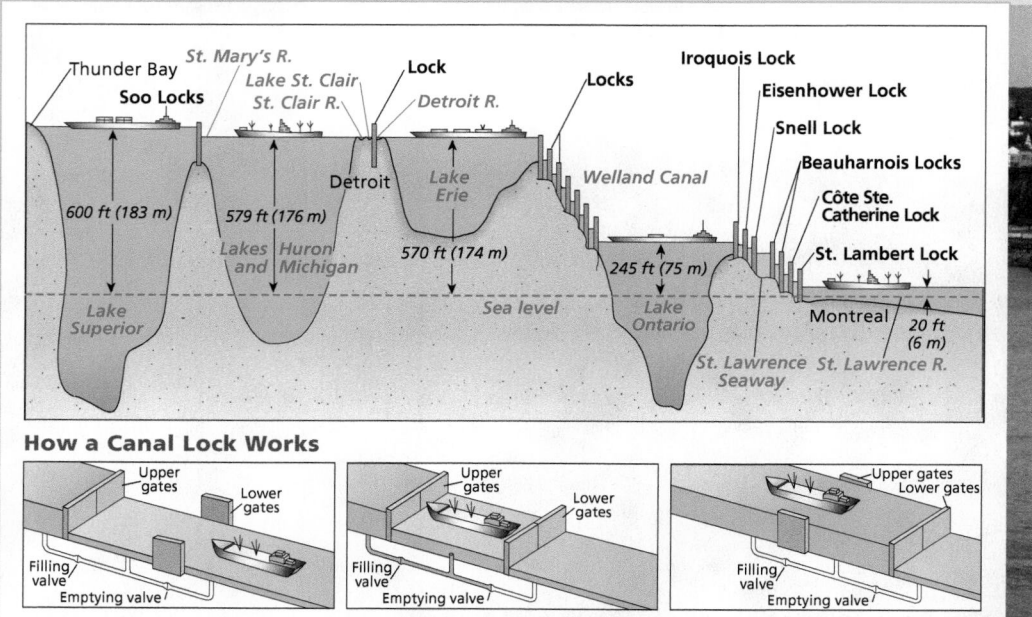

The Great Lakes and the St. Lawrence Seaway

How a Canal Lock Works

206 United States and Canada

Differentiated Instruction

For Advanced Readers **L3**
Assign students the long-term project *Mapping World Trade.* Ask students to work in pairs or small groups to find out where imported items come from, where goods produced in their community are exported to, and how worldwide trade shapes our lives and the lives of people everywhere.

Go Online
PHSchool.com
For: Long-term Integrated Projects: *Mapping World Trade*
Visit: PHSchool.com
Web Code: lhd-4206

To solve this problem, the United States and Canada built the St. Lawrence Seaway. Completed in 1959, it is a system of locks, canals, and dams that allows ships to move from one water level to another. A lock is an enclosed area on a canal that raises or lowers ships from one water level to another. Now, ships can travel from Duluth, Minnesota, on Lake Superior, all the way to the Atlantic Ocean. The St. Lawrence Seaway makes it much easier for the United States and Canada to trade with each other and with Europe. The St. Lawrence Seaway has been called Canada's highway to the sea because of the volume of goods that travels its length.

Trade What country is the biggest trading partner of the United States? It is Canada. And, the United States is Canada's largest trading partner, too. About three fourths of all of Canada's foreign trade—both exports and imports—is with the United States. Our economies are interdependent. That means that in order to be successful, each country needs to do business with the other.

▓ Diagram Skills

Ships traveling from the Atlantic Ocean to Lake Superior must go through a series of locks along the St. Lawrence Seaway. **Describe** How do the locks allow ships to make the great change in elevation between the Atlantic and the Great Lakes? **Identify Effects** How did building the St. Lawrence Seaway affect the economies of the United States and Canada?

Independent Practice
Ask students to complete the concept web with the information they have just learned.

Monitor Progress
■ Show *Section Reading Support Transparency USC 50* and ask students to check their graphic organizers individually. Go over key concepts and clarify key vocabulary as needed.

   📖 **United States and Canada Transparencies,** *Section Reading Support Transparency USC 50*

■ Tell students to fill in the last column of the *Reading Readiness Guide.* Probe for what they learned that confirms or invalidates each statement.

   All in One **United States and Canada Teaching Resources,** *Reading Readiness Guide,* p. 156

Differentiated Instruction

For English Language Learners L1
Encourage students to examine the prefixes *im- (in)*, *ex- (outside)*, and *inter- (between)*, as well as the base words *port* and *dependence*, to help understand the concepts *importing*, *exporting*, and *inter*dependence. Ask students to apply these concepts to their countries of origin, describing what the countries import and export, and identifying trade partners.

For Gifted and Talented L3
Assign students the *Book Project: Write a Children's Book*, encouraging them to use any person, place, event, or idea from Chapter 7 as the topic.

   All in One **United States and Canada Teaching Resources,** *Book Project: Write A Children's Book*, pp. 76–78

Assess and Reteach

Assess Progress `L2`

Have students complete the Section Assessment. Administer the *Section Quiz.*

 **United States and Canada Teaching Resources,** *Section Quiz,* p. 158

Reteach `L1`

If students need more instruction, have them read this section in the Reading and Vocabulary Study Guide.

Chapter 7, Section 5, **Western Hemisphere Reading and Vocabulary Study Guide,** pp. 78–80

Extend `L3`

Have students learn more about environmental issues by completing the activity *Energy and Resources: The Imbalance of Energy Consumption.* Assign students to work in groups to answer the questions.

Go Online
PHSchool.com

For: Environmental and Global Issues: *Energy and Resources: The Imbalance of Energy Consumption*
Visit: PHSchool.com
Web Code: lhd-4207

Answers

✓ Reading Check The main goals of the Organization of American States are to maintain peace in the Western Hemisphere and to prevent other countries from interfering in the region.

Section 5 Assessment

Key Terms
Students' sentences should reflect knowledge of each Key Term.

Target Reading Skill
Answers will vary, but should reflect that students understand the skill.

Comprehension and Critical Thinking
1. (a) water pollution, air pollution, and endangered forests **(b)** by creating treaties to clean up lakes, agreements to control air quality, and laws that set aside only specific parts of forests for the logging industry **(c)** Pollution in one country can cause acid rain in another country.

The emblem of the Organization of American States shows the furled flags of its member nations.

Since 1988, the United States and Canada have signed two important trade agreements. The Free Trade Agreement (FTA) put an end to **tariffs**, or fees charged on imported goods. Tariffs raise the cost of goods, so the amount of trade can be limited. By eliminating tariffs, Canada and the United States agreed to have **free trade**, trade without taxes on imported goods. In 1994, this agreement was expanded to include Mexico. The goal of the North American Free Trade Agreement (NAFTA) is to encourage trade and economic growth in all three countries. The agreement affects many major industries, including agriculture, trucking, and manufacturing. Since these agreements were made, trade among the three countries has increased. Although some jobs in the United States have been created because of increased imports, other jobs have been lost because American companies have moved to Mexico.

Interdependent Countries The United States and Canada are interdependent politically as well as economically. Both Canada and the United States belong to the Organization of American States, or OAS. This international organization was formed to promote cooperation among countries in the Western Hemisphere. The member countries work with one another to promote political, economic, military, and cultural cooperation. The main goals of OAS are to maintain peace in the Western Hemisphere and to prevent other countries from interfering within the region.

✓ Reading Check **What are the main goals of the member countries in the Organization of American States?**

 Section **5** Assessment

Key Terms
Review the key terms at the beginning of this section. Use each term in a sentence that explains its meaning.

 Target Reading Skill
What word or idea were you able to clarify by rereading or reading ahead?

Comprehension and Critical Thinking
1. (a) Explain What are some environmental problems the United States and Canada share?

(b) Summarize How have these two countries worked together to solve these problems?
(c) Identify Effects How can one nation's problems affect another?
2. (a) Note What country is the largest trading partner of the United States?
(b) Make Generalizations How has the St. Lawrence Seaway made trade easier for the United States and Canada?
(c) Identify the Main Idea What is the goal of NAFTA?

Writing Activity
Write a paragraph that explains the main reasons that Canada and the United States are important to each other.

Writing Tip Begin your paragraph with a topic sentence that states your main idea. Be sure to include examples, details, and facts that support your main idea.

---

208 United States and Canada

---

2. (a) Canada **(b)** The St. Lawrence Seaway allows ships to move from one water level to another through a system of locks, canals, and dams. It allows goods to be shipped easily between the United States and Canada. **(c)** to encourage trade and economic growth among Canada, the United States, and Mexico by ending tariffs on imported goods

Writing Activity
Use the *Rubric for Assessing a Writing Assignment* to evaluate students' paragraphs.

United States and Canada Teaching Resources, *Rubric for Assessing a Writing Assignment,* p. 183

7 Review and Assessment

◆ Chapter Summary

Native American artifact

Section 1: The Arrival of the Europeans
- The first Americans are called Native Americans.
- The lives of Native Americans changed after Europeans arrived.
- The 13 colonies won independence after the Revolutionary War.

Section 2: Growth and Conflict in the United States
- The United States doubled its size in 1803 with the Louisiana Purchase.
- The Industrial Revolution changed the way people in America lived.
- The Civil War pitted the North against the South.

Section 3: The United States on the Brink of Change
- The Industrial Revolution helped the rich but not the poor.
- The United States fought two world wars and became a superpower.
- After years of fighting various wars, Americans faced new terrorist threats.

Section 4: The History of Canada
- Britain fought France to gain control of Canada.
- Canadians won the right to control their own government.
- Today, Canada is completely independent of Great Britain.

Section 5: The United States and Canada Today
- The United States and Canada work together to solve environmental issues.
- The United States and Canada are each other's largest trading partners.

Civil War soldiers

◆ Key Terms

Each of the statements below contains a key term from the chapter. If the statement is true, write *true*. If it is false, rewrite the statement to make it correct.

1. A **missionary** is a person who must work for a period of years to gain freedom.
2. A **tariff** is a fee charged on imported goods.
3. **Acid rain** forms over millions of years from plant and animal remains.
4. The **Industrial Revolution** was a period of great tension between the United States and the Soviet Union.
5. A **dominion** is a self-governing area that is subject to the United States.
6. Canada is a **bilingual** country, meaning that it has two official languages.
7. A **boycott** is a refusal to buy or use goods and services.
8. An **abolitionist** is a person who moves to a new country in order to settle there.

Chapter 7 **209**

┌ Vocabulary Builder ─────

Revisit this chapter's high-use words:

theorize	conflict	cooperate
establish	slum	adopt
inspire	restore	maintain
spur	decisive	expand

Ask students to review the definitions they recorded on their *Word Knowledge* worksheets.

All in One **United States and Canada Teaching Resources,** *Word Knowledge,* p. 162

Consider allowing students to earn extra credit if they use the words in their answers to the questions in the Chapter Review and Assessment. The words must be used correctly and in a natural context to win the extra points.

Review and Assessment

Review Chapter Content

- Review and revisit the major themes of this chapter by asking students to classify what Guiding Question each bulleted statement in the Chapter Summary answers. Have students write the Chapter Summary on a separate piece of paper and complete the activity in pairs. Each pair should write the number of the Guiding Question next to each statement on their paper. Refer to p. 139 of the Student Edition for the text of Guiding Questions.

- Assign *Vocabulary Development* for students to review Key Terms.

  All in One **United States and Canada,** *Vocabulary Development,* p. 182

Answers

Key Terms

1. False. A missionary is a person who wants to convert others to his or her religion.
2. True
3. False. Wind picks up pollutants in the air where they combine with moisture to form acid rain.
4. False. The Industrial Revolution was a time when handmade items began to be produced by machines.
5. False. A dominion is a self-governing area.
6. True
7. True
8. False. An abolitionist is someone who wants to end slavery.

Comprehension and Critical Thinking

9. (a) The Spanish were interested in settling the land and gaining wealth by working the farms and the mines. The French were interested in fur trade along the St. Lawrence and Mississippi Rivers. **(b)** The Spanish enslaved the Native Americans, forcing them into harsh labor on farms and in the mines. The French wanted the help of Native Americans in order to build their fur trade and so they treated them with respect.

10. (a) It helped to increase the production of textiles by converting from handmade to machine-made goods. **(b)** The Industrial Revolution provided workers with more job opportunities in factories, but diminished the need for custom-made items.

11. (a) The act gave free land to settlers. **(b)** The railroads provided faster and cheaper access from the east to the west.

12. (a) Canada **(b)** Loyalists were people who opposed the colonies separating from Great Britain, so they would be likely to oppose Canadian independence as well.

13. (a) Parliamentary government; the monarch of Great Britain is head of state, the prime minister makes the laws. **(b)** Great Britain's **(c)** Answers will vary, students answers should show an understanding that the monarch's duties would be ceremonial.

14. (a) Because the United States and Canada have a long, open border, goods can travel easily between the two countries; Canada is the United States' largest trade partner and vice versa. **(b)** The United States and Canada share the English language and similar natural resources, which contribute to a strong trade partnership.

Skills Practice

Diagrams will vary, but should be labeled clearly and include accurate information.

Writing Activity: Language and Arts

Student answers will vary, but should include the different reasons why European settlers came to each land, the different strategies by which each country gained its independence from Great Britain, the similarities in the growth of each country, and each country's contribution to the major international events of the 20th century.

◆ Comprehension and Critical Thinking

9. (a) Compare Why were Spanish and French explorers interested in the Americas?
(b) Identify Cause and Effect How did the treatment of Native Americans reflect the different interests of the Spanish and the French explorers?

10. (a) Explain How did the Industrial Revolution change the textile industry?
(b) Draw Conclusions How might this change have affected workers?

11. (a) Identify What was the Homestead Act?
(b) Draw Inferences How did railroads help settle the American West more quickly?

12. (a) Name Where did some Loyalists move after the American Revolution?
(b) Identify Frame of Reference Why would Loyalists have opposed independence from Britain?

13. (a) Define What kind of government does Canada have?
(b) Name What system is the Canadian government modeled on?
(c) Draw Conclusions What duties might a monarch have, since he or she is not the head of the government?

14. (a) Describe How has geography contributed to the trade partnership between Canada and the United States?
(b) Draw Inferences What other factors might explain this strong trade relationship?

◆ Skills Practice

Interpreting Diagrams In the Skills for Life activity in this chapter, you learned how to interpret information in a diagram. You also learned that labels on a diagram often should be read in a certain order.

Review the steps you followed to learn this skill. Then reread the part of Section 5 called Improving Air Quality. Create a diagram showing the cycle of acid rain. Remember to label your diagram clearly.

◆ Writing Activity: Language Arts

Compare and contrast the histories of the United States and of Canada. Write a paragraph describing the ways in which the growth, settlement, and independence of the United States and Canada were similar and ways in which they were different.

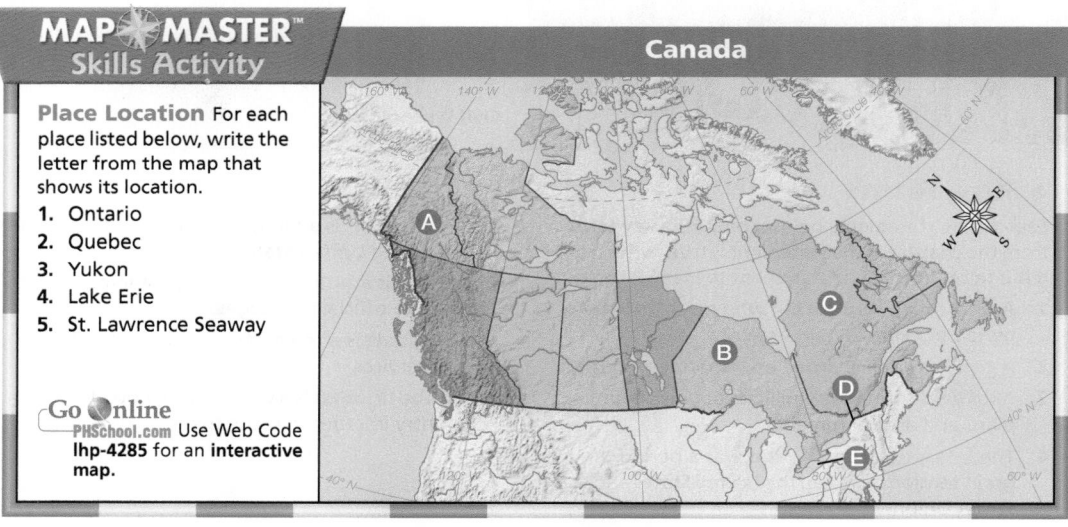

MAP MASTER Skills Activity

Place Location For each place listed below, write the letter from the map that shows its location.
1. Ontario
2. Quebec
3. Yukon
4. Lake Erie
5. St. Lawrence Seaway

Go Online
PHSchool.com Use Web Code lhp-4285 for an **interactive map.**

Canada

Use *Rubric for Assessing a Writing Assignment* to evaluate students' comparisons of the history of the United States and Canada.

All In One United States and Canada Teaching Resources, *Rubric for Assessing a Writing Assignment,* p. 183

Standardized Test Prep

Test-Taking Tips

Some questions on standardized tests ask you to analyze primary sources. Read the excerpt below from a famous United States document. Then follow the tips to answer the sample question.

"All legislative Powers herein granted shall be vested in a Congress of the United States, which shall consist of a Senate and House of Representatives. . . . The House of Representatives shall be composed of Members chosen every second Year by the People of the several states. . . . The Senate of the United States shall be composed of two Senators from each State for six Years; and each Senator shall have one Vote."

TIP Try to identify the main idea, or most important point, of the passage.

Pick the letter that best answers the question.

Which document does this extract come from?

A ~~Declaration of Independence~~

B United States Constitution

C Federalist Papers

D ~~Pledge of Allegiance~~

TIP Use what you already know about United States history and government to help you find the *best* answer.

Think It Through Start with the main idea of the extract: *The Congress is supposed to make laws.* Which document explains the powers of each branch of government? You can rule out A and D. The Pledge is a statement of loyalty. The Declaration of Independence explains why colonists cut their ties to England. That leaves B and C. Maybe you aren't sure about the Federalist Papers, but you probably know that the Constitution is the plan for our government—including Congress. The correct answer is B.

Practice Questions

Use the tips above and other tips in this book to help you answer the following questions.

1. Which event encouraged immigrants and farmworkers to look for jobs in cities?
   A the Civil War
   B the Industrial Revolution
   C the Louisiana Purchase
   D the Indian Removal Act

2. What was the result of the Seven Years' War?
   A Canada became independent.
   B France lost, but kept control over Quebec.
   C Great Britain gained control over all of Canada.
   D Canada became a dominion of Great Britain.

Read the excerpt on Article 102, and then answer the question that follows.

Article 102: Objectives
a) eliminate barriers to trade in, and facilitate the cross-border movement of, goods and services between the territories of the Parties;
b) promote conditions of fair competition in the free-trade area.

3. Which document does this excerpt most likely come from?
   A the British North America Act
   B the Treaty of Paris
   C NAFTA
   D the Quebec Act

Use Web Code lha-4205 for a Chapter 7 self-test.

Chapter 7 **211**

Cultures of the United States and Canada

Overview

Section **1** A Heritage of Diversity and Exchange
1. Explain how cultural patterns developed in the United States and Canada.
2. Discuss the cultural patterns that exist today in the United States and Canada.

Section **2** The United States: A Nation of Immigrants
1. Learn about the people of the United States.
2. Find out about the culture of the United States.

Section **3** The Canadian Mosaic
1. Find out about the people of Canada.
2. Learn about Canadian culture.

Technology Resources

Students use embedded Web codes to access Internet activities, chapter self-tests, and additional map practice. They may also access Dorling Kindersley's Online Desk Reference to learn more about each country they study.

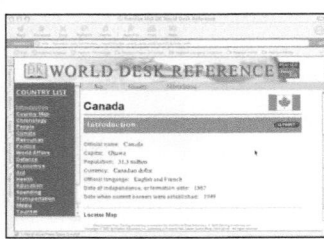

Use the Interactive Textbook to make content and concepts come alive through animations, videos, and activities that accompany the complete basal text—online and on CD-ROM.

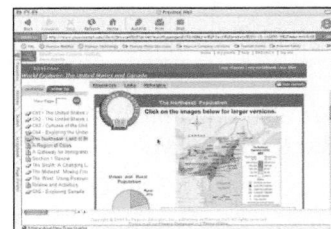

PRENTICE HALL

Use this complete suite of powerful teaching tools to make planning lessons and administering tests quicker and easier.

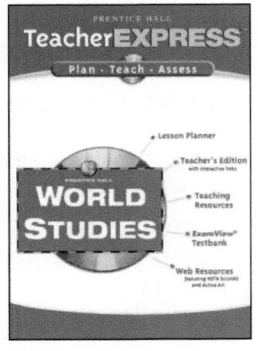

Reading and Assessment

Reading and Vocabulary Instruction

🔁 Model the Target Reading Skill

Main Idea Tell students that the main idea is the most important idea in a section. All of the details in a well-written paragraph should support the main idea. Write the paragraph below on the board. Point out that the main idea is that both the United States and Canada have diverse populations because of immigration. With students, identify and underline each supporting detail.

Because of immigration, both the United States and Canada have diverse populations. The first immigrants came mainly from West European countries, such as <u>Great Britain, France, Spain, and Germany</u>. <u>Many Africans were forced to come as slaves</u>. *Later waves of immigrants included* <u>Asians, Eastern Europeans, and Latin Americans</u>.

Ask yourself aloud: What do these details have in common? *(They all support the main idea that the populations of the United States and Canada are diverse because of immigration.)*

Use the following worksheets from All-in-One United States and Canada Teaching Resources (pp. 207–209) to support this chapter's Target Reading Skill.

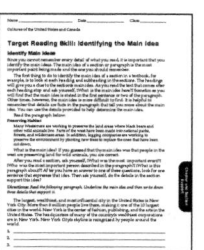 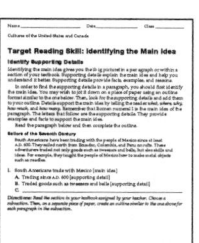 

Vocabulary Builder
High-Use Academic Words

Use these steps to teach this chapter's high-use words:

1. Have students rate how well they know each word on their Word Knowledge worksheets (All-in-One United States and Canada Teaching Resources, p. 210).

2. Pronounce each word and ask students to repeat it.

3. Give students a brief definition and sample sentence (provided on TE pp. 215, 223, and 228).

4. Work with students as they fill in the "Definition or Example" column of their Word Knowledge worksheets.

Assessment

Formal Assessment

Test students' understanding of core knowledge and skills.

Chapter Tests A and B, All-in-One United States and Canada Teaching Resources, pp. 226–231

Customize the Chapter Tests to suit your needs.
Exam*View*® **Test Bank CD-ROM**

Skills Assessment

Assess geographic literacy.
MapMaster Skills, Student Edition pp. 213, 215, 232

Assess reading and comprehension.
Target Reading Skills, Student Edition, pp. 217, 224, 229, and in Section Assessments

Chapter 8 Assessment, Western Hemisphere Reading and Vocabulary Study Guide, p. 91

Performance Assessment

Assess students' performance on this chapter's Writing Activities using the following rubrics from All-in-One United States and Canada Teaching Resources.

Rubric for Assessing a Student Poem, p. 222

Rubric for Assessing a Journal Entry, p. 223

Rubric for Assessing a Writing Assignment, p. 224

Rubric for Assessing a Circle Graph, p. 225

Assess students' work through performance tasks.

Small Group Activity: Producing a Concert, All-in-One United States and Canada Teaching Resources, pp. 213–216

Online Assessment

Have students check their own understanding.
Chapter Self-Test

Test Preparation

United States and Canada Benchmark Test 1, AYP Monitoring Assessments, pp. 89–92

Section 1 A Heritage of Diversity and Exchange

🕐 *3.5 periods, 1.75 blocks (includes Skills for Life)*

Social Studies Objectives

1. Explain how cultural patterns developed in the United States and Canada.
2. Discuss the cultural patterns that exist today in the United States and Canada.

Reading/Language Arts Objective

Learn to identify the main idea of a paragraph or section.

Prepare to Read	Instructional Resources	Differentiated Instruction
Build Background Knowledge Discuss diversity in the United States and Canada. **Set a Purpose for Reading** Have students evaluate statements on the *Reading Readiness Guide*. **Preview Key Terms** Teach the section's Key Terms. **Target Reading Skill** Introduce the section's Target Reading Skill of **identifying main ideas**.	**All in One United States and Canada Teaching Resources** L2 Reading Readiness Guide, p. 196 L2 Identify Main Ideas, p. 207	**Spanish Reading and Vocabulary Study Guide** L1 Chapter 8, Section 1, pp. 61–62 ELL

Instruct	Instructional Resources	Differentiated Instruction
Patterns of Culture Develop Ask questions about trading and interaction between the Native Americans and European settlers. **Cultural Patterns Today** Discuss immigration to a new country. **Target Reading Skill** Review **identifying main ideas**.	**All in One United States and Canada Teaching Resources** L2 Guided Reading and Review, p. 197 L2 Reading Readiness Guide, p. 196 **United States and Canada Transparencies** L2 Transparency B15: Outline L2 Section Reading Support Transparency USC 51	**All in One United States and Canada Teaching Resources** L1 Outline Map 12: Canada: Political, p. 217 ELL, LPR, SN L2 Skills for Life, p. 212 AR, GT, LPR, SN **Teacher's Edition** L1 For Less Proficient Readers, TE p. 218 L3 For Gifted and Talented, TE p. 218 **Spanish Support** L2 Guided Reading and Review (Spanish), p. 78 ELL

Assess and Reteach	Instructional Resources	Differentiated Instruction
Assess Progress Evaluate student comprehension with the section assessment and section quiz. **Reteach** Assign the Reading and Vocabulary Study Guide to help struggling students. **Extend** Extend the lesson by assigning an Enrichment activity.	**All in One United States and Canada Teaching Resources** L2 Section Quiz, p. 198 L3 Enrichment, p. 211 Rubric for Assessing a Student Poem, p. 222 **Reading and Vocabulary Study Guide** L1 Chapter 8, Section 1, pp. 82–84	**Teacher's Edition** L3 For Advanced Readers, TE p. 221 **United States and Canada Transparencies** L1 Transparency B17: Concept Web ELL, LPR, SN L3 Transparency B16: Venn Diagram AR, GT **Spanish Support** L2 Section Quiz (Spanish), p. 79 ELL

Key

L1 Basic to Average   L3 Average to Advanced   LPR Less Proficient Readers   GT Gifted and Talented
L2 For All Students   AR Advanced Readers   ELL English Language Learners
                                                       SN Special Needs Students

Section 2 The United States: A Nation of Immigrants

 *2 periods, 1 block*

Social Studies Objectives
1. Learn about the people of the United States.
2. Find out about the culture of the United States.

Reading/Language Arts Objective
Identify the supporting details of a main idea.

Prepare to Read	Instructional Resources	Differentiated Instruction
Build Background Knowledge Ask students to think about reasons immigrants come to the United States. **Set a Purpose for Reading** Have students begin to fill out the *Reading Readiness Guide*. **Preview Key Terms** Teach the section's Key Terms. **Target Reading Skill** Introduce the section's Target Reading Skill of **identifying supporting details**.	**All in One United States and Canada Teaching Resources** L2 Reading Readiness Guide, p. 200 L2 Identify Supporting Details, p. 208	**Spanish Reading and Vocabulary Study Guide** L1 Chapter 8, Section 2, pp. 63–64 ELL

Instruct	Instructional Resources	Differentiated Instruction
The People of the United States Ask questions that compare and contrast the first and second groups of immigrants that came to the United States. **Target Reading Skill** Review **identifying supporting details**. **United States Culture** Ask questions about and discuss reflections of diversity in the United States.	**All in One United States and Canada Teaching Resources** L2 Guided Reading and Review, p. 201 L2 Reading Readiness Guide, p. 200 **United States and Canada Transparencies** L2 Section Reading Support Transparency USC 52	**All in One United States and Canada Teaching Resources** L3 Small Group Activity: Producing a Concert, pp. 213–216 AR, GT L2 Doing Searches on the Internet, p. 220 AR, GT, LPR, SN **Teacher's Edition** L3 For Advanced Readers, TE p. 224 **Spanish Support** L2 Guided Reading and Review (Spanish), p. 80 ELL

Assess and Reteach	Instructional Resources	Differentiated Instruction
Assess Progress Evaluate student comprehension with the section assessment and section quiz. **Reteach** Assign the Reading and Vocabulary Study Guide to help struggling students. **Extend** Extend the lesson by having students read two poems by an American poet.	**All in One United States and Canada Teaching Resources** L2 Section Quiz, p. 202 L3 Mother to Son, p. 218 L3 Daybreak in Alabama, p. 219 Rubric for Assessing a Journal Entry, p. 223 **Reading and Vocabulary Study Guide** L1 Chapter 8, Section 2, pp. 85–87	**Spanish Support** L2 Section Quiz (Spanish), p. 81 ELL

Key
L1 Basic to Average L3 Average to Advanced
L2 For All Students

LPR Less Proficient Readers
AR Advanced Readers
SN Special Needs Students

GT Gifted and Talented
ELL English Language Learners

Section 3 The Canadian Mosaic

 4 periods, 2 blocks (includes Chapter Review and Assessment)

Social Studies Objectives
1. Find out about the people of Canada.
2. Learn about Canadian culture.

Reading/Language Arts Objective
Learn to identify the implied main idea.

Prepare to Read	**Instructional Resources**	**Differentiated Instruction**
Build Background Knowledge Have students think about things they already know about Canada. **Set a Purpose for Reading** Have students evaluate statements on the *Reading Readiness Guide*. **Preview Key Terms** Teach the section's Key Terms. **Target Reading Skill** Introduce the section's Target Reading Skill of **identifying main ideas.**	**All in One United States and Canada Teaching Resources** L2 Reading Readiness Guide, p. 204 L2 Identifying Implied Main Ideas, p. 209	**Spanish Reading and Vocabulary Study Guide** L1 Chapter 8, Section 3, pp. 65–66 ELL

Instruct	**Instructional Resources**	**Differentiated Instruction**
The People of Canada Discuss Canada's indigenous people. **Canadian Culture** Ask questions about and discuss Canadian culture. **Target Reading Skill** Review **identifying main ideas.**	**All in One United States and Canada Teaching Resources** L2 Guided Reading and Review, p. 205 L2 Reading Readiness Guide, p. 204 **United States and Canada Transparencies** L2 Section Reading Support Transparency USC 53	**Teacher's Edition** L3 For English Language Learners, TE p. 229 L1 For Special Needs Students, TE p. 229 **Student Edition on Audio CD** L1 Chapter 8, Section 3 ELL, LPR, SN **Spanish Support** L2 Guided Reading and Review (Spanish), p. 82 ELL

Assess and Reteach	**Instructional Resources**	**Differentiated Instruction**
Assess Progress Evaluate student comprehension with the section assessment and section quiz. **Reteach** Assign the Reading and Vocabulary Study Guide to help struggling students. **Extend** Extend the lesson by assigning a CD-ROM activity.	**All in One United States and Canada Teaching Resources** L2 Section Quiz, p. 206 Rubric for Assessing a Writing Assignment, p. 224 Rubric for Assessing a Circle Graph, p. 225 L2 Vocabulary Development, p. 221 L2 Word Knowledge, p. 210 L2 Chapter Tests A and B, pp. 226–231 **Reading and Vocabulary Study Guide** L1 Chapter 8, Section 3, pp. 88–90 **Passport to the World CD-ROM** L3 Canada: Photo Tour	**Spanish Support** L2 Section Quiz (Spanish), p. 83 ELL L2 Chapter Summary (Spanish), p. 84 ELL L2 Vocabulary Development (Spanish), p. 85 ELL

Key
L1 Basic to Average	L3 Average to Advanced	
L2 For All Students		
	LPR Less Proficient Readers	GT Gifted and Talented
	AR Advanced Readers	ELL English Language Learners
	SN Special Needs Students	

Summarizing

Research shows that students who know how to summarize are better at comprehending and recalling text. The key to being able to summarize is the ability to recognize main ideas and their supporting details. This allows readers to state important ideas briefly and in a way that is easy to remember.

Use the following steps to model how to write a summary:

1. Preview the selection, gathering information from such features as titles, bold-faced headings, and discussion questions. Take notes on the board.
2. Invite students to use these notes to make predictions about what they will learn from the selection.
3. Read the selection, modeling aloud how to decide on main ideas and supporting details. Record these on the board.
4. Group similar ideas, taking out any extra words to make the sentences as short as possible.
5. Write your summary. Delete more unnecessary words, modeling your thinking process as you do.

Encourage Active Participation

Help students become aware of their own learning strategies by comparing them with those of others in the classroom. Below are some sentence starters with which students can express their thoughts by measuring them against the ideas of others:

One way my method is similar to _____'s is that we both _____.
I agree with this point that _____ made: _____.
I would like to add this detail to _____'s description: _____.
I disagree with _____'s description in this way: _____.
I agree with _____ that _____.
From _____'s description of the way he or she summarizes, I conclude that _____.

World Studies Background

Canadian English

Though American English and Canadian English are much alike, there are some slight differences. For example, an English-speaking Canadian might say, "Please get me a serviette, I spilled my pop on the chesterfield!" Under the same circumstances, an American might say, "Please get me a napkin, I spilled my soda on the couch!"

Cooperative Organizations

Both Canada and the United States are members of the Organization of American States, which promotes friendship and cooperation among nations of the Western Hemisphere. According to the charter of the OAS, an act of aggression against one nation is considered an act against all American nations.

The Battle of Quebec

France's defeat at the battle of Quebec in 1759, during the French and Indian War, marked the end of the French Empire in North America and began Great Britain's dominance. Among the combatants in the war were British colonists who would one day employ the military skills they gained in this conflict against Great Britain itself. One of these was George Washington, future general of the American army during the Revolutionary War.

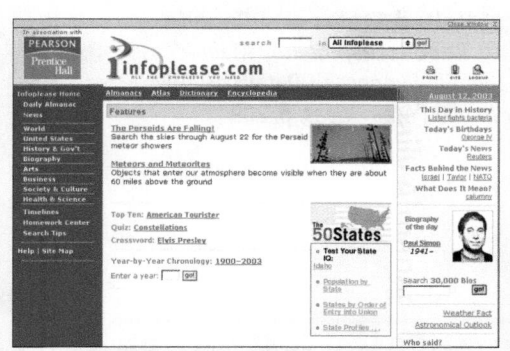

Infoplease® provides a wealth of useful information for the classroom. You can use this resource to strengthen your background on the subjects covered in this chapter. Have students visit this advertising-free site as a starting point for projects requiring research.

Use Web Code **lhd-4300** for **Infoplease®**.

Chapter 8 Cultures of the United States and Canada

Guiding Questions

Remind students about the Guiding Questions introduced at the beginning of this section.

Section 1 relates to **Guiding Question** ❷ **How have historical events affected the cultures of the United States and Canada?** *(The United States and Canada have a long history of diversity and cultural exchange beginning with the arrival of the Europeans. Immigrants from around the world continue to come to the two countries.)*

Section 2 relates to **Guiding Question** ❸ **How has the variety of people in the United States and Canada benefited and challenged the two nations?** *(The United States' mixture of ethnic groups produces a diversity of ideas and traditions.)*

Section 3 relates to **Guiding Question** ❸ **How has the variety of people in the United States and Canada benefited and challenged the two nations?** *(Because immigrants to Canada preserve many of their traditions and beliefs, there are many distinct ethnic groups with their own unique identities.)*

Target Reading Skill

In this chapter, students will learn and apply the reading skill of identifying the main idea. Use the following worksheets to help students practice this skill:

All in One United States and Canada Teaching Resources, *Identify Main Ideas,* p. 207; *Identify Supporting Details,* p. 208; *Identify Implied Main Ideas,* p. 209

Chapter Preview

This chapter will introduce you to the cultures of the United States and Canada.

Section 1
A Heritage of Diversity and Exchange

Section 2
The United States: A Nation of Immigrants

Section 3
The Canadian Mosaic

Target Reading Skill

Main Idea In this chapter you will focus on skills you can use to identify the main ideas as you read.

▶ Young people enjoy an amusement park ride in Orlando, Florida.

Differentiated Instruction

The following Teacher's Edition strategies are suitable for students of varying abilities.

Advanced Readers pp. 221, 224
English Language Learners p. 229
Gifted and Talented p. 218
Less Proficient Readers p. 218
Special Needs Students p. 229

Bibliography

For the Teacher
Mitic, Trudy Duivenvoorden. *People in Transition: Reflection on Becoming Canadian.* BPR Publishers, 2001.
Pang, Guek-Cheng. *Canada.* Cavendish, 1996.
Utter, Jack. *American Indians: Answers to Today's Questions, 2nd edition.* University of Oklahoma Press, 2002.

For the Student
L1 Herold, Maggie Rugg. *A Very Important Day.* Morrow, 1995.
L2 Kalman, Bobbie. *Canada: The People.* Crabtree Publishing, 2001.
L3 Bode, Janet. *The Colors of Freedom: Immigrant Stories.* Franklin Watts, Inc, 2000.

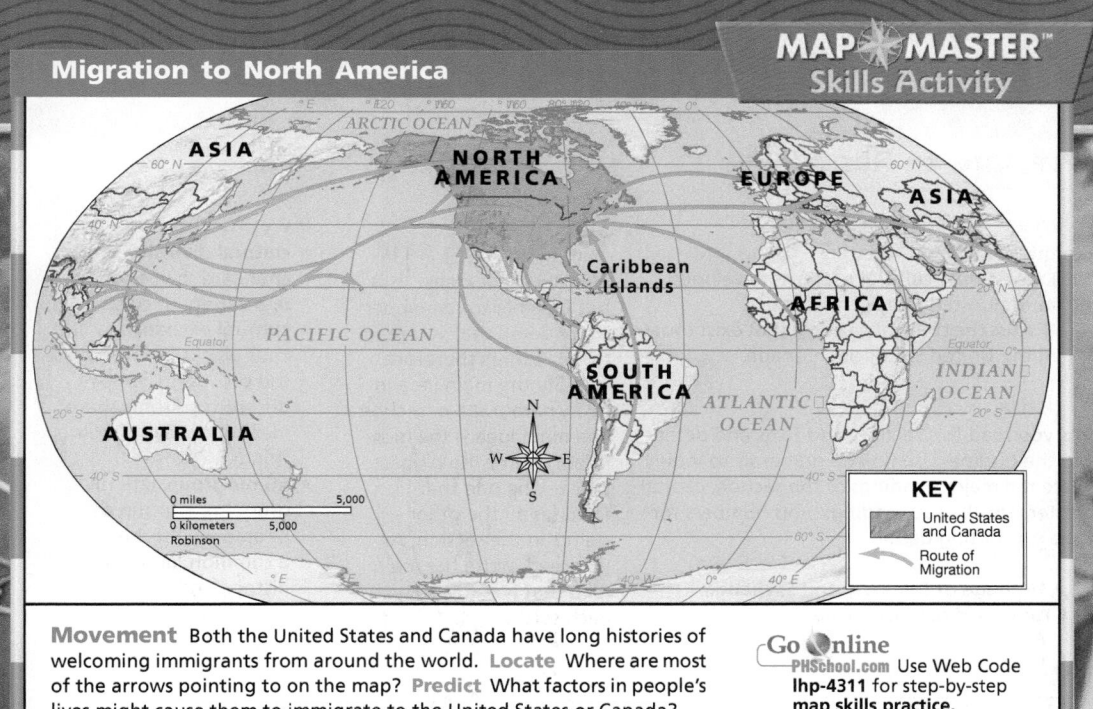

Migration to North America

MAP▪MASTER™
Skills Activity

ASIA
NORTH AMERICA
EUROPE
ASIA
Caribbean Islands
AFRICA
PACIFIC OCEAN
SOUTH AMERICA
ATLANTIC OCEAN
INDIAN OCEAN
AUSTRALIA

0 miles 5,000
0 kilometers 5,000
Robinson

N W E S

KEY
United States and Canada
Route of Migration

Movement Both the United States and Canada have long histories of welcoming immigrants from around the world. **Locate** Where are most of the arrows pointing to on the map? **Predict** What factors in people's lives might cause them to immigrate to the United States or Canada?

Go Online
PHSchool.com Use Web Code
lhp-4311 for step-by-step
map skills practice.

MAP▪MASTER™
Skills Activity

- Draw students' attention to the origins of the arrows. Ask them to identify a continent from which many arrows originate, such as Asia. Then ask them to identify which regions these arrows point to. (*Hawaii; the western, central, and eastern United States; western Canada*)

Go Online
PHSchool.com **Students may practice their map skills using the interactive online version of this map.**

Using the Visual L2

Reach Into Your Background Point out the photograph at left and its caption. Then tell students to read the section titles on p. 212. Discuss how the photograph illustrates what they will learn about in this chapter. (*The photograph shows the diversity of the United States' population.*)

Answers

MAP▪MASTER™
Skills Activity **Locate** Most of the arrows are pointing to the United States, particularly the northeastern region. **Predict** Possible answers: strife or poverty in their home countries, desire for a better standard of living or new opportunities

Chapter 8 **213**

⌐ Chapter Resources ¬

Teaching Resources
L2 Vocabulary Development, p. 221
L2 Skills for Life, p. 212
L2 Chapter Tests A and B, pp. 226–231

Spanish Support
L2 Spanish Chapter Summary, p. 84
L2 Spanish Vocabulary Development, p. 85

Media and Technology
L1 Student Edition on Audio CD
L1 Guided Reading Audiotapes, English and Spanish
L2 Social Studies Skills Tutor CD-ROM
ExamView Test Bank CD-ROM

PRENTICE HALL
Presentation EXPRESS™
Teach · Connect · Inspire

Teach this chapter's content using the PresentationExpress™ CD-ROM including:
- slide shows
- transparencies
- interactive maps and media
- *ExamView*® QuickTake Presenter

Section 1
Step-by-Step Instruction

Objectives

Social Studies
1. Explain how cultural patterns developed in the United States and Canada.
2. Discuss the cultural patterns that exist today in the United States and Canada.

Reading/Language Arts
Learn to identify the main idea of a paragraph or section.

Prepare to Read

Build Background Knowledge   L2
In this section students will learn more about the cultural diversity of the United States and Canada. Have students preview the headings and visuals in this section with the following question in mind: **Why can the cultures of the United States and Canada be described as a "heritage of diversity and exchange?"** Conduct an Idea Wave (TE, p. T35) to create a list.

Set a Purpose for Reading   L2
■ Preview the Objectives.

■ Read each statement in the *Reading Readiness Guide* aloud. Ask students to mark the statements true or false.

All in One **United States and Canada Teaching Resources,** *Reading Readiness Guide,* p. 196

■ Have students discuss the statements in pairs or groups of four, then mark their worksheets again. Use the Numbered Heads participation strategy (TE, p. T36) to call on students to share their group's perspective.

Vocabulary Builder
Preview Key Terms   L2
Pronounce each Key Term, then ask the students to say the term with you. Provide a simple explanation, such as, "A place with cultural diversity includes people who practice different traditions."

Prepare to Read

Objectives
In this section you will
1. Explain how cultural patterns developed in the United States and Canada.
2. Discuss the cultural patterns that exist today in the United States and Canada.

Taking Notes
As you read this section, add facts and details to the outline. Use Roman numerals to indicate the major headings of the section, capital letters for the subheadings, and numbers for the supporting details.

> **A Heritage of Diversity and Exchange**
> I. Patterns of culture develop
>   A.
>   B.
> II.

 **Target Reading Skill**

Identify Main Ideas   It is not possible to remember every detail that you read. Good readers therefore identify the main idea in every paragraph or section. The main idea is the most important or the biggest point—the one that includes all the other points in the section. As you read, write the main idea that is stated in each section.

Key Terms
• **cultural diversity** (KUL chur ul duh VUR suh tee) *n.* a variety of cultures
• **cultural exchange** (KUL chur ul eks CHAYNJ) *n.* the process by which different cultures share ideas and ways of doing things
• **ethnic group** (ETH nik groop) *n.* a group of people who share a common language, history, and culture

Fur traders at Fort Garry, present-day Winnipeg, in Manitoba, Canada

214 United States and Canada

By 1763, Canada and the eastern half of the present-day United States were one land, governed by Great Britain. When the Revolutionary War ended in 1783, new political boundaries were created. A new country, the United States, was born.

New political borders, however, did not divide cultural regions that already existed. The same patterns of **cultural diversity,** or a wide variety of cultures, continued.

> **By 1810, many . . . merchants were . . . immigrants, as were almost all the millers, mechanics, store-keepers, . . . and the majority of the farmers. . . . [They] had been lured by economic opportunities. . . .**
> —*D. W. Meinig, The Shaping of America*

This passage describes American immigrants to Canada. At that time, Americans in the northeastern United States were more comfortable with the culture of southern Canada than with some of the cultures within their own country.

 **Target Reading Skill**   L2

Identify Main Ideas Point out the Target Reading Skill. Tell students that being able to identify the main idea of a paragraph or section can help them remember what they have read.

Model reading the second paragraph on p. 214 to identify a main idea that is stated directly in the paragraph. Read the paragraph out loud and ask yourself "Which sentence speaks for the whole paragraph?"

(The first sentence: New political borders, however, did not divide cultural regions that already existed.)

Give students *Identify Main Ideas.* Have them complete the activity in their groups.

All in One **United States and Canada Teaching Resources,** *Identify Main Ideas,* p. 207

Patterns of Culture Develop

The United States and Canada have always been culturally diverse. Both countries are geographically diverse, too—that is, they have a variety of landforms, climates, and vegetation. The cultures of the first Americans reflected their environments. Native Americans near the ocean ate a great deal of fish and told stories about the sea. Native Americans in forests learned how to trap and hunt forest animals. They also traded with each other. When groups trade, they receive more than just goods. They also get involved in cultural exchange, or the process by which different cultures share ideas and ways of doing things.

Cultural Exchange When Europeans arrived in North America, they changed Native American life. Some changes came from things that Europeans brought with them. For example, there were no horses in the Americas before the Spanish explorers arrived. Once horses were introduced, they became an important part of Native American culture.

Native American in the Badlands of South Dakota

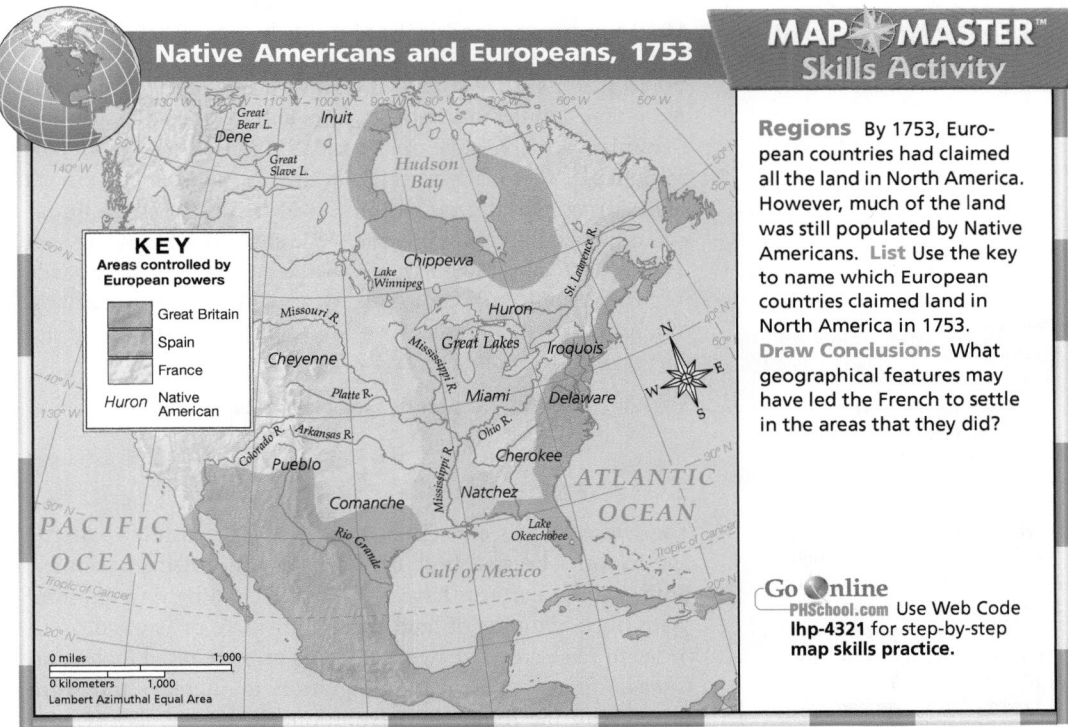

Native Americans and Europeans, 1753

MAP MASTER™ Skills Activity

KEY
Areas controlled by European powers

- Great Britain
- Spain
- France
- *Huron* Native American

Great Bear L.
Dene
Inuit
Great Slave L.
Hudson Bay
Lake Winnipeg
Chippewa
Missouri R.
Huron
St. Lawrence R.
Lake Winnipeg
Cheyenne
Great Lakes
Iroquois
Mississippi R.
Miami
Delaware
Platte R.
Ohio R.
Colorado R.
Arkansas R.
Cherokee
Pueblo
Mississippi R.
Natchez
Comanche
Lake Okeechobee
Rio Grande
ATLANTIC OCEAN
PACIFIC OCEAN
Gulf of Mexico
Tropic of Cancer

0 miles 1,000
0 kilometers 1,000
Lambert Azimuthal Equal Area

Regions By 1753, European countries had claimed all the land in North America. However, much of the land was still populated by Native Americans. **List** Use the key to name which European countries claimed land in North America in 1753. **Draw Conclusions** What geographical features may have led the French to settle in the areas that they did?

Go Online PHSchool.com Use Web Code **lhp-4321** for step-by-step map skills practice.

Chapter 8 Section 1 **215**

Vocabulary Builder

Use the information below to teach students this section's high-use words.

High-Use Word	Definition and Sample Sentence
diverse, p. 215	*adj.* different, varied He liked all styles of music, which illustrated his **diverse** taste.
contribution, p. 216	*n.* something given or shared Their research was a major **contribution** to the field of science.
tradition, p. 218	*n.* a way of doing things that is passed down over time Watching a football game is one of our Thanksgiving **traditions**.

Patterns of Culture Develop L2

Guided Instruction

- **Vocabulary Builder** Clarify the high-use words **diverse** and **contribution** before reading.

- Read Patterns of Culture Develop, using the Oral Cloze technique (TE, p. T33).

- Ask students **What happens when groups trade with each other?** *(They get goods and become involved in cultural exchange.)*

- Ask students **Why do you think both Native Americans and European settlers were willing to change some of their customs after they interacted?** *(They learned something useful to add to or replace customs they already had.)*

- Ask students to give one example of a cultural exchange between Europeans and Africans. *(Africans learned English and used European tools, while Europeans absorbed African music and food into their daily lives.)*

Independent Practice

Ask students to copy the Taking Notes graphic organizer onto a piece of paper. Using the *Outline Transparency,* briefly model how to distinguish between major headings and supporting details.

📖 **United States and Canada Transparencies,** *Transparency B15: Outline*

Monitor Progress

As students fill in the graphic organizer, make sure individuals are correctly identifying major headings and supporting details. Provide assistance as needed.

Answers

MAP MASTER Skills Activity **List** Great Britain, Spain, and France **Draw Conclusions** The French were interested in trading furs, so they settled near rivers that were good trade routes.

Go Online PHSchool.com Students may practice their map skills using the interactive online version of this map.

Cultural Patterns Today

L2

Guided Instruction

- **Vocabulary Builder** Clarify the high-use word **tradition** before reading.

- Read Cultural Patterns Today. As students read, circulate and make sure individuals can answer the Reading Check question.

- Ask students **Why do the United States and Canada share similar cultural patterns and histories?** *(They both were once British colonies.)*

- Discuss with students how immigration changes cultural patterns. Ask students **What are some reasons people immigrate to the United States and Canada?** *(Many come seeking political or religious freedom; others come to escape disease, famine, or overpopulation in their homeland. They come to improve their lives.)*

Links

Read the **Links to Math** on this page. Ask students **Why was it important for Native Americans to have a number system?** *(Having a number system is important in conducting trade and communicating.)*

Answers

Identify Causes The climate and fertile soil in the plains regions of the United States and Canada are good for farming.

✓ Reading Check Possible answers: Europeans brought horses to North America; Native Americans taught Europeans how to trap, survive in the forest, and grow local foods; Africans learned English and used European tools while African music and foods entered the lives of European Americans; Russian and Ukrainian settlers brought hardy wheat to Canada.

Harvesting Wheat
These farmers in Manitoba, Canada, are harvesting wheat with a horse-drawn reaper, which cuts grain.
Identify Causes *Why did farming attract many immigrants to the United States and Canada?*

Links to Math

Math

Using Your Fingers and Toes Native American groups developed number systems to help when conducting trade with others. The Chukchee, who hunted reindeer along the Bering Strait, used their fingers to count. The question *How many?* is translated "How many fingers?" Their word for *five* is "hand," for *ten,* "both hands," and for *twenty,* "man"—meaning both hands and both feet.

216 United States and Canada

Native Americans also contributed to European culture. The French learned how to trap and to survive in the forest. English families learned to grow local foods such as corn. Cultural exchange also took place between enslaved Africans and their owners. The Africans learned English and used European tools. African music and foods entered the daily lives of slave owners.

Immigrant Contributions This give-and-take happens every time immigrants come to a country. When Russian and Ukrainian settlers came to Canada's Prairie Provinces, they brought a kind of hardy wheat from their home country. Farmers soon learned that it grew well in Canada's climate. These immigrants helped the region become the leading wheat-growing area in Canada today. Members of other ethnic groups have made important contributions to American and Canadian cultures, too. An **ethnic group** is a group of people who share a common language, history, and culture.

✓ Reading Check **What are two examples of cultural exchange?**

Cultural Patterns Today

The United States and Canada share similar cultural patterns and histories because both of them were once British colonies. Both of their cultures have also been shaped by immigration. With huge amounts of land to be cultivated, or worked on in order to raise crops, the governments of the United States and Canada first encouraged immigration to increase the work force. With the Industrial Revolution, the end of slavery, and the rise of cities, the demand for workers was great.

Skills for Life **Skills Mini Lesson**

Drawing Inferences and Conclusions [L2]

1. Teach how to draw conclusions based on two or more inferences by discussing the following steps with students:
1) identify what you know to be true;
2) make an educated guess based on what you assume to be true; 3) use two or more inferences to draw a conclusion; 4) check the logic of the conclusion.

2. Help students practice the skill by drawing a conclusion about what life was like before horses arrived in the Americas. *(Possible answer: Native Americans probably traveled by foot.)*

3. Have students apply the skill by drawing a conclusion based on two inferences in the text.

Today, the United States and Canada continue to attract immigrants because they are wealthy nations with stable governments. Many immigrants come seeking political asylum, religious freedom, or economic opportunities. Others come to escape famine, disease, or overcrowding in their homelands. They all come looking to improve their lives.

Fitting In When immigrants move from their homeland to another country, they often have to make difficult decisions. As immigrants build a life in a new country, they must learn different laws and customs. Often they need to learn a new language, too. Some immigrants work hard to keep up the customs of their home culture as they settle in. Many feel torn between their cultural heritage and their new life.

For instance, when he was 14 years old, Herman immigrated to the United States from Guyana, a country in South America. Five years later, someone asked him if he felt Guyanese or American. He said, "I'm in between. Deep down inside, where I was born, that's what I am. You can't change a tiger['s] stripe."

Others, however, try to put as much of their old life behind them as they can. When Louisa and her husband immigrated to Saskatchewan, Canada, from Hong Kong, they were eager to start their new lives:

> **❝**It takes time to adapt to a new environment. It is sometimes difficult for one to change one's life abruptly. However, it is the reality that we must fit in. We are determined to succeed in overcoming the difficulties and to live a Canadian way of life.**❞**
>
> —Louisa, a Chinese immigrant

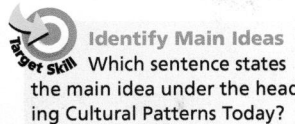

Identify Main Ideas Which sentence states the main idea under the heading Cultural Patterns Today?

Celebrating Cultures The dancers below march in a parade during Carnival Miami in Florida. The photo on the left is a busy street in Chinatown in Vancouver, British Columbia. **Analyze Images** In what ways do the photographs below show how immigrants have blended their traditional cultures with their new cultures?

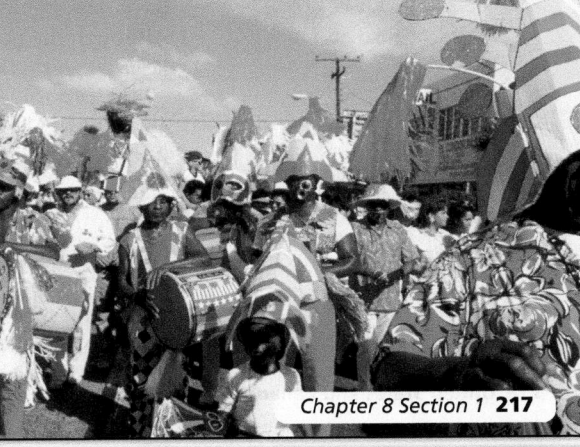

Chapter 8 Section 1 **217**

Assess and Reteach

Assess Progress `L2`

Have students complete the Section Assessment. Administer the *Section Quiz*.

All in One **United States and Canada Teaching Resources,** *Section Quiz,* p. 198

Reteach `L1`

If students need more instruction, have them read this section in the Reading and Vocabulary Study Guide.

Chapter 8, Section 1, **Western Hemisphere Reading and Vocabulary Study Guide,** pp. 82–84

Extend `L3`

Point out that the United States shares a common border with Mexico as well as Canada. The culture along this border blends those of Mexico and the United States. Have students complete *Enrichment* to learn more about this border culture.

All in One **United States and Canada Teaching Resources,** *Enrichment,* p. 211

Answers

Conclusions Canadians and Americans both enjoy professional baseball, which is a money-making business.

Play Ball!
Baseball is widely considered to be the "national pastime" of the United States. It is also a popular sport in Canada. One professional baseball team in Canada competes against American teams in the major leagues. **Conclusions** *How does professional baseball link the United States and Canada both culturally and economically?*

Maintaining Traditions Almost all immigrants cling to some of the things that remind them of their former homes. Many large cities in the United States and Canada have areas where certain ethnic groups live or conduct business, such as Chinatown in Vancouver and Little Havana in Miami.

Of course, people maintain traditions in their own homes as well. Think about your family or your friends' families. Do they use special phrases from the language they learned from their parents or grandparents? Do they eat special foods? Customs give people a sense of identity. They also enrich life in both the United States and Canada.

Cultural Ties The United States and Canada are historically and economically linked. They share a border, a continent, and have felt Britain's influence on their history and language. Although the population of the United States is nearly ten times larger than that of Canada, the people are very much alike.

At least three fourths of people in both countries live in urban areas. Most Canadians live within 200 miles (320 kilometers) of the United States' border. Canadians and Americans dress alike and eat similar foods. The majority of both Canadians and Americans are either Roman Catholic or Protestant. Both nations have long life expectancies and high rates of literacy, or the ability to read and write. Canadians and Americans often read the same books and magazines, listen to the same music, and watch many of the same movies and television shows.

218 United States and Canada

Differentiated Instruction

For Less Proficient Readers `L1`

Students may have difficulty understanding the concept that most Canadians live within 200 miles (320 kilometers) of the United States. Have them work with a partner to show the distance on the outline map of Canada.

All in One **United States and Canada Teaching Resources,** *Outline Map 12: Canada: Political,* p. 217

For Gifted and Talented `L3`

Invite students to interview a community member who immigrated to the United States. Have them query the interviewee on decisions he or she had to make once in the country. Students can share their interview by playing an audiotape or writing a feature article.

Economic Ties With vast resources and strong economies, both the United States and Canada have a high standard of living. A standard of living is a measure of the amount of goods, services, and leisure time people have. Their economies are linked, too. The total amount of trade that takes place each year between the United States and Canada is larger than it is between any other two countries. Changes in business trends in the United States are quickly reflected in the Canadian business sector. The two nations trade in manufactured goods, forestry products, and food items. They also trade heavily in energy, such as oil, coal, and electricity.

In addition, millions of Canadians travel to the United States each year. Nearly two million Canadians visit Florida alone, spending more than a billion dollars there. Most of these tourists, known as Snowbirds, come to escape Canada's long, cold winters. Likewise, most of Canada's tourists are American. Americans can travel to Canada almost as easily as they would to a different state.

✓ Reading Check **What cultural characteristics do the United States and Canada have in common?**

Tourists visit the Grand Canyon (upper photo) and Quebec City (lower photo).

Section 1 Assessment

Key Terms
Review the key terms at the beginning of this section. Use each term in a sentence that explains its meaning.

Target Reading Skill
State the main ideas in Section 1.

Comprehension and Critical Thinking
1. (a) Recall Describe how Native American cultures reflected their environments.

(b) Analyze How did the arrival of Europeans affect Native American cultures?
2. (a) List Note the similarities between the United States and Canada.
(b) Explore the Main Idea How are the economies of the United States and Canada linked?
(c) Draw Conclusions The economy of which country—the United States or Canada—is more dependent on the other's?

Writing Activity
Write a poem about a custom that is important to your family or the family of a friend. Start by listing words or phrases that describe the details of the family custom.

Writing Tip After you write a first draft of the poem, read it aloud. Circle words that do not offer a clear picture of the custom. Replace them with more lively words.

Chapter 8 Section 1 **219**

Objectives

Learn how to use a concept web to organize information and how to transfer information from text to a graphic.

Prepare to Read

Build Background Knowledge L2

Remind students that in Section 1, they took notes about the main ideas and details in the text by using an outline. Invite students to brainstorm other helpful ways to remember information they have read. Using an Idea Wave (TE, p. T35), ask students to share their thoughts on how being able to identify main ideas and supporting details helps them to remember information.

Instruct

Using Graphic Organizers L2

Guided Instruction

- Read the introduction with the class, then have students study the illustration.

- Have students learn the skill by reading the numbered list on p. 220.

- Model the skill by walking students through the steps under Practice the Skill on p. 221. Model each step in the activity by referring to the concept map. Using Think-Write-Pair-Share (TE, p. T36), invite students to add supporting details relating to family history and other topics.

Independent Practice

- Assign *Skills for Life* and have students complete it individually.

  All in One **United States and Canada Teaching Resources,** *Skills for Life,* p. 212

Monitor Progress

As students are completing the *Skills for Life* worksheet, circulate to be sure individuals are applying the skill steps correctly. Provide assistance as needed.

Using Graphic Organizers

"Today we're going to brainstorm," Ms. King told her social studies class. She drew a large circle at the center of the chalkboard, and inside it she wrote *Cultures of the United States.* "This is our topic. Now, give me the names of some important culture groups in our country."

The ideas flew fast. "European settlers!" "Before them, Native Americans." "Hispanics!" "African Americans!" "Asians!" Ms. King put each group in its own circle and connected it with a line to the center circle.

"Great start! Now give me details about each of these groups," she urged her students. "What ideas did Europeans bring here?"

She made several small circles and connected them to the large circle, saying, *"European settlers."* She filled in the circles as the students brainstormed the topic: *democracy . . . architecture . . . English language . . . banking . . . measurements . . . medicine. . . .*

By the time she finished, the chalkboard looked like a spider web. In fact, the connected circles made what is sometimes called a *web diagram.* It is also known as a *concept web.*

A concept web is a type of *graphic organizer,* a diagram that puts information into a graphic, or visual, form to make it easier to understand.

Learn the Skill

Like an outline, a concept web begins with a main topic and adds subtopics and details. Follow the steps below to learn about concept webs.

1 **Identify a main topic.** A main topic generally has at least two subtopics. Identify the subtopics.

2 **Draw a circle at the center of the concept map.** Label it with the main topic.

3 **For each subtopic, draw a circle.** Label the circles. Attach them to the main circle with lines to show that the subtopics are related to the main topic.

4 **If necessary, divide the subtopics even further.** Some subtopics have subtopics of their own. To show this, draw more circles, label them, and attach them to the circle with the subtopics.

220 United States and Canada

Background: Links Across Place

Coming to America The United States is home to many different cultures because of immigration. In the past, large numbers of people have immigrated to the United States from countries such as Ireland, Germany, and Russia. But where do immigrants come from today? In 2002, the largest number of immigrants—219,380— arrived from Mexico. The next largest group is from India, at 71,105. China is a major source of immigrants, with 61,282 people. In contrast to Mexico, people from our northern neighbor, Canada, immigrate to the United States in much smaller numbers—19,519 Canadians came to live in the United States in 2002.

Practice the Skill

Suppose you want to write a paper about your culture. Refer to the steps on the previous page and the concept web below to see how you might organize your thoughts.

1. Your topic is My Culture. You know that many factors affect a person's culture. Those factors will be your subtopics.

2. The concept web below shows My Culture in an oval at the center.

3. The ovals connected to the center show that religion, family history, languages, and the celebration of special occasions are parts of a person's culture.

4. Add supporting details that relate to family history and the other subtopics. These details go in the empty ovals shown below.

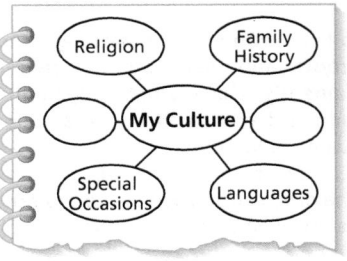

Today, many people can trace their family's history through photographs. This family has photographs of their grandfather (from top to bottom) as a baby, as a young man, with his wife and children, and with his grandson.

Apply the Skill

Choose a part of the text in Section 1. Using the steps for this skill, make a concept web that shows the main idea, subtopics, and details.

Section 2
Step-by-Step Instruction

Objectives

Social Studies

1. Learn about the people of the United States.
2. Find out about the culture of the United States.

Reading/Language Arts

Identify the supporting details of a main idea.

Prepare to Read

Build Background Knowledge L2

Tell students that in this section they will learn about the diversity of the American people. Have students revisit the reasons early settlers originally came to North America, such as escaping religious persecution or starting new lives. Then have students discuss if these are still reasons that immigrants move to the United States today and have them brainstorm other reasons that would cause people to immigrate. Ask students to share their ideas using the Think-Write-Pair-Share strategy (TE, p. T36).

Set a Purpose for Reading L2

- Preview the Objectives.

- Form students into pairs or groups of four. Distribute the *Reading Readiness Guide*. Ask students to fill in the first two columns of the chart. Use the Numbered Heads participation strategy (TE, p. T36) to call on students to share one piece of information they already know and one piece of information they want to know.

> **All in One** **United States and Canada Teaching Resources,** *Reading Readiness Guide,* p. 200

Vocabulary Builder
Preview Key Terms L2

Pronounce each Key Term, then ask the students to say the word with you. Provide a simple explanation, such as, "Some Native Americans live on reservations, or land set aside by the United States government for Native American use only."

Prepare to Read

Objectives

In this section you will
1. Learn about the people of the United States.
2. Find out about the culture of the United States.

Taking Notes

As you read this section, look for details about the cultural diversity of the United States. Copy the chart below and record your findings in it.

Causes	Event	Effects
• • •	The U.S. is culturally diverse	• • •

Target Reading Skill

Identify Supporting Details The main idea of a paragraph or section is supported by details that give further information about it. These details may explain the main idea or give examples or reasons. As you read, note the details that explain the main idea in this section: "The United States is a diverse nation."

Key Terms

- **reservation** (rez ur VAY shun) *n.* an area of land set aside for a special purpose
- **treaty** (TREE tee) *n.* a formal agreement, usually between two or more nations

The Statue of Liberty

222 United States and Canada

This view of life in the United States comes from an immigrant arriving in Ellis Island in 1920:

> **I feel like I had two lives. You plant something in the ground, it has its roots, and then you transplant it where it stays permanently. That's what happened to me. . . . All of a sudden, I started life new, amongst people whose language I didn't understand. . . . [E]verything was different . . . but I never despaired, I was optimistic. . . . [T]his is the only country where you're not a stranger, because we are all strangers. It's only a matter of time who got here first.**
>
> —*Lazarus Salamon, a Hungarian immigrant*

The People of the United States

The population of the United States has been growing steadily since the first national census was taken in 1790. About 4 million people lived in the nation then. Today, more than 280 million people live in the United States.

Target Reading Skill L2

Identify Supporting Details Call attention to the Target Reading Skill. Point out that supporting details give more information about the main idea.

Model reading the first paragraph under The People of the United States to identify the main idea and its supporting details: "The first sentence gives the main idea, that the population of the United States has been growing steadily." Then read each of the following sentences and ask students if the sentences supply supporting details. *(yes)*

Give students *Identify Supporting Details.* Have them complete the activity in their groups.

> **All in One** **United States and Canada Teaching Resources,** *Identify Supporting Details,* p. 208

Despite the vast size of the United States, its people share many common attitudes and traditions. These experiences help bring Americans together. At the same time, Americans are a diverse mix of races, ethnicities, and religions.

The First People Today's Native Americans are descendents of the first people to live in the Americas. Most experts believe that the first Americans migrated from Asia across the Bering Strait thousands of years ago. Gradually, the human population spread south across North America.

When European settlers arrived in North America, they often came into conflict with the Native Americans who were living there. As Europeans moved west, they forced the local Indians to move to land already occupied by other Native American groups.

The United States government pursued a general policy of supporting white settlement. They established reservations, or federal lands set aside for Native Americans, and forced Native Americans to relocate.

Conflict With Settlers From 1778 to 1871, the United States government wrote and signed hundreds of treaties, or formal agreements, with American Indian groups. In these treaties, Native Americans agreed to interact peacefully with settlers. They also agreed to give up much of their land. In return, the federal government promised to pay for that land and to protect them.

Most of these treaties were broken, often because settlers wanted to expand onto reservation lands. When settlers violated these treaties, Native Americans fought back. They were fighting not only for their land but for their resources and way of life. Native Americans fought more than 1,000 battles throughout the West between 1861 and 1891.

Native Americans Today In the 1960s, Native Americans began to seek economic and political equality. Several groups, including the American Indian Movement (AIM), formed to work for better living conditions and equal rights. They called on the government to address their concerns. The United States has since passed a series of reforms, giving money and land to Native American groups. Today, about 2.5 million people in the United States are Native American.

Fighting For Civil Rights
Dennis Banks, a leader in the American Indian Movement (AIM), leads a protest in South Dakota. **Draw Inferences** *Why do you think Banks chose Mount Rushmore as the site for the protest?*

Instruct

The People of the United States ⬜L2

Guided Instruction
- **Vocabulary Builder** Clarify the high-use words **attitude, violate,** and **reform** before reading.

- Read The People of the United States, using the Structured Silent Reading technique (TE, p. T34).

- Ask students to identify the first people who lived on the land that would become the United States. (*Native Americans*) Then ask **What conflicts arose between the Native Americans and the settlers?** (*Conflicts arose between the Native Americans and the settlers who broke federal government treaties and took Native American lands.*)

- Compare and contrast the first and second group of immigrants by asking students these questions. **From what part of Europe did the first wave of immigrants come?** (*mostly northern Europe*) **From what part of Europe did the second group of immigrants come?** (*southern and eastern Europe*) **What religion dominated the first group of immigrants?** (*Protestantism*) **What religions dominated the second group of immigrants?** (*Judaism, Catholicism, Greek Orthodox*)

Vocabulary Builder

Use the information below to teach students this section's high-use words.

High-Use Word	Definition and Sample Sentence
attitude, p. 223	*n.* opinion or feeling about something Ian studied, so he has a positive **attitude** about today's exam.
violate, p. 223	*v.* to break a promise or law They **violated** curfew by staying out after dark.
reform, p. 223	*n.* improvement or correction The mayor's **reforms** helped make the city a safer place.
enrich, p. 225	*n.* to improve the quality of something Viewing many artists' work has **enriched** my skill as an artist.

Answers

Draw Inferences Possible answers: Banks may have chosen the monument as the site for the protest to underline how Native Americans have not always shared in the freedom that the people depicted in the monument stand for.

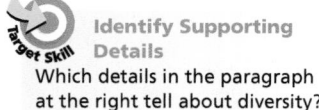

Target Reading Skill

Identify Supporting Details As a follow-up, ask students to answer the Target Reading Skill question in the Student Edition. *(The first major wave of immigration took place from 1830 to 1890. Immigrants were from England, Scotland, Scandinavia, and Germany. These groups continued to immigrate to the United States until World War II.)*

Independent Practice

Ask students to copy the Taking Notes graphic organizer onto a piece of paper. Briefly model how to identify which details to record.

Monitor Progress

As students fill in the graphic organizer, circulate and make sure individuals are choosing the correct details. Provide assistance as needed.

Identify Supporting Details
Which details in the paragraph at the right tell about diversity?

Graph Skills

Thousands of people attend the annual Ninth Avenue International Food Festival in New York City. The festival features food from nearly 30 countries along the mile-long celebration. **Identify** Where do most immigrants to the United States come from? **Draw Conclusions** What languages might the immigrants from those regions speak?

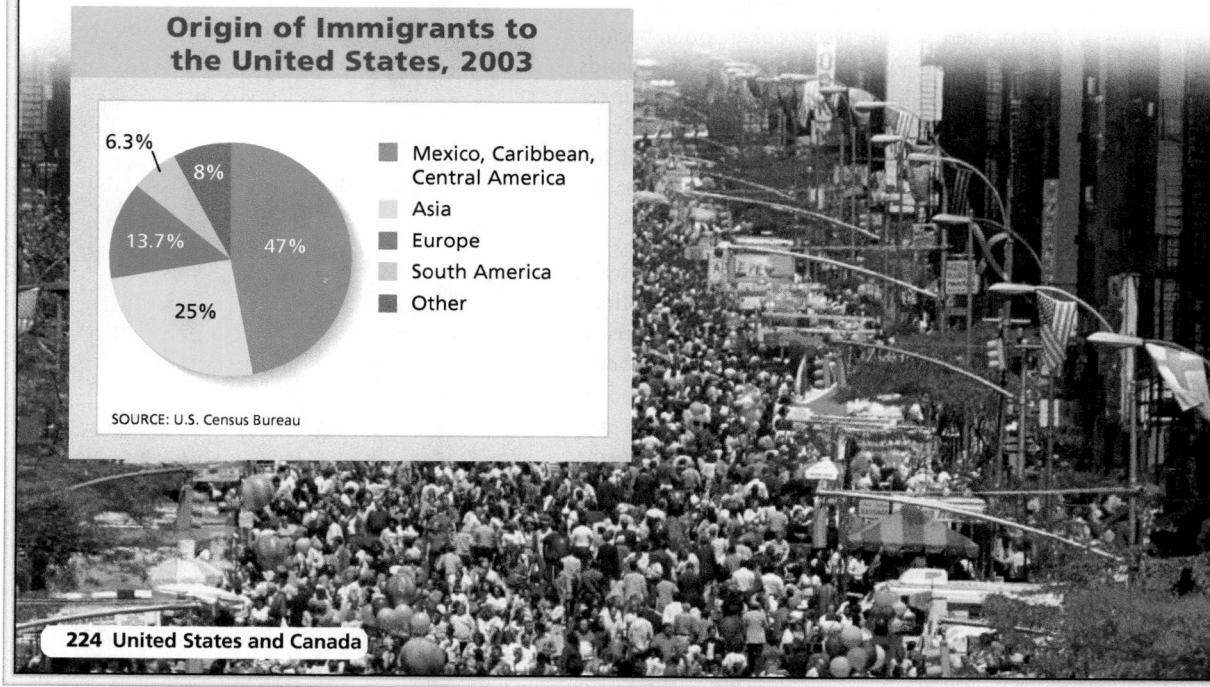

Origin of Immigrants to the United States, 2003

- 6.3%
- 8%
- 13.7%
- 47%
- 25%

- Mexico, Caribbean, Central America
- Asia
- Europe
- South America
- Other

SOURCE: U.S. Census Bureau

224 United States and Canada

Immigrants The United States has always been a nation of immigrants. However, the first major wave of immigration took place from 1830 to 1890. These immigrants were mainly Protestants from England, Scotland, Scandinavia, and Germany who came to farm the land. They adapted fairly easily to the American ways of life because of their similar backgrounds. These ethnic groups would continue to come to the United States in large numbers until World War I.

The first large influx of Chinese immigrants came in 1849, during the California Gold Rush. More Chinese arrived in the 1860s to lay track for the transcontinental railroad. They had a more difficult time than Europeans adjusting to life in the United States. Widespread unemployment and fierce competition for gold led to violence and discrimination against many Asian immigrants.

A Second Wave of Immigrants The second major wave of immigration took place from 1880 to 1920. Unlike the first wave, these immigrants went to work in factories, mills, and mines. Immigrants from southern and eastern Europe dominated the second wave: Jews from Russia and Poland, Roman Catholics from Poland and Italy, and some of the Greek Orthodox faith. Like the Asian immigrants before them, they dressed differently, ate different foods, and spoke different languages. They often worked in poor conditions for low wages.

Differentiated Instruction

For Advanced Readers
Have groups of students research the music of different groups of people in the United States or Canada by completing *Small Group Activity: Producing a Concert.* Ask students to create a poster to accompany their musical presentation. Display the posters around the classroom.

All in One United States and Canada Teaching Resources, *Small Group Activity: Producing a Concert,* pp. 213–216

Answers

Graph Skills Identify The largest group is from Mexico, the Caribbean, and Central America; the second largest, from Asia.
Draw Conclusions Possible answers: Spanish, Chinese, Korean, and many other languages

The writings of Zora Neale Hurston, Ralph Waldo Emerson, and Sandra Cisneros (from far left) reflect the diversity of the books that Americans read.

Immigrants Today   Non-Europeans form the largest immigrant groups coming to the United States today. Most immigrants arrive from Asia and Latin America. The hard work of these immigrants, and of those before them, have helped develop the United States agriculturally, industrially, and economically. They also helped create a culturally diverse nation.

✓ Reading Check   **Where do most immigrants arrive from today?**

United States Culture

Have you ever eaten bagels, tacos, dim sum, or spaghetti? Have you listened to music at a Caribbean carnival or watched a dragon parade on Chinese New Year? Diverse foods, books, music, and pastimes all enrich the lives of Americans.

Literature   A distinctly American literature emerged in the nineteenth century, as Ralph Waldo Emerson and others wrote about politics and nature. By the twentieth century, America's diversity had begun to influence its literature. Playwright Eugene O'Neill had an Irish background, while Zora Neale Hurston wrote novels about what it was like to be African American. Traditions such as Native American folk tales and slave narratives also gained importance. American literature is now more varied than ever before, reflecting the diversity in today's culture.

Musical Traditions   In addition to diverse literature, Americans listen to and create many different kinds of music, from classical to popular. Popular music includes country, rap, rock, reggae, and jazz. Although it has its roots in African rhythms, jazz developed in the South, in places like New Orleans, Louisiana. African American singers and musicians, such as Louis Armstrong and Duke Ellington, made jazz popular around the world.

Pianist and composer Duke Ellington and trumpeter Louis Armstrong rehearse their first recording together in a New York City recording studio in 1946.

United States Culture   L2

Guided Instruction

- **Vocabulary Builder**   Clarify the high-use word **enrich** before reading.

- Read United States Culture with students. As students read, circulate and make sure individuals can answer the Reading Check question.

- Ask students to name some foods that came from other countries that are now part of American culture. (*bagels, tacos, dim sum, spaghetti*)

- Ask students **What does the list of writers reveal about the culture of the United States today?** (*They reflect a society in which there is diversity.*)

- Have students discuss other elements not mentioned in the section that illustrate the diversity that makes up American culture. (*Possible answers: art, holidays, religion, language*)

Independent Practice

Have students complete the graphic organizer by filling in the details on the chart.

Monitor Progress

- Show *Section Reading Support Transparency USC 52* and ask students to check their graphic organizers individually. Go over key concepts and clarify key vocabulary as needed.

  📖 **United States and Canada Transparencies,** *Section Reading Support Transparency USC 52*

- Tell students to fill in the last column of the *Reading Readiness Guide*. Probe for what they learned that confirms or invalidates each statement.

  All in One **United States and Canada Teaching Resources,** *Reading Readiness Guide,* p. 200

Answer

✓ Reading Check   Today, most immigrants arrive from Latin America and Asia.

Assess and Reteach

Assess Progress   L2

Have students complete the Section Assessment. Administer the *Section Quiz.*

All in One **United States and Canada Teaching Resources,** *Section Quiz,* p. 202

Reteach   L1

If students need more instruction, have them read this section in the Reading and Vocabulary Study Guide.

Chapter 8, Section 2, **Western Hemisphere Reading and Vocabulary Study Guide,** pp. 85–87

Extend   L3

Have students learn more about American literature by reading *Mother to Son* and *Daybreak in Alabama,* by Langston Hughes. Ask students to create illustrations for each poem.

All in One **United States and Canada Teaching Resources,** *Mother to Son,* p. 218, *Daybreak in Alabama,* p. 219

Answers

✓ **Reading Check** baseball, basketball, and football

Section 2 Assessment

Key Terms

Students' sentences should reflect knowledge of each Key Term.

🔄 **Target Reading Skill**

Answers will vary. Students may note details on p. 225 that encompass foods, traditions, literature, and music.

Comprehension and Critical Thinking

1. (a) by establishing reservations and forcing Native Americans to relocate **(b)** Possible answer: because white settlers wanted valuable land **(c)** Possible answer: The U.S. government signed and broke treaties with Native Americans, and used its powerful army to fight Native Americans, finally placing them on reservations.

2. (a) in the nineteenth century **(b)** by the twentieth century; writers from different backgrounds **(c)** Possible answer: Immigrants helped to create a culturally diverse nation in areas such as literature, music, and sports.

Basketball was invented in 1891 and quickly gained popularity in schools and colleges throughout the country.

Probably the most popular style of music to originate in the United States is rock-and-roll. A combination of rhythm and blues, gospel, and country music, rock music first became popular in the 1950s. It created a sensation all over the country and quickly spread from the United States to Europe and Asia. It remains one of the most popular musical styles throughout the world today.

Sports Many Americans watch and participate in sports activities. Sports in North America go all the way back to Native American groups who played a form of lacrosse. In the late 1800s, sports such as tennis, hiking, and golf grew in popularity. Organized team sports also began to develop a following near the end of the 1800s.

Three major sports were invented in the United States: baseball, basketball, and football. Baseball soon became the national pastime, producing sports heroes like Babe Ruth in the early 1900s. Today, baseball's popularity has spread to Japan, the Caribbean, Russia, Mexico, and Central America.

✓ **Reading Check** **Which major sports were invented in the United States?**

✦ Section 2 Assessment

Key Terms

Review the key terms at the beginning of this section. Use each term in a sentence that explains its meaning.

🔄 **Target Reading Skill**

State the details that support the main idea on page 225 that the United States is diverse.

Comprehension and Critical Thinking

1. (a) Explain How did the United States government support white settlement in the West?

(b) Draw Inferences Why did the government send Native Americans to live on land that was not considered valuable?

(c) Analyze Information How were Native Americans at a disadvantage in their conflict with white settlers?

2. (a) Note When did American literature begin to have a distinct voice?

(b) Identify Causes When and how did American literature become more diverse?

(c) Synthesize Information How has the immigrant experience influenced American culture?

Writing Activity

Write an entry in your journal explaining how the literature and music of the United States reflect diverse cultures. When you write a journal entry, you can let your ideas flow without stopping to edit what you write.

For: An activity on Ellis Island
Visit: PHSchool.com
Web Code: lhd-4302

226 United States and Canada

Writing Activity

Use the *Rubric for Assessing a Journal Entry* to evaluate students' journals.

All in One **United States and Canada Teaching Resources,** *Rubric for Assessing a Journal Entry,* p. 223

Go Online PHSchool.com Typing in the Web Code when prompted will bring students directly to detailed instructions for this activity.

Prepare to Read

Objectives

In this section you will
1. Find out about the people of Canada.
2. Learn about Canadian culture.

Taking Notes

As you read this section, look for details that show why Canadians consider their society to be a mosaic. Copy the concept web below and record your findings in it.

The Mosaic of Canadian Society

🎯 Target Reading Skill

Identify Main Ideas
Identifying main ideas can help you remember the most important ideas that you read. Sometimes, the main ideas are not stated directly. All the details in a section add up to a main idea, but you must state the main idea yourself. Carefully read the details in the two paragraphs below. Then, state the main idea of these paragraphs.

Key Terms

- **melting pot** (MELT ing paht) *n.* a country in which many cultures blend together to form a single culture
- **reserve** (rih ZURV) *n.* an area of land set aside by the government

Over the years, Canada has been as welcoming to immigrants as the United States. However, one important difference between the countries is the way in which they view immigration. The United States considers itself to be a **melting pot**, or a country in which all cultures blend together to form a single culture. In this view, immigrants are encouraged to adopt American ways. Canadians view immigration in a slightly different way, as one Canadian journalist explains:

> **Canadians believe . . . in a mosaic of separate pieces, with each chunk becoming part of the whole physically but retaining its own separate identity, color, and tastes. This certainly makes for an interesting mix. Importantly, it provides Canadians with an identity peg, one major way to see themselves as different from Americans, as they must. And as they are.**
>
> —*Andrew H. Malcolm*

A crowd celebrates Canada Day.

🎯 Target Reading Skill

Identify Main Ideas Point out the Target Reading Skill. Tell students that when a main idea is not specifically expressed, readers can combine important details to express the main idea.

Model identifying the implied main idea in the first paragraph on p. 229 under the heading Immigrants. Point out that the first three sentences provide background to help set up the main idea. The information in the last two sentences can be used to identify the main idea. (*Many immigrants settled in Canada until the government restricted immigration during the Great Depression.*)

Give students *Identify Implied Main Ideas.* Have them complete the activity in their groups.

All in One United States and Canada Teaching Resources, *Identify Implied Main Ideas,* p. 209

Objectives

Social Studies
1. Find out about the people of Canada.
2. Learn about Canadian culture.

Reading/Language Arts
Learn to identify the implied main idea.

Prepare to Read

Build Background Knowledge 📘 L2

Ask students to list two pieces of information they know about Canada. Model the thought process by suggesting that they recall what they have read about the similarities and differences between Canada and the United States. Use the Give One, Get One strategy (TE, p. T37) to generate a list.

Set a Purpose for Reading 📘 L2

- Preview the Objectives.

- Read each statement in the *Reading Readiness Guide* aloud. Ask students to mark the statements true or false.

  All in One United States and Canada Teaching Resources, *Reading Readiness Guide,* p. 204

- Have students discuss the statements in pairs or groups of four, then mark their worksheets again. Use the Numbered Heads participation strategy (TE, p. T36) to call on students to share their group's perspective.

Vocabulary Builder

Preview Key Terms 📘 L2

Pronounce each Key Term, then ask the students to say the word with you. Provide a simple explanation, such as, "Many of Canada's native peoples live on reserves, while many Native Americans in the United states live on reservations."

Instruct

The People of Canada L2

Guided Instruction

■ **Vocabulary Builder** Clarify the high-use words **promote** and **restrict**.

■ Read The People of Canada, using the Paragraph Shrinking technique (TE, p. T34).

■ Ask students **What are Canada's indigenous peoples called?** *(First Nations)*

■ Discuss how the way the Canadian government treated First Nations was similar to the way the United States first treated Native Americans. *(European settlers took over the indigenous peoples' lands. Many indigenous peoples were sent to reserves in Canada while they were sent to reservations in the United States. Others were denied equal rights.)*

■ Ask students **Why has Canada's population doubled since World War II?** *(More workers were needed when the economy began to grow again after World War II. Millions of immigrants came to Canada to fill this need.)*

Independent Practice

Ask students to copy the Taking Notes graphic organizer onto a piece of paper. Briefly model how to use the concept web to record supporting details that show why Canadians consider their society to be a mosaic.

Monitor Progress

As students fill in the graphic organizer, circulate and make sure individuals are choosing the correct details. Provide assistance as needed.

Answers

Graph Skills Identify Asia and Oceania **Compare and Contrast** Similar—the areas of origin are similar; Different—the United States has a higher percentage of immigrants from Mexico, the Caribbean, and Central America than Canada, and Canada has a higher percentage of Asian immigrants.

The People of Canada

Today, Canada has a population of more than 31 million people. Many of them are immigrants. At first, Canada's leaders preferred Christian European settlers. At times, laws set limits on immigrants who were Jews, Asians, or Africans. But that has changed. Today, people of all ethnic groups move to Canada.

French Canadians Sometimes, the ties among Canadians are not as strong as those among Americans. People in the United States rarely talk about forming independent states or countries. Some Canadian groups do. French Canadians in Quebec are concerned about preserving their heritage. Special laws promote French culture and language. Street and advertising signs are written in both French and English. But many French Canadians want Quebec to become a separate country. To show their determination, they have license plates that read *Je me souviens,* or "I remember." This phrase refers to remembering their French heritage.

First Nations Canada's indigenous peoples, called First Nations, also want to preserve their culture. They are trying to fix past problems by working with existing governments.

In Canada, as in the United States, early European settlers took over the native peoples' lands. Many indigenous peoples were sent to reserves, or areas that the government set aside for them, similar to reservations in the United States. Others were denied equal rights. Recently, laws have been passed allowing First Nations to use their own languages in their schools.

■ Graph Skills

Canada is an ethnically diverse country. **Identify** Where do most immigrants to Canada come from? **Compare and Contrast** Compare the Origin of Immigrants to Canada chart here with the similar chart on page 224. How are they similar? How do they differ?

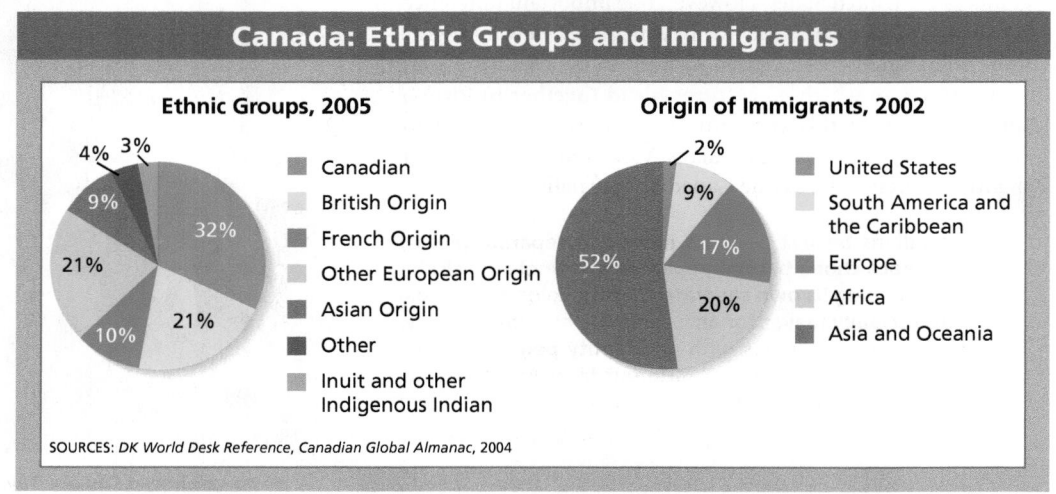

Canada: Ethnic Groups and Immigrants

Ethnic Groups, 2005
- 32%
- 21%
- 21%
- 10%
- 9%
- 4%
- 3%

Legend:
- Canadian
- British Origin
- French Origin
- Other European Origin
- Asian Origin
- Other
- Inuit and other Indigenous Indian

Origin of Immigrants, 2002
- 52%
- 20%
- 17%
- 9%
- 2%

Legend:
- United States
- South America and the Caribbean
- Europe
- Africa
- Asia and Oceania

SOURCES: *DK World Desk Reference, Canadian Global Almanac,* 2004

Vocabulary Builder

Use the information below to teach students this section's high-use words.

High-Use Word	Definition and Sample Sentence
promote, p. 228	*v.* to help with the growth of something Watering plants regularly helps to **promote** their growth.
restrict, p. 229	*v.* to keep within a certain amount Ann **restricts** the amount of food her dog eats so that he stays fit and healthy.

Inuits   Canada's Inuits (IN oo its) lived in the Arctic for centuries as nomadic hunters and gatherers. They had excellent survival skills and were fine craftworkers. They made everything they needed using available materials, such as snow, stone, animal bones, and driftwood. Modern technology, however, allows them to buy the clothes and tools they used to make. Many Inuits have lost their traditional skills. As a result, some feel they are losing their identity.

Immigrants   Because Britain and France were the first countries to colonize Canada, most Canadians were of British or French descent by the late 1800s. By the 1920s, many immigrants came from central and eastern Europe to farm the prairies in the west. But when the Depression hit in 1929, there was no longer a need for as many workers. The government restricted immigration.

After World War II, the economy began to grow again. With the need for more workers, millions of immigrants came to Canada. Many of them were from Africa, Asia, and Latin America and settled mainly in large urban areas. For example, many Asian immigrants settled in Vancouver and Toronto. Since World War II, Canada's population has more than doubled. Much of that growth is because of immigrants and their children.

√ Reading Check   **How has technology changed the way that Inuits live?**

Remembering Canada's History
The community of Chemainus, British Columbia, is famous for its collection of 35 larger-than-life historical murals. **Analyze Images**   *How does this mural honor the role that the country's indigenous peoples have played in Canada's history?*

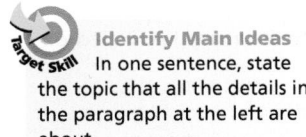 **Identify Main Ideas**   In one sentence, state the topic that all the details in the paragraph at the left are about.

Chapter 8 Section 3 **229**

Guided Instruction
- Read Canadian Culture with students.
- Ask students **What is one cultural issue that unites most Canadians?** *(They feel the United States has too much influence on their culture.)*
- Discuss Canadian literature and music. Ask students to name Canadian writers and musicians. Encourage them to include people not mentioned in the text. *(writers: Lucy Maud Montgomery, Margaret Atwood, Robertson Davies, Alice Munro, Michael Ondaatje; musicians: Bryan Adams, Sarah McLachlan, Shania Twain, Céline Dion)*

Independent Practice
Have students complete the graphic organizer by filling in the rest of the details on the concept web.

Monitor Progress
- Show *Section Reading Support Transparency USC 53* and ask students to check their graphic organizers individually. Go over key concepts and clarify key vocabulary as needed.

   United States and Canada Transparencies, *Section Reading Support Transparency USC 53*

- Tell students to fill in the last column of the *Reading Readiness Guide.* Probe for what they learned that confirms or invalidates each statement.

   All in One **United States and Canada Teaching Resources,** *Reading Readiness Guide,* p. 204

Target Reading Skill

Identify Main Ideas As a follow-up, ask students to perform the Target Reading Skill activity in the Student Edition. *(Since World War II, the population of Canada has grown significantly, which has occurred in part by an increase in immigration.)*

Answers
Analyze Images The presence of the mural in the collection acknowledges the importance of indigenous peoples in history.
√ Reading Check   They now can buy many of the things they used to make and many Inuits have lost their traditional skills.

For English Language Learners   L3
Some of the verbs used in this section may be confusing to students acquiring English as a second language. Point out irregular verbs in the section such as *made, sent,* and *came.* Help students to make a list of the section's past-tense verbs and their corresponding infinitives.

For Special Needs Students   L1
Have students read the section as they listen to the recorded version on the Student Edition on Audio CD. Check for comprehension by pausing the CD and asking students to share their answers to the Reading Checks.

◉ Chapter 8, Section 3, **Western Hemisphere Student Edition on Audio CD**

Assess and Reteach

Answers

✓ Reading Check the recording and sports industries

Section 3 Assessment

Key Terms
Students' sentences should reflect knowledge of each Key Term.

↻ **Target Reading Skill**
Possible answer: The population of Canada is made up of immigrants from all over the world and Canada's indigenous peoples. Canadians share a common culture and also express their own ethnic heritages. Literature, music, and sports are all important to Canadian culture.

Comprehension and Critical Thinking
1. (a) English and French **(b)** Special laws promote French culture and language, and street and advertising signs are in French and English. **(c)** Possible answer: They feel it is the best way to protect Quebec's French culture.

2. (a) through writing, music, and sports **(b)** Possible answer: They worry that the United States has too much influence on their culture.

Playing hockey on an outdoor ice rink

Canadian Culture

Canada has made a special effort to encourage people to be Canadian and to express their ethnic heritage at the same time. One cultural issue does unite most Canadians: They feel that the United States has too much influence on their culture. Even today, Canadians search for ways to express their unique culture.

Canadian writers have long been famous for their work. From Lucy Maud Montgomery's *Anne of Green Gables* to writers of today, such as Margaret Atwood and Alice Munro, Canadian literature is popular throughout the world.

Canadian singers have made contributions to cultural life as well. Popular Canadian singers include Shania Twain and Céline Dion. Many singers maintain their ties to Canada even though their jobs often require them to be elsewhere. Since the 1960s, the Canadian recording industry has become a billion-dollar business.

Another billion-dollar industry in Canada is sports. Ice hockey is Canada's national sport. Every year, hockey teams from the United States and Canada compete for the Stanley Cup, a Canadian prize. Hockey serves not only as a national pastime but also as an important symbol of national identity.

✓ Reading Check **Which industries bring billions of dollars into the Canadian economy?**

Section 3 Assessment

Key Terms
Review the key terms at the beginning of this section. Use each term in a sentence that explains its meaning.

↻ **Target Reading Skill**
State the main ideas in Section 3.

Comprehension and Critical Thinking
1. (a) List What are two languages spoken in Canada?

(b) Identify the Main Idea In what ways do French Canadians try to preserve their culture and language?
(c) Draw Conclusions Why do many French Canadians want Quebec to be an independent country?
2. (a) Explain How do Canadians try to express their culture?
(b) Make Generalizations Why do Canadians worry about the influence of the United States on their culture?

Writing Activity
Write a brief paragraph explaining why you think ice hockey developed in Canada.

For: An activity on immigrants
Visit: PHSchool.com
Web Code: lhd-4303

Writing Activity
Use the *Rubric for Assessing a Writing Assignment* to evaluate students' paragraphs.

All in One **United States and Canada Teaching Resources,** *Rubric for Assessing a Writing Assignment,* p. 224

Go Online PHSchool.com Typing in the Web Code when prompted will bring students directly to detailed instructions for this activity.

Review and Assessment

◆ Chapter Summary

Section 1: A Heritage of Diversity and Exchange

- Both the United States and Canada contain a wide variety of cultures.
- Immigrants have shaped the histories and cultures of the United States and Canada.
- The United States and Canada are important to each other for many reasons, including the cultural and economic ties that they share.

Section 2: The United States: A Nation of Immigrants

- The United States government fought many battles with Native Americans, pushing them westward.
- Millions of immigrants came to the United States to work on farms and railroads and in factories, mills, and mines.
- Diverse foods, literature, music, and sports help enrich life in the United States.

Section 3: The Canadian Mosaic

- Many immigrants come to Canada in search of a better life.
- First Nations, Inuits, and immigrants all add to the diversity of Canadian life.
- Canadians have made many contributions to the worlds of literature, music, and sports.

Quebec City

◆ Key Terms

Copy the lists of vocabulary words and definitions side by side on a sheet of paper. Then, draw a line from each term to its correct definition.

1. cultural diversity
2. cultural exchange
3. reservation
4. melting pot
5. ethnic group
6. treaty
7. reserve

A an area of land set aside for a special purpose

B an area of land set aside by the Canadian government

C a variety of cultures

D people who share a language, history, and culture

E a formal agreement

F the process in which different cultures share ideas and ways of doing things

G a country in which all cultures blend together to form a single culture

Chapter 8 **231**

┌ Vocabulary Builder ─

Revisit this chapter's high-use words:

diverse   attitude   enrich
contribution   violate   promote
tradition   reform   restrict

Ask students to review the definitions they recorded on their *Word Knowledge* worksheets.

All in One **United States and Canada Teaching Resources,** *Word Knowledge,* p. 210

Consider allowing students to earn extra credit if they use the words in their answers to the questions in the Chapter Review and Assessment. They must use the words correctly and in a natural context to win the extra points.

Review Chapter Content

- Review and revisit the major themes of this chapter by asking students to classify what Guiding Question each bulleted statement in the Chapter Summary answers. Have students work in groups to classify the statements. Use the Numbered Heads strategy (TE, p. T36) to have the groups share their answers in a class discussion. Refer to p. 139 in the Student Edition for text of Guiding Questions.

- Assign *Vocabulary Development* for students to review Key Terms.

  All in One **United States and Canada Teaching Resources,** *Vocabulary Development,* p. 221

Answers

Key Terms

1. C
2. F
3. A
4. G
5. D
6. E
7. B

Review and Assessment
Comprehension and Critical Thinking

8. (a) to increase the work force, to have people to cultivate land, raise crops, and work in cities **(b)** They attract immigrants because they are wealthy countries with stable governments. **(c)** Possible answer: They find it hard to keep customs of their original culture when they need to learn a new language, laws, and customs in their new country. They feel torn between their cultural heritage and their new life.

9. (a) Nearly two million Canadians visit Florida each year as tourists, supporting many tourism-related industries. **(b)** Possible answer: It would harm such businesses as hotels, restaurants, and amusement centers, resulting in many job losses.

10. (a) They had similar backgrounds and languages. **(b)** Their culture and traditions were different from those of the first wave of immigrants.

11. (a) Possible answer: Because American society is diverse, Americans listen to many kinds of music and new styles of music develop, such as jazz and rock-and-roll. **(b)** Possible answer: Both originated in the United States, growing out of traditional music styles. Jazz has roots in African rhythms and rock-and-roll is a combination of rhythm and blues, gospel, and country music.

12. (a) They are working with the government to fix past problems; they are using native languages in schools. **(b)** Possible answer: Canadian culture encourages people to retain their traditional identity rather than trying to blend into one single culture. **(c)** Possible answer: Canadians wish to express their own culture rather than be influenced by the culture of the United States.

Skills Practice
Concept webs will vary, but should be labeled clearly and include accurate information.

◆ Comprehension and Critical Thinking

8. (a) Explain Why did the United States and Canada first encourage immigration?
(b) Identify Causes Why do the United States and Canada continue to attract immigrants today?
(c) Identify Frame of Reference Why do some immigrants find it challenging to balance their cultural heritage with their new environment?

9. (a) Recall How do Canadians contribute to Florida's economy?
(b) Predict In what ways would Florida's economy be affected if these tourists vacationed somewhere else?

10. (a) Recall Why did most of the first wave of immigrants adapt fairly easily to life in the United States?
(b) Draw Conclusions Why was the second wave of immigrants discriminated against when the first wave of immigrants largely was not?

11. (a) Explain How does American society influence American music?
(b) Analyze What is it about jazz or rock-and-roll music that makes them uniquely American?

12. (a) Explain How are First Nations preserving their culture?
(b) Compare and Contrast Why is Canada characterized as a mosaic rather than as a melting pot?
(c) Identify Point of View Why is it important for Canadians to see themselves as different from Americans?

◆ Skills Practice

Using Graphic Organizers In the Skills for Life activity in this chapter, you learned how to use graphic organizers. You also learned that graphic organizers put information into a visual form.

Review the steps you followed to learn this skill. Then reread Cultural Patterns Today, beginning on page 216. Create a concept web about people's reasons for choosing to immigrate to the United States and Canada.

◆ Writing Activity: Math

In pairs or teams, research the different ethnic or cultural groups that are represented in your state. Calculate the results in percentage form. Then display the information as a circle graph. Write a brief summary of your findings.

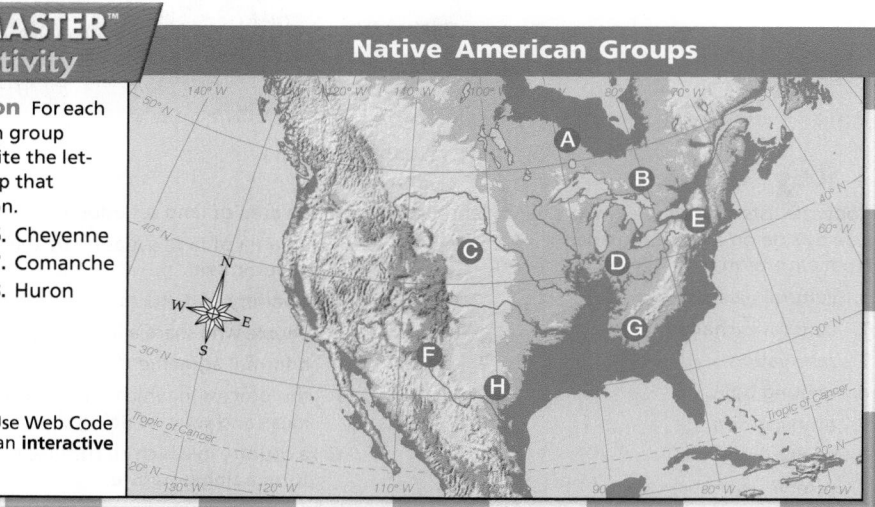

MAP MASTER™
Skills Activity

Native American Groups

Place Location For each Native American group listed below, write the letter from the map that shows its location.
1. Miami   6. Cheyenne
2. Chippewa   7. Comanche
3. Cherokee   8. Huron
4. Iroquois
5. Pueblo

Go Online
PHSchool.com Use Web Code **lhp-4333** for an **interactive map.**

Writing Activity: Math
Student answers should include a circle graph and an informative summary. Use *Rubric for Assessing a Circle Graph* to evaluate students' graphs.

All in One United States and Canada Teaching Resources, *Rubric for Assessing a Circle Graph,* p. 225

Standardized Test Prep

MAP★MASTER™
Skills Activity

1. D	**2.** A
3. G	**4.** E
5. F	**6.** C
7. H	**8.** B

Test-Taking Tips

Some questions on standardized tests ask you to analyze a passage to find a main idea. Read the passage below. Then follow the tips to answer the sample question.

One Toronto radio station broadcasts in thirty languages. . . . In many Vancouver neighborhoods the street signs are in . . . English and Chinese. Toronto's city government routinely prepares its annual property tax notices in six languages: English, French, Chinese, Italian, Greek, and Portuguese.

TIP Before reading the answer choices, think of a main idea that would cover each sentence in the passage. Then match your idea to one of the answer choices.

Pick the letter that best answers the question.

What is the main idea of this passage?

A Toronto's city government prepares tax notices in many languages.

B The Chinese are an important ethnic group in Toronto.

C Many people in Toronto are bilingual, or speak two languages.

D Toronto has a diverse mix of people and ethnic groups.

TIP Read all of the answer choices before making a final choice. You can't be sure you have the right answer until you have read each one.

Think It Through You can rule out answer A, because it applies only to one of the sentences in the passage. You can rule out answer B because though it may be true, the Chinese are only one of the ethnic groups mentioned in the passage. Both answers C and D sound like they might be correct. Read answer C carefully. It isn't right because though the passage describes many languages, it does not say that most people in Toronto are bilingual. The correct answer is D.

Practice Questions

Use the tips above and other tips in this book to help you answer the following questions.

1. When two groups of people share ideas and ways of doing things, they are practicing
   A trade.
   B cultural exchange.
   C cultural diversity.
   D immigration.

2. What kind of standard of living do the United States and Canada have?
   A Both countries have low standards of living.
   B Both countries have high standards of living.
   C The United States has a high standard of living, while Canada's is low.
   D Canada has a high standard of living, while that of the United States is low.

3. Which group in Canada often talks about forming an independent country?
   A the Chippewa
   B the British
   C the French Canadians
   D the Inuit

Read the passage below, and then answer the question that follows.

Culture here has been shaped by a history of British colonization. It has also been shaped by immigrants who have come here from all over the world, bringing their cultures with them. Music, literature, and sports are important parts of the culture.

4. Based on what you have read, which country could this passage be describing?
   A either the United States or Canada
   B the United States
   C Canada
   D neither the United States nor Canada

Go Online
PHSchool.com

Use Web Code **lha-4303** for a **Chapter 8 self-test.**

Chapter 8 **233**

Standardized Test Prep

Answers

1. B
2. B
3. C
4. A

Assessment Resources

Use *Chapter Tests A and B* to assess students' mastery of chapter content.

All in One **United States and Canada Teaching Resources,** *Chapter Tests A and B,* pp. 226–231

Tests are also available on the *ExamView®* *Test Bank CD-ROM.*

⊙ *ExamView® Test Bank CD-ROM*

Use a benchmark test to evaluate students' cumulative understanding of what they have learned in Chapters 6 through 8.

📄 *United States and Canada Benchmark Test 1,* **AYP Monitoring Assessments,** pp. 89–92

9 The United States

Overview

Introducing the United States
1. Look at a map and study the data to learn about the states of the United States.
2. Analyze data to compare the states.
3. Identify characteristics that most states share.
4. Find some of the key differences among the states.

Section 1

The Northeast: An Urban Center
1. Learn how the large cities of the Northeast contribute to the economy of the United States.
2. Find out how the Northeast has been a port of entry for many immigrants.

Section 2

The South: The Growth of Industry
1. Learn how the South's land is important to its economy.
2. Read about how the growth of industry is changing the South.

Section 3

The Midwest: Leaving the Farm
1. Read about how technology is changing life on farms.
2. Learn how changes in farming are affecting the development of cities.

Section 4

The West: Using and Preserving Resources
1. Learn about the natural resources of the West.
2. Read about the challenges facing the urban West.

Technology Resources

Students use embedded Web codes to access Internet activities, chapter self-tests, and additional map practice. They may also access Dorling Kindersley's Online Desk Reference to learn more about each country they study.

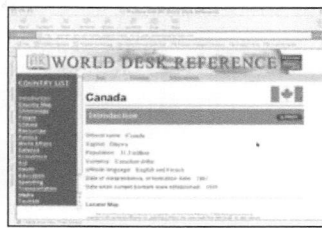

Use the Interactive Textbook to make content and concepts come alive through animations, videos, and activities that accompany the complete basal text—online and on CD-ROM.

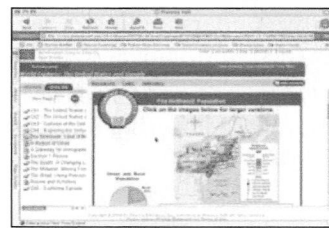

PRENTICE HALL

Use this complete suite of powerful teaching tools to make planning lessons and administering tests quicker and easier.

Reading and Assessment

CHAPTER 9

Reading and Vocabulary Instruction

🔄 Model the Target Reading Skill

Comparison and Contrast Explain that when you compare things, you observe how they are similar. When you contrast things, you observe how they are different. By comparing and contrasting, students can sort out and analyze information. Write the following on the board. Draw attention to the phrases marked with 1 for comparisons and those marked with 2 for contrasts.

❶

Both St. Louis and New York City are important urban centers

❶

in the United States. St. Louis, Missouri, is located on the

❶

Mississippi River. New York City is also on a river, the Hudson.

❷

While St. Louis is a banking and commercial center, New York—

❷

the country's largest, wealthiest, and most influential city—is the

❷

"money capital" of the United States.

Circle the words "both," "also," and "while" because they are signifiers of comparisons and contrasts.

Use the following worksheets from All-in-One United States and Canada Teaching Resources (pp. 251–253) to support this chapter's Target Reading Skill.

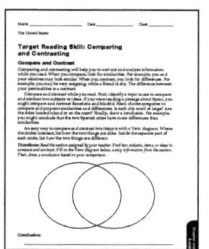 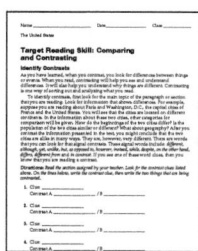

Vocabulary Builder
High-Use Academic Words
Use these steps to teach this chapter's high-use words:

1. Have students rate how well they know each word on their Word Knowledge worksheets (All-in-One United States and Canada Teaching Resources, p. 254).

2. Pronounce each word and ask students to repeat it.

3. Give students a brief definition and sample sentence (provided on TE pp. 249, 256, 265, and 272).

4. Work with students as they fill in the "Definition or Example" column of their Word Knowledge worksheets.

Assessment

Formal Assessment
Test students' understanding of core knowledge and skills.

Chapter Tests A and B, All-in-One United States and Canada Teaching Resources, pp. 275–280

Customize the Chapter Tests to suit your needs.
ExamView® Test Bank CD-ROM

Skills Assessment
Assess geographic literacy.

MapMaster Skills, Student Edition pp. 235, 249, 260, 269, 278

Regional Profile Map and Chart Skills, Student Edition pp. 250, 256, 265, 272

Assess reading and comprehension.

Target Reading Skills, Student Edition, pp. 251, 259, 267, 275, and in Section Assessments

Chapter 9 Assessment, Reading and Vocabulary Study Guide, p. 104

Performance Assessment
Assess students' performance on this chapter's Writing Activities using the following rubrics from All-in-One United States and Canada Teaching Resources.

Rubric for Assessing a Timeline, p. 272

Rubric for Assessing a Writing Assignment, p. 273

Rubric for Assessing a Newspaper Article, p. 274

Assess students' work through performance tasks.

Small Group Activity: Simulation: Town Meeting on Water Use, All-in-One United States and Canada Teaching Resources, pp. 257–260

Portfolio Suggestions, Teacher's Edition, p. 109

Online Assessment
Have students check their own understanding.

Chapter Self-Test

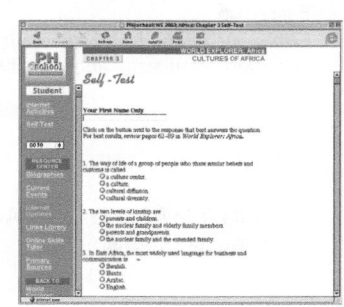

Section 1 The Northeast: An Urban Center

 2.5 periods, 1.25 blocks (includes Country Databank)

Social Studies Objectives
1. Learn how the large cities of the Northeast contribute to the economy of the United States.
2. Find out how the Northeast has been a port of entry for many immigrants.

Reading/Language Arts Objective
Compare and contrast to help sort out and analyze information.

Prepare to Read

Build Background Knowledge
Have students list characteristics of some major northeastern cities.

Set a Purpose for Reading
Have students begin to fill out the *Reading Readiness Guide.*

Preview Key Terms
Teach the section's Key Terms.

Target Reading Skill
Introduce the section's Target Reading Skill of **comparing and contrasting**.

Instructional Resources

All in One United States and Canada Teaching Resources
- L2 Reading Readiness Guide, p. 236
- L2 Compare and Contrast, p. 251

Differentiated Instruction

Spanish Reading and Vocabulary Study Guide
- L1 Chapter 9, Section 1, pp. 68–69 ELL

World Studies Video Program
- L2 The Geography of the United States AR, GT, LPR, SN

Instruct

A Region of Cities
Discuss the major cities of the Northeast.

Regional Profile
Ask students to derive information from maps, charts, and graphs.

Target Reading Skill
Review **comparing and contrasting**.

Eyewitness Technology
Have students read about and discuss skyscrapers.

Ports of Entry
Discuss the cities to which immigrants to the United States came.

Instructional Resources

All in One United States and Canada Teaching Resources
- L2 Guided Reading and Review, p. 237
- L2 Reading Readiness Guide, p. 236
- L2 Reading a Population Density Map, p. 263
- L2 Writing a Letter, p. 270

United States and Canada Transparencies
- L2 Section Reading Support Transparency USC 54
- L1 Transparency B16: Venn Diagram
- L2 Color Transparency USC 27: United States: Agricultural Regions

Differentiated Instruction

All in One United States and Canada Teaching Resources
- L2 Outline Map 11: The United States: Political, p. 267 AR, GT, LPR, SN

Teacher's Edition
- L1 For Less Proficient Readers, TE p. 237
- L3 For Advanced Readers, TE pp. 240, 253
- L3 For Gifted and Talented, TE p. 244
- L1 For English Language Learners, TE pp. 246, 252
- L1 For Special Needs Students, TE p. 252

PHSchool.com
- L3 For: Environmental and Global Issues: Nickel-and-Diming
  Web Code: lhd-4402 AR, GT

Assess and Reteach

Assess Progress
Evaluate student comprehension with the section assessment and section quiz.

Reteach
Assign the Reading and Vocabulary Study Guide to help struggling students.

Extend
Extend the lesson by having students create a television commercial about a city in the Northeast.

Instructional Resources

All in One United States and Canada Teaching Resources
- L2 Section Quiz, p. 238
  Rubric for Assessing a Writing Assignment, p. 273

Reading and Vocabulary Study Guide
- L1 Chapter 9, Section 1, pp. 92–94

Differentiated Instruction

All in One United States and Canada Teaching Resources
Rubric for Assessing a Timeline, p. 272
AR, GT, LPR, SN

Spanish Support
- L2 Section Quiz (Spanish), p. 87 ELL

Key
- L1 Basic to Average
- L3 Average to Advanced
- L2 For All Students

- LPR Less Proficient Readers
- AR Advanced Readers
- SN Special Needs Students

- GT Gifted and Talented
- ELL English Language Learners

Section 2 The South: The Growth of Industry

 3.5 periods, 1.75 blocks (includes Skills for Life)

Social Studies Objectives
1. Learn how the South's land is important to its economy.
2. Read about how the growth of industry is changing the South.

Reading/Language Arts Objective
Use signal words to find relationships among ideas or events.

Prepare to Read	Instructional Resources	Differentiated Instruction
Build Background Knowledge Discuss the industries and products associated with the South's diverse economy. **Set a Purpose for Reading** Have students evaluate statements on the *Reading Readiness Guide*. **Preview Key Terms** Teach the section's Key Terms. **Target Reading Skill** Introduce the section's Target Reading Skill of **using signal words**.	**All in One United States and Canada Teaching Resources** L2 Reading Readiness Guide, p. 240 L2 Compare and Contrast, p. 251	**Spanish Reading and Vocabulary Study Guide** L1 Chapter 9, Section 2, pp. 70–71 ELL

Instruct	Instructional Resources	Differentiated Instruction
Regional Profile Ask students to derive information from maps, charts, and graphs. **The Land of the South** Ask questions about the South's land and resources. **Target Reading Skill** Review **using signal words**. **Southern Cities and Industries** Ask questions about Southern cities and industries.	**All in One United States and Canada Teaching Resources** L2 Guided Reading and Review, p. 241 L2 Reading Readiness Guide, p. 240 **United States and Canada Transparencies** L2 Section Reading Support Transparency USC 55 **Social Studies Skills Tutor CD-ROM** L2 Transferring Information from One Medium to Another	**All in One United States and Canada Teaching Resources** L3 Reading an Economic Activity Map, p. 264 AR, GT L2 Skills for Life, p. 256 AR, GT, LPR, SN **Teacher's Edition** L1 For English Language Learners, TE p. 259 L3 For Gifted and Talented, TE p. 260 **Spanish Support** L2 Guided Reading and Review (Spanish), p. 88 ELL

Assess and Reteach	Instructional Resources	Differentiated Instruction
Assess Progress Evaluate student comprehension with the section assessment and section quiz. **Reteach** Assign the Reading and Vocabulary Study Guide to help struggling students. **Extend** Extend the lesson by assigning a research project.	**All in One United States and Canada Teaching Resources** L2 Section Quiz, p. 242 Rubric for Assessing a Writing Assignment, p. 273 **Reading and Vocabulary Study Guide** L1 Chapter 9, Section 2, pp. 95–97	**All in One United States and Canada Teaching Resources** L1 Reading a Circle Graph, p. 265 ELL, LPR, SN **Teacher's Edition** L3 For Advanced Readers, TE p. 263 L1 For Special Needs Students, TE p. 263 **Spanish Support** L2 Section Quiz (Spanish), p. 89 ELL **Social Studies Skills Tutor CD-ROM** L1 Analyzing Graphic Data ELL, LPR, SN

Key
L1 Basic to Average	L3 Average to Advanced	LPR Less Proficient Readers	GT Gifted and Talented
L2 For All Students		AR Advanced Readers	ELL English Language Learners
		SN Special Needs Students	

Section 3 The Midwest: Leaving the Farm

2 periods, 1 block

Social Studies Objectives
1. Read about how technology is changing life on farms.
2. Learn how changes in farming are affecting the development of cities.

Reading/Language Arts Objective
Contrast two situations to find out how they are different.

Prepare to Read

Build Background Knowledge
Have students brainstorm words they associate with a farm and refer to the list as they read the section.

Set a Purpose for Reading
Have students evaluate statements on the *Reading Readiness Guide.*

Preview Key Terms
Teach the section's Key Terms.

Target Reading Skill
Introduce the section's Target Reading Skill of **identifying contrasts.**

Instructional Resources

All in One United States and Canada Teaching Resources
- L2 Reading Readiness Guide, p. 244
- L2 Identify Contrasts, p. 252

Differentiated Instruction

Spanish Reading and Vocabulary Study Guide
- L1 Chapter 9, Section 3, pp. 72–73 ELL

Instruct

Regional Profile
Ask students to derive information from maps, charts, and graphs.

Technology Changes Farm Life
Discuss how advances in technology affected farms.

Target Reading Skill
Review **identifying contrasts.**

Cities Develop in the Midwest
Discuss some of the major cities of the Midwest.

Instructional Resources

All in One United States and Canada Teaching Resources
- L2 Guided Reading and Review, p. 245
- L2 Reading Readiness Guide, p. 244

United States and Canada Transparencies
- L2 Transparency B7: Cause and Effect Chart
- L2 Section Reading Support Transparency USC 56

Differentiated Instruction

All in One United States and Canada Teaching Resources
- L1 Reading a Table, p. 266 ELL, LPR, SN
- L3 Enrichment, p. 255 AR, GT

Teacher's Edition
- L2 For English Language Learners, TE p. 266
- L1 For Special Needs Students, TE p. 266
- L3 For Advanced Readers, TE p. 267
- L1 For Less Proficient Readers, TE pp. 267, 268
- L3 For Gifted and Talented, TE p. 268

United States and Canada Transparencies
- L3 Transparency B20: Timeline AR, GT

Assess and Reteach

Assess Progress
Evaluate student comprehension with the section assessment and section quiz.

Reteach
Assign the Reading and Vocabulary Study Guide to help struggling students.

Extend
Extend the lesson by showing a video.

Instructional Resources

All in One United States and Canada Teaching Resources
- L2 Section Quiz, p. 246
  Rubric for Assessing a Writing Assignment, p. 273

Reading and Vocabulary Study Guide
- L1 Chapter 9, Section 3, pp. 98–100

Differentiated Instruction

Spanish Support
- L2 Section Quiz (Spanish), p. 91 ELL

Key
- L1 Basic to Average
- L3 Average to Advanced
- L2 For All Students
- LPR Less Proficient Readers
- AR Advanced Readers
- SN Special Needs Students
- GT Gifted and Talented
- ELL English Language Learners

234e

Section 4 The West: Using and Preserving Resources

 4.5 periods, 2.25 blocks (includes Chapter Review and Assessment and Literature)

Social Studies Objectives
1. Learn about the natural resources of the West.
2. Read about the challenges facing the urban West.

Reading/Language Arts Objective
Make comparisons to see how two situations are the same.

Prepare to Read

Build Background Knowledge
Discuss recycling and conservation of natural resources.

Set a Purpose for Reading
Have students begin to fill out the *Reading Readiness Guide*.

Preview Key Terms
Teach the section's Key Terms.

Target Reading Skill
Introduce the section's Target Reading Skill of **making comparisons**.

Instructional Resources

All in One United States and Canada Teaching Resources
- L2 Reading Readiness Guide, p. 248
- L2 Make Comparisons, p. 253

Differentiated Instruction

Spanish Reading and Vocabulary Study Guide
- L1 Chapter 9, Section 4, pp. 74–75 ELL

Instruct

Regional Profile
Ask students to derive information from maps, charts, and graphs.

Natural Resources of the West
Discuss the use and management of resources in the West.

The Urban West
Discuss the issues of cities in the West.

Target Reading Skill
Review **making comparisons**.

Instructional Resources

All in One United States and Canada Teaching Resources
- L2 Guided Reading and Review, p. 249
- L2 Reading Readiness Guide, p. 248

United States and Canada Transparencies
- L2 Color Transparency USC 29: The United States: Annual Precipitation and Prevailing Winds
- L2 Section Reading Support Transparency USC 57

Differentiated Instruction

All in One United States and Canada Teaching Resources
- L1 Reading a Table, p. 266 ELL, LPR, SN
- L3 Activity Shop Lab: Making a Model River, pp. 261–262 AR, GT

Teacher's Edition
- L1 For Less Proficient Readers, TE p. 273
- L3 For Gifted and Talented, TE pp. 273, 275
- L1 For Special Needs Students, TE p. 275
- L3 For Advanced Readers, TE p. 282

Student Edition on Audio CD
- L1 Chapter 9, Section 4 ELL, LPR, SN

Assess and Reteach

Assess Progress
Evaluate student comprehension with the section assessment and section quiz.

Reteach
Assign the Reading and Vocabulary Study Guide to help struggling students.

Extend
Extend the lesson by assigning a Small Group Activity.

Instructional Resources

All in One United States and Canada Teaching Resources
- L2 Section Quiz, p. 250
- L3 Small Group Activity, pp. 257–260 Rubric for Assessing a Writing Assignment, p. 273
- L2 Vocabulary Development, p. 271
- L2 Word Knowledge, p. 254 Rubric for Assessing a Newspaper Article, p. 274
- L2 Chapter Tests A and B, pp. 275–280

Reading and Vocabulary Study Guide
- L1 Chapter 9, Section 4, pp. 101–103

Differentiated Instruction

All in One United States and Canada Teaching Resources
- L3 Personal Experience of Maria Antonia Pico, pp. 268–269 AR, GT

Spanish Support
- L2 Section Quiz (Spanish), p. 93 ELL
- L2 Chapter Summary (Spanish), p. 94 ELL
- L2 Vocabulary Development (Spanish), p. 95 ELL

Key
- L1 Basic to Average
- L3 Average to Advanced
- L2 For All Students
- LPR Less Proficient Readers
- AR Advanced Readers
- SN Special Needs Students
- GT Gifted and Talented
- ELL English Language Learners

Reading Background

Using the Choral Reading Technique Effectively

The Choral Reading technique ensures participation by all students, including English language learners, because it provides a non-threatening reading environment. To ensure success with this technique, choose shorter passages (less than 500 words), and encourage students to stay with your voice, so that everyone reads at the same rate. When students have finished reading in unison, allow time for students to reread the passage silently, focusing on new or unfamiliar words.

Reading Passage Strategies

In this chapter, students will use the ReQuest technique to read passages. It is important to help students ask their own questions while reading. This gives them a purpose for reading and helps them monitor their comprehension.

Model this technique using the following passage from page 260 of the Student Edition. After reading the passage aloud, begin by asking questions that have students recall information and progress to more interpretive questions.

A big part of the South's economy depends on moving goods and people into and out of the region. Most of the South's largest cities play important roles in this transportation industry. Miami, Florida, and New Orleans, Louisiana, are major ports. Miami is a center for goods and people going to and from Central and South America. New Orleans is a gateway between the Gulf of Mexico and the Mississippi River system. It is also an important port for oil tankers.

Let me make sure I understand the selection: What does much of the South's economy depend on? *(moving goods and people into and out of the region)* What exactly does that mean? *(importing and exporting of goods, and tourism)* What cities therefore play a big part in the South's economy? *(Miami and New Orleans)* Why is this so? *(Miami is far south and close to the Caribbean and South America. It is a major port, allowing easy access for ships. New Orleans is at the mouth of the Mississippi River and a major port on the Gulf of Mexico.)*

Continue in this manner, alternating between teacher- and student-proposed questions. As students become more proficient, you might partner them and have them write down their questions. Ask pairs to read their questions to the group so that others can answer them.

World Studies Background

Skyscrapers

The skyscraper owes its development to various mechanical advances in the last part of the nineteenth century. An important one was the perfection of the high-speed elevator. The invention of a system in which a metal framework supported both walls and floors was another. The first skyscraper, the Home Insurance Building in Chicago, was designed in 1883 by William Le Baron Jenney. It was followed by similar buildings in Chicago and in New York City.

Mining Town Revisited

Virginia City, Nevada, was one of the many towns that were quickly built during the gold and silver mining boom years. This town, in the Sierra Nevada Mountains, grew near the rich deposit of silver called the Comstock Lode, which was discovered in 1859. As miners poured in, Virginia City went from a temporary mining camp to a town with more permanent structures including homes and more than 100 saloons! The town's population grew to about 30,000. However, within 25 years the silver ran out, and the population declined. Today, Virginia City is a well-preserved town that attracts thousands of tourists during the summer months.

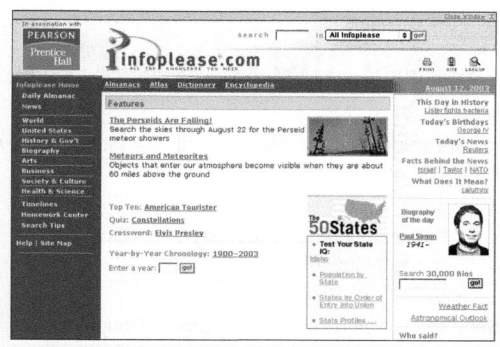

Infoplease® provides a wealth of useful information for the classroom. You can use this resource to strengthen your background on the subjects covered in this chapter. Have students visit this advertising-free site as a starting point for projects requiring research.

Use Web Code **lhd-4400** for **Infoplease®**.

Mapping Words

Research shows that the use of word maps can help students internalize word meanings and develop more comprehensive definitions of words (as opposed to simple one- or two-word definitions). Use the following steps to map word definitions:

1. Have students look at the Key Term *commute*. Ask them to answer the following questions:
   - What is it? *(traveling to get to work)*
   - What is it like? *(it can be long or short; travel can be by car, bus, subway, or train)*
   - What are some examples? *(taking the subway to work, driving from the suburbs to the city)*
2. Record responses to the questions on a word web.
3. Have students develop the answers in the word web into a definition: *(commuting is traveling to get to work, usually by car, bus, subway, or train. Driving from the suburbs to the city is one example of a commute.)*

Writing Paragraphs

It is important for students to be able to demonstrate what they have learned with strong writing skills. Help students practice writing an informative paragraph using the following steps. Model each step using the paragraph under the heading *The Land of the South*, on page 255 of the Student Edition.

1. Begin with a topic sentence.
   There are many different ways that people in the South can make a living.
2. Add three to five sentences to elaborate on the topic.
   The South's particular geography and climate make many of these jobs possible. The region has a warm climate, and most parts of it receive plenty of rain. The wide coastal plains along the Atlantic Ocean and the Gulf of Mexico have rich soil.
3. Include a summary sentence.
   Together, these features make much of the South an excellent place for growing crops and raising animals.

   Point out to students that the length of the sentences varies. Draw attention to the variety of sentence structure and transition words as well. Explain how the last sentence both summarizes the topic and adds new information.

George Washington Bridge

The George Washington Bridge, one of the longest suspension bridges in the world, spans the Hudson River. At 4,760 feet long (1,451 meters), it is one of several links between New York City and New Jersey. Other crossings include the Lincoln and Holland tunnels and railway tubes. The bridge was begun in 1927, and opened to vehicular traffic in 1931. A second level was opened in 1962.

The Sun Belt

The term "Sun Belt" gained popularity in the 1970s when there was a significant population shift to the southern part of the United States. After World War II, people of retirement age were attracted to this region by the warm climate. The relative lack of labor unions and a cheaper labor force encouraged manufacturers from the North to relocate to the region as well. The oil boom of the 1970s added to the region's wealth, as did an enormous tourism business. By the 1990s, cities in the Sun Belt, including Los Angeles, San Diego, Phoenix, and San Antonio, were among the ten largest cities in the country.

The United States

Guiding Questions

Remind students about the Guiding Questions introduced at the beginning of this section.

Section 1 relates to **Guiding Question 5**
How did the United States and Canada become two of the wealthiest nations in the world? *(The major cities of the Northeast are centers of trade, finance, manufacturing, and communications.)*

Section 2 relates to **Guiding Question 1**
How has physical geography affected the cultures of the United States and Canada? *(The warm climate of the South provides good conditions for farming.)*

Section 3 relates to **Guiding Question 5**
How did the United States and Canada become two of the wealthiest nations in the world? *(The Midwest is the agricultural center of the United States. Its major cities contribute to the country's economy.)*

Section 4 relates to **Guiding Question 1**
How has physical geography affected the cultures of the United States and Canada? *(The West is rich in natural resources, attracting people to the region for hundreds of years.)*

Target Reading Skill

In this chapter, students will learn and apply the reading skill of compare and contrast. Use the following worksheets to help students practice this skill:

All in One United States and Canada Teaching Resources, *Compare and Contrast,* p. 251; *Identify Contrasts,* p. 252; *Make Comparisons,* p. 253

Differentiated Instruction

The following Teacher's Edition strategies are suitable for students of varying abilities.

Advanced Readers pp. 240, 253, 263, 267, 282

English Language Learners pp. 246, 252, 259, 266

Gifted and Talented pp. 244, 260, 268, 273, 275

Less Proficient Readers pp. 237, 267, 268, 273

Special Needs Students pp. 252, 263, 266, 275

Chapter Preview

This chapter will introduce you to the four regions of the United States.

Country Databank
The Country Databank provides data on each of the fifty states.

Section 1
The Northeast
An Urban Center

Section 2
The South
The Growth of Industry

Section 3
The Midwest
Leaving the Farm

Section 4
The West
Using and Preserving Resources

Target Reading Skill

Comparison and Contrast In this chapter you will focus on using comparison and contrast to help you sort out and analyze information.

▶ Members of the California National Guard display an American flag.

234 United States and Canada

Bibliography

For the Teacher
Brands, H.W. *The Age of Gold: The California Gold Rush and the New American Dream.* Doubleday, 2002.

Bluestone, Barry and Mary Huff Stevenson. *The Boston Renaissance: Race, Space, and Economic Change in an American Metropolis.* Russell Sage Foundation, 2000.

Gannon, Michael. *Florida: A Short History.* University of Florida, 2003.

For the Student
L1 Ashabranner, Brent K. and Jennifer Ashabranner. *On the Mall in Washington, D.C.: A Visit to America's Front Yard.* 21st Century Books, 2002.

L2 Knowlton, Marylee and Dale Anderson. *Arriving at Ellis Island.* Gareth Stevens, 2002.

L3 Stein, R. Conrad. *Los Angeles (Cities of the World).* Children's Press, 2001.

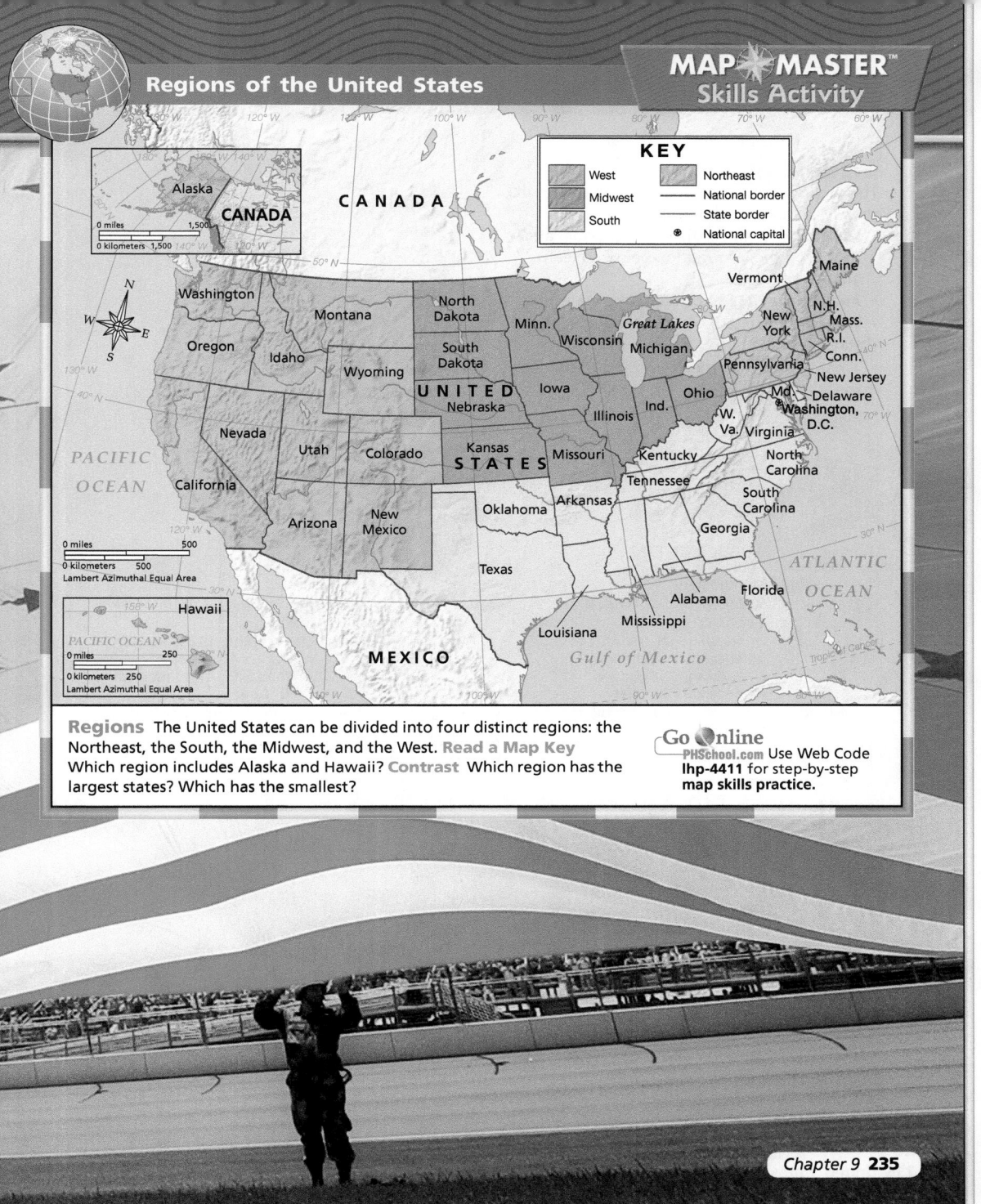

Regions of the United States

KEY

West	Northeast
Midwest	— National border
South	— State border
	⊛ National capital

CANADA

Alaska
CANADA
0 miles 1,500
0 kilometers 1,500

Washington
Montana
North Dakota
Minn.
Great Lakes
Maine
Vermont
N.H.
Mass.
New York
R.I.
Conn.

Oregon
Idaho
Wyoming
South Dakota
Wisconsin
Michigan
Pennsylvania
New Jersey

UNITED
Nebraska
Iowa
Ohio
Md.
Delaware
Washington, D.C.

Nevada
Utah
Colorado
Kansas
STATES
Missouri
Illinois
Ind.
W. Va.
Virginia

California
Kentucky
North Carolina

Arizona
New Mexico
Oklahoma
Arkansas
Tennessee
South Carolina

PACIFIC OCEAN

Texas
Georgia

0 miles 500
0 kilometers 500
Lambert Azimuthal Equal Area

Hawaii
PACIFIC OCEAN
0 miles 250
0 kilometers 250
Lambert Azimuthal Equal Area

MEXICO
Alabama
Mississippi
Louisiana
Florida
Gulf of Mexico

ATLANTIC OCEAN

Regions The United States can be divided into four distinct regions: the Northeast, the South, the Midwest, and the West. **Read a Map Key** Which region includes Alaska and Hawaii? **Contrast** Which region has the largest states? Which has the smallest?

Go Online
PHSchool.com Use Web Code **lhp-4411** for step-by-step **map skills practice.**

MAP MASTER™
Skills Activity

Ask students to locate their state on the map and identify the name of the region in which they live. Then ask them to identify bordering states. Are they in the same region? If not, what regions are they in?

Go Online
PHSchool.com Students may practice their map skills using the interactive online version of this map.

Using the Visual L2

Reach Into Your Background Draw students' attention to the photograph on pp. 234–235. Ask students to recall and discuss what they know about the meaning of the stars and stripes in the flag.

Answers

MAP MASTER
Skills Activity **Read a Map Key** the West
Contrast the West; the Northeast

Chapter Resources

Teaching Resources
- L2 Vocabulary Development, p. 271
- L2 Skills for Life, p. 256
- L2 Chapter Tests A and B, pp. 275–280

Spanish Support
- L2 Spanish Chapter Summary, p. 94
- L2 Spanish Vocabulary Development, p. 95

Media and Technology
- L1 Student Edition on Audio CD
- L1 Guided Reading Audiotapes, English and Spanish
- L2 Social Studies Skills Tutor CD-ROM
  ExamView Test Bank CD-ROM

PRENTICE HALL
Presentation EXPRESS™
Teach · Connect · Inspire

Teach this chapter's content using the PresentationExpress™ CD-ROM including:
- slide shows
- transparencies
- interactive maps and media
- *ExamView*® QuickTake Presenter

Objectives

- Look at a map and study the data to learn about the states of the United States.

- Analyze data to compare the states.

- Identify characteristics that most states share.

- Find some of the key differences among the states.

Prepare to Read

Build Background Knowledge L2

Invite students to describe what they know about the 50 states of the United States, and about their own state in particular. Ask students to share what new information they learned from the watching the World Studies Video. Conduct an Idea Wave (TE, p. T35) to generate a list of states and capitals. Keep a running list of responses on the board. See how many states and capitals students can name and tell them they will have a chance to complete the list after reading the United States Databank.

The Geography of the United States,
World Studies Video Program

Guide for Reading

This section provides an introduction to the fifty states that make up the United States.

- Look at the map on the previous page, and then read the information below to learn about each state.
- Analyze the data to compare the states.
- What are the characteristics that most of the states share?
- What are some of the key differences among the states?

Alabama

Year of Statehood	1819
Capital	Montgomery
Land Area	50,744 sq mi; 131,427 sq km
Population	4,447,100
Ethnic Group(s)	71.1% white; 26.0% African American; 1.7% Hispanic; 0.7% Asian; 0.5% Native American; 0.7% other
Agriculture	cotton, greenhouse products, peanuts
Industry	pulp, paper, chemicals, electronics

Alaska

Year of Statehood	1959
Capital	Juneau
Land Area	571,951 sq mi; 1,481,353 sq km
Population	626,932
Ethnic Group(s)	69.3% white; 15.6% Native American; 4.1% Hispanic; 4.0% Asian; 3.5% African American; 2.1% other
Agriculture	greenhouse products, barley, oats
Industry	petroleum, tourism, fishing

Geological formations of limestone, called tufa, in Mono Lake, California

236 United States and Canada

Arizona

Year of Statehood	1912
Capital	Phoenix
Land Area	113,635 sq mi; 294,315 sq km
Population	5,130,632
Ethnic Group(s)	75.5% white; 25.3% Hispanic; 5.0% Native American; 3.1% African American; 1.8% Asian; 11.7% other
Agriculture	cotton, lettuce, cauliflower
Industry	manufacturing, construction, tourism

Arkansas

Year of Statehood	1836
Capital	Little Rock
Land Area	52,068 sq mi; 134,856 sq km
Population	2,673,400
Ethnic Group(s)	80.0% white; 15.7% African American; 3.2% Hispanic; 0.8% Asian; 0.8% Native American; 1.6% other
Agriculture	poultry, cattle, rice, soybeans
Industry	manufacturing, agriculture, tourism, forestry

California

Year of Statehood	1850
Capital	Sacramento
Land Area	155,959 sq mi; 403,934 sq km
Population	33,871,648
Ethnic Group(s)	59.5% white; 32.4% Hispanic; 10.9% Asian; 6.7% African American; 1.0% Native American; 17.1% other
Agriculture	poultry, cattle, milk
Industry	agriculture, tourism, apparel

Colorado

Year of Statehood	1876
Capital	Denver
Land Area	103,718 sq mi; 268,630 sq km
Population	4,301,261
Ethnic Group(s)	82.8% white; 17.1% Hispanic; 3.8% African American; 2.2% Asian; 1.0% Native American; 7.3% other
Agriculture	poultry, cattle, corn, wheat
Industry	manufacturing, construction

Introducing the United States　L2

Guided Instruction

- Have students read the first two pages of data tables in the Country Databank using the Structured Silent Reading strategy (TE, p. T34).

- Ask students to identify several differences between Alabama and Alaska. Ask them to start with differences in the years of statehood and the size of each state. *(Alabama became a state in 1819; Alaska in 1959. Alaska is more than 10 times bigger than Alabama.)*

- Ask **What industries are important in both Arkansas and California?** *(agriculture, tourism)*

- Ask **Which state is more densely populated, Alabama or Alaska? How can you tell?** *(Alabama; it has far more people and a much smaller land area.)*

- Ask **In which state would you be more likely to find a cattle ranch, Colorado or Alaska? How can you tell?** *(Colorado, because cattle ranching is listed as an important agricultural activity.)*

Differentiated Instruction

For Less Proficient Readers　L1
Have students create a Venn Diagram showing the similarities and differences between California and Colorado. Ask them to focus on the agriculture and industry of these states. Display the *Venn Diagram* transparency to show students

how to sketch the organizer. Circulate to make sure students are filling in the organizers correctly.

📖 **United States and Canada Transparencies,** *Transparency B16: Venn Diagram*

Guided Instruction (continued)

- Point out the Ethnic Groups data on pp. 238–239. Ask students **Which state on these pages has the highest percentage of Asian residents?** *(Hawaii)* **Which has the highest percentage of African Americans?** *(Georgia)*

- Ask **In which of these states is tourism an important industry?** *(Florida, Hawaii, Idaho)*

- Have students look at the map on p. 235. Ask them to locate both Hawaii and Florida. Discuss why warm-weather crops such as citrus fruits and sugar might be important in these states. *(These states are located farther south than most of the other states, giving them warmer climates and a longer growing season, which allows warm-weather crops to be a major source of income for their economies.)*

Introducing The United States

Connecticut

Year of Statehood	1788
Capital	Hartford
Land Area	4,845 sq mi; 12,549 sq km
Population	3,405,565
Ethnic Group(s)	81.6% white; 9.1% African American; 9.4% Hispanic; 2.4% Asian; 0.3% Native American; 4.3% other
Agriculture	nursery stock, mushrooms, vegetables, sweet corn
Industry	manufacturing, retail trade, government

Delaware

Year of Statehood	1787
Capital	Dover
Land Area	1,954 sq mi; 5,061 sq km
Population	783,600
Ethnic Group(s)	74.6% white; 19.2% African American; 4.8% Hispanic; 2.1% Asian; 0.3% Native American
Agriculture	poultry, soybeans, potatoes, corn
Industry	chemicals, agriculture, finance

An alligator at Everglades National Park, Florida

Florida

Year of Statehood	1845
Capital	Tallahassee
Land Area	53,927 sq mi; 139,671 sq km
Population	15,982,378
Ethnic Group(s)	78.0% white; 16.8% Hispanic; 14.6% African American; 1.7% Asian; 0.3% Native American; 3.1% other
Agriculture	poultry, cattle, citrus fruits
Industry	tourism, agriculture, manufacturing

Georgia

Year of Statehood	1788
Capital	Atlanta
Land Area	57,906 sq mi; 149,977 sq km
Population	8,186,453
Ethnic Group(s)	65.1% white; 28.7% African American; 5.3% Hispanic; 2.1% Asian; 0.3% Native American; 2.5% other
Agriculture	poultry, cattle, peanuts, cotton
Industry	services, manufacturing, retail trade

Hawaii

Year of Statehood	1959
Capital	Honolulu
Land Area	6,423 sq mi; 16,636 sq km
Population	1,211,537
Ethnic Group(s)	41.6% Asian; 24.3% white; 9.4% Native Hawaiian or Pacific Islander; 7.2% Hispanic; 1.8% African American; 0.3% Native American; 1.3% other
Agriculture	sugar, pineapples
Industry	tourism, defense, sugar

Idaho

Year of Statehood	1890
Capital	Boise
Land Area	82,747 sq mi; 214,315 sq km
Population	1,293,953
Ethnic Group(s)	91.0% white; 7.9% Hispanic; 1.4% Native American; 0.9% Asian; 0.4% African American; 4.3% other
Agriculture	poultry, cattle, potatoes
Industry	manufacturing, agriculture, tourism

Illinois

Year of Statehood	1818
Capital	Springfield
Land Area	55,584 sq mi; 143,963 sq km
Population	12,419,293
Ethnic Group(s)	73.5% white; 15.1% African American; 12.3% Hispanic; 3.4% Asian; 0.2% Native American; 5.8% other
Agriculture	livestock, corn, soybeans, wheat
Industry	services, manufacturing, travel

Indiana

Year of Statehood	1816
Capital	Indianapolis
Land Area	35,867 sq mi; 92,896 sq km
Population	6,080,485
Ethnic Group(s)	87.5% white; 8.4% African American; 3.5% Hispanic; 1.0% Asian; 0.3% Native American; 1.6% other
Agriculture	livestock, corn, soybeans, wheat
Industry	manufacturing, services, agriculture

Iowa

Year of Statehood	1846
Capital	Des Moines
Land Area	55,869 sq mi; 144,701 sq km
Population	2,926,324
Ethnic Group(s)	93.9% white; 2.8% Hispanic; 2.1% African American; 1.3% Asian; 0.3% Native American; 1.3% other
Agriculture	livestock, poultry, grain, corn
Industry	agriculture, communications, construction

Winner of the Indianapolis 500 race in Indiana

Chapter 9 **239**

Guided Instruction (continued)

- Tell students that pages 238–239 include facts about some of the most important agricultural states in the country. Iowa leads the country in corn production, with Illinois and Indiana close behind. Ask students **In how many of these states is corn an important crop?** (*five: Connecticut, Delaware, Illinois, Indiana, Iowa*)

- Ask **Which industry is important to the economy of six of these states?** (*manufacturing*)

Background: Global Perspectives

Exporting Food The vast fertile plains of the Midwest have helped the United States become a major exporter of food. In fact, the United States is by far the world's leading exporter of wheat and corn, which grow very well in the Midwest. Overall, the United States has a trade deficit, meaning the country imports more than it exports. But in the area of agriculture, the United States has a trade surplus—the country exports more food than it imports. In 2001, the United States exported $53.7 billion worth of food, while food imports were valued at $39 billion. That amounts to a surplus of nearly $15 billion.

- Ask **What is the capital of Maine?** *(Augusta)* **Of what state is Lansing the capital?** *(Michigan)*

- Tell students that two of the states on this page were among the original 13 colonies. Ask them to use the information provided to determine which two they are. *(Maryland, Massachusetts)*

- Have students turn back to the map on p. 235. Ask **In terms of location, what do the states of Maine and Massachusetts have in common?** *(Both states border the Atlantic Ocean.)* Ask students to think about how the industries of these states might be affected by their location. *(Their location on the coast has helped promote industries such as fishing and trade.)*

Introducing The United States

Kansas

Year of Statehood	1861
Capital	Topeka
Land Area	81,815 sq mi; 211,901 sq km
Population	2,688,418
Ethnic Group(s)	86.1% white; 7.0% Hispanic; 5.7% African American; 1.7% Asian; 0.9% Native American; 3.4% other
Agriculture	livestock, poultry, wheat, sorghum
Industry	manufacturing, finance, insurance

Kentucky

Year of Statehood	1792
Capital	Frankfort
Land Area	39,728 sq mi; 10,896 sq km
Population	4,041,769
Ethnic Group(s)	90.1% white; 7.3% African American; 1.5% Hispanic; 0.7% Asian; 0.2% Native American; 0.6% other
Agriculture	poultry, cattle, tobacco, corn
Industry	manufacturing, services, finance

Louisiana

Year of Statehood	1812
Capital	Baton Rouge
Land Area	43,562 sq mi; 112,826 sq km
Population	4,468,976
Ethnic Group(s)	63.9% white; 32.5% African American; 2.4% Hispanic; 1.2% Asian; 0.6% Native American; 0.7% other
Agriculture	poultry, soybeans, sugar cane
Industry	wholesale and retail trade, tourism

Maine

Year of Statehood	1820
Capital	Augusta
Land Area	30,862 sq mi; 76,933 sq km
Population	1,274,923
Ethnic Group(s)	96.9% white; 0.7% Asian; 0.7% Hispanic; 0.6% Native American; 0.5% African American; 0.2% other
Agriculture	poultry, potatoes, aquaculture
Industry	manufacturing, agriculture, fishing

Maryland

Year of Statehood	1788
Capital	Annapolis
Land Area	9,774 sq mi; 25,315 sq km
Population	5,296,486
Ethnic Group(s)	64.0% white; 27.9% African American; 4.3% Hispanic; 4.0% Asian; 0.3% Native American; 1.8% other
Agriculture	poultry, greenhouse and nursery products
Industry	manufacturing, biotechnology

Massachusetts

Year of Statehood	1788
Capital	Boston
Land Area	7,840 sq mi; 20,306 sq km
Population	6,349,097
Ethnic Group(s)	84.5% white; 6.8% Hispanic; 5.4% African American; 3.8% Asian; 0.2% Native American; 3.7% other
Agriculture	cranberries, greenhouse products, vegetables
Industry	services, trade, manufacturing

240 United States and Canada

Differentiated Instruction

For Advanced Readers   L3

Have students do Internet or library research to find out more about the states listed on this page. Ask them to find the nickname of each state. Then have them choose one state nickname and ask them to find the story behind the nickname. Have students write a short essay describing why this nickname fits this state.

Michigan

Year of Statehood	1837
Capital	Lansing
Land Area	56,804 sq mi; 147,122 sq km
Population	9,938,444
Ethnic Group(s)	80.2% white; 14.2% African American; 3.3% Hispanic; 1.8% Asian; 0.6% Native American; 1.3% other
Agriculture	poultry, corn, wheat, soybeans
Industry	manufacturing, services, tourism, agriculture

Minnesota

Year of Statehood	1858
Capital	St. Paul
Land Area	79,610 sq mi; 206,190 sq km
Population	4,919,479
Ethnic Group(s)	89.4% white; 3.5% African American; 2.9% Asian; 2.9% Hispanic; 1.1% Native American; 1.3% other
Agriculture	livestock, poultry, corn, soybeans
Industry	agribusiness, forest products, mining

Mississippi

Year of Statehood	1817
Capital	Jackson
Land Area	46,907 sq mi; 121,489 sq km
Population	2,844,658
Ethnic Group(s)	61.4% white; 36.3% African American; 1.4% Hispanic; 0.7% Asian; 0.4% Native American; 0.5% other
Agriculture	cattle, poultry, cotton, rice
Industry	warehousing/distribution, services

Missouri

Year of Statehood	1821
Capital	Jefferson City
Land Area	68,886 sq mi; 178,415 sq km
Population	5,595,211
Ethnic Group(s)	84.9% white; 11.2% African American; 2.1% Hispanic; 1.1% Asian; 0.4% Native American; 0.9% other
Agriculture	livestock, poultry, soybeans, corn
Industry	agriculture, manufacturing, aerospace

Detroit, Michigan

Guided Instruction (continued)

- Have students identify the largest state on pages 240–241. (*Kansas*) Have them identify the smallest. (*Massachusetts*)

- Ask students to compare and contrast the industries of Maryland and Michigan. (*Similarities: manufacturing is important in both states. Differences: biotechnology is a major industry in Maryland, while services, tourism, and agriculture are important in Missouri.*)

- Ask **How can you tell that natural resources play an important part in Minnesota's economy?** (*Minnesota's industries—agribusiness, forest products, and mining—are all based on the use of natural resources.*)

Background: Links Across Place

Motown During the late 1950s, the city of Detroit in Michigan became an important center for rock music and African American musicians. It was here that Motown Records, named for Detroit's nickname, developed. Popular singing groups, such as the Temptations and Diana Ross and the Supremes, rose to stardom from Detroit neighborhoods. The "Motown Sound" developed into an energetic urban brand of rhythm and blues that remains popular today.

- Have students review the states on both of these pages. Ask **In which of these states is more than 40 percent of the population Hispanic?** (*New Mexico*)

- Tell students that the most densely populated state in the country is listed on one of these two pages. Ask them to use the data given to try to figure out which one it is. (*New Jersey, which students can see has a relatively small land area and a large population compared to other states.*)

Introducing The United States

Horses grazing in Montana

Montana

Year of Statehood	1889
Capital	Helena
Land Area	145,552 sq mi; 376,980 sq km
Population	902,195
Ethnic Group(s)	90.6% white; 6.2% Native American; 2.0% Hispanic; 0.5% Asian; 0.3% African American; 0.7% other
Agriculture	cattle, wheat, barley, sugar beets
Industry	agriculture, timber, mining, tourism

Nebraska

Year of Statehood	1867
Capital	Lincoln
Land Area	76,872 sq mi; 199,098 sq km
Population	1,711,263
Ethnic Group(s)	89.6% white; 5.5% Hispanic; 4.0% African American; 1.3% Asian; 0.9% Native American; 2.8% other
Agriculture	livestock, poultry, corn, sorghum
Industry	agriculture, manufacturing

Nevada

Year of Statehood	1864
Capital	Carson City
Land Area	109,826 sq mi; 284,449 sq km
Population	1,998,257
Ethnic Group(s)	75.2% white; 19.7% Hispanic; 6.8% African American; 4.5% Asian; 1.3% Native American; 8.4% other
Agriculture	hay, alfalfa seed, potatoes
Industry	tourism, mining, manufacturing

New Hampshire

Year of Statehood	1788
Capital	Concord
Land Area	8,968 sq mi; 23,227 sq km
Population	1,235,786
Ethnic Group(s)	96.0% white; 1.7% Hispanic; 1.3% Asian; 0.7% African American; 0.2% Native American; 0.6% other
Agriculture	dairy products, nursery and greenhouse products
Industry	tourism, manufacturing

242 United States and Canada

Background: Links Across Time

Santa Fe Santa Fe, New Mexico, is not only the highest state capital at 6,996 feet (2,132 meters) above sea level, it is also the oldest city to be a state capital. Santa Fe was founded by Spanish settlers in 1610. This region was home to the Pueblo Native Americans, who temporarily drove the Spanish out of New Mexico in the Pueblo Rebellion of 1680. Santa Fe became part of Mexico when Mexico gained independence from Spain in 1821. The city became part of the United States in 1848, as a result of the Mexican War. Santa Fe's art, food, and architecture reflect the diverse mix of cultures that have been part of this city for almost 400 years. The state's population also reflects this history, as can be seen in the large percentage of Hispanic and Native American residents.

New Jersey

Year of Statehood	1787
Capital	Trenton
Land Area	7,417 sq mi; 19,210 sq km
Population	8,414,350
Ethnic Group(s)	72.6% white; 13.6% African American; 13.3% Hispanic; 5.7% Asian; 0.2% Native American; 5.4% other
Agriculture	poultry, nursery and greenhouse products, tomatoes
Industry	pharmaceuticals, telecommunications

New Mexico

Year of Statehood	1912
Capital	Santa Fe
Land Area	121,356 sq mi; 314,312 sq km
Population	1,819,046
Ethnic Group(s)	66.8% white; 42.1% Hispanic; 9.5% Native American; 1.9% African American; 1.1% Asian; 17.1% other
Agriculture	cattle, hay, onions, chilies
Industry	government, services, trade

New York

Year of Statehood	1788
Capital	Albany
Land Area	47,214 sq mi; 122,284 sq km
Population	18,976,457
Ethnic Group(s)	67.9% white; 15.9% African American; 15.1% Hispanic; 5.5% Asian; 0.4% Native American; 7.1% other
Agriculture	cattle, poultry, apples, grapes
Industry	manufacturing, finance, communications

North Carolina

Year of Statehood	1789
Capital	Raleigh
Land Area	48,711 sq mi; 126,161 sq km
Population	8,049,313
Ethnic Group(s)	72.1% white; 21.6% African American; 4.7% Hispanic; 1.2% Native American; 2.3% other
Agriculture	livestock, poultry, tobacco, cotton
Industry	manufacturing, agriculture, tourism

The Exploris museum in Raleigh, North Carolina

■ Ask students to rank the four states on this page in terms of size, from largest to smallest. *(New Mexico, North Carolina, New York, New Jersey)*

■ Now ask students to rank these same states in terms of populations, from largest to smallest. *(New York, New Jersey, North Carolina, New Mexico)* Ask **What can be determined by comparing the size ranking and the population ranking?** *(The two largest states in size have significantly lower population densities.)*

Guided Instruction (continued)

- Tell students that the smallest state in the country is listed on one these two pages. Ask them to figure out which one it is. *(Rhode Island)*

- Ask **Do you think there are any very large cities in North Dakota? How can you tell?** *(No; the population of the entire state is just 642,200, so there cannot be any very large cities in the state.)*

- Ask **What is one thing that the economies of Ohio, Oklahoma, Oregon, Pennsylvania, and Rhode Island have in common?** *(Manufacturing is an important industry in all five states.)*

Introducing The United States

North Dakota

Year of Statehood	1889
Capital	Bismarck
Land Area	68,976 sq mi; 178,648 sq km
Population	642,200
Ethnic Group(s)	92.5% white; 4.9% Native American; 1.2% Hispanic; 0.6% African American; 0.6% Asian; 0.4% other
Agriculture	cattle, spring wheat, durum, barley
Industry	agriculture, mining, tourism

Ohio

Year of Statehood	1803
Capital	Columbus
Land Area	40,948 sq mi; 106,055 sq km
Population	11,353,140
Ethnic Group(s)	85.0% white; 11.5% African American; 1.9% Hispanic; 1.2% Asian; 0.2% Native American; 0.8% other
Agriculture	livestock, poultry, corn, hay
Industry	manufacturing, trade, services

Oklahoma

Year of Statehood	1907
Capital	Oklahoma City
Land Area	68,667 sq mi; 177,848 sq km
Population	3,450,654
Ethnic Group(s)	76.2% white; 7.9% Native American; 7.6% African American; 5.2% Hispanic; 1.4% Asian; 4.6% other
Agriculture	livestock, poultry, wheat, cotton
Industry	manufacturing, mineral and energy exploration

Oregon

Year of Statehood	1859
Capital	Salem
Land Area	95,997 sq mi; 248,632 sq km
Population	3,421,399
Ethnic Group(s)	86.6% white; 8.0% Hispanic; 1.6% African American; 3.0% Asian; 1.3% Native American; 4.4% other
Agriculture	cattle, poultry, greenhouse products
Industry	manufacturing, services, trade, finance

Pennsylvania

Year of Statehood	1787
Capital	Harrisburg
Land Area	44,817 sq mi; 116,076 sq km
Population	12,281,054
Ethnic Group(s)	85.4% white; 10.0% African American; 3.2% Hispanic; 1.8% Asian; 0.1% Native American; 1.5% other
Agriculture	livestock, poultry, corn, hay
Industry	agribusiness, manufacturing, health care

Rhode Island

Year of Statehood	1790
Capital	Providence
Land Area	1,045 sq mi; 2,707 sq km
Population	1,048,319
Ethnic Group(s)	85.0% white; 8.7% Hispanic; 4.5% African American; 2.3% Asian; 0.5% Native American; 5.1% other
Agriculture	nursery products, turf, vegetables
Industry	services, manufacturing

244 United States and Canada

Differentiated Instruction

For Gifted and Talented ▐L3▌

Have students make a resource map of one region of the United States. They should start by drawing a large map of that region on a poster-sized piece of paper. Then they can fill in the industries shown in the Country Databank, using a small symbol to represent each industry. The map should include a key, giving the meaning of each symbol. Encourage students to do additional research to add more industries to their map.

South Carolina

Year of Statehood	1788
Capital	Columbia
Land Area	30,109 sq mi; 77,982 sq km
Population	4,012,012
Ethnic Group(s)	67.2% white; 29.5% African American; 2.4% Hispanic; 0.9% Asian; 0.3% Native American; 1.0% other
Agriculture	poultry, tobacco, cotton, soybeans
Industry	tourism, agriculture, manufacturing

South Dakota

Year of Statehood	1889
Capital	Pierre
Land Area	75,885 sq mi; 196,542 sq km
Population	754,844
Ethnic Group(s)	88.7% white; 8.3% Native American; 1.4% Hispanic; 0.6% African American; 0.6% Asian; 0.5% other
Agriculture	livestock, poultry, corn, soybeans
Industry	agriculture, services, manufacturing

Congaree Swamp National Monument, South Carolina

Tennessee

Year of Statehood	1796
Capital	Nashville
Land Area	41,217 sq mi; 106,752 sq km
Population	5,689,283
Ethnic Group(s)	80.2% white; 16.4% African American; 2.2% Hispanic; 1.0% Asian; 0.3% Native American; 1.0% other
Agriculture	cattle, poultry, tobacco, cotton
Industry	manufacturing, trade, services

Texas

Year of Statehood	1845
Capital	Austin
Land Area	261,797 sq mi; 678,054 sq km
Population	20,851,820
Ethnic Group(s)	71.0% white; 32.0% Hispanic; 11.5% African American; 2.7% Asian; 0.6% Native American; 11.8% other
Agriculture	livestock, poultry, cotton
Industry	manufacturing, trade, oil and gas extraction

- Have students determine from the information provided which state is the youngest and which is the oldest on these two pages. *(Oklahoma is the youngest and Pennsylvania is the oldest.)*

- Ask students to describe the locations of South Carolina and South Dakota *(South Dakota is in the Midwest, not far from Canada. South Carolina is in the South, on the Atlantic coast.)* Ask **What are these two states south of?** *(their northern counterparts, North Dakota and North Carolina)*

Guided Instruction (continued)

- Ask **The economies of what states listed on these two pages rely on their mineral resources?** *(West Virginia, Wyoming)*

- Ask **What agricultural products do Vermont, West Virginia, and Washington have in common?** *(apples)*

- Ask **Which of Virginia's industries might be related to its location bordering Washington, D.C.?** *(government)*

Independent Practice

- Using the map of the United States on p. 235 as a model, have students fill in the names of each state on an outline map. Then ask them to use the Country Databank to help them create a map that shows whether each state joined the United States in the 1700s, 1800s, or 1900s. Tell students to choose different colors to represent each century. They should explain what each color represents in the map key.

  All In One **United States and Canada Teaching Resources,** *Outline Map 11: The United States: Political,* p. 267

Monitor Progress

Circulate to make sure students are filling in their maps correctly. Provide assistance as needed.

Assess and Reteach

Assess Progress   L2

Direct students' attention back to the lists of states and capitals on the board. Encourage them to use the Country Databank to complete these lists as a class. Then have students complete the Assessment questions.

Introducing The United States

Utah

Year of Statehood	1896
Capital	Salt Lake City
Land Area	82,144 sq mi; 212,753 sq km
Population	2,233,169
Ethnic Group(s)	89.2% white; 9.0% Hispanic; 1.7% Asian; 1.3% Native American; 0.8% African American; 4.9% other
Agriculture	poultry, hay, corn, wheat, barley
Industry	services, trade, manufacturing

Vermont

Year of Statehood	1791
Capital	Montpelier
Land Area	9,250 sq mi; 23,958 sq km
Population	608,827
Ethnic Group(s)	96.8% white; 0.9% Asian; 0.5% African American; 0.4% Native American; 1.2% other
Agriculture	dairy products, apples, maple syrup
Industry	manufacturing, tourism, agriculture

Rower in Seattle, Washington

Virginia

Year of Statehood	1788
Capital	Richmond
Land Area	39,594 sq mi; 102,548 sq km
Population	7,078,515
Ethnic Group(s)	72.3% white; 19.6% African American; 0.7% Hispanic; 3.7% Asian; 0.3% Native American; 0.1% Native Hawaiian or Pacific Islander; 2.0% other
Agriculture	cattle, poultry, tobacco
Industry	services, trade, government

Washington

Year of Statehood	1889
Capital	Olympia
Land Area	66,544 sq mi; 172,349 sq km
Population	5,894,121
Ethnic Group(s)	81.8% white; 7.5% Hispanic; 5.5% Asian; 3.2% African American; 1.6% Native American; 4.3% other
Agriculture	cattle, poultry, apples, potatoes
Industry	technology, aerospace, biotechnology

246 United States and Canada

Differentiated Instruction

For English Language Learners   L2

Tell students that each state also has a two-letter abbreviated name. List the abbreviated state names on one side of the board, and the full state names on the other. Help students identify the states and their corresponding abbreviations. If you wish, you can divide students into pairs and have each pair create a set of flash cards, with the full state name on one side of the card, and the abbreviation on the other. Then have students take turns quizzing each other.

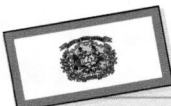

West Virginia

Year of Statehood	1863
Capital	Charleston
Land Area	24,078 sq mi; 62,362 sq km
Population	1,808,344
Ethnic Group(s)	95.0% white; 3.2% African American; 0.7% Hispanic; 0.5% Asian; 0.2% Native American; 0.2% other
Agriculture	apples, peaches, hay, tobacco
Industry	manufacturing, services, mining

Wisconsin

Year of Statehood	1848
Capital	Madison
Land Area	54,310 sq mi; 140,663 sq km
Population	5,363,675
Ethnic Group(s)	88.9% white; 5.7% African American; 3.6% Hispanic; 1.7% Asian; 0.9% Native American; 1.6% other
Agriculture	cattle, poultry, corn, hay
Industry	services, manufacturing, trade

Wyoming

Year of Statehood	1890
Capital	Cheyenne
Land Area	97,100 sq mi; 251,489 sq km
Population	493,782
Ethnic Group(s)	92.1% white; 6.4% Hispanic; 2.3% Native American; 0.8% African American; 0.6% Asian; 2.6% other
Agriculture	cattle, wheat, beans, barley
Industry	mineral extraction, oil, natural gas, tourism and recreation

SOURCE: U.S. Census; *World Almanac,* 2003
Note: Percentages may not total 100% due to rounding. The Hispanic population may be any race and is dispersed among racial categories.

Wisconsin dairy farm

Assessment

Comprehension and Critical Thinking

1. Compare and Contrast Compare the physical sizes and the population sizes of California and Rhode Island.

2. Draw Conclusions Are there characteristics that most of the states share? Explain.

3. Compare and Contrast What are some key differences among the states?

4. Categorize What are the major products of the South and the Midwest?

5. Make Generalizations Based on the data, make a generalization about industry in the United States.

6. Make a Timeline Create a timeline showing the year of statehood for 15 states.

Keeping Current

Access the **DK World Desk Reference Online** at **PHSchool.com** for up-to-date information about the United States.

Web Code: lhe-4401

Section 1
Step-by-Step Instruction

Objectives

Social Studies

1. Learn how the large cities of the Northeast contribute to the economy of the United States.

2. Find out how the Northeast has been a port of entry for many immigrants.

Reading/Language Arts

Compare and contrast to help sort out and analyze information.

Prepare to Read

Build Background Knowledge L2

Tell students that in this section they will learn more about the Northeast. Point out which part of the United States is the Northeast on the map on page 235. Write New York City, Philadelphia, and Boston on the board. Ask students to preview the photos in the section, reading each caption. Then have students brainstorm some characteristics of each city. Provide a few suggestions to get started. Conduct an Idea Wave (TE, p. T35) to generate a list.

Set a Purpose for Reading L2

■ Preview the Objectives.

■ Form students into pairs or groups of four. Distribute the *Reading Readiness Guide*. Ask students to fill in the first two columns of the chart. Use the Numbered Heads participation strategy (TE, p. T36) to call on students to share one piece of information they already know and one piece of information they want to know.

All in One United States and Canada Teaching Resources, *Reading Readiness Guide,* p. 236

Vocabulary Builder
Preview Key Terms L2

Pronounce each Key Term, then ask students to say the word with you. Provide a simple explanation such as, "Many people commute to work on a train."

Prepare to Read

Objectives

In this section, you will

1. Learn how the large cities of the Northeast contribute to the economy of the United States.

2. Find out how the Northeast has been a port of entry for many immigrants.

Taking Notes

As you read this section, look for details about Boston, Philadelphia, and New York City. Copy the chart below, and record your findings in it.

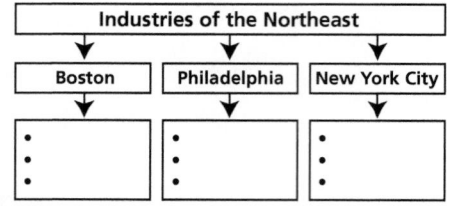

Industries of the Northeast		
Boston	Philadelphia	New York City
• • •	• • •	• • •

🎯 Target Reading Skill

Compare and Contrast
Comparing and contrasting can help you sort out and analyze information. When you compare, you examine the similarities between things. When you contrast, you look at the differences between things. As you read this section, compare and contrast the large cities of the Northeast.

Key Terms

• **commute** (kuh MYOOT) *v.* to travel to work

• **megalopolis** (meg uh LAHP uh lis) *n.* a number of cities and suburbs that blend into one very large urban area

• **population density** (pahp yuh LAY shun DEN suh tee) *n.* the average number of people per square mile or square kilometer

Rush hour in a New York City subway station

For more than a century, life in New York City has been crowded. One hundred years ago, horse-drawn carriages caused traffic jams. Today, more than 3 million riders squeeze into New York's subway cars every day. Others travel the many miles of bus lines or catch one of the city's 12,000 taxis. And many people drive their own cars through the city's busy streets.

New York City is not unique. Washington, D.C., Boston, Massachusetts, and Philadelphia, Pennsylvania, are also crowded. In these big cities, thousands of people **commute,** or travel to work, each day. Many drive to work from suburbs that are far from the city's center. Even people who live in the city must travel from one area to another to work.

🎯 Target Reading Skill L2

Compare and Contrast Point out the Target Reading Skill. Explain that students can compare, or find similarities, and contrast, or find differences, to help them analyze information.

Model the skill by reading the Philadelphia and New York City sections on pages 251 and 253 with students, and identifying the similarities and differences between the two cities. (*Both are large cities in the Northeast located near rivers. Philadelphia is an industrial powerhouse while New York City is more of a financial powerhouse.*)

Give students *Compare and Contrast.* Have them complete the activity in groups.

All in One United States and Canada Teaching Resources, *Compare and Contrast,* p. 251

A Region of Cities

A nearly unbroken chain of cities runs from Boston to New York to Washington, D.C. This coastal region of the Northeast is a megalopolis (meg uh LAHP uh lis). A **megalopolis** is a region where the cities and suburbs have grown so close together that they form one big urban area. Find this area on the map below.

The Northeast is the most densely populated region of the United States. **Population density** is the average number of people per square mile (or square kilometer). The population density of New Jersey is 10 times greater than the density of Kentucky.

The Northeast's economy is based on its cities. Many were founded in colonial times, along rivers or near the Atlantic Ocean. These cities began as transportation and trade centers. Today, manufacturing, finance, communications, and government employ millions of urban northeasterners.

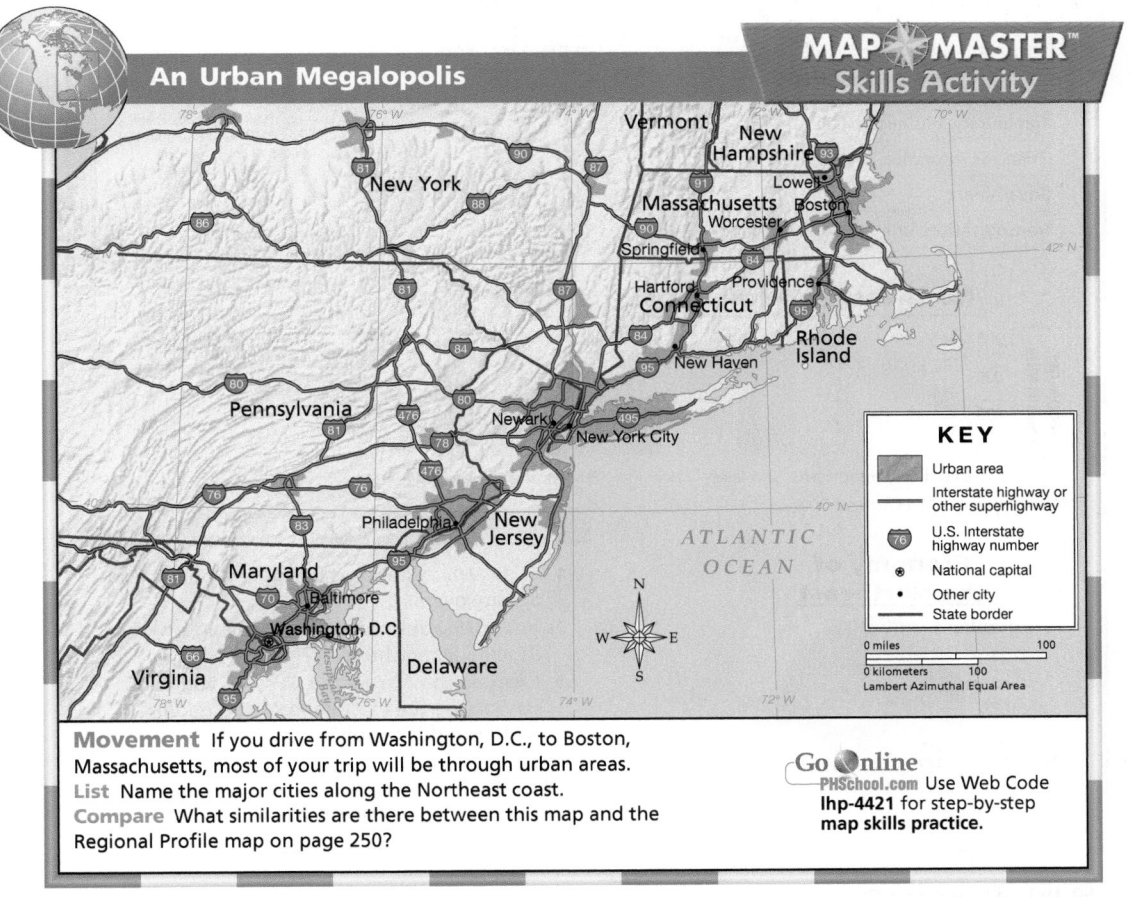

An Urban Megalopolis

MAP MASTER™ Skills Activity

KEY

- Urban area
- Interstate highway or other superhighway
- 76 U.S. Interstate highway number
- ⊛ National capital
- • Other city
- State border

0 miles 100
0 kilometers 100
Lambert Azimuthal Equal Area

Movement If you drive from Washington, D.C., to Boston, Massachusetts, most of your trip will be through urban areas.
List Name the major cities along the Northeast coast.
Compare What similarities are there between this map and the Regional Profile map on page 250?

Go Online PHSchool.com Use Web Code **lhp-4421** for step-by-step map skills practice.

Chapter 9 Section 1 **249**

Guided Instruction L2

- Ask students to read the text and study the map and charts on this page. As a class, answer the Map and Chart Skills questions.

- Discuss the concept of *services*. Ask students to give examples of a business or personal service. (*business—Web site developer; personal—hairdresser*)

Independent Practice

- Distribute *Reading a Population Density Map*. Have students work in pairs to complete the worksheet.

  All in One **United States and Canada Teaching Resources,** *Reading a Population Density Map,* p. 263

- Then have students return to the map on this page. Ask them to write a short paragraph explaining how they think the Northeast's population density affects its economy.

REGIONAL PROFILE
Focus on Economics

The Northeast

Although it is the nation's smallest region, the Northeast is the most heavily populated region in the United States. It has many large and old cities. New York is the center of international trade and finance, while Philadelphia was the birthplace of the Declaration of Independence and the United States Constitution. With so many people living in such a small area, services are an important part of the Northeast's economy. As you study the graphs and map, think about how population density affects an area's economy.

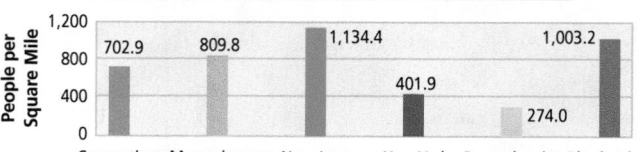

Types of Services

Community, business, personal
Financial, insurance, real estate
Government
Transportation, utilities, communication

The Northeast: Population Density
KEY

Persons per sq. mile	Persons per sq. kilometer
More than 519	More than 199
260–519	100–199
130–259	50–99
25–129	10–49
1–24	1–9

Urban Areas
- ■ More than 9,999,999
- □ 5,000,000–9,999,999
- ◉ 1,000,000–4,999,999
- • 500,000–999,999
- • Less than 500,000
- — National border
- — State border

Northeast Population Density, 2000

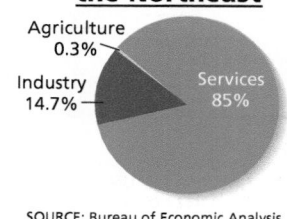

State	People per Square Mile
Connecticut	702.9
Massachusetts	809.8
New Jersey	1,134.4
New York	401.9
Pennsylvania	274.0
Rhode Island	1,003.2

SOURCE: *New York Times Almanac,* 2006

Economy of the Northeast

Agriculture 0.3%
Industry 14.7%
Services 85%

SOURCE: Bureau of Economic Analysis

Map and Chart Skills

1. **Note** Which state has the highest population density overall?
2. **Infer** Why did most major northeastern cities develop along the coast?
3. **Explore the Main Idea** Why do you think services are the most important economic activity in this region?

Use Web Code lhe-4411 to access the **DK World Desk Reference Online.**

Answers

Map and Chart Skills

1. New Jersey
2. They had good harbors for trade with Europe and other cities along the coast.
3. The area is heavily populated; people need services.

Go Online PHSchool.com Students can find more information about this topic on the DK World Desk Reference Online.

Skills for Life — Skills Mini Lesson

Synthesizing Information L2

1. Explain that when you synthesize something, you put together pieces of information to draw conclusions. For each piece of information, identify the main idea and supporting details. Next, look for links between the pieces of information. Finally, draw a conclusion.

2. Help students practice the skill by synthesizing the information given in the Types of Services table and the Economy of the Northeast circle graph.

3. Have students synthesize the information from the map and the bar graph to draw a conclusion about where people live in the Northeast.

Boston In colonial times, the city of Boston was called the "hub of the universe." Boston remains an important city in the Northeast. It is a city filled with history. The American Revolution began when British troops marched from Boston to Concord in 1775. You can still visit buildings that date from before the American Revolution, including Paul Revere's house, which is the oldest building in the downtown area. Yet you will find that Boston is a very modern city, too.

The Boston area is known worldwide for its leading research centers, including dozens of colleges and universities. Cambridge (KAYM brij) is the home of Harvard, which was founded in 1636 and is the oldest university in the United States. Cambridge is also home to the Massachusetts Institute of Technology (MIT).

Boston is noted for its medical, science, and technology centers as well. Some of the best medical schools and hospitals in the country are located in Boston. Many medical firsts took place here, including the use of anesthesia (an es THEE zhuh) during surgery. Boston's universities and scientific companies often work together to carry out research and to design new products.

Philadelphia Many people consider Philadelphia to be the "cradle of the nation" because, like Boston, it was an important city in our nation's early history. It was once the capital of the country. It was in Philadelphia that America's founders wrote the Declaration of Independence and the Constitution. By the late 1700s, Philadelphia had become the political, financial, and commercial center of the nation. Home to the country's leading seaport until it was surpassed by New York's in the 1820s, Philadelphia quickly became a major shipbuilding center as well.

Today, Philadelphia is an industrial center. It is located on the Delaware River. Important land and water transportation routes pass through there. Ships, trucks, and trains bring in raw materials from other parts of Pennsylvania and from all over the world. Many factories process food, produce medical supplies, and manufacture chemicals. Hundreds of products are then shipped out for sale. In addition, Philadelphia has become a center of the health care industry, due to its several medical, dental, and pharmacology schools.

Boston's outdoor market, Haymarket, is one of the city's most famous attractions.

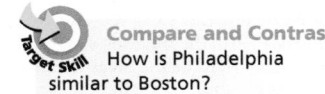
Compare and Contrast
How is Philadelphia similar to Boston?

The Skyscraper [L2]

Guided Instruction
Ask students to study The Skyscraper by reading the text and captions, and examining the photos and diagram. As a class, answer the Analyzing Images question. Allow students to briefly discuss their responses with a partner before sharing answers.

Independent Practice
Have students use cardboard or another medium of their choice to construct their own skyscraper. Provide them with a specific size for the base, such as one foot wide and one foot long. Tell them to try to make as many floors as they can without making the structure unstable.

Answer
ANALYZING IMAGES The building is very tall which allows more offices to fit in a smaller space.

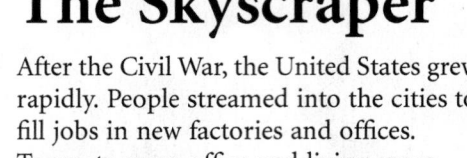

The Skyscraper

After the Civil War, the United States grew rapidly. People streamed into the cities to fill jobs in new factories and offices. To create more office and living space, architects used new technology to build taller and taller structures. By the 1930s, the skylines of all major American cities were dominated by tall skyscrapers. The Empire State Building, shown at right, was built in 1931. At 1,252 feet (382 meters), it is the tallest skyscraper in New York City.

Rockefeller Center, New York City
Most modern skyscrapers wear a glass skin of windows.

High-speed elevators travel as fast as 1,400 feet (426 meters) a minute.

The outside of the building is covered with ten million bricks.

60,000 tons of steel were used to make the skeleton that supports the building.

About ten minutes is all it takes for the fittest runners to race up the 1,576 steps from the lobby to the 86th floor, in the Fleet Empire State Run-Up.

More than 200 steel and concrete piles support the 365,000-ton building.

Construction workers
Workers rest during the construction of New York City's Chrysler Building. Built in 1930, the building's owner hoped it would be the tallest in the world—but even taller buildings were soon built.

ANALYZING IMAGES
How does the structure of this building allow more offices in less space?

252 United States and Canada

Differentiated Instruction

For English Language Learners [L1]
Students may find it difficult to pronounce some of the words in this section, such as *populated, finance, economy, density,* and *utilities.* Show students how to break down these words into smaller parts to help them sound out the pronunciation. Check to make sure students understand the meanings of the words as well.

For Special Needs Students [L1]
Preteach key concepts to students by showing *Section Reading Support Transparency USC 54* before reading. Go over the key points on the transparency.

 United States and Canada Transparencies, *Section Reading Support Transparency USC 54*

New York City The largest, wealthiest, and most influential city in the United States is New York City. More than 8 million people live there, making it one of the 10 largest cities in the world. The city covers an area of about 300 square miles (800 square kilometers) on islands and the mainland around the mouth of the Hudson River. Tunnels and bridges connect the various parts of the city.

New York is the center of fashion, publishing, advertising, and the arts in the United States. New York's Broadway is known for its plays and musicals, Fifth Avenue for its shopping, and Wall Street for its finance.

New York City is our nation's "money capital." About 350,000 New Yorkers work for banks and other financial institutions. The headquarters of many of the country's wealthiest corporations are in New York. The New York Stock Exchange is on Wall Street. Noted for its skyscrapers, New York City's skyline is recognized by people around the world.

On September 11, 2001, the city became a target of terrorists, who crashed two planes into the towers of the World Trade Center. The World Trade Center held government agencies and businesses that were involved in international trade. Nearly 3,000 people were killed as a result of the attack.

√ Reading Check **Which city is considered the financial capital of the United States?**

View From the Top
More than 30 million tourists visit New York City each year. Among the city's biggest tourist attractions are the theaters on 42nd Street (lower photo) and Central Park, which lies in the midst of a maze of skyscrapers (upper photo).
Identify Effects What effect does tourism have on New York's economy?

Ports of Entry L2

Guided Instruction
- **Vocabulary Builder** Clarify the high-use word **innumerable** before reading.

- Read about immigration to the Northeast in Ports of Entry.

- Discuss with students the meaning of a port of entry. *(the port where immigrants arrive in a country)* Ask **Which Northeast cities were ports of entry for immigrants?** *(New York, Boston, and Philadelphia)*

- Ask **How do you think this flow of immigrants helped the cities of the Northeast grow in importance?** *(They provided a workforce for factories and industry. They also brought diversity, new ideas, and skills.)*

Independent Practice
Partner students and have them write a letter that an immigrant arriving in a Northeast city might send to someone back home about his or her first impressions. Give students *Writing a Letter* to help them get started.

All in One **United States and Canada Teaching Resources,** *Writing a Letter,* p. 270

Monitor Progress
Tell students to fill in the last column of their *Reading Readiness Guides.* Ask them to evaluate if what they learned was what they had expected to learn.

All in One **United States and Canada Teaching Resources,** *Reading Readiness Guide,* p. 236

Differentiated Instruction

For Advanced Readers L3
Have students complete the *Nickel-and-Diming* Internet activity to learn about a city's infrastructure and how increased population can affect it. Ask students to find out whether the populations of Boston, Philadelphia, and New York City have increased, stayed the same, or decreased in recent years and what effect these changes have had on the infrastructure of each city.

Go Online
PHSchool.com

For: Environmental and Global Issues: *Nickel-and-Diming*
Visit: PHSchool.com
Web Code: lhd-4402

Answers

Identify Effects Tourism forms an important part of New York's economy.

√ Reading Check New York City

Assess and Reteach

Assess Progress [L2]

Have students complete the Section Assessment. Administer the *Section Quiz.*

All in One United States and Canada Teaching Resources, *Section Quiz,* p. 238

Reteach [L1]

If students need more instruction, have them read this section in the Reading and Vocabulary Study Guide.

Chapter 9, Section 1, **Western Hemisphere Reading and Vocabulary Study Guide,** pp. 92–94

Extend [L3]

Organize students into groups of four to design a television commercial urging people to visit one of the three major cities in the Northeast. Students should supplement information in the text with more research. Encourage groups to include cultural, economic, and recreational features of the city in their presentation.

Answer

✓ Reading Check   New York harbor

Section 1 Assessment

Key Terms

Students' sentences should reflect knowledge of each Key Term.

Target Reading Skill

Possible answer: Similarities—Most cities were founded in colonial times and began as transportation and trade centers. Differences—Northeastern cities vary in population size and in the businesses that fuel their economies.

Comprehension and Critical Thinking

1. (a) more than 8 million people **(b)** Although the Northeast is the smallest region in the nation, it is the most densely populated region. **(c)** Answers will vary, but may include that population density affects the types of homes people live in, the method they use to get to and from work, and the type of jobs available.

2. (a) New York City **(b)** Answers may vary, but may include that more jobs may have been available to incoming immigrants in the Northeast. **(c)** The cultures of immigrants have blended into that of the Northeast and enriched its diversity.

Immigrants arrive at Ellis Island in 1920.

Ports of Entry

Louis Waldman came to the United States in 1909, when he was seventeen years old. He landed at the Ellis Island immigration station in New York harbor:

> ❝ Behind me was the bustling harbor with its innumerable boats, the sight of which made me seasick all over again. Facing me were the tall buildings of lower Manhattan, buildings which were more magnificent and higher than any I had ever imagined, even in my wildest dreams. . . . ❞
>
> —*Russian immigrant Louis Waldman*

From 1892 to 1954, millions of immigrants came to the United States through Ellis Island. Today, Ellis Island is a national monument.

Although New York was the main port of entry, Boston and Philadelphia were also important gateways for immigrants. In the 1700s, more German immigrants entered the country through Philadelphia than through any other port. In the 1800s, many Irish immigrants entered through both Philadelphia and Boston.

After arriving in these port cities, many immigrants stayed and built new lives. Today, all three cities are rich in ethnic diversity. To get a real sense of this ethnic diversity, just look at the names in the phonebooks of these big cities.

✓ Reading Check   **Where is Ellis Island located?**

Section 1 Assessment

Key Terms

Review the key terms at the beginning of this section. Use each term in a sentence that explains its meaning.

Target Reading Skill

What are two ways that the cities of the Northeast are similar? What are two ways that they are different?

Comprehension and Critical Thinking

1. (a) Recall How many people live in New York City?

(b) Compare How does the population density of the Northeast compare with densities of other regions of the country?

(c) Cause and Effect How does population density affect the ways people live and work?

2. (a) Recall What city was the main port of entry for European immigrants in the 1800s?

(b) Identify the Main Idea Why might immigrants have chosen to live in the Northeast?

(c) Cause and Effect How have immigrants affected the culture of the Northeast?

Writing Activity

Which city described in this section are you most interested in learning more about? Make a list of things you would like to learn about this city. Then write a brief paragraph explaining why you want to learn these things.

For: An activity on mass transit systems
Visit: PHSchool.com
Web Code: lhd-4401

254 United States and Canada

Writing Activity

Use the *Rubric for Assessing a Writing Assignment* to evaluate students' paragraphs.

All in One United States and Canada Teaching Resources, *Rubric for Assessing a Writing Assignment,* p. 273

Go Online PHSchool.com Typing in the Web code when prompted will bring students directly to detailed instructions for this activity.

Prepare to Read

Objectives
In this section, you will
1. Learn how the South's land is important to its economy.
2. Read about how the growth of industry is changing the South.

Taking Notes
As you read this section, look for details about the growth of industry and how it has affected the economy. Copy the table below, and record your findings in it.

Industry	Products	Effects on Economy

Target Reading Skill

Use Signal Words Signal words point out relationships among ideas or events. Certain words, such as *however* or *like,* can signal a comparison or contrast. As you read this section, notice the contrast between what the South's economy was based on 50 years ago and what it is based on today. What signal words indicate the contrast?

Key Terms
- **petrochemical** (pet roh KEM ih kul) *n.* a substance such as plastic or paint that is made from petroleum
- **industrialization** (in dus tree ul ih ZAY shun) *n.* the process of building new industries in an area dominated by farming
- **Sun Belt** (sun belt) *n.* an area of the United States stretching from the southern Atlantic coast to the California coast

In 1895, at the age of fifteen, Catherine Evans Whitener had no idea that she was about to make history. Her friends and family liked the cotton bedspreads she made so much that she began to display them on her front porch in Dalton, Georgia. Her first sale earned her $2.50. After a large store placed an order for 24 bedspreads, an industry was born.

As interest in her work grew, Whitener began to train other girls to help produce the bedspreads. In 1917, she and her brother formed the Evans Manufacturing Company. Their company and others like it employed some 10,000 workers during the Great Depression. So many bedspreads were sold to travelers in the Dalton area that the highway through the town became known as "Bedspread Alley."

The Land of the South

There are many different ways that people in the South can make a living. The South's particular geography and climate make many of these jobs possible.

Catherine Evans Whitener

Objectives

Social Studies
1. Learn how the South's land is important to its economy.
2. Read about how the growth of industry is changing the South.

Reading/Language Arts
Use signal words to find relationships among ideas or events.

Prepare to Read

Build Background Knowledge　L2
In this section, students will learn about the southern part of the United States. Tell students to preview the visuals and headings in the section with these questions in mind: **What kinds of products are made in the South? What kinds of industries take place there?** Provide a few examples *(cotton, textiles, shipping).* Make a list on the board. Then tell the class that all of the above are part of the South's diverse economy.

Set a Purpose for Reading　L2
- Preview the Objectives.
- Read each statement in the *Reading Readiness Guide* aloud. Ask students to mark the statements true or false.
- Have students discuss the statements in pairs or groups of four, then mark their worksheets again. Use the Numbered Heads participation strategy (TE, p. T36) to call on students to share their group's perspectives.

  All in One United States and Canada Teaching Resources, *Reading Readiness Guide,* p. 240

Target Reading Skill　L2

Use Signal Words Draw students' attention to the Target Reading Skill. Tell them that signal words such as *however* and *like* can help them notice a comparison or contrast.

Model using signal words by writing the following sentence on the board and identifying the signal word: "Unlike the Northeast, the South has a warm, wet climate in which oranges grow well." *(The word* unlike *signals a contrast.)*

Give students *Compare and Contrast.* Have them complete the activity in groups.

All in One United States and Canada Teaching Resources, *Compare and Contrast,* p. 251

Vocabulary Builder
Preview Key Terms　L2
Pronounce each Key Term, then ask students to say the word with you. Provide a simple explanation such as, "Many people move to the Sun Belt, located in the southern United States, because of its warm climate."

Instruct

REGIONAL PROFILE
Focus on Culture

Guided Instruction L2

- Ask students to read and study the Regional Profile on this page. Work with the class to answer the Map and Chart Skills questions. Have students briefly discuss their responses with a partner before sharing answers.

- If you have not already done so, show the video *Miami's Little Havana* for Section 2 of this chapter. The video will provide an example of how Hispanic culture is thriving in the South. Ask students to write down at least three things that they learned from it.

  Miami's Little Havana, **World Studies Video Program**

Independent Practice

Ask students to summarize the information on one of the bar graphs in a short paragraph. If necessary, have students refer to *Transferring Information from One Medium to Another* on the Social Studies Skills Tutor CD-ROM.

  Transferring Information from One Medium to Another, **Social Studies Skills Tutor CD-ROM**

Answers

Map and Chart Skills

1. the Northeast
2. Texas and Florida
3. Possible answer: There may be more celebrations and traditions reflecting Hispanic and African American cultures.

Go Online PHSchool.com Students can find more information about this topic on the DK World Desk Reference Online.

The region has a warm climate, and most parts of it receive plenty of rain. The wide coastal plains along the Atlantic Ocean and the Gulf of Mexico have rich soil. In addition, the South has a long growing season. There are between 200 and 290 frost-free days every year. Together, these features make much of the South an excellent place for growing crops such as cotton, rice, tobacco, and sugar cane and raising animals.

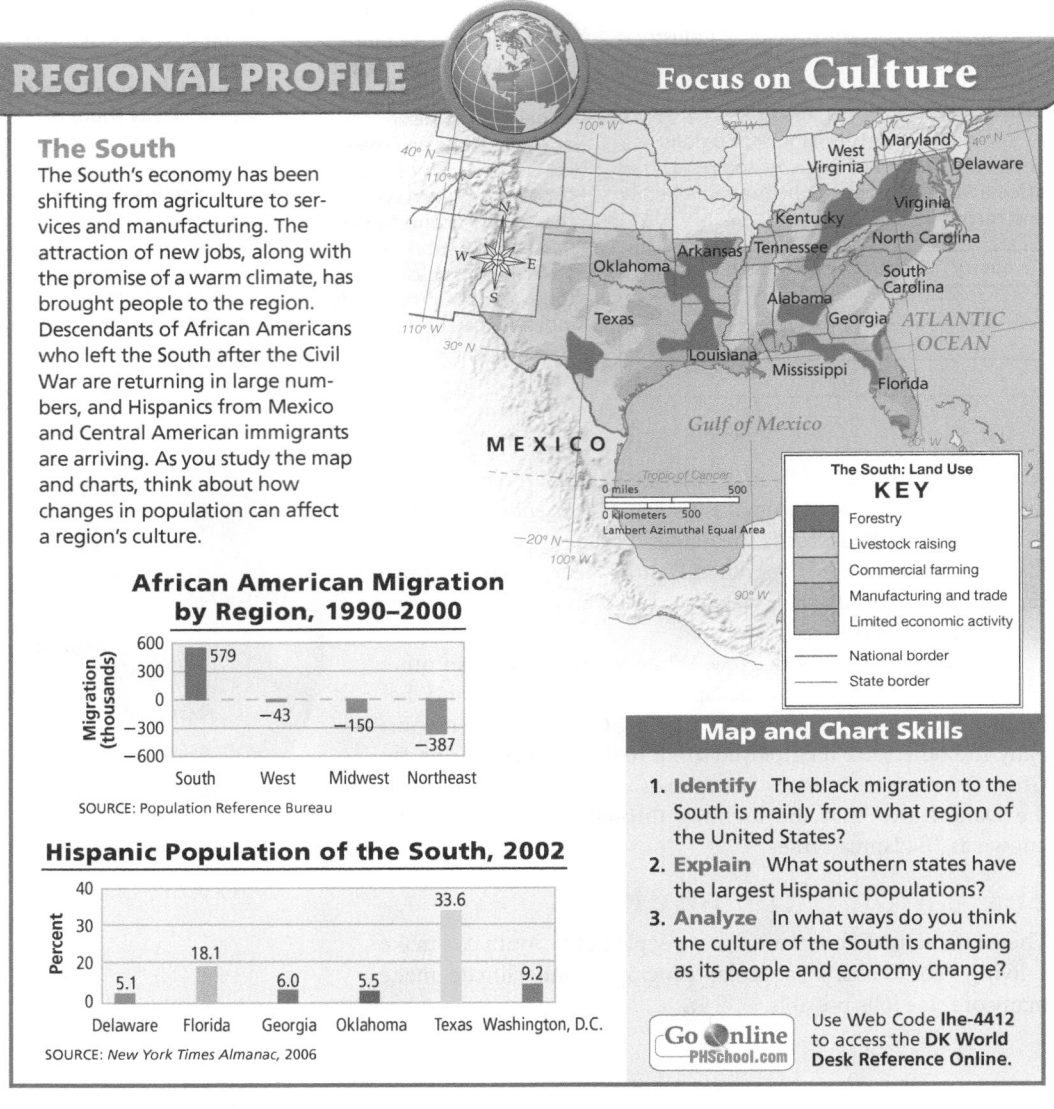

REGIONAL PROFILE   Focus on Culture

The South

The South's economy has been shifting from agriculture to services and manufacturing. The attraction of new jobs, along with the promise of a warm climate, has brought people to the region. Descendants of African Americans who left the South after the Civil War are returning in large numbers, and Hispanics from Mexico and Central American immigrants are arriving. As you study the map and charts, think about how changes in population can affect a region's culture.

The South: Land Use
KEY
- Forestry
- Livestock raising
- Commercial farming
- Manufacturing and trade
- Limited economic activity
- National border
- State border

African American Migration by Region, 1990–2000

Migration (thousands)

- South: 579
- West: −43
- Midwest: −150
- Northeast: −387

SOURCE: Population Reference Bureau

Hispanic Population of the South, 2002

Percent

- Delaware: 5.1
- Florida: 18.1
- Georgia: 6.0
- Oklahoma: 5.5
- Texas: 33.6
- Washington, D.C.: 9.2

SOURCE: *New York Times Almanac*, 2006

Map and Chart Skills

1. **Identify** The black migration to the South is mainly from what region of the United States?
2. **Explain** What southern states have the largest Hispanic populations?
3. **Analyze** In what ways do you think the culture of the South is changing as its people and economy change?

Go Online PHSchool.com Use Web Code lhe-4412 to access the **DK World Desk Reference Online.**

Vocabulary Builder

Use the information below to teach students this section's high-use words.

High-Use Word	Definition and Sample Sentence
consume, p. 257	*v.* to use up He **consumed** all of the milk and none was left for our cereal.
decade, p. 260	*n.* period of ten years She told him, "You're a **decade** old!" on his tenth birthday.

Farming One of the most important parts of the South's economy is farming. For years, the South's major crop was cotton. By the 1950s, bedspread factories in Georgia alone consumed 500,000 bales of cotton every year. Many southern farmers once depended on cotton as their only source of income. Today, cotton still brings much money to the South, especially to Alabama, Mississippi, and Texas, but King Cotton no longer rules this region. In the 1890s, the boll weevil (bohl WEE vul), a kind of beetle, began to attack cotton plants in the South. Over the next 30 years, it destroyed cotton crops across the region. Without money from cotton, many farmers went bankrupt. Today, most southern farmers raise more than one crop.

Growing Conditions Some of these crops need special growing conditions. Citrus fruits require year-round warmth and sunshine. Florida has plenty of both. More oranges, tangerines, grapefruits, and limes are grown here than in any other state. Rice needs warm, moist growing conditions. Farmers in Arkansas, Louisiana, and Mississippi take advantage of their climate by growing rice along the coast of the Gulf of Mexico and in the Mississippi River valley.

Agricultural Products Some areas of the South have become famous for their agricultural products. Georgia has taken one of its products as its nickname—the Peach State. Georgia is also known for its peanut and pecan crops. Texans raise more cattle than do farmers in any other state. All of these items are just a sample of the diversity of southern agriculture.

The Cotton Crop
Although cotton (below) is no longer the South's major crop, it is still important to the region's economy.
Identify Effects *How did boll weevils (above) affect the South's economy and way of farming?*

Guided Instruction

- **Vocabulary Builder** Clarify the high-use word **consume** before reading.

- Read The Land of the South using the Paragraph Shrinking strategy (TE, p. T34).

- Ask **How is the South's land important to its economy?** *(Farming is one of the most important parts of the South's economy. The wide coastal plains in the South have rich soil that is good for farming.)*

- Ask **How do mineral resources contribute to the South's economy?** *(Oil and natural gas are used for fuel and many products, including petrochemicals such as plastic and paint. Other useful minerals are also mined.)*

Background: Global Perspectives

Cotton Cotton is one of the most important crops in the world. China leads the world in cotton production, but the United States, India, Pakistan, Brazil, Egypt, and some of the countries that were once part of the former Soviet Union are also major producers. In addition to cloth, products from parts of the cotton plant include automobile tire cord, plastic reinforcing, packing materials, cellulose, pressed paper, and cardboard. Cottonseed oil is used to make cosmetics, cooking oil, and some detergents.

Answer

Identify Effects Over the course of 30 years, the boll weevil destroyed many farmers' cotton crops. This caused many farmers in the South to plant more than one crop. Cotton no longer rules the region.

Ask students to create the Taking Notes graphic organizer on a blank piece of paper. Then have them begin to fill in the table with information from these pages. Briefly model how to identify information to include.

Monitor Progress
As students fill in the graphic organizer, move around the room and make sure individuals are choosing the correct details. Provide assistance as needed.

Offshore Drilling
The rig provides a platform for oil drilling in the Gulf of Mexico. Draw Conclusions *Why is drilling for oil an important industry in the South?*

Drilling and Mining In some parts of the South, what is under the soil is as important as what grows in it. In Louisiana, Oklahoma, and Texas, companies drill for oil and natural gas. These can be used as fuel and made into **petrochemicals,** which are substances, such as plastics, paint, nylon, and asphalt, that come from petroleum. In Alabama, Kentucky, West Virginia, and Tennessee, miners dig for coal. The South also produces minerals that are not used for fuel, such as crushed stone, construction sand and gravel, and cement. Southern states are leading producers of salt, sulfur, and zinc.

Fishing and Forestry Many people in the South make a living in fishing and forestry. The Chesapeake Bay area of Maryland and Virginia is famous for its shellfish, including clams, crabs, and scallops. Mississippi leads the nation in catfish farming. However, the South's fishing industry is strongest in Louisiana, Texas, and Florida. The timber industry is active in most of the southern states. Softwood trees like southern pine are turned into lumber or paper. People use hardwood trees to make furniture. North Carolina has the nation's largest hardwood furniture industry.

✔ Reading Check **Name two kinds of crops that need special growing conditions.**

Background: Global Perspectives

Louisiana's Island Industry About 140 miles (84 kilometers) west of New Orleans lies tiny Avery Island, where the McIlhenny family has been producing Tabasco sauce for more than 130 years. The fiery red peppers that are the main ingredient of the sauce are native to Central America, but grow equally well on Avery Island. In fact, the name *Tabasco* comes from a Native American language and means "land where the soil is hot and humid." The sauce is almost entirely a product of the island. Not only are the peppers grown on the island, they are mixed with salt mined on the island. Once the sauce has been properly aged in oaken barrels, it is bottled and shipped to more than 105 countries.

Answers

Draw Conclusions Oil drilling companies employ many people, as do companies that process oil.

✔ Reading Check Citrus fruits and rice are crops that need special growing conditions.

Southern Cities and Industries

Some people still think of the South as it was in the early 1900s—a slow-moving, mostly rural region. But over the past 50 years, this region has gone through many changes. Although the South's rural areas are still important to its economy, most people in the South today live in cities. Some work in factories or in high-technology firms. Others work in tourism or in one of the other service industries in this region's growing economy. This change from an agriculture-based economy to an industry-based economy is called **industrialization.**

Textiles   One of the most important industries in the South is the textile industry. Textile mills make cloth. They were originally built in this region to use the South's cotton. Today, many mills still make cotton cloth. Others now make cloth from synthetic, or human-made, materials. The textile industry is strongest in Georgia, the Carolinas, and Virginia.

Technology   One expanding set of industries is in the field of high technology, or very specialized, complex technology. For example, workers develop computers and other electronics and figure out better ways to use them. Some centers of high technology are Raleigh-Durham, North Carolina, and Austin, Texas.

Another high-technology industry is the aerospace business. In Cape Canaveral, Florida, Houston, Texas, and Huntsville, Alabama, people work for the National Aeronautics and Space Administration (NASA). Some people train as astronauts, while others run the space shuttle program. Atlanta, Georgia, is now a center for the cable television industry.

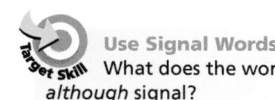
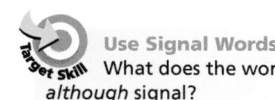
Use Signal Words
What does the word *although* signal?

Space Camp
Every year, people attend United States Space Camp in Huntsville, Alabama. As one student (left) sits in the cockpit of a space shuttle, other students (right) experiment with the feeling of being in outer space.
Analyze Images How do these photographs reflect the high-technology industry?

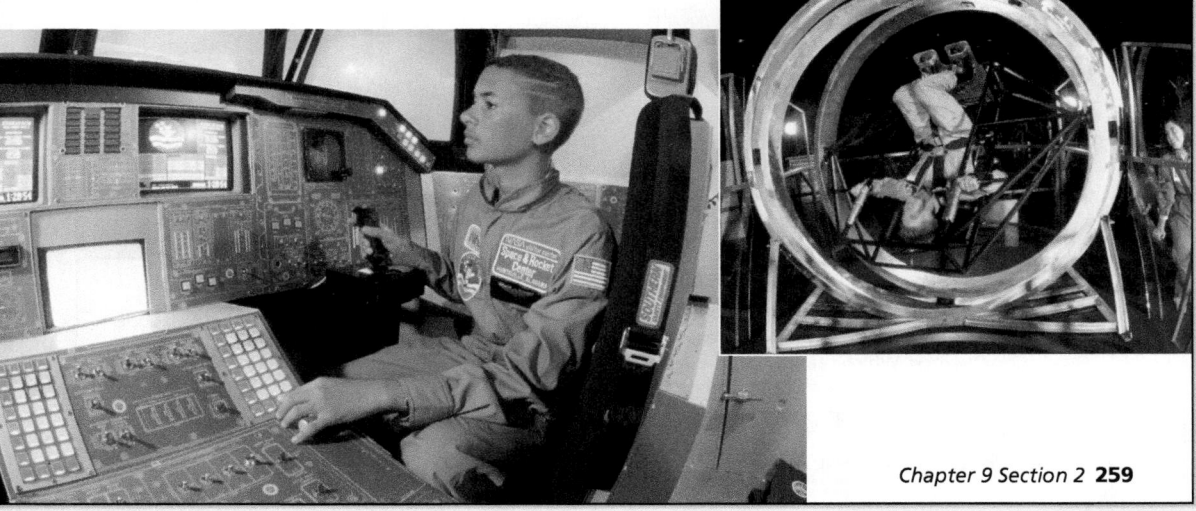

Differentiated Instruction

For English Language Learners   L1
Pair native English-speaking students with English learners to read the section. Encourage students to answer each other's questions about the material. You may wish to have Spanish-speaking students com-plete the *Guided Reading and Review* in Spanish for this section to further their understanding of the content.

📄 *Guided Reading and Review (Spanish),*
Spanish Support, p. 88

➔ Target Reading Skill   L2

Use Signal Words As a follow up, ask students to answer the Target Reading Skill question in the Student Edition. *(The word* although *signals a contrast.)*

Southern Cities and Industries   L2

Guided Instruction

- **Vocabulary Builder** Clarify the high-use word **decade** before reading.

- Read Southern Cities and Industries with students. As students read, circulate and make sure individuals can answer the Reading Check question.

- Ask students **Where do most people in the South live—in urban or rural areas?** *(Most people live in urban areas.)*

- Discuss with students how industrialization has changed the South. *(Although farming is still important to the South's economy, many people in the South now work in industries such as aerospace and tourism. Industrialization has helped the South's economy.)*

Answer

Analyze Images They show the aerospace business, which is a high-technology industry.

Guided Instruction (continued)
- Ask **Why does transportation play a large role in the South's economy?** *(Many southern cities are centers of transportation, moving goods in and out of the region.)*

Independent Practice
Have students complete the graphic organizer with additional information about the growth of industry and its effects on the economy.

Monitor Progress
- Show *Section Reading Support Transparency USC 55* and ask students to check their graphic organizers individually. Go over key concepts and clarify key vocabulary as needed.

📖 **United States and Canada Transparencies,** *Section Reading Support Transparency USC 55*

- Tell students to fill in the last column of their *Reading Readiness Guides.* Probe for what they learned that confirms or invalidates each statement.

All in One United States and Canada Teaching Resources, *Reading Readiness Guide,* p. 240

Transportation and Tourism A big part of the South's economy depends on moving goods and people into and out of the region. Most of the South's largest cities play important roles in this transportation industry. Miami, Florida, and New Orleans, Louisiana, are major ports. Miami is a center for goods and people going to and from Central and South America. New Orleans is a gateway between the Gulf of Mexico and the Mississippi River system. It is also an important port for oil tankers.

Some of the people the transportation industry brings to the South come to stay. Thousands come to work in the South's new industries. Thousands more choose to move to the South because of its climate. The South is part of the Sun Belt. The **Sun Belt** is the broad area of the United States that stretches from the southern Atlantic coast to the coast of California. It is known for its warm weather. The population of the Sun Belt has been rising for the past few decades. Some arrivals are older adults who want to retire to places without cold, snowy winters. Others come to take advantage of both the weather and the work that the Sun Belt offers.

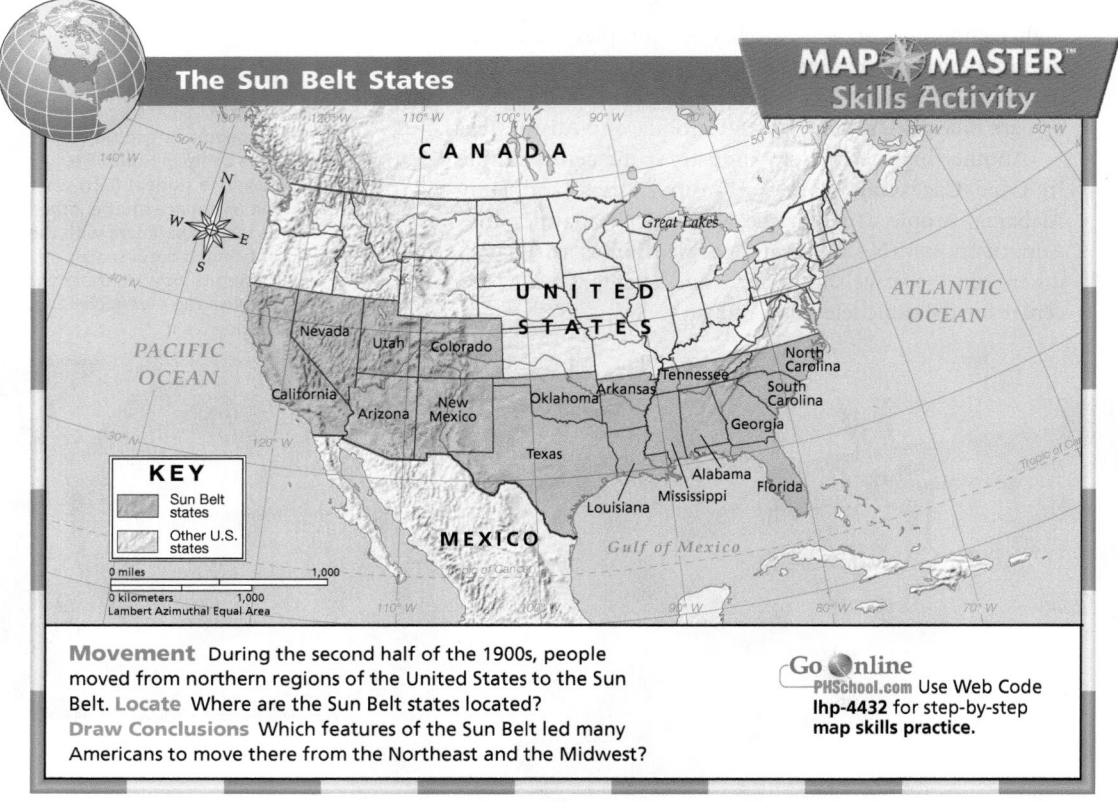

MAP MASTER Skills Activity

The Sun Belt States

KEY
- Sun Belt states
- Other U.S. states

0 miles 1,000
0 kilometers 1,000
Lambert Azimuthal Equal Area

Movement During the second half of the 1900s, people moved from northern regions of the United States to the Sun Belt. **Locate** Where are the Sun Belt states located? **Draw Conclusions** Which features of the Sun Belt led many Americans to move there from the Northeast and the Midwest?

Go Online PHSchool.com Use Web Code **lhp-4432** for step-by-step map skills practice.

260 United States and Canada

Answers

MAP MASTER Skills Activity **Locate** in the southern and southwestern United States **Draw Conclusions** The region's new industries and mild climate drew people to the Sun Belt.

Go Online PHSchool.com Students may practice their map skills using the interactive online version of this map.

Differentiated Instruction

For Gifted and Talented L3
Suggest that students choose one state in the South and create an economic activity map for it. Remind students to make a key for their map. Students can research their map in the library or on the Internet.

As a model, you might wish to have students first complete *Reading an Economic Activity Map.*

All in One United States and Canada Teaching Resources, *Reading an Economic Activity Map,* p. 264

Warm weather also brings to the South people who only plan to visit. These people fuel the region's tourist industry. In winter, tourists flock to the sunny beaches of Florida and the Gulf Coast. In the summer, they hike in the mountains of the Appalachians and Ozarks. Southern historic cities such as Charleston, South Carolina, or New Orleans, Louisiana, draw tourists at any time of the year. In states throughout the South, there are always fun and exciting things to see and to do.

The Nation's Capital   The city of Washington is not in a state. Instead, it is in the District of Columbia, which lies between the states of Maryland and Virginia. This area of land was chosen in 1790 as the site for the nation's capital. Located on the shore of the Potomac River, Washington, D.C., is a planned city. Many people consider Washington to be one of the most beautiful cities in the world. It has wide avenues, grand public buildings, and dramatic monuments, including the Supreme Court, the Library of Congress, the Washington Monument, and the Lincoln Memorial. The city's major avenues are named after the states. As the nation's capital, Washington is home to the nation's leaders and to hundreds of foreign diplomats.

Tourists on a paddleboat near the Jefferson Memorial in Washington, D.C.

√ Reading Check   **Where is the city of Washington located?**

Section 2 Assessment

Key Terms
Review the key terms at the beginning of this section. Use each term in a sentence that explains its meaning.

Target Reading Skill
Review the section Fishing and Forestry on page 258. Find the word that signals contrast in relation to the fishing industry.

Comprehension and Critical Thinking
1. (a) List Name five of the southern states.
(b) Draw Conclusions How have the geography and climate of the South shaped its economy?

(c) Summarize In what ways has the South's economy changed since the 1800s?
2. (a) Recall Why has the population of the Sun Belt been increasing?
(b) Explain Why have many people in the South moved from rural to urban areas?
(c) Identify Cause and Effect How has the South's economy affected this population growth?

Writing Activity
Suppose that you work in an advertising firm in Atlanta, Georgia; Houston, Texas; or Miami, Florida. Create an advertisement persuading people to move to your city or state. It can be designed for a newspaper or a magazine. It can also be for radio, television, or the Internet.

Go Online
PHSchool.com
For: An activity on oil
Visit: PHSchool.com
Web Code: lhd-4402

Chapter 9 Section 2 **261**

Writing Activity
Use the *Rubric for Assessing a Writing Assignment* to evaluate students' advertisements.

All in One **United States and Canada Teaching Resources,** *Rubric for Assessing a Writing Assignment,* p. 273

Go Online
PHSchool.com Typing in the Web code when prompted will bring students directly to detailed instructions for this activity.

Objective

Learn how to read and analyze circle graphs.

Prepare to Read

Build Background Knowledge `L2`

Ask students to describe a circle graph and note a recent one from their studies. Then invite students to explain how a circle graph could show weather data, such as the percentage of rainy days a city has in a year. *(The circle graph could show the percentage of days with rain and the percentage without rain.)* Encourage students to sketch an example of such a graph to share with the class.

Instruct

Understanding Circle Graphs `L2`

Guided Instruction

- Read the opening paragraphs with students. Discuss other kinds of data a circle graph might show.

- Read the steps to analyze and interpret a circle graph as a class and write them on the board.

- Practice the skill by following the steps on page 262 as a class. Model each step by reading aloud the questions on p. 263 and answering them. Point out that the purpose of the first circle graph on the page is to show the major ethnic groups in the United States, and the whole circle represents 100 percent of the population. Identify each portion of the graph. You might conclude that although more than 50 percent of the population is white the American population is ethnically diverse.

Independent Practice

Assign *Skills for Life* and have students complete it individually.

All in One **United States and Canada**
Teaching Resources, *Skills for Life,* p. 256

Understanding Circle Graphs

Chris walked across the playground with his new friend Kyung, who had just moved to Florida from Korea. Kyung looked up at the sun.

"It's really hot here. Does the entire United States get weather like this?"

"Let me think," said Chris. "In the Northwest it rains a lot, and I don't think it gets quite as hot as here. Arizona and New Mexico do, for sure. The Midwest has some really hot summers but freezing-cold winters. And then there's arctic Alaska—the summers don't get too hot there, even though the sun shines all night long. The United States gets a lot of different weather."

**Boston meteorologist
Mish Michaels**

M eteorologists collect an amazing variety of weather information from all over the country. One way they present data on temperatures, rainfall, and other weather information is to put it into graphs.

Learn the Skill

Follow the steps below to learn how to read and interpret a circle graph.

1 **Study the elements of the circle graph.** Read the title of the graph and all the labels. Make sure that you understand the purpose of the graph.

2 **Study the information shown in the graph.** The full circle represents 100 percent, or all, of something. Identify what the circle represents.

3 **Compare the portions within the graph.** Each division of the circle represents a certain percentage, or portion, of the whole. The portions should always add up to 100 percent. Notice which piece is the biggest—that is, the highest percentage. Which piece is the smallest?

4 **Draw conclusions from the graph.** Draw conclusions about the topic of the graph. Your conclusion should attempt to explain any differences or similarities in the sizes of the pieces of the circle.

Monitor Progress

Monitor the students doing the *Skills for Life* worksheet, checking to make sure they understand the skill steps.

Practice the Skill

Refer to the circle graph on the right and follow the steps for interpreting it.

1 After reading the title and labels of the graph, what do you think is its purpose?

2 What does the full circle represent—the circle is 100 percent of what?

3 What does each colored portion of the graph represent? Which is the largest portion? Which is the smallest portion?

4 Write a conclusion statement about the graph. Explain the meaning of the differences in the sizes of the portions.

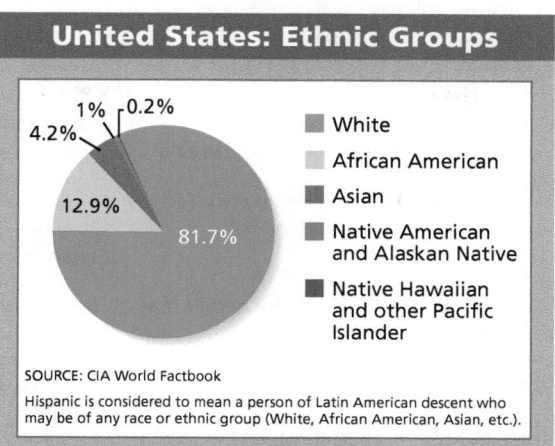

United States: Ethnic Groups

- 0.2%
- 1%
- 4.2%
- 12.9%
- 81.7%

- White
- African American
- Asian
- Native American and Alaskan Native
- Native Hawaiian and other Pacific Islander

SOURCE: CIA World Factbook

Hispanic is considered to mean a person of Latin American descent who may be of any race or ethnic group (White, African American, Asian, etc.).

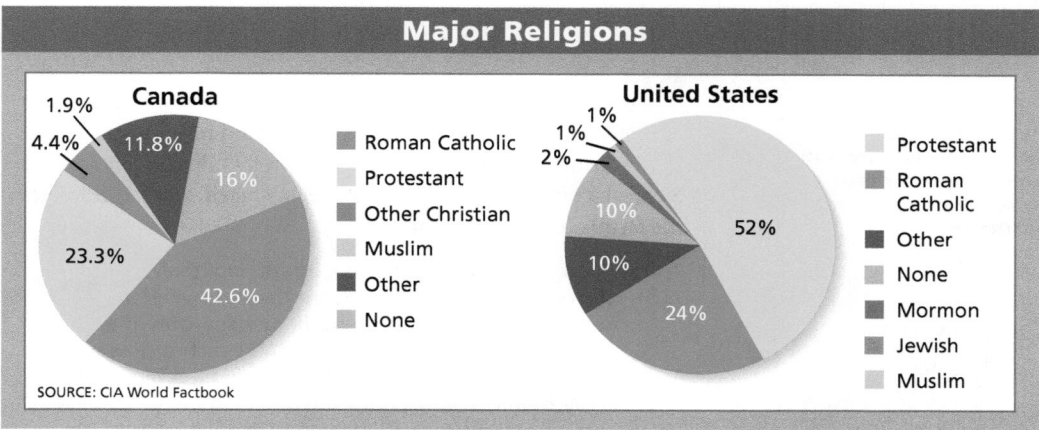

Major Religions

Canada
- 1.9%
- 4.4%
- 11.8%
- 16%
- 23.3%
- 42.6%

- Roman Catholic
- Protestant
- Other Christian
- Muslim
- Other
- None

United States
- 1%
- 1%
- 2%
- 10%
- 10%
- 52%
- 24%

- Protestant
- Roman Catholic
- Other
- None
- Mormon
- Jewish
- Muslim

SOURCE: CIA World Factbook

Apply the Skill

Study the two circle graphs above. Following the steps in this skill, write a conclusion statement about each graph. Then compare the graphs and write a conclusion about their similarities and differences.

Assess and Reteach

Assess Progress   L2
Ask students to do the Apply the Skill activity.

Reteach   L1
If students are having trouble applying the skill steps, have them review the skill using the interactive Social Studies Skills Tutor CD-ROM.

⊙ *Analyzing Graphic Data*, **Social Studies Skills Tutor CD-ROM**

Extend   L3
To extend the lesson, have students find the circle graphs showing the major ethnic groups in the United States and Canada in the DK World Desk Reference Online. Ask them to apply the skill steps to compare the two graphs and write a conclusion about their similarities and differences.

Differentiated Instruction

For Advanced Readers   L3
Ask students to find examples of circle graphs used in newspapers or news magazines. Have students work in pairs to apply the skill steps to analyze one of the graphs.

For Special Needs Students   L1
If students need further instruction on how to read a circle graph, have them complete the *Reading a Circle Graph* activity with a partner.

All in One **United States and Canada Teaching Resources,** *Reading a Circle Graph*, p. 265

Answer

Apply the Skill

Possible conclusion: The graphs are alike in that both show sizeable Roman Catholic and Protestant segments. In both countries a form of Christianity predominates, although Roman Catholics make up a larger portion of the population in Canada than in the United States. The graphs show larger Mormon and Jewish segments in the United States, and a slightly larger Muslim segment in Canada.

Section 3
Step-by-Step Instruction

Objectives
Social Studies
1. Read about how technology is changing life on farms.
2. Learn how changes in farming are affecting the development of cities.

Reading/Language Arts
Contrast two situations to find out how they are different.

Prepare to Read

Build Background Knowledge   L2
Tell students that the region they will study in this section has long been associated with farming. Brainstorm a list of words and phrases that come to mind when one thinks of a farm, such as crops and animals. Use an Idea Wave (TE, p. T35) to elicit ideas to write on the board. Have students note the ideas that the section supported and those it did not support as they read.

Set a Purpose for Reading   L2
- Preview the Objectives

- Read each statement in the *Reading Readiness Guide* aloud. Ask students to mark the statements true or false.

- Have students discuss the statements in pairs or groups of four, then mark their worksheets again. Use the Numbered Heads participation strategy (TE, p. T36) to call on students to share their group's perspectives.

All in One United States and Canada Teaching Resources, *Reading Readiness Guide,* p. 244

Vocabulary Builder
Preview Key Terms   L2
Pronounce each Key Term, then ask students to say the word with you. Provide a simple explanation such as, "During a recession, many people cut back on buying things they don't need because they may not be making as much money as they once had."

Section 3

The Midwest
Leaving the Farm

Prepare to Read

Objectives
In this section, you will
1. Read about how technology is changing life on farms.
2. Learn how changes in farming are affecting the development of cities.

Taking Notes
As you read this section, look for details that show how changes in agriculture have caused cities to grow. Copy the chart below, and record your findings in it.

Target Reading Skill
Identify Contrasts When you contrast two or more situations, you examine how they differ. In this section you will read about family farms and corporate farms. Although they both rely on technology, they differ in how they use it. As you read, list all of the differences between family farms and corporate farms.

Key Terms
- **mixed-crop farm** (mikst krahp fahrm) *n.* a farm that grows several different kinds of crops
- **recession** (rih SESH un) *n.* a decline in business activity and economic prosperity
- **corporate farm** (KAWR puh rit fahrm) *n.* a large farm that is run by a corporation, or an agricultural company

Present-day harvesting machines (below) work the land much faster than horse-driven plows once did (bottom).

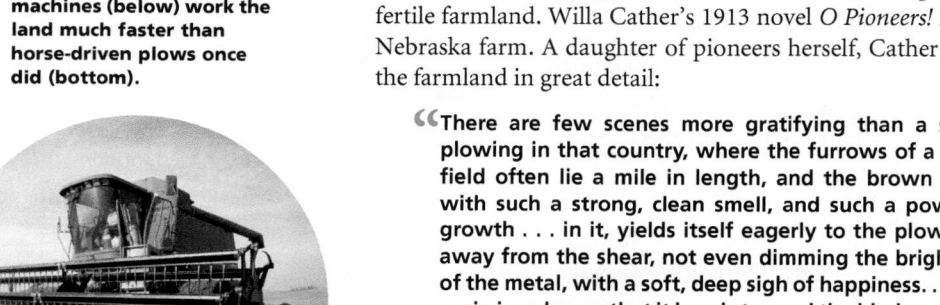

Nebraska is one of several states in the middle of the country that make up the Midwest. Nebraska is a land of vast prairies and fertile farmland. Willa Cather's 1913 novel *O Pioneers!* is set on a Nebraska farm. A daughter of pioneers herself, Cather describes the farmland in great detail:

" There are few scenes more gratifying than a spring plowing in that country, where the furrows of a single field often lie a mile in length, and the brown earth, with such a strong, clean smell, and such a power of growth . . . in it, yields itself eagerly to the plow; rolls away from the shear, not even dimming the brightness of the metal, with a soft, deep sigh of happiness. . . . The grain is so heavy that it bends toward the blade and cuts like velvet. "

—*Willa Cather,* O Pioneers!

264 United States and Canada

Target Reading Skill   L2

Identify Contrasts Point out the Target Reading Skill. Explain that students can contrast two situations to identify their differences.

Model identifying contrasts by reading the *O, Pioneers* excerpt on p. 264 aloud and identifying the differences between farming in Cather's time and farming today. (*Horse-drawn farming equipment was used in Cather's*

time while tractors are used today. Also, farms today have electricity and roads leading to them unlike the farms of Cather's time.)

Give students *Identify Contrasts.* Have them complete the activity in groups.

All in One United States and Canada Teaching Resources, *Identify Contrasts,* p. 252

Farming in the Midwest has changed since Cather's time. Tractors have replaced horse-drawn farm equipment. Electricity and roads have been brought out to rural farms. Today, technology continues to change the way people farm the land.

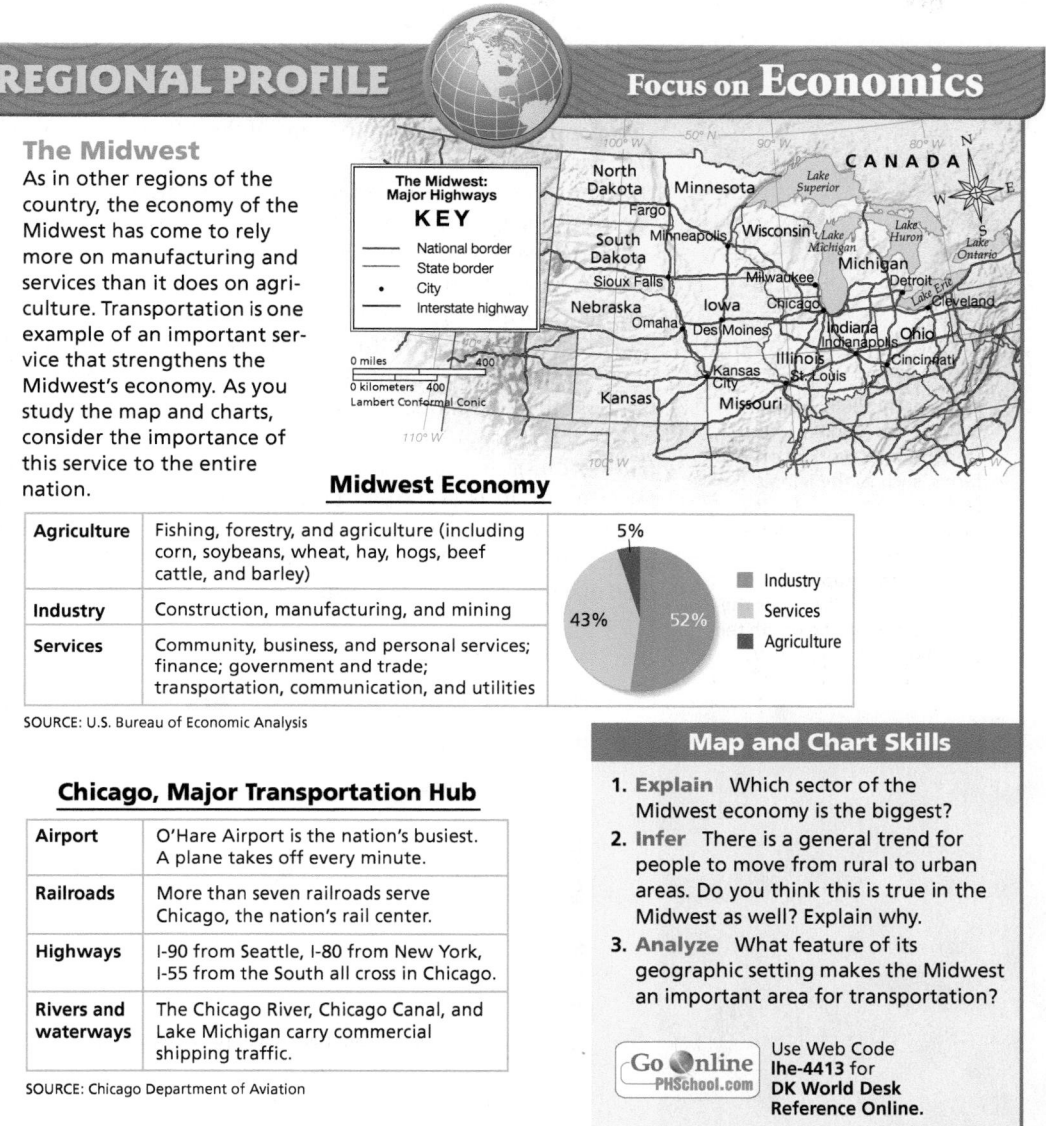

REGIONAL PROFILE — Focus on Economics

The Midwest

As in other regions of the country, the economy of the Midwest has come to rely more on manufacturing and services than it does on agriculture. Transportation is one example of an important service that strengthens the Midwest's economy. As you study the map and charts, consider the importance of this service to the entire nation.

The Midwest: Major Highways

KEY
- —— National border
- —— State border
- • City
- —— Interstate highway

0 miles 400
0 kilometers 400
Lambert Conformal Conic

Midwest Economy

Agriculture	Fishing, forestry, and agriculture (including corn, soybeans, wheat, hay, hogs, beef cattle, and barley)
Industry	Construction, manufacturing, and mining
Services	Community, business, and personal services; finance; government and trade; transportation, communication, and utilities

5%
Industry
Services
Agriculture
43% 52%

SOURCE: U.S. Bureau of Economic Analysis

Chicago, Major Transportation Hub

Airport	O'Hare Airport is the nation's busiest. A plane takes off every minute.
Railroads	More than seven railroads serve Chicago, the nation's rail center.
Highways	I-90 from Seattle, I-80 from New York, I-55 from the South all cross in Chicago.
Rivers and waterways	The Chicago River, Chicago Canal, and Lake Michigan carry commercial shipping traffic.

SOURCE: Chicago Department of Aviation

Map and Chart Skills

1. **Explain** Which sector of the Midwest economy is the biggest?
2. **Infer** There is a general trend for people to move from rural to urban areas. Do you think this is true in the Midwest as well? Explain why.
3. **Analyze** What feature of its geographic setting makes the Midwest an important area for transportation?

Go Online PHSchool.com Use Web Code lhe-4413 for **DK World Desk Reference Online.**

Vocabulary Builder

Use the information below to teach students this section's high-use words.

High-Use Word	Definition and Sample Sentence
technique, p. 266	*n.* method of accomplishing a desired aim The new **technique** was more effective than the old method.
prosper, p. 266	*v.* to achieve economic success The farmers **prospered** when they brought in a good crop.
efficiently, p. 267	*adv.* bringing about a result with the least waste of time She finished one project quickly and **efficiently** moved on to the next.
ethnic, p. 268	*adj.* relating to large groups of people who share a common cultural background His **ethnic** background was a mix of Swedish and Native American.

Instruct

REGIONAL PROFILE
Focus on Economics

Guided Instruction L2

Lead students in reading the text and reviewing the graphic material on this page. Work with the class to answer the Map and Chart Skills questions. Allow students to confer with a partner before sharing their responses.

Independent Practice

Partner students and have them each make up two questions for the other to answer. Questions should be based on the information in the Regional Profile.

Answers

Map and Chart Skills

1. Industry
2. Yes; as more people take jobs in businesses and industry, they move to urban areas where these economic activities are located.
3. It is in the center of the nation and it is near the Great Lakes, Mississippi River, and other bodies of water that are used for transportation.

Go Online PHSchool.com Students can find more information about this topic on the DK World Desk Reference Online.

Technology Changes Farm Life L2

Guided Reading

- **Vocabulary Builder** Clarify the high-use words **technique, prosper,** and **efficient** before reading.

- Read Technology Changes Farm Life using the ReQuest procedure (TE, p. T35).

- Have students name the technological advances that helped people build farms in the Midwest. *(steel plows, the windmill, barbed wire, and drilling equipment)*

- Discuss with students the reasons for the decline of the family farm. *(Farmers borrowed money from banks to buy more land and equipment. In the 1980s, a recession took place, decreasing the demand for farm products and increasing loan interest rates. Farmers were unable to pay loans so many sold or left their farms.)*

Answers

Graph Skills **Describe** decreasing from 1910 to 1990 and increasing slightly from 1990 to 2000 **Analyze Information** Today farming employs less than four million people, far less than it employed in the early 1900s.

Technology Changes Farm Life

The Midwest is often called the heartland because it is the agricultural center of our nation. The soil is rich, and the climate is suitable for producing corn, wheat, soybeans, and livestock. Inventions such as the steel plow, the windmill, and barbed wire helped settlers carve out farms on the plains. Drilling equipment helped to make wells deep enough to reach water. These tools also helped make farms productive. Technological advances continue to improve farming techniques today.

Family Farms Decline Until the 1980s, small family farms were common in the Midwest. Many of these farms were mixed-crop farms. On a **mixed-crop farm,** several different kinds of crops are grown. This was a sensible way for farmers to work. If one crop failed, the farm had others to fall back on.

In the 1960s and 1970s, family farms prospered. The world population was rising, and demand for American farm products was high. Farmers felt that they could increase their business if they enlarged their farms. To build bigger farms, farmers bought more land and equipment. But all of this cost money. Many farmers borrowed money from local banks.

In the early 1980s, there was a countrywide **recession** (rih SESH un), or a downturn in business activity. The demand for farm products decreased. Then, interest rates on bank loans increased. As a result, many farmers were not able to make enough money to pay their loans. Some families sold their farms. More than one million American farmers have left the land since 1980.

Graph Skills

In the early 1900s, about one third of the workers in the United States worked on farms, such as the Illinois farm shown below. **Describe** What is the pattern of the number of farm workers shown in the graph? **Analyze Information** What does the information on the graph tell you about farming today?

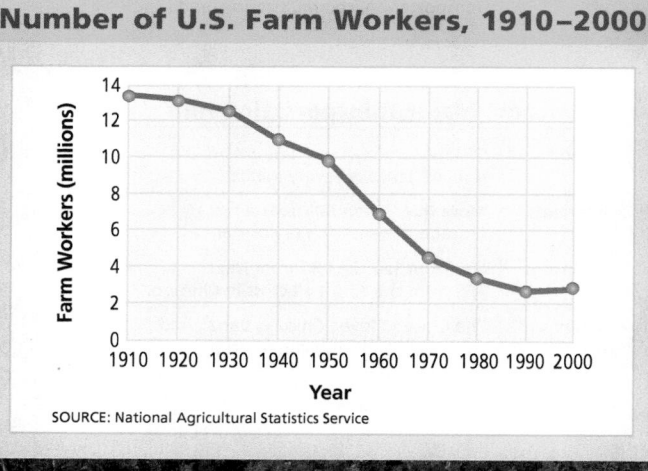

Number of U.S. Farm Workers, 1910–2000

SOURCE: National Agricultural Statistics Service

266 United States and Canada

Differentiated Instruction

For English Language Learners L2
Encourage native speakers to help non-native speakers use context clues to clarify words with multiple meanings in the Regional Profile, such as *rich* and *service.*

For Special Needs Students L1
Some students may require additional help to read and understand the tables illustrated in the Regional Profile. Have students work in pairs to complete *Reading a Table,* then as a class review the tables and discuss the process of determining the answers.

All in One **United States and Canada Teaching Resources,** *Reading a Table,* p. 266

Corporate Farms Rise A small number of agricultural companies bought many of these family farms. When these agricultural companies combine several small family farms into one large farm, it is called a **corporate farm.** Large corporations can afford to buy the expensive land and equipment that modern farming requires. These large farms are run efficiently and make a profit.

Corporate farmers rely on machines and computers to do much of the work. This means that corporate farms employ fewer workers. Kansas offers a good example of corporate farming, since it has fewer workers and larger farms. In Kansas, 90 percent of the land is farmland, but fewer than 1 percent of the people are farmers. Most of the people in Kansas live and work in cities such as Wichita.

Small family farms do still exist in the Midwest. But most of them struggle to earn enough money for supporting a family. Family farmers usually need to have another job as well. Many people look to the cities for more job opportunities.

✓ Reading Check **Why did so many families sell or leave their farms?**

Identify Contrasts
How are corporate farms different from family farms?

Chapter 9 Section 3 **267**

✎ Target Reading Skill   L2

Identify Contrasts As a follow up, ask students to answer the Target Reading Skill question in the Student Edition. *(Family farms are run by a small group of people, while corporate farms are run by large corporations. Family farms usually grow a smaller amount of crops than corporate farms. They also rely more on human labor while corporate farms often rely more on machines and computers to do the work.)*

Guided Instruction (continued)
■ Ask students **How might corporate farms benefit consumers?** *(Products grown and raised on corporate farms can be sold at a cheaper price because it costs less money to produce them with fewer workers to pay and more efficient farming equipment.)*

Independent Practice
Have students create the Taking Notes graphic organizer on a blank piece of paper. Use the *Cause and Effect Chart* transparency to model how to begin filling it in.

📖 **United States and Canada Transparencies,** *Transparency B7: Cause and Effect Chart*

Monitor Progress
While students work on their charts, circulate to make sure individuals are choosing the correct information to include. Provide assistance as needed.

Differentiated Instruction

For Advanced Readers   L3
Have students research a list of inventions that helped to change the nature of farming. Ask students to make a time line showing the dates of six of the most important inventions. Have students write a brief summary explaining how this technology affected farming. Use the *Time Line* transparency to model how to make a time line.

📖 **United States and Canada Transparencies,** *Transparency B20: Timeline*

For Less Proficient Readers   L1
Pair these students with more proficient readers and have them create an outline of the material as they read. Tell students to use the headings in the section as a framework.

Answer

✓ Reading Check There was a recession and the demand for farm products decreased while interest rates increased. Many farmers could not make their payments on loans and so they were forced to sell or leave their farms.

Cities Develop in the Midwest

L2

Guided Instruction

- **Vocabulary Builder** Clarify the high-use word **ethnic** before reading.

- Have students read Cities Develop in the Midwest. As students read, circulate to make sure individuals can answer the Reading Check question.

- Ask **What are some important cities in the Midwest?** *(Chicago, Detroit, St. Louis, Minneapolis, St. Paul)*

- Ask **How has being located near a body of water been important in the growth and development of these cities?** *(In some cases, farm products were shipped to other states via the Great Lakes. In others, people have used the lakes and rivers near these cities as points of departure. These activities have drawn people to the cities and helped them develop.)*

Links

Read the **Links Across the World** on this page. Ask students **Why do you think that the construction of buildings such as the Sears Tower did not occur until the twentieth century?** *(In order to construct such tall buildings, advances in architecture, construction, and materials were required. These technological advances did not occur until the twentieth century.)*

Cities Develop in the Midwest

Many Midwestern cities began as centers of transportation and processing. Farmers from the surrounding area would send their harvests and livestock to nearby cities to be processed and shipped east. The largest processing city was Chicago, Illinois.

Chicago Located on Lake Michigan, Chicago was surrounded by prairies and farms in the mid-1800s. Farmers sent corn, wheat, cattle, and hogs to the mills and meat-packing plants in the city. Here the raw materials were turned into foods and shipped east by way of the Great Lakes. When railroads were built, Chicago really boomed. By the late 1800s, it had become a steel-making and manufacturing center. What was one of the most important manufactured products made in Chicago? You probably guessed it: farm equipment.

Today, Chicago is the biggest city in the heartland. It is known for its ethnic diversity and lively culture. It is the hub of major transportation routes including highways, railroads, airlines, and shipping routes. Chicago is also the home of the first steel skyscraper—the Home Insurance Company Building—and many other architectural wonders. For a bird's-eye view of Chicago, go to the top of the Sears Tower, one of the tallest buildings in the world.

Links Across The World

Higher and Higher Until 1996, Chicago's Sears Tower, at 1,454 feet (443 meters), was the world's tallest building. The photo below shows the view from the Sears Tower. The twin Petronas Towers in Malaysia then held the title. In 2004, the Taipei 101 building in Taipei, Taiwan, gained the title of world's tallest building, topping out at 1,671 feet (509 meters). Today, even taller skyscrapers are being planned in cities around the world.

268 United States and Canada

Differentiated Instruction

For Gifted and Talented L3

Have students read about the Gateway Arch in the *Enrichment* worksheet. From the list provided, students should select another American memorial or monument to research. Then have them write a report on the site and present it to the class.

All in One United States and Canada Teaching Resources, *Enrichment,* p. 255

For Less Proficient Readers L1

Remind students to read the captions that appear with photographs or other visual material. Direct students' attention to the captions in this section. Have them reread them to find one noun that names the object in the photo. When students are finished, ask them to describe each item without referring to the caption.

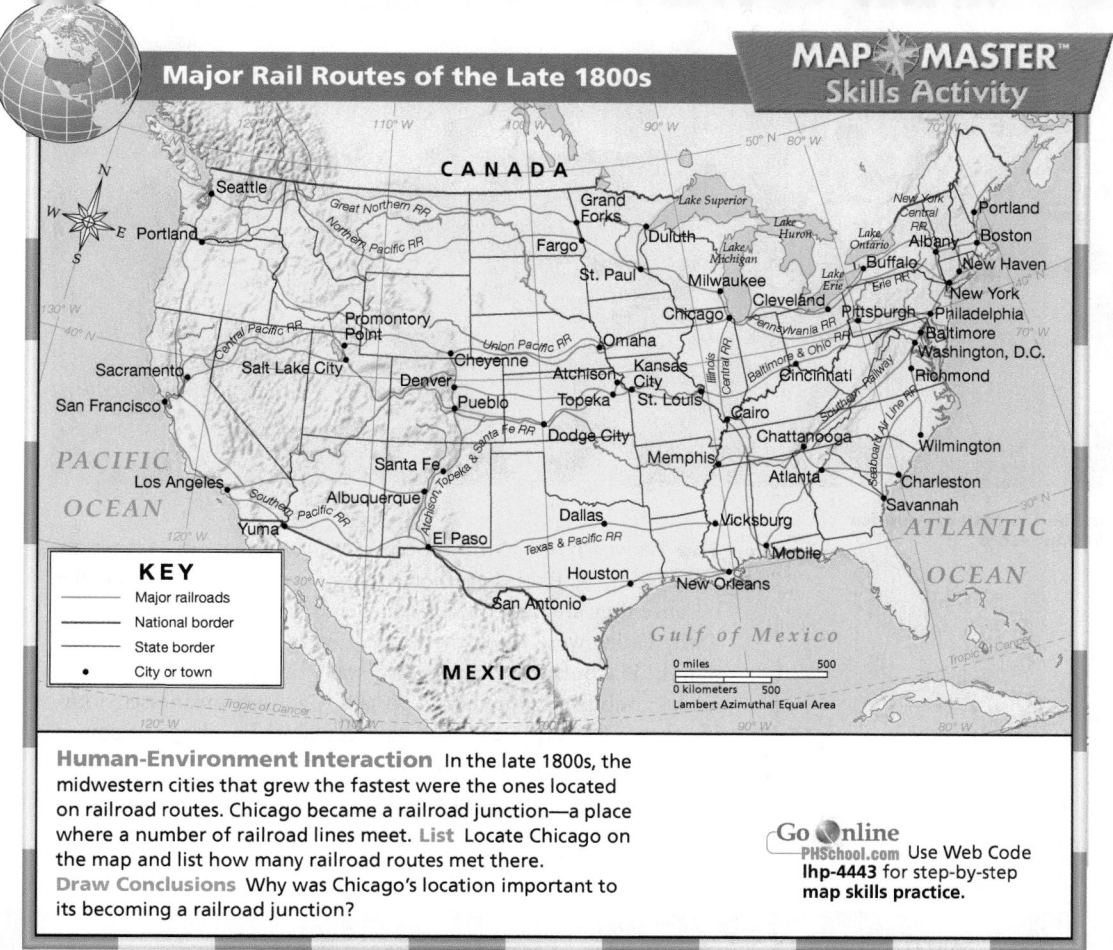

Major Rail Routes of the Late 1800s

MAP MASTER™ Skills Activity

KEY
— Major railroads
— National border
— State border
• City or town

0 miles 500
0 kilometers 500
Lambert Azimuthal Equal Area

Human-Environment Interaction In the late 1800s, the midwestern cities that grew the fastest were the ones located on railroad routes. Chicago became a railroad junction—a place where a number of railroad lines meet. **List** Locate Chicago on the map and list how many railroad routes met there.
Draw Conclusions Why was Chicago's location important to its becoming a railroad junction?

Go Online
PHSchool.com Use Web Code
lhp-4443 for step-by-step
map skills practice.

Detroit and St. Louis Two other large cities in the Midwest are Detroit, Michigan, and St. Louis, Missouri. They have both played an important role in the country's history. Why do you think Detroit is called the Motor City? You will find the head-quarters of America's automobile manufacturers here. General Motors, Ford, and Daimler Chrysler have their main offices and factories in the city.

Covered wagons, not cars, used to roll through St. Louis. Located on the Mississippi River, this city was the starting point for pioneers heading west. Its location on the banks of the Mississippi River made it an important city in the days before railroads. Today, a huge stainless steel arch beside the river marks St. Louis as the Gateway to the West. St. Louis is also a banking and commercial center.

Chapter 9 Section 3 **269**

Skills Mini Lesson

Using a Special Purpose Map

1. Explain that there are many different types of special purpose maps. Thematic maps focus on a specific topic, such as transportation routes. The key and the map title can help students identify the purpose of a map.

2. Help students practice the skill by reading the title of the map on p. 269 and identifying what the symbols in the key represent.

3. Have students apply the skill by tracing and describing two possible railroad routes from New York City to Denver.

Assess and Reteach

Assess Progress   L2

Have students complete the Section Assessment. Administer the *Section Quiz*.

All in One **United States and Canada Teaching Resources,** *Section Quiz,* p. 246

Reteach   L1

If students need more instruction, have them read this section in the Reading and Vocabulary Study Guide.

Chapter 9, Section 3, **Western Hemisphere Reading and Vocabulary Study Guide,** pp. 98–100

Extend   L3

If you have not already done so, show students *Taming the Mississippi* to help them learn more about this important transportation route that flows through the Midwest.

The Geography of the United States, **World Studies Video Program**

Answer

✓ **Reading Check** The world's first skycraper was located in Chicago.

Section 3 Assessment

Key Terms

Students' sentences should reflect knowledge of each Key Term.

Target Reading Skill

There were more prosperous family farms in the 1960s and 1970s. Farming technology has advanced since the 1980s so fewer workers are needed on farms.

Comprehension and Critical Thinking

1. (a) It is the agricultural center of the United States. **(b)** There was a recession that led to decreased demand for farm products and an increase in interest rates on farm loans. **(c)** Possible answer: There will probably continue to be fewer opportunities for farmers to own their own small farms.

2. (a) They began as centers of transportation and processing. **(b)** They helped cities grow by allowing them to ship the goods they produced faster and to more places. **(c)** It is in the middle of the country and on Lake Michigan so its location makes it a good transportation hub for people and goods.

Inside the Mall of America in Minnesota

The Twin Cities Minneapolis is the largest city in Minnesota, followed by St. Paul. Together, they are known as the Twin Cities because they are next to each other on the Mississippi River. The Twin Cities were once the flour-milling center of the United States. Pillsbury and Company was founded there in 1872. Today, publishing, medical, computer, and art businesses flourish there. The city's suburbs have replaced hundreds of square miles of fertile land once used for farming.

✓ **Reading Check** **Where was the world's first skyscraper located?**

Section 3 Assessment

Key Terms
Review the key terms at the beginning of this section. Use each term in a sentence that explains its meaning.

Target Reading Skill
What are two ways that farming in the 1960s and 1970s was different from farming since the 1980s?

Comprehension and Critical Thinking
1. (a) Explain Why is the Midwest called the nation's heartland?

(b) Explore the Main Idea Why did family farmers face hard times in the 1980s?
(c) Predict What do you think the future holds for family farmers?
2. (a) Recall How did some midwestern cities get their starts?
(b) Identify Effects How did railroads affect the growth of midwestern cities?
(c) Draw Inferences How might Chicago's location affect its growth today?

Writing Activity
Suppose that you are a farmer and you have decided to sell your farm and move to a city. Write a letter to a friend explaining your decision.

Go Online **PHSchool.com**
For: An activity on the automobile industry
Visit: PHSchool.com
Web Code: lhd-4403

Writing Activity
Use the *Rubric for Assessing a Writing Assignment* to evaluate students' letters.

All in One **United States and Canada Teaching Resources,** *Rubric for Assessing a Writing Assignment,* p. 273

Go Online **PHSchool.com** Typing in the Web code when prompted will bring students directly to detailed instructions for this activity.

The West
Using and Preserving Resources

Prepare to Read

Objectives
In this section you will
1. Learn about the natural resources of the West.
2. Read about the challenges facing the urban West.

Taking Notes
As you read this section, look for ways that natural resources are used and conserved in the West. Copy the table below, and record your findings in it.

Resources of the West	
Using Resources	Conserving Resources
•	•
•	•
•	•

🎯 Target Reading Skill

Make Comparisons Comparing two or more situations enables you to see how they are alike. As you read this section, compare how different parts of the West use and manage resources. Write the information in your Taking Notes table.

Key Terms
• **forty-niner** (FAWRT ee NY nur) *n.* the nickname for a miner who took part in the California Gold Rush of 1849
• **responsible development** (rih SPAHN suh bul dih VEL up munt) *n.* balancing the needs of the environment, community, and economy
• **mass transit** (mas TRAN sit) *n.* a system of subways, buses, and commuter trains used to transport large numbers of people

Objectives
Social Studies
1. Learn about the natural resources of the West.
2. Read about the challenges facing the urban West.

Reading/Language Arts
Make comparisons to see how two situations are the same.

Prepare to Read

Build Background Knowledge L2
Tell students that they will learn about how the people of the West are trying to use their natural resources wisely. Call on volunteers to describe some of their own recycling or conservation efforts. Discuss how it could make a difference if everyone in the country made efforts to conserve natural resources. Use the Give One, Get One participation strategy (TE, p. T37) to elicit student responses.

Set a Purpose for Reading L2
■ Preview the Objectives

■ Form students into pairs or groups of four. Distribute the *Reading Readiness Guide*. Ask students to fill in the first two columns of the chart. Use the Numbered Heads participation strategy (TE, p. T36) to call on students to share one piece of information they already know and one piece of information they want to know.

All in One United States and Canada Teaching Resources, *Reading Readiness Guide,* p. 248

Vocabulary Builder
Preview Key Terms L2
Pronounce each Key Term, then ask students to say the word with you. Provide a simple explanation such as, "Forty-niners were people who went to California to find gold in 1849."

From colonial days to the present, Americans have been drawn westward. Over time, explorers and settlers have pushed out the farthest boundaries of the western frontier. In the 1780s, the frontier was considered to be the land as far west as the Mississippi River. Twenty years later, it included all of the land to the Rocky Mountains. By the 1850s, the frontier was the region that we now think of as the West—the land from the Rocky Mountains to the Pacific Ocean. By the 1900s, it also included Alaska and Hawaii.

Although the boundaries of the West have changed dramatically over the years, one factor has remained the same: People are attracted westward by the promise of the land.

Rocky Mountains, Colorado

🎯 Target Reading Skill L2

Make Comparisons Point out the Target Reading Skill. Tell students that they can make comparisons to find the similarities between two situations.

Model the skill by reading this page aloud and identifying the similarity between the West in the 1780s and the West today. *(Its land still attracts people to move there.)*

Give students *Make Comparisons.* Have them complete the activity in groups.

All in One United States and Canada Teaching Resources, *Make Comparisons,* p. 253

Instruct

Guided Instruction   L2

Ask students to study the Regional Profile map and charts and read the text on this page. Work with the class to answer the Map and Chart Skills questions. Allow students to discuss their responses with a partner before sharing answers.

Independent Practice

Display *Color Transparency USC 29: The United States: Annual Precipitation and Prevailing Winds.* Ask students to compare and contrast the amount of precipitation that falls in the West with the amount that falls in the other United States regions.

📖 **United States and Canada Transparencies,** *Color Transparency USC 29: The United States: Annual Precipitation and Prevailing Winds*

Answers

Map and Chart Skills

1. The coasts of Washington and Oregon receive the most rain.

2. Washington

3. Some issues that might be addressed are water pollution and which bodies of water can be used to produce hydroelectric power.

Go Online
PHSchool.com **Students can find more information about this topic on the DK World Desk Reference Online.**

Natural Resources of the West

For well over 400 years, people have been drawn to the West by its wealth of natural resources. The Spanish had already settled in the Southwest when the Pilgrims arrived in New England in the 1620s. After Lewis and Clark's exploration of the Louisiana Territory in the early 1800s, more people moved westward.

REGIONAL PROFILE   Focus on Geography

The West

Water is an important resource of the West—more important even than gold. Farmers have always needed large quantities of water to irrigate their lands. Today, as large cities and their populations grow, people are demanding more and more water for everyday use. Study the map and charts, and think about how water availability and use are shaping this region.

California Cropland

Nonirrigated 11%

Irrigated 89%

SOURCE: National Agriculture Statistics Service

Leading Hydroelectric Power-Producing States, 2006

States	Thousands of Megawatt Hours
Washington	14,650
Oregon	7,854
California	8,088
New York*	4,173
Alabama*	1,913
Idaho	1,736
Tennessee*	1,557

SOURCE: Energy Information Administration, US Department of Energy
*not a western state

The West: Precipitation KEY

Inches		Millimeters
More than 59		More than 1,499
40–59		1,000–1,499
20–39		500–999
10–19		250–499
Less than 10		Less than 250

—— National border
—— State border

Map and Chart Skills

1. **Locate** Which areas of the West receive the most rain?
2. **Identify** What state produces the most hydroelectric power?
3. **Analyze** There is a category of law devoted to water use. What issues might be addressed by lawyers who specialize in water use?

Go Online
PHSchool.com **Use Web Code lhe-4414 to access the DK World Desk Reference Online.**

272 United States and Canada

Vocabulary Builder

Use the information below to teach students this section's high-use words.

High-Use Word	Definition and Sample Sentence
pollution, p. 274	*n.* the condition of being unclean; contamination **Pollution** made the lake too dirty to swim in.
site, p. 274	*n.* location The carpenter arrived at the work **site**.
junction, p. 274	*n.* a place where two roads or rivers meet A stop sign was put in at the **junction** of the two roads.

Mineral Resources Before gold was discovered in California, Native Americans and Spanish settlers lived in the region. With the California Gold Rush, the population exploded. The sleepy port of San Francisco boomed into a prosperous city. Its population grew from 800 people in 1848 to 25,000 just two years later. The first miners and prospectors of the Gold Rush were called **forty-niners** because they arrived in 1849. They arrived, bought supplies, and headed off to the Sierra Nevada expecting to strike it rich. Few of them succeeded, but many remained in the West.

A gold strike in 1858 in Colorado led to the founding of the city of Denver. Similar events took place in Nevada, Idaho, and Montana in the 1860s. Further discoveries of valuable minerals, including silver and copper, drew more and more people to the West. A mining town formed around each new discovery.

All of these new settlers needed homes, and the timber to build them with was in large supply in the the Pacific Northwest. After the Civil War, logging camps, sawmills, and paper mills sprang up in Washington, Oregon, and northern California. At first, the resources of the West seemed unlimited. The use of these resources created wealth and many jobs. However, it also brought with it new challenges.

The Cost of Mining
Merchants and traders supplied miners with food, clothing, and tools. Supplies were hauled from the river ports to the mining camps by wagons and mules. This caused increased prices. With the population boom and the difficulty of getting supplies up to the camps, the cost of living for miners was high. **Conclude** *Was trying to strike it rich worth the amount of time, effort, and money needed? Explain your answer.*

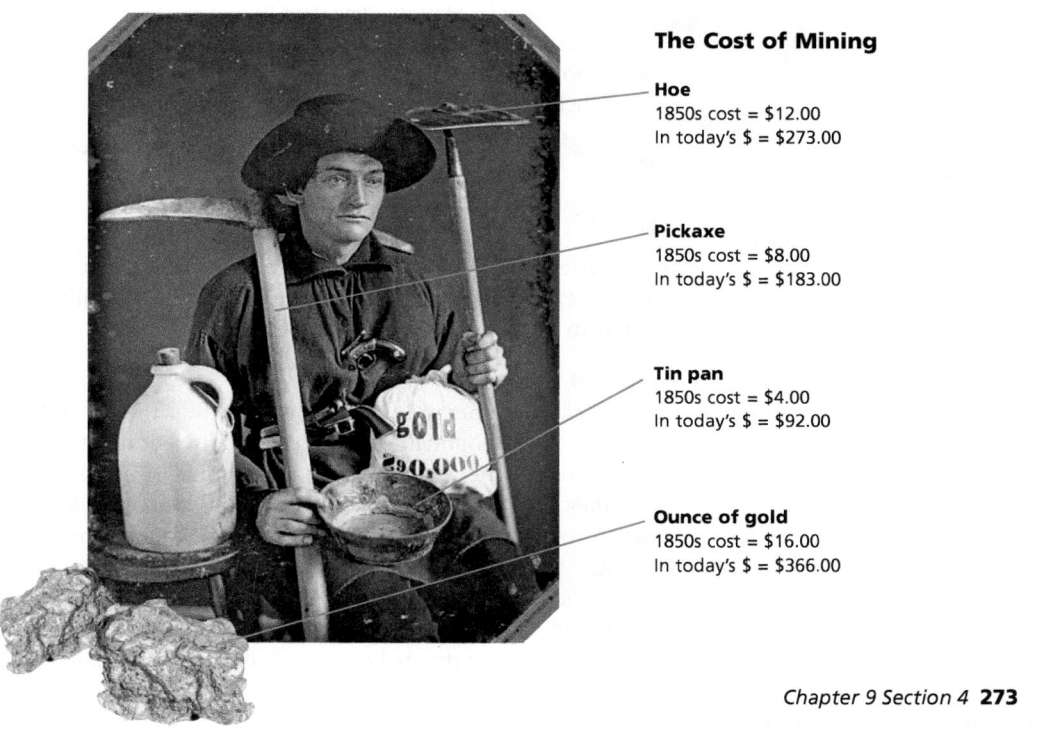

The Cost of Mining

Hoe
1850s cost = $12.00
In today's $ = $273.00

Pickaxe
1850s cost = $8.00
In today's $ = $183.00

Tin pan
1850s cost = $4.00
In today's $ = $92.00

Ounce of gold
1850s cost = $16.00
In today's $ = $366.00

Natural Resources of the West 〔L2〕

Guided Instruction

- **Vocabulary Builder** Clarify the high-use word **pollution** before reading.

- Read Natural Resources of the West with students, using the Choral Reading strategy (TE, p. T34).

- Ask **What useful minerals are found in the West?** (*gold, silver, copper*) **What are some useful non-mineral resources found in the West?** (*timber and water*)

- Lead a discussion on the ways people in the West are addressing the challenge of managing resources. (*Logging companies are replacing trees by planting new ones; power plants are using advanced technology to control pollution; the number of campers is being limited in national parks such as Yosemite.*)

Independent Practice
Have students create the Taking Notes graphic organizer on a blank piece of paper. Ask them to begin filling in the ways resources are used and conserved in the West. Fill in the first detail for each column with them to model how to choose the correct details.

Monitor Progress
As students work on their graphic organizers, circulate to make sure individuals comprehend key concepts. Provide assistance as needed.

Differentiated Instruction

For Less Proficient Readers 〔L1〕
To ensure that students understand the Regional Profile on the previous page, students may need further instruction on how to read a table. Distribute *Reading a Table* and have students complete the activity in pairs. It may also be helpful to explain the definition of a megawatt hour.

All in One **United States and Canada Teaching Resources,** *Reading a Table* p. 266

For Gifted and Talented 〔L3〕
To enhance students understanding of the Regional Profile on the previous page, have students choose three states from the table and do Internet or library research to find the sources of hydroelectric power in that state. Have them present their findings in a table.

Answer
Conclude Possible answers: Yes, it was worth it if you ended up finding gold; No, it was not worth it because the chance of striking it rich was so slim.

The Urban West L2

Guided Instruction

- **Vocabulary Builder** Clarify the high-use words **function** and **site** before reading.

- Read the Urban West as a class. As students read, circulate and make sure individuals can answer the Reading Check question.

- Ask **How has the work people do to earn a living changed in the West?** *(Most people are no longer farmers, loggers, and miners; they now have jobs in businesses in the cities.)*

- Ask **What is the second most populated city in the United States?** *(Los Angeles, California)*

- Have students brainstorm ways in which the Western states might better meet the challenge of air pollution. Conduct an Idea Wave (TE, p. T35) to generate a list of possibilities. *(Possible answers: build more mass transit systems; limit the size of cars people can own; develop better energy-saving vehicles.)*

Old Faithful is the best-known geyser in Yellowstone National Park, Wyoming.

Managing Resources California's population continued to grow after the Gold Rush. To meet the demand for new houses, loggers leveled many forests. Engineers built dams to pipe water through the mountains to coastal cities. Next to the dams, they built hydroelectric plants. Cities like San Francisco got water and power this way, but the dams flooded whole valleys of the Sierras.

To save parts of the West as natural wilderness, Congress created several national parks and forests. Yet these parks are not trouble-free. California's Yosemite (yoh SEM uh tee) National Park now gets so many visitors that it suffers from traffic jams and air pollution in the summer. Some of the scenic views in Montana's Glacier National Park are also reduced by hazy skies.

Some westerners are working on **responsible development**, or balancing the needs of the environment, the community, and the economy. For example, Yosemite now limits the number of campers in the park. Dam building has stopped. In addition, some logging companies are working to preserve the environment by planting new trees to replace the ones that have been cut down. Advanced technology, such as power plants with better pollution-control devices, can help meet energy and environmental needs.

✓ Reading Check **What caused California's population to grow in the 1800s?**

The Urban West

Most westerners today are not miners, farmers, or loggers. Rather, they live and work in cities. Their challenge is to figure out how to use natural resources wisely.

Portland, Oregon "Your town or mine?" two land developers asked each other in 1845. They were at the same site and predicted the development of a major port city. Located near the junction of the Willamette and Columbia rivers, how could they fail? Francis W. Pettygrove of Portland, Maine, won the coin toss. He named the site after his hometown in the East.

Portland became a trade center for lumber, fur, grain, salmon, and wool. In the 1930s, new dams produced cheap electricity. Portland attracted many manufacturing industries.

274 United States and Canada

Answer

✓ Reading Check The Gold Rush caused the population to soar.

Skills for Life — Skills Mini Lesson

Distinguishing Fact and Opinion

1. Introduce the skill by explaining that a fact can be proved true, while an opinion, which is an individual belief, cannot be proven.

2. To practice the skill, write the following statements on the board and have students determine which is a fact and which is an opinion: *San Jose is California's most beautiful city. (opinion) Many people moved to Los Angeles to work in the movie industry. (fact)*

3. To apply the skill, have each student write one fact and one opinion on a separate slip of paper, then switch with a partner and determine which is which.

Seattle, Washington The port city of Seattle was founded in the early 1850s. It was named after a Native American leader who helped the area's first settlers. Seattle has grown into a bustling city of more than half a million people.

Years of unchecked growth eventually led to problems. In the 1960s, a group of local citizens started a campaign to revitalize the local economy. A bridge was built across Lake Washington to help residents commute. Sewage was cleaned up from Lake Washington, and many neighborhood parks were created. The group also kept Pike Place Market from being destroyed. It is the oldest continuously run market in the country. Farmers have sold their crops and produce there since 1907.

San Jose, California Urban sprawl is a local challenge in San Jose. The area around San Jose was once known for its beautiful orchards and farms. Now it is called Silicon Valley because it is a part of the computer industry.

San Jose's most valuable resource is now its people. They come from all parts of the world. The greater population density has created crowded freeways and air pollution. To counter these problems, San Jose has built a light-rail mass transit system. A **mass transit** system replaces individual cars with energy-saving buses or trains.

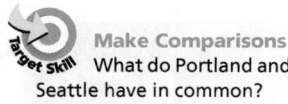
Make Comparisons What do Portland and Seattle have in common?

■ Graph Skills

The Internet boom of the 1990s saw between 7,000 and 10,000 Internet companies start up. It began to decline dramatically by the beginning of 2000. **Describe** In what year did the most Internet companies shut down? **Predict** If the number of company shutdowns continues, what would be the effect on urban sprawl?

Internet Company Shutdowns

Number of Companies vs. Year (2000, 2001, 2002)

SOURCE: Webmergers

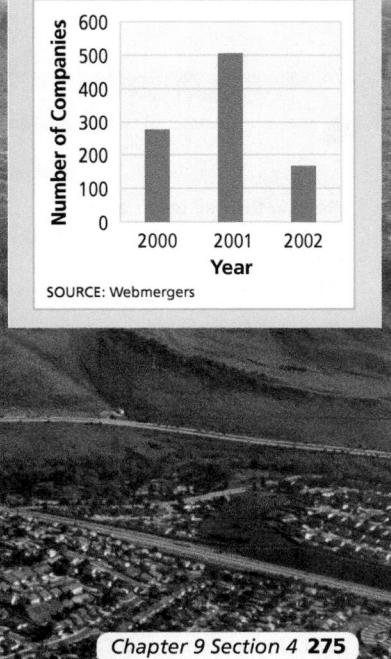

◕ Target Reading Skill   L2

Make Comparisons As a follow up, ask students to answer the Target Reading Skill question in the Student Edition. *(Both Portland and Seattle are port cities.)*

Independent Practice
Tell students to complete their graphic organizers with more information about using and conserving resources.

Monitor Progress
■ Show *Section Reading Support Transparency USC 57* and ask students to check their graphic organizers individually. Go over key concepts and clarify key vocabulary as needed.

📖 **United States and Canada Transparencies,** *Section Reading Support Transparency USC 57*

■ Tell students to fill in the last column of their *Reading Readiness Guides.* Ask students to evaluate if what they learned was what they had expected to learn.

📑 All in One **United States and Canada Teaching Resources,** *Reading Readiness Guide,* p. 248

⌐Differentiated Instruction¬

For Special Needs Students   L1
Have students read the section as they listen to the recorded version on the Student Edition on Audio CD. Check for comprehension by asking students to write one sentence about each city.

◉ Chapter 9, Section 4, **Student Edition on Audio CD**

For Gifted and Talented   L3
Assign students the *Making a Model River* activity. As they work, ask students to relate the project to the use of rivers in the West.

📑 All in One **United States and Canada Teaching Resources,** *Activity Shop Lab: Making a Model River,* pp. 261–262

Answers
Graph Skills Describe 2001
Predict Urban sprawl might slow down.

Assess and Reteach

Assess Progress `L2`

Have students complete the Section Assessment. Administer the *Section Quiz*.

> **All in One United States and Canada Teaching Resources,** *Section Quiz,* p. 250

Reteach `L1`

If students need more instruction, have them read this section in the Reading and Vocabulary Study Guide

> Chapter 9, Section 4, **Western Hemisphere Reading and Vocabulary Study Guide,** pp. 101–103

Extend `L3`

Have students complete the *Small Group Activity* to increase their understanding of the importance of water as a resource in the West and its various uses.

> **All in One United States and Canada Teaching Resources,** *Small Group Activity: Simulation: Town Meeting on Water Use,* pp. 257–260

Answer

✓ **Reading Check** San Jose needed a mass transit system to help address its problems with pollution and highway crowding.

Section 4 Assessment

Key Terms

Students' sentences should reflect knowledge of each Key Term.

Target Reading Skill

In the 1780s, Los Angeles was a small Mexican village. Today it is the second most populated city in the United States, and it is a center for banking, the aircraft industry, and the entertainment industry.

Comprehension and Critical Thinking

1. (a) the Gold Rush **(b)** Many people who came to the West during the Gold Rush stayed and established cities. **(c)** More people means the use of more resources. People in the West had to find ways to conserve and protect resources.

2. (a) A developer named it after his hometown of Portland, Maine. **(b)** Trees and the Columbia and Willamette rivers made it a good location for a city. **(c)** Possible answers: Trees that are cut for lumber may be replaced by newly planted trees; limits may be placed on fishing; pollution of the rivers may be prohibited.

Los Angeles, California Los Angeles is another California city whose people are its greatest resource. It has grown from a small Mexican village in the 1780s to the second-most-populated city in the United States. The Gold Rush and the building of the transcontinental railroad helped the city grow.

By the 1920s, the movie, petroleum, and manufacturing industries all brought more people to the city. Today, Los Angeles is a center for banking and aircraft manufacturing. But, it is most noted for its entertainment industry. In addition to the Hollywood movie industry, the headquarters of many of the country's recording companies and radio and television networks are located here. Many broadcasts are in foreign languages, especially Spanish. Hispanics are the largest ethnic group in the city, followed by Asians.

The Hollywood sign hovers over Los Angeles, California, and is a reminder that the city is home to the entertainment industry. Cameramen (lower photo) shoot a movie on a local set.

✓ **Reading Check** Why did San Jose need a mass transit system?

Section 4 Assessment

Key Terms

Review the key terms at the beginning of this section. Use each term in a sentence that explains its meaning.

Target Reading Skill

Compare Los Angeles today to what it was like in the 1780s.

Comprehension and Critical Thinking

1. (a) Recall What event took place in California in 1849?
(b) Identify Cause and Effect How did that event lead to the formation of towns and cities?

(c) Infer How did the population explosion affect the West's natural resources?
2. (a) Explain How did Portland, Oregon, get its name?
(b) Summarize What natural resources made Portland a good location for a city?
(c) Predict How might these resources be protected today?

Writing Activity

What natural resources are there in your community? In what ways do people use these natural resources? Write a paragraph describing the natural resources in your area and how they are used.

Go Online PHSchool.com

For: An activity on Denver
Visit: PHSchool.com
Web Code: lhd-4404

Writing Activity

Use the *Rubric for Assessing a Writing Assignment* to evaluate students' paragraphs.

> **All in One United States and Canada Teaching Resources,** *Rubric for Assessing a Writing Assignment,* p. 273

Go Online PHSchool.com Typing in the Web code when prompted will bring students directly to detailed instructions for this activity.

Review and Assessment

Review and Assessment
Review Chapter Content

- Review and revisit the major themes of this chapter by having students relate each bulleted statement in the Chapter Summary to a Guiding Question. Use the Think-Write-Pair-Share participation strategy (TE, p. T36) to have students determine the number of the Guiding Question that relates to each statement and then have students discuss their classifications with their partners. Refer to page 1 in the Student Edition for the text of the Guiding Questions.

- Assign *Vocabulary Development* for students to review Key Terms.

All in One **United States and Canada Teaching Resources,** *Vocabulary Development*, p. 271

◆ Chapter Summary

Section 1: The Northeast
- A chain of cities runs from Boston, Massachusetts, to Washington, D.C.
- The Northeast is the most densely populated region of the United States.
- Many immigrants entered the United States through one of the ports in the Northeast.

Section 2: The South
- The South's warm climate and abundant rainfall make it suitable for growing many crops.
- Drilling, mining, fishing, and forestry are important industries in the South.
- Many people have moved from rural towns to the cities for better job opportunities.

Section 3: The Midwest
- Technology has changed the way that American farms operate.
- Many small family farms have closed because they are unprofitable.
- Many Midwestern cities got their start as places that processed and shipped farm products.

Section 4: The West
- The West has a wide array of natural resources.
- Managing these natural resources is an important task for people in the West.
- People are some of the urban West's most valuable resources.

Haymarket in Boston, Massachusetts

◆ Key Terms

Use each key term below in a sentence that shows the meaning of the term.

1. commute
2. megalopolis
3. population density
4. petrochemical
5. industrialization
6. Sun Belt
7. mixed-crop farm

8. recession
9. corporate farm
10. forty-niner
11. mass transit

┌ Vocabulary Builder ─────────

Revisit this chapter's high-use words:

hub	decade	ethnic
institution	technique	pollution
innumerable	prosper	site
consume	efficiently	junction

Ask students to review the definitions they recorded on their *Word Knowledge* worksheet.

All in One **United States and Canada Teaching Resources,** *Word Knowledge*, p. 254

Consider allowing students to earn extra credit if they use the words in their answers to the questions in the Chapter Review and Assessment. The words must be used correctly and in a natural context to win the extra points.

Answers
Key Terms
1–11. Students' sentences should reflect knowledge of each Key Term.

Comprehension and Critical Thinking

12. (a) New York, Boston, and Philadelphia
(b) Answers will vary depending on cities selected. Possible answer: Boston and Philadelphia are both historic cities. Boston is known for its colleges and universities. It is a medical, science, and technology center while Philadelphia is an industrial center and a transportation center.

13. (a) New York City **(b)** Possible answer: It is the largest, wealthiest, and most influential city in the country.

14. (a) warm climate, plenty of rain, good soil, and wide plains along coast **(b)** cotton **(c)** Farmers might have continued to plant only cotton instead of a variety of crops.

15. (a) They make a living in mining, forestry, fishing, textiles, aerospace, technology, cable television, transportation, and tourism. **(b)** Georgia is one of the states in which the textile industry is the strongest.

16. (a) Demand for farm products decreased while interest rates for loans increased, leaving farmers unable to pay their loans and forcing them to leave or sell their farms. **(b)** Mixed-crop farms are run by small families and produce a small amount of crops, while corporate farms rely on machines and computers to do the work and produce larger amounts of crops.

17. (a) minerals, timber, and water **(b)** for mining, building homes, irrigating lands, and bringing water to cities **(c)** Today, people are trying to manage the use of resources to preserve them.

Skills Practice
Students' conclusions will vary.

Writing Activity: Science
Students' reports will vary, but should include mention of computers and large farm machines. Use *Rubric for Assessing a Newspaper Article* to evaluate students' reports. Tell students how many sources you would like them to use, if any, beyond the textbook.

All in One United States and Canada Teaching Resources, *Rubric for Assessing a Newspaper Article,* p. 274

◆ Comprehension and Critical Thinking

12. (a) List What are some of the large cities in the Northeast?
(b) Compare and Contrast Choose two of the Northeast's cities. How are they similar? How have they developed differently?

13. (a) Locate Which city in the Northeast was attacked by terrorists in 2001?
(b) Draw Conclusions Why might terrorists have targeted that city in particular?

14. (a) Explain What features make the South a good place for farming?
(b) Identify What was the South's most important crop until the 1900s?
(c) Predict How might farming in the South have been different without the boll weevil?

15. (a) Recall How do people in the South make a living other than by farming?
(b) Draw Conclusions How is Georgia important to the textile industry?

16. (a) Summarize How did the recession in the 1980s affect farmers?
(b) Compare and Contrast How are mixed-crop farming and corporate farming different?

17. (a) Name What are the main natural resources of the West?
(b) Summarize How have people used these natural resources?
(c) Compare and Contrast How has the way people manage natural resources in the West changed since the 1800s?

◆ Skills Practice

Understanding Circle Graphs In the Skills for Life activity in this chapter, you learned that information can be given in the form of circle graphs.

Review the steps you followed to learn this skill. Then reread the Regional Profile of the Midwest on page 265. Study the Midwest Economy circle graph on that page. Identify what percentage of the graph each part represents. Use the information in the circle graph to draw conclusions about the economy of the Midwest.

◆ Writing Activity: Science

Suppose that you are the science reporter for a newspaper covering the history of farming on the plains. Write a brief report about how advances in science and technology have contributed to successfully farming the land.

MAP MASTER™ Skills Activity

United States

Place Location Write the letter from the map that shows its location.
1. Boston
2. New York City
3. Washington, D.C.
4. Atlanta
5. Chicago
6. St. Louis
7. Portland
8. Los Angeles

Go Online
PHSchool.com Use Web Code **lhp-4444** for an interactive map.

278 United States and Canada

Standardized Test Prep

MAP★MASTER
Skills Activity

1. C   **2.** D
3. G   **4.** H
5. E   **6.** F
7. A   **8.** B

Test-Taking Tips

Some questions on standardized tests ask you to analyze graphs. Study the graph below. Then follow the tips to answer the sample question.

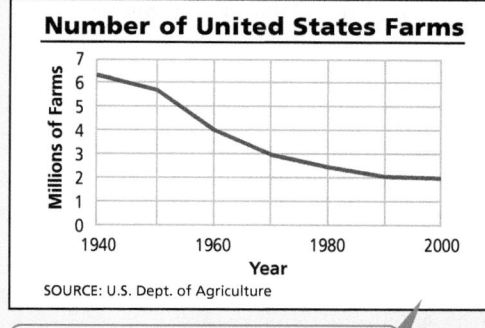

Number of United States Farms

SOURCE: U.S. Dept. of Agriculture

TIP When you study a graph, read the title to understand its subject. Then study information on the left side and bottom of the graph.

Based on this graph, it is clear that the

A size of farms has decreased since the 1940s.

B size of farms increased during the last half of the 1900s.

C number of farms steadily decreased during the last half of the 1900s.

D number of farms probably will increase during the first twenty years of the present century.

TIP Restate the question to make sure you understand what it is asking. "Based on the graph, what conclusion can you draw about United States farms?"

Think It Through Read the title of the graph. You can eliminate A and B because they are about the *size* of American farms. What does the graph show about the *number* of farms? The number line goes down after 1940, but there is no indication that the number of farms will increase in the 2000s. The correct answer is C.

Go Online
PHSchool.com Students may practice their map skills using the interactive online version of this map.

Standardized Test Prep

Answers

1. C

2. A

3. D

4. A

Go Online
PHSchool.com Students may use the Chapter 9 self-test on PHSchool.com to prepare for the Chapter Test.

Practice Questions

Use the tips above and other tips in this book to help you answer the following questions.

1. The most densely populated region of the United States is the

  A South.   **B** Midwest.

  C Northeast.   **D** West.

2. What caused San Francisco to grow into a large city?

  A the Gold Rush

  B hydroelectricity

  C the logging industry

  D Lewis and Clark's expedition

3. The Midwest's largest city is

  A Detroit, Michigan.   **B** St. Louis, Missouri.

  C Minneapolis, Minnesota.   **D** Chicago, Illinois.

Study the graph below, and then answer the question that follows.

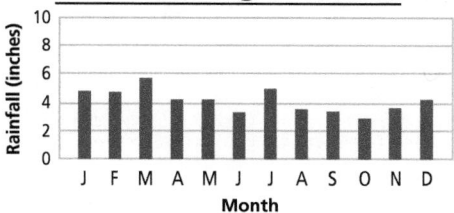

Atlanta, Georgia: Rainfall

SOURCE: *The World Almanac, 2001*

4. In which month is the average temperature highest in Atlanta? How much rain falls in that month?

  A March; 5.5 inches   **B** May; 6 inches

  C July; 6 inches   **D** September; 3 inches

Go Online
PHSchool.com

Use Web Code **lha-4404** for a **Chapter 9 self-test**

Chapter 9 **279**

Assessment Resources

Use *Chapter Tests A and B* to assess students' mastery of chapter content.

All in One **United States and Canada Teaching Resources,** *Chapter Tests A and B,* pp. 275–280

Tests are also available on the **ExamView®** **Test Bank CD-ROM.**

◉ **Exam*View*® Test Bank CD-ROM**

Objectives

- Learn how the town of Parmele changed over three generations.

- Identify elements that the memoirs of the three generations have in common.

- Determine the authors' purposes and points of view.

Prepare to Read

Build Background Knowledge [L2]

Discuss the concept of family history with students. Ask them how much they know about the lives of their grandparents and their parents' childhoods. Encourage students to think about how someone could find information to write a family history. Use an Idea Wave (TE, p. T35) to help students generate ideas.

Instruct

Childtimes [L2]

Guided Instruction

- Point out that some potentially unfamiliar words are defined for students in the margin. Clarify the meanings of these words before reading.

- Chunk each memoir into sections and have students use the Structured Silent Reading strategy (TE, p. T34) to read the passages. Point out that this selection includes the memories of three women representing three generations of a family.

- Have students describe Pattie's point of view. *(Pattie is writing about events that happened when she was very young. Her frame of reference is that of a black woman living in a growing southern town in the late 1800s. She mentions that she was too young to know what was going on at the time, but was told that the town developed quickly. Students should realize that her point of view was heavily influenced by those around her. For example, she seemed excited about the prospects of new jobs for people in town.)*

Answer

✔ Reading Check It was named after New Yorker Mr. Parmele who started a lumber company there.

From **Childtimes**

By Eloise Greenfield and Lessie Jones Little, with material by Pattie Ridley Jones

Prepare to Read

Background Information

How much do people know about the lives of their grandparents or their parents as children? Suppose someone wanted to write a history of his or her family. How could he or she find information?

You can learn a great deal from seeing how a single family lives through several generations. Every family history reflects the history of the place where that family lives. The following excerpts come from a memoir, or a story of personal experience, written by a mother, a daughter, and a grandmother. The book tells the story of their family, as well as the growth of their hometown, Parmele, North Carolina.

Objectives

In this section you will

1. Learn how and why the town of Parmele changed over three generations.

2. Identify elements that the memoirs of the three generations have in common.

About the Selection

Childtimes: A Three-Generation Memoir was published in 1979 by Thomas Y. Crowell.

✔ Reading Check

How did the town of Parmele get its name?

Pattie Frances Ridley Jones—born in Bertie County, North Carolina, December 15, 1884

Parmele, North Carolina

Towns build up around work, you know. People go and live where they can find jobs. And that's how Parmele got started.

At first, it was just a junction, a place where two railroads crossed. Two Atlantic Coast Line railroads, one running between Rocky Mount and Plymouth, and one running between Kinston and Weldon. Didn't too many people live around there then, and those that did were pretty much spread out.

Well, around 1888, a Yankee named Mr. Parmele came down from New York and looked the place over, and he saw all those big trees and decided to start a lumber company. Everybody knew what that meant. There were going to be jobs! People came from everywhere to get work. I was right little at that time, too little to know what was going on, but everybody says it was something to see how fast that town grew. All those people moving in and houses going up. They named the town after the man who made the jobs, and they called it *Pomma-lee*.

The lumber company hired a whole lot of people. They hired workers to lay track for those little railroads they call tram roads that they were going to run back and forth between the town and the woods. They hired lumberjacks to chop the trees down and cut them up into logs, and load them on the tram cars. They hired

Read Fluently

Form the class into partners. Choose a paragraph from the selection. Have students take turns reading the paragraph aloud. Ask them to underline words that give them trouble as they read. Then, have them decode the problem words with their partner. Provide assistance as needed. Have students reread the paragraph two more times to improve their reading speed. Remind them to stop at the commas and periods and to read with expression.

men to build the mill and put the machinery in, and millworkers to run the machines that would cut the logs into different sizes and dry them and make them nice and smooth. . . .

Lessie Blanche Jones Little—born in Parmele, North Carolina, October 1, 1906

Parmele

I used to hear Papa and Mama and their friends talking about the lumber mill that had been the center of life in Parmele before I was born, but there wasn't any mill when I was growing up. The only thing left of it was the sawdust from all the wood they had sawed there. The sawdust was about a foot thick on the land where the mill had been. I used to love to walk on it. It was spongy, and it made me feel like I was made of rubber. I'd take my shoes off and kind of bounce along on top of it. But that was all that was left of the mill.

My Parmele was a train town. The life of my town moved around the trains that came in and out all day long. About three hundred people lived in Parmele, most of them black. There were three black churches, a Baptist, a Methodist, and a Holiness, and one white church. Two black schools, one white. There wasn't even one doctor, and not many people would have had the money to pay one, if there had been. If somebody got down real bad sick, a member of the family would go by horse and buggy to a nearby town and bring the doctor back, or sometimes the doctor would ride on his own horse.

Most of the men and women in Parmele earned their living by farming. Some did other things like working at the tobacco factory in Robersonville, but most worked on the farms that were all around in the area, white people's farms usually. When I was a little girl, they earned fifty cents a day, a farm day, sunup to sundown, plus meals. After they got home, they had all their own work to do, cooking and cleaning, laundry, chopping wood for the woodstove, and shopping. . . .

A steam engine pulls a train through the countryside.

- Have students compare the entries by Lessie and Eloise. Ask them to identify the similarities in their memoirs. *(Both discuss how people in the town and people in their families made a living; both talk about the part the train station played in their lives; both include stories that hint at the state of the economy of the town at the time.)*

Independent Practice

Have students work with partners to brainstorm a list of questions about family life in Parmele that they would like to ask the authors of these memoirs.

Monitor Progress

Circulate to make sure students are communicating effectively while brainstorming. Make sure individuals understand the assignment as it relates to the literature selection. . . .

Pamlico Sound (PAM lih koh sownd) *n.* a long body of water off the coast of North Carolina that separates the Hatteras Islands from the mainland

✓ Reading Check

What kind of work did Eloise's father do before he went to Washington, D.C.?

Sharecroppers in the South

282 United States and Canada

Parmele had trains coming in and going out all day long. Passenger trains and freight trains. There was always so much going on at the station that I wouldn't know what to watch. People were changing trains and going in and out of the cafe and the restaurant. They came from big cities like New York and Chicago and Boston, and they were all wearing the latest styles. Things were being unloaded, like furniture and trunks and plows and cases of fruit and crates of clucking chickens, or a puppy, or the body of somebody who had died and was being brought back home. And every year around the last two weeks in May, a special train would come through. It had two white flags flying on the locomotive, and it was carrying one hundred carloads of white potatoes that had been grown down near <u>Pamlico Sound</u>, where everybody said the soil was so rich they didn't even have to fertilize it.

The train station was a gathering place, too. A lot of people went there to relax after they had finished their work for the day. They'd come downtown to pick up their mail, or buy a newspaper, and then they'd just stand around laughing and talking to their friends. And on Sundays fellas and their girls would come all the way from other towns, just to spend the afternoon at the Parmele train station. . . .

It was hard for Papa to find work. Not long after Sis Clara died, we moved to Mount Herman, a black section of Portsmouth, Virginia. Papa worked on the docks there, and even though he didn't make much money, the work was steady. But when we moved back to Parmele, it was hard for him to find any work at all. . . .

Eloise Glynn Little Greenfield—born in Parmele, North Carolina, May 17, 1929

Daddy Makes a Way

When I was three months old, Daddy left home to make a way for us. He went North, as thousands of black people had done, during slavery and since. They went North looking for safety, for justice, for freedom, for work, looking for a good life. Often one member of a family would go ahead of the others to make a way—to find a job and a place to live. And that's what my father did.

In the spring of 1926, Daddy had graduated from high school, Parmele Training School. He had been offered a scholarship by Knoxville College in Tennessee, but he hadn't taken it. He and Mama had gotten married that fall, and now they had Wilbur and me to take care of. Mama had been teaching school since her graduation from Higgs, but she had decided to stop.

Answer

✓ Reading Check   He did farm work harvesting potatoes and working in tobacco fields, packed and loaded at a tobacco warehouse, and moved houses.

Nineteen twenty-nine was a bad time for Daddy to go away, but a worse time for him not to go. The <u>Great Depression</u> was about to begin, had already begun for many people. All over the United States, thousands of people were already jobless and homeless.

In Parmele, there were few permanent jobs. Some seasons of the year, Daddy could get farm work, harvesting potatoes and working in the tobacco fields. Every year, from August to around Thanksgiving, he worked ten hours a day for twenty-five cents an hour at a tobacco warehouse in a nearby town, packing tobacco in huge barrels and loading them on the train for shipping. And he and his father were house movers. Whenever somebody wanted a house moved from one place to another, Daddy and Pa would jack it up and attach it to a windlass, the machine that the horse would turn to move the house. But it was only once in a while that they were called on to do that.

So, one morning in August 1929, Mama went with Daddy to the train station and tried to hold back her tears as the Atlantic Coast Line train pulled out, taking him toward Washington, D.C. Then she went home, sat in the porch swing, and cried.

In Washington, friends helped Daddy find a room for himself and his family to live in, and took him job hunting. He found a job as a dishwasher in a restaurant, and in a few weeks, he had saved enough money for our train fare.

Great Depression (grayt dee PRESH un) *n.* an economic collapse that began in 1929 and lasted throughout the 1930s, causing many people to lose their jobs

Review and Assessment

Thinking About the Selection

1. (a) Recall Why was the town located where it was? What caused the town to first begin to grow?
(b) Identify Why did building a sawmill attract more people to Parmele? How did they earn a living after the mill closed?
(c) Evaluate How did the life of a young person in Parmele compare with your own?
2. (a) Respond What do these memoirs tell you about how hard life in Parmele was at different time periods?

(b) Infer What aspect of their parents' lives most shaped the lives of these women when they were young girls?
(c) Compare and Contrast What do the three narrators have in common? How are they different?

Writing Activity

Write a Memoir Write a memoir of your own childhood. Use the point of view of yourself as an older person. Talk about the forces that have most shaped your life.

About the Author

Eloise Greenfield (b. 1929) was born in Parmele, North Carolina. She has received dozens of awards and honors for her more than thirty books of poetry, biography, and fiction. Greenfield's fiction often depicts strong, loving African American families and contains positive messages for all of her readers. She currently lives in Washington, D.C.

Literature **283**

Writing Activity

Use *Rubric for Assessing a Writing Assignment* to evaluate students' memoirs.

All in One United States and Canada Teaching Resources, *Rubric for Assessing a Writing Assignment,* p. 273

Assess Progress L2
Have students answer the assessment questions.

Reteach L1
Have students work in pairs to make a simple chart with the name of each writer in the selection as the column headings. Under each name students should list the main ideas the writer has presented in her part of the memoir. *(Pattie Frances Ridley Jones: how the town got its name and the start of the lumber company; Lessie Blanche Jones Little: the town as a train center and the life in a small town that was mostly black; Eloise Glynn Little Greenfield: how the town was affected by the Depression, her father's struggles to find work)*

Extend L3
Have students read *Personal Experience of Maria Antonia Pico,* a memoir from a woman who lived in another part of the United States in the 1800s. Have them answer the questions at the end of the selection. In addition, ask them to describe Pico's point of view.

All in One United States and Canada Teaching Resources, *Personal Experience of Maria Antonia Pico,* pp. 268–269

Review and Assessment

Thinking About the Selection

1. (a) It was located at the junction of two railroads where goods could easily be shipped to and from the town. It grew because of the lumber company that Mr. Parmele began. **(b)** It created more jobs. After it closed, people made a living mostly by farming. **(c)** Answers will vary, but students should mention the similarities and differences in jobs and size of community.

2. (a) People were happy just to get any kind of job, which shows how difficult it was to make a living in Parmele. Lessie suggests that people were so poor they could not even pay for a doctor if the town had one. **(b)** The issue of finding work to earn a living seemed to shape the girls' lives. **(c)** Possible answers: They all tell about the same place and the struggles to find work. Pattie's memoir recollects more positive things about work than the other memoirs because of the lumber company. Both Lessie and Eloise recall the difficulty their fathers had finding work.

Chapter Overview

Overview

Introducing Canada
1. Learn about the provinces and territories of Canada.
2. Analyze data to compare the provinces and territories of Canada.
3. Identify characteristics that most provinces and territories share.
4. Explain key differences among the provinces and territories.

Section 1

Ontario and Quebec: Bridging Two Cultures
1. Read about the seat of the Canadian government in Ontario.
2. Learn about the French cultural influence in Quebec.

Section 2

The Prairie Provinces: Canada's Breadbasket
1. Learn why many immigrants came to the Prairie Provinces in the 1800s.
2. Read about how Canadians celebrate their cultural traditions.

Section 3

British Columbia: Economic and Cultural Changes
1. Find out about the people and cultures of the Canadian West.
2. Learn what the economy and culture of British Columbia are like.

Section 4

The Atlantic Provinces: Relying on the Sea
1. Learn what life is like on the Atlantic coast.
2. Discover how maritime industries affect the provinces.

Section 5

The Northern Territories: New Frontiers
1. Discover what life is like for people in Canada's far north.
2. Find out about the remote region of the Yukon Territory.
3. Understand how the new territory of Nunavut was formed.

Technology Resources

Go Online
PHSchool.com

Students use embedded Web codes to access Internet activities, chapter self-tests, and additional map practice. They may also access Dorling Kindersley's Online Desk Reference to learn more about each country they study.

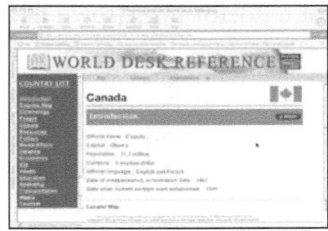

Interactive Textbook

Use the Interactive Textbook to make content and concepts come alive through animations, videos, and activities that accompany the complete basal text—online and on CD-ROM.

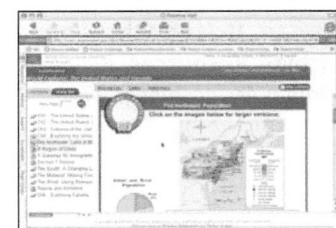

PRENTICE HALL
TeacherEXPRESS
Plan • Teach • Assess

Use this complete suite of powerful teaching tools to make planning lessons and administering tests quicker and easier.

Reading and Vocabulary Instruction

⟳ Model the Target Reading Skill

Context The context of a word is the surrounding words, phrases, and sentences that help reveal its meaning. Unless a definition is given, a reader must interpret a word's meaning by using context clues. Write the passage below, from page 290 of the Student Edition, on the board. Model using context clues to reveal the meaning of the word in quotation marks.

Canada's capital, Ottawa, is located in Ontario. But government functions spill over into the city of Hull, Quebec, located on the other end of the Macdonald-Cartier Bridge. Hull is considered Ottawa's "sister city" because a number of federal government office buildings dot its landscape.

Ask yourself aloud: What clues explain what it means for Hull to be Ottawa's *sister city? (The word* because *is a clue that a definition or explanation follows. The explanation says that Hull has government buildings, where some government functions from Ottawa are performed. So the two cities have something in common— they both have government buildings. Another thing they have in common is the bridge that connects them. They must be "sister cities" because they have enough in common to make them seem related.)* Have students choose another paragraph that contains an unfamiliar word and use context clues to decipher its meaning.

Use the following worksheets from All-in-One United States and Canada Teaching Resources (pp. 305–308) to support this chapter's Target Reading Skill.

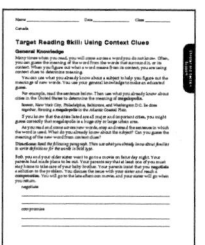 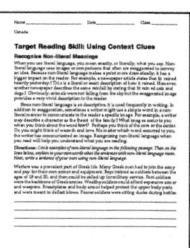 

Vocabulary Builder
High-Use Academic Words

Use these steps to teach this chapter's high-use words:

1. Have students rate how well they know each word on their Word Knowledge worksheets (All-in-One United States and Canada Teaching Resources, p. 309).
2. Pronounce each word and ask students to repeat it.
3. Give students a brief definition and sample sentence (provided on TE pp. 291, 299, 305, 312, and 319).
4. Work with students as they fill in the "Definition or Example" column of their Word Knowledge worksheets.

Assessment

Formal Assessment

Test students' understanding of core knowledge and skills.

Chapter Tests A and B, and Final Exams A and B
All-in-One United States and
Canada Teaching Resources,
pp. 329–334, 339–344

Customize the Chapter
Tests to suit your needs.
Exam*View*® **Test Bank CD-ROM**

Skills Assessment

Assess geographic literacy.

MapMaster Skills, Student Edition, pp. 285, 309, 314, 324

Regional Profile Map and Chart Skills, Student Edition, pp. 292, 296, 300, 306, 313, 320

Assess reading and comprehension.

Target Reading Skills, Student Edition, pp. 295, 302, 307, 314, 319, and in Section Assessments

Chapter 10 Assessment, Western Hemisphere Reading and Vocabulary Study Guide, p. 120

Performance Assessment

Assess students' performance using the following rubrics from All-in-One United States and Canada Teaching Resources.

Rubric for Assessing a Student Poster, p. 325

Rubric for Assessing a Performance on a Project, p. 328

Assess students' work through performance tasks.

Small Group Activity: Writing a Newspaper Feature, All-in-One United States and Canada Teaching Resources, pp. 312–315

Portfolio Suggestions, Teacher's Edition, p. 151

Online Assessment

Have students check their own understanding.

Chapter Self-Test

Test Preparation

United States and Canada Practice Tests A, B, and C, Test Prep Workbook, pp. 85–96

United States and Canada Benchmark Test 2 and Outcome Test, AYP Monitoring Assessments, pp. 93–96, 176–181

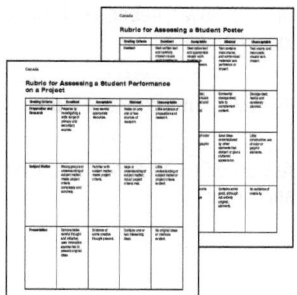

Section 1 Ontario and Quebec: Bridging Two Cultures

 2 periods, 1.25 blocks (includes Country Databank)

Social Studies Objectives
1. Read about the seat of the Canadian government in Ontario.
2. Learn about the French cultural influence in Quebec.

Reading/Language Arts Objective
Use context clues to determine the meaning of unfamiliar words.

Prepare to Read	**Instructional Resources**	**Differentiated Instruction**
Build Background Knowledge Discuss the different cultures of Ontario and Quebec. **Set a Purpose for Reading** Have students evaluate statements on the *Reading Readiness Guide.* **Preview Key Terms** Teach the section's Key Terms. **Target Reading Skill** Introduce the section's Target Reading Skill of **using context clues.**	**All in One United States and Canada Teaching Resources** L2 Reading Readiness Guide, p. 286 L2 Use Context Clues: General Knowledge, p. 305	**Spanish Reading and Vocabulary Study Guide** L1 Chapter 10, Section 1, pp. 77–78 ELL

Instruct	**Instructional Resources**	**Differentiated Instruction**
Ontario Discuss the governments and major cities of Ontario. **Regional Profile** Ask students to derive information from maps, charts, and graphs. **French Culture in Quebec** Discuss how Quebec's culture reflects both French and local influence. **Target Reading Skill** Review **using context clues.** **Regional Profile** Ask students to derive information from maps, charts, and graphs.	**All in One United States and Canada Teaching Resources** L2 Guided Reading and Review, p. 287 L2 Reading Readiness Guide, p. 286 L2 Reading a Population Density Map, p. 316 **United States and Canada Transparencies** L2 Section Reading Support Transparency USC 58	**All in One United States and Canada Teaching Resources** Rubric for Assessing a Student Poster, p. 325 ELL, LPR, SN L2 Outline Map 12: Canada: Political, p. 319 AR, GT, LPR, SN L3 Preparing for Presentations, p. 323 AR, GT L3 Enrichment, p. 310 AR, GT L3 Shadows on the Rock, pp. 320–322 AR, GT **Teacher's Edition** L3 For Advanced Readers, TE pp. 287, 296 L3 For English Language Learners, TE p. 292 L1 For Special Needs Students, TE p. 293 L3 For Gifted and Talented, TE p. 293 L1 For Less Proficient Readers, TE pp. 287, 296 **Student Edition on Audio CD** L1 Chapter 5, Section 1 ELL, LPR, SN

Assess and Reteach	**Instructional Resources**	**Differentiated Instruction**
Assess Progress Evaluate student comprehension with the section assessment and section quiz. **Reteach** Assign the Reading and Vocabulary Study Guide to help struggling students. **Extend** Extend the lesson by assigning a Small Group Activity.	**All in One United States and Canada Teaching Resources** L2 Section Quiz, p. 288 L3 Small Group Activity: Writing a Newspaper Feature, pp. 312–315 Rubric for Assessing a Writing Assignment, p. 326 **Reading and Vocabulary Study Guide** L1 Chapter 10, Section 1, pp. 105–107	**Spanish Support** L2 Section Quiz (Spanish), p. 97 ELL

Key

L1 Basic to Average   L3 Average to Advanced   LPR Less Proficient Readers   GT Gifted and Talented

L2 For All Students   AR Advanced Readers   ELL English Language Learners

                                      SN Special Needs Students

Section 2 The Prairie Provinces: Canada's Breadbasket

 *1.5 periods, 0.75 block*

Social Studies Objectives

1. Learn why many immigrants came to the Prairie Provinces in the 1800s.
2. Read about how Canadians celebrate their cultural traditions.

Reading/Language Arts Objective

Practice interpreting the meaning of nonliteral language.

Prepare to Read	**Instructional Resources**	**Differentiated Instruction**
Build Background Knowledge Show students the video *Canada's Prairie Provinces* and then discuss the main points. **Set a Purpose for Reading** Have students evaluate statements on the *Reading Readiness Guide*. **Preview Key Terms** Teach the section's Key Terms. **Target Reading Skill** Introduce the section's Target Reading Skill of **interpreting nonliteral meanings**.	**All in One United States and Canada Teaching Resources** L2 Reading Readiness Guide, p. 290 L2 Recognize Nonliteral Meanings, p. 306	**Spanish Reading and Vocabulary Study Guide** L1 Chapter 10, Section 2, pp. 79–80 ELL

Instruct	**Instructional Resources**	**Differentiated Instruction**
The Prairie Provinces Discuss people of the Canadian Plains and how settlements developed there. **Regional Profile** Ask students to derive information from maps, charts, and graphs. **Celebrating Traditions** Discuss traditional celebrations of the Prairie Provinces. **Target Reading Skill** Review **interpreting nonliteral meanings**.	**All in One United States and Canada Teaching Resources** L2 Guided Reading and Review, p. 291 L2 Reading Readiness Guide, p. 290 **United States and Canada Transparencies** L2 Section Reading Support Transparency USC 59	**Teacher's Edition** L3 For Gifted and Talented, TE pp. 300, 302 L3 For Advanced Readers, TE p. 300 L1 For English Language Learners, TE p. 301 L1 For Special Needs Students, TE p. 301 L1 For Less Proficient Readers, TE p. 302 **Student Edition on Audio CD** L1 Chapter 10, Section 2 ELL, LPR, SN **Spanish Support** L2 Guided Reading and Review (Spanish), p. 98 ELL

Assess and Reteach	**Instructional Resources**	**Differentiated Instruction**
Assess Progress Evaluate student comprehension with the section assessment and section quiz. **Reteach** Assign the Reading and Vocabulary Study Guide to help struggling students. **Extend** Extend the lesson by having students research different traditions of the Prairie Provinces.	**All in One United States and Canada Teaching Resources** L2 Section Quiz, p. 292 Rubric for Assessing a Student Poster, p. 325 **Reading and Vocabulary Study Guide** L1 Chapter 10, Section 2, pp. 108–110	**Spanish Support** L2 Section Quiz (Spanish), p. 99 ELL

Key

L1 Basic to Average   L3 Average to Advanced
L2 For All Students

LPR Less Proficient Readers
AR Advanced Readers
SN Special Needs Students

GT Gifted and Talented
ELL English Language Learners

British Columbia: Economic and Cultural Changes
Section 3

 1.5 periods, .75 block

Social Studies Objectives
1. Find out about the people and cultures of the Canadian West.
2. Learn what the economy and culture of British Columbia are like.

Reading/Language Arts Objective
Use context clues to determine the meaning of unfamiliar words.

Prepare to Read	Instructional Resources	Differentiated Instruction
Build Background Knowledge Have students brainstorm ways that the east and west coasts of Canada may differ. **Set a Purpose for Reading** Have students evaluate statements on the *Reading Readiness Guide*. **Preview Key Terms** Teach the section's Key Terms. **Target Reading Skill** Introduce the section's Target Reading Skill of **using context clues**.	**All in One United States and Canada Teaching Resources** L2 Reading Readiness Guide, p. 294 L2 Use Context Clues: General Knowledge, p. 305	**Spanish Reading and Vocabulary Study Guide** L1 Chapter 10, Section 3, pp. 81–82 ELL

Instruct	Instructional Resources	Differentiated Instruction
The People of the Canadian West Discuss the impact of gold miners, fur traders, and railroads on the people of the Canadian West. **Regional Profile** Ask students to derive information from maps, charts, and graphs. **Target Reading Skill** Review **using context clues**. **Economics and Culture** Ask questions about and discuss the economy and culture of British Columbia.	**All in One United States and Canada Teaching Resources** L2 Guided Reading and Review, p. 295 L2 Reading Readiness Guide, p. 294 L2 Analyzing Statistics, p. 317 **United States and Canada Transparencies** L2 Section Reading Support Transparency USC 60	**Teacher's Edition** L3 For Advanced Readers, TE p. 306 L1 For Less Proficient Readers, TE p. 307 L2 For English Language Learners, TE p. 307 L1 For Special Needs Students, TE p. 309 L3 For Gifted and Talented, TE p. 309 **PHSchool.com** L3 **For:** Environmental and Global Issues: Trade in a Global Economy **Web Code:** lhd-4506 AR, GT **Spanish Support** L2 Guided Reading and Review (Spanish), p. 100 ELL

Assess and Reteach	Instructional Resources	Differentiated Instruction
Assess Progress Evaluate student comprehension with the section assessment and section quiz. **Reteach** Assign the Reading and Vocabulary Study Guide to help struggling students. **Extend** Extend the lesson by having students write a newspaper editorial about the impact of gold miners on the Canadian West.	**All in One United States and Canada Teaching Resources** L2 Section Quiz, p. 296 Rubric for Assessing a Journal Entry, p. 327 **Reading and Vocabulary Study Guide** L1 Chapter 10, Section 3, pp. 111–113	**Spanish Support** L2 Section Quiz (Spanish), p. 101 ELL

Key
L1 Basic to Average L3 Average to Advanced
L2 For All Students

LPR Less Proficient Readers
AR Advanced Readers
SN Special Needs Students

GT Gifted and Talented
ELL English Language Learners

Section 4 The Atlantic Provinces: Relying on the Sea

 3 periods, 1.5 blocks (includes Skills for Life)

Social Studies Objectives
1. Learn what life is like on the Atlantic coast.
2. Discover how maritime industries affect the provinces.

Reading/Language Arts Objective
Learn how cause-and-effect clues can help you understand the meaning of an unfamiliar word.

Prepare to Read

Build Background Knowledge
Have students study the location of the Atlantic Provinces using a transparency.

Set a Purpose for Reading
Have students begin to fill out the *Reading Readiness Guide*.

Preview Key Terms
Teach the section's Key Terms.

Target Reading Skill
Introduce the section's Target Reading Skill of **using context clues**.

Instructional Resources

All in One United States and Canada Teaching Resources
- L2 Reading Readiness Guide, p. 298
- L2 Use Context Clues: Cause and Effect, p. 307

United States and Canada Transparencies
- L2 Color Transparency USC 40: Canada: Physical-Political

Differentiated Instruction

Spanish Reading and Vocabulary Study Guide
- L1 Chapter 10, Section 4, pp. 83–84 ELL

Instruct

Living on the Coast
Discuss the effects of location on the lives of the people living in the Atlantic Provinces.

Target Reading Skill
Review **using context clues**.

Regional Profile
Ask students to derive information from maps, charts, and graphs.

A Maritime Economy
Discuss the fishing industry in Canada.

Instructional Resources

All in One United States and Canada Teaching Resources
- L2 Guided Reading and Review, p. 299
- L2 Reading Readiness Guide, p. 298
- L2 Reading a Line Graph, p. 318

United States and Canada Transparencies
- L2 Section Reading Support Transparency USC 61

Differentiated Instruction

All in One United States and Canada Teaching Resources
- L2 Skills for Life, p. 311 AR, GT, LPR, SN

Teacher's Edition
- L1 For Less Proficient Readers, TE p. 313
- L1 For English Language Learners, TE p. 314
- L1 For Special Needs Students, TE p. 314

Spanish Support
- L2 Guided Reading and Review (Spanish), p. 102 ELL

Assess and Reteach

Assess Progress
Evaluate student comprehension with the section assessment and section quiz.

Reteach
Assign the Reading and Vocabulary Study Guide to help struggling students.

Extend
Extend the lesson by having students debate the ban on cod fishing.

Instructional Resources

All in One United States and Canada Teaching Resources
- L2 Section Quiz, p. 300
  Rubric for Assessing a Writing Assignment, p. 326

Reading and Vocabulary Study Guide
- L1 Chapter 10, Section 4, pp. 114–116

Differentiated Instruction

Teacher's Edition
- L3 For Advanced Readers, TE p. 317

Spanish Support
- L2 Section Quiz (Spanish), p. 103 ELL

Key
- L1 Basic to Average
- L2 For All Students
- L3 Average to Advanced
- LPR Less Proficient Readers
- AR Advanced Readers
- SN Special Needs Students
- GT Gifted and Talented
- ELL English Language Learners

Section 5 **The Northern Territories: New Frontiers**

3.5 periods, 1.75 blocks (includes Chapter Review and Assessment)

Social Studies Objectives

1. Discover what life is like for people in Canada's far north.
2. Find out about the remote region of the Yukon Territory.
3. Understand how the new territory of Nunavut was formed.

Reading/Language Arts Objective

Use context clues to determine the meaning of a familiar word when used in an unfamiliar way.

Prepare to Read	Instructional Resources	Differentiated Instruction
Build Background Knowledge Have students contrast the Northern Territories with Canada's other regions. **Set a Purpose for Reading** Have students evaluate statements on the *Reading Readiness Guide*. **Preview Key Terms** Teach the section's Key Terms. **Target Reading Skill** Introduce the section's Target Reading Skill of **using context clues**.	**All in One United States and Canada Teaching Resources** L2 Reading Readiness Guide, p. 302 L2 Use Context Clues: Definition/Description, p. 308	**Spanish Reading and Vocabulary Study Guide** L1 Chapter 10, Section 5, pp. 85–86 ELL

Instruct	Instructional Resources	Differentiated Instruction
The Far North Ask how the population of the Northern Territories is affected by their geography. **Target Reading Skill** Review **using context clues**. **Regional Profile** Ask students to derive information from maps, charts, and graphs. **Forming New Territories** Ask questions about the Yukon Territory and Nunavut.	**All in One United States and Canada Teaching Resources** L2 Guided Reading and Review, p. 303 L2 Reading Readiness Guide, p. 302 **United States and Canada Transparencies** L2 Section Reading Support Transparency USC 62	**Teacher's Edition** L1 For Less Proficient Readers, TE p. 320 **Spanish Support** L2 Guided Reading and Review (Spanish), p. 104 ELL

Assess and Reteach	Instructional Resources	Differentiated Instruction
Assess Progress Evaluate student comprehension with the section assessment and section quiz. **Reteach** Assign the Reading and Vocabulary Study Guide to help struggling students. **Extend** Extend the lesson by assigning a Long-Term Integrated Project.	**All in One United States and Canada Teaching Resources** L2 Section Quiz, p. 304 L2 Vocabulary Development, p. 324 Rubric for Assessing a Writing Assignment, p. 326 L2 Word Knowledge, p. 309 Rubric for Assessing Performance on a Project, p. 328 L2 Chapter Tests A and B, pp. 329–334 L2 Final Exams A and B, pp. 339–344 **Reading and Vocabulary Study Guide** L1 Chapter 10, Section 5, pp. 117–119	**Spanish Support** L2 Section Quiz (Spanish), p. 105 ELL L2 Chapter Summary (Spanish), p. 106 ELL L2 Vocabulary Development (Spanish), p. 107 ELL **PHSchool.com** L3 **For:** Long-Term Integrated Project: *Holding Community Meetings Under Different Forms of Government* **Web Code:** lhd-4507

Key

L1 Basic to Average   L3 Average to Advanced
L2 For All Students

LPR Less Proficient Readers
AR Advanced Readers
SN Special Needs Students

GT Gifted and Talented
ELL English Language Learners

Reading Background

Seed Discussions

Give students the opportunity to lead their own discussions about what they are reading in the chapter. Tell students that in order to lead a discussion, they will need a strong "seed" to start with.

Model a strong seed versus a weak seed. A strong seed might be an opinion, such as: "I believe that Quebec should (or should not) be independent from the rest of Canada." A weak seed might be a restatement of fact, such as: "Francophones make up about 80 percent of the population of Montreal and its surrounding areas."

Have the class list ideas for strong seeds, such as questions or opinions about what they have learned, or things in the chapter that surprised them. Once students are comfortable with the concept, have each student write a seed on a sheet of paper. Then have students form small groups. In each group, each person should take a turn leading a discussion from the seed he or she has written. Divide time equally so every person gets an equal opportunity as leader.

Author's Craft

The way an author presents information is as important as the information presented. Explain that as students read, they should ask themselves how the material is organized. This will clarify any uncertainty about what students are reading, as well as help them remember it. As an example, present the following selection from page 321:

After gold was discovered in a branch of the Klondike River in 1896, thousands of prospectors swarmed to the area. Within two years, the population of the town of Dawson swelled to about 30,000.

Guide students toward recognizing a framework for these sentences by asking questions. Did the author use dates or present a chronological sequence? Is the author comparing one thing to another? Can you see a cause and effect relationship? Students should recognize that the author organized these sentences chronologically. A cause and effect relationship is also represented; the population grew because many prospectors came to the area.

Have students work individually or in pairs as they reread sections of the chapter. As they read, have them jot down different techniques the author used by asking the same kinds of questions themselves. When students have finished taking notes, have the class discuss what techniques they have found.

World Studies Background

Canada's Ties to Britain

When Britain passed the British North America Act in 1867, the Canadian provinces, which were still British colonies, became unified into a dominion of Canada. The British Parliament continued to hold authority over Canada, however. The Act served as the dominion's constitution until Britain's Queen Elizabeth II proclaimed the Constitution Act of 1982. At that time, Canada formally became a sovereign nation and Britain no longer ruled it.

The Pacific Rim

The Pacific Rim is the name for the islands and countries that lie in and encircle the Pacific Ocean. Canada, the United States, Mexico, Japan, China, and South Korea, among others, are Pacific Rim countries. The cities of Los Angeles, Vancouver, Hong Kong, and Tokyo are all world economic leaders that are part of the Pacific Rim. In 1989, 21 Pacific Rim countries formed the Asia-Pacific Economic Cooperation to solidify their economic ties.

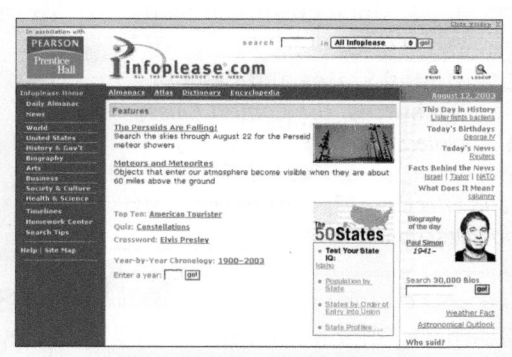

Infoplease® provides a wealth of useful information for the classroom. You can use this resource to strengthen your background on the subjects covered in this chapter. Have students visit this advertising-free site as a starting point for projects requiring research.

 Use Web code lhd-4500 for **Infoplease®**.

Guiding Questions

Remind students about the Guiding Questions at the beginning of this section.

Section 1 relates to Guiding Question ④ **How do the governments of the United States and Canada differ? How are they alike?** (*Canada has a monarch and a prime minister; both elect representatives*)

Section 2 relates to Guiding Question ② **How have historical events affected the cultures of the United States and Canada?** (*In the late 1870s, people of European descent began moving onto the Canadian prairie.*)

Section 3 relates to Guiding Question ⑤ **How did the United States and Canada become two of the wealthiest nations in the world?** (*British Columbia exports resources.*)

Section 4 relates to Guiding Question ① **How has physical geography affected the cultures of the United States and Canada?** (*Much of the Atlantic Provinces' economy depends on fishing and shipbuilding.*)

Section 5 relates to Guiding Question ③ **How has the variety of people in the United States and Canada benefited and challenged the two nations?** (*The northern territories have a variety of cultures and ethic groups.*)

⟳ Target Reading Skill

In this chapter, students will learn the skill of using context. Use the following to help students practice this skill:

All In One United States and Canada Teaching Resources, *Use Context Clues: General Knowledge, p. 305; Recognize Nonliteral Meanings, p. 306; Use Context Clues: Cause and Effect, p. 307; Use Context Clues: Definition/Description, p. 308*

Differentiated Instruction

These Teacher's Edition strategies are suitable for students of varying abilities.

Advanced Readers, pp. 287, 296, 300, 306, 317

English Language Learners, pp. 292, 301, 307, 314

Gifted and Talented, pp. 293, 300, 302, 309

Less Proficient Readers, pp. 287, 296, 302, 307, 313, 320

Special Needs Students, pp. 293, 301, 309, 314

Chapter 10 Canada

Chapter Preview

This chapter will introduce you to the provinces and territories of Canada.

Country Databank
The Country Databank provides data of each of the provinces and territories in Canada.

Section 1
Ontario and Quebec
Bridging Two Cultures

Section 2
The Prairie Provinces
Canada's Breadbasket

Section 3
British Columbia
Economic and Cultural Changes

Section 4
The Atlantic Provinces
Relying on the Sea

Section 5
The Northern Territories
New Frontiers

 Target Reading Skill

Context In this chapter, you will focus on using context to help you understand unfamiliar words. Context includes the words, phrases, and sentences surrounding the word.

▶ Lighthouse in Peggy's Cove, Nova Scotia, Canada

Bibliography

For the Teacher
Dickason, Olive Patricia. *Canada's First Nations: A History of Founding Peoples from Earliest Times.* Oxford University Press, 2001.

Molyneaux, Geoffrey. *British Columbia: An Illustrated History.* Raincoast Books, 2003.

Moogk, Peter. *La Nouvelle France: The Making of French Canada: A Cultural History.* Michigan State University Press, 2000.

For the Student
L1 Hancock, Lyn. *Nunavut.* Fitzhenry & Whiteside Ltd, 2003.

L2 Moore, Christopher. *The Big Book of Canada: Exploring the Provinces and Territories.* Tundra Books, 2002.

L3 Prophet, Elizabeth Clare. *Beginnings: Stories of Canada's Past.* Ronsdale Press, 2001.

Canada: Political

KEY
— National border
— Provincial or territorial border
⊛ National capital
★ Provincial or territorial capital
• Other city

0 miles 1,000
0 kilometers 1,000
Lambert Azimuthal Equal Area

Regions Canada is politically divided into ten provinces and three territories. **Locate** Describe the relative locations of Quebec, Saskatchewan, and British Columbia. **Draw Conclusions** Which of the three provinces do you think Europeans settled first? Explain your answer.

Go Online
PHSchool.com Use Web Code
lhp-4511 for step-by-step
map skills practice.

Chapter 10 **285**

Have students study the map, paying close attention to the title and the map key. Then have them list each province and territory on a separate sheet of paper. Have students write down one piece of information from the map about each province or territory, such as the capital, any large bodies of water, or what other provinces, territories, or country it borders. Create a table on the board with a column for each province, and then have students take turns coming up and adding facts from their lists.

Go Online
PHSchool.com Students may practice
their map skills using the interactive
online version of this map.

Using the Visual   L2

Reach Into Your Background Draw students' attention to the photo and its caption. Ask students, **What is a lighthouse used for? Looking at Nova Scotia's location on the map, why do you think lighthouses might be important there?** Conduct an Idea Wave (TE, p. T35) to generate a list of student responses.

Answers

**MAP MASTER
Skills Activity**   **Locate** Quebec is near the eastern coast of Canada; Saskatchewan is in Canada's interior; British Columbia is on Canada's west coast. **Draw Conclusions** Possible answer: Quebec, because it is located the closest to Europe.

Chapter Resources

Teaching Resources
- L2 Vocabulary Development, p. 324
- L2 Skills for Life, p. 311
- L2 Chapter Tests A and B, pp. 329–334
- L2 Final Exams A and B, pp. 339–344

Spanish Support
- L2 Spanish Chapter Summary, p. 106
- L2 Spanish Vocabulary Development, p. 107

Media and Technology
- L1 Student Edition on Audio CD
- L1 Guided Reading Audiotapes, English and Spanish
- L2 Social Studies Skills Tutor CD-ROM
  ExamView Test Bank CD-ROM

**PRENTICE HALL
Presentation EXPRESS™**
Teach Connect Inspire

Teach this chapter's content using the PresentationExpress™ CD-ROM including:
- slide shows
- transparencies
- interactive maps and media
- *ExamView®* QuickTake Presenter

Objectives

- Learn about the provinces and territories of Canada.

- Analyze data to compare the provinces and territories of Canada.

- Identify characteristics that most provinces and territories share.

- Explain key differences among the provinces and territories.

Prepare to Read

Build Background Knowledge

L2

Invite students to share what they know about the provinces and territories of Canada, and what they learned about the country from watching the video *The Geography of Canada*. Create a table on the board with the following columns: *Name, Province/Territory, Capital, Major Cities, Population Density—High or Low?* Conduct an Idea Wave (TE, p. T35) to generate a list of what students learned or know about each topic. Write their responses in the appropriate column on the board.

📼 *The Geography of Canada*, **World Studies Video Program**

Guide for Reading

This section provides an introduction to the ten provinces and three territories that make up Canada.

- Look at the map on the previous page, and then read the information below to learn about each province and territory.
- Analyze the data to compare the provinces and territories.
- What are the characteristics that most of the provinces and territories share?
- What are some of the key differences among the provinces and territories?

Alberta

Capital	Edmonton
Land Area	247,999 sq mi; 642,317 sq km
Population	3,101,561
Language(s)	English, Chinese, German, French
Agriculture	livestock, wheat, canola, dairy products, barley, poultry, potatoes, nurseries, vegetables, eggs, sugar beets, honey
Industry	manufacturing, construction, oil production and refinery

British Columbia

Capital	Victoria
Land Area	357,214 sq mi; 925,186 sq km
Population	4,118,141
Language(s)	English, Chinese, Punjabi, German, French
Agriculture	nurseries, livestock, dairy products, vegetables, poultry, fruit, potatoes, ginseng, canola, wheat
Industry	forestry, wood and paper, mining, tourism, agriculture, fishing, manufacturing

Odyssium is Edmonton, Alberta's space and science center.

286 United States and Canada

Manitoba

Capital	Winnipeg
Land Area	213,728 sq mi; 553,556 sq km
Population	1,150,038
Language(s)	English, German, French
Agriculture	wheat, livestock, canola, dairy products, potatoes, barley, poultry, eggs, nurseries, vegetables, corn, honey
Industry	manufacturing, agriculture, food industry, mining, construction

New Brunswick

Capital	Fredericton
Land Area	27,587 sq mi; 71,450 sq km
Population	756,939
Language(s)	English, French
Agriculture	potatoes, dairy products, poultry, nurseries, livestock, eggs, fruit
Industry	manufacturing, fishing, mining, forestry, pulp and paper, agriculture

Newfoundland and Labrador

Capital	St. John's
Land Area	144,362 sq mi; 373,872 sq km
Population	531,820
Language(s)	English, French
Agriculture	dairy products, eggs, nurseries, vegetables, potatoes, hogs
Industry	mining, manufacturing, fishing, logging and forestry, electricity production, tourism

Northwest Territories

Capital	Yellowknife
Land Area	456,789 sq mi; 1,183,085 sq km
Population	40,071
Language(s)	English, French, Inuktitut
Agriculture	potatoes, hay, nurseries, livestock
Industry	construction, mining, utilities, services, tourism

Nova Scotia

Capital	Halifax
Land Area	20,594 sq mi; 53,338 sq km
Population	943,497
Language(s)	English, French
Agriculture	dairy products, poultry, livestock, nurseries, fruit, eggs, vegetables
Industry	manufacturing, fishing and trapping, mining, agriculture, pulp and paper

Snowy owl

Instruct

Introducing Canada L2

Guided Instruction

- With students, read through each data table using the Structured Silent Reading strategy (TE, p. T34).

- Have students make a list of the provinces and territories in order of population, from highest to lowest. Ask **How do the populations of the territories differ from those of the provinces?** *(They are much smaller.)*

- Ask **Which language does all of Canada have in common?** *(English)* **What language is the second most common in Canada?** *(French)*

- Ask **Which industry do nearly all of the provinces share?** *(manufacturing)*

- Ask **Based on what you have learned about Canada's physical geography, why do you think fishing and mining are major industries in Canada?** *(Much of Canada is on the Pacific, Atlantic, and Arctic Oceans, which provide fish; many inland areas are on the Canadian Shield, which is rich in minerals.)*

Differentiated Instruction

For Advanced Readers L3
To gain a deeper understanding about the French heritage of the province of Quebec, have students read *Shadows on the Rock*, and then answer the assessment questions.

All in One **United States and Canada Teaching Resources,** *Shadows on the Rock,* pp. 320–322

For Less Proficient Readers L1
Form students into pairs to create a poster highlighting one province or territory. Posters should include the capital and major industies of the province or territory, and a picture of its flag. Use *Rubric for Assessing a Student Poster* to evaluate students' work.

All in One **United States and Canada Teaching Resources,** *Rubric for Assessing a Student Poster,* p. 325

Independent Practice

Have students show the agricultural products of each province and territory on *Outline Map 12: Canada: Political.* Tell students to use symbols to represent each product, and to include a map key explaining their symbols. Tell students to give the map an appropriate title.

All in One **United States and Canada Teaching Resources,** *Outline Map 12: The United States and Canada: Political,* p. 319

Monitor Progress

Circulate to be sure students are making the map key correctly and that they have chosen an appropriate map title.

Introducing Canada

Nunavut

Capital	Iqaluit
Land Area	747,533 sq mi; 1,936,113 sq km
Population	29,016
Language(s)	Inuktitut, English
Industry	mining, tourism, shrimp and scallop fishing, hunting and trapping, arts and crafts production

Ontario

Capital	Toronto
Land Area	354,340 sq mi; 917,741 sq km
Population	11,977,360
Language(s)	English, French, Chinese, Italian, German, Portuguese, Polish, Spanish, Punjabi
Agriculture	livestock, dairy products, nurseries, vegetables, poultry, soybeans, corn, tobacco, eggs, fruit, wheat, ginseng, maple products
Industry	manufacturing, construction, agriculture, forestry, mining

Prince Edward Island

Capital	Charlottetown
Land Area	2,185 sq mi; 5,660 sq km
Population	135,294
Language(s)	English, French
Agriculture	potatoes, dairy products, livestock, vegetables
Industry	agriculture, tourism, fishing, manufacturing

Cape Tryon on Prince Edward Island

288 United States and Canada

Background: Daily Life

The Inuit Nunavut is the largest territory in Canada in land area, but one of the smallest in population. The majority of the population there is Inuit, an indigenous group of northern Canada that has been living in this region for more than 4,000 years. Originally the Inuit were nomads, moving from place to place, and hunting and fishing in the Arctic waters. They built houses from snow in the winter and lived in tents made from animal skins in the summer. Today, however, the lifestyle of many Inuit has changed. Most live in permanent homes in towns and cities. Hunting and fishing have remained important, but are often part of the commercial economy, rather than for subsistence.

Quebec

Capital	Quebec
Land Area	594,860 sq mi; 1,365,128 sq km
Population	7,432,005
Language(s)	French, English, Italian
Agriculture	dairy products, livestock, poultry, vegetables, corn, nurseries, maple products, fruit, potatoes, soybeans, barley, tobacco, wheat
Industry	manufacturing, electric power, mining, pulp and paper, transportation equipment

Saskatchewan

Capital	Regina
Land Area	251,866 sq mi; 591,670 sq km
Population	1,001,224
Language(s)	English, German, Cree, Ukrainian, French
Agriculture	wheat, livestock, canola, barley, lentils, dairy products, poultry, potatoes, nurseries, eggs, honey
Industry	agriculture, mining, manufacturing, electric power, construction, chemical production

Musicians in Montreal, Quebec

Yukon Territory

Capital	Whitehorse
Land Area	186,661 sq mi; 474,391 sq km
Population	29,552
Language(s)	English, German, French
Agriculture	nurseries, vegetables, poultry
Industry	mining, tourism

SOURCES: *CIA World Factbook*, 2002; *World Almanac*, 2003; *Canadian Global Almanac*, 2003, Canada Census, 2001

Assessment

Comprehension and Critical Thinking

1. Compare and Contrast Compare Nunavut and Ontario based on physical size and population size.

2. Draw Conclusions What characteristics do the three territories share?

3. Contrast How has geographic location affected the populations and industries of Canada's provinces and territories?

4. Categorize What are the major products in Canada?

5. Infer What can you infer about Nunavut if there are no agricultural products listed?

6. Make a Bar Graph Create a bar graph showing the population of the provinces and territories of Canada.

Keeping Current

Access the **DK World Desk Reference Online** at **PHSchool.com** for up-to-date information about Canada.

Web Code: **lhe-4501**

Assess and Reteach

Assess Progress   L2

Direct students' attention back to the columns on the board. Encourage them to suggest additional information to fill in under each heading based on what they learned from the Country Databank. Also, create new columns entitled *Land Area*, *Languages*, *Agriculture*, and *Industry*, and have students add the appropriate information. Then have students answer the Assessment questions.

Reteach   L2

Ask students to create a table on a large piece of poster board that shows the data for all of the provinces and territories in the Country Databank. Have them list the categories across the top of the table and the names of the regions along the side. Model filling in the information for one of the provinces on the board.

Extend   L3

Portfolio Activity Divide students into groups, and assign each group a data category for each province or territory that is not listed in the Country Databank, such as percentage of ethnic groups or exports and imports. Have students do research to find this information for each province or territory, and create a circle graph or bar graph that shows this information. Then have students add their work to their portfolios.

Answers

Assessment

1. Nunavut has over twice the land area as Ontario, while Ontario has over 400 times the population of Nunavut.

2. Characteristics they share include: small populations; English as at least one of their languages; mining and tourism as industries.

3. Location affects Canada's climate. Few people have settled in the colder areas where not many crops will grow. Canada's industries are affected by the natural resources of each area.

4. livestock, vegetables, eggs, and dairy products

5. that the land is not suitable to raise crops or livestock

6. Students' graphs will vary, but their bar graphs should reflect the correct populations of each province and territory.

Section 1
Step-by-Step Instruction

Objectives

Social Studies
1. Read about the seat of the Canadian government in Ontario.
2. Learn about the French cultural influence in Quebec.

Reading/Language Arts
Use context clues to determine the meaning of unfamiliar words.

Prepare to Read

Build Background Knowledge L2
Ask students to suppose that while visiting Canada, they travel across the MacDonald-Cartier Bridge, which connects Ontario and Quebec. Tell them that the road signs on the Ontario side of the bridge are primarily in English, and the road signs on the Quebec side are primarily in French. Have students brainstorm the possible benefits and challenges of living in a country where neighboring regions speak different languages and have different cultures. Have students use the Give One, Get One participation strategy (TE, p. T37) to generate a list.

Set a Purpose for Reading L2
- Preview the Objectives.
- Read each statement in the *Reading Readiness Guide* aloud. Ask students to mark the statements true or false.
- Have students discuss the statements in pairs or groups of four, then mark their worksheets again. Use the Numbered Heads participation strategy (TE, p. T36) to call on students to share their group's perspectives.

All in One United States and Canada Teaching Resources, *Reading Readiness Guide,* p. 286

Vocabulary Builder
Preview Key Terms L2
Pronounce each Key Term, then ask students to say the word with you. Provide a simple explanation such as, "A Francophone is a person who learned to speak French before any other language."

Prepare to Read

Objectives
In this section you will
1. Read about the seat of the Canadian government in Ontario.
2. Learn about the French cultural influence in Quebec.

Taking Notes
As you read this section, look for ways that people in Quebec are preserving and celebrating their culture. Copy the concept web below, and record your findings in it.

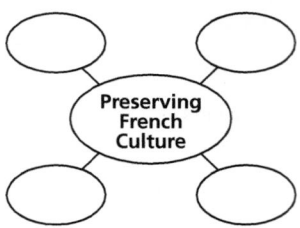

Preserving French Culture

Target Reading Skill

Use Context Clues When you come across an unfamiliar word, you can often figure out its meaning from clues in the context. The context refers to the surrounding words, phrases, and sentences. Sometimes the context will define the word. In this example, the phrase in italics explains what a tariff is: Both countries charged tariffs, or *fees,* on imported goods.

Key Terms
- **federation** (fed ur AY shun) *n.* a union of states, groups, provinces, or nations
- **Francophone** (FRANG koh fohn) *n.* a person who speaks French as his or her first language
- **Quiet Revolution** (KWY ut rev uh LOO shun) *n.* a peaceful change in the government of Quebec
- **separatist** (SEP ur uh tist) *n.* a person who wants Quebec to become an independent country

The Macdonald-Cartier Bridge

290 United States and Canada

Much of the border between Ontario and Quebec is formed by the Ottawa River. The Macdonald-Cartier Bridge stretches across the river, connecting the two provinces. The bridge is named for two Canadian political leaders, one an English speaker and one a French speaker. While the bridge links the two provinces, its very name characterizes the differences between the provinces—people in Ontario speak English primarily, while people in Quebec mostly speak French.

In spite of this significant distinction, Ontario and Quebec have much in common. They are home to Canada's two largest cities—Toronto, Ontario, and Montreal, Quebec. They are the two most populous provinces in Canada. Canada's capital, Ottawa, is located in Ontario. But government functions spill over into the city of Hull, Quebec, located on the other end of the Macdonald-Cartier Bridge. Hull is considered Ottawa's "sister city" because a number of federal government office buildings dot its landscape.

Target Reading Skill L2

Use Context Clues Point out the Target Reading Skill. Tell students that terms and phrases surrounding an unknown word can provide clues to the unfamiliar word's meaning.

Model using context clues to find the meaning of *primarily* in the following sentence from p. 290: "While the bridge links the two provinces, its very name characterizes the differences between the provinces—people in Ontario speak English primarily, while people in Quebec mostly speak French." *(The surrounding information and the word* mostly *provide clues that* primarily *also means "mostly.")*

Give students *Use Context Clues: General.* Have them complete the activity in their groups.

All in One United States and Canada Teaching Resources, *Use Context Clues: General Knowledge,* p. 305

Ontario

The province of Ontario is perhaps Canada's most diverse province geographically. Located on the United States border, it reaches from Hudson Bay in the north to the Great Lakes in the south. Ontario's northern region is part of the Canadian Shield, the region of ancient rock that covers about half of Canada. The Canadian Shield has rocky terrain, rugged winters, and is sparsely populated. Ontario's southern lowlands have milder winters and warm summers. About one third of Canada's entire population lives in this southern area.

Canada's Federal Government

Canada is a federation, or union, of 10 provinces and 3 territories. In the Canadian federation, each province has its own government. Each of these governments shares power with Canada's central government, located in Ottawa.

Although Canada's formal head of state is the monarch of Britain, Canada has complete power over its own government. The head of state, represented by the governor general, performs mainly ceremonial duties, such as hosting politicians from other countries, supporting charitable causes, and honoring the achievements of Canadians. Unlike the United States, in which the president is head of state as well as head of government, Canada has a separate head of government, called the prime minister. The prime minister leads the government and is part of Canada's central legislature—the Canadian Parliament.

Ottawa Ottawa has been a capital city since the middle of the nineteenth century, when Upper and Lower Canada—present-day Ontario and Quebec—formed the Province of Canada. Ottawa was selected as the capital because it was located on the border of the two territories. In 1867, Nova Scotia and New Brunswick joined Ontario and Quebec to become the Dominion of Canada, an autonomous, or self-governing, member of the British Empire.

The Canadian Government

```
                    Sovereign
                       |
                  Governor
                  General
                       |
PARLIAMENT      Prime Minister        JUDICIARY

House of                          Supreme Court
Commons    Senate                 of Canada
                                  Federal Court
                                  of Canada
```

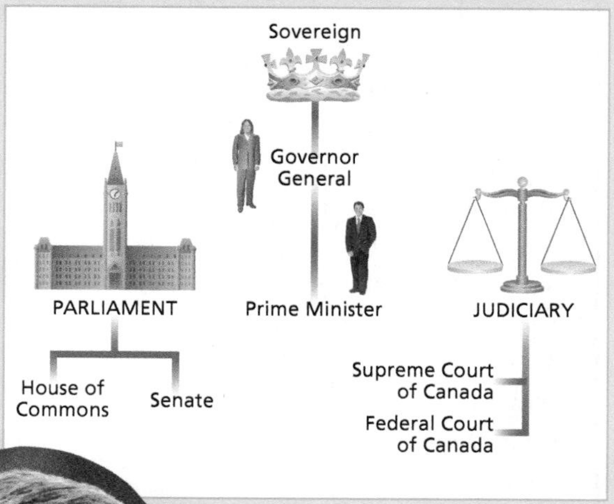

■ Diagram Skills

In the Canadian government structure, the executive, or prime minister, proposes laws; the legislature, Parliament, adopts laws; and the judiciary interprets laws. Stephen Harper, shown at left, was elected as Canadian prime minister in 2006. **Identify** Name the two houses of Parliament. **Contrast** How does Canada's head of state differ from the President of the United States?

Vocabulary Builder

Use the information below to teach students this section's high-use words.

High-Use Word	Definition and Sample Sentence
structure, p. 293	*n.* something (such as a building) that has been built "That's the largest **structure** in town," he said, pointing to a tall building.
mature, p. 293	*v.* to reach a final state Over the years, the sapling **matured** into a beautiful, tall tree.
issue, p. 295	*n.* something that is being discussed or debated, a problem to be talked over They debated the **issue** until it was time to go to bed.
margin, p. 295	*n.* the amount of the difference between two quantities It was almost a tie—John won by a very small **margin**.

Instruct

Ontario L2

Guided Instruction

- **Vocabulary Builder** Clarify the high-use words **structure** and **mature** before reading.

- Read Ontario, using the Choral Reading technique (TE, p. T34).

- Discuss Canada's head of state and its head of government, pointing out who fills each role and how their functions differ. *(Canada's head of state is the monarch of Britain, while the country's head of government is the prime minister. The head of state is a ceremonial figure who hosts politicians from other countries and honors the achievements of Canadians. The head of government leads the government and is part of Canada's central legislature.)*

- Ask students to compare and contrast Ottawa and Toronto. *(Both cities are in Ontario, and both are capitals. Ottawa is the country's capital, while Toronto is the province's capital. Ottawa is Canada's center of government, while Toronto is Canada's largest city and its main commercial and financial center.)*

Independent Practice L2

Assign *Guided Reading and Review.*

All in One **United States and Canada Teaching Resources,** *Guided Reading and Review,* p. 287

Monitor Progress L2

Monitor the students as they complete the *Guided Reading and Review,* checking to make sure they understand and can answer the questions on the worksheet.

Answers

Diagram Skills **Identify** the House of Commons and the Senate **Contrast** Canada's head of state performs mainly ceremonial duties, while the President of the United States is both head of state and head of government.

Guided Instruction

Ask students to study the Regional Profile on this page. Remind them to read the map key to fully understand the population density map of Ontario. Also encourage them to study the table and think about the information each provides. As a class, answer the Map and Chart Skills questions. Allow students to briefly discuss their responses with a partner before sharing answers.

Independent Practice

Distribute *Reading a Population Density Map*. Discuss the differences between the map on the worksheet and the one of Ontario on page 292. Have students work in pairs to complete the worksheet.

All in One United States and Canada Teaching Resources, *Reading a Population Density Map,* p. 316

Ontario

Canada separated from England very gradually. It went from a dependent colony of England, to a dominion, and finally to an independent nation with ties to Great Britain through the British Commonwealth of Nations. As you study the map and charts, compare and contrast Canada's government with that of the United States.

Ontario: Population Density

KEY

Persons per sq. mile	Persons per sq. kilometer
More than 129	More than 49
25–129	10–49
1–24	1–9
Less than 1	Less than 1

Urban Areas
- More than 4,999,999
- 1,000,000–4,999,999
- 500,000–999,999
- Less than 500,000
- National border
- Provincial or territorial border

The House of Commons

Province or Territory	Seats
Alberta	28
British Columbia	36
Manitoba, Saskatchewan	14
New Brunswick	10
Newfoundland and Labrador	7
Northwest Territories, Nunavut, Yukon Territory	1
Nova Scotia	11
Ontario	106
Prince Edward Island	4
Quebec	75

SOURCE: *Canadian Global Almanac, 2003*

Structure of Government

	Canada	United States
Head of State (ceremonial)	Queen of England / Governor General (the Queen's representative)	President (elected by the voters)
Head of Government (political)	Prime Minister (PM, the leader of the majority party in the House of Commons)	President
Legislature	Parliament • House of Commons (elected by the voters) • Senate (appointed by PM)	Congress • House of Representatives (elected) • Senate (elected)
Districts	Provinces and territories	States

Map and Chart Skills

1. **Note** Where is most of Ontario's population located?
2. **Explain** How does population affect the number of seats a province or territory has in the House of Commons?
3. **Analyze** What is the difference in the roles of the voters in Canada and in the United States?

 **Go Online PHSchool.com** Use Web Code **lhe-4511** for **DK World Desk Reference Online.**

Answers

Map and Chart Skills

1. southern Ontario
2. Territories and provinces with larger populations have more seats; those with smaller populations have fewer.
3. Voters in the United States have a more direct role in electing government leaders.

Go Online PHSchool.com Students can find more information about this topic on the DK World Desk Reference Online.

Differentiated Instruction

For English Language Learners L3
Check for students' comprehension of the term *cultural mosaic,* which appears in the second paragraph on p. 293. Have students read the Spanish Support section of the United States and Canada Teaching Resources. Then ask them to write in their own words what it means that "Toronto has matured into a cultural mosaic with a very diverse population." Have pairs of students read their explanations to each other and discuss whether they both understand the term to mean the same thing. If they do not agree about the term, mediate a discussion between them about the possible meanings.

Guided Reading and Review (Spanish), **Spanish Support,** p. 96

Guided Instruction

- **Vocabulary Builder** Clarify the high-use words **issue** and **margin** before reading.

- Ask students to read about the role French history and culture has played in Quebec in French Culture in Quebec. As students read, circulate and make sure individuals can answer the Reading Check question.

- Discuss some of the peaceful ways in which the French separatist movement in Quebec took shape. *(Early on, the government helped the French separatist movement take shape peacefully by creating better job opportunities for Francophones. Later, the government made French the official language of Quebec and required immigrants to Quebec to learn the language. Additionally, the question of whether or not Quebec should become a separate nation was decided by voting rather than by fighting.)*

Toronto Each of Canada's provinces has a capital. Toronto is the capital of Ontario. It is also Canada's largest city and its commercial and financial center. Founded in 1793, Toronto was first known as York. Its location on Lake Ontario made it a major trade and transportation center. Toronto has come to be identified by its Canadian National (CN) Tower, which, at 1,815 feet (553 meters), is the world's tallest freestanding structure.

Toronto has matured into a cultural mosaic with a very diverse population—nearly half of its residents are foreign-born. After World War II, a large number of Europeans immigrated to Canada, with many settling in Toronto.

The most recent wave of immigrants included a large number of Asians. About 10 percent of Toronto's residents are of Chinese ethnicity. British, Italian, First Nations, Portuguese, East Indian, Greek, German, Ukrainian, Polish, and French are among the other ethnic groups that make up Toronto's population.

✓ Reading Check **Where is Canada's federal government located?**

Toronto Cityscape
The CN Tower (right) dominates Toronto's skyline. The large aerial photo taken from the tower shows Rogers Centre (formerly the SkyDome), home of the Toronto Blue Jays baseball team. It was the first domed stadium built with a roof that opens and closes.
Draw Conclusions *Why would a domed stadium be needed in Toronto?*

Differentiated Instruction

For Special Needs Students   L1
Have students read the section as they listen to the recorded version on the Student Edition on Audio CD. Then have them write a summary of French Culture in Quebec as they read the section to themselves again.

  ◉ Chapter 10, Section 1, **Student Edition on Audio CD**

For Gifted and Talented   L3
Have students conduct research to find five aspects of French-Canadian culture that are not in the text. Have them use *Preparing for Presentations*, to help them present their findings to the class.

  All in One **United States and Canada Teaching Resources,** *Preparing for Presentations,* p. 323

Answers

Draw Conclusions so baseball can be played in bad weather

✓ Reading Check Ottawa, Ontario

Ask students to give examples of how Quebec's culture reflects a mix of French and local influences. (*People have added local ingredients such as maple syrup to French-style cooking. Quebec's architecture is also a mix of French and Canadian styles.*)

Independent Practice

Ask students to create the Taking Notes graphic organizer on a blank piece of paper. Then ask them to fill in the ovals with the information they have just learned. Briefly model how to fill in separate pieces of information in each oval.

French Culture in Quebec

French culture first reached Quebec in the 1500s, when Jacques Cartier (zhahk kahr tee AY), a French explorer, sailed along the St. Lawrence River and landed in a village called Stadacona (stad uh KOH nuh). The Iroquois, the native people of the area, inhabited the village. Today, the site of that village is the city of Quebec, capital of the province of Quebec.

Cartier claimed the region we now know as Quebec for France and named it Canada. Great Britain, however, was also interested in the region. French and British forces fought for the land in four separate wars over a period of nearly 80 years. The last of the battles were part of the French and Indian War. In 1759, the British captured the city of Quebec. Within four years, France surrendered all of its North American land east of the Mississippi River to the British.

Despite Great Britain's victory, tens of thousands of French colonists remained in the region, and their descendants make up the majority of Quebec's population today. They are called **Francophones** (FRANG koh fohnz), or people who speak French as their first language. In Quebec's largest city, Montreal, and its surrounding areas, more than 65 percent of the population are Francophones.

French Influence in Quebec
French culture reached Quebec hundreds of years ago, and it still exists in the capital city today.
Analyze Images *How can the influence of French culture be seen in this street in Quebec City?*

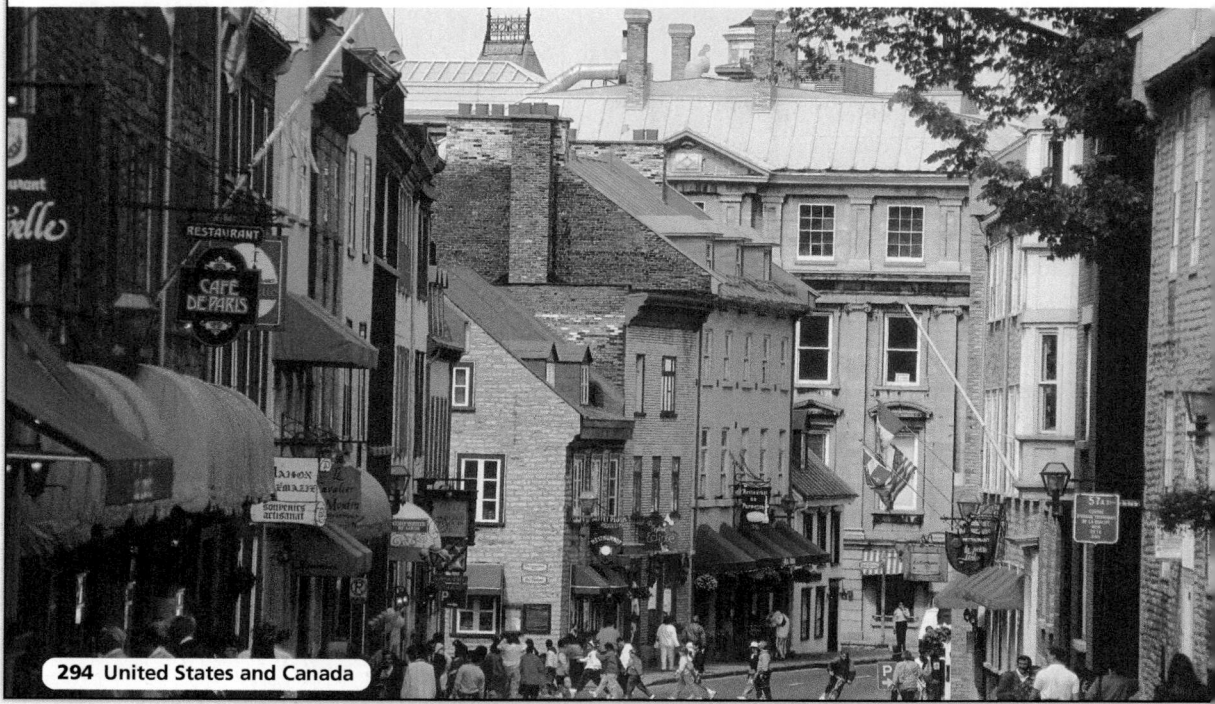

294 United States and Canada

Skills for Life — Skills Mini Lesson

Recognizing Bias　L2

1. Teach the skill by explaining that a biased statement expresses a slanted opinion that is not supported by facts and often used loaded words.

2. Have students practice the skill by assessing if the following statement if biased: *French Canadian separatists wanted the beautiful, expressive French language to* be Quebec's official language and the charming French-Canadian traditions to be maintained.

3. Have students apply the skill by rewriting the sentence above to make it more fair. Students should eliminate any loaded words (*beautiful, expressive, charming*) and be sure the statement can be supported with facts from the chapter.

Answer

Analyze Images Signs are written in French.

Francophones Seek Rights

In the 1960s, many Francophones began to express concern that their language and culture might die, because English was spoken in the schools and at work. They also believed that opportunities for Francophones in Quebec were not equal to those for English speakers. For the most part, Francophones got jobs with lower pay. So they set out to create change, in a movement that was similar to the civil rights movement in the United States in the 1960s. In 1960, the Liberal party, which supported Francophones, came to power in Quebec. Prime Minister Jean Lesage led the government in creating better job opportunities for Francophones and in modernizing education and health care in Quebec. This change in the government became known as the **Quiet Revolution** because great changes were brought about peacefully.

INDÉPENDA

Disagreement on Separation
A Quebec resident (left) displays her opposition to separation. Other people carrying signs calling for independence and sovereignty rally to support the split from Canada (above). **Analyze Images** *What evidence is there that the woman at the left is against the Separatist Movement?*

The Separatist Movement

During the Quiet Revolution, the separatist movement began to grow. **Separatists** are people who want to see Quebec break away from the rest of Canada and become an independent country. French-Canadian separatists saw important victories in the 1970s as French became the official language of Quebec and the children of immigrants to the province were required to learn French. But still, Quebec remained a province of Canada.

Not everyone in Quebec supported the idea of separation from Canada. In 1980, the provincial government held a referendum. In a referendum, voters cast ballots for or against an issue. This referendum asked voters whether Quebec should become a separate nation. A majority voted no.

In 1995, Quebec held another referendum. Again, Quebec's people voted to remain part of Canada. But this time the margin was very slim—50.6 percent voted against separation while 49.4 percent voted for it. Since then, separatists have lost power and positions in government, but they vow that they will continue to fight for Quebec's independence.

Use Context Clues
If you do not know what a referendum is, look for a context clue. Here, the sentence following *referendum* is a definition of the term. What is a referendum?

- As students fill in the graphic organizer, circulate and make sure individuals are choosing logical details to place in the concept web. Provide assistance as needed.

- Show *Section Reading Support Transparency USC 58* and ask students to check their graphic organizers individually. Go over key concepts and clarify key vocabulary as needed.

  United States and Canada Transparencies, *Section Reading Support Transparency USC 58*

- Tell students to fill in the last column of the *Reading Readiness Guide.* Probe for what they learned that confirms or invalidates each statement.

  All in One **United States and Canada Teaching Resources,** *Reading Readiness Guide,* p. 286

Target Reading Skill

Use Context Clues As a follow up, ask students to answer the Target Reading Skill question in the Student Edition. *(In a referendum, voters cast ballots for or against an issue.)*

Skills Mini Lesson

Supporting a Position

1. Teach the skill by explaining that one supports a position by identifying reasons, supporting each with facts, and drawing a valid conclusion.

2. Help students practice the skill by reading the passages about Quebec and its separatist movement on pp. 294–295 and stating the position of separatists in Quebec. *(The separatists want Quebec to break away from the rest of Canada.)*

3. Have students apply the skill by determining the reasons why many Francophones became separatists. *(They feared their language and culture would die out, and they felt they did not have equal opportunities.)*

Answer

Analyze Images The woman is holding the Canadian flag and has the Canadian maple leaf painted on her face. She also has a sticker that reads "No" in English on her forehead.

Guided Instruction `L2`

Ask students to study the Regional Profile on this page. Encourage students to study the map, circle graph, and time lines carefully. As a class, answer the Map and Chart Skills questions. Allow students to briefly discuss their responses with a partner before sharing answers.

Independent Practice

Ask students to consider the circle graph on this page. It shows how Montreal's population is divided among different languages. Ask students to write a paragraph comparing the percentages of Montreal residents who speak English, French, both, and neither. Encourage students to include a comment on how this breakdown relates to Quebec's history.

Answers

Map and Chart Skills

1. in southern Quebec and along the St. Lawrence River

2. The names of some provinces and bodies of water reflect Canada's early history. City names in Quebec reflect French heritage.

3. Possible answer: the language law may have made some separatists more willing to have Quebec remain part of Canada.

Go Online PHSchool.com Students can find more information about this topic on the DK World Desk Reference Online.

Quebec

Like much of Canada, Quebec's early history was shaped by two countries—Great Britain and France. Unlike the rest of the nation, however, French influence has remained particularly strong in Quebec. The province's recent history reflects the importance of the French legacy in the region. As you study the map, chart, and timelines, think about how history and culture have interacted in Quebec throughout its history.

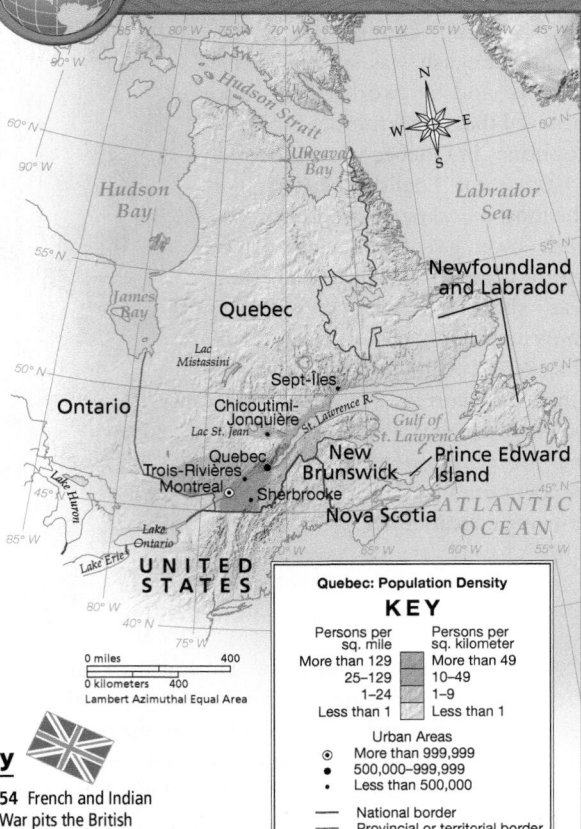

Languages Spoken in Montreal

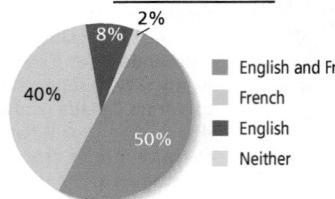

- 2%
- 8%
- 40%
- 50%

- English and French
- French
- English
- Neither

SOURCE: *Canadian Global Almanac, 2003*

Quebec: Population Density KEY

Persons per sq. mile	Persons per sq. kilometer
More than 129	More than 49
25–129	10–49
1–24	1–9
Less than 1	Less than 1

Urban Areas
- ◉ More than 999,999
- ● 500,000–999,999
- · Less than 500,000

— National border
— Provincial or territorial border

0 miles 400
0 kilometers 400
Lambert Azimuthal Equal Area

Early Canadian History

1608 Samuel de Champlain builds a fort at Quebec for the French fur trade.

1663 King Louis XIV declares New France a royal colony.

1754 French and Indian War pits the British against the French.

1600	1650	1700	1750	1800

1610 English explorer Henry Hudson charts Hudson Bay.

1670 Hudson's Bay Company is set up in England.

1763 The Treaty of Paris ends French control of Canada.

Recent Quebec History

1968 Interest grows in a separate French-speaking province.

1976 Parti Québécois (PQ) takes power under Premier René Lévesque.

1980 In a referendum, Quebec votes to stay a part of federal Canada.

1965	1970	1975	1980

1977 French becomes the official language of Quebec.

Map and Chart Skills

1. **Identify** Where is most of Quebec's population located?

2. **Infer** How do the place names on the map reflect early Canadian history?

3. **Analyze** What effect do you think the language law had on those who wanted Quebec to be a separate country?

 Use Web Code lhe-4521 for DK World Desk Reference Online.

Differentiated Instruction

For Advanced Readers `L3`

Have students read the quotations on the *Enrichment* worksheet. Then ask students to write a summary titled "The Canadian Identity" using both the *Enrichment* sheet and the Regional Profile.

All in One **United States and Canada Teaching Resources,** *Enrichment,* p. 310

For Less Proficient Readers `L1`

Pair students with more proficient readers to read *Shadows on the Rock*. Have students take turns reading the paragraphs aloud. Then have the pairs answer the questions at the end of the reading.

All in One **United States and Canada Teaching Resources,** *Shadows on the Rock,* pp. 320–322

Celebrating Quebec's Culture One of the ways in which Quebec's people celebrate their culture is through festivals. The Quebec Winter Carnival lasts 17 days. Fantastic ice sculptures adorn Quebec City, and canoe races take place among the ice floes in the St. Lawrence River.

Another Quebec festival honors St. Jean-Baptiste (zhahn bah TEEST), or John the Baptist, the patron saint, or special guardian, of French Canadians. This festival is held June 24. All over the province, people celebrate with bonfires, firecrackers, and street dances.

French style and cooking flourish in Quebec—with Quebec variations. Sugar pie, for example, uses maple sugar from the province's forests. Quebec also has French architecture. The people of Quebec take pride in preserving their lively culture.

√ Reading Check **What is the official language of Quebec?**

An ice slide sculpture at Quebec City's Winter Carnival

 Section **1** Assessment

Key Terms
Review the key terms at the beginning of this section. Use each key term in a sentence that explains its meaning.

Target Reading Skill
Find the word *autonomous* on page 291. Use context to figure out its meaning. What clue helped you figure out its meaning?

Comprehension and Critical Thinking
1. (a) Identify Who is the head of state in Canada?

(b) Contrast How does the head of state differ from the head of government?
(c) Analyze What are the possible benefits of this kind of system?
2. (a) Recall How many people in and around Montreal are Francophones?
(b) Make Generalizations Why are French-Canadians concerned with preserving their heritage?
(c) Summarize What has the Canadian government done to meet the demands of French-Canadians?

Writing Activity
You have read that some people in Quebec want to remain a part of Canada while others want Quebec to become a separate country. Write a paragraph giving your opinion on the subject. Be sure to give reasons for your point of view.

For: An activity on Quebec
Visit: PHSchool.com
Web Code: lhd-4501

Writing Activity
Use the *Rubric for Assessing a Writing Assignment* to evaluate students' paragraphs.

All in One **United States and Canada Teaching Resources,** *Rubric for Assessing a Writing Assignment,* p. 326

Go Online PHSchool.com Typing in the Web code when prompted will bring students directly to detailed instructions for this activity.

Assess and Reteach

Assess Progress
L2
Have students complete the Section Assessment. Administer the *Section Quiz.*

All in One **United States and Canada Teaching Resources,** *Section Quiz,* p. 288

Reteach
L1
If students need more instruction, have them read this section in the Reading and Vocabulary Study Guide.

Chapter 10, Section 1, **Western Hemisphere Reading and Vocabulary Study Guide,** pp. 105–107

Extend
L3
Have students learn more about French Canadians and Quebec by completing the *Small Group Activity: Writing a Newspaper Feature.*

All in One **United States and Canada Teaching Resources,** *Small Group Activity: Writing a Newspaper Feature,* pp. 312–315

Answers

√ Reading Check French

Section 1 Assessment

Key Terms
Students' sentences should reflect knowledge of each Key Term.

Target Reading Skill
Autonomous means self-governing. This definition is given in the sentence.

Comprehension and Critical Thinking
1. (a) the monarch of Britain **(b)** The head of state is a ceremonial figure, while the head of government—the prime minister—leads the government and is part of Canada's central legislature. **(c)** Answers will vary, but may include the possible benefit that each leader can focus solely on his or her specific duties.

2. (a) more than 80 percent **(b)** As a minority in Canada, French Canadians are concerned that their language and culture might be lost. **(c)** It has created better job opportunities for French Canadians, modernized education and health care in Quebec, and made French the official language of Quebec.

Objectives

Social Studies

1. Learn why many immigrants came to the Prairie Provinces in the 1800s.
2. Read about how Canadians celebrate their cultural traditions.

Reading/Language Arts

Practice interpreting the meaning of non-literal language.

Prepare to Read

Build Background Knowledge L2

Tell students that they will learn about the Canadian plains in this section. The Canadian plains are part of the same prairie that makes up much of the Midwest region of the United States. Have students watch the video *Canada's Prairie Provinces* and note two to three similarities between the Canadian prairie and the American prairie they learned about in the last chapter. Ask students to share their ideas using the Numbered Heads participation strategy (TE, p. T36).

📼 *Canada's Prairie Provinces*, **World Studies Video Program**

Set a Purpose for Reading L2

■ Preview the Objectives.

■ Read each statement in the *Reading Readiness Guide* aloud. Ask students to mark the statements true or false.

All in One **United States and Canada Teaching Resources,** *Reading Readiness Guide,* p. 290

■ Have students discuss the statements in pairs or groups of four, then mark their worksheets again. Use the Numbered Heads participation strategy (TE, p. T36) to call on students to share their group's perspectives.

Vocabulary Builder
Preview Key Terms L2

Pronounce each Key Term, then ask students to say the word with you. Provide a simple explanation such as, "If you have immunity to a disease, you will not catch the disease."

Prepare to Read

Objectives

In this section you will
1. Learn why many immigrants came to the Prairie Provinces in the 1800s.
2. Read about how Canadians celebrate their cultural traditions.

Taking Notes

As you read this section, looks for details about European immigration to the Prairie Provinces. Copy the chart below, and record your findings in it.

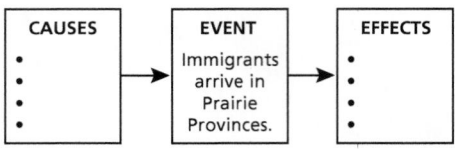

Target Reading Skill

Interpret Nonliteral Meanings Literal language means exactly what it says. Nonliteral language uses images to communicate an idea. Sometimes nonliteral language communicates a point more vividly than literal language. In this section, you will read about "Canada's Breadbasket." When you see these words, ask yourself: How does nonliteral language make a point about the Prairie Provinces region?

Key Terms

• **descent** (dee SENT) *n.* a person's ancestry
• **immunity** (ih MYOO nuh tee) *n.* a natural resistance to disease

---

Sheets of floating ice in Hudson Bay

298 United States and Canada

One day in 1821, after a difficult journey, about 200 Swiss immigrants reached Hudson Bay in northern Canada. They wanted to become farmers in the region that now includes Saskatchewan (sas KACH uh wahn), Alberta, and Manitoba. Stories of good land and an excellent climate attracted the settlers to the vast plains. But no shelter, food, or supplies awaited them. The settlers survived only because the native people of the region, the Saulteaux (sawl TOH), helped them.

The winters were harsh. In summer they had to put up with drought, floods, and swarms of grasshoppers. With few trees on the plains, people built homes out of prairie sod—strips of grass with thick roots and soil attached. They cut it into blocks, which they piled up to make walls in the same way that American settlers did in the Midwest. "Soddies" were cheap, but if it rained, the roofs leaked. Few settlers had farming experience, and they did not anticipate such hardships.

Target Reading Skill L2

Interpret Nonliteral Meanings Point out the Target Reading Skill. Tell students that nonliteral language often uses images to vividly communicate an idea.

Model how to interpret nonliteral meanings by reading the first paragraph on page 302. Point out that the information in this paragraph helps make it clear that "boomed" is a nonliteral way of saying "grew very quickly."

Give students *Recognize Nonliteral Meanings.* Have them complete the activity in their groups.

All in One **United States and Canada Teaching Resources,** *Recognize Nonliteral Meanings,* p. 306

The Prairie Provinces

Manitoba, Saskatchewan, and Alberta are located on the largest prairie in the world, stretching across the three provinces and down into the central United States. As a result, they are often called the Prairie Provinces. These provinces occupy lands where indigenous peoples have lived for thousands of years.

A Way of Life Ends The Cree and Saulteaux were among the indigenous peoples who lived on the plains in present-day Manitoba. The Cree, Blackfoot, and Assiniboine (uh SIN uh boyn) lived in present-day Alberta. The Chipewyan (chip uh WY un) and Sioux, also called Dakota, are native to Saskatchewan.

These native peoples were deeply connected to the plants and animals of their lands. Buffalo, in particular, were the foundation of their daily lives. Buffalo meat provided food, and buffalo hides were made into clothing. Regina, now the capital of Saskatchewan, was once a place the Cree called *Wascana*, which means "pile of bones." Here people made buffalo bones into tools. Despite their dependence on the buffalo, however, native peoples only used what they needed. Huge numbers of buffalo remained.

In the late 1870s, however, that changed. People of European **descent,** or ancestry, moved into the region and began killing off the buffalo herds that blanketed the region. People killed the buffalo both for sport and for their hides. In a few years, nearly all the buffalo were gone. At the same time, the government of Canada began to take over the indigenous peoples' land. Most agreed to give up their land and live on reserves. The ways of life of many indigenous peoples in the Plains region of North America had come to an end.

A Buffalo Hunt
By the 1730s, Plains Indians were able to trade for horses. *Analyze Images How did horses help the Plains Indians to hunt buffalo more effectively?*

Instruct

The Prairie Provinces L2

Guided Instruction

- **Vocabulary Builder** Clarify the high-use word **occupy** before reading.

- Read The Prairie Provinces, using the Structured Silent Reading technique (TE, p. T34).

- Ask students **In what ways did indigenous people on the plains rely on the buffalo?** (*The buffalo provided indigenous people with meat, hides for clothing, and bones to use to make tools.*)

- Then ask **How did the arrival of European settlers change life for indigenous people on the plains?** (*Settlers killed nearly all the buffalo and most indigenous people were moved onto reserves. Plains Indians were also affected by diseases brought by Europeans.*)

Vocabulary Builder

Use the information below to teach students this section's high-use word.

High-Use Word	Definition and Sample Sentence
occupy, p. 299	*v.* to take up space, fill Someone already **occupied** the seat next to Rita.

Answer

Analyze Images Horses allowed hunters to get closer to the buffalo, and to follow buffalo herds for longer distances.

Guided Instruction $L2$

Ask students to study the Regional Profile on this page. Remind them to read the map key to understand what the different symbols on the map represent. Also encourage them to study the graphs carefully. As a class, answer the Map and Chart Skills questions. Allow students to briefly discuss their responses with a partner before sharing answers.

Independent Practice

- Help students read the line graph by asking them to list approximately how many farms were in the Prairie Provinces in each of the five years shown on the graph. Then have students write a sentence stating whether the number of farms increased or decreased over time.

- Help students read the bar graph by asking them to fill in the following sentence for each product: "_____% of Canadian _____ is grown in the Prairie Provinces." Ask them to summarize the three sentences with a conclusion about whether the Prairie Provinces produce most of or only a little of Canada's wheat, barley, rye, and oats.

Answers

Map and Chart Skills

1. wheat, barley, rye, oats

2. about 200 acres larger

3. The Prairie Provinces still have the best land in Canada for raising wheat, barley, rye, and oats and new technologies have helped increase crops.

Go Online PHSchool.com Students can find more information about this topic on the DK World Desk Reference Online.

REGIONAL PROFILE
Focus on Economics

Prairie Provinces

Canada is the world's second-largest exporter of wheat, after the United States. Although the size of farms in Canada is growing larger, there are fewer of them. Farmers take advantage of science and new technology to increase their crop production. But the new methods are expensive, so corporate farms are replacing small family farms. As you study the map and charts, think about where the food you eat comes from.

Number of Farms in Prairie Provinces

SOURCE: Statistics Canada

Average Size of Farms in Prairie Provinces

SOURCE: Statistics Canada

Percent of Canadian Grains Grown in Prairie Provinces

Wheat 95% | Barley and rye 90% | Oats 75%

SOURCE: *Canadian Wheat Board, Canadian Global Almanac, 2004*

Prairie Provinces: Land Use
KEY
- Forestry
- Livestock raising
- Commercial agriculture
- Manufacturing and trade
- Limited economic activity
- National border
- Provincial or territorial border

Northwest Territories — Nunavut — Hudson Bay — Alberta — Manitoba — Saskatchewan — Ontario — British Columbia — UNITED STATES

0 miles 500
0 kilometers 500
Lambert Azimuthal Equal Area

Map and Chart Skills

1. **Identify** What important crops are grown in the Prairie Provinces?

2. **Note** How much larger was a Prairie Province farm in 2001 than in 1981?

3. **Draw Conclusions** How is it possible that the number of farms has decreased but the Prairie Provinces produce most of Canada's wheat, barley, rye, and oats?

Go Online PHSchool.com Use Web Code lhe-4511 for DK World Desk Reference Online.

Differentiated Instruction

For Gifted and Talented $L3$

Have students research crops other than wheat that Canada produces. Ask students to make a poster showing where each is grown.

For Advanced Readers $L3$

Have students research to learn more about the role of wheat production in Canada's economy. Ask them to write a summary of their findings, including at least three pieces of information that they did not learn in the textbook.

Increasing Immigration The population of the indigenous peoples also began to shrink. This happened, in part, because European immigrants brought diseases to which the Plains Indians did not have **immunity**, or natural resistance. At the same time, the European population swelled. The settlers were eager to farm the prairie. The Canadian government encouraged people to settle on the Plains. Newcomers would help the economy grow. In the late 1800s and early 1900s, Canada advertised free land in European newspapers. The advertisements worked, and immigration increased. From 1900 to 1910, the population of Alberta alone increased by more than 500 percent.

Until the early 1900s, nearly all Canadians were indigenous peoples or people of French or British descent. That quickly changed. German, French, Belgian, Ukrainian, Hungarian, and Scandinavian immigrants all came to the Prairie Provinces. These immigrants farmed, mined, ranched, and participated in the fur trade.

Links to Science

Sanctuary Visitors to Saskatchewan's Grasslands National Park see some of North America's last untouched prairies. Ancient grasses called wheat grass, spear grass, and sage blow in the wind. The park is also home to 12 endangered and threatened species. They include hawks, burrowing owls, and short-horned lizards (below).

Prairie wheat grows in Saskatchewan, Canada.

Guided Instruction (continued)

- Ask **What did the Canadian government do to encourage immigration to Canada?** (*The government advertised free land in European newspapers.*)

- Ask **What effect did these advertisements have on Canada's population and economy?** (*European immigration increased, causing the population to grow. Immigrants contributed to the economy by farming, ranching, mining, and trading furs.*)

Independent Practice
Ask students to create the Taking Notes graphic organizer on a blank piece of paper. Then ask them to fill in causes and effects from the information they have just learned. Briefly model how to distinguish between a cause and an effect.

Monitor Progress
As students fill in the graphic organizer, circulate and make sure individuals are correctly placing causes in the Causes box and effects in the Effects box. Provide assistance as needed.

Links
Read the **Links to Science** on this page. Ask students **Why do you think it is necessary to create sanctuaries such as Saskatchewan's Grasslands National Park?** (*Answers will vary, but may include the need to ensure that animals and plants are preserved from extinction.*)

Differentiated Instruction

For English Language Learners [L1]
Pair students with native English speakers to read the Links to Science. Ask both students in each pair to read the box aloud, with the English language learner reading first. Then have the students work together to write a summary of the box in their own words.

For Special Needs Students [L1]
Have students read the section as they listen to the recorded version on the Student Edition on Audio CD. Check for comprehension of concepts such as *ancestry* and *immunity* by pausing the CD and asking students to try to describe them aloud.

⊙ Chapter 10, Section 2, **Student Edition on Audio CD**

Celebrating Traditions L2

Guided Instruction

- Ask students to read Celebrating Traditions. As students read, circulate and make sure individuals can answer the Reading Check question.

- Ask students to name the different celebrations that take place in the Prairie Provinces, the city each occurs in, and the heritage each commemorates. *(The Calgary Stampede in Calgary, Alberta, commemorates the area's ranching heritage. Klondike Days in Edmonton, Alberta, commemorates the area's gold rush. Festival du Voyageur in Winnipeg, Manitoba, commemorates the area's fur-trading heritage. The Weyburn Wheat Festival in Weyburn, Saskatchewan, commemorates the area's wheat crop.)*

Independent Practice

Have students complete the graphic organizer by filling in the last few effects of immigrants arriving in the Prairie Provinces.

Monitor Progress

- Show *Section Reading Support Transparency USC 59* and ask students to check their graphic organizers individually. Go over key concepts and clarify key vocabulary as needed.

  📖 **United States and Canada Transparencies,** *Section Reading Support Transparency USC 59*

- Tell students to fill in the last column of the *Reading Readiness Guide.* Probe for what they learned that confirms or invalidates each statement.

  All in One United States and Canada Teaching Resources, *Reading Readiness Guide,* p. 290

🎯 Target Reading Skill L2

Interpret Nonliteral Meanings As a follow up, ask students to answer the Target Reading Skill question in the Student Edition. *(the region that produces most of the country's wheat)*

Answers

✓ **Reading Check** because it produces so much wheat

Compare The Midwest is similar to the Prairie Provinces of Canada because the regions share similar types of farmland.

Interpret Nonliteral Meanings
What does the phrase *Canada's Breadbasket* mean?

Harvesting Wheat
This farmer harvests wheat near Saskatoon, Saskatchewan. Saskatchewan has more farmland than any other Canadian province. It is also Canada's largest producer of wheat. **Compare** *What part of the United States is similar to this part of Canada? Explain why.*

Farming the Land Many of the European immigrants who arrived became wheat farmers. In 1886, the completion of the Canadian Pacific Railway allowed settlers to reach the Prairie Provinces more easily. Better transportation also meant that wheat could be carried more quickly from farms to Canadian ports and then to the rest of the world. The wheat economy of Canada boomed.

Today, more than three fourths of Canada's farmland is in the Prairie Provinces. Wheat is still the major crop. Every year since the mid-1930s, Saskatchewan has produced more than half of Canada's wheat crop. This has helped Canada to become one of the world's leading exporters of wheat. It is no wonder then, that the region is known as Canada's Breadbasket. Although corporate farming is increasing, there are still more family-run farms in Canada than there are in the United States.

✓ **Reading Check** **Why is this region known as Canada's Breadbasket?**

302 United States and Canada

Differentiated Instruction

For Less Proficient Readers L1
Pair less proficient readers with more advanced readers and ask each pair to make a chart titled "Prairie Province Celebrations." Students should use the following column headings for their charts: *Name of Celebration, Location, What it Commemorates,* and *Events Involved.*

For Gifted and Talented L3
Ask students to select a Prairie Province celebration that interests them, such as the Calgary Stampede or Klondike Days. Have them write a fictional account of attending the celebration. Students should use details from at least two sources other than the textbook.

Celebrating Traditions

Each year, cities of the Prairie Provinces celebrate their ethnic or cultural heritage. In Calgary, Alberta, the Calgary Stampede commemorates the area's ranching legacy. This ten-day rodeo event has been held in Calgary since 1912. It offers a large variety of events such as chuck-wagon races, cow-milking contests, and bull riding. For ten days every July, the city of Edmonton, Alberta, celebrates the gold rush with its Klondike Days. Popular events include the raft race and the sourdough pancake breakfast. (During the gold rush many prospectors ate sourdough bread and biscuits).

Festival du Voyageur is held each February in Winnipeg, the capital of Manitoba. It honors the French Canadian fur-trading heritage of the area and features traditional food, arts and crafts, and exhibits. And in Weyburn, Saskatchewan, residents pay tribute to wheat as the area's most important crop with the Weyburn Wheat Festival. A great deal of fun at this festival comes from harvesting competitions and plant shows. The smell of fresh-baked bread from outdoor ovens adds to the atmosphere.

Rodeo events take place during the Calgary Stampede in Calgary, Alberta.

✓ Reading Check **Which Canadian festival celebrates ranching?**

Section 2 Assessment

Key Terms
Review the key terms at the beginning of this section. Use each key term in a sentence that explains its meaning.

Target Reading Skill
Find the phrase "buffalo herds that blanketed the region" on page 299. Explain in your own words what it means.

Comprehension and Critical Thinking
1. (a) List Which three provinces make up the Prairie Provinces?
(b) Explain What attracted thousands of European immigrants to the Canadian Prairie Provinces?

(c) Identify Effects How did the lives of indigenous people in the Canadian plains change after Europeans arrived?
2. (a) Recall Name two ways that Canadians celebrate their cultural heritage.
(b) Identify Effects How have European immigrants influenced the life and culture of the Prairie Provinces?
(c) Draw Conclusions What do you think were the advantages and disadvantages of moving to the Canadian plains in the 1800s?

Writing Activity
Suppose that it is the year 1900, and you work for Canada's government. The government will give 160 acres of land to people willing to come to the Prairie Provinces to start farms. Make a poster advertising free land. Describe conditions that would make settlers want to come.

Go Online
PHSchool.com

For: An activity on Saskatchewan
Visit: PHSchool.com
Web Code: lhd-4502

Chapter 10 Section 2 **303**

Writing Activity
Use the *Rubric for Assessing a Student Poster* to evaluate students' posters advertising free land.

All in One **United States and Canada Teaching Resources,** *Rubric for Assessing a Student Poster,* p. 325

Go Online
PHSchool.com Typing in the Web code when prompted will bring students directly to detailed instructions for this activity.

Assess Progress L2
Have students complete the Section Assessment. Administer the *Section Quiz.*

All in One **United States and Canada Teaching Resources,** *Section Quiz,* p. 292

Reteach L1
If students need more instruction, have them read this section in the Reading and Vocabulary Study Guide.

Chapter 10, Section 2, **Western Hemisphere Reading and Vocabulary Study Guide,** pp. 108–110

Extend L3
Have student groups organize a fair that celebrates the different cultural groups of the Prairie Provinces. Each group should research one cultural group. Encourage students to find out about traditional crafts, dances, clothes, and art. Suggest that they obtain recordings of music or prepare food that represents the cultural group they are presenting.

Answers

✓ Reading Check the Calgary Stampede

Section 2 Assessment

Key Terms
Students' sentences should reflect knowledge of each Key Term.

Target Reading Skill
Possible answer: the herds of buffalo were large and covered vast areas of land.

Comprehension and Critical Thinking
1. (a) Alberta, Manitoba, and Saskatchewan
(b) The Canadian government offered free land to settlers. **(c)** The buffalo that the indigenous people relied on were killed off. Most indigenous people agreed to give up their land and live on reserves. However, many died because of diseases brought by the immigrants.

2. (a) Canadians celebrate their heritage with festivals that include contests and traditional foods and crafts. **(b)** by bringing new industries, skills, and traditions **(c)** Answers will vary. Advantages include free farm land and new opportunities. Disadvantages include lack of food and supplies, harsh winters, and few trees for building.

Section 3
Step-by-Step Instruction

Objectives

Social Studies

1. Find out about the people and cultures of the Canadian West.
2. Learn what the economy and culture of British Columbia are like.

Reading/Language Arts

Use context clues to determine the meaning of unfamiliar words.

Prepare to Read

Build Background Knowledge L2

Tell students that most people in British Columbia live closer to Asia than to the east coast of their own country. Encourage them to think about how this might affect life in British Columbia. Ask students to think back to what they learned about French Canada in Section 1, then use the Give One, Get One participation strategy (TE, p. T37) to brainstorm a list of ways that the cultures of the east and west coasts of Canada might differ.

Set a Purpose for Reading L2

- Preview the Objectives.

- Read each statement in the *Reading Readiness Guide* aloud. Ask students to mark the statements true or false.

  All in One **United States and Canada Teaching Resources,** *Reading Readiness Guide,* p. 294

- Have students discuss the statements in pairs or groups of four, then mark their worksheets again. Use the Numbered Heads participation strategy (TE, p. T36) to call on students to share their group's perspectives.

Vocabulary Builder
Preview Key Terms L2

Pronounce each Key Term, then ask students to say the word with you. Provide a simple explanation such as, "During the gold rush, boomtowns grew quickly as places where gold miners could live and buy the things they needed."

Section 3
British Columbia
Economic and Cultural Changes

Prepare to Read

Objectives

In this section you will

1. Find out about the people and cultures of the Canadian West.
2. Learn what the economy and culture of British Columbia are like.

Taking Notes

As you read this section, look for details about the history of British Columbia. Copy the table below, and record your findings in it.

Events in British Columbian History	
10,000 years ago	
1700s	
1800s	
Today	

Target Reading Skill

Use Context Clues When you come across an unfamiliar word, you can sometimes figure out its meaning by using context—the surrounding words, phrases, and sentences. Sometimes the meaning of a word may not be clear until you have read an entire passage. However, you can infer the meaning of the unfamiliar word using general context clues and evaluating the information in the reading passage.

Key Terms

- **totem pole** (TOHT um pohl) *n.* a tall, carved pole containing the symbols of a particular Native American group, clan, or family
- **boomtown** (boom town) *n.* a settlement that springs up quickly to serve the needs of miners

Dancers at Chinese New Year in Vancouver, British Columbia

A visitor starts her day at a tiny coffee shop. All around her, people are speaking Dutch, Japanese, Spanish, German, and English. After having breakfast, the visitor gets into her car. On the radio, she hears country music—sung in French. Driving downtown, she passes street signs in Chinese, Indian men wearing turbans, a Korean travel agency, and a Thai restaurant. Where in the world is she? It may seem like the United Nations. But it is Vancouver (van KOO vur), British Columbia—a truly international city. As the largest city in British Columbia, Vancouver is the province's major center of industry, transportation, commerce, and culture.

304 United States and Canada

Target Reading Skill L2

Use Context Clues Point out the Target Reading Skill. Remind students that context clues are pieces of information that help you find the meaning of an unfamiliar word.

Model the skill by reading this sentence on p. 308: "There were countless obstacles—soaring mountains, steep valleys, and glaciers." Explain that students can use clues in the sentence to find the meaning of

obstacles. (*This sentence gives examples which help show that obstacles are things that can block progress.*)

Give students *Use Context Clues: General Knowledge.* Have them complete the activity in their groups.

All in One **United States and Canada Teaching Resources,** *Use Context Clues: General Knowledge,* p. 305

The People of the Canadian West

The first people came to present-day British Columbia at least 10,000 years ago. They belonged to several ethnic groups and spoke many different languages. Each group had its own customs and a complex society. The people along the coast caught fish, whales, and shellfish. They also carved giant **totem poles,** or tall, carved poles containing the symbols of a particular group, clan, or family. Other groups lived and hunted game in the dense inland forests. Some people traded with one another and got along well. Others fought.

New Arrivals In the late 1700s, Spanish, British, and Russian explorers arrived in the area to trade. In 1778, James Cook, a British explorer, sailed to Vancouver Island, off the coast of British Columbia. A group of Nootka (NOOT kuh) people met the British and agreed to trade. These coastal people wanted iron tools, while the British wanted furs. When the British built a fur-trading post on the island, trade between the two groups began to flourish.

Trade changed the indigenous peoples' lives a great deal. Although fur traders did not permanently settle the area, they introduced tools, European-style clothing, and ideas. In 1858, everything changed. Gold was discovered along the Fraser River.

Indigenous Carvings
The Haida sculptor (below) works on a small totem pole. Large totem poles (right) are sometimes used to tell the history of a family or tribe. **Analyze Images** *What does this totem pole tell you about the lives of the indigenous people who carved it?*

Vocabulary Builder

Use the information below to teach students this section's high-use word.

High-Use Word	Definition and Sample Sentence
benefit, p. 310	*v.* to gain something useful; to help The extra time to study **benefited** the whole class.

The People of the Canadian West L2

Guided Instruction

- Read The People of the Canadian West, using the Paragraph Shrinking strategy (TE, p. T34).

- Ask students **When fur traders went to what is now British Columbia, how did they affect the lives of indigenous people? How was this different from the impact of gold miners on indigenous people?** *(The fur traders did not settle permanently; they came and went. The gold miners settled towns and pushed indigenous people onto reserves.)*

Answer

Analyze Images Possible answer: The fact that the figure in the totem pole is holding fish may mean that fishing was an important part of the lives of the people who carved it.

Guided Instruction L2

Ask students to study the Regional Profile on this page. As a class, answer the Map and Chart Skills questions. Allow students to briefly discuss their responses with a partner before sharing answers.

Independent Practice

To give students more practice working with data, distribute *Analyzing Statistics*. Have students work in pairs to complete the worksheet. Encourage them to use the table on page 168 as a model for their tables.

All in One United States and Canada Teaching Resources, *Analyzing Statistics,* p. 317

REGIONAL PROFILE   Focus on Geography

British Columbia

More than 90 percent of British Columbia is owned by the government, which manages the land and its resources. The government sets certain rules about where and how forests can be cut, and then leases the land to private companies and loggers. More than 260,000 British Columbians depend on forestry for their jobs. British Columbia is the largest single exporter of softwood lumber in the world. As you study the map and charts, think about the importance of the provinces' natural resources.

British Columbia: Natural Resources

KEY
- Gold
- Silver
- Copper
- Iron
- Lead
- Zinc
- Coal
- Petroleum
- Natural gas
- Hydroelectric power
- Forested area
- Barren land
- Cropland and urban area
- — National border
- Provincial or territorial border

0 miles 200
0 kilometers 200
Lambert Azimuthal Equal Area

Yukon Territory · Northwest Territories · Gulf of Alaska · ALASKA (U.S.) · Finlay River · Peace River · British Columbia · Queen Charlotte Islands · Fraser River · Columbia River · Alberta · PACIFIC OCEAN · Vancouver Island · UNITED STATES · 140°W · 135°W · 130°W · 125°W · 120°W · 55°N · 50°N

Income From Mining in British Columbia, 2005

Mineral	Dollars (millions)
Copper	$1,130
Zinc	$528
Gold	$255
Lead	$87

SOURCE: *Price Waterhouse Coopers, Canada*

Canadian Wood and Paper Products Production

- 3%
- 21%
- 5%
- 31%
- 26%
- 14%

- Quebec
- British Columbia
- Ontario
- New Brunswick
- Alberta
- Other

SOURCE: *Canadian Global Almanac, 2004*

Map and Chart Skills

1. **Identify** Look at the map to describe the location of British Columbia's forests.
2. **Analyze Information** What is the total income British Columbia received in 2005 from mining copper, gold, zinc, and lead?
3. **Draw Conclusions** What do the charts tell you about the importance of forest products to the economy of British Columbia?

 Use Web Code lhe-4513 for **DK World Desk Reference Online.**

Answers

Map and Chart Skills

1. Forests are located inland, and cover most of British Columbia.

2. $2 billion

3. British Columbia is among the leading producers of wood and paper products in Canada, so many people in British Columbia depend on the industry for jobs.

Go Online PHSchool.com Students can find more information about this topic on the DK World Desk Reference Online.

Differentiated Instruction

For Advanced Readers L3

Have students learn more about trade by completing the online activity *Trade in a Global Economy*. As they complete the activity, have students pay attention to Canada's role as one of the world's major exporters.

Go Online PHSchool.com
For: Environmental and Global Issues: *Trade in a Global Economy*
Visit: PHSchool.com
Web Code: lhd-4506

- Ask students to describe the reaction of indigenous peoples to the arrival of gold miners. *(They were angry that their land was being taken. They protested.)*

- Ask: **What recent actions have the indigenous peoples of British Columbia taken?** *(They have found new pride in their culture and they are gaining new rights and land.)*

⊙ **Target Reading Skill** L2

Use Context Clues As a follow up, ask students to answer the Target Reading Skill question in the Student Edition. *(a large boat that is powered by a turning wheel)*

The Gold Rush A few years earlier, the British had established Victoria, a trading village on Vancouver Island. It was a small town of traders and farmers. Then, one Sunday morning in April 1858, an American paddlewheeler entered Victoria's harbor. It dropped off more than 400 men. They carried packs, blankets, spades, pickaxes, knives, and pistols. These rugged-looking characters had come to mine gold in the area. In a single morning, Victoria's population more than doubled.

Within weeks, tens of thousands more miners had arrived. Victoria quickly became a "stumptown"—all of its great trees had been chopped down to build shacks and boats. The town served as a supply center for the miners who were looking for gold on the Fraser River.

Two years later, miners also struck gold in the Cariboo Mountains in eastern British Columbia. Another wave of miners came from China, Europe, and the United States. The region was far from the coast and hard to reach, so the government built a 400-mile (644-kilometer) highway to it. Almost overnight, **boomtowns,** or settlements that were built to serve the needs of the miners, sprang up along the road. When the gold rush was over, many boomtowns died out.

Changes for Indigenous Peoples The thousands of settlers who arrived were taking gold from indigenous people's land—even taking over the land itself. In 1888, the British government took steps to confine some indigenous peoples to a small reserve. The indigenous peoples protested. The reserve was located on land that they had always lived on. How, they asked, could the government now "give" it to them?

Mining for Gold
This photograph, taken in 1900, shows a group of people looking for gold at Pine Creek, British Columbia. *Analyze Information Why would most people choose to mine gold from creeks and streams rather than by digging deep into the ground?*

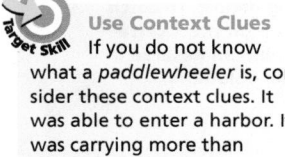

Use Context Clues If you do not know what a *paddlewheeler* is, consider these context clues. It was able to enter a harbor. It was carrying more than 400 passengers. Therefore, a paddlewheeler is _____.

Differentiated Instruction

For Less Proficient Readers L1
To help students keep track of the many cultural groups that have come to British Columbia over time, ask them to make a list as they read. Each time they read about a new cultural group, have them record the name of the group and the reason(s) why those people came to British Columbia.

For English Language Learners L2
Have students complete *Guided Reading and Review (Spanish)*. Then pair them with native English speakers and ask the partners to discuss the meaning of the words *stumptown* and *boomtown* and write a short description of both words.

   Guided Reading and Review (Spanish), **Spanish Support,** p. 100

Answer

Analyze Information Mining gold from creeks probably was safer and required less equipment than digging.

Ask students **Why did immigration to British Columbia increase even more once the building of the Canadian Pacific Railway began?** *(Immigrants from all over the world went to Canada to help build the railroad.)*

Independent Practice

Ask students to create the Taking Notes graphic organizer on a blank piece of paper. Then have students fill in the events that match each date as they read.

Monitor Progress

As students fill in the graphic organizer, circulate and make sure individuals are correctly listing events beside the time periods in which they occurred. Provide assistance as needed.

An indigenous man uses a gaff, an iron hook with a long handle, to catch salmon on the Morice-town Indian Reserve in British Columbia.

Like indigenous peoples throughout Canada, they had little choice. In a few short years, native people had gone from being the great majority to being the smallest minority of the population. They were pushed onto small reserves. The government passed laws banning many of their customs, religions, and languages. Authorities took children from their parents and placed them in government-run schools.

Recently, the indigenous peoples of British Columbia have found new pride in their history and culture. Their art is thriving. They are also demanding political rights and land. As a result, tension has developed between indigenous peoples and other British Columbians. For example, in 1999 the Sechelt Indians were awarded thousands of acres of land northwest of Vancouver and more than $40 million Canadian dollars. Many people felt that these terms were too generous. In July 2002, residents of British Columbia voted to place limits on native land claims.

The Canadian Pacific Railway British Columbia officially joined Canada in 1871. One of the conditions of joining was that a transcontinental railroad would be built within 10 years. Construction began in 1875, but little progress was made until 1881. That spring, Canadians began work on the enormous project of building a railroad that would stretch from Montreal to Vancouver. The goal of the project was to unite Canada. Look at the physical map of Canada on page 142 and you can see what a huge task this was. There were countless obstacles—soaring mountains, steep valleys, and glaciers. Workers built bridges and blasted long tunnels through the mountains.

The railroad project brought more change to Canada. There were not enough workers available to complete the railway on schedule. Thousands of immigrants, particularly from Ireland and China, came to work on the railroad. Towns grew up along the railroad, and more newcomers moved in. In a few short years, British Columbia changed from a sparsely inhabited region to a settled one, complete with cities.

✓ Reading Check **Why was the Canadian Pacific Railway built?**

Background: Links Across Time

The North West Mounted Police
Today, Canada's federal police force is the Royal Canadian Mounted Police. When the force was founded in 1873 in Alberta, it was called the North West Mounted Police and was the only authority to patrol the vast western stretches of Canada. The original Mounties, as they were called, took on a variety of tasks. For example, they were responsible for ensuring the fair treatment of indigenous people by fur traders, and for providing wilderness survival tips to immigrants. In 1920, the Mounties became a national police force called by the name they use today.

Answer

✓ Reading Check The Canadian Pacific Railway was built to unite Canada.

Economics and Culture

Although the Canadian Pacific Railroad connects all of Canada, the mountains are a barrier between British Columbia and the rest of the country. Today, most British Columbians live along the coast, west of the mountains. Many of them feel that their economic future lies with other countries more than with the rest of Canada.

The Pacific Rim Many British Columbians feel a link between their province and the Pacific Rim countries—nations that border the Pacific Ocean. One link is British Columbia's diverse people. More than 15 percent have Asian ancestors.

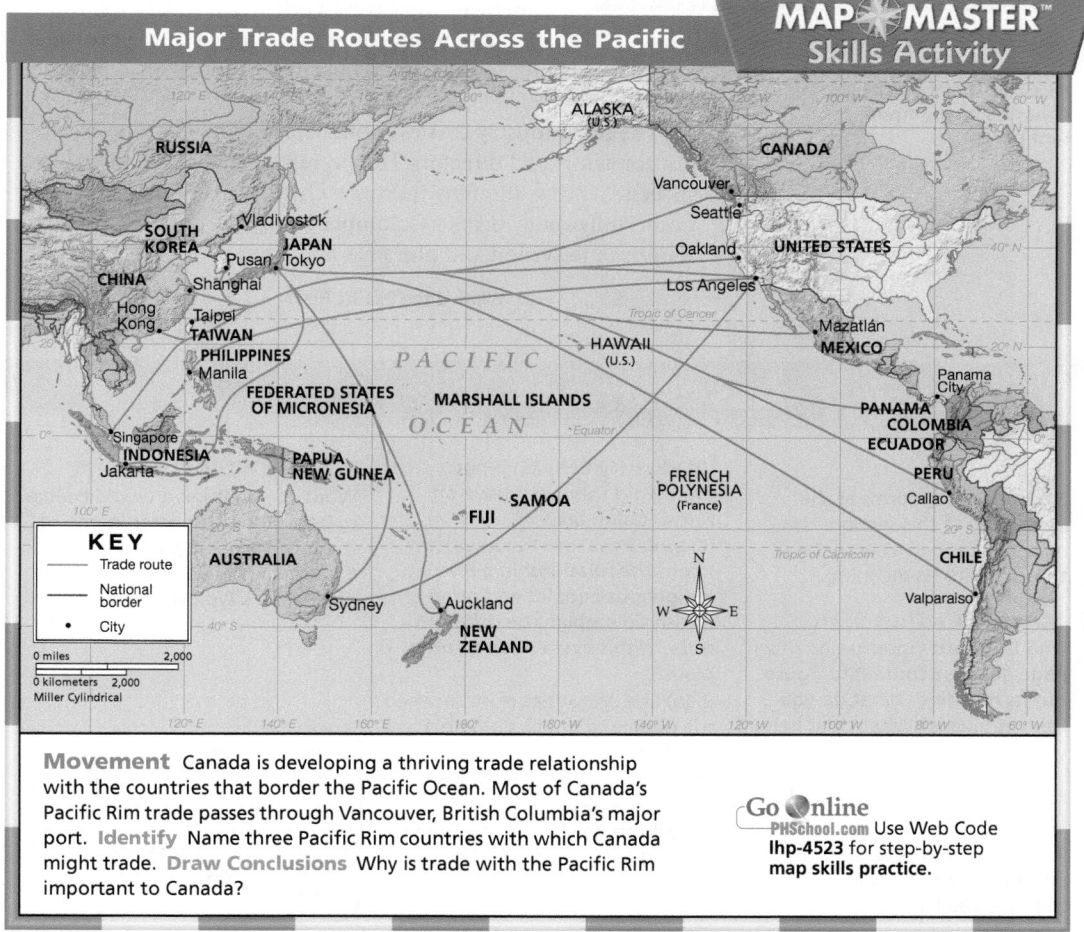

Major Trade Routes Across the Pacific

MAP MASTER™ Skills Activity

KEY
— Trade route
— National border
• City

0 miles 2,000
0 kilometers 2,000
Miller Cylindrical

Movement Canada is developing a thriving trade relationship with the countries that border the Pacific Ocean. Most of Canada's Pacific Rim trade passes through Vancouver, British Columbia's major port. **Identify** Name three Pacific Rim countries with which Canada might trade. **Draw Conclusions** Why is trade with the Pacific Rim important to Canada?

Go Online
PHSchool.com Use Web Code lhp-4523 for step-by-step map skills practice.

Chapter 10 Section 3 **309**

Assess and Reteach

Assess Progress [L2]

Have students complete the Section Assessment. Administer the *Section Quiz.*

> **All in One United States and Canada Teaching Resources,** *Section Quiz,* p. 296

Reteach [L1]

If students need more instruction, have them read this section in the Reading and Vocabulary Study Guide.

> Chapter 10, Section 3, **Western Hemisphere Reading and Vocabulary Study Guide,** pp. 111–113

Extend [L3]

Have each student write a newspaper editorial from the point of view of a townsperson about the consequences of thousands of gold miners arriving in Victoria. Encourage students to consider questions such as the following before writing: In what different ways might citizens of Victoria react to the newcomers? Would they be excited, wary, angry, or welcoming? How would the population increase affect the community's businesses? Who might benefit and who might be hurt?

Answers

> ✔ Reading Check The Pacific Rim is made up of the countries that border the Pacific Ocean.

Section 3 Assessment

Key Terms
Students' sentences should reflect knowledge of each Key Term.

Target Reading Skill
Possible answer: "international" means of many different countries. The paragraph describes languages from many different countries.

Comprehension and Critical Thinking
1. (a) gold mining **(b)** The population of British Columbia more than doubled, and indigenous people were forced onto reserves and had many of their customs, religions, and languages banned. **(c)** Answers will vary. Students may say that the relationship would be better today if so many newcomers had not arrived in such a short time period and forced so much change on the indigenous people.

The water in Vancouver's harbor does not freeze. As a result, it's one of Canada's most important ports.

Trade is still another link between British Columbia and the Pacific Rim. Forty percent of the province's trade is with Asian countries. British Columbia wants good relationships with them. As a result, in British Columbian schools, students learn Asian languages. They learn Japanese, Cantonese Chinese, or Mandarin Chinese. Some even learn Punjabi (pun JAH bee), a language of India and Pakistan.

The Film Industry The television and film industry is another example of British Columbia's strong link to other countries. British Columbia is the third-largest film production center in North America—after New York and Los Angeles. More than 200 productions were filmed in the province in 2002, bringing more than $800 million Canadian dollars to the region.

The film industry creates about 50,000 jobs. The jobs are not just for actors and directors. Hotels, restaurants, and gas stations all benefit from the film industry. Only a two-hour plane ride from Hollywood, British Columbia is a good option for many American television and film projects.

> ✔ Reading Check **What is the Pacific Rim?**

✦ Section 3 Assessment

Key Terms
Review the key terms at the beginning of this section. Use each key term in a sentence that explains its meaning.

Target Reading Skill
Find the word "international" on page 304. Use context to figure out its meaning. What do you think it means? What clues helped you arrive at a meaning?

Comprehension and Critical Thinking
1. (a) Recall What brought people to British Columbia in the late 1800s?

(b) Identify Effects What effects did this event have on British Columbia?
(c) Link Past and Present How might the relationship between indigenous peoples and other British Columbians be different today if this event hadn't taken place?
2. (a) List What ties exist between the people of British Columbia and the Pacific Rim?
(b) Analyze How does British Columbia's geography contribute to its economic and cultural ties with the Pacific Rim?

Writing Activity
What do you think it would be like to be a gold prospector in one of the gold rushes in Canada? Write a journal entry describing a gold prospector's typical workday.

> **Go Online**
> **PHSchool.com**
> **For:** An activity on totem poles
> **Visit:** PHSchool.com
> **Web Code:** lhd-4503

310 United States and Canada

---

2. (a) heritage, language, and trade **(b)** British Columbia's nearness to the other Pacific Rim countries has led to cultural exchange and valuable trading relationships.

Writing Activity
Use the *Rubric for Assessing a Journal Entry* to evaluate students' journal entries.

> **All in One United States and Canada Teaching Resources,** *Rubric for Assessing a Journal Entry,* p. 327

Go Online PHSchool.com Typing in the Web code when prompted will bring students directly to detailed instructions for this activity.

The Atlantic Provinces
Relying on the Sea

Prepare to Read

Objectives
In this section you will
1. Learn what life is like on the Atlantic coast.
2. Discover how maritime industries affect the provinces.

Taking Notes
As you read this section, look for the causes and effects of overfishing. Copy the chart below, and record your findings in it.

CAUSES	EVENT	EFFECTS
• •	Cod fishing ban	• •

Target Reading Skill

Use Context Clues Context, the words and phrases surrounding a word, can help you understand a word you may not know. One context clue to look for is cause and effect. The context clues show how the unfamiliar word is related to the cause or is the result of an action or idea. Clues to look for include *because, since, therefore,* and *so.*

Key Terms
- **exile** (EK syl) *v.* to force someone to leave his or her native land or home
- **maritime** (MA rih tym) *adj.* having to do with navigation or shipping on the sea
- **aquaculture** (AHK wuh kul chur) *n.* the cultivation of fish or water plants

Modern-day Norwegian explorer Helge Ingstad was aboard a ship in 1960 that stopped at a rocky peninsula in Newfoundland. The land formation was similar to what he had seen on ancient maps, and the scenery reminded him of the descriptions in Viking legends. After spotting what appeared to be the outlines of old building foundations, Ingstad believed he might be at the site of the first known Viking settlement in North America. Eight years of archaeological digs proved that Ingstad had unearthed a Viking settlement—possibly the very one that Leif Ericsson reached and named Vinland around the year 1000. Many artifacts were found at the site, including fireplaces, and a pit where iron may have been heated and formed into tools. The Viking settlement is now called L'Anse aux Meadows (lahns oh meh DOH). Viking buildings and artifacts have been reconstructed, and the historic site has become a popular tourist attraction.

From the time of the Vikings until today, the location of the Atlantic Provinces has had a huge influence on the region.

Some historians believe that Leif Ericsson may have landed here at L'Anse aux Meadows about 1,000 years ago.

Target Reading Skill

Use Context Clues Point out the Target Reading Skill. Explain that students can use cause-and-effect clues in the text to help them find the meaning of unfamiliar words.

Model the skill by asking students to use cause-and-effect clues to help find the meaning of *archaeologist* in this sentence: Archaeologists dug in Newfoundland because they wanted to find the remains of a very old Viking settlement.

Point out the context clues that can help students infer the meaning of archaeologist.

Give students *Use Context Clues: Cause and Effect.* Have them complete the activity in their groups.

United States and Canada Teaching Resources, *Use Context Clues: Cause and Effect,* p. 307

Objectives
Social Studies
1. Learn what life is like on the Atlantic coast.
2. Discover how maritime industries affect the provinces.

Reading/Language Arts
Learn how cause-and-effect clues can help you understand the meaning of an unfamiliar word.

Prepare to Read

Build Background Knowledge
Tell students that they will learn how the people of Canada's Atlantic Provinces rely on the sea in this section. Ask students to study the location of the Atlantic Provinces on *Color Transparency USC 40.* Point out that these provinces each border a large length of ocean. Using Think-Write-Pair-Share (TE, p. T36), challenge students to make a list of industries that are likely to thrive along an ocean coastline *(fishing, shipping, tourism).*

United States and Canada Transparencies, *Color Transparency USC 40: Canada: Physical-Political*

Set a Purpose for Reading
- Preview the Objectives.
- Read each statement in the *Reading Readiness Guide* aloud. Ask students to mark the statements true or false.
- Have students discuss the statements in pairs or groups of four, then mark their worksheets again. Use the Numbered Heads participation strategy (TE, p. T36) to call on students to share their group's perspectives.

United States and Canada Teaching Resources, *Reading Readiness Guide,* p. 298

Vocabulary Builder
Preview Key Terms
Pronounce each Key Term, then ask students to say the word with you. Provide a simple explanation such as, "Aquaculture is also known as fish farming."

Instruct

Living on the Coast ▢L2

Guided Instruction

- **Vocabulary Builder** Clarify the high-use word **neutral** before reading.

- Read Living on the Coast, using the Oral Cloze reading strategy (TE, p. T33).

- Ask students **How has location influenced life in the Atlantic Provinces?** *(Because the provinces border the Atlantic Ocean, they have developed a strong fishing industry. Also, Newfoundland and Labrador is an important transatlantic transportation and communications center.)*

- Ask **What happened to Acadians when the British controlled Acadia in 1755?** *(Acadians were exiled. Some moved to Quebec, others to Louisiana.)*

Independent Practice

Ask students to create the Taking Notes graphic organizer on a blank piece of paper. Then ask them to fill in causes and effects from the information they have just learned. Briefly model how to distinguish between a cause and an effect.

Monitor Progress

As students fill in the graphic organizer, circulate and make sure individuals are placing causes in the Causes box and effects in the Effects box. Provide assistance as needed.

⊙ Target Reading Skill ▢L2

Use Context Clues As a follow up, ask students to answer the Target Reading Skill question in the Student Edition. *(something that crosses the Atlantic Ocean)*

Living on the Coast

Today, Newfoundland and Labrador, along with Prince Edward Island, New Brunswick, and Nova Scotia, make up the Atlantic Provinces. These provinces are located in eastern Canada, where they all share at least part of their border with the Atlantic Ocean. Many of the people in these provinces live on the coast. One exception is Prince Edward Island, where the population is evenly spread across the island. The people in the Atlantic Provinces are mainly of English, Irish, Scottish, and French descent.

Newfoundland and Labrador Five hundred years after the Vikings left their colony in Vinland, John Cabot rediscovered the island in 1497. He called it the *New Found Land.* About 100 years later, the island became England's first overseas colony. It was used mainly as a fishing station until settlers moved there permanently in the early 1600s. In 2001, the province's name officially changed from Newfoundland to Newfoundland and Labrador.

The province of Newfoundland and Labrador is the easternmost part of North America. Because of its location, the province is an important transatlantic transportation and communications center. It was here in 1901 that Guglielmo Marconi (goo lee EL moh mahr KOH nee) received the first wireless telegraph signals from across the Atlantic Ocean. More importantly, the province is located next to the Grand Banks, which at one time were the best fishing grounds in the world.

Use Context Clues If you do not know what *transatlantic* means, look for a context clue. Use the cause and effect context clue and the surrounding sentences to figure out its meaning. What does *transatlantic* mean?

Northern gannets fly around Avalon Peninsula, Newfoundland and Labrador.

┌ Vocabulary Builder ─────────

Use the information below to teach students this section's high-use words.

High-Use Word	Definition and Sample Sentence
neutral, p. 314	*adj.* not taking one side or the other in a quarrel or war My brother stayed **neutral** in the fight between my sister and me.
focus, p. 315	*n.* center of attention The teacher was the **focus** of the class when she announced the day of the next test.

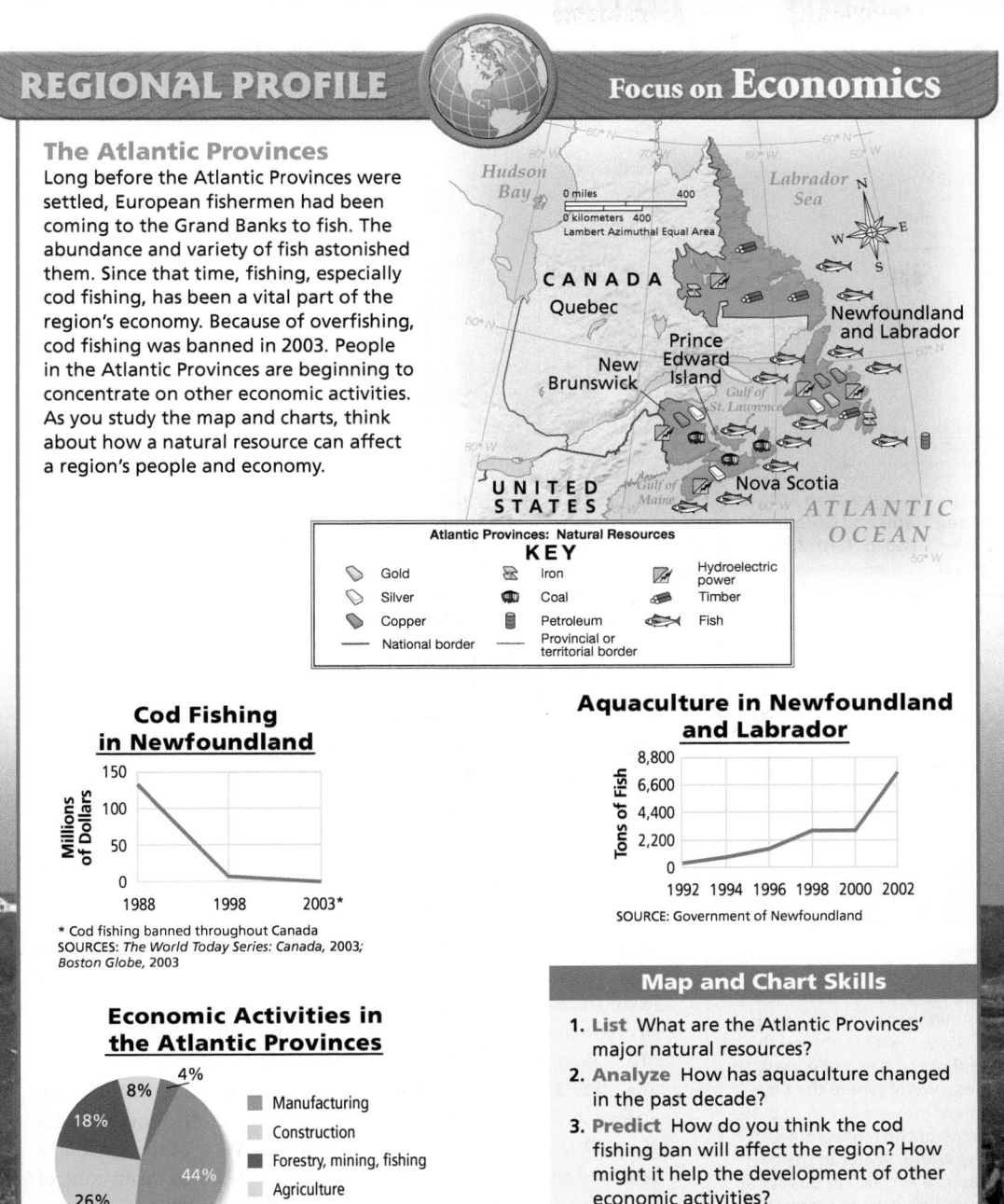

The Atlantic Provinces

Long before the Atlantic Provinces were settled, European fishermen had been coming to the Grand Banks to fish. The abundance and variety of fish astonished them. Since that time, fishing, especially cod fishing, has been a vital part of the region's economy. Because of overfishing, cod fishing was banned in 2003. People in the Atlantic Provinces are beginning to concentrate on other economic activities. As you study the map and charts, think about how a natural resource can affect a region's people and economy.

Atlantic Provinces: Natural Resources

KEY

Gold	Iron	Hydroelectric power
Silver	Coal	Timber
Copper	Petroleum	Fish
— National border	— Provincial or territorial border	

Cod Fishing in Newfoundland

* Cod fishing banned throughout Canada
SOURCES: *The World Today Series: Canada, 2003; Boston Globe, 2003*

Aquaculture in Newfoundland and Labrador

SOURCE: Government of Newfoundland

Economic Activities in the Atlantic Provinces

- 44% Manufacturing
- 26% Construction
- 18% Forestry, mining, fishing
- 8% Agriculture
- 4% Utilities

SOURCE: *Canadian Global Almanac, 2003*

Map and Chart Skills

1. **List** What are the Atlantic Provinces' major natural resources?
2. **Analyze** How has aquaculture changed in the past decade?
3. **Predict** How do you think the cod fishing ban will affect the region? How might it help the development of other economic activities?

Go Online
PHSchool.com
Use Web Code lhe-4514 for DK World Desk Reference Online.

Chapter 10 Section 4 **313**

Guided Instruction L2

Ask students to study the Regional Profile on this page. Encourage them to study the map and the graphs on the page and think about the information each provides. As a class, answer the Map and Chart Skills questions. Allow students to briefly discuss their responses with a partner before sharing answers.

Independent Practice

- To help students understand the information given in the line graphs, distribute *Reading a Line Graph*. Have students work in pairs to complete the worksheet.

  All in One **United States and Canada Teaching Resources,** *Reading a Line Graph,* p. 318

- Ask students to study the line graphs on this page. Ask **Which line graph shows an increase over time?** *(the aquaculture graph)* **Which one shows a decrease over time?** *(the cod fishing graph)*

Answers

Map and Chart Skills

1. Fish, coal, and timber
2. It has increased from producing almost no fish to producing about 8,000 tons of fish per year.
3. Possible answer: The ban may cause financial hardship to people who make their living from cod fishing. The ban will force people in the region to focus on other economic activities, such as manufacturing, construction, or utilities. This should help those economic activities to grow.

Go Online
PHSchool.com Students can find more information about this topic on the DK World Desk Reference Online.

Differentiated Instruction

For Less Proficient Readers L1

Remind students that it is important to read the title and labels of each line graph to understand the information it provides. Similarly, remind them to read the keys on the circle graph and the map to ensure that they comprehend all the information on these visuals. Have students practice reading graphs by copying the data from a graph into a table. For the cod fishing graph, for example, have students complete a table such as this:

Year	Millions of dollars
1988	
1998	
2003	

A Maritime Economy [L2]

Guided Instruction

- **Vocabulary Builder** Clarify the high-use word **focus** before reading.

- Read about the economy of the Atlantic Provinces in A Maritime Economy. As students read, make sure individuals can answer the Reading Check question.

- Discuss the way a booming fishing industry led to the development of other industries in the Atlantic Provinces. *(Fishing required fishing vessels, so a shipbuilding industry emerged. The shipbuilding industry needed wood with which to build ships, so the forestry industry grew.)*

Independent Practice

Have students continue to fill in the boxes in their graphic organizers with causes and effects of overfishing.

Monitor Progress

- Show *Section Reading Support Transparency USC 61.* Go over key concepts and clarify key vocabulary as needed.

    📖 **United States and Canada Transparencies,** *Section Reading Support Transparency USC 61*

- Tell students to fill in the last column of the *Reading Readiness Guide.* Probe for what they learned that confirms or invalidates each statement.

    All in One United States and Canada Teaching Resources, *Reading Readiness Guide,* p. 298

Links

Read the **Links to Science** on this page. Ask students **How would the unique shape of the Bay of Fundy affect the region's economy?** *(Answers may include that it allows for a greater variety and availability of fish.)*

Answers

MAP MASTER Skills Activity **Read a Map Key** Britain, Spain, and France **Draw Conclusions** Britain

✓ **Reading Check** in 1763

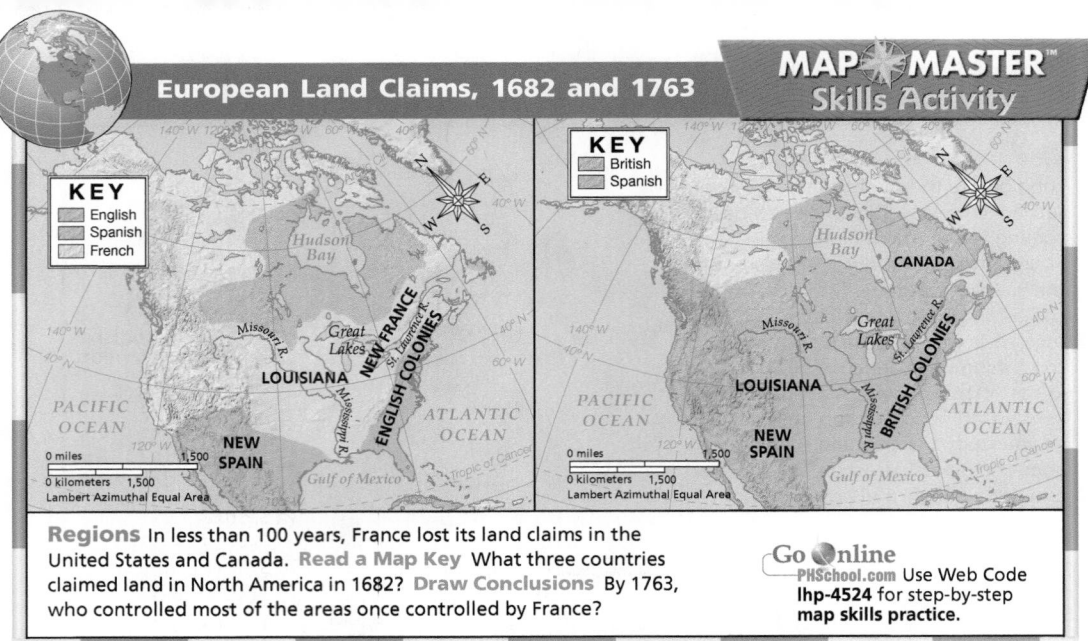

MAP MASTER Skills Activity

European Land Claims, 1682 and 1763

KEY
- English
- Spanish
- French

KEY
- British
- Spanish

Regions In less than 100 years, France lost its land claims in the United States and Canada. **Read a Map Key** What three countries claimed land in North America in 1682? **Draw Conclusions** By 1763, who controlled most of the areas once controlled by France?

Go **Online** PHSchool.com Use Web Code **lhp-4524** for step-by-step map skills practice.

Links to Science

High Tide The Bay of Fundy lies between New Brunswick and Nova Scotia. Its unique funnel shape—narrow with shallow water at the north end of the bay and wide with deep water where the bay opens into the ocean—causes some of the highest tides in the world. Water in the bay can rise as much as 60 feet at high tide. These exceptional tides carry about 100 billion tons of water in and out of the bay each day.

Acadia Eastern Canada was once almost entirely populated by people of French descent. Nova Scotia, New Brunswick, and Prince Edward Island were part of Acadia. Here, in the early 1600s, the French established their first permanent North American settlement. French control of the area, however, did not last long. The English wanted this land, and the two countries fought over it many times. The area shifted from one country's control to the other's more than once. During the fighting, Acadians remained neutral.

In 1755, a time when Britain controlled the area, Britain feared that the French inhabitants of Acadia might secretly be loyal to France. As a result, Acadians were **exiled**, or forced to leave the area. Some exiled Acadians settled in Quebec or New Brunswick, while others moved to France, the West Indies, and other French colonies. Still others moved to present-day Louisiana, then a French settlement, where their descendants today are known as Cajuns. Britain gained permanent control over Acadia in 1763 at the end of the Seven Years' War. Many Acadians returned to the area only to find that the British had taken control of the fertile lands they had once farmed. So they took up fishing and lumbering instead to support themselves.

✓ **Reading Check** When did Britain gain permanent control over Acadia?

314 United States and Canada

Differentiated Instruction

For English Language Learners [L1]
Check for students' comprehension of the terms *maritime* and *aquaculture.* Have students read this section in the Spanish Reading and Vocabulary Study Guide to reinforce these and other concepts for them.

📖 Chapter 10, Section 4, **Western Hemisphere Spanish Reading and Vocabulary Study Guide,** pp. 83–84

For Special Needs Students [L1]
After students have read about Acadia and watched the video *Cultures of the Atlantic Provinces,* ask them to work in pairs to write a paragraph summarizing the experience of Acadians during the 1700s.

📼 *Cultures of the Atlantic Provinces,* **World Studies Video Program**

A Maritime Economy

Maritime means related to navigation or commerce on the sea. No term better sums up the focus of life in the Atlantic Provinces. The Atlantic Provinces are often called the Maritime Provinces. Much of the economy there depends on fishing.

In the 1800s, the demand for fishing vessels brought about the growth of the shipbuilding industry. The region led Canada in ship construction through most of the 1800s. The forestry industry in the area kept shipbuilders well supplied. Both industries helped the region's economy boom. Shipbuilding is still a major employer in the region, particularly in Nova Scotia.

Fishing is another major industry. However, the fishing industry has changed. In Newfoundland and Labrador, cod had been the primary catch until cod fishing was partially banned in 1992 and completely banned in 2003. The government banned cod fishing because the waters had been overfished. Tens of thousands of fishing jobs have been lost as a result of the ban.

Today, the province has turned its attention toward other types of fish to make up for loss of revenue from cod. Fish farming, or **aquaculture,** is a growing industry. Mussels are grown on Canada's eastern coast, and salmon farms are operating off the shores of New Brunswick.

Fishing village on Cape Breton Island, Nova Scotia

√ Reading Check **Which Atlantic Province is a leader in the shipbuilding industry?**

Section 4 Assessment

Key Terms
Review the key terms at the beginning of this section. Use each key term in a sentence that explains its meaning.

Target Reading Skill
Find the word *overfished* on page 315. Use context to figure out its meaning. What clue helped you?

Comprehension and Critical Thinking
1. (a) **List** Name the provinces that make up the Atlantic Provinces.

(b) **Explain** Where are the Atlantic Provinces located?
(c) **Analyze** How has the location of Newfoundland and Labrador made it an important communications center?
2. (a) **Recall** What industries did fishing help to grow in the 1800s?
(b) **Summarize** How has the fishing industry in the Atlantic Provinces changed in recent years?
(c) **Predict** What role might the fishing industry play in the Atlantic Provinces' economy in the future?

Writing Activity
Suppose that you are a French farmer living in Acadia in 1755. The British have told you that you must move to Louisiana. Write a paragraph describing how you feel about the move.

Go Online
PHSchool.com

For: An activity on Nova Scotia
Visit: PHSchool.com
Web Code: lhd-4504

Go Online
PHSchool.com Typing in the Web code when prompted will bring students directly to detailed instructions for this activity.

Assess and Reteach

Extend L3
Discuss with students the partial ban on cod fishing in Newfoundland and Labrador. Remind students that beginning in the 1880s, the region's shipbuilding industry declined, while fishing remained important to the economy. Divide the class into two groups and organize a debate. Ask one group to argue for the ban and the other to argue against it. Suggest that students do research to find information that supports their group's side.

Section 4 Assessment

Key Terms
Students' sentences should reflect knowledge of each Key Term.

Target Reading Skill
Possible answer: *overfished* means fished too much. The fact that the government banned cod fishing is a clue to this meaning.

Comprehension and Critical Thinking
1. (a) Newfoundland and Labrador, Prince Edward Island, New Brunswick, and Nova Scotia (b) in eastern Canada, along the Atlantic Ocean (c) Newfoundland and Labrador is the eastern-most part of North America, so it helps connect the two sides of the Atlantic.

2. (a) shipbuilding and forestry (b) In some provinces, processing fish is now a big industry, in addition to or replacing catching fish. Also, cod fishing has been banned in Newfoundland and Labrador because of overfishing. (c) Answers will vary. Students may say that with the development of aquaculture and the increased importance of fish processing, the fishing industry will stay strong. Others may say that the overfishing of the waters of the Atlantic will cause the fishing industry to become less important.

Objective
Learn how to write a summary.

Prepare to Read

Build Background Knowledge L2
Ask students to brainstorm instances in which they chose to give a summary of something rather than all the details. Ask whether any students have recently described a movie they saw or a trip they took. Encourage students to explain why they gave a summary rather than a detailed explanation.

Instruct

Writing a Summary L2

Guided Instruction
- Read the steps to writing a summary as a class and write them on the board.

- Practice the skill by following the steps on p. 316 as a class. Model each step in the activity by choosing a sample vacation to summarize *(a visit to a national park)*, stating the main ideas *(On my vacation, we had good weather, saw lots of animals, and hiked through beautiful woods and over rocky mountains.)*, identifying what the main ideas have in common *(Everything about my vacation was great.)*, and writing a summary paragraph *(My vacation was great because of all the interesting things we got to see and do. We had good weather, saw lots of animals, and hiked through beautiful woods and over rocky mountains.)*.

Independent Practice
Assign *Skills for Life* and have students complete it individually.

All in One United States and Canada Teaching Resources, *Skills for Life,* p. 311

Monitor Progress
As students are completing the *Skills for Life* worksheet, circulate to make sure students understand the skill steps. Provide assistance as needed.

 # Writing a Summary

> "Hey, how was your weekend?"
> If your friend asked you this question, would you tell him everything that happened over the weekend? Of course you wouldn't. You would pick a few major events and state them as a conclusion. For instance, "I went to the ball game on Saturday afternoon and the movies on Saturday night. I was really busy."
> When you're asked to summarize information, you find the main ideas and weave them into a conclusion. Being able to summarize information is a school survival skill. You need it to take tests, write essays, have debates, and understand what you read.

Learn the Skill
You can summarize many types of information: a novel, a news report, a movie—even a museum exhibit. These steps show you how to sum up information.

1 **Find and state the main idea of each paragraph or section of information you want to summarize.** You can often find a main idea in the topic sentence of a paragraph. If you are summarizing a large piece of information, you might want to jot down the main ideas.

2 **Identify what the main ideas have in common.** Look for the logic in how the ideas are presented. You might find events in chronological order. You might find causes and effects or comparisons. You can also look for main ideas that describe parts of a whole topic.

3 **Write a summary paragraph beginning with a topic sentence.** The topic sentence should draw together the main ideas you are summarizing. The main ideas on your list will become the supporting details of your summary.

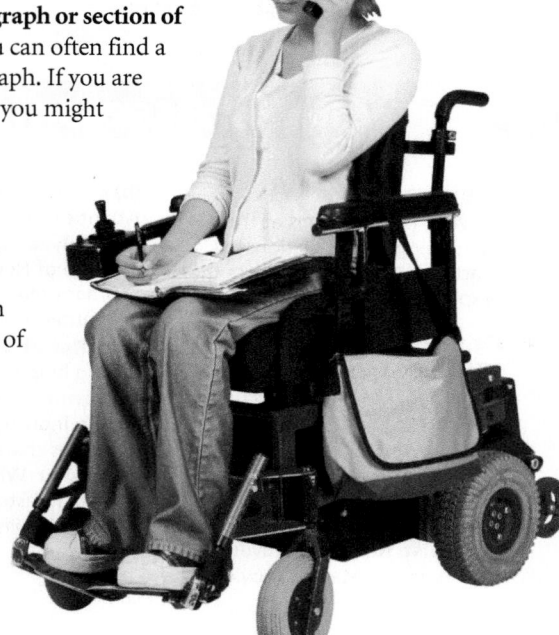

Practice the Skill

Reread pages 294–295. Follow the steps on the previous page in order to summarize the text.

1 Read the heading and subheadings of this passage. List the main idea of each paragraph. For example, in the first paragraph, the first half of the topic sentence provides a strong main idea: "French culture first reached Quebec in the 1500s. . . ." If no one sentence states the whole main idea, you should form a statement in your own words. Now write down the main idea for the other paragraphs in this passage.

2 The main ideas in this passage are mostly in chronological order. In what other ways are they related?

3 One possible topic sentence for your summary might be this: "The province of Quebec has struggled to preserve its French heritage in a country dominated by English culture." Use this topic sentence, or write your own, and then complete the summary paragraph by adding explanations and details. The details will come from the main ideas on your list.

A welcome-to-Quebec sign in English and French.

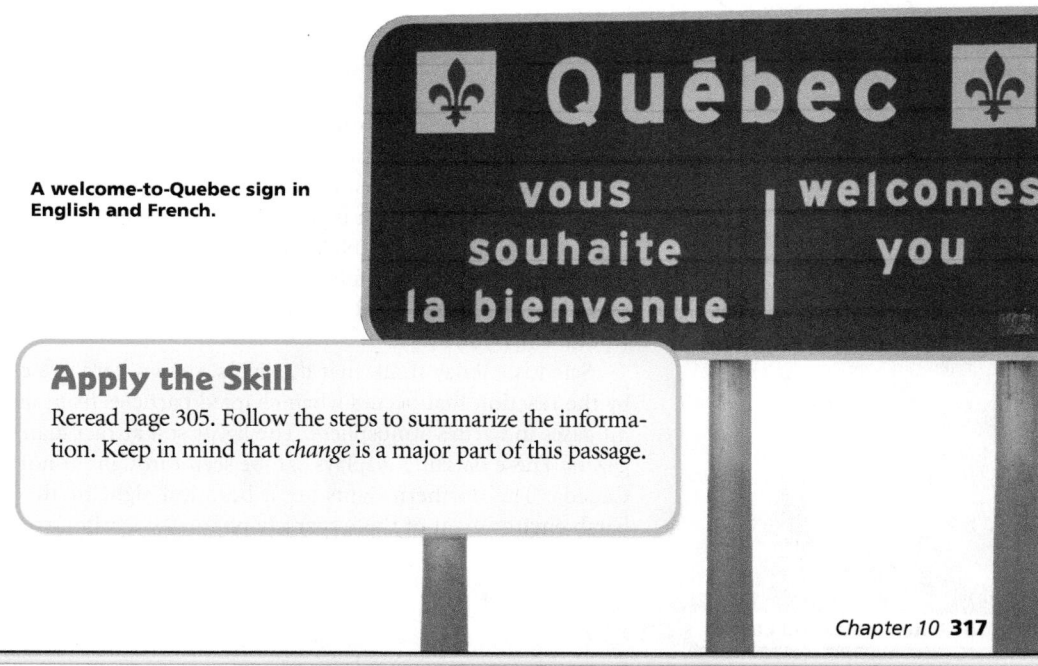

Apply the Skill

Reread page 305. Follow the steps to summarize the information. Keep in mind that *change* is a major part of this passage.

Chapter 10 **317**

Differentiated Instruction

For Advanced Readers L3
Ask students to select another passage from the textbook and write a summary of it. Then have students trade summaries with a partner and challenge each student to identify the passage that the other student summarized. Allow students to revise their summaries based on their partner's responses.

Assess and Reteach

Assess Progress L2
Ask students to do the Apply the Skill activity.

Reteach L1
If students are having trouble applying the skill steps, have them review the skill by working in pairs to write a summary of The Prairie Provinces section.

Extend L3
To extend the lesson, have pairs of students select something they have both read, seen, or participated in recently and write a summary about it. Ask each student in a pair to write his or her own summary and to include at least two paragraphs. Then have partners trade their summaries and identify differences. Students may revise their summaries after seeing their partner's summary if they wish.

Answer
Apply the Skill
Answers will vary, but should show that students understand the skill steps.

Chapter 10 **317**

Section 5
Step-by-Step Instruction

Section 5
The Northern Territories
New Frontiers

Objectives

Social Studies

1. Discover what life is like for people in Canada's far north.

2. Find out about the remote region of the Yukon Territory.

3. Understand how the new territory of Nunavut was formed.

Reading/Language Arts

Use context clues to determine the meaning of a familiar word when used in an unfamiliar way.

Prepare to Read

Build Background Knowledge L2

Tell students that in this section, they will learn about the Northern Territories of Canada. Ask them to preview the section's headings and photos with this question in mind: **How are the Northern Territories different from other regions of Canada?** Have students share responses using an Idea Wave (TE, p. T35).

Set a Purpose for Reading L2

■ Preview the Objectives.

■ Read each statement in the *Reading Readiness Guide* aloud. Ask students to mark the statements true or false.

   All in One United States and Canada Teaching Resources, *Reading Readiness Guide,* p. 302

■ Have students discuss the statements in pairs or groups of four, then mark their worksheets again. Use the Numbered Heads participation strategy (TE, p. T36) to call on students to share their group's perspectives.

Vocabulary Builder
Preview Key Terms L2

Pronounce the Key Term, then ask students to say the word with you. Provide a simple explanation such as, "The aurora borealis is a colorful, natural light show in the sky of the far north."

Prepare to Read

Objectives

In this section you will

1. Discover what life is like for people in Canada's far north.

2. Find out about the remote region of the Yukon Territory.

3. Understand how the new territory of Nunavut was formed.

Taking Notes

As you read the section, look for details about the government of the Northern Territories. Copy the concept web below, and record your findings in it.

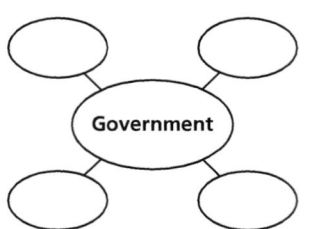

Target Reading Skill

Use Context Clues Words and phrases can take on different meanings in different situations. For example, if you are watching a play, and someone says that the *cast* is very talented, you would know that *cast* means the group of actors. But *cast* can also mean "to throw a fishing line" or "something you put on a broken arm." The information surrounding a word—whether it is a few other words, or phrases and sentences—is the context of that word.

Key Terms

• **aurora borealis** (aw RAWR uh bawr ee AL us) *n.* the colorful bands of light that can be seen in the skies of the Northern Hemisphere

• **Inuktitut** (ih NOOK tih toot) *n.* the native language of the Inuit

Named for the Latin word for dawn, the **aurora borealis** (aw RAWR uh bawr ee AL us), or northern lights, is a colorful band of light that can be seen in the Northern Hemisphere. The farther north you travel, the better is your chance of seeing these colorful bands of light. Some of Canada's indigenous peoples believed the lights were spirits. One folktale described the lights as spirits playing games. Others said that if you whistled loudly, the spirits would whisk you away.

Scientists today think that the lights, shown here, are caused by the reaction that occurs when charged particles from the sun hit gases in Earth's atmosphere. The lights still attract many skygazers. These dazzling displays can be seen throughout northern Canada. The northern lights are a beautiful sight in the often harsh environment of these sparsely populated territories.

318 United States and Canada

Target Reading Skill L2

Use Context Clues Point out the Target Reading Skill. Tell students that words can have different meanings in different contexts. In this case, the context surrounding a word can provide clues to the word's meaning.

Model using context clues by finding the meaning of "pass" in this sentence from p. 321: "The end of the pass narrowed to less than three feet wide and became very steep."

(The context helps show that "pass" here means a narrow passage through mountains.)

Give students *Use Context Clues: Definition/Description.* Have them complete the activity in their groups.

   All in One United States and Canada Teaching Resources, *Use Context Clues: Definition/Description,* p. 308

The Far North

In addition to its provinces, Canada has three territories—the Northwest Territories, Yukon Territory, and Nunavut (NOO nuh voot). The territories make up more than one third of Canada's total land area and stretch far north into the Arctic Ocean. Despite the region's size, the people there comprise less than one percent of the nation's population. The main reason for the low population is the region's rugged terrain and harsh climate. The area is made up of tundra with little vegetation, icy waters, and subarctic forests.

Modern Inuits
This modern Inuit family travels on a snowmobile on Ellesmere Island. **Draw Conclusions** *How does technology influence Inuit life?*

People of the Far North Another characteristic unique to this region is the large number of indigenous people who live there. In the Northwest Territories, almost 50 percent of the population is made up of indigenous peoples such as the Dene, Métis, and Inuit. In Nunavut, about 85 percent of the population are Inuit. In contrast, only about 14 percent of the Yukon population is made up of native people. The rest of the population is of European or other ancestry.

Contact with Europeans has changed many of the ways in which indigenous peoples live. Technology has played a major role. For example, seal hunting is an important part of Inuit life. Today, Inuit hunters use snowmobiles instead of dogsleds to cross the frozen land.

A Different Form of Government Members of the House of Commons, a part of the Canadian Parliament, represent both territories and provinces in the federal government. Each territory has its own legislative, or law-making, body similar to those of the provinces.

But, the federal government exercises more authority over the territories. While territories do have control over many of the same local concerns as provinces, such as education, the federal government controls other areas, such as some natural resources. Territories also have less power to tax than the provinces do.

✓ **Reading Check** What percentage of Nunavut's population is Inuit?

Target Skill — Use Context Clues You know that *exercise* often refers to physical activity or putting something in action. Use part of that definition to help you understand *exercises authority*. What does *exercise* mean in this context? What is the meaning of the phrase *exercises authority*?

Vocabulary Builder

Use the information below to teach students this section's high-use words.

High-Use Word	Definition and Sample Sentence
environment, p. 318	*n.* natural surroundings We wore coats and hats to protect us from the cold **environment**.
despite, p. 319	*prep.* regardless of We played outside **despite** the cold weather.
portion, p. 322	*n.* part or section I ate my **portion** of the orange, while my friend ate the other part.
resident, p. 322	*n.* someone who lives in a place A **resident** of the neighborhood invited us to a barbecue in her backyard.

Instruct

The Far North L2

Guided Instruction

- **Vocabulary Builder** Clarify the high-use words **environment** and **despite** before reading.

- Read The Far North, using the Structured Silent Reading strategy (TE, p. T34).

- Ask students to describe the difference between provinces and territories. *(In the territories, the federal government has more authority over such things as taxes and natural resources than in the provinces.)*

- Ask students **What factors contribute to the low population of these territories?** *(the rugged terrain and harsh climate)*

Independent Practice

Ask students to create the Taking Notes graphic organizer on a blank piece of paper. Then ask students to fill in the ovals with the information the have just learned. Briefly model how to fill in each separate detail in a different oval.

Monitor Progress

As students fill in the graphic organizer, circulate and make sure individuals are choosing the correct details. Provide assistance as needed.

Target Reading Skill L2

Use Context Clues As a follow up, ask students to answer the Target Reading Skill question in the Student Edition. *(Exercise means putting something in action in this context. The phrase* exercises authority *means to put into action or use authority.)*

Answers

Draw Conclusions Possible answer: Technology has changed many aspects of Inuit life. In the photo, the snowmobile may make crossing the frozen land easier.

✓ **Reading Check** about 85 percent

Guided Instruction

Ask students to study the Regional Profile on this page. Encourage them to look at the map, graphs, and on the page and think about the information each provides. As a class, answer the Map and Chart Skills questions. Allow students to briefly discuss their responses with a partner before sharing answers.

Independent Practice

- Help students read the bar graphs by asking them to fill in the following sentence for each territory: "_____ has a population of _____ people and an area of _____ square miles."

- Then ask students whether a larger land area means a larger population. Help them see that the Northwest Territories has a larger land area and population than the Yukon, but Nunavut has a larger land area and smaller population than the Yukon—so there is not a direct relationship between land area and population.

Answers

Map and Chart Skills

1. Inuit

2. Possible answer: It is easier to come to agreement when sitting in a circle because there is no clear divide between members, everyone is equal.

3. Possible answers: It would work because a vote can take place no matter how parties are seated; it would not work because representing a population as large as the whole country requires parties to be more organized.

Go Online
PHSchool.com Students can find more information about this topic on the DK World Desk Reference Online.

Northern Territories

Three territories—Nunavut, the Northwest Territories, and Yukon—make up this region. As territories, they have a different status from Canada's provinces. All three territories have legislatures, but there are no political parties. Decisions are made by agreement rather than by majority vote. Most of the territories' public land is controlled by the government in Ottawa. As you study the map and graphs, think about why and how Canada's territories are different from the nation's provinces.

Northern Territories: Native North American Groups KEY

- Champagne and Aishihik
- Gwich'in
- Inuit
- Inuvialuit
- Nacho Nyak Dun
- Sahtu Dene and Métis
- ——— National border
- ——— Provincial or territorial border
- ★ Provincial or territorial capital
- • Other town

0 miles — 1,000
0 kilometers — 1,000
Lambert Azimuthal Equal Area

Population and Area of Northern Canada

SOURCE: Statistics Canada

SOURCE: *Encyclopaedia Britannica*

Nunavut Legislature

Most provincial legislatures meet in a divided chamber. The party in power sits on one side, and the opposition sits on the other. The Nunavut legislature sits in a circle.

Map and Chart Skills

1. **Identify** What is the main ethnic group in Nunavut?
2. **Infer** How does the circular seating of the legislature serve the Nunavut decision-making process?
3. **Analyze** Would the organization of Nunavut's legislature work for the Canadian federal government in Ottawa? Explain why or why not.

Go Online
PHSchool.com
Use Web Code lhe-4515 for **DK World Desk Reference Online.**

Differentiated Instruction

For Less Proficient Readers

As students read the Regional Profile, have them make a two-column chart to help them keep track of the differences between provinces and territories. Have them label the first column *Territories* and the second column *Differences from Provinces.* Explain that they should use the first column to record details given about territories, such as that they have legislatures. They should use the second column to record ways that territories are different from provinces, such as that they do not have political parties.

Forming New Territories

All of Canada's northern land used to be one giant territory—the Northwest Territories. Over time, this vast land was split up into three separate territories.

Yukon Territory The Yukon Territory was once a district of the Northwest Territories. In 1898, an act of Parliament made it a separate territory. Many people are familiar with the Yukon Territory because of the Klondike Gold Rush. After gold was discovered in a branch of the Klondike River in 1896, thousands of prospectors swarmed to the area. Within two years, the population of the town of Dawson swelled to about 30,000. Saloons, banks, theaters, and dance halls sprang up there.

It was amazing that so many people were able to get to the area, because one of the main routes was the treacherous Chilkoot Pass, known as "the meanest 32 miles in the world." The end of the pass narrowed to less than three feet wide and became very steep. But the Yukon's era of prosperity was short-lived. By the end of 1898, the rush began to slow, and the population of the settlement declined quickly. Today, fewer than 1,300 people live in Dawson.

Building a New Capital
A new building was constructed in Iqaluit to house Nunavut's legislature. **Draw Conclusions** *How might the construction of a new capital have helped Nunavut's economy?*

Guided Instruction

- **Vocabulary Builder** Clarify the high-use words **portion** and **resident** before reading.

- Read Forming New Territories. As students read, circulate and make sure individuals can answer the Reading Check question.

- Ask students **Why, during the 1890s, were many people willing to brave the Chilkoot Pass to get to the Yukon Territory?** *(to mine the gold found there)*

- Ask students **What do you think was the most important factor that allowed for the creation of Nunavut?** *(the large percentage of Inuit people in the area; when the matter came to a vote, the Inuit population was large enough to determine the outcome)*

Independent Practice

Have students complete the graphic organizer by filling in details about the government of Nunavut.

Monitor Progress

- Show *Section Reading Support Transparency USC 62* and ask students to check their graphic organizers individually.

  United States and Canada Transparencies, *Section Reading Support Transparency USC 62*

- Tell students to fill in the last column of the *Reading Readiness Guide.* Probe for what they learned that confirms or invalidates each statement.

  All in One United States and Canada Teaching Resources, *Reading Readiness Guide,* p. 302

Answers

Draw Conclusions by providing work for people in the construction industry and boosting local businesses

---

Skills Mini Lesson

Sequencing L2

1. Teach the skill by explaining that a timeline is a useful tool for keeping track of what happened and when.

2. Help students practice the skill by reading Forming New Territories and determining the topic, the time span, and the events that relate to the topic. *(topic: the creation of new territories; time span: 1898 to 1999; events: the creation of the Yukon Territory, the vote for a new territory, the carving out of Nunavut, and making Nunavut a territory)*

3. Have students apply the skill by asking students to make a timeline that has a beginning date and an end date, equal sections, and labels identifying each event.

Assess and Reteach

Assess Progress `L2`

Have students complete the Section Assessment. Administer the *Section Quiz*.

 **United States and Canada Teaching Resources,** *Section Quiz,* p. 304

Reteach `L1`

If students need more instruction, have them read this section in the Reading and Vocabulary Study Guide.

📖 Chapter 10, Section 5, **Western Hemisphere Reading and Vocabulary Study Guide,** pp. 117–119

Extend `L3`

Now that students have learned how the government of Nunavut differs from the governments of Canada and its provinces, have them learn about other kinds of government by starting the *Holding Community Meetings Under Different Forms of Government* Long-Term Integrated Project. Assign students to groups to do the activity.

Go Online
PHSchool.com

For: Long-Term Integrated Project: *Holding Community Meetings Under Different Forms of Government*
Visit: PHSchool.com
Web Code: lhd-4507

Answer

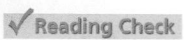 the Northwest Territories

Section 5 Assessment

Key Terms

Students' sentences should reflect knowledge of each Key Term.

🎯 Target Reading Skill

Possible answer: in this context, *bands* are thin strips.

Comprehension and Critical Thinking

1. (a) the Northwest Territories, Yukon Territory, and Nunavut **(b)** similar: they all have their own legislative bodies; different: the federal government has more control over the territories' governments than it does over the provinces'

This stop sign is in Inuktitut and English.

Nunavut In 1993, the area now known as Nunavut was carved out of the eastern portion of the Northwest Territories. A constitutional act officially made Nunavut the third Canadian territory on April 1, 1999. A decades-long dream of the Inuit people to have their own self-governing territory became reality.

The Inuit, who make up most of Nunavut's population, proposed the formation of Nunavut in the 1970s. Nunavut means "our land" in **Inuktitut** (ih NOOK tih toot), the native language of the Inuit. When the matter came to a vote in 1982, residents overwhelmingly favored the creation of their own territory.

The construction of Nunavut's new capital, Iqaluit (ee KAH loo eet), provided many jobs for people. But Nunavut still faces several challenges. Leaders in the territory must work to keep its economy strong in spite of its remote location and harsh climate. The modernization of the area, which now has an Internet provider, a television broadcaster, and cellular phone service, may be a step in the right direction.

✓ **Reading Check** **Present-day Nunavut was once a part of which territory?**

★ Section 5 Assessment

Key Terms

Review the key terms at the beginning of this section. Use each key term in a sentence that explains its meaning.

🎯 Target Reading Skill

Find the word *bands* on page 318. Use your own knowledge and the surrounding words and phrases to explain what *bands* means in this context.

Comprehension and Critical Thinking

1. (a) List Which three territories make up the Northern Territories?

(b) Compare and Contrast How do the governments of provinces and territories differ? How are they the same?

2. (a) Recall What event made the Yukon Territory famous?
(b) Identify Effects How did that event cause the town of Dawson to grow?

3. (a) Recall What is the newest territory in Canada?
(b) Identify Point of View Why might Inuits have wanted to create a self-governing territory?

Writing Activity

Suppose that you are Inuit, and you have always been a part of a minority in a larger territory. Describe what it might be like living for the first time in a territory where you are part of the majority.

Go Online
PHSchool.com

For: An activity on Nunavut
Visit: PHSchool.com
Web Code: lhd-4505

---

2. (a) the Klondike Gold Rush **(b)** by causing thousands of prospectors to swarm to the area

3. (a) Nunavut **(b)** Answers will vary. Students may say that Inuit people might have wanted to create a self-governing territory because they have a different heritage, traditions, and beliefs than other Canadians and wanted to be able to represent and govern in accordance with their culture.

Writing Activity

Use the *Rubric for Assessing a Writing Assignment* to evaluate students' descriptions.

 **United States and Canada Teaching Resources,** *Rubric for Assessing a Writing Assignment,* p. 326

Go Online
PHSchool.com Typing in the Web code when prompted will bring students directly to detailed instructions for this activity.

10 Review and Assessment

◆ Chapter Summary

Section 1: Ontario and Quebec
- Canada's central government is located in Ottawa, Ontario.
- Toronto is Canada's financial center and largest city.
- French Canadians are concerned about preserving their cultural heritage, and some think that Quebec should become an independent country.

Section 2: The Prairie Provinces
- Manitoba, Saskatchewan, and Alberta are called the Prairie Provinces.
- Many European immigrants settled the Canadian plains in the late 1800s.
- Disease and the destruction of the buffalo in the late 1800s led to the end of many indigenous peoples' way of life.

Section 3: British Columbia
- Following the discovery of gold in 1858, the population of British Columbia grew rapidly.
- Indigenous peoples were pushed onto small reserves and were not allowed to practice many of their customs.
- British Columbia has geographic, economic, and cultural ties to foreign countries, especially those of the Pacific Rim.

Section 4: The Atlantic Provinces
- Newfoundland and Labrador, Prince Edward Island, New Brunswick, and Nova Scotia make up the Atlantic Provinces.
- The location of the Atlantic Provinces has shaped the history, culture, and economy of the people there.
- The economy of the Atlantic Provinces is dependent on the fishing industry.

Section 5: The Northern Territories
- The Northern Territories—made up of the Northwest Territories, Yukon Territories, and Nunavut—are the least-populated regions in Canada.
- The Northern Territories have a different form of government from that of Canada's provinces.
- Nunavut is the homeland of the Inuit, and Canada's newest territory.

Totem pole

◆ Key Terms

Each of the statements below contains a key term from the chapter. If the statement is true, write *true*. If it is false, rewrite the statement to make it true.

1. A **separatist** is a person who speaks French as his or her first language.

2. A **boomtown** is a settlement that springs up to serve the needs of miners.

3. Colorful bands of light that can be seen in the Northern Hemisphere are the **aurora borealis**.

4. **Descent** is a natural resistance to disease.

5. **Aquaculture** has to do with navigation or shipping on the sea.

6. After the **Quiet Revolution**, Nunavut became a separate territory.

7. An **exile** is someone who is forced to leave his or her homeland.

8. A **federation** is a union of states, groups, provinces, or nations.

Chapter 10 **323**

┌ Vocabulary Builder ─

Revisit this chapter's high-use words:

structure	occupy	environment
mature	benefit	despite
issue	neutral	portion
margin	focus	resident

Ask students to review the definitions they recorded on their *World Knowledge* worksheets.

 **United States and Canada Teaching Resources,** *Word Knowledge,* p. 309

Consider allowing students to earn extra credit if they use the words in their answers to the questions in the Chapter Review and Assessment. The words must be used correctly and in a natural context to win the extra points.

Review Chapter Content

- Review and revisit the major themes of this chapter by asking students to classify what Guiding Question each bulleted statement in the Chapter Summary answers. Write the Chapter Summary on the board and divide the class into groups to complete the activity. Then have a member from each group write the numbers they selected next to each statement on the board. Refer to page 139 in the Student Edition for the text of Guiding Questions.

- Assign *Vocabulary Development* for students to review Key Terms.

  All in One **United States and Canada Teaching Resources,** *Vocabulary Development,* p. 324

Answers

Key Terms

1. False. A separatist is a person who wants Quebec to break away from Canada and become an independent country.

2. True

3. True

4. False. Descent is an individual's ancestry.

5. False. Aquaculture is a method of farming fish.

6. False. The Quiet Revolution was a time during which great changes in Quebec's government were brought about peacefully.

7. True

8. True

Chapter 10 **323**

Review and Assessment

Comprehension and Critical Thinking

9. (a) The British monarch is Canada's head of state; his or her duties are purely ceremonial. **(b)** The United States President is head of state and head of government, whereas the British monarch is Canada's head of state and the Canadian prime minister is head of government.

10. (a) The people voted for Quebec to remain part of Canada. **(b)** Many people in Quebec want to separate from Canada in order to preserve their French heritage and culture, which they worry will die out in an English-dominated country.

11. (a) Buffalo meat was used for food, hides were used for clothes, and bones were used for tools. **(b)** The traditional ways of life of the indigenous peoples of the plains came to an end.

12. (a) Spain, Britain, Russia **(b)** The indigenous people and the early explorers traded with each other. **(c)** The miners set up towns and quickly doubled the population of British Columbia, taking over the land and forcing the indigenous people onto reserves.

13. (a) Acadia **(b)** Exiled Acadians returned to find the British had taken over the land they had once farmed. Acadians then took up fishing and lumbering instead of farming.

14. (a) because of the region's rugged terrain and harsh climate **(b)** Answers will vary. Students may say that the harsh climate determines the economic activities that are available to people or that it prevents many newcomers from arriving, allowing the culture to remain mainly indigenous.

Skills Practice

Students' summaries will vary, but answers should reflect understanding of the skill and should include a topic sentence and main ideas drawn from Section 3 of this chapter.

Writing Activity: Language and Arts

Students' storyboards will vary but should include real events from British Columbia's history. Dates should be given along with clear indications of what occurred and why it is interesting.

Use *Rubric for Assessing a Performance on a Project* to evaluate students' storyboards. Tell

◆ Comprehension and Critical Thinking

9. (a) Explain What is the role of the British monarch in Canadian government?
(b) Compare and Contrast How does the Canadian government differ from that of the United States?

10. (a) Recall What were the results of the 1980 and 1995 referendums on Quebec's independence?
(b) Analyze Why do so many people in Quebec want to separate from Canada?

11. (a) List In what ways was the buffalo important to indigenous peoples on the Plains?
(b) Identify Effects How might the destruction of the buffalo have affected the native people who lived there?

12. (a) List In the late 1700s, which countries sent explorers to present-day British Columbia?
(b) Summarize What was the relationship between the early explorers and the indigenous people of the region?
(c) Compare and Contrast How and why did the miners' relationship with native peoples differ from that of the early explorers?

13. (a) Locate Where was the first French settlement in North America?

(b) Summarize How did the lives of Acadians change after the British gained control over the region in 1763?

14. (a) Explain Why are the Northern Territories not heavily populated?
(b) Predict How does climate affect culture in the Northern Territories?

◆ Skills Practice

Writing a Summary Review the steps you followed in the Skills for Life activity in this chapter. Then reread the part of Section 3 under the heading Economics and Culture. Find and state the main idea of each paragraph. Then, identify what the main ideas have in common. Finally, write a summary paragraph that begins with a topic sentence.

◆ Writing Activity: Language Arts

Suppose that you have been asked to develop a proposal for a film to be set in British Columbia. You may choose to make a documentary or a historical film. Outline the events or the plot of the film on a storyboard—a series of sketches that show the sequence of major scenes in the film.

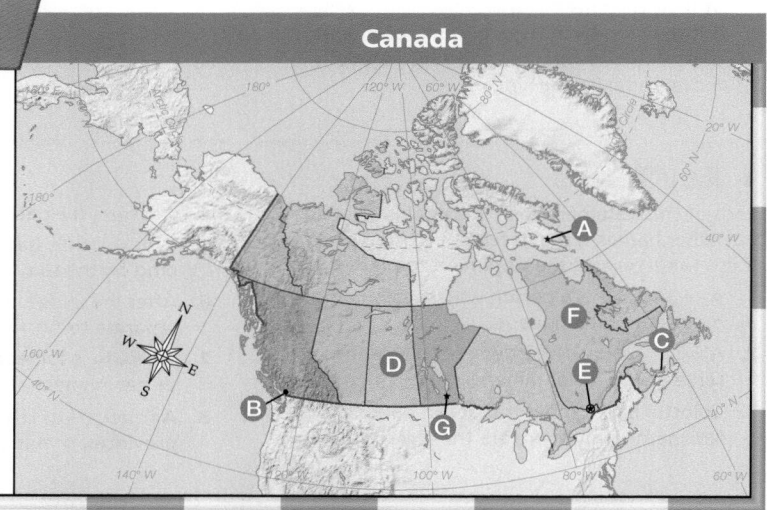

MAP MASTER™ Skills Activity

Place Location For each place listed below, write the letter from the map that shows its location.

1. Quebec
2. Ottawa
3. Saskatchewan
4. Winnipeg
5. Vancouver
6. Prince Edward Island
7. Iqaluit

Go Online
PHSchool.com Use Web Code
lhp-4555 for an
interactive map.

Canada

students how many sources you would like them to use, if any, beyond the textbook.

All in One United States and Canada Teaching Resources, *Rubric for Assessing a Performance on a Project,* p. 328

MAP MASTER™ Skills Activity

1. F	**2.** E
3. D	**4.** G
5. B	**6.** C
7. A	

Go Online
PHSchool.com Students may practice their map skills using the interactive online version of this map.

Standardized Test Prep

Test-Taking Tips

Some questions on standardized tests ask you to analyze a reading selection. Read the passage below. Then, follow the tips to answer the sample question.

> **TIP** Read for key words that may help you answer the question. In this case, the key word is *Nunavut*.

In 1982, citizens of Canada's Northwest Territories were about to vote on whether to allow the creation of a self-governing homeland. It would be known as Nunavut and would be carved out of the territories. Someone argued, "We're asking for a share in the resources. We don't want to appear as beggars dependent on government handouts, but we are now being denied the resources that we so willingly gave up to support this nation."

Who might have made this argument?

> **TIP** Try to answer the question before you look at the answer choices. Doing so may help you find the BEST answer.

- **A** a descendant of a French fur trader
- **B** a descendant of an English farmer
- **C** a descendant of an Inuit hunter
- **D** a descendant of a German logger

Think It Through The key word *Nunavut* will help you answer the question. What does the passage have to do with Nunavut? The speaker says the government owes his people resources that had been taken away. Which group wants a separate homeland that would give them control over their own resources? You can eliminate B and D. That leaves A and C. Some French in Quebec do want their own homeland. But, their resources and land were not taken away. The answer is C.

Practice Questions

Use the tips above and other tips in this book to help you answer the following questions.

1. Who is Canada's head of state?
   - **A** the monarch of Britain
   - **B** the prime minister
   - **C** the governor of Ontario
   - **D** the president

Read the passage below, and then answer the question that follows.

In the late 1800s, life changed for a group of people who lived on Canada's plains. They could not hunt the way they always had, and their lands were taken away by new settlers. They also began to get sick in large numbers from new diseases.

2. Who does this passage describe?
   - **A** French Canadians
   - **B** Scandinavian immigrants
   - **C** Native Americans
   - **D** German immigrants

3. British Columbia has special economic and cultural ties to
   - **A** Russia.
   - **B** the rest of Canada.
   - **C** the northeastern United States.
   - **D** the Pacific Rim.

4. Who first settled Canada's Atlantic Provinces in large numbers?
   - **A** the French
   - **B** the British
   - **C** the Vikings
   - **D** Americans

Go Online
PHSchool.com
Use Web Code lha-4505
for a **Chapter 10 self-test.**

Chapter 10 **325**

Standardized Test Prep

Answers

1. A
2. C
3. D
4. B

> Go Online
> PHSchool.com Students may use the Chapter 10 self-test on PHSchool.com to prepare for the Chapter Test.

⌐ Assessment Resources ⌐

Teaching Resources
Chapter Tests A and B, pp. 329–334
Final Exams A and B, pp. 339–344

Test Prep Workbook
United States and Canada Study Sheet, pp. 124–127
United States and Canada Practice Tests A, B, and C, pp. 85–96

AYP Monitoring Assessments
United States and Canada Benchmark Test 2, pp. 93–96
United States and Canada Outcome Test, pp. 176–181

Technology
⊙ Exam*View*® Test Bank CD-ROM

- Students can further explore the Guiding Questions by completing hands-on projects.

- Three pages of structured guidance in All-in-One United States and Canada Teaching Resources support each of the projects described on this page.

  All in One **United States and Canada Teaching Resources,** *Book Project: Set Up a Weather Station,* pp. 73–75; *Book Project: Make a Timeline of Local History,* pp. 79–81

- There are also two additional projects introduced, explained, and supported in the All-in-One United States and Canada Teaching Resources.

  All in One **United States and Canada Teaching Resources,** *Book Project: Write a Children's Book,* pp. 76–78; *Book Project: Create a Diorama,* pp. 82–84

- Go over the four project suggestions with students.

- Ask each student to select one of the projects, or design his or her own. Work with students to create a project description and a schedule.

Projects

Create your own projects to learn more about the United States and Canada. At the beginning of this book, you were introduced to the Guiding Questions for studying the chapters and special features. But you can also find answers to these questions by doing projects on your own or with a group.

1 **Geography** How has physical geography affected the cultures of the United States and Canada?

2 **History** How have historical events affected the cultures of the United States and Canada?

3 **Culture** How has the variety of people in the United States and Canada benefited and challenged the two nations?

4 **Government** How do the governments of the United States and Canada differ? How are they alike?

5 **Economics** How did the United States and Canada become two of the wealthiest nations in the world?

Project
RESEARCH YOUR LOCAL HISTORY

Make a Timeline
Read about the history of your community at the local public library. Write down dates and descriptions of between 10 and 20 important events. Then, make a timeline large enough to hang on the wall of your classroom. Draw a picture of each event and place it next to its description on the timeline. Add several major events of United States history.

Project
SET UP A WEATHER STATION

Create a Weather Log
Set up a weather station to measure and record your local weather as you read this book. Measure the temperature each day at the same time. Also record the amount of precipitation and the wind direction. Record all of your findings in a weather log.

Each day, compare your local weather with the weather in other parts of the country. You can get this information from television, radio, the newspaper, or the Internet. When you have finished your measurements and recordings, create graphs to display your local readings. Then, compare your findings with the climate map in the Regional Overview.

- Post project schedules and monitor student progress by asking for progress reports.

- Assess student projects using rubrics from the All-in-One United States and Canada Teaching Resources.

  All in One **United States and Canada Teaching Resources,** *Rubric for Assessing Student Performance on a Project,* p. 85; *Rubric for Assessing Performance of an Entire Group,* p. 86; *Rubric for Assessing Individual Performance in a Group,* p. 87

  Portfolio Activity Tell students they can add their completed Book Project as the final item in their portfolios. Assess student portfolios with *Rubric for Assessing a Student Portfolio.*

  All in One **United States and Canada Teaching Resources,** *Rubric for Assessing Student Portfolio,* p. 88

327

Teaching the Target Reading Skills

The Prentice Hall *World Studies* program has interwoven essential reading skills instruction throughout the Student Edition, Teacher's Edition, and ancillary resources. In Latin America, students will learn six reading skills.

Student Edition The *World Studies* Student Edition provides students with reading skills instruction, practice, and application opportunities in each chapter within the program.

Teacher's Edition The *World Studies* Teacher Edition supports your teaching of each skill by providing full modeling in each chapter's interleaf and modeling of the specific sub-skills in each section lesson.

All in One Teaching Resources The *World Studies* All-in-One Teaching Resources provides a worksheet explaining and supporting the elements of each Target Reading Skill. Use these to help struggling students master skills, or as more practice for every student.

Target Reading Skills

The Target Reading Skills introduced on this page will help you understand the words and ideas in this section on Latin America and in other social studies reading you do. Each chapter focuses on one of these reading skills. Good readers develop a bank of reading strategies, or skills. Then they draw on the particular strategies that will help them understand the text they are reading.

Chapter 11 Target Reading Skill
Using the Reading Process Previewing can help you understand and remember what you read. In this chapter you will practice using these previewing skills: setting a purpose for reading, predicting what the text will be about, and asking questions before you read.

Chapter 12 Target Reading Skill
Clarifying Meaning If you do not understand something you are reading right away, you can use several skills to clarify the meaning of the word or idea. In this chapter you will practice these strategies for clarifying meaning: rereading, reading ahead, paraphrasing, and summarizing.

Chapter 13 Target Reading Skill
Using Cause and Effect Recognizing cause and effect will help you understand relationships among the situations and events you are reading about. In this chapter you will practice these skills: identifying cause and effect, recognizing multiple causes, and understanding effects.

Chapter 14 Target Reading Skill
Using Context Using the context of an unfamiliar word can help you understand its meaning. Context includes the words, phrases, and sentences surrounding a word. In this chapter you will practice using these context clues: definitions, contrast, and your own general knowledge.

Chapter 15 Target Reading Skill
Identifying the Main Idea Since you cannot remember every detail of what you read, it is important to identify the main ideas. The main idea of a section or paragraph is the most important point, the one you want to remember. In this chapter you will practice these skills: identifying both stated and implied main ideas, and identifying supporting details.

Chapter 16 Target Reading Skill
Comparing and Contrasting You can use comparison and contrast to sort out and analyze the information you are reading. Comparing means examining the similarities between things. Contrasting is looking at differences. In this chapter you will practice these skills: comparing and contrasting, identifying contrasts, and making comparisons.

328 Latin America

Assessment Resources

Use the diagnosing readiness tests from **AYP Monitoring Assessments** to help you identify problems before students begin to study Latin America.

Determine students' reading level and identify challenges:

- *Screening Tests,* pp. 1–10

Evaluate students' verbal skills:

- *Critical Thinking and Reading Tests,* pp. 25–34
- *Vocabulary Tests,* pp. 45–52
- *Writing Tests,* pp. 53–60

LATIN AMERICA

The early peoples of Latin America created great civilizations from the riches of their land and their own ideas and skills. Their descendants have mixed with newcomers from around the world to create modern societies that blend the old and the new into vibrant and distinctive cultures.

Guiding Questions

The text, photographs, maps, and charts in this book will help you discover answers to these Guiding Questions.

1. **Geography** What are the main physical features of Latin America?

2. **History** How has Latin America been shaped by its history?

3. **Culture** What factors have affected cultures in Latin America?

4. **Government** What types of government have existed in Latin America?

5. **Economics** How has geography influenced the ways in which Latin Americans make a living?

Project Preview

You can also discover answers to the Guiding Questions by working on projects. Several project possibilities are listed on page 526 of this book.

Guiding Questions

- This section was developed around five Guiding Questions about Latin America. They appear on the reduced Student Edition page to the left. The Guiding Questions are intended as an organizational focus for the section. The Guiding Questions act as a kind of umbrella under which all of the material falls.

- You may wish to add your own Guiding Questions to the list in order to tailor them to your particular course.

- Draw students' attention to the Guiding Questions. Ask them to write the questions in their notebooks for future reference.

- In the Teacher's Edition, each section's themes are linked to a specific Guiding Question at the beginning of each chapter. Then, an activity at the end of the chapter returns to the Guiding Questions to review key concepts.

Project Preview

- The projects for this book are designed to provide students with hands-on involvement in the content area. Students are introduced to some projects on pages 526–527.

- *Book Projects* give students directions on how to complete these projects, and more.

  All in One Latin America Teaching Resources, *Book Project: Visions of Latin America,* pp. 73–75; *Book Project: Latin America in the News,* pp. 76–78; *Book Project: A Latin American Concert,* pp. 79–81; *Book Project: Explorer's Dictionary,* pp. 82–84

- Assign projects as small group activities, whole-class projects, or individual projects. Consider assigning a project at the beginning of the course.

Assess students' social studies skills:

- *Geographic Literacy Tests,* pp. 13–20
- *Visual Analysis Tests,* pp. 21–24
- *Communications Tests,* pp. 35–44

The *World Studies* program provides instruction and practice for all of these skills. Use students' test results to pinpoint the skills your students have mastered and the skills they need to practice. Then use *Correlation to Program Resources* to prescribe skills practice and reinforcement.

- *Correlation to Program Resources,* pp. 64–77

Objectives

- Describe the relative location and size of Latin America.

- Investigate the major languages of Latin America.

- Examine the physical features of Latin America.

- Explain why Latin America is ideal for hydroelectricity plants.

Prepare to Read

Build Background Knowledge   L2

Have students brainstorm a list of words or impressions related to Latin America and write them on the board. Tell students that they will either confirm or revise these impressions during their study of the region.

Instruct

Investigate Latin America   L2

Guided Instruction

- Read the introductory, Location, and Regions paragraphs as a class. Divide the class into small groups of three or four.

- Hand out the *Regional Overview* worksheet. Direct students to fill in the worksheet as they study the Regional Overview.

  All in One Latin America Teaching Resources, *Regional Overview,* pp. 89–91

Independent Practice

Ask the groups to write a statement describing Latin America's location and size in comparison to the United States.

Monitor Progress

Circulate and make sure the groups are communicating effectively.

Answers

LOCATION Santiago and Brasília–opposite seasons; Mexico City–same seasons

REGIONS Latin America's Pacific Coast is almost four times longer.

Investigate Latin America

Latin America is a vibrant region in the midst of change. The region's northern edge is marked by the boundary between the United States and Mexico. To the south, it extends to the tip of South America. Latin America covers about 14 percent of Earth's surface.

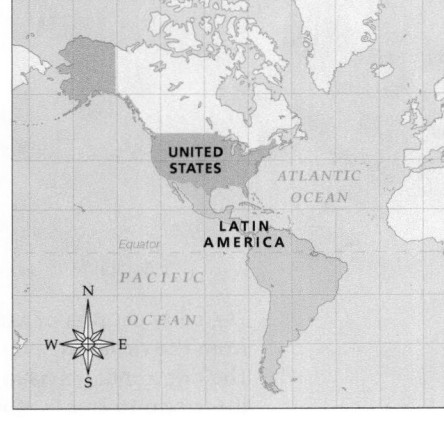

▲ San Cristóbal de las Casas, Mexico

LOCATION

1 Explore Latin America's Location

Recall from the MapMaster Skills Handbook that when it's winter north of the Equator it's summer south of the Equator, and vice versa. Trace the line of the Equator on the map above with your finger. Next, break into small groups. Tell each other in what season your birthdays fall. Work together to figure out in what season your birthdays would be if you all lived in Santiago, Chile. What would the seasons be if you lived in Brasília, Brazil? If you lived in Mexico City, Mexico?

REGIONS

2 Compare the Size of Latin America and the United States

How does Latin America's length compare to the length of the continental United States? Take a piece of string and curve it along the west coast of the United States from the border with Canada to the border with Mexico. Cut the string the same length as the coast. Now see how many string lengths fit along the west coast of Latin America. Start at northern Mexico. Finish at the southern tip of South America. How many times longer is Latin America's Pacific Coast than the coast of the United States?

330 Latin America

Mental Mapping

Everything in Its Place List the names of some Middle American, South American, and Caribbean countries on the board. Include Mexico, Panama, Haiti, Brazil, Puerto Rico, Peru, Guatemala, Cuba, Chile, and Venezuela.

Distribute *Outline Map 4: Latin America: Physical.* Ask students to locate as many countries on the maps as they can from

memory, without looking in their textbooks. Tell them to write the names of the countries they cannot locate on the water area of the map near the correct landmass. They can update their outline maps as they study the region.

All in One Latin America Teaching Resources, *Outline Map 4: Latin America: Physical,* p. 92

Political Latin America

Key
- — National border
- ⊛ National capital
- ★ Other capital
- • Other city

▲ **Rio de Janeiro, Brazil**
As a result of a treaty signed in 1494, the Portuguese settled Brazil. Brazilians still speak Portuguese today.

MOVEMENT

3 Investigate the Languages of Latin America

When people move, they bring their native language with them. Look at the Country Databanks to find a country in Latin America where there is more than one official language. Why might a country have two or more official languages?

Differentiated Instruction

For Special Needs Students L2
If possible, show students the Latin America flyover segment on the Passport to the World CD-ROM. Ask students to list several of the region's major landforms on the board after viewing the segment.

⊙ *Flyover segment,* **Passport to the World CD-ROM**

Guided Instruction

- Read the Movement paragraph. Refer students to the Country Databanks on pages 426–429, 456–461, and 488–493 to review the languages spoken in Latin America. Ask students to write on the board the countries that have more than one official language.

- Ask students to continue completing the Regional Overview worksheet.

  All in One Latin America Teaching Resources, *Regional Overview,* pp. 89–91

- Discuss why a country might have two or more official languages.

Independent Practice

Provide students with the *Outline Map 5: Latin America: Political.* Have students label each country in Latin America and color in the countries according to the official language spoken there. Remind them to include a key.

All in One Latin America Teaching Resources, *Outline Map 5: Latin America: Political,* p. 93

Monitor Progress

Circulate while students complete their maps and provide assistance where needed.

Answers

MOVEMENT Haiti, Bolivia, and Peru all have more than one official language.

A country might have two or more official languages because its population might be bilingual; many people might speak one language, while many others speak another; it might have ties to a European language as well as an indigenous language

Physical Latin America L2

Guided Instruction
- Read the Place paragraph. Have students study the physical map of Latin America. Ask them to use the map key to determine the highest altitudes in Latin America, as well as the Amazon Basin's elevation.

- Ask students to continue completing the *Regional Overview* worksheet.
  All In One Latin America Teaching Resources, *Regional Overview,* p. 89–91

Independent Practice
- Have students explore the physical features of Latin America by creating a bar graph.

- Give them the following statistics:

Peak	Elevation
Aconcagua, Argentina	22,831ft [6,959m]
Ojos del Salado, Argentina-Chile	22,572 ft [6,880m]
Bonete, Argentina	22,546 ft [6872m]

Tell students that these are the three highest peaks in Latin America.

- Ask students to create a bar graph comparing the heights of these mounts to the highest peak in the United States: Mt. McKinley, Alaska, at an elevation of 20,320 ft [6,194m].

- Ask: **What do the bar graphs show?** *(Even the third highest peak in Latin America is taller than the highest peak in the United States.)*

Monitor Progress
Make sure students are creating their graphs correctly. If individuals are having trouble, guide them in setting up the graphs with the names of the mountains on the x-axis and the intervals of feet on the y-axis. Suggest they mark off intervals of 5,000 feet. Point out that they must plan ahead to have enough room on the y-axis to show the largest number of feet on their graphs.

Answers
PLACE The Andes Mountains have the highest altitude in the Latin America. The Amazon Basin is zero to 650 feet above sea level. Climbing boots would probably not be necessary there.

Physical Latin America

▲ **Popocatépetl Volcano, Mexico**
Snow-capped Popocatépetl is a volcano with a crater more than half a mile wide. People work in the fields below the volcano.

Key

ELEVATION

Feet	Meters
More than 13,000	More than 3,960
6,500–13,000	1,980–3,960
1,600–6,500	480–1,980
650–1,600	200–480
0–650	0–200

—— National border

PLACE
4 Examine the Physical Features of Latin America

Latin America has many extremes of elevation. The colors on the map key tell you which parts of Latin America have the highest altitude, and which have the lowest. What landform is located in the part of Latin America with the highest elevation? Now find the Amazon Basin. How many feet above sea level is it?

Background: Daily Life

Elevation Elevation is an important factor in everyday life in Latin America because elevation influences climate. Assuming that air is not moving, air is 3.5°F (1.9°C) cooler for every 1,000 feet (305 meters) one climbs. Thus, while the city of Guayaquil on the coast of Ecuador may be very hot and sticky, the city of Quito is almost cold. That is because Quito is located high in the Andes Mountains.

Major Hydroelectric Plants

Electricity generated from water power is called hydroelectricity. One way to build a hydroelectric plant is to dam a river. The dam creates a large lake. When the dam gates open, water gushes from the lake to the river, turning huge paddles that create electricity. If you live in a region near a large river, your electricity may be generated in this way.

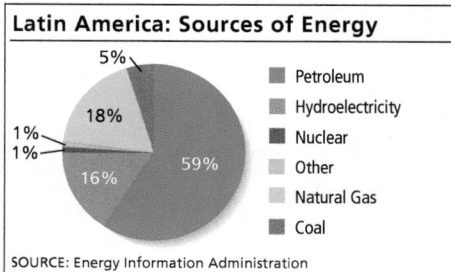

▲ **Itaipú Dam, Brazil/Paraguay**
Water surges through the gate at the Itaipú Dam. This dam supplies electricity to large areas of Brazil and Paraguay.

LOCATION

5 Investigate Latin America's Use of Hydroelectricity

The world's largest hydroelectric plant is located on the border of Brazil and Paraguay. Look at the circle graph below. How much of its power does Latin America get from hydroelectricity? From what energy source does Latin America get most of its power?

Latin America: Sources of Energy

- 5%
- 18%
- 1%
- 1%
- 16%
- 59%

Legend:
- Petroleum
- Hydroelectricity
- Nuclear
- Other
- Natural Gas
- Coal

SOURCE: Energy Information Administration

PRACTICE YOUR GEOGRAPHY SKILLS

1. You are taking a trip through Latin America. You board your ship in Puerto Rico. You want to reach Panama. In which direction should you sail?

2. You are traveling through the Andes in Peru, looking for a large lake. What is it called?

3. You have traveled north again. You are looking for a hydroelectric plant in the far north of Brazil, near the coast. What is the plant called?

▲ **Lake Titicaca, Peru**

Regional Overview **333**

Differentiated Instruction

For Gifted and Talented   L3
Challenge students to create a model of how a hydroelectric plant works. Have them research more details about how dams help create hydroelectric power, or explore alternate methods, such as harnessing the power of waterfalls or tides.

Major Hydroelectric Plants   L2

Guided Instruction

- Read the introductory paragraph and the Location paragraph and study the map.

- Ask students: **What country has the most hydroelectric plants?** *(Brazil)*

- Ask students: **Where do you think new hydroelectric plants could be built?** *(Possible answers: along the Amazon River in Brazil, where rivers drain in Ecuador)* **Which countries will be affected by the construction of these new plants?** *(Students should note that the new plants will affect the countries in which the river flows.)*

- Ask students to study the circle graph. Ask: **What are the top three sources of energy in Latin America?** *(petroleum, natural gas, and hydroelectricity)* **How much more energy comes from petroleum than hydroelectricity?** *(43% more energy comes from petroleum than hydroelectricity)* Ask students to predict some of the benefits of hydroelectricity compared to the other top sources. *(renewable resource, less pollution)*

- Direct students to finish the *Regional Overview* worksheet.
  All in One Latin America Teaching Resources, *Regional Overview*, pp. 89–91

Independent Practice

Ask students to study the maps on pages 332 and 333 and write a brief statement on why Latin America is an ideal place for hydroelectric plants.

Monitor Progress

If students are having trouble with their statements, ask them: **Would you describe Latin America as "a region with plenty of rivers?"** *(Looking at the maps, yes. Almost every country in South America has at least one major river.)*

Answers

LOCATION sixteen percent; petroleum

PRACTICE YOUR GEOGRAPHY SKILLS

1. south southwest
2. Lake Titicaca
3. Tucuruí

Focus on Countries in Latin America L2

Guided Instruction
- Have students pick a number (1–5) from a hat and divide the class according to the numbers they selected.

- Have each group read the text on the country relative to their group number and note down important details.

Independent Practice
Have each group use the Country Databanks (pp. 426–429, 456–461, and 488–493), DK Compact Atlas of the World, and the DK World Desk Reference Online (see student pages for web code) to research the country they have been assigned. Focus their efforts on the geography, climate, government and people of the countries. Then, have each group report to the class the information they have gathered.

Monitor Progress
If students' oral reports veer off the main topic, offer prompts to get them back on track.

Focus on Countries in Latin America

Now that you've investigated the geography of Latin America, take a closer look at some of the countries that make up this region. The map shows all the countries of Latin America. The ten countries that you will study in depth in the second half of this book are shown in yellow on the map.

Go Online PHSchool.com Use Web Code lfp-1010 for the interactive maps on these pages.

◄ **Mexico**
Mexico is the United States's southern neighbor. Its capital, Mexico City, is one of the largest cities on the planet. Many of the people who live and work in Mexico City have moved there from the countryside.

▲ **Haiti**
Haiti lies on the western third of the island of Hispaniola. It is the only nation in the Americas formed as a result of a successful revolt by enslaved Africans.

◄ **Peru**
Peru is a mountainous country that is home to many species of animals, including the llama. Llamas thrive in the mountains and their wool is used for clothing.

334 Latin America

Background: Links Across Time

Place Names American Indian place names often describe a region's physical characteristics. For example, *Panama* meant "abundance of fish" to the people who lived there before Europeans arrived.

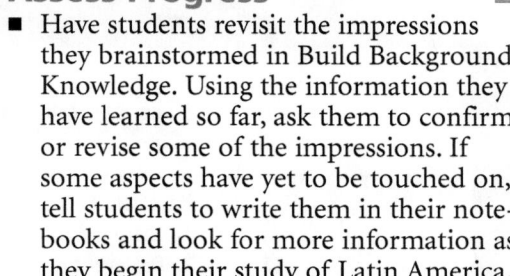

▲ Brazil
Brazil is the largest country in Latin America and is the home of São Paulo, the fastest-growing city in the world. Yet more than half of the country is made up of the Amazon rain forest, home to many diverse Native American groups who have lived there for thousands of years.

Key

——	National border
☐	Countries with in-depth coverage
▨	Non-feature countries

0 miles 1,000
0 kilometers 1,000
Lambert Azimuthal Equal Area

Chile ▶
Chile is a long, narrow country with a dramatic, mountainous landscape. In some parts of Chile, people still live much as their ancestors did.

Regional Overview **335**

Assess and Reteach

Assess Progress [L2]

- Have students revisit the impressions they brainstormed in Build Background Knowledge. Using the information they have learned so far, ask them to confirm or revise some of the impressions. If some aspects have yet to be touched on, tell students to write them in their notebooks and look for more information as they begin their study of Latin America.

- Ask students to complete Practice Your Geography Skills on p. 333.

Reteach [L1]

For more exploration of the region, have students view the Latin America portion of the Passport to the World CD-ROM and complete the Customs Quiz.

⊙ *Latin America,* **Passport to the World CD-ROM**

Extend [L3]

Portfolio Activity One way of assessing student accomplishments is by having them build a portfolio of their best work. To begin their portfolios for Latin America, have students choose another of the Latin American countries mentioned on pages 334–335. Then, assign a project on this country. Students can choose what type of project they would like to do. Options include collages, maps, stories, paragraphs, dioramas, and more.

- Give students *Learning More About a Topic* to help them get started on their research.

All in One Latin America Teaching Resources, *Learning More About a Topic,* p. 94

Overview

Section 1

Land and Water
1. Learn where Latin America is located.
2. Discover the important landforms of Latin America.
3. Find out how Latin America's waterways have affected the region.

Section 2

Climate and Vegetation
1. Find out what kinds of climate Latin America has.
2. Learn what factors influence climate in Latin America.
3. Understand how climate and vegetation influence the ways people live.

Section 3

Resources and Land Use
1. Find out what Latin America's most important natural resources are.
2. Learn why depending on a one-resource economy has been a problem for Latin American nations.

Technology Resources

Students use embedded Web codes to access internet activities, chapter self-tests, and additional map practice. They may also access Dorling Kindersley's Online Desk Reference to learn more about each country they study.

Use the Interactive Textbook to make content and concepts come alive through animations, videos, and activities that accompany the complete basal text—online and on CD-ROM.

PRENTICE HALL

Use this complete suite of powerful teaching tools to make planning lessons and administering tests quicker and easier.

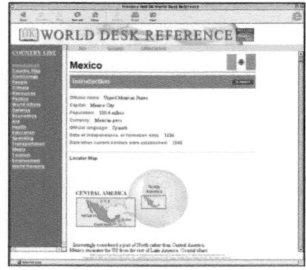

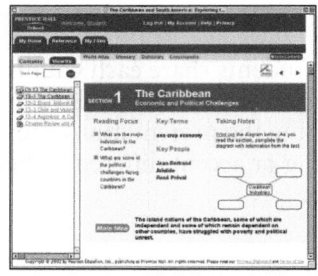

Reading and Assessment

Reading and Vocabulary Instruction

🔁 Model the Target Reading Skill

Reading Process Explain to students that reading actively will help them retain knowledge and become better readers. One way of reading actively is to preview and think about the text *before reading*.

Model this skill by thinking about this chapter aloud:

This chapter's title is *Latin America: Physical Geography*. So I'll be learning about what the physical features of Latin America are like when I read the chapter.

The first section is called *Land and Water*. I wonder how the land and water of Latin America are different from those of the United States? I'll read the section to find out.

The second section is called *Climate and Vegetation*. What does vegetation mean exactly? It sounds like the word "vegetable," so maybe it has something to do with plants. When I read that section, I'll find out what "vegetation" means.

The third section is called *Resources and Land Use*. I'm not sure about resources, but land use must mean how people use the land. I predict that in this section, I'll learn about interaction between humans and the environment in Latin America.

Use the following worksheets from All-in-One Latin America Teaching Resources, (pp. 110, 111, and 112) to support this chapter's Target Reading Skill.

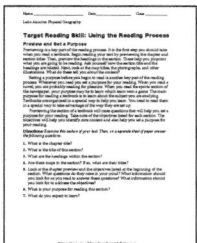
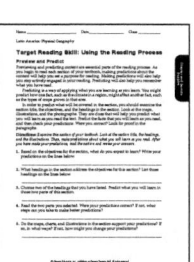

Vocabulary Builder

High-Use Academic Words

Use these steps to teach this chapter's high-use words:

1. Have students rate how well they know each word on their Word Knowledge worksheets (All-in-One Latin America Teaching Resources, p. 113).
2. Pronounce each word and ask students to repeat it.
3. Give students a brief definition and sample sentence (provided on TE pp. 339, 344, and 353).
4. Work with students as they fill in the "Definition or Example" column of their Word Knowledge worksheets.

Assessment

Formal Assessment

Test students' understanding of core knowledge and skills.

Chapter Tests A and B, All-in-One Latin America Teaching Resources, pp. 130–135

Customize the Chapter Tests to suit your needs.

ExamView® Test Bank CD-ROM

Skills Assessment

Assess geographic literacy.

MapMaster Skills, Student Edition, pp. 337, 339, 344, 348, 353, 360

Assess reading and comprehension.

Target Reading Skills, Student Edition, pp. 341, 347, 357, and in Section Assessments

Chapter 11 Assessment, Western Hemisphere Reading and Vocabulary Study Guide, p. 131

Performance Assessment

Assess students' performance on this chapter's Writing Activities using the following rubric from All-in-One Latin America Teaching Resources.

Rubric for Assessing a Writing Assignment, p. 129

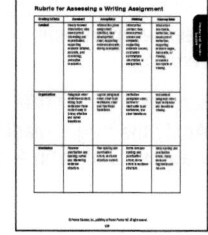

Assess students' work through performance tasks.

Small Group Activity: Making a Relief Map, All-in-One Latin America Teaching Resources, pp. 116–119

Online Assessment

Have students check their own understanding.

Chapter Self-Test

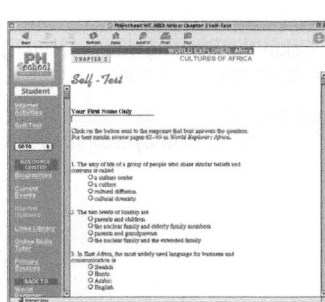

Test Preparation

Assess students' skills and diagnose problems as students begin their study of this region.

Screening and Diagnosing Readiness Tests, AYP Monitoring Assessments, pp. 1–63

Section 1 Land and Water

1.5 periods, .75 block

Social Studies Objectives

1. Learn where Latin America is located.
2. Discover the important landforms of Latin America.
3. Find out how Latin America's waterways have affected the region.

Reading/Language Arts Objective

Preview to set a purpose for reading.

Prepare to Read	Instructional Resources	Differentiated Instruction
Build Background Knowledge Name countries, landforms and waterways in Latin America. **Set a Purpose for Reading** Have students evaluate statements on the *Reading Readiness Guide*. **Preview Key Terms** Teach the section's Key Terms using a "See It—Remember It" chart. **Target Reading Skill** Introduce the section's Target Reading Skill of **previewing and setting a purpose for reading.**	**All in One Latin America Teaching Resources** L2 Reading Readiness Guide, p. 99 L2 Preview and Set a Purpose, p. 110	**Spanish Reading and Vocabulary Study Guide** L2 Chapter 11, Section 1, pp. 90–91 ELL

Instruct	Instructional Resources	Differentiated Instruction
Where is Latin America? Using the map, discuss the location of Latin America. **Landforms of Latin America** Discuss landforms and their effects on the region's people. **Target Reading Skill** Review **previewing and setting a purpose for reading.** **Latin America's Waterways** Apply the target reading skill while discussing the waterways of Latin America.	**All in One Latin America Teaching Resources** L2 Guided Reading and Review, p. 100 L2 Reading Readiness Guide, p. 99 **Latin America Transparencies** L2 Section Reading Support Transparency LA 28	**Spanish Support** L2 Guided Reading and Review (Spanish), p. 122 ELL

Assess and Reteach	Instructional Resources	Differentiated Instruction
Assess Progress Evaluate student comprehension with the section assessment and section quiz. **Reteach** Assign the Reading and Vocabulary Study Guide to help struggling students. **Extend** Extend the lesson by assigning a map worksheet.	**All in One Latin America Teaching Resources** L2 Section Quiz, p. 101 L3 Reading a Physical Map, p. 122 Rubric for Assessing a Writing Assignment, p. 129 **Reading and Vocabulary Study Guide** L1 Chapter 11, Section 1, pp. 122–124	**Spanish Support** L2 Section Quiz (Spanish), p. 123 ELL

Key

L1 Basic to Average	L3 Average to Advanced	LPR Less Proficient Readers	GT Gifted and Talented
L2 For All Students		AR Advanced Readers	ELL English Language Learners
		SN Special Needs Students	

336c

Section 2 Climate and Vegetation

2.5 periods, 1.25 blocks (includes Skills For Life)

Social Studies Objectives

1. Find out what kind of climates Latin America has.
2. Learn what factors influence climate in Latin America.
3. Understand how climate and vegetation influence the way people live.

Reading/Language Arts Objective

Make predictions about a text to help set a purpose for reading.

Prepare to Read	Instructional Resources	Differentiated Instruction
Build Background Knowledge Discuss how climate affects people's lives. **Set a Purpose for Reading** Have students begin to fill out the *Reading Readiness Guide.* **Preview Key Terms** Teach the section's Key Terms. **Target Reading Skill** Introduce the section's Target Reading Skill of **previewing and predicting.**	**All in One Latin America Teaching Resources** L2 Reading Readiness Guide, p. 103 L2 Preview and Predict, p. 111	**Spanish Reading and Vocabulary Study Guide** L2 Chapter 11, Section 2, pp. 92–93 ELL

Instruct	Instructional Resources	Differentiated Instruction
The Climates of Latin America Have students consider effects of different climates. **What Factors Affect Climate?** Ask students key questions about factors affecting climate. **Target Reading Skill** Review **previewing and predicting.** **Climate, Plants, and People** Discuss the relationship between the climate and economy of Latin America.	**All in One Latin America Teaching Resources** L2 Guided Reading and Review, p. 104 L2 Reading Readiness Guide, p. 103 **Latin America Transparencies** L2 Section Reading Support Transparency LA 29 L2 Color Transparency LA 26: Mexico: Physical-Political	**All in One Latin America Teaching Resources** L2 Skills for Life, p. 115 AR, GT, LPR, SN **Teacher's Edition** L3 For Advanced Readers, TE p. 345 L1 For English Language Learners, p. 347 L3 For Gifted/Talented Students, TE p. 348 L1 For Special Needs Students, TE p. 351 **Spanish Support** L2 Guided Reading and Review (Spanish), p. 124 ELL

Assess and Reteach	Instructional Resources	Differentiated Instruction
Assess Progress Evaluate student comprehension with the section assessment and section quiz. **Reteach** Assign the Reading and Vocabulary Study Guide to help struggling students. **Extend** Extend the lesson by assigning a Small Group Activity.	**All in One Latin America Teaching Resources** L2 Section Quiz, p. 105 L3 Small Group Activity, pp. 116–119 Rubric for Assessing a Writing Assignment, p. 129 **Reading and Vocabulary Study Guide** L1 Chapter 11, Section 2, pp. 125–127	**All in One Latin America Teaching Resources** L3 Activity Shop Interdisciplinary, pp. 120–121 GT **Social Studies Skills Tutor CD-ROM** L1 Analyzing and Interpreting Special-Purpose Maps SN, LPR

Key

L1 Basic to Average	L3 Average to Advanced	LPR Less Proficient Readers	GT Gifted and Talented
L2 For All Students		AR Advanced Readers	ELL English Language Learners
		SN Special Needs Students	

Section 3 Resources and Land Use

4 periods, 2 blocks (includes Chapter Review and Assessment, and Literature)

Social Studies Objectives

1. Find out what Latin America's most important natural resources are.
2. Learn why depending on a one-resource economy has been a problem for Latin American nations.

Reading/Language Arts Objective

Create questions to help you understand and remember what you read.

Prepare to Read	Instructional Resources	Differentiated Instruction
Build Background Knowledge Discuss what students predict Latin America's natural resources might be. **Set a Purpose for Reading** Have students evaluate statements on the *Reading Readiness Guide.* **Preview Key Terms** Teach the section's Key Terms. **Target Reading Skill** Introduce the section's Target Reading Skill of **previewing and asking questions**.	**All in One Latin America Teaching Resources** L2 Reading Readiness Guide, p. 107 L2 Preview and Ask Questions, p. 112	**Spanish Reading and Vocabulary Study Guide** L2 Chapter 11, Section 3, pp. 94–95 ELL

Instruct	Instructional Resources	Differentiated Instruction
Latin America's Resources Ask students key questions about Latin America's resources. **Resources and the Economy** Discuss the relationship between the resources and economies of Latin American nations. **Target Reading Skill** Review **previewing and asking questions**.	**All in One Latin America Teaching Resources** L2 Guided Reading and Review, p. 108 L2 Reading Readiness Guide, p. 107 **Latin America Transparencies** L2 Section Reading Support Transparency LA 30	**All in One Latin America Teaching Resources** L3 Message from the Rain Forest Amerindians, p. 123 AR L2 Structuring Paragraphs, p. 126 AR, GT, LPR, SN L2 Creating Paragraph Outlines, p. 127 AR, GT, LPR, SN **Teacher's Edition** L1 For Less Proficient Readers, TE p. 354 L3 For Advanced Readers, TE p. 355 L1 For Special Needs Students, TE p. 357

Assess and Reteach	Instructional Resources	Differentiated Instruction
Assess Progress Evaluate student comprehension with the section assessment and section quiz. **Reteach** Assign the Reading and Vocabulary Study Guide to help struggling students. **Extend** Extend the lesson by assigning an Enrichment activity.	**All in One Latin America Teaching Resources** L2 Section Quiz, p. 109 L3 Enrichment, p. 114, Rubric for Assessing a Writing Assignment, p. 129 L2 Vocabulary Development, p. 128 L2 Word Knowledge, p. 113 L2 Chapter Tests A & B, pp. 130–135 **Reading and Vocabulary Study Guide** L1 Chapter 11, Section 3, pp. 128–130	**All in One Latin America Teaching Resources** L3 My Friend the Painter, pp. 124–125 AR, GT **Spanish Support** L2 Section Quiz (Spanish), p. 127 ELL L2 Chapter Summary (Spanish), p. 128 ELL L2 Vocabulary Development (Spanish), p. 129 ELL **Student Edition on Audio CD** L1 Chapter 11, Section 3 SN

Key

L1 Basic to Average	L3 Average to Advanced	LPR Less Proficient Readers	GT Gifted and Talented
L2 For All Students		AR Advanced Readers	ELL English Language Learners
		SN Special Needs Students	

Reading Background

Previewing and Prereading

This chapter's Target Reading Skill asks students to preview each section and set a purpose for reading. Students who do a brief, preliminary reading of complex material are in a strategic position to take control of their learning and comprehension.

Previewing helps students consider what they already know about a topic they will be studying and gives some idea of what a text selection is about before they read it. Previewing also helps students identify the text structure and develop a mental framework for ideas to be encountered in the text. This can help them in formulating a more realistic reading and study plan.

Follow the steps below to teach students how to preview and pre-read.

1. Tell students that previewing will help them identify the text structure and develop a mental outline of ideas they will encounter in the text.

2. List the various text features you will be previewing in the order in which you would like students to examine them: section title, text headings, introduction, list of key terms, questions or tasks in the reading selection, photographs, drawings, maps, charts and other visuals in the text. Focus students' attention on some of these items, or ask them to look at all of them.

3. Prompt students to reflect after examining various text features. They may ask themselves questions such as: What is this reading selection about? What are some key words I will learn? How should I tackle this reading and divide up the task?

Language Strategies for Predicting

In this chapter, students will use the ReQuest (Reciprocal Questioning) Procedure to share their ideas. As part of this activity, students are asked to make predictions about the reading. Students may feel more comfortable actively participating if they have some sample language strategies to use in framing their predictions. Offer students the following language strategies:

> I guess/predict/imagine that . . .
>
> Based on . . . I infer that . . .
>
> I hypothesize that . . .

Remind students that their predictions may differ from other students', and that they may build on others' predictions to help strengthen their own.

World Studies Background

Exploring the Amazon

The Amazon River has fascinated people for hundreds of years. Perhaps its most famous explorer was Theodore Roosevelt. In 1913, the former President was part of the first group to officially explore the rain forests of Brazil between the Amazon River and the Río de la Plata. For over 40 days, Roosevelt and his companions overcame insects, disease, lack of food, and high rapids in order to map this area.

Volcano of the Andes

The Andes Mountains contain many volcanoes, some of which are quite dangerous. On November 13, 1985, the Nevado del Ruiz volcano in northern Colombia erupted for the first time since 1845. This caused one of the worst natural disasters

in South American history. The heat of the volcanic eruption melted glacial ice that had accumulated on top of the volcano. As lahar, or volcanic mud, flowed furiously down from the volcano, 14 towns and villages in the area were destroyed, causing over 20,000 deaths.

The Silver River

The Río de la Plata, which means Silver River in Spanish, is the largest estuary in South America. An estuary is a partially enclosed area where seawater and fresh water meet, and a valuable environment for wildlife. The river provides a home to many species, including the La Plata, or Franciscana, dolphin, which is unique because it can live in the fresh water river and in the salt water of the ocean.

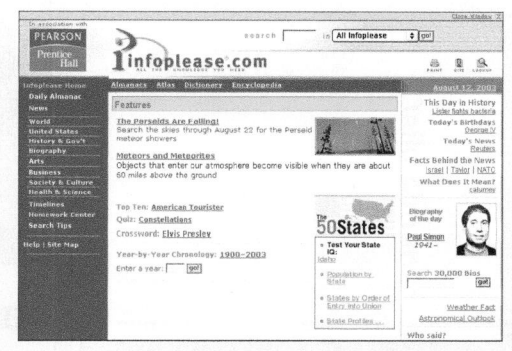

Infoplease® provides a wealth of useful information for the classroom. You can use this resource to strengthen your background on the subjects covered in this chapter. Have students visit this advertising-free site as a starting point for projects requiring research.

Use Web code **lfd-1100** for **Infoplease.®**

Guiding Questions

Remind students about the Guiding Questions introduced at the beginning of this section.

Section 1 relates to **Guiding Question** ①
What are the main physical features of Latin America? *(Latin America has mountains, plateaus, islands, tropical rain forests, and rivers.)*

Section 2 relates to **Guiding Question** ⑤
How has geography influenced the ways in which Latin Americans make a living? *(Temperature, rainfall, and elevation affect what kinds of crops Latin Americans can grow and sell.)*

Section 3 relates to **Guiding Question** ⑤
How has geography influenced the ways in which Latin Americans make a living? *(Some Latin American countries have many natural resources that can be sold, while others have limited resources to cultivate and sell.)*

⊙ Target Reading Skill

In this chapter, students will learn and apply the reading skill of compare and contrast. Use the following worksheets to help students practice this skill:

All in One **Latin America Teaching Resources**, *Preview and Set a Purpose,* p. 110; *Preview and Predict,* p. 111; *Preview and Ask Questions,* p. 112

Latin America: Physical Geography

Chapter Preview

This chapter will introduce you to the geography of Latin America and show how geography affects the people who live there.

Section 1
Land and Water

Section 2
Climate and Vegetation

Section 3
Resources and Land Use

⊙ Target Reading Skill

Reading Process In this chapter you will focus on the reading process by using previewing to help you understand and remember what you read.

▶ Stepping stones through a rain forest in Costa Rica

336 Latin America

Differentiated Instruction

The following Teacher Edition strategies are suitable for students of varying abilities.

Advanced Readers, pp. 345, 355
English Language Learners, p. 347
Gifted and Talented, p. 347
Less Proficient Readers, pp. 354, 364
Special Needs Students, pp. 351, 357

Bibliography

For the Teacher
The Eyewitness Atlas of the World. Dorling Kindersley, 1994.
Goulding, Michael. *Smithsonian Atlas of the Amazon.* Smithsonian Institution Press, 2003.
Schlessinger, Andrew. *The Rainforest.* Schlessinger, 1993. Video.

For the Student
L1 Albert, Toni. *The Remarkable Rainforest: An Active-Learning Book for Kids.* Trickle Creek Books, 1996.
L2 *National Geographic Student Atlas of the World.* National Geographic, 2001.
L3 Bernhard, Brendan. *Pizarro, Orellana, and the Exploration of the Amazon.* Chelsea, 1991.

MAP MASTER™ Skills Activity

Latin America: Physical

Place Latin America's geography is varied, but some landforms are found throughout the region. **Locate** Find the main mountain ranges in Latin America. Where are they located? **Compare and Contrast** How does the eastern part of South America compare to the western coastal region?

Go Online
PHSchool.com Use Web Code **lfp-1121** for step-by-step **map skills practice.**

KEY
ELEVATION

Feet	Meters
More than 13,000	More than 3,960
6,500–13,000	1,980–3,960
1,600–6,500	480–1,980
650–1,600	200–480
0–650	0–200

National border

0 miles 1,500
0 kilometers 1,500
Lambert Azimuthal Equal Area

Chapter 11 **337**

MAP MASTER™ Skills Activity

- Point out to students the shape of South America. Encourage students to trace the outline of the region, while describing its shape.

- Write Amazon Basin, Brazil Highlands, Atacama Desert, and Andes Mountains on the board. Call on students to write the elevation range of each physical feature on the board, using the map key.

Go Online
PHSchool.com Students may practice their map skills using the interactive online version of this map.

Using the Visual · L2

Reach Into Your Background Ask students to study the photograph on pages 336 and 337, and read the caption on page 336. Ask them to note details about the image, then share their ideas with the class. Ask **Why do you think these stepping stones exist?** Point out that rain forests get a lot of rainfall. Some areas might be impassable after a heavy rain. Ask students if they can relate this image to their own lives. Allow them to share memories and ideas.

Answers

MAP MASTER Skills Activity **Locate** The Andes are on the Pacific coast of South America. The Sierra Madre Occidental and Sierra Madre Oriental cover much of Mexico. **Compare and Contrast** The eastern part has a lower elevation than the western and coastal region.

Chapter Resources

Teaching Resources
Letter Home, p. 97
- L2 Vocabulary Development, p. 128
- L2 Skills for Life, p. 115
- L2 Chapter Tests A and B, pp. 130–135

Spanish Support
Spanish Letter Home p. 121
- L2 Spanish Chapter Summary, p. 128

- L2 Spanish Vocabulary Development, p. 129

Media and Technology
- L1 Student Edition on Audio CD
- L1 Guided Reading Audiotapes, English and Spanish
- L2 Social Studies Skills Tutor CD-ROM
ExamView® Test Bank CD-ROM

PRENTICE HALL
Presentation EXPRESS™
Teach · Connect · Inspire

Teach this chapter's content using the PresentationExpress™ CD-ROM including:
- slide shows
- transparencies
- interactive maps and media
- *ExamView*® QuickTake Presenter

Objectives

Social Studies

1. Learn where Latin America is located.
2. Discover the important landforms of Latin America.
3. Find out how Latin America's waterways have affected the region.

Reading/Language Arts

Preview to set a purpose for reading.

Prepare to Read

Build Background Knowledge `L2`

Tell students that they will start their study of Latin America by learning about its land and water. Show the Discovery Channel School video. Ask students to note three to five facts about Latin America's land and water as they watch. Have students engage in a Give One, Get One activity (TE, p. T37) to share their answers.

 *The Geography of Latin America,*
World Studies Video Program

Set a Purpose for Reading `L2`

■ Preview the Objectives.

■ Read each statement in the *Reading Readiness Guide* aloud. Ask students to mark the statements true or false.

Have students discuss the statements in pairs or groups of four, then mark their worksheets again. Use the Numbered Heads participation structure (TE, p. T36) to call on students to share their group's perspectives.

All in One Latin America Teaching Resources, *Reading Readiness Guide,* p. 99

Vocabulary Builder
Preview Key Terms `L2`

Create a three-column "See It—Remember It" chart of the Key Terms on the board. Write a term in the first column, a short definition in the second column, and a sketch in the third column. Guide students as they copy and complete the chart.

Land and Water

Prepare to Read

Objectives

In this section you will

1. Learn where Latin America is located.
2. Discover the important landforms of Latin America.
3. Find out how Latin America's waterways have affected the region.

Taking Notes

As you read this section, look for the main ideas about the geography of Latin America. Copy the table below and record your findings in it.

Geography of Latin America		
Region	**Landforms**	**Waterways**
Middle America		
Caribbean		
South America		

 Target Reading Skill

Preview and Set a Purpose When you set a purpose for reading, you give yourself a focus. Before you read this section, look at the headings, photos, and maps to see what the section is about. Then set a purpose for reading, such as learning about Latin America's geography. Now read to meet your purpose.

Key Terms

• **Middle America** (MID ul uh MEHR ih kuh) *n.* Mexico and Central America

• **plateau** (pla TOH) *n.* a large raised area of mostly level land

• **isthmus** (IS mus) *n.* a strip of land with water on both sides that joins two larger bodies of land

• **pampas** (PAM puz) *n.* flat grasslands in South America

• **rain forest** (rayn FAWR ist) *n.* a dense evergreen forest that has abundant rainfall year-round

• **Amazon River** (AM uh zahn RIV ur) *n.* a long river in northern South America

• **tributary** (TRIB yoo tehr ee) *n.* a river or stream that flows into a larger river

La Paz, Bolivia

What would it be like to land at the highest major airport in the world? Many visitors to La Paz, Bolivia, do just that. They land at El Alto airport. *El Alto* (el AL toh) means "the high one" in Spanish. It is a good name for this airport, which is located more than 13,000 feet (3,962 meters) up in the Andes Mountains.

Shortly after leaving the plane, some visitors may get mountain sickness. The "thin" air of the Andes contains less oxygen than most people are used to. Oxygen starvation makes visitors' hearts beat faster and leaves them short of breath. Later on in the day, the visitors may get terrible headaches. It takes a few days for newcomers' bodies to get used to the mountain air. But the people who live in the Andes do not have these problems. Their bodies are used to the mountain environment.

Target Reading Skill `L2`

Preview and Set a Purpose for Reading
Point out the Target Reading Skill. Explain to students that passages containing new information are often easier if you have a reason for reading before you begin.

Model setting a purpose for reading using the heading and passage on page 342. Tell students that your purpose for reading Latin America's Waterways is to find out the names of the major waterways of Latin America.

Ask students to read the passage with this purpose in mind. While students are reading, write the waterways mentioned in the passage on the board. Allow students to ask questions about setting a purpose for reading if they are unsure of how to use the skill.

Give students *Preview and Set a Purpose.* Have them complete the activity in groups.

All in One Latin America Teaching Resources, *Preview and Set a Purpose,* p. 110

Where Is Latin America?

When visitors land in La Paz, Bolivia, they have arrived in South America, one of the regions of Latin America. Find Bolivia on the map titled Political Latin America on page 3. As you can see, Latin America is located in the Western Hemisphere, south of the United States. Notice that Latin America includes all the nations from Mexico to the tip of South America. It also includes the islands that dot the Caribbean (ka ruh BEE un) Sea.

Geographic features divide Latin America into three smaller regions, as you can see in the map below. They are Mexico and Central America, which is also called **Middle America;** the Caribbean; and South America. South America is so large that geographers classify it as a continent.

✓ Reading Check **What three regions make up Latin America?**

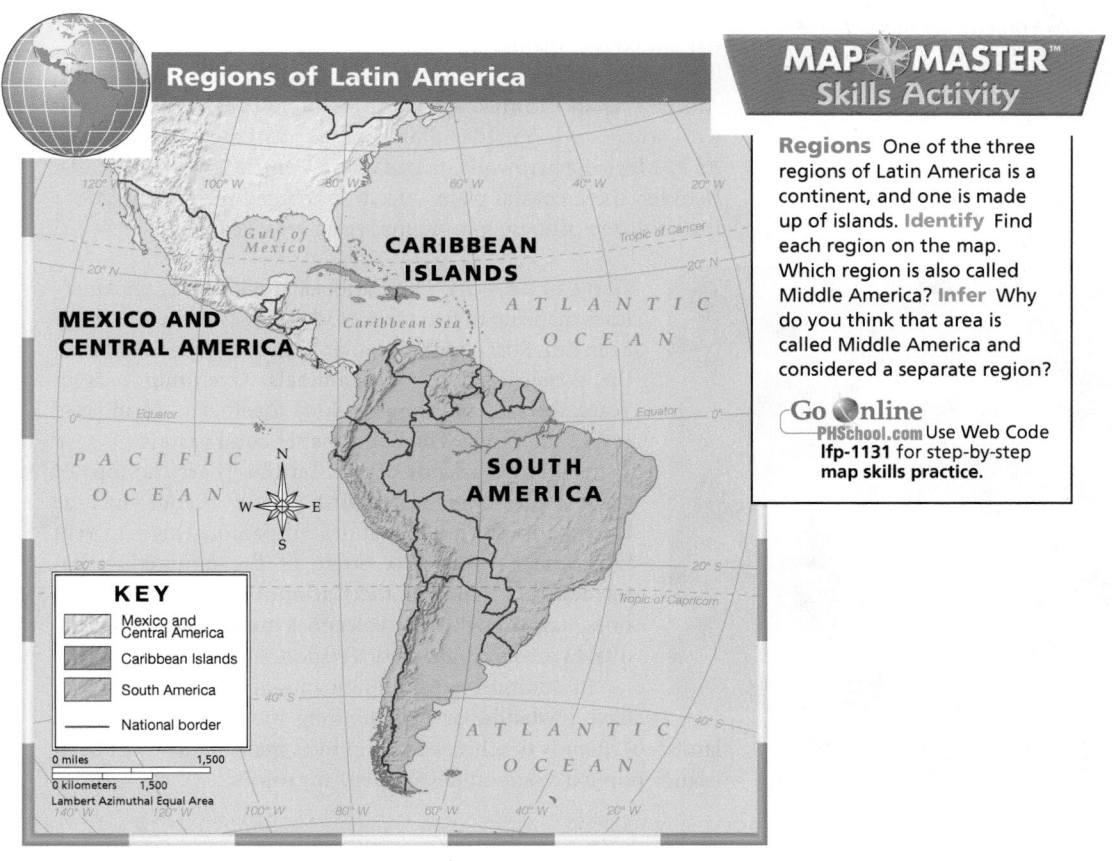

Regions of Latin America

MAP☀MASTER™
Skills Activity

Regions One of the three regions of Latin America is a continent, and one is made up of islands. **Identify** Find each region on the map. Which region is also called Middle America? **Infer** Why do you think that area is called Middle America and considered a separate region?

Go Online
PHSchool.com Use Web Code **lfp-1131** for step-by-step map skills practice.

KEY

▨ Mexico and Central America

▨ Caribbean Islands

▨ South America

— National border

0 miles 1,500
0 kilometers 1,500
Lambert Azimuthal Equal Area

Guided Instruction

- **Vocabulary Builder** Clarify the high-use word **classify** before reading.
- Read Where Is Latin America? using the Structured Silent Reading strategy (TE, p. T34).
- Ask students to use the map on this page to identify the continents spanned by Latin America, and the major bodies of water that border the three regions. *(North America and South America; Pacific Ocean, Caribbean Sea, Atlantic Ocean, and Gulf of Mexico)*

Independent Practice

Assign *Guided Reading and Review*.

🔲 All in One **Latin America Teaching Resources,** *Guided Reading and Review*, p. 100

Monitor Progress

As students begin *Guided Reading and Review*, circulate to answer questions and provide assistance as needed.

Answers

✓ Reading Check Middle America (Mexico and Central America), the Caribbean, and South America.

MAP☀MASTER Skills Activity **Identify** Mexico and Central America **Infer** The region falls in the middle of the Western Hemisphere between North America and South America. It has different characteristics from the other two Latin American regions.

Go Online PHSchool.com Student may practice their map skills using the interactive online version of this map.

Vocabulary Builder

Use the information below to teach students this section's high-use words.

High-Use Word	Definition and Sample Sentence
classify, p. 339	*v.* to arrange by putting into groups The librarian **classifies** books by author, title, and subject.
dominate, p. 340	*v.* to be most powerful or important; to tower over That huge building **dominates** the rest of the block.
impressive, p. 341	*adj.* having a strong effect on the mind or emotions The colorful display of fireworks was **impressive.**

Read the **Links Across Time** on this page. Ask students **What do the regions of Latin America have in common?** *(People from Latin America share a language based on the European language of Latin.)*

Landforms of Latin America

L2

Guided Instruction

- **Vocabulary Builder** Clarify the meaning of the high-use words **dominate** and **impressive** before reading.

- Ask students to read Landforms of Latin America. Circulate to make sure that students can answer the Reading Check question.

- Ask students **What landforms would they find in Central America?** *(an isthmus, coastal plains, mountains, and volcanoes)* **In South America?** *(huge mountains, rolling highlands, plains, rain forest)*

- Ask students **How does the mountainous land of Middle America affect the lives of people in the region?** *(Travel is difficult.)*

Independent Practice

Ask students to create the Taking Notes graphic organizer on a blank piece of paper. Then have them fill in the "Landforms" column with the information they have just learned. Briefly model how to choose details, reminding students that "Middle America" is another name for Mexico and Central America.

Monitor Progress

As students complete the "Landforms" column, walk around the room to ensure that students are recording the right details. Answer individual questions and offer help as needed.

Links Across Time

Why "Latin" America?
Why are three distinct regions called by one name, Latin America? About 500 years ago, Europeans sailed to the Americas. Most of those who settled in what is now called Latin America came from Spain and Portugal. These European colonists brought their own languages and ways of life with them. Today, most Latin Americans speak Spanish, Portuguese, or French. These languages have their roots in the ancient European language of Latin. As a result, the entire region is known as Latin America.

A parrotfish swims by a coral reef in the Caribbean Sea.

Landforms of Latin America

Picture mountains that pierce the clouds, and grassy plains that never seem to end. Imagine wet, dense forests and sun-baked deserts. This is Latin America, a region of variety and contrast.

Mexico and Central America Mexico and Central America stretch 2,500 miles (4,023 kilometers) from the United States border to South America. This distance is almost equal to the width of the United States from Los Angeles to New York City. Mountains dominate Middle America. These mountains are part of a long system of mountain ranges that extends from Canada through the United States all the way to the tip of South America.

Mexico's central plateau lies between two mountain ranges. A **plateau** (pla TOH) is a large raised area of mostly level land. Most of Mexico's people live there. However, the surrounding mountains make it difficult for people to travel to and from the central plateau. Along the east and west coasts of Mexico are narrow coastal plains.

Central America, located south of Mexico and north of South America, is an isthmus. An **isthmus** (IS mus) is a strip of land with water on both sides that joins two larger bodies of land. As in Mexico, narrow plains run along Central America's coasts. Between these coastal plains are steep, rugged mountains. More than a dozen of these mountains are active volcanoes.

The Caribbean The Caribbean region of Latin America is made up of two types of islands located in the Caribbean Sea. Some of the smaller islands are made of coral, the skeletons of tiny sea animals. Over hundreds of years, the skeletons have melded together to form large reefs and islands. The Bahamas are coral islands.

The larger islands of the Caribbean are the tops of huge underwater mountains. These islands include Cuba, Jamaica (juh MAY kuh), Hispaniola (his pun YOH luh), and Puerto Rico. Some of the mountains that formed the islands of the Caribbean were once volcanoes, and a few of the volcanoes are still active. Earthquakes are common in this region.

In addition to mountain ranges, these islands also have lowlands, or plains, along their coasts. Beautiful landscapes, sandy beaches, and coral reefs make many Caribbean islands popular vacation destinations for tourists.

Skills for Life — Skills Mini Lesson

Making Valid Generalizations **L2**

1. A generalization is a conclusion based on a few examples. Generalizations help people to see patterns and similarities. To make a generalization, you must gather specific facts, identify similarities, and draw conclusions about the similarities.

2. Model the skill by reading Mexico and Central America on page 340. Note the sentences "Along the east and west coasts of Mexico are narrow coastal plains" and "As in Mexico, narrow plains run along Central America's coasts." A generalization could be: *Narrow plains are found along the coast of many countries in Middle America.*

3. Have students apply the skill by reading The Caribbean and South America and then creating a generalization about all of Latin America.

South America The continent of South America has many types of landforms, but the Andes Mountains are probably the most impressive. The Andes run some 5,500 miles (8,900 kilometers) along the western coast of South America. In some places, the Andes rise to heights of more than 20,000 feet (6,100 meters). That's about as high as twenty 100-story buildings stacked one on top of another. Except for the Himalayan Mountains in Asia, the Andes are the highest mountains in the world.

The Andes are steep and difficult to cross. Even so, many people farm in this region. East of the Andes are rolling highlands. These highlands spread across parts of Brazil, Venezuela (ven uh ZWAY luh), Guyana (gy AN uh), and other South American countries. Farther south are the **pampas** (PAM puz), a large region of flat grasslands that stretches through Argentina (ahr jun TEE nuh) and Uruguay (YOOR uh gway). The pampas are similar to the Great Plains of the United States.

The eastern highlands and the Andes surround the Amazon River Basin. The Amazon River Basin contains the largest tropical rain forest in the world. A **rain forest** is a dense evergreen forest that has abundant rainfall throughout the year. This rain forest covers more than a third of the continent.

√ Reading Check **Describe the Andes mountain range.**

Preview and Set a Purpose
If your purpose is to learn about the geography of Latin America, how does the paragraph at the left help you meet your goal?

Latin American Cowboys
These cowboys are herding cattle in the Patagonia region of Argentina. **Analyze Images** *What details in the photo suggest that this scene is not taking place in the United States?*

Preview and Set a Purpose As a follow up, ask students to answer the Target Reading Skill question in the Student Edition. (*This paragraph describes the most prominent landform of South America, the Andes Mountains, which is one important piece of information regarding the geography of Latin America.*)

Latin America's Waterways L2

Guided Instruction
- Have students read Latin America's Waterways on page 342.
- Ask students to describe ways that rivers are important to people in South America. (*for transportation, food, and electric power*)

Independent Practice
Have students complete the graphic organizer by filling in the "Waterways" column.

Monitor Progress
- Show *Section Reading Support Transparency LA 28* and ask students to check their graphic organizers individually. Go over key concepts and clarify key vocabulary as needed.

  📄 **Latin America Transparencies,** *Section Reading Support Transparency LA 28*

- Tell students to fill in the last column of the *Reading Readiness Guide*. Probe for what they learned that confirms or invalidates each statement.

  All in One **Latin America Teaching Resources,** *Reading Readiness Guide,* p. 99

Background: Global Perspectives

Asia's Mighty Himalaya Mountains
Only the Himalaya, a mountain system in Asia, stand taller than the Andes. The Himalaya make up the tallest range in the world. They extend along the India-Tibet border and through Pakistan, Nepal, China, and Bhutan. The tallest peak of this range is the well-known—and often-climbed—Mount Everest. At 29,035 feet (8,850 meters) above sea level, Everest stands more than a mile higher than the tallest peak in the Andes (and the Western Hemisphere), Aconcagua, which is 22,835 feet (6,960 meters) high.

Answers

√ Reading Check The Andes Mountains are about 5,500 miles long and rise to about 20,000 feet at their highest. They are not easy to travel across, but many people farm in the region. **Analyze Images** The gauchos use horses to herd cattle and wear traditional clothing.

Assess and Reteach

Assess Progress `L2`

Have students complete the Section Assessment. Administer the *Section Quiz*.

 Latin America Teaching Resources, *Section Quiz,* p. 101

Reteach `L1`

For more instruction, have students read this section in the Reading and Vocabulary Study Guide.

Chapter 11, Section 1, **Western Hemisphere Reading and Vocabulary Study Guide,** pp. 122–124

Extend `L3`

To extend the lesson, have students study the physical map of Latin America on *Reading a Physical Map.* Ask students to complete the worksheet individually or in pairs.

 Latin America Teaching Resources, *Reading a Physical Map,* p. 54

Answers

Infer The fishers will probably sell their catch locally because they are using small boats to transport a small number of fish.

✓ Reading Check The Paraná, Paraguay, and Uruguay Rivers form the Río de la Plata system.

Section 1 Assessment

Key Terms

Students' sentences should reflect knowledge of each Key Term.

Target Reading Skill

Students should be able to state a reasonable purpose for reading, such as "To learn about the landforms and waterways of Latin America" or "To be able to locate Latin America and name its regions." Students' answers will vary according to whether or not their purpose was accomplished. If not, students should be able to state a different, more appropriate purpose.

Comprehension and Critical Thinking

1. (a) Middle America, the Caribbean, and South America. **(b)** Middle America lies just south of the United States. The Caribbean is east of Middle America. South America is south of the Caribbean.

Fishing the Rivers of Brazil
The families of these Brazilian fishers could not survive without their catch. **Infer** *Do you think these fishers sell their catch locally or send it to other countries? Use details from the photo to explain your answer.*

Latin America's Waterways

Latin America has some of the longest and largest bodies of water in the world. These waterways are important to the people of the region. Rivers serve as natural highways in places where it is hard to build roads. Fish from the rivers provide food. Rushing water from large rivers provides power to generate electricity.

Latin America's **Amazon** (AM uh zahn) **River** is the second-longest river in the world. Only the Nile in Africa is longer. The Amazon flows 4,000 miles (6,437 kilometers) from Peru across Brazil into the Atlantic Ocean. It carries more water than any other river in the world—about 20 percent of all the fresh river water on Earth! The Amazon gathers power from more than 1,000 tributaries that spill into it. **Tributaries** are the rivers and streams that flow into a larger river. With its tributaries, the Amazon drains an area of more than two million square miles.

The Paraná (pah rah NAH), Paraguay, and Uruguay rivers form the Río de la Plata system, which separates Argentina and Uruguay. In Venezuela, people travel on the Orinoco River and Lake Maracaibo (mar uh KY boh). Up in the Andes Mountains, Lake Titicaca is the highest lake in the world on which ships can travel. It lies 12,500 feet (3,810 kilometers) above sea level.

✓ Reading Check **What rivers form the Río de la Plata system?**

 **Section 1 Assessment**

Key Terms

Review the key terms at the beginning of this section. Use each term in a sentence that explains its meaning.

 Target Reading Skill

What was your purpose for reading this section? Did you accomplish it? If not, what might have been a better purpose?

Comprehension and Critical Thinking

1. (a) Name What are the three regions of Latin America?

(b) Synthesize Where are the regions located in relation to one another?

2. (a) Recall What are the main landforms of Latin America?

(b) Identify Cause and Effect How do mountain ranges affect life in Latin America?

3. (a) Identify Which is the largest river in Latin America?

(b) Analyze Information What are three important characteristics of that river?

(c) Generalize How do countries benefit from their waterways?

Writing Activity

If your family were planning to move to Latin America, which of its three regions would you prefer to live in? Write a paragraph explaining your choice.

> **Writing Tip** Begin your paragraph with a topic sentence that states your main idea—your choice of region. Give at least two reasons for your choice. Support each reason with a specific detail.

---

2. (a) The main landforms of Latin America are mountains, plains, rain forests, plateaus, highlands, and deserts. **(b)** Mountains make it difficult to travel, but some people are able to farm in the region.

3. (a) Amazon **(b)** It carries 20 percent of all fresh water on Earth, has more than 1,000 tributaries, and drains more than two million square miles. **(c)** People use rivers for travel, electricity, and as a source of food.

Writing Activity

Use the *Rubric for Assessing a Writing Assignment* to evaluate students' paragraphs.

 Latin America Teaching Resources, *Rubric for Assessing a Writing Assignment,* p. 129

Prepare to Read

Objectives

In this section you will
1. Find out what kinds of climate Latin America has.
2. Learn what factors influence climate in Latin America.
3. Understand how climate and vegetation influence the ways people live.

Taking Notes

As you read this section, look for the ways different factors affect climate and vegetation. Copy the table below and record your findings in it.

Factor	Effect on Climate	Effect on Vegetation

Target Reading Skill

Preview and Predict Making predictions about your text helps you set a purpose for reading and remember what you read. Before you begin, look at the headings, photos, and anything else that stands out. Then predict what the text might be about. For example, you might predict that this section will tell about Latin America's climate and plants. As you read, if what you learn doesn't support your prediction, revise your prediction.

Key Terms

- **El Niño** (el NEEN yoh) *n.* a warming of the ocean water along the western coast of South America
- **elevation** (el uh VAY shun) *n.* the height of land above sea level
- **economy** (ih KAHN uh mee) *n.* the ways that goods and services are produced and made available to people

Every few years, something strange happens off the western coast of South America. Fish that usually thrive in the cold waters of the Pacific Ocean are driven away. At the same time, other changes occur on land. Areas that usually have dry weather get heavy rains, and low-lying regions are flooded. In other parts of Latin America, drought plagues the land and the people.

What brings this disaster to Latin America? It is El Niño (el NEEN yoh), a warming of the ocean water along the western coast of South America. It occurs every few years and influences global weather patterns. El Niño is Spanish for "the little boy." Peruvian fishermen gave it this name, which refers to the baby Jesus, because the warm water currents usually reach Peru around Christmas time. El Niño is one of many factors that affect climate in Latin America.

The warm water current of El Niño appears red in this view from space.

Target Reading Skill L2

Preview and Predict Point out the Target Reading Skill. Tell students that to predict what the reading will be about, they should make an educated guess about the content based on clues. Clues might include photos, headings, maps, or even boldfaced words in the passage. Explain to students that once they make a prediction, they can read the passage with the purpose of finding out whether their prediction is correct or needs to be revised.

As an example, ask students to look at the head and the diagram on page 346 of the Student Edition. Using those clues, make this prediction: "This passage will explain what vertical climate zones are and how height affects climate."

Give students *Preview and Predict*. Have them complete the activity in groups.

All in One Latin America Teaching Resources, *Preview and Predict,* p. 111

Objectives
Social Studies

1. Find out what kinds of climate Latin America has.
2. Learn what factors influence climate in Latin America.
3. Understand how climate and vegetation influence the way people live.

Reading/Language Arts

Make predictions about a text to help set a purpose for reading.

Prepare to Read

Build Background Knowledge L2

In this section, students will learn about the climate and plant life of Latin America. Tell them that climate is a place's weather conditions over a number of years. Ask students to list examples of how climate affects their lives. Model a statement such as "When it is rainy, I don't like to sit outside." Conduct an Idea Wave (TE, p. T35) so that students can share their answers.

Set a Purpose for Reading L2

- Preview the Objectives.
- Form students into pairs or groups of four. Distribute the *Reading Readiness Guide.* Ask the students to fill in the first two columns of the chart. Use the Numbered Heads participation structure (TE, p. T36) to call on students to share one piece of information they already know and one piece of information they want to know.

All in One Latin America Teaching Resources, *Reading Readiness Guide,* p. 99

Vocabulary Builder
Preview Key Terms L2

Pronounce each Key Term, then ask the students to say the word with you. Provide a simple explanation for each term such as, "As you climb to the top of a mountain, the elevation increases."

The Climates of Latin America

Guided Instruction

- **Vocabulary Builder** Clarify the meaning of the high-use word **vary** before reading.
- Read The Climates of Latin America with students, using the Oral Cloze technique (TE, p. T33).
- Have students look at the map on page 344 and tell which climate in Latin America most resembles the climate where they live and why. *(Answers will vary depending on where students live.)*

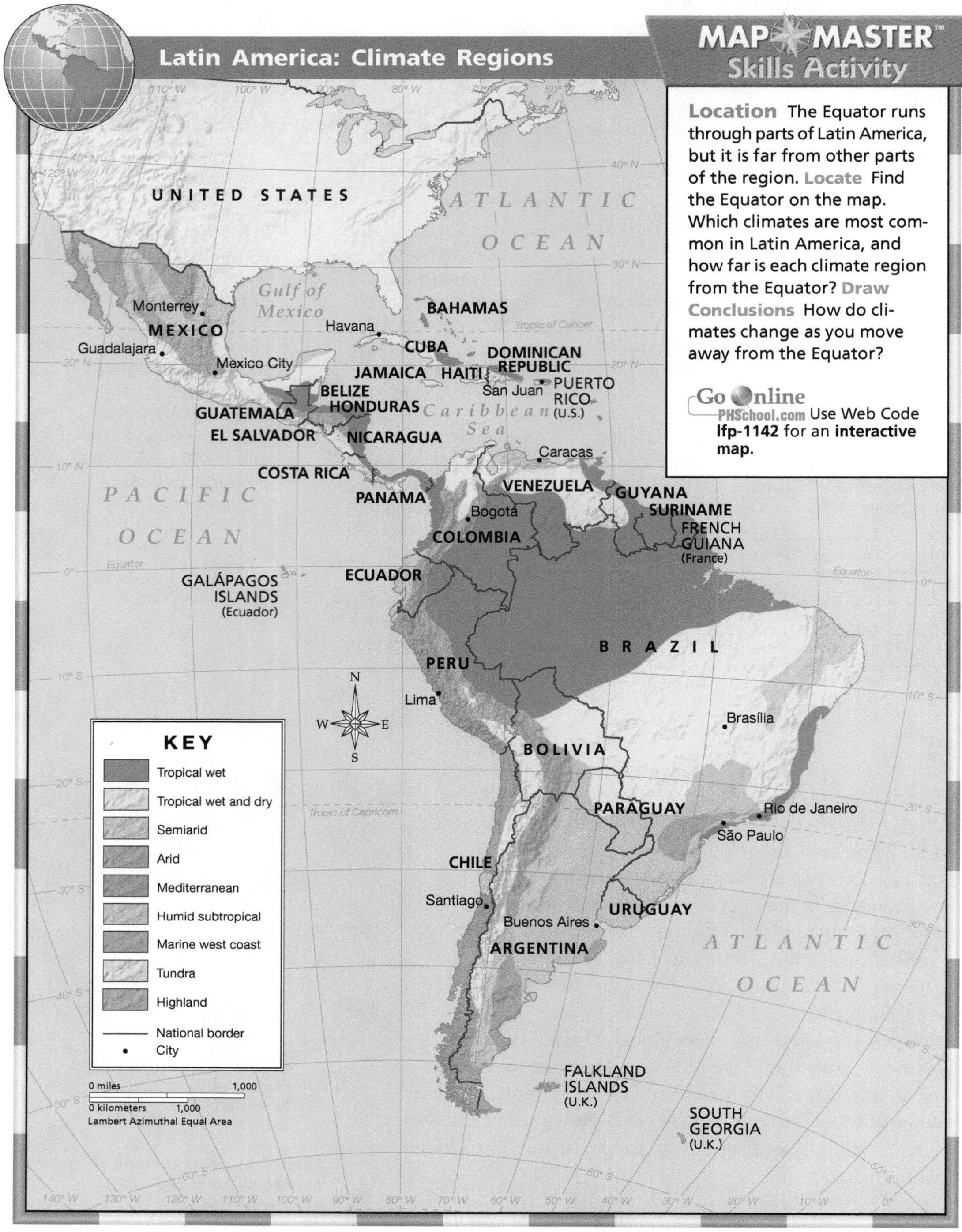

Latin America: Climate Regions

MAP MASTER™ Skills Activity

Location The Equator runs through parts of Latin America, but it is far from other parts of the region. **Locate** Find the Equator on the map. Which climates are most common in Latin America, and how far is each climate region from the Equator? **Draw Conclusions** How do climates change as you move away from the Equator?

Go Online PHSchool.com Use Web Code lfp-1142 for an **interactive map**.

UNITED STATES

ATLANTIC OCEAN

Gulf of Mexico

Monterrey
MEXICO
Guadalajara
Mexico City
Havana
BAHAMAS
CUBA
JAMAICA   HAITI
DOMINICAN REPUBLIC
San Juan   PUERTO RICO (U.S.)
BELIZE
GUATEMALA   HONDURAS
EL SALVADOR   NICARAGUA
Caribbean Sea
Caracas
COSTA RICA
PANAMA
VENEZUELA
GUYANA
SURINAME
FRENCH GUIANA (France)
Bogotá
COLOMBIA
PACIFIC OCEAN
GALÁPAGOS ISLANDS (Ecuador)
ECUADOR
BRAZIL
PERU
Lima
Brasília
BOLIVIA
PARAGUAY
Rio de Janeiro
São Paulo
CHILE
Santiago
Buenos Aires
URUGUAY
ARGENTINA
ATLANTIC OCEAN
FALKLAND ISLANDS (U.K.)
SOUTH GEORGIA (U.K.)

KEY

- Tropical wet
- Tropical wet and dry
- Semiarid
- Arid
- Mediterranean
- Humid subtropical
- Marine west coast
- Tundra
- Highland
- ⎯ National border
- • City

0 miles   1,000
0 kilometers   1,000
Lambert Azimuthal Equal Area

Answers

MAP MASTER™ Skills Activity **Locate** The most common climates in Latin America are tropical wet, and tropical wet and dry. Both types of climate are found on or near the Equator. **Draw Conclusions** As you move farther away from the Equator, climates generally become cooler and drier.

Go Online PHSchool.com Students may practice their map skills using the interactive online version of this map.

Vocabulary Builder

Use the information below to teach students this section's high-use words.

High-Use Word	Definition and Sample Sentence
vary, p. 345	*v.* to change The weather **varied** from hard rain to sunny skies.
moderate, p. 346	*adj.* not extreme A **moderate** breeze cooled her hot forehead.
abundant, p. 349	*adj.* existing in ample supply Her hair was thick and **abundant**.
irregular, p. 349	*adj.* not according to the usual pattern or rules; unpredictable The weather person could not predict the **irregular** weather.

The Climates of Latin America

What is the climate like where you live? Is it hot? Cold? Rainy? Dry? If you lived in Latin America, the climate might be any of these. Climate in Latin America can vary greatly even within the same country.

Hot, Cold, Wild, and Mild In parts of the Andes, below-zero temperatures can set your teeth chattering. Travel to the Amazon Basin, and you may be sweating in 90°F (32°C) heat. And don't forget your umbrella! This part of Latin America receives more than 80 inches (203 centimeters) of rain each year. If you prefer dry weather, visit the Atacama (ah tah KAH mah) Desert in Chile or the Sonoran Desert in Mexico. These areas are two of the driest places on Earth.

The weather in the Caribbean is usually sunny and warm. From June to November, however, the region is often hit with fierce hurricanes. In 2005, Hurricane Wilma shattered the sunny Caribbean weather with a wild blast. Winds howled at more than 185 miles per hour (300 kilometers per hour). Waves nearly 20 feet (6 meters) high smashed into the coast. The storm tore roofs off houses, shattered windows, and yanked huge trees from the ground. Wilma turned out to be the most intense hurricane ever recorded in the region.

Hurricanes are a part of life for people living in the Caribbean. But people in other parts of Latin America have to deal with other climates. For example, people who live in the mountains need to protect themselves against the cold. That's because the higher up the mountains you go, the cooler it gets.

Climate Regions of Latin America Look at the map titled Latin America: Climate Regions. You will notice that many parts of Latin America have a tropical wet climate. A tropical wet climate means hot, humid, and rainy weather all year round.

Other parts of Latin America have a tropical wet and dry climate. These areas are equally hot, but the rainy season does not last all year long. Parts of Mexico and Brazil and most of the Caribbean have a tropical wet and dry climate.

Much of Argentina, Uruguay, and Paraguay has a humid sub-tropical climate. Here, the summers are hot and wet while the winters are cool and damp. Farther south, the climate turns arid, or dry. This colder, drier area is called Patagonia (pat uh GOH nee uh).

√ Reading Check **Describe a tropical wet and dry climate.**

Links to Science

What is a Hurricane?
A hurricane is a strong tropical storm with winds of 73 miles per hour (117 kilometers per hour) or more. Hurricanes get their energy from warm, humid air at the ocean's surface. As the warm air rises and forms clouds, more air is pulled into the developing storm. The winds spiral inward. As the storm grows, it creates very high winds and heavy rains. At the center of the hurricane is the "eye," an area of calm. After the eye passes over an area, the hurricane resumes. It can still cause serious damage, as Hurricane Mitch did in 1998 in countries such as Honduras and Nicaragua (photo below).

Guided Instruction (continued)

- Have students consider what life would be like in a region that is often hit hard by hurricanes, such as the Caribbean islands. Ask **What parts of life would be affected by a hurricane?** (*Hurricanes can destroy homes, devastate fields full of crops, cause roads to flood and become impassable, and knock down electrical wires.*)

- **How would you contrast the climate in northern Brazil with the climate in Patagonia?** (*The climate in northern Brazil is hot, humid, and rainy all year round, whereas the climate in Patagonia is cold and dry.*)

Independent Practice
Assign *Guided Reading and Review.*

All in One **Latin America Teaching Resources,** *Guided Reading and Review,* p. 104

Monitor Progress
Circulate among students as they begin the worksheet to answer questions and provide assistance as needed.

Links

Read the **Links to Science** on this page. Ask students **What makes hurricanes so dangerous?** (*The high winds of a hurricane can destroy homes and towns, and the heavy rains can cause flooding.*)

Differentiated Instruction

For Advanced Readers L3
Have students read more about hurricanes using the library or approved Internet resources. Working in pairs or small groups, ask students to research one hurricane and its effect on the area it hit. Students can use the information they find to create a short oral report to present to the class.

Answers

√ Reading Check A tropical wet and dry climate has hot weather all year long, with a humid, rainy season and a drier season.

What Factors Affect Climate?

L2

Guided Instruction

- **Vocabulary Builder** Clarify the meaning of the high-use word **moderate** before reading.

- Read about elevation, location, and wind patterns in What Factors Affect Climate? As students read, circulate and make sure that they can answer the Reading Check question.

- Ask students to apply the information they have just learned by answering these questions: **How do you think these three factors affect the climate in the region where we live? Is elevation an important factor? How far are we from the Equator? What kind of wind patterns do we have?** (*Answers will depend on region.*)

Independent Practice

Ask students to create the Taking Notes graphic organizer on a sheet of paper. Have them complete the "Factor" and "Effect on Climate" columns using the information in the reading. Model identifying a factor and an effect. Record each detail in the organizer.

Monitor Progress

As students work on the graphic organizer, walk around the classroom to answer questions and assist those who are having trouble identifying the correct details.

Answers

✓ Reading Check Regions near the Equator usually have a warm climate unless the region's elevation is high.

Diagram Skills **Identify** The elevation of the tree line is 10,000 feet (3,048 meters). Above 14,000 feet (4,267 meters) snow will not melt. **Draw Conclusions** Above the snow line, there is not sufficient grass for grazing, and below the tree line, farmers grow crops that they do not want the animals to eat.

What Factors Affect Climate?

Have you ever hiked in the mountains? If so, you've probably noticed that as you climbed higher the temperature dropped.

One key factor affecting the climate of mountainous Latin America is **elevation**, the height of land above sea level. Look at the diagram titled Vertical Climate Zones. It shows how elevation affects climate. As you can see, the higher the elevation, the colder the temperature. Near the Equator, it may be a warm 80°F (27°C) at sea level. But above 10,000 feet (3,048 meters), the temperature may remain below freezing—too cold for people to live.

Location also affects Latin America's climate. Regions close to the Equator are generally warmer than those farther away. Look at the map titled Latin America: Climate Regions on page 344. Find the Equator. Which parts of Latin America are closest to the Equator? These regions are likely to have the warmest weather.

Wind patterns affect climate too. Winds move cold air from the North and South poles toward the Equator. They also move warm air from the Equator toward the poles. In the Caribbean, sea breezes help to keep temperatures moderate. Winds also affect rainfall in the Caribbean. More rain falls on the sides of islands facing the wind than on the sides facing away.

✓ Reading Check How does nearness to the Equator affect climate?

■ Diagram Skills

Even near the Equator, temperature varies with elevation. Notice the tree line. Above the tree line, it is too cold and windy for trees to grow. **Identify** What is the elevation of the tree line? Above what elevation is there snow year-round? **Draw Conclusions** Why is land between the tree line and the snow line used for grazing?

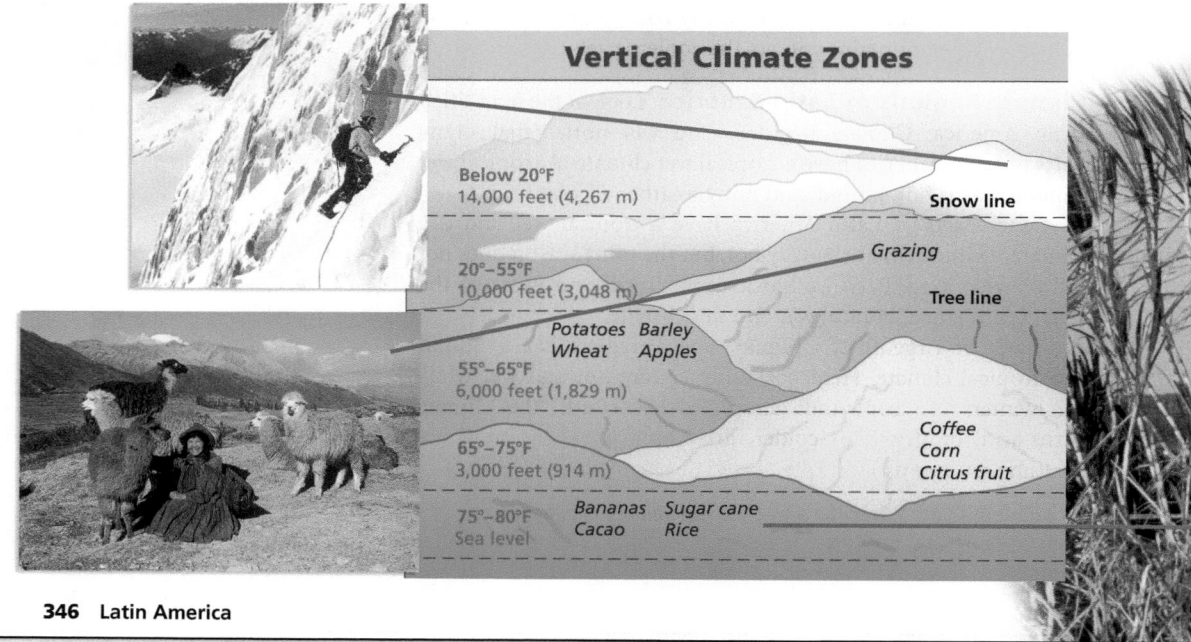

Vertical Climate Zones

Below 20°F 14,000 feet (4,267 m)	Snow line
20°–55°F 10,000 feet (3,048 m)	Grazing / Tree line
55°–65°F 6,000 feet (1,829 m)	Potatoes Barley Wheat Apples
65°–75°F 3,000 feet (914 m)	Coffee Corn Citrus fruit
75°–80°F Sea level	Bananas Sugar cane Cacao Rice

346 Latin America

Skills Mini Lesson

Analyzing Photographs

L2

1. Point out that by examining a photograph closely and asking questions about it, students can gain more information about a topic.

2. Help students practice the skill by looking at the large photograph on page 347. Have them read the caption and ask them to identify what location is being shown.

3. Have students apply the skill by asking themselves other questions about the photo. (*For example: What feeling do I get from this photograph? What would life be like here?*)

Climate, Plants, and People

Imagine a forest so dense and lush that almost no sunlight reaches the ground. Broad green leaves, tangled vines, and thousands of species of trees and plants surround you. The air is hot and heavy with moisture. Welcome to the Amazon rain forest.

Now, suppose you have traveled to the coast of northern Chile. You're in the Atacama Desert. Winds carry no moisture to this barren land, and there are few signs of life. The Andes shield this parched region from rain. Parts of the desert have not felt a single raindrop in hundreds of years.

Vegetation Regions Latin America's varied climate and physical features make such extremes possible. Look at the map titled Latin America: Vegetation Regions on the next page. Notice which countries in Latin America have areas of tropical rain forest. Now, find these countries on the climate map. How do the tropical climate and heavy rainfall in these countries influence the vegetation that grows there?

Of course, not all of Latin America is either rain forest or desert. Many regions of Latin America with less extreme climates have different kinds of vegetation. For example, the pampas of Argentina and Uruguay are grassy plains where cattle are raised. Herding is also a way of life on grasslands high in the Andes Mountains, where Native Americans have raised llamas for centuries. Llamas are used mostly as pack animals. Their relatives, alpacas and vicuñas, provide fine wool.

Preview and Predict Based on what you've read so far, is your prediction on target? If not, revise or change your prediction now.

Life in the Climate Zones
A mountain climber ascends above the snow line in Argentina (facing page, top), and llamas graze above the tree line (facing page, bottom). In the photo on this page, a woman harvests sugar cane in Barbados. *Generalize* *At what elevations would you expect to find most farms? Explain why.*

Differentiated Instruction

For English Learners　L1
To help students with the basic concepts that are assumed in this section, ask them what words they know that are related to the words *vegetation* and *moisture* on page 347 (*vegetable, moist*). Guide them to use the related words to work out the meanings of *vegetation* and *moisture*.

Background: Links Across Time

Mummies of the Atacama Desert
The Chinchorro, a people who lived in what is today Chile more than 5,000 years ago, preserved their dead as mummies—long before the Egyptians did so. The Atacama Desert is so dry that the bodies could be preserved without decay for thousands of years.

Target Reading Skill　L2
Preview and Predict As a follow up, ask students to answer the Target Reading Skill question in the Student Edition. *(Answers will vary, but students should be able to recognize whether their prediction is accurate.)*

Climate, Plants, and People　L2

Guided Instruction
- **Vocabulary Builder** Clarify the meaning of the high-use words **abundant** and **irregular** before reading.
- Read Climate, Plants, and People with students.
- Engage students in a discussion about the relationship between climate and economy. Ask questions such as **What might happen to the gauchos of Argentina and Uruguay in a year of drought?** *(Gauchos would not be able to adequately feed their cattle in a year of drought and might lose income.)*
- **Why would a sugar cane farmer not want to live at the top of a mountain?** *(Sugar cane requires warm temperatures to grow, and temperatures would be too cool at high elevations.)*

Independent Practice
Have students complete the graphic organizer by filling in the "Effect on Vegetation" column using the information on pages 347–349.

Monitor Progress
- Show *Section Reading Support Transparency LA 29* and ask students to check their graphic organizers individually. Go over key concepts and clarify key vocabulary as needed.

  Latin America Transparencies, *Section Reading Support Transparency LA 29*

- Tell students to fill in the last column of *Reading Readiness Guide*. Probe for what they learned that confirms or invalidates each statement.

  All in One Latin America Teaching Resources, *Reading Readiness Guide*, p. 103

Answers

Generalize between sea level and 10,000 feet (3,048 meters)

Assess and Reteach

Assess Progress L2

Have students complete the Section Assessment. Administer the *Section Quiz.*

All in One **Latin America Teaching Resources,** *Section Quiz,* p. 105

Reteach L1

For more instruction, have students read this section in the Reading and Vocabulary Study Guide.

Chapter 11, Section 2, **Western Hemisphere Reading and Vocabulary Study Guide,** pp. 122–124

Extend L3

Have students work together in small groups to complete the *Small Group Activity: Making a Relief Map.* Try to group students of varying abilities together.

All in One **Latin America Teaching Resources,** *Small Group Activity: Making a Relief Map,* pp. 116–119

Latin America: Vegetation Regions

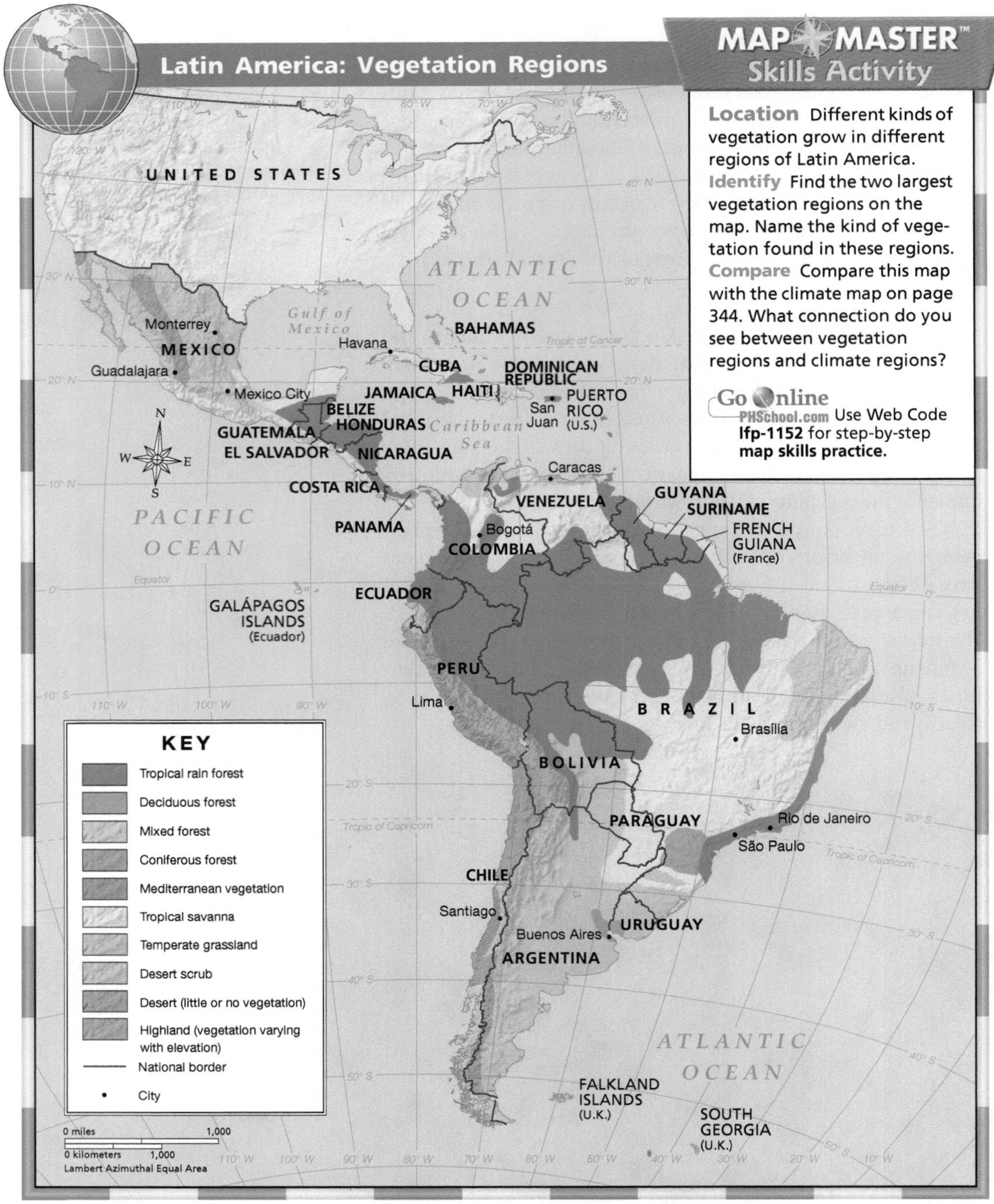

UNITED STATES
ATLANTIC OCEAN
Gulf of Mexico
BAHAMAS
Tropic of Cancer
Monterrey
MEXICO
Havana
CUBA
DOMINICAN REPUBLIC
Guadalajara
Mexico City
JAMAICA
HAITI
PUERTO RICO (U.S.)
San Juan
BELIZE
HONDURAS
Caribbean Sea
GUATEMALA
EL SALVADOR
NICARAGUA
COSTA RICA
Caracas
PACIFIC OCEAN
PANAMA
VENEZUELA
GUYANA
SURINAME
FRENCH GUIANA (France)
Bogotá
COLOMBIA
Equator
GALÁPAGOS ISLANDS (Ecuador)
ECUADOR
PERU
Lima
BRAZIL
Brasília
BOLIVIA
PARAGUAY
Rio de Janeiro
São Paulo
Tropic of Capricorn
CHILE
Santiago
Buenos Aires
URUGUAY
ARGENTINA
ATLANTIC OCEAN
FALKLAND ISLANDS (U.K.)
SOUTH GEORGIA (U.K.)
KEY
Tropical rain forest
Deciduous forest
Mixed forest
Coniferous forest
Mediterranean vegetation
Tropical savanna
Temperate grassland
Desert scrub
Desert (little or no vegetation)
Highland (vegetation varying with elevation)
National border
City
0 miles 1,000
0 kilometers 1,000
Lambert Azimuthal Equal Area

MAP MASTER™ Skills Activity

Location Different kinds of vegetation grow in different regions of Latin America. **Identify** Find the two largest vegetation regions on the map. Name the kind of vegetation found in these regions. **Compare** Compare this map with the climate map on page 344. What connection do you see between vegetation regions and climate regions?

Go Online PHSchool.com Use Web Code **lfp-1152** for step-by-step **map skills practice.**

Answers

MAP MASTER™ Skills Activity **Identify** The two largest vegetation regions in Latin America are tropical rain forest and tropical savanna. **Compare** The outlines of vegetation regions are, in many cases, similar to climate regions. For example, the tropical wet climate region is also the region in which tropical rain forests are found.

Go Online PHSchool.com Students may practice their map skills using the interactive online version of this map.

Differentiated Instruction

For Gifted and Talented L3

To help students expand their knowledge of the vegetation of Latin America, have them complete the *Activity Shop Interdisciplinary: Rain Forest Resources.*

All in One **Latin America Teaching Resources,** *Activity Shop Interdisciplinary: Rain Forest Resources,* pp. 120–121

Crops and Climate Temperature and rainfall affect not only what plants grow naturally in a region, but also what crops people can grow there. Sugar cane, coffee, and bananas require warm weather and abundant rainfall. These crops are important to the economies of many countries around the Caribbean Sea. The **economy** is the ways that goods and services are produced and made available to people. Look again at the climate map on page 344. Why do you think the area around the Caribbean is well suited to growing these crops?

Elevation and Vegetation Elevation also affects vegetation. For example, palm trees and fruit trees that grow well in the coastal plains of Mexico and Central America would not survive high in the Andes. To grow at higher elevations, plants must be able to withstand cooler temperatures, strong winds, and irregular rainfall.

Look again at the diagram on page 346 titled Vertical Climate Zones. Notice the tree line and the snow line. It is too cold and windy for trees to grow above the tree line, but plants that grow low to the ground, such as grasses, are found in this area. Birds, bats, mice, foxes, and llamas also live here. Above the snow line, snow does not melt, and there is almost no wildlife.

Harvesting bananas in Honduras

 **Reading Check** Describe how elevation affects the vegetation of a region.

Section 2 Assessment

Key Terms
Review the key terms at the beginning of this section. Use each term in a sentence that explains its meaning.

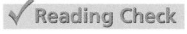 **Target Reading Skill**
What did you predict about this section? How did your prediction guide your reading?

Comprehension and Critical Thinking
1. (a) **Recall** Describe Latin America's climate regions.

(b) **Synthesize** How does climate affect the ways that Latin Americans live?
2. (a) **Identify** Name three factors that affect climate.
(b) **Apply Information** Why might two areas near the Equator have very different climates?
3. (a) **Name** What two factors affect the kinds of vegetation that grow in a region?
(b) **Infer** Why do some farmers in Argentina raise apples while farmers in other parts of the country raise sheep?

Writing Activity
Would you pack differently for trips to the Atacama Desert and the Andes Mountains? Write a paragraph describing what you would take to each place and why.

For: An activity on the rain forest
Visit: PHSchool.com
Web Code: lfd-1102

Answers

✓ Reading Check Only vegetation that can withstand cold temperatures and irregular rainfall grows well at higher elevations; plants that need warm temperatures and steady rainfall thrive at lower elevations.

Section 2 Assessment

Key Terms
Students' sentences should reflect knowledge of each key term.

Target Reading Skill
Students' predictions should be appropriate to the section content, such as: "This section will contain information about how climate in Latin America influences the lives of people who live there." Thought-provoking predictions guide students' reading by helping them to stay focused. Students can read to find out if their predictions are on target or if they need to revise their predictions.

Comprehension and Critical Thinking
1. (a) The climate regions of Latin America include: tropical wet—hot, humid, and rainy all year; tropical wet and dry—hot and rainy during part of the year, and hot and dry the rest of the year; humid subtropical—hot and wet summers, cool and damp winters; and arid—dry. (b) Climate affects the variety and success of crops and the type of clothing and shelter needed to survive.

2. (a) elevation, location, and wind patterns (b) One area may have a higher elevation and thus a colder climate than the other.

3. (a) temperature and amount of rainfall (b) Apples grow best in the cool climate found in parts of northern and central Argentina, while sheep are raised in drier, colder climates in other parts of the country.

Writing Activity
Use the *Rubric for Assessing a Writing Assignment* to evaluate students' paragraphs.

All in One **Latin America Teaching Resources,** *Rubric for Assessing a Writing Assignment,* p. 129

Go Online PHSchool.com Typing in the Web code when prompted will bring students directly to detailed instructions for this activity.

Objective

Learn how to analyze and interpret special-purpose maps.

Prepare to Read

Build Background Knowledge [L2]

Ask students to think about times they have needed to use a map. Ask them what kinds of maps they have used. Create a list on the board.

Analyzing and Interpreting Special-Purpose Maps [L2]

Guided Instruction

- Read the steps to analyze and interpret a special-purpose map as a class and write them on the board.
- Practice the skill by following the steps on p. 350 as a class. Model each step in the activity by choosing a sample vacation activity *(warm water surfing)*, identifying what climate the activity requires *(tropical wet, tropical wet and dry, or humid subtropical, located on the ocean)*, then find some locations on the map that meet your requirements *(any island in the Caribbean, most of the Atlantic coast of South America through the southern border of Uruguay, most of the Pacific and Atlantic coasts of Central America and parts of Mexico.)*
- Ask students to choose at least three of the vacation activities they brainstormed earlier. Then have students follow the steps to determine where in Latin America they should visit to do each activity.

Analyzing and Interpreting Climate Maps

Travel agent: Thanks for calling South America Travel Service. May I help you?

Customer: I'd like to visit South America, but I can't decide where to go. Could you send me brochures of places you recommend?

Travel agent: Certainly. And you might want to visit our Web site, which features a climate map of South America. You'll see that the region has many climates, offering activities from water skiing to snow skiing.

A special purpose map shows information about a particular topic. The climate map on the next page is a type of special purpose map. The travel agent knows that for most people, climate is an important factor in deciding where to vacation.

Learn the Skill

Use these steps to analyze and interpret a climate map.

1. **Read the map title and look at the map to get a general idea of what it shows.** Notice the area for which climate is being shown.

2. **Read the key to understand how the map uses symbols, colors, and patterns.** A climate map usually uses colors to represent different climates.

3. **Use the key to interpret the map.** Look for the different colors on the map. Notice where different climates are located, and what landforms and waterways are also in those locations.

4. **Draw conclusions about what the map shows.** Facts you discover when you analyze a climate map can help you draw conclusions about a place: what kinds of plants and animals live there or how the people make a living.

Independent Practice

Assign *Skills for Life* and have students complete it individually.

 Latin America Teaching Resources, *Skills for Life,* p. 115

Monitor Progress

As students are completing *Skills for Life*, circulate to make sure individuals are applying the skill steps effectively. Provide assistance as needed.

Practice the Skill

If you were the caller on page 350, where would you want to go on your vacation? List your favorite vacation activities, and then use the map on this page to identify several places you would like to visit.

1 Jot down the purpose of the map. What does it show?

2 Look at the key to see the different climates in South America. Identify the climates in which you could probably do the vacation activities on your list.

3 On the map, find the places that have the climates you have identified.

4 Use the climate map to draw conclusions about each place you found. Might the place have ocean views? Rock walls to climb? Forests with fascinating wildlife? Write your conclusions for each place, and choose a vacation destination.

South America: Climate Regions

KEY
- Tropical wet
- Tropical wet and dry
- Semiarid
- Arid
- Mediterranean
- Humid subtropical
- Marine west coast
- Tundra
- Highland
- National border
- City

0 miles 1,500
0 kilometers 1,500
Lambert Azimuthal Equal Area

Apply the Skill

Now take the role of the travel agent. You get an e-mail from an author. "I am writing a book that takes place in a desert region of South America that is also near the ocean. Where should I go to do my research?"

Turn to your map. **(a)** In what climate are you likely to find a desert? **(b)** What places in South America have that type of climate? **(c)** Among those places, which is closest to the ocean? Write a reply to the author. Suggest a location and explain why it will suit her needs.

Chapter 11 **351**

Differentiated Instruction

For Special Needs Students L1
Partner special needs students with more proficient students to do Level 1 of the *Analyzing and Interpreting Special-Purpose Maps* lesson on the Social Studies

Skills Tutor CD-ROM together. When the students feel more confident, they can move onto Level 2 alone.

⊙ *Analyzing and Interpreting Special-Purpose Maps,* **Social Studies Skills Tutor CD-ROM**

Assess and Reteach

Assess Progress L2
Ask students to do the Apply the Skill activity.

Reteach L1
If students are having trouble applying the skill steps, have them review the skill using the interactive Social Studies Skills Tutor CD-ROM.

⊙ *Analyzing and Interpreting Special-Purpose Maps,* **Social Studies Skills Tutor CD-ROM**

Extend L3
- To extend the lesson, ask students to apply the skill steps to the physical map of Mexico on *Color Transparency LA 26*. Instead of analyzing climate regions, however, the students will analyze Mexico's elevation.

- Ask them to identify what the colors on the map key indicate *(the elevation of land)*. Then ask them to identify what part of Mexico has an elevation of 5,000 to 10,000 feet *(the Plateau of Mexico)*. What parts of Mexico have an elevation of 0 to 1,000 feet? *(both coasts)* Finally, remind students higher elevation usually causes lower temperatures. What conclusion can they draw about the temperature of the Plateau of Mexico? *(It will be cooler there than in areas with lower elevation.)*

  📖 **Latin America Transparencies,** *Color Transparency LA 26: Mexico: Physical-Political*

Answers
Apply the Skill

(a) arid

(b) northern Mexico including Baja California; inland Argentina and the southern half of Argentina's Atlantic coast; a strip of land along the Pacific Coast in Peru and northern Chile

(c) Baja California; the southern part of Argentina's Atlantic coast; land along the Pacific Coast in Peru and northern Chile. Students' replies should describe the locations of these arid regions near the ocean.

Section 3
Step-by-Step Instruction

Objectives
Social Studies

1. Find out what Latin America's most important natural resources are.

2. Learn why depending on a one-resource economy has been a problem for Latin American nations.

Reading/Language Arts

Create questions to help you understand and remember what you read.

Prepare to Read

Build Background Knowledge · L2

Tell students that they will learn about the natural resources of Latin America in this section. Ask students to briefly preview the headings and visuals, then predict what some of the region's natural resources might be. Conduct an Idea Wave (TE, p. T35) to elicit responses.

Set a Purpose for Reading · L2

■ Preview the Objectives.

■ Read each statement in the *Reading Readiness Guide* aloud. Ask students to mark the statements true or false.

■ Have students discuss the statements in pairs or groups of four, and then mark their worksheets again. Use the Numbered Heads participation structure (TE, p. T36) to call on students to share their group's perspectives.

All in One Latin America Teaching Resources, *Reading Readiness Guide,* p. 107

Vocabulary Builder
Preview Key Terms · L2

Pronounce each Key Term, and then ask the students to say the word with you. Provide a simple explanation, such as, "When you plant different kinds of crops instead of just one crop, you diversify your farming."

Section 3
Resources and Land Use

Prepare to Read

Objectives
In this section you will
1. Find out what Latin America's most important natural resources are.
2. Learn why depending on a one-resource economy has been a problem for Latin American nations.

Taking Notes
As you read this section, look for the major resources of each region of Latin America. Copy the chart below and record your findings in it.

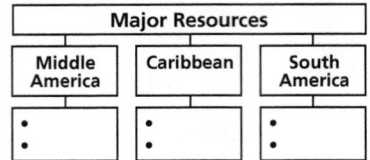

```
            Major Resources
    ┌───────────┬───────────┬───────────┐
    Middle       Caribbean    South
    America                   America
    • ___        • ___        • ___
    • ___        • ___        • ___
```

Target Reading Skill
Preview and Ask Questions Before you read this section, preview the headings and illustrations to see what the section is about. Then write two questions that will help you understand or remember something important in the section. For example, you might ask, "What are the resources of Middle America?" Then read to answer your questions.

Key Terms
• **natural resources** (NACH ur ul REE sawrs uz) *n.* things found in nature that people can use to meet their needs
• **hydroelectricity** (hy droh ee lek TRIS ih tee) *n.* electric power produced by rushing water
• **one-resource economy** (wun REE sawrs ih KAHN uh mee) *n.* a country's economy based largely on one resource or crop
• **diversify** (duh VUR suh fy) *v.* to add variety

Quechua Indian women sort ore at a Bolivian tin mine.

Bolivia has long depended on its mineral resources for wealth. At first, silver helped to bring money into Bolivia's treasury. Soon, however, tin became even more important. For many years, Bolivia enjoyed the wealth that tin brought to the economy. Then, in the 1920s and 1930s, a worldwide economic crisis hit. Industries stopped buying tin, as well as other natural resources. Bolivia suffered as its main resource failed to bring in money. This economic crisis hit all of Latin America hard. It brought home a problem that many Latin American nations have: They rely too much on one resource.

Latin America's Resources

What do the following things have in common: fish, petroleum, water, silver, and forests? They are all natural resources of Latin America. **Natural resources** are things found in nature that people can use to meet their needs. Latin America's resources are as varied as its physical features and climate.

Target Reading Skill · L2
Preview and Ask Questions Point out the Target Reading Skill. Explain that creating questions about the reading is an effective way to read with a focus. Model previewing and asking questions using the subhead on page 355. Show students that South America: A Wealth of Resources can be rephrased as the question: "What resources are found in South America?"

Ask students to read the passage on page 355 with that question in mind. Then model answering the question by mentioning these resources: minerals, oil, forests, fish, rich soil.

Give students *Preview and Ask Questions*. Have them complete the activity in groups.

All in One Latin America Teaching Resources, *Preview and Ask Questions,* p. 112

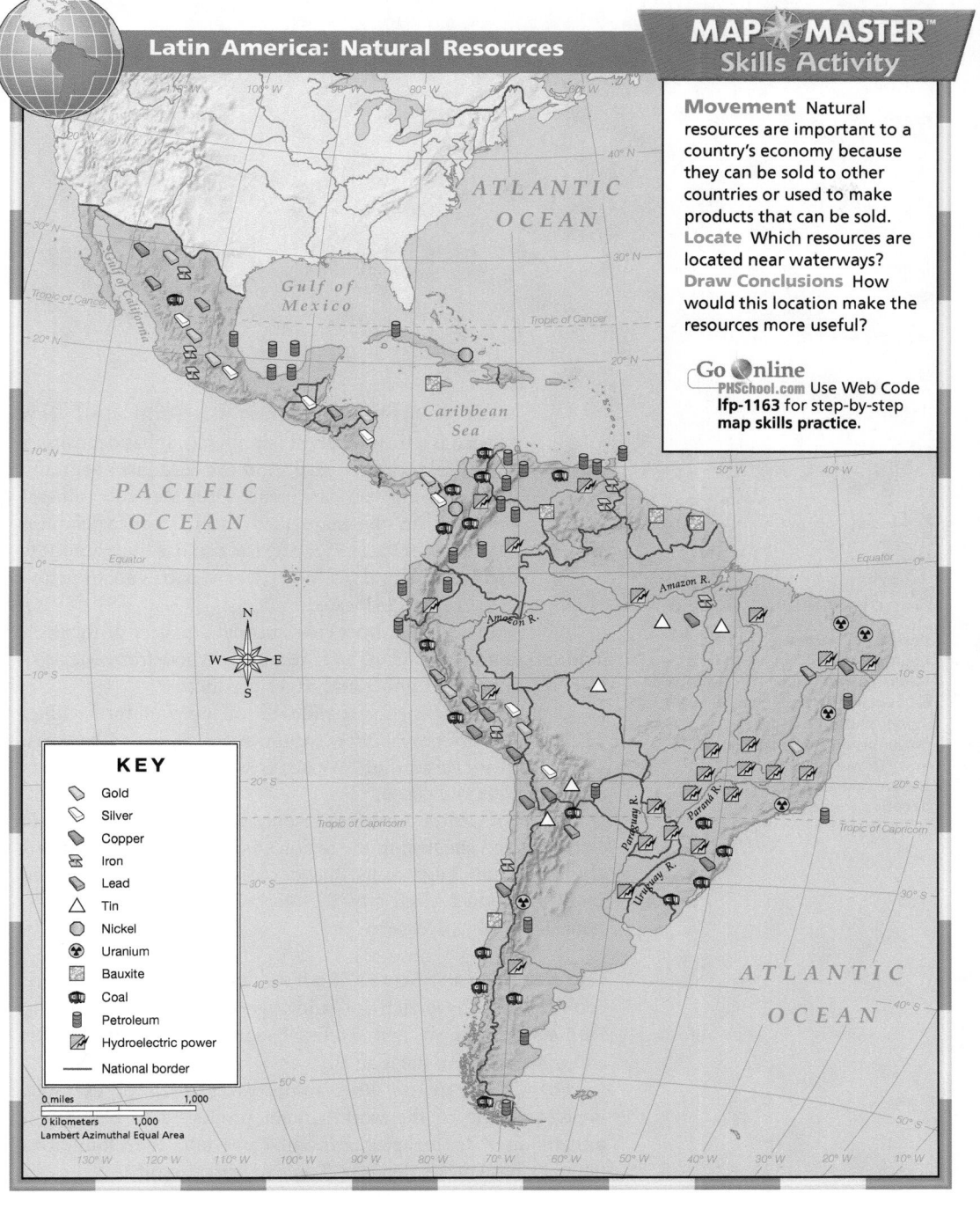

Latin America: Natural Resources

Movement Natural resources are important to a country's economy because they can be sold to other countries or used to make products that can be sold. **Locate** Which resources are located near waterways? **Draw Conclusions** How would this location make the resources more useful?

Go Online
PHSchool.com Use Web Code **lfp-1163** for step-by-step map skills practice.

KEY

- Gold
- Silver
- Copper
- Iron
- Lead
- △ Tin
- ○ Nickel
- ☢ Uranium
- ▨ Bauxite
- Coal
- Petroleum
- ▨ Hydroelectric power
- — National border

0 miles 1,000
0 kilometers 1,000
Lambert Azimuthal Equal Area

Latin America's Resources

L2

Guided Instruction

- **Vocabulary Builder** Clarify the meaning of the high-use word **deposit** before reading.

- Read Latin America's Resources using the ReQuest Procedure (TE, p. T35). As students engage in the silent reading portion of the technique, circulate to ensure that students are able to answer the Reading Check question.

- Ask students **What are some uses that you can think of for the different kinds of minerals found in Middle America and the Caribbean?** (*Coal and oil are used for fuel; copper and iron can be found in household items such as pots and pans; bauxite is used to make aluminum; gold and silver are precious metals sometimes found in jewelry.*)

- Ask students to identify three natural resources of the Caribbean. **Which resources does the Caribbean have in common with Mexico?** (*Three resources of the Caribbean are rich soil, minerals, and oil; all three are also found in Mexico.*)

Vocabulary Builder

Use the information below to teach students this section's high-use words.

High-Use Word	Definition and Sample Sentence
deposit, p. 354	*n.* a natural supply Finding the **deposit** of gold made the prospector rich.
factor, p. 357	*n.* something that actively brings about a result The heat of the sun was a **factor** in my decision to move inside.
dependence, p. 357	*n.* trust or reliance Nina's **dependence** on Jane for rides may be a problem if Jane is ever out sick.

Answers

MAP★MASTER Skills Activity **Locate** All of the resources are located near waterways. **Draw Conclusions** because resources can be transported easily to other countries

Go Online
PHSchool.com **Students may practice their map skills using the interactive online version of this map.**

- Direct students' attention to the sentence on page 355 that says, "For example, coffee is a key crop in Brazil and Colombia." Ask students to discuss what they think "key crop" means. *(Students should suggest that a key crop is one that many farmers in those countries grow, and the sale of which accounts for a large piece of the economy in those countries.)*

- Ask students **Since there are so many possible uses for the trees in South America's rain forests, what problems or issues might come up in relation to this resource?** *(Possible answers: Some people want to cut down trees to use for firewood or to make furniture. Others want to protect the rain forests as a source of food and as a natural resource that is home to many kinds of unique plants and wildlife.)* **What would happen if all of the trees were cut down?** *(If the rain forests were cut down completely, it would affect plants, animals, and humans. Many species of plants and wildlife would be lost. Such a large change might also affect the climate.)*

Varied Resources
Countries depend on a variety of resources, from commercially grown cabbage in the Dominican Republic (upper photo) to hydroelectric power produced by this dam in Brazil (lower photo). **Generalize** *Explain how each resource could benefit a country's economy.*

Middle America: Riches of Land and Sea
Mexico is a treasure chest of minerals. It has deposits of silver, gold, copper, coal, iron ore, and just about any other mineral you can name. Find Mexico's mineral resources on the map titled Latin America: Natural Resources on page 353. Mexico also has huge amounts of oil and natural gas. Where are Mexico's oil, or petroleum, resources located?

In addition, trees cover nearly a quarter of Mexico's land. Trees are another natural resource. Wood from Mexico's trees is turned into lumber and paper products.

Central America's climate and rich soil are good for farming. The people there grow coffee, cotton, sugar cane, and bananas. They also plant cacao (kuh KAY oh) trees. Cacao seeds are made into chocolate and cocoa.

Not all of Central America's resources are on land. The people catch fish and shellfish in the region's waters. Central Americans also have built huge dams that harness the power of rushing water to produce electricity. Electric power created by rushing water is called **hydroelectricity.**

The Caribbean: Sugar, Coffee, and More Caribbean countries also have rich soil and a good climate for farming. Farmers grow sugar cane, coffee, bananas, cacao, citrus fruits, and other crops on the islands.

The Caribbean has other resources as well. For example, Jamaica is one of the world's main producers of bauxite—a mineral used to make aluminum. Cuba and the Dominican Republic have nickel deposits. Trinidad is rich in oil.

354 Latin America

Answers

Generalize The commercially grown cabbage is exported to other countries, bringing money into the Dominican Republic. Hydroelectric power created by the dam in Brazil could be used in Brazil, or exported to other countries for a profit.

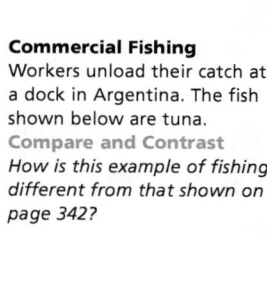

Commercial Fishing
Workers unload their catch at a dock in Argentina. The fish shown below are tuna.
Compare and Contrast
How is this example of fishing different from that shown on page 342?

South America: A Wealth of Resources Like Mexico, South America is rich in minerals. It has gold, copper, tin, bauxite, and iron ore. Look again at the map titled Latin America: Natural Resources on page 353. Where are these resources located? South America also has oil. Much of South America's oil is found in Venezuela.

South America's plants and fish are natural resources, too. Forests cover about half the continent. Trees from these forests provide everything from wood for building to coconuts for eating. Mahogany and rosewood are used to make fine furniture. Some woods are used by local people for fuel. The rain forests of South America contain a wide variety of trees and other vegetation. Some of these plants are used to make medicines. Scientists are studying other plants to see if they, too, might have medical uses.

The people of South America harvest many kinds of fish. Tuna, anchovies, and other species of fish are plentiful in the waters off the Pacific coast. Shellfish, such as shrimp, are also important to the region's economy. Freshwater fish, those found in rivers, are an important food source in South America.

Like other parts of Latin America, South America has rich soil. Farmers grow many different crops there. For example, coffee is a key crop in Brazil and Colombia. Wheat is important in Argentina. Many South American economies rely on the production of sugar cane, cotton, and rice.

✓ Reading Check **What kinds of products are made from South America's forests?**

Have students create the Taking Notes graphic organizer on a blank piece of paper. Ask them to fill in the information for "Middle America" and "Caribbean." Briefly model how to choose the correct details. Then have students complete the graphic organizer by filling in the "South America" section.

Monitor Progress
Show *Section Reading Support Transparency LA 30* and ask students to check their graphic organizers individually. Go over key concepts and clarify key vocabulary as needed.

📖 **Latin America Transparencies,** *Section Reading Support Transparency LA 30*

Differentiated Instruction

For Advanced Readers [L3]
Have these students continue learning about the important natural resources of the Latin American forests by reading the primary source *Message from the Rain Forest Amerindians*. Ask these students to share what they have learned with the class, as well as any opinions they may have developed as a result of the reading.

All in One **Latin America Teaching Resources,** *Message from the Rain Forest Amerindians*, p. 123

Answers

✓ Reading Check Trees and plants from South America's forests are used to make buildings and furniture, supply coconuts and other food products, as a source of medicines, and for research. **Compare and Contrast** A large quantity of fish is being packed and loaded onto large ships, while on page 342, fewer fish are placed into a small boat for transport.

Resources and the Economy

Guided Instruction

- **Vocabulary Builder** Clarify the meaning of the high-use words **factor** and **dependence** before reading.

- Read Resources and the Economy with students, asking them to pay special attention to the vocabulary in the section.

- Ask students why a nation might develop a one-resource economy. *(When a country is rich in one resource, many people and companies may want to profit from that resource. If all of the companies turn to one industry, the nation slips into a one-resource economy.)*

- Ask students **Which resources and crops have some countries become too dependent on in Latin America?** *(oil, coffee, bananas, sugar)*

- Ask students how weather can affect a country's economy if it is too dependent on one crop. *(For example, if El Niño kills plants that fish depend on, a country that is too dependent on fishing can suffer.)*

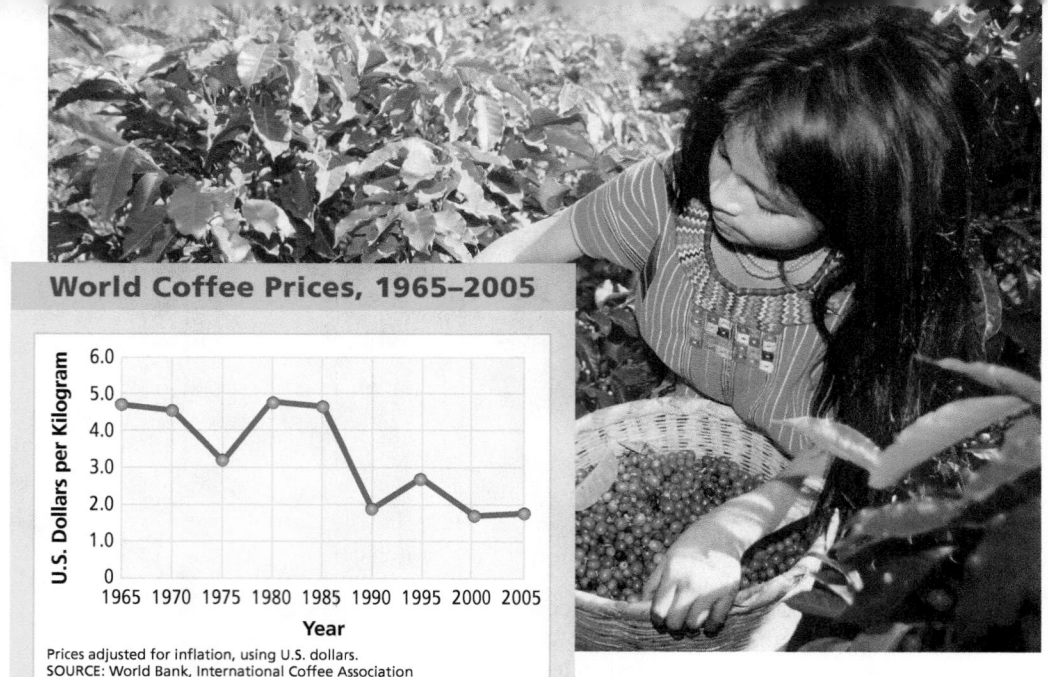

World Coffee Prices, 1965–2005

Prices adjusted for inflation, using U.S. dollars.
SOURCE: World Bank, International Coffee Association

■ Graph Skills

World coffee prices affect not only the economies of many Latin American countries but also ordinary people, such as this Guatemalan coffee-picker. **Describe** What is the pattern of coffee prices over the 40 years shown in the graph above? **Analyze Information** What years were good years for coffee growers? What year might have been the worst? Explain your answer.

Resources and the Economy

Not every country shares equally in the wealth of Latin America's resources. Some Latin American countries have many resources, while others have few. Some countries do not have the money they need to develop all of their resources. Even when countries do develop their resources, not everyone in that country always enjoys the benefits. And sometimes countries rely too much on one resource or crop.

Problems of a One-Resource Economy Sometimes having a great deal of a valuable resource can lead to economic problems. That's because some countries then develop what is called a **one-resource economy,** an economy that depends largely on one resource or crop. Why is this a problem? Here is an example: When world copper prices are high, the copper mining industry is very successful. But suppose copper prices drop sharply. Then copper exports are not worth as much. When this happens, the mining industry loses money. Mining workers may lose their jobs. People and businesses—even a whole country—can go into debt. Chile is the leading producer of copper in the world. When prices plunge, Chile's whole economy suffers.

356 Latin America

Answers

Graph Skills **Describe** Prices have gone down over the 40 years shown on the graph, with many highs and lows. **Analyze Information** The spans 1965–1970 and 1980–1985 were good years for coffee growers. The year 1990 was probably the worst, because the prices dropped quickly after a number of good years.

The World Economy Oil is one of Latin America's most valuable resources. But world oil prices go up and down, sometimes very suddenly. Mexico and Venezuela are major oil producers. In the mid-1980s, oil companies produced more oil than the world needed. As a result, prices dropped. Mexico earned much less income than it had expected.

Many people in Latin America make their living by farming. Some Latin American countries depend on only one or two crops, such as coffee, bananas, or sugar. Certain factors outside the country—such as increased production of coffee by other countries—may cause the price of the crop to drop. When the price of a crop goes down, exports of that crop bring less money into the country.

Weather Effects Weather brings challenges, too. Hurricanes, droughts, and plant diseases may damage crops. Weather can also hurt the fishing industry. Usually, the cold water of the Pacific supports a large number of small water plants on which fish feed. But when El Niño strikes, the warm water kills the plants and the fish die or move to other areas. The fishing industry of Peru has suffered great economic losses due to El Niño effects.

In each case described above, dependence on a particular resource—copper, oil, one particular crop, or fishing—has hurt the economy of the country that depended on it. That is because, if something unexpected happens to the major resource of a country with a one-resource economy, that country is left with few other sources of income.

Preview and Ask Questions
Ask a question that will help you learn something important from the paragraph at the left. Now read the paragraph and answer your question.

At the Mercy of the Weather
In 2001, a severe drought in Guatemala caused many crops to dry up. This man is sowing beans on top of his failed corn crop.
Predict *What might be the result if this farmer depended only on corn?*

Preview and Ask Questions As a follow up, ask students to answer the Target Reading Skill question in the Student Edition. *(Students' questions will vary, but should relate to farming in Latin America. Possible questions include "What are some crops that Latin American countries depend on to bring in money?" or "What outside factors affect how much money Latin American farmers can make for their crops?")*

Guided Instruction (continued)
■ Discuss how and why Latin American countries are trying to diversify their economies. *(How—by encouraging manufacturing of a variety of products and raising of different kinds of crops. Why—to protect the economies of Latin American nations from sudden and uncontrollable crises.)*

Independent Practice
Assign *Guided Reading and Review.*
　All in One **Latin America Teaching Resources,** *Guided Reading and Review,* p. 108

Monitor Progress
Tell students to fill in the last column of the *Reading Readiness Guide.* Probe for what they learned that confirms or invalidates each statement.
　All in One **Latin America Teaching Resources,** *Reading Readiness Guide,* p. 107

Differentiated Instruction

For Special Needs Students   L1
Have students listen to the recorded version of the section on the Student Edition on Audio CD, following along with the text as they listen. Ask students to work in pairs to answer the Reading Check questions as they appear. Pause the CD to give students time to answer, and ask them to share their answers with you.
　◉ Chapter 11, Section 3, **Student Edition on Audio CD**

Answers

Predict The farmer would have lost his whole season's crop, losing any money he would have made from it.

Assess and Reteach

Assess Progress `L2`

Have students complete the Section Assessment. Administer the *Section Quiz.*

 Latin America Teaching Resources, *Section Quiz,* p. 109

Reteach `L1`

For more instruction, have students read this section in the Reading and Vocabulary Study Guide.

Chapter 11, Section 3, **Western Hemisphere Reading and Vocabulary Study Guide,** pp. 128–130

Extend `L3`

Have students learn more about crops grown in Latin America by completing the *Enrichment* activity.

 Latin America Teaching Resources, *Enrichment,* p. 114

Answers

✓ Reading Check Brazil is diversifying its economy by making machinery, steel, and chemicals.

Section 3 Assessment

Key Terms
Students' sentences should reflect knowledge of each Key Term.

Target Reading Skill
Students' questions and answers will vary, but should reflect an understanding of the section's important concepts.

Comprehension and Critical Thinking
1. (a) *Middle America*: minerals, oil, natural gas, trees, rich soil, fish, rushing water. *Caribbean*: fertile soil, bauxite, nickel, oil; *South America*: minerals, oil, trees, plants, fish, fertile soil. **(b)** Middle America and South America both have minerals, oil, trees, and fertile soil. **(c)** They enable a region to grow crops like coffee, corn, citrus fruit, potatoes, barley, wheat, and apples, which all benefit an economy.

2. (a) Venezuela has depended on oil, while El Salvador depended mainly on coffee. **(b)** No—both Venezuela's and El Salvador's economies were hurt by depending on one resource. **(c)** If a disease destroyed El Salvador's coffee crop, coffee plantation workers

---

An automobile factory in Quito, Ecuador

Latin America Begins to Diversify

Because Latin American nations have learned the risks of depending on one resource or crop, they began to diversify their economies in the 1960s and 1970s. To **diversify** is to add variety. Many Latin American nations are building factories. Factories make products that can be sold to bring more money into the economy. Factories also provide jobs.

Rather than depending so much on oil, Venezuela has been promoting investment in its agriculture, steel, and tourism industries. The island nation Trinidad and Tobago also has large deposits of natural resources such as oil and natural gas. However, tourism and international business are also important parts of the economy.

El Salvador used to depend too heavily on its coffee crop. Now, cotton, sugar, corn, and other crops play an important role in the nation's economy. Brazil, too, has been building up its industries so that it does not have to depend so much on agriculture. In addition to farm products, Brazil now exports machinery, steel, and chemicals. The governments of Latin America continue to look for ways to protect their nations from the hazards of a one-resource economy.

✓ Reading Check **How is Brazil diversifying its economy?**

 **Section 3 Assessment**

Key Terms
Review the key terms at the beginning of this section. Use each term in a sentence that explains its meaning.

Target Reading Skill
What questions helped you learn something important from this section? What are the answers to your questions?

Comprehension and Critical Thinking
1. (a) Identify Name the important natural resources of each region of Latin America.

(b) Compare How are the resources of South America similar to those of Middle America?
(c) Draw Conclusions How can rich soil and a mild climate benefit the economy of a region?
2. (a) Recall What resources have Venezuela and El Salvador depended on in the past?
(b) Synthesize Was depending on these resources good for the economies of these countries?
(c) Identify Cause and Effect Suppose a disease destroyed El Salvador's coffee crop. How would this loss affect coffee-plantation workers and the economy of El Salvador? Explain your answer.

Writing Activity
Suppose you are the president of a Latin American country. Your nation depends on sugar cane for nearly all of its income. Outline the arguments you would use in a speech to persuade your people of the need to diversify. Then write an introduction to your speech.

> **Writing Tip** A persuasive speech is like a persuasive essay. Be sure you have three reasons to support your main idea. Use persuasive language to introduce those ideas in your opening paragraph.

---

would suffer, but El Salvador's economy as a whole would not be harmed as much as in the past, because the country has diversified and grows other crops.

Writing Activity
Use the *Rubric for Assessing a Writing Assignment* to evaluate students' paragraphs.

Latin America Teaching Resources, *Rubric for Assessing a Writing Assignment,* p. 129

Review and Assessment

◆ Chapter Summary

Section 1: Land and Water
- Latin America is located south of the United States and is made up of three regions.
- Mountain ranges and rain forests dominate Latin America, but there are also islands, plains, plateaus, and deserts.
- Waterways such as the Amazon River provide transportation, food, and electric power to the people of Latin America.

Section 2: Climate and Vegetation
- Latin America has a wide range of climate regions.
- Climate is shaped by elevation, nearness to the Equator, and wind patterns.
- Latin America's diverse climate regions affect vegetation patterns and how people live.

Section 3: Resources and Land Use
- Latin America's resources include minerals, good farmland, forests, and fish.
- Depending on only a few resources, such as one crop or mineral, can lead to economic problems.
- Latin American countries are now diversifying their economies.

Argentina

Honduras

Brazil

◆ Key Terms

Each of the statements below contains a key term from the chapter. Decide whether each statement is true or false. If it is true, write *true*. If it is false, rewrite the sentence to make it true.

1. A plateau is a narrow strip of land that has water on both sides and joins two larger bodies of land.

2. A tributary is smaller than the river into which it flows.

3. Pampas are flat grasslands.

4. Rain forests thrive in hot, dry climates.

5. Elevation is the distance from the Equator.

6. The goods a country produces are its natural resources.

7. Hydroelectricity is electric power produced from rushing water.

8. To diversify an economy is to produce more of one resource.

Chapter 11   **359**

⌐ Vocabulary Builder ¬

Revisit this chapter's high-use words:

classify	dominate	impressive
vary	moderate	deposit
abundant	irregular	
factor	dependence	

Ask students to review the definitions they recorded on their *Word Knowledge* work-sheets.

All in One Latin America Teaching Resources, *Word Knowledge,* p. 113

Consider allowing students to earn extra credit if they use the words in their answers to the questions in the Chapter Review and Assessment. The words must be used correctly and in a natural context to win the extra points.

Review and Assessment

Review Chapter Content
- Review the important themes of this chapter by asking students to classify what Guiding Question each bulleted statement in the Chapter Summary answers. Have students do this activity together as a class. Refer to page 329 in the Student Edition for the text of the Guiding Questions.
- Assign *Vocabulary Development* for students to review Key Terms.

All in One Latin America Teaching Resources, *Vocabulary Development,* p. 128

Answers

Key Terms

1. False. A plateau is a large raised area of mostly level land.

2. True

3. True

4. False. Rain forests thrive in hot, wet climates.

5. False. Elevation is the altitude above sea level.

6. False. The things found in nature that people can use are its natural resources.

7. True

8. False. To diversify an economy is to add variety by producing more than one kind of product or resource.

Review and Assessment

Comprehension and Critical Thinking

9. (a) on the central plateau **(b)** That part of Mexico is a raised area of level land surrounded by mountains. **(c)** The surrounding mountains make travel difficult.

10. (a) the Andes Mountains **(b)** The high elevation causes some parts of South America to have a very cold climate; only vegetation that can withstand cooler or cold temperatures can survive. The Andes are difficult for people to cross, but many people farm there. **(c)** Possible answers: Help—the Andes are a fertile farming area and a sight that attracts tourists. Hurt—the Andes have isolated some communities of South America.

11. (a) a warming of the ocean water along the western coast of South America that occurs every few years and influences global weather patterns **(b)** El Niño drives cold-water fish away, causes heavy rains in dry areas, floods in low-lying areas, and drought. **(c)** Commercial fisherman cannot work, property is destroyed through flooding, and tourism declines.

12. (a) the higher the elevation, the cooler the temperatures **(b)** Possible answer: Hot, wet, tropical regions give rise to rain forests; arid regions are usually deserts with little vegetation; areas with more moderate temperatures and rainfall contain grasslands or other kinds of vegetation. **(c)** People's jobs often depend on climate and vegetation: for example, farmers can only raise crops that tolerate the climate.

13. (a) minerals, oil, natural gas, trees, rich soil for farming, and abundant waters that produce electricity and contain fish and shell fish **(b)** The rushing waters of rivers are harnessed to produce hydroelectric power. **(c)** The prices of the resource fall sharply and economies that depend solely on that resource go into crisis.

14. (a) one that depends largely on one resource or crop **(b)** Possible answers: Venezuela is creating more factories and farms and improving its mines. Brazil is exporting machinery, steel, and chemicals. El Salvador and Trinidad are encouraging farmers to diversify their crop production. **(c)** One-resource economies are vulnerable to outside factors that can leave the country with few or no sources of income.

◆ Comprehension and Critical Thinking

9. (a) Recall In what part of Mexico do most Mexicans live?
(b) Describe What is this part of Mexico like?
(c) Identify Causes What makes travel to and from this area difficult?

10. (a) Identify What is the major mountain range in South America?
(b) Identify Effects Describe two effects this mountain range has on the climate, the vegetation, or the people.
(c) Evaluate Do you think that the mountains help or hurt South America? Explain.

11. (a) Define What is El Niño?
(b) Identify Effects What are some of El Niño's effects on land and sea?
(c) Synthesize How can El Niño affect the economy of Latin America?

12. (a) Recall How does elevation affect climate?
(b) Contrast How are the different vegetation regions in Latin America shaped by their climates?
(c) Infer How do climate and vegetation affect how people live and work?

13. (a) Identify What are the major resources of Middle America?
(b) Categorize Which of these resources helps produce power?
(c) Analyze Explain what happens when too much of one resource is produced worldwide.

14. (a) Define What is a one-resource economy?
(b) Summarize Describe how one Latin American country is diversifying its economy.
(c) Generalize Why is it important for countries to diversify their economies?

◆ Skills Practice

Analyzing and Interpreting Climate Maps
In the Skills for Life activity in this chapter, you analyzed and interpreted a climate map. The skill you learned can be applied to other special-purpose maps.

Review the steps you followed to learn the skill. Then turn to the map titled Latin America: Vegetation Regions on page 348. Take the role of the travel agent again. This time respond to

two people: one who wants to visit a rain forest and another who wants to visit grassy plains to observe Latin American cowboys.

◆ Writing Activity: Science

Suppose you are the television meteorologist for a small Caribbean island. As part of your weather report, you are doing an overview of the weather for the past three months. Explain to your broadcast audience why one side of your island has been rainy and the other side has been sunny. You can create a mental picture or a map of the geography of your island (including mountains and rivers) to aid in your explanation.

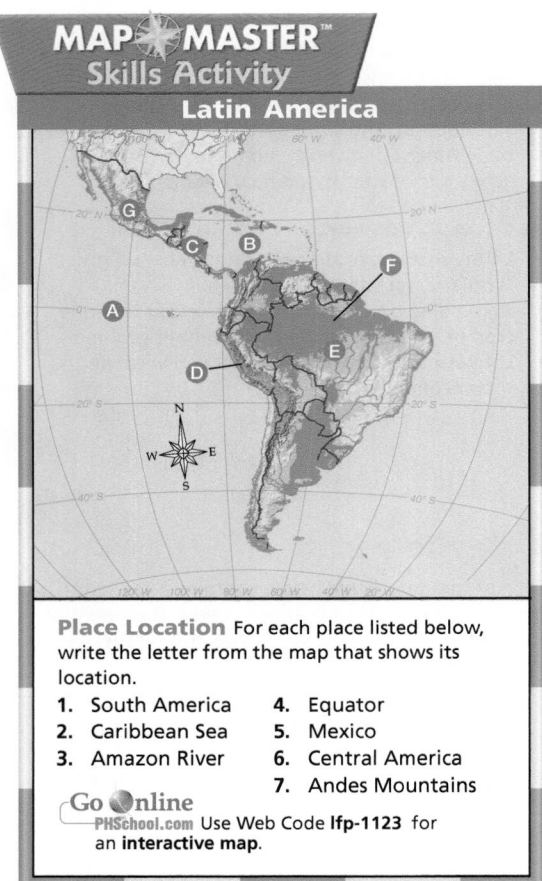

MAP ★ MASTER™
Skills Activity
Latin America

Place Location For each place listed below, write the letter from the map that shows its location.

1. South America
2. Caribbean Sea
3. Amazon River
4. Equator
5. Mexico
6. Central America
7. Andes Mountains

Go Online
PHSchool.com Use Web Code lfp-1123 for an **interactive map**.

Skills Practice

Possible response to someone who wants to visit a rain forest: Visit the Amazon rain forest.

Possible response to someone who wants to visit grassy plains: Visit the pampas of Argentina or Uruguay.

Writing Activity: Science

Students' answers should note that more rain falls on the side of an island that faces the wind than on the side that faces away from the wind.

Use the *Rubric for Assessing a Writing Assignment* to evaluate students' overviews.

All in One **Latin America Teaching Resources,** *Rubric for Assessing a Writing Assignment,* p. 129

Standardized Test Prep

Test-Taking Tips

Some questions on standardized tests ask you to make mental maps. Read the passage below. Then follow the tips to answer the question.

> **TIP** Try to picture the locations of the Southern Hemisphere and the Amazon River in your mind. Think of maps you have seen.

Pick the letter that best answers the question.

Zach's geography teacher asked his class to write clues for a game called What Country Is It? Zach wrote the following set of clues:

This country is mostly in the Southern Hemisphere. The Amazon River runs through it. It is larger than Argentina.

A ~~Mexico.~~
B Brazil.
C ~~Canada.~~
D Peru.

> **TIP** First rule out answer choices that don't make sense. Pick the BEST answer from the remaining choices.

Think It Through Canada and Mexico are both in the Northern Hemisphere, so you can rule out answers A and C. The Amazon River runs across northern South America, including both Peru and Brazil. But Peru is smaller than Argentina. That leaves Brazil, answer B.

Practice Questions

Choose the letter of the best answer.

1. What two bodies of land does the isthmus of Central America connect?
   A the Caribbean and South America
   B Mexico and the United States
   C Mexico and the Caribbean
   D South America and North America

2. Which of the following factors does NOT affect a region's climate?
   A hurricanes
   B elevation
   C location
   D wind patterns

3. Throughout much of Latin America, people use rushing water to create
   A wells.
   B swimming pools.
   C water parks.
   D hydroelectricity.

4. The largest tropical rain forest in the world is located in
   A Mexico's central plateau.
   B the Amazon River Basin.
   C the isthmus of Central America.
   D the coral reefs of the Caribbean.

Read the following passage and answer the question that follows.

Yoshi is writing clues for a game called Name That Region. He wrote the following set of clues:
This region in Latin America is located in the Northern Hemisphere. It is made up of islands. Farming is especially good in this region.

5. What region do Yoshi's clues describe?
   A South America
   B the Caribbean
   C Mexico
   D North America

Use Web Code **lfa-1101** for a **Chapter 11 self-test.**

MAP★MASTER™
Skills Activity

1. E
2. B
3. F
4. A
5. G
6. C
7. D

Go Online PHSchool.com Students may practice their map skills using the interactive online version of this map.

Standardized Test Prep

Answers

1. D
2. A
3. D
4. B
5. B

Go Online PHSchool.com Students may use the Chapter 11 self-test on PHSchool.com to prepare for the Chapter Test.

Assessment Resources

Use *Chapter Tests A and B* to assess students' mastery of chapter content.

All In One **Latin America Teaching Resources,** *Chapter Tests A and B,* pp. 130–135

Tests are also available on the *ExamView® Test Bank CD-ROM.*

⊙ *ExamView® Test Bank CD-ROM*

Objectives

1. Discover how a story from the past can shape the present.
2. Learn how geography can have an important effect on people's lives.
3. Analyze the effectiveness of plot elements such as setting, conflict, and resolution.

Prepare to Read

Build Background Knowledge `L2`

Ask students to read the title of the story and the definition of *surveyor* in the margin. Invite students to predict what the story will be about and how geography might affect it. Point out that the title "The Surveyor" could have more than one meaning. Lead an Idea Wave (TE, p. T35) to help students share their ideas.

The Surveyor `L2`

Guided Instruction

- Point out that some potentially unfamiliar words are defined for students in the margin. Clarify the meanings of the words before reading.

- Partner students and have them read the selection. Ask them to write the answers to each Reading Check as they read. Do a brief survey of their answers to make sure they understand the passage as they read.

- Ask students **What distinction does the author make about Latin American family life?** (*The author explains that Latin American families tend to expand family boundaries to include people who share time and significant experiences with the family.*) **Félix Caballero is not related by blood or marriage to the author, but Ada considers him part of her family. Why?** (*Felix spends a lot of time with the family, so he is part of the author's extended family.*)

The Surveyor
By Alma Flor Ada

Prepare to Read

Background Information
Do people in your family tell you stories about their past? Are some of those stories repeated many times? What stories do you remember the best? What do you learn from these stories?

The stories that family members tell each other become a part of a family's history. They are important because they teach us about our cultural heritage. They connect us to events, to places, and to people. They show us the world from a particular, personal point of view.

Alma Flor Ada (AL muh flawr AY duh) grew up in Cuba. The following selection shows what Ada learned from one of the stories her father used to tell her.

Objectives
In this selection you will
1. Discover how a story from the past can shape the present.
2. Learn how geography can have an important effect on people's lives.

surveyor (sur VAY ur) *n.* a person who measures land and geographic features

Small farmers in Cuba live in villages like this one.

My father, named Modesto after my grandfather, was a <u>surveyor</u>. Some of the happiest times of my childhood were spent on horseback, on trips where he would allow me to accompany him as he plotted the boundaries of small farms in the Cuban countryside. Sometimes we slept out under the stars, stringing our hammocks between the trees, and drank fresh water from springs. We always stopped for a warm greeting at the simple huts of the neighboring peasants, and my eyes would drink in the lush green forest crowned by the swaying leaves of the palm trees.

Read Fluently

Partner students and have them choose a paragraph from the selection. Have students take turns reading the paragraph aloud. Ask them to underline words that give them trouble as they read. Then, have them decode the problem words with their partner. Provide assistance as needed. Have them reread the paragraph two more times to improve their reading speed. Remind them to stop at the commas and periods and to read with expression.

Since many surveying jobs called for dividing up land that a family had inherited from a deceased parent or relative, my father's greatest concern was that justice be achieved. It was not enough just to divide the land into equal portions. He also had to ensure that all parties would have access to roads, to water sources, to the most fertile soil. While I was able to join him in some trips, other surveying work involved large areas of land. On these jobs, my father was part of a team, and I would stay home, eagerly awaiting to hear the stories from his trip on his return.

Latin American families tend not to limit their family boundaries to those who are born or have married into it. Any good friend who spends time with the family and shares in its daily experiences is welcomed as a member. The following story from one of my father's surveying trips is not about a member of my blood family, but instead concerns a member of our extended family.

Félix Caballero, a man my father always liked to <u>recruit</u> whenever he needed a team, was rather different from the other surveyors. He was somewhat older, unmarried, and he kept his thoughts to himself. He came to visit our house daily. Once there, he would sit silently in one of the living room's four rocking chairs, listening to the lively conversations all around him. An occasional nod or a single word were his only contributions to those conversations. My mother and her sisters sometimes made fun of him behind his back. Even though they never said so, I had the impression that they questioned why my father held him in such high regard.

Then one day my father shared this story.

"We had been working on foot in mountainous country for most of the day. Night was approaching. We still had a long way to go to return to where we had left the horses, so we decided to cut across to the other side of the mountain, and soon found ourselves facing a deep <u>gorge</u>. The gorge was <u>spanned</u> by a railroad bridge, long and narrow, built for the sugarcane trains. There were no side rails or walkways, only a set of tracks resting on thick, heavy crossties suspended high in the air.

"We were all upset about having to climb down the steep gorge and up the other side, but the simpler solution, walking across the bridge, seemed too dangerous. What if a cane train should appear? There would be nowhere to go. So we all began the long descent . . . all except for Félix. He decided to risk

Surveyors use instruments like this one to help them take measurements.

recruit (rih KROOT) *v.* to enlist or hire to join a group

gorge (gawrj) *n.* a narrow canyon with steep walls
span (span) *v.* to extend across a space

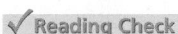 Reading Check

What kind of work does Ada's father do?

Literature **363**

Guided Instruction (continued)

- Ask students: **What is Ada's father's profession?** (*He is a surveyor.*) **How is his profession related to geography?** (*He measures land and geographic features.*)

- Ask students to describe the setting of the story. (*rural Cuba, a mountainous gorge with a railroad bridge*)

- Ask **What are the two main problems in the story?** (*Félix is in danger when a train comes as he is crossing the railroad bridge above the gorge; Félix's inclusion in the family is awkward and not understood.*)

- Ask **How is Félix's problem on the bridge resolved?** (*To survive, Félix rests his surveyor poles on the ties and hangs below the railroad tracks until the train passes.*)

- **How does the story about Félix's past adventure affect Ada's opinion about him?** (*She decides that underneath Félix's quiet manner is a very courageous man. She understands why her father admires Félix.*)

Answers

√ Reading Check Ada's father is a surveyor. He measures land and geographic features.

Independent Practice

Partner students and ask them to write a brief paragraph explaining how the saying "Actions speak louder than words" relates to this story. Instruct them to brainstorm ideas together before writing, and then write their paragraphs individually. Give them *Structuring Paragraphs* and *Creating Paragraph Outlines* to help them get started.

Latin America Teaching Resources, *Structuring Paragraphs,* p. 126; *Creating Paragraph Outlines,* p. 127

Monitor Progress

As students brainstorm, circulate and make sure the partners are communicating effectively. If some are having trouble brainstorming, ask them the following questions: **What does Félix say in the story?** *(not very much)* **What does Félix do in Ada's father's story?** *(He thinks quickly and acts bravely in a dangerous situation.)*

---

dissuade (dis SWAYD) *v.* to persuade not to do something

ominous (AHM uh nus) *adj.* threatening

resilient (rih ZIL yunt) *adj.* able to withstand shock and bounce back from changes

---

walking across the railroad bridge. We all tried to <u>dissuade</u> him, but to no avail. Using an old method, he put one ear to the tracks to listen for vibrations. Since he heard none, he decided that no train was approaching. So he began to cross the long bridge, stepping from crosstie to crosstie between the rails, balancing his long red-and-white surveyor's poles on his shoulder.

"He was about halfway across the bridge when we heard the <u>ominous</u> sound of a steam engine. All eyes rose to Félix. Unquestionably he had heard it, too, because he had stopped in the middle of the bridge and was looking back.

"As the train drew closer, and thinking there was no other solution, we all shouted, 'Jump! Jump!', not even sure our voices would carry to where he stood, so high above us. Félix did look down at the rocky riverbed, which, as it was the dry season, held little water. We tried to encourage him with gestures and more shouts, but he had stopped looking down. We could not imagine what he was doing next, squatting down on the tracks, with the engine of the train already visible. And then, we understood. . . .

"Knowing that he could not manage to hold onto the thick wooden crossties, Félix laid his thin but <u>resilient</u> surveyor's poles across the ties, parallel to the rails. Then he let his body slip down between two of the ties, as he held onto the poles. And there he hung, below the bridge, suspended over the gorge but safely out of the train's path.

A train on a narrow railroad bridge travels high above the trees.

Differentiated Instruction

For Less Proficient Readers L1

Explain to students that "The Surveyor" contains a story within a story. The story that forms the framework of the selection is about Ada's family, particularly her father. The story within the story describes Félix Caballero's courageous actions. To help students with this concept, have them create a chart and label one column "Framework story" and the other "Internal story," then have them take notes in the appropriate column as they read.

"The cane train was, as they frequently are, a very long train. To us, it seemed interminable. . . . One of the younger men said he counted two hundred and twenty cars. With the approaching darkness, and the smoke and shadows of the train, it was often difficult to see our friend. We had heard no human sounds, no screams, but could we have heard anything at all, with the racket of the train crossing overhead?

"When the last car began to curve around the mountain, we could just make out Félix's lonely figure still hanging beneath the bridge. We all watched in relief and amazement as he pulled himself up and at last finished walking, slowly and calmly, along the tracks to the other side of the gorge."

After I heard that story, I saw Félix Caballero in a whole new light. He still remained as quiet as ever, prompting a smile from my mother and her sisters as he sat silently in his rocking chair. But in my mind's eye, I saw him crossing that <u>treacherous</u> bridge, stopping to think calmly of what to do to save his life, emerging all covered with soot and smoke but triumphantly alive—a lonely man, hanging under a railroad bridge at dusk, suspended from his surveyor's poles over a rocky gorge.

If there was so much courage, such an ability to calmly confront danger in the quiet, aging man who sat rocking in our living room, what other wonders might lie hidden in every human soul?

treacherous (TRECH ur us) *adj.* dangerous

☑ Reading Check

What makes Félix think he will be safe?

About the Author

Alma Flor Ada (b. 1938) was born in Camagüey (kah mah GWAY), Cuba. Her relatives were great storytellers. Their stories—part truth, part fiction—and her own childhood experiences are woven into her writing. Dr. Ada now lives in California where she is a professor at the University of San Francisco and an author and translator.

Review and Assessment

Thinking About the Selection

1. (a) Respond What is your reaction to what Félix did?
(b) Infer What qualities did Ada's father see in Félix that shaped his opinion of the man?
2. (a) Recall How did Ada's mother and her sister treat Félix?
(b) Analyze Why did the women have such a response to Félix?
3. (a) Recall What parts of the story tell us about Ada and her father?

(b) Evaluate Information What has Ada learned and from whom did she learn it? What did you learn?

Writing Activity
Write a Short Story Choose a story you have heard from a friend or a family member, or a story that you have told about an event that was important or meaningful to you. Write the story. Include an introduction and a conclusion that explain why the story is important to you.

Literature **365**

Review and Assessment

Thinking About the Selection
1. (a) Students may say they admire Félix for his actions, as Ada did, or they think he made a bad decision to cross the bridge instead of climbing down the gorge. **(b)** Ada's father saw that Félix was brave and resourceful.

2. (a) Ada's mother and her sisters made fun of Félix behind his back. **(b)** Félix visited every day, but was very quiet.

3. (a) In the beginning of the story, Ada shares memories of accompanying her father on surveying trips and listening to his stories. **(b)** Ada learns to look beneath the surface of people to get a true measure of their characters from her father; student answers will vary.

Assess and Reteach

Assess Progress L2
Have students answer the assessment questions.

Reteach L1
- If students are having trouble analyzing and interpreting the actions of the characters in the story, have them list each character and the information they know about them. (*Ada's father—works as a surveyor, tries to divide land fairly, respects Félix; Félix Caballero—works with Ada's father, his quietness hides courage and the ability to take decisive action; Ada's mother—makes fun of Félix behind his back, wonders why her husband admires him; Ada—loves her father's stories, has a new appreciation of Félix after her father's story*)

- Work with the students until their lists are complete, and then ask them to answer the assessment questions again.

Extend L3
To extend the lesson, ask students to read the selection *My Friend the Painter* and answer the questions at the end.

 Latin America Teaching Resources, *My Friend the Painter,* pp. 124–125

Answers

☑ Reading Check   Félix trusts the strength of his surveyor's poles to hold him suspended under the bridge.

Writing Activity
Use *Rubric for Assessing a Writing Assignment* to evaluate students' stories.

 Latin America Teaching Resources, *Rubric for Assessing a Writing Assignment,* p. 129

Overview

Section 1
Early Civilizations of Middle America
1. Find out what Mayan civilization was like.
2. Learn how the Aztecs built their empire and understand what kind of society they created.

Section 2
The Incas: People of the Sun
1. Find out how the Incas created their empire.
2. Understand what Incan civilization was like.
3. Learn how the descendants of the Incas live today.

Section 3
European Conquest
1. Learn why Europeans sailed to the Americas.
2. Find out how the conquistadors conquered the Aztecs and the Incas.
3. Understand how the Spanish empire was organized and how colonization affected the Americas.

Section 4
Independence
1. Learn what events inspired revolutions in Latin America.
2. Find out how Mexico gained its independence.
3. Discover how Bolívar and San Martín helped bring independence to South America.

Section 5
From Past to Present
1. Learn how Latin American caudillos and foreign involvement contributed to the region's troubled past.
2. Find out how Latin American nations are struggling to improve their economies and the welfare of their people.

Technology Resources

Students use embedded Web codes to access Internet activities, chapter self-tests, and additional map practice. They may also access Dorling Kindersley's Online Desk Reference to learn more about each country they study.

Use the Interactive Textbook to make content and concepts come alive through animations, videos, and activities that accompany the complete basal text—online and on CD-ROM.

Use this complete suite of powerful teaching tools to make planning lessons and administering tests quicker and easier.

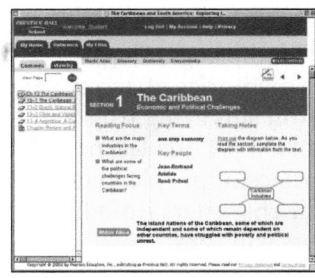

Reading and Assessment

Reading and Vocabulary Instruction

CHAPTER 12

⟲ Model the Target Reading Skill

Clarifying Meaning When rereading and reading ahead, students look within the text for the meaning of unfamiliar words and terms. Paraphrasing helps students restate ideas in words they better understand and remember. When summarizing, students state the main points of the passage.

Model techniques for clarifying meaning by thinking aloud about this text from page 369:

The Great Mystery of the Mayas *About* A.D. *900 the Mayan cities began to decline. No one knows why. Crop failures, war, disease, drought, or famine may have killed many Mayas. Or perhaps people rebelled against the control of the priests and nobles. The Mayas stayed in the region, however. Millions of Mayas still live in Mexico, Belize, Guatemala, Honduras, and El Salvador.*

I'm not sure what the mystery in the subhead is. I'll read ahead to find out. In the first two sentences, I see the mystery—no one is sure why the Mayan cities declined. The third sentence lists many possible explanations, so I'll reread it and think about each one. The fourth sentence seems complicated, so I'll restate it: "Maybe the Mayas got tired of the rules made by their leaders." Finally, I'll finish the paragraph and summarize it: "No one is sure why Mayan cities declined in A.D. 900, but their descendants still live in the area."

Use the following worksheets from All-in-One Latin America Teaching Resources, (pp. 159, 160, and 161) to support this chapter's Target Reading Skill.

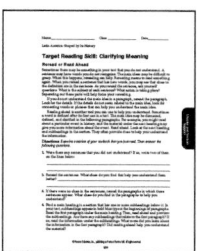 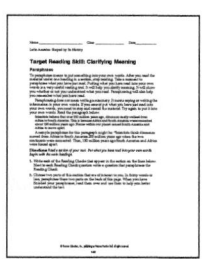 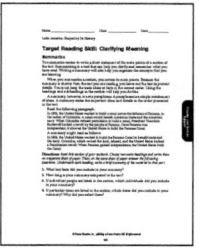

Vocabulary Builder
High-Use Academic Words

Use these steps to teach this chapter's High-Use Words:

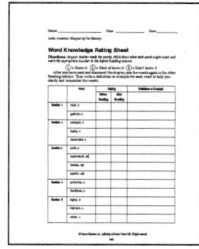

1. Have students rate how well they know each word on their Word Knowledge worksheets (All-in-One Latin America Teaching Resources, p. 162).
2. Pronounce each word and ask students to repeat it.
3. Give students a brief definition or sample sentence (provided on TE pp. 369, 374, 379, and 393).
4. Work with students as they fill in the "Definition or Example" column of their Word Knowledge worksheets.

Assessment

Formal Assessment

Test students' understanding of core knowledge and skills.

Chapter Tests A and B, All-in-One Latin America Teaching Resources, pp. 177–182

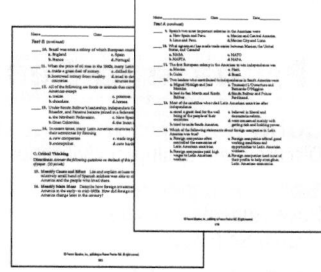

Customize the Chapter Tests to suit your needs.

ExamView Test Bank CD-ROM

Skills Assessment

Assess geographic literacy.

MapMaster Skills, Student Edition pp. 367, 398

Assess reading and comprehension.

Target Reading Skills, Student Edition, pp. 370, 374, 382, 387, 394 and in Section Assessments

Chapter 12 Assessment, Western Hemisphere Reading and Vocabulary Study Guide, p. 147

Performance Assessment

Assess students' performance on this chapter's Writing Activities using the following rubrics from All-in-One Latin America Teaching Resources.

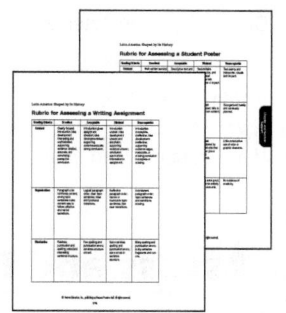

Rubric for Assessing a Writing Assignment, p. 174

Rubric for Assessing a Student Poster, p. 175

Assess students' work through performance tasks.

Small Group Activity: Mayan Math Bowl, All-in-One Latin America Teaching Resources, pp. 165–168

Online Assessment

Have students check their own knowledge.

Chapter Self-Test

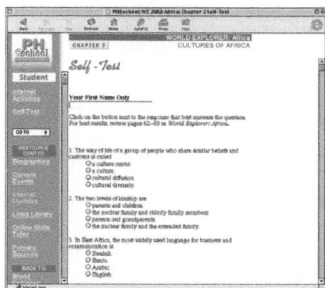

Section 1 Early Civilizations of Middle America

1.5 period, .75 block

Social Studies Objectives

1. Find out what Mayan civilization was like.
2. Learn how the Aztecs built their empire and understand what kind of society they created.

Reading/Language Arts Objective

Reread to better understand words and ideas in the text.

Prepare to Read	Instructional Resources	Differentiated Instruction
Build Background Knowledge Discuss the meaning of civilization. **Set a Purpose for Reading** Have students evaluate statements on the *Reading Readiness Guide.* **Preview Key Terms** Teach the section's Key Terms using a "See It—Remember It" chart. **Target Reading Skill** Introduce the section's Target Reading Skill of **rereading**.	**All In One Latin America Teaching Resources** L2 Reading Readiness Guide, p. 140 L2 Reread or Read Ahead, p. 159	**Spanish Reading and Vocabulary Study Guide** L1 Chapter 12, Section 1, pp. 97–98 ELL

Instruct	Instructional Resources	Differentiated Instruction
The Mayas Discuss aspects of Mayan civilization. **The Aztec Empire** Discuss how the Aztec empire worked. **Target Reading Skill** Review **rereading**. **Eyewitness Technology** Have students read about and discuss Aztec Farming.	**All In One Latin America Teaching Resources** L2 Guided Reading and Review, p. 141 L2 Reading Readiness Guide, p. 140 **Latin America Transparencies** L2 Section Reading Support Transparency LA 31	**Teacher's Edition** L3 For Gifted and Talented Students, TE p. 371 **Spanish Support** L2 Guided Reading and Review (Spanish), p. 130 ELL

Assess and Reteach	Instructional Resources	Differentiated Instruction
Assess Progress Evaluate student comprehension with the section assessment and section quiz. **Reteach** Assign the Reading and Vocabulary Study Guide to help struggling students. **Extend** Extend the lesson by assigning a small group activity.	**All In One Latin America Teaching Resources** L2 Section Quiz, p. 142 L3 Small Group Activity: Mayan Math Bowl, pp. 165–168 Rubric for Assessing a Writing Assignment, p. 174 **Reading and Vocabulary Study Guide** L1 Chapter 12, Section 1, pp. 132–134	**Spanish Support** L2 Section Quiz (Spanish), p. 13 ELL

Key

L1 Basic to Average	L3 Average to Advanced	LPR Less Proficient Readers	GT Gifted and Talented
L2 For All Students		AR Advanced Readers	ELL English Language Learners
		SN Special Needs Students	

Section 2 The Incas: People of the Sun

1.5 period, .75 block

Social Studies Objectives

1. Find out how the Incas created their empire.
2. Understand what Incan civilization was like.
3. Learn how the descendants of the Incas live today.

Reading/Language Arts Objective

Read ahead to help clarify a word or an idea.

Prepare to Read	**Instructional Resources**	**Differentiated Instruction**
Build Background Knowledge Discuss uses of interstate highways. **Set a Purpose for Reading** Have students begin to fill out the *Reading Readiness Guide*. **Preview Key Terms** Teach the section's Key Terms. **Target Reading Skill** Introduce the section's Target Reading Skill of **reading ahead**.	**All in One Latin America Teaching Resources** L2 Reading Readiness Guide, p. 144 L2 Reread or Read Ahead, p. 159	**Spanish Reading and Vocabulary Study Guide** L1 Chapter 12, Section 2, pp. 99–100 ELL

Instruct	**Instructional Resources**	**Differentiated Instruction**
The Rise of the Incas Discuss how the Incan empire developed. **Target Reading Skill** Review **reading ahead**. **Incan Civilization** Discuss aspects of Incan civilization. **The Quechua: Descendants of the Incas** Ask students how the Quechua continue Incan traditions.	**All in One Latin America Teaching Resources** L2 Guided Reading and Review, p. 145 L2 Reading Readiness Guide, p. 144 **Latin America Transparencies** L2 Section Reading Support Transparency LA 32	**Teacher's Edition** L3 For Gifted and Talented Students, TE p. 375 **Spanish Support** L2 Guided Reading and Review (Spanish), p. 132 ELL

Assess and Reteach	**Instructional Resources**	**Differentiated Instruction**
Assess Progress Evaluate student comprehension with the section assessment and section quiz. **Reteach** Assign the Reading and Vocabulary Study Guide to help struggling students. **Extend** Extend the lesson by assigning a Long-Term Integrated Project.	**All in One Latin America Teaching Resources** L2 Section Quiz, p. 146 Rubric for Assessing a Writing Assignment, p. 174 **Reading and Vocabulary Study Guide** L1 Chapter 12, Section 2, pp. 135–137	**Spanish Support** L2 Section Quiz (Spanish), p. 133 ELL **PHSchool.com** L3 For: Long-Term Integrated Projects: Building Models of Housing Around the World Web code: lfd-1202

Key

L1 Basic to Average
L2 For All Students
L3 Average to Advanced

LPR Less Proficient Readers
AR Advanced Readers
SN Special Needs Students

GT Gifted and Talented
ELL English Language Learners

Section 3 European Conquest

1.5 period, .75 block

Social Studies Objectives

1. Learn why Europeans sailed to the Americas.

2. Find out how the conquistadors conquered the Aztecs and the Incas.

3. Understand how the Spanish empire was organized and how colonization affected the Americas.

Reading/Language Arts Objective

Paraphrase to understand and remember what you have read.

Prepare to Read	Instructional Resources	Differentiated Instruction
Build Background Knowledge Discuss reasons for exploring the unknown. **Set a Purpose for Reading** Have students begin to fill out the *Reading Readiness Guide.* **Preview Key Terms** Teach the section's Key Terms. **Target Reading Skill** Introduce the section's Target Reading Skill of **paraphrasing**.	**All in One** Latin America **Teaching Resources** L2 Reading Readiness Guide, p. 148 L2 Paraphrase, p. 160	**Spanish Reading and Vocabulary Study Guide** L2 Chapter 12, Section 3, pp. 101–102 ELL

Instruct	Instructional Resources	Differentiated Instruction
Europeans Arrive in the Americas Ask students key questions about the beginnings of American exploration. **The Success of the Conquistadors** Discuss the actions of the conquistadors with students. **Colonization** Discuss the colonization of Latin America. **Target Reading Skill** Review **paraphrasing**.	**All in One** Latin America **Teaching Resources** L2 Guided Reading and Review, p. 149 L2 Reading Readiness Guide, p. 148 **Latin America Transparencies** L2 Section Reading Support Transparency LA 33	**All in One** Latin America **Teaching Resources** L3 The Talking Stone, pp. 169–171 **Teacher's Edition** L2 For English Language Learners, TE p. 381 L2 For Advanced Readers, TE p. 381 **Spanish Support** L2 Guided Reading and Review (Spanish), p. 134 ELL

Assess and Reteach	Instructional Resources	Differentiated Instruction
Assess Progress Evaluate student comprehension with the section assessment and section quiz. **Reteach** Assign the Reading and Vocabulary Study Guide to help struggling students. **Extend** Extend the lesson by showing and discussing a video.	**All in One** Latin America **Teaching Resources** L2 Section Quiz, p. 150 Rubric for Assessing a Writing Assignment, p. 174 **Reading and Vocabulary Study Guide** L1 Chapter 12, Section 3, pp. 138–140	**Spanish Support** L2 Section Quiz (Spanish), p. 135 ELL

Key

L1 Basic to Average	L3 Average to Advanced	LPR Less Proficient Readers	GT Gifted and Talented
L2 For All Students		AR Advanced Readers	ELL English Language Learners
		SN Special Needs Students	

Section 4 Independence

 3 periods, 1.5 blocks (includes Skills for Life)

Social Studies Objectives

1. Learn what events inspired revolutions in Latin America.
2. Find out how Mexico gained its independence.
3. Discover how Bolívar and San Martín helped bring independence to South America.

Reading/Language Arts Objective

Summarize to understand the main points you have read in the correct order.

Prepare to Read	Instructional Resources	Differentiated Instruction
Build Background Knowledge Discuss the ideas behind the Fourth of July. **Set a Purpose for Reading** Have students evaluate statements on the *Reading Readiness Guide.* **Preview Key Terms** Teach the section's Key Terms. **Target Reading Skill** Introduce the section's Target Reading Skill of **summarizing.**	**All in One Latin America Teaching Resources** L2 Reading Readiness Guide, p. 152 L2 Summarize, p. 161	**Spanish Reading and Vocabulary Study Guide** L2 Chapter 12, Section 4, pp. 103–104 ELL

Instruct	Instructional Resources	Differentiated Instruction
The Seeds of Revolution Discuss the events that inspired revolutions in Latin America. **Independence in Mexico** Teach students how Mexico gained its independence. **South American Independence** Discuss how revolutionary leaders brought about independence in Latin America. **Target Reading Skill** Review **paraphrasing.**	**All in One Latin America Teaching Resources** L2 Guided Reading and Review, p. 153 L2 Reading Readiness Guide, p. 152 **Latin America Transparencies** L2 Section Reading Support Transparency LA 34	**All in One Latin America Teaching Resources** Rubric for Assessing a Student Poster, p. 175 AR L2 Skills for Life, p. 164 GT, AR, LPR, SN **Teacher's Edition** L1 For Less Proficient Readers, TE p. 387 L3 For Advanced Readers, TE p. 387 **Reading and Vocabulary Study Guide** L1 Chapter 12, Section 4, pp. 141–143 LPR

Assess and Reteach	Instructional Resources	Differentiated Instruction
Assess Progress Evaluate student comprehension with the section assessment and section quiz. **Reteach** Assign the Reading and Vocabulary Study Guide to help struggling students. **Extend** Assign students to groups to prepare a talk show based on Latin American revolutionary leaders.	**All in One Latin America Teaching Resources** L2 Section Quiz, p. 154 Rubric for Assessing a Writing Assignment, p. 174 **Reading and Vocabulary Study Guide** L1 Chapter 12, Section 4, pp. 141–143	**Teacher's Edition** L2 For Special Needs Students, TE p. 391 **Spanish Support** L2 Section Quiz (Spanish), p. 137 ELL **Social Studies Skills Tutor CD-ROM** L1 Sequencing SN, LPR, ELL

Key

L1 Basic to Average	L3 Average to Advanced	LPR Less Proficient Readers	GT Gifted and Talented
L2 For All Students		AR Advanced Readers	ELL English Language Learners
		SN Special Needs Students	

Section 5 From Past to Present

 3.5 periods, 1.75 blocks (includes Chapter Review and Assessment)

Social Studies Objectives

1. Learn how Latin American caudillos and foreign involvement contributed to the region's troubled past.
2. Find out how Latin American nations are struggling to improve their economies and the welfare of their people.

Reading/Language Arts Objective

Reread or read ahead to help understand words and ideas in the text.

Prepare to Read

Build Background Knowledge
Have students predict the problems Latin America faced after independence.

Set a Purpose for Reading
Have students evaluate statements on the *Reading Readiness Guide*.

Preview Key Terms
Teach the section's Key Terms.

Target Reading Skill
Introduce the section's Target Reading Skill of **rereading or reading ahead.**

Instructional Resources

All in One Latin America Teaching Resources

- L2 Reading Readiness Guide, p. 156
- L2 Reread or Read Ahead, p. 159

Differentiated Instruction

Spanish Reading and Vocabulary Study Guide

- L2 Chapter 12, Section 5, pp. 105–106 ELL

Instruct

A Troubled Past
Discuss how caudillos and foreign involvement affected the newly independent Latin America.

The Struggle Continues
Discuss the economic challenges of Latin America.

Target Reading Skill
Review **rereading or reading ahead.**

Instructional Resources

All in One Latin America Teaching Resources

- L2 Guided Reading and Review, p. 157
- L2 Reading Readiness Guide, p. 156

Latin America Transparencies

- L2 Section Reading Support Transparency LA 35

Differentiated Instruction

Spanish Support

- L2 Guided Reading and Review (Spanish), p. 20 ELL

Assess and Reteach

Assess Progress
Evaluate student comprehension with the section assessment and section quiz.

Reteach
Assign the Reading and Vocabulary Study Guide to help struggling students.

Extend
Extend the lesson by assigning an Enrichment worksheet.

Instructional Resources

All in One Latin America Teaching Resources

- L2 Section Quiz, p. 158
- L3 Enrichment, p. 163
  Rubric for Assessing a Writing Assignment, p. 174
- L2 Vocabulary Development, p. 173
- L2 Word Knowledge, p. 162
- L2 Chapter Tests A and B, pp. 177–182

Reading and Vocabulary Study Guide

- L1 Chapter 12, Section 5, pp. 144–146

Differentiated Instruction

Teacher's Edition

- L1 For Special Needs Students, TE p. 395
- L1 For English Language Learners, TE p. 395

Spanish Support

- L2 Section Quiz (Spanish), p. 139 ELL
- L2 Chapter Summary (Spanish), p. 140 ELL
- L2 Vocabulary Development (Spanish), p. 141 ELL

Student Edition on Audio CD

- L1 Chapter 12, Section 5 SN, LPR, ELL

Key

- L1 Basic to Average
- L2 For All Students
- L3 Average to Advanced
- LPR Less Proficient Readers
- AR Advanced Readers
- SN Special Needs Students
- GT Gifted and Talented
- ELL English Language Learners

Reading Background

Using the Choral Reading Technique Effectively

The Choral Reading Technique ensures participation by all learners, including English Language Learners, because it provides a non-threatening reading environment. To ensure success with this technique, choose shorter passages (less than 500 words), and encourage students to stay with your voice, so that everyone reads at the same rate. When students have finished reading in unison, allow time for students to reread the passage silently, focusing on new or unfamiliar words.

Pre-Teaching Vocabulary

Research literature on academic vocabulary instruction indicates that effective strategies require students to go beyond simply looking up dictionary definitions or examining the context. Vocabulary learning must be based on the learner's dynamic engagement in constructing understanding.

If students are not retaining the meaning of the Key Terms or high-use words, use this extended vocabulary sequence to engage them in learning new words.

1. Present the word in writing and point out the part of speech.
2. Pronounce the word and have students pronounce the word.
3. Provide a range of familiar synonyms (or "it's like" words) before offering definitions.
4. Provide an accessible definition and concrete examples, or "showing sentences."
5. Rephrase the simple definition or example sentence, asking students to complete the statement by substituting the word aloud.
6. Check for understanding by providing an application task/question requiring critical thinking.

Sample instructional sequence:

1. *Dictator* is a noun, a word that names a person, place, or thing.
2. Say the word *dictator* after me. (Students repeat.)
3. A *dictator* is like a *tyrant* or a *despot*.
4. The word *dictator* means *a ruler with complete power.* The *dictator* declared that every Friday would be a holiday celebrating his rule.
5. By the _____'s order, every Friday was a holiday celebrating his rule. (Students substitute missing word.)
6. Is the president of the United States a *dictator*? Yes-No-Why? (Students answer the question.)

World Studies Background

Uncovering the World of the Maya

A huge volcanic eruption that occurred around the year A.D. 595 in modern-day El Salvador covered Cerén, a Mayan village, with volcanic ash and left it frozen in time. Archaeologists have found mud-preserved adobe buildings that were once homes, kitchens, and ceremonial buildings. Objects such as deer skull headdresses and red paste were probably used in religious ceremonies. Food that the Maya ate, such as corn and squash, has been found. Even footprints in the dirt were preserved. As they discover more clues in Cerén, researchers become more convinced of the sophistication of the Mayan civilization.

Brazil's Revolution

Although Brazil's fight for independence lacked the violence of other Latin American revolutions, freedom did not come easily. Groups of Brazilian rebels began working toward independence in the late 1700s, but the Portuguese government stopped them. In 1817, a northeastern region of Brazil tried to form its own colony, but again, the rebels were stopped. Brazilians were finally able to move toward independence when the Emperor Pedro I came to rule Portugal. Despite pressure from many Portuguese officials to keep Brazil as a colony, Pedro refused. Instead, he set Brazil free in September 1822, with a written statement titled "Independence or Death."

Guiding Questions

Remind students about the Guiding Questions introduced at the beginning of this section.

Section 1 relates to **Guiding Question** ②
How has Latin America been shaped by its history? *(The Mayas and the Aztecs made scientific and agricultural discoveries that are still important in Latin America today.)*

Section 2 relates to **Guiding Question** ③
What factors have affected cultures in Latin America? *(Descendants of the Incas still use farming methods similar to those of their ancestors.)*

Section 3 relates to **Guiding Question** ②
How has Latin America been shaped by its history? *(The European conquest helped lead to the decline of the Native American population and increased European cultural influence in Latin America.)*

Section 4 relates to **Guiding Question** ④
What types of governments have existed in Latin America? *(In the early 1800s, many countries in Latin America struggled to become independent of European rule.)*

Section 5 relates to **Guiding Question** ④
What types of government have existed in Latin America? *(In the 1960s and 1970s, military regimes seized power in many Latin American countries. By the 1980s, some of these were replaced by elected governments.)*

⤺ Target Reading Skill

In this chapter, students will learn and apply the reading skill of clarifying meaning. Use the following worksheets to help students practice this skill:

> **All in One** **Latin America Teaching Resources,** *Reread or Read Ahead,* p. 159; *Paraphrase,* p. 160; *Summarize,* p. 161

Differentiated Instruction

The following Teacher Edition strategies are suitable for students of varying abilities.

Advanced Readers, pp. 381, 387
English Language Learners, pp. 381, 395
Gifted and Talented, pp. 371, 375
Less Proficient Readers, p. 387
Special Needs Students, pp. 391, 395

Chapter Preview

This chapter presents the history of Latin America and shows how that history affects the region to this day.

Section 1
Early Civilizations of Middle America

Section 2
The Incas: People of the Sun

Section 3
European Conquest

Section 4
Independence

Section 5
From Past to Present

⤺ **Target Reading Skill**

Clarifying Meaning In this chapter you will focus on skills you can use to clarify meaning as you read.

▶ Decorated wall of a Mayan building at Uxmal, Mexico

366 Latin America

Bibliography

For the Teacher
Arnold, Caroline. *City of the Gods: Mexico's Ancient City of Teotihuacán.* Clarion, 1994.
Baquedano, Elizabeth. *Aztec, Inca, and Maya* (Eyewitness Books). Knopf, 1993.
Thomson, Hugh. *The White Rock: An Exploration of the Inca Heartland.* Overlook Press, 2003.

For the Student
L1 Defrates, Joanna. *What Do We Know About the Aztecs?* Bedrick, 1995.
L2 Kimmel, Eric. *Montezuma and the Fall of the Aztecs.* Holiday House, 2000.
L3 Green, Jen. *The Encyclopedia of the Ancient Americans: Explore the Wonders of the Aztec, Maya, Inca, North American Indian and Arctic Peoples.* Southwater, 2001.

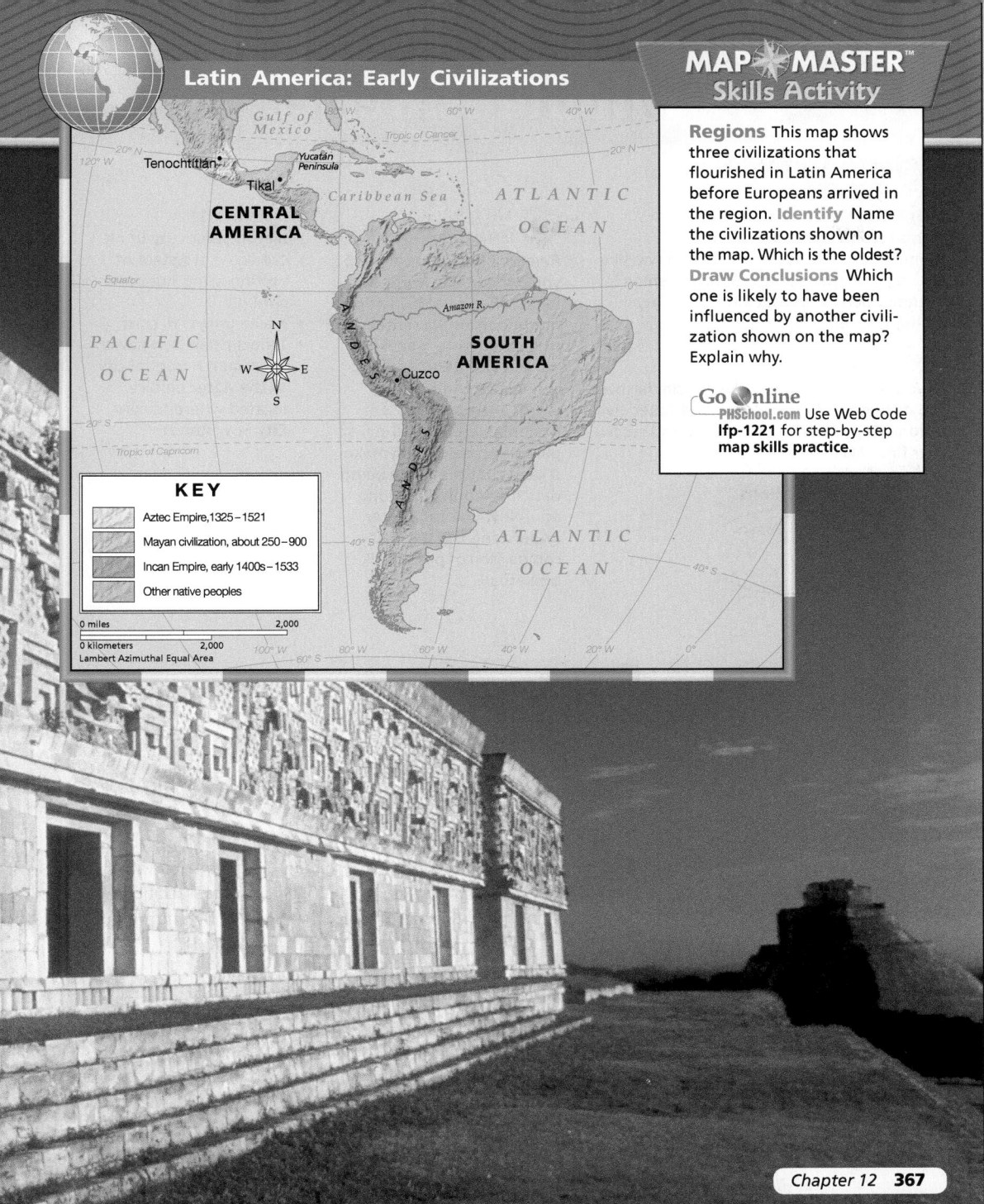

Latin America: Early Civilizations

Tenochtitlán
Yucatán Peninsula
Tikal
CENTRAL AMERICA
Gulf of Mexico
Tropic of Cancer
Caribbean Sea
ATLANTIC OCEAN
PACIFIC OCEAN
Equator
Amazon R.
SOUTH AMERICA
ANDES
Cuzco
Tropic of Capricorn
ATLANTIC OCEAN

KEY
- Aztec Empire, 1325–1521
- Mayan civilization, about 250–900
- Incan Empire, early 1400s–1533
- Other native peoples

0 miles 2,000
0 kilometers 2,000
Lambert Azimuthal Equal Area

MAP MASTER™ Skills Activity

Regions This map shows three civilizations that flourished in Latin America before Europeans arrived in the region. **Identify** Name the civilizations shown on the map. Which is the oldest? **Draw Conclusions** Which one is likely to have been influenced by another civilization shown on the map? Explain why.

Go Online
PHSchool.com Use Web Code lfp-1221 for step-by-step map skills practice.

MAP MASTER™ Skills Activity

- Point out to students that each shaded area on the map represents a different civilization. Call on students to identify the colors and which civilizations they represent.

- Ask students to use the map's scale to measure the approximate length of the territory held by each civilization, and compare them. Ask **Which civilization had the largest area?** (*Incan Empire*) **Which had the smallest?** (*Mayan civilization*) **How do you think size of a civilization might have affected its inhabitants?** (*Possible answer: Larger civilizations might have needed more rulers in different areas; smaller civilizations might have needed less.*)

Go Online
PHSchool.com Students may practice their map skills using the interactive online version of this map.

Using the Visual L2

Reach Into Your Background Draw students' attention to the caption and photo on pages 366–367. Discuss the visual with students, and have them identify the items in the photo. Ask **Do you think that these are modern buildings? Why or why not? What kinds of clues can they see in the photo that might tell them what the building was used for or where it was located?**

Answers

MAP MASTER Skills Activity **Identify** Aztec, Mayan, and Incan; Mayan **Draw Conclusions** The Aztec and Mayan Empires likely influenced one another since they existed in nearby areas.

Chapter 12 **367**

Chapter Resources

Teaching Resources
- L2 Vocabulary Development, p. 173
- L2 Skills for Life, p. 164
- L2 Chapter Tests A and B, pp. 177–182

Spanish Support
- L2 Spanish Chapter Summary, p. 140
- L2 Spanish Vocabulary Development, p. 141

Media and Technology
- L1 Student Edition on Audio CD
- L1 Guided Reading Audiotapes, English and Spanish
- L2 Social Studies Skills Tutor CD-ROM
  ExamView Test Bank CD-ROM

PRENTICE HALL Presentation EXPRESS™
Teach · Connect · Inspire

Teach this chapter's content using the PresentationExpress™ CD-ROM including:
- slide shows
- transparencies
- interactive maps and media
- *ExamView®* QuickTake Presenter

Objectives

Social Studies

1. Find out what Mayan civilization was like.
2. Learn how the Aztecs built their empire and understand what kind of society they created.

Reading/Language Arts

Reread to better understand words and ideas in the text.

Prepare to Read

Build Background Knowledge `L2`

Tell students that they will now study the history of Latin America, starting with the oldest civilizations we know about. Ask students to name some features of American civilization. Model the thought process by encouraging them to think about cities, the arts, the sciences, and the system of education. Use the Give One and Get One participation strategy (TE, p. T37) to generate a list.

Set a Purpose for Reading `L2`

- Preview the Objectives.
- Read each statement in the *Reading Readiness Guide* aloud. Ask students to mark the statements true or false.

   All in One Latin America Teaching Resources, *Reading Readiness Guide,* p. 140

- Have students discuss the statements in pairs or groups of four, then mark their worksheets again. Use the Numbered Heads participation structure (TE, p. T36) to call on students to share their group's perspectives.

Vocabulary Builder
Preview Key Terms `L2`

Create a three column "See It—Remember It" chart of the Key Terms on the board. Write a term in the first column, a short definition in the second column, and a sketch in the third column. Guide students as they copy and complete the chart.

Early Civilizations of Middle America

Prepare to Read

Objectives

In this section you will
1. Find out what Mayan civilization was like.
2. Learn how the Aztecs built their empire and understand what kind of society they created.

Taking Notes

As you read this section, look for similarities and differences in the Mayan and Aztec civilizations. Copy the diagram below and record your findings in it.

Ancient Civilizations

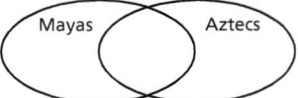

Mayas   Aztecs

Target Reading Skill

Reread Rereading can help you understand words and ideas in the text. If you do not understand a sentence or a paragraph, read it again to look for connections among the words and sentences. For example, rereading the first paragraph below can make it clear that the game being described took place long ago. Now you can better understand the surprising comparison of pok-ta-tok to basketball.

Key Terms

- **hieroglyphics** (hy ur oh GLIF iks) *n.* a system of writing using signs and symbols
- **maize** (mayz) *n.* corn
- **Tenochtitlán** (teh nawch tee TLAHN) *n.* capital city of the Aztec empire, located where Mexico City now stands

Fans cheered as the players brought the ball down the court. Suddenly, the ball flew into the air and sailed through the hoop. Fans and players shouted and screamed. Although this may sound like a championship basketball game, it is actually a moment in a game played more than 1,000 years ago. The game was called pok-ta-tok.

Pok-ta-tok was a game played by the ancient Mayas. Using only their leather-padded hips and elbows, players tried to hit a four-pound (1.9 kilogram), six-inch (15.2 centimeter) rubber ball through a stone hoop mounted 30 feet (9.1 meters) above the ground.

The Mayas

How do we know about this ancient game? Crumbling ruins of pok-ta-tok courts and ancient clay statues of players have been found at sites in Central America and southern Mexico. In these areas, Mayan civilization thrived from about A.D. 250 to A.D. 900. By studying ruins, scientists have learned much about Mayan civilization.

Target Reading Skill `L2`

Reread Point out the Target Reading Skill. Tell students that rereading a sentence or a paragraph will help them to better understand words and ideas in the text.

Model rereading by reading and rereading the first paragraph on page 369. Tell students that rereading can help them better under-

stand where Mayan cities were located and how they served as religious centers.

Give students *Reread or Read Ahead*. Have them complete the activity in groups.

   All in One Latin America Teaching Resources, *Reread or Read Ahead,* p. 159

Mayan Civilization The Mayas built great cities, such as Copán (koh PAHN) in the present-day country of Honduras, and Tikal (tee KAHL) in present-day Guatemala. Mayan cities were economic, political, and religious centers. Large pyramid-shaped temples often stood in the middle of Mayan cities. Rival Mayan cities also engaged in frequent warfare with one another.

Mayan priests studied the stars and planets. They developed two calendars. They used one to schedule religious celebrations and the other, as we do today, to follow the seasons. The Mayas also developed a system of writing using signs and symbols called **hieroglyphics** (hy ur oh GLIF iks). Hieroglyphics found in books and in carvings have helped scientists understand Mayan culture.

Farmers worked in fields surrounding the cities. Their most important crop was maize, or corn, the main food of the Mayas. They also grew beans, squash, peppers, avocados, and papayas.

The Great Mystery of the Mayas About A.D. 900, the Mayan cities began to decline. No one knows why. Crop failures, war, disease, drought, or famine may have killed many Mayas. Or perhaps people rebelled against the control of the priests and nobles. The Mayas stayed in the region, however. Millions of Mayas still live in Mexico, Belize, and Guatemala.

✓ Reading Check **What is the "great mystery of the Mayas"?**

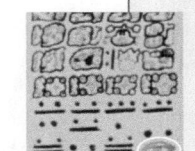

Links to
Math

The Concept of Zero
The Mayas created a number system that included zero. Zero is important in math because it is a symbol that shows that there is none of something. For example, to write the number 308, you need a symbol to show that there are no tens. The idea of zero, which also developed in Asia, is considered to be one of the greatest inventions in mathematics. In the Mayan book above, the zero looks like a shell (circled above). Other numbers are made up of bars and dots.

Mayan Ruins
The Mayan city of Chichén Itzá had a pok-ta-tok court as well as this huge temple. **Infer** *What does this great temple suggest about Mayan culture and technology?*

Chapter 12 Section 1 **369**

Vocabulary Builder

Use the information below to teach students this section's high-use words.

High-Use Word	Definition and Sample Sentence
ritual, p. 370	*n.* a ceremony or regularly performed practice Going to the baseball game had become a **ritual** in her family.
garment, p. 370	*n.* any article of clothing He had to wash the **garment** by hand.

Instruct

The Mayas

Guided Instruction

- Read The Mayas with students, using the Choral Reading technique (TE, p. T34). As students read, circulate and make sure individuals can answer the Reading Check question.

- Discuss some aspects of Mayan civilization. *(Mayan cities were economic, political, and religious centers. Mayan priests studied the stars and planets. The Mayas developed a system of writing called hieroglyphics and Mayan farmers grew crops, such as maize, in fields surrounding the cities.)*

- Ask students **What types of jobs did the Mayas have? Are they similar to or different from jobs that people have today?** *(builders, priests, and farmers; similar)*

Independent Practice

Ask students to create the Taking Notes graphic organizer on a blank piece of paper. Then have them fill in the "Mayas" circle with the information they have just learned. Briefly model how to identify which details to record.

Monitor Progress

As students fill in the graphic organizer, circulate and make sure individuals are choosing the correct details. Provide assistance as needed.

Answers

✓ Reading Check The "great mystery of the Mayas" is why their cities began to decline around A.D. 900.

Infer The great temple suggests that the Mayas had an advanced culture and technology.

The Aztec Empire

Guided Instruction

- **Vocabulary Builder** Clarify the high-use words **ritual** and **garment** before reading.

- Read The Aztec Empire with students.

- Discuss how the Aztecs built their empire. *(The Aztecs gained land and riches from the people they conquered.)*

- Have students describe the different roles and positions in Aztec society. *(The Aztec emperor ruled over all Aztec lands; nobles helped the emperor govern; soldiers fought in wars to expand the empire and protected trade routes; priests were religious leaders and were important in government; many Aztecs were farmers.)*

Independent Practice

Have students complete the graphic organizer by filling in the "Aztecs" circle and then adding the aspects common to both civilizations in the overlapping circle.

Monitor Progress

- Show *Section Reading Support Transparency LA 31* and ask students to check their graphic organizers individually. Go over key concepts and clarify key vocabulary as needed.

  Latin America Transparencies, *Section Reading Support Transparency LA 31*

- Tell students to fill in the last column of the *Reading Readiness Guide*. Probe for what they learned that confirms or invalidates each statement.

  All in One Latin America Teaching Resources, *Reading Readiness Guide,* p. 140

Target Reading Skill L2

Reread As a follow up, ask students to answer the Target Reading Skill question in the Student Edition. *(Aztec astronomers predicted eclipses and the movements of planets, and kept records using hieroglyphics.)*

Aztec calendar
The face of the Aztec sun god is shown in the center of this stone calendar. The symbols surrounding the face represent the twenty days in each Aztec month. **Draw Conclusions** *Why would the Aztec sun god be associated with the calander?*

Reread
Read the paragraph at the right again to find out two things Aztec astronomers did.

The Aztec Empire

In the 1400s, another great civilization arose in Middle America. It was created by the Aztecs, who had arrived in the Valley of Mexico in the 1100s.

The Aztecs settled on an island in Lake Texcoco in 1325. They changed the swampy lake into a magnificent city. **Tenochtitlán** (teh nawch tee TLAHN), the Aztec capital, stood on the site of present-day Mexico City. When Europeans explored the area in the 1500s, they found the Aztecs ruling a rich empire from the city of Tenochtitlán.

Building an Empire In the 1400s, Aztec warriors began conquering the other people in the region. They forced the conquered people to pay tribute, or taxes. Tribute could be paid in food, cotton, gold, or slaves. The Aztecs grew rich from the tribute.

The Aztec emperor ruled over all Aztec lands. Nobles helped the emperor to govern. Soldiers fought in wars to expand the empire. They also protected the empire's trade routes. Priests were not only religious leaders, but were also important in society. People of the upper classes wore feathered garments and carried feathered fans as symbols of their status.

Farming Most of the people in the Aztec empire were farmers. The Aztecs used irrigation, or artificial systems for watering crops. As you can see in Eyewitness Technology: Aztec Farming on the next page, they also created new farmland by constructing artificial floating gardens called chinampas. Aztec farmers grew corn, squash, and beans on these chinampas.

Culture and Religion Tenochtitlán was a magnificent capital city. It had huge temples, busy markets, wide streets and canals, and floating gardens. It even had a zoo. The markets were filled with food, gold and silver jewelry, feathers, and fine crafts. The emperor and nobles lived in splendid palaces and had many slaves to serve them.

In the temples, priests performed rituals, including human sacrifice, or the offering of human lives, to please their gods. Aztec priests also used an advanced calendar based on the Maya calendar. Aztec astronomers also predicted eclipses and the movements of planets. They kept records using hieroglyphics similar to those used by the Mayas.

Background: Global Perspectives

Hieroglyphics The term *hieroglyph*, meaning "sacred carving," was used by the Greeks to describe the characters on Egyptian monuments. Eventually, *hieroglyphic* was applied to the picture-writing of other cultures, such as the Mayas. The Mayan writing system is pictorial, but bears no other relation to Egyptian hieroglyphics.

Answer

Draw Conclusions The sun was an important element in determining the calendar.

Aztec Farming

The Aztec city of Tenochtitlán, in central Mexico, grew quickly. The Aztecs soon used up all the farmland that was available on the island. To grow more crops, they learned how to create new farmland. At the outskirts of town, Aztec farmers dug canals through the marshy land to make small plots called *chinampas,* or "floating beds." People could paddle canoes through the many canals running among the chinampas.

The Floating City: Tenochtitlán
This painting shows what Tenochtitlán looked like. Built on a small island in the middle of a lake, it grew to a city of 200,000 people.

2 Mud and vegetation are piled onto mats that rest on the water's surface.

1 Wooden posts are set up to hold the sides of each plot in place.

3 Willow trees are planted to keep the mud in place. Over time, their roots will anchor the chinampas to the bottom of the lake.

4 Woven reeds are placed along the sides of the mud and vegetation to hold them in.

5 More layers of mud and fertile manure are added until the land is ready to plant.

6 Maize grows tall on a fully developed chinampa.

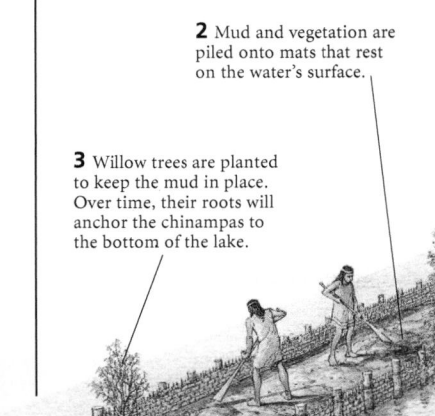

Modern-Day Living
Today, most of the lakes used by the Aztecs have been drained and covered by city growth. However, some chinampas are still used as farmland. The photo at the left shows Mexicans farming chinampas today.

> **ANALYZING IMAGES**
> How did the planting of willow trees make the Aztecs' chinampas more stable?

 Differentiated Instruction

For Gifted and Talented L3
Read the following quotation from Bernal Díaz del Castillo, one of the first Spaniards to see Tenochtitlán:
"Some of the soldiers among us who had been in many parts of the world, in Constantinople, and all over Italy, and in Rome, said that so large a market place and so full of people ... they had never beheld before."

Ask students **What can you conclude about the population of the Aztec capital from this eyewitness account? How do you think the Spanish might have felt when they first saw the city of Tenochtitlán?** *(The population must have been very large. The Spanish might have been in awe of the city, impressed by its wealth, or might have felt intimidated by so many people.)*

Aztec Farming

Guided Instruction L2
Have students read the first paragraph on this page. As a class, look at the diagram and read the numbered captions. Then have students discuss their answers to the Analyzing Images question. Then direct students' attention to the photos and their captions.

Independent Practice
Have students work in pairs to create an "Instruction Manual" for growing a crop using the Aztec Farming method. Students should create a list of the numbered steps, and include drawings of each step.

Assess and Reteach

Assess Progress L2
Have students complete the Section Assessment. Administer the *Section Quiz.*

   All in One Latin America Teaching Resources, *Section Quiz,* p. 142

Reteach L1
If students need more instruction, have them read this section in the Reading and Vocabulary Study Guide.

   Chapter 12, Section 1, **Western Hemisphere Reading and Vocabulary Study Guide,** pp. 132–134

Answers

ANALYZE IMAGES Over time, the roots of the willow trees anchored the chinampas to the bottom of the lake.

Extend

L3

Have students further explore the Mayan civilization by doing this chapter's *Small Group Activity* about the Mayan mathematic system.

AllinOne Latin America Teaching Resources, *Small Group Activity: Mayan Math Bowl,* p. 165–168

Answers

Generalize Students may answer that people are fascinated by the ancient culture.

✓ Reading Check The Aztecs traded crops, crafts, weapons, tools and luxury goods. Porters carried the goods because the Aztecs had no pack animals. Trade was usually done by barter.

Section 1 Assessment

Key Terms

Students' sentences should reflect knowledge of each Key Term.

Target Reading Skill

Students should be able to identify a difficult or unfamiliar word or unclear idea and explain how rereading helped their comprehension.

Comprehension and Critical Thinking

1. (a) Mayas built great cities, many of which were religious centers. Mayan farmers grew many crops; the most important was maize. Mayas designed an accurate calendar and wrote using hieroglyphics. **(b)** Their civilization was advanced with highly educated people in science and technology. **(c)** The Mayan civilization had people who were highly skilled mathematicians.

2. (a) The emperor ruled over the people; nobles and priests helped the emperor rule; warriors fought battles; traders carried goods; craftspersons created works of art. Most people were farmers. **(b)** 1100s—the Aztec arrived in the Valley of Mexico; 1325 —they settled on an island in Lake Texcoco, and built the city of Tenochtitlán; 1400s— warriors began conquering other people in the region **(c)** Answers will vary but should include that conquered people were probably unhappy about being forced to work for and pay tribute to the Aztecs.

Past Meets Present
This girl is sketching an Aztec statue at the site of the Great Temple of the Aztecs in Mexico City. **Generalize** *Why do you think people still flock to see and study Aztec ruins?*

Aztec Medicine Aztec doctors were able to make more than 1,000 medicines from plants. They used the medicines to lower fevers, cure stomachaches, and heal wounds. Aztec doctors also set broken bones and practiced dentistry.

Trade Because of the power of the Aztec army, traders could travel long distances in safety. Crops from distant parts of the empire were brought to the capital and to other cities. Crafts, weapons, and tools were also carried throughout the empire and beyond. Luxury goods such as jaguar skins, cacao beans, and fine jewelry were also traded. These goods were carried by people called porters, because the Aztecs did not have pack animals to carry loads. Trade was usually done by barter, or the exchange of goods without the use of money.

The End of the Aztec Empire The Aztecs did not abandon their fine cities as the Mayas had done. Instead, they were conquered by newcomers from a faraway land. You will read about how the Aztec empire fell later in this chapter.

✓ Reading Check How was trade carried out in the Aztec empire?

 Section **1** Assessment

Key Terms
Review the key terms at the beginning of this section. Use each term in a sentence that explains its meaning.

Target Reading Skill
What word or idea were you able to clarify by rereading? Explain how rereading helped.

Comprehension and Critical Thinking
1. (a) Identify Describe the main features of Mayan civilization.

(b) Conclude What do the facts that Mayas created accurate calendars and great cities tell about their civilization?
(c) Infer What can you infer about the mathematical skills of the Mayas?
2. (a) Describe How was Aztec society organized?
(b) Sequence Tell how the Aztecs created their large and powerful empire.
(c) Infer How do you think the conquered peoples felt about being ruled by the Aztecs? Explain your answer.

Writing Activity
If you could interview an ancient Maya or Aztec about his or her life, what would you ask? Write some questions that would help you understand one of these civilizations. Organize your questions into at least three different topics.

Writing Tip First decide which civilization to focus on. Then use the blue headings in the section to help you decide on topics. Reread the text under the headings to get ideas for your questions.

372   Latin America

Writing Activity
Use the *Rubric for Assessing a Writing Assignment* to evaluate students' interview questions.

AllinOne Latin America Teaching Resources, *Rubric for Assessing a Writing Assignment,* p. 174

Prepare to Read

Objectives
In this section you will
1. Find out how the Incas created their empire.
2. Understand what Incan civilization was like.
3. Learn how the descendants of the Incas live today.

Taking Notes
As you read this section, look for details of Incan civilization. Copy the web below and fill in the ovals with information about the Incas.

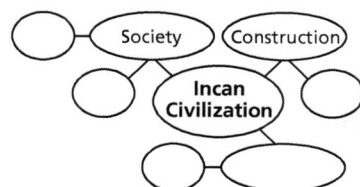

 Target Reading Skill

Read Ahead Reading ahead can help you understand something you are not sure of in the text. If you do not understand a certain word or passage, keep reading. The word or idea may be clarified further on. For example, at first you may not understand why a second runner begins running beside the first one in the first paragraph below. Read the second paragraph to find the term *relay runners*. That will help you understand the idea in paragraph one.

Key Terms
- **Cuzco** (KOOS koh) *n.* capital of the Incan empire
- **Topa Inca** (TOH puh ING kuh) *n.* emperor of the Incas, who expanded their empire
- **census** (SEN sus) *n.* an official count of all the people in an area
- **quipu** (KEE poo) *n.* knotted strings on which the Incas recorded information
- **aqueduct** (AK wuh dukt) *n.* a pipe or channel that carries water from a distant source

The runner sped along the mountain road. He lifted a horn made from a shell to his lips and blew. A second runner appeared and began running beside him. Without stopping, the first runner gave the second runner the message he carried. The second runner was gone like the wind. He would not stop until he reached the next runner.

The Incas used relay runners to spread news from one place in their empire to another. Incan messengers carried news at a rate of 250 miles (402 kilometers) a day. Without these runners, controlling the vast empire would have been very difficult.

An Incan runner blowing a conch shell and carrying a quipu

 Target Reading Skill [L2]
Read Ahead Point out the Target Reading Skill. Tell students to keep reading if a word or an idea in a paragraph is not clear because it may be clarified further on.

Model reading ahead by reading the first sentence under the subhead Government and Records from p. 375: "The government of the Incan empire was carefully organized." Tell students to read ahead to the next paragraph to clarify how the emperor governed and kept track of his empire.

Give students *Reread or Read Ahead*. Have them complete the activity in their groups.

All in One **Latin America Teaching Resources,** *Reread or Read Ahead,* p. 159

Objectives
Social Studies
1. Find out how the Incas created their empire.
2. Understand what Incan civilization was like.
3. Learn how the descendants of the Incas live today.

Reading/Language Arts
Read ahead to help clarify a word or an idea.

Prepare to Read

Build Background Knowledge [L2]
In this section, students will learn about an ancient civilization located in South America. Ask students to quickly preview the headings and visuals in the section with this question in mind: **How does the Incan civilization differ from the Mayan and Aztec civilizations?** Provide a few simple examples to get students started. Conduct an Idea Wave (TE, p. T35) to generate a list.

Set a Purpose for Reading [L2]
- Preview the Objectives.
- Form students into pairs or groups of four. Distribute the *Reading Readiness Guide*. Ask students to fill in the first two columns of the chart. Use the Numbered Heads participation structure (TE, p. T36) to call on students to share one piece of information they already know and one piece of information they want to know.

All in One **Latin America Teaching Resources,** *Reading Readiness Guide,* p. 144

Vocabulary Builder
Preview Key Terms [L2]
Pronounce each Key Term, then ask students to say the word with you. Provide a simple explanation such as "Every ten years the United States takes a census to count how many people live in our country."

Instruct

The Rise of the Incas L2

Guided Instruction

- **Vocabulary Builder** Clarify the high-use words **conquest** and **loyalty** before reading.

- Have students read The Rise of the Incas using the Partner Paragraph Shrinking technique. (TE, p. T34). As students read, circulate and make sure individuals can answer the Reading Check question.

- Discuss how the Inca were able to acquire a vast empire. *(through wars and conquest, by demanding loyalty from conquered peoples)*

- Ask students **Why do you think it was important to Pachacuti that conquered peoples were loyal to the Incas?** *(If conquered people were disloyal, they might rebel and try to fight against Pachacuti and the Incas. Pachacuti would then have to divide his forces to fight the rebellions.)*

Independent Practice

Ask students to create the Taking Notes graphic organizer on a blank piece of paper. Then have them fill in a few of the circles with the information they have just learned. Briefly model how to identify which details to record.

Monitor Progress

As students fill in the graphic organizer, circulate and make sure individuals are choosing the correct details. Provide assistance as needed.

⊙ Target Reading Skill L2

Read Ahead As a follow up, ask students to answer the Target Reading Skill question in the Student Edition. *(The Incan Empire was over 2,500 miles [4,023 kilometers] long and had 12 million people. The answer is found in the third paragraph on the page.)*

Answers

☑ Reading Check   by forcing those who were disloyal to leave their land and replacing them with people who were loyal

Chart Skills Identify The Mayan civilization lasted more than 600 years, the Incan civilization only 97 years. Analyze Information The two early dates show important milestones in the growth of the Aztec civilization before it became an empire.

Read Ahead The paragraph at the right says that the Incan empire was "large and powerful." Read ahead to find out how big it was. Where did you find the answer?

■ **Timeline Skills**

Three great civilizations are shown on the timeline. Vertical lines indicate specific events. Horizontal brackets show periods of time. **Identify** Which civilization lasted the longest? Which empire lasted the shortest time? **Analyze Information** Why does the timeline show two dates for the Aztecs before the beginning of their empire?

The Rise of the Incas

The large and powerful empire of the Incas had small beginnings. In about 1200, the Incas settled in **Cuzco** (KOOS koh), a village in the Andes that became the Incan capital city. It is now a city in the country of Peru. Most Incas were farmers. They grew maize and other crops. Through wars and conquest, the Incas won control of the entire Cuzco Valley, one of many valleys that dot the Andes Mountains.

In 1438, Pachacuti (pahch ah KOO tee) became ruler of the Incas. The name Pachacuti means "he who shakes the earth." Pachacuti conquered the people of the Andes and the Pacific coast, from Lake Titicaca north to the city of Quito in present-day Ecuador. Pachacuti demanded loyalty from the people he conquered. If they were disloyal, he forced them off their land. He replaced them with people loyal to the Incas.

Later, Pachacuti's son, **Topa Inca,** became emperor of the Incas. He expanded the empire. In time, it stretched some 2,500 miles (4,023 kilometers) from what is now Ecuador south along the Pacific coast through Peru, Bolivia, Chile, and Argentina. The 12 million people ruled by the Incas lived mostly in small villages.

☑ **Reading Check**   **How did Pachacuti make sure conquered peoples were loyal to the Incas?**

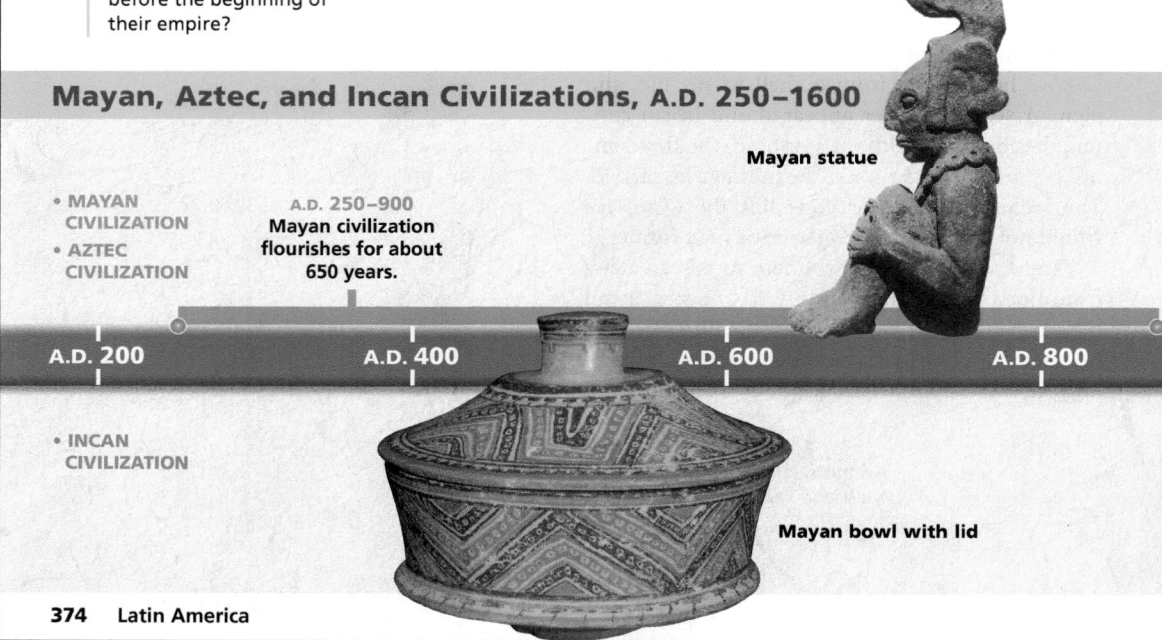

Mayan, Aztec, and Incan Civilizations, A.D. 250–1600

Mayan statue

- MAYAN CIVILIZATION
- AZTEC CIVILIZATION

A.D. 250–900 Mayan civilization flourishes for about 650 years.

- INCAN CIVILIZATION

| A.D. 200 | A.D. 400 | A.D. 600 | A.D. 800 |

Mayan bowl with lid

374 Latin America

Vocabulary Builder

Use the information below to teach students this section's high-use words.

High-Use Word	Definition and Sample Sentence
conquest, p. 374	*n.* the act of gaining something by using force. After its **conquest,** the Spanish had to rebuild the country.
loyalty, p. 374	*n.* the quality or state of being faithful. Her dog showed his **loyalty** by barking when the doorbell rang.
descendant, p. 377	*n.* a person who comes from an ancestor or group of ancestors. The Quechuas are **descendants** of the ancient Incas.

Incan Civilization

The Incas were excellent farmers, builders, and managers. The Incan capital, Cuzco, was the center of government, trade, learning, and religion. In the 1500s, one of the first Spaniards to visit Cuzco described it as "large enough and handsome enough to compare to any Spanish city."

The emperor, along with the nobles who helped him run the empire, lived in the city near the central plaza. Nobles wore special headbands and earrings that showed their high rank. Most of the farmers and workers outside Cuzco lived in mud-brick huts.

Government and Records The government of the Incan empire was carefully organized. The emperor chose nobles to govern each province. Each noble conducted a census so that people could be taxed. A **census** is an official count of all the people in an area. Local officials collected some of each village's crops as a tax. The villagers also had to work on government building projects. However, the government took care of the poor, the sick, and the elderly.

The Incas did not have a written language. Incan government officials and traders used **quipus** (KEE pooz), knotted strings on which they recorded information. Each quipu had a main cord with several colored strings attached to it. Each color represented a different item, and knots of different sizes at certain distances stood for numbers.

Keeping Count
Incan quipus like this one recorded information about births, deaths, trade, and taxes. **Generalize** What would be some advantages and disadvantages of this system of record keeping?

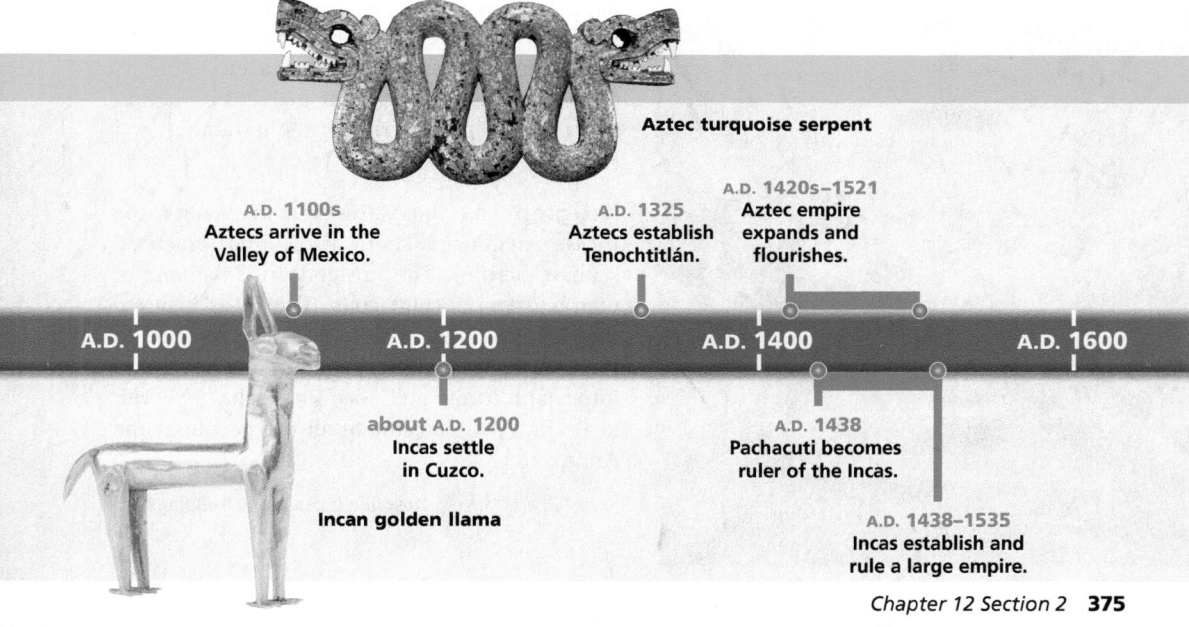

Aztec turquoise serpent

A.D. 1100s
Aztecs arrive in the Valley of Mexico.

A.D. 1325
Aztecs establish Tenochtitlán.

A.D. 1420s–1521
Aztec empire expands and flourishes.

A.D. 1000   A.D. 1200   A.D. 1400   A.D. 1600

about A.D. 1200
Incas settle in Cuzco.

Incan golden llama

A.D. 1438
Pachacuti becomes ruler of the Incas.

A.D. 1438–1535
Incas establish and rule a large empire.

Chapter 12 Section 2 **375**

Differentiated Instruction

For Gifted and Talented L3
The peoples of Central and South America did not have the wheel, yet they overcame major physical barriers to build great cities. Have students research how the Aztecs and Incas constructed cities without the wheel. Students may present their findings in the form of an illustrated report or by building models of some of the technology used.

Incan Civilization   L2

Guided Instruction
- Read about the achievements of the Inca in Incan Civilization.
- Ask students to discuss what aspects of Incan civilization are similar to the community in which they live. (*The government is responsible for conducting a census, collecting taxes, and taking care of the poor, the sick, and the elderly; public buildings are used as government or religious centers; roads and bridges transport goods, information, and people; aqueducts carry water to city centers and farms.*)
- Have students discuss the most important aspects of Incan religion. (*The Incas worshipped many gods and practiced human sacrifice; Inti and Viracocha were two important Inca gods.*)

Independent Practice
Have students complete the graphic organizer by filling in the remaining circles about Incan civilization.

Monitor Progress
- Show *Section Reading Support Transparency LA 32* and ask students to check their graphic organizers individually. Go over key concepts and clarify key vocabulary as needed.

  Latin America Transparencies, *Section Reading Support Transparency LA 32*

Answers
Generalize Advantages—could record a lot of information on quipus, quipus might last longer than paper; Disadvantages—quipus take up a lot of space, hard to learn

The Quechua: Descendants of the Incas L2

Guided Instruction

- **Vocabulary Builder** Clarify the high-use word **descendant** before reading.

- Read how Incan descendants combine ancient and modern traditions in The Quechua: Descendants of the Incas.

- Ask students **What traditions do the Quechua maintain that reflect their Incan heritage?** (*farming methods, spinning and weaving, distinctive clothing style*)

Independent Practice
Assign *Guided Reading and Review*.

All In One **Latin America Teaching Resources,** *Guided Reading and Review,* p. 145

Monitor Progress
Tell students to fill in the last column of the *Reading Readiness Guide*. Ask them to evaluate if what they learned was what they had expected to learn.

All In One **Latin America Teaching Resources,** *Reading Readiness Guide,* p. 144

Answers

Reading Check Incan buildings were constructed without modern tools. Stoneworkers cut stones so that they fit together perfectly without mortar or cement.

Roads, Bridges, and Aqueducts The Incas built more than 14,000 miles (22,530 kilometers) of roads. The roads went over some of the most mountainous land in the world. The road system helped the Incas to govern their vast empire. Not only did runners use the roads to deliver messages, but Incan armies and trade caravans also used the roads for speedy travel.

In addition to roads, the Incas needed bridges to span the deep gorges of the Andes Mountains. Gorges are narrow passes or valleys between steep cliffs. In the Andes, swift-moving rivers often flow through gorges. The Incas developed rope bridges to carry people safely over these dangerous spaces. The bridges were made of braided vines and reeds. Similar bridges are still in use today in the Andes.

The Incas also built canals and aqueducts to carry water to dry areas. An **aqueduct** is a pipe or channel that carries water from a distant source. One stone aqueduct carried water from a mountain lake almost 500 miles (805 kilometers) to its destination. The system of canals and aqueducts allowed the Incas to irrigate land that was otherwise too dry to grow crops.

Incan Buildings The Incas were masters of building with stone. They constructed cities, palaces, temples, and fortresses without the use of modern tools. Using only hammers and chisels, Incan stoneworkers cut large stones so precisely that they fit together without mortar or cement. The stones fit together so tightly that even today a piece of paper cannot be slipped between them. Many Incan structures can still be seen in Peru. The most famous Incan ruin is Machu Picchu (MAH choo PEEK choo), a city that includes buildings, stairs carved into the side of the mountain, and roads cut into bare rock.

Religion Like the Mayas and the Aztecs, the Incas worshipped many gods and practiced human sacrifice. The sun god, Inti, was one of their most important gods. The Incas believed that Inti was their parent, and they referred to themselves as "children of the sun." Another important Incan god was Viracocha (vee ruh KOH chuh), the creator of all the people of the Andes.

√ Reading Check **Describe Incan stone buildings.**

The Quechua: Descendants of the Incas

The Spanish conquered the Incan empire in the 1500s. However, descendants of the Incas still live in present-day Peru, Ecuador, Bolivia, Chile, and Colombia. They speak Quechua (KECH wuh), the Incan language.

Today, many of the Quechua live high in the Andes. Although they are isolated from many aspects of modern life, they have been influenced by it. For example, their religion combines elements of Roman Catholic and traditional practices.

Most Quechua who live in the mountains grow only enough food to feed their families. They continue to use farming methods similar to those of the ancient Incas. They also continue the weaving traditions of the Incas. They spin wool and weave fabric much as their ancestors did. They use this brightly colored cloth with complex patterns for their own clothing and also sell it to outsiders. Their clothing styles, such as the distinctive poncho, also reflect their Incan heritage.

Terrace Farming
The Incas built terraces into the sides of steep slopes to increase their farmland and to keep soil from washing down the mountains.
Infer *Why do you think terrace farming is still used in the Andes Mountains today?*

✓ **Reading Check** **How do the Quechua preserve Incan culture?**

Section 2 Assessment

Key Terms
Review the key terms at the beginning of this section. Use each term in a sentence that explains its meaning.

Target Reading Skill
What word or idea were you able to clarify by reading ahead? Where did you find this clarification?

Comprehension and Critical Thinking
1. (a) Recall Where and when did the Incas create their empire?

(b) Sequence List the major events in the creation of the Incan empire in order.
2. (a) Identify What were the major achievements of Incan civilization?
(b) Draw Conclusions Why were a good network of roads and record keeping important to the Incan empire?
3. (a) Describe How do the descendants of the Incas live now?
(b) Infer Why do you think the Quechua still do many things the way their ancestors did?

Writing Activity
Which of the Incan achievements do you think was most important in creating their large and rich empire? Explain your choice in a paragraph. Give at least two reasons for your choice.

Go Online
PHSchool.com

For: An activity on the Incas
Visit: PHSchool.com
Web Code: lfd-1202

Assess Progress L2
Have students complete the Section Assessment. Administer the *Section Quiz.*

 Latin America Teaching Resources, *Section Quiz, p. 146*

Reteach L1
If students need more instruction, have them read this section in the Reading and Vocabulary Study Guide.

Chapter 12, Section 1, **Western Hemisphere Reading and Vocabulary Study Guide,** pp. 135–137

Extend L3
Have students discover more about Incan building methods by completing the *Long Term Integrated Project: Building Models of Housing Around the World.* Assign students to work groups to work on the project.

Go Online
PHSchool.com **For:** Long Term Integrated Project: *Building Models of Housing Around the World*
Visit: PHSchool.com
Web Code: lfd-1202

Answers

Infer The people of the Andes still need to farm as much land as possible.

✓ **Reading Check** The Quechua preserve their Incan culture by continuing to use farming methods and weaving traditions similar to those of the ancient Incas.

Writing Activity
Use the *Rubric for Assessing a Writing Assignment* to evaluate students' paragraphs.

 **Latin America Teaching Resources,** *Rubric for Assessing a Writing Assignment,* p. 174

Section 2 Assessment

Key Terms
Students' sentences should reflect knowledge of each Key Term.

Target Reading Skill
Students should identify a word or idea they were uncertain about and indicate where they found clarification.

Comprehension and Critical Thinking
1. (a) The Incas created their empire in about 1200 in Cuzco, a village in the Andes of what is today Peru. **(b)** 1200—settled in Cuzco; 1438—Pachacuti conquered the people of the Andes and the Pacific coast; later Topa Inca expanded the empire even more; 1500s—the Spaniards conquered the Incas.

2. (a) a well-organized government; earthquake-proof buildings; roads and bridges; canals and aqueducts; the quipu **(b)** Roads connected all parts of the empire and made travel easier. Good record keeping made the government efficient.

3. (a) The Quechua live in the Andes and practice farming and weaving traditions similar to those of the ancient Incas. **(b)** The Quechua are subsistence farmers who are isolated from many aspects of modern life.

Objectives

Social Studies

1. Learn why Europeans sailed to the Americas.

2. Find out how the conquistadors conquered the Aztecs and the Incas.

3. Understand how the Spanish empire was organized and how colonization affected the Americas.

Reading/Language Arts

Paraphrase to understand and remember what you have read.

Prepare to Read

Build Background Knowledge `L2`

Tell students that in this section they will learn about the Europeans' effect on the history of Latin America. Show *Pizzaro and the Empire of Gold*, then ask students what they think will happen when Europeans arrive in Latin America. Use an Idea Wave (TE, p. T35) to solicit answers.

📼 *Pizarro and the Empire of Gold,*
World Studies Video Program

Set a Purpose for Reading `L2`

■ Preview the Objectives.

■ Form students into pairs or groups of four. Distribute the *Reading Readiness Guide.* Ask students to fill in the first two columns of the chart. Use the Numbered Heads participation structure (TE, p. T36) to call on students to share one piece of information they already know and one piece of information they want to know.

All in One Latin America Teaching Resources, *Reading Readiness Guide,* p. 148

Vocabulary Builder
Preview Key Terms

Pronounce each Key Term, then ask students to say the word with you. Provide a simple explanation such as, "In Brazil, farmers grow banana trees or coffee beans on large haciendas made up of hundreds of acres of land."

Prepare to Read

Objectives

In this section you will

1. Learn why Europeans sailed to the Americas.

2. Find out how the conquistadors conquered the Aztecs and the Incas.

3. Understand how the Spanish empire was organized and how colonization affected the Americas.

Taking Notes

As you read this section, look for the major events in the European conquest of Latin America. Copy the timeline below, and record the events in the proper places on it.

Columbus arrives
in the Americas.

```
  |----+--------+--------|
1490 1492
```

Target Reading Skill

Paraphrase When you paraphrase, you restate what you have read in your own words. This process can help you understand and remember what you read.

Key Terms

• **Moctezuma** (mahk tih ZOO muh) *n.* ruler of the Aztec empire at the time the Spanish arrived there

• **Christopher Columbus** (KRIS tuh fur kuh LUM bus) *n.* Italian explorer sponsored by Spain who landed in the West Indies in 1492

• **conquistador** (kahn KEES tuh dawr) *n.* one of the conquerors who claimed and ruled land in the Americas for the Spanish government in the 1500s

• **Hernán Cortés** (hur NAHN kohr TEZ) *n.* conquistador who conquered the Aztec empire

• **Francisco Pizarro** (frahn SEES koh pea SAHR oh) *n.* conquistador who conquered the Incas

• **mestizo** (meh STEE zoh) *n.* in Latin America, a person of mixed Spanish and Native American ancestry

• **hacienda** (hah see EN dah) *n.* a large farm or plantation

One day in 1519, the Aztec ruler **Moctezuma** (mahk tih ZOO muh) received startling news. Something strange had appeared offshore. He sent spies to find out about it. The spies reported back to Moctezuma:

> ❝We must tell you that we saw a house in the water, out of which came white men, with white hands and faces, and very long, bushy beards, and clothes of every color: white, yellow, red, green, blue, and purple, and on their heads they wore round hats.❞
>
> —*An Aztec spy*

The white men with round hats were a Spanish military force. They had sailed to the coast of Mexico in search of treasure. They would bring great changes to the land of the Aztecs.

Cortés meets Moctezuma, in a 1976 mural by Roberto Cueva del Rio.

378 Latin America

Target Reading Skill `L2`

Paraphrase Point out the Target Reading Skill. Tell students that paraphrasing, or restating what they have read in their own words, can help them understand and remember what they have read.

Model using paraphrasing by restating the quotation in the second paragraph of this page. (*The spies said they saw what looked like a house in water and strange white men with colorful clothes and round hats.*)

Give students *Paraphrase*. Have them complete the activity in groups.

All in One Latin America Teaching Resources, *Paraphrase,* p. 160

Tabula nouarum infularum, quas diuerfis refpectibus Occidentales & Indianas uocant.

> Columbus thought he had reached these islands in 1492.

> Many explorers set sail from Spain.

> This flag shows that Spain claimed this land.

> This flag shows Portugal's claim to this land.

Europeans Arrive in the Americas

In the 1400s, the European nations of Spain and Portugal were searching for new trade routes to Asia. They knew that in Asia they would find goods such as spices and silks. These goods could be traded for huge profits in Europe.

Columbus Reaches America Christopher Columbus, an Italian explorer, thought he could reach Asia by sailing west across the Atlantic Ocean. Columbus knew the world was round, as did most educated Europeans. But Columbus believed the distance around the world was shorter than it is. First Columbus asked Portugal to sponsor his voyage. Portugal refused. Then he asked Spain. Queen Isabella of Spain finally agreed.

Columbus set sail in early August, 1492. Some 10 weeks later, on October 12, he spotted land. Columbus thought he had reached the East Indies in Asia, so he called the people he met Indians.

Mapping the Americas
This 1540 map is based on information supplied by Columbus and other explorers. Also shown is an astrolabe, a navigational instrument from the 1500s. Infer *Find the islands Columbus was looking for, and the Caribbean islands he found instead. Why do you think he thought they were the same?*

Instruct

Europeans Arrive in the Americas L2

Guided Instruction

■ **Vocabulary Builder** Clarify the high-use word **profit** before reading.

■ Read Europeans Arrive in the Americas using the Structured Silent Reading technique (TE, p. T34).

■ Ask students **Why did European nations begin exploring other parts of the world?** *(They were searching for new trade routes to Asia.)*

■ Ask students **How did Spain and Portugal divide the continent of South America?** *(The Treaty of Tordesillas set the Line of Demarcation that gave Spain land and the right to trade west of the line and Portugal the same east of the line.)*

■ Ask students to locate the Line of Demarcation on the map on p. 382. Then ask **What country benefited the most from the Line of Demarcation? Why?** *(Spain; it received the right to settle and trade on much more land than Portugal.)*

Independent Practice

Ask students to create the Taking Notes graphic organizer on a blank piece of paper. Then have them fill in the time line with dates and events they have just learned.

Monitor Progress

As students fill in the graphic organizer, circulate and make sure individuals did not miss any dates or events and that they are written in chronological order.

Answers

Infer Columbus may have thought he had found the right islands because the ones he did find were in a similar harbor.

The Success of the Conquistadors

L2

Guided Instruction

- **Vocabulary Builder** Clarify the high-use words **supernatural** and **fearless** before reading.

- Ask students to read about how Cortés and Pizarro defeated two of the most powerful empires in the Americas in The Success of the Conquistadors. As students read, circulate and make sure individuals can answer the Reading Check question.

- Ask students **Why were Spanish explorers interested in conquering kingdoms in the Americas?** *(They were in search of gold and other treasures.)*

- Ask students to predict what might have happened if Moctezuma and the Aztecs defeated Cortés and his army. Allow students to share answers with a partner before responding. *(Possible answers include: Cortés and his men may have been forced to pay tribute to Moctezuma; more Spaniards may have come from Spain to continue fighting the Aztecs.)*

Dividing a Continent Spain and Portugal each sent explorers to the Americas and tried to stop the other country from claiming land there. In 1494, the two nations signed an important treaty. (A treaty is an agreement in writing made between two or more countries.) The Treaty of Tordesillas (tawr day SEE yahs) set an imaginary line from the North Pole to the South Pole at about 50°W longitude, called the Line of Demarcation. It gave Spain the right to settle and trade west of the line. Portugal could do the same east of the line. The only part of South America that is east of the line is roughly the eastern half of present-day Brazil. Because of the Treaty of Tordesillas, the language and background of Brazil are Portuguese.

✓ Reading Check **Why did Spain and Portugal become rivals?**

The Success of the Conquistadors

Spanish explorers heard stories of wealthy kingdoms in the Americas. They hoped to find gold and other treasures there. Spanish rulers did not pay for the expeditions of the explorers. Instead, they gave the conquistadors (kahn KEES tuh dawrs), or conquerors, the right to hunt for treasure and to settle in the Americas. In exchange, conquistadors agreed to give Spain one fifth of any treasures they found.

Sculpture of the Aztec god Quetzalcoatl

Cortés Conquers the Aztecs Aztec rulers demanded heavy tribute from the peoples they had conquered. When the conquistador **Hernán Cortés** arrived in Mexico in 1519, he found many of these groups willing to help him against the Aztecs.

Cortés headed for Tenochtitlán with 500 soldiers and 16 horses. Aztec spies saw them coming. They had never seen horses before. Moctezuma's spies described the Spanish as "supernatural creatures riding on hornless deer, armed in iron, fearless as gods."

Moctezuma thought Cortés might be the god Quetzalcoatl (ket sahl koh AHT el). Quetzalcoatl had promised to return and rule the Aztecs. With a heavy heart, Moctezuma welcomed Cortés and his soldiers. Cortés tried to convince Moctezuma to surrender to Spain and then seized him as a hostage. After a brief period of peace, Spanish soldiers killed some Aztecs. Then the Aztecs rebelled against the Spanish. By the end of the fighting, Moctezuma was dead, and Cortés and his army barely escaped.

With the help of the Aztecs' enemies, Cortés defeated the Aztecs in 1521. By then, about 240,000 Aztecs had been killed and so had 30,000 of Cortés's allies. Tenochtitlán and the Aztec empire lay in ruins, but the region had been claimed for Spain.

Answers

✓ Reading Check Spain and Portugal became rivals because each country sent explorers to the Americas and tried to stop one another from claiming land there.

Skills Skills Mini Lesson
for Life

Analyzing Primary Sources

1. Teach the skill by telling students that a primary source is an eyewitness account or observation of an event. It can include facts as well as opinions. Primary sources include letters, diaries, interviews, speeches, photographs, paintings, and newspapers.

2. Have students practice this skill by analyzing the second paragraph on page 378.

Ask students if they think this is a primary source and why. Have students identify the eyewitnesses to this event and explain how they know.

3. Have students apply the skill by reading Christopher Columbus' *Journal Entry*. Ask them to identify and analyze the primary source.

All in One **Latin America Teaching Resources,** *Journal Entry*, p. 172

Pizarro Conquers the Incas Francisco Pizarro (frahn SEES koh pea SAHR oh) was also a Spanish conquistador. He heard stories about the rich Incan empire. In 1531, Pizarro sailed to the Pacific coast of South America with a force of 180 Spanish soldiers. The Spanish captured and killed the Incan emperor and many other Incan leaders. By 1535, Pizarro had conquered most of the Incan empire, including the capital, Cuzco.

In only 15 years, the conquistadors had defeated the two most powerful empires in the Americas. How did they do it? The Spanish had guns and cannons and horses, all of which the Native Americans had never seen. Native American weapons were far less powerful. The Europeans also carried diseases such as smallpox, measles, and chicken pox. The Native Americans had never been exposed to these diseases, and entire villages got sick and died. Also, because of local rivalries, some Native Americans were eager to help the Spanish conquistadors.

✓ **Reading Check** What are two reasons the conquistadors were able to conquer the Aztecs and the Incas?

Advantages of the Conquistadors
This illustration shows conquistadors using guns ❶ to fight Aztec soldiers armed with spears ❷ . For protection, the Spanish have metal helmets, ❸ while the Aztecs use feather and animal skin shields ❹ .
Contrast *What other items in the picture might have contributed to the Spanish victory?*

■ Ask students **How were the Spanish able to defeat the Native Americans?** *(They had guns and horses, which the Native Americans had never seen; Native American weapons were far less powerful; the Spanish carried diseases that sickened and killed entire villages; they were able to use local rivalries to enlist the help of some Native American groups.)*

Independent Practice
Have students continue to fill in the graphic organizer with dates and events from The Success of the Conquistadors.

Monitor Progress
As students fill in the graphic organizer, circulate and make sure individuals are choosing the correct details. Provide assistance as needed.

Differentiated Instruction

For English Language Learners 🔲2️⃣
Students may have difficulty pronouncing some of the longer words in this section, such as *supernatural, surrounded, surrendered*, and *diseases*. Encourage students to break down these words into smaller parts and sound out the pronunciations.

For Advanced Readers 🔲3️⃣
Give students the Aztec story *The Talking Stone* to learn more about Moctezuma and the Aztec culture.

All in One Latin America Teaching Resources, *The Talking Stone*, pp. 169–171

Answers
Contrast The picture shows that the conquistadors also have full body armor and a crossbow. Both items would have helped the conquistadors to defeat the Aztecs.

✓ **Reading Check** Possible answers: The conquistadors had guns, cannons, and horses; they carried diseases that wiped out entire villages; they received help from enemies of the Aztecs and Incas.

Colonization

Guided Instruction

- **Vocabulary Builder** Clarify the meaning of the high-use word **superior** before reading.

- Ask students to read Colonization and review the map and diagram on pages 382 and 383.

- Ask students to explain how Spain organized its territory. *(The territory was divided into provinces that were ruled by viceroys appointed by the king.)*

- Discuss with students how Spain's colonization of Latin America affected the region. *(European culture became an influence in the region; Christianity was introduced; Native Americans were enslaved and affected by disease; new industries were introduced; the new products influenced trade.)*

Independent Practice

Have students complete the graphic organizer with dates and events from Colonization.

Target Reading Skill

Paraphrase As a follow up, ask students to answer the Target Reading Skill question in the Student Edition. *(Possible answer: Settlers from many European nations came to Latin America to 1) spread the Christian religion, 2) find gold and riches, 3) farm. The settlers created colonies that would benefit them.)*

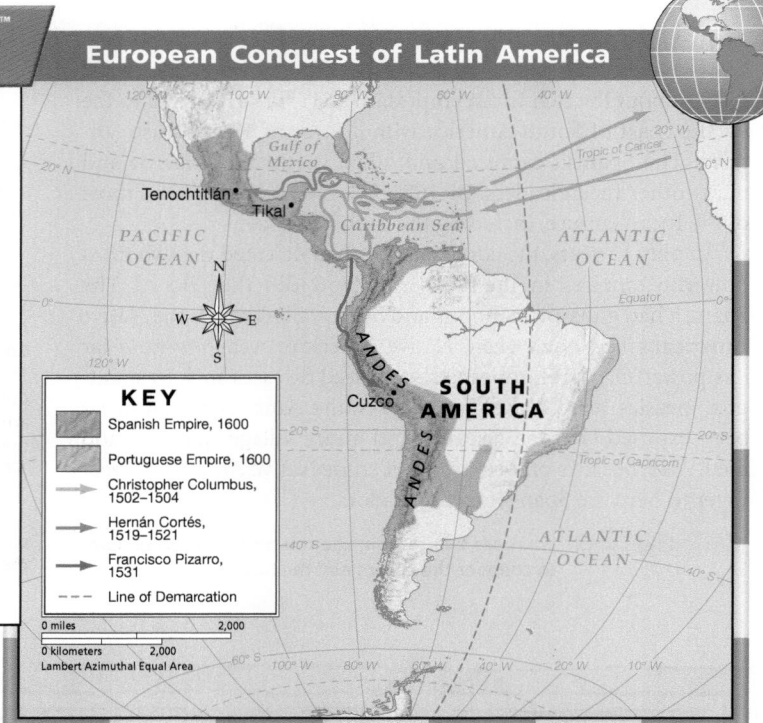

MAP MASTER™ Skills Activity

European Conquest of Latin America

Movement The map shows Columbus's last voyage from Spain and the voyages of the conquistadors who conquered the Aztecs and the Incas. **Locate** Cortés and Pizarro were already in Latin America when they began their conquests. Find their starting points. **Identify Causes** Why were much of the Portuguese and Spanish empires located along the coasts? Why might the Spanish Empire have extended inland in certain areas?

Go Online PHSchool.com Use Web Code **lfp-1213** for **an interactive map.**

KEY

- Spanish Empire, 1600
- Portuguese Empire, 1600
- Christopher Columbus, 1502–1504
- Hernán Cortés, 1519–1521
- Francisco Pizarro, 1531
- Line of Demarcation

0 miles 2,000
0 kilometers 2,000
Lambert Azimuthal Equal Area

Colonization

By the 1600s, Spain claimed land throughout much of the Americas. Spain's lands stretched from southern South America all the way north into the present-day United States, and included some islands in the Caribbean Sea. Later, the French and English also claimed some Caribbean islands. Portugal claimed Brazil.

European Settlers Arrive Settlers from Spain, Portugal, and other European nations began arriving in what came to be called Latin America. Some of them were missionaries, sent by the Catholic Church to spread Christianity to the peoples of the Americas. Others came to look for gold and other mineral riches. Still others wanted to settle and farm the land. If the Native American people resisted, the newcomers used their superior force to suppress them. The Europeans created the kinds of colonies that would benefit them and the countries from which they had come.

Paraphrase
Read the paragraph at the right carefully and then paraphrase it, or restate it in your own words. In your paraphrase, you might number the reasons people came to the Americas.

Answers

MAP MASTER™ Skills Activity **Locate** Cortés started in present-day Cuba; Pizarro in present-day Panama. **Identify Causes** The coasts were accessible by sailing vessel; the Spanish may have used rivers to extend inland.

Go Online PHSchool.com Students may practice their map skills using an online version of this map.

Skills Mini Lesson

Skills for Life

Recognizing Bias

1. Teach the skill by telling students that bias, or prejudice, involves judging what a person is like based on assumptions or a stereotype, rather than on that person's individual qualities.

2. Practice the skill by discussing how European actions, such as demanding taxes or labor from Native Americans, show that Europeans prejudged the Native Americans.

3. Apply the skill by asking **What kinds of biases or opinions might the Spanish have had about the Native Americans that led to this treatment?** *(Europeans might have thought that their culture and ways of life were superior to that of the Native Americans.)*

Spain Organizes Its Empire Spain controlled the largest portion of the Americas south of what is now the United States. The king of Spain wanted to keep strict control over his empire, so the territory was divided into provinces. The king appointed viceroys, or representatives who ruled the provinces in the king's name. Other settlers who had been born in Spain helped the viceroys rule. Meanwhile, a council in Spain supervised the colonial officials to make sure they did not become too powerful.

The two most important provinces in Spain's American empire were New Spain and Peru. The capital of New Spain was Mexico City. Lima became the capital of Peru.

Spanish social classes determined where people lived in Lima. The most powerful citizens lived in the center of the city. They either came from Spain or had Spanish parents. Mestizos, people of mixed Spanish and Native American ancestry, lived on the outskirts of Lima. Many mestizos were poor, but some were middle class or even quite wealthy. Native Americans were the least powerful class. Most Native Americans continued to live in the countryside. The Spanish forced them to work on haciendas. A hacienda (hah see EN dah) was a plantation owned by Spaniards or the Catholic Church.

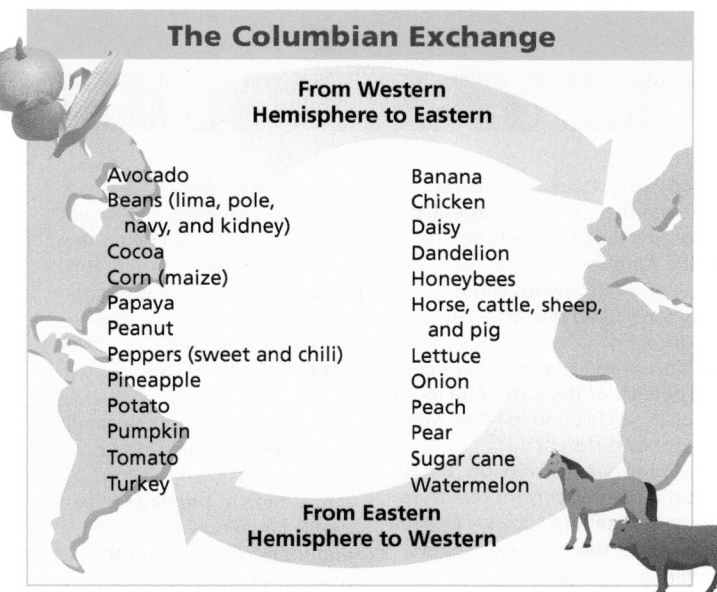

The Columbian Exchange

From Western Hemisphere to Eastern

Avocado
Beans (lima, pole, navy, and kidney)
Cocoa
Corn (maize)
Papaya
Peanut
Peppers (sweet and chili)
Pineapple
Potato
Pumpkin
Tomato
Turkey

Banana
Chicken
Daisy
Dandelion
Honeybees
Horse, cattle, sheep, and pig
Lettuce
Onion
Peach
Pear
Sugar cane
Watermelon

From Eastern Hemisphere to Western

■ **Diagram Skills**
Goods, as well as people, crossed the Atlantic Ocean in the years after Columbus's voyages. Identify Which animals were part of the exchange? Infer Which animal had the potential for making the greatest change in its new home? Explain your answer.

Monitor Progress
- Show *Section Reading Support Transparency LA 33* and ask students to check their graphic organizers individually. Go over key concepts and clarify key vocabulary as needed.

  Latin America Transparencies, *Section Reading Support Transparency LA 33*

- Tell students to fill in the last column of the *Reading Readiness Guide.* Ask them to evaluate if what they learned was what they had expected to learn.

  All in One Latin America Teaching Resources, *Reading Readiness Guide,* p. 148

Assess and Reteach

Assess Progress L2
Have students complete the Section Assessment. Administer the *Section Quiz.*

  All in One Latin America Teaching Resources, *Section Quiz,* p. 150

Reteach L1
If students need more instruction, have them read this section in the Reading and Vocabulary Study Guide.

  Chapter 12, Section 3, **Western Hemisphere Reading and Vocabulary Study Guide,** pp. 138–140

Extend L3
Show students *Pizarro and the Empire of Gold.* Have them paraphrase how Pizarro and his small army were able to defeat the much larger Incan army.

  Pizarro and the Empire of Gold, **World Studies Video Program**

┌─ **Background: Biography** ─

Defender of the Indians
Bartolomé de Las Casas, born in Seville, Spain, in 1474, was a Spanish missionary and historian who spoke out against the Europeans' harsh treatment of Native Americans. He had witnessed the abuses that Native Americans had suffered and worked to improve their conditions. Las Casas' work helped Spain pass the New Laws in 1542, which brought about some improvements in the lives of the Native Americans in the Spanish colonies. Las Casas also contributed to our knowledge of Spanish colonies in America through his writings in *History of the Indies.* He died in Madrid in July 1566.

Answers

Diagram Skills Identify Chickens, honeybees, horses, cattle, sheep, pigs Infer Horses had the potential to make great changes because the people in the Western Hemisphere had no domesticated animals capable of carrying people and goods as well as horses.

Answers

Explain Diseases weakened Native American resistance to Spanish rule.

✓ Reading Check The Native American population declined because of overwork, malnutrition, and European diseases.

Section 3 Assessment

Key Terms
Students' sentences should reflect knowledge of each Key Term.

⟳ Target Reading Skill
During the first 50 years of Spanish rule the Native American population declined greatly. Because they needed more workers, the Spanish began importing enslaved Africans. Meanwhile, European demand for products from the Americas grew.

Comprehension and Critical Thinking
1. (a) Europeans reached the Americas while searching for new trade routes to Asia; once in the Americas they searched for gold and other treasures, and wanted to spread Christianity. **(b)** It divided the land; land west of the line was settled by Spain; land east of the line was settled by Portugal.

2. (a) Hernán Cortés conquered the Aztecs; Francisco Pizarro conquered the Incas. **(b)** Similar: Both were conquered by the Spanish; their enemies helped the conquistadors; their emperors were killed; Different: At first Cortés was welcomed by Moctezuma, but then the Aztecs revolted and were ultimately defeated by Cortés; the Incan emperor was immediately killed by Pizarro and his men; Tenochtitlán was in ruins after it was conquered; Cuzco was preserved. **(c)** Answers will vary, but possible answers include: The conquistadors had weapons and horses; they carried diseases that wiped out entire villages; they received help from both empires' enemies.

3. (a) The territory was divided into provinces; the king of Spain appointed viceroys to rule the provinces; Spanish settlers helped the viceroys rule; a council in Spain supervised the colonial officials to curb their power. **(b)** The Spanish forced Native Americans to work on haciendas and in mines. Many died from overwork, malnutrition, and disease. Then the Spanish brought millions of enslaved Africans to work in the Americas.

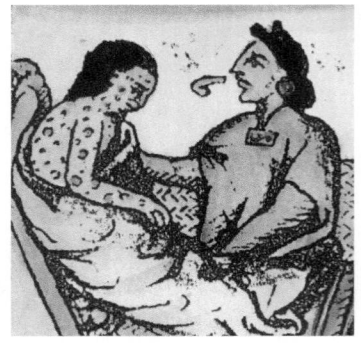

Devastating Diseases
This 1500s illustration shows a medicine man treating an Aztec for smallpox. Native Americans had never been exposed to European diseases. **Explain** *How did these diseases contribute to the success of Spanish rule?*

The Effect of European Rule Spain gave its settlers encomiendas (en koh mee EN dahs), which were rights to demand taxes or labor from Native Americans. At first, the Native Americans were forced to work only on the haciendas. But when silver was discovered in Mexico and Peru, the Spanish forced them to work in the mines as well. Many Native Americans died from overwork, malnutrition, and European diseases. Others rebelled unsuccessfully against the Spanish.

In the first 50 years of Spanish rule, the Native American population of New Spain declined from an estimated 25 million to 3 million. The Spanish now needed more workers for their haciendas and mines. They began importing enslaved Africans in large numbers. In Europe, the demand for products from the Americas continued to grow. Even more workers were needed. Millions more slaves were brought from Africa.

Brazil The situation was somewhat different in Brazil, which was a colony of Portugal. Most settlers remained near the coast. They took land from the Native Americans for sugar plantations and cattle ranches. Brazil also came to depend on the forced labor of Native Americans and enslaved Africans.

✓ Reading Check **Why did the Native American population decline?**

 Section 3 Assessment

Key Terms
Review the key terms at the beginning of this section. Use each term in a sentence that explains its meaning.

⟳ Target Reading Skill
Paraphrase the second paragraph on this page. Present ideas in the order they appear in the paragraph.

Comprehension and Critical Thinking
1. (a) Recall Explain why Europeans came to the Americas in the 1500s.

(b) Identify Cause and Effect How did the Treaty of Tordesillas affect the European settlement of the Americas?
2. (a) Identify Which conquistadors conquered the Aztecs and the Incas?
(b) Compare In what ways were the defeats of the Aztec and Incan empires similar, and in what ways were they different?
(c) Evaluate Information What was the most important reason for the conquistadors' success? Explain.
3. (a) Describe How was Spain's empire organized?
(b) Draw Conclusions How did the Spanish conquest affect Native Americans and Africans?

Writing Activity
Review how Moctezuma's spies described the Spanish when they saw them for the first time. How do you think those spies might have described you and your friends? Write a brief description from their point of view.

> **Writing Tip** Notice the details in the description by Moctezuma's spies. Then focus on similar details. Use descriptive words for color, size, texture, and sound. Remember the point of view of the speaker: a Native American of the 1500s.

Writing Activity
Use the *Rubric for Assessing a Writing Assignment* to evaluate students' descriptions.

All in One **Latin America Teaching Resources,** *Rubric for Assessing a Writing Assignment,* p. 174

Independence

Prepare to Read

Objectives
In this section you will
1. Learn what events inspired revolutions in Latin America.
2. Find out how Mexico gained its independence.
3. Discover how Bolívar and San Martín helped bring independence to South America.

Taking Notes
As you read the section, look for the ways revolutionary leaders helped bring independence to Latin America. Copy the table below and use it to record the name and accomplishments of each person.

Leader	Country	Accomplishment

Target Reading Skill

Summarize When you summarize, you restate the main points you have read in the correct order. Because you leave out less important details, a summary is shorter than the original text. Summarizing is a good technique to help you comprehend and study. As you read, pause to summarize occasionally.

Key Terms
- **Toussaint L'Ouverture** (too SAN loo vehr TOOR) *n.* leader of Haiti's fight for independence
- **revolution** (rev uh LOO shun) *n.* overthrow of a government, with another taking its place
- **criollo** (kree OH yoh) *n.* a person with Spanish parents who was born in Latin America
- **Simón Bolívar** (see MOHN boh LEE vahr) *n.* a South American revolutionary leader
- **José de San Martín** (hoh SAY deh sahn mahr TEEN) *n.* a South American revolutionary leader
- **caudillo** (kaw DEE yoh) *n.* a military officer who rules a country very strictly

On August 24, 1791, the night sky over Saint-Domingue (san duh MAYNG) glowed red and gold. The French Caribbean colony was on fire. The slaves were sick of being mistreated by their white masters. They finally had rebelled. Now they were burning every piece of white-owned property they could find. This Night of Fire was the beginning of the first great fight for freedom in Latin America. Toussaint L'Ouverture (too SAN loo vehr TOOR), a former slave, led the people of Saint-Domingue in this fight for independence for more than 10 years. Eventually they won, and they founded the independent country of Haiti (HAY tee) in 1804.

The Seeds of Revolution

The flame of liberty lit in Haiti soon spread across Latin America. By 1825, most of the region was independent. Latin Americans would no longer be ruled by Europe.

Toussaint L'Ouverture

Target Reading Skill

Summarize Point out the Target Reading Skill. Tell students that when summarizing a paragraph or section they should include only the main points in the correct order and omit the less important details.

Model the skill by summarizing the first paragraph on this page. "The Night of Fire was the first battle for independence in Latin America. Toussaint L'Ouverture led the people of Saint-Domingue in their fight for independence for more than 10 years. Eventually Haiti became an independent country in 1804."

Give students *Summarize*. Have them complete the activity in their groups.

All in One **Latin America Teaching Resources,** *Summarize,* p. 161

Objectives
Social Studies

1. Learn what events inspired revolutions in Latin America.
2. Find out how Mexico gained its independence.
3. Discover how Bolívar and San Martín helped bring independence to South America.

Reading/Language Arts

Summarize to understand the main points you have read in the correct order.

Prepare to Read

Build Background Knowledge   `L2`

Tell students that they will learn how the countries of Latin America won their independence in this section. Remind students about how Americans celebrate their independence on the Fourth of July. Ask **Why is independence so important to Americans?** Use the Idea Wave participation strategy (TE, p. T35) to generate a list.

Set a Purpose for Reading   `L2`

- Preview the Objectives.
- Read each statement in the *Reading Readiness Guide* aloud. Ask students to mark the statements true or false.

    All in One **Latin America Teaching Resources,** *Reading Readiness Guide,* p. 152

- Have students discuss the statements in pairs or groups of four, then mark their worksheets again. Use the Numbered Heads participation structure (TE, p. T36) to call on students to share their group's perspectives.

Vocabulary Builder
Preview Key Terms   `L2`

Pronounce each Key Term, then ask students to say the word with you. Provide a simple explanation such as, "The American colonists fought the American Revolution to free themselves from British rule."

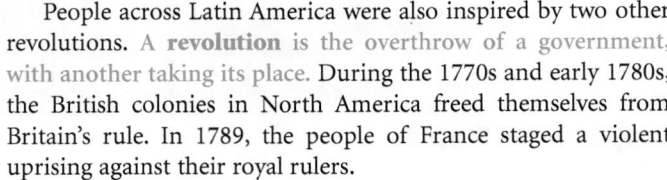

Instruct

The Seeds of Revolution
L2

Guided Instruction
- Read The Seeds of Revolution using the Re Quest Procedure (TE, p. T35).

- Ask students **Who were the criollos?** *(Latin Americans who had Spanish parents; they were often the wealthiest and best-educated people in the Spanish colonies, but had little political power.)*

- Ask students **What effect did the American and French revolutions have on Latin Americans?** *(They inspired ideas of independence in many Latin Americans.)*

Independent Practice
Ask students to create the Taking Notes table on a blank piece of paper. Then have them fill in the columns with information about Toussaint L'Ouverture.

Monitor Progress
As students fill in the table, circulate and make sure individuals summarize L'Ouverture's accomplishments, omitting the less important details.

Answers

✓ Reading Check The American and French Revolutions inspired ideas of independence in Latin America. **Analyze Images** Some of the people behind Hidalgo seem to be Native Americans, while others are dressed as farmers or soldiers. The painter may be suggesting that Hidalgo was supported by many different groups of people.

People across Latin America were also inspired by two other revolutions. A **revolution** is the overthrow of a government, with another taking its place. During the 1770s and early 1780s, the British colonies in North America freed themselves from Britain's rule. In 1789, the people of France staged a violent uprising against their royal rulers.

Criollos (kree OH yohz) paid particular attention to these events. A **criollo** had Spanish parents, but had been born in Latin America. Criollos often were the best-educated and wealthiest people in the Spanish colonies, but they had little political power. Only people born in Spain could hold government office. Many criollos attended school in Europe. There, they learned about the ideas that inspired revolution in France and the United States.

The criollos especially liked the idea that people had the right to govern themselves. However, they were frightened by the slave revolt in Haiti. The criollos wanted independence from Spain but power for themselves.

✓ Reading Check Which revolutions inspired ideas of independence in Latin America?

Cry of Dolores
This section of a mural by Juan O'Gorman shows Hidalgo and his followers. **Analyze Images** Look carefully at the people behind Hidalgo. What does the painter suggest about the Mexican Revolution by showing these people?

Independence in Mexico

Mexico began its struggle for self-government in 1810. That's when Miguel Hidalgo (mee GEL hee DAHL goh), a criollo priest, began planning the Mexican revolution. He appealed to local mestizos and Native Americans.

The "Cry of Dolores" In September 1810, the Spanish government discovered Hidalgo's plot. But before the authorities could arrest him, Hidalgo took action. He wildly rang the church bells in the town of Dolores. A huge crowd gathered. "Recover from the hated Spaniards the land stolen from your forefathers," he shouted.

Hidalgo's call for revolution became known as the "Cry of Dolores." It attracted some 80,000 fighters, mostly mestizos and Native Americans. The rebels won some victories, but their luck soon changed. By the beginning of 1811, they were in full retreat. Hidalgo tried to flee the country, but government soldiers soon captured him. He was convicted of treason and then executed by firing squad in July 1811.

386　Latin America

Vocabulary Builder

Use the information below to teach students this section's high-use words.

High-Use Word	Definition and Sample Sentence
authorities, p. 386	*n.* persons in command The **authorities** looked into the incident.
forefathers, p. 386	*n.* ancestors My **forefathers** came from Spain.

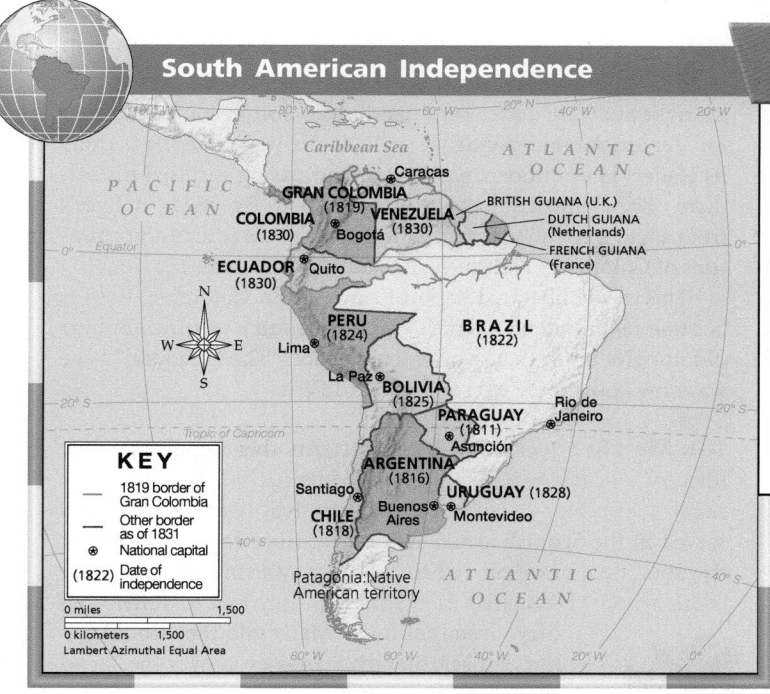

Regions After freeing themselves from Spain, several former colonies formed Gran Colombia, modeled after the United States. **Identify** Which modern nations were part of Gran Colombia? **Compare** Look at the map of South America on page 331. Compare Peru's modern borders to those of 1831.

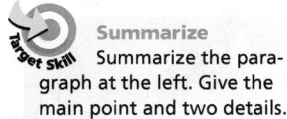

Go Online
PHSchool.com Use Web Code **lfp-1214** for step-by-step **map skills practice**.

Mexico Becomes Independent The Spanish could execute the revolution's leaders, but they could not kill its spirit. Small rebel groups kept fighting. Then a high-ranking officer in the Spanish army, Agustín de Iturbide (aw guh STEEN deh ee toor BEE day), joined the rebels. Many wealthy people who had viewed Hidalgo as a dangerous hothead trusted Iturbide to protect their interests. He was a criollo and an army officer. They decided to support the rebellion. In 1821, Iturbide declared Mexico independent.

✓ Reading Check **What groups made up most of Hidalgo's army?**

South American Independence

Simón Bolívar (see MOHN boh LEE vahr), one of South America's most important revolutionary leaders, was born in Venezuela in 1783. His family was one of the richest and most important families in Latin America. When Bolívar was at school in Spain, he met Prince Ferdinand, the heir to the Spanish throne. He played a game similar to present-day badminton with the prince. Custom required that Bolívar show respect for the prince by losing. Instead, Bolívar played hard and tried to win. He even knocked the prince's hat off with his racquet! The angry prince demanded an apology. Bolívar refused. He claimed it was an accident.

Target Skill

Summarize
Summarize the paragraph at the left. Give the main point and two details.

Chapter 12 Section 4 **387**

Independence in Mexico and South American Independence L2

Guided Instruction

- **Vocabulary Builder** Clarify the high-use words **authorities** and **forefathers** before reading.

- Read how Latin America became free from Spain's rule in Independence in Mexico and South American Independence. As students read, circulate and make sure individuals can answer the Reading Check questions.

- Ask students **What was the "Cry of Dolores?"** (*Miguel Hidalgo's call for revolution against Spain in Mexico*)

- Ask students **How did Mexico become independent in 1821?** (*Agustín de Iturbide, a criollo leader in the Spanish army, joined with mestizo and Native American rebel forces to declare independence.*)

- Ask students to brainstorm what qualities they think make a hero. Do the qualities of a hero fit the description of the leaders they have read about? Who? Why? Use a Numbered Heads participation strategy (TE, p. T36) to have students answer these questions.

- Ask students **What challenges might the newly independent countries face?** (*Possible challenges: remaining unified, organizing their governments, finding good leaders, rebuilding their economies.*)

Target Reading Skill L2

Summarize As a follow up, ask students to answer the Target Reading Skill question in the Student Edition. (*Possible answer: Símon Bolívar as a young man defied authority. He refused to lose a game to Prince Ferdinand and even knocked Ferdinand's hat off.*)

Differentiated Instruction

For Less Proficient Readers L1
Have students read the section in the Reading and Vocabulary Study Guide. This version provides basic-level instruction in an interactive format with questions and write-on lines.

📖 Chapter 12, Section 4, **Western Hemisphere Reading and Vocabulary Study Guide**, pp. 141–143

For Advanced Readers L3
Have students work in pairs to create posters for or against seeking independence from Spanish rule. The posters should urge people to support their position. Use the *Rubric for Assessing a Student Poster* to evaluate students' posters.

All in One **Latin America Teaching Resources**, *Rubric for Assessing a Student Poster*, p. 175

Answers

✓ Reading Check Mestizo and Native American groups made up most of Hidalgo's army.

MAP MASTER Skills Activity **Identify** the modern nations of Colombia, Panama, Venezuela, and Ecuador **Compare** Peru used to extend further inland, but had less land along the coast to the South.

Independent Practice

Have students complete the table of leaders and their accomplishments.

Monitor Progress

■ Show *Section Reading Support Transparency LA 34* and ask students to check their graphic organizers individually. Go over key concepts and clarify key vocabulary as needed.

📖 **Latin America Transparencies,** *Section Reading Support Transparency LA 34*

■ Tell students to fill in the last column of the *Reading Readiness Guide*. Probe for what they learned that confirms or invalidates each statement.

All in One **Latin America Teaching Resources,** *Reading Readiness Guide,* p. 152

Citizen Heroes

Read **Citizen Heroes** on this page. Ask students **How do Martí's efforts to free his country from Spain compare to those of San Martín?** *(Martí, like San Martín, dedicated his life to fighting for independence from Spanish rule.)*

Assess and Reteach

Assess Progress   L2

Have students complete the Section Assessment. Administer the *Section Quiz.*

All in One **Latin America Teaching Resources,** *Section Quiz,* p. 154

Reteach   L1

If students need more instruction, have them read this section in the Reading and Vocabulary Study Guide.

📖 Chapter 12, Section 4, **Western Hemisphere Reading and Vocabulary Study Guide,** pp. 141–143

Citizen Heroes

To Be a Leader: José Martí

José Martí grew up in Cuba when it was still a Spanish colony. At the age of 16, he started a newspaper dedicated to Cuban independence. After he supported an 1868 uprising, Martí was sent to prison. He spent many years in exile, working for Cuban freedom by writing and publishing, and by helping to form a revolutionary party. In 1895, Martí led an invasion of Cuba to free the island from Spanish rule. He was killed on the battlefield a month later—seven years before Cuba achieved independence. This statue of Martí is in New York City's Central Park.

388 Latin America

Bolívar, The Liberator Many years later, Bolívar and Ferdinand faced off again. This time, Bolívar knocked Spanish America right out from under Ferdinand's feet. Bolívar joined the fight for Venezuelan independence in 1807. Six years later he became its leader. His confidence, courage, and daring inspired his soldiers. They enjoyed victory after victory. By 1822, Bolívar's troops had freed a large area from Spanish rule (the future countries of Colombia, Venezuela, Ecuador, and Panama).

This newly liberated region formed Gran Colombia. Bolívar became its president. Even though his country was free, Bolívar did not give up the cause of independence. "The Liberator," as he was now known, turned south toward Peru.

San Martín Fights for Freedom Another important revolutionary leader was **José de San Martín** (hoh SAY deh sahn mahr TEEN). He was an Argentine who had lived in Spain and served in the Spanish army. When Argentina began its fight for freedom, he quickly offered to help. San Martín took good care of his troops. He shared each hardship they had to suffer, and they loved him for it. Many said they would follow San Martín anywhere—even over the snow-capped Andes Mountains.

In 1817, his soldiers had to do just that. San Martín led them through high passes in the Andes into Chile. This bold action took the Spanish completely by surprise. In a matter of months, Spain was defeated. San Martín declared Chile's independence. Then he, too, turned his attention to Peru.

Again, San Martín planned a surprise. This time, he attacked from the sea. The Spanish were not prepared, and their defenses quickly collapsed. In July 1821, San Martín pushed inland and seized Lima, the capital of Peru.

An Important Meeting A year later, San Martín met with Bolívar to discuss the fight for independence. Historians do not know what happened in that meeting. But afterward, San Martín suddenly gave up his command. He left Bolívar to continue the fight alone. Eventually, Bolívar drove the remaining Spanish forces out of South America altogether. By 1825, only Cuba and Puerto Rico were still ruled by Spain.

Background: Links Across Time

African Independence Although Europe is closer to Africa than Latin America, most Europeans began to colonize Africa later. Many Europeans established formal colonies in Africa in the late 1800s. Like the people of Latin America, many people in Africa later were inspired by the ideas of self-government and independence. African countries began to achieve independence in the 1950s, 1960s, and 1970s.

Brazil Takes a Different Route Portugal's colony, Brazil, became independent without fighting a war. In the early 1800s, during a war in Europe, French armies invaded Spain and Portugal. Portugal's royal family fled to Brazil for safety. The king returned to Portugal in 1821. However, he left his son, Dom Pedro, to rule the colony. Dom Pedro took more power than the king expected. He declared Brazil independent in 1822. Three years later, Portugal quietly admitted that Brazil was independent.

Independence Brings Challenges Simón Bolívar dreamed of uniting South America as one country, a "United States of South America." Gran Colombia was the first step. But Bolívar found that his dream was impossible. Latin America was a huge area, divided by the Andes and dense rain forests. Also, the leaders of the countries in Gran Colombia wanted little to do with Bolívar. In poor health, he retired from politics.

Even though he did not remain in office, Bolívar set the standard for Latin American leaders. Most were **caudillos** (kaw DEE yohz), military officers who ruled very strictly. Bolívar cared about the people he governed. However, many caudillos did not. These later caudillos only wanted to stay in power and get rich. You will read about how these caudillos affected the nations they governed in the next section.

This July 2000 parade in Bogotá celebrates 181 years of Colombian independence.

✔ **Reading Check** What are two reasons that South America was not united into one country?

Section 4 Assessment

Key Terms
Review the key terms at the beginning of this section. Use each term in a sentence that explains its meaning.

Target Reading Skill
Write a summary of the last two paragraphs on this page. Include a main point and several details from each paragraph.

Comprehension and Critical Thinking
1. (a) Identify What events inspired independence movements in Latin America?

(b) Identify Cause and Effect Why were many criollos in favor of independence?

2. (a) Describe How did Hidalgo begin the Mexican Revolution?
(b) Analyze Information Explain why Iturbide was successful and Hidalgo was not.

3. (a) Recall What were the achievements of Bolívar, San Martín, and Dom Pedro?
(b) Infer What do you think Bolívar had in mind when he wanted to create the "United States of South America"?

Writing Activity
Suppose you are a soldier in Bolívar's or San Martín's army. Describe what you are doing, why you are doing it, and how you feel about your commander.

> **Writing Tip** Remember to write your description in the first person, using the pronouns *I* or *we*. Use vivid words, such as *terrified, exhausted,* or *thrilled,* to describe your feelings.

Chapter 12 Section 4 **389**

Writing Activity
Use the *Rubric for Assessing a Writing Assignment* to evaluate students' descriptions.

All in One **Latin America Teaching Resources,** *Rubric for Assessing a Writing Assignment,* p. 174

Extend   L3
Assign students to work groups to prepare a talk show featuring the heroes of the Latin American independence movement as guests. Individual group members should: prepare questions to ask the heroes, create props, write the script, assign roles for heroes and talk show host, and rehearse the show. Call on groups to present their shows to the class.

Answers

✔ Reading Check   South America was a huge area, divided by the Andes and dense rain forests. Also, the leaders of the countries in Gran Colombia did not want to unite South America as one country.

Section 4 Assessment

Key Terms
Students' sentences should reflect an understanding of each Key Term.

Target Reading Skill
Bolívar dreamed of uniting South America as one country, but found his dream was impossible. South America was too large, and leaders of the Gran Colombia countries did not want to have anything to do with him. Bolívar became the model for Latin American leaders. He was a caudillo, but he cared about the people he governed. Other caudillos that followed only wanted to have power and get rich.

Comprehension and Critical Thinking
1. (a) the American and French Revolutions
(b) The criollos wanted independence from Spain because they wanted political power.
2. (a) In 1810 Hidalgo's "Cry of Dolores" attracted 80,000 fighters, mostly mestizos and Native Americans. **(b)** Many people viewed Hidalgo as dangerous, but they trusted Iturbide who was a criollo and a high-ranking officer in the Spanish army. As a result, they supported the rebellion.
3. (a) Bolívar and San Martín were liberators who fought against the Spanish for the independence of countries in South America. Dom Pedro peacefully gained independence for Brazil from Portugal. **(b)** Possible answers: Bolívar wanted to unite all the countries under one central government; he also might have wanted to create a government like that of the United States.

Objective

Learn how to sequence and make a timeline.

Prepare to Read

Build Background Knowledge `L2`

Ask students to think about one activity they have done each day over the last five days. Then ask how they might show these activities in the order in which they occurred.

Instruct

Sequencing Making a Timeline `L2`

Guided Instruction

■ Read the steps to make a timeline as a class and write them on the board.

■ Practice the skill by following the steps on p. 390 as a class. If students are uncomfortable disclosing events from their past, tell them that they are free to make up entries. No one will call them on incorrect events. Model each step in the activity by suggesting a name for the timeline (*History of the First 10 Years of My Life*) and providing simple examples of events. (*moving to a new place, starting a new school, or learning to ride a bicycle*)

■ Have students write their events on separate index cards. Make sure that students choose beginning and end dates that will encompass all their entries. Ask students to put all their events in chronological order. Then have students construct their timelines on a sheet of paper. Before students mark their entries on their timelines, make sure that their dates are evenly spaced.

Making a Timeline

If you want to show where cities and towns are located along a certain route, you can draw a road map. But how do you show when events occurred? In that case, you can draw a timeline.

You might say that a timeline is a map of time. It has a beginning date and an ending date. It shows when events occurred during that time period, and in what order. Look at pages 374 and 375 for an example of a historical timeline. Use a timeline whenever you need to organize a series of dates.

Golden bird made by the Incas

Learn the Skill

Use these steps to make a timeline.

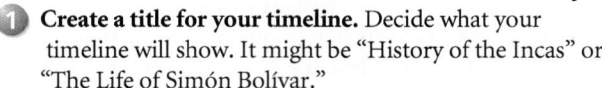 **Create a title for your timeline.** Decide what your timeline will show. It might be "History of the Incas" or "The Life of Simón Bolívar."

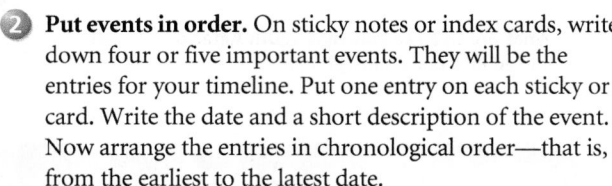 **Put events in order.** On sticky notes or index cards, write down four or five important events. They will be the entries for your timeline. Put one entry on each sticky or card. Write the date and a short description of the event. Now arrange the entries in chronological order—that is, from the earliest to the latest date.

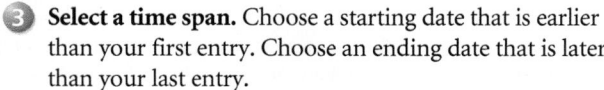 **Select a time span.** Choose a starting date that is earlier than your first entry. Choose an ending date that is later than your last entry.

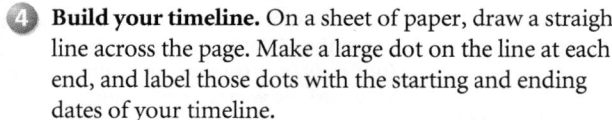 **Build your timeline.** On a sheet of paper, draw a straight line across the page. Make a large dot on the line at each end, and label those dots with the starting and ending dates of your timeline.

5 **Mark the divisions of time periods.** Divide your timeline into equal time periods. Label each one.

6 **Put your entries on the timeline.** Put a dot at the appropriate place on the timeline for each entry. From each dot, draw a straight line upward or downward. Write the text of the entry next to the straight line.

Portrait of Simón Bolívar

390 Latin America

Independent Practice

Assign *Skills for Life* and have students complete it individually.

All In One **Latin America Teaching Resources,** *Skills for Life,* p. 164

Monitor Progress

As students are completing *Skills for Life,* circulate to make sure individuals are applying the skill steps effectively. Provide assistance as needed.

Practice the Skill

Now make a timeline of your own life, the life of someone you know, or the life of someone famous. Create the timeline by following the steps below.

1 Your timeline can cover an entire life or some portion of it. Choose a title that reflects the topic and the time span.

2 Decide which important events you want to include. Write the events with their dates on sticky notes or index cards, and arrange them chronologically, that is, from the earliest to the latest date.

3 Choose starting and ending dates that include all your entries.

4 Draw your timeline and mark the starting and ending dates.

5 Add the time periods to your drawing. For instance, if you used 1995 as your starting date, your next date might be 1998 or 2000. Make sure the dates are equally spaced along the line.

6 Add your entries to the appropriate places on your timeline.

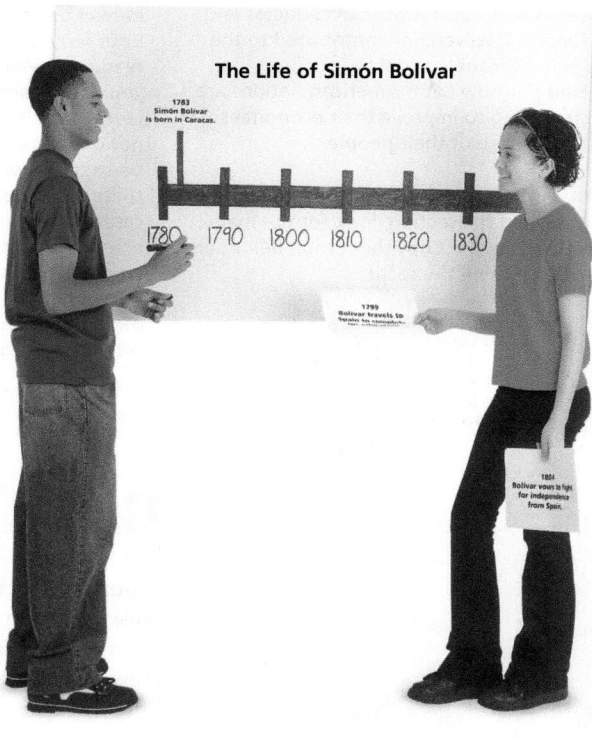

Apply the Skill

Identify what you think are the most important events in Section 4, Independence. Then create a timeline of the major events in the section, using no more than five entries.

Differentiated Instruction

For Special Needs Students L1

Partner special needs students with more proficient students to do Level 1 of the Sequencing lesson on the Social Studies Skills Tutor CD-ROM together. When students feel more confident, they can move onto Level 2 alone.

⊙ *Sequencing,* Social Studies Skills Tutor CD-ROM

Assess and Reteach

Assess Progress L2

Ask students to do the Apply the Skill activity.

Reteach L1

If students are having trouble applying the skill steps, have them review the skill using the interactive Social Studies Skills Tutor CD-ROM.

⊙ *Sequencing,* Social Studies Skills Tutor CD-ROM

Extend L3

To extend the lesson, ask students to research the life of one of the people they read about in Section 4. Then have them make a timeline of up to eight events in that person's life.

Answers
Apply the Skill

Answers will vary, but students' timelines should include dates and events from Section 4 in chronological order.

Objectives
Social Studies

1. Learn how Latin American caudillos and foreign involvement contributed to the region's troubled past.
2. Find out how Latin American nations are struggling to improve their economies and the welfare of their people.

Reading/Language Arts

Reread or read ahead to help understand words and ideas in the text.

Prepare to Read

Build Background Knowledge L2

In this section, students will read about Latin America's history from independence to the present. Write this statement on the board: After independence, the biggest problems facing Latin American nations were _____. Have students preview the section, then predict answers to the statement. Conduct an Idea Wave (TE, p. T35) to generate a list.

Set a Purpose for Reading L2

■ Preview the Objectives.

■ Read each statement in the *Reading Readiness Guide* aloud. Ask students to mark the statements true or false

> **All in One Latin America Teaching Resources,** *Reading Readiness Guide,* p. 156

■ Have students discuss the statements in pairs or groups of four, then mark their worksheets again. Use the Numbered Heads participation structure (TE, p. T36) to call on students to share their group's perspectives.

Vocabulary Builder
Preview Key Terms L2

Pronounce each Key Term, then ask students to say the word with you. Provide a simple explanation such as, "The dictator took away people's right to freedom of speech and freedom of religion."

Prepare to Read

Objectives

In this section you will
1. Learn how Latin American caudillos and foreign involvement contributed to the region's troubled past.
2. Find out how Latin American nations are struggling to improve their economies and the welfare of their people.

Taking Notes

As you read the section, look for the main ideas and details. Copy the format below, and use it to outline the section.

> I. A troubled past
>   A. Colonial legacy
>   1.
>   2.
>   3.
>   B. Foreign involvement

Slaves building a street in Rio de Janeiro, from an 1824 lithograph

392   Latin America

🎯 Target Reading Skill

Reread or Read Ahead
Both rereading and reading ahead can help you understand words and ideas in the text. If you do not understand a word or passage, use one or both of these techniques. In some cases, you may wish to read ahead first to see if the word or idea is clarified later on. If not, try going back and rereading the original passage.

Key Terms

- **dictator** (DIK tay tur) *n.* a ruler with complete power
- **export** (eks PAWRT) *v.* to send products from one country to be sold in another
- **import** (im PAWRT) *v.* to bring products into one country from another
- **foreign debt** (FAWR in det) *n.* money owed by one country to other countries
- **regime** (ruh ZHEEM) *n.* a particular administration or government

Before independence, when Latin America was ruled by European nations, many of the ordinary people of the region were very poor. In the Spanish colonies, people born in Spain held government office. Criollos were often wealthy and owned large haciendas, or plantations. However, most mestizos and Native Americans owned little land. African Americans were slaves.

A Troubled Past

Latin America has changed a great deal since the nations of the region became independent. On the other hand, many problems with their roots in the colonial past still remain today.

Colonial Legacy After Spain's Latin American colonies became independent, the criollos gained political power. However, most mestizos and Native Americans remained poor. Many continued to work on the haciendas as they had before. Even after slavery was ended, former slaves had little opportunity for a better life.

🎯 Target Reading Skill L2

Reread or Read Ahead Point out the Target Reading Skill. Tell students to reread or read ahead to help them understand unfamiliar words or clarify ideas.

Model rereading using the second paragraph on page 395. Tell students that rereading can help clarify what reformers in South American countries wanted to do. Then tell students that reading ahead to the next paragraph will help them understand what happened as reformers made their demands to the governments of South American countries.

Give students *Reread or Read Ahead.* Have them complete the activity in their groups.

> **All in One Latin America Teaching Resources,** *Reread or Read Ahead,* p. 159

Many of the new Latin American countries were ruled by caudillos. These "strongmen" ignored the democratic constitutions that had been established by their new nations. They became dictators, or rulers with complete power. There were revolts, and some dictators were overthrown. Often they were replaced by other caudillos. Life changed little for the ordinary people.

Before independence, Latin American colonies exported farm products, minerals, and other resources to Spain and Portugal. To export is to send products from one country to be sold in another. The colonies bought manufactured products from the European countries that ruled them. After independence, the new nations of Latin America were free to trade with other countries. The United States became an important trading partner for Latin America. But Latin American countries still relied on exporting farm products and minerals. And they still imported manufactured goods. To import is to bring products into one country from another.

Working on the Railroad
This railroad linking El Salvador to Guatemala was built in the 1920s by an American company, using local laborers. Identify Causes *Why do you think an American company was interested in building a railroad there?*

Instruct

A Troubled Past L2

Guided Instruction

- **Vocabulary Builder** Clarify the meaning of the high-use words **legacy** and **intervene** before reading.

- Have students read A Troubled Past using the Structured Silent Reading technique (TE, p. T34). As students read, circulate and make sure individuals can answer the Reading Check question.

- Ask students **What problems arose under the rule of the Latin American caudillos, and what happened to the ordinary people as a result?** *(They ignored the democratic constitutions established by their new nations and became dictators; as a result, independence changed little for ordinary people.)*

- Ask students **How did foreign involvement affect the newly independent countries of Latin America?** *(Latin American countries were free to trade with other countries; foreign governments also became involved in Latin American policies.)*

Independent Practice

Ask students to create the Taking Notes outline on a blank piece of paper. Then have them fill in the main ideas and details from the information they have just learned. Briefly model how to identify which details to record.

Monitor Progress

As students fill in the outline, circulate and make sure individuals are choosing the correct details. Provide assistance as needed.

Vocabulary Builder

Use the information below to teach students this section's high-use words.

High-Use Word	Definition and Sample Sentence
legacy, p. 392	*n.* anything handed down from an ancestor The ring was a **legacy** from her grandmother.
intervene, p. 394	*v.* to come or be in between His mother **intervened** and stopped the fight between him and his brother.
censor, p. 395	*v.* to remove or suppress material The government **censored** some of the official papers.

Answers

Identify Causes to transport goods between El Salvador and Guatemala

Target Reading Skill

L2

Reread or Read Ahead As a follow up, ask students to answer the Target Reading Skill question in the Student Edition. *(Answers will vary, but students should either indicate that rereading or reading ahead helped them clarify what they read.)*

The Struggle Continues

L2

Guided Instruction

- **Vocabulary Builder** Clarify the high-use word **censor** before reading.

- Together with students, read about the challenges faced by Latin American countries as they strive to advance their economies in The Struggle Continues.

- Help students to recognize the cycle that is perpetuated by borrowing and owing money. Ask students **How does the inability to pay back foreign debt make it difficult for countries to improve their economies?** *(To pay their debts countries must cut back on some services; foreign ownership of business increases, sending revenue outside of the country.)*

- Ask students to brainstorm ways in which the people in Latin American countries might address these challenges in the future. Conduct a Give One, Get One participation strategy (TE, p. T37) to generate a list of possibilities. *(Answers will vary but might include borrowing less money from other countries, increasing trade between countries, trying to export more goods and import fewer manufactured goods, and creating more jobs.)*

Answers

√ Reading Check President Roosevelt thought that the United States should keep law and order in Latin America and force Latin American nations to pay their foreign debt.

Graph Skills Identify highest – Brazil, lowest – Paraguay; **Identify Cause and Effect** The industrialized countries might have borrowed large sums of money to help them build up industries.

Reread or Read Ahead Reread or read ahead to see why the United States became involved in Latin America. Which technique helped you clarify what you reread?

Foreign Involvement Foreign companies began to buy large farms, mines, and other land in Latin America. They built seaports and railroads that made it easier to export their products. These companies were interested in taking resources out of Latin America. The United States and other foreign nations supported Latin American governments that helped these companies.

In 1903, the United States wanted to build a canal across the Isthmus of Panama, in the nation of Colombia. A canal would benefit American trade and the American navy. When Colombia refused permission to build a canal, U.S. President Theodore Roosevelt backed a revolt by the people of Panama against Colombia. Once Panama was independent, it allowed the United States to build the Panama Canal.

As owner of the Panama Canal, the United States had even more interest in Latin America. In 1904, President Roosevelt claimed that the United States had a right to keep law and order there. He also said the United States could force Latin American nations to pay their **foreign debt,** or money they owed to other countries. For the next 20 years, the United States used Roosevelt's policy to intervene in Latin America.

√ Reading Check **What role did President Roosevelt think the United States should have in Latin America?**

Graph Skills

Many Latin American nations have gone into debt to foreign countries and to world organizations. **Identify** Which country in the graph has the highest foreign debt? Which has the lowest? **Identify Cause and Effect** Brazil, Mexico, and Argentina are among the most industrialized Latin American countries. Why might building industries lead to debt?

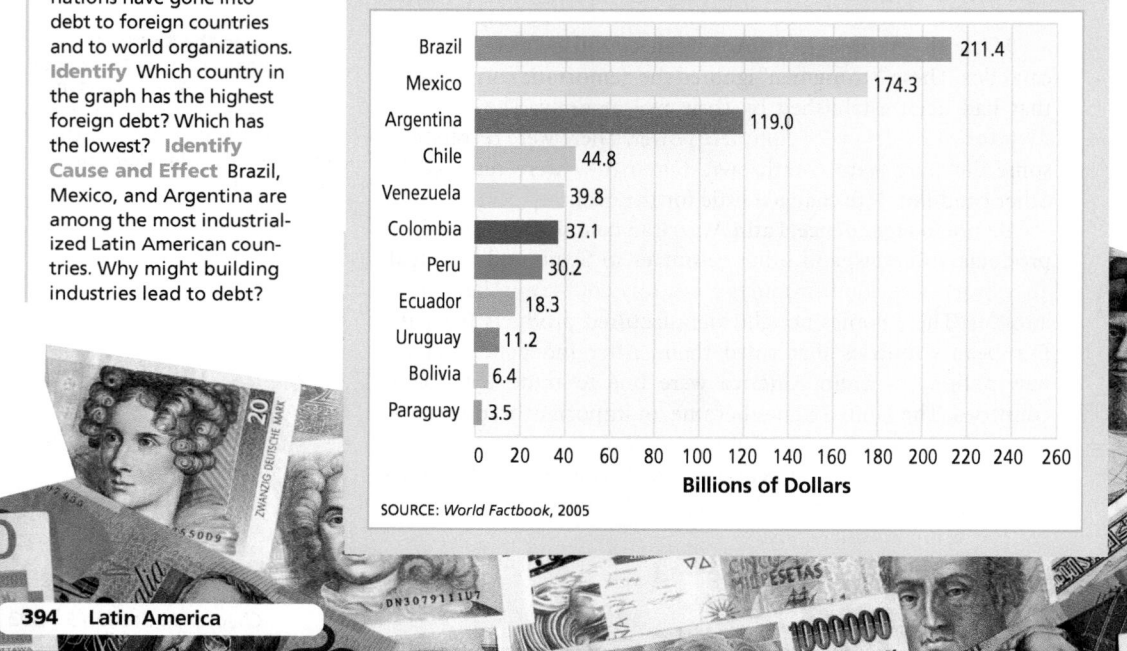

Foreign Debt of Latin American Nations, 2005

Country	Billions of Dollars
Brazil	211.4
Mexico	174.3
Argentina	119.0
Chile	44.8
Venezuela	39.8
Colombia	37.1
Peru	30.2
Ecuador	18.3
Uruguay	11.2
Bolivia	6.4
Paraguay	3.5

SOURCE: *World Factbook*, 2005

Skills Mini Lesson

Analyzing Graphic Data

1. Tell students that charts and graphs can help them see information quickly, and can also help them draw conclusions.

2. Refer students to the bar graph *Foreign Debt of Latin American Nations, 2005* on this page. Have them practice the skill by identifying the title of the graph, the labels, and any similarities or differences they notice in the information being presented in the graph. Then have them draw a conclusion about the countries and their foreign debts shown on the graph. *(Larger countries such as Brazil, Mexico, and Argentina have larger amounts of foreign debt than smaller countries.)*

3. Have students apply the skill by identifying the parts of the graph on page 405 entitled *The World's Five Largest Urban Areas, 2003* and drawing conclusions from the information illustrated on the graph.

The Struggle Continues

In the mid-1900s, there were still big gaps between the few who were rich and the many who were poor. Most of Latin America's land was owned by a small percentage of the people. Many businesses were owned by foreign companies.

The Beginnings of Reform At the same time, some groups wanted to improve conditions for the poor. Reformers of the 1930s and 1940s wanted to divide the land more equally and to diversify the economies of their countries. Some Latin American countries did begin to make reforms.

As demands for reform continued in the 1960s and 1970s, military regimes seized power in many Latin American countries. A regime is a particular administration or government. These military regimes ruled harshly. They censored the press, outlawed political parties, and imprisoned—or even killed—those who opposed them.

By the 1980s, however, some of these harsh regimes were replaced by elected governments. But problems still remained. Some elected leaders abused their power. President Alberto Fujimori of Peru, for example, dissolved Peru's legislature and later dismissed the high court justices when they disagreed with him. And many Latin American nations still had huge economic problems. One of these problems was foreign debt.

Foreign Debt Latin American countries had borrowed money to improve their economies. In the 1980s, oil prices went up at the same time that prices of many Latin American products fell. Latin American countries had to spend more money, but they were making less and less. To make up the difference, they borrowed money from wealthy countries such as the United States. Then they had to borrow more money to pay off their debts.

Although Mexico was a major oil producer, it too suffered an economic crisis. In the 1970s, Mexico began to rely more and more on oil exports to fuel its economy. But in the 1980s, more oil was being produced than the world needed. In 1982, Mexico found that it could not repay its debt.

Protests in Buenos Aires
In Argentina, foreign debt contributed to an economic crisis. In this 2003 protest, unemployed Argentines lift shovels as they march to demand jobs. **Apply Information** *Use the text to help explain how foreign debt might lead to unemployment.*

Chapter 12 Section 5 **395**

Independent Practice

Have students complete their outlines by adding main ideas and details. Tell them to continue their outlines with "II. The struggle continues," and items that fall underneath that heading.

Monitor Progress

- Show *Section Reading Support Transparency LA 35* and ask students to check their graphic organizers individually. Go over key concepts and clarify key vocabulary as needed.

  Latin America Transparencies, *Section Reading Support Transparency LA 35*

- Tell students to fill in the last column of the *Reading Readiness Guide*. Probe for what they learned that confirms or invalidates each statement.

  All in One Latin America Teaching Resources, *Reading Readiness Guide*, p. 156

Assess and Reteach

Assess Progress   L2

Have students complete the Section Assessment. Administer the *Section Quiz*.

All in One Latin America Teaching Resources, *Section Quiz*, p. 158

Reteach   L1

If students need more instruction, have them read this section in the Reading and Vocabulary Study Guide.

Chapter 12, Section 5, **Western Hemisphere Reading and Vocabulary Study Guide**, pp. 144–146

Extend   L3

Have students learn more about the history of Latin America by completing the *Enrichment* worksheet in the Latin America Teaching Resources.

All in One Latin America Teaching Resources, *Enrichment*, p. 163

Answers

Apply Information Foreign debt may lead the government to cut jobs.

Answers

☑ Reading Check When Mexico could not pay its debt, two international organizations, the World Bank and the International Monetary Fund, lent Mexico money under strict conditions.

Section 5 Assessment

Key Terms
Students' sentences should reflect knowledge of each Key Term.

⟳ Target Reading Skill
Students should identify any unfamiliar words or unclear ideas that they clarified by rereading or reading ahead.

Comprehension and Critical Thinking
1. (a) Caudillos often ignored the democratic constitutions adopted by their countries and ruled as dictators. **(b)** Latin American governments that allowed foreign companies to remove resources from Latin America were supported by the United States and other foreign countries. The United States helped Panama become independent from Colombia in order to gain permission to build the Panama Canal. **(c)** After gaining independence, the new Latin American nations were free to trade with other countries. However, they still relied on exporting farm products and minerals, and importing manufactured goods.

2. (a) Mexico borrowed money to improve its economy. When Mexico could not pay its foreign debt, it borrowed more money from the World Bank and the International Monetary Fund. As a result, the debt grew larger. **(b)** Powerful groups probably resist reform because they do not want to risk losing any of their power, wealth, or land.

Writing Activity
Use the *Rubric for Assessing a Writing Assignment* to evaluate students' paragraphs.

All in One Latin America Teaching Resources, *Rubric for Assessing a Writing Assignment,* p. 174.

Plaza in Montevideo, Uruguay
Although Latin American countries are still working to improve their economies, they do have large, thriving modern cities.

Two international organizations stepped in. The World Bank and the International Monetary Fund lent Mexico money—but there were strict conditions. Mexico found that it had to cut back on programs that helped the poor. Other Latin American countries also borrowed under these strict conditions. They had to allow more foreign ownership of businesses and farms. In Argentina, debt, unemployment, and other economic problems caused riots in the streets. In 2000, the president of Argentina was forced to resign.

Looking Toward the Future Recently, Latin American countries have tried to improve their economies by joining trade organizations. In 1994, another trade treaty came into effect—the North American Free Trade Agreement (NAFTA). It made trade easier among Mexico, the United States, and Canada.

Efforts to improve the economies and the welfare of people in Latin America continue. You will read more about these efforts in the Focus on Countries chapters later in this book.

☑ Reading Check **What happened when Mexico could not pay its debt?**

 Section 5 Assessment

Key Terms
Review the key terms at the beginning of this section. Use each term in a sentence that explains its meaning.

⟳ Target Reading Skill
What words or ideas in this section were you able to clarify by rereading or reading ahead?

Comprehension and Critical Thinking
1. (a) Describe How did caudillos rule their countries?

(b) Explain Describe foreign involvement in Latin America.
(c) Compare and Contrast How did Latin America's economy change after independence? How did it remain the same?
2. (a) Recall How did Mexico end up with a large foreign debt?
(b) Draw Conclusions The powerful groups that own the most land also run the governments of some Latin American countries. Why do you think these groups resist reform?

Writing Activity
What do you think is the most important challenge facing Latin America today? Write a paragraph explaining your choice.

For: An activity on Venezuela
Visit: PHSchool.com
Web Code: lfd-1205

Go Online PHSchool.com Typing in the Web code when prompted will bring students directly to detailed instructions for this activity.

Review and Assessment

◆ Chapter Summary

Section 1: Early Civilizations of Middle America

- The Mayas built great cities, created an advanced number system and calendars, and then mysteriously abandoned their cities.
- The Aztecs of central Mexico ruled a rich empire from their capital at Tenochtitlán, which was a center of trade and learning.

Section 2: The Incas

- The Incas built a huge empire based in what is now Peru.
- The Incas built excellent roads and aqueducts, and used quipus rather than a written language to manage their empire.
- The descendants of the Incas still live in the Andes Mountains.

Section 3: European Conquest

- Europeans came to the Americas for riches and for land.
- The conquistadors conquered the Aztecs and Incas in 15 years.
- Spain ruled a large empire in the Americas, bringing disease and enslavement to the Native Americans and importing enslaved Africans.

Mexico

Section 4: Independence

- Revolutions in North America, France, and Haiti helped inspire Latin Americans to seek independence.
- Mexico's revolution began with Hidalgo's "Cry of Dolores" and was completed by Iturbide.
- Bolívar and San Martín were the liberators of South America.

Section 5: From Past to Present

- Many problems in Latin America are the result of the region's colonial past, foreign involvement, and undemocratic governments.
- Reform movements are working to help the poor, elected governments have replaced military ones, and nations are struggling with their foreign debt.

◆ Key Terms

Define each of the terms below.

1. hieroglyphics
2. maize
3. census
4. regime
5. conquistador
6. mestizo

7. hacienda
8. revolution
9. criollo
10. caudillo
11. import
12. foreign debt

┌ Vocabulary Builder ─

Revisit this chapter's high-use words:

ritual	profit	forefathers
garment	supernatural	legacy
conquest	fearless	intervene
loyalty	superior	censor
descendant	authorities	

Ask students to review the definitions they recorded on their *Word Knowledge* worksheets.

All in One Latin America Teaching Resources, *Word Knowledge,* p. 162

Consider allowing students to earn extra credit if they use the words in their answers to the questions in the Chapter Review and Assessment. The words must be used correctly and in a natural context to earn extra points.

Review and Assessment

Review Chapter Content

- Review and revisit the major themes of this chapter by asking students to classify what Guiding Question each bulleted statement in the Chapter Summary answers. Have students work together in groups to classify the sentences. Refer to page 1 in the Student Edition for the text of the Guiding Questions.

- Assign *Vocabulary Development* for students to review Key Terms.

  All in One Latin America Teaching Resources, *Vocabulary Development,* p. 173

Answers

Key Terms

1–12. Make sure students' definitions accurately reflect the definition of each Key Term.

Comprehension and Critical Thinking

13. (a) Mayans built great cities, designed an accurate calendar and used a system of writing. **(b)** Similar: Both groups conquered other groups to build large empires, used irrigation to water their crops, used nobles to help the emperors govern, and were conquered by the Spanish. Different: Aztecs constructed artificial floating gardens, while Incas farmed the surrounding land; Incas built roads, bridges, tunnels and aqueducts; Aztecs had a written language, the Incas did not; descendants of the Incas live in the Andes today. **(c)** having strong leaders and large and powerful armies to conquer other groups and control vast lands

14. (a) Christopher Columbus, Hernán Cortés, and Francisco Pizarro **(b)** They hoped to find gold and other treasures. **(c)** They disliked the Aztecs because they demanded heavy tribute from them.

15. (a) The territory was divided into provinces. Viceroys appointed by the Spanish King ruled the provinces. Other settlers who had been born in Spain helped the viceroys rule. A council in Spain supervised the colonial officials to make sure they did not become too powerful. **(b)** rights given to the Spanish settlers to demand taxes or labor from Native Americans; Native Americans were forced to work on haciendas and later in mines. **(c)** The Native American population dropped from 25 million to 3 million and the Spanish needed more workers. European demand for more products from the Americas meant that more enslaved workers were needed.

16. (a) Miguel Hidalgo **(b)** People of each country wanted to be free to govern themselves. Enslaved or poor workers who were oppressed supported the revolutions. **(c)** After independence criollos gained political power while life for Native Americans remained the same as before.

17. (a) Caudillos were "strongmen" who often ignored the democratic constitutions established by their new nations and instead became dictators. **(b)** Railroads and seaports made it easier for foreign companies to export their products. **(c)** When it borrows money to improve its economy, prices for its products fall, and it has to borrow more money to pay off existing debts.

◆ Comprehension and Critical Thinking

13. (a) Recall Describe Mayan civilization.
(b) Compare How were the Aztec and Incan civilizations similar and different?
(c) Generalize What lessons in empire-building can be learned from the Aztecs and the Incas?

14. (a) Name Which Europeans were the first to explore Central and South America?
(b) Identify Causes Why did the Spanish want to explore the Americas?
(c) Conclude Why did many Native Americans help Hernán Cortés defeat the Aztecs?

15. (a) Recall How did Spain organize its empire?
(b) Explain What were encomiendas and what effect did they have on Native Americans?
(c) Identify Causes Why did the Spanish start to import enslaved Africans to the Americas? Why did this practice increase over time?

16. (a) Identify Who led the Mexican Revolution?
(b) Compare Compare the ways Mexico, Haiti, and Peru gained their independence.
(c) Draw Conclusions How did independence affect criollos? Native Americans?

17. (a) Recall Describe how caudillos ruled their countries.
(b) Identify Causes Why did foreign nations build seaports and railroads in Latin America?
(c) Explain What is one way a nation can develop foreign debt?

◆ Writing Activity: Math

Look again at the photo of the quipu on page 375. Suppose you have five strings of different colors to record the number of people in your class: girls, boys, and the teacher. How would you show this information? Use string or make a drawing with colored pencils. Now write directions for using the mathematical system you just invented. Have another student read and follow your directions. Evaluate how well your partner used your mathematical system.

◆ Skills Practice

Making a Timeline In the Skills for Life activity in this chapter, you learned to create a timeline. Review the steps you followed to learn the skill.

Use an encyclopedia or other reliable source to research one of the people you read about in this chapter. Then make a timeline of the important events in that person's life.

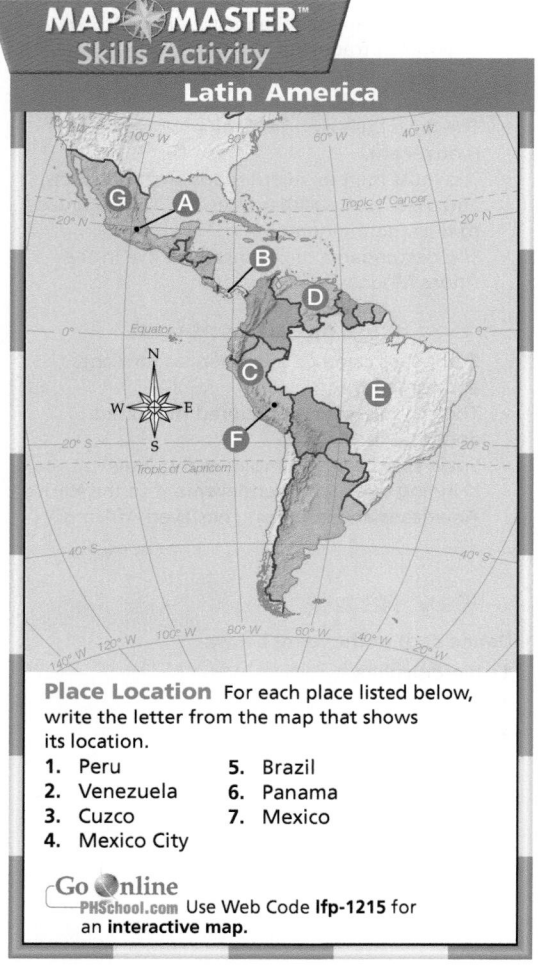

MAP MASTER™
Skills Activity

Latin America

Place Location For each place listed below, write the letter from the map that shows its location.
1. Peru
2. Venezuela
3. Cuzco
4. Mexico City
5. Brazil
6. Panama
7. Mexico

Go Online
PHSchool.com Use Web Code **lfp-1215** for an **interactive map**.

Skills Practice
Students' timelines should accurately reflect the dates and events of the life of the person they chose.

Writing Activity: Math
Students' drawings and directions for their mathematical system will vary, but should accurately record the number of people in the class.

Standardized Test Prep

Test-Taking Tips

Some questions on standardized tests ask you to analyze a point of view. Read the paragraph below. Then follow the tips to answer the sample question.

Pick the letter that best answers the question.
In 1519, the Spanish conquistador Hernán Cortés marched toward the great Aztec capital, Tenochtitlán, with 500 soldiers. Somebody watching the troops whispered: *This is a happy day! These white gods could mean the end to Moctezuma and his bloodthirsty followers. Let us help them on their way.*

Which onlooker might have made those comments?
- **A** a spy of Moctezuma
- **B** a soldier of Francisco Pizarro
- **C** a Native American neighbor of the Aztecs
- **D** a wife of Moctezuma

TIP Make sure you understand the question. Restate it in your own words: *The person who said those words was probably _____.*

TIP Use what you know about history along with common sense to choose the BEST answer.

Think It Through Moctezuma's own spies would not want an end to him or call themselves bloodthirsty. The same would be true for his wife. Francisco Pizarro was a conqueror who didn't arrive in South America until years after Cortés. A neighbor of the Aztecs might have been happy to see Cortés, because Moctezuma was a powerful enemy who conquered many of his neighbors. So the best answer is C.

Practice Questions

Choose the letter of the best answer.

1. Unlike the Incas and Aztecs, the Mayas did NOT have
   - **A** an emperor.
   - **B** a calendar.
   - **C** cities.
   - **D** a form of writing.

2. Brazil's language and culture—Portuguese—were established by
   - **A** the voyage of Columbus.
   - **B** Pizarro's conquest.
   - **C** the Treaty of Tordesillas.
   - **D** the encomienda system.

3. What is one way that Latin American countries have been trying to improve their economies?
   - **A** by cooperating with one another
   - **B** by increasing their foreign debt
   - **C** by giving more land to large companies
   - **D** by depending on one resource

Read the following passage and answer the question that follows.

The following is taken from a speech made by someone living in Latin America in the early 1800s: "I love my country, but I deserve to govern myself. I learned plenty about governing when I attended school in Europe!"

4. Who most likely made this speech?
   - **A** the king of Spain
   - **B** a criollo
   - **C** a poor mestizo
   - **D** a Native American

Use Web Code **lfa-1201**
for a **Chapter 12 self-test.**

MAP MASTER
Skills Activity

1. C
2. D
3. F
4. A
5. E
6. B
7. G

Go Online PHSchool.com Students may practice their map skills using the interactive online version of this map.

Standardized Test Prep

Answers

1. A
2. C
3. A
4. B

Go Online PHSchool.com Students may use the Chapter 12 self-test on PHSchool.com to prepare for the Chapter Test

---

Assessment Resources

Use *Chapter Tests A and B* to assess students' mastery of chapter content.

All in One Latin America Teaching Resources, *Chapter Tests A and B,* pp. 177-182

Tests are also available on the *ExamView®* *Test Bank CD-ROM.*

⊙ *ExamView®* Test Bank CD-ROM

Overview

1 Section

Cultures of Mexico and Central America
1. Discover the cultural heritage of the people of Middle America.
2. Find out why many people in this region have been moving away from the countryside.

2 Section

The Cultures of the Caribbean
1. Find out what ethnic groups make up the people of the Caribbean.
2. Learn how the different cultures of the region blended to create Caribbean food, music, and celebrations.

3 Section

The Cultures of South America
1. Find out what ethnic groups are represented in the four cultural regions of South America.
2. Learn what life is like in the countryside and in the cities of South America.

Technology Resources

Students use embedded Web codes to access Internet activities, chapter self-tests, and additional map practice. They may also access Dorling Kindersley's Online Desk Reference to learn more about each country they study.

Use the Interactive Textbook to make content and concepts come alive through animations, videos, and activities that accompany the complete basal text—online and on CD-ROM.

PRENTICE HALL

Use this complete suite of powerful teaching tools to make planning lessons and administering tests quicker and easier.

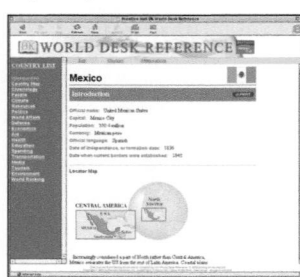

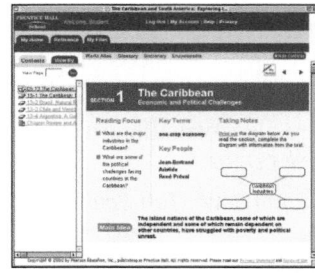

Reading and Vocabulary Instruction

🔄 Model the Target Reading Skill

Cause and Effect Explain to students that understanding cause and effect will help them to better understand the events that they read about. By identifying causes and effects, understanding that some effects are the results of multiple causes, and analyzing effects in context, students become more adept at seeing patterns both within and beyond the reading.

Model this skill by thinking aloud about these statements concerning the cultures of the Caribbean from page 411 of the Student Edition:

> *Many people came to the Caribbean as colonists, slaves, or immigrants.*

> *The area has great ethnic variety.*

One of these sentences states a cause, and the other one states an effect. How will I decide which is which? Let me set up the statements in two ways, using a connection word like "because," to see which makes more sense. 1) "Because many people came to the Caribbean as colonists, slaves, or immigrants, the Caribbean now has great ethnic variety." 2) "Because the Caribbean has great ethnic variety, many people came to the Caribbean as colonists, slaves, or immigrants."

My first statement makes more sense. People coming to the Caribbean as colonists, slaves, and immigrants happened first, and it caused the variety of ethnicities, which is the effect.

Use the following worksheets from All-in-One Latin America Teaching Resources (pp. 199, 200, and 201) to support this chapter's Target Reading Skill.

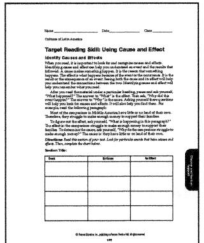 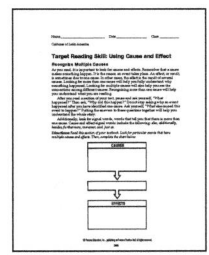 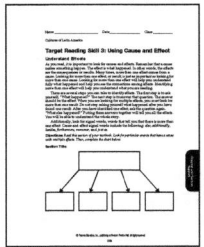

Vocabulary Builder

High-Use Academic Words

Use these steps to teach this chapter's high-use words:

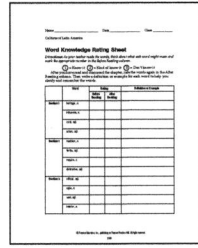

1. Have students rate how well they know each word on their Word Knowledge worksheets (All-in-One Latin America Teaching Resources, p. 202.)
2. Pronounce each word and ask students to repeat it.
3. Give students a brief definition or sample sentence (provided on TE pp. 403, 411, and 416.)
4. Work with students as they fill in the "Definition or Example" column of their Word Knowledge worksheets.

Assessment

Formal Assessment

Test students' understanding of core knowledge and skills.

Chapter Tests A and B, All-in-One Latin America Teaching Resources, pp. 218–223

Customize the Chapter Tests to suit your needs.
ExamView® Test Bank CD-ROM

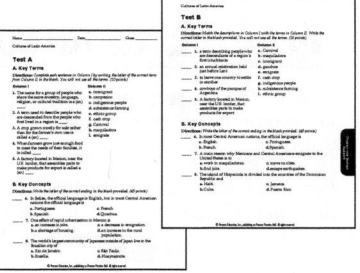

Skills Assessment

Assess geographic literacy.
MapMaster Skills, Student Edition pp. 401, 422

Assess reading and comprehension.
Target Reading Skills, Student Edition, pp. 405, 411, 415, and in Section Assessments
Chapter 13 Assessment, Reading and Vocabulary Study Guide, p. 157

Performance Assessment

Assess students' performance on this chapter's Writing Activities using the following rubrics from All-in-One Latin America Teaching Resources.

Rubric for Assessing a Journal Entry, p. 215
Rubric for Assessing a Writing Assignment, p. 216
Rubric for Assessing a Newspaper Article, p. 217

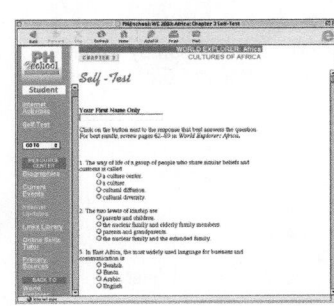

Assess students' work through performance tasks.

Small Group Activity: Share the Music, All-in-One Latin America Teaching Resources, pp. 205–208

Online Assessment

Have students check their own understanding.
Chapter Self-Test

Test Preparation

Latin America Benchmark Test 1, AYP Monitoring Assessments, pp. 97–100

Section 1 Cultures of Mexico and Central America

 *3 periods, 1.5 blocks (includes Skills for Life)*

Social Studies Objectives

1. Discover the cultural heritage of the people of Middle America.

2. Find out why many people in this region have been moving away from the countryside.

Reading/Language Arts Objective

Identify causes and effects to understand the relationships among situations and events.

Prepare to Read	**Instructional Resources**	**Differentiated Instruction**
Build Background Knowledge Brainstorm things that represent culture. **Set a Purpose for Reading** Have students evaluate statements on the *Reading Readiness Guide.* **Preview Key Terms** Teach the section's Key Terms. **Target Reading Skill** Introduce the section's Target Reading Skill of **identifying causes and effects.**	**All in One Latin America Teaching Resources** L2 Reading Readiness Guide, p.188 L2 Identify Causes and Effects, p. 199	**Spanish Reading and Vocabulary Study Guide** L2 Chapter 13, Section 1, pp. 108–109 ELL

Instruct	**Instructional Resources**	**Differentiated Instruction**
Cultural Heritage Discuss the different elements that make up Middle American culture. **Leaving the Countryside** Discuss why people are leaving rural areas. **Target Reading Skill** Review **identifying causes and effects.**	**All in One Latin America Teaching Resources** L2 Guided Reading and Review, p. 189 L2 Reading Readiness Guide, p. 188 **Latin America Transparencies** L2 Section Reading Support Transparency LA 36	**All in One Latin America Teaching Resources** L3 We Live in Mexico (Lugo), pp. 209–210 AR, GT L3 A Huge Black Umbrella, pp. 211–213 AR, GT L2 Skills for Life, p. 204 GT, AR, LPR, SN **Teacher's Edition** L1 For Less Proficient Readers, TE p. 405 L3 For Advanced Readers, TE p. 405 **Spanish Support** L2 Guided Reading and Review (Spanish), p. 142 ELL

Assess and Reteach	**Instructional Resources**	**Differentiated Instruction**

Assess Progress
 Evaluate student comprehension with the section assessment and section quiz.
 	
 Reteach
 Assign the Reading and Vocabulary Study Guide to help struggling students.
 	
 Extend
 Extend the lesson by assigning an activity from *Environmental and Global Issues.*
	All in One Latin America Teaching Resources
	 L2 Section Quiz, p. 190
	    Rubric for Assessing a Journal Entry, p. 215
	
	 Reading and Vocabulary Study Guide
	 L1 Chapter 13, Section 1, pp. 148–150
	
	 PHSchool.com
	 L3 For: Environmental and Global Issues, *Nickel-and-Diming*
	    Web code: lfd-1304
		Spanish Support
		 L2 Section Quiz (Spanish), p. 143 ELL
		
		 Teacher's Edition
		 L1 For Special Needs Students, p. 409
		 L1 For Less Proficient Readers, p. 409
		
		 Social Studies Skills Tutor CD-ROM
		 L1 Distinguishing Fact from Opinion SN, LPR, ELL

Key

L1 Basic to Average
L2 For All Students
L3 Average to Advanced

LPR Less Proficient Readers
AR Advanced Readers
SN Special Needs Students

GT Gifted and Talented
ELL English Language Learners

400c

Section 2 The Cultures of the Caribbean

 1.5 periods, .75 block

Social Studies Objectives

1. Find out what ethnic groups make up the people of the Caribbean.
2. Learn how the different cultures of the region blended to create Caribbean food, music, and celebrations.

Reading/Language Arts Objective

Recognize multiple causes to understand the development of complex events.

Prepare to Read	**Instructional Resources**	**Differentiated Instruction**
Build Background Knowledge Fill in a word web with information about the Caribbean. **Set a Purpose for Reading** Have students evaluate statements on the *Reading Readiness Guide*. **Preview Key Terms** Teach the section's Key Terms. **Target Reading Skill** Introduce the section's Target Reading Skill of **recognizing multiple causes**.	**All in One Latin America Teaching Resources** L2 Reading Readiness Guide, p. 192 L2 Recognize Multiple Causes, p. 200	**Spanish Reading and Vocabulary Study Guide** L2 Chapter 13, Section 2, pp. 110–111 ELL

Instruct	**Instructional Resources**	**Differentiated Instruction**
The People of the Caribbean Discuss the major ethnic groups of the Caribbean. **Target Reading Skill** Review **recognizing multiple causes**. **A Blend of Cultures** Identify how cultures blended in the Caribbean.	**All in One Latin America Teaching Resources** L2 Guided Reading and Review, p. 193 L2 Reading Readiness Guide, p. 192 **Latin America Transparencies** L2 Section Reading Support Transparency LA 37	**Spanish Support** L2 Guided Reading and Review (Spanish), p. 144 ELL

Assess and Reteach	**Instructional Resources**	**Differentiated Instruction**
Assess Progress Evaluate student comprehension with the section assessment and section quiz. **Reteach** Assign the Reading and Vocabulary Study Guide to help struggling students. **Extend** Extend the lesson by having students watch a Discovery Channel World Studies Video.	**All in One Latin America Teaching Resources** L2 Section Quiz, p. 194 Rubric for Assessing a Writing Assignment, p. 216 **Reading and Vocabulary Study Guide** L1 Chapter 13, Section 2, pp. 151–153	**Spanish Support** L2 Section Quiz (Spanish), p. 147 ELL

Key

 Basic to Average    Average to Advanced   **LPR** Less Proficient Readers   **GT** Gifted and Talented

 For All Students   **AR** Advanced Readers   **ELL** English Language Learners

SN Special Needs Students

Section 3 The Cultures of South America

 3.5 periods, 1.75 blocks (includes Chapter Review and Assessment)

Social Studies Objectives

1. Find out what ethnic groups are represented in the four cultural regions of South America.
2. Learn what life is like in the countryside and in the cities of South America.

Reading/Language Arts Objective

Understand how one cause can bring about multiple effects.

Prepare to Read

Build Background Knowledge
Have students predict the cultural elements shared by South America and other regions of Latin America.

Set a Purpose for Reading
Have students evaluate statements on the *Reading Readiness Guide*.

Preview Key Terms
Teach the section's Key Terms.

Target Reading Skill
Introduce the section's Target Reading Skill of **understanding effects.**

Instructional Resources

All in One Latin America Teaching Resources

L2 Reading Readiness Guide, p. 196
L2 Understand Effects, p. 201

Differentiated Instruction

Spanish Reading and Vocabulary Study Guide

L2 Chapter 13, Section 3, pp. 112–113 ELL

Instruct

The People of South America
Ask students about the four cultural regions of South America.

Target Reading Skill
Review **understanding effects.**

Country and City Life
Discuss country and city life in South America.

Instructional Resources

All in One Latin America Teaching Resources

L2 Guided Reading and Review, p. 197
L2 Reading Readiness Guide, p. 196

Latin America Transparencies

L2 Section Reading Support Transparency LA 38

Differentiated Instruction

Teacher's Edition

L3 For Gifted and Talented Students, TE p. 418
L1 For Less Proficient Readers, p. 418
L1 For Special Needs Students, TE p. 419
L2 For English Language Learners, p. 419

Passport to the World CD-ROM

L1 LPR, SN, ELL

Student Edition on Audio CD

L1 Chapter 13, Section 1, SN, LPR, ELL

Spanish Support

L2 Guided Reading and Review (Spanish), p. 146 ELL

Assess and Reteach

Assess Progress
Evaluate student comprehension with the section assessment and section quiz.

Reteach
Assign the Reading and Vocabulary Study Guide to help struggling students.

Extend
Extend the lesson by assigning an activity about art in Latin America.

Instructional Resources

All in One Latin America Teaching Resources

L2 Section Quiz, p. 198
Rubric for Assessing a Newspaper Article, p. 217
L2 Vocabulary Development, p. 214
L2 Word Knowledge, p. 202
L2 Chapter Tests A and B, pp. 218–223

Reading and Vocabulary Study Guide

L1 Chapter 13, Section 3, pp. 154–156

Differentiated Instruction

Spanish Support

L2 Section Quiz (Spanish), p. 147 ELL
L2 Chapter Summary (Spanish), p. 148 ELL
L2 Vocabulary Development (Spanish), p. 149 ELL

Key

L1 Basic to Average
L2 For All Students
L3 Average to Advanced

LPR Less Proficient Readers
AR Advanced Readers
SN Special Needs Students

GT Gifted and Talented
ELL English Language Learners

Reading Background

Mapping Word Definitions

Mapping definitions can extend students' understanding of vocabulary and high-use words. Have students create word maps by answering each of these questions about each word: What is it? What is it like or not like? What are some examples?

Model mapping the key term *cash crop* from section 3 of this chapter:

What is it? *(a crop grown for sale or export rather than for the farmer's own use)* What is it like? *(It is the opposite of subsistence farming, in which farmers grow only enough to use themselves.)* What are some examples? *(coffee, sugar, cocoa, and bananas)*

Another way to map words is to develop a graphic organizer that shows the word, its definition, a synonym, and a sentence using the word. Put this example of an organizer on the board:

Term	*cash crop*
Definition	*crop grown for sale or export rather than for the farmer's own use*
Synonym	*profitable harvest*
Sentence	*Farmers in South America grow bananas as a cash crop to export to other countries.*

Summarizing

Help students to engage with the text by asking them to summarize as they read. Model how to summarize by using the B-head section "Leaving the Countryside" on page 405 of this chapter. Ask students to read silently and actively take notes. At the same time, write notes about the section on the board, such as "rapid population growth"; "seeking work in factories"; and "growing cities have trouble providing services." Have students add to the notes on the board. Then ask students to choose which sentence provides a better summary of the passage based on the notes written on the board:

1. Because of rapid population growth in Mexico and Central America, many people must leave rural areas to find jobs in cities. The cities are growing so fast that there are often not enough services for all of the people.

2. The population of Mexico and Central America will double in 30 years. Some people in Mexico move to the border with the United States to work in factories.

Students should recognize that option 1 provides a more effective summary, because it applies more of the information in the passage.

World Studies Background

The Children of Mexico

As the population of Mexico rapidly increases, children under 18 become a greater percentage of the population. In fact, about 40 percent of Mexico's total population is now under 18 years of age.

Because youth makes up such a large part of the population, in 2000 and 2003 children were invited by UNICEF to participate in a survey about how to improve their country. Their main concerns were violence and poverty.

Sharing Caribbean Culture

The poetry and plays of Nobel Prize winner Derek Walcott have helped teach the world about the Caribbean. His work focuses on themes of his Caribbean heritage—slavery (his ancestors were slaves), violence, and finding identity in a country that was once a colony. Born in St. Lucia, Walcott writes in English but sometimes includes other languages, such as Creole.

Cash Crops in South America

In much of South America, the processing and exporting of cash crops creates jobs for city dwellers. For this reason, many crops are grown on large farms closer to cities where they can be immediately processed. Agriculture made up only 12 percent of the gross domestic product in the 1990s, but workers involved in the agriculture industry made up more than 20 percent of the total workforce.

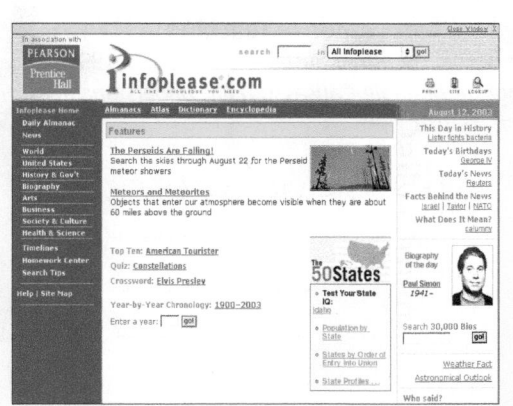

Infoplease® provides a wealth of useful information for the classroom. You can use this resource to strengthen your background on the subjects covered in this chapter. Have students visit this advertising-free site as a starting point for projects requiring research.

Use Web Code **lfd-1300** for **Infoplease®**

Guiding Questions

Remind students about the Guiding Questions introduced at the beginning of this section.

Section 1 relates to Guiding Question **3**
What factors have affected cultures in Latin America? *(The cultures of Mexico and Central America have been affected by the regions' ethnic diversity, religion, and the migration of much of the population from the countryside to towns and cities.)*

Section 2 relates to Guiding Question **2**
How has Latin America been shaped by its history? *(The Caribbean is ethnically and culturally diverse because of the many groups that settled there as colonists, immigrants, or slaves.)*

Section 3 relates to Guiding Question **3**
What factors have affected culture in Latin America? *(The cultures of South America have been affected by the ethnic variety, geography, and local history of the different cultural regions.)*

Target Reading Skill

In this chapter, students will learn and apply the reading skill of cause and effect. Use the following worksheets to help students practice this skill:

 Latin America Teaching Resources, *Identify Causes and Effects,* p. 199; *Recognize Multiple Causes,* p. 200; *Understand Effects,* p. 201

Chapter Preview

This chapter will introduce you to the cultures of the three regions of Latin America.

Section 1
The Cultures of Mexico and Central America

Section 2
The Cultures of the Caribbean

Section 3
The Cultures of South America

Target Reading Skill

Cause and Effect In this chapter you will focus on recognizing cause and effect in the text you are reading. Recognizing cause and effect will help you understand relationships among situations or events.

▶ A boy playing steel drums during a Carnival celebration in St. Thomas

400 Latin America

Bibliography

For the Teacher
Barlow, Genevieve. *Stories from Latin America: Historias de Latinoamerica.* McGraw Hill/Contemporary Books, 1995.
Gutmann, Matthew C. *Perspectives on Las Americas: A Reader in Culture, History, and Representation.* Blackwell Publishers, 2003.
Machado, Ana Maria. *Exploration into Latin America.* New Discovery, 1995.

For the Student
L1 Dorros, Arthur. *Tonight Is Carnaval.* Dutton, 1992.
L2 Despain, Pleasant. *The Emerald Lizard: Fifteen Latin American Tales to Tell in English and Spanish.* August House, 1999.
L3 Hernandez, Romel. *Caribbean Islands: Facts and Figures.* Mason Crest Publishers, 2002.

Differentiated Instruction

The following Teacher Edition strategies are suitable for students of varying abilities.

Advanced Readers, p. 405
English Language Learners, p. 419
Gifted and Talented Students, p. 418
Less Proficient Readers, pp. 405, 409, 418
Special Needs Students, pp. 409, 419

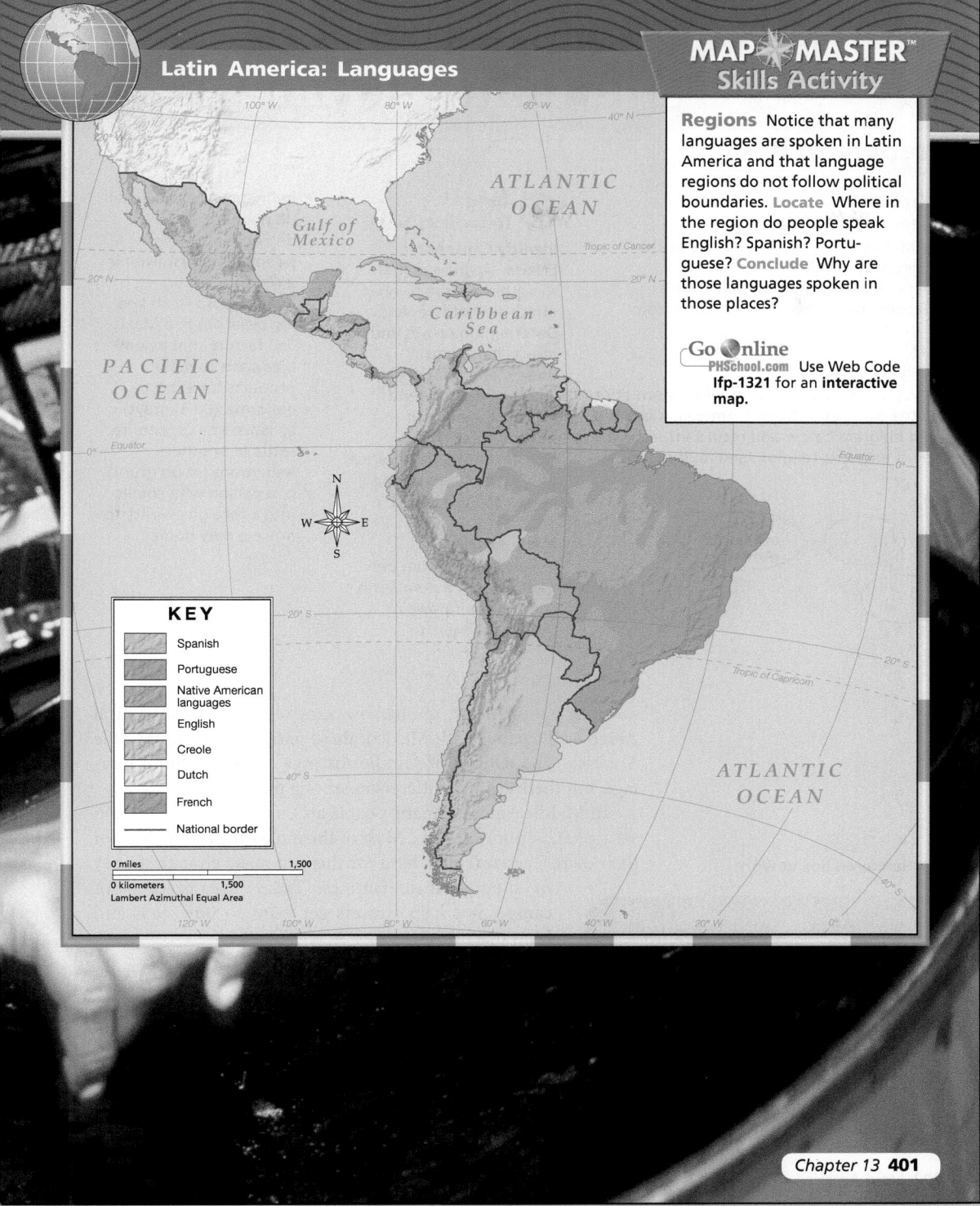

Latin America: Languages

Regions Notice that many languages are spoken in Latin America and that language regions do not follow political boundaries. **Locate** Where in the region do people speak English? Spanish? Portuguese? **Conclude** Why are those languages spoken in those places?

Go Online
PHSchool.com Use Web Code **Ifp-1321** for an **interactive map.**

ATLANTIC OCEAN

Gulf of Mexico

Tropic of Cancer

Caribbean Sea

PACIFIC OCEAN

Equator

ATLANTIC OCEAN

Tropic of Capricorn

KEY

- Spanish
- Portuguese
- Native American languages
- English
- Creole
- Dutch
- French
- — National border

0 miles 1,500
0 kilometers 1,500
Lambert Azimuthal Equal Area

Chapter 13 **401**

- Point out to students the map title, key, and scale. Encourage students to study the map and list the languages spoken in Latin America.

- Refer students to the political map of Latin America on page 331 of the Student Edition. They can use the map to help them with the MapMaster Skills Activity.

Go Online
PHSchool.com **Students may practice their map skills using the interactive online version of this map.**

Using the Visual   L2

Reach Into Your Background Draw students attention to the caption accompanying the picture on pages 400–401. Discuss the photograph with students. Have them discuss what details stand out to them. Can they relate the celebration pictured to their own lives? Encourage students to share their ideas with the class.

Answers

Locate English is spoken in parts of Central America, parts of the Caribbean islands, and a small area in northern South America. Spanish is spoken in Mexico, much of Central America, the Caribbean, and parts of South America, especially in the south. Portuguese is spoken mainly in Brazil. **Conclude** The languages spoken in a region are affected by its history, culture, and the ethnic groups who live there.

Chapter Resources

Teaching Resources
- L2 Vocabulary Development, p. 214
- L2 Skills for Life, p. 204
- L2 Chapter Tests A and B, pp. 218–223

Spanish Support
- L2 Spanish Chapter Summary, p. 148
- L2 Spanish Vocabulary Development, p. 149

Media and Technology
- L1 Student Edition on Audio CD
- L1 Guided Reading Audiotapes, English and Spanish
- L2 Social Studies Skills Tutor CD-ROM
- *ExamView Test Bank CD-ROM*

PRENTICE HALL
Presentation EXPRESS™
Teach · Connect · Inspire

Teach this chapter's content using the PresentationExpress™ CD-ROM including:
- slide shows
- transparencies
- interactive maps and media
- *ExamView*® QuickTake Presenter

 **Section 1** Cultures of Mexico and Central America

Objectives
Social Studies

1. Discover the cultural heritage of the people of Middle America.
2. Find out why many people in this region have been moving away from the countryside.

Reading/Language Arts

Identify causes and effects to better understand the relationships among situations and events.

Prepare to Read

Build Background Knowledge L2

Tell students that knowing about the geography and history of Latin America will help them as they learn about the region's cultures. Ask students to quickly preview the section headings and photographs with this question in mind: **What makes up a culture?** Point out the artwork on p. 403 and explain that art is one facet of culture. Use the Give One and Get One strategy (TE, p. 37) to generate a list.

Set a Purpose for Reading L2

- Preview the Objectives.
- Read each statement from the *Reading Readiness Guide* aloud. Ask students to mark the statements true or false.

  All in One Latin America Teaching Resources, *Reading Readiness Guide*, p. 188

- Have students discuss the statements in pairs or groups of four, then mark their worksheets again. Use the Numbered Heads participation structure (TE, p. T36) to call on students to share their group's perspectives.

Vocabulary Builder
Preview Key Terms

Pronounce each Key Term, and then ask students to say the word with you. Provide a simple explanation such as, "Native American groups, such as the Cherokee and Sioux, are indigenous people living in the United States."

Prepare to Read

Objectives

In this section you will
1. Discover the cultural heritage of the people of Middle America.
2. Find out why many people in this region have been moving away from the countryside.

Reading to Learn

As you read this section, look for information on the cultures of Middle America. Copy the web diagram below and record information about ancestry, religion, and language.

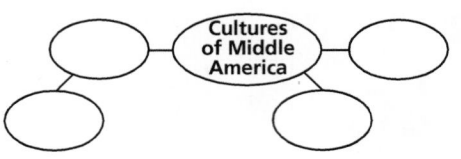

Target Reading Skill

Identify Causes and Effects A cause makes something happen. An effect is what happens. Determining causes and effects helps you understand relationships among situations and events. As you read this section, think of the cultures of Middle America as effects. What are the causes of these effects?

Key Terms

- **campesino** (kahm peh SEE noh) *n.* a poor Latin American farmer or farm worker
- **indigenous people** (in DIJ uh nus PEA pul) *n.* descendants of the people who first lived in a region
- **maquiladora** (mah kee luh DOHR ah) *n.* a Mexican factory that assembles parts to make products for export
- **emigrate** (EM ih grayt) *v.* to leave one country to settle in another
- **immigrant** (IM uh grunt) *n.* a person who comes into a foreign country to make a new home

A Honduran boy at work

402 Latin America

Seven nations form the narrow, crooked isthmus of Central America. Together with Mexico, these nations make up Middle America. The nations of Middle America share a cultural heritage, but there are also differences among them.

In Middle America, many people are **campesinos** (kahm peh SEE nohz), or poor farmers. Most of them have little or no land of their own. Therefore, it is hard for them to make enough money to support their families. Today, organizations of campesinos help farmers get loans to buy seeds and farm machinery.

Cultural Heritage

There is much diversity, or variety, among the people of Middle America. Many people are mestizo. That means they have both Spanish and indigenous ancestors. **Indigenous people** are descendants of the people who first lived in a region. In Latin America, indigenous people are also called Native Americans or Indians.

Target Reading Skill L2

Identify Causes and Effects Point out the Target Reading Skill. Tell students that being able to identify causes and effects will help them to understand how and why events occur or situations develop.

Model identifying the causes and effect in this passage on p. 404: "The Spanish settlers who came to the region were Roman Catholic. In the 1500s and 1600s, Spanish missionaries converted many Native Americans to Christianity. The Catholic Church has been important to this region every since." (*Causes—Spanish settlers were Catholic and Catholic missionaries converted many Native Americans. Effect—The Catholic Church has long been important to the region.*)

Give students *Identify Causes and Effects.* Have them complete the activity in groups.

All in One Latin America Teaching Resources, *Identify Causes and Effects*, p. 199

One Region, Many Faces In Honduras, most of the people are mestizo. About one third of Guatemala's people are mestizo. Another 60 percent are indigenous. Many Costa Ricans are direct descendants of Spaniards. And more than 40 percent of the people of Belize are of African or mixed African and European descent.

The countries of Central America have many languages, too. Guatemala is home to more than 20 languages. Spanish is the language of government and business, but the indigenous people in Guatemala speak their own languages. So do indigenous people in Panama, El Salvador, and Nicaragua. Spanish is the main language in six of the seven countries. People in Belize speak English.

Mexico also blends Native American and Spanish influences. Spanish is the first language for most Mexicans, but some Mexicans speak Native American languages as well. About 30 percent of the people of Mexico are indigenous, and about 60 percent of the population are mestizos.

Art of Middle America Art made by Native Americans before the arrival of Europeans is called Pre-Columbian art. Archaeologists have found beautiful wall paintings and painted vases, sculptures, and metalwork in Mexico and Central America. Gold jewelry was a specialty of the Mixtec people, while the Olmecs created huge stone heads and lovely figures made of jade.

This 1930 self-portrait is by the Mexican artist Frida Kahlo.

Mexican History
This detail of *Sugar Cane* (1931) by Diego Rivera shows some people hard at work. Because the Aztecs and Mayas had painted murals, these more recent artworks revived a Native American art form. **Infer** *Which people are not hard at work? What do you learn about Mexican history from these details?*

Vocabulary Builder

Use the information below to teach students this section's high-use words.

High-use Word	Definition and Sample Sentence
heritage, p. 402	*n.* culture or traditions handed down from one's ancestors or the past He was very proud of his **heritage**.
influence, p. 403	*n.* the power of persons or things to affect others She hoped her sister would not use her **influence** to get her into the club.
rural, p. 405	*adj.* of, or related to, the countryside I love the **rural** atmosphere of the farm.
urban, p. 405	*adj.* of, or related to, the city Living in an **urban** area can be exciting.

Cultural Heritage L2

Guided Instruction

- **Vocabulary Builder** Clarify the high-use words **heritage** and **influence** before reading.

- Read Cultural Heritage using the Structured Silent Reading technique (TE, p. T34).

- Ask students to identify and discuss the main "ingredients" that blended to create the culture of Middle America. (*Native American beliefs, customs, languages, and art mixed with those of the Spanish settlers to form a unique and diverse cultural blend. The Catholic Church has also been an important influence on the culture of this region.*)

Answers

Infer The man in the hammock and the guards are not hard at work. The man in the hammock is probably a Spanish settler who owns the sugar-cane plantation. The guards are probably mestizo. This shows that Spanish settlers took over Mexico and had more power than the indigenous people. They had to hire guards to force people to work. It also shows that Mexican society was split into classes based on a person's ancestry.

Independent Practice

Ask students to create the Taking Notes graphic organizer on a blank piece of paper. Then have them label the ovals "Ancestry," "Art," "Religion," and "Language." Students can then fill in the ovals with information they have just learned. Briefly model labeling the ovals and recording details.

Monitor Progress

As students fill in the graphic organizer, circulate and make sure that individuals are choosing the correct details. Provide assistance as needed.

Show *Section Reading Support Transparency LA 36* and ask students to check their graphic organizers individually. Go over key concepts and clarify key vocabulary as needed.

Latin America Transparencies, *Section Reading Support Transparency LA 36*

A Blend of Cultures
Indigenous people attend a church service in the Mexican state of Chiapas. **Infer** *What evidence is there in the photo that these people have blended Christianity with their traditional culture?*

The art of Mexico reflects both its Spanish and its Native American cultures. In the 1920s, the government invited Mexican artists to create murals on public buildings. Murals are large pictures painted directly on walls. The murals by such artists as Diego Rivera (dee AY goh rih VEHR uh) and José Clemente Orozco (ho SAY kleh MEN teh oh ROHS koh) show the history of Mexico, including the contributions of the indigenous people to the nation.

The Church Religion is important to the people of Mexico and Central America. The Spanish settlers who came to the region were Roman Catholic. In the 1500s and 1600s, Spanish missionaries converted many Native Americans to Christianity. The Catholic Church has been important to this region ever since. Most of the people are Catholic. Native Americans have blended many elements of their religions with Christianity.

Fighting Injustice In Middle America, priests and bishops have spoken out against injustice. Following the Church's lead, citizens have taken steps to end poverty and injustice. Ordinary people have started health clinics, farms, and organizations.

Elvia Alvarado (el VEE uh al vuh RAH doh) works for one of these organizations, and her work is not easy. "The communities we work in are hard to get to," she says. "Sometimes I don't eat all day, and in the summertime the streams dry up and there's often no water to drink." Sometimes Alvarado does not get paid. "But I couldn't be happy if my belly was full while my neighbors didn't have a plate of beans and tortillas to put on the table," she says.

✓ **Reading Check** **Name two ways people have worked to fight poverty and injustice.**

Background: Biography

Oscar Arnulfo Romero y Galdamez
Oscar Arnulfo Romero y Galdamez, archbishop of El Salvador, was born in Ciudad Barrios, El Salvador, in 1917. Ordained as a priest in 1942, he was appointed archbishop in 1977. At first, Romero avoided political affairs. Later, he thought the church should help its people obtain social justice. Romero spoke out against the human rights abuses and violence committed against the poor by the military regime. In 1980, while celebrating mass, Romero was assassinated.

Answers

Infer The people in the photo are wearing brightly colored traditional clothing as they head into the Christian church to worship.

✓ **Reading Check** Officials of the Catholic Church have spoken out against injustice, and ordinary citizens have started organizations to help the poor, such as health clinics and farms.

Leaving the Countryside

The population of Mexico and Central America is growing rapidly. This rapid population growth has made it hard for young people in rural areas to find jobs. Many have left their homes to look for work in the cities. Today, most people in Middle America live in cities.

In Mexico, some people move to towns and cities along the border with the United States. There, they can work in factories owned by American companies. These companies place their factories in Mexico because wages and other costs are lower there. Border factories that assemble imported parts to make products for export are called **maquiladoras** (mah key luh DOHR ahs).

Other urban areas in the region also offer jobs and other opportunities. Many rural people have moved to large cities such as Mexico City in Mexico, Panama City and Colón in Panama, and San José, the capital of Costa Rica. As a result, these cities have grown rapidly and often have trouble providing housing and services for new arrivals.

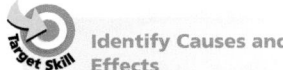

Identify Causes and Effects
What factor makes it difficult for young people in rural areas to find jobs? List that as a cause. What is the result of this unemployment? List that as an effect.

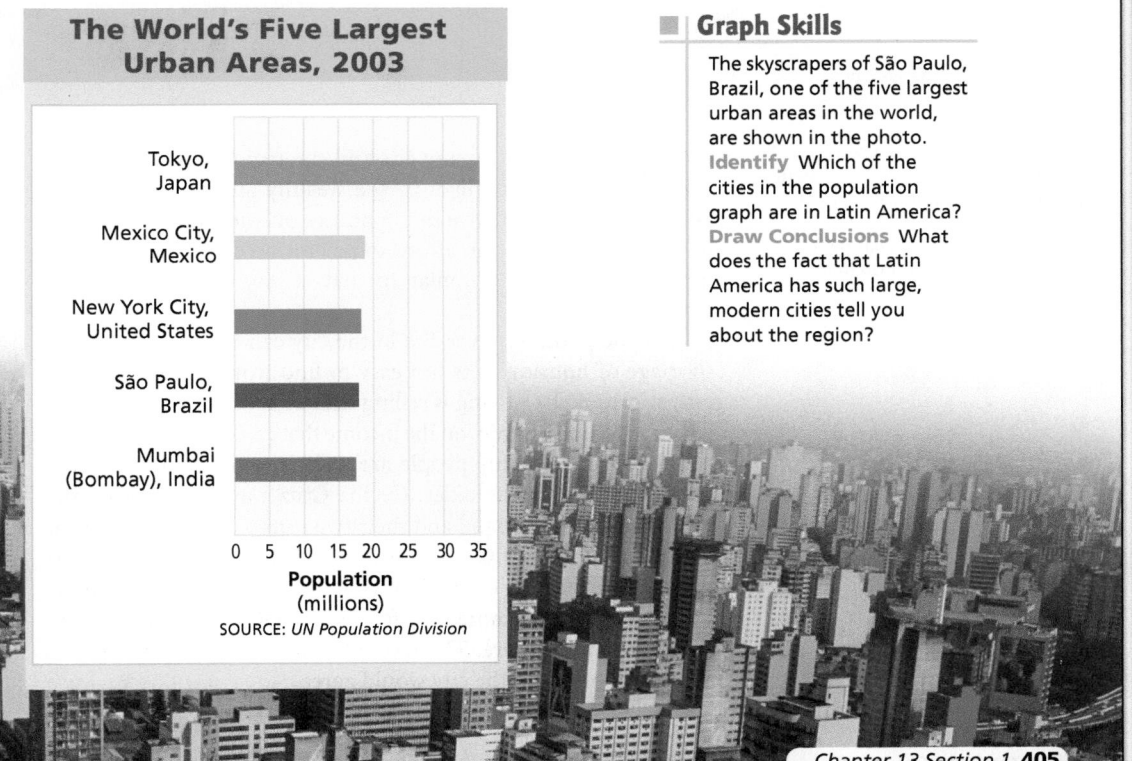

The World's Five Largest Urban Areas, 2003

Population (millions) — cities listed: Tokyo, Japan; Mexico City, Mexico; New York City, United States; São Paulo, Brazil; Mumbai (Bombay), India. Scale 0 5 10 15 20 25 30 35.

SOURCE: UN Population Division

Graph Skills

The skyscrapers of São Paulo, Brazil, one of the five largest urban areas in the world, are shown in the photo. **Identify** Which of the cities in the population graph are in Latin America? **Draw Conclusions** What does the fact that Latin America has such large, modern cities tell you about the region?

Chapter 13 Section 1 **405**

Target Reading Skill L2

Identify Causes and Effects As a follow up, ask students to answer the Target Reading Skill question in the Student Edition. *(Cause—rapid population growth; Effect—Many young people have left their homes in the countryside to find work in the cities.)*

Leaving the Countryside L2

Guided Instruction

- **Vocabulary Builder** Clarify the high-use words **rural** and **urban** before reading.

- With students, read about the changes in population distribution in Middle America in Leaving the Countryside. As students read, circulate and make sure that individuals can answer the Reading Check question.

- Ask students **Why are many rural people in Middle America moving to the cities? What might be some drawbacks to living in the cities?** *(Because of a huge growth in population, there are few jobs in the countryside. This forces many young people to leave their homes to look for work in the cities. The cities provide jobs and a better education than the countryside does. However, many people who go to the cities end up living in crowded conditions and in poverty.)*

- Discuss with students the reasons why some people from Middle America emigrate to other countries. *(because they want a better life in a new land or to earn good money before returning home)*

Answers

Graph Skills Identify Mexico City, São Paulo **Draw Conclusions** It is an urbanized region, with a large percentage of the population living in cities.

Independent Practice

Assign *Guided Reading and Review.*

 Latin America Teaching Resources, *Guided Reading and Review,* p. 189

Monitor Progress

Tell students to fill in the last column of the *Reading Readiness Guide.* Probe for what they learned that confirms or invalidates each statement.

 Latin America Teaching Resources, *Reading Readiness Guide,* p. 188

Assess and Reteach

Assess Progress   L2

Have students complete the Section Assessment. Administer the *Section Quiz.*

 Latin America Teaching Resources, *Section Quiz,* p. 190

Reteach   L1

If students need more instruction, have them read this section in the Reading and Vocabulary Study Guide.

Chapter 13, Section 1, **Western Hemisphere Reading and Vocabulary Study Guide,** pp. 148–150

Extend   L3

Have students investigate the challenges of living in a growing city by completing *Nickel-and-Diming* from Environmental and Global Issues. After they discuss the questions in pairs, have volunteers share their ideas with the class.

Go Online PHSchool.com **For:** Environmental and Global Issues: *Nickel-and-Diming*
Visit: PHSchool.com
Web Code: lfd-1304

Answer

Analyze Images The people are wearing similar clothes that feature colorful patterns. This type of clothing is probably traditional. The food for sale appears to be a native fruit, and it is probably a common part of their diet.

A Market in Guatemala
Guatemalans shop at a traditional market in Totonicapán, one of the country's largest cities.
Analyze Images *What details in this photo reflect Guatemalan culture?*

Life in the City In many cities in the region, there are sharp contrasts between the lives of the wealthy and the lives of the poor. Wealthy people live in big houses on wide streets. They go to good schools and can afford to pay for medical care. Many of them have a lifestyle similar to that of wealthy people in the United States.

For the poor, however, life in the city can be hard. There is a shortage of housing. It is not easy to find work. Sometimes, the only way to make a living is selling fruit or soda on street corners. It is hard to feed a family on the income that can be earned this way.

Nevertheless, many people are willing to live with the hardships they find in the cities. Cecilia Cruz can explain why. She moved with her husband and their two sons to Mexico City from the southern state of Oaxaca (wah HAH kah). They live in a two-room house made of cinder blocks. It is on the outermost boundary of the city. "We came here for the schools," says Cruz. "There are more choices here. The level of education is much higher." Most newcomers to the city would agree.

406 Latin America

 Skills Mini Lesson

Making Predictions   L2

1. Point out to students that if they understand how certain causes produce certain effects, they can use that knowledge to make predictions.

2. Help students practice the skill by reading the following pair of sentences and determining which is the cause and which is the effect.

   ■ Thousands of young people in the countryside cannot find jobs. *(cause)*

   ■ Thousands move to cities to find work. *(effect)*

3. Have students apply the skill by answering these questions: People moved away from the countryside because they could not find jobs. What if new industries developed in the countryside? What might happen to the population? *(People might move back to the countryside to get jobs in the new industries.)*

Moving to the United States Most people in Mexico and Central America move somewhere else within their own country if they cannot find work. However, there are also thousands of people who emigrate. To **emigrate** is to leave one country and settle in another. Most leave to find jobs. Many of them emigrate to the United States.

Fermin Carrillo (fehr MEEN kah REE yoh) is one worker who did just that. He left his home town of Huaynamota (wy nah MOH tah), Mexico. There were no more jobs at home, and his parents needed food and medical care. Carrillo moved to a town in Oregon. Now he works in a fish processing plant. He sends most of the money he earns home to his parents. Carrillo hopes one day to become an American citizen.

Other immigrants are different. An **immigrant** is a person who has moved into one country from another. These immigrants want to return home after earning some money to help their families.

Building a Better Life Many Mexicans and Central Americans, like Fermin Carrillo, have left the region in search of a better life. Many more have followed Elvia Alvarado's example. You read about Alvarado's work with community groups in Honduras. She helps poor farmers get seeds, farm machinery, and more land. Like Alvarado, many Middle Americans have stayed at home and begun to build a better life for themselves and their neighbors.

A modern Tarahumara Indian of Mexico wearing traditional clothing

✓ Reading Check **Why do many Mexicans move to the United States?**

![compass star] **Section 1 Assessment**

Key Terms
Review the key terms at the beginning of this section. Use each term in a sentence that explains its meaning.

Target Reading Skill
What are three effects of the Spanish colonization of Middle America?

Comprehension and Critical Thinking
1. (a) Identify What are the main languages and religions of the people of Middle America?

(b) Identify Cause and Effect How do the languages and religions of Middle America reflect the region's history?
(c) Predict How might this diversity lead to challenges for the region?
2. (a) Recall Describe life in the countryside and in the city.
(b) Identify Causes What is one reason that rural people in Mexico and Central America are moving to the cities?
(c) Predict What impact might the emigration of many Mexicans have on their country?

Writing Activity
Write a journal entry from the point of view of one of the people you read about in this section. Think about what life is like for that person. Include his or her hopes, dreams, and experiences.

Go Online
PHSchool.com

For: An activity on indigenous peoples
Visit: PHSchool.com
Web Code: lfd-1301

Chapter 13 Section 1 **407**

Writing Activity
Use the *Rubric for Assessing a Journal Entry* to evaluate students' journal entries.
![All in One] **Latin America Teaching Resources,** *Rubric for Assessing a Journal Entry,* p. 215

Go Online
PHSchool.com Typing in the Web code when prompted will bring students directly to detailed instructions for this activity.

Answers

✓ Reading Check Many Mexicans come to the United States to improve their way of life, to earn money to help support their families, and to find better jobs than they could find at home.

Section 1 Assessment

Key Terms
Students' sentences should reflect an understanding of each Key Term.

Target Reading Skill
Three effects of Spanish colonization of Middle America are: Spanish is the major language in the region; Catholicism is the main religion in the region; and a large number of the people are of Spanish descent or of mixed Spanish and Native-American descent.

Comprehension and Critical Thinking
1. (a) Although some indigenous languages still exist, Spanish is the main language in the region. Catholicism, with some elements of Native American beliefs, is the main religion in the region. **(b)** The languages and religions vary within the region, reflecting the fact that different groups have lived there over time. However, the fact that Spanish and Catholicism are the main language and main religion reflects that the Spanish conquered the indigenous people. **(c)** Some groups of indigenous people might want to gain back their lands or fight to have other rights. Indigenous groups may resent people of Spanish descent. People of Spanish descent might be prejudiced against mestizo or indigenous people.

2. (a) In the countryside, the population is growing rapidly. This is leading to unemployment. Young people leave their towns to go to the cities to find work. In the cities, people are crowded together and often live in poverty, although there are more jobs and schools are usually better than in the countryside. **(b)** The rapid rise in the population is leading to unemployment in the rural areas, forcing people to move to the cities to find jobs. **(c)** If too many people emigrate from Mexico, the country would lose people with skills that are important for its economy. Also, if people work in other countries, they pay taxes there, so Mexico loses tax money when workers leave the country.

Skills for Life

Objective

Learn how to distinguish fact and opinion.

Prepare to Read

Build Background Knowledge   L2

On the board, write a statement of fact and a statement of opinion. (For example: *Fact*—"Our community's population is 15,000." *Opinion*—"Our community is the prettiest in the state.") Ask volunteers to identify which statement is a fact and which is an opinion, and then label each statement accordingly. Discuss what makes each statement a fact or an opinion, and then ask students to write short definitions of fact and opinion.

Instruct

Distinguishing Fact and Opinion   L2

Guided Practice

- Read the steps to analyze statements in the sample paragraph and determine if the statements are facts or opinions.

- Practice the skill by following the steps on p. 408 as a class. Model each step in the activity by choosing a sample fact from the paragraph (*Urbanization takes place when people move from rural areas to urban areas*), and explaining how that fact could be proven true (*by looking the word up in a dictionary*). Then identify a word in the paragraph that judges (*bad*), and any words that signal personal feeling in that statement (*I believe*), and decide if the statement could be proven true or false. (*The words* I believe *signal that this is an opinion, not a fact. However, it might be possible to prove that the belief is a fact if enough evidence can be found that supports that opinion.*)

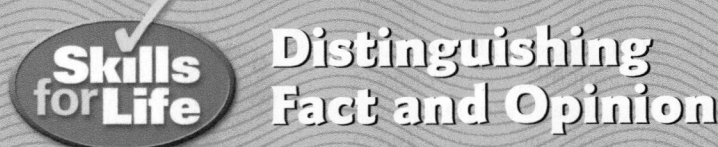

Skills for Life — Distinguishing Fact and Opinion

Kate was excited. She was going to Papantla, Mexico. Lila had just been there. "The bus ride is very long and boring," she told Kate. "The town is not interesting. You should skip that trip!"

Kate's guidebook said that Papantla is near the ruins of an ancient Indian city and that traditional dances are still performed there. The bus schedule said it was a three-hour ride. Her map showed that the bus traveled through the mountains.

Kate hurried off to buy a ticket. She relied on facts rather than opinions. That the bus ride is three hours long is a **fact**. Lila's statement that the bus ride "is very long and boring" is an **opinion**.

Distinguishing fact from opinion is something you need to do almost every day. You do it as you—like Kate—reach your own decisions.

Learn the Skill

To distinguish fact from opinion, use the following steps.

1 **Look for facts by asking what can be proved true or false.** A fact usually tells who, what, when, where, or how much.

2 **Ask how you could check whether each fact is true.** Could you do your own test by measuring or counting? Could you find information in an encyclopedia?

3 **Look for opinions by identifying personal beliefs or value judgments.** Look for words that signal personal feelings, such as *I think*. Look for words that judge, such as *beautiful* and *ugly* or *should* and *ought to*. An opinion cannot be proved true *or* false.

4 **Ask whether each opinion is supported by facts or good reasons.** A well-supported opinion can help you make up your own mind—as long as you recognize it as an opinion and not a fact.

Independent Practice

Assign *Skills for Life* and have students complete it individually.

All in One **Latin America Teaching Resources,** *Skills for Life,* p. 204

Monitor Progress

As students complete the *Skills for Life* worksheet, circulate to make sure they understand the skills steps.

Practice the Skill

Read the paragraph in the box at the right until you are sure that you understand its meaning. Then read for facts and opinions.

1 Identify facts in the paragraph that tell how much, what, where, or when.

2 Explain how each fact you identified could be proven true or false.

3 (a) Identify two words that judge. Could the statements containing these words be proved true or false? (b) Identify one example of words that signal personal feelings. Could this statement be proved true or false?

4 The second sentence of the paragraph expresses an opinion. Is the opinion well supported with facts and reasons?

> Urbanization takes place when people move from rural areas to urban areas. I believe that urbanization in Mexico is bad. First, the cities are already too crowded. There are thousands of homeless people in urban areas. Many people can't find jobs. Second, the city streets were not designed for so many cars. Traffic jams are a huge headache. Finally, the water and electrical systems do not have the capacity to serve more people. I think the time has come for the government to stop urbanization.

Apply the Skill

Look at the travel brochure above. List three facts and two opinions from the brochure. Are the opinions well supported? How useful would this brochure be if you were planning a trip? Explain your answer.

Differentiated Instruction

For Special Needs Students L1
Partner special needs students with proficient readers to do Level 1 of the *Distinguishing Fact and Opinion* lesson on the Social Studies Skills Tutor CD-ROM together. When the students feel more confident, they can move onto Level 2 alone.

⊙ *Distinguishing Fact and Opinion,* **Social Studies Skills Tutor CD-ROM**

For Less Proficient Readers L1
Have less proficient readers think of a topic that interests them, such as sports or computer games. Then have them make a two-column chart, with their topic written at the top. The first column is labeled *Facts* and the second is labeled *Opinions.* Have students fill in the chart with at least three facts and three opinions about the topic.

Assess and Reteach

Assess Progress L2
Ask students to do the Apply the Skill activity.

Reteach L1
If students are having trouble applying the skill steps, have them review the skill using the interactive Social Studies Skills Tutor CD-ROM.

⊙ *Distinguishing Fact and Opinion,* **Social Studies Skills Tutor CD-ROM**

Extend L3
To extend the lesson, ask students to apply the skill steps to identify fact and opinion in a short newspaper or magazine article. Ask students to identify at least three facts in the article and explain how each one could be proven true or false. Then ask students to identify at least two opinions, if applicable. They should point out any words that signal a personal feeling, and tell if and how, the statements could be proved true or false. Point out to students that when reporters write straight news articles, they try to avoid expressing their personal opinion. An editorial, on the other hand, is an expression of someone's opinion.

Answers
Apply the Skill

Facts: 1. Costa Rica has rain forests and beaches. **2.** Costa Rica has volcanoes. **3.** The weather is warm all year round.

Opinions: 1. Costa Rica is the most beautiful country in Latin America. **2.** Costa Rica's beaches are "relaxing;" the rain forests are "beautiful;" the volcanoes are "amazing."

The opinions are not well supported, since there are no facts provided to back them up. Some students may feel that the brochure would be helpful in planning a vacation; others may feel that the brochure does not offer enough facts to be useful.

Section 2
Step-by-Step Instruction

Objectives
Social Studies

1. Find out what ethnic groups make up the people of the Caribbean.
2. Learn how the different cultures of the region blended to create Caribbean food, music, and celebrations.

Reading/Language Arts

Recognize multiple causes to understand the development of complex events.

Prepare to Read

Build Background Knowledge
L2

In this section, students will learn about Caribbean cultures. Draw the beginnings of a word web on the board. In the center oval write "Caribbean." Ask students to quickly preview the section then ask them what they know about the Caribbean. Conduct an Idea Wave (TE, p. T35) to elicit student ideas, and add relevant responses to the word web.

Set a Purpose for Reading
L2

- Preview the Objectives.
- Read each statement from the *Reading Readiness Guide* aloud. Ask students to mark the statements true or false.

   All in One Latin America Teaching Resources, *Reading Readiness Guide,* p. 192

- Have students discuss the statements in pairs or groups of four, then mark their worksheets again. Use the Numbered Heads participation structure (TE, p. T36) to call on students to share their group's perspectives.

Vocabulary Builder
Preview Key Terms
L2

Pronounce each Key Term, and then ask students to say the word with you. Provide a simple explanation such as, "The West Indies is another name for the region called the Caribbean."

Section 2
The Cultures of the Caribbean

Prepare to Read

Objectives
In this section you will
1. Find out what ethnic groups make up the people of the Caribbean.
2. Learn how the different cultures of the region blended to create Caribbean food, music, and celebrations.

Taking Notes
As you read the section, look for the main ideas and details about Caribbean culture. Copy the format below and use it to outline the section.

> I. The people of the Caribbean
> A. The first people of the Caribbean
>   1.
>   2.
>   3.
> B. People in the Caribbean today

Target Reading Skill

Recognize Multiple Causes A cause makes something happen. An effect is what happens. Sometimes an effect can have more than one cause. For example, the distinctive quality of Caribbean food is an effect with several causes, including local fishing and farming as well as the cultural heritage of the West Indian people. As you read this section, identify multiple causes for other characteristics of Caribbean culture.

Key Terms
- **West Indies** (west IN deez) *n.* the Caribbean islands
- **ethnic group** (ETH nik groop) *n.* a group of people who share the same ancestry, language, religion, or cultural traditions
- **Carnival** (KAHR nuh vul) *n.* a lively annual celebration just before Lent in Latin America

The Caribbean islands are spread across more than 2,000 miles (3,219 kilometers), from Florida to the northeast coast of South America. There are more than a dozen different nations in the Caribbean region. As you might expect, a variety of peoples with many different cultures live within this large area.

This watercolor showing the Arawaks was painted in the 1800s.

The People of the Caribbean

The Caribbean islands are also called the **West Indies** because Christopher Columbus, when he first arrived there, thought he had reached the Indies in Asia. That's why he called the people of the islands *Indians*.

410 Latin America

Target Reading Skill
L2

Recognize Multiple Causes Point out the Target Reading Skill. Tell students that, often, an event or problem has more than one cause. To understand a complex situation, it is important to recognize if it has various causes and what they might be.

Model recognizing multiple causes using this passage on p. 411: "Because so many people came to the Caribbean as colonists, slaves, or immigrants, the area has a rich ethnic variety." (*Effect*—The Caribbean has great ethnic diversity. *Causes*—Colonists from European countries settled in the region; Africans were brought to the region as slaves; immigrants from countries such as China arrived.)

Give students *Recognize Multiple Causes.* Have them complete the activity in groups.

   All in One Latin America Teaching Resources, *Recognize Multiple Causes,* p. 200

410 *Latin America*

The First People of the Caribbean Long before Columbus arrived, the first people to live on these islands were a Native American group called the Ciboney (see buh NAY). The Ciboney lived in the region for thousands of years. In about 300 B.C., they were joined by another indigenous group, the Arawaks (AH rah wahks), who came from South America. In about 1000, the Caribs (KAR ibz), another South American group, arrived.

The Caribs gave the region its name. They lived in the Caribbean for more than 400 years before the first Europeans arrived. Christopher Columbus and other Spaniards enslaved the Native Americans. Almost all of the Caribs, Arawaks, and other indigenous groups died either of overwork or of diseases the Spanish brought with them. Today, there are just a few hundred Caribs. They live on the island of Dominica.

Other Europeans followed the Spanish. They hoped to make money from the region's wealth of natural resources. In the 1600s, Dutch, French, and English colonists began claiming territory. They built large sugar plantations and brought many enslaved Africans to work on them.

Most of the Caribbean people today are descended from these Africans. Immigrants from China, India, and the Middle East have also come to the region to work.

People in the Caribbean Today Because so many people came to the Caribbean as colonists, slaves, or immigrants, the area has a rich ethnic variety. An **ethnic group** is a group of people who share the same ancestry, language, religion, or cultural traditions. The ethnic groups of the Caribbean are Native American, African, European, Asian, and Middle Eastern.

Recognize Multiple Causes
There are very few Native Americans left on the Caribbean islands. What causes of this effect are given in the paragraph at the left?

Caribbean Diversity
These teenagers are students in the French West Indies. **Generalize** *How does this group reflect the population of the Caribbean?*

Chapter 13 Section 2 **411**

Depending on their island's history, the people of a Caribbean island may speak one of several European languages. Their language may also be a mixture of European and African languages. For example, two countries and two cultures exist on the island of Hispaniola. On the eastern half is one country, the Dominican Republic. Its population is Spanish-speaking and mostly mestizo. West of the Dominican Republic is the country of Haiti. Nearly all of Haiti's people are descended from Africans. They speak French and Haitian Creole, a French-based language with some African and Spanish words.

Most West Indians are Christians, but there are also small groups of Hindus, Muslims, and Jews. Some people practice traditional African religions.

Life on the Islands Most of the Caribbean islands have very fertile soil, and many people in the region make their living farming. Dorothy Samuels is a ten-year-old from Jamaica, one of the Caribbean islands. Her family are farmers. They plant yams and other vegetables and fruits. They also plant cacao beans. Every Saturday, Dorothy's mother and grandmother take their fruits and vegetables to the market to sell. All the traders at their market are women.

Dorothy is a good student. She hopes one day to go to college in Kingston, Jamaica's capital city. Jamaican laws require that women have as much opportunity for education as men have. Equality for women is important in Jamaican culture because many Jamaican women are independent farmers and business owners.

✓ **Reading Check** How are women's rights and opportunities protected in Jamaica?

Skills Mini Lesson

Answers

✓ **Reading Check** The right of Jamaican women to equal opportunities in education is protected by law. Equality for women is important in Jamaica because so many women are independent farmers and business owners.

A Blend of Cultures

The rich culture of the Caribbean has a variety of sources. West Indians enjoy many kinds of music and dance, celebrations, and food. They also play a variety of sports. Baseball, soccer, and track and field are popular. On some islands, people also play cricket, which is a British game similar to baseball. Dominoes—although not a sport—is a popular game throughout the region.

Carnival Many people in the Caribbean observe the Roman Catholic tradition of Lent, which is the period of 40 days before Easter Sunday. Because Lent is a very solemn time, these people have a lively public festival called **Carnival** just before Lent.

Different countries celebrate Carnival in different ways. In Trinidad and Tobago, for example, people spend all year making costumes and floats for the celebration. Lent always starts on a Wednesday. At 5 A.M. the Monday before, people go into the streets in their costumes. Calypso bands play. Thousands of fans follow the bands through the streets, dancing and celebrating. At the stroke of midnight on Tuesday, the party stops. Lent has begun.

Carnival Celebration
The dancers below are Carnival performers in Port of Spain, Trinidad, while the girl on the facing page has dressed up for the celebration. *Draw Inferences What do the costumes and props indicate about how much time and effort goes into preparing for this celebration?*

Background: Links Across Time

Calypso In the early 1800s, enslaved West Africans in Trinidad developed the Caribbean musical style *calypso*. Often forbidden to communicate with each other, the enslaved Africans developed a folk form using a call-and-response style brought from Africa. The songs expressed the slaves' feelings about slave masters and other local figures. After the abolition of slavery in 1838, calypso groups began competing during the Carnival season before Lent.

In the 1940s and 1950s, calypso moved on to the world stage, via popular recordings. An example of a very famous calypso recording is Harry Belafonte's *Banana Boat Song (Day-O)*. Calypso was also the basis for more recent Caribbean musical styles, such as reggae and soca.

Guided Instruction (continued)

■ Have students identify elements of blended Caribbean culture in religion, food, and music. (*Religion—Carnival is celebrated before Lent, which is a Roman Catholic practice brought from Europe. The celebration has characteristics of other cultures, such as Calypso music, which has African roots. Food—Caribbean cooking blends local foods and recipes from various cultures, including African, Indian, British, and Chinese. Music—Caribbean music is a blend of both African and European musical traditions.*)

Independent Practice

Have students complete the Taking Notes outline by jotting down details from A Blend of Cultures.

Monitor Progress

■ When students are finished with their outlines, show *Section Reading Support Transparency LA 37* and ask students to check their outlines individually. Go over key concepts and clarify key vocabulary as needed.

　📖 **Latin America Transparencies,** *Section Reading Support Transparency LA 37*

■ Tell students to fill in the last column of the *Reading Readiness Guide*. Probe for what they learned that confirms or invalidates each statement.

　All in One **Latin America Teaching Resources,** *Reading Readiness Guide*, p. 192

Answers

Draw Inferences The props and costumes show that a lot of time and effort went into preparing for the celebration.

Assess and Reteach

Assess Progress `L2`

Have students complete the Section Assessment. Administer the *Section Quiz*.

> **All in One** **Latin America Teaching Resources,** *Section Quiz*, p. 194

Reteach `L1`

If students need more instruction, have them read this section in the Reading and Vocabulary Study Guide.

> Chapter 13, Section 2, **Western Hemisphere Reading and Vocabulary Study Guide,** pp. 151–153

Extend `L3`

Remind students about the different types of music they learned about in the video *Caribbean Music: It's All in the Mix*. Make the music of Latin America come alive for students by having them create simple percussion instruments. *Small Group Activity: Share the Music* gives students complete instructions for creating some instruments used in the region.

> *Caribbean Music: It's All in the Mix,* **World Studies Video Program**

> **All in One** **Latin America Teaching Resources,** *Small Group Activity: Share the Music,* pp. 205–208

Answers

> ✓ **Reading Check** Calypso songs have humorous lyrics and a distinctive beat. Reggae from Jamaica has a strong rhythm with a "chunking" sound at the end of each measure, and the lyrics are sometimes political.

Section 2 Assessment

Key Terms

Students' sentences should reflect an understanding of each Key Term.

Target Reading Skill

Causes include: Europeans colonizing islands in the region; Africans being brought to the islands as slaves to work on plantations; more recently, new groups, such as Chinese, Indians, and people from the Middle East immigrating to the Caribbean.

Comprehension and Critical Thinking

1. (a) The Ciboney, Arawaks, and Caribs. **(b)** They died of overwork or Spanish diseases.

This waiter in Grenada shows a variety of Caribbean dishes.

Food Caribbean food is a mixture that represents the different cultures of the islands. It also makes use of the rich natural resources of the region. Caribbean people can enjoy many types of seafood that are not found in United States waters. For instance, the people of Barbados love to eat flying fish and sea urchin eggs. Bammy—a bread made from the cassava plant—is still made the way the African slaves made it. West Indians also cook spicy curries from India, sausages from England, and Chinese dishes. Many tropical fruits grow on the islands. The fruits are used to make many juices and other drinks that are not readily available in the United States.

Music Caribbean music, which has both African and European sources, is famous around the world. Calypso is a form of song that uses humorous lyrics and has a distinctive beat. Reggae (REHG ay) music and ska come from Jamaica. Reggae songs have a strong rhythm with a "chunking" sound at the end of each measure. The lyrics of traditional reggae songs often have political messages.

Another distinctive Caribbean musical sound is that made by steel drums. These instruments are made from recycled oil drums. A steel drum can be tuned so that different parts of it play different notes. Players strike the instruments with rubberized drumsticks.

> ✓ **Reading Check** **Describe two types of Caribbean music.**

Section 2 Assessment

Key Terms

Review the key terms at the beginning of this section. Use each term in a sentence that explains its meaning.

Target Reading Skill

What are three reasons, or causes, for the diversity of ethnic groups and cultures in the Caribbean?

Comprehension and Critical Thinking

1. (a) Identify Who were the first inhabitants of the Caribbean islands?
(b) Explain What happened to those people? Why?
(c) Identify Causes Why do West Indians speak a variety of languages today?
2. (a) Recall What kinds of activities do Caribbean people enjoy?
(b) Categorize Which traditions have these activities come from?
(c) Draw Conclusions Why is there more of a cultural blend in the Caribbean than in Middle America?

Writing Activity

Select one aspect of Caribbean culture, such as food, music, or celebrations. Write a paragraph comparing and contrasting that aspect of Caribbean culture with the cultural practices where you live.

> **Writing Tip** Before you begin, decide how you will organize your paragraph. One way is to cover all the similarities first and then all the differences.

(c) West Indians speak a variety of languages because so many different groups came to live there.

2. (a) Caribbean people enjoy festivals, cooking and eating, music and dance, and sports and games. **(b)** Most of these activities are a blend of African and European traditions, but also include traditions from Chinese, Indian, and other cultures. **(c)** because many more types of people came to the Caribbean to conquer the area, to farm it, and to work there, than came to Middle America

Writing Activity

Use the Rubric for *Assessing a Writing Assignment* to evaluate students' paragraphs.

> **All in One** **Latin America Teaching Resources,** *Rubric for Assessing a Writing Assignment,* p. 216

The Cultures of South America

Prepare to Read

Objectives

In this section you will
1. Find out what ethnic groups are represented in the different cultural regions of South America.
2. Learn what life is like in the countryside and the cities of South America.

Taking Notes

As you read this section, look for information about the cultural regions of South America. Copy the table below and record your findings in it.

Location of Region	Countries	Characteristics
Caribbean Coast		

Target Reading Skill

Understand Effects An effect is what happens as the result of a specific cause or factor. For example, you can see in the paragraph below that the geography of the Lake Titicaca region has had several effects on the way the Native Americans there live. This section discusses the effects of geography and colonization on different regions of South America. As you read, note the effects of each of these factors on the way South Americans live today.

Key Terms

- **gauchos** (GOW chohz) *n.* cowboys of the pampas of Argentina
- **subsistence farming** (sub SIS tuns FAHR ming) *n.* growing only enough food to meet the needs of the farmer's family
- **cash crop** (kash krahp) *n.* a crop grown mostly for sale rather than for the farmer's own use

---

Between Peru and Bolivia is the deep lake called Lake Titicaca. It lies high in the Andes Mountains. This area is cool and dry. There are few trees. Native Americans here make their living from totora reeds, a kind of thick, hollow grass that grows on the lakeshore. They use these reeds to make houses, mats, hats, ropes, sails, toys, roofs, and floors. They eat the reeds, feed them to livestock, and brew them into tea. Totora reeds can even be made into medicine.

Long ago, a number of Native American groups built floating islands with totora reeds. They used the islands to hide from the Incas. Today, some Native Americans still live on floating islands on Lake Titicaca.

Native Americans who live on Lake Titicaca make their boats out of totora reeds.

Chapter 13 Section 3 **415**

Objectives

Social Studies

1. Find out what ethnic groups are represented in the four cultural regions of South America.
2. Learn what life is like in the countryside and in the cities of South America.

Reading/Language Arts

Understand how one cause can bring about multiple effects.

Prepare to Read

Build Background Knowledge   `L2`

In this section, students will learn about the cultures of South America. Explain that, along with Middle America and the Caribbean, the Spanish also colonized much of South America. Based on what they have learned from Sections 1 and 2 of this chapter, have students predict what South American cultures might have in common with the other regions of Latin America. Conduct an Idea Wave (TE, p. T35) to elicit responses.

Set a Purpose for Reading   `L2`

- Preview the Objectives.
- Distribute the worksheet and read each statement from the *Reading Readiness Guide* aloud. Ask students to mark the statements true or false.

    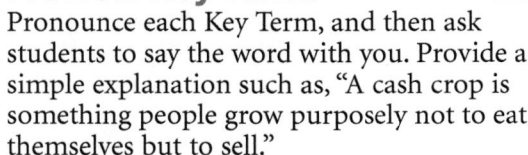 **Latin America Teaching Resources,** *Reading Readiness Guide,* p. 196

- Have students discuss the statements in pairs or groups of four, then mark their worksheets again. Use the Numbered Heads participation structure (TE, p. 36) to call on students to share their group's perspectives.

Target Reading Skill   `L2`

Understand Effects Point out the Target Reading Skill. Tell students that it is important to understand what the effects of different causes are, and how those effects change and shape the world.

Model understanding effects using this passage on p. 419: "Export farming uses so much land for cash crops that South America has to import food for its own people to eat." (*The effect of South American countries using so much farm land for growing cash crops is that many South American countries import food to eat.*)

Give students *Understand Effects.* Have them complete the activity in groups.

 **Latin America Teaching Resources,** *Understand Effects,* p. 201

Vocabulary Builder

Preview Key Terms   `L2`

Pronounce each Key Term, and then ask students to say the word with you. Provide a simple explanation such as, "A cash crop is something people grow purposely not to eat themselves but to sell."

Target Reading Skill

Understand Effects As a follow up, ask students to answer the Target Reading Skill question in the Student Edition. *(Many people in South America speak Spanish and are Catholic.)*

Instruct

The People of South America

Guided Instruction

- **Vocabulary Builder** Clarify the high-use words **official** and **style** before reading.
- Read The People of South America using the Structured Silent Reading technique (TE, p. T34).
- Ask students **What are the four cultural regions of South America?** *(northern South America; the Andean region; Argentina, Chile, Paraguay, and Uruguay; and Brazil.)*
- Ask students **How has history influenced the culture of the Caribbean coast?** *(The languages, religions, and ethnic groups of each country have been influenced by the countries that colonized the area.)*

Answers

Conclude The land in the photo seems to be suitable for raising llamas, but might be difficult to farm.

416 *Latin America*

Understand Effects What two effects of Spanish colonization are described in the paragraph at the right?

An Ancient Way of Life
Toco Indians in Peru wear traditional clothing and herd llamas much as their ancestors did. **Conclude** *Look at the setting of the photo. How do you think geography has contributed to these people keeping their traditional way of life?*

416 Latin America

The People of South America

Most South Americans today are descended from Native Americans, Africans, or Europeans. In this way, they are like the people of Mexico and Central America. Like its neighbors to the north, South America, too, was colonized mainly by Spain. Today, many South Americans speak Spanish and are Catholic, yet different regions within South America have their own unique cultures.

Caribbean South America There are four cultural regions in South America. The first region includes Colombia, Venezuela, Guyana, Suriname, and French Guiana. These countries are in northern South America, on or near the Caribbean Sea. Their cultures are similar to those of the Caribbean islands.

Local history has also influenced the cultures of each nation. Colombia and Venezuela were Spanish colonies, and their people are mainly mestizo. Their official language is Spanish, and most of the people are Roman Catholic. On the other hand, Guyana, Suriname, and French Guiana were colonized by different European nations. Guyana was once an English colony, and its official language is English. Suriname was a Dutch colony until 1975, and the people there still speak Dutch. In both countries, many people are Muslim or Hindu. French Guiana is not an independent nation; it is an overseas department of France. While its official language is French, many of its people are of mixed African and European descent.

Vocabulary Builder

Use the information below to teach students this section's high-use words.

High-Use Word	Definition and Sample Sentence
official, p. 416	*adj.* lawful; having authority The document had an **official** seal on it.
style, p. 418	*n.* way or manner She wore her hair in an attractive **style.**
vast, p. 419	*adj.* very large and wide The auditorium was so **vast** that it could have seated a thousand people.
interior, p. 420	*n.* remote, inner part or area, especially of a country If you dislike the coast, try visiting the **interior** of the country.

■ Ask students **How do the Quechua and the Aymará keep their cultural traditions alive?** *(They speak their own languages and follow the ways of their ancestors.)*

■ Discuss Chile's geographic diversity with students. *(Chile has mountains, beaches, deserts, forests, and polar regions.)*

■ Ask students **How is the traditional lifestyle of the gauchos changing?** *(Cattle ranching is still important, but wheat fields are begin to replace grazing lands.)*

■ Ask students **What ethnic groups live in Brazil?** *(Native Americans, people of African and European descent, and people of mixed descent)*

The Andean Countries and the South To the south and west, the culture is very different. Peru, Ecuador, and Bolivia are Andean countries. Many Native Americans live high in the Andes Mountains. In Bolivia, there are more indigenous people than mestizos. The Quechua and Aymara (eye muh RAH) peoples speak their own languages and follow the traditional ways of their ancestors.

Cityscapes
This avenue in Buenos Aires, Argentina (left photo) is said to be the widest boulevard in the world. Signs in São Paulo, Brazil, (right photo) are in Portuguese and Japanese. **Draw Conclusions** *What can you conclude about South America's cities and culture from these two photos?*

The third cultural region consists of Chile, Argentina, Paraguay, and Uruguay. The long, narrow country of Chile has mountains, beaches, deserts, forests, and even glaciers. Although its geography is diverse, its people are not. Most people in Chile are mestizos. In Argentina and Uruguay, however, the big cities are very diverse. Many different ethnic groups live there.

Another culture exists on Argentina's pampas, or plains. The pampas are the traditional home of the **gauchos** (GOW chohz), the Argentinean cowboys. While cattle raising is still important, wheat fields are beginning to replace grazing lands on the pampas, and the day of the gaucho may be coming to an end.

Brazil South America's largest country was once a colony of Portugal, and today its people speak Portuguese. However, Brazil is culturally diverse. Many Native Americans live in Brazil, as do people of African and European descent. Some Brazilians are of mixed descent. Many people have moved to Brazil from other countries. Brazil's largest city, São Paulo (sow PAW loh), is home to more Japanese than any other place in the world except Japan.

Chapter 13 Section 3 **417**

Pampas Beef Industry The pampas, like the Great Plains in the United States, is an important source of beef for countries around the world. Argentina exports its beef to the European Union (its largest customer), the United States, and Canada, among many other countries. In 2002, the United States imported over 20,000 metric tons of processed beef from Argentina, worth $128 million, and representing 9 percent of Argentina's production. Argentina exported a total of 223,403 tons of beef in 2002, making it the eighth largest beef exporter in the world.

Answers

Draw Conclusions The larger photo shows a large and modern city. The smaller photo shows signs in different languages. From these photos, one can conclude that South America's cities are large, modern, and diverse.

Read **Citizen Heroes** with students. Ask **How did these women achieve their leadership role?** (*The Mothers of the "Disappeared" became leaders by continuing to protest when their government refused to account for their children's disappearances.*)

Guided Instruction (continued)

■ Ask students **How are South American women fighting for their rights?** (*Some are getting bank loans to start small businesses.*)

■ Ask students to list the South American writers discussed in the text along with what country they are from. (*Possible answers: Gabriela Mistral, Chile; Pablo Neruda, Chile; Gabriel Garcia Marquez, Colombia; Isabel Allende, Chile*)

Independent Practice

Ask students to create the Taking Notes chart on a blank piece of paper. Students then fill the chart in with information they have just read. Briefly model by filling in the first box.

Monitor Progress

As students fill in the graphic organizer, circulate and make sure that individuals are choosing the correct details. Provide assistance as needed.

Show *Section Reading Support Transparency LA 38* and ask students to check their graphic organizers individually. Go over key concepts and clarify key vocabulary as needed.

Latin America Transparencies, *Section Reading Support Transparency LA 38*

Answers

√ Reading Check South American women are fighting for equal rights in the areas of education, jobs, access to health care, and political power.

Citizen Heroes

Mothers of the "Disappeared"

In 1976, a military government took control of Argentina and began arresting people who opposed their regime. Other opponents of the government simply "disappeared"—kidnapped by unidentified armed men. Fourteen mothers of these "disappeared" demanded information about their children. When the government did not respond, the women began to march in front of the presidential palace every Thursday at 3:30 P.M. They became know as the Mothers of Plaza de Mayo (PLAH zuh day MY oh). Their peaceful protests brought worldwide attention to their cause. As one observer put it, "These are women who moved from being housewives in Argentina to being global leaders for justice."

South American Literature South America has produced many famous writers. Gabriela Mistral (gah bree AY lah mees TRAHL), a poet from Chile, was the first Latin American to win the Nobel Prize for Literature. Her poetry reflects her love of children, and so does her second career as a teacher. When she was a school principal, she encouraged the young Chilean poet Pablo Neruda (PAH bloh neh ROO duh). He went on to win the Nobel Prize in 1971. When he was a young man, Neruda composed complex poems. Toward the end of his life, however, he wrote about simple, everyday objects, such as onions and socks.

Another South American winner of the Nobel Prize for Literature was the Colombian novelist Gabriel García Márquez (gah bree EL gahr SEE ah MAHR kes). He is best known for novels in the style of magic realism, which mixes fantasy with historical facts and realistic stories. Isabel Allende (EES uh bel ah YEN day), a novelist from Chile, also uses magic realism in many of her novels and stories. She is also known for her "letters" to members of her family, which were published as books.

The Role of Women In some ways, women do not yet play a role equal to that of men in South America. Women in South America are more likely than men to be poor. They also do not attend school for as many years as men do.

More and more women in South America today are fighting to make a living for themselves and their children. They are demanding equal rights. Women are struggling for the rights to go to school, to work in all types of jobs, to have good health care, and to have a voice in government. Some women are getting bank loans to start small businesses. These businesses are sometimes based on traditional skills such as sewing, weaving, or preparing food.

√ Reading Check **What rights are women fighting for?**

Differentiated Instruction

For Gifted and Talented [L3]

Have students research and write a biography of one of the authors mentioned on Student Edition p. 418. Have students give brief outlines of their subjects' lives as oral reports to the class, including a poem or brief excerpt of the author's work. If students are Spanish speakers, have them read the work in Spanish first and then in English.

For Less Proficient Readers [L1]

Have students use the Passport to the World CD-ROM to enrich and extend their knowledge of Brazil. They can take the Photo Tour and examine the Timeline of the country.

Brazil, **Passport to the World CD-ROM**

Country and City Life

South America has cities with millions of people, but it also has vast areas with almost no people at all. Many South Americans still live in the countryside, but others are leaving farms and moving to cities.

Farming in South America Outside of Argentina, Chile, and Uruguay, most rural people with land of their own do **subsistence farming.** That means they grow only enough food to meet their families' needs. They have only small plots of land. These farmers plant corn, beans, potatoes, and rice.

Very large farms grow crops to export to other countries. The main export cash crops of South America are coffee, sugar, cacao, and bananas. **Cash crops** are crops grown mostly for sale rather than for the farmer's own use. Export farming uses so much land for cash crops that South America has to import food for its own people to eat.

South America's Cities The cities of South America illustrate the region's mix of cultures. Many major cities—Lima, Peru, and Buenos Aires, Argentina, for example—were founded by Spanish colonists more than 400 years ago. Much of their architecture is Spanish in style. Some buildings in even older cities follow Native American designs.

Two Ways to Farm
The top photo shows a banana processing plant on a plantation in Ecuador. Below is a small family-owned coffee farm in Colombia.
Infer *Why might plantation owners not be interested in farming the area in the lower photo? How easy do you think it is to make a living there?*

Country and City Life L2

Guided Instruction

- **Vocabulary Builder** Clarify the high-use words **vast** and **interior** before reading.

- With students, read about the characteristics of the urban and rural experience in South America in Country and City Life. As students read, circulate and make sure that individuals can answer the Reading Check question.

- Ask students to list the characteristics of South America's countryside and the characteristics of South America's cities. (*Countryside—Many people still live there, but some areas have almost no people; in most countries rural people practice subsistence farming; cash crops use much of the land and keep countries from growing enough food to feed the people. Cities— have a cultural mix; architecture is Spanish and modern, with some Native-American buildings; some cities have slums called* favelas *or* ranchos; *rural people are moving to cities; cities are crowded and resources are under great pressure; some governments cannot provide enough water and electricity.*)

Independent Practice
Assign *Guided Reading and Review.*

All in One **Latin America Teaching Resources,** *Guided Reading and Review,* p. 197

Monitor Progress
Tell students to fill in the last column of the *Reading Readiness Guide.* Probe for what they learned that confirms or invalidates each statement.

All in One **Latin America Teaching Resources,** *Reading Readiness Guide,* p. 196

Differentiated Instruction

For Special Needs Students L1
Have students read the section as they listen to the recording on the Student Edition on Audio CD. Check for comprehension by pausing the CD and asking students to share their answers to the Reading Check questions.

⊙ **Chapter 13, Section 3, Student Edition on Audio CD**

For English Language Learners L2
Before students read, have them skim the section and select two to four words which are unfamiliar to them, or which interest them. Have students write each word with its part of speech and definition, and then write a sentence using the word. Partner them with native English speakers to review the information and sentences.

Answer
Infer because the area is hilly and looks inaccessible; it is probably hard to make a living there

Assess and Reteach

Assess Progress

Have students complete the Section Assessment. Administer the *Section Quiz.*

 Latin America Teaching Resources, *Section Quiz,* p. 198

Reteach

If students need more instruction, have them read this section in the Reading and Vocabulary Study Guide.

Chapter 13, Section 3, **Western Hemisphere Reading and Vocabulary Study Guide,** pp. 154–156

Extend

Have students learn more about the art of Latin America by completing the *Enrichment* activity.

 Latin America Teaching Resources, *Enrichment,* p. 203

Answers

√ Reading Check buildings in the Spanish colonial style, new, modern structures of concrete, steel, and glass; and some of Native American design

Infer electricity

Section 3 Assessment

Key Terms

Students' sentences should reflect an understanding of each Key Term.

Target Reading Skill

Many still follow the traditional ways of their ancestors and speak their own languages.

Comprehension and Critical Thinking

1. (a) Cultural regions of South America: Northern—very diverse area; includes many different groups and colonial histories. Andean—many indigenous people still live here and ancient languages and traditions are still alive. Chile, Argentina, Paraguay, and Uruguay—mostly mestizos and Spanish speaking, although large cities are diverse. Brazil—official language is Portuguese; Native Americans, people of African and European descent, and Japanese live there. **(b)** Native Americans have been able to maintain their cultures in remote areas like the Andes Mountains. Argentineans developed a ranching culture on the plains of the pampas.

City of Contrasts
This view of Buenos Aires shows poor neighborhoods in the foreground while the modern downtown rises in the distance. **Infer** *What city services do the people in the foreground seem to lack?*

In contrast, modern office blocks and apartment buildings of concrete, steel, and glass tower above the downtown areas of many South American cities. One or two cities were built quite recently. Brasília, the Brazilian capital, was constructed in the 1950s. It was a completely planned city, designed to draw people to the country's interior.

On the other hand, the slums of many South American cities have certainly been unplanned. They are called *favelas* (fuh VEH lus) in Brazil and *ranchos* in Venezuela. The population of South America is booming. Like Mexicans and Central Americans, South Americans cannot find enough jobs in rural areas. Every day, thousands of rural people move to the cities looking for work. Usually they end up in poor neighborhoods. City governments try to provide electricity and running water to everyone. But people move into cities so quickly that it is hard for city governments to keep up.

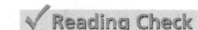 √ Reading Check **What types of buildings are found in South American cities?**

Section 3 Assessment

Key Terms
Review the key terms at the beginning of this section. Use each term in a sentence that explains its meaning.

Target Reading Skill
What are two effects of the fact that many Native Americans still live high in the Andes Mountains?

Comprehension and Critical Thinking
1. (a) Recall Describe two cultural regions of South America.

(b) Identify Cause and Effect Explain two ways in which the geography of South America has shaped how people live.
2. (a) Identify Describe two different kinds of farms in South America.
(b) Compare and Contrast How are city life and rural life similar and different?
(c) Analyze Information How does the movement of people from the countryside to urban areas put pressure on cities?

Writing Activity
Suppose you were a newspaper reporter visiting Argentina in 1976. Write a short article about the Mothers of Plaza de Mayo for your American readers.

For: An activity on South America
Visit: PHSchool.com
Web Code: lfd-1303

2. (a) Subsistence farming is done by individual families to raise food to survive. Cash crops are raised on large farms to be sold. **(b)** Similar—the poor struggle to survive on very little; different—some areas of the countryside are empty, while the cities are crowded. **(c)** Cities must increase services such as water and electricity. Housing can be in short supply, leading to the development of slums and homelessness.

Writing Activity
Use the *Rubric for Assessing a Newspaper Article* to evaluate students' articles.

 Latin America Teaching Resources, *Rubric for Assessing a Newspaper Article,* p. 217

Go Online PHSchool.com Typing in the Web code when prompted will bring students directly to detailed instructions for this activity.

Review and Assessment

◆ Chapter Summary

Section 1: The Cultures of Middle America

- Many different cultural groups live in Middle America, and the languages and arts of the region reflect this diversity.
- Population growth and lack of jobs have caused many rural Middle Americans to move to the cities or to emigrate to the United States.

Section 2: The Cultures of the Caribbean

- The people of the Caribbean are made up of many ethnic groups, including descendants of Africans and Europeans.
- West Indian sports, food, music, and celebrations reflect the blend of cultures in the Caribbean.

Section 3: The Cultures of South America

- Life in the different cultural regions of South America is influenced by geography and by the ethnic groups that settled there.
- South America has both large farms that export their crops and small subsistence farms.
- South American cities are overcrowded with poor rural people coming to look for work.

Mexico

French West Indies

Ecuador

◆ Key Terms

Match the definitions in Column I with the key terms in Column II.

Column I
1. a group of people who share ancestry, language, religion, or cultural traditions
2. descendants of the people who first lived in a region
3. growing only enough food to meet the needs of their families
4. a person who has moved from one country to settle in another
5. a poor farmer who owns little or no land

Column II

A indigenous people

B campesino

C immigrant

D ethnic group

E subsistence farming

Chapter 13 **421**

Review Chapter Content

- Revisit the Guiding Questions on p. 329 of the Student Edition. Then have students review the major themes of this chapter by deciding what Guiding Question each bulleted statement in the Chapter Summary answers. Write the statements on the board and have students work in groups to classify them.
- Assign *Vocabulary Development* for students to review Key Terms.

  All in One **Latin America Teaching Resources,** *Vocabulary Development,* p. 214

Answers

Key Terms

1. **D, ethnic group** *(a group of people who share ancestry, language, religion, or cultural traditions)*

2. **A, indigenous people** *(descendants of the people who first lived in a region)*

3. **E, subsistence farming** *(growing only enough food to meet the needs of their families)*

4. **C, immigrant** *(a person who has moved from one country to another)*

5. **B, campesino** *(a poor farmer who owns little or no land)*

⌐ Vocabulary Builder ─────

Revisit this chapter's high-use words:

heritage	influence	rural
urban	fertile	require
distinctive	festival	tradition
official	style	vast
interior		

Ask students to review the definitions they recorded on their *Word Knowledge* worksheets.

All in One **Latin America Teaching Resources,** *Word Knowledge,* p. 202

Consider allowing students to earn extra credit if they use the words in their answers to the questions in the chapter Review and Assessment. The words must be used correctly and in a natural context to earn extra points.

Review and Assessment

Comprehension and Critical Thinking

6. (a) In general, the population is rising in Middle America. **(b)** The rise in population is making jobs scarce, especially in rural areas, so many people in those regions are moving to cities.

7. (a) The Ciboney were the first people to live in the Caribbean; later the Arawak and Carib people also populated the region. **(b)** When the Spanish colonized the Caribbean, most Native Americans were enslaved and died of overwork or from European diseases. **(c)** The Caribbean has been colonized by many different European groups, who also brought enslaved Africans there to work on plantations. In modern times, people from other parts of the world, such as China, India, and the Middle East, have also come to the Caribbean to live and work.

8. (a) Carnival is a festival celebrated by Roman Catholics just before the fasting period of Lent. **(b)** In the Caribbean, this festival occurs before Lent and includes elements of West Indian cultures, such as African-influenced music and costumes.

9. (a) Portuguese **(b)** Unlike the rest of South America, which was mainly colonized by Spain, Brazil was colonized by Portugal, and Brazil's language and culture reflect this.

10. (a) *Ranchos* is the word for "slums" in Brazil; *favelas* is the word for "slums" in Venezuela. **(b)** Many rural people have gone to the cities to look for jobs, and they often end up in these very poor areas. **(c)** Because there are not enough jobs in the countryside, people flock to the cities, where governments have a difficult time keeping up with the demand for services, such as water and electricity.

11. (a) Cash crops are crops that are grown to sell, not to feed a farm family. **(b)** Huge amounts of land are used to grow cash crops for export, and not to grow food to feed the people.

Skills Practice
Facts: "There is so much variety from the different cultures in the area."; "There are also lots of tropical fruits and juices."; "A lot of food is quite spicy"; "The Carib Heaven Restaurant will give you a chance to try. . . cuisine."

◆ Comprehension and Critical Thinking

6. (a) Recall Describe population growth in Middle America.
(b) Identify Effects How has population growth affected the movement of people in that region?

7. (a) Identify Who were the first people to inhabit the Caribbean islands?
(b) Identify Cause and Effect What happened to those people, and why?
(c) Draw Conclusions Why is there such cultural diversity in the Caribbean today?

8. (a) Define What is Carnival?
(b) Identify Cause and Effect How does Carnival reflect both West Indian culture and Roman Catholic traditions?

9. (a) Describe What language is spoken in Brazil?
(b) Identify Effects Why are Brazil's culture and language different from the rest of South America's?

10. (a) Define What are *ranchos* and *favelas*?
(b) Identify Causes Why are they growing?
(c) Draw Conclusions How do conditions in the countryside affect these city neighborhoods?

11. (a) Define What are cash crops?
(b) Conclude Why does export farming cause problems for some South American countries?

◆ Skills Practice

Distinguishing Fact and Opinion In the Skills for Life activity in this chapter, you learned how to distinguish facts from opinions. You also learned how to use facts and well-supported opinions to help you make decisions.

Read the paragraph below. List the facts and the opinions. Explain how this paragraph could help you decide whether to try the Carib Heaven Restaurant.

> Caribbean food is the best in the world. There is so much variety from the different cultures of the area. There are also lots of tropical fruits and juices. A lot of the food is quite spicy—just the way I like it! The Carib Heaven Restaurant will give you a chance to try this great cuisine.

◆ Writing Activity: Geography

Suppose you are a writer for a travel magazine. Write an article about one of the places you "visited" in this chapter. Include descriptions of the landforms, waterways, climate, and vegetation. Explain how geography has affected the way people live in that place.

Refer to the maps in the Regional Overview and in Chapter 11 as well as to the information in this chapter. You can also do additional research if you wish.

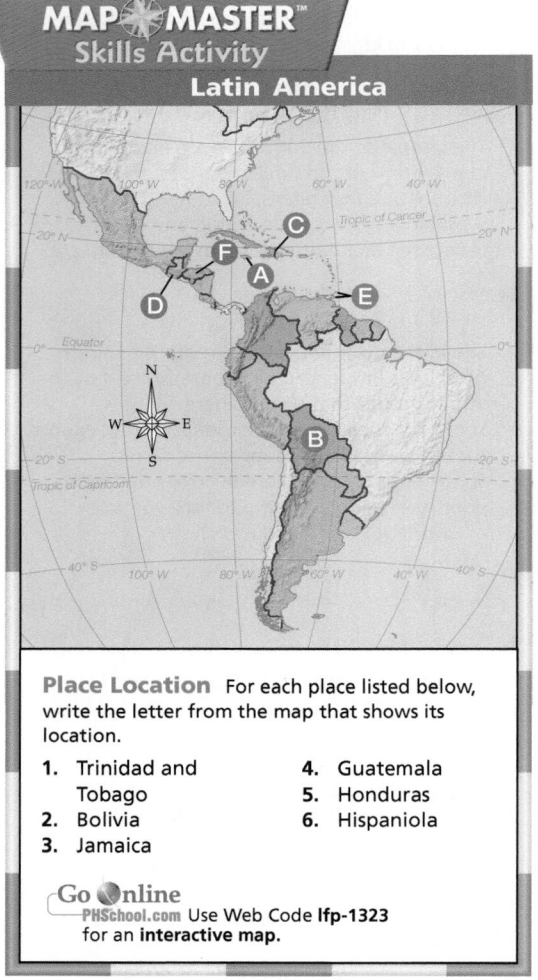

MAP MASTER™
Skills Activity
Latin America

Place Location For each place listed below, write the letter from the map that shows its location.

1. Trinidad and Tobago
2. Bolivia
3. Jamaica
4. Guatemala
5. Honduras
6. Hispaniola

Go Online
PHSchool.com Use Web Code lfp-1323 for an **interactive map**.

Opinions: "Caribbean food is the best in the world"; "just the way I like it (spicy)"; "this is great cuisine"

Students' answers will vary. Students may focus on a particular detail about food served by the restaurant, such as the fact that the food is spicy, in deciding whether they would want to try eating there.

Writing Activity: Geography
Students' answers will vary, but should focus on one of the places described in the chapter, and include information about landforms, waterways, climate, and vegetation.

Use *Rubric for Assessing a Newspaper Article* to evaluate students' reports.

All in One Latin America Teaching Resources, *Rubric for Assessing a Newspaper Article*, p. 217

Standardized Test Prep

Test-Taking Tips

Some questions on standardized tests ask you to analyze graphs and charts. Look at the circle graph at the right. Then follow the tips to answer the sample question.

Think It Through Because only one percent of Mexicans are Protestant, you can eliminate answer D. You can also eliminate A easily, because England had little influence on Mexico. You know from the text that the Aztec influence was important, but you can see from the graph that the Aztec religion does not play a large role in Mexico today. That leaves the Roman Catholic country of Spain, which makes sense when you consider Mexico's history. Therefore, the correct answer is B.

TIP Draw your own conclusions about the graph before you look at the answer choices.

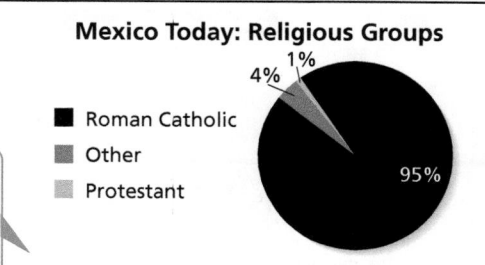

Mexico Today: Religious Groups

- ■ Roman Catholic
- ■ Other
- ■ Protestant

1%
4%
95%

Pick the letter that best answers the question.

The information in the graph could be used to show the influence of

- **A** England on the development of modern Mexico.
- **B** Spain on the development of modern Mexico.
- **C** Ancient Aztecs on the development of modern Mexico.
- **D** Protestantism on the development of modern Mexico.

TIP Look for the BEST answer, as more than one answer choice may seem to fit.

Practice Questions

Choose the letter of the best answer.

1. Most of the people of Mexico and Central America are
   - **A** indigenous or of mixed ancestry.
   - **B** European or Spanish.
   - **C** indigenous or European.
   - **D** Spanish or of mixed ancestry.

2. Rapid population growth in Mexico and Central America has caused all of the following EXCEPT
   - **A** migration to cities.
   - **B** emigration to other countries.
   - **C** fewer jobs for everyone.
   - **D** better living conditions in the cities.

3. The Andean countries of South America include
   - **A** Bolivia, Peru, and Ecuador.
   - **B** Peru, Brazil, and Bolivia.
   - **C** Brazil, Argentina, and Chile.
   - **D** Bolivia, Ecuador, and Argentina.

Study the circle graphs and answer the question that follows.

Venezuela Population: 1950

Rural 47%
Urban 53%

Venezuela Population: 2002

Rural 13%
Urban 87%

4. Which sentence best describes the population trend in Venezuela?
   - **A** The rural population has steadily increased.
   - **B** The urban and rural populations have remained the same.
   - **C** The urban population has steadily increased.
   - **D** The urban population has steadily decreased.

Go Online PHSchool.com

Use Web Code lfa-1301 for a **Chapter 13 self-test.**

Chapter 13 **423**

MAP MASTER Skills Activity

1. E	**2.** B
3. A	**4.** D
5. F	**6.** C

Go Online PHSchool.com Students may practice their map skills using the interactive online version of this map.

Standardized Test Prep

Answers

1. A
2. D
3. A
4. C

Go Online PHSchool.com Students may use the Chapter 13 self-test on PHSchool.com to prepare for the Chapter Test.

Assessment Resources

Use *Chapter Tests A and B* to assess students' mastery of chapter content.

All in One Latin America Teaching Resources, *Chapter Tests A and B,* pp. 218–223

Tests are also available on the *ExamView® Test Bank CD-ROM.*

⦿ *ExamView® Test Bank CD-ROM*

Use a benchmark test to evaluate students' cumulative understanding of what they have learned in Chapters 1 through 3.

📄 *Latin America Benchmark Test 1,* **AYP Monitoring Assessments,** pp. 97–100

Overview

Introducing Mexico and Central America
1. Use data to compare countries.
2. Learn what characteristics Mexico and most Central American countries share.
3. Name some key differences among the countries.

Section **1**

Mexico: Moving to the City
1. Learn what life is like for people in rural Mexico.
2. Find out why many Mexicans have been moving from the countryside to the cities.
3. Understand why the growth of Mexico City presents challenges for the people and the environment.

Section **2**

Guatemala: Descendants of an Ancient People
1. Learn why there is a struggle for land in Guatemala.
2. Find out how the Mayas lost their land.
3. Discover how groups are working to improve the lives of Guatemala's indigenous people.

Section **3**

Panama: An Important Crossroads
1. Find out why people wanted to build a canal across the Isthmus of Panama.
2. Learn how the Panama Canal was built.
3. Understand how the canal has affected the nation of Panama.

Technology Resources

Students use embedded web codes to access internet activities, chapter self-tests, and additional map practice. They may also access Dorling Kindersley's Online Desk Reference to learn more about each country they study.

Use the Interactive Textbook to make content and concepts come alive through animations, videos, and activities that accompany the complete basal text—online and on CD-ROM.

PRENTICE HALL

Use this complete suite of powerful teaching tools to make planning lessons and administering tests quicker and easier.

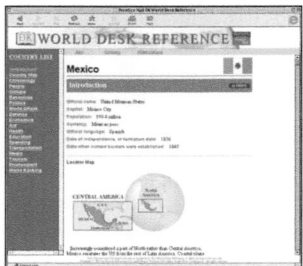

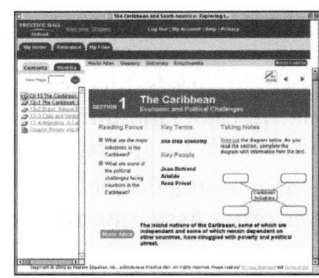

Reading and Assessment

Reading and Vocabulary Instruction

🔁 Model the Target Reading Skill

Context Understanding how to derive meaning from context clues can help students become more confident and better readers.

Model using context clues to better understand unfamiliar words by thinking aloud about this sentence from page 430: *Mexico's population has risen dramatically over the last 30 years.*

This sentence uses the word *dramatically.* I think this is an important word, but I'm not completely sure of its meaning. Because it is right next to the word *risen,* I am going to guess that *dramatically* describes how or how much the population of Mexico has risen. Maybe something in the next sentence will give me another clue. The next sentence says: *The country's population is growing at one of the highest rates in the world.* That's a great clue. Now I can see that *dramatically* in this context must mean a lot, or a great deal.

Use the following worksheets from All-in-One Latin America Teaching Resources (pp. 239–241) to support this chapter's Target Reading Skill.

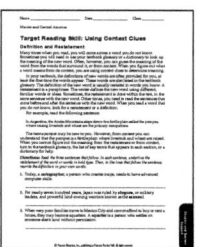 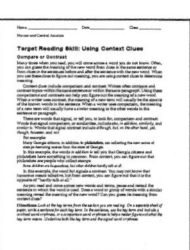 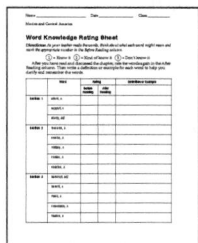

Vocabulary Builder
High-Use Academic Words
Use these steps to teach this chapter's high-use words:

1. Have students rate how well they know each word on their Word Knowledge worksheets (All-in-One Latin America Teaching Resources, p. 242).

2. Pronounce each word and ask students to repeat it.

3. Give students a brief definition or sample sentence (provided in TE pp. 431, 438, and 445.)

4. Work with students as they fill in the "Definition or Example" column of their Word Knowledge worksheets.

Assessment

Formal Assessment
Test students' understanding of core knowledge and skills.

> **Chapter Tests A and B,**
> All-in-One Latin America
> Teaching Resources, pp. 265–270

Customize the Chapter Tests
to suit your needs.
> **Exam *View*® Test Bank
> CD-ROM**

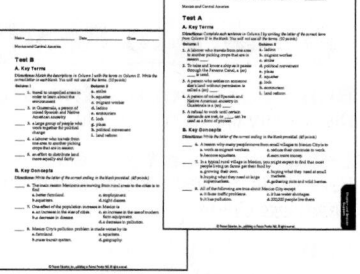

Skills Assessment
Assess geographic literacy.

> **MapMaster Skills,** Student Edition pp. 425, 434, 445, 452
> **Country Profile Map and Chart Skills,** Student Edition pp. 432, 439, 446

Assess reading and comprehension.

> **Target Reading Skills,** Student Edition, pp. 435, 438, 448 and in Section Assessments
> **Chapter 14 Assessment,** Reading and Vocabulary Study Guide, p. 167

Performance Assessment
Assess students' performance on this chapter's Writing Activities using the following rubrics from All-in-One Latin America Teaching Resources.

> **Rubric for Assessing a Bar Graph,** p. 260
> **Rubric for Assessing a Journal Entry,** p. 261
> **Rubric for Assessing a Report,** p. 262
> **Rubric for Assessing a Writing Assignment,** p. 263
> **Rubric for Assessing a Newspaper Article,** p. 264

Assess students' work through performance tasks.

> **Small Group Activity: Simulation: Who Should Control the Panama Canal?** All-in-One Latin America Teaching Resources, pp. 245–248
> **Portfolio Activity,** Teacher Edition, p.101

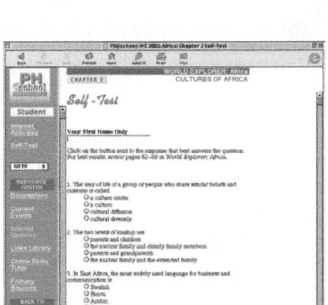

Online Assessment
Have students check their own understanding.

> **Chapter Self-Test**

Section 1 Mexico: Moving to the City

 2.5 periods, 1.25 block (includes Country Databank)

Social Studies Objectives
1. Learn what life is like for people in rural Mexico.
2. Find out why many Mexicans have been moving from the countryside to the cities.
3. Understand why the growth of Mexico City presents challenges for people and the environment.

Reading/Language Arts Objective
Use context clues to determine the meaning of unfamiliar words.

Prepare to Read

Build Background Knowledge
Discuss city life vs. country life.

Set a Purpose for Reading
Have students evaluate statements on the *Reading Readiness Guide*.

Preview Key Terms
Teach the section's Key Terms.

Target Reading Skill
Introduce the section's Target Reading Skill of **using context clues**.

Instructional Resources

All in One Latin America Teaching Resources
- L2 Reading Readiness Guide, p. 228
- L2 Use Context Clues: Definition/Description, p. 239

Differentiated Instruction

Spanish Reading and Vocabulary Study Guide
- L2 Chapter 14, Section 1, pp. 115–116 ELL

Discovery Channel World Studies Video Program
- L2 Mexico and Central America: Navigating the Highs and Lows ELL, LPR, SN

Instruct

Life in Rural Mexico
Ask students key questions about life in rural Mexico.

Country Profile
Direct students to derive information from maps, charts, and graphs.

Moving to Mexico City
Discuss why people are moving to Mexico City.

Opportunities and Challenges
Discuss pollution in Mexico City.

Target Reading Skill
Review **using context clues**.

Instructional Resources

All in One Latin America Teaching Resources
- L2 Guided Reading and Review, p. 229
- L2 Reading Readiness Guide, p. 228
- L2 Reading a Population Distribution Map, p. 251

Latin America Transparencies
- L2 Section Reading Support Transparency LA 39

Differentiated Instruction

All in One Latin America Teaching Resources
- L2 Outline Map 6: Mexico, p. 253 AR, GT, LPR, SN
- L2 Outline Map 7: Central America and the Caribbean, p. 254 AR, GT, LPR, SN

Latin America Teacher's Edition
- L1 For Special Needs Students, TE p. 428, 433
- L1 For Less Proficient Readers, TE p. 428, 433
- L3 For Advanced Readers, TE p. 434

Student Edition on Audio CD
- L1 Chapter 14, Section 1 SN, ELL, LPR
- L1 **Passport to the World CD-ROM** SN, LPR, ELL

Assess and Reteach

Assess Progress
Evaluate student comprehension with the section assessment and section quiz.

Reteach
Assign the Reading and Vocabulary Study Guide to help struggling students.

Extend
Extend the lesson by assigning an *Enrichment* activity.

Instructional Resources

All in One Latin America Teaching Resources
- L2 Section Quiz, p. 230
- L3 Enrichment, p. 243
  Rubric for Assessing a Journal Entry, p. 261

Reading and Vocabulary Study Guide
- L1 Chapter 14, Section 1, pp. 158–160

Differentiated Instruction

All in One Latin America Teaching Resources
  Rubric for Assessing a Bar Graph, p. 260

Spanish Support
- L2 Section Quiz (Spanish), p. 151 ELL

Key
- L1 Basic to Average
- L2 For All Students
- L3 Average to Advanced
- LPR Less Proficient Readers
- AR Advanced Readers
- SN Special Needs Students
- GT Gifted and Talented
- ELL English Language Learners

Section 2 Guatemala: Descendants of an Ancient People

 3 periods, 1.5 blocks (includes Skills for Life)

Social Studies Objectives

1. Learn why there is a struggle for land in Guatemala.
2. Find out how the Mayas lost their land.
3. Discover how groups are working to improve the lives of Guatamala's indigenous people.

Reading/Language Arts Objective

Use context clues that show contrast to determine the meaning of unfamiliar words.

Prepare to Read	**Instructional Resources**	**Differentiated Instruction**
Build Background Knowledge Use photographs to brainstorm about the Maya. **Set a Purpose for Reading** Have students evaluate statements on the *Reading Readiness Guide.* **Preview Key Terms** Teach the section's Key Terms. **Target Reading Skill** Introduce the section's Target Reading Skill of **using context clues**.	**All in One Latin America Teaching Resources** L2 Reading Readiness Guide, p. 232 L2 Use Context Clue: Compare and Contrast, p. 240	**Spanish Reading and Vocabulary Study Guide** L2 Chapter 14, Section 2, pp. 117–118 ELL

Instruct	**Instructional Resources**	**Differentiated Instruction**
The Struggle for Land Discuss the ownership and distribution of land. **Target Reading Skill** Review **using context clues**. **The Mayas Lose Their Land** Discuss the challenges facing the Mayas' ownership of land. **Country Profile** Direct students to derive information from maps, charts, and graphs. **Working for a Better Life** Discuss how the Mayas are improving their situation.	**All in One Latin America Teaching Resources** L2 Guided Reading and Review, p. 233 L2 Reading Readiness Guide, p. 232 L2 Reading a Circle Graph, p. 252 **Latin America Transparencies** L2 Section Reading Support Transparency LA 40	**All in One Latin America Teaching Resources** L2 Skills for Life, p. 244 AR, GT, LPR, SN **Latin America Teacher's Edition** L1 For English Language Learners, TE p. 440 L3 For Gifted and Talented Students, TE p. 440 **Student Edition on Audio CD** L1 Chapter 14, Section 2 ELL, LPR, SN **Spanish Support** L2 Guided Reading and Review (Spanish), p. 152 ELL

Assess and Reteach	**Instructional Resources**	**Differentiated Instruction**
Assess Progress Evaluate student comprehension with the section assessment and section quiz. **Reteach** Assign the Reading and Vocabulary Study Guide to help struggling students. **Extend** Extend the lesson by assigning a Book Project.	**All in One Latin America Teaching Resources** L2 Section Quiz, p. 234 L3 Book Project: Latin America in the News, pp. 76–78 Rubric for Assessing a Report, p. 262 **Reading and Vocabulary Study Guide** L1 Chapter 14, Section 2, pp. 161–163	**Latin America Teacher's Edition** L1 For Special Needs Students, p. 443 L3 For Gifted and Talented, TE p. 443 **Social Studies Skills Tutor CD-ROM** L1 Drawing Inferences and Conclusions LPR, SN, ELL

Key

L1 Basic to Average	L3 Average to Advanced	LPR Less Proficient Readers	GT Gifted and Talented
L2 For All Students		AR Advanced Readers	ELL English Language Learners
		SN Special Needs Students	

424d

Section 3 Panama: An Important Crossroads

3.5 periods, 1.75 blocks (includes Chapter Review and Assessment)

Social Studies Objectives

1. Find out why people wanted to build a canal across the Isthmus of Panama.
2. Learn how the Panama Canal was built.
3. Understand how the canal has affected the nation of Panama.

Reading/Language Arts Objective

Use context clues and your own knowledge to determine the meaning of unfamiliar words.

Prepare to Read	Instructional Resources	Differentiated Instruction
Build Background Knowledge Discuss aspects of Panama. **Set a Purpose for Reading** Have students begin to fill out the *Reading Readiness Guide.* **Preview Key Terms** Teach the section's Key Terms. **Target Reading Skill** Introduce the section's Target Reading Skill of **using context clues.**	**All in One Latin America Teaching Resources** L2 Reading Readiness Guide, p. 236 L2 Use Context Clues: General Knowledge, p. 241	**Spanish Reading and Vocabulary Study Guide** L2 Chapter 14, Section 3, pp. 119–120 ELL

Instruct	Instructional Resources	Differentiated Instruction
Why Build a Canal? Discuss the reasons for building the Panama Canal. **Country Profile** Direct students to derive information from maps, charts, and graphs. **Building the Canal: A Heroic Effort** Ask questions about how the canal was built. **Target Reading Skill** Review **using context clues.** **Panama and Its Canal** Ask questions about the control of the Panama Canal. **Eyewitness Technology** Teach students more about the Panama Canal.	**All in One Latin America Teaching Resources** L2 Guided Reading and Review, p. 237 L2 Reading Readiness Guide, p. 236 L2 Outline Map 7: Central America and the Caribbean, p. 254 L2 Doing Searches on the Internet, p. 258 L2 Activity Shop Lab: Making a Model Canal Lock, pp. 249–250 **Latin America Transparencies** L2 Section Reading Support Transparency LA 41	**All in One Latin America Teaching Resources** L3 Locks, Crocs, and Skeeters, pp. 255–256 AR, GT L3 Beyond the Chagres, p. 257 AR, GT **Latin America Teacher's Edition** L1 For Less Proficient Readers, TE p. 447 L3 For Advanced Readers, TE p. 447 L1 For Special Needs Students, TE p. 448 **Spanish Support** L2 Guided Reading and Review (Spanish), p. 155 ELL

Assess and Reteach	Instructional Resources	Differentiated Instruction
Assess Progress Evaluate student comprehension with the section assessment and section quiz. **Reteach** Assign the Reading and Vocabulary Study Guide to help struggling students. **Extend** Extend the lesson by assigning a Small Group Activity about who should control the Panama Canal.	**All in One Latin America Teaching Resources** L2 Section Quiz, p. 238 L3 Small Group Activity: pp. 245–248 Rubric for Assessing a Newspaper Article, p. 264 L2 Vocabulary Development, p. 259 L2 Chapter Tests A and B , p. 265–270	**Spanish Support** L2 Section Quiz (Spanish), p. 155 ELL L2 Chapter Summary (Spanish), p. 156 ELL L2 Vocabulary Development (Spanish), p. 157 ELL **Reading and Vocabulary Study Guide** L2 Chapter 14, Section 3, pp. 164–166

Key

L1 Basic to Average
L2 For All Students
L3 Average to Advanced

LPR Less Proficient Readers
AR Advanced Readers
SN Special Needs Students

GT Gifted and Talented
ELL English Language Learners

Reading Background

Applying New Words Outside the Classroom

Expand students' understanding of this chapter's vocabulary by assigning an activity which applies the chapter's Key Terms and high-use words to real life. Choose five or six vocabulary words from the chapter, such as *plaza, support, political movement, erosion,* and *benefit,* and ask students to list them in their notebooks.

Next, ask students where they might *see* these words outside of their textbook. List the responses on the board. Suggestions might include signs, newspapers, magazines, history books, fiction books, and biographies. Then ask students where they might *hear* these words. Answers might include television or radio news broadcasts, conversations with parents or other adults, and political speeches. Finally, ask students how they might *use* these words. Students can suggest sample sentences or topics of conversation.

Have students keep a log for one week in which they record where and how they see their selected words printed or spoken. Have students share their logs at the end of the week.

Encourage Active Participation

In this chapter, students will use an Idea Wave to share their ideas. Remind students that if their idea is closely related to another person's idea, they should acknowledge the other person's idea when they share theirs. Below are some language strategies for active classroom participation:

> *My idea is similar to _____'s idea.*
>
> *As _____ already pointed out, it seems like . . .*
>
> *I don't agree with _____ because . . .*

Be sure that students understand that it is acceptable and desirable for them to build on their classmates' ideas, using these strategies.

World Studies Background

Mexico's Cities

Mexico City is one of the biggest cities in the world, alongside Tokyo, Japan, São Paolo, Brazil, and New York City. Besides Mexico City, Mexico has two other large metropolitan areas—Guadalajara and Monterrey. Guadalajara is called "the most Mexican of cities." It has a rich history and plentiful cultural events. Monterrey, in the Sierra Madres, is considered Mexico's industrial powerhouse.

Political Unrest in Guatemala

Civil war erupted in Guatemala in the 1960s when leftist guerrilla movements challenged the harsh military regime. During the civil war, the government ruled through the heavy hand of "death squads" that routinely tortured and murdered critics, including students and labor leaders. More than 150,000 people were killed and another 40,000 "disappeared." The civil war finally ended in 1996.

Malaria

Although the malaria problem that plagued the building of the Panama Canal was eventually resolved by technological advancements, the disease is still a growing problem. Some three million people die each year as a result of malaria. Quinine was effective in treating malaria for many years. However, some strains of malaria have now grown resistant to the quinine cure. This factor, among others, is one cause of the latest rise of malaria.

Guiding Questions

Remind students about the Guiding Questions introduced at the beginning of this section.

Section 1 relates to **Guiding Question** ⑤ **How has geography influenced the ways in which Latin Americans make a living?** *(The dependence of rural Mexicans on farming is changing as more Mexicans move to cities.)*

Section 2 relates to **Guiding Question** ② **How has Latin America been shaped by its history?** *(The Mayas of Guatemala have been struggling to keep their land and their culture intact for five hundred years.)*

Section 3 relates to **Guiding Question** ⑤ **How has geography influenced the ways in which Latin Americans make a living?** *(The location of the isthmus in Panama spurred the building of the canal, which is a large part of Panama's economy.)*

⟳ Target Reading Skill

In this chapter, students will learn and apply the reading skill of using context clues. Use the following worksheets to help students practice this skill:

 Latin America Teaching Resources, *Use Context Clues: Definition/Description*, p. 239; *Use Context Clues: Compare and Contrast*, p. 240; *Use Context Clues: General Knowledge*, p. 241

Chapter Preview

This chapter will introduce you to the northernmost region of Latin America: Mexico and Central America.

Country Databank
The Country Databank provides data and descriptions of each of the countries in the region: Belize, Costa Rica, El Salvador, Guatemala, Honduras, Mexico, Nicaragua, and Panama.

Section 1
Mexico
Moving to the City

Section 2
Guatemala
Descendants of an Ancient People

Section 3
Panama
An Important Crossroads

⟳ Target Reading Skill

Context In this chapter you will focus on using context to help you understand unfamiliar words. Context includes the words, phrases, and sentences surrounding the word.

▶ A Guatemalan woman walking home from a rural market

Differentiated Instruction

The following Teacher Edition strategies are suitable for students of varying abilities.

Advanced Readers, pp. 434, 447
English Language Learners, p. 440
Gifted and Talented Students, pp. 440, 443
Less Proficient Readers, pp. 428, 433, 447
Special Needs Students, pp. 428, 433, 443, 448

Bibliography

For the Teacher
Ancona, George. *The Piñata Maker: El Piñatero.* Harcourt, 1994.
Nye, Naomi Shihab, ed. *The Tree is Older Than You Are: A Bilingual Gathering of Poems and Stories from Mexico with Paintings by Mexican Artists.* Simon, 1995.
St. George, Judith. *Panama Canal: Gateway to the World.* Putnam, 1989.

For the Student
L1 Herrera, Juan Felipe. *Calling the Doves/El canta de las palomas.* Children's Book Press, 1995.
L2 Rummel, Jack. *Mexico.* Chelsea, 1990.
L3 Castañada, Omar S. *Among the Volcanoes.* Lodestar, 1992.

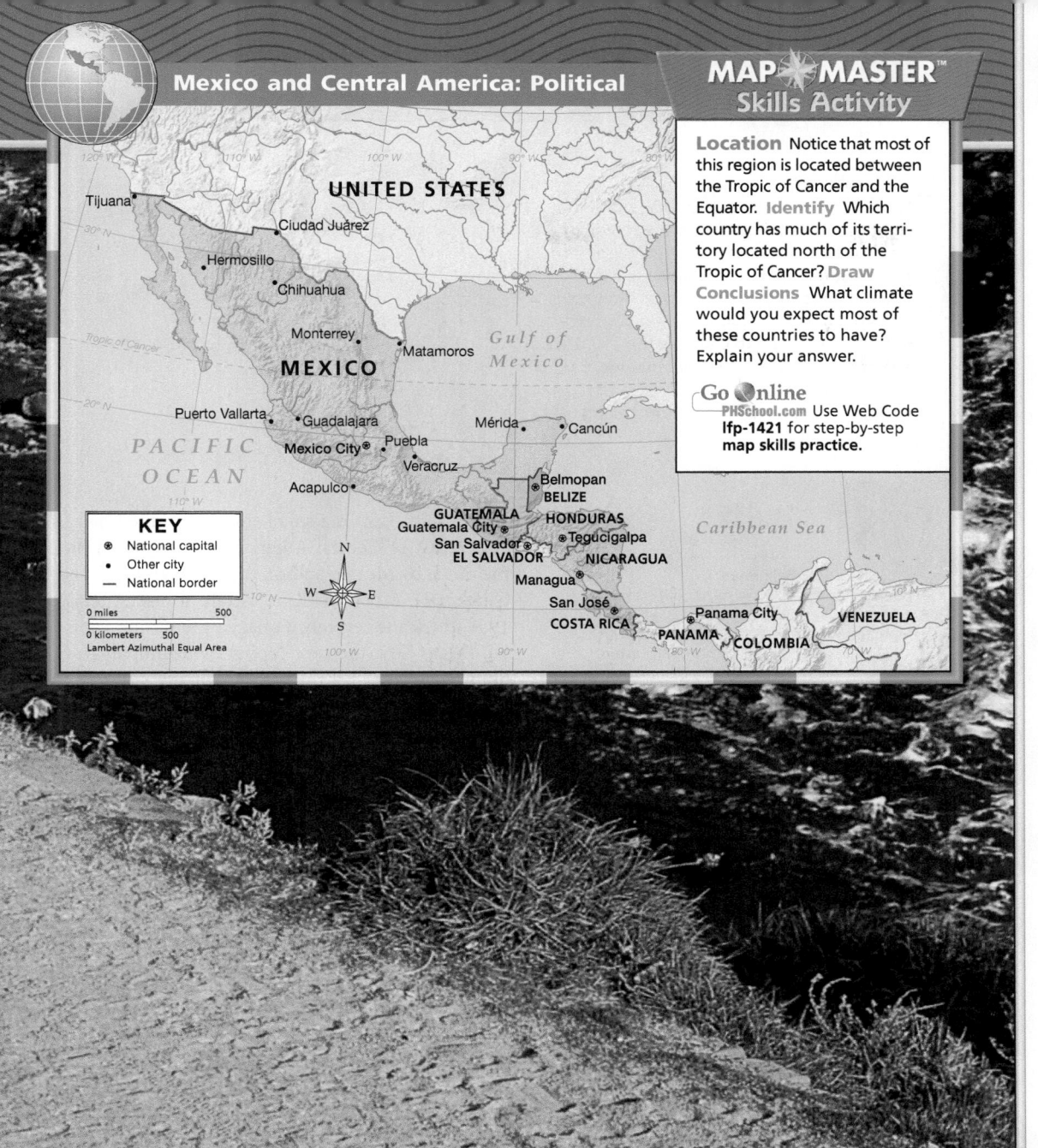

Mexico and Central America: Political

UNITED STATES

Tijuana
Ciudad Juárez
Hermosillo
Chihuahua
Monterrey
Matamoros
Gulf of Mexico
MEXICO
Puerto Vallarta
Guadalajara
Mérida
Cancún
PACIFIC OCEAN
Mexico City⊛
Puebla
Veracruz
Acapulco
Belmopan
BELIZE
GUATEMALA
Guatemala City⊛
HONDURAS
San Salvador⊛
Tegucigalpa
EL SALVADOR
NICARAGUA
Caribbean Sea
Managua
San José
Panama City
VENEZUELA
COSTA RICA
PANAMA
COLOMBIA

KEY
⊛ National capital
• Other city
— National border

0 miles 500
0 kilometers 500
Lambert Azimuthal Equal Area

N W E S

MAP ★ MASTER™ Skills Activity

Location Notice that most of this region is located between the Tropic of Cancer and the Equator. **Identify** Which country has much of its territory located north of the Tropic of Cancer? **Draw Conclusions** What climate would you expect most of these countries to have? Explain your answer.

Go Online
PHSchool.com Use Web Code lfp-1421 for step-by-step **map skills practice.**

Chapter 14 **425**

- Point out to students the shape of Mexico and Central America. Encourage students to trace the outline of the region, while describing its funnel shape.

- Write *Mexico* and the names of each country in Central America on the board. Then call on students to write the names of the capital cities next to the appropriate countries on the board. Point out that the map key provides a symbol for national capitals.

Go Online
PHSchool.com Students may practice their map skills using the interactive online version of this map.

Using the Visual   L2

Reach Into Your Background Draw students' attention to the caption accompanying the picture on pages 424–425. Discuss the visual with students. What interests them about this photo? Encourage students to share details about the woman and the landscape. Have them describe the scene in the photo. Why are markets important in all countries? Have students share their ideas.

Answers

MAP ★ MASTER Skills Activity **Identify** Mexico
Draw Conclusions Most of the countries have a warm climate because they are close to the Equator.

Chapter Resources

Teaching Resources
L2 Vocabulary Development, p. 259
L2 Skills for Life, p. 244
L2 Chapter Tests A and B, pp. 265–270

Spanish Support
L2 Spanish Chapter Summary, p. 156
L2 Spanish Vocabulary Development, p. 157

Media and Technology
L1 Student Edition on Audio CD
L1 Guided Reading Audiotapes, English and Spanish
L2 Social Studies Skills Tutor CD-ROM
ExamView Test Bank CD-ROM

PRENTICE HALL
Presentation EXPRESS™
Teach · Connect · Inspire

Teach this chapter's content using the PresentationExpress™ CD-ROM including:
- slide shows
- transparencies
- interactive maps and media
- *ExamView*® QuickTake Presenter

Objectives

- Use data to compare countries.
- Learn what characteristics Mexico and most Central American countries share.
- Name some key differences among the countries.

Prepare to Read

Build Background Knowledge   L2

Tell students that they will learn about Mexico and each country in Central America as they read the Country Databank. Show the World Studies video, telling students to note two or three facts about Mexico and Central America as they watch. Ask students to share what they know about Mexico and Central America and what they found interesting in the World Studies Video Overview. List the students' ideas on the board. Tell them that what they learn in this chapter may overturn some of their ideas about the region.

Mexico and Central America: Navigating the Highs and Lows, **World Studies Video Program**

Guide for Reading

This section provides an introduction to the eight countries that make up the region of Mexico and Central America.

- Look at the map on the previous page and then read the paragraphs below to learn about each nation.
- Analyze the data to compare the countries.
- What are the characteristics that most of the countries share?
- What are some key differences among the countries?

Belize

Capital	Belmopan
Land Area	8,805 sq mi; 22,806 sq km
Population	262,999
Ethnic Group(s)	mestizo, Creole, Maya, Garifuna
Religion(s)	Roman Catholic, Protestant
Government	parliamentary democracy
Currency	Belizean dollar
Leading Exports	sugar, bananas, citrus, clothing, fish products, molasses, wood
Language(s)	English (official), English Creole, Spanish, Mayan, Garifuna (Carib)

Belize (buh LEEZ) is a small country on the Caribbean coast of Central America. It is bordered on the north by Mexico and on the south and west by Guatemala. Much of Belize is rain forest. After a 1961 hurricane severely damaged the former capital, Belize City, the new capital of Belmopan was built. However, Belize City is still the country's largest and most important city. Formerly known as British Honduras, Belize was the last British colony in North America. It didn't become independent until 1981. Today, its government is based on the British model.

Jaguar in Belize

426 Latin America

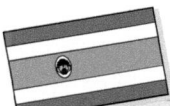

Costa Rica

Capital	San José
Land Area	19,560 sq mi; 50,660 sq km
Population	3.8 million
Ethnic Group(s)	white, mestizo, black, indigenous Indian, East Asian
Religion(s)	Roman Catholic, Protestant
Government	democratic republic
Currency	Costa Rican colón
Leading Exports	coffee, bananas, sugar, pineapples, textiles, electronics
Language(s)	Spanish (official), English Creole, Bribri, Cabecar

Costa Rica (KAHS tah REE kuh) is a narrow country located between the Pacific Ocean and the Caribbean Sea. It is bordered by Nicaragua and Panama. Even though its name means "rich coast," few riches were found there, and the Spanish colony grew slowly. Costa Rica gained its independence in 1838. Today it is known for its stable government, democratic traditions, and the fact that its army was abolished in 1948. Wealth is more evenly divided in Costa Rica than in other countries in the region, and more government resources go to education and public welfare.

El Salvador

Capital	San Salvador
Land Area	8,000 sq mi; 20,720 sq km
Population	6.4 million
Ethnic Group(s)	mestizo, indigenous Indian, white
Religion(s)	Roman Catholic, Protestant
Government	republic
Currency	Salvadoran colón, U.S. dollar
Leading Exports	offshore assembly exports, coffee, sugar, shrimp, textiles, chemicals, electricity
Language(s)	Spanish (official)

Small and densely populated, El Salvador (el SAL vuh dawr) is one of the poorest countries in the region. It is bordered by Guatemala, Honduras, and the Pacific Ocean. A row of volcanoes runs through El Salvador. In 2001, violent earthquakes killed many people and shattered the economy. El Salvador also suffered from political unrest and a bloody civil war from 1979 to 1992. For much of its history, El Salvador's economy depended on coffee, but manufacturing increased in the 1960s when El Salvador joined the Central American Common Market.

Guatemala

Capital	Guatemala City
Land Area	41,865 sq mi; 108,430 sq km
Population	13.3 million
Ethnic Group(s)	mestizo, indigenous Indian, white
Religion(s)	Roman Catholic, Protestant, traditional beliefs
Government	constitutional democratic republic
Currency	quetzal
Leading Exports	coffee, sugar, bananas, fruits and vegetables, cardamom, meat, apparel, petroleum, electricity
Language(s)	Spanish (official), Quiché, Cakchiquel, Kekchi

One third of the people in Central America live in Guatemala (gwaht uh MAH luh), and Guatemala City is the largest city in Central America. Guatemala is bordered by Mexico, Belize, Honduras, and El Salvador as well as the Caribbean Sea and the Pacific Ocean. Earthquakes, volcanic eruptions, and hurricanes have caused repeated disasters. Guatemala was once home to the ancient Mayan civilization. More recently, it has suffered from harsh military dictatorships, civil war, and discrimination against its large indigenous population.

Chapter 14 **427**

Instruct

Introducing Mexico and Central America L2

Guided Instruction

- Read each country paragraph as a class using the Oral Cloze strategy (TE, p. T33). Then, ask students to read through each data table.

- Ask **Which country has the largest land area?** *(Mexico, with 742,486 sq mi/ 1,923,040 sq km)* **Which has the smallest land area?** *(El Salvador, with 8,000 sq mi/ 21,720 sq km)*

- Discuss the religions listed for each country. **What religions do almost all of the countries share?** *(Roman Catholic and Protestant)* **What countries are exceptions?** *(Some Guatemalans hold traditional beliefs.)*

- Ask **Which country does not use Spanish as its official language?** *(The official language of Belize is English.)* Have students study the information on Belize, then speculate why Belize uses English instead of Spanish. *(Belize has strong ties to Great Britain. It was a British colony rather than a Spanish colony, and did not become independent until 1981.)*

- Ask **How is Costa Rica different from other countries in the region?** *(Costa Rica gained independence early; has abolished its army; and allows wealth to be distributed more evenly.)*

Background: Link Across Time

The Quiché Maya of Guatemala

The Quiché Maya lived in Guatemala as early as 1500 B.C. During that time they had an advanced civilization that included political, social, and class structures. Their history and beliefs are written in the Quiché language in the *Popol Vuh,* which includes a list of their kings until 1550. Today, the Quiché language is spoken by about 700,000 people, more than any other Mayan language.

Independent Practice

- Give students *Outline Maps 6 and 7*.

    All in One **Latin America Teaching Resources,** *Outline Map 6: Mexico; Outline Map 7: Central America and the Caribbean,* pp. 253–254

- Ask them to choose one type of data in the Country Databank (such as Government or Official Language) and express it on their maps. Guide them to avoid Ethnic Groups and Leading Exports. Refer them to p. 425 for a map of the region.

- Remind them to create a map key that clearly explains the meaning of any colors or symbols on their maps.

- Students should also include the capital of each country on their maps.

Monitor Progress

Circulate to make sure students have chosen appropriate data and are expressing it correctly.

Introducing Mexico and Central America

Honduras

Capital	Tegucigalpa
Land Area	43,201 sq mi; 111,890 sq km
Population	6.6 million
Ethnic Group(s)	mestizo, indigenous Indian, black, white
Religion(s)	Roman Catholic, Protestant
Government	democratic constitutional republic
Currency	Lempira
Leading Exports	coffee, bananas, shrimp, lobster, meat, zinc, lumber
Language(s)	Spanish (official), Black Carib, English Creole

Honduras (hahn DOOR us) stretches from the Caribbean Sea to the Pacific Ocean. It is also bordered by Guatemala, El Salvador, and Nicaragua. Much of the country is mountainous, and the Mosquito Coast on the Caribbean has few people. Most of the population lives in the central highlands. During the early 1900s, foreign-owned banana plantations dominated the economy, and Honduras was ruled by a series of military governments. There was a return to democracy in 1984, and diversification of the economy began. In 2005, the country was devastated by Hurricane Stan, and it is still recovering from this disaster.

Mayan statue at Copán in Honduras

***The Flower Carrier* (1935) by Mexican artist Diego Rivera**

Mexico

Capital	Mexico City
Land Area	742,486 sq mi; 1,923,040 sq km
Population	103.4 million
Ethnic Group(s)	mestizo, Amerindian, European
Religion(s)	Roman Catholic, Protestant
Government	federal republic
Currency	Mexican peso
Leading Exports	manufactured goods, oil and oil products, silver, fruits, vegetables, coffee, cotton
Language(s)	Spanish (official), Nahuatl, Mayan, Zapotec, Mixtec

Mexico (MEK sih koh) is located south of the United States and northwest of Central America. It stretches from the Pacific Ocean to the Gulf of Mexico and the Caribbean Sea. Like the United States, Mexico is a federal republic. It has 31 states. The election of President Vicente Fox in 2000 and subsequent elections reflected a move toward greater democracy and the growth of a multiparty system. Mexico is a major oil producer, but also has considerable foreign debt.

428 Latin America

Differentiated Instruction

For Special Needs Students **L1**

Have students become more familiar with the region through the flyover, time line, and photographs for this region on the Passport to the World CD ROM.

 Passport to the World CD-ROM

For Less Proficient Readers **L1**

If students are having trouble comparing the data, have them create a chart that will show all of the information in one place. Have them complete the charts in groups of two or three.

Nicaragua

Capital	Managua
Land Area	46,430 sq mi; 120,254 sq km
Population	5.2 million
Ethnic Group(s)	mestizo, white, black, indigenous Indian
Religion(s)	Roman Catholic, Protestant
Government	republic
Currency	Córdoba oro
Leading Exports	coffee, shrimp and lobster, cotton, tobacco, beef, sugar, bananas, gold
Language(s)	Spanish (official), English Creole, Miskito

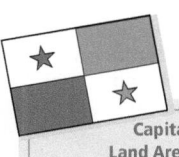

Panama

Capital	Panama City
Land Area	29,340 sq mi; 75,990 sq km
Population	2.9 million
Ethnic Group(s)	mestizo, mixed black and indigenous Indian, white, indigenous Indian
Religion(s)	Roman Catholic, Protestant
Government	constitutional democracy
Currency	Balboa
Leading Exports	bananas, shrimp, sugar, coffee, clothing
Language(s)	Spanish (official), English Creole, indigenous Indian languages

SOURCES: DK World Desk Reference Online; *CIA World Factbook; The World Almanac,* 2003

Nicaragua (nik uh RAH gwuh) stretches across Central America from the Caribbean Sea to the Pacific Ocean. It is bordered on the north by Honduras and on the south by Costa Rica. Like its neighbors, Nicaragua has a row of volcanoes and has experienced many eruptions and earthquakes. After the overthrow of a 40-year dictatorship in 1979, Nicaragua was plunged into civil war, which ended in 1990. In 2005, the country was devastated by Hurricane Stan and is still recovering from the aftermath of the hurricane and the years of civil war.

The narrow country of Panama (PAN uh mah) has been both a barrier and a bridge between the Atlantic and Pacific oceans. It is bordered on the west by Costa Rica and on the east by the South American nation of Colombia. At first, Panama's rough terrain and rain forests hindered travel across the isthmus. The Panama Canal, which opened in 1914, made Panama a main shipping route and led to its economic growth. Most Panamanians live near the canal. Panama City is located at the canal's Pacific entrance. Another major city, Colón, is found near the Caribbean entrance to the canal.

Assessment

Comprehension and Critical Thinking

1. Compare and Contrast Compare the physical size and the population size of Honduras and Guatemala.

2. Draw Conclusions What are the characteristics that most of the countries share?

3. Compare and Contrast What are some key differences among the countries?

4. Categorize What kinds of products are the major exports of this region?

5. Infer What can you infer about a country if many of its exports are made in factories?

6. Make a Bar Graph Create a bar graph showing the population of the countries in the region.

Keeping Current

Access the **DK World Desk Reference Online** at **PHSchool.com** for up-to-date information about all eight countries in this chapter.

Web Code: **lfe-1410**

Assess and Reteach

Assess Progress [L2]

- Ask students to return to the list of their impressions about Mexico and Central America. How many of them turned out to be untrue?
- Ask students to answer the Assessment questions.

Reteach [L1]

If students are having trouble analyzing the data, ask them to concentrate on only two countries. Have them create a simple table with the following heads: **Similarities** and **Differences.** Have them study the two countries they have chosen and record similarities between them in one column and differences in another. Then ask them to write one sentence summarizing the similarities and another sentence explaining the differences.

Extend [L3]

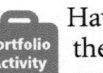

Have students choose one country in the Country Databank. Ask them to research the country, using the DK World Desk Reference Online as a starting point. Then, have them create a paragraph, short story, chart, graph, map, or illustration about the country to add to their portfolios.

Answers

Assessment

1. The two countries are roughly the same size, but Guatemala has 6.7 million more people.
2. Most of the countries share the Roman Catholic and Protestant religions and have had political upheavals.
3. Belize uses English as its official language; Costa Rica has had less political turmoil.
4. crops such as coffee or bananas
5. The country is fairly industrialized.
6. Students' bar graphs should reflect the countries' populations accurately. Use *Rubric for Assessing a Bar Graph* to evaluate students' work.

 Latin America Teaching Resources, *Rubric for Assessing a Bar Graph,* p. 260

Objectives

Social Studies

1. Learn what life is like for people in rural Mexico.
2. Find out why many Mexicans have been moving from the countryside to the cities.
3. Understand why the growth of Mexico City presents challenges for the people and the environment.

Reading/Language Arts

Use context clues to determine the meaning of unfamiliar words.

Prepare to Read

Build Background Knowledge `L2`

Tell students that they will learn about life in Mexico in this section. Ask students to list two ideas about country life and two ideas about city life. Model the thought process by encouraging them to think about housing, transportation, jobs, and schools. Conduct an Idea Wave (TE, p. T35) to generate a list.

Set a Purpose for Reading `L2`

■ Preview the Objectives.

■ Read each statement in the *Reading Readiness Guide* out loud. Ask students to mark the statements true or false.

> **All in One Latin America Teaching Resources,** *Reading Readiness Guide,* p. 228

■ Have the groups discuss the statements in pairs or groups of four, then mark their guides again. Use the Numbered Heads participation structure (TE, p. T36) to call on students to share their group's perspectives.

Vocabulary Builder

Preview Key Terms `L2`

Pronounce each Key Term and then ask the students to say the word with you. Provide a simple explanation, such as "A migrant worker might be hired to pick tomatoes in one place and apples in another."

Mexico
Moving to the City

Prepare to Read

Objectives

In this section you will
1. Learn what life is like for people in rural Mexico.
2. Find out why many Mexicans have been moving from the countryside to the cities.
3. Understand why the growth of Mexico City presents challenges for people and the environment.

Taking Notes

As you read this section, look for ways that life is similar and different in rural and in urban Mexico. Copy the Venn diagram below and record your findings in it.

Life in Mexico

Rural   Urban

Target Reading Skill

Use Context Clues When you come across an unfamiliar word, you can often figure out its meaning from clues in the context. The context refers to the surrounding words, phrases, and sentences. Sometimes the context will define the word. In this example, the phrase in italics explains what smog is: "Smog, *a low-lying layer of polluted air,* hung over the city."

Key Terms

- **migrant worker** (MY grunt WUR kur) *n.* a laborer who travels from one area to another, picking crops that are in season
- **plaza** (PLAH zuh) *n.* a public square at the center of a village, a town, or a city
- **squatter** (SKWAHT ur) *n.* a person who settles on someone else's land without permission

---

Using oxen to plow a field

Most farm families in Mexico are poor. Many are campesinos. Some work their own small farms. They often plow the land and harvest their crops by hand because they cannot afford expensive farm machinery. Other campesinos do not own land. They work on large farms owned by rich landowners. These **migrant workers** travel from one area to another, picking the crops that are in season.

Mexico's population has risen dramatically over the last 30 years. The country's population is growing at one of the highest rates in the world. There is not enough farm work for so many people. A large family cannot support itself on a small farm. And there are not enough jobs for all the migrant workers.

Many rural Mexicans are moving from the countryside to Mexico City. Why are they making this move? How does moving to the city change their lives? How is this trend changing the country of Mexico?

Target Reading Skill `L2`

Use Context Clues Point out the Target Reading Skill. Tell students that information surrounding an unknown word can provide clues to the word's meaning.

Model using context clues to find the meaning of the word *support* in this sentence: "Ramiro works to support, or provide for,

his family." (The phrase *or provide for* explains what support means.)

Give students *Use Context Clues: Definition/Description.* Have them complete the activity in their groups.

> **All in One Latin America Teaching Resources,** *Use Context Clues: Definition/ Description,* p. 239

Life in Rural Mexico

Find the Plateau of Mexico on the map titled Physical Latin America on page 332. The southern part of the plateau has Mexico's best farmland. Throughout much of this region, life has changed little over many years.

Rural Villages Nearly every village in the Mexican countryside has a church and a market. At the center of most villages is a public square called a **plaza.** Farm families grow their own food. If they have extra food, they sell it at the market in the plaza. Rural people buy nearly everything they need—clothing, food, toys, and housewares—at the market rather than in stores.

Farm Work Ramiro Avila (rah MEE roh ah VEE luh) grew up in the state of Guanajuato (gwah nah HWAH toh), in central Mexico. In his small village, Ramiro knew everyone and everyone knew him.

Ramiro's family were campesinos who owned no land. Even as a young child, Ramiro had to work to help support his family. He and his father had jobs as farm laborers. They worked on someone else's farm. They made less than a dollar a day. When Ramiro was 13, his parents decided to move to Mexico City. They joined many other Mexicans who were making this move.

√ Reading Check **What is life like in rural Mexican villages?**

A Village Market in Mexico
Like many Mexican markets, this one sells a wide variety of goods.
Infer *Why do you think markets like this one become the center of village life?*

Vocabulary Builder

Use the information below to teach students this section's high-use words.

High-Use Word	Definition and Sample Sentence
support, p. 431	*v.* to hold up or provide for The table legs **support** the tabletop.
afford, p. 433	*v.* to be able to do without serious risks (usually used in terms of money) I could not **afford** to buy a ticket to the movie.
sturdy, p. 433	*adj.* strongly built, firm I packed the heavy books in a strong, **sturdy** box.

Instruct

Life in Rural Mexico L2

Guided Instruction

■ **Vocabulary Builder** Clarify the high-use word **support** before reading.

■ Read Life in Rural Mexico, using the Oral Cloze technique (TE p. T33).

■ Discuss good aspects of living in the country, then possible reasons for leaving. Use the Numbered Heads participation strategy to elicit responses. *(Good—good farmland so families can grow their own food, community gatherings at plaza, everyone knows each other; Reasons for leaving— hard work, can't own their own land, poor wages as farm laborers)*

■ Ask students: **Do you think the good aspects of life in rural Mexico outweigh the bad? Why?** *(Possible answers: Good—living in a community where people know you; Bad—staying poor even if you work hard, not having enough food or medicine to keep your family healthy)*

Independent Practice

Ask students to create the Taking Notes graphic organizer on a blank piece of paper. Then have them fill in the "Rural" circle with the information they have just learned. Briefly model how to identify which details to record.

Monitor Progress

As students fill in the graphic organizer, circulate and make sure individuals are choosing the correct details. Provide assistance as needed.

Answers

Infer People can get many of the things they need there; it is a central place where the community gathers.

√ Reading Check Life in rural areas is good because people can grow their own food and people know each other. However, life can be difficult because many people work as farm laborers and do not make much money.

Guided Instruction L2

Ask students to study the Country Profile on this page. As a class, answer the Map and Chart Skills questions. Allow students to briefly discuss their responses with a partner before sharing answers.

Independent Practice

- Distribute *Reading a Population Distribution Map.* Have students work with partners to complete the worksheet.

  All In One **Latin America Teaching Resources,** *Reading a Population Distribution Map,* p. 251

- Tell students that the map of Mexico on the worksheet shows where the people of Mexico live. Ask them to compare the map on this page of the Student Edition with the map on the worksheet. Coach students to see that the population distribution map shows that more people live in Mexico's cities, where the industrial businesses are located.

Answers

Map and Chart Skills

1. in and around cities

2. Mexico exports the most goods to the United States. The location of the United States along Mexico's border fosters this trade partnership.

3. People tend to live near where they can get jobs to support themselves. If most economic activity takes place in a country's cities, jobs and people will follow.

Go Online PHSchool.com Students can find more information about this topic on the DK World Desk Reference Online.

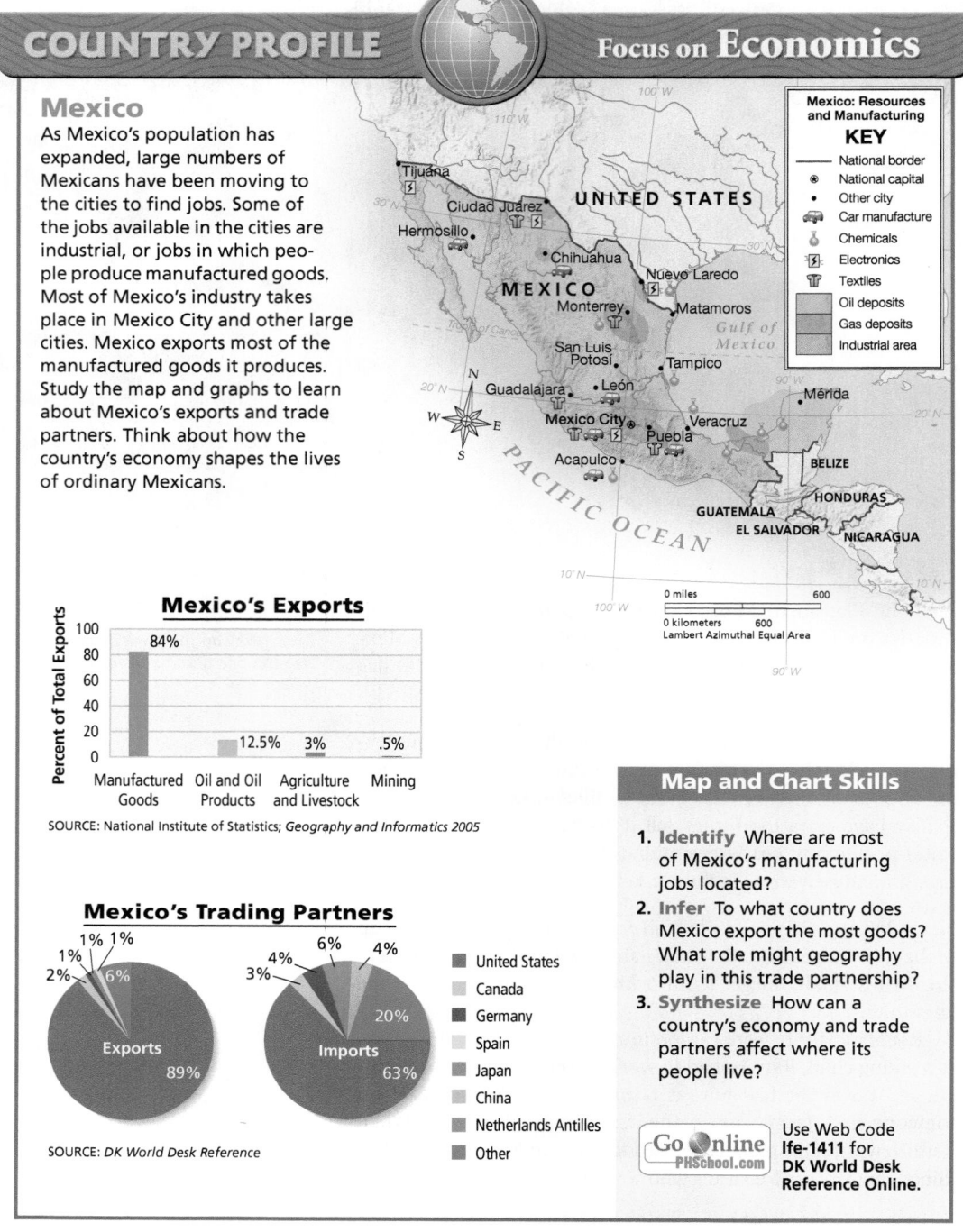

Mexico

As Mexico's population has expanded, large numbers of Mexicans have been moving to the cities to find jobs. Some of the jobs available in the cities are industrial, or jobs in which people produce manufactured goods. Most of Mexico's industry takes place in Mexico City and other large cities. Mexico exports most of the manufactured goods it produces. Study the map and graphs to learn about Mexico's exports and trade partners. Think about how the country's economy shapes the lives of ordinary Mexicans.

Mexico: Resources and Manufacturing
KEY
— National border
⊛ National capital
• Other city
🚗 Car manufacture
Chemicals
Electronics
Textiles
Oil deposits
Gas deposits
Industrial area

Mexico's Exports

84%   12.5%   3%   .5%

Manufactured Goods   Oil and Oil Products   Agriculture and Livestock   Mining

Percent of Total Exports

SOURCE: National Institute of Statistics; *Geography and Informatics 2005*

Mexico's Trading Partners

Exports: 89%, 6%, 1%, 1%, 2%, 1%
Imports: 63%, 20%, 6%, 4%, 4%, 3%

- United States
- Canada
- Germany
- Spain
- Japan
- China
- Netherlands Antilles
- Other

SOURCE: *DK World Desk Reference*

Map and Chart Skills

1. **Identify** Where are most of Mexico's manufacturing jobs located?
2. **Infer** To what country does Mexico export the most goods? What role might geography play in this trade partnership?
3. **Synthesize** How can a country's economy and trade partners affect where its people live?

Go Online PHSchool.com Use Web Code **lfe-1411** for **DK World Desk Reference Online.**

Skills Mini Lesson

Using Cartographer's Tools L2

1. Teach the skill by pointing out to students that there are certain elements common to most maps. These include a scale and a compass rose.
2. Help students practice the skill by looking at the map on this page and determining how many miles Ciudad Juarez is from Chihuahua. *(a little over 200 miles or 320 kilometers)*
3. Have students apply the skill by answering this question: How far is Hermosillo from the United States border? *(about 175 miles or 280 kilometers)*

Life in the City
New arrivals to Mexico City often live in temporary houses (left). But the children still have a chance to attend school (right). **Infer** *Using clues from the photos, describe what life is like for the family shown washing clothes outdoors.*

Moving to Mexico City

Many rural people move to the cities because they cannot find work in the countryside. They hope they can make a better living in urban areas such as Mexico City. They also hope that their children will get a better education in city schools. Although city life will be very different from life in the countryside, these families leave their familiar villages behind to make a new start in the city.

Housing in the City Like thousands of other campesino families coming to the city, Ramiro's family did not have much money. When they arrived in Mexico City, they could not afford a house. They went to live in Colonia Zapata, one of many neighborhoods where poor people become squatters. A **squatter** is a person who settles on someone else's land without permission.

Many small houses built by squatters cling to the sides of a steep hill in the Colonia. The older houses near the bottom of the hill are built of concrete. However, most people cannot afford to make sturdy houses when they first arrive. Therefore many of the newer houses higher up the hill are constructed of scrap metal. Most squatter families hope that they will soon be able to buy land from the government. Then they can build their own permanent houses and even have a garden and a patio.

Work and School Once they settle in Mexico City, many families discover that it is still difficult to find work. Sometimes the men of the family look for jobs across the border, in the United States. They often work as farm laborers in states near the Mexican border, such as Texas and California. These men leave their families behind in Mexico, but many of them send money home every month.

Moving to Mexico City L2

Guided Instruction

- **Vocabulary Builder** Clarify the high-use words **afford** and **sturdy** before reading.

- Read the portrait of life in Mexico City presented in Moving to Mexico City with students. As students read, circulate and make sure individuals can answer the Reading Check question.

- Ask students to list reasons why many rural people move to the cities. *(to find better jobs, to get a better education for their children)*

Independent Practice

Have students complete the graphic organizer by filling in the "Urban" circle and adding the aspects common to rural and urban life where the circles overlap.

Monitor Progress

Show *Section Reading Support Transparency LA 39* and ask students to check their graphic organizers individually. Go over key concepts and clarify key vocabulary as needed.

Latin America Transparencies, *Section Reading Support Transparency LA 39*

Answer

Infer Life looks difficult for these people. They look like they are crowded into a very small space. They must use the small space around their temporary house to clean, cook, and dry their clothes after washing.

Opportunities and Challenges

Guided Instruction

- Ask students to read Opportunities and Challenges. Review the map and diagram on pp. 434 and 435 with students.

- Ask students **On the site of what city was Mexico City built?** *(the Aztec capital Tenochtitlán)* **When was Mexico city the capital of New Spain?** *(during colonial times)* **Have students describe Mexico City today.** *(It is the capital of Mexico. About 20 million people live there, and it is one of the largest cities in the world.)*

Answer

✓ Reading Check Older children may have to hold down jobs when they move from the country to the city. They may also have to cope with fathers being away for much of the year.

MAP★MASTER Skills Activity **Use the Map Key** purple **Synthesize** Students may respond that the increased size of Mexico City adds to the city's transportation problems.

Go Online PHSchool.com Students may practice their map skills using the interactive online version of this map.

Children in these families not only have to get used to city life. They must also adjust to being without their fathers for months at a time. The older children have many new responsibilities. Sometimes they care for the younger children. Or they may work at low-paying jobs in the daytime to help support their families and then go to school at night.

✓ Reading Check **What new responsibilities might older children face when they move to Mexico City?**

Opportunities and Challenges

Large cities in Mexico—and around the world—share many problems as well as many advantages. Even so, each city is unique. Take a closer look at Mexico City.

Mexico's Capital City Mexico City was built on the site of the Aztec capital, Tenochtitlán. During colonial times, it was the capital of New Spain. Today, it is the capital of the modern nation of Mexico.

Much of Mexico's urban population lives in Mexico City. If you count the people in outlying areas, Mexico City has nearly 20 million people. It is one of the largest cities in the world.

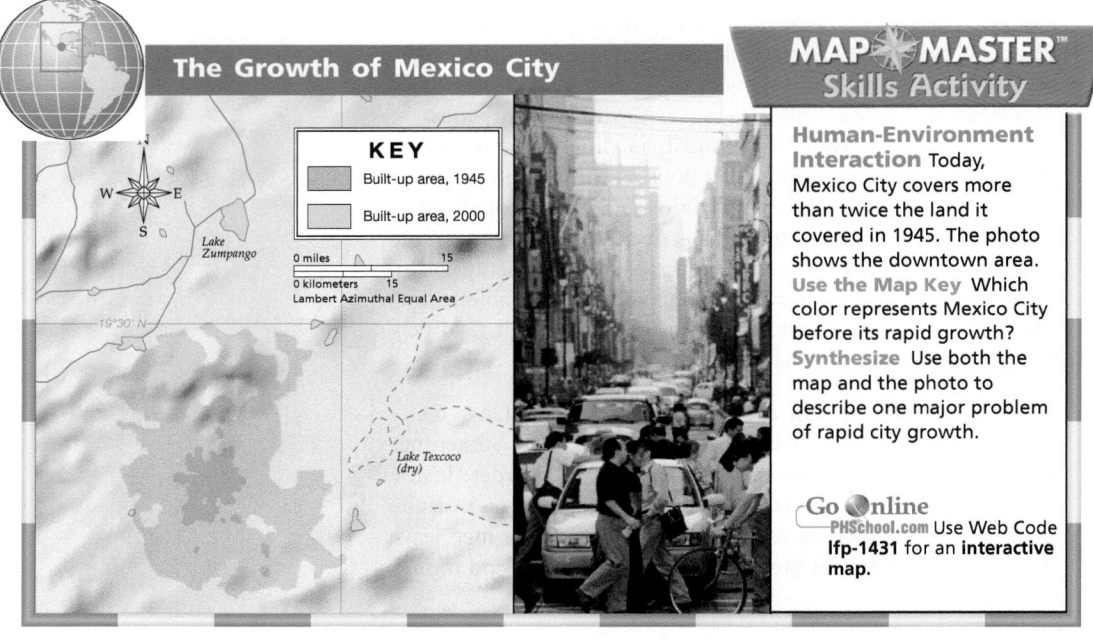

The Growth of Mexico City

MAP★MASTER Skills Activity

KEY
- Built-up area, 1945
- Built-up area, 2000

0 miles 15
0 kilometers 15
Lambert Azimuthal Equal Area

Lake Zumpango

Lake Texcoco (dry)

19°30' N

Human-Environment Interaction Today, Mexico City covers more than twice the land it covered in 1945. The photo shows the downtown area. **Use the Map Key** Which color represents Mexico City before its rapid growth? **Synthesize** Use both the map and the photo to describe one major problem of rapid city growth.

Go Online PHSchool.com Use Web Code **lfp-1431** for an **interactive map.**

434 Latin America

Differentiated Instruction

For Advanced Readers **L3**
Have students choose one aspect about Mexico City that intrigues them. The aspect could be daily life in the city, the history of the place, or its geographical make-up. Ask them to read more about their chosen angle, and create a brief oral report to deliver to the class.

Smog in Mexico City

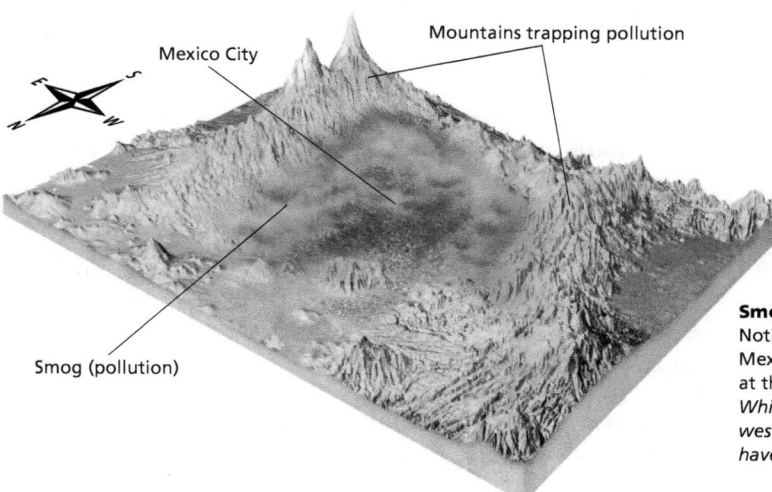

Mexico City

Mountains trapping pollution

Smog (pollution)

Smog Alert
Notice the mountains surrounding Mexico City, and study the compass at the far left. **Analyze Images** *Which part of Mexico City—east, west, north, or south—seems to have the least smog? Explain why.*

Old and New, Rich and Poor Mexico City has both modern skyscrapers and older, historic areas with two- and three-story buildings. Wide avenues and highways along with narrower side streets can barely handle the traffic of this sprawling city. The subway, the underground railroad system, carries more than four million people each day.

Small neighborhoods of very wealthy people are tucked away from the rest of the city. But most of Mexico City's residents are not wealthy. The poorest live on the outskirts of the city. Some of them must travel several hours a day just to get to their jobs.

Pollution and Geography Because of their rapid population growth, many of Mexico's large cities face problems of traffic, pollution, and water shortages. In Mexico City, millions of cars and trucks jam the streets. They compete with taxis, trolleys, and buses. The exhaust fumes from these vehicles pollute the air. Mexico City has also outgrown its fresh water supply. The city must now pump in water from sources as far as 100 miles away.

Mexico City's geography makes its pollution problem worse. The city spreads across a bowl-shaped valley. The surrounding mountains trap automobile exhaust, factory smoke, and other kinds of pollution near the city. The resulting smog cannot blow away, and it hangs over Mexico City as a brown cloud.

 Use Context Clues
If you do not know what a subway is, look in the surrounding words for a context clue. Here, the phrase following *subway* is a definition of the term. What is a subway?

Background: Global Perspectives

Earthquakes in Urban Centers
Although the volcanoes that ring Mexico City are dormant, the land is still seismically active. One of Mexico's most destructive earthquakes occurred in Mexico City in 1985. Other cities that are located on earthquake faults include San Francisco; Tokyo, Japan; and Kathmandu, Nepal.

Guided Instruction (continued)

- Ask students to describe the factors contributing to air pollution in Mexico City. Allow students to share answers with a partner before responding. (*growing population, traffic, pollution, mountains*)

- Ask students to brainstorm ways in which the people of Mexico could address the challenges of air pollution. Conduct an Idea Wave (TE, p. T35) to generate a list of possibilities. (*improve public transportation, improve the roads, better emission standards*)

- Ask students **How do people make a living in large cities such as Mexico City?** (*working in factories or offices, selling goods from stalls on the street*)

- Ask students **What effects has NAFTA had in Mexico?** (*NAFTA increased manufacturing and exports in Mexico, but new industrial development has increased pollution in cities.*)

Independent Practice
Assign *Guided Reading and Review*.

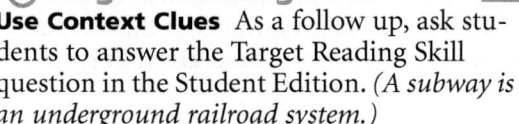 **Latin America Teaching Resources,** *Guided Reading and Review*, p. 229

Monitor Progress
Tell students to fill in the last column of the *Reading Readiness Guide*. Probe for what they learned that confirms or invalidates each statement.

All in One Latin America Teaching Resources, *Reading Readiness Guide*, p. 228

Target Reading Skill L2
Use Context Clues As a follow up, ask students to answer the Target Reading Skill question in the Student Edition. (*A subway is an underground railroad system.*)

Answers

Analyze Images The northern part of Mexico City has less smog because the northern edge of the city is not hemmed in by mountains.

Assess and Reteach

Assess Progress `L2`

Have students complete the Section Review. Administer the *Section Quiz*.

 Latin America Teaching Resources, *Section Quiz*, p. 230

Reteach `L1`

If students need more instruction, have them read this section in the Reading and Vocabulary Study Guide.

Chapter 14, Section 1, **Western Hemisphere Reading and Vocabulary Study Guide**, pp. 168–170

Extend `L3`

Have students learn more about Mexico today by completing the *Enrichment* activity. Assign students to work in groups to complete the project.

 Latin America Teaching Resources, *Enrichment*, p. 243

Answers

√ **Reading Check** Mexico recently became a member of NAFTA, which helped to increase manufacturing and exports.

Section 1 Assessment

Key Terms

Students' sentences should reflect knowledge of each Key Term.

Target Reading Skill

Because the text mentions that Mexico City has modern skyscrapers as well as older buildings, you can assume that the city has grown and will continue to grow, or sprawl.

Comprehension and Critical Thinking

1. (a) Most people who live in Mexican villages are farmers. They buy most of their goods at the village market. **(b)** Most people are poor and do not own the land they farm. Farming is hard work. People can earn more money working in a city.

2. (a) Poor people in Mexico City live in temporary housing and work as much as possible to make ends meet. **(b)** Rural Mexicans face housing problems, transportation problems, and possible separation from family members.

The 2000 election of President Vicente Fox, of the National Action Party, was a historic change in Mexico.

Making a Living In spite of all their problems, large cities offer many ways to make a living. Millions of people work in factories and offices. Thousands more sell goods from stalls in the street. These street vendors are an important part of city life. For example, some vendors sell juice or bottled water.

Looking to the Future Two events have recently brought changes to Mexico. One of these was the signing of the North American Free Trade Agreement (NAFTA) in 1994. As you read in Chapter 12, the purpose of NAFTA was to improve trade among Canada, the United States, and Mexico.

In Mexico, manufacturing and exports did increase. So did foreign investment. But some say that poor Mexican farmers and factory workers did not benefit from NAFTA. Their incomes actually went down. What's more, new industrial development has increased pollution in Mexico's cities.

In 2000, Mexicans elected Vicente Fox president. Until Fox's election, one political party, the Institutional Revolutionary Party (PRI), had ruled Mexico for 71 years. During his six years as president, Fox focused on improving the economy and strengthening Mexico's relationship with the United States. Elections in 2006 revealed a deep divide within the country, and for months, the results of the close presidential election remained contested.

√ **Reading Check** What changes has Mexico recently gone through?

Section 1 Assessment

Key Terms

Review the key terms at the beginning of this section. Use each term in a sentence that explains its meaning.

Target Reading Skill

Find the word *sprawling* on page 435. Use context to figure out its meaning. What clue helped you figure out its meaning?

Comprehension and Critical Thinking

1. (a) Recall Describe life in a Mexican village.

(b) Identify Causes Why do so many rural Mexicans move to the cities?

2. (a) Describe How do poor people live in Mexico City?

(b) Synthesize What new problems do rural Mexicans face when they move to the city?

3. (a) Describe What is Mexico City like?

(b) Identify Causes What factors cause pollution in Mexico City?

(c) Evaluate Information Identify the benefits and drawbacks of moving to Mexico City.

Writing Activity

Write an entry in your journal comparing Mexico City with your hometown. How are the two places similar and how are they different? How would your life be different if you lived in a place like Mexico City?

For: An activity on Mexico City
Visit: PHSchool.com
Web Code: lfd-1401

436 Latin America

---

3. (a) Mexico City is large, with a huge population and pollution problems. **(b)** Traffic volume, high emissions, and geographic factors cause pollution in Mexico City. **(c)** Benefits—more jobs, better pay, more opportunities for education; Drawbacks—crowding, inadequate housing, and pollution.

Writing Activity

Use the *Rubric for Assessing a Journal Entry* to evaluate students' journal entries.

Latin America Teaching Resources, *Rubric for Assessing a Journal Entry*, p. 261

Go Online PHSchool.com Typing in the web code when prompted will bring students directly to detailed instructions for this activity.

Guatemala
Descendants of an Ancient People

Prepare to Read

Objectives

In this section you will
1. Learn why there is a struggle for land in Guatemala.
2. Find out how the Mayas lost their land.
3. Discover how groups are working to improve the lives of Guatemala's indigenous people.

Taking Notes

As you read this section, look for details about the Mayas' struggle for their rights. Copy the chart below, and record your findings in it.

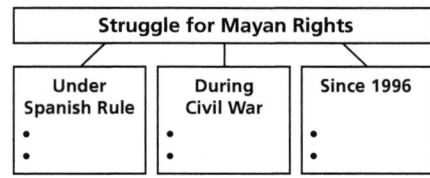

Struggle for Mayan Rights

Under Spanish Rule	During Civil War	Since 1996
•	•	•
•	•	

🎯 Target Reading Skill

Use Context Clues Context, the words and phrases surrounding a word, can help you understand a new word. One context clue is contrast, a word or words that have the opposite meaning of the unfamiliar word. In this example, the contrast with the newly arrived Spanish helps explain the word *indigenous*: "The struggle of the indigenous people of Guatemala to keep their land began when the Spanish first arrived."

Key Terms

• **ladino** (luh DEE noh) *n.* a mestizo, or person of mixed Spanish and Native American ancestry in Guatemala
• **land reform** (land ree FAWRM) *n.* the effort to distribute land more equally and fairly
• **political movement** (puh LIT ih kul MOOV munt) *n.* a large group of people who work together for political change
• **strike** (stryk) *n.* a refusal to work until certain demands of workers are met

In Guatemala, Native Americans make up the majority of the population. They form 23 ethnic groups. Even though the indigenous groups of Guatemala are related to one another, each group is different. Each one has its own language and customs. The largest group is the Quiché Maya.

Mayan families are often poor. They raise corn on tiny plots of land, but can barely earn enough money to survive. Children often work to help support their families. Mayan girls do weaving to bring in extra money. One Mayan girl described her childhood as similar to the childhoods of "all Indian girls, at the side of my mother, making tortillas and learning to weave and embroider."

Like many other indigenous people, the Mayas have found it difficult to get an education and escape poverty. They have also struggled to preserve their traditional culture as they become part of modern Guatemala.

Modern Mayan women weave much as their ancestors did.

Chapter 14 Section 2 **437**

🎯 Target Reading Skill

Use Context Clues Point out the Target Reading Skill. Tell students that information surrounding an unfamiliar word can provide clues to the word's meaning. Explain that sometimes a paragraph may contain words that contrast, or are opposite in meaning to, an unfamiliar word in the paragraph.

Model how to use context clues to figure out the meaning of the word *rebel* in this sentence from page 440: "Then government military forces fought **rebel** groups that were living in the highlands." (The word *rebel* contrasts with *government military forces*.)

Give students *Use Context Clues: Compare and Contrast*. Have them complete the activity in their groups.

All in One **Latin America Teaching Resources,** *Use Context Clues: Compare and Contrast,* p. 240

Objectives
Social Studies

1. Learn why there is a struggle for land in Guatemala.
2. Find out how the Mayas lost their land.
3. Discover how groups are working to improve the lives of Guatemala's indigenous people.

Reading/Language Arts

Use context clues that show contrast to determine the meaning of unfamiliar words.

Prepare to Read

Build Background Knowledge   L2

Ask students to preview the photographs in this section and to write down what these photographs show about the Mayas. Conduct an Idea Wave (TE, p. T35) to allow students to share their ideas.

Set a Purpose for Reading   L2

■ Preview the Objectives.

■ Read each statement in the *Reading Readiness Guide* aloud. Ask students to mark the statements true or false.

  All in One **Latin America Teaching Resources,** *Reading Readiness Guide,* p. 232

■ Have students discuss the statements in pairs or groups of four, then mark their worksheets again. Use the Numbered Heads participation structure (TE, p. T36) to call on students to share their group's perspectives.

Vocabulary Builder
Preview Key Terms   L2

Pronounce each Key Term, then ask the students to say the word with you. Provide a simple explanation such as, "During a strike, workers may stop working until they get better wages or working conditions."

The Struggle for Land L2

Guided Instruction

- **Vocabulary Builder** Clarify the high-use words **resource** and **erosion** before reading.

- Read The Struggle for Land using the Structured Silent Reading technique (TE, p. T34).

- Discuss with students why Mayan families in Guatemala are unable to produce good crops on their land. *(Much of the land in Guatemala belongs to a few rich families and the only land available to the Mayas is in the mountains. The soil of the Guatemalan highlands is not very good and soil erosion makes farming difficult.)*

- Ask students **Why do you think that wealthy landowners have resisted land reform?** *(The wealthy landowners probably do not want to give up their land to poorer farmers. They may want to protect what they have.)*

Independent Practice

Assign *Guided Reading and Review*.

All in One **Latin America Teaching Resources,** *Guided Reading and Review,* p. 233

Monitor Progress

Make sure that students are correctly completing the *Guided Reading and Review* worksheet. Provide assistance as necessary.

Target Reading Skill L2

Use Context Clues As a follow up, ask students to answer the Target Reading Skill question in the Student Edition. *(A hacienda is a big farm, or plantation, where crops are grown to sell abroad.)*

Answers

Analyze Images The people who live on this farm may be able to raise only enough food for themselves, possibly with some left over to sell to others.

✓ Reading Check The best land is used for haciendas, where crops are grown to sell abroad. Campesinos grow crops on small farms in the highlands. These crops are often sold locally.

438 *Latin America*

Farming in the Mountains
This small Mayan farm clings to a Guatemalan hillside. **Analyze Images** *Look carefully at the buildings and the fields. What do these details tell you about making a living on this farm?*

Use Context Clues If you do not remember what *hacienda* means, consider these context clues. A hacienda is "where crops are grown to sell abroad." Haciendas are also contrasted with small farms. Therefore a hacienda is _____.

The Struggle for Land

Land is a valuable resource in Guatemala, as it is in all of Latin America. Fair distribution of the land is a serious problem throughout the region.

The People and the Land Much of the land in Guatemala belongs to a few rich families. The rich landowners of Guatemala are **ladinos** (luh DEE nohz), mestizos who are descended from Native Americans and Spaniards. Native Americans who follow European ways are also considered to be ladinos.

For many years, most Mayas have lived in the mountains because it was the only land available to Native Americans. Although Mayan families work hard on their farms, they often fail to produce good crops. The soil of the Guatemalan highlands is not very good. Soil erosion makes farming even more difficult.

Land Distribution In many Latin American countries, the best land is used for haciendas where crops are grown to sell abroad. Guatemalan haciendas produce coffee, cotton, sugar cane, and bananas. In contrast, campesinos grow maize, beans, and squash on small farms in the highlands. These crops are often sold in village markets and provide food for the local population.

Since the 1930s, **land reform,** the effort to distribute land more equally, has been a major goal of many reform and political groups. The wealthy landowners, who have the greatest political power in many Latin American countries, have often resisted these reforms. Clashes between those in favor of reform and those against it have even led to violence and civil war. You will read about the Guatemalan civil war later in this section.

✓ Reading Check How is land distributed in many Latin American countries?

438 Latin America

Vocabulary Builder

Use the information below to teach students this section's high-use words.

High-Use Word	Definition and Sample Sentence
resource, p. 438	*n.* a supply of something useful
	Iron is a useful natural **resource**.
erosion, p. 438	*n.* the slow wearing away by water and wind
	Tree roots hold down soil and stop **erosion**.
civilian, p. 440	*n.* a person who is not a member of the armed forces
	I am a **civilian**, not a soldier.
violation, p. 441	*n.* the breaking of a rule, law, or promise
	Speeding is a **violation** of the law.

The Mayas Lose Their Land

In order to get enough land to make a living—or even to keep the land they have—the Mayas of Guatemala have faced many challenges. One challenge relates to their culture. Indigenous people do not always think of themselves as citizens of the country in which they live. A Mayan woman is more likely to think of herself as a Maya than as a Guatemalan.

COUNTRY PROFILE

Focus on **Culture**

Guatemala

Guatemala today has two distinct cultures: indigenous and ladino. Ladinos speak Spanish, the country's official language, and live mainly in the cities. The majority of Guatemala's population, however, are Mayas. Most Mayas live in villages and towns in the country's highlands. From town to town, Mayan groups speak slightly different languages and create unique art. Their art includes distinctive fabric patterns woven by each group. Study the map and charts to learn more about Guatemalan culture.

Guatemala: Languages
KEY

Spanish
Native American
⊙ National capital
• Other city

MEXICO
BELIZE
GUATEMALA
San Juan Cotzal
Cobán
Puerto Barrios
Chichicastenango
Rabinal
Patzún
⊙ Guatemala City
San José
HONDURAS
EL SALVADOR
Caribbean Sea
PACIFIC OCEAN

0 miles 100
0 kilometers 100
Mercator

Ethnic Groups

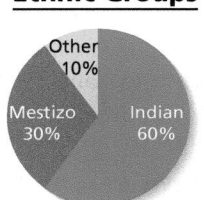

Other 10%
Mestizo 30%
Indian 60%

SOURCE: *DK World Desk Reference*

Mayan Towns

Town Name	Language	Sample Fabric
Patzún	Cakchiquel	
Cobán	Kekchí	
Chichicastenango	Quiché	
San Juan Cotzal	Ixil	
Rabinal	Pokomchi	

Map and Chart Skills

1. Identify In what parts of the country is Spanish spoken? What language would you expect the people in Rabinal to speak?

2. Infer What advantages and disadvantages result from having so many languages in one country?

 Go Online PHSchool.com

Use Web Code lfe-1412 for **DK World Desk Reference Online.**

Guided Instruction

■ **Vocabulary Builder** Clarify the high-use word **civilian** before reading.

■ Read The Maya Lose Their Land.

■ Discuss with students why Native Americans were left with little political power or land after the Spanish invasion. (*The Spanish conquistadors claimed the country's land. The Spanish had political power.*)

Independent Practice

Ask students to create the Taking Notes graphic organizer on a blank piece of paper. Have them fill in the first two segments.

Monitor Progress

As students fill in the graphic organizer, circulate and make sure that individuals are choosing the correct details.

COUNTRY PROFILE
Focus on **Culture**

Guided Instruction [L2]

Ask students to study the Country Profile on this page. As a class, answer the Map and Chart Skills questions.

Independent Practice

For practice in reading circle graphs, have students complete *Reading a Circle Graph* in pairs.

 Latin America Teaching Resources, *Reading a Circle Graph*, p. 252

 **Skills Mini Lesson**

Problem Solving [L2]

1. Teach the skill by reviewing with students the problem of unfair distribution of land in Guatemala.

2. Have students practice the skill by brainstorming possible solutions to the problem.

3. Have students apply the skill by evaluating the possible solutions. Which would be the most effective? Why? Have them choose the most effective solution.

Answers

Map and Chart Skills

1. in northern Guatemala and in southern Guatemala; Pokomchi.

2. Advantages: Creates diversity and keeps traditions alive. Disadvantages: Causes communication problems.

Working for a Better Life

L2

Guided Instruction

- **Vocabulary Builder** Clarify the high-use word **violation** before reading.

- Have students read Working for a Better Life. As students read, circulate and make sure they can answer the Reading Check question.

- Have students look at the photo on this page. Ask how these demonstrators are voicing their opinion. *(by organizing in a group and carrying signs)*

- Ask **Why are Mayan language radio programs, books, and newspapers important?** *(They give the Mayas access to current events, literature, and information.)*

Independent Practice

Ask students to fill in the last segment of their graphic organizers.

Monitor Progress

- Show *Section Reading Support Transparency LA 40* and ask students to check their graphic organizers individually. Go over key concepts and clarify key vocabulary as needed.

    Latin America Transparencies, *Section Reading Support Transparency LA 40*

- Tell students to fill in the last column of the *Reading Readiness Guide.* Probe for what they learned that confirms or invalidates each statement.

    All in One Latin America Teaching Resources, *Reading Readiness Guide,* p. 232

Answers

✓ Reading Check Some Mayas were killed or forced to leave the country. Soldiers claimed their land and many Mayas lost their belongings.

Citizen Heroes

Justina Tzoc: A Voice for Change

For many years, Justina Tzoc (hoo STEE nah tsohk) has worked to help Mayan women in remote areas of Guatemala. She calls her effort "the kind of work that has no beginning and no end." During the Guatemalan civil war, Tzoc faced many dangers as she helped these women organize to fight for their rights. Although the civil war is over, Tzoc's work goes on. According to Tzoc, the indigenous women of Guatemala will continue to work "so that we are recognized—have a voice and a vote."

440 Latin America

A political demonstration in Guatemala City

In addition, the majority of Native Americans in Guatemala cannot read or write. For these two reasons, most Mayas have not filed any papers with the government showing that they own land. Even after they have worked hard for many years to grow crops on a piece of land, a Mayan family often has no way to prove that their land belongs to them.

A 500-Year-Old Struggle The indigenous people of Guatemala have fought to keep both their land and their culture for more than 500 years. This struggle began when the Spanish first arrived in the Americas.

The Spanish conquistadors conquered the Native Americans by force. Many were killed. Others died of hunger or the hardships of slavery. Still others died from European diseases. In many Latin American countries, there are few indigenous people left. In contrast, Guatemala is largely Native American. However, the Native Americans have little political power or land.

Civil War Beginning around 1960, a civil war raged in Guatemala for more than 30 years. First, an elected leader who favored land reform was overthrown by the military. Then government military forces fought rebel groups that were living in the highlands. Armed fighters were not the only ones killed in the fighting. Thousands of civilians were also killed, and many others fled the country. Those who fought for human rights or opposed the government were treated harshly by a series of military rulers.

The Mayas suffered during the civil war. In hundreds of villages throughout Guatemala, soldiers came to claim the Mayas' land. Many Mayas lost all of their belongings and were forced out of their villages. Some had to move to other countries to live.

✓ Reading Check **What happened to the Mayas during the civil war?**

Working for a Better Life

Some Mayas remained in Guatemala during the civil war. They started **political movements,** which are large groups of people who work together for political change. One such movement, called Nukuj Akpop (nooh KOO ahk POHP), still works to fight poverty and bring human rights to Mayas.

Defending Campesino Rights Today, Mayan political movements seek to defend campesino rights. They help villages plan ways to protect themselves. They teach people the history of their land and how to read. They also help organize meetings, protests, and strikes. A **strike** is a refusal to work until certain demands of workers are met. Above all, these political movements defend Native American land rights.

Changes Come to Guatemala These efforts brought change in Guatemala. For the first time, Mayas gained a voice in their government. Mayan priests were appointed to advise government officials about Mayan culture. Radio programs were broadcast in Mayan languages, and Mayan-language books and newspapers also appeared.

In 1996, agreements were signed ending the civil war. Among these was a promise that indigenous communities would be rebuilt. However, not all of these agreements have been carried out. Violations of human rights by the government increased again in 2000, and many Guatemalans protested in the streets. The fight for the rights of the Mayas—and for all the ordinary people of Guatemala—continues.

Some political movements in Guatemala are geared toward helping indigenous people, such as the man above.

✓ **Reading Check** How do political movements try to help the Mayas?

Section 2 Assessment

Key Terms
Review the key terms at the beginning of this section. Use each term in a sentence that explains its meaning.

⟳ Target Reading Skill
Find the word *civilians* on page 440. Look for a contrast near the word. How does this contrast help you define *civilians*?

Comprehension and Critical Thinking
1. (a) Describe How is land used in Guatemala?
(b) Identify Causes Why do the Mayas often fail to earn a living from their land?

2. (a) Recall What are two reasons the Mayas lost their land?
(b) Synthesize Explain how the Mayas have been at a disadvantage in their struggle against their rulers.
3. (a) Identify What are two ways that political movements work to help the Mayas?
(b) Summarize What kinds of changes have these groups brought about?
(c) Predict Do you think life will improve for the Mayas in the decades ahead? Explain.

Writing Activity
Suppose you are a reporter for a radio news program. Write a report on the situation of the Mayas in Guatemala. Present background information about Mayan culture and history. Then tell your listeners about current conditions. Be sure that your report can be read in two to three minutes.

> **Writing Tip** Introduce your report with a "hook," an interesting event or observation that will make your listeners stay tuned.

Chapter 14 Section 2 **441**

Assess and Reteach

Assess Progress　L2
Have students complete the Section Assessment. Administer the *Section Quiz*.

  All in One **Latin America Teaching Resources,** *Section Quiz, p. 234*

Reteach　L1
If students need more instruction, have them read this section in the Reading and Vocabulary Study Guide.

  📖 Chapter 14, Section 2, **Western Hemisphere Reading and Vocabulary Study Guide,** pp. 161–163

Extend　L3
Have students extend their knowledge by completing the *Book Project: Latin America in the News.*

  All in One **Latin America Teaching Resources,** *Book Project: Latin America in the News,* pp. 76–78

Answers

✓ **Reading Check** by seeking to defend their rights, especially land rights.

Writing Activity
Use the *Rubric for Assessing a Report* to evaluate students' reports.

  All in One **Latin America Teaching Resources,** *Rubric for Assessing a Report,* p. 262

Section 2 Assessment

Key Terms
Students' sentences should reflect knowledge of each Key Term.

⟳ Target Reading Skill
A contrast near the word *civilians* is *armed fighters.* This contrast shows that a civilian is someone who is not a member of the armed forces.

Comprehension and Critical Thinking
1. (a) Guatemalan haciendas produce crops to sell abroad, while campesinos and Native Americans grow crops on small farms. **(b)** Poor soil and erosion make farming difficult.

2. (a) Possible answers: the invasion of the Spanish conquistadors; civil war in the 1950s; lack of proper paperwork. **(b)** The Mayas have a historical disadvantage; also many cannot read or write.

3. (a) Possible answers: defending campesino rights and Native American land rights; teaching people their history and how to read; organizing meetings, protests, and strikes. **(b)** Mayas have gained a voice in their government; Mayan-language books and newspapers have been created. **(c)** Students' opinions will vary, but should reflect what they have learned in this section.

Objective
Learn how to infer and draw conclusions.

Prepare to Read

Build Background Knowledge `L2`
Ask students to suppose that a friend has asked them on an outing to a surprise location, telling them to bring a towel, sunscreen, sunglasses, and a bathing suit. Then ask what they can infer from these items and how these inferences help them to conclude where their friend is taking them. (*A towel and bathing suit indicate swimming; sunglasses and sunscreen indicate outdoors; therefore they are probably going to the beach or an outdoor pool.*)

Instruct

Drawing Inferences and Conclusions `L2`

Guided Instruction
- Read the passage, then read the steps to drawing inferences and conclusions as a class and write them on the board.
- Practice the skill by following the steps on p. 443 as a class. Model each step in the activity by walking through how to build inferences from facts about the Mayas in Guatemala, use the facts to draw inferences, and come to a conclusion from those inferences.

Independent Practice
Assign *Skills for Life* and have students complete it individually.

    All in One **Latin America Teaching Resources,** *Skills for Life,* p. 244

Monitor Progress
Check to make sure students understand the skill steps as they complete the *Skills for Life* worksheet.

Skills for Life — Drawing Inferences and Conclusions

When Mr. Macintosh walked into the classroom, Tina watched him carefully.
  "Uh-oh," she said quietly. "Looks like a pop quiz." Tina started flipping through the pages of last night's homework assignment.
  Miguel heard Tina. "Why do you think there's going to be a quiz?" he whispered to Tina.
  "For starters, it's Friday. He tends to give quizzes at the end of the week. And do you see that blue notebook he's got in his hand?" Miguel saw it. "He always writes test questions in it. Whenever he pulls it out, we have a test."
  Just then Mr. Macintosh said, "Good morning, class. Please close your books for a pop quiz."
  Tina was correct that the class would have a pop quiz. You can understand why. She drew good inferences and a strong conclusion.

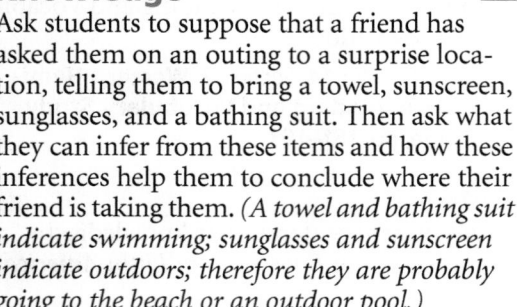

An inference is an educated guess based on facts or evidence. A conclusion is a judgment. Conclusions are often based on several inferences.

Learn the Skill
Use the steps below to draw logical inferences and a strong conclusion.

1. **Identify what you know or assume to be true.** Tina stated these facts: First, it was Friday. Mr. Macintosh tends to give quizzes at the end of the week. Second, he was carrying his blue notebook in which he writes test questions.

2. **Use the facts to draw inferences.** Inferences can usually be stated as an "if . . . then" sentence. The "if" part is the facts you know. The "then" part is an educated guess that follows logically from the facts.

3. **Use two or more inferences to draw a reasoned judgment or conclusion.** From her two inferences, Tina was able to draw this conclusion: The class was about to have a pop quiz.

A protest by Mayas in Guatemala City

Practice the Skill

Read the passage titled Working for a Better Life on pages 440 and 441. Then use the steps below to draw inferences and a conclusion about the situation of the Mayas in Guatemala.

1. Answer these questions in order to help you find facts: What have political movements done to improve life for Guatemalans? What changes have occurred in Guatemala?

2. Use the facts to create at least two inferences, or educated guesses. State your inferences as "if . . . then" sentences. For example: If Mayas learn to read, then they will be more successful at defending their rights.

3. Using the inferences you have written, what conclusion can you draw about the Mayas in Guatemala?

Smog in Mexico City

> ### Apply the Skill
>
> Turn to Section 1 of Chapter 14 and reread the passage titled Opportunities and Challenges on pages 434 and 435. Use the steps of this skill to draw inferences and a conclusion about some aspect of life in Mexico City, such as traffic or pollution.

Chapter 14 **443**

Assess and Reteach

Assess Progress L2
Ask students to do the Apply the Skill activity.

Reteach L1
If students are having trouble applying the skills steps, have them review the skill using the interactive Social Studies Skills Tutor CD-ROM.

⊙ *Drawing Inferences and Conclusions,* **Social Studies Skills Tutor CD-ROM**

Extend L3
Have students find an article in a newspaper or magazine about current events and use the skill steps to draw inferences and conclusions from facts in the article.

Answers
Apply the Skill
A possible answer is that because the underground railroad carries more than four million people a day *(fact)*, and roads cannot handle the amount of traffic the city has *(fact)*, you can infer that the underground railroad is very crowded and traffic on the roads moves slowly. Therefore, it must take a long time to travel from one place to another in Mexico City *(conclusion)*.

Section 3
Step-by-Step Instruction

Objectives
Social Studies

1. Find out why people wanted to build a canal across the Isthmus of Panama.
2. Learn how the Panama Canal was built.
3. Understand how the canal has affected the nation of Panama.

Reading/Language Arts
Use context clues and your own knowledge to determine the meaning of unfamiliar words.

Prepare to Read

Build Background Knowledge   L2
Tell students that they will learn how Panama became an important crossroads in this section. Ask students to quickly preview the headings, photos, and maps in the section. As they preview, ask students to note two or three ideas about Panama. Then ask **What makes Panama different from Guatemala and Mexico?** Use the Idea Wave participation strategy (TE, p. T35) to allow students to share their ideas.

Set a Purpose for Reading   L2
■ Preview the Objectives.

■ Form students into pairs or groups of four. Distribute the *Reading Readiness Guide.* Ask students to fill in the first two columns of the chart. Use the Numbered Heads participation structure (TE, p. T36) to call on students to share one piece of information they already know and one piece of information they want to know.

 All in One **Latin America Teaching Resources**, *Reading Readiness Guide*, p. 236

Vocabulary Builder
Preview Key Terms   L2
Pronounce each Key Term, and then ask students to say the word with you. Provide a simple explanation such as, "Ecotourism has sprung up because many people like to travel to different places to learn about and observe wildlife."

Section 3 — Panama
An Important Crossroads

Prepare to Read

Objectives
In this section you will
1. Find out why people wanted to build a canal across the Isthmus of Panama.
2. Learn how the Panama Canal was built.
3. Understand how the canal has affected the nation of Panama.

Taking Notes
As you read this section, look for the problems the builders of the Panama Canal faced and how they solved those problems. Copy the table below, and record your findings in it.

Building the Panama Canal

Problem	Solution

Target Reading Skill
Use Context Clues
Sometimes you come across a word you know that is being used in an unfamiliar way. You can use context clues and your own general knowledge to understand the new use of the word. For example, you may know that *vessel* often means "ship," and that a cargo ship carries cargo. Therefore, a water vessel is probably a container that holds, or carries, water.

Key Terms
- **Panama Canal** (PAN uh mah kuh NAL) *n.* a shipping canal across the Isthmus of Panama, linking the Atlantic Ocean to the Pacific Ocean
- **lock** (lahk) *n.* a section of waterway in which ships are raised or lowered by adjusting the water level
- **Canal Zone** (kuh NAL zohn) *n.* a 10-mile strip of land along the Panama Canal, once governed by the United States
- **ecotourism** (ek oh TOOR iz um) *n.* travel to unspoiled areas in order to learn about the environment

Statue of Vasco Nuñez de Balboa in Panama City, Panama

444 Latin America

Ever since Christopher Columbus first explored the Isthmus of Panama, the Spanish had been looking for a water route through it. They wanted to be able to sail west from Spain all the way to Asia. The Spanish were also looking for gold. In 1513, the conquistador Vasco Nuñez de Balboa heard of "a mighty sea beyond the mountains" of what is now Panama. He also heard that the streams flowing into that sea were filled with gold.

Balboa organized an expedition of Spaniards and Indians. They struggled across the isthmus, through very difficult country, for over a month. Finally Balboa waded into the Pacific Ocean, which he claimed for Spain. Balboa went on to explore the Pacific coast and found gold and other treasure there.

Balboa still hoped that a water route could be found through the isthmus. But if not, he said, "it might not be impossible to make one." The effort to create this waterway has shaped the history of the isthmus and led to the creation of the nation of Panama. Even today, geography has a major effect on Panama.

Target Reading Skill   L2
Use Context Clues Point out the Target Reading Skill. Tell students that information surrounding an unknown word as well as their own knowledge can provide clues to that word's meaning.

Model using context clues to find the meaning of the word *hub* in this sentence from p. 122: "Panama is also a communications *hub*. Five international fiber-optic networks cross through Panama. Fiber-optic networks are used for long-distance telephone lines and computer networks." (*Panama is a communications center because five fiber-optic networks cross through the country.* Hub *must mean the center or core of something.*)

Give students *Use Context Clues: General Knowledge.* Have them complete the activity in groups.

 All in One **Latin America Teaching Resources,** *Use Context Clues: General Knowledge,* p. 241

Why Build a Canal?

The **Panama Canal,** a manmade waterway across the Isthmus of Panama, is a shortcut through the Western Hemisphere. It is the only way to get from the Pacific Ocean to the Atlantic Ocean by ship without going all the way around South America. Sailors had dreamed of a canal through Central America since the 1500s. A canal could shorten the trip from the Atlantic to the Pacific by 7,800 miles (12,553 kilometers), saving both time and money. But it was not until the 1900s that engineers had the technology to make such a canal.

Crossing the Isthmus By 1534, the Spanish had built a seven-foot-wide stone road across the isthmus. It was used to carry treasure to the Atlantic coast for shipment to Spain. More than 300 years later, during the California Gold Rush, prospectors wanted to get from the east coast of the United States to California as quickly as possible. However, there was not yet a transcontinental railroad in the United States, and travel by horse and wagon was slow and difficult. Instead, many prospectors traveled by boat to Panama, trekked across the isthmus, and took another boat to California.

Passing Through the Canal
Special Panama Canal pilots steer ships through the canal. Here, the captain and first mate of a ship consult with a pilot. **Infer** *Why do you think the passage of ships through the canal is controlled so carefully?*

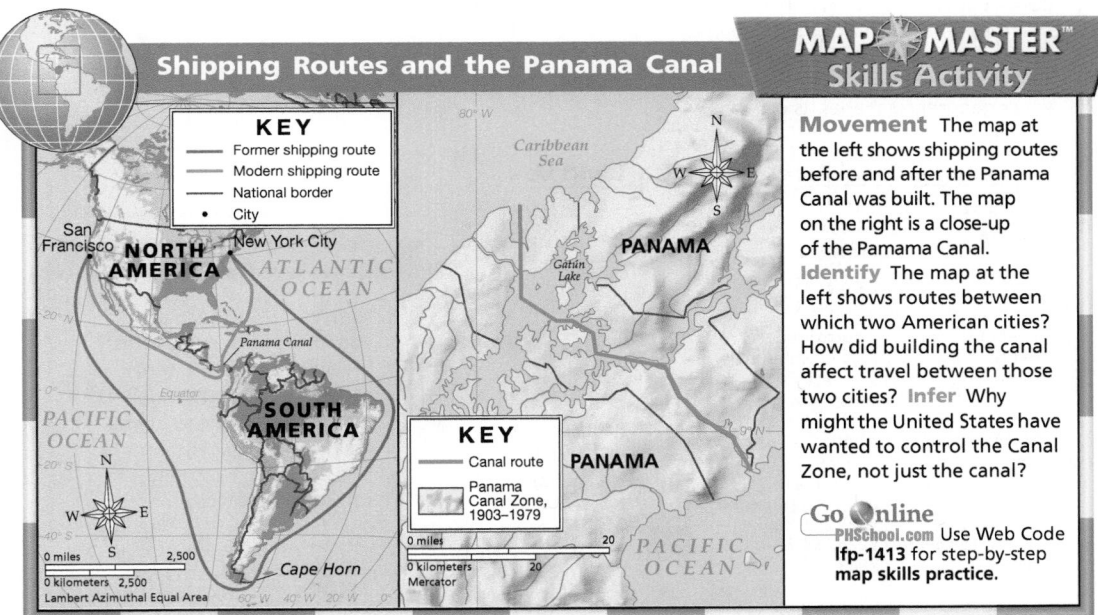

Shipping Routes and the Panama Canal

MAP MASTER™ Skills Activity

KEY
— Former shipping route
— Modern shipping route
— National border
• City

San Francisco • NORTH AMERICA • New York City • ATLANTIC OCEAN • Panama Canal • PACIFIC OCEAN • SOUTH AMERICA • Equator • Cape Horn
0 miles 2,500
0 kilometers 2,500
Lambert Azimuthal Equal Area

Caribbean Sea • Gatún Lake • PANAMA

KEY
— Canal route
▢ Panama Canal Zone, 1903–1979
PANAMA
0 miles 20
0 kilometers 20
Mercator

Movement The map at the left shows shipping routes before and after the Panama Canal was built. The map on the right is a close-up of the Pamama Canal.
Identify The map at the left shows routes between which two American cities? How did building the canal affect travel between those two cities? **Infer** Why might the United States have wanted to control the Canal Zone, not just the canal?

Go Online PHSchool.com Use Web Code **lfp-1413** for step-by-step **map skills practice.**

Vocabulary Builder

Use the information below to teach students this section's high-use words.

High-Use Word	Definition and Sample Sentence
bankrupt, p. 446	*adj.* unable to pay one's debts, or bills
	The **bankrupt** company could not pay its bills and went out of business.
benefit, p. 447	*v.* to be good for
	A good night's rest would **benefit** the team before the game.
crossroads, p. 448	*n.* a place where roads meet
	Meet me at the **crossroads**.
finance, p. 448	*n.* the management and use of money
	She was good with money, so she chose a career in **finance**.

Instruct

Why Build a Canal? L2

Guided Instruction
- **Vocabulary Builder** Clarify the high-use words **bankrupt** and **benefit** before reading.
- Have students read Why Build a Canal? using the Oral Cloze strategy (TE, p. T33). Review the map on p. 445 with students.
- Discuss with students why President Roosevelt wanted to build a canal across the Isthmus of Panama. *(It would speed trade between the Atlantic and Pacific coasts and allow the American navy mobility.)*
- Ask students **Do you think that the United States should have helped Panama to revolt against Colombia? Why or why not?** *(Yes: The United States needed to help Panama so that it could be a free country and so that the United States could build the canal. No: The United States should not have interfered with Panama and Colombia just so that it could build a canal. It should have tried further negotiations with Colombia.)*

Independent Practice
Ask students to create the Taking Notes graphic organizer on a blank piece of paper. Then have them fill in the "Problem" column with the information they have just learned.

Monitor Progress
As students fill in the graphic organizer, circulate and make sure individuals are choosing the correct details. Provide assistance as needed.

Answers

Infer probably to avoid delays and damage to the canal and to ships

MAP MASTER Skills Activity **Identify** New York City and San Francisco; it shortened the shipping routes between them **Infer** perhaps to protect the canal, control who used the canal, and to charge admittance fees

Go Online PHSchool.com Students may practice their map skills using the interactive online version of this map.

Guided Instruction L2

Ask students to study the Country Profile. Point out the map, chart, and circle graph. As a class, answer the Map and Chart Skills questions. Allow students to briefly discuss their responses with a partner before sharing answers.

Independent Practice

Distribute *Outline Map 7: Central America and the Caribbean.* Have students locate and label Panama, the Atlantic Ocean, and the Pacific Ocean on their maps. Then, using the map on p. 446 as a reference, have students mark and label the approximate location of the Panama Canal on their outline maps. Assist students as necessary.

All in One Latin America Teaching Resources, *Outline Map 7: Central America and the Caribbean,* p. 254

The French Begin a Canal In 1881, when Panama was part of Colombia, a French company gained the rights to build a canal through Panama. However, the builders had to struggle with mud slides, a mountain range, and a dense tropical forest. Tropical diseases killed many workers. After several years of digging and blasting, the French company went bankrupt. Work on the canal stopped.

In 1902, the United States government bought the French company's equipment. Then, the United States began negotiating with Colombia for the rights to continue building a canal.

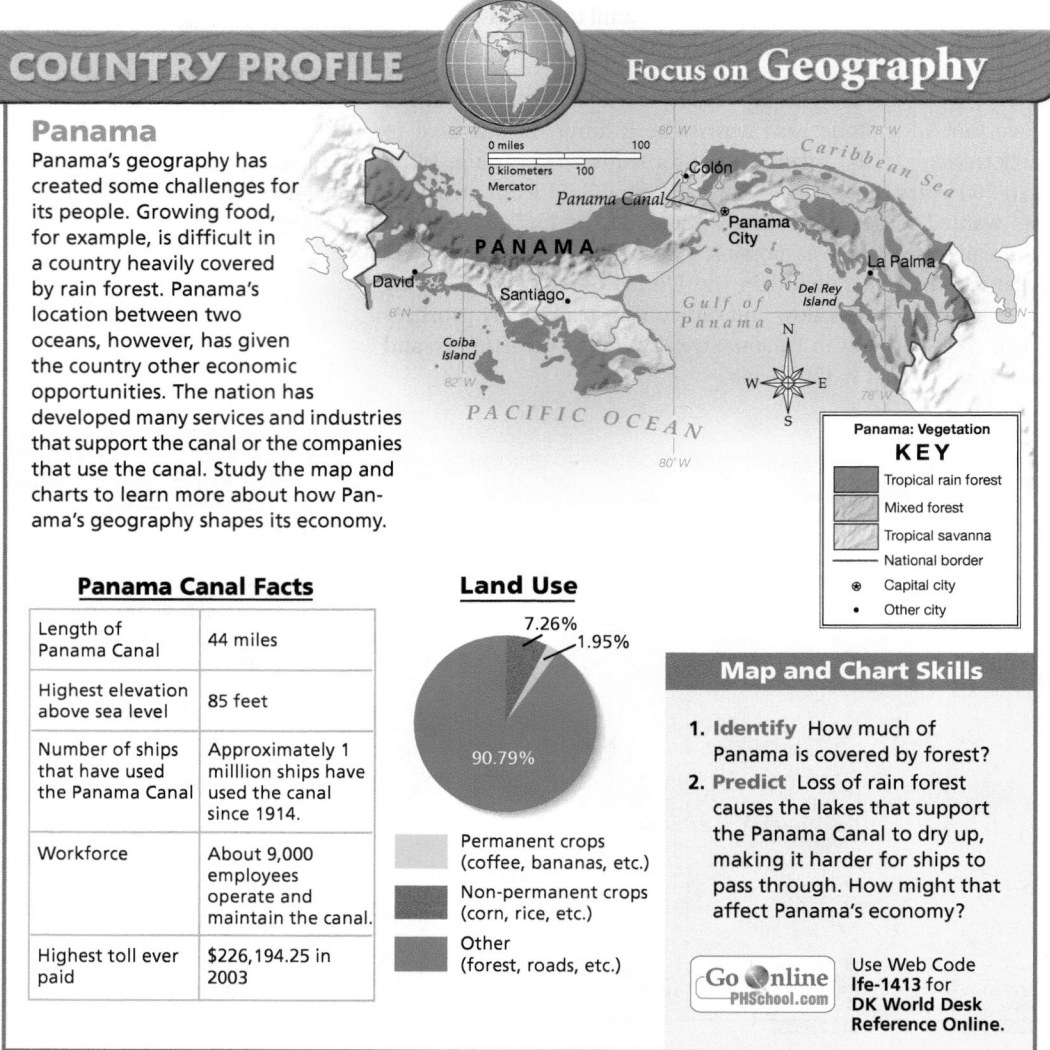

COUNTRY PROFILE Focus on **Geography**

Panama

Panama's geography has created some challenges for its people. Growing food, for example, is difficult in a country heavily covered by rain forest. Panama's location between two oceans, however, has given the country other economic opportunities. The nation has developed many services and industries that support the canal or the companies that use the canal. Study the map and charts to learn more about how Panama's geography shapes its economy.

Panama: Vegetation
KEY
- Tropical rain forest
- Mixed forest
- Tropical savanna
- National border
- ⊛ Capital city
- • Other city

Panama Canal Facts

Length of Panama Canal	44 miles
Highest elevation above sea level	85 feet
Number of ships that have used the Panama Canal	Approximately 1 milllion ships have used the canal since 1914.
Workforce	About 9,000 employees operate and maintain the canal.
Highest toll ever paid	$226,194.25 in 2003

Land Use

7.26%
1.95%
90.79%

- Permanent crops (coffee, bananas, etc.)
- Non-permanent crops (corn, rice, etc.)
- Other (forest, roads, etc.)

Map and Chart Skills

1. **Identify** How much of Panama is covered by forest?
2. **Predict** Loss of rain forest causes the lakes that support the Panama Canal to dry up, making it harder for ships to pass through. How might that affect Panama's economy?

Go Online PHSchool.com Use Web Code **lfe-1413** for **DK World Desk Reference Online.**

Answers

Map and Chart Skills

1. About three-quarters to two-thirds of Panama's land is covered by forest.
2. Industries related to the canal would suffer financially.

Go Online PHSchool.com Students can find more information about this topic on the DK World Desk Reference Online.

Skills Mini Lesson

Using Reliable Information L2

1. Point out to students that some sources are more reliable than others. To evaluate reliability, one must consider the source's accuracy, time period, authority, and bias.
2. Help students practice the skill by comparing two Internet or print sources about the Panama Canal.
3. Have students apply the skill by asking them to complete *Doing Searches on the Internet.* Ask them to evaluate the reliability of some of their favorite Web sites.

All in One Latin America Teaching Resources, *Doing Searches on the Internet,* p. 258

The New Nation of Panama Colombia refused to grant the United States rights to build a canal. But business people in Panama thought a canal would benefit the local economy. Also, many Panamanians wanted to be free of Colombia's rule. They saw the canal as an opportunity to win independence.

At the same time, President Theodore Roosevelt felt that the canal was important for the United States. It would speed trade between the Atlantic and Pacific coasts. It would also allow the American navy to move back and forth in case of war. Roosevelt did not wait for events to unfold. He took action. In November 1903, the United States helped Panama revolt against Colombia. Two weeks after Panama declared its independence, the United States received the rights to build the canal.

✓ Reading Check   Why did Panamanians want a canal?

Building the Canal: A Heroic Effort

The Americans faced the same challenges of moving earth and rock that the French had faced. In addition, the project called for a dam to be built to form a lake. There were locks to design and build. A **lock** is a section of waterway in which ships are raised or lowered by adjusting the water level.

While the work on the canal was difficult and slow, by far the biggest problem was disease. Some 20,000 workers had died of malaria and yellow fever while the French worked on the canal. Scientists did not know what caused these diseases, so they could do little to prevent them.

Digging the Canal
Canal workers wore the badges shown above. In the photo at the left, they use steam shovels and trains to build the Panama Canal.
Draw Conclusions *From what you see in the photo, how were trains used in the construction?*

Guided Instruction

- Have students read Building the Canal: A Heroic Effort.

- Ask students **Why did workers need to build a dam and locks in order for the canal to work?** *(A dam stops the flow of water across a river or stream and creates a reservoir; locks allow ships to be raised and lowered to compensate for the different water levels connected by the canal.)*

- Ask students **What challenges were faced by the workers building the canal?** *(The French faced mudslides, diseases, difficulty clearing the forest, bankruptcy; Americans faced disease and resistance from Colombia for the rights to build the canal.)*

Independent Progress

Have students complete the graphic organizer by filling in the "Solution" column.

Monitor Progress

Show *Section Reading Support Transparency LA 41* and ask students to check their graphic organizers individually. Go over key concepts and clarify key vocabulary as needed.

📖 **Latin America Transparencies,** *Section Reading Support Transparency LA 41*

Differentiated Instruction

For Less Proficient Readers   L1
Ask students to find photographs of words or terms with which they may not be familiar, such as "dams" and "locks," in print or on the Internet. To search for terms on the Internet, have students type in the unfamiliar word along with the word "photograph" to get the best results.

For Advanced Readers   L3
Have students read *Locks, Crocs, and Skeeters* and *Beyond the Chagres*. Then, ask students to create their own dictionaries of the selections' key words or terms, with illustrations.

All In One **Latin America Teaching Resources,** *Locks, Crocs, and Skeeters,* pp. 255–256; *Beyond the Chagres,* p. 257

Answer

✓ Reading Check Panamanians wanted a canal because they thought that it would benefit the local economy. Some Panamanians wanted a canal because they saw it as a way to win independence from Colombia.

Draw Conclusions The trains in the photograph appear to be hauling supplies to the building site, or carrying rubble out of the building site.

Use Context Clues As a follow up, ask students to answer the Target Reading Skill question in the Student Edition. (*Standing water is water that does not move.*)

Panama and Its Canal L2

Guided Instruction

- **Vocabulary Builder** Clarify the meaning of the high-use words **crossroads** and **finance** before reading.

- Read Panama and Its Canal. As students read, circulate and make sure individuals can answer the Reading Check question.

- Ask students **Why did Panamanians riot in the 1960s and 1970s?** (*They rioted to protest American control of the Panama Canal and the Canal Zone.*)

- Ask students **Do you think the United States should have given Panama control of the canal? Why or why not?** (*Yes—The people of Panama deserve control over their own land. No—Panama's original treaty with the United States was forever. The United States needs to be near to the canal to protect it.*)

- Discuss how the canal has affected Panama's economy. (*It has made Panama a hub for communication and international trade, increased the numbers of factories, boosted ecotourism.*)

Independent Practice

Assign *Guided Reading and Review.*

All in One Latin America Teaching Resources, *Guided Reading and Review,* p. 237

Monitor Progress

Tell students to fill in the last column of the *Reading Readiness Guide.* Ask them to evaluate if what they learned was what they expected to learn.

All in One Latin America Teaching Resources, *Reading Readiness Guide,* p. 236

Answer

✓ Reading Check Workers fought the mosquitoes by burning sulfur in houses, covering water vessels with mesh, and filling in swampy breeding grounds with dirt.

 **Use Context Clues** You know that *standing* often refers to a person "staying still in an upright position." Use part of that definition to help you understand *standing water.* Ask yourself, can water stand still? What does *standing* mean in this context? What is *standing water?*

Panama City at night

In the early 1900s, doctors discovered that malaria and yellow fever were both carried by mosquitoes. The mosquitoes bred in standing water. In 1904, the Panama Canal Company hired a doctor and a large crew to deal with the mosquito problem. It took more than a year to complete the job. Workers burned sulfur in every house to kill mosquitoes. They covered every water vessel with mesh to keep mosquitoes out. They filled in swampy breeding grounds with dirt. Without these efforts, the Panama Canal probably could not have been built.

It took eight years and more than 70,000 workers, mostly Caribbean islanders, to build the Panama Canal. It remains one of the greatest engineering feats of modern times.

✓ Reading Check **How did workers fight the mosquitoes?**

Panama and Its Canal

When the United States gained the rights to build a canal, it signed a treaty with Panama. The treaty gave the United States the right to build the Panama Canal and to control it forever.

The Canal Zone The United States also controlled an area called the Canal Zone. The **Canal Zone** was an area containing the canal, the land on either side of the canal, the ports, the port cities, and the railroad. The treaty allowed the United States to govern the Canal Zone according to its laws and gave the United States the right to invade Panama to protect the canal. The United States built 14 military bases in the Canal Zone and stationed thousands of soldiers there.

Many Panamanians felt the United States had too much power in Panama. For years, Panama held talks with the United States about transferring control of the canal to Panama. In the 1960s and 1970s, angry Panamanians rioted to protest American control.

A Change of Ownership In 1977, after years of talks, President Jimmy Carter signed two new treaties with Panama's government. These treaties gave Panama more control over the canal. In 1999, Panama finally gained full control of the Panama Canal.

Panama Today The Panama Canal dominated life in Panama for much of the 1900s, and it continues to be extremely important today. Because of the canal, Panama has become an international crossroads for trade. The ships that pass through the Panama Canal each day pay tolls according to their weight. International trade is very important to Panama's economy. The canal has made Panama a leading banking and finance center.

Differentiated Instruction

For Special Needs Students L1
Help students review the major events that led to Panamanian control of the canal by creating time lines. Have pairs draw a line on a piece of paper. Ask students to look for dates on this page under "The Canal Zone" and "A Change of Ownership" and to write them on their time lines. Then have students look for the events that go with the dates, and write those events next to the dates on their time lines. (*1960s—Panamanians protest American control of the canal; 1970s—Panamanians continue to protest; 1978—President Carter signs new treaties giving Panama more control; 1999—Panama gains control of the canal.*)

The Panama Canal

Every day, an average of 33 ships pass through the Panama Canal. It takes each ship around nine hours to cross from one ocean to the other. The Panama Canal is like a water elevator with lakes. Ships are raised and lowered in the locks as they travel from one ocean to the other.

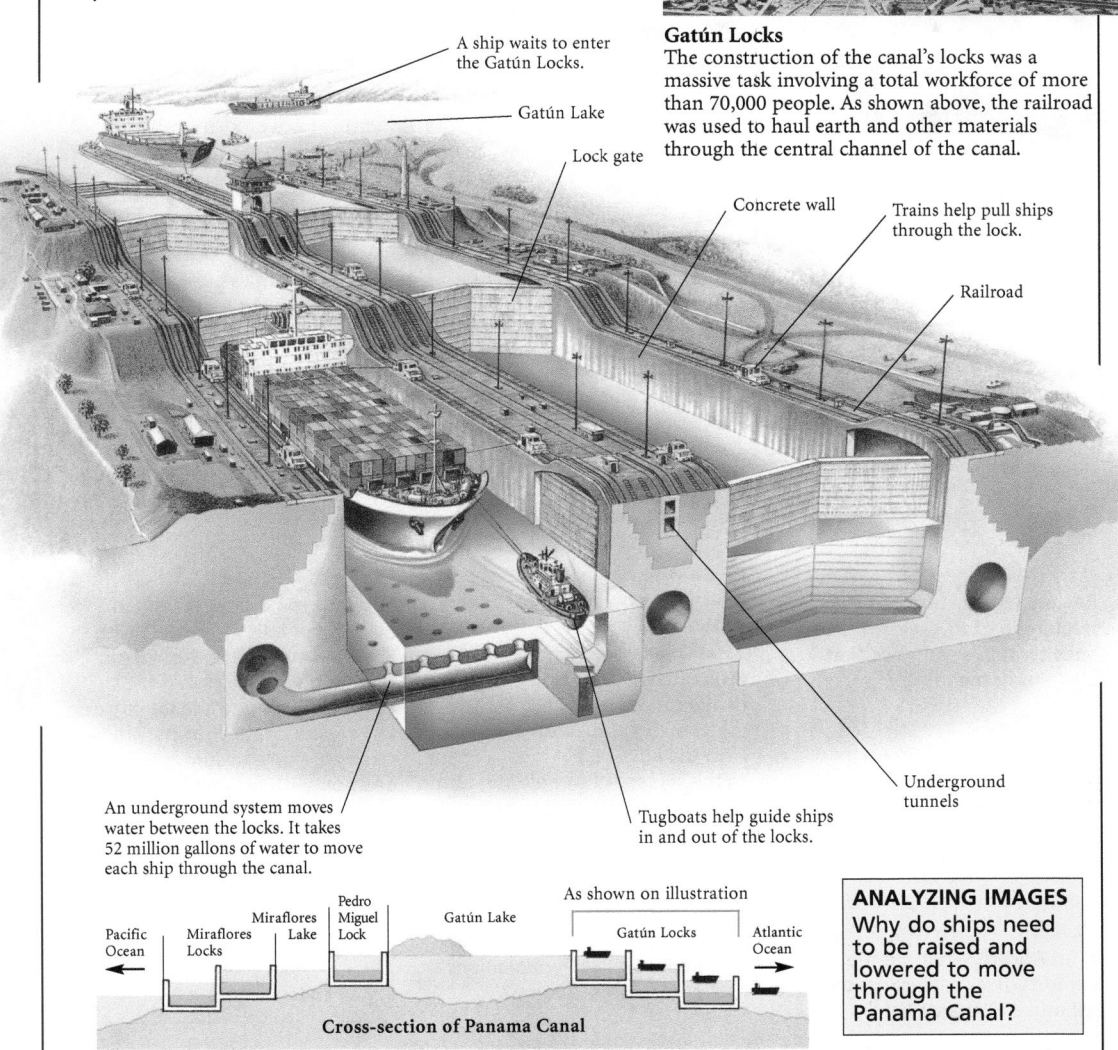

Gatún Locks
The construction of the canal's locks was a massive task involving a total workforce of more than 70,000 people. As shown above, the railroad was used to haul earth and other materials through the central channel of the canal.

A ship waits to enter the Gatún Locks.

Gatún Lake

Lock gate

Concrete wall

Trains help pull ships through the lock.

Railroad

Underground tunnels

An underground system moves water between the locks. It takes 52 million gallons of water to move each ship through the canal.

Tugboats help guide ships in and out of the locks.

Pacific Ocean — Miraflores Locks — Miraflores Lake — Pedro Miguel Lock — Gatún Lake — As shown on illustration — Gatún Locks — Atlantic Ocean

Cross-section of Panama Canal

ANALYZING IMAGES
Why do ships need to be raised and lowered to move through the Panama Canal?

Background: Links Across Place

The Suez Canal Like the Panama Canal, the Suez Canal is one of the world's busiest canals. The Suez Canal, which extends across the Isthmus of Suez in Egypt, connects the Mediterranean and the Red Seas and is a major link between Europe and Asia. Unlike the Panama Canal, which contains many locks, the Suez Canal does not contain locks because the levels of the Mediterranean and Red Seas are similar. Before the Suez Canal was built, ships from Great Britain and other parts of Europe had to travel around the southern coast of Africa to get to India.

The Panama Canal L2

Guided Instruction
Ask students to study the diagrams of the Panama Canal on this page. Help students to see which parts of the detailed diagram on the top of the page correspond to the cross section below it. As a class, answer the question at the bottom of the page. Allow students to briefly discuss their responses with a partner before sharing their ideas.

Independent Practice
Have students learn more about how the Panama Canal works by completing the *Activity Shop Lab: Making a Model Canal Lock.*

> **All in One Latin America Teaching Resources,** *Activity Shop Lab: Making a Model Canal Lock,* pp. 249–250

Answer

ANALYZING IMAGES The Gatún Lake, in the middle of the canal, has a higher elevation than the sea on both sides of the canal. People designed locks to allow the ships to pass from sea level to Gatún Lake and back to sea level again.

Assess and Reteach

Assess Progress L2

Have students complete the Section Assessment. Administer the *Section Quiz*.

 Latin America Teaching Resources, *Section Quiz,* p. 238

Reteach L1

If students need more instruction, have them read this section in the Reading and Vocabulary Study Guide.

Chapter 14, Section 3, **Western Hemisphere Reading and Vocabulary Study Guide,** pp. 164–166

Extend L3

Have students learn more about issues surrounding the Panama Canal works by completing the *Small Group Activity: Simulation: Who Should Control the Panama Canal?*

 Latin America Teaching Resources, *Small Group Activity: Simulation: Who Should Control the Panama Canal?,* pp. 245–248

Answers

✓Reading Check Because of the canal, Panama is an international trading center, a leading banking and finance center, and a communications and tourist center.

Section 3 Assessment

Key Terms
Students' sentences should reflect knowledge of each Key Term.

Target Reading Skill
The word *unfold* means "to become known." The words *wait* and *took action* provide clues to the word's meaning. The fact that Roosevelt *took action,* not waiting for events to *unfold,* shows that *unfold* has a less active meaning.

Comprehension and Critical Thinking
1. (a) It shortens the trip between the Atlantic and Pacific Oceans, saving both time and money. **(b)** Possible answer: Colombia refused to grant the United States permission to build the canal; the United States helped Panama revolt against Colombia to gain independence; Panama gave the United States the right to build the canal.

New Industries Traffic through the canal has also encouraged warehousing and manufacturing. Many factories in Panama are similar to the maquiladoras in Mexico. They assemble parts imported from abroad and then export the finished products. Materials for these factories come from Hong Kong, the United States, and Japan as well as other countries. Most finished products are shipped to Latin American nations or are sold within Panama itself.

Panama is also a communications hub. International fiber-optic networks cross through Panama. Fiber-optic networks are used for long-distance telephone lines and computer networks.

Tourism Another important industry in Panama is tourism. Many tourists come to travel through the canal. They also visit Panama's rain forests. Look at the map in the Country Profile on page 446 to see how much of Panama is covered by rain forests. Tourism in unspoiled areas to observe wildlife and learn about the environment is called **ecotourism**. Ecotourists come to see the wide variety of plants and animals in the rain forest. These include howler monkeys, sloths, harpy eagles, and capybaras—huge rodents that look like guinea pigs. Panama's government has recently invested millions of dollars to promote ecotourism in its rain forests.

An ecotourist riding through Panama's rain forest

✓ Reading Check Why is the canal important to Panama today?

Section 3 Assessment

Key Terms
Review the key terms at the beginning of this section. Use each term in a sentence that explains its meaning.

Target Reading Skill
Find the word *unfold* on page 447. Use your own knowledge and the surrounding words and phrases to explain what *unfold* means in this context.

Comprehension and Critical Thinking
1. (a) Recall What are the benefits of a canal across the Isthmus of Panama?

(b) Sequence List three events, in order, that led to the building of the canal.
2. (a) Describe What kinds of difficulties did the builders of the canal face?
(b) Identify Cause and Effect How did advances in medicine lead to the successful completion of the Panama Canal?
3. (a) Define What was the Canal Zone?
(b) Explain How was the Canal Zone governed?
(c) Draw Conclusions Why was it so important to Panamanians to gain control of the canal?

Writing Activity
Suppose you are an American newspaper editor in the 1970s. Write an editorial either for or against giving control of the Panama Canal and the Canal Zone to Panama. State your position clearly. Be sure to support your position with reasons and facts.

For: An activity on Panama
Visit: PHSchool.com
Web Code: lfd-1403

450 Latin America

---

2. (a) Difficulties included: moving earth and rock, building a dam to form a lake, designing and building locks, and battling disease. **(b)** The discovery that mosquitoes carried malaria and yellow fever allowed workers to take measures to control mosquitoes, which lessened disease.

3. (a) an area containing the Panama Canal, the land on either side of the canal, the ports, the port cities, and the railroad **(b)** according to United States laws **(c)** Many Panamanians believed that the United States had too much power in Panama.

Writing Activity
Use the *Rubric for Assessing a Newspaper Article* to evaluate students' editorials.

Latin America Teaching Resources, *Rubric for Assessing a Newspaper Article,* p. 264

Go Online PHSchool.com Typing in the web code when prompted will bring students directly to detailed instructions for this activity.

Review and Assessment

◆ Chapter Summary

Section 1: Mexico
- Many farmers in Mexico are poor, and jobs in the countryside are scarce.
- Many rural Mexicans move to the cities to look for work, but they find that city life is hard and very different from life in the countryside.
- Mexico City is a huge city that is facing overcrowding and pollution problems.

Section 2: Guatemala
- Most of the land in Guatemala is owned by only a few wealthy ladino families who grow crops for export.
- The Mayas lost much of their land to their Spanish conquerors and later they lost more land during the civil war.
- Today, political movements are working to improve life for the Mayas.

Section 3: Panama
- The Panama Canal shortens sea travel between the Atlantic Ocean and the Pacific Ocean.
- After the French could not complete the canal, the United States overcame engineering challenges and disease to build it.
- The Panama Canal is a key water route today and is important to Panama's economy.

Mexico

Guatemala

Panama

Review Chapter Content
- Review and revisit the major themes of this chapter by asking students to classify what Guiding Question each bulleted statement in the Chapter Summary answers. Form students into groups of three or four to complete the activity. Refer to page 1 in the Student Edition for the text of the Guiding Questions.
- Assign *Vocabulary Development* to help students review the Key Terms.

All in One **Latin America Teaching Resources,** *Vocabulary Development,* p. 259

◆ Key Terms

Each of the statements below contains a key term from the chapter. If the statement is true, write *true*. If it is false, rewrite the statement to make it true.

1. A migrant worker is a person who settles on someone else's land without permission.

2. A plaza is an open field in the countryside.

3. A canal uses a series of locks to raise and lower ships by adjusting the water level.

4. Land reform is a new and better way of farming the land.

5. When people strike, they stop working in order to achieve a goal.

6. Ecotourism can involve visiting the rain forest to learn about its environment.

7. A ladino is any person from Latin America.

8. The Panama Canal shortens the route ships must travel between the Atlantic Ocean and the Pacific Ocean.

Chapter 14 **451**

◆ Vocabulary Builder

Revisit this chapter's High-Use Words:

support	erosion	benefit
afford	civilian	crossroads
sturdy	violation	finance
resource	bankrupt	

Ask students to review the definitions they recorded on their *Word Knowledge* worksheets.

All in One **Latin America Teaching Resources,** *Word Knowledge,* p. 242

Consider allowing students to earn extra credit if they use the words in their answers to the questions in the Chapter Review and Assessment. The words must be used correctly and in a natural context to win the extra points.

Answers

Key Terms
1. False. A migrant worker is a laborer who travels from one area to another, picking crops that are in season.
2. False. A plaza is a public square at the center of a village, a town, or a city.
3. True.
4. False. Land reform is the effort to distribute land more equally and fairly.
5. True.
6. True
7. False. A ladino is a mestizo, or person of mixed Spanish and Native America ancestry in Guatemala.
8. True.

Comprehension and Critical Thinking

9. (a) Mexico City and the United States **(b)** because it is difficult to support their families in the country

10. (a) Mexico's population is growing rapidly. **(b)** Population growth causes crowding and increased pollution in Mexico's cities.

11. (a) The Mayas lost more of their land. **(b)** Good farmland in Guatemala is scarce. Powerful people have tried to force Mayas off their land because the Mayas have little political power.

12. (a) Political movements are working to improve life for Mayas. **(b)** The political movements use protests and strikes as methods to bring about change. These methods bring about changes by forcing authorities to recognize the Mayas' rights.

13. (a) France **(b)** Difficulties such as disease and thick vegetation caused France's efforts to fail. **(c)** The canal saves time and money for travelers by shortening the trip from the Atlantic Ocean to the Pacific Ocean by almost 8,000 miles.

14. (a) Many Panamanians wanted the United States to build the canal, but Colombia blocked the negotiations. The United States helped Panama become independent from Colombia. **(b)** Panamanians thought that the canal would benefit the local economy. **(c)** The canal brings international trade to Panama and encourages many other businesses, including tourism.

Skills Practice
Students answers will vary.

Possible inferences Panama was unhappy as part of Colombia. The opportunities the canal presented were more important to some Panamanians than remaining part of Colombia. The United States helped Panama gain independence to win the right to build the canal.

Possible conclusion The United States and Panama fought jointly for Panamanian independence because leaders in both countries felt that building the canal would serve their country's interests.

Writing Activity: Science
Student answers will vary, but should include the scientific discovery that mosquitoes carried malaria and yellow fever.

◆ Comprehension and Critical Thinking

9. (a) Identify Name two places many rural Mexicans go when they leave the countryside.
(b) Generalize Why do so many people make these moves?

10. (a) Recall Describe population growth in Mexico.
(b) Identify Effects How does population growth affect Mexico's cities?

11. (a) Summarize What happened to the Mayas during the Guatemalan civil war?
(b) Synthesize Why have so many Mayas been forced from their land?

12. (a) Identify What groups are working to improve life for the Mayas?
(b) Identify Cause and Effect What are two methods these groups use, and how might these methods bring about change?

13. (a) Identify What country first tried to build a canal across Panama?
(b) Identify Causes Why did that country fail to complete the canal?
(c) Draw Conclusions How does the whole world benefit from the Panama Canal?

14. (a) Summarize How did Panama become an independent nation?
(b) Identify Causes Why did Panama want the United States to build the Panama Canal?
(c) Identify Effects What benefits has the Panama Canal brought to Panama?

◆ Skills Practice

Drawing Inferences and Conclusions In the Skills for Life activity in this chapter, you learned how to draw inferences. You also learned how to draw a conclusion, or make a reasoned judgment, using two or more inferences.

Review the steps you followed to learn this skill. Then reread The New Nation of Panama on page 447. List several inferences you can draw about the events described there. Finally, use your inferences to draw a conclusion about those events.

◆ Writing Activity: Science

Suppose you were the science reporter for a newspaper covering the building of the Panama Canal. Write a brief report about how advances in science contributed to the successful completion of the Panama Canal.

MAP MASTER™ Skills Activity

Place Location For each place listed below, write the letter from the map that shows its location.

1. Mexico
2. Guatemala
3. Panama
4. Nicaragua
5. Mexico City
6. Panama Canal

Go Online
PHSchool.com Use Web Code lfp-1423 for step-by-step map skills practice.

Mexico and Central America

Use Rubric for Assessing a Newspaper Article to evaluate students' reports. Tell students how many sources you would like them to use, if any beyond the textbook.

All in One Latin America Teaching Resources, *Rubric for Assessing a Newspaper Article,* p. 264

Standardized Test Prep

Test-Taking Tips

Some questions on standardized tests ask you to analyze a reading selection. Study the passage below. Then follow the tips to help you answer the sample question.

> Many people have moved to Mexico City to find jobs in factories. Cars and buses clog the city streets. In addition, the city is located in a valley surrounded by mountains, and pollution gets trapped there. <u>Because</u> of its geography and heavy traffic, Mexico City has one of the worst cases of air pollution in the world.

TIP Look for words that signal causes or reasons, such as the word *because* in the last sentence.

Pick the letter that best completes the statement.

Mexico City's air pollution problem is made worse by

A ~~smog from South America.~~

B its location.

C its textile factories.

D ~~its lack of rain.~~

TIP First cross out answers that you know are wrong. Then consider each remaining choice before selecting the best answer.

Think It Through Look at the remaining answer choices. Answer C might be correct, but the passage does not mention textile factories. Remember the signal word *because*. The sentence beginning with *because* gives geography as one reason for Mexico City's pollution. Geography includes location, so B is the correct answer.

Practice Questions

Use the tips above and other tips in this book to help you answer the following questions.

1. Which of the following was not a problem for the builders of the Panama Canal?
   A disease carried by mosquitoes
   B mudslides
   C blizzards
   D a mountain range blocking the route

2. In Guatemala, most of the land is owned by
   A Native Americans.
   B Spanish conquerors.
   C a few wealthy ladino families.
   D the Mayas.

3. What is one result of rapid population growth in Mexico?
   A Farms are getting overcrowded.
   B The economy is improving because there are more people to buy things.
   C Rural people are moving to the cities to find work.
   D Factories are shutting down.

Use the circle graph below to answer Question 4. Choose the letter of the best answer to the question.

Population of Guatemala

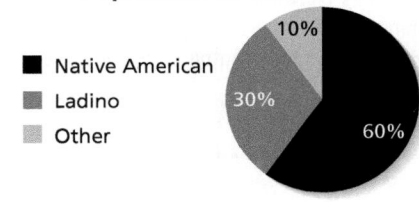

- Native American
- Ladino
- Other

4. According to the circle graph, which of the following statements is true?
   A Most people in Guatemala are descended from Europeans and Native Americans.
   B Half of Guatemala's population is ladino.
   C Most Guatemalans are Native American.
   D There are more Spaniards than ladinos in Guatemala.

PHSchool.com
Use Web Code lfa-1401 for a **Chapter 14 self-test.**

Chapter 14 **453**

Standardized Test Prep
Answers

1. C

2. C

3. C

4. C

Assessment Resources

Use *Chapter Tests A and B* to assess students' mastery of chapter content.

All in One **Latin America Teaching Resources,** *Chapter Tests A and B,* pp. 265–270

Tests are also available on the **ExamView Test Bank CD-ROM.**

◉ **Exam***View*® **Test Bank CD-ROM**

Overview

Introducing The Caribbean

1. Find out the location and important facts about each country.

2. Analyze the data to compare countries.

3. Learn what characteristics countries share.

4. Discover key differences among countries.

Section **1**

Cuba: Clinging to Communism

1. Find out how Cuba's history led to thousands of Cubans leaving their homeland.

2. Discover how Cuban exiles feel about their lives in the United States and about their homeland.

3. Learn what changes have recently come to Cuba.

Section **2**

Haiti: A Struggle for Democracy

1. Find out how democracy has been threatened in Haiti.

2. Learn what life is like for the people of Haiti, both in the countryside and in the cities.

Section **3**

Puerto Rico: An American Commonwealth

1. Understand how the people of Puerto Rico are both American and Puerto Rican.

2. Find out what life is like on the island of Puerto Rico.

3. Learn about the three kinds of political status Puerto Ricans are considering for their future.

Go Online
PHSchool.com

Students use embedded Web codes to access Internet activities, chapter self-tests, and additional map practice. They may also access Dorling Kindersley's Online Desk Reference to learn more about each country they study.

Interactive Textbook

Use the Interactive Textbook to make content and concepts come alive through animations, videos, and activities that accompany the complete basal text—online and on CD-ROM.

PRENTICE HALL
TeacherEXPRESS
Plan • Teach • Assess

Use this complete suite of powerful teaching tools to make planning lessons and administering tests quicker and easier.

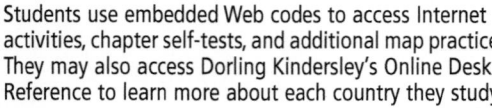

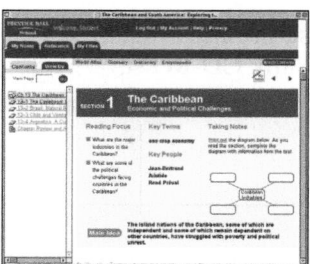

Reading and Assessment

Reading and Vocabulary Instruction

⤵ Model the Target Reading Skill

Main Idea Tell students that finding the main idea can help them understand their reading and remember key concepts. The main idea is the most important point in the reading. It is supported by the details in the passage. Model this skill by thinking aloud about the main idea of Section 2 of this chapter.

I am going to look for clues to the main idea on the first page of the section. The title of the section is *Haiti: A Democracy in Progress.* This probably means that the main idea will have to do with the ongoing political issues in Haiti.

The first sentence of the section says: *Jean Bertrand Aristide was elected president of Haiti in 1990, but he served for only seven months!* Because this sentence includes very specific details about one person, it is a detail, not the main idea.

The next paragraph starts like this: *Haiti's history has been a continuing struggle for democracy.* This sentence is more general. It talks about all of Haiti and about a process that is continuing. It also relates to the title of the section. I think I have found the main idea.

Use the following worksheets from All-in-One Latin America Teaching Resources, (pp. 287, 288, and 289) to support this chapter's Target Reading Skill.

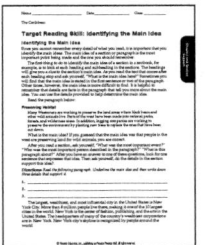 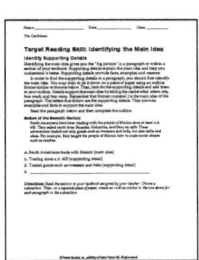 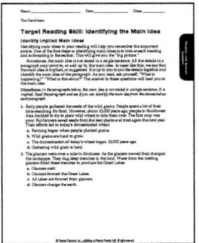

Vocabulary Builder

High-Use Academic Words

Use these steps to teach this chapter's high-use words:

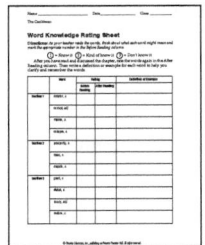

1. Have students rate how well they know each word on their Word Knowledge worksheets (All-in-One Latin America Teaching Resources, p. 290).
2. Pronounce each word and ask students to repeat it.
3. Give students a brief definition or sample sentence (provided on TE pp. 463, 471, and 477.)
4. Work with students as they fill in the "Definition or Example" column of their Word Knowledge worksheets.

Assessment

Formal Assessment

Test students' understanding of core knowledge and skills.

Chapter Tests A and B, All-in-One Latin America Teaching Resources, pp. 306–311

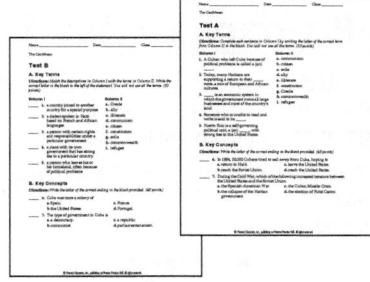

Customize the Chapter Tests to suit your needs.

Exam*View*® Test Bank CD-ROM

Skills Assessment

Assess geographic literacy.

MapMaster Skills, Student Edition pp. 455, 484

Country Profile Map and Chart Skills, Student Edition pp. 465, 472, 479

Assess reading and comprehension.

Target Reading Skills, Student Edition, pp. 464, 474, 478, and in Section Assessments

Chapter 15 Assessment, Reading and Vocabulary Study Guide, p. 177

Performance Assessment

Assess students' performance on this chapter's Writing Activities using the following rubrics from All-in-One Latin America Teaching Resources.

Rubric for Assessing a Bar Graph, p. 302

Rubric for Assessing a Writing Assignment, p. 303

Rubric for Assessing a Newspaper Article, p. 304

Rubric for Assessing a Journal Entry, p. 305

Assess students' work through performance tasks.

Small Group Activity: Creating a Magazine Story, All-in-One Latin America Teaching Resources, pp. 293–296

Portfolio Activity, Teacher Edition, p. 132

Online Assessment

Have students check their own understanding.

Chapter Self-Test

Section 1 Cuba: Clinging to Communism

3.5 periods, 1.75 blocks (includes Country Databank and Skills for Life)

Social Studies Objectives
1. Find out how Cuba's history led to thousands of Cubans leaving their homeland.
2. Discover how Cuban exiles feel about their lives in the United States and about their homeland.
3. Learn what changes have recently come to Cuba.

Reading/Language Arts Objective
Identify main ideas in each section or paragraph.

Prepare to Read	Instructional Resources	Differentiated Instruction

Build Background Knowledge
Preview the section and then brainstorm how Cuba's government affects life in Cuba.

Set a Purpose for Reading
Have students begin to fill out the *Reading Readiness Guide*.

Preview Key Terms
Teach the section's Key Terms.

Target Reading Skill
Introduce the section's Target Reading Skill of **identifying main ideas**.

All in One Latin America Teaching Resources
- L2 Reading Readiness Guide, p. 276
- L2 Identify Main Ideas, p. 287

Spanish Reading and Vocabulary Study Guide
- L2 Chapter 15, Section 1, pp. 122–123 ELL

Discovery Channel World Studies Video Program
- L2 The Caribbean: Dynamic Lands and Cultures ELL, LPR, SN

Instruct	Instructional Resources	Differentiated Instruction

Cuba's History
Discuss Castro's government.

Target Reading Skill
Review **identifying main ideas**.

Cuban Exiles
Discuss successes and difficulties faced by Cuban exiles.

Country Profile
Ask students to derive and use information from maps, charts, and graphs.

Changes Come to Cuba
Describe changes in Cuba since the 1990s.

All in One Latin America Teaching Resources
- L2 Guided Reading and Review, p. 277
- L2 Reading Readiness Guide, p. 276

Latin America Transparencies
- L2 Section Reading Support Transparency LA 42

All in One Latin America Teaching Resources
- L3 Morning Girl, pp. 298–300
- L2 Outline Map 7: Central America and the Caribbean, p. 297 AR, GT, LPR, SN
- L2 Skills for Life, p. 292 AR, GT, LPR, SN

Western Hemisphere Teacher's Edition
- L1 For Less Proficient Readers, TE p. 457, 464
- L3 For Advanced Readers, TE p. 457
- L1 For Special Needs Students, TE p. 464

Assess and Reteach	Instructional Resources	Differentiated Instruction

Assess Progress
Evaluate student comprehension with the section assessment and section quiz.

Reteach
Assign the Reading and Vocabulary Study guide to help struggling students.

Extend
Extend the lesson by assigning an *Enrichment* activity.

All in One Latin America Teaching Resources
- L2 Section Quiz, p. 278
- L3 Enrichment, p. 291
  Rubric for Assessing a Writing Assignment, p. 303

Reading and Vocabulary Study Guide
- L1 Chapter 15, Section 1, pp. 168–170

All in One Latin America Teaching Resources
Rubric for Assessing a Bar Graph, p. 302

Latin America Transparencies
- L1 Color Transparency LA 23: Central America and the Caribbean: Political LPR, SN, ELL

Social Studies Skills Tutor CD-ROM
- L1 Comparing and Contrasting SN, LPR, ELL

Key
- L1 Basic to Average
- L2 For All Students
- L3 Average to Advanced
- LPR Less Proficient Readers
- AR Advanced Readers
- SN Special Needs Students
- GT Gifted and Talented
- ELL English Language Learners

Section 2 Haiti: A Struggle for Democracy

1.5 periods, .75 block

Social Studies Objectives
1. Find out how democracy has been threatened in Haiti.
2. Learn what life is like for the people of Haiti, both in the countryside and in the cities.

Reading/Language Arts Objective
Identify supporting details of a main idea.

Prepare to Read

Build Background Knowledge
Have students list countries where people speak French.

Set a Purpose for Reading
Have students evaluate statements on the *Reading Readiness Guide*.

Preview Key Terms
Teach the section's Key Terms.

Target Reading Skill
Introduce the section's Target Reading Skill of **identifying supporting details.**

Instructional Resources

All In One Latin America Teaching Resources
- L2 Reading Readiness Guide, p. 280
- L2 Identify Supporting Details, p. 288

Differentiated Instruction

Spanish Reading and Vocabulary Study Guide
- L2 Chapter 15, Section 2, pp. 124–125 ELL

Instruct

Democracy in Danger
Ask questions about the hardships with which Haitians have struggled.

Country Profile
Ask students to derive information from maps, charts, and graphs.

The People of Haiti
Discuss the people of Haiti.

Target Reading Skill
Review **identifying supporting details.**

Instructional Resources

All In One Latin America Teaching Resources
- L2 Outline Map 7: Central America and the Caribbean, p. 297
- L2 Guided Reading and Review, p. 281
- L2 Reading Readiness Guide, p. 280

Latin America Transparencies
- L2 Section Reading Support Transparency LA 43

Differentiated Instruction

Western Hemisphere Teacher's Edition
- L3 For Gifted and Talented, TE p. 472
- L3 For Advanced Readers, TE p. 472
- L1 For English Language Learners, TE p. 473
- L1 For Special Needs Students, TE p. 473

Student Edition on Audio CD
- L1 Chapter 15, Section 2 SN, LPR, ELL

Spanish Support
- L2 Guided Reading and Review (Spanish), p. 160 ELL

Assess and Reteach

Assess Progress
Evaluate student comprehension with the section assessment and section quiz.

Reteach
Assign the Reading and Vocabulary Study Guide to help struggling students.

Extend
Extend the lesson by assigning a *Small Group Activity*.

Instructional Resources

All In One Latin America Teaching Resources
- L2 Section Quiz, p. 282
- L3 Small Group Activity: Creating a Magazine Story, pp. 293–296

   Rubric for Assessing a Newspaper Article, p. 304

Reading and Vocabulary Study Guide
- L1 Chapter 15, Section 2, pp. 171–173

Differentiated Instruction

Spanish Support
- L2 Section Quiz (Spanish), p. 161 ELL

Key
 Basic to Average   Average to Advanced   LPR Less Proficient Readers   GT Gifted and Talented
L2 For All Students   AR Advanced Readers   ELL English Language Learners
                                                                              SN Special Needs Students

Section 3 Puerto Rico: An American Commonwealth

4 periods, 2 blocks (includes Chapter Review and Assessment)

Section Lesson Planner

Social Studies Objectives

1. Understand how the people of Puerto Rico are both American and Puerto Rican.

2. Find out what life is like on the island of Puerto Rico.

3. Learn about the three kinds of political status Puerto Ricans are considering for their future.

Reading/Language Arts Objective

Identify implied main ideas in the text.

Prepare to Read

Build Background Knowledge
Think about Latin American countries' struggle for independence.

Set a Purpose for Reading
Have students begin to fill out the *Reading Readiness Guide*.

Preview Key Terms
Teach the section's Key Terms.

Target Reading Skill
Introduce the section's Target Reading Skill of **identifying implied main ideas**.

Instructional Resources

All In One Latin America Teaching Resources

- **L2** Reading Readiness Guide, p. 284
- **L2** Identify Implied Main Ideas, p. 289

Differentiated Instruction

Spanish Reading and Vocabulary Study Guide

- **L2** Chapter 15, Section 3, pp. 126–127 ELL

Instruct

Puerto Rican and American
Compare and contrast Puerto Ricans and citizens who live in the United States.

Life on the Island
Discuss what the island of Puerto Rico is like.

Country Profile
Ask students to derive information from maps, charts, and graphs.

Seeking a New Direction
Discuss the possibility of Puerto Rico becoming part of the United States.

Target Reading Skill
Review **identifying implied main ideas**.

Instructional Resources

All In One Latin America Teaching Resources

- **L2** Guided Reading and Review, p. 285
- **L2** Reading Readiness Guide, p. 284

Latin America Transparencies

- **L2** Section Reading Support Transparency LA 44

Differentiated Instruction

Western Hemisphere Teacher's Edition

- **L3** For Advanced Readers, TE p. 478
- **L1** For English Language Learners, TE p. 478
- **L1** For Less Proficient Readers, TE p. 481
- **L3** For Gifted and Talented, TE p. 481

Reading and Vocabulary Study Guide

- **L1** Chapter 15, Section 3, pp. 174–176 LPR, SN, ELL

Spanish Support

- **L2** Guided Reading and Review (Spanish), p. 162 ELL

Assess and Reteach

Assess Progress
Evaluate student comprehension with the section assessment and section quiz.

Reteach
Assign the Reading and Vocabulary Study Guide to help struggling students.

Extend
Extend the lesson by analyzing information from a Discovery Channel World Studies video.

Instructional Resources

All In One Latin America Teaching Resources

- **L2** Section Quiz, p. 286
  Rubric for Assessing a Journal Entry, p. 305
- **L2** Vocabulary Development, p. 301
- **L2** Word Knowledge, p. 290
- **L2** Chapter Tests A and B, pp. 306–311

Reading and Vocabulary Study Guide

- **L1** Chapter 15, Section 3, pp. 174–176

Differentiated Instruction

Spanish Support

- **L2** Section Quiz (Spanish), p. 163 ELL
- **L2** Chapter Summary (Spanish), p. 164 ELL
- **L2** Vocabulary Development (Spanish), p. 165 ELL

Key

L1 Basic to Average	**L3** Average to Advanced	**LPR** Less Proficient Readers	**GT** Gifted and Talented
L2 For All Students		**AR** Advanced Readers	**ELL** English Language Learners
		SN Special Needs Students	

Reading Background

Summarizing

Showing students how to summarize can help them comprehend and recall text.

Good summarizers make notes on the text and reread as they write. Poor summarizers read the text once and begin writing. Share this information with your students, then model how to create a one-sentence summary. In this type of summary, students must organize their ideas in the briefest possible way.

Use the following steps to model how to write a one-sentence summary:

1. Read the selection aloud.

2. List four or five ideas from the selection.

3. Show how to combine these ideas into one sentence.

4. Take out any extra words to make the sentence as short as possible.

If students are new to summarizing this way, give them the following sentence frames:

Section 1: *Compare and Contrast*

Cuba's government and economy in the 1800s and in 1994 are similar in that they both _____, but in the 1800s, _____ while in 1994, _____.

Section 2: *Description*

Haiti's political situation has always been _____.

Section 3: *Problem/Solution*

Puerto Rico is_____, but_____, so_____.

Seed Discussions

Give students the opportunity to lead their own discussions about what they are reading in the chapter. Tell students that in order to lead a discussion with their classmates, they will need a strong "seed" to start with. Have the class list ideas for strong seeds, such as questions or opinions about what they have learned, or things in the chapter that surprised them.

Model a strong seed versus a weak seed. A strong seed might be an opinion, such as: "I believe Puerto Rico should become a state of the United States." A weak seed might be a restatement of fact, such as: "Puerto Ricans adopted their constitution in 1951."

Once students are comfortable with the concept of a strong seed, have each student write a seed on a sheet of paper. Then have students form small groups. In each group, students should take turns leading a discussion from the seed they have written. Divide time equally so every person gets an equal opportunity as leader.

World Studies Background

The Spanish-American War

In the late 1800s, when Cuba was fighting for independence from Spain, the American government sent the battleship *Maine* to Cuba to protect Americans living there. On February 15, 1898, the *Maine* exploded and 266 people died. Although no one knew what caused the explosion, many Americans called for the President to "Remember the *Maine!*" and go to war with Spain. The Spanish-American War ended after four months, with Spain having to give up its colonies.

The Island of Hispaniola

The nations of Haiti and the Dominican Republic have had intertwined histories. The countries began as Spanish colonies.

Later, Spain and France traded possession back and forth for years. Haiti declared its independence from France in 1804, and the Dominican Republic won its independence from Spain 40 years later.

Puerto Rico's Baseball Hero

Roberto Clemente, from Puerto Rico, was one of the first Latin American superstars in baseball. He was famous not only for baseball but also for his desire to help others. In 1972 Clemente was on his way to assist with earthquake relief efforts in Nicaragua when his plane crashed, killing everyone aboard. A sports center was built in Puerto Rico as a reminder of Clemente's contributions.

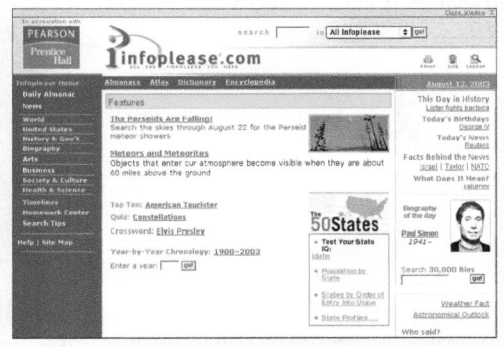

Infoplease® provides a wealth of useful information for the classroom. You can use this resource to strengthen your background on the subjects covered in this chapter. Have students visit this advertising-free site as a starting point for projects requiring research.

Use Web Code **lfd-1500** for **Infoplease**.

Chapter 15 The Caribbean

Guiding Questions

Remind students about the Guiding Questions introduced at the beginning of this section.

Section 1 relates to **Guiding Question** ❹ **What types of government have existed in Latin America?** *(After Fidel Castro took power in 1959, Cuba became a communist country.)*

Section 2 relates to **Guiding Question** ❷ **How has Latin America been shaped by its history?** *(Haiti, the only nation in the Americas formed from a successful revolt of enslaved Africans, has struggled through years of dictatorship while striving toward democracy.)*

Section 3 relates to **Guiding Question** ❸ **What factors have affected cultures in Latin America?** *(Puerto Rico's relationship with the United States as a commonwealth has resulted in a mix of cultures between the two places.)*

⊙ Target Reading Skill

In this chapter, students will learn and apply the reading skill of identifying the main idea. Use the following worksheets to help students practice this skill.

All in One Latin America Teaching Resources, *Identify Main Ideas, p. 287; Identify Supporting Details, p. 288; Identify Implied Main Ideas, p. 289*

Chapter Preview

This chapter will introduce you to 13 island nations and one commonwealth of the Caribbean.

Country Databank
The Country Databank provides data and descriptions of the commonwealth and each of the countries in the region: Antigua and Barbuda, The Bahamas, Barbados, Cuba, Dominica, Dominican Republic, Grenada, Haiti, Jamaica, Saint Kitts and Nevis, Saint Lucia, Saint Vincent and the Grenadines, and Trinidad and Tobago.

Section 1
Cuba
Clinging to Communism

Section 2
Haiti
A Struggle for Democracy

Section 3
Puerto Rico
An American Commonwealth

⊙ **Target Reading Skill**

Main Idea In this chapter you will focus on finding and remembering the main idea, or the most important point, of sections and paragraphs.

▶ Rowboats on a Curaçao beach

Bibliography

For the Teacher
Arthur, Charles. *Haiti in Focus: A Guide to the People, Politics, and Culture.* Interlink Publishing Group, 2002.

Martinez-Fernandez, Luis et al. *Encyclopedia of Cuba: People, History, Culture* (2 Volumes). Oryx Press, 2003.

Trias, Monge. *Puerto Rico: The Trials of the Oldest Colony in the World.* Yale University Press, 1999.

For the Student
L1 Banting, Erinn. *Puerto Rico: The People and Culture (Lands, Peoples, Cultures).* Crabtree Publishing, 2003.

L2 Crouch, Clifford W. *Cuba (Major World Nations).* Chelsea House Publishers, 1997.

L3 Ngcheong-Lum. *Haiti (Cultures of the World).* Benchmark Books, 1997.

Differentiated Instruction

The following Teacher Edition strategies are suitable for students of varying abilities.

Advanced Readers, pp. 457, 478
English Language Learners, pp. 473, 478
Gifted and Talented, pp. 472, 481
Less Proficient Readers, pp. 457, 464, 481
Special Needs Students, pp. 464, 473

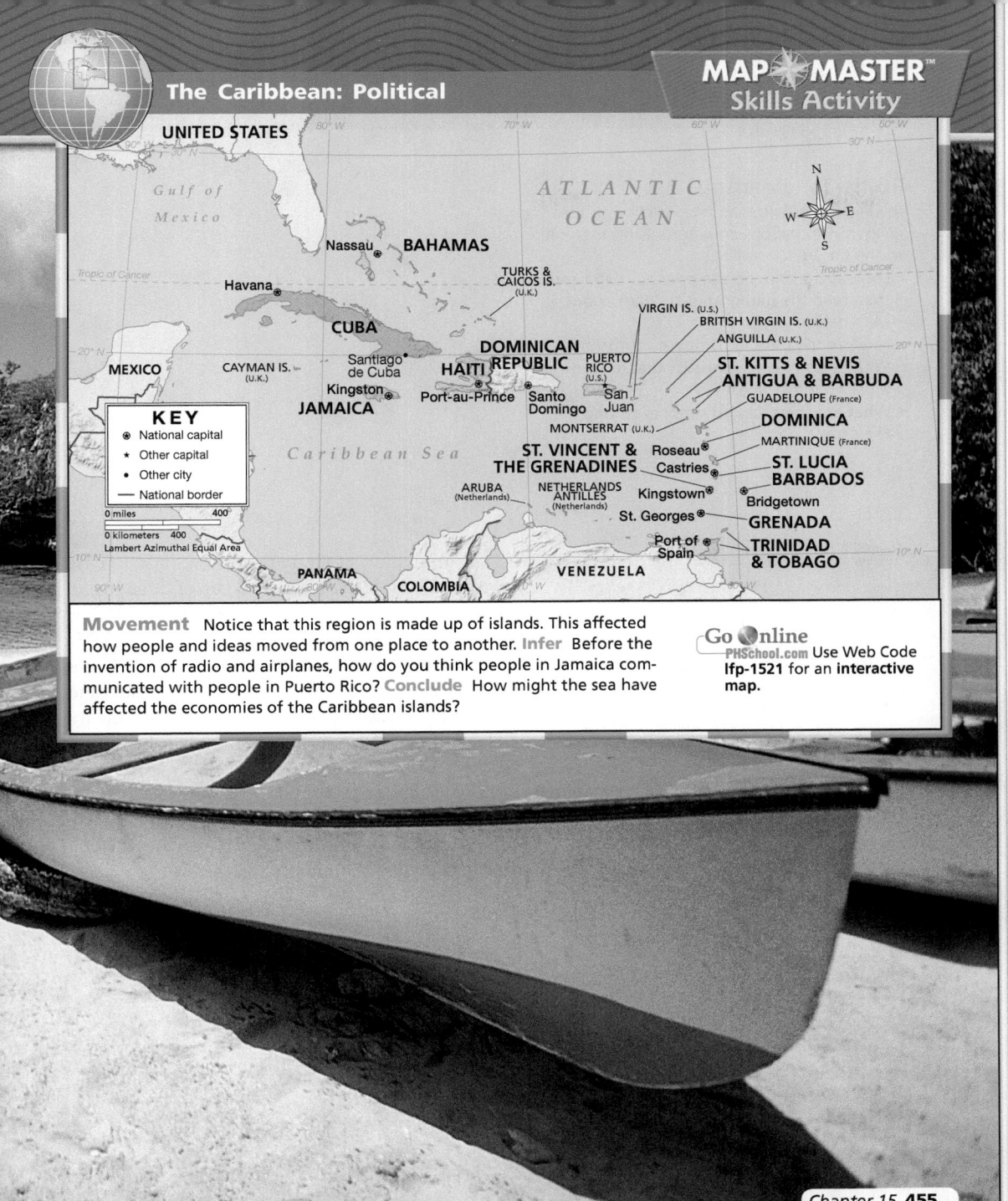

The Caribbean: Political

UNITED STATES

Gulf of Mexico

ATLANTIC OCEAN

Tropic of Cancer

Nassau • BAHAMAS

Havana •

CUBA

TURKS & CAICOS IS. (U.K.)

VIRGIN IS. (U.S.)
BRITISH VIRGIN IS. (U.K.)
ANGUILLA (U.K.)

MEXICO

CAYMAN IS. (U.K.)

Santiago de Cuba

DOMINICAN REPUBLIC

HAITI

PUERTO RICO (U.S.)

San Juan

ST. KITTS & NEVIS
ANTIGUA & BARBUDA

Kingston •

Port-au-Prince

Santo Domingo

GUADELOUPE (France)

JAMAICA

MONTSERRAT (U.K.)

DOMINICA

MARTINIQUE (France)

Caribbean Sea

ST. VINCENT & THE GRENADINES

Roseau
Castries

ST. LUCIA
BARBADOS

KEY
⊛ National capital
★ Other capital
• Other city
— National border

0 miles 400
0 kilometers 400
Lambert Azimuthal Equal Area

ARUBA (Netherlands)

NETHERLANDS ANTILLES (Netherlands)

Kingstown ⊛

St. Georges ⊛

Bridgetown

GRENADA

PANAMA

COLOMBIA

VENEZUELA

Port of Spain

TRINIDAD & TOBAGO

Movement Notice that this region is made up of islands. This affected how people and ideas moved from one place to another. **Infer** Before the invention of radio and airplanes, how do you think people in Jamaica communicated with people in Puerto Rico? **Conclude** How might the sea have affected the economies of the Caribbean islands?

Go Online PHSchool.com Use Web Code **lfp-1521** for an **interactive map.**

■ Point out the map of the Caribbean on page 455. Tell students that the words in capital letters show the names of the countries, while the words with upper and lower case letters identify cities in the countries, mostly the capitals. Show students how the leaders, or lines, connect a label with a place on the map. Point out that when a country's name appears in parentheses, it means that it has a connection to the place under whose name it appears. Ask students to find examples of places on the map with connections to other countries.

Go Online PHSchool.com Students may practice their map skills using the interactive online version of this map.

Using the Visual   L2

Reach Into Your Background Draw students' attention to the caption accompanying the picture on pages 454–455.

Have students share details about the scene. What might the weather in this region be like? How might the boats be used? Have students provide examples of ways that location and climate can affect a nation's economy.

Answers

MAP MASTER Skills Activity **Infer** in person or by mail
Conclude People of the Caribbean islands may have traded products found in the sea, such as fish.

Chapter Resources

Teaching Resources
L2 Vocabulary Development, p. 301
L2 Skills for Life, p. 292
L2 Chapter Tests A and B, pp. 306–311

Spanish Support
L2 Spanish Chapter Summary, p. 164
L2 Spanish Vocabulary Development, p. 165

Media and Technology
L2 Student Edition on Audio CD
L2 Guided Reading Audiotapes, English and Spanish
L2 Social Studies Skills Tutor CD-ROM
ExamView Test Bank CD-ROM

PRENTICE HALL
Presentation **EXPRESS**™
Teach · Connect · Inspire

Teach this chapter's content using the PresentationExpress™ CD-ROM including:
■ slide shows
■ transparencies
■ interactive maps and media
■ *ExamView*® QuickTake Presenter

Objectives

- Learn about the nations of the Caribbean.
- Analyze data to compare Caribbean countries.
- Identify characteristics that countries share.
- Discover key differences among countries.

Prepare to Read

Build Background Knowledge L2

Tell students that in this section they will be learning about the countries that make up the Caribbean region of Latin America. Show the World Studies video. Ask students to note three to five facts about the Caribbean countries as they watch. Have students engage in a Give One, Get One activity (TE, p. T37) to share the facts they noted.

 The Caribbean: Dynamic Lands and Cultures, **World Studies Video Program**

Guide for Reading

This section provides an introduction to the 13 countries and one commonwealth that make up the Caribbean region.

- Look at the map on the previous page and then read the paragraphs to learn about each nation.
- Analyze the data to compare countries.
- What are the characteristics that most of these countries share?
- What are some key differences among the countries?

Antigua and Barbuda

Capital	Saint John's
Land Area	171 sq mi; 442 sq km
Population	67,448
Ethnic Group(s)	black, white, Southwest Asian
Religion(s)	Protestant, Roman Catholic, traditional beliefs
Government	constitutional monarchy
Currency	East Caribbean dollar
Leading Exports	petroleum products, manufactured goods, machinery and transport equipment, food and live animals
Language(s)	English (official), English Creole

The tiny nation of Antigua and Barbuda (an TIG wuh and bahr BOO dah) is made up of three islands located in the eastern Caribbean Sea. Christopher Columbus landed on the main island, Antigua, in 1493. English settlers began arriving there in the 1630s. They raised tobacco and then sugar cane. Enslaved Africans were imported to work on the plantations. However, slavery was abolished in the British colony in 1834. In 1981, Antigua joined with neighboring Barbuda and with Redonda, a nearby uninhabited island, to become an independent nation. Today, tourism is the nation's main source of income.

English Harbor, Antigua

The Bahamas

Capital	Nassau
Land Area	3,888 sq mi; 10,070 sq km
Population	308,529
Ethnic Group(s)	black, white, Asian, Hispanic
Religion(s)	Anglican, Baptist, Roman Catholic, Methodist, Church of God
Government	constitutional parliamentary democracy
Currency	Bahamian dollar
Leading Exports	fish and crawfish, rum, salt, chemicals, fruits and vegetables
Language(s)	English (official), English Creole, French Creole

More than 700 islands make up the nation called The Bahamas (buh HAH muz), but fewer than 30 of them are inhabited. The island chain stretches southward off the east coast of Florida to within 50 miles (80.5 kilometers) of Cuba. It is thought that Christopher Columbus first landed in the Americas on the Bahamian island of San Salvador. The Bahamas are generally flat, with a mild climate and beautiful beaches, so it is not surprising that tourism is a major industry. Banking has also become important. Once a British colony, The Bahamas now has a government based on the British parliamentary model.

Barbados

Capital	Bridgetown
Land Area	166 sq mi; 431 sq km
Population	276,607
Ethnic Group(s)	black, white, mixed white and black
Religion(s)	Protestant, Roman Catholic
Government	parliamentary democracy
Currency	Barbados dollar
Leading Exports	sugar and molasses, rum, other foods and beverages, chemicals, electrical components, clothing
Language(s)	English (official), Bajan

Barbados (bahr BAY dohs) is a triangular-shaped island in the eastern Caribbean Sea. It was settled by the British in the 1600s and gained its independence in 1966. Today, both the culture and the government of Barbados reflect its British colonial heritage. In the past, much of Barbados was used for sugar plantations. Today, the government promotes smaller farms that grow food for the local population. The government spends approximately 20 percent of its budget on education, and 98 percent of the people can read and write.

Cuba

Capital	Havana
Land Area	42,803 sq mi; 110,860 sq km
Population	11.2 million
Ethnic Group(s)	mixed white and black, white, black, East Asian
Religion(s)	Roman Catholic, Protestant
Government	communist state
Currency	Cuban peso
Leading Exports	sugar, nickel, tobacco, fish, medical products, citrus, coffee
Language(s)	Spanish

Cuba (KYOO buh) is the largest country in the Caribbean region. Its main island lies south of Florida in the Caribbean Sea near the Gulf of Mexico. The island has many beaches, bays, and harbors. In 1903, the United States leased Guantánamo Bay from Cuba for use as a naval base, and it is still under American control today. The rest of the island is a communist state headed by Fidel Castro, who has governed Cuba since the revolution of 1959. Cuban culture reflects its Spanish colonial past and African influences.

Chapter 15 **457**

Instruct

Introducing the Caribbean L2

Guided Instruction

- Read each country paragraph as a class using the Choral Reading technique (TE, p. T34). Then direct students to study each data table.

- Discuss the size of these countries. **Which country is the largest in land area?** *(Cuba)* **How do you think this has affected this country's population?** *(Cuba is the largest country in land area and population; more land means that more people can live there and use the land for its resources.)*

- Ask **What religions do almost all the countries share?** *(Roman Catholic and some form of Protestant)* **In what country would you find Hindus and Muslims?** *(Trinidad and Tobago)*

- Ask **In which countries is English not an official language?** *(Cuba, Dominican Republic, Haiti)* **What do you think is the reason for this?** *(The majority of the other countries in the Caribbean have British or American influence, whereas these countries have a strong Spanish or French influence.)*

Differentiated Instruction

For Advanced Readers L3
Have students read the Primary Source and Literature Reading, *Morning Girl*, to experience the arrival of the Europeans from the perspective of a young Bahamian girl. Then have students answer the questions provided.

All in One Latin America Teaching Resources, *Morning Girl*, pp. 298–300

For Less Proficient Readers L1
To help students access and compare the data, have them create a set of charts using different categories in the Databank such as religions, leading exports, official languages, population and land area. Students can complete the charts in small groups.

- Ask students to identify the different types of governments of the Caribbean nations. **Which country is a commonwealth?** *(Puerto Rico)* **Which country has a communist government?** *(Cuba)* **Which countries have governments that are constitutional monarchies?** *(Antigua and Barbuda, Grenada, Saint Kitts and Nevis)* **What form of government do most of the other countries have?** *(some type of democracy)*

- Ask **What language do Dominica and the Dominican Republic share?** *(French Creole)*

- Ask **Why is Grenada sometimes called the Isle of Spice?** *(It produces nutmeg, cinnamon, cloves, ginger, and vanilla.)*

COUNTRY DATABANK

Introducing The Caribbean

Dominica

Capital	Roseau
Land Area	291 sq mi; 754 sq km
Population	73,000
Ethnic Group(s)	black, mixed white and black, white, Southwest Asian, Carib
Religion(s)	Roman Catholic, Protestant
Government	parliamentary democracy
Currency	East Caribbean dollar
Leading Exports	bananas, soap, bay oil, vegetables, grapefruit, oranges
Language(s)	English (official), French Creole

Dominica (dahm uh NEE kuh) lies between Guadeloupe and Martinique in the Caribbean Sea. The island was formed by volcanic activity. Hot springs, such as those that feed Boiling Lake, are still active. In spite of its rich soil and pleasant climate, Dominica is very poor. Hurricanes often destroy crops. Tourism is hampered by poor transportation and lack of hotels. Dominica is one of the few Caribbean islands on which Carib Indians still live and continue to practice the cultural traditions of their ancestors.

Dominican Republic

Capital	Santo Domingo
Land Area	18,679 sq mi; 48,380 sq km
Population	8.7 million
Ethnic Group(s)	mixed white and black, white, black
Religion(s)	Roman Catholic
Government	representative democracy
Currency	Dominican Republic peso
Leading Exports	ferronickel, sugar, gold, silver, coffee, cocoa, tobacco, meats, consumer goods
Language(s)	Spanish (official), French Creole

The Dominican Republic (doh MIN ih kun rih PUB lik) occupies the eastern two thirds of Hispaniola. The island was first colonized by Spain. In 1697, France acquired the western third of Hispaniola. That part of the island became the independent country of Haiti in 1804. The remaining portion—which later became the Dominican Republic—was controlled by France, Spain, and Haiti at various times. It also suffered many revolutions and dictatorships. Today, its government is stable. Agriculture and tourism are important to the economy of the Dominican Republic.

Grenada

Capital	Saint George's
Land Area	133 sq mi; 344 sq km
Population	89,211
Ethnic Group(s)	black, mixed white and black, white, South Asian, Carib
Religion(s)	Roman Catholic, Protestant
Government	constitutional monarchy
Currency	East Caribbean dollar
Leading Exports	bananas, cocoa, nutmeg, fruits and vegetables, clothing, mace
Language(s)	English (official), English Creole

Nutmeg, Grenada

Grenada (gruh NAY duh) is an oval-shaped island in the eastern Caribbean Sea. It has forested mountains as well as highlands with many rivers and streams. Bays, natural harbors, and beaches dot the southern coast. Grenada is sometimes called the Isle of Spice because of its production of nutmeg, cinnamon, cloves, ginger, and vanilla. Agricultural exports and tourism support the economy. Once governed by France and later by Great Britain, Grenada is now an independent nation.

Background: Links Across Place

Reggae This popular music dates to the 1960s when it developed among poor Jamaicans in Kingston, the country's capital. Its roots include ska, a Jamaican and British dance-hall music, traditional Jamaican and African folk music, and American soul music. Reggae features strong accents off the beat and instrumentation including electric guitars, organ, piano, and drums. The words to many reggae songs reflect Rastafarian beliefs. The singer Bob Marley and his group, the Wailers, helped to spread reggae, and it gained international popularity.

Haiti

Capital	Port-au-Prince
Land Area	10,641 sq mi; 27,560 sq km
Population	7.1 million
Ethnic Group(s)	black, mixed white and black, white
Religion(s)	Roman Catholic, Protestant, traditional beliefs
Government	elected government
Currency	gourde
Leading Exports	manufactured goods, coffee, oils, cocoa
Language(s)	French (official), French Creole (official)

Occupying the western third of the island of Hispaniola, Haiti (HAY tee) was once heavily forested. Today, there are few woodlands left, and much of the land is no longer able to support farming due to soil erosion. Even so, most of Haiti's people are farmers, although they have little modern machinery or fertilizers. Haiti is one of the most densely populated nations in the world and the poorest in the Western Hemisphere. Numerous revolutions and dictatorships have plagued Haiti since its hopeful beginning as the first independent nation in Latin America.

Jamaica

Capital	Kingston
Land Area	4,182 sq mi; 10,831 sq km
Population	2.7 million
Ethnic Group(s)	black, mixed white and black, South Asian, white, East Asian
Religion(s)	Protestant, Roman Catholic, traditional beliefs
Government	constitutional parliamentary democracy
Currency	Jamaican dollar
Leading Exports	alumina, bauxite, sugar, bananas, rum
Language(s)	English (official), English Creole

Jamaica (juh MAY kuh) is a mountainous island located 90 miles (145 kilometers) south of Cuba in the Caribbean Sea. Tourism is vital to the economy of this beautiful island. Most of the population lives on the coastal plains, and more than half of Jamaicans live in cities. The island was first colonized by the Spanish and then by the British. Enslaved Africans were brought to Jamaica to work on the sugar and coffee plantations. Today, Jamaica's population is diverse, including Asian and Arab immigrants as well as people of European and African descent.

Puerto Rico

Capital	San Juan
Land Area	3,459 sq mi; 8,959 sq km
Population	4.0 million
Ethnic Group(s)	white, black, indigenous Indian, Asian, mixed white and black
Religion(s)	Roman Catholic, Protestant
Government	commonwealth
Currency	U.S. dollar
Leading Exports	pharmaceuticals, electronics, apparel, canned tuna, beverage concentrates, medical equipment
Language(s)	Spanish and English (official)

The self-governing commonwealth of Puerto Rico (PWEHR tuh REE koh) lies approximately 50 miles (80 kilometers) east of the Dominican Republic in the Caribbean Sea. The northern shore of the main island faces the Atlantic Ocean. Several smaller islands are also part of the commonwealth. The island's economy originally depended on sugar. In the mid-1900s, however, industry and trade became more important. Today, Puerto Rico has a more diverse economy than any of the other Caribbean islands.

Guided Instruction (continued)

- Ask **What are some characteristics of the population of Haiti?** *(They are black, mixed white and black, and white; belong to Roman Catholic or Protestant religions or practice traditional beliefs. Most are farmers.)*
- Ask students **How does the size and make-up of the population of Haiti compare with those of Puerto Rico?** *(Sample answer: Puerto Rico's population is slightly less than half the size of Haiti's, but it has more ethnic groups.)*

Independent Practice

- Provide students with *Outline Map 7: Central America and the Caribbean.*

  All in One **Latin America Teaching Resources,** *Outline Map 7: Central America and the Caribbean,* p. 297

- Have students put the capital of each country on the map. Students can refer to the map on page 455.
- Next, have students choose one of the following types of data—religion, government, or language(s)—to show on their maps. Remind them to make a map key with colors or symbols that match the information on their maps.

Monitor Progress

As students work, circulate to make sure they are converting the data to use on their maps in an appropriate way.

Assess and Reteach

Introducing **The Caribbean**

St. Kitts and Nevis

Capital	Basseterre
Land Area	101 sq mi; 261 sq km
Population	38,736
Ethnic Group(s)	black, white, Southwest Asian
Religion(s)	Roman Catholic, Protestant
Government	constitutional monarchy
Currency	East Caribbean dollar
Leading Exports	machinery, food, electronics, beverages, tobacco
Language(s)	English (official), English Creole

Two small islands located in the eastern Caribbean Sea make up the Federation of St. Kitts and Nevis (saynt kits and NEE vis). They gained their independence from Great Britain in 1983, and are now part of the British Commonwealth. The islands are of volcanic origin, and a dormant volcano is the highest point on St. Kitts. The beaches of that island have black, volcanic sands. Nevis is known for its hot and cold springs, and is surrounded by coral reefs. St. Kitts and Nevis have become popular tourist destinations.

St. Lucia

Capital	Castries
Land Area	234 sq mi; 606 sq km
Population	160,145
Ethnic Group(s)	black, mixed white and black, South Asian, white
Religion(s)	Roman Catholic, Protestant
Government	parliamentary democracy
Currency	East Caribbean dollar
Leading Exports	bananas, clothing, cocoa, vegetables, fruits, coconut oil
Language(s)	English (official), French Creole

The island nation of St. Lucia (saynt LOO shuh) is located in the eastern Caribbean Sea. Its geography is marked by wooded mountains and fertile valleys as well as by two huge pyramids of rock, called the Twin Pitons, which rise more than 2,400 feet (731.5 kilometers) from the sea. In the crater of a dormant volcano are boiling sulphur springs, which attract many tourists. St. Lucia's rain forests are also a major tourist attraction. Sugar cane was the most important crop on the island until 1964, when most of the land was converted to raising bananas.

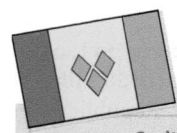

St. Vincent and the Grenadines

Capital	Kingstown
Land Area	150 sq mi; 389 sq km
Population	116,394
Ethnic Group(s)	black, mixed white and black, South Asian, Carib
Religion(s)	Protestant, Roman Catholic, Hindu
Government	parliamentary democracy
Currency	East Caribbean dollar
Leading Exports	bananas, eddoes and dasheen, arrowroot starch, tennis racquets
Language(s)	English (official), English Creole

The nation of St. Vincent and the Grenadines (saynt VIN sunt and thuh GREN uh deenz) is made up of the island of St. Vincent and a string of islands called the Grenadines. They are located in the eastern Caribbean Sea, between St. Lucia and Grenada. St. Vincent has forested volcanic mountains. Its tallest volcano, Soufrière, last erupted in 1979, causing extensive damage. However, the volcanic ash has also made the soil fertile. The Grenadines are made up of coral reefs and have fine beaches. Therefore, it is not surprising that agriculture and tourism play important roles in the nation's economy.

460 Latin America

Trinidad and Tobago

Capital	Port-of-Spain
Land Area	1,980 sq mi; 5,128 sq km
Population	1.2 million
Ethnic Group(s)	black, South Asian, mixed white and black, white, East Asian
Religion(s)	Roman Catholic, Hindu, Muslim, Protestant
Government	parliamentary democracy
Currency	Trinidad and Tobago dollar
Leading Exports	petroleum and petroleum products, chemicals, steel products, fertilizer, sugar, cocoa, coffee, citrus, flowers
Language(s)	English (official), English Creole, Hindi, French, Spanish

SOURCES: DK World Desk Reference Online; *CIA World Factbook*, 2002; *World Almanac*, 2003

Green honeycreeper, Trinidad and Tobago

Trinidad and Tobago (TRIN ih dad and toh BAY goh) are located close to the South American coast, northeast of Venezuela. Trinidad, the larger island, has mountains with spectacular waterfalls as well as swampy areas. Tobago is surrounded by coral reefs. The reefs have rich marine life, and are popular tourist attractions. The bird sanctuary at Caroni Swamp also attracts tourists. Trinidad has a very diverse population, with Spanish, French, African, English, East Indian, and Chinese influences, and many languages are spoken there. Trinidad is known for its calypso and steel-drum music.

Assessment

Comprehension and Critical Thinking

1. Compare and Contrast Compare the physical size and population of Cuba to those of the Dominican Republic.

2. Draw Conclusions What are the characteristics that most Caribbean countries share?

3. Compare and Contrast What are some key differences among the countries?

4. Categorize Which countries rely on agricultural products as their major exports? Which rely on other products?

5. Infer How has geography influenced the economies of the Caribbean countries?

6. Make a Bar Graph Use your answer to Question 1 to make a bar graph. What does the graph reveal about the population densities of Cuba and the Dominican Republic?

Keeping Current

Access the **DK World Desk Reference Online** at **PHSchool.com** for up-to-date information about all the countries in this chapter.

Web Code: **lfe-1510**

Answers

Assessment

1. Cuba has more than twice the land area of the Dominican Republic and has almost three million more people.

2. They are islands; they are small in land size, have fine beaches and tourist appeal; most have a democratic government, English as an official language, and Roman Catholicism and Protestantism as main religions.

3. Possible answers: Some countries are made up of more than one island, while others consist of only one island; their people speak different languages such as English, French, and Spanish; they use different forms of money such as the East Caribbean dollar, the Bahamian dollar, or the Dominican Republic peso; they have different forms of government such as constitutional monarchies, a communist state, and a representative democracy.

4. Answers will vary because most countries have a combination of agricultural and other products for export. Mostly agricultural: Dominica, Grenada, St. Lucia, Saint Vincent and the Grenadines; Mostly other products: Antigua and Barbuda, Bahamas, Barbados, Cuba, Dominican Republic, Haiti, Jamaica, Puerto Rico, Saint Kitts and Nevis, Trinidad and Tobago.

5. Many rely on tourism because of their climate, beaches, and beautiful waters. The climate is also an asset for growing crops.

6. Students should conclude that the Dominican Republic is more densely populated because it is a much smaller country in terms of land. Use *Rubric for Assessing a Bar Graph* to evaluate students' work.

All in One **Latin America Teaching Resources,** *Rubric for Assessing a Bar Graph*, p. 302

Section 1
Step-by-Step Instruction

Objectives

Social Studies

1. Find out how Cuba's history led to thousands of Cubans leaving their homeland.
2. Discover how Cuban exiles feel about their lives in the United States and about their homeland.
3. Learn what changes have recently come to Cuba.

Reading/Language Arts

Identify main ideas in a section or paragraph.

Prepare to Read

Build Background Knowledge L2

In this section, students will learn about the political and economic history of Cuba. Ask students to preview the headings and visuals in the section with this question in mind: **How has the government in Cuba affected the lives of the Cuban people?** Provide a few simple examples to get students started. Have students engage in a Think-Pair-Share activity (TE, p. T36) to share their answers.

Set a Purpose for Reading L2

- Preview the Objectives.
- Form students into pairs or groups of four. Distribute the *Reading Readiness Guide*. Ask students to fill in the first two columns of the chart. Use the Numbered Heads participation structure (TE, p. T36) to call on students to share one piece of information they already know and one piece of information they want to know.

All in One Latin America Teaching Resources, *Reading Readiness Guide,* p. 276

Vocabulary Builder
Preview Key Terms L2

Pronounce each Key Term, then ask students to say the word with you. Provide a simple explanation, such as, "Someone who is illiterate cannot read a newspaper or a book."

Section 1
Cuba
Clinging to Communism

Prepare to Read

Objectives
In this section you will
1. Find out how Cuba's history led to thousands of Cubans leaving their homeland.
2. Discover how Cuban exiles feel about their lives in the United States and about their homeland.
3. Learn about recent changes in Cuba.

Taking Notes
As you read this section, look for details about life in communist Cuba. Copy the web diagram below, and record your findings in it.

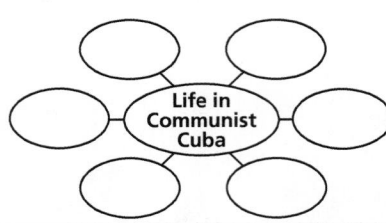

Target Reading Skill

Identify Main Ideas It is impossible to remember every detail that you read. Good readers identify the main idea in every section or paragraph. The main idea is the most important point—the one that includes all the other points. For example, the first sentence under the red heading Cuban Exiles, on page 465, states the main idea of that portion of text.

Key Terms
- **Fidel Castro** (fih DEL KAS troh) *n.* the leader of Cuba's government
- **communism** (KAHM yoo niz um) *n.* an economic system in which the government owns all large businesses and most of the country's land
- **illiterate** (ih LIT ur ut) *adj.* unable to read and write
- **ally** (AL eye) *n.* a country joined to another country for a special purpose
- **exile** (EK syl) *n.* a person who leaves his or her homeland for another country, often for political reasons

Cubans in a makeshift raft set out for the United States.

In the summer of 1994, more than 20,000 Cubans took to the sea. They sailed on anything that would float—rubber tires, old boats, and homemade rafts. One hope kept them going. It was the thought of making it to the United States. They wanted desperately to live in the United States as immigrants.

These Cubans left their homeland for two main reasons. One reason was Cuba's struggling economy. People often did not have enough to eat. Clothing, medicine, and other basic necessities were also hard to get. A desire for freedom was even more important to many Cubans. Cuba's leader, **Fidel Castro** (fih DEL KAS troh), was a dictator. He did not allow Cubans to speak out against government policies they disagreed with.

Political and economic changes in Cuba caused many of its citizens to leave their country. How and why did these changes occur? How has Cuba changed since then?

462 Latin America

Target Reading Skill L2

Identifying Main Ideas Draw attention to the Target Reading Skill. Remind students that the main idea is the most important point in a section or paragraph. The other information in the section or paragraph tells more about the main idea.

Model identifying the main idea using the first paragraph on page 464. The main idea is the first sentence: "At the same time, Castro's government brought some improvements to Cuba." (The rest of the paragraph gives two examples of these improvements—improved literacy and access to health care.)

Give students *Identify Main Ideas.* Have them complete the activity in their groups.

All in One Latin America Teaching Resources, *Identify Main Ideas,* p. 287

Cuba's History

Cuba's government and economy had once been very different than they were in 1994. Although it is a small country, Cuba has many advantages. It has fertile farmland. It is located at the entrance to the Gulf of Mexico, and has excellent harbors. The map titled The Caribbean: Political, at the beginning of this chapter, shows why Cuba's location makes it a good place for trade with the United States and other parts of the Caribbean.

Cuban Independence When the United States won the Spanish-American War in 1898, Cuba gained its independence from Spain. In the years that followed, Cuba became the richest country in the Caribbean. Sugar planters made money selling to people in the United States. Hotels were built, and tourists came to Cuba to enjoy its beautiful beaches and wonderful climate. Many Cubans became businesspeople, teachers, doctors, and lawyers.

Not all Cubans shared in the country's wealth, however. Most farm and factory workers earned low wages. Cuba also had many harsh leaders who ruled as dictators. In the 1950s, Fulgencio Batista (fool HEN see oh bah TEE stah) ruled Cuba. Rebel groups began forming. They wanted to remove the corrupt Batista regime and change the country.

Communism in Cuba A young lawyer named Fidel Castro led one of these small rebel groups. After two attempts to overthrow the government, he was finally successful in 1959.

Fidel Castro still holds power in Cuba today. Castro's government is communist. Under **communism,** the government owns all large businesses and most of the country's land. After Castro took power, the Cuban government nationalized, or took over, private businesses and land. Further, Castro said that newspapers and books could print only information supporting his government. Anyone who disagreed with government policy was put in jail. Huge numbers of Cubans fled the island. Many settled in Miami, Florida, in a neighborhood that came to be called Little Havana, named after the capital of Cuba.

An Important Vote
Fulgencio Batista, "strong man" of Cuba, casts his vote in the 1940 presidential election. **Infer** *Why do you think dictators hold "elections"?*

Vocabulary Builder

Use the information below to teach students this section's high-use words.

High-Use Word	Definition and Sample Sentence
dictator, p. 462	*n.* a ruler with complete power The **dictator** would not allow any kind of music to be played in his country.
corrupt, p. 463	*adj.* dishonest, crooked We do not do business with them because they seem **corrupt**.
missile, p. 464	*n.* a weapon that shoots into the air The **missile** soared overhead as it flew to reach its target.
collapse, p. 467	*n.* breakdown The **collapse** of the bridge occurred when the support columns crumbled.

Cuba's History   L2

Guided Instruction

- **Vocabulary Builder** Clarify the high-use words **dictator**, **corrupt**, and **missile** before reading.

- Read Cuba's History, using Partner Paragraph Shrinking (TE, p. T34).

- Discuss the changes that Fidel Castro's government brought to Cuba. *(Many Cubans fled the country. Castro's government took over the land and businesses of people, suppressed information that didn't support the government, and jailed those who opposed it. The government also improved literacy and provided health care.)*

- Ask students: **Why do you think Castro has been able to stay in power for so long?** *(Possible answer: Castro has a tight hold on Cuba. The government owns most of the businesses. Castro was backed by the Soviet Union with money and supplies for a long time.)*

Independent Practice

Have students create the Taking Notes graphic organizer on a blank piece of paper. Then have them begin to fill in the circles on the web with information about life in communist Cuba.

Monitor Progress

As students fill in the graphic organizer, circulate and make sure individuals are choosing relevant details. Provide assistance as needed.

Answers

Infer Possible answer: Dictators may hold elections to give the impression that the government is democratic.

Target Reading Skill

Identify Main Ideas As a follow-up, ask students to answer the Target Reading Skill question in the Student Edition. *(The United States viewed communist Cuba as a threat to American interests in the region.)*

Cuban Exiles

Guided Instruction

- Read the stories in Cuban Exiles with students. Then ask students to read Links Across the World.
- Ask students to name some successes and difficulties faced by Cuban exiles in the United States. *(Successes—Many have become successful in business in Florida, serve as elected officials, and influence government policy. Difficulties—At times, exiles have been unable to communicate with their families in Cuba; some have disturbing memories of their former lives and trips to the United States.)*

Independent Practice

Have students continue to fill in their graphic organizers.

Monitor Progress

Circulate to make sure students are filling in their graphic organizers correctly. Provide assistance as needed.

The Cold War Heats Up
The photograph above shows Fidel Castro (left) and Nikita Khrushchev (right), the Soviet premier. At the right, an American patrol plane flies over a Soviet freighter during the Cuban Missile Crisis. **Infer** *What kind of relationship did Cuba and the Soviet Union have in the 1960s?*

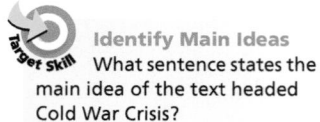 **Identify Main Ideas**
What sentence states the main idea of the text headed Cold War Crisis?

At the same time, Castro's government brought some improvements to Cuba. In the 1960s and 1970s, many Cubans were **illiterate**, or unable to read and write. Castro sent teachers into the countryside, and literacy improved dramatically. Today, about 97 percent of Cubans can read and write. The government also provides basic health care for all.

As a communist country, Cuba became an ally of the Soviet Union. An **ally** is a country joined with another country for a special purpose. The Soviet Union was the most powerful communist nation in the world. It wanted to spread communism worldwide. The Soviets sent money and supplies to Cuba. Relations between Cuba and the United States grew worse when the United States openly welcomed the people who fled from Cuba.

Cold War Crisis The United States viewed communist Cuba as a threat to American interests in the region. This was a period of tension between the United States and the Soviet Union and their allies. It was called the Cold War as the conflict did not involve "hot," or military, action. It lasted from 1945 to 1991.

In the 1960s, the Soviets began sending military support to Cuba. Then, in 1962, photographs taken by American aircraft revealed the construction of Soviet atomic-missile sites in Cuba. Those missiles, if fired, would be able to reach the United States.

U.S. President John F. Kennedy demanded the missiles be removed, and sent the American navy to prevent Soviet ships from going to Cuba. He said that an attack from Cuba would be viewed as an attack by the Soviet Union. After a week of tension called the Cuban Missile Crisis, Soviet Premier Nikita Khrushchev agreed to remove the missiles if the United States promised not to invade Cuba. A "hot" war was prevented, but the Cold War continued.

✓ **Reading Check** **What was the Cuban Missile Crisis?**

464 Latin America

Answers

Infer Possible answer: Cuba and the Soviet Union were allies against the United States.

✓ **Reading Check** It was a situation created when the United States learned that the Soviet Union had sent atomic missiles to Cuba, a country within striking distance of the United States. The United States called out its navy to prevent Soviet ships from going to Cuba, and after a week of tension the Soviet Union agreed to remove the missiles if the United States would promise not to invade Cuba.

Differentiated Instruction

For Less Proficient Readers

Students who are less proficient readers may have trouble absorbing the information in this section. Have students work in pairs to create an outline of the material. They should use the headings in the section as a framework.

For Special Needs Students

Partner students with more able students. Have students write on a sheet of paper the three headings of Cuba's History. As each pair reads this section, have them determine the main idea of the text related to the heading. Then have students write a sentence on their sheet of paper stating the main idea for each.

Cuban Exiles

Cubans have been leaving their country ever since Castro took power. They have become exiles. An **exile** is a person who leaves his or her homeland for another country, usually for political reasons. A large number of Cuban exiles have come to the United States to live.

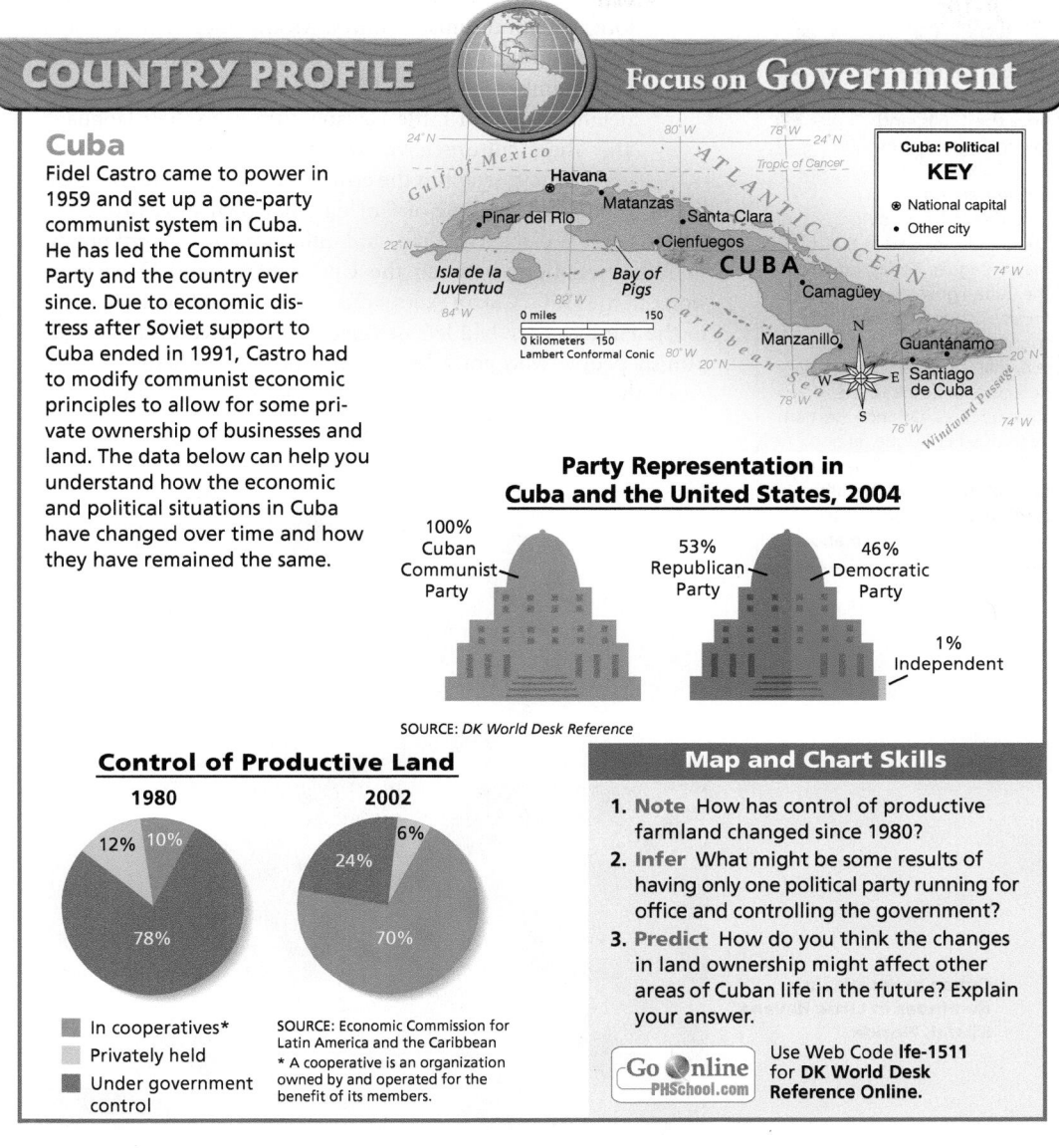

COUNTRY PROFILE
Focus on Government

Cuba

Fidel Castro came to power in 1959 and set up a one-party communist system in Cuba. He has led the Communist Party and the country ever since. Due to economic distress after Soviet support to Cuba ended in 1991, Castro had to modify communist economic principles to allow for some private ownership of businesses and land. The data below can help you understand how the economic and political situations in Cuba have changed over time and how they have remained the same.

Cuba: Political
KEY
⊛ National capital
• Other city

Party Representation in Cuba and the United States, 2004

100% Cuban Communist Party

53% Republican Party
46% Democratic Party
1% Independent

SOURCE: *DK World Desk Reference*

Control of Productive Land

1980
12%
10%
78%

2002
6%
24%
70%

■ In cooperatives*
■ Privately held
■ Under government control

SOURCE: Economic Commission for Latin America and the Caribbean
* A cooperative is an organization owned by and operated for the benefit of its members.

Map and Chart Skills

1. **Note** How has control of productive farmland changed since 1980?
2. **Infer** What might be some results of having only one political party running for office and controlling the government?
3. **Predict** How do you think the changes in land ownership might affect other areas of Cuban life in the future? Explain your answer.

Go Online PHSchool.com Use Web Code **lfe-1511** for **DK World Desk Reference Online.**

COUNTRY PROFILE
Focus on Government

Guided Instruction   L2

Ask students to study the text and visuals in the Country Profile on this page. As a class, answer the Map and Chart Skills questions. Allow students to discuss their responses with a partner before sharing.

Independent Practice

Ask students to represent on a circle graph the number of people in 2003's National Assembly of the People's Power who belonged to the Cuban Communist Party. (*It would show one circle with no sections to represent 100 percent.*)

Answers

Map and Chart Skills

1. Less is under government control and more is in cooperatives or is privately held.
2. There would be little opposition to government policies in a one-party system.
3. As people gain more control in one area, they might want it in others.

Go Online PHSchool.com Students can find more information about this topic on the DK World Desk Reference Online.

Skills Mini Lesson

Decision Making   L2

1. Point out to students that they often make decisions. First, they identify the problem. Then they think of possible options. Next they evaluate each option. Finally, they choose an option.
2. Have students practice the skill by reading the Links Across the World feature on page 466. Tell them to identify the problem facing some Cuban baseball players. (*Should they defect to the U.S.?*) Ask students to list options and note the pros and cons for each.
3. Have students apply the skill by deciding what they would do if they were a Cuban baseball player.

Changes Come to Cuba

L2

Guided Instruction

- **Vocabulary Builder** Clarify the high-use word **collapse** before reading.

- Ask students to read about and describe the changes in Cuba beginning in the 1990s. Allow students to share answers with a partner before responding. (*Private ownership of some businesses has been allowed; tourism has been encouraged; the United States has loosened travel restrictions; American businesspeople and farmers hope to trade in Cuba; the Cuban economy is improving and there is more interest in trade.*)

Independent Practice

Have students complete the graphic organizer.

Monitor Progress

- Show *Section Reading Support Transparency 5.1* and ask students to check their graphic organizers individually. Go over key concepts and clarify key vocabulary as needed. Provide assistance as needed.

  📖 **Latin America Transparencies,** *Section Reading Support Transparency LA 42*

- Tell students to fill in the last column of the *Reading Readiness Guide.* Ask them to evaluate if what they learned was what they had expected to learn.

  All in One **Latin America Teaching Resources,** *Reading Readiness Guide,* p. 276

A New Life Lydia Martin left Cuba in 1970 when she was only six years old. Her mother had grown tired of the limits on freedom and lack of opportunity in communist Cuba. She wanted to take Lydia to the United States. Lydia's father begged them to stay. He asked them, "Have you stopped to think you may never see me again?"

Like Lydia, many Cuban exiles left family members behind. They dream of returning to Cuba—once it is no longer a communist country. Meanwhile, many Cubans have made successful new lives in the United States. A large number have settled in Miami, Florida. In the Cuban neighborhood of Little Havana, they keep their language and their culture alive. At the same time, they have become important in the economic, cultural, and political life of Miami and the state of Florida. They own successful businesses, serve as elected officials, and influence government policy.

When relations between the United States and Cuba grew worse in the 1970s, Cuban exiles suffered. They could not even write to the families they had left behind. Castro's government might punish people who got a letter from the United States. What's more, the United States did not allow Americans to visit Cuba.

Cuban exiles playing dominoes in Little Havana, Miami, Florida

466 Latin America

Background: Link Across Time

Cash Crop The chief crop grown in Cuba is sugar cane, the plant from which refined sugar and cane sugar come. Sugar cane plants, originally from Asia, were introduced to the Americas by Spanish and Portuguese explorers in the fifteenth and sixteenth centuries. In a tropical climate, such as that of Cuba, the plant, once a costly luxury or medicine, thrived. Today, Cuba and India produce a large percentage of the world's cane sugar.

Another Wave of Exiles In 1991, the government of the Soviet Union collapsed and could no longer help Cuba. Food, medicine, tools, and other necessities became even more scarce in Cuba. Many families had little more than rice to eat.

As the situation in Cuba worsened, more people wanted to leave the island. Vanesa Alonso (vah NES uh ah LOHN soh) was one of them. In 1994, Vanesa and her family left Cuba on a rickety raft. Today, Vanesa lives in Miami, just a few miles from the ocean, but she hardly ever goes to the beach. The blue waves and roaring surf remind her of her terrifying trip from Cuba to the United States. That memory still gives her bad dreams.

✓ Reading Check **What caused another wave of exiles?**

Changes Come to Cuba

In the 1990s, when Cuba's economy was near collapse, Castro began allowing private ownership of some businesses. In addition, the Cuban government began encouraging tourism. The United States also loosened some restrictions on travel to Cuba. American businesspeople and farmers have begun to visit Cuba, hoping to sell their products there. The Cuban economy is improving. Castro has ruled Cuba for more than 40 years. Many Cuban exiles hope that the regime that follows Castro's will encourage better relations with the United States. They hope that they will be able to return home or to visit there in freedom.

✓ Reading Check **What changes did Castro make in the 1990s?**

New Visitors
Tourism increased in Cuba during the 1990s. **Analyze Images** *Judging from this photo of Havana, why might tourists want to visit Cuba?*

Section **1** Assessment

Key Terms
Review the key terms at the beginning of this section. Use each term in a sentence that explains its meaning.

Target Reading Skills
One important main idea of this section is stated on the first page. What is it?

Comprehension and Critical Thinking
1. (a) Describe How did Castro come to power in Cuba?

(b) Identify Effects How did life for Cubans change—for better and for worse—under Castro's rule?
(c) Synthesize What role did the Soviet Union play in Cuba?
2. (a) Define What is Little Havana?
(b) Find Main Ideas How have many Cubans adapted to life in the United States?
3. (a) Recall What do Cuban exiles hope will happen in Cuba in the near future?
(b) Predict What changes do you think are in store for Cuba? Explain your answer.

Writing Activity
Write a letter to a relative in Cuba from the point of view of a Cuban exile in the United States. Have another student write a response from the point of view of the Cuban relative. The relatives should exchange information about their daily lives and their hopes for the future.

> **Writing Tip** Before you begin, decide on the age, gender, and personality of the person writing the letter.

Chapter 15 Section 1 **467**

Objective

Learn how to compare and contrast information.

Prepare to Read

Build Background Knowledge L2

Ask students to think of the variety of countries in the Caribbean region and have them select two or three that they might like to visit. Then ask how comparing and contrasting these places might help them decide where to go.

Instruct

Comparing and Contrasting L2

Guided Instruction

■ Read the steps as a class to learn how to compare and contrast. Then write them on the board.

■ Practice the skill by following the steps on page 469 as a class. Model each step in the activity. Show students how to choose a topic and categories for comparison, note details about each place, identify similarities and differences, and draw a conclusion about which vacation spot they might prefer.

Independent Practice

Assign *Skills for Life* and have students complete it individually.

 Latin America Teaching Resources, *Skills for Life,* p. 292

Monitor Progress

The teacher should monitor the students doing the *Skills for Life* worksheet, checking to make sure they understand the skills steps.

Skills for Life   Comparing and Contrasting

"Come to the Caribbean," say the TV ads. But which Caribbean will you choose: an island with a Spanish culture or one with Native American, African, British, or French heritage? Do you want a luxury resort or a small village?
To plan your trip, you'd have to think about what you want to see and do and about which islands have these characteristics.
Then you would use the skill of comparing and contrasting to decide which country to visit.

To compare and contrast means to look for similarities and differences. It is a skill you use often, but you can learn to use it even more effectively by following the steps below.

Learn the Skill

Follow the steps below to learn the skill of comparing and contrasting.

1. **Identify a topic and purpose.** What do you want to compare, and why? Some examples of a purpose are to make a choice, to understand a topic, and to discover patterns.

2. **Select some categories for comparison.** For example, if you wanted to choose between two cars, your categories might be model, cost, and power seats.

3. **Make notes or a chart about the categories you're comparing.** A category such as power seats calls for a *yes* or a *no*. For other categories, such as model or cost, you need to note specific details.

4. **Identify the similarities and differences.** For each category, are the things you are comparing the same or different? What are the differences? Which differences are most important for your purpose?

5. **Draw conclusions.** Use the similarities and differences you found to answer an important question about your topic or to make a choice.

468 Latin America

Fun in the Sun

Winter Fun

Practice the Skill

Suppose you are planning a January vacation. Use the postcards above to help you decide between two possible vacation spots: one in the Caribbean and one in the northern United States. Follow the steps on the previous page to compare and contrast the two choices.

Scenery

Weather

Activities

1. In this example, the purpose is provided for you: to make a choice. What is the topic?

2. Ask yourself, "What aspects of these two places could I compare based on the postcards?" Jot down ideas. These ideas will be your categories.

3. Use your categories to jot down notes about each place.

4. For each category, decide whether the two vacation spots are similar or different. In what ways are they different?

5. Draw a conclusion. Are the two vacation spots basically similar or different? Which differences are important to your decision? Write a conclusion stating where you want to spend your vacation and why.

A Jamaican family

Apply the Skill

Turn to the Country Databank at the beginning of Chapter 14 or 15. Choose two countries, each from a different region. Compare and contrast the two countries and draw a conclusion about them.

Assess and Reteach

Assess Progress L2
Ask students to do the Apply the Skill activity.

Reteach L1
If students are having trouble applying the skills steps, have them review the skill using the interactive Social Studies Skills Tutor CD-ROM.

 Comparing and Contrasting, **Social Studies Skills Tutor CD-ROM**

Extend L3
- To extend the lesson, ask students to look back at the Country Databank on pages 456–461 of the Student Edition. Have students identify the five countries with the largest populations in the region. Then have them create a simple bar graph using this information. Point out to students that looking at a bar graph is an easy way to compare information.

Differentiated Instruction

For Special Needs Students L1
Partner special needs students with proficient readers to do Level 1 of the *Comparing and Contrasting* lesson on the Social Studies Skills Tutor CD-ROM together.

When the students feel more confident, they can move onto Level 2 alone.

Comparing and Contrasting, **Social Studies Skills Tutor CD-ROM**

Answers
Apply the Skill Students' comparisons should include relevant information for each country, and students' conclusions should be based on that information.

Objectives

Social Studies

1. Find out how democracy has been threatened in Haiti.
2. Learn what life is like for the people of Haiti, both in the countryside and in the cities.

Reading/Language Arts

Identify supporting details of a main idea.

Prepare to Read

Build Background Knowledge L2

In this section, students will learn about the country of Haiti and the difficulties it is striving to overcome. Show the World Studies video. Ask students to note three to five facts about Haiti as they watch. Conduct an Idea Wave (TE, p. T35) for students to share the facts they gathered.

📼 *Haiti: A Striving Nation,* **World Studies Video Program**

Set a Purpose for Reading L2

■ Preview the Objectives.

■ Read each statement in the *Reading Readiness Guide* aloud. Ask students to mark the statements true or false.

> All In One **Latin America Teaching Resources,** *Reading Readiness Guide,* p. 280

■ Have students discuss the statements in pairs or groups of four, then mark their worksheets again. Use the Numbered Heads participation structure (TE, p. 36) to call on students to share their group's perspectives.

Vocabulary Builder

Preview Key Terms L2

Pronounce each Key Term, then ask the students to say the word with you. Provide a simple explanation such as, "A refugee often finds shelter from danger by traveling to another country, especially in times of war."

Prepare to Read

Objectives

In this section you will

1. Find out how democracy has been threatened in Haiti.
2. Learn what life is like for the people of Haiti, both in the countryside and in the cities.

Taking Notes

As you read this section, look for the events in Haiti's struggle for democracy. Copy the timeline below, and record the events in the appropriate places on it.

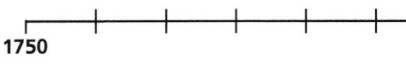

1750

🎯 Target Reading Skill

Identify Supporting Details The main idea of a paragraph or section is supported by details that give further information about it. These details may explain the main idea or give examples or reasons. The main idea of the portion of text titled The Boat People is "The Haitians who fled by sea became known as the Haitian boat people." As you read, notice how the example that follows helps explain who the boat people were and why they fled.

Key Terms

● **Jean-Bertrand Aristide** (zhan behr TRAHN ah rees TEED) *n.* former president of Haiti

● **refugee** (ref yoo JEE) *n.* someone who leaves his or her homeland to protect personal safety and escape persecution

● **Creole** (KREE ohl) *n.* a person of mixed African and European descent; in Haiti, a language that mixes French and African languages

In 2004, armed rebels (left) forced Haitian president Jean-Bertrand Aristide to leave office.

470 Latin America

Over the years, Haiti's military and its wealthy elite have used violence to block the country's attempts at democracy and economic improvement. One percent of Haiti's population controls nearly 50 percent of the country's wealth. This small, wealthy group is prepared to use violence when its control is challenged.

In 2006, though, with the support of the country's poor majority, René Préval was elected Haiti's president. Préval was already an important Haitian leader. In the 1970s, he had helped get rid of Haiti's military dictator. In the 1990s, he also worked closely with Jean-Bertrand Aristide (zhan behr TRAHN ah rees TEED), who ruled at various times. They both wanted to fight poverty in Haiti. However, in 2004, armed groups overthrew Aristide and took control. The year 2006 marked the first presidential election since that time.

🎯 Target Reading Skill L2

Identify Supporting Details Point out the Target Reading Skill. Review with students what they learned about identifying the main idea in Section 1 of this chapter. Then explain that supporting details tell more about the main idea.

Model identifying a supporting detail using the first paragraph on page 470. The main idea is that a small group of people is willing to use violence to keep influence in the Haitian government. Point out that the following sentence supports this idea: "Over the years, Haiti's military and its wealthy elite have used violence to block the country's attempts at democracy and economic improvement."

Give students *Identify Supporting Details.* Have them complete the activity in their groups.

> All In One **Latin America Teaching Resources,** *Identify Supporting Details,* p. 288

Democracy in Danger

Haiti's problems in 2004 were not unusual. The country has a long history of tensions between rich and poor, political instability, and violence. For example, Aristide was first elected president in 1990 but was forced out after only seven months in office.

The Boat People Thousands of Aristide's supporters had to flee Haiti's capital, Port-au-Prince (pawrt oh PRANS). Many of them fled by sea. They became known as the Haitian boat people. Because they left their homeland to protect their own personal safety and escape persecution, they are called **refugees.** Many Haitian boat people headed for the United States.

The Beaubrun (boh BRUN) family was among those refugees. Bazelais (bah zuh LAY) Beaubrun had spoken out against the military government in Haiti. After soldiers threatened him, he knew his life was in danger if he stayed. First Bazelais went into hiding. Then he took his family onto a crowded boat that was headed for the United States.

The U. S. Coast Guard stopped the boat and took the Haitians to an American military base. If Bazelais was really in danger for his political beliefs, he and his family could immigrate to the United States. After three months, the Beaubruns were allowed to enter the United States. Some families were not so lucky. U. S. officials sent them back to Haiti.

Refugees
The Beaubrun family escaped from Haiti and now live in Brooklyn, New York. **Infer** *Why would it be particularly difficult for a family like the Beaubruns, with young children, to make the journey described here?*

The Birth of Haiti The overthrow of the elected government in 2004 does not mean that most Haitians did not want democracy. Their country was born out of a desperate struggle for freedom. Haiti is the only nation in the Americas formed from a successful revolt of enslaved Africans.

As you can see on the map of Haiti on the next page, Haiti lies on the western third of the island of Hispaniola. It was once a colony of France. Europeans brought enslaved Africans to Haiti to work on sugar cane and coffee plantations. In the 1790s, slave revolts began. The Haitian leader Toussaint L'Ouverture helped banish slavery from Haiti in 1801. He also offered Haitians a new way of life, based on the idea that all people could live as equals.

Vocabulary Builder

Use the information below to teach students this section's high-use words.

High-Use Word	Definition and Sample Sentence
equality, p. 473	*n.* the state or quality of being equal The Constitution provides for the **equality** of all Americans under the law.
prosperity, p. 473	*n.* the condition of being wealthy, successful The increase in employment illustrates the company's **prosperity**.
dispute, p. 475	*n.* a quarrel or argument A **dispute** developed between the umpire and the batter.

Instruct

Democracy in Danger L2

Guided Instruction

- **Vocabulary Builder** Clarify the high-use words **equality** and **prosperity** before reading.

- Read Democracy in Danger using the Oral Cloze technique (TE, p. T33).

- Discuss the problems that the Beaubruns faced in leaving Haiti and immigrating to the United States. *(They were threatened by Haitian soldiers and had to go into hiding; they took a crowded boat to the United States and waited three months for approval for entry.)*

- Ask **Why do you think Haitians have been willing to undergo hardships to get to the United States?** *(The constant military struggles and harsh dictators have caused upheaval and persecution and have ruined the economy.)*

Answer

Infer Possible answer: Rafts may be unsafe for ocean travel and some children may not know how to swim.

Guided Instruction L2

Ask students to study the Country Profile on this page. Have them read the text and study the visual material. As a class, answer the Map and Chart Skills questions. Allow students to discuss their responses with a partner before sharing answers.

Independent Practice

- Distribute *Outline Map 7: Central America and the Caribbean.* Have students work with partners to label the bodies of water, Haiti, the Dominican Republic, the Bahamas, and the United States. Ask students to trace possible routes that boat people from Haiti might take as they try to reach the United States.

  All in One Latin America Teaching Resources, *Outline Map 7: Central America and the Caribbean,* p. 297

- Have partners write a statement suggesting how events listed on the timeline may have caused hardships for Haitians.

Answers

Map and Chart Skills

1. Dominican Republic

2. to the United States, Canada, the Bahamas, France, and the Dominican Republic

3. France controlled Haiti until Haiti gained independence in 1804.

4. Unemployment is high, the ratio of doctors to people is low, and life expectancy is low.

5. Students may answer that Haitians might want to return to Haiti if there were peace, opportunities to work, and improved health conditions.

Go Online PHSchool.com Students can find more information about this topic on the DK World Desk Reference Online.

Haiti

Haiti has a stormy history of colonization, revolution, and dictatorships. The nation's European and African roots can still be seen in its vibrant Creole language and heritage. Yet Haiti's history has shaped the country in other ways as well. Today, Haiti is the poorest country in Latin America. Years of political and economic unrest have caused many Haitians to leave the country. Study the map, timeline, and charts. Think about how Haiti's history affects the life of an ordinary Haitian.

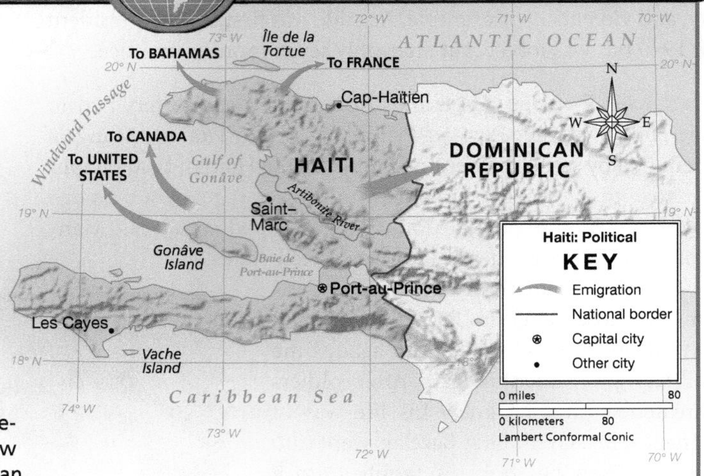

Haiti: Political KEY
- Emigration
- National border
- ⊛ Capital city
- • Other city

0 miles 80
0 kilometers 80
Lambert Conformal Conic

Foreign Influence in Haiti Since Independence

1800	1900	2000

1804 Haiti expels the French and gains independence.

1915 United States occupies Haiti.

1957 A series of brutal dictatorships begins.

1990 Aristide is elected president.

1994 International pressure allows Aristide to return.

2004 Aristide leaves the country.

About One in Seven Haitians Has Emigrated

Haiti Today

Unemployment	Ratio of Doctors to People	Life Expectancy
70%	1 doctor per 5,000 people	52 years

SOURCE: *DK World Desk Reference*

Map and Chart Skills

1. **Identify** Haiti shares an island with which country?
2. **Locate** Where do Haitians go when they leave their country?
3. **Identify Causes** What information in the timeline helps explain why Haiti's culture has French influences?
4. **Infer** What data in the table show why some Haitians choose to leave?
5. **Predict** What changes in Haiti might encourage Haitians who have emigrated to return to their country?

 Use Web Code lfe-1512 for **DK World Desk Reference Online.**

Differentiated Instruction

For Gifted and Talented L3

Have students choose one of Haiti's past leaders. Ask students to learn more about this person and his or her impact on the country. Have students prepare a brief oral report to deliver to the class.

Years of Dictatorship In the years that followed, Toussaint L'Ouverture's goal of freedom and equality was never fully realized. Most of Haiti's presidents became dictators once they got into power. One of the worst was François Duvalier (frahn SWAH doo vahl YAY), who took power in 1957. Because Duvalier had been a country doctor, Haitians called him "Papa Doc." Papa Doc was followed by his son, Jean-Claude Duvalier (zhan KLAWD doo vahl YAY), or "Baby Doc." Both were cruel leaders who stole government funds and used violence to keep power.

In 1986, rebels forced Baby Doc to leave the country. Many Haitians thought a period of freedom and prosperity was about to begin. Instead, Haiti was ruled by one military dictator after another.

A Brief Period of Hope Aristide's election in 1990 briefly brought hope to Haitians. However, these hopes were dashed when yet another military uprising forced Aristide to flee the country. The United States and other nations pressured the military to give power back to Aristide. In 1994, Aristide returned to Haiti, restoring democratic government. Haitians rejoiced, believing that peace and progress would follow.

In national elections held in 2000, it seemed that Aristide's supporters had won control of the legislature, and Aristide again assumed the presidency. But the election results were challenged. Armed rebels began to attack government offices. In early 2004, after rebel groups gained control of much of Haiti, Aristide left the country. Democracy in Haiti was threatened again. It took two years to organize new elections. Finally in 2006, René Préval was elected president.

√ Reading Check **What were the results of the 2000 elections?**

Citizen Heroes

Loune Viaud: Winner of Human Rights Award

Loune Viaud (loon vee OH) has been fighting injustice for a long time. During "Baby Doc's" regime, she courageously spoke out for human rights. Today she fights for all Haitians to have the right to healthcare—no matter how poor or sick they are. Viaud runs a clinic and works to ensure safe drinking water. When she received the 2002 Robert F. Kennedy Human Rights Award, Viaud called herself "a humble foot soldier in the struggle for health and human rights."

The dictator Jean-Claude "Baby Doc" Duvalier ruled Haiti from 1971 to 1986.

Guided Instruction (continued)

■ Ask students **What has been a main cause of Haiti's lack of success in achieving democracy?** *(Haiti hasn't had the right kind of leadership for a democracy. The military holds too much power.)*

Independent Practice

Ask students to copy the Taking Notes graphic organizer on a blank piece of paper. Then have them fill in events that they have read about. Briefly model how to decide which events to include.

Monitor Progress

■ Show *Section Reading Support Transparency LA 43* and have students check their graphic organizers individually. Go over key concepts and clarify key vocabulary as needed.

📖 **Latin America Transparencies,** *Section Reading Support Transparency LA 43*

Links

Read the **Citizen Heroes** on this page. Ask students **Why do you think Viaud was courageous during "Baby Doc's" regime?** *(She was probably in danger because she spoke out for human rights.)*

Answers

√ Reading Check The election results were challenged and armed rebels began to attack government offices.

Identify Supporting Details As a follow-up, ask students to answer the Target Reading Skill question in the Student Edition. *(Most Haitians are descended from enslaved Africans, and Creole, based on French and African languages, is spoken in Haiti.)*

The People of Haiti `L2`

Guided Instruction

- **Vocabulary Builder** Clarify the high-use word **dispute** before reading.

- Read The People of Haiti with students. As students read, circulate and make sure individuals can answer the Reading Check question.

- Ask students **Which traditions blend to create the culture of Haiti?** *(French, African, and West Indian traditions)*

- Ask students to explain how people in rural parts of Haiti often trade one kind of poverty for another when they move to the city. *(People in the countryside are usually farmers who struggle to grow enough food on small plots. When they go to the city looking for work, they end up in poor neighborhoods.)*

Independent Practice

Assign *Guided Reading and Review.*

All In One **Latin America Teaching Resources,** *Guided Reading and Review,* p. 281

Monitor Progress

Have students fill in the last column of the *Reading Readiness Guide.* Probe for what they learned that confirms or invalidates each statement.

All In One **Latin America Teaching Resources,** *Reading Readiness Guide,* p. 280

Answer

Synthesize Rural Haitians use resources from the sea and build their homes with local resources.

What details in the paragraph at the right are examples that support this idea: Haitian culture blends African, French, and West Indian traditions?

The People of Haiti

The Haitian people have suffered a great deal. Nevertheless, Haitian refugees remember many good things about their homeland: the warm weather, children playing soccer with their friends, dressing up for church, and many festivals. Haitian culture blends African, French, and West Indian traditions. Nearly all of Haiti's people are descended from the enslaved Africans who were brought to Haiti during colonial times. Haitians of mixed African and European ancestry are referred to as **Creole.** They are a minority in Haiti, but they have much of the wealth and power. Creole also refers to the language spoken in Haiti, which is based on both French and African languages.

Rural Life Today, Haiti is the poorest country in the Western Hemisphere. About two thirds of the people struggle to make a living farming small plots of land. But the land has been overused. Most trees have been cut. Rains wash the topsoil into the sea. When farmer Pierre Joseph stands on his small farm, he can see the calm waters of the Caribbean. When he looks down, he sees the dry, cracked earth of his one-acre field. Joseph is thin because he rarely gets enough to eat. "The land just doesn't yield enough," he says. He points to the few rows of corn and beans that he can grow on his one acre.

Fishing and Farming
A rural fisherman casts his net (above). The homes in the photo at the right have adobe walls and thatched roofs.
Synthesize *What can you learn about rural life in Haiti from these photos?*

⟲ Skills Mini Lesson

Supporting a Position `L2`

1. Point out that people generally have a position, or view, on subjects. Explain that reasons, supported by evidence such as facts, statistics, and statements from experts, help to support a position.

2. Have students practice the skill by taking a position on whether or not Haitians should leave the countryside for the city. Have students list evidence for their position.

3. Have students apply the skill by writing a paragraph stating a position and supporting it with evidence.

City Life Because of rural poverty, many people have left the countryside for the cities. They come to Port-au-Prince looking for work. Most poor people from the country cannot afford decent housing. They live in the poorest neighborhoods. These areas are dirty and crowded. The streets are not paved, so the rain turns them to mud. Many of the tiny homes are made of crumbling concrete. At the same time, the wealthy live in large wooden houses on the hills overlooking the city. There is also a small middle class of doctors, lawyers, teachers, and owners of small businesses. These people live fairly well. But the overwhelming majority of Haitians—in the city as well as in the countryside—are poor.

What Lies Ahead Recent election disputes and political violence have put Haitian democracy at risk once again. And these conditions have hurt the economy as well. Most people in Haiti are still poor. Many live in cities where violence is common. And many still try to leave their homeland, in search of a better life.

✓ Reading Check **Describe the poor neighborhoods of Port-au-Prince.**

Colorful Culture
Haitians often decorate buses and trucks in bright colors. **Analyze Images** *What can you learn about city life in Haiti from this photo of Port-au-Prince?*

Section 2 Assessment

Key Terms
Review the key terms at the beginning of this section. Use each term in a sentence that explains its meaning.

Target Reading Skills
State the details that support the main idea on page 473: *Toussaint L'Ouverture's goal of freedom and equality was never fully realized.*

Comprehension and Critical Thinking
1. (a) Define Who are the Haitian boat people?

(b) Sequence List the major events of Haiti's history in the order they occurred.
(c) Identify Cause and Effect How did the events of Haiti's history lead to the migration of the boat people?
2. (a) Describe What is rural life like for many Haitians?
(b) Compare and Contrast How is life in the city similar to and different from life on a farm?
(c) Find Main Ideas What are the major problems facing Haiti today?

Writing Activity
Suppose you were an American newspaper reporter in Haiti in 2004. Write an article about conditions in Haiti immediately after President Aristide was forced from power. Include the experiences of individual Haitians.

PHSchool.com

For: An activity on Haiti
Visit: PHSchool.com
Web Code: lfd-1502

Chapter 15 Section 2 **475**

Section 2 Assessment

Key Terms
Students' sentences should reflect knowledge of each Key Term.

Target Reading Skill
Most of Haiti's presidents became dictators. François Duvalier and his son, Jean-Claude, were cruel leaders who used violence to stay in power. After Jean-Claude was forced to leave Haiti, more dictators came to power.

Comprehension and Critical Thinking
1. (a) refugees from Haiti who fled Haiti by sea **(b)** Arawaks live in Haiti when Spanish arrive; Spanish bring enslaved Africans; Toussaint L'Ouverture helps Haiti become independent; United States occupies Haiti; a series of dictatorships beginning with Papa Doc; President Aristide forced to leave by military but returns in 1994; disputed elections continue to trouble Haiti; Aristide forced to leave again after rebel groups gain control. **(c)** In 1990, the military forced out

---

Assess and Reteach

Assess Progress [L2]
Have students complete the Section Assessment. Then administer the *Section Quiz.*

All in One Latin America Teaching Resources, *Section Quiz, p. 282*

Reteach [L1]
If students need more instruction, have them read this section in the Reading and Vocabulary Study Guide.

Chapter 15, Section 2, **Western Hemisphere Reading and Vocabulary Study Guide,** pp. 171–173

Extend [L3]
Have students learn more about the countries of the Caribbean by completing the *Small Group Activity: Creating a Magazine Story.*

All in One Latin America Teaching Resources, *Small Group Activity: Creating a Magazine Story,* pp. 293–296

Answers

✓ Reading Check They are dirty and crowded with no decent housing. The streets are unpaved, and the concrete homes are tiny and crumbling.

Analyze Images Port-au-Prince is very crowded with much traffic.

Writing Activity
Use the *Rubric for Assessing a Assessing a Newspaper Article* to evaluate students' articles.

All in One Latin America Teaching Resources, *Rubric for Assessing a Newspaper Article,* p. 304

Go Online PHSchool.com Typing in the web code when prompted will bring students directly to detailed instructions for this activity.

an elected ruler. Some of the ruler's supporters fled Haiti.

2. (a) It is a struggle to make a living farming on small overused plots of poor land. **(b)** Alike—poor people live in bad conditions; Different—those in the country are farmers; city dwellers look for other kinds of work. **(c)** election disputes, a poor economy, poverty, and violence.

Section 3
Step-by-Step Instruction

Objectives

Social Studies
1. Understand how the people of Puerto Rico are both American and Puerto Rican.
2. Find out what life is like on the island of Puerto Rico.
3. Learn about the three kinds of political status Puerto Ricans are considering for their future.

Reading/Language Arts
Identify implied main ideas in the text.

Prepare to Read

Build Background Knowledge L2

In this section, students will learn about Puerto Rico and the benefits and detriments of being a commonwealth of the United States. Remind students about the variety of struggles for independence fought by the countries of Latin America. Have students engage in a Think-Pair-Share activity (TE, p. T36) to create a list of reasons why a country would desire to be independent.

Set a Purpose for Reading L2

- Preview the Objectives.
- Form students into pairs or groups of four. Distribute the *Reading Readiness Guide*. Ask students to fill in the first two columns of the chart. Use the Numbered Heads participation structure (TE, p. T36) to call on students to share one piece of information they already know and one piece of information they want to know.

All in One Latin America Teaching Resources, *Reading Readiness Guide*, p. 284

Vocabulary Builder
Preview Key Terms L2
Pronounce each Key Term, then ask students to say the word with you. Provide an example such as, "A citizen of the United States enjoys many rights and privileges under our government."

Section 3
Puerto Rico
An American Commonwealth

Prepare to Read

Objectives
In this section you will
1. Understand why the people of Puerto Rico are both American and Puerto Rican.
2. Find out what life is like on the island of Puerto Rico.
3. Learn about the three kinds of political status Puerto Ricans are considering for their future.

Taking Notes
As you read this section, look for ways that life is similar and different in Puerto Rico and on the mainland United States. Copy the Venn diagram below, and record your findings in it.

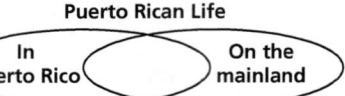

Puerto Rican Life

In Puerto Rico   On the mainland

Target Reading Skill

Identify Implied Main Ideas Identifying main ideas can help you remember the most important points you read. Sometimes the main idea is not stated directly. All the details in that portion of text add up to a main idea, but you must state the main idea yourself. For example, you could state the main idea of the text headed A Mix of Cultures this way: *Puerto Rico shows influences of Spanish, African, Caribbean, and United States mainland culture.*

Key Terms
- **constitution** (kahn stuh TOO shun) *n.* a statement of a country's basic laws and values
- **citizen** (SIT uh zun) *n.* a person with certain rights and responsibilities under a particular government
- **commonwealth** (KAHM un welth) *n.* a self-governing political unit that has strong ties to a particular country

A government building in Puerto Rico

476 Latin America

Puerto Rico was once a Spanish colony. When the United States defeated Spain in the Spanish-American War, Spain ceded, or gave, Puerto Rico to the United States. The United States slowly granted Puerto Rico more control of its own government and affairs. In 1951, Puerto Ricans voted to adopt their own constitution. A **constitution** is a statement of a country's basic laws and values. This gave Puerto Rico its own lawmakers. But it was still connected to the United States.

What is the nature of Puerto Rico's connection to the United States? How does that relationship affect life in Puerto Rico? And why do some Puerto Ricans want to change the nature of their island's relationship to the United States?

Target Reading Skill L2

Identify Implied Main Ideas Point out the Target Reading Skill. Review what students have learned about main ideas, then explain that sometimes the main idea is not stated directly, but is implied by details in a passage. In this case a reader must determine the main idea from the details.

Model identifying implied main ideas with this sentence about the first paragraph

on this page: *Although it has its own constitution, Puerto Rico is still connected to the United States.* Point out the details in the paragraph that support this idea, even though it is not explicitly stated.

Give students *Identify Implied Main Ideas*. Have them complete the activity in their groups.

All in One Latin America Teaching Resources, *Identify Implied Main Ideas*, p. 289

Puerto Ricans in the Mainland United States, 2000

Population	
Total	3,406,178
Northeast	2,074,574
South	759,305
Midwest	325,363
West	246,936

SOURCE: United States Census Bureau

Distribution by Region

7.2%
9.6%
22.3%
60.9%

- Northeast
- South
- Midwest
- West

Puerto Rican and American

People move from Puerto Rico to the United States mainland and back again very easily because Puerto Rico is part of the United States. Puerto Ricans are American citizens. **Citizens** are individuals with certain rights and responsibilities under a particular government. But Puerto Rico is not a state of the Union. It has a different status.

The Commonwealth of Puerto Rico Today, Puerto Rico is a commonwealth of the United States. A **commonwealth** is a self-governing political unit that has strong ties to a particular country. Although Puerto Ricans are American citizens, they cannot vote in presidential elections. They do not pay United States taxes. And they have only a nonvoting representative in the United States Congress. However, Puerto Ricans do serve in the armed forces of the United States.

Puerto Ricans on the Mainland Many Puerto Ricans have moved to the mainland United States. Most settle in cities in the Northeast. Life is very different there. While Puerto Rico has a warm Caribbean climate, winters in Northern cities can be cold and harsh. And cities like New York are much bigger than any city in Puerto Rico. The language of the mainland is English, while people speak Spanish in Puerto Rico. There is a lot to get used to.

■ Chart Skills

This market is in an area of New York City called Spanish Harlem, where many Puerto Ricans have settled. **Identify** According to the graph, which region has the largest Puerto Rican population? The smallest? **Infer** Why do you think that people tend to settle in areas where there are already many people from their former homes?

Instruct

Puerto Rican and American L2

Guided Instruction

- **Vocabulary Builder** Clarify the high-use words **grant** and **status** before reading.
- Read about the people of Puerto Rico in Puerto Rican and American, using the Choral Reading technique (TE, p. T34).
- Ask students **What are three ways that Puerto Ricans living in Puerto Rico are different from Americans who live in the United States mainland?** *(People living in Puerto Rico can't vote in presidential elections, don't pay United States taxes, and only have a non-voting representative in Congress.)*
- Ask students **Suppose that you are moving from the mainland United States to Puerto Rico. What would you like about moving there? What would you dislike?** *(Answers will vary. Students may say that they would like the warm weather, but would have trouble learning Spanish and miss their friends.)*

Independent Practice

Ask students to create the Taking Notes graphic organizer on a blank piece of paper. Then have them begin to fill in the sections of the Venn diagram. Briefly model how to fill in the diagram.

Monitor Progress

While students fill in the graphic organizer, move around the room and make sure individuals are choosing the correct details. Provide assistance as needed.

┌ Vocabulary Builder ─

Use the information below to teach students this section's high-use words.

High-Use Word	Definition and Sample Sentence
grant, p. 476	*v.* to allow to have The principal **granted** the students use of the gym for the dance.
status, p. 477	*n.* state of affairs or condition Due to the **status** of the injury, he will not be able to compete.
luxury, p. 480	*n.* great comfort It was a **luxury** driving to the prom in a limousine.
restore, p. 480	*v.* to bring back to an earlier condition The museum **restored** the damaged painting.

Answers

Chart Skills Identify Northeast; West
Infer Possible answer: It may be easier to adjust to new surroundings with people who share the same language and traditions.

Guided Instruction

- **Vocabulary Builder** Clarify the high-use words **luxury** and **restore** before reading.
- Read Life on the Island with students.
- Ask students to explain why they think people have moved back to Puerto Rico from the United States mainland. *(Possible answer: Puerto Rico was their original homeland and they miss the mountains, sea, vegetation, and Puerto Rican lifestyle.)*

Esmeralda Santiago

Coming to New York City Esmeralda Santiago (ez mehr AHL dah sahn tee AH goh) moved from Puerto Rico to New York City when she was 13 years old. At first, she found life on the mainland strange and confusing. One problem was that to succeed in school, she had to improve her English. She also found that Puerto Ricans living in New York were different from her friends on the island. Instead of the salsa and merengue music she loved, they preferred rock music. Most of the time they spoke neither pure Spanish nor English, but a mixture of the two that they called "Spanglish." Although they were Puerto Rican, Esmeralda felt different from them. Eventually, she learned their ways. She became more like them and thought less about her old life on the island.

✓ Reading Check **When Puerto Ricans move to New York City, what kinds of differences do they find?**

Life on the Island

Many people travel back and forth between the mainland and Puerto Rico. They live for a while in each place. Many Puerto Ricans moved to the mainland during the 1950s. However, since 1965, just as many Puerto Ricans have been moving back to their island as are leaving it.

Returning Home Julia de Jesus Chaparro (HOO lee ah day HAY soos chah PAH roh) moved back to a small mountain village in Puerto Rico after spending more than 14 years in Boston, Massachusetts. To explain why, she takes visitors to her back porch. From there, she can see a row of steep mountains. Peeking between them is the bright blue of the Caribbean Sea. The mountain slopes steeply down from Julia's back porch, but she has managed to clear some land. Her garden of mangoes, coconuts, grapefruit, and lemons thrives in the sun. Behind a nearby tree, a hen and six chickens are pecking in the dirt.

Puerto Rican Hillside
This hilly region is in the Central Mountains of Puerto Rico. **Draw Conclusions** *What can you learn about the geography, climate, and land use of this region from the photograph?*

478 Latin America

Answers

✓ Reading Check There are differences in climate, population density, language, music, and customs.

Draw Conclusions This region has hills, has a warm climate, and is used for farming.

Much of Puerto Rico is made up of hills and mountains—the kind of landscape you would see from Julia's back porch. In the hills, Puerto Rican cowhands, called *jíbaros* (HEE bahr ohs), raise cattle. They also hunt, fish, and raise chickens and pigs. On other parts of the island, farmers ride horses through fields of tall sugar cane. To the southwest, where the land is lower, fishing villages dot the coast.

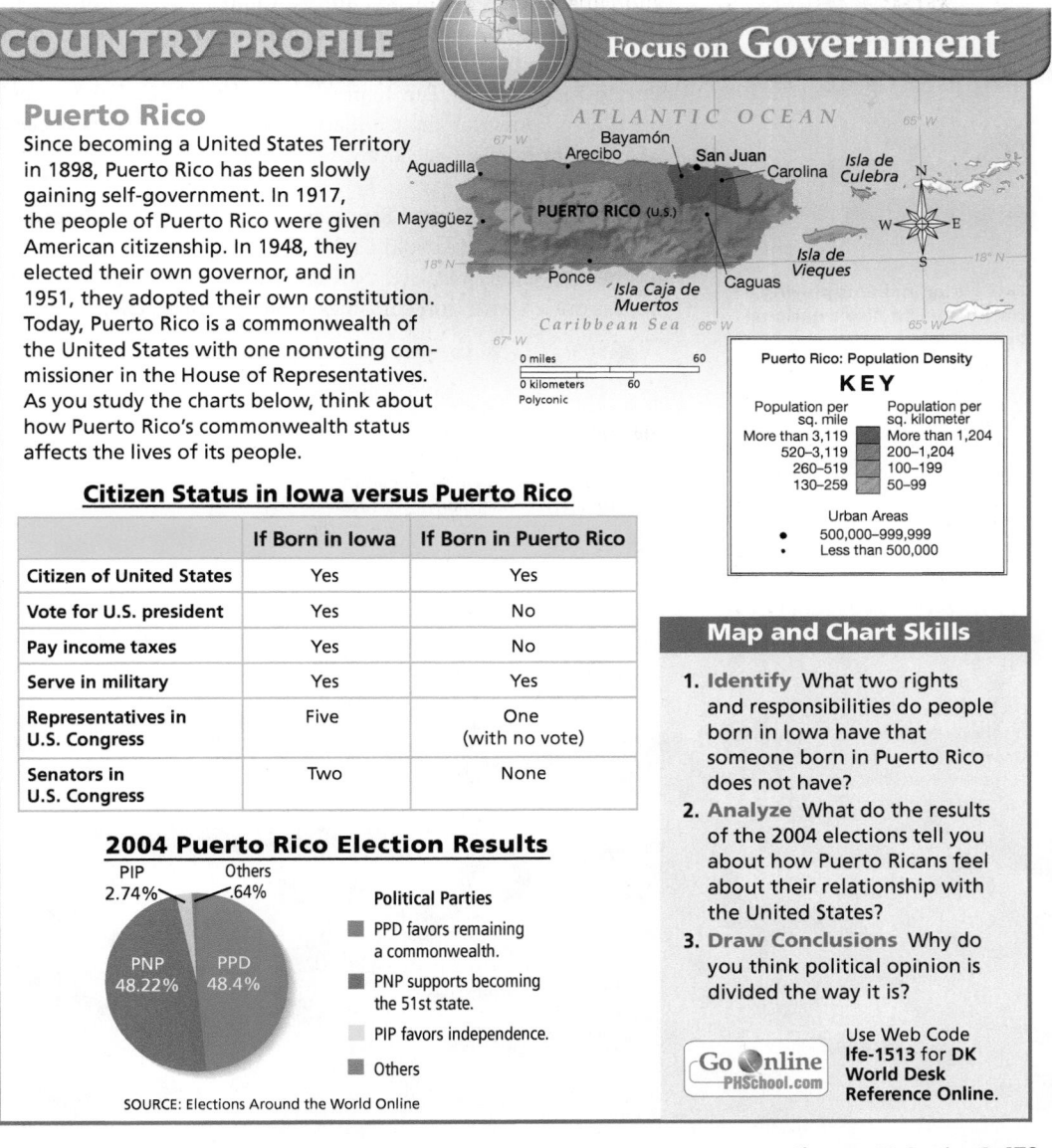

COUNTRY PROFILE — Focus on Government

Puerto Rico

Since becoming a United States Territory in 1898, Puerto Rico has been slowly gaining self-government. In 1917, the people of Puerto Rico were given American citizenship. In 1948, they elected their own governor, and in 1951, they adopted their own constitution. Today, Puerto Rico is a commonwealth of the United States with one nonvoting commissioner in the House of Representatives. As you study the charts below, think about how Puerto Rico's commonwealth status affects the lives of its people.

Puerto Rico: Population Density

KEY

Population per sq. mile	Population per sq. kilometer
More than 3,119	More than 1,204
520–3,119	200–1,204
260–519	100–199
130–259	50–99

Urban Areas
- 500,000–999,999
- Less than 500,000

Citizen Status in Iowa versus Puerto Rico

	If Born in Iowa	If Born in Puerto Rico
Citizen of United States	Yes	Yes
Vote for U.S. president	Yes	No
Pay income taxes	Yes	No
Serve in military	Yes	Yes
Representatives in U.S. Congress	Five	One (with no vote)
Senators in U.S. Congress	Two	None

2004 Puerto Rico Election Results

PIP 2.74%   Others .64%
PNP 48.22%   PPD 48.4%

Political Parties
- PPD favors remaining a commonwealth.
- PNP supports becoming the 51st state.
- PIP favors independence.
- Others

SOURCE: Elections Around the World Online

Map and Chart Skills

1. **Identify** What two rights and responsibilities do people born in Iowa have that someone born in Puerto Rico does not have?
2. **Analyze** What do the results of the 2004 elections tell you about how Puerto Ricans feel about their relationship with the United States?
3. **Draw Conclusions** Why do you think political opinion is divided the way it is?

Go Online PHSchool.com — Use Web Code **Ife-1513** for **DK World Desk Reference Online**.

COUNTRY PROFILE
Focus on Government

Guided Instruction   L2

Direct students to read the Country Profile text about Puerto Rico and to study the visuals on this page. As a class, answer the Map and Chart Skills questions. Allow students to discuss their responses with a partner before sharing answers.

Independent Practice

Ask students to use the information in the text on this page to create a timeline showing how the government in Puerto Rico has changed over time.

Answers

Map and Chart Skills

1. the right to vote for President and to have voting representatives in Congress
2. Most favor remaining a commonwealth or becoming a state; only a small percentage want to end their relationship with the United States.
3. Possible answer: There are compelling advantages and disadvantages to Puerto Rico becoming a state.

Go Online PHSchool.com Students can find useful information about this topic on the DK World Desk Reference Online.

Guided Instruction (continued)

- Ask students **How do some people living in Puerto Rico's cities make their living?** (*They work in factories and hotels and restaurants that draw tourists.*)

Independent Practice

Have students complete the graphic organizer by filling in the Venn diagram.

Monitor Progress

Show *Section Reading Support Transparency LA 44* and ask students to check their graphic organizers individually. Go over key concepts and clarify key vocabulary as needed

Latin America Transparencies, *Section Reading Support Transparency LA 44*

This guitar maker is playing a cuatro, Puerto Rico's national instrument.

A Mix of Cultures As people travel back and forth, they bring customs and products with them. If you visited Puerto Rico, you would see many influences from the United States mainland. You would also see that in Puerto Rico, there is a strong cultural connection to the Caribbean. Most people are a mix of Spanish and African ancestry.

Puerto Rican cities show influences of Spanish, Caribbean, and United States mainland culture. About 75 percent of Puerto Ricans live in cities. Many city people work in factories. Others work in the hotels and restaurants that draw many tourists. Puerto Rico's capital, San Juan (san HWAHN), has a large waterfront area known as the Condado (kohn DAH do). It is packed with luxury hotels. Not far away, modern skyscrapers pierce the brilliant sky.

In the old section of San Juan, Spanish-style buildings are everywhere. A 450-year-old Catholic church built by the Spanish has been carefully restored. Not far from the church sit ancient houses graced with iron balconies in lacy Spanish style.

√ Reading Check **Compare old and new San Juan.**

Old and New
The San Geronimo Fortress, built in the 1500s by the Spanish, stands in sharp contrast to the modern hotels of San Juan. **Infer** *How do you think the fortress might contribute to the current economy of San Juan?*

480 Latin America

Answers

√ Reading Check San Juan, Puerto Rico's capital, is on a waterfront called the Condado. It has many luxury hotels and skyscrapers. It also has an old section with Spanish-style buildings, including a 450-year-old Catholic church and old houses with Spanish-style iron balconies.
Infer Many tourists may come to Puerto Rico to see the fortress and other examples of Puerto Rico's Spanish history.

Seeking a New Direction

Puerto Rico is bound by many United States laws, and Puerto Ricans have many questions about this situation. Is it good for Puerto Rico? Should Puerto Rico become independent? Or should it become a state of the United States?

Commonwealth or Statehood?   Puerto Ricans have many disagreements over what the status of their island should be. Many feel that having "one foot" in Puerto Rico and "one foot" in the United States can lead to problems. Others point out how the relationship with the United States has helped Puerto Rico. American businesses on the island have raised the standard of living. Each year, the United States government sends millions of dollars to the island to help people in need.

Some people still feel that Puerto Rico is at a disadvantage because Puerto Ricans cannot vote in United States elections. They say Puerto Rico should try to become a state. But if it does, it will become the poorest state in the union. Puerto Ricans earn more money than people in other Caribbean countries. However, they earn less than people on the United States mainland. Also, if Puerto Rico becomes a state, Puerto Ricans will have to pay United States taxes. This could lower the earnings of many people who have little to spare. For these reasons, in 1993 and again in 1998, Puerto Ricans voted not to become the 51st state of the United States.

Statehood Now!
These people are rallying for Puerto Rican statehood in a 1996 demonstration. **Transfer Information** *What arguments in favor of statehood might these demonstrators give?*

 **Identify Implied Main Ideas**
In one sentence, state what all the details in the paragraph at the left are about.

Guided Instruction
- Read Seeking a New Direction with students. As students read, circulate and make sure that individuals can answer the Reading Check question.
- Discuss with students how life would change for Puerto Ricans if Puerto Rico became a state of the United States. *(Puerto Ricans would be allowed to vote in the United States elections, but would have to pay taxes.)*
- Ask students **Do you think Puerto Rico should become the fifty-first state? Why or why not?** *(Answers will vary. Yes—If Puerto Rico becomes a state, its citizens will have all the benefits of American citizenship. Paying taxes is worth the advantage. No—Puerto Ricans should wait until their economy improves before joining the United States so that taxation will not be a hardship on people.)*

Independent Practice
Assign *Guided Reading and Review.*

All in One **Latin America Teaching Resources,** *Guided Reading and Review,* p. 285

Monitor Progress
Tell students to fill in the last column of the *Reading Readiness Guide.* Ask them to evaluate if what they learned was what they had expected to learn.

All in One **Latin America Teaching Resources,** *Reading Readiness Guide,* p. 284

Target Reading Skill L2
Identify Implied Main Ideas As a follow up, ask students to answer the Target Reading Skill question in the Student Edition. *(So far economic reasons have kept Puerto Ricans from voting to become a state.)*

| **Differentiated Instruction** |

For Less Proficient Readers L1
Have students read the section in the Reading Vocabulary and Study Guide. This version provides basic-level instruction in an interactive format with questions and write-on lines.
Chapter 15, Section 3, **Western Hemisphere Reading and Vocabulary Study Guide,** pp. 174–176

For Gifted and Talented L3
Ask students to find photographs of various aspects of life and scenery in Puerto Rico. Encourage students to prepare short captions or statements about the photos and share these with the class.

Answer
Transfer Information They might argue that statehood would give them more influence over laws in the United States.

Assess and Reteach

Assess Progress L2

Have students complete the Section Assessment. Administer the *Section Quiz.*

 Latin America Teaching Resources, *Section Quiz,* p. 286

Reteach L1

If students need more instruction, have them read this section in the Reading and Vocabulary Study Guide.

 Chapter 15, Section 3, **Western Hemisphere Reading and Vocabulary Study Guide,** pp. 174–176

Extend L3

Remind students of the World Studies video, *Puerto Rico: Past and Present,* that they watched earlier. Have students make a chart comparing either rural or urban regions of Puerto Rico or New and Old San Juan. You may wish to reshow the video if students are having trouble recalling data.

 Puerto Rico: Past and Present, **World Studies Video Program**

Answers

Predict Answers will vary but should reflect knowledge of facts from the lesson.

✓ **Reading Check** They feel Puerto Rico's identity as a Caribbean nation with Spanish culture is threatened by its association with the United States.

Section 3 Assessment

Key Terms
Students' sentences should reflect knowledge of each Key Term.

Target Reading Skill
Answers will vary, but should reflect important main ideas from the section.

Comprehension and Critical Thinking
1. (a) It is a commonwealth of the United States. **(b)** Puerto Ricans adopted their own constitution in 1951.

2. (a) Possible answer: In the mountains and hills people hunt, fish, and raise animals; in other parts of the island farmers grow sugar cane; along the coast people fish. **(b)** Most people are of African and Spanish ancestry, speak Spanish, and live in cities with skyscrapers.

3. (a) commonwealth, statehood, and a separate nation **(b)** commonwealth benefit—helped by American businesses and government, drawback—cannot vote in U.S. elections; statehood benefit—people can vote, drawback—will be poorest state, have to pay taxes; separate nation benefit—clear identity, drawback—might lose some U.S. aid

---

Rally for Independence
This rally of the Independenista Party was held in 1980. **Predict** *Do you think these demonstrators or those on the previous page will ever get their wish for Puerto Rico? Explain your answer.*

The Question of Independence Some people who voted against statehood have even bigger dreams for Puerto Rico. They want it to become a separate nation. If it does not, they fear that Puerto Ricans will become confused about their identity. They stress Puerto Rico's connection to other Caribbean nations. They want to make sure that Puerto Ricans always identify with the Spanish language and Spanish culture. But for now, Puerto Rico will keep its links to the mainland. Many Puerto Ricans hope that their relationship with the United States will lead to a profitable and peaceful future.

✓ **Reading Check** **Why do some people favor Puerto Rican independence?**

 ## Section 3 Assessment

Key Terms
Review the key terms at the beginning of this section. Use each term in a sentence that explains its meaning.

Target Reading Skills
State two main ideas of Section 3.

Comprehension and Critical Thinking
1. (a) Explain What is Puerto Rico's relationship to the United States?
(b) Sequence How did Puerto Rico gain more control over its own affairs?

2. (a) Describe List three different regions of Puerto Rico, and tell how people earn a living in each one.
(b) Synthesize How does Puerto Rican culture show Spanish, Caribbean, and mainland influences?
3. (a) List What are the three options Puerto Ricans consider for the future of their relationship with the United States?
(b) Analyze What are the benefits and drawbacks of each option?

Writing Activity
Write a journal entry from the point of view of either Julia or Esmeralda. Discuss your feelings about life on the mainland and in Puerto Rico. Explain where you would prefer to live and why.

For: An activity on San Juan
Visit: PHSchool.com
Web Code: lfd-1503

Writing Activity
Use the *Rubric for Assessing a Journal Entry* to evaluate students' journal entries.

 Latin America Teaching Resources, *Rubric for Assessing a Journal Entry,* p. 305

Go Online
PHSchool.com Typing in the web code when prompted will bring students directly to detailed instructions for this activity.

Review and Assessment

◆ Chapter Summary

Section 1: Cuba

- Cuba became a communist country under Fidel Castro and then became an ally of the Soviet Union.
- During the Cold War, relations between Cuba and the United States worsened.
- Many Cubans have fled Cuba for the United States, where they have made successful new lives, but some dream of returning to a free and democratic Cuba.
- Recently Castro has allowed some private ownership of businesses and is encouraging tourism and trade.

Cuba

Section 2: Haiti

- Haiti has struggled for democracy since independence, but has enjoyed only short periods of elected government.
- The election of President Aristide brought a brief period of hope, but then a military takeover caused many Haitians to flee their country.
- The people of Haiti are poor. Farmers struggle on land that has been overused, crowded city slums do not have basic services, and political violence is a fact of life.

Section 3: Puerto Rico

- Puerto Rico is a commonwealth of the United States. Puerto Ricans are American citizens, and many of them move to the United States mainland.
- Life in Puerto Rico blends Caribbean and mainland influences.
- Puerto Ricans disagree over whether they should become a state, become independent, or remain a commonwealth.

◆ Key Terms

Match the definitions in Column I with the key terms in Column II.

Column I

1. a statement of a country's basic laws and values
2. a country joined to another country for a special purpose
3. a place that has its own government but also has strong ties to another country
4. those who leave their homeland for their own personal safety and to escape persecution
5. individuals with certain rights and responsibilities under a particular government

Column II

A citizens
B ally
C commonwealth
D constitution
E refugees

┌ Vocabulary Builder ┐

Revisit this chapter's high-use words:

dictator	equality	status
corrupt	prosperity	luxury
missile	dispute	restore
collapse	grant	

Ask students to review the definitions they recorded on their *Word Knowledge* worksheets.

 **Latin America Teaching Resources,** *Word Knowledge,* p. 290

Consider allowing students to earn extra credit if they use the words in their answers to the questions in the Chapter Review and Assessment. The words must be used correctly and in a natural context to win the extra points.

Review and Assessment

Review Chapter Content

- Review and revisit the major themes of this chapter by asking students to classify what Guiding Question each bulleted statement in the Chapter Summary answers. Have students complete this activity as a class. Refer to page 1 in the Student Edition for the text of the Guiding Questions.

- Assign *Vocabulary Development* for students to review Key Terms.

All in One Latin America Teaching Resources, *Vocabulary Development,* p. 301

Answers

Key Terms

1. D
2. B
3. C
4. E
5. A

Review and Assessment

Comprehension and Critical Thinking

6. (a) Possible answers: fertile farmland, located at entrance to the Gulf of Mexico, excellent harbors, good beaches, pleasant climate. **(b)** Its location made it a good place for trade with the United States and other parts of the Caribbean; its farmland provided money from sugar cane; its beaches and climate drew tourists. **(c)** Castro's communist government took over private businesses and land.

7. (a) During Batista's rule many farm and factory workers earned low wages and didn't share the country's wealth. **(b)** The government took over businesses and land; people couldn't speak out against government; many people fled the island; literacy and healthcare improved. **(c)** The country's economy and living conditions worsened without the help of the Soviet Union. Castro allowed some private ownership of businesses and encouraged tourism to bolster the economy.

8. (a) France **(b)** L'Overture wanted all people to live as equals and enjoy freedom. His ideals were not fulfilled during the rule of the Duvaliers, cruel dictators who used violence to keep power and who stole government money.

9. (a) a Catholic priest who was elected president of Haiti **(b)** elected in 1990, forced to leave the country by the military, returned in 1994, elected again in 2000 under cloud of cheating and fraud resulting in the halt of international aid, called on to resign by some Haitians in 2002 **(c)** People who supported Aristide had to hide because they were attacked by the military. Many fled; some became boat people and headed for the United States.

10. (a) Puerto Ricans can move easily between Puerto Rico and the mainland, serve in armed forces, have nonvoting representative in Congress **(b)** Many move to the mainland for jobs and services but move back to the island for the beautiful geography and because of family and cultural ties.
(c) Advantages: self-government, U.S. government aid, no taxes, better standard of living. Disadvantages: nonvoting representative in Congress, unable to vote in presidential elections.

◆ Comprehension and Critical Thinking

6. (a) Name What are two advantages Cuba has because of its geography?
(b) Identify Cause and Effect How did these advantages lead to Cuba's prosperity?
(c) Synthesize Information How did Cuba change from a prosperous country to a poor one?

7. (a) Recall Why did revolutionary leaders like Fidel Castro gain support in Cuba?
(b) Describe What is life like under Castro's communist government of Cuba?
(c) Identify Effects What happened in Cuba when the communist regime of the Soviet Union collapsed? Explain why.

8. (a) Name Haiti was a colony of which European country?
(b) Synthesize Describe Toussaint L'Ouverture's ideals for Haiti, and explain whether or not the rule of the Duvaliers fulfilled those ideals.

9. (a) Identify Who is Jean-Bertrand Aristide?
(b) Sequence What are the main events of Aristide's struggle for power?
(c) Draw Conclusions How did what happened to Aristide affect ordinary people who supported him? Explain why.

10. (a) List What rights and responsibilities of United States citizenship do Puerto Ricans have?
(b) Find Main Ideas Explain why so many Puerto Ricans move back and forth between their island and the mainland.
(c) Compare What are the advantages and disadvantages of commonwealth status for Puerto Rico?

◆ Skills Practice

Comparing and Contrasting In the Skills for Life activity in this chapter, you learned how to compare and contrast. Review the steps of this skill.

Now look again at the first two sections of this chapter. As you recall, people from both Cuba and Haiti have fled their countries to come to the United States. What kinds of countries did they leave behind? How are Cuba and Haiti similar and different? Use a chart to compare the two countries. Then write a conclusion sentence on the topic.

◆ Writing Activity: Math

Review the charts in Country Profile: Haiti on page 472. Also consider the current population of Haiti, which is approximately 8 million. Use this information and your math skills to write a paragraph about Haiti's loss of population. You may wish to convert numbers into percentages or explain ratios in your paragraph.

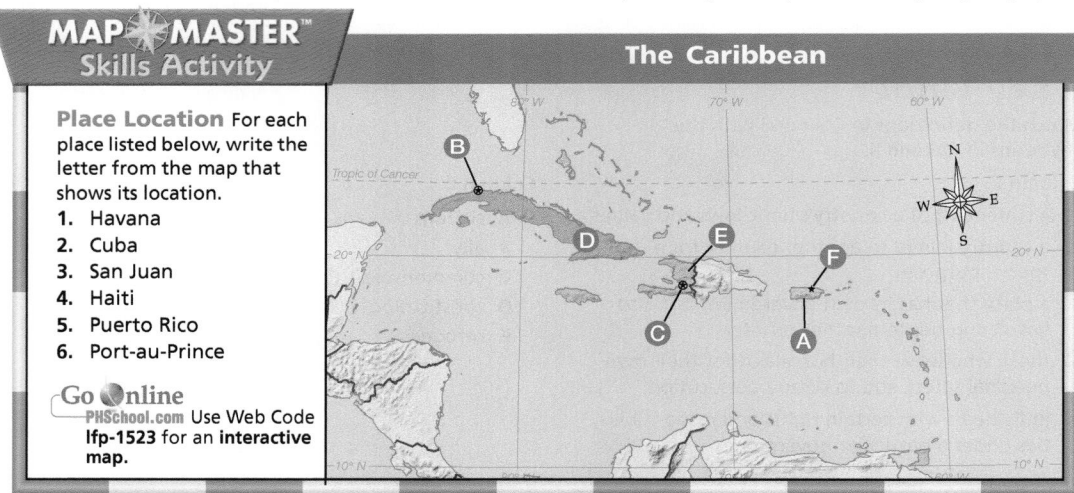

MAP MASTER™ Skills Activity

The Caribbean

Place Location For each place listed below, write the letter from the map that shows its location.
1. Havana
2. Cuba
3. San Juan
4. Haiti
5. Puerto Rico
6. Port-au-Prince

Go Online
PHSchool.com Use Web Code lfp-1523 for an interactive map.

484 Latin America

Skills Practice

Students should create a chart comparing and contrasting Cuba and Haiti using appropriate information from the text.

Possible conclusion: Both are former colonies that were ruled by dictators and have poor economies. Haiti is poorer and more volatile than Cuba.

Standardized Test Prep

Test-Taking Tips

Some questions on standardized tests ask you to sequence information. Study the timeline below. Then follow the tips to answer the sample question.

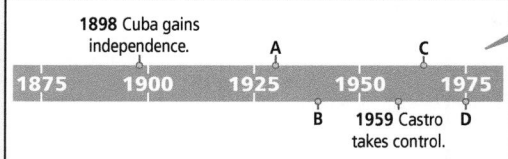

1898 Cuba gains independence.

| 1875 | 1900 | 1925 | 1950 | 1975 |

A   C

B   1959 Castro   D
     takes control.

TIP Notice that the leader lines connect events to their dates on the timeline. See which dates are closest to each answer choice.

Pick the letter that best answers the question.

At which point on the timeline did large numbers of Cuban exiles <u>begin</u> going to the United States?

A point A
B point B
C point C
D point D

TIP Preview the question first. Look for information relating to the question as you examine the timeline.

Think It Through Notice the key word *begin* in the question. You know that many Cubans left Cuba for the United States because they opposed Castro's government. Therefore, they must have *started* leaving after Castro came to power. So you can rule out choices A and B. Although exiles may still have been leaving Cuba in 1975, the exile movement most likely *began* shortly after Castro's new government was formed. So the correct answer is C.

Practice Questions

Choose the letter of the best answer.

1. Before Cuba gained independence, it was a colony of
   A France.
   B Spain.
   C the United States.
   D Portugal.

2. Which of the following nations was formed from a revolt of enslaved Africans?
   A Haiti
   B Cuba
   C Puerto Rico
   D Hispaniola

3. Which of the following statements best describes Puerto Rico's relationship with the United States?
   A It is a colony of the United States.
   B It is a state of the United States.
   C It is a country with special ties to the United States.
   D It is a commonwealth of the United States.

Study the timeline below and answer the question that follows.

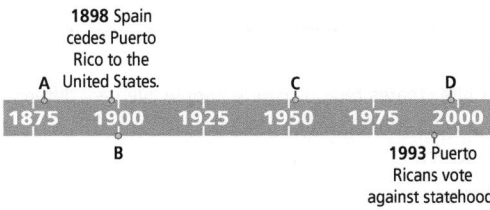

1898 Spain cedes Puerto Rico to the United States.

A

| 1875 | 1900 | 1925 | 1950 | 1975 | 2000 |

C   D

B

1993 Puerto Ricans vote against statehood.

4. At which point on the timeline did Puerto Rico become a commonwealth?
   A point A
   B point B
   C point C
   D point D

Go Online
PHSchool.com

Use Web Code lfa-1501 for a **Chapter 15 self-test.**

Assessment Resources

Use *Chapter Tests A and B* to assess students' mastery of chapter content.

All in One Latin America Teaching Resources, *Chapter Tests A and B,* pp. 306–311

Tests are also available on the **ExamView® Test Bank CD-ROM.**

⊙ **ExamView® Test Bank CD-ROM**

Writing Activity: Math
Answers will vary, but students should mention the flight of Haitians in their paragraph as one reason for population loss.

Use *Rubric for Assessing a Writing Assignment* to evaluate students' paragraphs. Tell students how many sources you would like them to use, if any, beyond the textbook.

All in One Latin America Teaching Resources, *Rubric for Assessing a Writing Assignment,* p. 303

MAP MASTER
Skills Activity

1. B	**2.** D
3. F	**4.** E
5. A	**6.** C

Go Online
PHSchool.com Students may practice their map skills online using the interactive version of this map.

Standardized Test Prep
Answers

1. B
2. A
3. D
4. C

Go Online
PHSchool.com Students may use the Chapter 15 self-test on PHSchool.com to prepare for the Chapter Test.

Overview

Introducing South America

1. Use data to compare countries.
2. Learn what characteristics the countries of South America share.
3. Name some key differences among the countries.

Section 1

Brazil: Geography Shapes a Nation

1. Learn about the geography of Brazil.
2. Discover why the rain forests are important to Brazil and to the whole world.
3. Find out what groups make up the people of Brazil and how they live.

Section 2

Peru: An Ancient Land Looks to the Future

1. Learn how geography has affected the way people live in the three regions of Peru.
2. Discover what life is like in the cities and towns of the Altiplano.

Section 3

Chile: Land of Contrasts

1. Find out how the geography of Chile creates regions where people live very differently.
2. Learn how Chile's people live and what products they produce.
3. Find out how Chile restored democracy.

Section 4

Venezuela: Oil Powers the Economy

1. Find out how Venezuela was made wealthy by oil.
2. Learn how the ups and downs of oil prices affected the economy and people of Venezuela.
3. Understand how Venezuela is changing.

Technology Resources

Students use embedded web codes to access internet activities, chapter self-tests, and additional map practice. They may also access Dorling Kindersley's Online Desk Reference to learn more about each country they study.

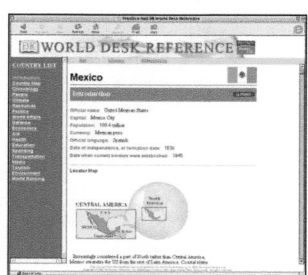

Use the Interactive Textbook to make content and concepts come alive through animations, videos, and activities that accompany the complete basal text—online and on CD-ROM.

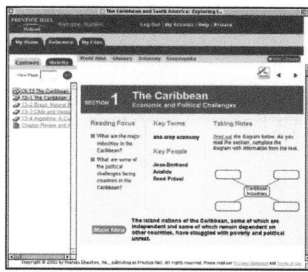

PRENTICE HALL

TeacherEXPRESS™
Plan • Teach • Assess

Use this complete suite of powerful teaching tools to make planning lessons and administering tests quicker and easier.

Reading and Assessment

Reading and Vocabulary Instruction

⤾ Model the Target Reading Skill

Compare and Contrast Tell students that comparing and contrasting can be a helpful tool both for clarifying and remembering information. Comparing allows students to see patterns of similarities, and contrasting elucidates patterns of difference.

Model comparing and contrasting by thinking aloud about the following paragraph:

There are three distinct geographic regions in Peru. The mountain region is often very cold. Native Americans live in the mountains, surviving by farming and selling wool. The coastal region is dry. It was once home to Native Americans, but is now an urban region, with a mixture of cultural groups. The forests are hot and humid. Some Native Americans live in the forests, but there are few towns or roads.

Think aloud: The subject of this paragraph is the three geographic regions in Peru. To be more specific, the paragraph discusses the climate and people of these geographic regions. How are these regions similar? At one point in time, Native Americans lived in all three regions. How are these regions different? They have different climates.

Use the following worksheets from All-in-One Latin America Teaching Resources, (pp. 331, 332, and 333) to support this chapter's Target Reading Skill.

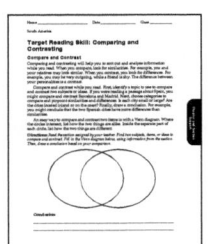 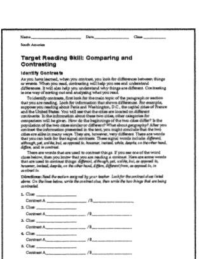 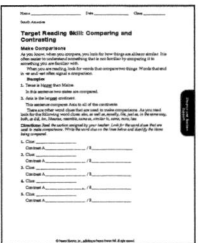

Vocabulary Builder
High-Use Academic Words

Use these steps to teach this chapter's High-Use words:

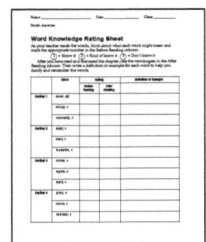

1. Have students rate how well they know each word on their Word Knowledge worksheets (All-in-One Latin American Teaching Resources, p. 334).
2. Pronounce each word and ask students to repeat it.
3. Give students a brief definition or sample sentence (provided on TE pp. 495, 502, 508, and 517.)
4. Work with students as they fill in the "Definition or Example" column of their Word Knowledge worksheets.

Assessment

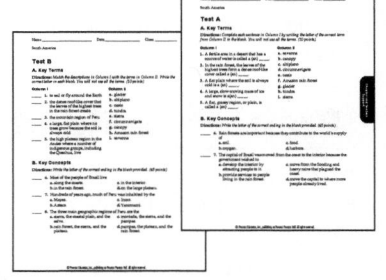

Formal Assessment

Test students' understanding of core knowledge and skills.

> **Chapter Tests A and B,** All-in-One Latin America Teaching Resources, pp. 353–358

Customize the Chapter Tests to suit your needs.
ExamView® Test Bank CD-ROM

Skills Assessment

Assess geographic literacy.

> **MapMaster Skills,** Student Edition pp. 487, 524
> **Country Profile Map and Chart Skills,** Student Edition pp. 498, 502, 508, 518

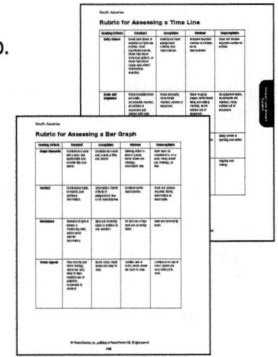

Assess reading and comprehension.

> **Target Reading Skills,** Student Edition, pp. 497, 505, 509, 519, and in Section Assessments
> **Chapter 16 Assessment,** Western Hemisphere Reading and Vocabulary Study Guide, p. 190

Performance Assessment

Assess students' performance on this chapter's Writing Activities using the following rubrics from All-in-One Latin America Teaching Resources.

> **Rubric for Assessing a Bar Graph,** p. 348
> **Rubric for Assessing a Timeline,** p. 351

Assess students' work through performance tasks.

> **Small Group Activity: Making a Mural,** All-in-One Latin America Teaching Resources, pp. 337–340
> **Portfolio Activity,** Teacher Edition, p. 165

Online Assessment

Have students check their own understanding.
> **Chapter Self-Test**

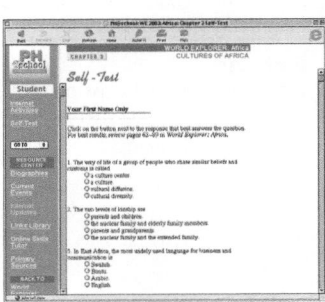

Test Preparation

> **Latin America Practice Tests A, B and C,** Test Prep Workbook, pp. 61–72
> **Latin America Benchmark Test 2 and Outcome Test,** AYP Monitoring Assessments, pp. 101–104, 182–187

Section 1 Brazil: Geography Shapes a Nation

3 periods, 1.5 blocks (includes Country Databank)

Social Studies Objectives
1. Learn about the geography of Brazil.
2. Discover why the rain forests are important to Brazil and to the whole world.
3. Find out what groups make up the people of Brazil and how they live.

Reading/Language Arts Objective
Compare and contrast things to analyze and sort out information.

Prepare to Read	**Instructional Resources**	**Differentiated Instruction**
Build Background Knowledge Have students discuss the effects of Brazil's geography on its people. **Set a Purpose for Reading** Have students evaluate statements on the *Reading Readiness Guide.* **Preview Key Terms** Teach the section's Key Terms. **Target Reading Skill** Introduce the section's Target Reading Skill of **comparing and contrasting.**	**All in One Latin America Teaching Resources** **L2** Reading Readiness Guide, p. 316 **L2** Compare and Contrast, p. 331	**Spanish Reading and Vocabulary Study Guide** **L2** Chapter 16, Section 1, pp. 129–130 ELL **Discovery Channel World Studies Video Program** **L2** South America: Adapting to a Varied Landscape LPR, SN, ELL **Latin America Transparencies** **L1** Transparency B16: Venn Diagram LPR, SN, ELL

Instruct	**Instructional Resources**	**Differentiated Instruction**
The Geography of Brazil Discuss the geography of Brazil. **The Importance of the Rain Forest** Discuss the dangers threatening the Amazon rain forest. **Target Reading Skill** Review **comparing and contrasting.** **Country Profile** Direct student to derive information from maps, charts, and graphs, followed by an activity and a discussion. **The People of Brazil** Discuss Brazil's people and how they live.	**All in One Latin America Teaching Resources** **L2** Guided Reading and Review, p. 317 **L2** Reading Readiness Guide, p. 316 **L2** Reading a Population Density Map, p. 341 **Latin America Transparencies** **L2** Section Reading Support Transparency LA 45	**All in One Latin America Teaching Resources** **L3** Enrichment, p. 335 AR, GT **L1** Outline Map 8: South America, p. 343 AR, GT, LPR, SN **Western Hemisphere Teacher's Edition** **L1** For Less Proficient Readers, TE p. 489 **L1** For English Language Learners, TE p. 489, 496 **L3** For Gifted and Talented Students, TE p. 492, 496 **L3** For Advanced Readers, TE p. 490, 497 **L1** For Special Needs Students, TE p. 497

Assess and Reteach	**Instructional Resources**	**Differentiated Instruction**
Assess Progress Evaluate student comprehension with the section assessment and section quiz. **Reteach** Assign the Reading and Vocabulary Study Guide to help struggling students. **Extend** Extend the lesson by assigning a Small Group Activity.	**All in One Latin America Teaching Resources** **L2** Section Quiz, p. 318 **L3** Small Group Activity: Making a Mural, pp. 337–340 Rubric for Assessing a Writing Assignment, p. 349 **Reading and Vocabulary Study Guide** **L1** Chapter 16, Section 1, pp. 178–180	**All in One Latin America Teaching Resources** Rubric for Assessing a Bar Graph, p. 348 AR, GT, ELL **Spanish Support** **L2** Section Quiz (Spanish), p. 167 ELL

Key

L1 Basic to Average	**L3** Average to Advanced	**LPR** Less Proficient Readers	**GT** Gifted and Talented
L2 For All Students		**AR** Advanced Readers	**ELL** English Language Learners
		SN Special Needs Students	

486c

Section 2 Peru: An Ancient Land Looks to the Future

 *1.5 periods, .75 block*

Social Studies Objectives
1. Learn how geography has affected the way people live in the three regions of Peru.
2. Discover what life is like in the cities and towns of the altiplano.

Reading/Language Arts Objective
Contrast two regions to find out how they are different.

Prepare to Read	**Instructional Resources**	**Differentiated Instruction**
Build Background Knowledge Show a video to help students brainstorm about life in Peru. **Set a Purpose for Reading** Have students evaluate statements on the *Reading Readiness Guide*. **Preview Key Terms** Teach the section's Key Terms. **Target Reading Skill** Introduce the section's Target Reading Skill of **identifying contrasts**.	**All in One Latin America Teaching Resources** L2 Reading Readiness Guide, p. 320 L2 Identify Contrasts, p. 332	**Spanish Reading and Vocabulary Study Guide** L2 Chapter 16, Section 2, pp. 131–132 ELL

Instruct	**Instructional Resources**	**Differentiated Instruction**
Country Profile Ask students to derive information from maps, charts, and graphs. **The Regions and People of Peru** Discuss why the people of Peru live where they do. **Life in the Altiplano** Discuss how the altiplano reflects the past. **Target Reading Skill** Review **identifying contrasts**.	**All in One Latin America Teaching Resources** L2 Guided Reading and Review, p. 321 L2 Reading Readiness Guide, p. 320 L2 Reading a Table, p. 342 **Latin America Transparencies** L2 Section Reading Support Transparency LA 46	**All in One Latin America Teaching Resources** L3 A Women's Prison in London, pp. 344–345 GT, AR **Western Hemisphere Teacher's Edition** L3 For Gifted and Talented Students, TE p. 503 L1 For Less Proficient Readers, TE p. 504 L3 For Advanced Readers, TE p. 504 **Spanish Support** L2 Guided Reading and Review (Spanish), p. 168 ELL

Assess and Reteach	**Instructional Resources**	**Differentiated Instruction**
Assess Progress Evaluate student comprehension with the section assessment and section quiz. **Reteach** Assign the Reading and Vocabulary Study Guide to help struggling students. **Extend** Extend the lesson by showing a Discovery Channel School Video.	**All in One Latin America Teaching Resources** L2 Section Quiz, p. 322 Rubric for Assessing a Writing Assignment, p. 349 **Reading and Vocabulary Study Guide** L1 Chapter 16, Section 2, pp. 181–183	**Spanish Support** L2 Section Quiz (Spanish), p. 169 ELL

Key

L1 Basic to Average	L3 Average to Advanced	LPR Less Proficient Readers AR Advanced Readers SN Special Needs Students	GT Gifted and Talented ELL English Language Learners

Section 3 Chile: Land of Contrasts

 3 periods, 1.5 blocks (includes Skills for Life)

Social Studies Objectives

1. Find out how the geography of Chile creates regions where people live very differently.
2. Learn how Chile's people live and what products they produce.
3. Find out how Chile restored democracy.

Reading/Language Arts Objective

Compare and contrast things to analyze and sort out information.

Prepare to Read

Build Background Knowledge
Discuss with students how geography has influenced the cultures of Chile.

Set a Purpose for Reading
Have students evaluate statements on the *Reading Readiness Guide*.

Preview Key Terms
Teach the section's Key Terms.

Target Reading Skill
Introduce the section's Target Reading Skill of **comparing and contrasting**.

Instructional Resources

All in One Latin America Teaching Resources

- L2 Reading Readiness Guide, p. 324
- L2 Compare and Contrast, p. 331

Differentiated Instruction

Spanish Reading and Vocabulary Study Guide

- L2 Chapter 16, Section 3, pp. 133–134 ELL

Instruct

Country Profile
Ask students to derive information from maps, charts, and graphs.

Target Reading Skill
Review **comparing and contrasting**.

The Geography of Chile
Discuss the differences between Chile's regions.

Chile's People and Products
Have students describe how Chile's natural resources affect its economy.

Restoring Democracy
Discuss Chile's political struggles.

Instructional Resources

All in One Latin America Teaching Resources

- L2 Guided Reading and Review, p. 325
- L2 Reading Readiness Guide, p. 324

Latin America Transparencies

- L2 Section Reading Support Transparency LA 47

All in One Latin America Teaching Resources

- L2 Skills for Life, p. 336 AR, GT, LPR, SN

Differentiated Instruction

Western Hemisphere Teacher's Edition

- L3 For Advanced Readers, TE p. 509, 511
- L1 For Less Proficient Readers, TE p. 510
- L1 For Special Needs Students, TE p. 510
- L1 For English Language Learners, TE p. 511

PHSchool.com

- L3 **For**: Environmental and Global Issues: *Trade in a Global Economy*
Web code: lfd-1606 AR, GT

Student Edition on Audio CD

- L1 Chapter 16, Section 3 SN, LPR, ELL

Assess and Reteach

Assess Progress
Evaluate student comprehension with the section assessment and section quiz.

Reteach
Assign the Reading and Vocabulary Study Guide to help struggling students.

Extend
Extend the lesson by assigning an online activity.

Instructional Resources

All in One Latin America Teaching Resources

- L2 Section Quiz, p. 326
  Rubric for Assessing a Journal Entry, p. 350

Reading and Vocabulary Study Guide

- L1 Chapter 16, Section 3, pp. 184–186

PHSchool.com

- L3 **For**: Environmental and Global Issues: *Analysis of Human Rights Violations*
Web code: lfd-1607

Differentiated Instruction

Latin America Transparencies

- L2 Color Transparency LA 9: The World: Annual Precipitation AR, GT, LPR, SN

Spanish Support

- L2 Section Quiz (Spanish), p. 171 ELL

Social Studies Skills Tutor CD-ROM

- L1 Synthesizing Information SN, LPR, ELL

Key

- L1 Basic to Average
- L2 For All Students
- L3 Average to Advanced
- LPR Less Proficient Readers
- AR Advanced Readers
- SN Special Needs Students
- GT Gifted and Talented
- ELL English Language Learners

Section 4 Venezuela: Oil Powers the Economy

3 periods, 1.75 blocks (includes Chapter Review and Assessment)

Social Studies Objectives
1. Find out how Venezuela was made wealthy by oil.
2. Learn how the ups and downs of oil prices affected the economy and people of Venezuela.
3. Understand how Venezuela is changing.

Reading/Language Arts Objective
Make comparisons to find out how two things are alike.

Prepare to Read

Build Background Knowledge
Discuss the economy of Venezuela.

Set a Purpose for Reading
Have students evaluate statements on the *Reading Readiness Guide.*

Preview Key Terms
Teach the section's Key Terms.

Target Reading Skill
Introduce the section's Target Reading Skill of **making comparisons**.

Instructional Resources

All in One Latin America Teaching Resources

- L2 Reading Readiness Guide, p. 328
- L2 Make Comparisons, p. 333

Differentiated Instruction

Spanish Reading and Vocabulary Study Guide

- L2 Chapter 16, Section 4, pp. 135–136 ELL

Instruct

A Land Made Wealthy by Oil
Ask questions about how oil has affected Venezuela's economy.

Country Profile
Ask students to derive information from maps, charts, and graphs.

Target Reading Skill
Review **making comparisons**.

The Economy and the People
Ask questions about how oil has affected the people of Venezuela.

A Change in Government
Discuss Venezuela's changes under Hugo Chavez.

Instructional Resources

All in One Latin America Teaching Resources

- L2 Guided Reading and Review, p. 329
- L2 Reading Readiness Guide, p. 328

Latin American Transparencies

- L2 Section Reading Support Transparency LA 48

Differentiated Instruction

All in One Latin America Teaching Resources

Rubric for Assessing a Timeline, p. 351 LPR, SN, ELL

Western Hemisphere Teacher's Edition

- L1 For Less Proficient Readers, TE p. 519, 521
- L1 For Special Needs Students, TE p. 519, 521
- L2 For English Language Learners, TE p. 520

Reading and Vocabulary Study Guide

- L1 Chapter 16, Section 4, pp. 187–189 SN, ELL, LPR

Assess and Reteach

Assess Progress
Evaluate student comprehension with the section assessment and section quiz.

Reteach
Assign the Reading and Vocabulary Study Guide to help struggling students.

Extend
Extend the lesson by assigning a writing activity.

Instructional Resources

All in One Latin America Teaching Resources

- L2 Section Quiz, p. 330
- L3 Writing to Persuade, p. 346
  Rubric for Assessing a Writing Assignment, p. 349
- L2 Vocabulary Development, p. 347
- L2 Word Knowledge Rating Form, p. 334
  Rubric for Assessing a Report, p. 352
- L2 Chapter Tests A and B, pp. 353–358

Differentiated Instruction

Spanish Support

- L2 Section Quiz (Spanish), p. 173 ELL
- L2 Chapter Summary (Spanish), p. 174 ELL
- L2 Vocabulary Development (Spanish), p. 175 ELL

Key

L1 Basic to Average	L3 Average to Advanced	LPR Less Proficient Readers	GT Gifted and Talented
L2 For All Students		AR Advanced Readers	ELL English Language Learners
		SN Special Needs Students	

Reading Background

Numbered Heads Strategy

In this chapter, students will use the Numbered Heads engagement strategy to come up with and share their responses to questions. Numbered Heads allows students to become more confident of their individual responses by sharing them with a smaller group before facing the whole class. Because students are then called on at random to speak for the group, they alternate opportunities to take on a leadership role, and all students are responsible for paying attention to the team's ideas.

Remind students that it is a good idea to compare and contrast their responses with those of other teams. Below are sample language strategies to help students achieve this goal.

> Our answer was (similar to/different from) that of team _____ because _____.
>
> We agree with team _____ that...
>
> As team _____ already pointed out, it seems like...
>
> Team _____ already mentioned..., but I would like to add that...

Evaluating similarities and differences between the teams' responses is also a good way to practice this chapter's Target Reading Skill of comparing and contrasting.

Author's Craft

Encourage students to notice not only the *what* of the reading, but the *how*. That is, ask them to pay special attention to how the author presents information. Explain that by exploring the structure of the reading, they can better analyze and remember the information presented. As an example, present the following paragraph from page 517 of the Student Edition:

> During the 1970s, the price of oil went up. An oil boom began. The standard of living of many Venezuelans went up, too. That is when the government started spending huge sums of money. Many people were hired to run government-owned businesses. The government built expensive subways and high-quality roads. Then the government began to borrow money so that it could spend even more.

Guide students toward recognizing a framework for these sentences by asking questions. *Did the author use dates or present a chronological sequence? Is the author comparing one thing to another? Can you see a cause and effect relationship?* Students should recognize a chronological sequence. One clue is the fact that the author begins by setting up a time frame: *During the 1970s....* Other clues are the use of the words *That is when* and *Then*. These are all phrases that have to do with time.

Have students work individually or in pairs as they reread sections of the chapter. As they read, have them identify different techniques the author used by asking the same kinds of questions

World Studies Background

Fighting for the Brazilian Rain Forest

Tensions over how best to use the Brazilian rain forest have sometimes led to violence. Francisco "Chico" Mendes lived his entire life in the forest, and made his living by collecting rubber from rubber trees. He led the Rural Workers Union, a group whose purpose was to stop ranchers and other people from cutting down trees. In December 1988, Mendes was shot and killed by a rancher with whom Mendes had previously argued. The rancher had hoped to clear a road to his property, and the Rural Workers Union had protested. Brazil continues to work to find a balance between the need to use the forest's resources to support the nation's economy and maintaining the forest and the way of life of its indigenous peoples.

The Quechua Language

It is estimated that about 10 million people in South America speak the Quechua language—more than any other native language on the continent. So many Peruvians speak Quechua that in 1975, the government made Quechua and Spanish both official languages of the country. Quechua spread across the continent as a trade language before the early 1400s, when the Inca adopted it. When the Spanish colonists arrived, they integrated some Quechua words into their own speech. Variations on some of those words have entered into the English we speak today, such as *condor* (a type of bird), *puma* (cougar), and *jerky* (dried meat.)

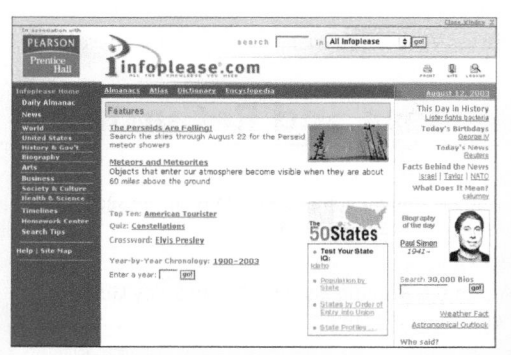

Infoplease® provides a wealth of useful information for the classroom. You can use this resource to strengthen your background on the subjects covered in this chapter. Have students visit this advertising-free site as a starting point for projects requiring research.

Use Web Code lfd-1600 for **Infoplease**.

of themselves. When students have finished taking notes, have the class discuss what techniques they have found.

Questions and Answers

Encourage students to be aware of the fact that there are many different kinds of questions. Questions that require you to:

1. remember a specific fact from the reading

2. synthesize or analyze information from different places in the reading

3. think beyond the reading to make an inference or assumption

4. find the answer somewhere completely outside of the reading

Model this concept by listing the following questions on the board and asking students to state what type of question each is, and where the answer could be found in relation to this chapter.

■ What is the largest country in South America?

(Specific fact; Brazil: page 495)

■ What are some threats to the Brazilian rain forest?

(Synthesize or analyze; Cutting down timber, smuggling, and pollution: page 497)

■ Why might Daniel Monteiro Costa want to be called Daniel Munduruku?

(Inference or assumption; To raise people's awareness about the culture and heritage of Munduruku Indians: inference from information on page 499)

■ How has Brazil recently been featured in the news?

(Outside the reading; could be answered by looking at recent newspapers and magazines)

After discussing these examples, have students work in teams to develop one question of each type based on the information in each chapter. Challenge students to trade their finished questions with another group and try to identify each type of question and how to answer it.

The Chilean Government

After the 1988 election in which the people of Chile voted to end the reign of military leader Augusto Pinochet, the government was returned to a democratic structure set out in a constitution of 1981. Like the United States, the government of Chile has an executive, legislative, and judicial branch. The president is elected for a four-year term, the National Congress has two houses, and a 17-member Supreme Court presides over the judicial system. Although political parties were outlawed under Pinochet, they were brought back in 1987 and now are an integral part of the democratic process.

Tourism in Venezuela

Although a distant second to the oil industry, on which Venezuela's economy heavily relies, tourism is the next-most profitable industry in the country. Just as is true of oil prices, income from tourism is vulnerable to change. Because of recent political turmoil in Venezuela, tourism—along with the rest of the nation's economy—has suffered, dropping almost 10 percent between 1995 and 2000.

One possible way to expand tourism in Venezuela would be to promote ecotourism, or environmental and adventure trips that promote sensitivity for local people and environments.

Chapter **16** South America

Guiding Questions

Remind students about the Guiding Questions introduced at the beginning of this section.

Section 1 relates to **Guiding Question** **What are the main physical features of Latin America?** *(The Amazon rain forest takes up more than one third of Brazil.)*

Section 2 relates to **Guiding Question** ❷ **How has Latin America been shaped by its history?** *(Many Quechuas, Uros, and other Native Americans living in Peru follow traditions that are hundreds of years old. The ruins of Incan cities still stand in parts of Peru.)*

Section 3 relates to **Guiding Question** ❸ **What factors have affected cultures in Latin America?** *(Chile's geography creates three regions in which people have very different cultures.)*

Section 4 relates to **Guiding Question** ❺ **How has geography influenced the ways in which Latin Americans make a living?** *(Venezuela's land is rich with oil. Many Venezuelans make a living in the oil industry.)*

⤺ Target Reading Skill

In this chapter, students will learn and apply the reading skill of comparison and contrast. Use the following worksheets to help students practice this skill.

All in One **Latin America Teaching Resources,** *Compare and Contrast,* p. 331; *Identify Contrasts,* p. 332; *Make Comparisons,* p. 333

Differentiated Instruction

The following Teacher Edition strategies are suitable for students of varying abilities.

Advanced Readers, pp. 490, 497, 504, 509, 511
English Language Learners, pp. 489, 496, 511, 520
Gifted and Talented, pp. 492, 496, 503, 515
Less Proficient Readers, pp. 489, 504, 510, 519, 521
Special Needs Students, pp. 497, 510, 513, 519, 521

Chapter Preview

This chapter will introduce you to the countries of the continent of South America.

Country Databank
The Country Databank provides data and descriptions of each of the countries in the region: Argentina, Bolivia, Brazil, Chile, Colombia, Ecuador, Guyana, Paraguay, Peru, Suriname, Uruguay, and Venezuela.

Section 1
Brazil
Geography Shapes a Nation

Section 2
Peru
An Ancient Land Looks to the Future

Section 3
Chile
Land of Contrasts

Section 4
Venezuela
Oil Powers the Economy

⤺ **Target Reading Skill**

Comparison and Contrast In this chapter you will focus on using comparison and contrast to help you sort out and analyze information.

▶ A plaza in Rio de Janeiro, Brazil

486 Latin America

Bibliography

For the Teacher
Allende, Isabel and Margaret Sayers Peden. *My Invented Country: A Nostalgic Journey Through Chile.* HarperCollins Publishers, 2003.
Bishop, Nathaniel H. *The Pampas and Andes: A Thousand Miles Walk Across South America.* The Narrative Press, 2003.

For the Student
L1 Goodman, Susan E. *Adventures in the Amazon Rain Forest (Ultimate Field Trip 1).* Bt Bound, 1999.
L1 Handau, Elaine. *Peru (True Book).* Children's Book Press, 2000.
L2 Black, Carolyn and Malika Hollander. *Brazil: The Land.* Crabtree Publishing, 2003.

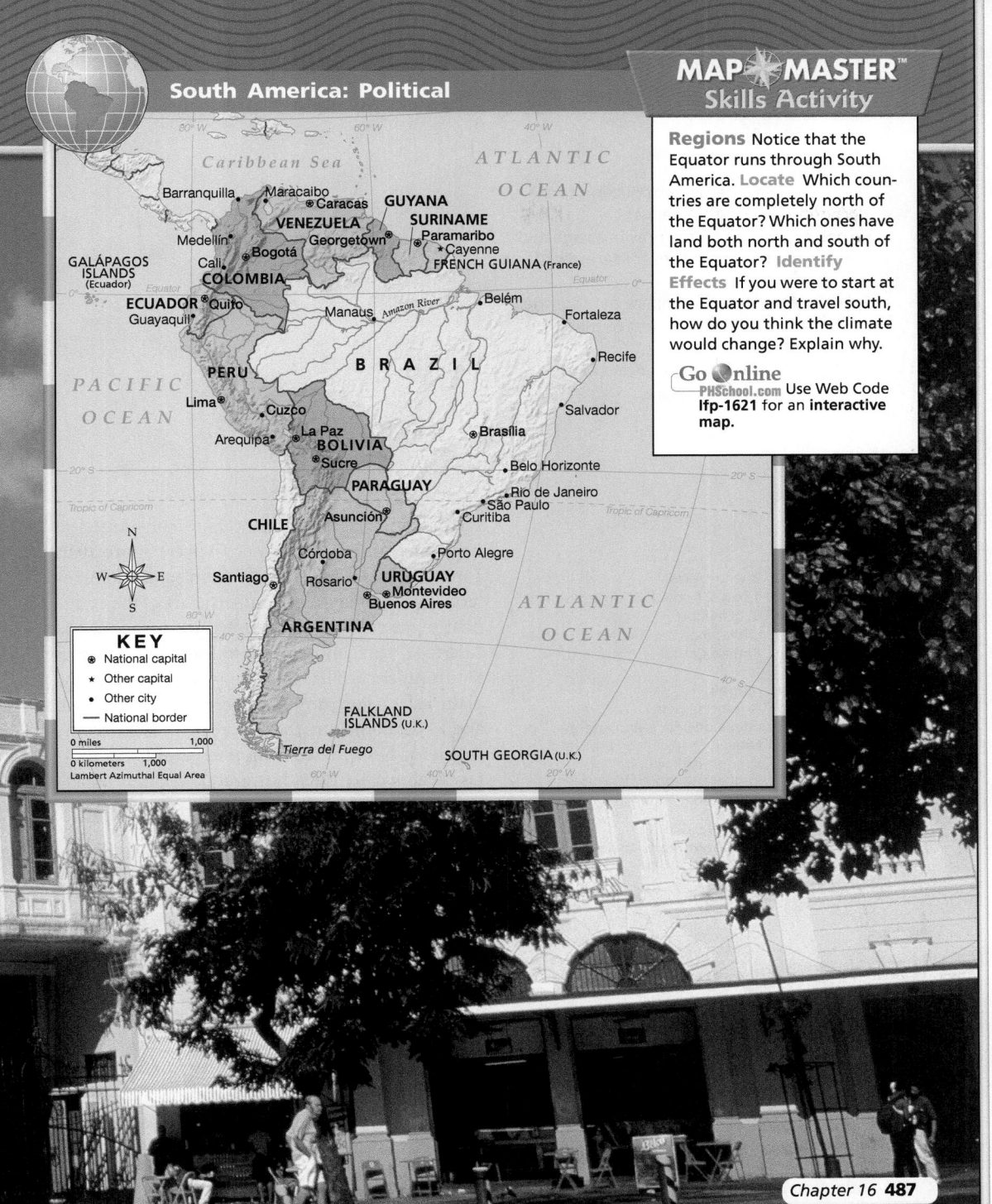

South America: Political

MAP MASTER™
Skills Activity

Regions Notice that the Equator runs through South America. **Locate** Which countries are completely north of the Equator? Which ones have land both north and south of the Equator? **Identify Effects** If you were to start at the Equator and travel south, how do you think the climate would change? Explain why.

Go Online
PHSchool.com Use Web Code **lfp-1621** for an **interactive map.**

Caribbean Sea

ATLANTIC OCEAN

Barranquilla • Maracaibo • Caracas
GUYANA
VENEZUELA SURINAME
Medellín • Georgetown • Paramaribo
GALÁPAGOS ISLANDS (Ecuador) Cali • Bogotá • Cayenne
COLOMBIA FRENCH GUIANA (France)
Equator
ECUADOR • Quito • Belém
Guayaquil Manaus *Amazon River*
Fortaleza
PACIFIC OCEAN
PERU B R A Z I L
Lima • Recife
• Cuzco
Arequipa • La Paz • Salvador
BOLIVIA • Brasília
• Sucre
PARAGUAY • Belo Horizonte
• Rio de Janeiro
CHILE Asunción • São Paulo
Curitiba
Córdoba • Porto Alegre
Santiago • Rosario URUGUAY
ARGENTINA • Montevideo
Buenos Aires
ATLANTIC OCEAN
Tropic of Capricorn

KEY
⊛ National capital
★ Other capital
• Other city
— National border

0 miles 1,000
0 kilometers 1,000
Lambert Azimuthal Equal Area

FALKLAND ISLANDS (U.K.)
Tierra del Fuego SOUTH GEORGIA (U.K.)

N W E S

MAP MASTER™
Skills Activity

- Have students locate the mountain chain in the western part of the continent. Point out that these are the Andes Mountains. Ask students **How do you think the Andes Mountains may have affected political boundaries in South America?** (*Some political boundaries seem to have been drawn along the mountains. For example, the mountains separate Argentina and Chile.*) **L3**

Go Online
PHSchool.com Students may practice their map skills using the interactive online version of this map.

Using the Visual **L2**

Reach Into Your Background Draw students' attention to the photograph (pp. 486–487) and its caption (p. 487). Discuss the visual. What interests students about this photograph? Is the scene something they would or would not expect to find in Rio de Janeiro, Brazil? Ask students to observe details in the photograph and share them with the class. Ask them to reach into their own background: have they ever seen buildings similar to those shown in the photograph? If so, where? Encourage students to discuss ideas.

Answers

MAP MASTER™
Skills Activity

Locate Venezuela, Guyana, Suriname, French Guiana; Ecuador, Colombia, Brazil
Identify Effects The climate would get cooler the farther south you traveled from the Equator.

Chapter Resources

Teaching Resources
- **L2** Vocabulary Development, p. 347
- **L2** Skills for Life, p. 336
- **L2** Chapter Tests A and B, pp. 353–358

Spanish Support
- **L2** Spanish Chapter Summary, p. 174
- **L2** Spanish Vocabulary Development, p. 175

Media and Technology
- **L1** Student Edition on Audio CD
- **L1** Guided Reading Audiotapes, English and Spanish
- **L2** Social Studies Skills Tutor CD-ROM
  ExamView Test Bank CD-ROM

PRENTICE HALL
Presentation EXPRESS™
Teach · Connect · Inspire

Teach this chapter's content using the PresentationExpress™ CD-ROM including:
- slide shows
- transparencies
- interactive maps and media
- *ExamView®* QuickTake Presenter

Objectives

■ Use data to compare countries.

■ Learn what characteristics South American countries share.

■ Identify some key differences among the countries.

Prepare to Read

Build Background Knowledge `L2`

Invite students to share what they know about South America and what they learned about the continent's geography from watching the World Studies Video Overview. Write the following headings on the chalkboard: *Climate, Vegetation, Population, Natural Resources*. Conduct an Idea Wave (TE, p. T35) to generate a list of what students learned or know about each topic. Write their responses under the appropriate heading on the board.

Guide for Reading

This section provides an introduction to the 12 countries of South America.

• Look at the map on the previous page and then read the paragraphs to learn about each nation.

• Analyze the data to compare the countries.

• What characteristics do most of these countries share?

• What are some key differences among the countries?

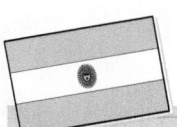

Argentina

Capital	Buenos Aires
Land Area	1,056,636 sq mi; 2,736,690 sq km
Population	37.8 million
Ethnic Group(s)	white, mestizo, indigenous Indian
Religion(s)	Roman Catholic, Protestant, Jewish
Government	republic
Currency	Argentine peso
Leading Exports	edible oils, fuels and energy, cereals, feed, motor vehicles
Language(s)	Spanish (official), Italian, indigenous Indian languages

The second-largest country in South America, Argentina (ahr jun TEE nuh) covers more than 1 million square miles (2.7 million square kilometers). It is located in the southern part of the continent, between the Andes Mountains and the Atlantic Ocean, and extends to the southern tip of South America. The Andes slope down to a fertile plain called the pampas, where raising livestock and wheat dominates the culture and the economy. Argentina has suffered from a series of harsh military regimes. In 1983, however, the nation established a democratic government.

Albatross chicks, Diego Ramirez Islands, Chile

488 Latin America

Bolivia

Capitals	La Paz and Sucre
Land Area	418,683 sq mi; 1,084,390 sq km
Population	8.5 million
Ethnic Group(s)	Quechua, mestizo, Aymara, white
Religion(s)	Roman Catholic, Protestant
Government	republic
Currency	boliviano
Leading Exports	soybeans, natural gas, zinc, gold, wood
Language(s)	Spanish (official), Quechua (official), Aymara (official)

Bolivia (buh LIV ee uh) is a landlocked country in central South America. Much of its population lives in the Altiplano, or high plateau region, which Bolivia shares with Peru. This plain lies between two ranges of the Andes Mountains. Mountains and rain forests isolate the Altiplano from the sea and from the rest of South America. Although Bolivia has rich mineral resources, mining is difficult at high altitudes. It is also difficult to transport the minerals to market. So, in spite of its resources, Bolivia has remained poor. More than half of Bolivians are indigenous people.

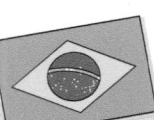

Brazil

Capital	Brasília
Land Area	3,265,059 sq mi; 8,456,510 sq km
Population	176 million
Ethnic Group(s)	white, mixed white and black, black, Asian, Arab, indigenous Indian
Religion(s)	Roman Catholic
Government	federal republic
Currency	real
Leading Exports	manufactured goods, iron ore, soybeans, footwear, coffee, autos
Language(s)	Portuguese (official), German, Italian, Spanish, Polish, Japanese, indigenous Indian languages

Brazil (bruh ZIL) is the largest country in South America. It occupies the eastern-central region of the continent, bordering the Atlantic Ocean. Brazil is known as the home of the huge Amazon rain forest and for its vibrant culture. The influence of its Portuguese colonial past can still be seen in Brazil's language, culture, and architecture. However, other groups have also made contributions to a distinctive Brazilian culture. These groups include the native Indians, Africans originally brought to Brazil as slaves, and immigrants from northern Europe and Japan.

Chile

Capital	Santiago
Land Area	289,112 sq mi; 748,800 sq km
Population	15.5 million
Ethnic Group(s)	white, mestizo, indigenous Indian
Religion(s)	Roman Catholic, Protestant
Government	republic
Currency	Chilean peso
Leading Exports	copper, fish, fruits, paper and pulp, chemicals
Language(s)	Spanish (official), indigenous Indian languages

Chile (CHIL ee) is a long, narrow country. It lies along the western coast of South America, from its northern border with Peru to the southern tip of the continent. Chile has varied landforms and climates, from deserts in the north and central fertile plains, to its rainy, stormy southern tip. Mountains, lakes, and glaciers complete the picture. Most Chileans live in the fertile valley of central Chile. About one third of Chile's people live in the vibrant capital of Santiago.

Chapter 16 **489**

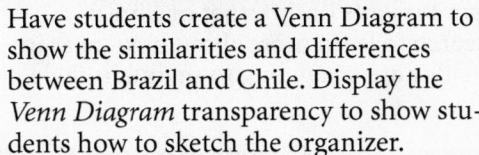
Instruct

Introducing South America L2

Guided Instruction
- Read each country paragraph as a class using the Structured Silent Reading technique (TE, p. T34). Then, ask students to read through each data table.
- Ask students **What groups have contributed to Brazil's culture?** *(Portuguese, native Indians, Africans, northern Europeans, and Asians)*
- Have students identify the similarities between Argentina and Bolivia. Remind them to use both the paragraphs and the data beside them. *(Similarities: Spanish as their official language, whites and mestizos as major ethnic groups, Roman Catholicism and Protestantism as major religions, and located near the Andes Mountains)*
- Ask students **How is Chile's long seacoast reflected in its economy?** *(The data shows that ocean resources are important to Chile's economy—fish is one of Chile's leading exports.)*

- Ask **Where is Colombia located? Why do you think its location would be important to its economy?** *(Colombia is located at the intersection of Central and South America. People and goods traveling by land between Central America and South America must pass through Colombia. Colombia's economy can benefit from the traffic of tourists and trade.)*

- Ask students **What leading exports do Colombia and Ecuador have in common?** *(petroleum and coffee)* Have students look at the map on p. 487. Discuss why the two countries might both produce and export these products. *(Ecuador and Colombia are located next to each other, therefore the resources found in the ground such as petroleum are similar. They are both located on the Equator so they both a have a warm, wet climate that is good for growing coffee beans.)*

Introducing **South America**

Colombia

Capital	Bogotá
Land Area	401,042 sq mi; 1,038,700 sq km
Population	41 million
Ethnic Group(s)	mestizo, white, mixed white and black, mixed black and indigenous Indian, indigenous Indian
Religion(s)	Roman Catholic
Government	republic
Currency	Colombian peso
Leading Exports	petroleum, coffee, coal, apparel, bananas, cut flowers
Language(s)	Spanish (official), indigenous Indian languages

Located on the northwest corner of South America, Colombia (kuh LUM bee uh) has coastlines on both the Pacific Ocean and the Caribbean Sea. To the northwest, it is bordered by Panama, which was once part of its territory. Colombia is located at the intersection of Central and South America and near the Panama Canal. This location makes it important to transportation and communication between the regions. Three ranges of the Andes Mountains divide the country. Most of Colombia's people live in the central valley or the hot, wet western region.

Ecuador

Capital	Quito
Land Area	106,888 sq mi; 276,840 sq km
Population	13.5 million
Ethnic Group(s)	mestizo, indigenous Indian, white, black
Religion(s)	Roman Catholic
Government	republic
Currency	U.S. dollar
Leading Exports	petroleum, bananas, shrimp, coffee, cocoa, cut flowers, fish
Language(s)	Spanish (official), Quechua, other indigenous Indian languages

Once part of the Incan empire, Ecuador (EK wuh dawr) was colonized by Spain in 1533 and became independent in 1830. A small country on the Pacific Coast, Ecuador has three regions. The lowland coastal region is the industrial center as well as the farm belt of Ecuador. Subsistence farming is the main economic activity in the highlands of the Andes Mountains. This is the region where the descendants of the Incas live and struggle to maintain their languages and traditional ways of life. The inland region benefits from large deposits of oil.

Giant tortoise, Ecuador

490 Latin America

Differentiated Instruction

For Advanced Readers [L3]
Have students do Internet or library research to learn more about how Incas in Ecuador are struggling to maintain their traditional ways of life. What are their traditional ways of life? What is threatening them? Have students write a short essay summarizing their findings.

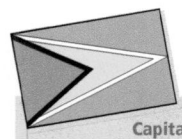

Guyana

Capital	Georgetown
Land Area	76,004 sq mi; 196,850 sq km
Population	698,209
Ethnic Group(s)	South Asian, black, indigenous Indian, white, East Asian, mixed white and black
Religion(s)	Christian, Hindu, Muslim
Government	republic
Currency	Guyanese dollar
Leading Exports	sugar, gold, bauxite/alumina, rice, shrimp, molasses, rum, timber
Language(s)	English (official), English Creole, Hindi, Tamil, indigenous Indian languages

Guyana (gy AN uh) lies on the northeast coast of South America. It is similar to its Caribbean island neighbors. Guyana was originally colonized by the Dutch, who imported enslaved Africans to work on their plantations. It became a British colony in 1814. After slavery ended in 1838, the British brought workers from India to do farm work. The descendants of these Africans and Indians form the largest ethnic groups in Guyana today. Most of the population lives on the narrow, wet coastal plain. The interior of the country is covered with dense rain forests.

Paraguay

Capital	Asunción
Land Area	153,398 sq mi; 397,300 sq km
Population	5.9 million
Ethnic Group(s)	mestizo
Religion(s)	Roman Catholic, Protestant
Government	constitutional republic
Currency	guaraní
Leading Exports	soybeans, feed, cotton, meat, edible oils, electricity
Language(s)	Spanish (official), Guaraní (official)

A small landlocked country, Paraguay (PA ruh gway) is bordered by Brazil, Argentina, and Bolivia. The Paraguay River divides the country into two sections. Much of the population is clustered in the fertile plains and hills of the eastern region. The west is sparsely populated. Most of the people of Paraguay are descended from the Spanish and the Guaraní, an indigenous group. In the cities, both Spanish and Guaraní are spoken, but in the countryside most people speak Guaraní.

Peru

Capital	Lima
Land Area	494,208 sq mi; 1,280,000 sq km
Population	28 million
Ethnic Group(s)	indigenous Indian, mestizo, white, black, East Asian
Religion(s)	Roman Catholic
Government	constitutional republic
Currency	nuevo sol
Leading Exports	fish and fish products, gold, copper, zinc, crude petroleum and byproducts, lead, coffee, sugar, cotton
Language(s)	Spanish (official), Quechua (official), Aymara

Peru (puh ROO) lies along the Pacific coast of South America, south of Colombia and Ecuador, and north of Chile. The Andes Mountains run the length of the country. A high plateau called the Altiplano is home to descendants of the Incas and other indigenous groups. Many of them live much as their ancestors did and speak Indian languages. The economic center of Peru is Lima, on the coast. Peru has been slow to modernize and industrialize. It has also suffered from military dictatorships and government corruption, but today it has an elected democratic government.

Chapter 16 **491**

Independent Practice

■ Distribute the outline map of South America.

 Latin America Teaching Resources, *Outline Map 8: South America,* p. 343

■ Have students create a map that shows the types of government of all of the South American countries. Tell students to choose a color to represent each government that will be displayed on the map. They should explain what each color represents in the map key. Then have students fill in each country with the color that corresponds to its type of government and have them locate and name the country's capital on the map.

■ Tell students to give the map an appropriate title.

Monitor Progress

■ Circulate to be sure students are making the map key, coloring in the countries, and locating the capitals correctly and that they have chosen an appropriate map title.

Assess and Reteach

Assess Progress   L2

Direct students attention back to the lists on the chalkboard. Encourage them to suggest more information to fill in under each topic based on what they learned from the Country Databank.

Introducing South America

Suriname

Capital	Paramaribo
Land Area	62,344 sq mi; 161,470 sq km
Population	436,494
Ethnic Group(s)	South Asian, Creole, Javanese, Maroon, indigenous Indian, East Asian, white
Religion(s)	Christian, Hindu, Muslim, traditional beliefs
Government	constitutional democracy
Currency	Suriname guilder or florin
Leading Exports	alumina, crude oil, lumber, shrimp and fish, rice, bananas
Language(s)	Dutch (official), Sranan, Javanese, Sarnami Hindi, Saramaccan, Chinese, Carib

Suriname (soor ih NAHM) is a small country on the northern coast of South America. Mountains and rain forest dominate its geography. Most of the people live on a narrow coastal plain. Suriname was settled by the Dutch, who imported enslaved Africans to work their coffee and sugar cane plantations. After slavery ended, workers from India, Java, and China were brought to work in the fields. The result is an ethnically mixed population. Suriname became independent in 1975. A series of military regimes followed, but democratic rule was established in 1987.

A gaucho in Uruguay

Uruguay

Capital	Montevideo
Land Area	67,108 sq mi; 173,620 sq km
Population	3.4 million
Ethnic Group(s)	white, mestizo, black
Religion(s)	Roman Catholic, Protestant, Jewish
Government	constitutional republic
Currency	Uruguayan peso
Leading Exports	meat, rice, leather products, wool, vehicles, dairy products
Language(s)	Spanish (official)

Uruguay (YOOR uh gway) is a small country located between two large ones: Brazil to the north and Argentina to the west. The capital, Montevideo, is situated where the River Platte empties into the Atlantic Ocean, making the city an important port for international trade. Most of Uruguay is made up of grassy plains and low hills. Raising cattle and sheep are the main occupations of that region. Tourism has become important along the country's sandy coastal beaches. Banking and other service industries also contribute to the economy.

492 Latin America

Differentiated Instruction

For Gifted and Talented   L3

To learn more about the coat of arms of the countries of Bolivia, Brazil, and Peru, have students complete the *Enrichment* worksheet in the Latin America Teaching Resources.

 Latin America Teaching Resources, *Enrichment,* p. 335

Venezuela

Capital	Caracas
Land Area	340,560 sq mi; 882,050 sq km
Population	24.3 million
Ethnic Group(s)	white, Southwest Asian, black, indigenous Indian
Religion(s)	Roman Catholic, Protestant
Government	federal republic
Currency	bolívar
Leading Exports	petroleum, bauxite and aluminum, steel, chemicals, agricultural products, basic manufactured goods
Language(s)	Spanish (official), indigenous Indian languages

SOURCES: DK World Desk Reference Online; *CIA World Factbook*, 2002 and 2006; *World Almanac*, 2003

Venezuela (ven uh ZWAY luh) is located on the northern coast of South America, along the Caribbean Sea. The government has encouraged both agriculture and industry in an effort to diversify the economy. However, Venezuela still depends largely on its huge deposits of oil. Most of Venezuela's people live in cities, primarily in the northern part of the country. Some of the country's indigenous population lives in isolated areas of rain forest. Once a Spanish colony, Venezuela freed itself from Spain in 1821 and then became part of Gran Colombia. Venezuela became an independent republic in 1830.

Caraballeda, Venezuela

Assessment

Comprehension and Critical Thinking

1. Compare and Contrast Which is the largest country in South America? Which is the smallest? What do these two countries have in common, in spite of their difference in size?

2. Categorize What characteristics do the countries south of the Equator share?

3. Contrast How have such contrasting geographic features as rolling, grassy plains and high altitudes affected the cultures and economies of the countries in which they are found?

4. Draw Conclusions Which countries have the most diverse populations? Explain how you reached that conclusion.

5. Make a Bar Graph Create a population graph of the five most populous countries of South America.

Keeping Current

Access the **DK World Desk Reference Online** at **PHSchool.com** for up-to-date information about all the countries in this chapter.

Go Online
PHSchool.com

Web Code: lfe-1433

Chapter 16 **493**

Reteach L2

Ask students to create a table on a large piece of poster board that shows the data for all of the countries in the Country Databank. Have them list the categories across the top of the table and the names of the countries along the side. Model filling in the information for one country on the chalkboard.

Extend L2

Portfolio Activity

Have students choose two countries in the Country Databank. Ask them to do library or Internet research to learn more about each country. Then have them write a short essay or create a table to explain the differences and similarities between the two countries. Have students add their work to their portfolios.

Answers

Assessment

1. Brazil is the largest country and Suriname is the smallest country. Both have rain forests and a diverse population.

2. They all have a form of republican government, and Roman Catholicism is a major religion in all countries.

3. Answers will vary. Students' responses should reflect that the geography of an area affects how people make a living and influences local traditions and cultures.

4. Guyana, Suriname, and Brazil have the most diverse populations. The data show that these countries have the largest numbers of ethnic groups. The text also explains that these countries are very diverse.

5. Students' bar graphs should reflect the correct populations of each country. Use *Rubric for Assessing a Bar Graph* to evaluate students' graphs.

All in One Latin America Teaching Resources, *Rubric for Assessing a Bar Graph*, p. 348

Section 1
Step-by-Step Instruction

Objectives

Social Studies
1. Learn about the geography of Brazil.
2. Discover why the rain forests are important to Brazil and to the whole world.
3. Find out what groups make up the people of Brazil and how they live.

Reading/Language Arts
Compare and contrast things to analyze and sort out information.

Prepare to Read

Build Background Knowledge L2

In this section, students will learn about the people and resources of Brazil. Ask students to preview the headings and visuals in the section with this question in mind: **How have the people of Brazil been affected by the country's natural resources?** Provide a few examples to get students started. Have students engage in a Think-Pair-Share activity (TE, p. T36) to generate their list of possible effects.

Set a Purpose for Reading L2
- Preview the Objectives.
- Read each statement in the *Reading Readiness Guide* aloud. Ask students to mark the statements true or false.

  All in One **Latin America Teaching Resources,** *Reading Readiness Guide,* p. 316

- Have students discuss the statements in pairs or groups of four, then mark their worksheets again. Use the Numbered Heads participation structure (TE, p. T36) to call on students to share their group's perspectives.

Vocabulary Builder
Preview Key Terms L2
Pronounce each Key Term, then ask students to say the word with you. Provide a simple explanation such as, "The canopy of the rain forest is made up of the leaves and branches at the very top of the forest."

Section 1

Brazil
Geography Shapes a Nation

Prepare to Read

Objectives
In this section you will
1. Learn about the geography of Brazil.
2. Discover why the rain forests are important to Brazil and to the whole world.
3. Find out what groups make up the people of Brazil and how they live.

Taking Notes
As you read this section, look for information about the rain forest. Copy the flowchart below and record your findings in it.

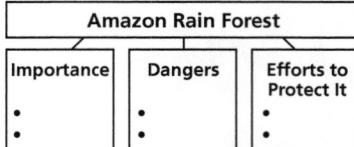

Target Reading Skill

Compare and Contrast When you compare, you examine the similarities between things. When you contrast, you look at the differences. Comparing and contrasting can help you sort out and analyze information. As you read this section, look for similarities and differences in the geographic regions, cultures, and cities of Brazil.

Key Terms
- **canopy** (KAN uh pea) *n.* the dense mass of leaves and branches that form the top layer of a rain forest
- **Amazon rain forest** (AM uh zahn rayn FAWR ist) *n.* a large tropical rain forest occupying the Amazon Basin in northern South America
- **Rio de Janeiro** (REE oh day zhuh NEHR oh) *n.* a large city in Brazil
- **Brasília** (bruh ZIL yuh) *n.* Brazil's new capital city
- **savanna** (suh VAN uh) *n.* a flat, grassy region, or plain

A toucan from Brazil's rain forest

Deep in Brazil's rain forest, the light barely penetrates. At the top of the trees, the leaves form a dense mass called a **canopy.** Sun and rain beat down upon the canopy. But on the ground, it is almost chilly. The cool, moist air is filled with sounds, such as the calls of birds, monkeys, and insects.

The **Amazon rain forest** is a large area of abundant rainfall and dense vegetation in northern Brazil. It occupies the Amazon Basin, the land drained by the Amazon River and its tributaries. Find the Amazon River and the Amazon Basin on the map titled Physical Latin America on page 332. The Amazon rain forest gets more than 80 inches (200 centimeters) of rain each year and has an average temperature of 80°F (27°C). It has millions of species of plants and animals, including orchids, jaguars, and toucans.

The dense foliage makes travel through the rain forest difficult, and few people live there. Even so, the Amazon rain forest is very important to the people of Brazil. It is also important to the rest of the world. Find out what Brazil is doing to protect and develop its rain forest resources.

Target Reading Skill L2

Compare and Contrast Point out the Target Reading Skill. Explain to students that you look for similarities when you compare things, and you look for differences when you contrast things. Tell them that comparing and contrasting can help them analyze information.

Model the skill by comparing and contrasting Brazil's interior and coast from the information given on p. 167. Point out a similarity (*Both are inhabited by people, although the coast has more.*) and a difference. (*The interior is mostly covered with rain forest, while the coast is a flat plateau.*)

Give students *Compare and Contrast.* Have them complete the activity in groups.

All in One **Latin America Teaching Resources,** *Compare and Contrast,* p. 331

The Geography of Brazil

Brazil, the largest country in South America, is nearly as big as the United States. It is also one of the richest countries in the world in land and resources. Until recently, its immense rain forests remained undisturbed. Only the few indigenous groups that had lived in them for centuries ever explored them.

Rain Forest and More Brazil's rain forests take up more than a third of the country. Look at the map titled Latin America: Vegetation Regions on page 348. In the southeast, the forests give way to a large plateau divided by mountain ranges and river valleys. The plateau reaches Brazil's long coast. Many harbors lie along the coast. **Rio de Janeiro** (REE oh day zhuh NEHR oh), Brazil's former capital, is one of many Brazilian cities that grew up around these coastal harbors. Most of Brazil's people live near the coast, far from the rain forests.

Brazil's New Capital: Brasília In the 1950s, the government of Brazil wanted to develop Brazil's interior region using the resources of the rain forest. But few Brazilians wanted to move to the interior of the country. How could the government tempt Brazilians to move?

The government's solution was to build a new capital city called **Brasília** in the interior, near the rain forest. They chose a site on the vast interior plain, or **savanna,** called the Cerrado (suh RAH doh). Work started in 1957, and the government began to move to the partly-completed capital in 1960. Today, Brasília has a population of nearly 2 million people, and many of Brazil's companies and organizations have their headquarters there.

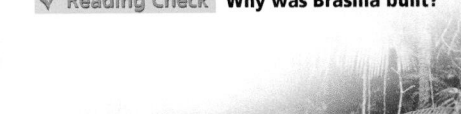 ✓ **Reading Check** Why was Brasília built?

Links to Science

The Photosynthesis "Factory" What is the source of the oxygen we breathe? The food we eat? The fuels we burn? They all begin with photosynthesis. This process is carried out by green plants. They transform water, sunlight, carbon dioxide, and other minerals into energy-rich substances. Plants store these substances for their own nourishment. But animals eat the plants as food. And people eat those animals, as well as eating plants directly. At the same time, the process of photosynthesis releases oxygen into the air. The Amazon rain forest, with its wealth of green plants, is such an important source of oxygen that it is sometimes called "the lungs of Earth."

And there's more. Fuels such as coal and oil are the remains of ancient plants. So photosynthesis, in a way, powers the world.

Vocabulary Builder

Use the information below to teach students this section's high-use words.

High-Use Word	Definition and Sample Sentence
dense, p. 494	*adj.* packed tightly together The **dense** crowd made it hard to get a good view of the parade.
occupy, p. 494	*v.* to take up or fill up, such as time or space Studying for the test **occupied** our entire evening.
community, p. 499	*n.* a group of people forming a smaller social unit within a larger one, and sharing common interests, work, identity, and location The athletic **community** was thrilled about the new gym.

The Geography of Brazil L2

Guided Instruction

■ **Vocabulary Builder** Clarify the high-use words **dense** and **occupy** before reading.

■ Read The Geography of Brazil, using the Partner Paragraph Shrinking technique (TE, p. T34).

■ Ask students **Why do you think many Brazilians live on the coast?** (*Many Brazilians live along the coast because the harbors provide access to people and goods from other places. The interior does not offer that access.*)

■ Discuss the features that make up Brazil's interior. (*The rain forest covers more than a third of the country. It gives way to a plateau in the southeast that is divided by mountains and river valleys.*)

Independent Practice

Have students create the Taking Notes graphic organizer on a blank piece of paper. Then have them begin to fill in a few details about the Amazon rain forest. Briefly model how to identify which details to record.

Monitor Progress

As students fill in the graphic organizer, circulate and make sure individuals are choosing the correct details. Encourage students to add bullets as needed. Provide assistance as needed.

Links

Read the **Links to Science** on this page. Have students explain why some people say that photosynthesis powers the world. (*Photosynthesis provides the necessary energy and nutrients for vegetation to survive. In turn, the oxygen created by photosynthesis and the vegetation itself provides the air and nutrients for animals and humans to survive.*)

Answers

✓ Reading Check Brasília was built because the government thought that having a capital city in the interior of the country would encourage Brazilians to move to that region.

The Importance of the Rain Forest

Guided Instruction

- Read about the importance of the Amazon rain forest in Brazil and on Earth in The Importance of the Rain Forest. As students read, circulate and make sure individuals can answer the Reading Check question.

- Ask students **What makes the Amazon rain forest so important?** (*The Amazon rain forest helps provide about one third of the world's oxygen; it is home to several million species of plants, animals, and insects; many modern medicines have been made from its plants; and it holds about one fifth of the world's fresh water.*)

- Discuss the dangers against which Brazil's government has to protect the Amazon rain forest. Ask students to consider the reasons why these dangers exist. (*The Amazon rain forest is in danger of having too many trees cut down, too many animals smuggled out, and too much pollution created within it. These dangers exist because people, such as loggers, furniture-makers, and miners, want to use the resources of the rain forest in their industries.*)

Answers

Graph Skills Transfer Information
Manaus; Manaus **Contrast** Possible answer: Brasília and Manaus would be surrounded by different types of vegetation, which could lead to different industries being based in each city.

The Importance of the Rain Forest

The rain forest is very important to life all over the world. Scientists estimate that rain forests produce about one third of the world's oxygen. They also calculate that the Amazon rain forest has several million different species of plants, animals, and insects—some that have not even been discovered yet. That is more species than any other region in the world.

Using Rain Forest Resources Many modern medicines have been made from rain forest plants, and scientists hope to discover even more species that have practical uses. The rain forest also holds about one fifth of the world's fresh water. But many scientists think that when people begin to use the resources of the rain forest, they upset the delicate balance of nature.

For example, in the past, Brazil made efforts at land reform by moving poor farmers to the Amazon rain forest and giving them land there. The farmers burned down trees to clear the land for their crops. After a few years, the soil in the rain forest became unfit for farming.

Graph Skills

Differences in temperature and rainfall create different environments for plants, animals, and people. **Transfer Information** Which city shown in the graphs gets more rainfall? Which has the higher temperatures? **Contrast** Use these climate differences to infer how life might be different in Brasília and Manaus.

Two Cities, Two Climates

Brasília

Manaus

Brasília: A City of the Savanna
Manaus: A City of the Rain Forest

Differentiated Instruction

For English Language Learners L2
Pair students with native English speakers to read the Links to Science on page 495. Then have the students work together to draw a diagram showing the process of photosynthesis.

For Gifted and Talented L3
Have students make posters showing the process of photosynthesis in which plants, animals, and people transform water, sunlight, carbon dioxide, and minerals into oxygen. Encourage them to do further reading on the subject if they want to add details beyond those given in the text to their poster.

Threats to the Amazon Rain Forest

Today, Brazil's leaders are trying to control development of the rain forest. They want to find ways to help the economy and the farmers while protecting this important resource. They are working to protect the rain forest from the following dangers:

First, if too much timber is cut down, there will not be enough trees to absorb the carbon dioxide in the atmosphere. The buildup of carbon dioxide may trap heat near Earth's surface, altering the world's climate. When part of the forest is destroyed, the animals and plants that live there may not survive. Plants that might produce important medicines could be destroyed before they are even discovered.

Smuggling is another problem. Approximately 12 million animals are smuggled out of Brazil each year. Many are endangered, and it is illegal to capture or kill them. There are also laws to slow down the logging of mahogany, a wood used to make furniture. But these laws are being broken. Illegal logging continues to threaten the rain forest.

Pollution caused by mining is a third problem. In the late 1980s, the mercury used in gold mining polluted streams in the forest. It made people in several Native American villages sick. The government of Brazil passed strict laws about mining in the rain forest. Sometimes the government insisted that the miners leave. At times, military police had to be called in to make sure they did.

Threats to Traditional Ways of Life Threats to the Amazon rain forest are also threats to the people who have traditionally lived there. The difficulty of traveling in the rain forest had kept many indigenous peoples isolated. They continued their ancient ways of life. Once the rain forest was opened to development, however, miners, farmers, and land speculators arrived. These newcomers brought diseases the Indians had not been exposed to before, and many died. Conflicts between the developers and the Indians were sometimes violent, and Indians were killed. And the isolated culture of the indigenous people began to change as it was brought into contact with modern ways.

✓ Reading Check **Describe three dangers threatening the rain forest.**

Illegal Logging
The small boat is towing a long raft of illegally cut logs down the Amazon River. **Analyze Images** *Which details in the photo suggest why logging might be difficult in the rain forest? Which details suggest why it might be easy?*

 Compare and Contrast What are some differences between the way the indigenous people lived before the development of the rain forest and the way they live now?

Have students complete the graphic organizer.

Monitor Progress

Show *Section Reading Support Transparency LA 45* and ask students to check their graphic organizers individually. Go over key concepts and clarify key vocabulary as needed.

📖 **Latin America Transparencies,** *Section Reading Support Transparency LA 45*

Target Reading Skill [L2]

Compare and Contrast As a follow up, ask students to answer the Target Reading Skill question in the Student Edition. *(Many still live in traditional communities, but their way of life is threatened. Modern ways have been introduced to the people there. Some have moved to the cities.)*

Differentiated Instruction

For Special Needs Students [L1]

Have students read the section as they listen to the recorded version on the Student Edition on Audio CD. Pause the CD after each subsection and ask the students if they have any questions about what they have read.

⦿ Chapter 16, Section 1, **Student Edition on Audio CD**

For Advanced Readers [L3]

Ask students to consider the three threats to the rain forest discussed in the text. Then have them write a possible solution to each problem. Encourage them to solve the problem while still allowing the rain forest's vast resources to be used.

Answers

Analyze Images Dense foliage makes getting trees out of the forest difficult, but the wide river makes passage easy.

✓ Reading Check The dangers threatening the Amazon rain forest include too much logging, the smuggling of animals out of the rain forest, and pollution caused by mining.

Guided Instruction L2

Ask students to study the Country Profile on this page. Remind them to read the map key to help them understand the population density map. Also encourage them to study each photograph on the page and think about the information it provides. As a class, answer the Map and Chart Skills questions. Allow students to briefly discuss their responses with a partner before sharing answers.

Independent Practice

■ Distribute *Reading a Population Density Map.* Have students work in pairs to complete the worksheet.

> **All in One** **Latin America Teaching Resources,** *Reading a Population Density Map,* p. 341

■ Now ask students to consider the map on p. 498. It, too, shows a country in which most of the population lives along or near the coastline and rivers. Ask students to use this knowledge as well as the other information given in the Country Profile to discuss reasons why the indigenous Indian culture is distinct from the culture of Brazil's cities.

Answers

Map and Chart Skills

1. Most Brazilians live near the coast or the major rivers.

2. Possible answer: Many Brazilians live on the coast because it provides access to harbors, and the flat, coastal plateau provides for easier living conditions than the dense rain forest of the country's interior.

3. Possible answer: Most of Brazil's population lives in coastal cities. People who come to Brazil from other countries probably feel there are more opportunities in these cities than in the rain forests of the interior.

> **Go Online** **PHSchool.com** Students can find more information about this topic in the DK World Desk Reference Online.

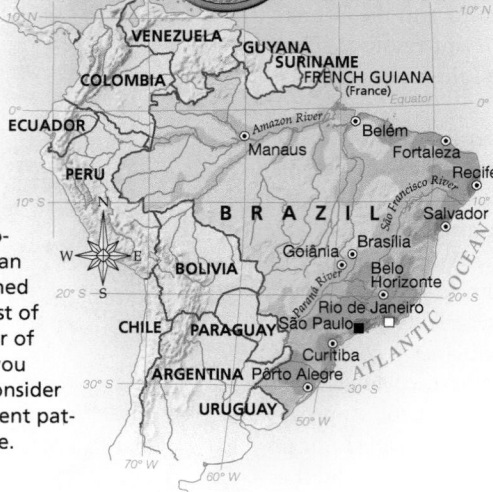
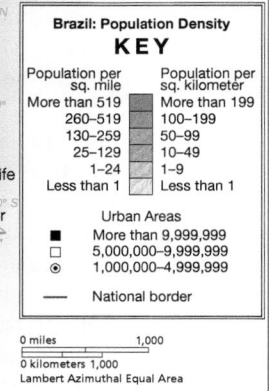

Brazil

Brazil's culture is vibrant and diverse. Portuguese and African influences are evident in Brazilian architecture, religion, music, and food. They also shape the culture of Brazil's cities, where 82 percent of the people live. The indigenous Indian culture, however, has remained largely separate from the rest of Brazil, isolated in the interior of the Amazon rain forest. As you study the map and charts, consider how geography and settlement patterns shape a nation's culture.

Brazil: Population Density
KEY

Population per sq. mile	Population per sq. kilometer
More than 519	More than 199
260–519	100–199
130–259	50–99
25–129	10–49
1–24	1–9
Less than 1	Less than 1

Urban Areas
■ More than 9,999,999
□ 5,000,000–9,999,999
◉ 1,000,000–4,999,999
— National border

0 miles 1,000
0 kilometers 1,000
Lambert Azimuthal Equal Area

Cultural Regions of Brazil

The Northeast
Sugar plantations shaped the culture of the northeast. Enslaved Africans imported to work on the plantations brought their culture with them. Today, the area is rich in art and music. The dance called the samba (shown above) was born here.

SOURCE: *Encyclopedia Britannica*

The South
European immigrants shaped the culture of the south. People mainly of Portuguese descent brought cattle ranching, wheat farming, and coffee production to the region. A distinct diet based on meat products developed here.

The Rain Forests
European immigrants had little contact with Brazil's indigenous peoples. These peoples continued to lead traditional lives, isolated in Brazil's rain forests. Some 230 groups live here today. Among them are the Yanomami, who are hunter-gatherers.

The Cities
In urban centers such as Rio de Janeiro (above) and São Paulo, African and European cultures blended together. For example, the Brazilian celebration called Carnival mixes Catholic and African traditions.

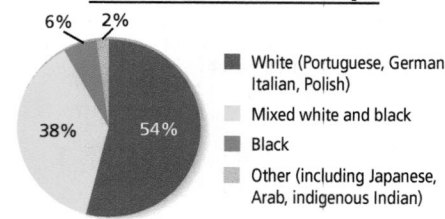

Brazil's Ethnic Groups

6% 2%
38% 54%

- White (Portuguese, German, Italian, Polish)
- Mixed white and black
- Black
- Other (including Japanese, Arab, indigenous Indian)

SOURCE: *CIA World Factbook*

Map and Chart Skills

1. **Identify** Where do most Brazilians live?

2. **Identify Causes** What are some of the reasons why Brazilians live where they do?

3. **Draw Conclusions** Why do you think Brazil's cities are more culturally diverse than the interior rain forest?

 Use Web Code **lfe-1611** for **DK World Desk Reference Online.**

Skills Mini Lesson

Transferring Information from One Medium to Another L2

1. Teach the skill by pointing out that sometimes you need to transfer information from one form to another to present ideas more clearly.

2. Help students practice the skill by suggesting another way to present the information shown on the population density map. *(A table is a good option.)*

3. Have students apply the skill by compiling a table that shows the name of each city on the map and the population range it is in.

The People of Brazil

The Native Americans living in the rain forest were some of the first people to live in Brazil. Today, many Brazilians are a mix of Native American, African, and European heritages. The Yanomami (yah noh MAH mee) are one of the larger Native American groups. They still live in traditional communities in the rain forest. As the rain forest is threatened, however, so too is the Yanomami way of life. Some Native Americans have left the rain forest for the cities.

The Different Cultures of Brazil Daniel Monteiro Costa is a writer and teacher who lives in São Paulo, Brazil. He is also known as Daniel Munduruku (mun duh ROO koo). Daniel is a Munduruku Indian. Many Munduruku still live in small villages in the rain forest. Daniel was born in the city of Belém (buh LEM), but he often visited his relatives in a nearby village. There, he heard stories the Munduruku people told about their history and culture. When he was growing up, Daniel saw that Indians were often treated with disrespect. He began studying the indigenous peoples of Brazil and became proud of his heritage. Now, Daniel works to keep Munduruku stories alive and to end discrimination against Indians in Brazil.

Native Americans are not the only cultural groups in Brazil. Many features of African culture also flourish there. The most African of Brazilian cities, Salvador, lies on the coastal plain. Most of the people who live here are descendants of the millions of Africans brought to Brazil as slaves.

Many Brazilians also have a European heritage. Some are descended from the Portuguese who colonized the area. Other more recent immigrants come from countries such as Italy. There are also Asian immigrants from Japan.

Working on Farms and in Factories In Brazil, most of the land that is suitable for growing crops is owned by only a few people. Sometimes they choose not to farm their land. About one third of Brazil's farmland, approximately 300 million acres (122 million hectares), is unused.

In the 1990s, Brazil's government gave some of this unused land to poor farmers. People began starting small farms just north of Rio de Janeiro. The farms allow them to support themselves.

Modern and Traditional
In the top photo, Brazilian soccer star Sissi participates in the 1999 Women's World Cup competition. The photo above shows a Kaiapo Indian from the rain forest.
Synthesize *Use the text to help you describe the two very different Brazilian ways of life represented by the photos.*

Background: Daily Life

Capoeira Capoeira, a Brazilian combination of dance and martial arts, developed in the northeastern part of the country. The dance form was created by enslaved Africans. Forbidden to fight each other, the slaves developed a form of fighting to music that looked like dancing. Music was played on drums and on a *beribau* made from a bow and gourd. Today, boys and some girls study capoeira, just as American young people study karate, judo, and other martial arts.

Instruct

The People of Brazil [L2]

Guided Instruction
- **Vocabulary Builder** Clarify the high-use word **community** before reading.
- Ask students to read about the lives of Brazilians in The People of Brazil.
- Have students list the various heritages of people in Brazil. (*People in Brazil have Native American, African, European, and Asian heritages.*)
- Engage students in a discussion about possible reasons why Brazil's government gave some of the country's unused land to poor farmers. (*The government was probably trying to help poor families support themselves and earn money from their crops.*)

Independent Practice
Assign *Guided Reading and Review*.

All in One Latin America Teaching Resources, *Guided Reading and Review,* p. 317

Monitor Progress
Tell students to fill in the last column of the *Reading Readiness Guide*. Probe for what they learned that confirms or invalidates each statement.

All in One Latin America Teaching Resources, *Reading Readiness Guide,* p. 316

Answers
Synthesize Many Brazilians enjoy a very modern lifestyle, while some Native Americans still maintain traditional ways of life.

Assess and Reteach

Assess Progress `L2`

Have students complete the Section Assessment. Then administer the *Section Quiz*.

All in One **Latin America Teaching Resources,** *Section Quiz,* p. 318

Reteach `L1`

If students need more instruction, have them read this section in the Reading and Vocabulary Study Guide.

Chapter 16, Section 1, **Western Hemisphere Reading and Vocabulary Study Guide,** pp. 178–180

Extend `L3`

Have students work together in small groups to complete the *Small Group Activity: Making a Mural.* Try to group students of varying abilities together.

All in One **Latin America Teaching Resources,** *Small Group Activity: Making a Mural,* pp. 337–340

Answers

✓Reading Check Rio de Janeiro is a city on the coast that is surrounded by mountains. Parts of the city are wealthy, with hotels, shops, and old palaces and government buildings. Other parts are poor; some homes have no electricity or running water.

Section 1 Assessment

Key Terms

Students' sentences should reflect knowledge of each Key Term.

Target Reading Skill

Both Brasília and Rio de Janeiro are large cities that are home to both the rich and the poor. Both are also home to many of Brazil's factories and businesses. The cities are different in that Rio de Janeiro is located on the coast while Brasília is located inland, and the population of Rio de Janeiro is about 10 million people while the population of Brasília is smaller at about two million people.

Comprehension and Critical Thinking

1. (a) rain forest, a large plateau, mountain ranges, and river valleys **(b)** Possible answer: Brazilians may have thought there would be

---

The plantations, or large farms, of Brazil produce crops for export. Brazil is the largest coffee producer in the world. But Brazilians know that they cannot depend on only one or two crops. The government has discouraged coffee production and tried to diversify the economy by building more factories. Today, Brazil produces iron and steel, cars, and electrical equipment. Since 1960, about 30 million people have left farms and plantations and moved into the cities to get jobs in these new industries.

A Brazilian City: Rio de Janeiro Brazilian cities are home to both the rich and the very poor. Rio de Janeiro is a good example of these contrasts. It lies on the Atlantic coast, surrounded by huge mountains that dip to the sea. If you climbed to the top of one, you could see the whole city. To the south, you would see expensive hotels and shops for tourists. In the downtown area, you would see old palaces and government buildings. Rio de Janeiro was Brazil's capital from 1822 to 1960.

But to the north, you would see clusters of small houses where factory workers live. On the slopes of the mountains are neighborhoods crowded with homes that have no electricity or running water. About 20 percent of Rio's more than 10 million people live in these *favelas*, or slums. However, most of Rio's people live in well-built houses with electricity and running water.

✓ Reading Check **What is Rio de Janeiro like?**

Rio de Janeiro

Section 1 Assessment

Key Terms

Review the key terms at the beginning of this section. Use each term in a sentence that explains its meaning.

Target Reading Skills

What are two ways Brasília and Rio de Janeiro are similar? What are two ways they are different?

Comprehension and Critical Thinking

1. (a) Name What are the main features of Brazil's geography?

(b) Infer Why do you think many people moved to Brasília?

2. (a) Identify Effects Why are Brazil's rain forests important to the whole world?

(b) Analyze Explain why it is difficult for Brazil to protect its rain forest and improve its economy at the same time.

3. (a) Identify What is the cultural heritage of Brazilians?

(b) Draw Conclusions How does unequal land distribution affect the economy and people of Brazil?

Writing Activity

Suppose you lived in a Brazilian city, such as Rio de Janeiro or Salvador, in 1960. Would you have moved to the new city of Brasília if you had been given the chance? Write a letter to a friend explaining why you are planning to move to Brasília or why you are not moving there.

> **Writing Tip** State your choice clearly. Then give three reasons to support your choice.

500 Latin America

---

new opportunities in a new city and in a new region.

2. (a) Brazil's rain forests help provide much of the world's oxygen, are home to several million species of plants, animals, and insects, and are the source of many medicines. **(b)** Many of the activities that would help the economy hurt the rain forest.

3. (a) Native American, African, European, with some Asian immigrants **(b)** Many poor Brazilians have no land to farm—and thus

aren't growing food for their families to eat or sell—while many rich Brazilians have land they could farm but do not.

Writing Activity

Use the *Rubric for Assessing a Writing Assignment* to evaluate students' letters to their friends.

All in One **Latin America Teaching Resources,** *Rubric for Assessing a Writing Assignment,* p. 349

Prepare to Read

Objectives
In this section you will
1. Learn how geography has affected the way people live in the three regions of Peru.
2. Discover what life is like in the cities and towns of the Altiplano.

Taking Notes
As you read this section, look for the ways that people live in the three regions of Peru. Copy the table below and record your findings in it.

Region	Geography	How People Live
	• •	• •

Target Reading Skill

Identify Contrasts When you contrast two regions, you examine how they are different. In this section you will read about the three geographic regions of Peru and about the ways people have adapted to them. As you read, list the differences between the regions and the ways people live there.

Key Terms
- **Altiplano** (al tih PLAH noh) *n.* a high plateau in the Andes Mountains
- **sierra** (see EHR uh) *n.* the mountain region of Peru
- **oasis** (oh AY sis) *n.* a fertile area in a desert that has a source of water

When people on Tribuna, an island in Lake Titicaca, play soccer, they are very careful. That's because the island is made of straw. The ground is uneven, and when they walk on it they can feel the water shifting below. "It seems crazy to play soccer on water," says Luis Colo, who lives on Tribuna. "We don't jump on each other after a goal, or we'd probably fall through the field."

Tribuna is one of about 70 islands made by the Uros (oo ROHS). The Uros have adapted to the geography of Lake Titicaca. As you read in Chapter 13, they make their islands out of totora reeds. They join the floating roots together and then lay cut reeds on top. This process creates an island that is firm enough to support small communities of people with huts and livestock. When the Uros need more land, they simply build another island.

From the time of the Incas, the people of Peru—like people everywhere—have adapted to their geography. The Uros are only one example. You will read about other examples of how geography has affected culture in this section.

Reed boats moored by a totora-reed island

Chapter 16 Section 2 **501**

Target Reading Skill
Identify Contrasts Point out the Target Reading Skill. Explain that students can contrast two regions to see how they are different.

Model the skill by helping students identify a contrast between the sierra and the selva using the information on p. 175. (*The sierra is cold while the selva is hot and humid.*)

Give students *Identify Contrasts*. Have them complete the activity in their groups.

All in One **Latin America Teaching Resources,** *Identify Contrasts,* p. 332

Section 2
Step-by-Step Instruction

Objectives
Social Studies
1. Learn how geography has affected the way people live in the three regions of Peru.
2. Discover what life is like in the cities and towns of the Altiplano.

Reading/Language Arts
Contrast two regions to find out how they are different.

Prepare to Read

Build Background Knowledge L2
Tell student that in this section they will learn how the geography and cultures of Peru have influenced the way Peruvians live. Show the World Studies video. Ask students to note three to five facts about the way people earn a living in Peru as they watch the video. Have students engage in a Give One, Get One activity (TE, p. T37) to share the information that have collected.

Making a Living in Peru, **World Studies Video Program**

Set a Purpose for Reading L2
- Preview the Objectives.
- Read each statement in the *Reading Readiness Guide* aloud. Ask students to mark the statements true or false.

  All in One **Latin America Teaching Resources,** *Reading Readiness Guide,* p. 320

- Have students discuss the statements in pairs or groups of four, then mark their worksheets again. Use the Numbered Heads participation structure (TE, p. T36) to call on students to share their group's perspectives.

Vocabulary Builder
Preview Key Terms L2
Pronounce each Key Term, then ask students to say the word with you. Provide a simple explanation such as, "Someone walking in the desert might feel great relief if he came across an oasis where there is water."

Guided Instruction **L2**

Ask students to study the Country Profile on this page. Remind them to read the map key to understand what the different colors on the map mean. Also encourage them to study the table and line graph carefully. As a class, answer the Map and Chart Skills questions. Allow students to briefly discuss their responses with a partner before sharing answers.

Independent Practice

- Distribute *Reading a Table*. Have students work in pairs to complete the worksheet.

  All In One Latin America Teaching Resources, *Reading a Table*, p. 342

- Now ask students to consider the table on p. 502. It gives information about the physical geography and the people of Peru. Help students identify the relationship between the geographic information and the cultural information. (*Geography influences aspects of culture, such as how people earn a living.*)

Answers

Map and Chart Skills

1. In the coastal region, people earn a living with professional jobs or jobs in manufacturing, refining, and agriculture. In the sierra, people have jobs in farming, herding, and tourism. In the selva, people earn a living by fishing, hunting, and gathering.

2. the coastal region; the sierra

3. The sierra may have lost population because of the lack of variety in occupations.

Peru

Peru is a country of geographic extremes. In the high mountains of the sierra, the air is almost too thin to breathe. The coast is largely desert except for scattered oases where rivers flow down from the mountains to the Pacific. Rain forest covers much of the eastern half of the country, or selva. As you study the map and charts below, think about how geography and climate affect the lives of Peruvians.

Peru: Three Regions

KEY

ELEVATION

Feet	Meters
More than 13,000	More than 3,960
6,500–13,000	1,980–3,960
1,600–6,500	480–1,980
650–1,600	200–480
0–650	0–200

Division between regions

—— National border

⊛ National capital

• Other city

Characteristics of Three Regions

Characteristic	Coastal Region	Sierra	Selva
Land area	11%	26%	63%
Dominant feature	Desert and oases	Mountains	Rain forest
Yearly precipitation	2 inches	Varies	75–125 inches
Main language	Spanish	Quechua	Varied indigenous languages
Major occupations	Professional; manufacturing and refining; agriculture	Farming and herding; tourism	Fishing; hunting and gathering

SOURCES: *Peru, Country Study, Department of the Army Handbook*, 1981; *Encyclopaedia Britannica*; *The World Today Series, Latin America 2002*; Library of Congress online

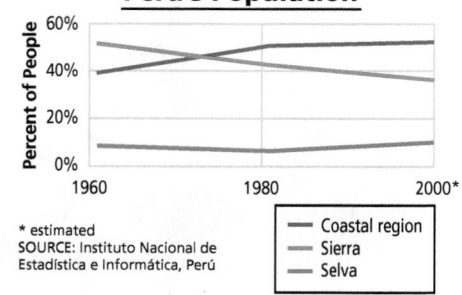

Peru's Population

Percent of People: 60%, 40%, 20%, 0% / 1960, 1980, 2000*

* estimated
SOURCE: Instituto Nacional de Estadística e Informática, Perú

—— Coastal region
—— Sierra
—— Selva

Map and Chart Skills

1. **Identify** How do people earn a living in different parts of Peru?

2. **Analyze** What region of Peru has the most people? What region has lost population?

3. **Infer** What information in the map and charts indicates why these changes in population might have occurred?

 Use Web Code lfe-1612 for **DK World Desk Reference Online**.

502 Latin America

Vocabulary Builder

Use the information below to teach students this section's high-use words.

High-Use Word	Definition and Sample Sentence
dwell, p. 504	*v.* to live as a resident
	Many fishermen in the northeast **dwell** along the Atlantic coast.
foundation, p. 504	*n.* the base on which something rests
	The house is more secure because its **foundation** is made of concrete.
adapt, p. 506	*v.* to make fit by changing or adjusting
	Animals **adapt** to the winter weather by growing a heavier coat of fur.

The Regions and People of Peru

The Uros live on Lake Titicaca. Find Lake Titicaca on the map of Peru in the Country Profile. Lake Titicaca is in Peru's **Altiplano** (al tih PLAH noh), a high plateau in the Andes Mountains. The Altiplano is about 12,000 feet (3,658 meters) above sea level. It is located in southern Peru near the Bolivian border.

Peru's Three Geographic Regions   The Andes Mountains, which run from northwest to southeast Peru, divide the country into three geographic regions. The mountain region, including the Andes and the Altiplano, is known as the **sierra.** Much of this region is so high that lower layers of the soil remain frozen all year. This kind of treeless plain, which supports only low-growing vegetation, is called tundra. Even so, people have lived in this region for centuries. The Incas built their empire in the Altiplano, with Cuzco as its capital. Today, some descendants of the Incas live much as their ancestors did. In addition to farming, these Native Americans herd sheep, cattle, llamas, and alpacas. Wool is one of the major products of the region.

The coastal region of Peru is very different from the sierra. This dry area is dotted with oases. An **oasis** is a fertile area in a desert that has a source of water. Before Europeans arrived, indigenous groups settled by these oases. Later, the Spanish also built cities along the coast. Today, this area is the economic center of Peru. In Lima (LEE muh), Peru's capital, historic Spanish buildings from the 1600s and 1700s stand next to modern skyscrapers. More than 6 million people—more than a quarter of Peru's population—live in Lima.

The third region of Peru is the large forested area that stretches from the lower slopes of the mountains to the lowlands of northeast Peru. Here, the weather is hot and humid all year. This isolated region is called the selva. It has few roads connecting it to the sierra and the coast. Little modern development has occurred here. Some Native American groups live in this rain forest much as their ancestors did.

A modern skyscraper stands beside a Spanish-style home in Lima.

A Peruvian Oasis
This small fertile area is surrounded by desert. **Draw Inferences** *Why do you think people settled by oases in this area of Peru?*

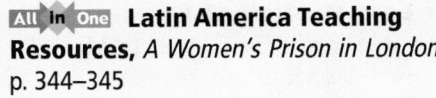
Differentiated Instruction

For Gifted and Talented   L3
Have students read the primary source reading *A Women's Prison in London* to learn more about the experiences of Flora Tristan, the niece of one of Peru's presidents.

All in One Latin America Teaching Resources, *A Women's Prison in London,* p. 344–345

Instruct

The Regions and People of Peru   L2

Guided Instruction

- Read The Regions and People of Peru, using the Structured Silent Reading technique (TE, p. T34).

- Ask students **Why do you think many people live in Peru's coastal region?** *(The climate of the coastal region is not as harsh as the other regions; the land is fertile for farming; people have access to ports on the coast.)*

- Ask students to consider which regions of Peru are mainly inhabited only by Native Americans. Then ask **Why do you think Native Americans live in these regions but most other Peruvians do not?** *(The sierra and the selva are mainly inhabited only by Native Americans. Native Americans probably live there because that is where their ancestors lived and their culture developed. Other Peruvians probably have not moved there because the high mountains and cold air of the sierra, the rain forest, and few roads of the selva make them harder places to live than the coastal region.)*

Independent Practice
Ask students to create the Taking Notes graphic organizer on a blank piece of paper. Then ask them to fill in the table with the information they have just learned about how people live in Peru's three regions. Briefly model how to fill in information in the appropriate column.

Monitor Progress
As students fill in the graphic organizer, circulate and make sure individuals are choosing the correct details and placing them in the correct columns of the table. Help students as needed.

Answers
Draw Inferences The surrounding area is dry desert so they needed to settle in a place where water was available.

Life in the Altiplano L2

Guided Instruction

- **Vocabulary Builder** Clarify the high-use words **dwell**, **foundation**, and **adapt** before reading.

- Read Life in the Altiplano. As students read, circulate and make sure individuals can answer the Reading Check question.

- Have students describe one difference and one similarity between the Altiplano's cities and its villages. *(Possible answer: A difference is that in the cities, most people have telephones; in the villages, there are no telephones. A similarity is that there are Incan ruins in both places.)*

- Ask students **How do you think Peruvians today feel about encountering Incan remains in their daily life?** Encourage students to think of a variety of responses Peruvians might have to this evidence of the past. *(While some Peruvians may not care strongly about remains from the past, many Peruvians probably respond to these remains by feeling pride about their heritage. As more Peruvians move to cities and as the villages of the Altiplano change, the physical remains of the past help people remember their cultural origins. Also, some Peruvians may see these remains as inspiration for their own ideas and pursuits—for example, the Incan suspension bridges offer a good method of crossing the deep gorges of the Altiplano.)*

Answers

√ Reading Check Native Americans and mestizos make up the majority of Peruvians.
Conclude They built staircases to travel up and down the mountain and built an aqueduct to transport water there.

Peru's People Native Americans make up almost half of Peru's population. Most Native Americans living in Peru are Quechua. Another third of Peru's people are mestizo. The remaining Peruvians are of European, African, and Asian descent. Even though Native Americans are such a large part of the population of Peru, until recently many of them have remained isolated from the modern world.

√ Reading Check **Which two groups make up the majority of Peruvians?**

Life in the Altiplano

Many Quechuas, Uros, and other Native Americans living on the Altiplano follow traditions that are hundreds of years old. Their communities, however, are slowly changing. Thousands of Native Americans have left for jobs in the city. And life is changing even for those who stay in their villages.

Old and New The past is constantly present in the Altiplano. The ruins of Incan cities, such as Machu Picchu, are found in the countryside. Even in modern cities, the old mixes with the new. Most city dwellers in the Altiplano have electricity. The streets are paved, and there are telephones. But there are also remnants of the past. In Cuzco, for example, parts of the old Incan wall that once surrounded the city are still standing. Modern houses are made of adobe and have red tile roofs, but their foundations are the remains of Incan stonework. There are also buildings constructed by the Spanish colonists.

Lost City of the Incas
The ruins of Machu Picchu were "discovered" in 1911 when a local guide led American scholars to the site. It has stone buildings, walkways, and staircases, as well as agricultural terraces that were once watered by an aqueduct. **Conclude** *How did the Incan builders adapt their city to the mountain site?*

504 Latin America

A Day in a Quechua Village Village life is very different from city life. In the isolated towns of the Altiplano, there are no telephones. Few buses drive through the villages. Most people are Quechua or Aymara.

Like their Incan ancestors, many Quechua rely on raising animals for their wool. The Incas tamed wild llamas and alpacas, and then they raised them to use as pack animals and as a source of wool. Today, many Quechua families keep sheep instead. Sheep are not native to the region but were brought to the Americas by European settlers.

Modesto Mamani (moh DES toh MUH mahn ee) is a 13-year-old Quechua boy. He wakes before dawn to the freezing mountain air and eats breakfast as soon as the sun comes up. Breakfast is always the same: a few rolls, coffee with sugar, and whole wheat kernels that can be eaten like popcorn. His only other meal may be lunch. It is usually potato and barley soup with *chunos*—freeze-dried potato skins.

On some days, Modesto spends much of his time working in the field with his father and brothers. On other days, he looks after the sheep or goes with his mother to the market. Even with school and chores, Modesto finds time to play soccer on the tundra in back of his house.

Like many other children who live in Altiplano villages, Modesto's life mixes the modern and the traditional. He wants to study to become an engineer so he can bring technology to the Altiplano. Meanwhile, much of his time revolves around the sheep his family raises. Not only does Modesto tend the sheep, he also uses their wool to knit sweaters.

School, Work, and Play
Modesto attends school—with his soccer ball! (left), and shows off one of his family's sheep (right). **Infer** *Why do you think people raise sheep in the region seen in the photo?*

Identify Contrasts What are two ways that life in a Quechua village differs from life in Cuzco?

Chapter 16 Section 2 **505**

Independent Practice
Have students complete the graphic organizer by filling in any new information about the Altiplano that they have just learned.

Monitor Progress
- Show *Section Reading Support Transparency LA 46* and ask students to check their graphic organizers individually. Go over key concepts and clarify key vocabulary as needed.

  Latin America Transparencies, *Section Reading Support Transparency LA 46*

- Tell students to fill in the last column of the *Reading Readiness Guide*. Probe for what they learned that confirms or invalidates each statement.

  All in One Latin America Teaching Resources, *Reading Readiness Guide*, p. 320

Target Reading Skill L2
Identify Contrasts As a follow up, ask students to answer the Target Reading Skill question in the Student Edition. (*Possible answers: In Cuzco, people have telephones, there is a lot of traffic, and most people are not Quechua or Aymara.*)

Skills Mini Lesson

Identifying Frame of Reference and Point of View L2

1. Teach the skill by explaining that point of view is an opinion or perspective on a topic and frame of reference is a person's background. Frame of reference often affects point of view.

2. Help students practice the skill by identifying the point of view of Modesto in the following scenario: Modesto's father tells Modesto to spend more time tending the sheep. Modesto is unhappy about this decision.

3. Have students apply the skill by identifying Modesto's frame of reference in the same scenario.

Answer
Infer The land looks suited to sheep grazing.

Assess and Reteach

Assess Progress L2
Have students complete the Section Assessment. Then administer the *Section Quiz*.

All in One **Latin America Teaching Resources,** *Section Quiz,* p. 322

Reteach L1
If students need more instruction, have them read this section in the Reading and Vocabulary Study Guide.

Chapter 16, Section 2, **Western Hemisphere Reading and Vocabulary Study Guide,** pp. 181–183

Extend L3
If you have not already done so, show students *Making a Living in Peru.* After students watch the video, ask them to write a brief summary describing the experiences of one of the Peruvians featured.

Making a Living in Peru, **World Studies Video Program**

Answers

√Reading Check Possible answer: Quechua families have adapted to the tundra by raising sheep, animals that are well-suited to that environment.

Analyze The bridge helps people travel across the gorges of the Altiplano.

Section 2 Assessment

Key Terms
Students' sentences should reflect knowledge of each Key Term.

Target Reading Skill
The selva is hot while the sierra is cool. The coast is much drier than the sierra. The coastal region is more populated than both the sierra and the selva.

Comprehension and Critical Thinking
1. (a) The three regions of Peru are the mountain region, or sierra, the coastal region, and the forested region, or selva. Students should draw their descriptions from information provided on pp. 503–504 of the text.
(b) The coastal plain has easy access to the outside world. It is an easier region to live in than the mountains or the rain forest.

Modern Suspension Bridge
Tourists stand on a modern suspension bridge that is based on a design developed by the Incas. **Analyze** *How does this type of bridge suit its environment?*

Geography and Culture You have seen how the Uros adapted to their environment by living on islands they create themselves, much as their ancestors did. But they are also modern people who play soccer. In another part of the Altiplano, Quechua families raise sheep, animals that are suited to the tundra. But their children learn about technology in school.

Long ago, the Incas solved a problem of their mountain environment: how to cross the deep gorges between mountain peaks. They invented suspension bridges. Modern versions of these bridges are still used in the Andes today. They are one more example of how geography and the past influence the present in Peru.

√ Reading Check **Explain how one group of Peruvians has adapted to their environment.**

Section 2 Assessment

Key Terms
Review the key terms at the beginning of this section. Use each term in a sentence that explains its meaning.

Target Reading Skills
How are the three geographic regions of Peru different?

Comprehension and Critical Thinking
1. (a) Describe What are the three regions of Peru, and what are they like?

(b) Identify Cause and Effect Why is the coastal plain the economic center of Peru?
2. (a) Describe How does Cuzco represent both old and new?
(b) Compare How is life for the Quechua similar to and different from life for the Uros?
(c) Predict Do you think the Uros and Quechua will preserve their traditional ways of life in this century? Explain.

Writing Activity
Write a letter that Modesto might send to a friend in Cuzco, inviting the friend to visit him in his village. Have Modesto describe what his friend might see and do on his visit.

Go Online
PHSchool.com

For: An activity on Peru
Visit: PHSchool.com
Web Code: lfd-1602

506 Latin America

2. (a) Cuzco has modern houses with foundations built by the Incas as well as buildings constructed by the Spanish colonists. **(b)** Similarities: Both have had to adapt to living in the Altiplano, both have taken on some modern activities, such as playing soccer and learning about technology. Differences: The Uros live along a lake, while the Quechua live on the tundra. **(c)** Answers will vary. Students should support their opinions with

facts from the section and from their personal knowledge.

Writing Activity
Use the *Rubric for Assessing a Writing Assignment* to evaluate students' letters to Modesto's friend.

All in One **Latin America Teaching Resources,** *Rubric for Assessing a Writing Assignment,* p. 349

Chile
Land of Contrasts

Prepare to Read

Objectives
In this section you will
1. Find out how the geography of Chile creates regions where people live very differently.
2. Learn how Chile's people live and what products they produce.
3. Find out how Chile restored democracy.

Taking Notes
As you read this section, look for the main ideas and details and how they relate to each other. Use the format below to create an outline of the section.

> I. The geography of Chile
>   A. The longest, narrowest country
>   1. Only 100 miles wide
>   2.

 Target Reading Skill

Compare and Contrast One way to understand regions is to compare and contrast them, or identify similarities and differences. When you compare, you look at similarities between things. When you contrast, you look at differences. As you read this section, compare and contrast the geographic regions and lifestyles of Chile.

Key Terms
- **Ferdinand Magellan** (FUR duh nand muh JEL un) *n.* Portuguese explorer sailing for Spain, whose expedition first circumnavigated the globe
- **circumnavigate** (sur kum NAV ih gayt) *v.* to sail or fly all the way around something, such as Earth
- **glacier** (GLAY shur) *n.* a large, slow-moving mass of ice and snow
- **Augusto Pinochet Ugarte** (ah GOO stoh pea noh SHAY oo gahr TAY) *n.* military dictator of Chile from 1973 to 1988

When Ferdinand Magellan first saw the Pacific Ocean in 1520, tears ran down his cheeks. **Ferdinand Magellan** was a Portuguese explorer sailing for Spain. He was searching for a way around or through the Americas. Ever since Christopher Columbus had failed to find a westward sea route all the way to Asia, explorers had been looking for one. But the continents of North and South America were in the way.

Magellan sailed from Spain in 1519 and worked his way south along the coast of South America. Bad weather forced him to spend the winter on the stormy southern coast. His crew threatened to rebel, but Magellan kept exploring. Finally, he found a way through the islands at the "bottom" of South America. His ships sailed through this narrow, dangerous passage to the Pacific Ocean. Magellan wept when he realized his great accomplishment. He knew that now he could sail to Asia—and all the way around the world.

The passage that Magellan discovered is in present-day Chile. It allowed European sailors to explore the western coast of South America.

Magellan's ship nears the strait that bears his name.

Chapter 16 Section 3 **507**

 Target Reading Skill L2

Compare and Contrast Point out the Target Reading Skill. Explain to students that you look for similarities when you compare things, and you look for differences when you contrast things. Tell them that comparing and contrasting can help them analyze information.

Model the skill by helping students identify the similarities and differences between northern and central Chile that are given on pp. 509–510. *(Similarity—Mining is important in both regions; Difference—Few plants can survive in the north while the central region has high grasses and dense forests.)*

Give students *Compare and Contrast*. Have them complete the activity in groups.

All in One Latin America Teaching Resources, *Compare and Contrast,* p. 331

Objectives

Social Studies
1. Find out how the geography of Chile creates regions where people live very differently.
2. Learn how Chile's people live and what products they produce.
3. Find out how Chile restored democracy.

Reading/Language Arts
Compare and contrast things to analyze and sort out information.

Prepare to Read

Build Background Knowledge L2
In this section, students will learn about the vivid contrasts that exist in the geography and cultures of Chile. Ask students to preview the headings and visuals in the section with this question in mind: **What factors of geography have influenced the cultures of Chile?** Provide a few examples to get students started. Conduct an Idea Wave (TE, p. T35) to generate a list.

Set a Purpose for Reading L2
- Preview the Objectives.
- Read each statement in the *Reading Readiness Guide* aloud. Ask students to mark the statements true or false.

  All in One Latin America Teaching Resources, *Reading Readiness Guide,* p. 324

- Have students discuss the statements in pairs or groups of four, then mark their worksheets again. Use the Numbered Heads participation structure (TE, p. T36) to call on students to share their group's perspectives.

Vocabulary Builder
Preview Key Terms L2
Pronounce each Key Term, then ask students to say the word with you. Provide a simple explanation such as, "When a space shuttle circumnavigates the Earth, it flies all the way around it."

Guided Instruction `L2`

Ask students to study the Country Profile on this page. Remind them to read the map key to understand what the different symbols on the map represent. Also encourage them to study the line graph carefully. As a class, answer the Map and Chart Skills questions. Allow students to briefly discuss their responses with a partner before sharing answers.

Independent Practice

Have students do an in-depth study on one of the following products and resources shown on the map of Chile: manufacturing, fish, or fruits. Ask students to do research to make a list of at least three types of fish that are caught, fruits that are grown, or manufactured items that are produced in Chile. Allow students to work in pairs to complete the activity.

Answers

Map and Chart Skills

1. Copper is found in northern Chile.

2. Fruits and fish

3. Agricultural and seafood exports make up 14 percent of Chile's total exports, while copper exports account for 36 percent.

4. Chile's economy improved at a faster rate than that of Latin America between 1990 and 2004.

5. Possible answer: Chile's economy has been steadily improving for over ten years, and none of its exports account for more than half of the total exports, so Chile has been able to create a stable, diversified economy.

Go Online PHSchool.com Students can find more information about this topic in the DK World Desk Reference Online.

Chile

Chile produces more copper than any other country in the world. To avoid relying too much on one resource, however, the government of Chile has encouraged agriculture and new industry. The United States is Chile's largest trade partner. About 18 percent of Chile's exports are sold to the United States. Today, Chile's economy is seen as strong and stable. Study the map and charts. Think about how Chile's location and resources have affected its economy.

Chile: Products and Resources

KEY

- Copper
- Petroleum
- Manufacturing
- Fruits
- Fish
- National border
- ⊛ National capital
- • Other city

0 miles 800
0 kilometers 800
Lambert Azimuthal Equal Area

Average Annual Income per Citizen

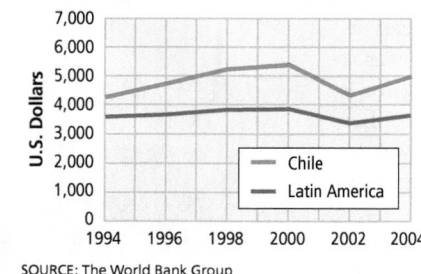

SOURCE: The World Bank Group

Chile's Exports

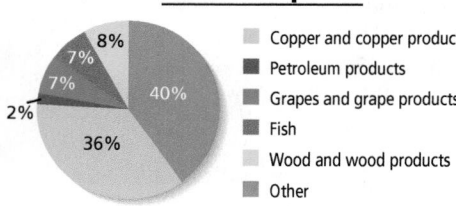

- Copper and copper products
- Petroleum products
- Grapes and grape products
- Fish
- Wood and wood products
- Other

SOURCE: Economic Commission of Latin America and the Caribbean

Map and Chart Skills

1. **Locate** Where are Chile's mineral resources found?

2. **Identify** Which economic resources are found in most parts of the country?

3. **Compare** How do Chile's agricultural and seafood exports compare to its copper exports?

4. **Analyze Information** What do you learn about Chile's economy from the line graph?

5. **Draw Conclusions** Do you think Chile has been successful in using its resources to create a diversified economy? Explain your answer.

 Use Web Code Ife-1613 for **DK World Desk Reference Online.**

Vocabulary Builder

Use the information below to teach students this section's high-use words.

High-Use Word	Definition and Sample Sentence
survive, p. 509	v. to continue to live after, or in spite of The plant did not **survive** because it did not get enough water.
regime, p. 513	n. a form of government or rule A new **regime** came to power after the votes were counted.
reject, p. 513	v. to refuse to take He **rejected** the idea of exchanging sandwiches because he didn't like peanut butter and jelly.

The Geography of Chile

The passage that Magellan discovered is now named after him. Find the Strait of Magellan on the map of Chile in the Country Profile. It is a major sea lane to this day. Although it is dangerous to sail through, the Strait of Magellan is safer than going all the way around Cape Horn to the south. Many ships have been lost in the Strait's stormy waters. While Magellan was lucky to get through the Strait, he was not lucky enough to return to Spain. He died during the voyage. Of the five ships that started Magellan's expedition, only one returned all the way to Spain. But it was the first ship to **circumnavigate,** or go all the way around, the globe.

The Longest, Narrowest Country Look at the map titled Physical Latin America on page 332. Find the Andes Mountains. They run down the whole length of Chile like a giant spine. Chile is narrow and shaped like a string bean. On average, it is only about 100 miles (161 kilometers) wide, but it is extremely long. It runs 2,650 miles (4,265 kilometers) down the Pacific Coast all the way to the tip of South America. It is the longest, narrowest country in the world.

The Driest Place in the World Chile contains an amazing variety of landforms and climates. In the north is the Atacama Desert, the driest region in the world. Not many plants or animals can survive there. But the desert is rich in copper, so the region is dotted with mines. Chile exports more copper than any country in the world.

Compare and Contrast
How is sailing through the Strait of Magellan different from sailing around Cape Horn? How is it similar?

A man examines salt formations in the Atacama Desert (above). Magellanic penguins (left) sometimes come ashore near the Strait of Magellan.

Compare and Contrast As a follow up, ask students to answer the Target Reading Skill question in the Student Edition. *(Both routes are dangerous to sail, but sailing through the Strait of Magellan is less dangerous and faster than sailing around Cape Horn.)*

Instruct

The Geography of Chile　　L2

Guided Instruction

- **Vocabulary Builder** Clarify the high-use word **survive** before reading.
- Read The Geography of Chile, using the Oral Cloze Reading technique (TE, p. T33).
- Discuss the features of northern and southern Chile. **Why do they make these regions undesirable places to live?** *(The northern third of Chile is a desert—the driest area in the world. Neither humans nor most plants and animals can live there well. The southern third of Chile is cold, wet, and stormy and thus also not an easy place to live.)*

Differentiated Instruction

For Advanced Readers　　L3

Have students complete the *Trade in a Global Economy* Internet activity. Then challenge them to do Internet or library research to create a circle graph that shows world exporters of copper and the percentage of the total world copper output for each.

Go Online
PHSchool.com **For:** Environmental and Global Issues: *Trade in a Global Economy.*
Visit: PHSchool.com
Web Code: lfd-1606

Independent Practice

Ask students to create the Taking Notes graphic organizer on a blank piece of paper. Briefly model how to identify a main idea and its supporting details. Then have students fill in the supporting details they have just read.

Monitor Progress

As students fill in the graphic organizer, circulate and make sure individuals are choosing details that support the main idea. Provide assistance as needed.

Varied Landscapes Chile's long central valley has rolling hills, high grasses, and dense forests. This is the region where most of the people live and where the capital of Chile, Santiago, is located. Both farming and mining are important here. In the southern part of central Chile is the beautiful Lakes Region, with forests, waterfalls, and mountains topped by glaciers. A glacier is a huge mass of slowly moving ice and snow. Many of the mountains of this region are volcanoes, and volcanic eruptions and earthquakes occur often in Chile.

The southern third of Chile is cold and wet and often stormy. Far to the south, the Strait of Magellan separates the mainland of Chile from the islands of Tierra del Fuego (tee EHR uh del FWAY goh), which are divided between Chile and Argentina. Tierra del Fuego is Spanish for "Land of Fire." When Magellan sailed past these islands, he saw smoke from the fires of the indigenous people who lived there. Because of the smoke, he called the large island Tierra del Fuego. This region is only about 600 miles (970 kilometers) from Antarctica. Icebergs dot the sea, and penguins come ashore.

✓ Reading Check **Describe the central region of Chile.**

Land of Contrasts
Icebergs float away from a glacier off Chile's southern coast (small photo). Below, a waterfall cascades in the central forest region. Draw Conclusions *What accounts for this difference in Chile's waterways?*

510 Latin America

Answers

Draw Conclusions The climate is colder in southern Chile.

✓ Reading Check The central region of Chile is a long valley with rolling hills, high grasses, and dense forests. The southern part of the region has lakes, forests, waterfalls, and mountains topped by glaciers. Some of the mountains are volcanoes. Most of Chile's population lives in the central region, and the capital city, Santiago, is located there. Farming and mining are important industries in the region.

Chile's People and Products

The lifestyles of Chileans vary from region to region. In the far south, sheep herders in heavy wool sweaters brave the strong winds. Farther north in the central valley, farmers grow wheat, potatoes, sugar beets, corn, tomatoes, and many fruits. In the cities, people in business suits hurry in and out of tall skyscrapers. Few people live in the Atacama Desert of the far north. While mining continues today, there are also ghost towns, or abandoned mining settlements, in the Atacama.

The People of Chile Chile's early Spanish settlers married Native Americans already living there. Today, mestizos make up more than 90 percent of the population. Only about 10 percent of Chileans are Native Americans.

Tonino Fuentes (toh NEE noh FWEN tays) lives in the countryside near Santiago. His family is mestizo. They work on a farm owned by a wealthy man of Spanish descent. Tonino's father trains horses that will appear in rodeos. He is teaching Tonino to be a rodeo rider. But Tonino has other things he must do. Every morning at sunrise, he and his mother milk their two cows. Then Tonino does his homework. That's because his school is in the afternoon, from 2:00 P.M. until 6:00 P.M. In the evening, Tonino often plays soccer with his friends.

Chile's Cities Today, more than 80 percent of Chile's people live in cities. Many rural Chileans have come to Santiago. In this capital city, old Spanish buildings stand near gleaming skyscrapers. The city is in the valley of the central plain, so the altitude is low enough to allow mild weather. The sea makes the air humid. Palm trees grow in the public parks. The snowcapped Andes lie to the east.

Unfortunately, the beautiful sights of Santiago are sometimes blocked by a thick layer of smog. The city is surrounded by mountains on three sides. The mountains trap exhaust from vehicles and smoke from factories in the valley. This is especially true in the winter, when there is not much wind. Pollution has become so bad that it makes many small children and elderly people sick. On a bad day, people wear surgical masks in order to breathe, or they press scarves to their faces.

The Spanish designed many of Chile's cities around a central square. Their buildings could not withstand Chile's earthquakes, however. Few colonial structures remain in Valparaiso, an important port. Chile's second-largest city, Concepción, was moved several miles inland in 1754 to protect it from tsunamis.

Chapter 16 Section 3 **511**

Links to
Language Arts

The "Real" Robinson Crusoe Many people have read the adventure story *Robinson Crusoe,* but few have visited the island named for this fictional character. The 1719 novel by Daniel Defoe is about a man named Robinson Crusoe who is stranded on a tropical island. It is based on the true story of Alexander Selkirk. In 1704, Selkirk, a Scottish sailor, quarreled with his captain and asked to be put ashore on one of the Juan Fernández Islands. He lived alone there until he was discovered by an English ship in 1709. Today, these islands are part of Chile. The largest island is named Robinson Crusoe and the second-largest is called Alexander Selkirk. An N. C. Wyeth illustration of the novel is shown below.

Guided Instruction

■ Read about the people who live in Chile and the goods they produce in Chile's People and Products. As students read, circulate and make sure individuals can answer the Reading Check question.

■ Ask students to describe the ways people make a living in the different regions of Chile. (*In the north, people mine. In the south, many people herd sheep. In the central valley, some people farm while others work in business.*)

■ Ask students to list the various mining and agricultural products of Chile. Then ask if students think these items represent enough diversification to keep Chile's economy healthy. (*Chilean products include wool, wheat, potatoes, sugar beets, corn, tomatoes, fruits, and copper. Some students may think the economy is diverse enough because there are so many different products. Other students may think that Chile needs to produce a wider variety of products, including products in technology and other modern businesses.*)

Independent Practice

Have students continue to fill in the graphic organizer by adding the information in this section to their outlines.

Monitor Progress

As students continue to fill in their outlines, circulate to make sure students are organizing the information correctly. Provide assistance as needed.

Links

Read the **Links to Language Arts** on this page. Have students find the Juan Fernández Island on the map at the beginning of this chapter. Ask students **What do you think living there would be like?** (*Answers will vary, but students should refer to the remoteness of these tiny islands that lie a good distance off the coast of Chile.*)

Differentiated Instruction

For Advanced Readers [L3]
Have students do research to answer at least two of the following questions: What is smog? How is it produced? What harm can it do? How can we prevent smog? Ask each student to present a brief oral report to the class on his or her findings.

For English Language Learners [L1]
Check for students' comprehension of terms on this page. If appropriate, have students read the section in the Spanish Reading and Vocabulary Study Guide to reinforce the concepts in this section.

Chapter 16, Section 3, **Western Hemisphere Spanish Reading and Vocabulary Study Guide,** pp. 133–134

Restoring Democracy L2

Guided Instruction

- **Vocabulary Builder** Clarify the high-use words **regime** and **reject** before reading.

- Ask students to read about Chile's struggle to maintain a democratic government in Restoring Democracy.

- Discuss the actions taken during Pinochet's control of Chile that were un-democratic. (*Under Pinochet's control, the Chilean congress could not meet, opposition political parties were banned, and people who spoke out against the regime were killed, imprisoned, or "disappeared"—all of these actions indicated a lack of democracy.*)

- Ask students **How was democracy re-stored?** (*In 1988, even though Pinochet's name was the only one on the election ballot, the people of Chile voted "no" and democra-cy was restored.*)

Independent Practice

Have students complete the graphic organiz-er by filling in the supporting details they identify in this section.

Monitor Progress

- Show *Section Reading Support Transparen-cy LA 47* and ask students to check their graphic organizers individually. Go over key concepts and clarify key vocabulary as needed.

   Latin America Transparencies, *Section Reading Support Transparency LA 47*

- Tell students to fill in the last column of the *Reading Readiness Guide*. Probe for what they learned that confirms or invalidates each statement.

   All in One Latin America Teaching Resources, *Reading Readiness Guide,* p. 325

Answers

Identify Effects Farming creates jobs that involve shipping and processing farm prod-ucts. People also have jobs making farming equipment.

Chile's Agricultural Revolution When copper prices fell in the 1980s, Chile realized that it must diversify its economy. One way was to sell more crops. By the late 1980s, agriculture had become a billion-dollar industry, providing jobs for about 900,000 Chileans. Chile shipped wheat, potatoes, and other vege-tables and fruits around the world.

The United States, Japan, and Europe are especially good markets for Chilean produce. From October through May, it is cold in the Northern Hemisphere but warm in the Southern Hemisphere. Chile provides fruits and vegetables to the United States during the months when American farmers cannot.

Another reason that Chilean produce is welcome in other countries is that Chile's fruits and vegetables are free of many common plant pests. Chile's farming regions are protected by the Andes Mountains, so some of the insect pests and ani-mal diseases that plague other countries never reach Chile. The government wants to make sure that Chilean produce remains this way. Customs inspectors at Chile's airports search baggage carefully. They are checking that no plant or animal matter from foreign places is allowed into the country because it might bring disease to Chile's crops.

✓ Reading Check **Why is Chilean produce free of many plant pests?**

Farming Fuels the Economy Grapes are harvested (below) and then shipped around the world from ports like this one in Valparaiso (bot-tom photo). **Identify Effects** *How does farming create jobs for people other than farm workers?*

512 Latin America

✓ Reading Check The Chilean produce is free of many plant pests because the Andes Mountains protect Chile's farming region, keeping out some of the pests that plague other countries. Officials at Chile's airports also help prevent pests from entering the country by checking bags to make sure that no plant or animal matter from a foreign place is allowed in.

Restoring Democracy

Today, Chile has a democratic government. But a dark cloud from its past still hangs over the country. In 1973, the armed forces took control of the government. They were led by General **Augusto Pinochet Ugarte** (ah GOO stoh pea noh SHAY oo gahr TAY), who became a brutal dictator. The Chilean congress could not meet during his rule. Opposition political parties were banned. People who spoke out against the military regime were killed, imprisoned, or "disappeared."

Nevertheless, there were national days of protest. The Catholic Church spoke out against the human rights abuses of the government. In the 1988 elections—even though Pinochet's name was the only one on the ballot—the people of Chile rejected him by voting "no." Democratic government was restored. Pinochet, however, remained an army general.

In 1998, at the age of 82, Pinochet went to London, England, for medical treatment. The government of Spain issued a warrant for his arrest for crimes against humanity. This caused an international crisis. Eventually, Pinochet was declared unfit for trial, and he returned to Chile. Some Chileans wanted him prosecuted; others did not. There is still controversy over bringing to trial those responsible for the abuses of the Pinochet regime.

Anti-Pinochet demonstrators gathered in London when the former dictator was there for medical treatment.

✓ **Reading Check** How did Pinochet's rule end?

Section 3 Assessment

Key Terms
Review the key terms at the beginning of this section. Use each term in a sentence that explains its meaning.

Target Reading Skills
What are two ways that Tonino's life in the countryside is different from life in Santiago?

Comprehension and Critical Thinking
1. (a) Identify Describe Chile's geographic regions.

(b) Identify Cause and Effect How does Chile's geography contribute to its variety of climates and vegetation?

2. (a) Name What kinds of crops are grown in Chile?
(b) Identify Causes Why is Chilean produce so popular in foreign countries?

3. (a) Recall Describe life in Chile when Pinochet was in power.
(b) Evaluate Information Do you think Pinochet should be brought to trial? Explain.

Writing Activity
How do you think Magellan's crew must have felt during their exploration of Tierra del Fuego? Write a journal entry that one of the crew might have written about the experience.

Go Online
PHSchool.com

For: An activity on Chile
Visit: PHSchool.com
Web Code: lfd-1603

Chapter 16 Section 3 **513**

Section 3 Assessment

Key Terms
Students' sentences should reflect knowledge of each Key Term.

Target Reading Skill
Implied contrasts include: Tonino works on a farm; his school is from 2:00 P.M. to 6:00 P.M.; his father trains horses, all of which differs from life in a big city.

Comprehension and Critical Thinking
1. (a) Northern region: Atacama Desert, the driest region in the world; very few plants and animals; provides a lot of copper. Central valley: covered in hills, grasses, and forests; farming and mining take place there; and most of Chile's people live there. Southern region: cold, wet, and stormy. **(b)** Chile's long and thin shape, its nearness to the Pacific Ocean and South Pole, and the fact that the Andes run through it lead to a great variety in climate and vegetation

---

Assess and Reteach

Assess Progress L2
Have students complete the Section Assessment. Then administer the *Section Quiz*.

All in One Latin America Teaching Resources, *Section Quiz*, p. 326

Reteach L1
If students need more instruction, have them read this section in the Reading and Vocabulary Study Guide.

 Chapter 16, Section 3, **Western Hemisphere Reading and Vocabulary Study Guide,** pp. 184–186

Extend L3
Remind students that Pinochet was accused of committing crimes against humanity during his rule. Have students complete the *Analysis of Human Rights Violations* activity.

Go Online
PHSchool.com **For:** Environmental and Global Issues: *Analysis of Human Rights Violations*
Visit: PHSchool.com
Web Code: lfd-1607

Answers

✓ **Reading Check** Pinochet's rule ended when the Chilean people voted against his reelection.

Writing Activity
Use the *Rubric for Assessing a Journal Entry* to evaluate students' journal entries .

All in One Latin America Teaching Resources, *Rubric for Assessing a Journal Entry,* p. 350

Go Online
PHSchool.com Typing in the web code when prompted will bring students directly to detailed instructions for this activity.

2. (a) wheat, potatoes, sugar beets, corn, tomatoes, and many fruits. **(b)** Chilean produce is free of many common plant pests.

3. (a) Congress was not allowed to meet, opposition political parties were not allowed to form, and many people were harshly punished or killed if they spoke out against the regime. **(b)** Students' opinions will vary.

Objective

Learn how to synthesize information.

Prepare to Read

Build Background Knowledge   L2

Encourage students to think about instances in their own lives when they have to put together more than one type of information to understand something. Offer some examples such as museums where the exhibits involve visuals, texts, and audio recordings. Then ask students to provide their own examples.

Instruct

Synthesizing Information   L2

Guided Instruction

- Read the steps to synthesize information as a class and write them on the board.

- Practice the skill by following the steps on p. 514 as a class. Model each step in the activity by choosing a photograph from Section 2 to analyze *(suspension bridge photograph on p. 506)*, identifying its main idea *(Peruvians have adapted to the deep gorges of the altiplano by building suspension bridges.)*, and identifying details that support the main ideas. *(The bridge shown is high up in the trees; no land below can be seen.)* Repeat these steps with the photograph of the Uros' reed islands on p. 501. *(The main idea is that the Uros adapted to their lake environment by building reed islands to live on. The supporting details are the lake and the huts on the island.)* Then ask students to list connections between the two main ideas *(Both reveal ways that people have adapted to their surroundings.)* and their conclusions. *(The people of Peru have found ways to live in many environments.)*

Synthesizing Information

When Madelyn returned from Chile, she entertained the class with a wonderful presentation—a map of the route she had taken, a slide show of the Andes Mountains, and a videotape she had made of life in a small village. She had even managed to ask the villagers a couple of questions in Spanish.

When she finished, the class applauded. Her teacher beamed.

"Madelyn, the amount of information you have gathered is stunning," Mr. Rishell said. "Now perhaps you could synthesize all this material for us."

"Sure!" Madelyn replied. Then she paused. "Um . . . how do you synthesize something?"

When you synthesize information, you find the main ideas of several different sources and use them to draw a conclusion. This skill is particularly useful when you are doing research for a report.

Learn the Skill

To synthesize information, follow these steps.

1. **Identify the main idea of each of your sources.** Main ideas are broad, major ideas that are supported by details.

2. **Identify details that support each main idea.** Look in each source for supporting details. Jot them down or create a chart.

3. **Look for connections between pieces of information.** These connections may be similarities, differences, causes, effects, or examples.

4. **Draw conclusions based on the connections you found.** Be sure to use all of your sources.

514 Latin America

Independent Practice

Assign *Skills for Life* and have students complete it individually.

All in One Latin America Teaching Resources, *Skills for Life,* p. 336

Monitor Progress

The teacher should monitor the students doing the *Skills for Life* worksheet, checking to make sure they understand the skills steps.

Peru		
Main Ideas	**Supporting Details**	
1. Peru has three distinct geographic regions:	• Coastal Region—Desert and oases	
	• Sierra—Mountains	
	• Selva—Rain forest	
2. Peruvians speak different languages:	•	
	•	
	•	

Practice the Skill

Use the steps on page 514 to synthesize information about Peru. Use these sources: the text under the heading The Regions and People of Peru and the Country Profile of Peru on page 502. Make a table like the one started above.

1 Study the information about Peru in the text as well as in the map and charts in the Country Profile. Add at least two main ideas to the first column of the table.

2 Now write details that support each main idea. You may find details that support one idea in several different sources.

3 Do the main ideas show contrasts or similarities within Peru's geographic regions? Jot down connections.

4 Your main ideas should help you write a one- or two-sentence conclusion that answers a question such as, "What have I learned about the regions of Peru?"

Brasília, Brazil

Apply the Skill

Use the steps you have just practiced to synthesize information about Brazil. Select information from text, maps, photographs, captions, and other sources beginning on page 494. Do not try to summarize everything you read about Brazil, but choose a major topic, such as city life.

Chapter 16 **515**

Assess Progress `L2`

Ask students to complete the Apply the Skill activity.

Reteach `L1`

If students are having trouble applying the skill steps, have them review the skill using the interactive Social Studies Skills Tutor CD-ROM.

 Synthesizing Information, **Social Studies Skills Tutor CD-ROM**

Extend `L3`

■ To extend the lesson, ask students to use *Color Transparency LA 9: The World: Annual Precipitation* to locate a place with high annual precipitation. Have them then find a book in the library or in the classroom about that place. What activities do people participate in? How do they make a living? Then have them draw a conclusion as to whether or not high amounts of precipitation affect what kinds of activities people do and how they make a living.

Latin America Transparencies, *Color Transparency LA 9: The World: Annual Precipitation*

■ Ask students to reread Section 3 and choose two or more pieces of information to synthesize using the steps they just learned. Have them create a chart like the one on page 187. *(Answers will vary, but be sure students have correctly completed the chart, choosing the appropriate main idea and supporting details for their pieces. Also, be sure they have drawn an appropriate conclusion.)*

Differentiated Instruction

For Special Needs Students `L1`

Partner special needs students with more proficient students to do Level 1 of the *Synthesizing Information* lesson on the Social Studies Skills Tutor CD-ROM together. When the students feel more confident, they can move on to Level 2 alone.

Synthesizing Information, **Social Studies Skills Tutor CD-ROM**

For Gifted and Talented `L3`

Challenge students to find three of their own sources of information that can be synthesized to give one main idea about Chile.

Answers

Apply the Skill

Students' summaries should include accurate information drawn from more than one source.

Section 4
Step-by-Step Instruction

Objectives

Social Studies

1. Find out how Venezuela was made wealthy by oil.

2. Learn how the ups and downs of oil prices affected the economy and people of Venezuela.

3. Understand how Venezuela is changing.

Reading/Language Arts

Make comparisons to find out how two situations are alike.

Prepare to Read

Build Background Knowledge L2

Tell students that in this section they will learn more about the economy of Venezuela. Have students preview the headings and visuals in this section with the following question in mind: **How has relying on one resource affected the economy and citizens of Venezuela?** Provide a few simple examples to get students started. Conduct an Idea Wave (TE, p. T35) to generate a list.

Set a Purpose for Reading L2

■ Preview the Objectives.

■ Read each statement in the *Reading Readiness Guide* aloud. Ask students to mark the statements true or false.

All In One Latin America Teaching Resources, *Reading Readiness Guide,* p. 328

■ Have students discuss the statements in pairs or groups of four, then mark their worksheets again. Use the Numbered Heads participation structure (TE, p. T36) to call on students to share their group's perspectives.

Vocabulary Builder

Preview Key Terms L2

Pronounce each Key Term, then ask students to say the word with you. Provide a simple explanation such as, "When a group of people try to remove their country's government and take power themselves, they have attempted a coup."

Section 4
Venezuela
Oil Powers the Economy

Prepare to Read

Objectives

In this section you will

1. Find out how Venezuela was made wealthy by oil.

2. Learn how the ups and downs of oil prices affected the economy and people of Venezuela.

3. Understand how Venezuela is changing.

Taking Notes

As you read this section, look for ways that oil prices affect Venezuela. Copy the cause-and-effect chain below and record your findings in it. Add boxes as needed.

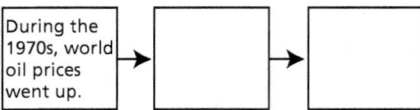

During the 1970s, world oil prices went up. → ☐ → ☐

 Target Reading Skill

Make Comparisons

Comparing two or more situations enables you to see how they are alike. As you read this section, compare life in Venezuela before and after the oil boom. Consider the economy, the government, and the lives of ordinary people.

Key Terms

- **Caracas** (kuh RAH kus) *n.* the capital of Venezuela
- **boom** (boom) *n.* a period of business growth and prosperity
- **privatization** (pry vuh tih ZAY shun) *n.* the government's sale of land or industries it owns to private businesses or individuals
- **coup** (koo) *n.* the overthrow of a ruler or government by an organized group, which then takes power

Caracas, Venezuela

516 Latin America

Welcome to **Caracas** (kuh RAH kus), the capital and largest city of Venezuela. The view from a high-rise apartment building can be breathtaking. At night, thousands of lights dot the surrounding hills. Steep mountains rise in the distance. Now look down at street level. During the day, well-dressed people walk to their jobs in modern office buildings. Others may be going to a museum or to one of the city's public gardens. Later, they may stroll by on their way to dinner or the theater or a concert.

Outside, the air is balmy. It is also clean. Caracas is in a valley that runs from east to west. Winds blow through it. They sweep the exhaust of the city's many cars, buses, and taxis out of Caracas. The subway system also helps by transporting many people who would otherwise have to drive.

Of course, not everyone in Caracas is wealthy and well dressed. The city—and the whole nation of Venezuela—went through a period of rapid growth and prosperity. However, much of the country's population lives in poverty. The contrast between rich and poor has led to political tensions in Venezuela.

Target Reading Skill L2

Make Comparisons Point out the Target Reading Skill. Explain that making comparisons can help students find the similarities between two situations.

Model the skill by drawing students' attention to the first sentence on page 517. Ask students to identify a similarity between Venezuela and the Persian Gulf region. *(Both have some of the world's largest oil reserves.)*

Give students *Make Comparisons.* Have them complete the activity in groups.

All In One Latin America Teaching Resources, *Make Comparisons,* p. 333

A Land Made Wealthy by Oil

Except for the Persian Gulf region, Venezuela has the largest oil reserves in the world. The map of Venezuela in the Country Profile on page 190 shows where Venezuela's vast supplies of oil are located. Venezuela's oil has earned millions of dollars on the world market. In the 1970s, many Venezuelans migrated from the countryside to work for the oil companies. They helped maintain the giant oil rigs in Lake Maracaibo (mar uh KY boh). They also worked in oil refineries.

Both the government and private corporations own oil companies in Venezuela. They have grown rich pumping, processing, and selling oil. In the early 1980s, Venezuela was the richest country in Latin America. Much of the money went to Caracas, the economic center of Venezuela. At that time, there seemed to be no end to the money that could be made in the oil industry.

Ups and Downs of Oil Prices During the 1970s, the price of oil went up. An oil **boom** began. **A boom** is a period of business growth and prosperity. The government spent huge sums of money and hired people to run government agencies and build roads and subways. Many people moved from the countryside to the cities to take these jobs. But from the mid-1980s through the 1990s, oil exporting countries produced more oil than the world needed. The price of oil fell, and many Venezuelans lost their jobs.

This economic downturn continued through the early twenty-first century. In 2002 and 2003, thousands of Venezuelan oil workers went on strike. Oil production and exports came to a standstill. The crisis kept about 200 million barrels of oil and gasoline from the world market. Soon after, oil prices began to rise. By 2004, oil prices were at their highest point in 20 years. They continued to soar into 2006.

Graph Skills

Oil pumped in Venezuela is important not only to that country but also to the United States. **Describe** According to the graph, what is the overall pattern of American imports of Venezuelan oil? **Predict** What do you think might happen to both countries if oil production were interrupted?

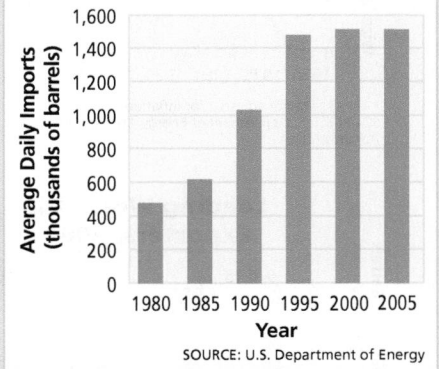

U.S. Petroleum Imports From Venezuela, 1980–2005

SOURCE: U.S. Department of Energy

Vocabulary Builder

Use the information below to teach students this section's high-use words.

High-Use Word	Definition and Sample Sentence
policy, p. 520	*n.* a plan or course of action intended to influence and determine decisions or actions
	The government had a strict **policy** on importing fruits and vegetables.
occur, p. 520	*v.* to take place
	Halloween always **occurs** on October 31st.
individual, p. 520	*n.* a single human considered apart from a society or community
	Five **individuals** can fit comfortably in that car.

Instruct

A Land Made Wealthy by Oil [L2]

Guided Instruction
- Read A Land Made Wealthy by Oil, using the Choral Reading technique (TE, p. T34).
- Ask students **How did oil help increase Venezuela's wealth?** *(Both the government and private corporations in Venezuela mined, processed, and sold the country's oil to countries around the world.)*
- Ask students **How did oil then lead to great poverty in Venezuela?** *(Venezuela and other oil-producing countries were producing more oil than the world needed. Prices dropped and Venezuela began making less and less money. Companies could not afford to keep all the workers they had hired. Many people lost their jobs and became poor.)*

Independent Practice
Ask students to create the Taking Notes graphic organizer on a blank piece of paper. Then have them fill in the boxes with the appropriate causes and their effects. Briefly model how to identify events that cause other events.

Monitor Progress
As students fill in the graphic organizer, circulate and make sure individuals are choosing events that cause or are caused by other events. Provide assistance as needed.

Answers

Graph Skills **Describe** Overall, the United States seems to be importing more oil from Venezuela every year. **Predict** Possible answer: Venezuela would lose money and the United States would export more oil from other oil producing countries.

Guided Instruction
L2

Ask students to study the Country Profile on this page. Encourage them to study the map and the graphs on the page and think about the information each provides. As a class, answer the Map and Chart Skills questions. Allow students to briefly discuss their responses with a partner before sharing answers.

Independent Practice

Ask students to study the graphs, then reread the section's text. Have them write a paragraph using this topic sentence "Oil is extremely important in Venezuela." Allow students to brainstorm ideas in pairs.

Answers

Map and Chart Skills

1. World oil prices fluctuated between about $10 and $25 per barrel between 1990 and 2000. Between 2000 and 2005 oil prices increased dramatically to about $50 per barrel.

2. The bar graph shows that Venezuela is one of the world's leading oil exporters, which tells us that oil is important to its economy. The circle graph shows how much of Venezuela's earnings from exports are due to oil.

3. When oil prices are high, Venezuela's economy flourishes. When prices are low, the economy suffers and people in the oil industry may lose their jobs.

4. Most of Venezuela's oil is located in the north so the large number of people who work for the oil industry probably want to live nearby.

Go Online PHSchool.com **Students can find more information about this topic in the DK World Desk Reference Online.**

Venezuela

Venezuela's economy is dominated by oil. Much of this oil lies under Lake Maracaibo, but there are also large deposits in the northeastern part of the country and near the Orinoco River. Venezuela also has large amounts of coal, iron ore, and minerals. In addition, Venezuela has large areas of rain forest that have less economic value. As you examine the map and graphs, notice where Venezuela's resources are located. Think about how resources and their location can shape a nation's economy and culture.

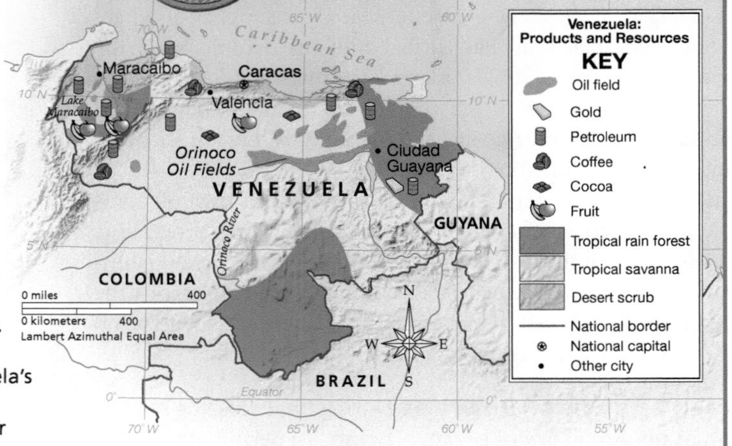

Venezuela: Products and Resources

KEY
- Oil field
- Gold
- Petroleum
- Coffee
- Cocoa
- Fruit
- Tropical rain forest
- Tropical savanna
- Desert scrub
- National border
- National capital
- Other city

World Crude Oil Prices, 1970–2005

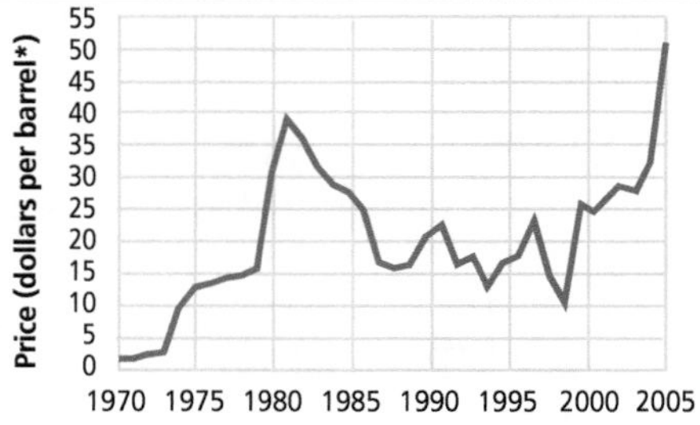

Price (dollars per barrel*)

1970 1975 1980 1985 1990 1995 2000 2005

* Figures are not adjusted for inflation.
SOURCE: U.S. Department of Energy, Energy Information Administration

Venezuela: Earnings from Exports, 2005

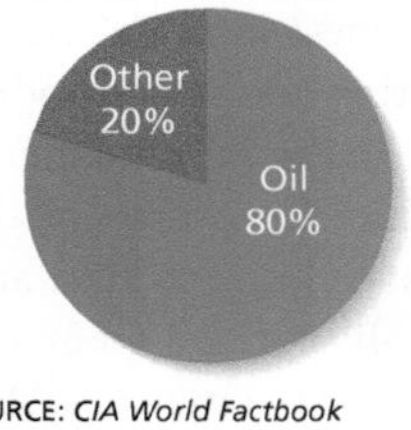

Other 20%
Oil 80%

SOURCE: CIA World Factbook

Leading World Oil Exporters, 2004

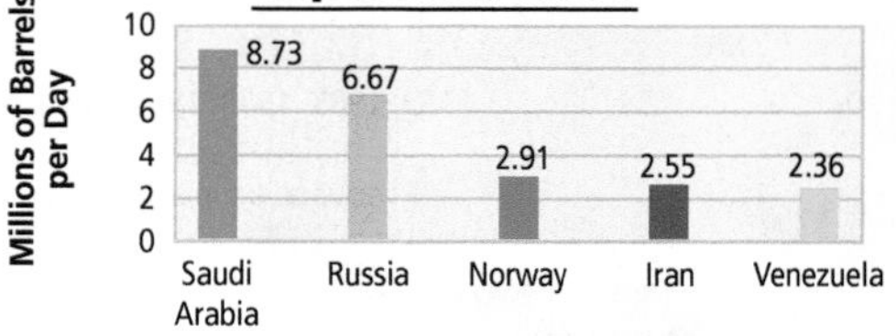

Millions of Barrels per Day

Saudi Arabia	Russia	Norway	Iran	Venezuela
8.73	6.67	2.91	2.55	2.36

SOURCE: U.S. Department of Energy, Energy Information Administration

Map and Chart Skills

1. Describe What is the pattern of the world price of oil from 1990 to 2005?

2. Synthesize Information How do two of the graphs show the importance of oil to Venezuela?

3. Predict In what ways could changes in the world price of oil affect Venezuela?

4. Draw Conclusions More than 80 percent of Venezuela's people live in cities. Use the information on the map and graphs to explain why Venezuela's cities are located in the north of the country.

Go Online PHSchool.com **Use Web Code lfe-1614 for DK World Desk Reference Online.**

— Background: Global Perspectives —

World Oil Powers Venezuela was a founding member of the Organization of Petroleum Exporting Countries (OPEC), which formed in 1960. Members coordinate policies regarding the sale of oil and share economic aid with one another. In late 1973, OPEC twice raised oil prices. While at first OPEC profited greatly from the price increases, Western countries soon found other ways to access oil, forcing OPEC to bring its prices back down. Recent decades have seen more price fluctuations but never again to the extent of the 1970s. Today, OPEC membership includes Iran, Iraq, Kuwait, Libya, Saudi Arabia, Qatar, and the United Arab Emirates in Southwest Asia; Algeria and Nigeria in Africa; and Indonesia in Asia. Ecuador in South America and Gabon in Africa are former members.

The New Poverty Despite growing prosperity from high oil prices, poverty remains a major problem in Venezuela. People who came from conditions of poverty in the countryside often moved to areas in the cities that lacked basic services, such as roads, hospitals, and permanent housing. Although the poverty rate began to decline in the early 2000s, it remained well above 30 percent in 2006.

✓ Reading Check **Why did many people lose their jobs in the 1980s and 1990s?**

The Economy and the People

During the oil boom, Venezuela changed from a traditional culture based on agriculture to a modern urban country. Now more than 80 percent of the population lives in cities.

Venezuelans and the Oil Economy This change can be seen in the story of Juan Varderi's family. Juan's grandfather raised sheep on a ranch east of Lake Maracaibo. He made a fairly good living selling wool and meat to people in Caracas. But Juan's father left the countryside and went to work on an oil rig that was owned by the government. By the time Juan was born, the family was living in Caracas in a small apartment. His father was making enough money for the family to have a television.

Juan loved living in the city, playing baseball in the street, and watching American television programs. "In the early 1980s, we thought we could live just like rich Americans seemed to live. We didn't understand it was only taking place on TV," Juan says. "We didn't know what was going to happen to us in just a few years."

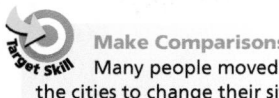

Make Comparisons Many people moved to the cities to change their situation. How was their situation in the countryside similar to their situation after they moved to the cities?

Play Ball!
Boys enjoying a baseball game in Caracas **Infer** Why do you think these boys are playing in this empty lot rather than on a baseball field?

Chapter 16 Section 4 **519**

Make Comparisons As a follow up, ask students to answer the Target Reading Skill question in the Student Edition. *(When the oil industry laid off workers, those that moved to the city to work in the oil industry experienced poverty similar to that which they suffered when they lived in rural areas.)*

The Economy and the People L2

Guided Instruction

- **Vocabulary Builder** Clarify the high-use words **policy**, **occur**, and **individual** before reading.

- Read about the effect of oil prices on Venezuelans in The Economy and the People. As students read, circulate and make sure individuals can answer the Reading Check question.

- Ask students **How did the oil boom change the culture of Venezuela?** *(The oil boom changed Venezuela from a traditional culture based on agriculture into a modern urban culture in which 80 percent of the people live in cities.)*

- Discuss the ways life changed for many Venezuelans after the oil boom ended. *(Many Venezuelans lost their jobs. Once the oil industry became privatized, people did have the opportunity to get hired again, but they were paid lower salaries.)*

Answers

✓ Reading Check Many people lost their jobs in the 1980s and 1990s because the oil-producing countries of the world began producing more oil than was needed. This caused the price of oil to fall.
Infer Possible answer: The city may not have been able to afford to build a baseball field in this part of the city.

Independent Practice

Have students continue to fill in the boxes of their graphic organizers with the causes and effects of events discussed.

Monitor Progress

Circulate and check students' graphic organizers to make sure they are identifying all the events in Venezuela that fit into the cause-and-effect chain. Provide assistance to any students who need it.

When Juan turned 15, oil prices suddenly fell. Juan's father was one of the many who lost their jobs. And like many other Venezuelan families, Juan's family was in danger of losing their apartment. Things looked bleak for those who had depended on the oil industry for their living.

Government Businesses Go Public In the late 1980s and the 1990s, the government sold some of its businesses to private corporations. **Privatization** (pry vuh tih ZAY shun) occurs when the government sells its industries to individuals or private companies. Under this policy, the government hoped the private companies would make big profits and hire more workers. The companies were able to hire many workers, but employees received less pay than they did when they worked for the government. This is what happened to Juan's father.

The Role of Weather The economic crisis grew in 1999 when Venezuela was hit by massive floods and mudslides. In some areas, unstable shacks were swept away or buried in mud, and many people were killed or made homeless. The destruction was so great that reconstruction and resettling of the homeless went on for years.

✓ Reading Check **How did salaries compare before and after privatization?**

Disaster!
In 1999, flooding and landslides caused devastation around Caracas (left), and destroyed much of the town of Macuto (right). **Draw Conclusions** *Explain how a major disaster like this would probably affect a country's economy.*

520 Latin America

Answers

Draw Conclusions A major disaster like this would probably devastate a country's economy. But, it might also create some new jobs related to rebuilding the city.

✓ Reading Check Salaries were lower after privatization.

A Change in Government

In 1998, Hugo Chavez was elected president of Venezuela on a platform to help the poor. Many of his new programs caused deep political divisions between the rich and poor, and Chavez survived many challenges to his presidency. In April 2002, he was forced out of office for two days during a failed coup attempt. A coup (koo) is the overthrow of a ruler or government by an organized group, which then takes power. In 2002 and 2003, Chavez dealt with protests to his administration and the strike that halted oil production. In August 2004, a referendum, or vote, was called to remove him from office. The referendum failed when 59 percent of voters supported Chavez.

Supporters and Opponents Many of Chavez's supporters defended the programs that were designed to help people living in poverty. Under the programs, oil revenues began to be used to provide health care, clean water, low cost food, electricity, and other basic services to the country's poor. The government also built new schools and created literacy programs.

Chavez's critics did not agree with many of his government policies, though. They denounced the government's increased military spending and interference in business. People in the international community condemned Chavez's strict control over the media. Many of Chavez's policies damaged the relationship between Venezuela and the United States.

A Change in Government L2

Guided Instruction

■ Ask students to read about Hugo Chavez and the changes he's made in Venezuela in A Change in Government.

■ Discuss the challenges to Chavez's rule. *(Many of President Chavez's economic programs caused deep political divisions between the rich and poor; and he has survived many challenges to his presidency including protests, strikes, and a failed coup attempt.)*

■ In pairs, ask students to list reasons why people support Chavez. *(His programs help people in poverty.)* Next, have them list reasons why people criticize Chavez. *(He controls the media; military spending has increased; his government interferes with businesses.)* Then, have them summarize people's reactions to his rule.

Independent Practice

Have students complete the graphic organizer by filling in the final of the causes and effects they learned in this section.

Monitor Progress

■ Show *Section Reading Support Transparency LA 48* and ask students to check their graphic organizers individually. Go over key concepts and clarify key vocabulary as needed.

📖 **Latin America Transparencies,** *Section Reading Support Transparency LA 48*

■ Tell students to fill in the last column of the *Reading Readiness Guide*. Probe for what they learned that confirms or invalidates each statement.

All in One **Latin America Teaching Resources,** *Reading Readiness Guide,* p. 328

Differentiated Instruction

For Less Proficient Readers L1

Help students understand the ups and downs of Venezuela's economy by having pairs create a time line showing the changes. Use the *Rubric for Assessing a Timeline* to evaluate students' timelines.

All in One **Latin America Teaching Resources,** *Rubric for Assessing a Timeline,* p. 351

For Special Needs Students L1

Have students read the section in the Reading and Vocabulary Study Guide. This version provides a summary of section content with interactive questions and activities to help students read.

📖 Chapter 16, Section 4, **Western Hemisphere Reading and Vocabulary Study Guide,** pp. 187–189

Assess and Reteach

Section 4 Assessment

Key Terms
Students' sentences should reflect knowledge of each Key Term.

Target Reading Skill
Both crises caused an economic setback in Venezuela; both caused people to lose their homes; both hit the poor the hardest.

Comprehension and Critical Thinking
1. (a) The government responded by spending huge sums of money—by hiring many people to run government agencies and government-owned businesses and by building expensive subways and roads. **(b)** The country relied so heavily on that one industry.

2. (a) In the 1970s, many people from the countryside moved to the cities to get jobs in the growing oil industry. **(b)** The oil boom affected oil workers by allowing them to earn

---

Some Venezuelans support Hugo Chavez (left), while others oppose his government (right).

Recent improvements Chavez faces another presidential election in December 2006. The slow upturn in the economy may help Chavez's chances in the election. Since 2003, the number of people living in poverty has gradually declined. The unemployment rate decreased from 17% in 2004 to 14% in 2005.

Because of the recent spike in oil prices, Venezuela earned $36 billion from its oil industry in 2005-triple the amount received in 1998. Today oil accounts for 80% of Venezuelan exports. Oil prices will probably continue to control Venezuela's economy for some time. Whatever the country's future is, one thing is certain. The oil boom brought Venezuela into the modern world.

✓ **Reading Check** **What are some recent signs that Venezuela's economy is improving?**

Section 4 Assessment

Key Terms
Review the key terms at the beginning of this section. Use each term in a sentence that explains its meaning.

Target Reading Skills
How were the effects of the fall of oil prices in the 1980s similar to the effects of the torrential rainstorms of 1999?

Comprehension and Critical Thinking
1. (a) Describe How did the government of Venezuela react to the oil boom?

(b) Draw Conclusions Why did the drop in oil prices affect Venezuela so much?
2. (a) Recall What brought many people from the countryside to the cities in the 1970s?
(b) Identify Effects How did the oil boom and then privatization affect oil workers?
3. (a) Sequence How did Hugo Chavez gain power?
(b) Infer Why do you think that most Venezuelans supported Chavez in the 2004 referendum?

Writing Activity
Juan Varderi learned about American families from television programs. Write the first scene of a television script about a Venezuelan family. First choose a time and place for your program, such as the 1970s in Caracas or today in the countryside. Then think about how a family would live in that setting.

> **Writing Tip** List the setting and characters first. Then use the correct form to write dialogue and stage directions.

522 Latin America

---

enough money to live comfortably. Privatization affected oil workers by giving them jobs after losing the government jobs, but with lower salaries.

3. (a) He was elected president after leading an unsuccessful coup against the government. **(b)** Answers will vary. Students might say that by 2004, the unemployment rate was starting to decline, which worked in his favor.

Writing Activity
Use the *Rubric for Assessing a Writing Assignment* to evaluate students' scripts.

🔲 **All In One** **Latin America Teaching Resources,** *Rubric for Assessing a Writing Assignment,* p. 349

16 Review and Assessment

Review and Assessment

◆ **Chapter Summary**

Section 1: Brazil

- The geography of Brazil includes rain forests, plateaus, and savannas.
- Rain forests are important to Brazil and affect the whole world, but they face many dangers.
- Most Brazilians live in cities along the coast, but some live on farms and in the rain forest.

Section 2: Peru

- Most Peruvians live in the modern cities of the coastal plain.
- Many Native Americans still lead traditional lives in the mountain and forest regions.
- Old and new ways of life exist side by side in the Altiplano, the high plateau in the Andes Mountains.

Section 3: Chile

- The regions of Chile have distinct types of climate and geography, and people live very differently in each region.
- Although most of Chile's people live in cities, agriculture is very important to Chile's economy.
- Chileans voted out a dictator and replaced his brutal regime with a democratic government.

Section 4: Venezuela

- Oil production made Venezuela rich.
- A decrease in oil prices caused problems for Venezuela's economy and for ordinary people.
- Venezuela's president, Hugo Chavez, has worked against poverty and supported many controversial policies.

Brazil

◆ **Key Terms**

Define each of the following terms.

1. Altiplano
2. sierra
3. oasis
4. boom
5. savanna
6. coup
7. canopy
8. Brasília
9. circumnavigate
10. privatization
11. Caracas
12. glacier
13. Rio de Janeiro
14. Amazon rain forest

Vocabulary Builder

Revisit this chapter's high-use words:

occupy   foundation   reject
dense   adapt   policy
community   survive   occur
dwell   regime   individual

Ask students to review the definitions they recorded on their *Word Knowledge* worksheets.

All in One Latin America Teaching Resources, *Word Knowledge,* p. 334

Consider allowing students to earn extra credit if they use the words in their answers to the questions in the Chapter Review and Assessment. The words must be used correctly and in a natural context to win the extra points.

Review Chapter Content

- Review and revisit the major themes of this chapter by asking students to identify which Guiding Question each bulleted statement in the Chapter Summary answers. Have students write each statement down and work in groups to determine which statement applies to which Guiding Question. Refer to page 329 in the Student Edition for the text of Guiding Questions.

- Assign *Vocabulary Development* for students to review Key Terms.

  All in One Latin America Teaching Resources, *Vocabulary Development,* p. 347

Answers

Key Terms

1. The Altiplano is the high plateau in the Andes Mountains of Peru.
2. The sierra is the mountain region of Peru, which includes the altiplano and the Andes Mountains.
3. An oasis is a place in the desert that has water and is fertile.
4. A boom is a period of business growth and prosperity.
5. A savanna is a flat, grassy region, or plain.
6. A coup is the overthrow of a ruler or government by an organized group that then takes power.
7. The canopy is the dense mass of leaves at the top of the tree in a rain forest.
8. Brasília is Brazil's new capital city.
9. To circumnavigate something is to go all the way around it.
10. Privatization occurs when the government sells its industries to individuals or private companies.
11. Caracas is the capital of Venezuela.
12. A glacier is a huge mass of slowly moving ice and snow.
13. Rio de Janeiro is a large city located on Brazil's coast.
14. The Amazon rain forest is a large tropical rain forest occupying the Amazon Basin in northern South America.

Comprehension and Critical Thinking

15. (a) A rain forest is hot, humid, and gets heavy rainfall. Plants grow abundantly and many different kinds of animals live there. **(b)** The Amazon rain forest helps produce about one third of the world's oxygen, it is home to millions of species of plants, animals, and insects, and many modern medicines have been made from plants there.

16. (a) along or near the coast and along rivers **(b)** to help the country use the resources of the rain forest to develop that region **(c)** Answers will vary slightly but should identify the areas along coasts and rivers as more accessible than the areas in the interior of the country. Also, the climate and terrain make it easier to live on the coast.

17. (a) The mountain region, or sierra, includes the Andes Mountains and the cold altiplano. Native Americans live and herd animals there. The coastal region is dry and dotted with oases. There are many cities in this region, which is the economic center of the country. The forested region, or selva, stretches from the base of the mountains to northeast Peru. It includes rain forest and is hot and humid. It has few roads to the other regions and little modern development. Some Native Americans live there. **(b)** Possible answer: They may begin to move away from some of their traditional ways of life and adopt more modern ways.

18. (a) Magellan discovered the strait when he was trying to find a way to sail around or through the Americas from Spain. The journey was difficult and Magellan did not make it back to Spain. **(b)** The mountains trap exhaust and smoke, creating pollution problems; Chile is in the Southern Hemisphere and can grow and sell produce when it is winter in the Northern Hemisphere; Chile's farming regions are protected by the Andes Mountains, which help keep out some insect pests and animal diseases that plague other countries. **(c)** Possible answer: There may be a great difference in culture between people in the north and people in the south because they are very far apart.

19. (a) Venezuela has one of the world's largest supplies of oil and has mined, processed, and sold it around the world. **(b)** Chile's and Venezuela's economic histories have been different in that Chile has not gone through the tremendous economic downturn that Venezuela has.

◆ **Comprehension and Critical Thinking**

15. (a) Describe What are the characteristics of a rain forest?
(b) Apply Information Why is the Amazon rain forest important even to countries far from Brazil?

16. (a) Identify Where do most of Brazil's people live?
(b) Identify Causes Why did the Brazilian government want people to move to the interior of the country?
(c) Analyze Why do you think Brazil's population is distributed the way it is?

17. (a) Identify Describe the three geographical regions of Peru.
(b) Predict How do you think the coming of modern conveniences such as electricity will change life for the indigenous people of Peru? Explain.

18. (a) Summarize Describe Magellan's discovery of the strait that bears his name.
(b) Identify Effects How does Chile's geography contribute to both its pollution problem and its agricultural boom?
(c) Infer How might the fact that Chile is so long and narrow affect Chilean society?

19. (a) Describe How did Venezuela grow rich from oil?
(b) Contrast In what ways have Chile's and Venezuela's economic histories been different?

◆ **Skills Practice**

Synthesizing Information In the Skills for Life activity in this chapter, you learned how to synthesize information from many sources. You also learned how to use what you found out to draw a conclusion about a particular topic.

Review the steps you followed to learn the skill. Then use those steps to synthesize information about Venezuela's economy from different sources within Section 4. Finally, draw a conclusion that pulls together what you learned.

◆ **Writing Activity: Science**

Suppose you are a science reporter for a local television station in Santiago, Chile. Santiago has been experiencing a week of very bad smog. Write a report explaining why the smog is so bad this week and suggesting how people might protect themselves from the pollution. Make sure your report can be read in two to three minutes.

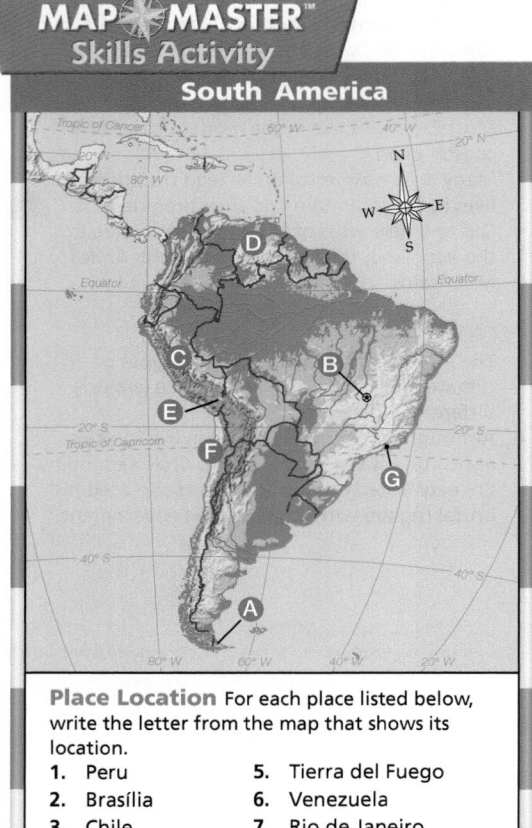

MAP MASTER™ Skills Activity

South America

Place Location For each place listed below, write the letter from the map that shows its location.
1. Peru
2. Brasília
3. Chile
4. Lake Titicaca
5. Tierra del Fuego
6. Venezuela
7. Rio de Janeiro

Go Online
PHSchool.com Use Web Code lfp-1301 for an **interactive map**.

Skills Practice
Students' answers will vary.

Possible conclusion Venezuela's economy has been negatively affected by relying heavily on one resource.

Writing Activity: Science
Students' answers will vary but should use the information provided in the section as well as information from other sources.

Use the Rubric for Assessing a Report to evaluate students' reports.

All in One **Latin America Teaching Resources,** *Rubric for Assessing a Report,* p. 352

Standardized Test Prep

MAP MASTER
Skills Activity

1. C   **2.** B
3. F   **4.** E
5. A   **6.** D
7. G

Go Online
PHSchool.com Students may practice their map skills using the interactive online version of this map.

Standardized Test Prep
Answers
1. B
2. D
3. C

Go Online
PHSchool.com Students may use the Chapter 16 self-test on PHSchool.com to prepare for the Chapter Test.

Test-Taking Tips

Some questions on standardized tests ask you to analyze a reading selection to find the main ideas. Read the passage below. Then follow the tips to answer the sample question.

> Brazil is a major world coffee grower. Brazil's farms and plantations also grow soybeans, wheat, rice, corn, sugar cane, cacao, oranges, and lemons. The country's factories make many goods. Cars, iron, steel, shoes, textiles, and electrical equipment are all important industries.

This paragraph concerns which basic economic question?

  A What goods does Brazil produce?
  B What services does Brazil produce?
  C How are goods and services produced in Brazil?
  D Who will buy these goods and services?

TIP Read the whole passage to understand the main idea. Notice that it lists two kinds of goods from Brazil, those that grow and those made in factories.

Think It Through Notice that three of the answers contain the word *produce* or *produced*. You know that the main idea of the paragraph is that Brazil produces two kinds of goods—crops grown on farms and goods made in factories. The passage does not describe how the goods are produced (answer C) or who buys them (answer D). There is nothing in the paragraph about services (answer B). Therefore the answer is A.

TIP Look for key words in the passage and in the answer choices to help you answer the question. *Grow* and *make* both mean "produce."

Practice Questions

Choose the letter of the best answer.

1. Chilean produce has a large market in the United States from October through May because
  A Americans eat more produce over the winter.
  B less produce is grown in the United States during the winter than in the summer.
  C Chileans do not consume as much of their own produce during those months.
  D it is easiest to transport goods during those months.

2. What caused Venezuela's oil industry to decline in the mid-1980s?
  A The oil fields began to dry up.
  B People weren't driving cars as much.
  C The country began to focus on steel production.
  D World oil prices fell.

Read the passage below and answer the question that follows.

Peru has three distinct geographic regions: the cold, mountainous sierra; the dry coastal plain; and the warm, forested selva. The ways people live in these regions are very different. For example, many people on the coastal plain live in cities, while most people in the sierra live in small villages.

3. Which statement best expresses the main idea of the passage?
  A Peru's geography is varied.
  B Peru's sierra is mountainous and cold.
  C Peru's geography affects the lives of its people.
  D There are no cities in Peru's sierra region.

Go Online
PHSchool.com
Use Web Code lfa-1601
for a **Chapter 16 self-test.**

Assessment Resources

Teaching Resources
Chapter Tests A and B, pp. 353–358
Final Exams A and B, pp. 363–368

Test Prep Workbook
Latin America Study Sheet, pp. 180–185
Latin America Practice Tests A, B, C, pp. 61–72

AYP Monitoring Assessments
Latin America Benchmark Test, pp. 101–104
Latin America Outcome Test, pp. 182–187

Technology
◉ *ExamView® Test Bank CD-ROM*

- Students can further explore the Guiding Questions by completing hands-on projects.

- Three pages of structured guidance in **All-in-One Latin America Teaching Resources** support each of the projects described on this page.

  All in One **Latin America Teaching Resources,** *Book Project: Latin America in the News,* pp. 76–78; *Book Project: A Latin American Concert,* pp. 79–81

- There are also two additional projects introduced, explained, and supported in the **All-in-One Latin America Teaching Resources.**

  All in One **Latin America Teaching Resources,** *Book Project: Visions of Latin America,* pp. 73–75; *Book Project: Explorer's Dictionary,* pp. 82–84

- Go over the four project suggestions with students.

- Ask each student to select one of the projects, or design his or her own. Work with students to create a project description and a schedule.

- Post project schedules and monitor student progress by asking for progress reports.

Projects

Create your own projects to learn more about Latin America. At the beginning of this section, you were introduced to the Guiding Questions for studying the chapters and special features. But you can also find answers to these questions by doing projects on your own or with a group. Use the questions to find topics you want to explore further. Then try the projects described on this page or create your own.

1 **Geography** What are the main physical features of Latin America?

2 **History** How has Latin America been shaped by its history?

3 **Culture** What factors have affected cultures in Latin America?

4 **Government** What types of government have existed in Latin America?

5 **Economics** How has geography influenced the ways in which Latin Americans make a living?

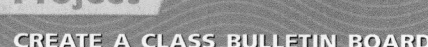

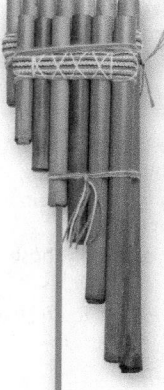

Project

CREATE A CLASS BULLETIN BOARD

Latin America in the News
As you read about Latin America, keep a class bulletin board display called Latin America in the News. Look in magazines and newspapers for articles about Latin American culture and current events. Print out articles from reliable online news sources. Choose a time, such as once a week, for the class to review and discuss the articles. You might have several students present the information to the class as a radio or television news report.

Project

RESEARCH LATIN AMERICAN MUSIC

A Latin American Concert
As you study Latin America, find out about the music of each region. Research the kinds of instruments people play and what they are made of. Learn how history and geography influenced the development of different kinds of music. Did you know, for example, that people in the Andes make a kind of rattle out of the hooves of llamas? That reggae developed as political protest? Find some examples of recorded Latin American music in the library, play them for your class, and report on what you learned about the music.

527

- Assess student projects using rubrics from the **All-in-One Latin America Teaching Resources.**

  All-in-One Latin America Teaching Resources, *Rubric for Assessing Student Performance on a Project,* p. 85; *Rubric for Assessing the Performance of an Entire Group,* p. 86; *Rubric for Assessing Individual Performance in a Group,* p. 87

Portfolio Activity Tell students they can add their completed Book Project as the final item in their portfolios. Assess student portfolios with *Rubric for Assessing a Student Portfolio.*

All-in-One Latin America Teaching Resources, *Rubric for Assessing a Student Portfolio,* p. 88

527

Reference

Table of Contents

Atlas **530**
The World: Political 530
The World: Physical 532
North and South America: Political 534
North and South America: Physical 535
United States: Political 536
Europe: Political 538
Europe: Physical 539
Africa: Political 540
Africa: Physical 541
Asia: Political 542
Asia: Physical 543
Oceania 544
The Arctic 545
Antarctica 545

Country Databank **546**

Glossary of Geographic Terms **554**

Gazetteer **556**

Glossary **562**

Index **576**

Acknowledgments **605**

The World: Political

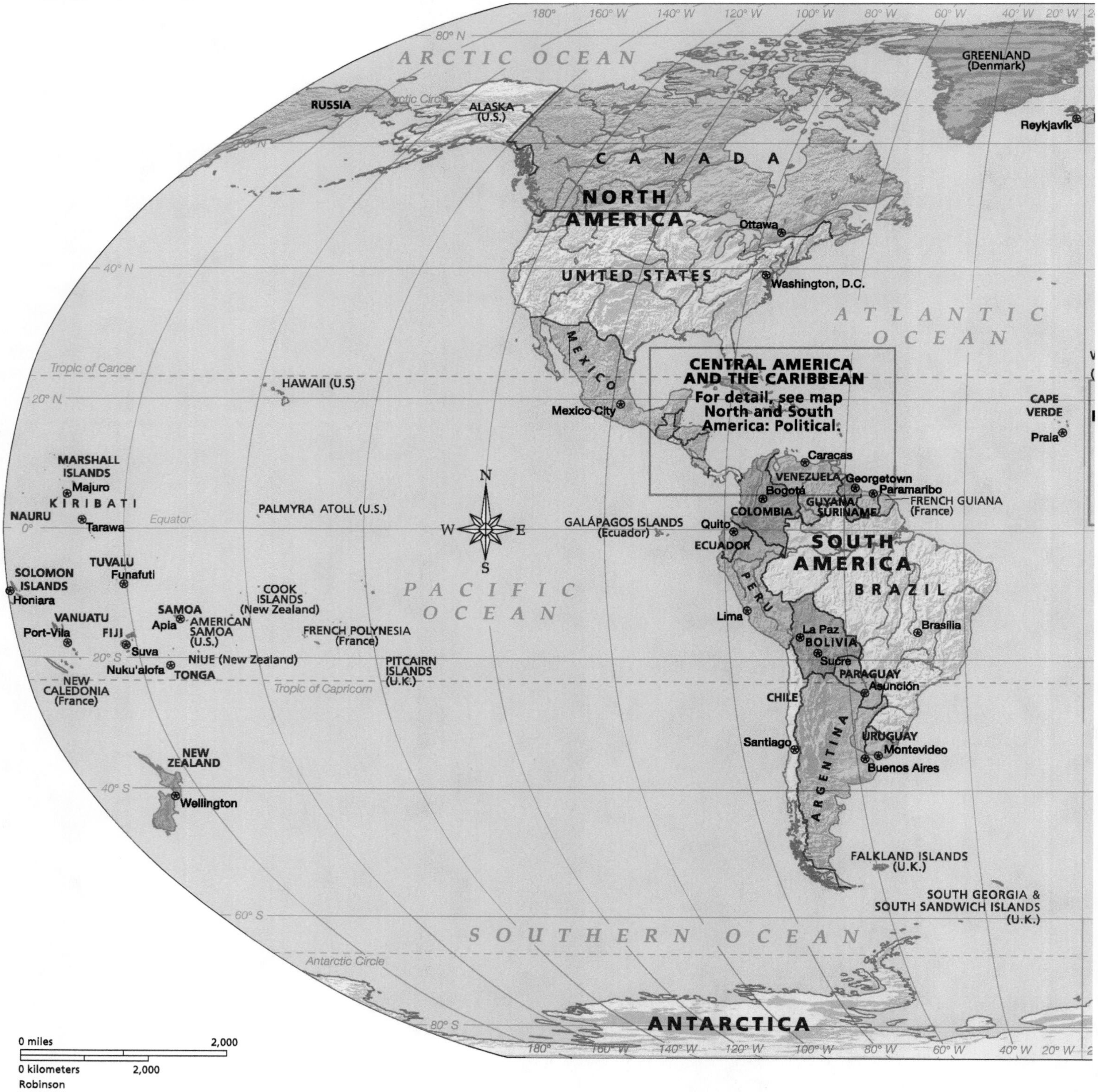

ARCTIC OCEAN

GREENLAND
(Denmark)

RUSSIA

ALASKA
(U.S.)

Reykjavík

CANADA

NORTH
AMERICA

Ottawa

UNITED STATES

Washington, D.C.

ATLANTIC
OCEAN

Tropic of Cancer

HAWAII (U.S)

MEXICO

CENTRAL AMERICA
AND THE CARIBBEAN
For detail, see map
North and South
America: Political.

CAPE
VERDE

20° N

Mexico City

Praia

MARSHALL
ISLANDS
Majuro

Caracas

K I R I B A T I

PALMYRA ATOLL (U.S.)

VENEZUELA Georgetown
Bogotá   Paramaribo
GUYANA   FRENCH GUIANA
COLOMBIA SURINAME (France)

NAURU

Equator

GALÁPAGOS ISLANDS
(Ecuador)

Quito

Tarawa

ECUADOR

SOUTH
AMERICA

TUVALU
Funafuti

PERU

B R A Z I L

SOLOMON
ISLANDS

COOK
ISLANDS
(New Zealand)

PACIFIC

Lima

Honiara

VANUATU

SAMOA
Apia AMERICAN
SAMOA
(U.S.)

OCEAN

La Paz
BOLIVIA

Brasília

Port-Vila

FIJI

FRENCH POLYNESIA
(France)

Suva

20° S

NIUE (New Zealand)

Sucre

Nuku'alofa TONGA

PITCAIRN
ISLANDS
(U.K.)

PARAGUAY

NEW
CALEDONIA
(France)

Tropic of Capricorn

CHILE

Asunción

URUGUAY

Santiago

Montevideo
Buenos Aires

NEW
ZEALAND

40° S

Wellington

FALKLAND ISLANDS
(U.K.)

SOUTH GEORGIA &
SOUTH SANDWICH ISLANDS
(U.K.)

60° S

SOUTHERN   OCEAN

Antarctic Circle

80° S

ANTARCTICA

0 miles   2,000

0 kilometers   2,000
Robinson

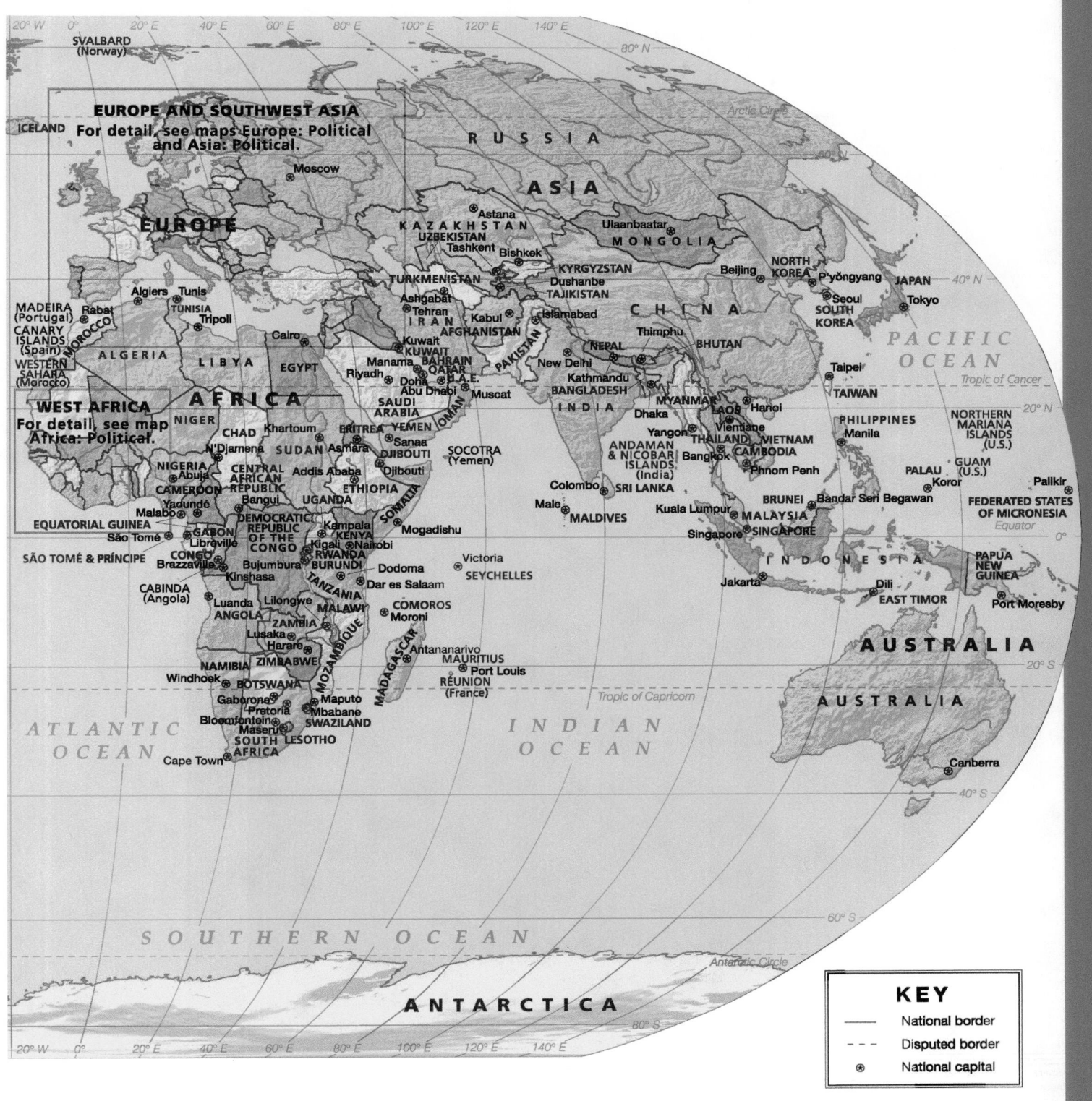

SVALBARD
(Norway)

EUROPE AND SOUTHWEST ASIA
For detail, see maps Europe: Political
and Asia: Political.

ICELAND

EUROPE

R U S S I A

Arctic Circle

80° N

Moscow

A S I A

⊛ Astana

K A Z A K H S T A N

Ulaanbaatar ⊛

UZBEKISTAN

M O N G O L I A

Tashkent ⊛ ⊛ Bishkek

Beijing ⊛

NORTH
KOREA

40° N

TURKMENISTAN

KYRGYZSTAN
Dushanbe
TAJIKISTAN

P'yŏngyang ⊛

JAPAN

Algiers Tunis

TUNISIA

Ashgabat ⊛

⊛ Tehran

Kabul ⊛

⊛ Seoul

SOUTH
KOREA

⊛ Tokyo

PACIFIC
OCEAN

MADEIRA
(Portugal)

Rabat ⊛

I R A N

AFGHANISTAN

Islamabad ⊛

C H I N A

CANARY
ISLANDS
(Spain)

MOROCCO

ALGERIA

LIBYA

EGYPT

Cairo ⊛

Kuwait ⊛
KUWAIT
BAHRAIN
Manama ⊛ QATAR

Thimphu ⊛

NEPAL

BHUTAN

New Delhi ⊛

Taipei ⊛

Tropic of Cancer

WESTERN
SAHARA
(Morocco)

A F R I C A

Riyadh ⊛

Doha ⊛
Abu Dhabi ⊛

U.A.E.
Muscat ⊛

Kathmandu ⊛

BANGLADESH

TAIWAN

20° N

WEST AFRICA
For detail, see map
Africa: Political.

NIGER

CHAD

Khartoum ⊛

ERITREA

SAUDI
ARABIA

OMAN

YEMEN

I N D I A

Dhaka ⊛

MYANMAR
LAOS ⊛ Hanoi

PHILIPPINES

NORTHERN
MARIANA
ISLANDS
(U.S.)

N'Djamena ⊛

SUDAN

Asmara ⊛
DJIBOUTI

Sanaa ⊛

SOCOTRA
(Yemen)

Yangon ⊛

Vientiane ⊛
THAILAND
Bangkok ⊛

VIETNAM
CAMBODIA

Manila ⊛

GUAM
(U.S.)

NIGERIA
Abuja ⊛

CENTRAL
AFRICAN
REPUBLIC

Addis Ababa ⊛

Djibouti ⊛

PALAU

Palikir ⊛

CAMEROON

Bangui ⊛

ETHIOPIA

Phnom Penh ⊛

Koror ⊛

FEDERATED STATES
OF MICRONESIA

Yaoundé ⊛

UGANDA

SOMALIA

Colombo ⊛

SRI LANKA

BRUNEI

Bandar Seri Begawan ⊛

Malabo ⊛

EQUATORIAL GUINEA

DEMOCRATIC
REPUBLIC
OF THE
CONGO

Kampala ⊛

KENYA

Male ⊛

MALDIVES

Kuala Lumpur ⊛
MALAYSIA

Equator

São Tomé ⊛

GABON
Libreville ⊛

Kigali ⊛
RWANDA

⊛ Nairobi

Mogadishu ⊛

Singapore ⊛ SINGAPORE

0°

SÃO TOMÉ & PRÍNCIPE

CONGO
Brazzaville ⊛

Bujumbura ⊛
BURUNDI

Victoria ⊛
SEYCHELLES

I N D O N E S I A

PAPUA
NEW
GUINEA

Kinshasa ⊛

TANZANIA

Dodoma ⊛

Dar es Salaam ⊛

Jakarta ⊛

Dili ⊛

⊛ Port Moresby

CABINDA
(Angola)

Luanda ⊛

Lilongwe ⊛
MALAWI

COMOROS
Moroni ⊛

EAST TIMOR

ANGOLA

ZAMBIA

Lusaka ⊛

Harare ⊛

MOZAMBIQUE

MADAGASCAR

Antananarivo ⊛
MAURITIUS

A U S T R A L I A

NAMIBIA

ZIMBABWE

⊛ Port Louis

20° S

Windhoek ⊛

BOTSWANA

RÉUNION
(France)

Tropic of Capricorn

A U S T R A L I A

Gaborone ⊛

Maputo ⊛

ATLANTIC
OCEAN

Pretoria ⊛
Bloemfontein ⊛
Maseru ⊛

Mbabane ⊛
SWAZILAND

INDIAN
OCEAN

SOUTH
Cape Town ⊛ AFRICA

LESOTHO

Canberra ⊛

40° S

SOUTHERN OCEAN

60° S

Antarctic Circle

80° S

ANTARCTICA

20° W   0°   20° E   40° E   60° E   80° E   100° E   120° E   140° E

The World: Physical

0 miles   2,000

0 kilometers   2,000

Robinson

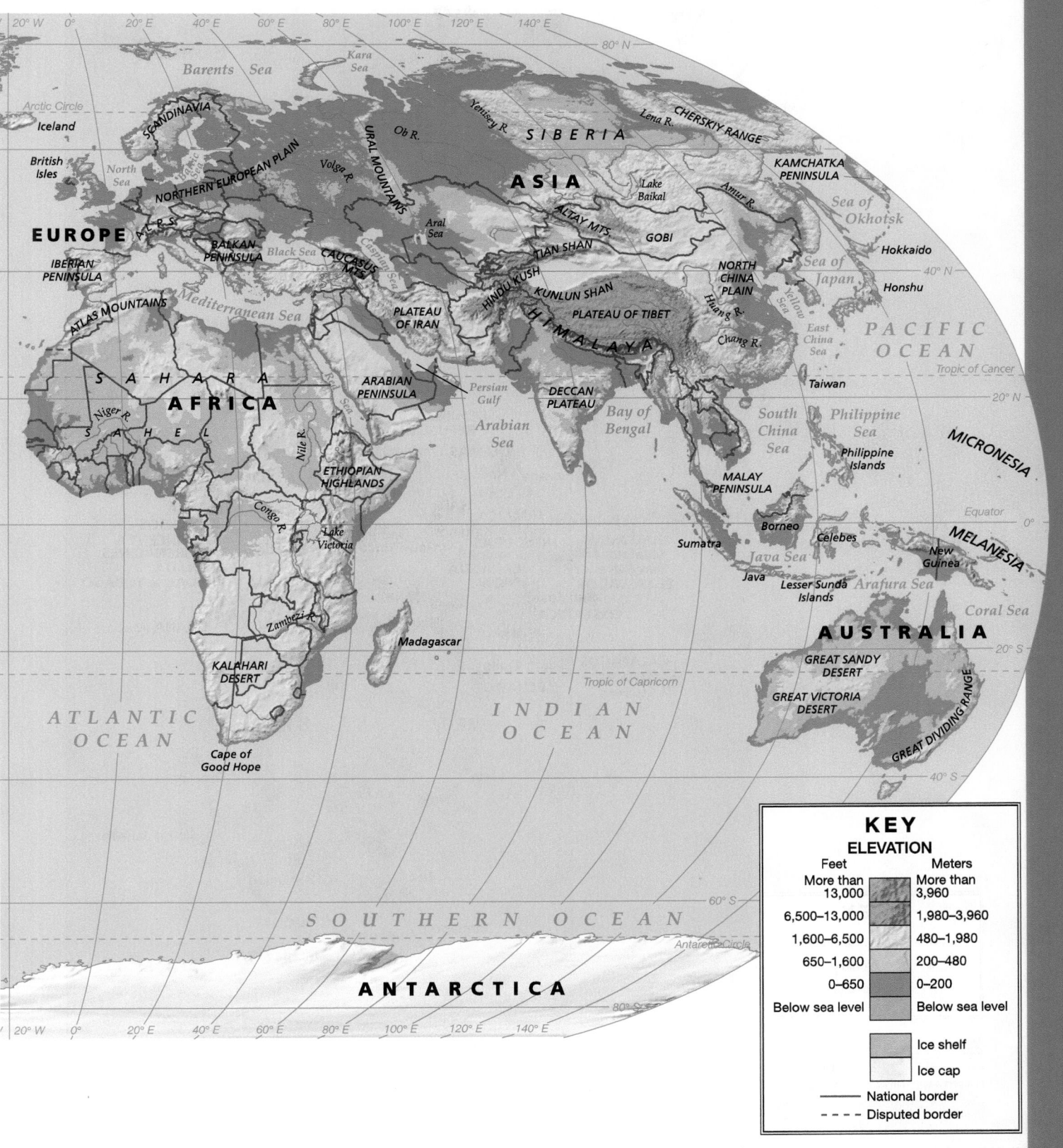

KEY

ELEVATION

Feet		Meters
More than 13,000		More than 3,960
6,500–13,000		1,980–3,960
1,600–6,500		480–1,980
650–1,600		200–480
0–650		0–200
Below sea level		Below sea level

Ice shelf

Ice cap

——— National border

- - - Disputed border

North and South America: Political

KEY

— National border

⊗ National capital

• Other city

0 miles   2,000

0 kilometers   2,000

Lambert Azimuthal Equal Area

534 Reference

North and South America: Physical

ASIA

ARCTIC OCEAN

EUROPE

Bering Strait

Beaufort Sea

Bering Sea

Aleutian Islands

Mt. McKinley 20,320 ft (6,194 m)

Alaska Range

Gulf of Alaska

Mackenzie R.

Great Bear Lake

Great Slave Lake

Greenland

Baffin Bay

Davis Strait

Baffin Island

Labrador Sea

ROCKY MOUNTAINS

GREAT PLAINS

Lake Winnipeg

CANADIAN SHIELD

Great Lakes

Newfoundland

Missouri R.

Colorado R.

Mississippi R.

Ohio R.

Appalachian Mts.

ATLANTIC OCEAN

Tropic of Cancer

Baja California

Rio Grande

Sierra Madre Oriental

Sierra Madre Occidental

Gulf of California

Tropic of Cancer

Gulf of Mexico

Yucatán Peninsula

Cuba

Greater Antilles

Hispaniola

Lesser Antilles

Caribbean Sea

PACIFIC OCEAN

Isthmus of Panama

Galápagos Islands

Orinoco R.

Guiana Highlands

Amazon R.

Equator

Equator

AMAZON BASIN

São Francisco R.

ANDES

Brazilian Highlands

Lake Titicaca

Gran Chaco

Paraguay R.

Paraná R.

Tropic of Capricorn

Tropic of Capricorn

Aconcagua 22,834 ft (6,960 m)

Pampas

Río de la Plata

Patagonia

ATLANTIC OCEAN

Falkland Islands

Tierra del Fuego

Cape Horn

KEY
ELEVATION

Feet	Meters
More than 13,000	More than 3,960
6,500–13,000	1,980–3,960
1,600–6,500	480–1,980
650–1,600	200–480
0–650	0–200

Ice cap

National border

0 miles 2,000

0 kilometers 2,000

Lambert Azimuthal Equal Area

N W E S

United States: Political

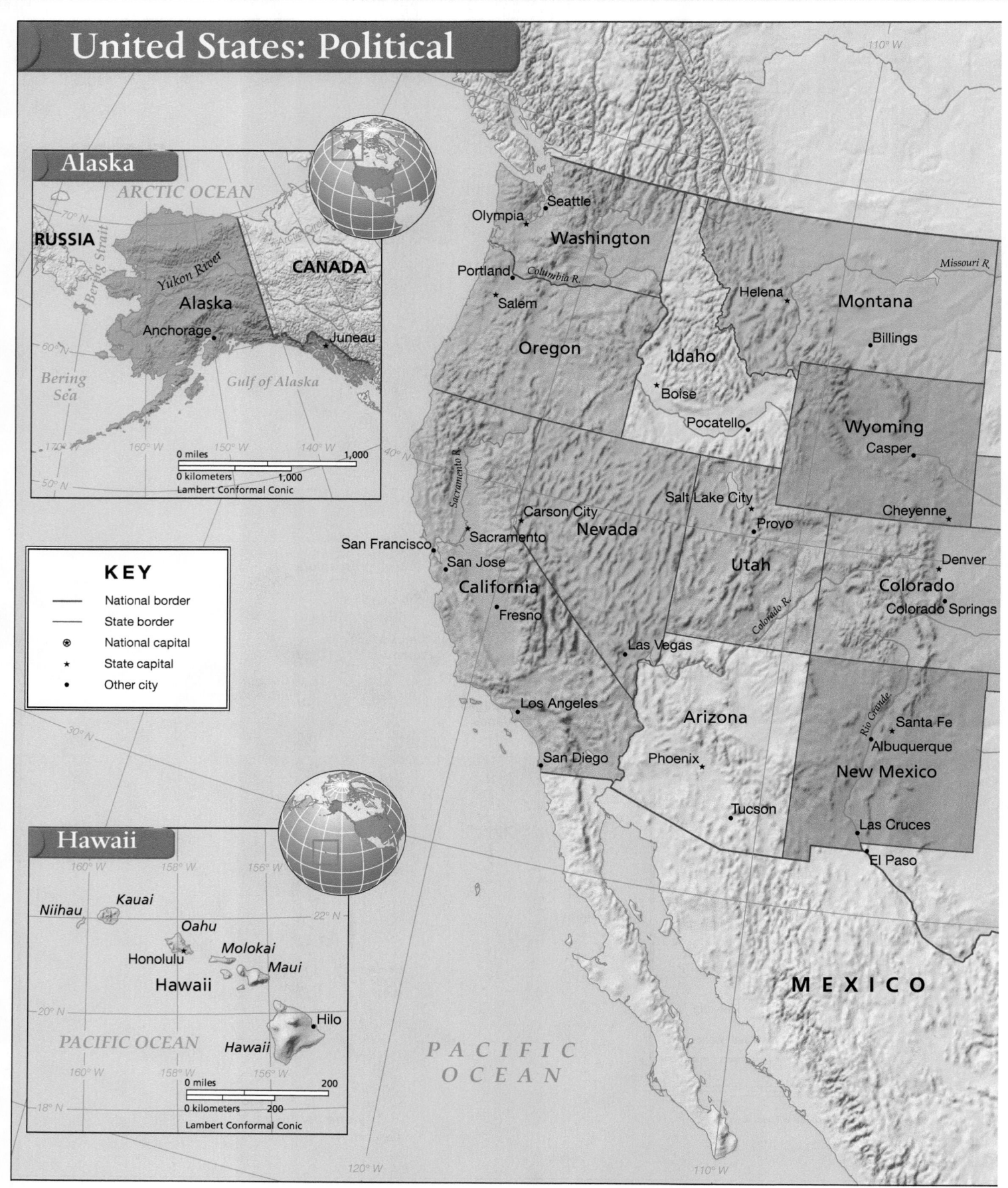

Alaska

ARCTIC OCEAN

RUSSIA

Bering Strait

70° N

Yukon River

CANADA

Arctic Circle

Alaska

60° N

Anchorage

Juneau

Bering Sea

Gulf of Alaska

170° W   160° W   150° W   140° W

50° N

0 miles   1,000

0 kilometers   1,000

Lambert Conformal Conic

KEY

————— National border

——— State border

⊛ National capital

★ State capital

• Other city

Hawaii

160° W   158° W   156° W

Niihau   Kauai

Oahu   22° N

Honolulu   Molokai

Hawaii   Maui

20° N

Hilo

PACIFIC OCEAN   Hawaii

160° W   158° W   156° W

18° N

0 miles   200

0 kilometers   200

Lambert Conformal Conic

110° W

Seattle
Olympia
Washington

Missouri R.

Portland   Columbia R.
Salem   Helena   Montana

Oregon   Idaho   Billings

Boise

Pocatello   Wyoming

Casper

40° N

Sacramento R.

Salt Lake City
Carson City   Cheyenne
San Francisco   Sacramento   Nevada   Provo

San Jose   Utah   Denver

California   Colorado

Fresno   Colorado Springs

Colorado R.

Las Vegas

Los Angeles   30° N

Arizona   Rio Grande

Santa Fe

San Diego   Phoenix   Albuquerque

New Mexico

Tucson   Las Cruces

El Paso

120° W

PACIFIC
OCEAN

MEXICO

110° W

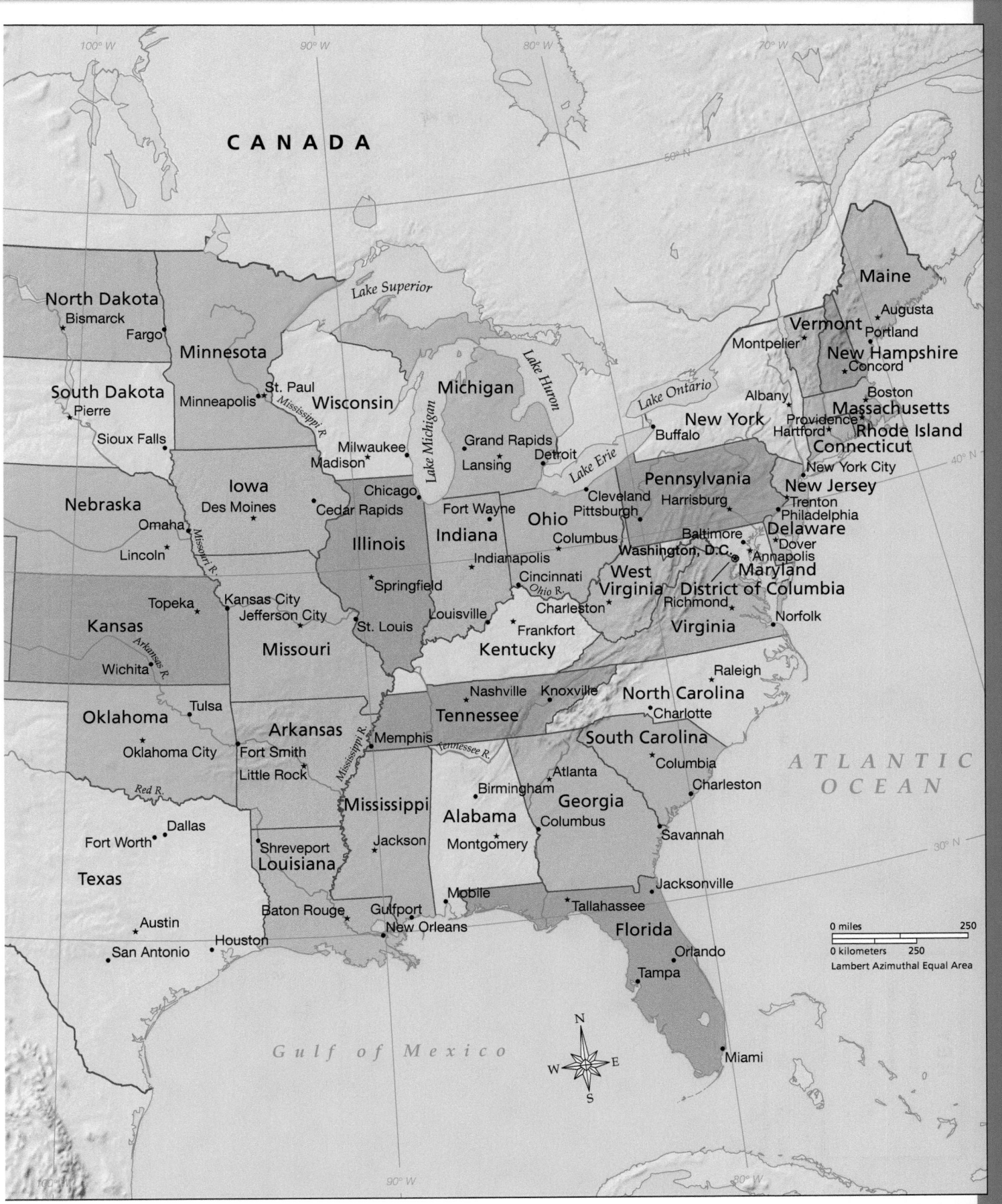

CANADA

North Dakota
Bismarck
Fargo
Minnesota
South Dakota
Pierre
Sioux Falls
Minneapolis
St. Paul
Wisconsin
Lake Superior
Michigan
Lake Huron
Maine
Augusta
Portland
Vermont
Montpelier
New Hampshire
Concord
Boston
Albany
Massachusetts
New York
Buffalo
Lake Ontario
Providence
Hartford
Rhode Island
Connecticut

Milwaukee
Madison
Lake Michigan
Grand Rapids
Lansing
Detroit
Lake Erie
Cleveland
Pittsburgh
Pennsylvania
Harrisburg
New York City
New Jersey
Trenton
Philadelphia

Nebraska
Omaha
Lincoln
Iowa
Des Moines
Cedar Rapids
Chicago
Illinois
Fort Wayne
Indiana
Ohio
Columbus
Indianapolis
Springfield
Cincinnati
Ohio R.
Baltimore
Washington, D.C.
Annapolis
Delaware
Dover
Maryland
West Virginia
District of Columbia

Missouri R.
Topeka
Kansas City
Jefferson City
St. Louis
Louisville
Charleston
Richmond
Virginia
Norfolk

Kansas
Arkansas R.
Wichita
Missouri
Frankfort
Kentucky
Raleigh
North Carolina

Oklahoma
Tulsa
Arkansas
Nashville
Knoxville
Tennessee
Charlotte
Memphis
Tennessee R.
South Carolina
Columbia

Oklahoma City
Fort Smith
Little Rock
Mississippi R.
Atlanta
Birmingham
Georgia
Charleston
Savannah

Red R.
Dallas
Fort Worth
Mississippi
Jackson
Alabama
Montgomery
Columbus

Texas
Shreveport
Louisiana
Baton Rouge
Gulfport
New Orleans
Mobile
Tallahassee
Jacksonville

Austin
San Antonio
Houston

Florida
Orlando
Tampa

Gulf of Mexico
N
W E
S
Miami

ATLANTIC
OCEAN

0 miles 250
0 kilometers 250
Lambert Azimuthal Equal Area

Europe: Political

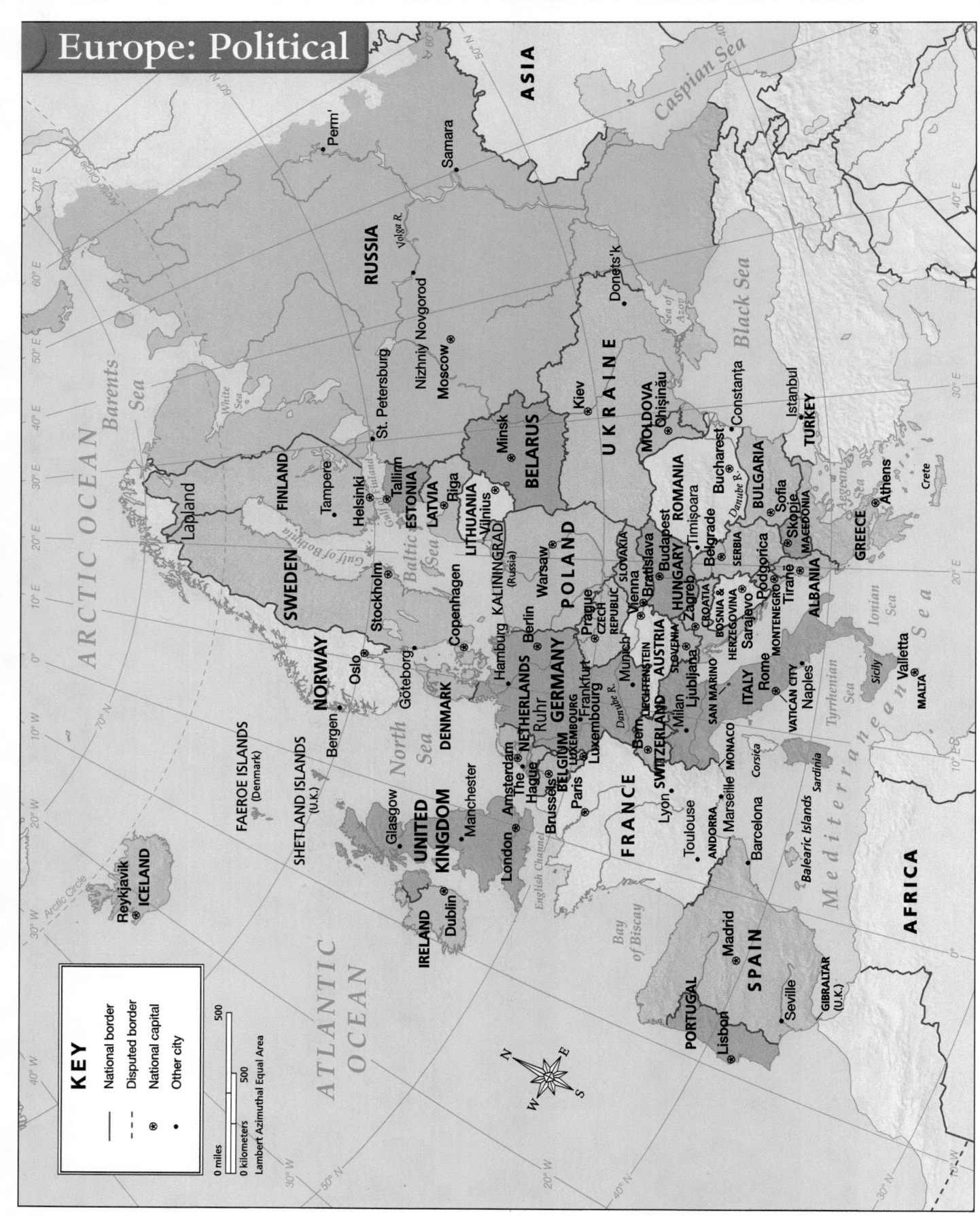

ASIA

Caspian Sea

Perm'

Samara

RUSSIA

Volga R.

Nizhniy Novgorod

Donets'k

Moscow

Sea of Azov

UKRAINE

Kiev

St. Petersburg

Black Sea

MOLDOVA
Chișinău

Minsk

BELARUS

Constanța

Istanbul

TURKEY

FINLAND

Tampere

Helsinki

Tallinn
ESTONIA
LATVIA
Riga

LITHUANIA
Vilnius

KALININGRAD
(Russia)

Warsaw

ROMANIA

Bucharest

BULGARIA

Sofia

Skopje

MACEDONIA

Athens

GREECE

Crete

Aegean Sea

Lapland

Gulf of Bothnia

SWEDEN

Baltic Sea

Gulf of Finland

White Sea

Barents Sea

ARCTIC OCEAN

Stockholm

Copenhagen

Berlin

POLAND

Prague
CZECH
REPUBLIC

SLOVAKIA

Bratislava
Budapest
HUNGARY

Timișoara

Belgrade

SERBIA

Podgorica

MONTENEGRO

Tiranë

ALBANIA

Ionian Sea

NORWAY

Oslo

Göteborg

DENMARK

Hamburg

GERMANY

Munich

Vienna

AUSTRIA

LIECHTENSTEIN

SLOVENIA

Ljubljana

Zagreb

CROATIA

BOSNIA &
HERZEGOVINA

Sarajevo

Rome

ITALY

Naples

Tyrrhenian Sea

Sicily

Valletta

MALTA

Mediterranean Sea

Bergen

North Sea

FAEROE ISLANDS
(Denmark)

SHETLAND ISLANDS
(U.K.)

Glasgow

Manchester

UNITED
KINGDOM

London

Amsterdam

NETHERLANDS

The
Hague

Brussels

BELGIUM

LUXEMBOURG

Luxembourg

Frankfurt

Ruhr

Danube R.

Bern

SWITZERLAND

Milan

Danube R.

SAN MARINO

MONACO

VATICAN CITY

Corsica

Sardinia

Paris

FRANCE

Lyon

Toulouse

Marseille

ANDORRA

Barcelona

Balearic Islands

English Channel

Reykjavik

ICELAND

IRELAND

Dublin

Bay
of Biscay

ATLANTIC
OCEAN

Madrid

SPAIN

Seville

GIBRALTAR
(U.K.)

PORTUGAL

Lisbon

AFRICA

N
W   E
S

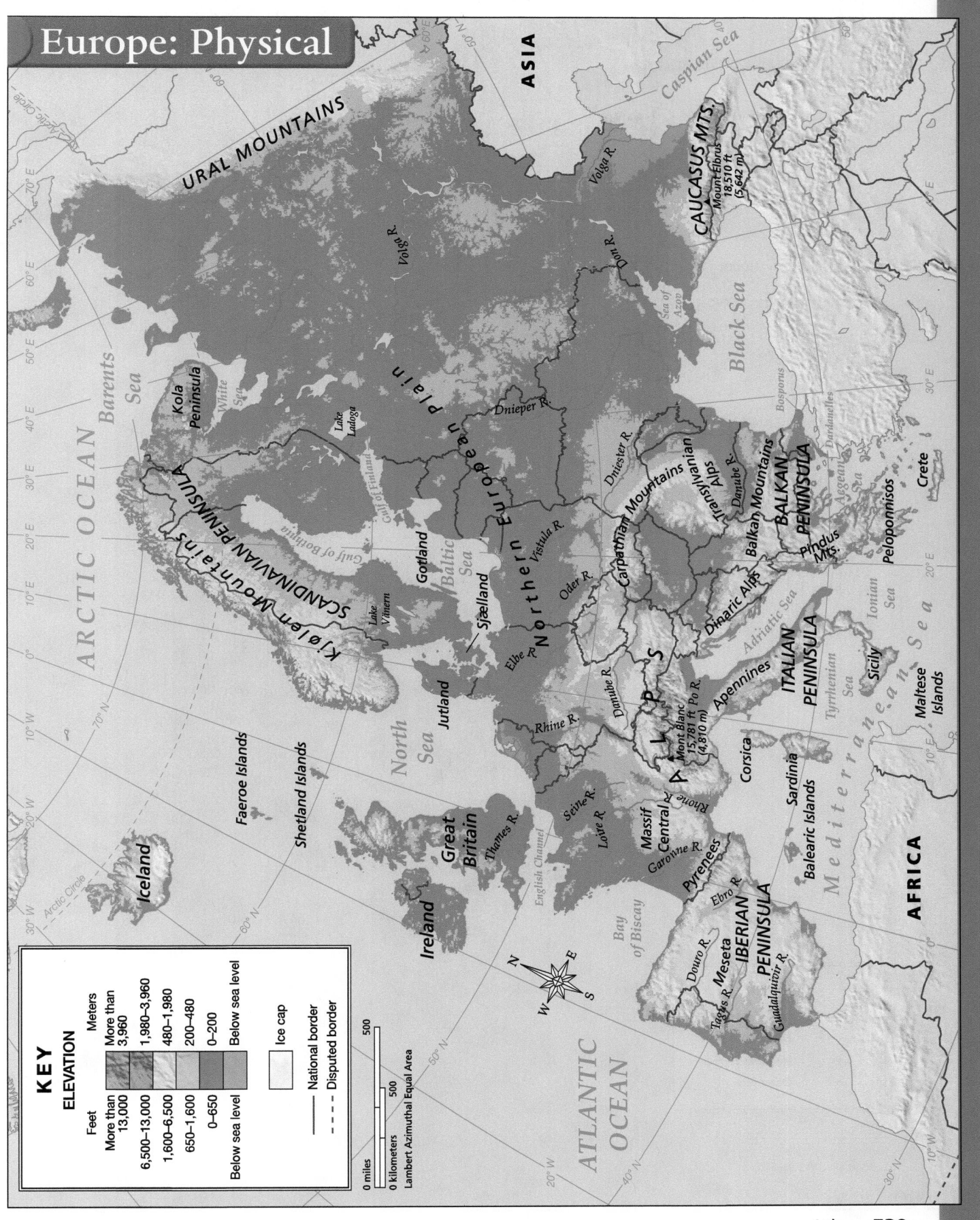

Europe: Physical

ASIA

URAL MOUNTAINS

ARCTIC OCEAN

Barents Sea

Kola Peninsula

White Sea

Caspian Sea

Volga R.

Volga R.

Don R.

CAUCASUS MTS.

Mount Elbrus
18,510 ft
(5,642 m)

Sea of Azov

Black Sea

Lake Ladoga

Dnieper R.

Northern European Plain

Dniester R.

Bosporus

Dardanelles

SCANDINAVIAN PENINSULA

Kjølen Mountains

Gulf of Finland

Gulf of Bothnia

Gotland

Baltic Sea

Vistula R.

Oder R.

Carpathian Mountains

Transylvanian Alps

Danube R.

Balkan Mountains

BALKAN PENINSULA

Aegean Sea

Crete

Peloponnisos

Pindus Mts.

Dinaric Alps

Lake Vänern

Sjælland

Elbe R.

Danube R.

Adriatic Sea

ITALIAN PENINSULA

Apennines

Ionian Sea

Sicily

Maltese Islands

Mediterranean Sea

North Sea

Jutland

Rhine R.

A L P S

Mont Blanc
15,781 ft
(4,810 m)

Po R.

Corsica

Tyrrhenian Sea

Sardinia

Balearic Islands

Great Britain

Thames R.

English Channel

Seine R.

Loire R.

Massif Central

Rhône R.

Garonne R.

Pyrenees

Ebro R.

AFRICA

Faeroe Islands

Shetland Islands

Iceland

Ireland

Arctic Circle

Bay of Biscay

Douro R.

Meseta

IBERIAN PENINSULA

Guadalquivir R.

Tagus R.

ATLANTIC OCEAN

KEY

ELEVATION

Feet	Meters
More than 13,000	More than 3,960
6,500–13,000	1,980–3,960
1,600–6,500	480–1,980
650–1,600	200–480
0–650	0–200
Below sea level	Below sea level

Ice cap

National border
Disputed border

N
E
W
S

0 miles 500
0 kilometers 500
Lambert Azimuthal Equal Area

Atlas **539**

Africa: Political

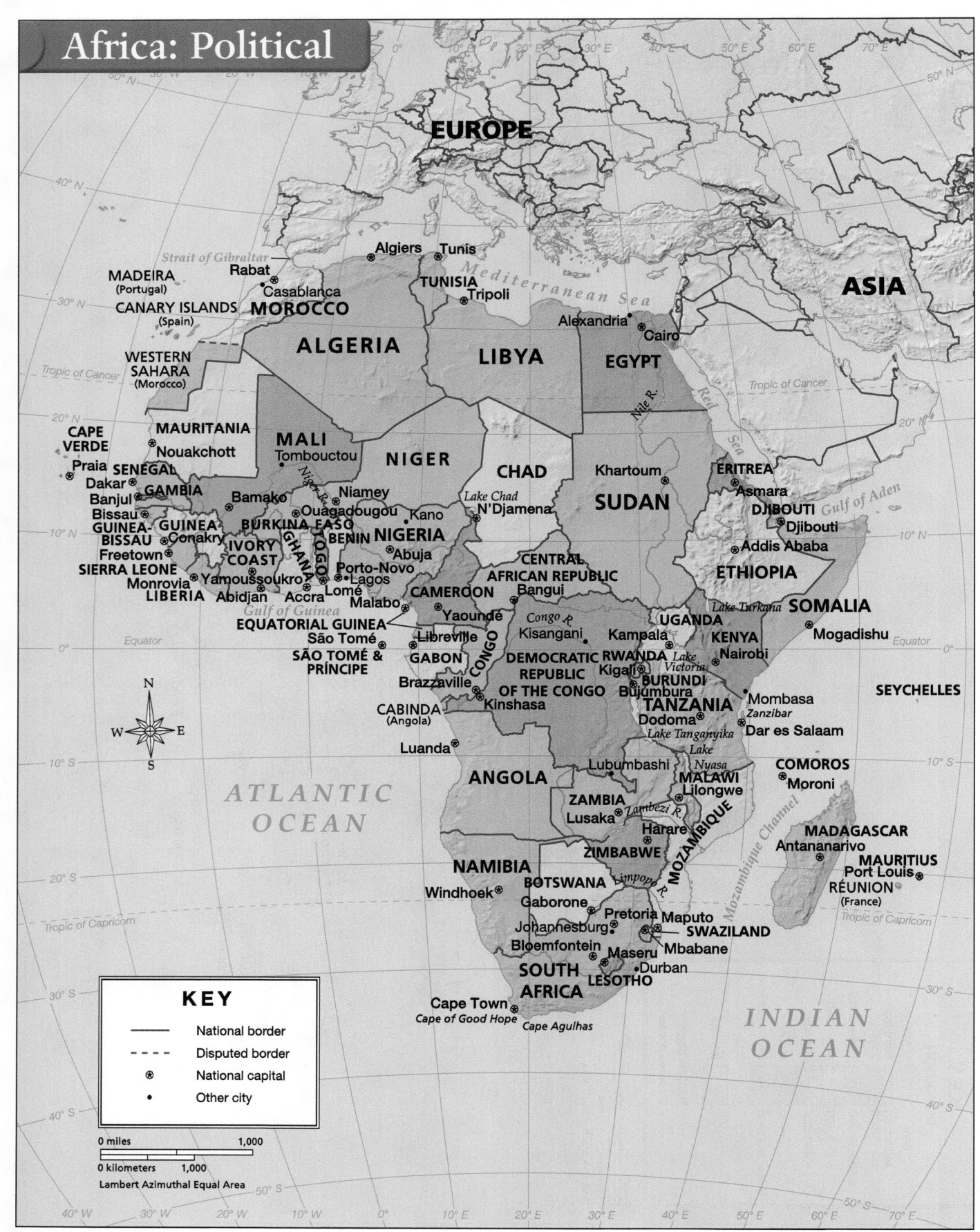

EUROPE

ASIA

Strait of Gibraltar

Mediterranean Sea

Algiers • Tunis

Rabat
• Casablanca
MOROCCO
TUNISIA
• Tripoli

Alexandria •
⊛ Cairo

MADEIRA
(Portugal)
CANARY ISLANDS
(Spain)

ALGERIA
LIBYA
EGYPT

Tropic of Cancer
Tropic of Cancer

WESTERN
SAHARA
(Morocco)

Nile R.

Red Sea

CAPE
VERDE
⊛ Nouakchott
MAURITANIA
MALI
Tombouctou
NIGER
CHAD
Khartoum ⊛
ERITREA
⊛ Asmara

Praia •
Dakar ⊛ **SENEGAL**
GAMBIA
Banjul ⊛
Bamako ⊛
⊛ Niamey
Kano •
Lake Chad
N'Djamena •
SUDAN
DJIBOUTI
⊛ Djibouti

Bissau •
GUINEA-
BISSAU ⊛ Conakry
GUINEA
Ouagadougou ⊛
BURKINA FASO
BENIN
NIGERIA
• Addis Ababa

Freetown ⊛
SIERRA LEONE
Monrovia ⊛
LIBERIA
Yamoussoukro ⊛
IVORY
COAST
GHANA
TOGO
Abidjan
Accra
Lomé
⊛ Abuja
Porto-Novo
• Lagos
Malabo
CAMEROON
CENTRAL
AFRICAN REPUBLIC
Bangui •
ETHIOPIA
SOMALIA

Gulf of Guinea
⊛ Yaoundé
Congo R.
UGANDA
Lake Turkana

EQUATORIAL GUINEA
São Tomé •
Libreville ⊛
Kisangani •
Kampala ⊛
KENYA
Mogadishu •
Equator

Equator
SÃO TOMÉ &
PRÍNCIPE
GABON
CONGO
DEMOCRATIC
REPUBLIC
OF THE CONGO
RWANDA
Kigali ⊛
Lake
Victoria
Nairobi ⊛

SEYCHELLES

Brazzaville ⊛
BURUNDI
Bujumbura ⊛
Kinshasa ⊛
CABINDA
(Angola)
Lubumbashi •
TANZANIA
Dodoma ⊛
Zanzibar •
Mombasa •
Dar es Salaam •
Lake Tanganyika

Luanda ⊛
Lake
Nyasa
COMOROS
• Moroni

ATLANTIC
OCEAN
ANGOLA
ZAMBIA
Lusaka ⊛
Zambezi R.
MALAWI
Lilongwe ⊛
MADAGASCAR
Antananarivo ⊛

NAMIBIA
BOTSWANA
Harare ⊛
ZIMBABWE
MOZAMBIQUE
Limpopo R.
Mozambique Channel
MAURITIUS
Port Louis ⊛
RÉUNION
(France)

Windhoek ⊛
Gaborone ⊛
Pretoria ⊛ Maputo ⊛
Johannesburg •
SWAZILAND
Tropic of Capricorn

Tropic of Capricorn
Bloemfontein •
Maseru ⊛
Mbabane ⊛
Durban •

SOUTH
AFRICA
LESOTHO

Cape Town ⊛
Cape of Good Hope
Cape Agulhas
INDIAN
OCEAN

KEY

——	National border
- - -	Disputed border
⊛	National capital
•	Other city

0 miles	1,000

0 kilometers	1,000

Lambert Azimuthal Equal Area

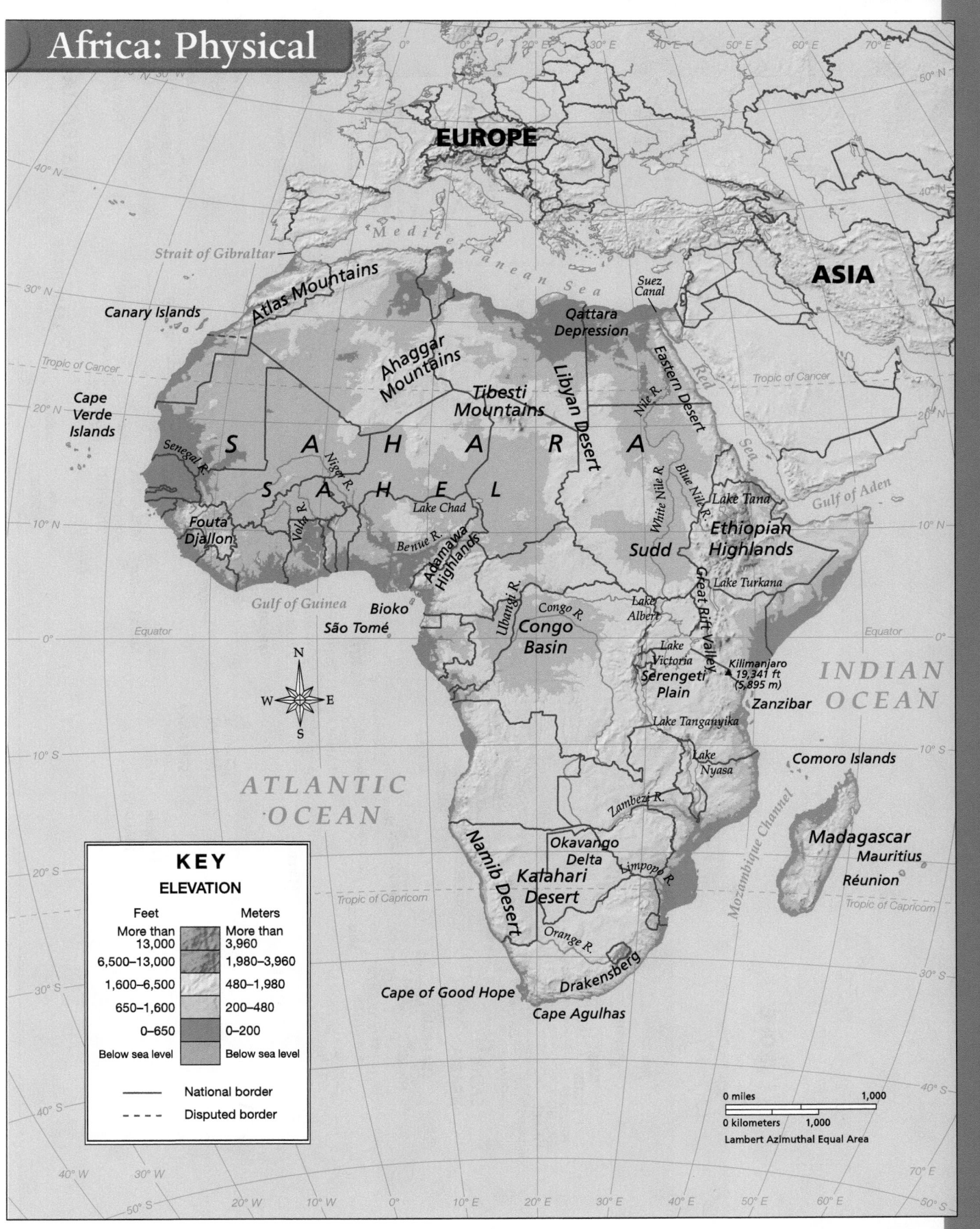

Africa: Physical

EUROPE

ASIA

Mediterranean Sea

Strait of Gibraltar

Canary Islands

Atlas Mountains

Qattara Depression

Suez Canal

Cape Verde Islands

Ahaggar Mountains

Tibesti Mountains

Libyan Desert

Eastern Desert

Nile R.

Red Sea

Tropic of Cancer

S A H A R A

Senegal R.

Niger R.

S A H E L

Lake Chad

White Nile R.

Blue Nile R.

Lake Tana

Gulf of Aden

Fouta Djallon

Volta R.

Benue R.

Adamawa Highlands

Ethiopian Highlands

Sudd

Lake Turkana

Gulf of Guinea

Bioko

São Tomé

Ubangi R.

Congo R.

Congo Basin

Lake Albert

Great Rift Valley

Equator

Lake Victoria

Serengeti Plain

Kilimanjaro
▲ 19,341 ft
(5,895 m)

Zanzibar

INDIAN OCEAN

Lake Tanganyika

Lake Nyasa

Comoro Islands

ATLANTIC OCEAN

Zambezi R.

Madagascar

Mauritius

Réunion

Okavango Delta

Limpopo R.

Mozambique Channel

Namib Desert

Kalahari Desert

Tropic of Capricorn

Orange R.

Cape of Good Hope

Drakensberg

Cape Agulhas

KEY

ELEVATION

Feet	Meters
More than 13,000	More than 3,960
6,500–13,000	1,980–3,960
1,600–6,500	480–1,980
650–1,600	200–480
0–650	0–200
Below sea level	Below sea level

———— National border

– – – – Disputed border

N W E S

0 miles 1,000
0 kilometers 1,000
Lambert Azimuthal Equal Area

Asia: Political

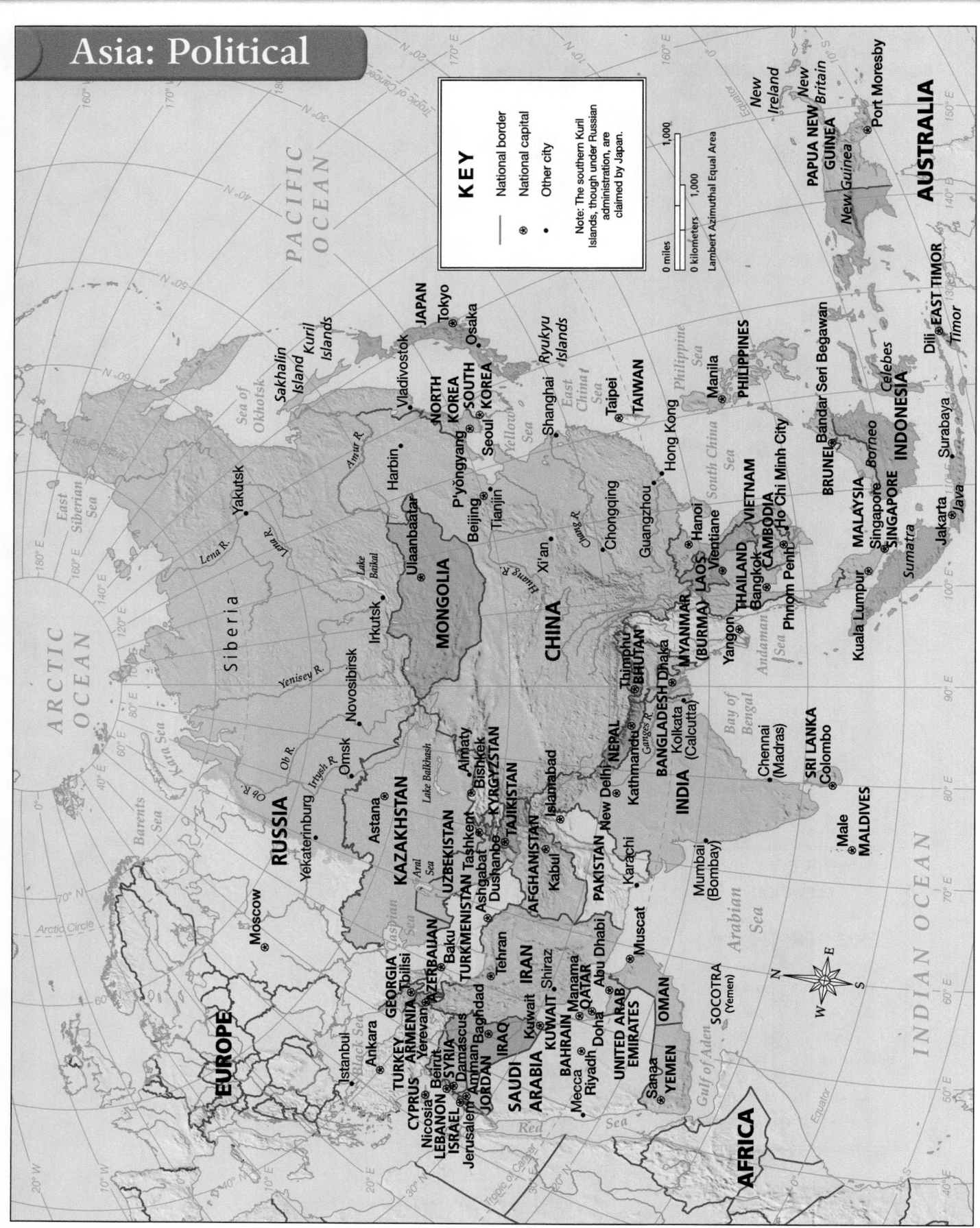

KEY

— National border

⊛ National capital

• Other city

Note: The southern Kuril Islands, though under Russian administration, are claimed by Japan.

0 miles 1,000

0 kilometers 1,000

Lambert Azimuthal Equal Area

Asia: Physical

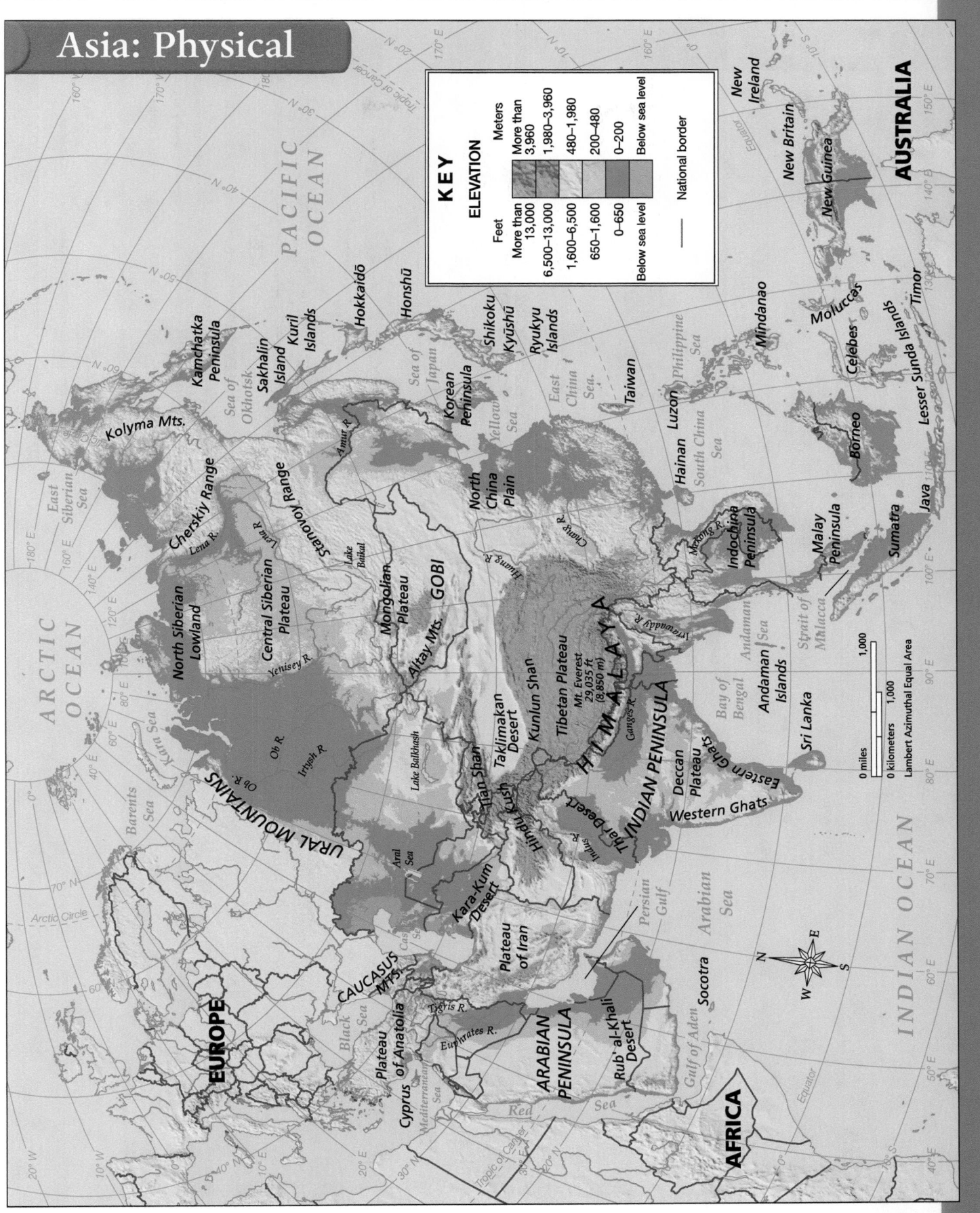

KEY

ELEVATION

Feet	Meters
More than 13,000	More than 3,960
6,500–13,000	1,980–3,960
1,600–6,500	480–1,980
650–1,600	200–480
0–650	0–200
Below sea level	Below sea level

—— National border

PACIFIC OCEAN

ARCTIC OCEAN

INDIAN OCEAN

EUROPE

AFRICA

AUSTRALIA

New Ireland
New Britain
New Guinea
Mindanao
Moluccas
Celebes
Lesser Sunda Islands
Timor
Borneo
Java
Sumatra
Malay Peninsula
Luzon
Philippine Sea
Hainan
South China Sea
Taiwan
East China Sea
Ryukyu Islands
Kyūshū
Shikoku
Honshū
Hokkaidō
Sea of Japan
Yellow Sea
Korean Peninsula
North China Plain
Sakhalin Island
Kuril Islands
Sea of Okhotsk
Kamchatka Peninsula
Kolyma Mts.
Cherskiy Range
Stanovoy Range
Lena R.
Amur R.
Lake Baikal
Mongolian Plateau
Altay Mts.
GOBI
Central Siberian Plateau
North Siberian Lowland
Yenisey R.
Ob R.
Irtysh R.
Lake Balkhash
Aral Sea
Tian Shan
Taklimakan Desert
Kunlun Shan
Tibetan Plateau
Mt. Everest 29,035 ft (8,850 m)
HIMALAYA
Hindu Kush
Thar Desert
Indus R.
Ganges R.
INDIAN PENINSULA
Deccan Plateau
Eastern Ghats
Western Ghats
Sri Lanka
Bay of Bengal
Andaman Islands
Andaman Sea
Strait of Malacca
Irrawaddy R.
Mekong R.
Chang R.
Huang R.
Indochina Peninsula
URAL MOUNTAINS
Ob R.
Barents Sea
Kara Sea
East Siberian Sea
Plateau of Iran
Kara-Kum Desert
CAUCASUS MTS.
Caspian Sea
Black Sea
Plateau of Anatolia
Cyprus
Mediterranean Sea
Tigris R.
Euphrates R.
ARABIAN PENINSULA
Rub' al-Khali Desert
Persian Gulf
Arabian Sea
Gulf of Aden
Socotra
Red Sea

Arctic Circle
Tropic of Cancer
Equator

0 miles 1,000
0 kilometers 1,000
Lambert Azimuthal Equal Area

N E S W

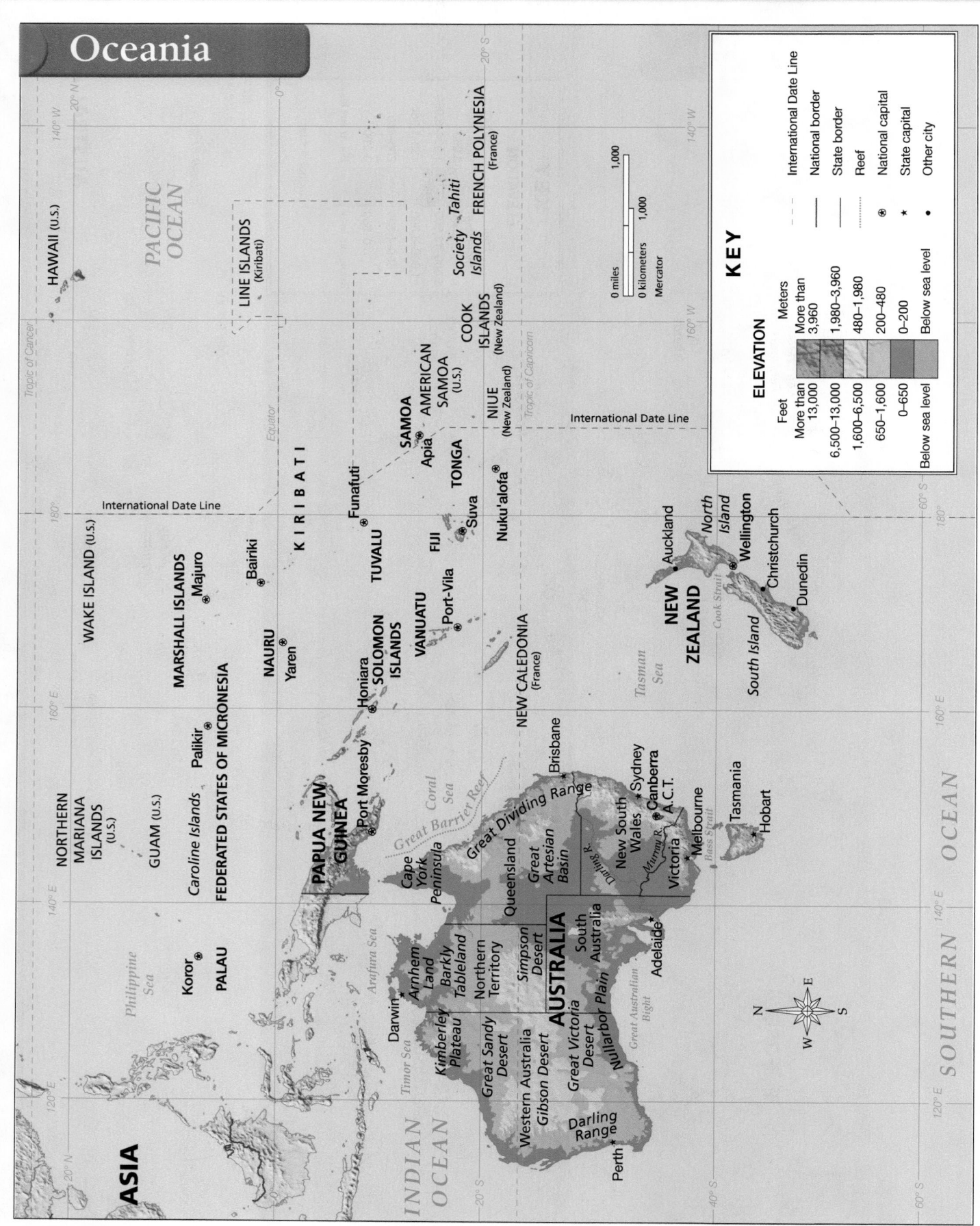

Oceania

ASIA

PACIFIC OCEAN

HAWAII (U.S.)

LINE ISLANDS
(Kiribati)

FRENCH POLYNESIA
(France)

Society
Islands   Tahiti

COOK
ISLANDS
(New Zealand)

SAMOA
Apia   AMERICAN
SAMOA
(U.S.)

TONGA

NIUE
(New Zealand)

International Date Line

KIRIBATI

Funafuti

TUVALU

FIJI   Suva

Nuku'alofa

Bairiki

Majuro

MARSHALL ISLANDS

WAKE ISLAND (U.S.)

International Date Line

VANUATU
Port-Vila

NAURU
Yaren

SOLOMON
ISLANDS
Honiara

NEW CALEDONIA
(France)

NORTHERN
MARIANA
ISLANDS
(U.S.)

GUAM (U.S.)

Caroline Islands   Palikir

FEDERATED STATES OF MICRONESIA

PAPUA NEW
GUINEA

Port Moresby

Coral
Sea

Great Barrier Reef

Brisbane

NEW
ZEALAND

North
Island

Auckland

Wellington
Christchurch
Dunedin

South Island

Cook Strait

Tasman
Sea

Koror   PALAU

Philippine
Sea

Arafura Sea

Timor Sea

Cape
York
Peninsula

Great Dividing Range

Queensland

Great
Artesian
Basin

New South
Wales   Sydney
Canberra
A.C.T.

Darling R.

Murray R.   Victoria   Melbourne

Tasmania
Hobart

Bass Strait

Darwin

Arnhem
Land

Barkly
Tableland

Northern
Territory

Simpson
Desert

South
Australia

Adelaide

Great Australian
Bight

Nullarbor Plain

AUSTRALIA

Kimberley
Plateau

Great Sandy
Desert

Western Australia
Gibson Desert

Great Victoria
Desert

Darling
Range

Perth

INDIAN
OCEAN

SOUTHERN   OCEAN

KEY

ELEVATION

Feet	Meters
More than 13,000	More than 3,960
6,500–13,000	1,980–3,960
1,600–6,500	480–1,980
650–1,600	200–480
0–650	0–200
Below sea level	Below sea level

- - - International Date Line
——— National border
——— State border
········· Reef
⊛ National capital
★ State capital
• Other city

0 miles   1,000
0 kilometers   1,000
Mercator

Tropic of Cancer

Equator

Tropic of Capricorn

20° N
0°
20° S

140° E   160° E   180°   160° W   140° W   120° W
120° E   140° E   160° E   180°

20° N

20° S
40° S
60° S

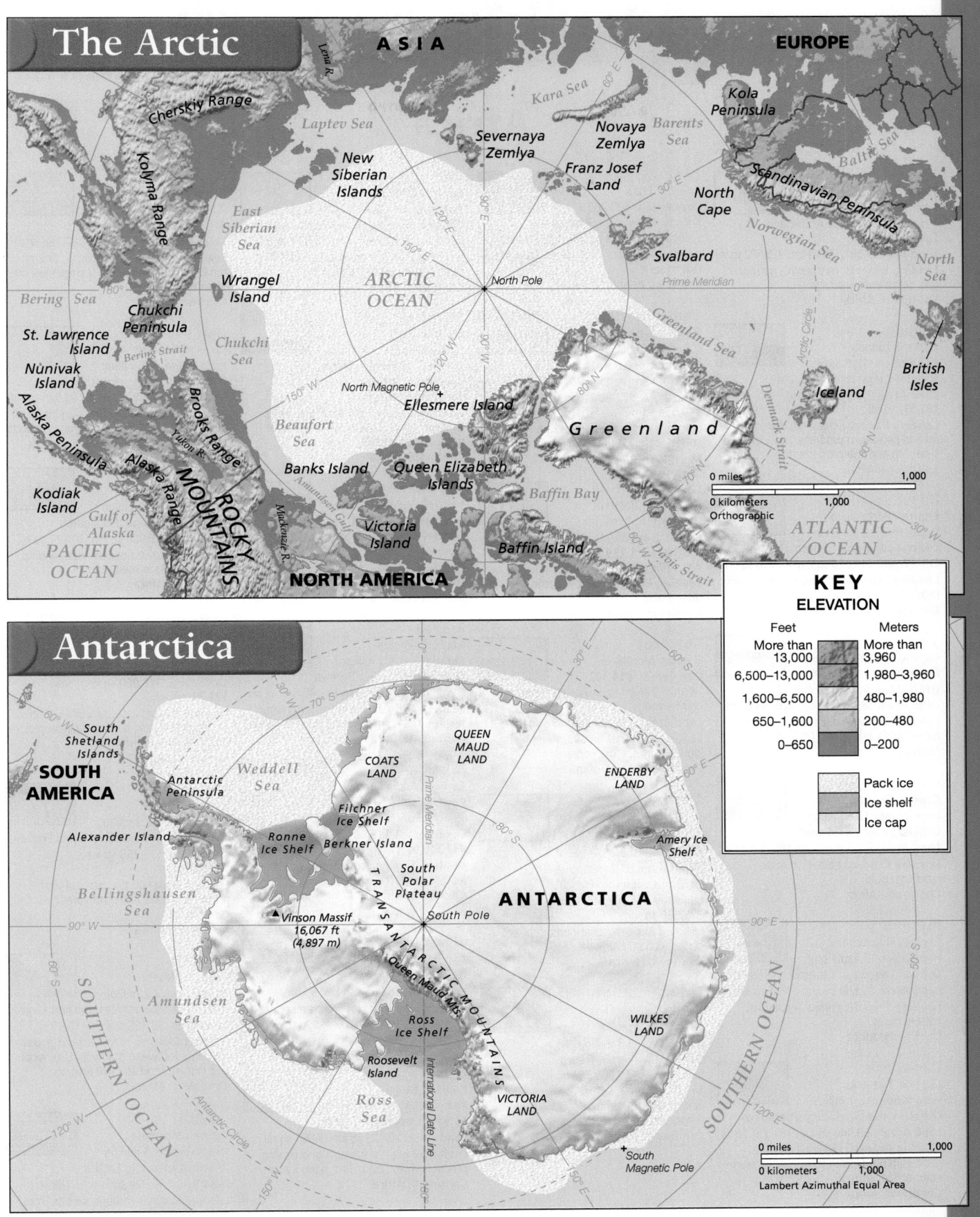

The Arctic

ASIA   EUROPE

Lena R.
Cherskiy Range
Kolyma Range
Laptev Sea
Kara Sea
Severnaya Zemlya
Novaya Zemlya
Franz Josef Land
Kola Peninsula
Barents Sea
Baltic Sea
New Siberian Islands
Scandinavian Peninsula
North Cape
East Siberian Sea
ARCTIC OCEAN
North Pole
Svalbard
Norwegian Sea
Bering Sea
Wrangel Island
Prime Meridian
North Sea
Chukchi Peninsula
Chukchi Sea
Greenland Sea
Arctic Circle
St. Lawrence Island
Bering Strait
North Magnetic Pole
Ellesmere Island
Iceland
British Isles
Nunivak Island
Beaufort Sea
Greenland
Denmark Strait
Alaska Peninsula
Brooks Range
Yukon R.
Banks Island
Queen Elizabeth Islands
Baffin Bay
Kodiak Island
Alaska Range
ROCKY MOUNTAINS
Amundsen Gulf
Mackenzie R.
Victoria Island
Baffin Island
Davis Strait
ATLANTIC OCEAN
Gulf of Alaska
PACIFIC OCEAN
NORTH AMERICA

0 miles 1,000
0 kilometers 1,000
Orthographic

Antarctica

South Shetland Islands
SOUTH AMERICA
Antarctic Peninsula
Weddell Sea
COATS LAND
QUEEN MAUD LAND
ENDERBY LAND
Alexander Island
Filchner Ice Shelf
Ronne Ice Shelf
Berkner Island
Prime Meridian
Amery Ice Shelf
Bellingshausen Sea
South Polar Plateau
ANTARCTICA
Vinson Massif 16,067 ft (4,897 m)
TRANSANTARCTIC MOUNTAINS
Queen Maud Mts.
South Pole
Amundsen Sea
Ross Ice Shelf
WILKES LAND
SOUTHERN OCEAN
Roosevelt Island
International Date Line
VICTORIA LAND
Ross Sea
Antarctic Circle
South Magnetic Pole

0 miles 1,000
0 kilometers 1,000
Lambert Azimuthal Equal Area

KEY
ELEVATION

Feet		Meters
More than 13,000		More than 3,960
6,500–13,000		1,980–3,960
1,600–6,500		480–1,980
650–1,600		200–480
0–650		0–200

Pack ice
Ice shelf
Ice cap

Country Databank

Africa

Algeria
Capital: Algiers
Population: 32.3 million
Official Languages: Arabic and Tamazight
Land Area: 2,381,740 sq km; 919,590 sq mi
Leading Exports: petroleum, natural gas, petroleum products
Continent: Africa

Angola
Capital: Luanda
Population: 10.6 million
Official Language: Portuguese
Land Area: 1,246,700 sq km; 481,551 sq mi
Leading Exports: crude oil, diamonds, refined petroleum products, gas, coffee, sisal, fish and fish products, timber, cotton
Continent: Africa

Benin
Capital: Porto-Novo
Population: 6.9 million
Official Language: French
Land Area: 110,620 sq km; 42,710 sq mi
Leading Exports: cotton, crude oil, palm products, cocoa
Continent: Africa

Botswana
Capital: Gaborone
Population: 1.6 million
Official Language: English
Land Area: 585,370 sq km; 226,011 sq mi
Leading Exports: diamonds, copper, nickel, soda ash, meat, textiles
Continent: Africa

Burkina Faso
Capital: Ouagadougou
Population: 12.6 million
Official Language: French
Land Area: 273,800 sq km; 105,714 sq mi
Leading Exports: cotton, animal products, gold
Continent: Africa

Burundi
Capital: Bujumbura
Population: 6.4 million
Official Languages: Kirundi and French
Land Area: 25,650 sq km; 9,903 sq mi
Leading Exports: coffee, tea, sugar, cotton, hides
Continent: Africa

Cameroon
Capital: Yaoundé
Population: 16.1 million
Official Languages: English and French
Land Area: 469,440 sq km; 181,251 sqmi
Leading Exports: crude oil and petroleum products, lumber, cocoa, aluminum, coffee, cotton
Continent: Africa

Cape Verde
Capital: Praia
Population: 408,760
Official Language: Portuguese
Land Area: 4,033 sq km; 1,557 sq mi
Leading Exports: fuel, shoes, garments, fish, hides
Location: Atlantic Ocean

Central African Republic
Capital: Bangui
Population: 3.6 million
Official Language: French
Land Area: 622,984 sq km; 240,534 sq mi
Leading Exports: diamonds, timber, cotton, coffee, tobacco
Continent: Africa

Chad
Capital: N'Djamena
Population: 9 million
Official Languages: Arabic and French
Land Area: 1,259,200 sq km; 486,177 sq mi
Leading Exports: cotton, cattle, gum arabic
Continent: Africa

Comoros
Capital: Moroni
Population: 614,382
Official Languages: Arabic, Comoran, and French
Land Area: 2,170 sq km; 838 sq mi
Leading Exports: vanilla, ylang-ylang, cloves, perfume oil, copra
Location: Indian Ocean

Congo, Democratic Republic of the
Capital: Kinshasa
Population: 55.2 million
Official Language: French
Land Area: 2,267,600 sq km; 875,520 sq mi
Leading Exports: diamonds, copper, coffee, cobalt, crude oil
Continent: Africa

Congo, Republic of the
Capital: Brazzaville
Population: 3.3 million
Official Language: French
Land Area: 341,500 sq km; 131,853 sq mi
Leading Exports: petroleum, lumber, sugar, cocoa, coffee, diamonds
Continent: Africa

Djibouti
Capital: Djibouti
Population: 472,810
Official Languages: Arabic and French
Land Area: 22,980 sq km; 8,873 sq mi
Leading Exports: reexports, hides and skins, coffee (in transit)
Continent: Africa

Egypt
Capital: Cairo
Population: 70.7 million
Official Language: Arabic
Land Area: 995,450 sq km; 384,343 sq mi
Leading Exports: crude oil and petroleum products, cotton, textiles, metal products, chemicals
Continent: Africa

Equatorial Guinea
Capital: Malabo
Population: 498,144
Official Languages: Spanish and French
Land Area: 28,050 sq km; 10,830 sq mi
Leading Exports: petroleum, timber, cocoa
Continent: Africa

Eritrea
Capital: Asmara
Population: 4.5 million
Official Language: Tigrinya
Land Area: 121,320 sq km; 46,842 sq mi
Leading Exports: livestock, sorghum, textiles, food, small manufactured goods
Continent: Africa

Ethiopia
Capital: Addis Ababa
Population: 67.7 million
Official Language: Amharic
Land Area: 1,119,683 sq km; 432,310 sq mi
Leading Exports: coffee, qat, gold, leather products, oilseeds
Continent: Africa

Gabon
Capital: Libreville
Population: 1.2 million
Official Language: French
Land Area: 257,667 sq km; 99,489 sq mi
Leading Exports: crude oil, timber, manganese, uranium
Continent: Africa

Gambia
Capital: Banjul
Population: 1.5 million
Official Language: English
Land Area: 10,000 sq km; 3,861 sq mi
Leading Exports: peanuts and peanut products, fish, cotton lint, palm kernels
Continent: Africa

Ghana
Capital: Accra
Population: 20.2 million
Official Language: English
Land Area: 230,940 sq km; 89,166 sq mi
Leading Exports: gold, cocoa, timber, tuna, bauxite, aluminum, manganese ore, diamonds
Continent: Africa

Guinea
Capital: Conakry
Population: 7.8 million
Official Language: French
Land Area: 245,857 sq km; 94,925 sq mi
Leading Exports: bauxite, alumina, gold, diamonds, coffee, fish, agricultural products
Continent: Africa

Guinea-Bissau
Capital: Bissau
Population: 1.4 million
Official Language: Portuguese
Land Area: 28,000 sq km; 10,811 sq mi
Leading Exports: cashew nuts, shrimp, peanuts, palm kernels, lumber
Continent: Africa

Ivory Coast
Capital: Yamoussoukro
Population: 16.8 million
Official Language: French
Land Area: 318,000 sq km; 122,780 sq mi
Leading Exports: cocoa, coffee, timber, petroleum, cotton, bananas, pineapples, palm oil, cotton, fish
Continent: Africa

Kenya
Capital: Nairobi
Population: 31.3 million
Official Languages: Swahili and English
Land Area: 569,250 sq km; 219,787 sq mi
Leading Exports: tea, horticultural products, coffee, petroleum products, fish, cement
Continent: Africa

Lesotho
Capital: Maseru
Population: 2.2 million
Official Languages: Sesotho and English
Land Area: 30,355 sq km; 11,720 sq mi
Leading Exports: manufactured goods (clothing, footwear, road vehicles), wool and mohair, food and live animals
Continent: Africa

Liberia
Capital: Monrovia
Population: 3.3 million
Official Language: English
Land Area: 96,320 sq km; 37,189 sq mi
Leading Exports: rubber, timber, iron, diamonds, cocoa, coffee
Continent: Africa

Libya
Capital: Tripoli
Population: 5.4 million
Official Language: Arabic
Land Area: 1,759,540 sq km; 679,358 sq mi
Leading Exports: crude oil, refined petroleum products
Continent: Africa

Madagascar
Capital: Antananarivo
Population: 16.5 million
Official Languages: French and Malagasy
Land Area: 581,540 sq km; 224,533 sq mi
Leading Exports: coffee, vanilla, shellfish, sugar, cotton cloth, chromite, petroleum products
Location: Indian Ocean

Malawi
Capital: Lilongwe
Population: 10.7 million
Official Languages: English and Chichewa
Land Area: 94,080 sq km; 36,324 sq mi
Leading Exports: tobacco, tea, sugar, cotton, coffee, peanuts, wood products, apparel
Continent: Africa

Mali
Capital: Bamako
Population: 11.3 million
Official Language: French
Land Area: 1,220,000 sq km; 471,042 sq mi
Leading Exports: cotton, gold, livestock
Continent: Africa

Mauritania
Capital: Nouakchott
Population: 2.8 million
Official Language: Arabic
Land Area: 1,030,400 sq km; 397,837 sq mi
Leading Exports: iron ore, fish and fish products, gold
Continent: Africa

Mauritius
Capital: Port Louis
Population: 1.2 million
Official Language: English
Land Area: 2,030 sq km; 784 sq mi
Leading Exports: clothing and textiles, sugar, cut flowers, molasses
Location: Indian Ocean

Morocco
Capital: Rabat
Population: 31.2 million
Official Language: Arabic
Land Area: 446,300 sq km; 172,316 sq mi
Leading Exports: phosphates and fertilizers, food and beverages, minerals
Continent: Africa

Mozambique
Capital: Maputo
Population: 19.6 million
Official Language: Portuguese
Land Area: 784,090 sq km; 302,737 sq mi
Leading Exports: prawns, cashews, cotton, sugar, citrus, timber, bulk electricity
Continent: Africa

Namibia
Capital: Windhoek
Population: 1.8 million
Official Language: English
Land Area: 825,418 sq km; 318,694 sq mi
Leading Exports: diamonds, copper, gold, zinc, lead, uranium, cattle, processed fish, karakul skins
Continent: Africa

Niger
Capital: Niamey
Population: 11.3 million
Official Language: French
Land Area: 1,226,700 sq km; 489,073 sq mi
Leading Exports: uranium ore, livestock products, cowpeas, onions
Continent: Africa

Nigeria
Capital: Abuja
Population: 129.9 million
Official Language: English
Land Area: 910,768 sq km; 351,648 sq mi
Leading Exports: petroleum and petroleum products, cocoa, rubber
Continent: Africa

Rwanda
Capital: Kigali
Population: 7.4 million
Official Languages: Kinyarwanda, French, and English
Land Area: 24,948 sq km; 9,632 sq mi
Leading Exports: coffee, tea, hides, tin ore
Continent: Africa

São Tomé and Príncipe
Capital: São Tomé
Population: 170,372
Official Language: Portuguese
Land Area: 1,001 sq km; 386 sq mi
Leading Exports: cocoa, copra, coffee, palm oil
Location: Atlantic Ocean

Senegal
Capital: Dakar
Population: 10.6 million
Official Language: French
Land Area: 192,000 sq km; 74,131 sq mi
Leading Exports: fish, groundnuts (peanuts), petroleum products, phosphates, cotton
Continent: Africa

Seychelles
Capital: Victoria
Population: 80,098
Official Languages: English and French
Land Area: 455 sq km; 176 sq mi
Leading Exports: canned tuna, cinnamon bark, copra, petroleum products (reexports)
Location: Indian Ocean

Sierra Leone
Capital: Freetown
Population: 5.6 million
Official Language: English
Land Area: 71,620 sq km; 27,652 sq mi
Leading Exports: diamonds, rutile, cocoa, coffee, fish
Continent: Africa

Somalia
Capital: Mogadishu
Population: 7.8 million
Official Languages: Somali and Arabic
Land Area: 627,337 sq km; 242,215 sq mi
Leading Exports: livestock, bananas, hides, fish, charcoal, scrap metal
Continent: Africa

South Africa
Capital: Cape Town, Pretoria, and Bloemfontein
Population: 43.6 million
Official Languages: Eleven official languages: Afrikaans, English, Ndebele, Pedi, Sotho, Swazi, Tsonga, Tswana, Venda, Xhosa, and Zulu
Land Area: 1,219,912 sq km; 471,008 sq mi
Leading Exports: gold, diamonds, platinum, other metals and minerals, machinery and equipment
Continent: Africa

Sudan
Capital: Khartoum
Population: 37.1 million
Official Language: Arabic
Land Area: 2,376,000 sq km; 917,374 sq mi
Leading Exports: oil and petroleum products, cotton, sesame, livestock, groundnuts, gum arabic, sugar
Continent: Africa

Swaziland
Capital: Mbabane
Population: 1.1 million
Official Languages: English and siSwati
Land Area: 17,20 sq km; 6,642 sq mi
Leading Exports: soft drink concentrates, sugar, wood pulp, cotton yarn, refrigerators, citrus and canned fruit
Continent: Africa

Tanzania
Capital: Dar es Salaam and Dodoma
Population: 37.2 million
Official Languages: Swahili and English
Land Area: 886,037 sq km; 342,099 sq mi
Leading Exports: gold, coffee, cashew nuts, manufactured goods, cotton
Continent: Africa

Togo
Capital: Lomé
Population: 5.2 million
Official Language: French
Land Area: 54,385 sq km; 20,998 sq mi
Leading Exports: cotton, phosphates, coffee, cocoa
Continent: Africa

Tunisia
Capital: Tunis
Population: 9.8 million
Official Language: Arabic
Land Area: 155,360 sq km; 59,984 sq mi
Leading Exports: textiles, mechanical goods, phosphates and chemicals, agricultural products, hydrocarbons
Continent: Africa

Uganda
Capital: Kampala
Population: 24.7 million
Official Language: English
Land Area: 199,710 sq km; 77,108 sq mi
Leading Exports: coffee, fish and fish products, tea, gold, cotton, flowers, horticultural products
Continent: Africa

Zambia
Capital: Lusaka
Population: 10.1 million
Official Language: English
Land Area: 740,724 sq km; 285,994 sq mi
Leading Exports: copper, cobalt, electricity, tobacco, flowers, cotton
Continent: Africa

Zimbabwe
Capital: Harare
Population: 11.3 million
Official Language: English
Land Area: 386,670 sq km; 149,293 sq mi
Leading Exports: tobacco, gold, iron alloys, textiles and clothing
Continent: Africa

Asia and the Pacific

Afghanistan
Capital: Kabul
Population: 27.8 million
Official Languages: Pashtu and Dari
Land Area: 647,500 sq km; 250,000 sq mi
Leading Exports: agricultural products, hand-woven carpets, wool, cotton, hides and pelts, precious and semiprecious gems
Continent: Asia

Armenia
Capital: Yerevan
Population: 3.3 million
Official Language: Armenian
Land Area: 29,400 sq km; 10,965 sq mi
Leading Exports: diamonds, scrap metal, machinery and equipment, brandy, copper ore
Continent: Asia

Australia
Capital: Canberra
Population: 19.6 million
Official Language: English
Land Area: 7,617,930 sq km; 2,941,283 sq mi
Leading Exports: coal, gold, meat, wool, alumina, iron ore, wheat, machinery and transport equipment
Continent: Australia

Azerbaijan
Capital: Baku
Population: 7.8 million
Official Language: Azerbaijani
Land Area: 86,100 sq km; 33,243 sq mi
Leading Exports: oil and gas, machinery, cotton, foodstuffs
Continent: Asia

Bahrain
Capital: Manama
Population: 656,397
Official Language: Arabic
Land Area: 665 sq km; 257 sq mi
Leading Exports: petroleum and petroleum products, aluminum, textiles
Continent: Asia

Bangladesh
Capital: Dhaka
Population: 133.4 million
Official Language: Bengali
Land Area: 133,910 sq km; 51,705 sq mi
Leading Exports: garments, jute and jute goods, leather, frozen fish and seafood
Continent: Asia

Bhutan
Capital: Thimphu
Population: 2.1 million
Official Language: Dzongkha
Land Area: 47,000 sq km; 18,147 sq mi
Leading Exports: electricity, cardamom, gypsum, timber, handicrafts, cement, fruit, precious stones, spices
Continent: Asia

Brunei
Capital: Bandar Seri Begawan
Population: 350,898
Official Language: Malay
Land Area: 5,270 sq km; 2,035 sq mi
Leading Exports: crude oil, natural gas, refined products
Continent: Asia

Cambodia
Capital: Phnom Penh
Population: 12.8 million
Official Language: Khmer
Land Area: 176,520 sq km; 68,154 sq mi
Leading Exports: timber, garments, rubber, rice, fish
Continent: Asia

China
Capital: Beijing
Population: 1.29 billion
Official Languages: Mandarin and Chinese
Land Area: 9,326,410 sq km; 3,600,927 sq mi
Leading Exports: machinery and equipment, textiles and clothing, footwear, toys and sports goods, mineral fuels
Continent: Asia

Cyprus
Capital: Nicosia
Population: 767,314
Official Languages: Greek and Turkish
Land Area: 9,240 sq km; 3,568 sq mi
Leading Exports: citrus, potatoes, grapes, wine, cement, clothing and shoes
Location: Mediterranean Sea

East Timor
Capital: Dili
Population: 952,618
Official Languages: Tetum and Portuguese
Land Area: 15,007 sq km; 5,794 sq mi
Leading Exports: coffee, sandalwood, marble
Continent: Asia

Fiji
Capital: Suva
Population: 856,346
Official Language: English
Land Area: 18,270 sq km; 7,054 sq mi
Leading Exports: sugar, garments, gold, timber, fish, molasses, coconut oil
Location: Pacific Ocean

Georgia
Capital: Tbilisi
Population: 5 million
Official Languages: Georgian and Abkhazian
Land Area: 69,700 sq km; 26,911 sq mi
Leading Exports: scrap metal, machinery, chemicals, fuel reexports, citrus fruits, tea, wine, other agricultural products
Continent: Asia

India
Capital: New Delhi
Population: 1.05 billion
Official Languages: Hindi and English
Land Area: 2,973,190 sq km; 1,147,949 sq mi
Leading Exports: textile goods, gems and jewelry, engineering goods, chemicals, leather manufactured goods
Continent: Asia

Indonesia
Capital: Jakarta
Population: 231.3 million
Official Language: Bahasa Indonesia
Land Area: 1,826,440 sq km; 705,188 sq mi
Leading Exports: oil and gas, electrical appliances, plywood, textiles, rubber
Continent: Asia

Iran
Capital: Tehran
Population: 66.6 million
Official Language: Farsi
Land Area: 1,636,000 sq km; 631,660 sq mi
Leading Exports: petroleum, carpets, fruits and nuts, iron and steel, chemicals
Continent: Asia

Iraq
Capital: Baghdad
Population: 24.7 million
Official Language: Arabic
Land Area: 432,162 sq km; 166,858 sq mi
Leading Exports: crude oil
Continent: Asia

Israel
Capital: Jerusalem
Population: 6.0 million
Official Language: Hebrew, Arabic
Land Area: 20,330 sq km; 7,849 sq mi
Leading Exports: machinery and equipment, software, cut diamonds, agricultural products, chemicals, textiles and apparel
Continent: Asia

Japan
Capital: Tokyo
Population: 127 million
Official Language: Japanese
Land Area: 374,744 sq km; 144,689 sq mi
Leading Exports: motor vehicles, semiconductors, office machinery, chemicals
Continent: Asia

Jordan
Capital: Amman
Population: 5.3 million
Official Language: Arabic
Land Area: 91,971 sq km; 35,510 sq mi
Leading Exports: phosphates, fertilizers, potash, agricultural products, manufactured goods, pharmaceuticals
Continent: Asia

Kazakhstan
Capital: Astana
Population: 16.7 million
Official Language: Kazakh
Land Area: 2,669,800 sq km; 1,030,810 sq mi
Leading Exports: oil and oil products, ferrous metals, machinery, chemicals, grain, wool, meat, coal
Continent: Asia

Kiribati
Capital: Bairiki (Tarawa Atoll)
Population: 96,335
Official Language: English
Land Area: 811 sq km; 313 sq mi
Leading Exports: copra, coconuts, seaweed, fish
Location: Pacific Ocean

Korea, North
Capital: Pyongyang
Population: 22.3 million
Official Language: Korean
Land Area: 120,410 sq km; 46,490 sq mi
Leading Exports: minerals, metallurgical products, manufactured goods (including armaments), agricultural and fishery products
Continent: Asia

Korea, South
Capital: Seoul
Population: 48.3 million
Official Language: Korean
Land Area: 98,190 sq km; 37,911 sq mi
Leading Exports: electronic products, machinery and equipment, motor vehicles, steel, ships, textiles, clothing, footwear, fish
Continent: Asia

Kuwait
Capital: Kuwait City
Population: 2.1 million
Official Language: Arabic
Land Area: 17,820 sq km; 6,880 sq mi
Leading Exports: oil and refined products, fertilizers
Continent: Asia

Kyrgyzstan
Capital: Bishkek
Population: 4.8 million
Official Languages: Kyrgyz and Russian
Land Area: 191,300 sq km; 73,861 sq mi
Leading Exports: cotton, wool, meat, tobacco, gold, mercury, uranium, hydropower, machinery, shoes
Continent: Asia

Laos
Capital: Vientiane
Population: 5.8 million
Official Language: Lao
Land Area: 230,800 sq km; 89,112 sq mi
Leading Exports: wood products, garments, electricity, coffee, tin
Continent: Asia

Lebanon
Capital: Beirut
Population: 3.7 million
Official Language: Arabic
Land Area: 10,230 sq km; 3,950 sq mi
Leading Exports: foodstuffs and tobacco, textile, chemicals, precious stones, metal and metal products, electrical equipment and products, jewelry, paper and paper products
Continent: Asia

Malaysia
Capital: Kuala Lumpur and Putrajaya
Population: 22.7 million
Official Language: Bahasa Malaysia
Land Area: 328,550 sq km; 126,853 sq mi
Leading Exports: electronic equipment, petroleum and liquefied natural gas, wood and wood products, palm oil, rubber, textiles, chemicals
Continent: Asia

Maldives
Capital: Malé
Population: 320,165
Official Language: Dhivehi (Maldivian)
Land Area: 300 sq km; 116 sq mi
Leading Exports: fish, clothing
Location: Indian Ocean

Marshall Islands
Capital: Majuro
Population: 73,360
Official Languages: Marshallese and English
Land Area: 181.3 sq km; 70 sq mi
Leading Exports: copra cake, coconut oil, handicrafts
Location: Pacific Ocean

Micronesia, Federated States of
Capital: Palikir (Pohnpei Island)
Population: 135,869
Official Language: English
Land Area: 702 sq km; 271 sq mi
Leading Exports: fish, garments, bananas, black pepper
Location: Pacific Ocean

Mongolia
Capital: Ulaanbaatar
Population: 2.6 million
Official Language: Khalkha Mongolian
Land Area: 1,555,400 sq km; 600,540 sq mi
Leading Exports: copper, livestock, animal products, cashmere, wool, hides, fluorspar, other nonferrous metals
Continent: Asia

Myanmar (Burma)
Capital: Rangoon (Yangon)
Population: 42.2 million
Official Language: Burmese (Myanmar)
Land Area: 657,740 sq km; 253,953 sq mi
Leading Exports: apparel, foodstuffs, wood products, precious stones
Continent: Asia

Nauru
Capital: Yaren District
Population: 12,329
Official Language: Nauruan
Land Area: 21 sq km; 8 sq mi
Leading Exports: phosphates
Location: Pacific Ocean

Nepal
Capital: Kathmandu
Population: 25.9 million
Official Language: Nepali
Land Area: 136,800 sq km; 52,818 sq mi
Leading Exports: carpets, clothing, leather goods, jute goods, grain
Continent: Asia

New Zealand
Capital: Wellington
Population: 3.8 million
Official Languages: English and Maori
Land Area: 268,680 sq km; 103,737 sq mi
Leading Exports: dairy products, meat, wood and wood products, fish, machinery
Location: Pacific Ocean

Oman
Capital: Muscat
Population: 2.7 million
Official Language: Arabic
Land Area: 212,460 sq km; 82,030 sq mi
Leading Exports: petroleum, reexports, fish, metals, textiles
Continent: Asia

Pakistan
Capital: Islamabad
Population: 147.7 million
Official Languages: Urdu and English
Land Area: 778,720 sq km; 300,664 sq mi
Leading Exports: textiles (garments, cotton cloth, and yarn), rice, other agricultural products
Continent: Asia

Palau
Capital: Koror
Population: 19,409
Official Languages: English and Palauan
Land Area: 458 sq km; 177 sq mi
Leading Exports: shellfish, tuna, copra, garments
Location: Pacific Ocean

Papua New Guinea
Capital: Port Moresby
Population: 5.2 million
Official Language: English
Land Area: 452,860 sq km; 174,849 sq mi
Leading Exports: oil, gold, copper ore, logs, palm oil, coffee, cocoa, crayfish, prawns
Location: Pacific Ocean

Philippines
Capital: Manila
Population: 84.5 million
Official Languages: Filipino and English
Land Area: 298,170 sq km; 115,123 sq mi
Leading Exports: electronic equipment, machinery and transport equipment, garments, coconut products
Continent: Asia

Qatar
Capital: Doha
Population: 793,341
Official Language: Arabic
Land Area: 11,437 sq km; 4,416 sq mi
Leading Exports: petroleum products, fertilizers, steel
Continent: Asia

Samoa
Capital: Apia
Population: 178,631
Official Languages: Samoan and English
Land Area: 2,934 sq km; 1,133 sq mi
Leading Exports: fish, coconut oil cream, copra, taro, garments, beer
Location: Pacific Ocean

Saudi Arabia
Capital: Riyadh and Jiddah
Population: 23.5 million
Official Language: Arabic
Land Area: 1,960,582 sq km; 756,981 sq mi
Leading Exports: petroleum and petroleum products
Continent: Asia

Singapore
Capital: Singapore
Population: 4.5 million
Official Languages: Malay, English, Mandarin, Chinese, and Tamil
Land Area: 683 sq km; 264 sq mi
Leading Exports: machinery and equipment (including electronics), consumer goods, chemicals, mineral fuels
Continent: Asia

Solomon Islands
Capital: Honiara
Population: 494,786
Official Language: English
Land Area: 27,540 sq km; 10,633 sq mi
Leading Exports: timber, fish, copra, palm oil, cocoa
Location: Pacific Ocean

Sri Lanka
Capital: Colombo
Population: 19.6 million
Official Language: Sinhala, Tamil, and English
Land Area: 64,740 sq km; 24,996 sq mi
Leading Exports: textiles and apparel, tea, diamonds, coconut products, petroleum products
Continent: Asia

Syria
Capital: Damascus
Population: 17.2 million
Official Language: Arabic
Land Area: 184,050 sq km; 71,062 sq mi
Leading Exports: crude oil, textiles, fruits and vegetables, raw cotton
Continent: Asia

Taiwan
Capital: Taipei
Population: 22.5 million
Official Language: Mandarin Chinese
Land Area: 32,260 sq km; 12,456 sq mi
Leading Exports: machinery and electrical equipment, metals, textiles, plastics, chemicals
Continent: Asia

Tajikistan
Capital: Dushanbe
Population: 6.7 million
Official Language: Tajik
Land Area: 142,700 sq km; 55,096 sq mi
Leading Exports: aluminum, electricity, cotton, fruits, vegetables, oil, textiles
Continent: Asia

Thailand
Capital: Bangkok
Population: 62.5 million
Official Language: Thai
Land Area: 511,770 sq km; 197,564 sq mi
Leading Exports: computers, transistors, seafood, clothing, rice
Continent: Asia

Tonga
Capital: Nuku'alofa
Population: 106,137
Official Languages: Tongan and English
Land Area: 718 sq km; 277 sq mi
Leading Exports: squash, fish, vanilla beans, root crops
Location: Pacific Ocean

Turkey
Capital: Ankara
Population: 67.3 million
Official Language: Turkish
Land Area: 770,760 sq km; 297,590 sq mi
Leading Exports: apparel, foodstuffs, textiles, metal manufactured goods, transport equipment
Continent: Asia

Turkmenistan
Capital: Ashgabat
Population: 4.7 million
Official Language: Turkmen
Land Area: 488,100 sq km; 188,455 sq mi
Leading Exports: gas, oil, cotton fiber, textiles
Continent: Asia

Asia and the Pacific (continued)

Tuvalu

Capital: Fongafale
Population: 10,800
Official Language: English
Land Area: 26 sq km; 10 sq mi
Leading Exports: copra, fish
Location: Pacific Ocean

United Arab Emirates
Capital: Abu Dhabi
Population: 2.4 million
Official Language: Arabic
Land Area: 82,880 sq km; 32,000 sq mi
Leading Exports: crude oil, natural gas, reexports, dried fish, dates
Continent: Asia

Uzbekistan

Capital: Tashkent
Population: 25.5 million
Official Language: Uzbek
Land Area: 425,400 sq km; 164,247 sq mi
Leading Exports: cotton, gold, energy products, mineral fertilizers, ferrous metals, textiles, food products, automobiles
Continent: Asia

Vanuatu
Capital: Port-Vila
Population: 196,178
Official Languages: English, French, and Bislama
Land Area: 12,200 sq km; 4,710 sq mi
Leading Exports: copra, kava, beef, cocoa, timber, coffee
Location: Pacific Ocean

Vietnam
Capital: Hanoi
Population: 81.1 million
Official Language: Vietnamese
Land Area: 325,320 sq km; 125,621 sq mi
Leading Exports: crude oil, marine products, rice, coffee, rubber, tea, garments, shoes
Continent: Asia

Yemen
Capital: Sanaa
Population: 18.7 million
Official Language: Arabic
Land Area: 527,970 sq km; 203,849 sq mi
Leading Exports: crude oil, coffee, dried and salted fish
Continent: Asia

Europe and Russia

Albania
Capital: Tiranë
Population: 3.5 million
Official Language: Albanian
Land Area: 27,398 sq km; 10,578 sq mi
Leading Exports: textiles and footwear, asphalt, metals and metallic ores, crude oil, vegetables, fruits, tobacco
Continent: Europe

Andorra
Capital: Andorra la Vella
Population: 68,403
Official Language: Catalan
Land Area: 468 sq km; 181 sq mi
Leading Exports: tobacco products, furniture
Continent: Europe

Austria
Capital: Vienna
Population: 8.2 million
Official Language: German
Land Area: 82,738 sq km; 31,945 sq mi
Leading Exports: machinery and equipment, motor vehicles and parts, paper and paperboard, metal goods, chemicals, iron and steel, textiles, foodstuffs
Continent: Europe

Belarus
Capital: Minsk
Population: 10.3 million
Official Languages: Belarussian and Russian
Land Area: 207,600 sq km; 80,154 sq mi
Leading Exports: machinery and equipment, mineral products, chemicals, textiles, food stuffs, metals
Continent: Europe

Belgium
Capital: Brussels
Population: 10.3 million
Official Languages: Dutch and French
Land Area: 30,230 sq km; 11,172 sq mi
Leading Exports: machinery and equipment, chemicals, metals and metal products
Continent: Europe

Bosnia and Herzegovina
Capital: Sarajevo
Population: 4.0 million
Official Language: Serbo-Croat
Land Area: 51,129 sq km; 19,741 sq mi
Leading Exports: miscellaneous manufactured goods, crude materials
Continent: Europe

Bulgaria
Capital: Sofía
Population: 7.6 million
Official Language: Bulgarian
Land Area: 110,550 sq km; 42,683 sq mi
Leading Exports: clothing, footwear, iron and steel, machinery and equipment, fuels
Continent: Europe

Croatia
Capital: Zagreb
Population: 4.4 million
Official Language: Croatian
Land Area: 56,414 km; 21,781 sq mi
Leading Exports: transport equipment, textiles, chemicals, foodstuffs, fuels
Continent: Europe

Czech Republic
Capital: Prague
Population: 10.3 million
Official Language: Czech
Land Area: 78,276 sq km; 29,836 sq mi
Leading Exports: machinery and transport equipment, intermediate manufactured goods, chemicals, raw materials and fuel
Continent: Europe

Denmark
Capital: Copenhagen
Population: 5.4 million
Official Language: Danish
Land Area: 42,394 sq km; 16,368 sq mi
Leading Exports: machinery and instruments, meat and meat products, dairy products, fish, chemicals, furniture, ships, windmills
Continent: Europe

Estonia
Capital: Tallinn
Population: 1.4 million
Official Language: Estonian
Land Area: 43,211 sq km; 16,684 sq mi
Leading Exports: machinery and equipment, wood products, textiles, food products, metals, chemical products
Continent: Europe

Finland
Capital: Helsinki
Population: 5.2 million
Official Languages: Finnish and Swedish
Land Area: 305,470 sq km; 117,942 sq mi
Leading Exports: machinery and equipment, chemicals, metals, timber, paper, pulp
Continent: Europe

France
Capital: Paris
Population: 59.8 million
Official Language: French
Land Area: 545,630 sq km; 310,668 sq mi
Leading Exports: machinery and transportation equipment, aircraft, plastics, chemicals, pharmaceutical products, iron and steel, beverages
Continent: Europe

Germany
Capital: Berlin
Population: 83 million
Official Language: German
Land Area: 349,223 sq km; 134,835 sq mi
Leading Exports: machinery, vehicles, chemicals, metals and manufactured goods, foodstuffs, textiles
Continent: Europe

Greece
Capital: Athens
Population: 10.6 million
Official Language: Greek
Land Area: 130,800 sq km; 50,502 sq mi
Leading Exports: food and beverages, manufactured goods, petroleum products, chemicals, textiles
Continent: Europe

Holy See (Vatican City)

Capital: Vatican City
Population: 900
Official Languages: Latin and Italian
Land Area: 0.44 sq km; 0.17 sq mi
Leading Exports: no information available
Continent: Europe

Hungary
Capital: Budapest
Population: 10.1 million
Official Language: Hungarian
Land Area: 92,340 sq km; 35,652 sq mi
Leading Exports: machinery and equipment, other manufactured goods, food products, raw materials, fuels and electricity
Continent: Europe

Iceland
Capital: Reykjavík
Population: 279,384
Official Language: Icelandic
Land Area: 100,250 sq km; 38,707 sq mi
Leading Exports: fish and fish products, animal products, aluminum, diatomite, ferrosilicon
Location: Atlantic Ocean

Ireland
Capital: Dublin
Population: 3.9 million
Official Languages: Irish Gaelic and English
Land Area: 68,890 sq km; 26,598 sq mi
Leading Exports: machinery and equipment, computers, chemicals, pharmaceuticals, live animals, animal products
Continent: Europe

Italy
Capital: Rome
Population: 57.7 million
Official Language: Italian
Land Area: 294,020 sq km; 113,521 sq mi
Leading Exports: fruits, vegetables, grapes, potatoes, sugar beets, soybeans, grain, olives, beef, diary products, fish
Continent: Europe

Latvia
Capital: Riga
Population: 2.4 million
Official Language: Latvian
Land Area: 63,589 sq km; 24,552 sq mi
Leading Exports: wood and wood products, machinery and equipment, metals, textiles, foodstuffs
Continent: Europe

Liechtenstein
Capital: Vaduz
Population: 32,842
Official Language: German
Land Area: 160 sq km; 62 sq mi
Leading Exports: small specialty machinery, dental products, stamps, hardware, pottery
Continent: Europe

Lithuania
Capital: Vilnius
Population: 3.6 million
Official Language: Lithuanian
Land Area: 65,200 sq km; 25,174 sq mi
Leading Exports: mineral products, textiles and clothing, machinery and equipment, chemicals, wood and wood products, foodstuffs
Continent: Europe

Luxembourg
Capital: Luxembourg
Population: 448,569
Official Languages: Luxembourgish, French, and German
Land Area: 2,586 sq km; 998 sq mi
Leading Exports: machinery and equipment, steel products, chemicals, rubber products, glass
Continent: Europe

Macedonia, The Former Yugoslav Republic of
Capital: Skopje
Population: 2.1 million
Official Languages: Macedonian and Albanian
Land Area: 24,856 sq km; 9,597 sq mi
Leading Exports: food, beverages, tobacco, miscellaneous manufactured goods, iron and steel
Continent: Europe

Malta
Capital: Valletta
Population: 397,499
Official Languages: Maltese and English
Land Area: 316 sq km; 122 sq mi
Leading Exports: machinery and transport equipment, manufactured goods
Location: Mediterranean Sea

Moldova
Capital: Chişinău
Population: 4.4 million
Official Language: Moldovan
Land Area: 33,371 sq km; 12,885 sq mi
Leading Exports: foodstuffs, textiles and footwear, machinery
Continent: Europe

Monaco
Capital: Monaco
Population: 31,987
Official Language: French
Land Area: 1.95 sq km; 0.75 sq mi
Leading Exports: no information available
Continent: Europe

Montenegro
Capital: Podgorica
Population: 620,145
Official Language: Serbian
Land Area: 13,812 sq km; 5,333 sq mi
Leading Exports: food products
Continent: Europe

Netherlands
Capital: Amsterdam and The Hague
Population: 16.1 million
Official Language: Dutch
Land Area: 33,883 sq km; 13,082 sq mi
Leading Exports: machinery and equipment, chemicals, fuels, foodstuffs
Continent: Europe

Norway
Capital: Oslo
Population: 4.5 million
Official Language: Norwegian
Land Area: 307,860 sq km; 118,865 sq mi
Leading Exports: petroleum and petroleum products, machinery and equipment, metals, chemicals, ships, fish
Continent: Europe

Poland
Capital: Warsaw
Population: 38.6 million
Official Language: Polish
Land Area: 304,465 sq km; 117,554 sq mi
Leading Exports: machinery and transport equipment, intermediate manufactured goods, miscellaneous manufactured goods, food and live animals
Continent: Europe

Portugal
Capital: Lisbon
Population: 10.1 million
Official Language: Portuguese
Land Area: 91,951 sq km; 35,502 sq mi
Leading Exports: clothing and footwear, machinery, chemicals, cork and paper products, hides
Continent: Europe

Romania
Capital: Bucharest
Population: 22.3 million
Official Language: Romanian
Land Area: 230,340 sq km; 88,934 sq mi
Leading Exports: textiles and footwear, metals and metal products, machinery and equipment, minerals and fuels
Continent: Europe

Russia
Capital: Moscow
Population: 145 million
Official Language: Russian
Land Area: 16,995,800 sq km; 6,592,100 sq mi
Leading Exports: petroleum and petroleum products, natural gas, wood and wood products, metals, chemicals, and a wide variety of civilian and military manufactured goods
Continents: Europe and Asia

San Marino
Capital: San Marino
Population: 27,730
Official Language: Italian
Land Area: 61 sq km; 24 sq mi
Leading Exports: building stone, lime, wood, chestnuts, wheat, wine, baked goods, hides, ceramics
Continent: Europe

Serbia
Capital: Belgrade
Population: 9.4 million
Official Language: Serbian
Land Area: 88,361 sq km; 34,116 sq mi
Leading Exports: food and live animals, manufactured goods, raw materials
Continent: Europe

Slovakia
Capital: Bratislava
Population: 5.4 million
Official Language: Slovak
Land Area: 48,800 sq km; 18,842 sq mi
Leading Exports: machinery and transport equipment, intermediate manufactured goods, miscellaneous manufactured goods, chemicals
Continent: Europe

Slovenia
Capital: Ljubljana
Population: 1.9 million
Official Language: Slovene
Land Area: 20,151 sq km; 7,780 sq mi
Leading Exports: manufactured goods, machinery and transport equipment, chemicals, food
Continent: Europe

Spain
Capital: Madrid
Population: 40.1 million
Official Languages: Spanish, Galician, Basque, and Catalan
Land Area: 499,542 sq km; 192,873 sq mi
Leading Exports: machinery, motor vehicles, foodstuffs, other consumer goods
Continent: Europe

Europe and Russia (continued)

Sweden
Capital: Stockholm
Population: 8.9 million
Official Language: Swedish
Land Area: 410,934 sq km; 158,662 sq mi
Leading Exports: machinery, motor vehicles, paper products, pulp and wood, iron and steel products, chemicals
Continent: Europe

Switzerland
Capital: Bern
Population: 7.3 million
Official Languages: German, French, and Italian
Land Area: 39,770 sq km; 15,355 sq mi
Leading Exports: machinery, chemicals, metals, watches, agricultural products
Continent: Europe

Ukraine
Capital: Kiev
Population: 48.4 million
Official Language: Ukrainian
Land Area: 603,700 sq km; 233,090 sq mi
Leading Exports: ferrous and nonferrous metals, fuel and petroleum products, machinery and transport equipment, food products
Continent: Europe

United Kingdom
Capital: London
Population: 59.8 million
Official Languages: English and Welsh
Land Area: 241,590 sq km; 93,278 sq mi
Leading Exports: manufactured goods, fuels, chemicals, food, beverages, tobacco
Continent: Europe

Latin America

Antigua and Barbuda
Capital: Saint John's
Population: 67,448
Official Language: English
Land Area: 442 sq km; 171 sq mi
Leading Exports: petroleum products, manufactured goods, machinery and transport equipment, food and live animals
Location: Caribbean Sea

Argentina
Capital: Buenos Aires
Population: 37.8 million
Official Language: Spanish
Land Area: 2,736,690 sq km; 1,056,636 sq mi
Leading Exports: edible oils, fuels and energy, cereals, feed, motor vehicles
Continent: South America

Bahamas
Capital: Nassau
Population: 300,529
Official Language: English
Land Area: 10,070 sq km; 3,888 sq mi
Leading Exports: fish and crawfish, rum, salt, chemicals, fruit and vegetables
Location: Caribbean Sea

Barbados
Capital: Bridgetown
Population: 276,607
Official Language: English
Land Area: 431 sq km; 166 sq mi
Leading Exports: sugar and molasses, rum, other foods and beverages, chemicals, electrical components, clothing
Location: Caribbean Sea

Belize
Capital: Belmopan
Population: 262,999
Official Language: English
Land Area: 22,806 sq km; 8,805 sq mi
Leading Exports: sugar, bananas, citrus, clothing, fish products, molasses, wood
Continent: North America

Bolivia
Capital: La Paz and Sucre
Population: 8.5 million
Official Language: Spanish, Quechua, and Aymara
Land Area: 1,084,390 sq km; 418,683 sq mi
Leading Exports: soybeans, natural gas, zinc, gold, wood
Continent: South America

Brazil
Capital: Brasília
Population: 176 million
Official Language: Portuguese
Land Area: 8,456,510 sq km; 3,265,059 sq mi
Leading Exports: manufactured goods, iron ore, soybeans, footwear, coffee, autos
Continent: South America

Chile
Capital: Santiago
Population: 15.5 million
Official Language: Spanish
Land Area: 748,800 sq km; 289,112 sq mi
Leading Exports: copper, fish, fruits, paper and pulp, chemicals
Continent: South America

Colombia
Capital: Bogotá
Population: 41 million
Official Language: Spanish
Land Area: 1,038,700 sq km; 401,042 sq mi
Leading Exports: petroleum, coffee, coal, apparel, bananas, cut flowers
Continent: South America

Costa Rica
Capital: San José
Population: 3.8 million
Official Language: Spanish
Land Area: 51,660 sq km; 19,560 sq mi
Leading Exports: coffee, bananas, sugar, pineapples, textiles, electronic components, medical equipment
Continent: North America

Cuba
Capital: Havana
Population: 11.2 million
Official Language: Spanish
Land Area: 110,860 sq km; 42,803 sq mi
Leading Exports: sugar, nickel, tobacco, fish, medical products, citrus, coffee
Location: Caribbean Sea

Dominica
Capital: Roseau
Population: 73,000
Official Language: English
Land Area: 754 sq km; 291 sq mi
Leading Exports: bananas, soap, bay oil, vegetables, grapefruit, oranges
Location: Caribbean Sea

Dominican Republic
Capital: Santo Domingo
Population: 8.7 million
Official Language: Spanish
Land Area: 48,380 sq km; 18,679 sq mi
Leading Exports: ferronickel, sugar, gold, silver, coffee, cocoa, tobacco, meats, consumer goods
Location: Caribbean Sea

Ecuador
Capital: Quito
Population: 13.5 million
Official Language: Spanish
Land Area: 276,840 sq km; 106,888 sq mi
Leading Exports: petroleum, bananas, shrimp, coffee, cocoa, cut flowers, fish
Continent: South America

El Salvador
Capital: San Salvador
Population: 6.4 million
Official Language: Spanish
Land Area: 20,720 sq km; 8,000 sq mi
Leading Exports: offshore assembly exports, coffee, sugar, shrimp, textiles, chemicals, electricity
Continent: North America

Grenada
Capital: Saint George's
Population: 89,211
Official Language: English
Land Area: 344 sq km; 133 sq mi
Leading Exports: bananas, cocoa, nutmeg, fruit and vegetables, clothing, mace
Location: Caribbean Sea

Guatemala
Capital: Guatemala City
Population: 13.3 million
Official Language: Spanish
Land Area: 108,430 sq km; 41,865 sq mi
Leading Exports: coffee, sugar, bananas, fruits and vegetables, cardamom, meat, apparel, petroleum, electricity
Continent: North America

Guyana
Capital: Georgetown
Population: 698,209
Official Language: English
Land Area: 196,850 sq km; 76,004 sq mi
Leading Exports: sugar, gold, bauxite/alumina, rice, shrimp, molasses, rum, timber
Continent: South America

Haiti
Capital: Port-au-Prince
Population: 7.1 million
Official Language: French and French Creole
Land Area: 27,560 sq km; 10,641 sq mi
Leading Exports: manufactured goods, coffee, oils, cocoa
Location: Caribbean Sea

Honduras
Capital: Tegucigalpa
Population: 6.6 million
Official Language: Spanish
Land Area: 111,890 sq km; 43,201 sq mi
Leading Exports: coffee, bananas, shrimp, lobster, meat, zinc, lumber
Continent: North America

Jamaica
Capital: Kingston
Population: 2.7 million
Official Language: English
Land Area: 10,831 sq km; 4,182 sq mi
Leading Exports: alumina, bauxite, sugar, bananas, rum
Location: Caribbean Sea

Mexico
Capital: Mexico City
Population: 103.4 million
Official Language: Spanish
Land Area: 1,923,040 sq km; 742,486 sq mi
Leading Exports: manufactured goods, oil and oil products, silver, fruits, vegetables, coffee, cotton
Continent: North America

Nicaragua
Capital: Managua
Population: 5 million
Official Language: Spanish
Land Area: 120,254 sq km; 46,430 sq mi
Leading Exports: coffee, shrimp and lobster, cotton, tobacco, beef, sugar, bananas, gold
Continent: North America

Panama
Capital: Panama City
Population: 2.9 million
Official Language: Spanish
Land Area: 75,990 sq km; 29,340 sq mi
Leading Exports: bananas, shrimp, sugar, coffee, clothing
Continent: North America

Paraguay
Capital: Asunción
Population: 5.9 million
Official Language: Spanish
Land Area: 397,300 sq km; 153,398 sq mi
Leading Exports: electricity, soybeans, feed, cotton, meat, edible oils
Continent: South America

Peru
Capital: Lima
Population: 28 million
Official Languages: Spanish and Quechua
Land Area: 1,280,000 sq km; 494,208 sq mi
Leading Exports: fish and fish products, gold, copper, zinc, crude petroleum and byproducts, lead, coffee, sugar, cotton
Continent: South America

Saint Kitts and Nevis
Capital: Basseterre
Population: 38,736
Official Language: English
Land Area: 261 sq km; 101 sq mi
Leading Exports: machinery, food, electronics, beverages, tobacco
Location: Caribbean Sea

Saint Lucia
Capital: Castries
Population: 160,145
Official Language: English
Land Area: 606 sq km; 234 sq mi
Leading Exports: bananas, clothing, cocoa, vegetables, fruits, coconut oil
Location: Caribbean Sea

Saint Vincent and the Grenadines
Capital: Kingstown
Population: 116,394
Official Language: English
Land Area: 389 sq km; 150 sq mi
Leading Exports: bananas, eddoes and dasheen, arrowroot starch, tennis racquets
Location: Caribbean Sea

Suriname
Capital: Paramaribo
Population: 436,494
Official Language: Dutch
Land Area: 161,470 sq km; 62,344 sq mi
Leading Exports: alumina, crude oil, lumber, shrimp and fish, rice, bananas
Continent: South America

Trinidad and Tobago
Capital: Port-of-Spain
Population: 1.2 million
Official Language: English
Land Area: 5,128 sq km; 1,980 sq mi
Leading Exports: petroleum and petroleum products, chemicals, steel products, fertilizer, sugar, cocoa, coffee, citrus, flowers
Location: Caribbean Sea

Uruguay
Capital: Montevideo
Population: 3.4 million
Official Language: Spanish
Land Area: 173,620 sq km; 67,100 sq mi
Leading Exports: meat, rice, leather products, wool, vehicles, dairy products
Continent: South America

Venezuela
Capital: Caracas
Population: 24.3 million
Official Language: Spanish
Land Area: 882,050 sq km; 340,560 sq mi
Leading Exports: petroleum, bauxite and aluminum, steel, chemicals, agricultural products, basic manufactured goods
Continent: South America

United States and Canada

Canada
Capital: Ottawa
Population: 31.9 million
Official Languages: English and French
Land Area: 9,220,970 sq km; 3,560,217 sq mi
Leading Exports: motor vehicles and parts, industrial machinery, aircraft, telecommunications equipment, chemicals, plastics, fertilizers, wood pulp, timber, crude petroleum, natural gas, electricity, aluminum
Continent: North America

United States
Capital: Washington, D.C.
Population: 281.4 million
Official Language: English
Land Area: 9,158,960 sq km; 3,536,274 sq mi
Leading Exports: capital goods, automobiles, industrial supplies and raw materials, consumer goods, agricultural products
Continent: North America

SOURCE: CIA World Factbook Online, 2002 and 2006

Glossary of Geographic Terms

basin
an area that is lower than surrounding land areas; some basins are filled with water

bay
a body of water that is partly surrounded by land and that is connected to a larger body of water

butte
a small, high, flat-topped landform with cliff-like sides

▲ **butte**

canyon
a deep, narrow valley with steep sides; often with a stream flowing through it

cataract
a large waterfall or steep rapids

◀ **cataract**

delta
a plain at the mouth of a river, often triangular in shape, formed where sediment is deposited by flowing water

flood plain
a broad plain on either side of a river, formed where sediment settles during floods

glacier
a huge, slow-moving mass of snow and ice

hill
an area that rises above surrounding land and has a rounded top; lower and usually less steep than a mountain

island
an area of land completely surrounded by water

isthmus
a narrow strip of land that connects two larger areas of land

mesa
a high, flat-topped landform with cliff-like sides; larger than a butte

mountain
a landform that rises steeply at least 2,000 feet (610 meters) above surrounding land; usually wide at the bottom and rising to a narrow peak or ridge

▶ **glacier**

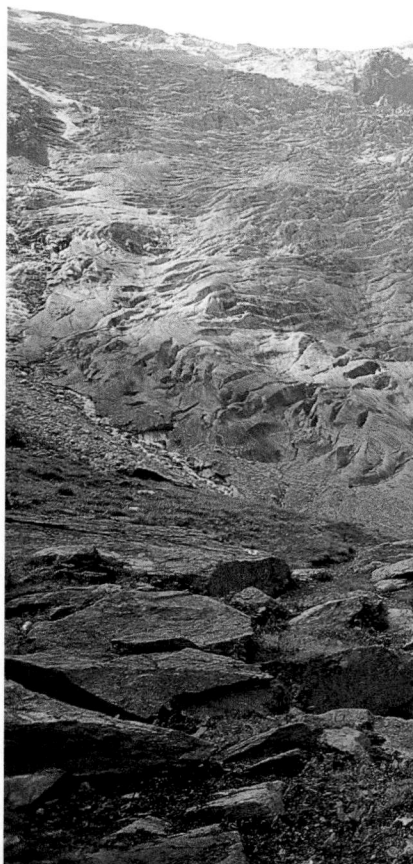

◀ **delta**

mountain pass
a gap between mountains

peninsula
an area of land almost completely surrounded by water but connected to the mainland

plain
a large area of flat or gently rolling land

plateau
a large, flat area that rises above the surrounding land; at least one side has a steep slope

river mouth
the point where a river enters a lake or sea

strait
a narrow stretch of water that connects two larger bodies of water

tributary
a river or stream that flows into a larger river

valley
a low stretch of land between mountains or hills; land that is drained by a river

volcano
an opening in Earth's surface through which molten rock, ashes, and gases escape from the interior

▶ **volcano**

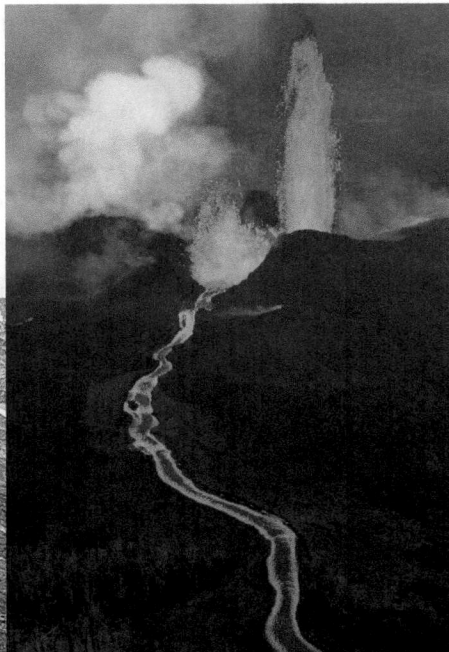

Gazetteer

A

Acadia (51° N, 110° W) the first permanent French settlement in North America, p. 314

Africa (10° N, 22° E) the world's second-largest continent, surrounded by the Mediterranean Sea, the Atlantic Ocean, the Indian Ocean, and the Red Sea, p. 15

Amazon rain forest (0° S, 49° W) a large tropical rain forest in the drainage basin of the Amazon River in northern South America, p. 494

Amazon River (0° S, 49° W) the longest river in South America, flowing across Brazil into the Atlantic Ocean, p. 342

Andes Mountains (20° S, 67° W) a mountain system extending along the western coast of South America, p. 341

Antarctic Circle (66°30′ S) a line of latitude around Earth near the South Pole, p. 32

Antarctica (87° S, 60° E) the continent that contains the South Pole; almost completely covered by an ice sheet, p. 35

Antofagasta (23°39′ S, 70°24′ W) a coastal city in Chile, p. 43

Appalachian Mountains (41° N, 77° W) a mountain system in eastern North America, p. 39

Arctic Circle (66°30′ N) a line of latitude around Earth near the North Pole, p. 30

Arctic a region located around the North Pole, p. 31

Argentina (34° S, 64° W) a country in South America, p. 488

Asia (50° N, 100° E) the world's largest continent, the main part of the Eurasian landmass, surrounded by the Arctic Ocean, the Pacific Ocean, the Indian Ocean, the Mediterranean Sea, and Europe, p. 54

Atacama Desert (25° S, 69° W) a desert in Chile, South America, p. 345

Atlanta (33°44′ N, 84°23′ W) the capital of the state of Georgia, p. 259

Australia (25° S, 135° E) a continent in the Southern Hemisphere, the world's smallest continent; also a country including the continent and Tasmania, p. 68

B

Bangladesh (24° N, 90° E) a country located in South Asia, p. 66

Bolivia (17° S, 65° W) a country in South America, p. 489

Boston (42°21′ N, 71°3′ W) the capital of the state of Massachusetts, p. 251

Brasília (15°47′ S, 47°55′ W) the capital city of Brazil, p. 495

Brazil (10° S, 55° W) the largest country in South America, p. 71

C

Calgary (51° N, 114° W) a city in southern Alberta, Canada, p. 303

Canada (60° N, 95° W) a large country in North America, p. 63

Canadian Shield a region of rocky, rugged land that covers about half of Canada, p. 151

Canal Zone (9° N, 80° W) a 10-mile strip of land along the Panama Canal, stretching from the Atlantic Ocean to the Pacific Ocean, once governed by the United States, p. 448

Caracas (10°30′ N, 66°56′ W) the capital city of Venezuela, p. 516

Caribbean Sea (15° N, 73° W) a sea bounded by the West Indies, Central America, and South America. It is part of the Atlantic Ocean. p. 340

Cariboo Mountains (59° N, 116° W) a mountain range in eastern British Columbia, Canada; a place where prospectors discovered gold in the 1800s, p. 307

Central America (11° N, 80° W) the part of Latin America south of Mexico and north of South America. It includes the seven republics of Guatemala,

Central America (11° N, 80° W) the part of Latin America south of Mexico and north of South America. It includes the seven republics of Guatemala, Honduras, El Salvador, Nicaragua, Costa Rica, Panama, and Belize. p. 103

Chicago (41°51′ N, 87°39′ W) a major city in the state of Illinois, on Lake Michigan, p. 268

Chile (30° S, 71° W) a country in South America, p. 507

China (35° N, 105° E) a large country in East Asia, officially the People's Republic of China, p. 20

Coast Ranges (55° N, 129° W) a series of mountain ranges along the Pacific coast of North America, p. 150

Colombia (4° N, 72° W) a country in South America, p. 490

Cuba (22° N, 80° W) the largest island country in the Caribbean Sea, p. 68

Cuyahoga River (41° N, 82° W) a river in northeastern Ohio, p. 203

Cuzco (13°31′ S, 71°59′ W) a city in Peru; capital of the Incan empire, p. 374

D

Dawson (64°4′ N, 139°25′ W) a city located in western Yukon Territory, Canada, p. 321

Death Valley (36° N, 116° W) the hottest, driest region of North America, located in southeastern California, p. 150

Denmark (56° N, 10° E) a country in northern Europe, p. 118

Detroit (42°20′ N, 83°3′ W) a city in the state of Michigan, p. 269

E

Egypt (27° N, 30° E) a country in North Africa, p. 60

El Salvador (13° N, 88° W) a country in Central America, p. 427

Equator (0°) a line of latitude that circles Earth at the center of the tropics, midway between the North and South poles, along which days and nights are always equal in length, p. 11

Europe (50° N, 28° E) the world's second-smallest continent, a peninsula of the Eurasian landmass bounded by the Arctic Ocean, the Atlantic Ocean, the Mediterranean Sea, and Asia, p. 43

F

Florida (28° N, 82° W) a state in the southeastern United States that is largely a peninsula, p. 12

Fraser River (49° N, 123° W) a major river of western North America, mainly in British Columbia, p. 152

G

Genoa (44°25′ N, 8°57′ E) a seaport city of Italy, p. 104

Georgia (33° N, 83° W) a state in the southeastern United States, p. 12

Germany (51° N, 10° E) a country in Western Europe, p. 97

Great Lakes a group of five large lakes in central North America: lakes Superior, Michigan, Huron, Erie, and Ontario, p. 151

Great Plains (42° N, 100° W) a semiarid plain located in North America, stretching from the Rio Grande at the U. S.-Mexico border in the south to the Mackenzie River Delta in the north, and from the Canadian Shield in the east to the Rocky Mountains in the west, p. 128

Greece (39° N, 22° E) a country in southeastern Europe, p. 93

Greenland (70° N, 40° W) a self-governing island in the northern Atlantic Ocean; Earth's largest island, a possession of Denmark, p. 18

Greenwich (51°28′ N, 0°) a borough of London, England, and location of the Royal Greenwich Observatory, whose site serves as the basis for longitude and for setting standard time, p. 12

Guatemala (15° N, 90° W) a country in Central America, p. 437

Gulf Stream a warm ocean current in the North Atlantic, flowing northeastward off the North American coast, p. 43

H

Haiti (19° N, 72° W) a country in the Caribbean Sea, on the island of Hispaniola, p. 470

Hispaniola (19° N, 71° W) an island in the Caribbean Sea, divided between Haiti in the west and the Dominican Republic in the east, p. 412

I

India (20° N, 77° E) a large country occupying most of the Indian subcontinent in South Asia, p. 13

Indonesia (5° S, 120° E) a country in Southeast Asia consisting of many islands, p. 93

Iqaluit (63°44' N, 68°28' W) the capital of Nunavut, Canada, p. 322

Iran (32° N, 53° W) a country in Southwest Asia, p. 118

Isthmus of Panama (9° N, 79° W) the narrow strip of land in Panama that separates the Atlantic Ocean and the Pacific Ocean, p. 444

Italy (43° N, 13° E) a boot-shaped country in southern Europe, p. 104

J

Jakarta (6°10' S, 106°48' E) the capital and largest city of Indonesia, p. 71

Jamaica (18° N, 77° W) an island country in the Caribbean Sea, p. 459

Jamestown (37°30' N, 75°55' W) the first permanent English settlement in North America, located in Virginia; now a site of historic preservation, p. 178

Japan (36° N, 138° E) an island country in the Pacific Ocean off the east coast of Asia, consisting of four main islands, p. 63

L

L'Anse aux Meadows (51°36' N, 55°32' W) the earliest known North American Viking settlement, located on Newfoundland, p. 311

Lake Titicaca (16° S, 69° W) the world's highest lake on which vessels can travel, located in the Andes Mountains in South America, p. 415

Libya (27° N, 17° E) a country in North Africa, p. 82

Lima (12°3' S, 77°3' W) the capital city of Peru, p. 503

London (51°30' N, 0°10' W) the capital and largest city of the United Kingdom, p. 22

Los Angeles (34°3' N, 118°14' W) a major city on the southwest coast of the state of California, p. 276

M

Mackenzie River (69° N, 134° W) a large river in the Northwest Territories of Canada, flowing northwest from the Great Slave Lake into the Beaufort Sea, p. 152

Mexico (23° N, 102° W) a country in North America, south of the United States, p. 67

Mexico City (19°24' N, 99°9' W) the capital of and largest city in Mexico; one of the largest urban areas in the world, p. 433

Miami (25°46' N, 80°11' W) a city on the southeast coast of Florida, p. 12

Middle America (11° N, 80° W) another term for Mexico and Central America, p. 339

Milky Way a galaxy consisting of several billions of stars, including the sun, p. 28

Minneapolis and St. Paul (44°58' N, 93°15' W) two cities in Minnesota; also called the Twin Cities, p. 270

Mississippi River (29° N, 89° W) a large river in the central United States flowing south from Minnesota to the Gulf of Mexico, p. 152

Missouri River (39° N, 90° W) a large river in the west central United States flowing southeast from Montana into the Mississippi River, p. 152

Montreal (45°31′ N, 73°34′ W) the largest city in the province of Quebec, Canada, p. 294

Mount Everest (27°59′ N, 86°56′ E) the highest point on Earth, located in the Himalayas on the border between Nepal and China, p. 54

Myanmar (22° N, 98° E) a country in Southeast Asia, also known as Burma, p. 82

N

Nepal (28° N, 83° E) a country in South Asia, p. 54

New York (43° N, 75° W) a state in the northeastern United States, p. 132

New York City (40°43′ N, 74°1′ W) a large city and port at the mouth of the Hudson River in the state of New York, the largest city in the United States, p. 84

New Zealand (41° S, 174° E) an island country in the Pacific Ocean, p. 122

Niagara Falls (43°5′ N, 79°4′ W) a waterfall on the Niagara River between Ontario, Canada, and New York state, p. 206

Nile Valley the fertile land located on both sides of the Nile River in northeastern Africa; site of one of the earliest civilizations, p. 63

North America (45° N, 100° W) the world's third-largest continent, consisting of Canada, the United States, Mexico, Central America, and many islands, p. 17

North Atlantic Current a warm ocean current in the North Atlantic, flowing eastward toward western and northern Europe, p. 43

North Korea (40° N, 127° E) a country in East Asia, officially the Democratic People's Republic of Korea, p. 82

North Pole (90° N) the northernmost end of Earth's axis, located in the Arctic Ocean, p. 11

Northwest Territories (65° N, 120° W) a region of northern Canada, p. 319

Norway (62° N, 10° E) a country in northern Europe, p. 118

Nunavut (70° N, 95° W) a Canadian territory in the northern part of Canada; home to a large Inuit population, p. 319

O

Ontario (50° N, 88° W) the second-largest province in Canada, p. 291

Ottawa (45°25′ N, 75°42′ W) the capital city of Canada, located in Ontario, p. 291

P

Pacific Northwest the region in the northwestern United States that includes Oregon, Washington, and northern California, p. 273

Panama (9° N, 80° W) a country in Central America, p. 444

Panama Canal (9° N, 79° W) an important shipping canal across the Isthmus of Panama, linking the Caribbean Sea (and the Atlantic Ocean) to the Pacific Ocean, p. 445

Pangaea according to scientific theory, a single landmass that broke apart to form today's separate continents; thought to have existed about 180 million years ago, p. 38

Paraguay (23° S, 58° W) a country in South America, p. 491

Pennsylvania Colony a colony in America founded in 1682 by William Penn, p. 178

Peru (10° S, 76° W) a country in South America, p. 501

Peru Current a cold-water current of the southeast Pacific Ocean; flows northward between 40° S and 4° S, p. 43

Philadelphia (39°57' N, 75°9' W) a city and port in Pennsylvania, on the Delaware River, p. 251

Philippines (13° N, 122° E) an island country located near Southeast Asia, p. 67

Port-au-Prince (18°32' N, 72°20' W) the capital city and chief port of Haiti, p. 471

Portland (45°31' N, 122°40' W) the largest city in the state of Oregon, p. 274

Puerto Rico (18° N, 64° W) an island commonwealth of the United States in the Caribbean Sea, p. 476

Q

Quebec (52° N, 72° W) a province in eastern Canada, p. 295

R

Ring of Fire a circle of volcanic mountains that surrounds the Pacific Ocean, including those on the islands of Japan and Indonesia, in the Cascades of North America, and in the Andes of South America, p. 33

Rio de Janeiro (22°55' S, 43°30' W) a major city in Brazil, p. 495

Rocky Mountains (48° N, 116° W) the major mountain range in western North America, extending from central New Mexico to northeastern British Columbia, p. 12

Rotterdam (51°55' N, 4°28' E) a seaport city in the Netherlands, p. 131

Russia (60° N, 80° E) a country stretching across eastern Europe and northern Asia, the largest country in the world, p. 3

S

Sahara the largest desert in the world, covering almost all of North Africa, p. 53

St. Lawrence River (49° N, 67° W) a river in eastern North America; the second-longest river in Canada, p. 153

St. Lawrence Seaway (46° N, 73° W) a navigable seaway from the Atlantic Ocean to the western end of the Great Lakes, p. 206

St. Louis (38°37' N, 90°11' W) a major city in Missouri, on the Mississippi River, p. 45

San Francisco (37°46' N, 122°25' W) a coastal city in California, p. 45

San Jose (37°20' N, 121°53' W) a city in western California, p. 275

San Juan (18°28' N, 66°7' W) the capital and largest city in Puerto Rico, p. 480

Santiago (33°27' S, 70°40' W) the capital city of Chile, p. 511

São Paulo (23°32' S, 46°37' W) the largest city in Brazil, p. 48

Saudi Arabia (25° N, 45° E) a country in Southwest Asia, p. 101

Seattle (47°36' N, 122°19' W) a city in the state of Washington on Puget Sound, p. 275

Sierra Nevada a mountain range in California in the western United States, p. 150

South Africa (30° S, 26° E) a country in Southern Africa, p. 70

South America (15° S, 60° W) the world's fourth-largest continent, bounded by the Caribbean Sea, the Atlantic Ocean, and the Pacific Ocean, and linked to North America by the Isthmus of Panama, p. 17

South Korea (37° N, 128° E) a country in East Asia, p. 67

South Pole (90° S) the southernmost end of Earth's axis, located in Antarctica, p. 12

Strait of Magellan (54° S, 71° W) a waterway separating mainland South America from the islands of Tierra del Fuego, at the southernmost tip of South America, p. 507

Switzerland (47° N, 8° E) a country in central Europe, p. 78

T

Tenochtitlán (19°24' N, 99°9' W) the capital of the Aztec Empire, located on the site of present-day Mexico City, p. 370

Texas (32° N, 99° W) a state in the south-central United States, p. 68

Tierra del Fuego (54° S, 67° W) an archipelago, or chain of islands, at the southernmost tip of South America, separated from the mainland by the Strait of Magellan, p. 508

Tokyo (35°42' N, 139°46' E) the capital and largest city of Japan, also the largest city in the world, p. 63

Toronto (43°39' N, 79°23' W) the largest and most populous city in Canada; the capital of the province of Ontario, p. 293

Trinidad and Tobago (11° N, 61° W) a republic of the West Indies, on the two islands called Trinidad and Tobago, p. 461

Tropic of Cancer (23°30' N) the northern boundary of the tropics, or the band of Earth that receives the most direct light and heat energy from the sun. Such a region lies on both sides of the Equator, p. 30

Tropic of Capricorn (23°30' S) the southern boundary of the tropics, p. 31. *See also* Tropic of Cancer.

U

United States (38° N, 97° W) a large country in North America, p. 12

V

Valley of Mexico (19° N, 99° W) the area in central Mexico where Mexico City is located and where most of the population lives, p. 370

Vancouver (49°16' N, 123°7' W) a city in south-western British Columbia, Canada, p. 304

Vatican City (41°54' N, 12°27' E) a nation-state of southern Europe, the smallest nation-state in the world, completely surrounded by the city of Rome, Italy, p. 81

Venezuela (8° N, 66° W) a country in northern South America, p. 516

Victoria (48°25' N, 123°22' W) the capital of British Columbia, Canada, p. 307

Vietnam (16° N, 108° E) a country located in Southeast Asia, p. 67

W

Washington, D.C. (38°53' N, 77°2' W) the capital city of the United States, located between Maryland and Virginia on the Potomac River, p. 261

West Indies (19° N, 70° W) the islands of the Caribbean, p. 410

Y

Yukon (64° N, 135° W) a territory in northwestern Canada, p. 319

Glossary

A

abolitionist (ab uh LISH un ist) *n.* a person who believed that enslaving people was wrong and who wanted to end the practice, p. 185

absolute location (AB suh loot loh KAY shun) *n.* the exact position of a place on Earth, p. 12

absolute monarchy (AB suh loot MAHN ur kee) *n.* a system of complete control by a king or queen who inherits the throne by birth, p. 82

acculturation (uh kul chur AY shun) *n.* the process of accepting new ideas from one culture and fitting them into another culture, p. 106

acid rain (AS id rayn) *n.* a rain, containing acid, that is harmful to plants and trees, often formed when pollutants from cars and factories combine with moisture in the air, p. 204

aerial photograph (EHR ee ul FOHT uh graf) *n.* a photographic image of Earth's surface taken from the air, p. 17

agribusiness (AG ruh biz niz) *n.* a large company that runs huge farms to produce, process, and distribute agricultural products, p. 164

agriculture (AG rih kul chur) *n.* farming, including growing crops and raising livestock, p. 94

alliance (uh LY uns) *n.* a formal agreement to pursue common interests formed between governments, often for military purposes, p. 180

alluvial soil (uh LOO vee ul soyl) *n.* soil deposited by water; fertile topsoil left by rivers after a flood, p. 164

ally (AL eye) *n.* a country joined with another for a special purpose, p. 464

Altiplano (al tih PLAH noh) *n.* a high plateau in the Andes, p. 503

Amazon rain forest (AM uh zahn rayn FAWR ist) *n.* a large tropical rain forest occupying the Amazon basin in northern South America, p. 494

Amazon River (AM uh zahn RIV ur) *n.* a long river in northern South America, p. 342

Andes (AN deez) *n.* a mountain system extending along the western coast of South America, p. 341

aquaculture (AHK wuh kul chur) *n.* the cultivation of fish and water plants, p. 315

aqueduct (AK wuh dukt) *n.* a pipe or channel used to carry water from a distant source, p. 376

arid (A rid) *adj.* dry, p. 44

Aristide, Jean-Bertrand (ah rees TEED, zhan behr TRAHN) *n.* former president of Haiti, p. 470

atmosphere (AT muh sfeer) *n.* a layer of gases surrounding a planet, p. 35

aurora borealis (aw RAWR uh bawr ee AL us) *n.* colorful bands of light that can be seen in northern skies, p. 318

axis (AK sis) *n.* an imaginary line around which a planet turns. Earth's axis runs through its center from the North Pole to the South Pole, p. 29

B

barometer (buh RAHM uh tur) *n.* an instrument for forecasting changes in the weather; anything that indicates a change, p. 89

bilingual (by LIN gwul) *adj.* speaking two languages; having two official languages, p. 197

biodiversity (by oh duh VUR suh tee) *n.* a large variety of living things in a region, p. 129

birthrate (BURTH rayt) *n.* the number of live births each year per 1,000 people, p. 64

bison (BY sun) *n.* the American buffalo, p. 175

blizzard (BLIZ urd) *n.* a heavy snowstorm with strong winds, p. 47

Bolívar, Simón (boh LEE vahr, see MOHN) *n.* a leader in the fight to free South America from Spanish rule, p. 387

boom (boom) *n.* a period of business growth and prosperity, p. 517

boomtown (boom town) *n.* a settlement that springs up quickly, often to serve the needs of miners, p. 307

boycott (BOY kaht) *n.* a refusal to buy or use goods and services, p. 179

Brasília (bruh ZIL yuh) *n.* capital of Brazil, founded in the 1950s to encourage people to move to the interior of the country, p. 495

C

campesino (kahm peh SEE noh) *n.* a poor Latin American farmer or farm worker, p. 402

Canal Zone (kuh NAL zohn) *n.* a ten-mile-wide strip of land along the Panama Canal, once governed by the United States, p. 448

canopy (KAN uh pea) *n.* the dense mass of leaves and branches forming the top layer of a forest, p. 52

capitalism (KAP ut ul iz um) *n.* an economic system in which private individuals or private groups of people own most businesses, p. 75

Caracas (kuh RAH kus) *n.* the capital of Venezuela, p. 516

cardinal directions (KAHR duh nul duh REK shunz) *n.* north, east, south, and west, p. 11

Carnival (KAHR nuh vul) *n.* a lively annual celebration just before Lent in Latin America, similar to Mardi Gras in the United States, p. 413

cash crop (kash krahp) *n.* a crop grown mostly for sale rather than for the needs of the farmer's family, p. 419

Castro, Fidel (KAS troh, fih DEL) *n.* the leader of Cuba's government, p. 462

caudillo (kaw DEE yoh) *n.* a military officer who rules a country very strictly, p. 389

census (SEN sus) *n.* an official count of all the people in an area, p. 375

circumnavigate (sur kum NAV ih gayt) *v.* to sail or fly all the way around something, such as Earth, p. 509

citizen (SIT uh zun) *n.* a person with certain rights and responsibilities under a particular government, p. 477

city-state (SIH tee stayt) *n.* a small, city-centered state, p. 81

civil engineering (SIV ul en juh NIHR ing) *n.* technology for building structures that alter the landscape, such as dams, roads, and bridges, p. 131

civilization (sih vuh luh ZAY shun) *n.* an advanced culture with cities and the use of writing, p. 94

civil rights (SIV ul ryts) *n.* the basic rights due to all citizens, p. 191

Civil War (SIV ul wawr) *n.* the war between the northern and southern states in the United States, which began in 1861 and ended in 1865, p. 185

African American soldiers fighting in the Civil War

climate (KLY mut) *n.* the average weather of a place over many years, p. 40

Cold War (kohld wawr) *n.* a period of great tension between the United States and the Soviet Union, which lasted for more than 40 years after World War II, p. 191

colonization (kahl uh nih ZAY shun) *n.* the movement of settlers and their culture to a new country, p. 125

Columbus, Christopher (kuh LUM bus, KRIS tuh fur) *n.* Italian explorer sponsored by Spain, who landed in the West Indies in 1492, p. 379

commercial farmer (kuh MUR shul FAHR mur) *n.* a farmer who grows most of his or her food for sale rather than for the needs of his or her family, p. 76

commonwealth (KAHM un welth) *n.* a self-governing political unit with strong ties to a particular country, p. 477

San Juan, the capital of
the commonwealth of Puerto Rico

communism (KAHM yoo niz um) *n.* an economic system in which the government owns all large businesses and most of a country's land; a political system in which the central government controls all aspects of citizens' lives, p. 75

commute (kuh MYOOT) *v.* to travel regularly to and from a place, particularly to and from a job, p. 248

compass rose (KUM pus rohz) *n.* a diagram of a compass showing direction on a map, p. 21

conformal map (kun FAWR mul map) *n.* a flat map of the entire Earth, which shows correct shapes but not true distances or sizes; also known as a Merca-

tor projection after geographer Gerardus Mercator, p. 18

coniferous tree (koh NIF ur us tree) *n.* a tree that produces cones that carry seeds, p. 52

conquistador (kahn KEES tuh dawr) *n.* one of a group of conquerors who claimed and ruled land in the Americas for the Spanish king in the 1500s, p. 380

constitution (kahn stuh TOO shun) *n.* a set of laws that defines and limits a government's power, p. 83

constitutional monarchy (kahn stuh TOO shun ul MAHN ur kee) *n.* a government in which the power of the king or queen is limited by law, p. 83

consumer (kun SOOM ur) *n.* a person who buys and uses goods and services, p. 74

Continental Divide (kahn tuh NEN tul duh VYD) *n.* the boundary that separates rivers flowing toward opposite sides of North America, located in the Rocky Mountains, p. 152

copse (kahps) *n.* a thicket of small trees or shrubs, p. 89

core (kawr) *n.* the ball of hot metal at the center of Earth, p. 34

corporate farm (KAWR puh rit fahrm) *n.* a large farm run by a corporation, often consisting of many smaller farms, p. 267

Cortés, Hernán (kohr TEZ, hur NAHN) *n.* conquistador who conquered the Aztecs, p. 380

coup (koo) *n.* short for *coup d'état* (koo day TAH), a French term meaning the overthrow of a ruler or government by an organized group that takes power, p. 521

Creole (KREE ohl) *n.* a person of mixed European and African descent; in Haiti, a language that mixes French and African languages, p. 474

criollo (kree OH yoh) *n.* a person with Spanish parents who was born in the Spanish colonies in Latin America, p. 386

crust (krust) *n.* the thin layer of rocks and minerals that surrounds Earth's mantle, p. 34

crust (krust) *n.* the thin layer of rocks and minerals that surrounds Earth's mantle, p. 34

cultural diffusion (KUL chur ul dih FYOO zhun) *n.* the movement of customs and ideas from one culture to another, p. 106

cultural diversity (KUL chur ul duh VUR suh tee) *n.* a wide variety of cultures, p. 214

cultural exchange (KUL chur ul eks CHAYNJ) *n.* a process in which different cultures share ideas and ways of doing things, p. 215

cultural landscape (KUL chur ul LAND skayp) *n.* the parts of a people's environment that they have shaped and that reflect their culture, p. 93

cultural trait (KUL chur ul trayt) *n.* a skill, custom, idea, or way of doing things that forms part of a culture, p. 92

culture (KUL chur) *n.* the way of life of a people, including their language, beliefs, customs, and practices, p. 92

Cuzco (KOOS koh) *n.* the capital of the Incan Empire; a city in modern Peru, p. 374

D

death rate (deth rayt) *n.* the number of deaths each year per 1,000 people, p. 64

deciduous tree (dee SIJ oo us tree) *n.* a tree that loses its leaves in the fall, p. 52

deforestation (dee fawr uh STAY shun) *n.* a loss of forest cover in a region, p. 129

degrees (dih GREEZ) *n.* units that measure angles; units that measure temperature, p. 11

demography (dih MAH gruh fee) *n.* the scientific study of population change and population distribution, p. 60

dependency (dee PEN dun see) *n.* a region that belongs to another state, p. 81

descendant (dee SEN dunt) *n.* a child, grandchild, great-grandchild (and so on) of an ancestor, p. 294

descent (dee SENT) *n.* ancestry, p. 299

desert (DEZ urt) *n.* a hot, dry region with little vegetation, p. 52

desert scrub (DEZ urt skrub) *n.* desert vegetation that needs little water, p. 52

developed nation (dih VEL upt NAY shun) *n.* a nation with many industries and advanced technology, p. 76

developing nation (dih VEL up ing NAY shun) *n.* a nation with few industries and simple technology, p. 76

dictator (DIK tay tur) *n.* a ruler of a country with complete power, p. 82

direct democracy (duh REKT dih MAHK ruh see) *n.* a form of government in which all adults take part in decisions, p. 82

discrimination (dih skrim ih NAY shun) *n.* the practice of treating certain groups of people unfairly, p. 191

distortion (dih STAWR shun) *n.* loss of accuracy. Every map projection causes some distortion of shape or size. p. 17

diversify (duh VUR suh fy) *v.* to add variety, p. 358

diversity (duh VUR suh tee) *n.* variety, p. 402

dominion (duh MIN yun) *n.* a self-governing area subject to Great Britain; for example, Canada prior to 1939, p. 196

E

economy (ih KAHN uh mee) *n.* a system for producing, distributing, consuming, and owning goods, services, and wealth, p. 74

ecotourism (ek oh TOOR iz um) *n.* travel to unspoiled areas in order to observe wildlife and learn about the environment, p. 450

elevation (el uh VAY shun) *n.* the height of land above sea level, p. 346

El Niño (el NEEN yoh) *n.* a warming of the ocean water along the western coast of South America; a current that influences global weather patterns, p. 343

emigrate (EM ih grayt) *v.* to leave one country to settle in another, p. 407

empire (EM pyr) *n.* a state containing several countries, p. 81

encomienda (en koh mee EN dah) *n.* the right of Spanish colonists to demand taxes or labor from Native Americans, granted by the Spanish government, p. 384

energy (EN ur jee) *n.* usable heat or power; capacity for doing work, p. 115

enslave (en SLAYV) *v.* to force someone to become a slave, p. 177

environment (en VY run munt) *n.* natural surroundings, p. 120

equal-area map (EEK wul EHR ee uh map) *n.* a map showing landmasses with the correct sizes, but with altered shapes, p. 19

Equator (ee KWAYT ur) *n.* the line of latitude around the middle of the globe, p. 11

equinox (EE kwih nahks) *n.* one of two days in the year when the sun is directly over the Equator and the days are almost exactly as long as the nights; known as spring and fall equinoxes, p. 30

erosion (ee ROH zhun) *n.* a process in which water, ice, or wind removes pieces of rock, p. 39

ethics (ETH iks) *n.* the standards or code of moral behavior distinguishing between right and wrong, p. 101

ethnic group (ETH nik groop) *n.* a group of people who share the same ancestry, language, religion, or cultural traditions, p. 216

exile (EK syl) *n.* a person who leaves or is forced to leave his or her homeland for another country, often for political reasons, p. 465; *v.* to force to leave an area, p. 314

A barge on the St. Lawrence Seaway carries goods for export.

export (eks PAWRT) *v.* to send products from one country to be sold in another country, p. 393; (EKS pawrt) *n.* a product that is sold in another country, p. 207

extended family (ek STEN did FAM uh lee) *n.* a family that includes several generations, p. 97

F

fault (fawlt) *n.* a crack in Earth's crust, p. 37

federation (fed ur AY shun) *n.* a union of states, groups, provinces, or nations, p. 291

foreign debt (FAWR in det) *n.* money owed by one country to another country or a foreign financial institution, p. 394

forty-niner (FAWRT ee NY nur) *n.* a miner of the California Gold Rush of 1849, p. 273

fossil fuel (FAHS ul FYOO ul) *n.* a fuel formed over millions of years, from animal and plant remains, including coal, petroleum, and natural gas, p. 117

Francophone (FRANG koh fohn) *n.* a person who speaks French as his or her first language, p. 294

free trade (free trayd) *n.* trade with no tariffs, or taxes, on imported goods, p. 208

fugitive (FYOO jih tiv) *n.* a runaway; someone who runs from danger, p. 184

G

gaucho (GOW choh) *n.* a cowboy of the pampas of South America, p. 417

geographic information systems (jee uh GRAF ik in fur MAY shun SIS tumz) *n.* computer-based systems that store and use information linked to geographic locations, p. 17

geography (jee AHG ruh fee) *n.* the study of Earth, p. 10

glacier (GLAY shur) *n.* a large, slow-moving mass of ice and snow, p. 150

globe (glohb) *n.* a model of Earth with the same round shape as Earth itself, p. 16

goods (gudz) *n.* physical products, p. 75

government (GUV urn munt) *n.* a system that creates and enforces laws in a region, p. 80

grassland (GRAS land) *n.* a region of flat or rolling land covered with grasses, p. 159

Great Lakes (grayt layks) *n.* the world's largest group of freshwater lakes, located between the United States and Canada; the five lakes Erie, Huron, Michigan, Ontario, and Superior, p. 151

Green Revolution (green rev uh LOO shun) *n.* the increased use of chemicals, machinery, and new crop varieties in agriculture since the 1950s that has greatly increased the world's food supply. It has also created environmental challenges. p. 65

H

hacienda (hah see EN dah) *n.* a large farm or plantation, often growing cash crops for export, p. 383

haze (hayz) *n.* dust, smoke, or other materials dispersed in air, which reduce visibility; often caused by pollution, p. 204

hemisphere (HEM ih sfeer) *n.* one half of Earth, p. 11

hemlock (HEM lahk) *n.* an evergreen tree with drooping branches and short, flat needles, p. 89

hieroglyphics (hy ur oh GLIF iks) *n.* a system of writing made up of signs and symbols, used by the Maya, the ancient Egyptians, and other cultures, p. 369

high latitudes (hy LAT uh toodz) *n.* the areas north of the Arctic Circle and south of the Antarctic Circle, p. 32

hill (hil) *n.* a landform with a rounded top that rises above the surrounding land but is lower and less steep than a mountain, p. 35

Holocaust (HAHL uh kawst) *n.* the killing of millions of Jews and others by the Nazis in World War II, p. 190

Homestead Act (HOHM sted akt) *n.* a law passed by the U. S. Congress in 1862 giving 160 acres (65 hectares) of land on the Midwestern plains to any adult willing to live on and farm it for five years, p. 188

human-environment interaction (HYOO mun en VY run munt in tur AK shun) *n.* how people affect the environment and the physical characteristics of their surroundings and how the environment affects them, p. 13

humid continental climate (HYOO mid kahn tuh NENT ul KLY mut) *n.* a climate with moderate to hot summers but very cold winters, supporting grasslands and forests, p. 51

hurricane (HUR ih kayn) *n.* a violent tropical storm, or cyclone, that forms over the Atlantic Ocean, p. 47

hydroelectricity (hy droh ee lek TRIH suh tee) *n.* electric power produced by rushing water, p. 165

I

illiterate (ih LIT ur ut) *adj.* unable to read or write, p. 464

immigrant (IM uh grunt) *n.* a person who moves to a new country in order to settle there, p. 67

immunity (ih MYOO nuh tee) *n.* a natural resistance to disease, p. 301

import (im PAWRT) *v.* to bring products into one country from another, p. 393; (IM pawrt) *n.* a product brought to one country from another for sale, p. 207

indentured servant (in DEN churd SUR vunt) *n.* a person who, in exchange for benefits received, must work for a period of years to gain freedom, p. 178

indigenous (in DIJ uh nus) *adj.* belonging to a certain place, p. 175

indigenous people (in DIJ uh nus PEA pul) *n.* people who are descended from the people who first lived in a region, p. 402

industrialization (in dus tree ul ih ZAY shun) *n.* the development of manufacturing in an economy, p. 125

Industrial Revolution (in DUS tree ul rev uh LOO shun) *n.* the change from making goods by hand to making them by machine, p. 183

institution (in stuh TOO shun) *n.* a custom or organization with social, educational, or religious purposes, p. 95

interdependent (in tur dee PEN dunt) *adj.* dependent on one another, p. 79

international (in tur NASH uh nul) *adj.* involving more than one nation, p. 84

Inuktitut (ih NOOK tih toot) *n.* the native language of the Inuit, p. 322

irrigation (ihr uh GAY shun) *n.* supplying dry land with water, p. 94

isthmus (IS mus) *n.* a narrow strip of land that has water on both sides and joins two larger bodies of land, p. 340

K

key (kee) *n.* the section of a map that explains the symbols and shading on the map, p. 21

L

labor force (LAY bur fawrs) *n.* the workers in a country or region, p. 188

Ladino (luh DEE noh) *n.* a mestizo, or person of mixed Spanish and Native American ancestry in Guatemala, p. 438

land bridge (land brij) *n.* a bridge formed by a narrow strip of land connecting one landmass to another, p. 175

landform (LAND fawrm) *n.* a shape or type of land, p. 35

landmass (LAND mas) *n.* a large area of land, p. 19

land reform (land ree FAWRM) *n.* the effort to distribute land more equally and fairly, p. 438

latitude (LAT uh tood) *n.* the distance north or south of the Equator, measured in units called degrees, p. 11

lichen (LY kun) *n.* a plant that is a combination of a fungus and an alga that grows and spreads over rocks and tree trunks, p. 39

life expectancy (lyf ek SPEK tun see) *n.* the average number of years that people live, p. 65

literacy (LIT ur uh see) *n.* the ability to read and write, p. 218

lock (lahk) *n.* an enclosed section of a canal used to raise or lower a ship to another level, p. 153

longitude (LAHN juh tood) *n.* the distance east or west of the Prime Meridian, measured in degrees, p. 11

Louisiana Purchase (loo ee zee AN uh PUR chus) *n.* the sale of land in 1803 by France to the United States; all the land between the Mississippi River and the eastern slope of the Rocky Mountains, p. 181

L'Ouverture, Toussaint (loo vehr TOOR, too SAN) *n.* a former slave who led the people of Haiti in their fight for independence, p. 385

lowland (LOH land) *n.* a land that is lower than the surrounding land, p. 151

low latitudes (loh LAT uh toodz) *n.* the area between the Tropic of Cancer and the Tropic of Capricorn, p. 32

M

Magellan, Ferdinand (muh JEL un, FUR duh nand) *n.* a Portuguese explorer sailing for Spain whose expedition was the first to circumnavigate the globe, p. 507

magma (MAG muh) *n.* soft, hot, molten rock, p. 36

maize (mayz) *n.* corn, p. 369

Manifest Destiny (MAN uh fest DES tuh nee) *n.* a belief that the United States had a right to own all the land from the Atlantic Ocean to the Pacific Ocean, p. 183

mantle (MAN tul) *n.* the thick, rocky layer around Earth's core, p. 34

manufacturing (man yoo FAK chur ing) *n.* processing raw materials to make a finished product, p. 123

maquiladora (mah kee luh DOHR ah) *n.* a factory that assembles imported parts to make products for export, often located in Mexico near the United States border, p. 405

marine west coast climate (muh REEN west kohst KLY mut) *n.* moderate climate occurring in areas cooled by ocean currents, supporting forests more often than grasses, p. 51

maritime (MA rih tym) *adj.* having to do with navigation or shipping on the sea, p. 315

mass transit (mas TRAN sit) *n.* a system of subways, buses, and commuter trains used to transport large numbers of people, p. 275

Mediterranean climate (med uh tuh RAY nee un KLY mut) *n.* moderate climate that receives most of its rain in winter and has hot and dry summers, supporting plants with leathery leaves that hold water, p. 51

megalopolis (meg uh LAHP uh lis) *n.* a number of cities and suburbs that blend into one very large urban area, p. 249

melting pot (MELT ing paht) *n.* a country in which all cultures blend together to form a single culture, p. 227

meridian (muh RID ee un) *n.* a line of longitude, p. 12

mestizo (meh STEE zoh) *n.* in Latin America, a person of mixed Spanish and Native American ancestry, p. 383

Mexico City (MEK sih koh SIT ee) *n.* the capital and largest city of Mexico, p. 433

Middle America (MID ul uh MEHR ih kuh) *n.* Mexico and Central America, p. 339

middle latitudes (MID ul LAT uh toodz) *n.* the areas between the high latitudes and the low latitudes, p. 32

migrant worker (MY grunt WUR kur) *n.* a laborer who travels from one area to another, picking crops that are in season, p. 430

Migrant workers in Mexico

migration (my GRAY shun) *n.* the movement of people from one country or region to another in order to make a new home, p. 67

mineral (MIN ur ul) *n.* a natural resource that is obtained by mining, such as gold, iron, or copper, p. 114

missionary (MISH un ehr ee) *n.* a person who tries to convert others to his or her religion, p. 177

mixed-crop farm (mikst krahp fahrm) *n.* a farm that grows several different kinds of crops, p. 266

Moctezuma (mahk tih ZOO muh) *n.* ruler of the Aztec empire at the time the Spanish arrived there, p. 378

mountain (MOWN tun) *n.* a steep landform that rises usually more than 2,000 feet (610 m) above sea level or the surrounding flatlands, p. 35

N

NAFTA (NAF tuh) *n.* North American Free Trade Agreement, signed in 1994 by Canada, the United States, and Mexico to establish mutual free trade, p. 208

nation-state (NAY shun stayt) *n.* a state that is independent of other states, p. 81

natural resource (NACH ur ul REE sawrs) *n.* a material found in nature that people use to meet their needs, p. 114

navigate (NAV uh gayt) *v.* to plot or direct the course of a ship or aircraft, p. 153

nomadic (noh MAD ik) *adj.* frequently moving from one place to another in search of food or pastureland, p. 229

nonrenewable resource (nahn rih NOO uh bul REE sawrs) *n.* a resource that cannot be replaced, p. 116

nuclear family (NOO klee ur FAM uh lee) *n.* a mother, a father, and their children, p. 97

An oasis in the Sahara

O

oasis (oh AY sis) *n.* a fertile area, in a desert, that has a source of water, p. 503

ocean current (OH shun KUR unt) *n.* a moving stream of water in the ocean created by uneven heating of Earth's surface, p. 42

oligarchy (AHL ih gahr kee) *n.* a government controlled by a small group of people, p. 82

one-resource economy (wun REE sawrs ih KAHN uh mee) *n.* a country's dependence largely on one resource or crop for income, p. 356

orbit (AWR bit) *n.* the path one body makes as it circles around another body, p. 28

P

Pacific Rim (puh SIF ik rim) *n.* the group of countries bordering on the Pacific Ocean, p. 309

pampas (PAM puz) *n.* the flat grasslands in the southern part of South America; a region similar to the Great Plains in the United States, p. 341

Panama Canal (PAN uh mah kuh NAL) *n.* a shipping canal across the Isthmus of Panama, linking the Caribbean Sea (and the Atlantic Ocean) to the Pacific Ocean, p. 445

parallel (PA ruh lel) *n.* in geography, a line of latitude, p. 12

permafrost (PUR muh frawst) *n.* a permanently frozen layer of ground below the top layer of soil, p. 159

petrochemical (pet roh KEM ih kul) *n.* a substance, such as a plastic, paint, or asphalt, that is made from petroleum, p. 258

petroleum (puh TROH lee um) *n.* an oily substance found under Earth's crust; the source of gasoline and other fuels; an energy resource, p. 116

Pinochet Ugarte, Augusto (pea noh SHAY oo gahr TAY, ah GOO stoh) *n.* military dictator of Chile from 1973 to 1988, p. 513

Pizarro, Francisco (pea SAHR oh, frahn SEES koh) *n.* conquistador who conquered the Incas, p. 381

plain (playn) *n.* a large area of flat or gently rolling land, p. 35

plantation (plan TAY shun) *n.* a large, one-crop farm with many workers, common in the southern United States before the Civil War, p. 178

plate (playt) *n.* in geography, a huge section of Earth's crust, p. 36

plateau (pla TOH) *n.* a large, mostly flat area that rises above the surrounding land, p. 35

plaza (PLAH zuh) *n.* a public square at the center of a village, a town, or a city, p. 431

polar climate (POH lur KLY mut) *n.* a climate of the high latitudes that is cold all year and has short summers, p. 50

political movement (puh LIT ih kul MOOV munt) *n.* a large group of people who work together for political change, p. 440

pollution (puh LOO shun) *n.* waste, usually made by people, which makes a place's air, water, or soil less clean, p. 132

population (pahp yuh LAY shun) *n.* total number of people in an area, p. 60

population density (pahp yuh LAY shun DEN suh tee) *n.* the average number of people per square mile or square kilometer, p. 62

population distribution (pahp yuh LAY shun dis trih BYOO shun) *n.* the way the population is spread out over an area, p. 60

prairie (PREHR ee) *n.* a region of flat or rolling land covered with tall grasses, p. 159

precipitation (pree sip uh TAY shun) *n.* water that falls to the ground as rain, sleet, hail, or snow, p. 40

Prime Meridian (prym muh RID ee un) *n.* the meridian that runs through Greenwich, England; 0° longitude, p. 11

prime minister (prym MIN is tur) *n.* the chief official in a government with a parliament, p. 291

privatization (pry vuh tih ZAY shun) *n.* a government's sale of land or industries it owns, to individuals or private companies, p. 520

producer (pruh DOOS ur) *n.* a person who makes products that are used by other people, p. 74

projection (proh JEK shun) *n.* method of mapping Earth on a flat surface, p. 18

province (PRAH vins) *n.* a political division of land in Canada, similar to a state in the United States, p. 159

push-pull theory (push pul THEE uh ree) *n.* a theory of migration claiming that difficulties "push" people to leave their old homes, while a hope for better living conditions "pulls" them to a new country, p. 68

Q

Quiet Revolution (KWY ut rev uh LOO shun) *n.* a peaceful change in the government of Quebec, Canada, in which the Parti Québécois won control of the legislature and made French the official language, p. 295

quipu (KEE poo) *n.* knotted strings on which the Incas recorded information, p. 375

R

rain forest (rayn FAWR ist) *n.* a dense evergreen forest that has abundant rainfall throughout the year, p. 341

rain shadow (rayn SHAD oh) *n.* an area on the side of a mountain away from the wind, which receives little rainfall, p. 157

raw materials (raw muh TIHR ee ulz) *n.* natural resources that must be processed to be useful, p. 114

recession (rih SESH un) *n.* a downturn in business activity and economic prosperity, not as severe as a depression, p. 266

Reconstruction (ree kun STRUK shun) *n.* the United States plan for rebuilding the nation after the Civil War, including a period when the South was governed by the United States Army, p. 186

referendum (ref uh REN dum) *n.* a ballot or vote in which voters decide for or against a particular issue, p. 295

refugee (ref yoo JEE) *n.* a person who leaves his or her homeland for personal safety or to escape persecution, p. 471

regime (ruh ZHEEM) *n.* a particular administration or government, p. 395

region (REE jun) *n.* an area with a unifying characteristic such as climate, land, population, or history, p. 12

relative location (REL uh tiv loh KAY shun) *n.* the location of a place described in relation to places near it, p. 12

renewable resource (rih NOO uh bul REE sawrs) *n.* a natural resource that can be replaced, p. 115

representative democracy (rep ruh ZEN tuh tiv dih MAHK ruh see) *n.* a government run by representatives that the people choose, p. 83

reservation (rez ur VAY shun) *n.* land set aside for a specific purpose, as by the United States government for Native Americans, p. 223

reserve (rih ZURV) *n.* land set aside for a specific purpose, as by the Canadian government for indigenous peoples, p. 228

responsible development (rih SPAHN suh bul dih VEL up munt) *n.* balancing the needs of the environment, community, and economy against one another, p. 274

revolution (rev uh LOO shun) *n.* a circular journey, p. 1; the overthrow of an existing government, with another government taking its place, p. 28

Revolutionary War (rev uh LOO shun ehr ee wawr) *n.* the war in which 13 American colonies won their independence from Britain, fought from 1775 to 1781, p. 179

Rio de Janeiro (REE oh day zhuh NEHR oh) *n.* a large city in Brazil, p. 495

Protesting a regime's policies in Argentina

Rocky Mountains (RAHK ee MOWN tunz) *n.* the major mountain range in western North America, extending south from Alberta, Canada, through the western United States to Mexico, p. 149

rotation (roh TAY shun) *n.* a complete turn, p. 29

rural (ROOR ul) *adj.* having to do with the countryside, p. 71

S

sanitation (san uh TAY shun) *n.* disposal of sewage and waste, p. 65

San Martín, José de (sahn mahr TEEN, hoh SAY deh) *n.* a leader in the fight to free South America from Spanish rule, p. 388

satellite image (SAT uh lyt IM ij) *n.* an image of Earth's surface taken from a satellite in orbit, p. 17

savanna (suh VAN uh) *n.* a flat, grassy region, or open plain with scattered trees and thorny bushes, p. 52

scale (skayl) *n.* relative size, p. 16

segregate (SEG ruh gayt) *v.* to set apart and force to use separate schools, housing, parks, and so on because of race or religion, p. 186

semiarid climate (sem ee A rid KLY mut) *n.* a hot, dry climate with little rain, supporting only shrubs and grasses, p. 44

separatist (SEP ur uh tist) *n.* someone who wants the province of Quebec to break away from the rest of Canada, p. 295

services (SUR vih siz) *n.* work done for other people that does not produce goods, p. 123

sierra (see EHR uh) *n.* a range of mountains, such as the one that runs from northwest to southeast Peru, p. 503

slum (slum) *n.* a usually crowded area of a city, often with poverty and poor housing, p. 187

social class (SOH shul klas) *n.* a grouping of people based on rank or status, p. 97

social structure (SOH shul STRUK chur) *n.* a pattern of organized relationships among groups of people within a society, p. 96

society (suh SY uh tee) *n.* a group of people sharing a culture and social structure, p. 96

sod (sahd) *n.* the top layer of soil containing grass plants and their roots, p. 298

solstice (SAHL stis) *n.* one of two days in the year when the sun is directly overhead at its farthest point from the Equator. Summer solstice, in the hemisphere where the sun is overhead, is the longest day and shortest night of the year. Winter solstice, on the same day in the opposite hemisphere, is the shortest day and longest night of the year. p. 30

squatter (SKWAHT ur) *n.* a person who settles on someone else's land without permission, p. 433

standard of living (STAN durd uv LIV ing) *n.* the level at which a person or nation lives, as measured by the availability of food, clothing, shelter, and so forth, p. 219

state (stayt) *n.* a region that shares a government, p. 80

strike (stryk) *n.* a refusal to work until certain demands of workers are met, p. 441

subarctic climate (sub AHRK tik KLY mut) *n.* a continental dry climate with cool summers and cold winters, p. 51

subsistence farmer (sub SIS tuns FAHR mur) *n.* a farmer who raises his or her food and animals mainly to feed his or her own family, p. 77

subsistence farming (sub SIS tuns FAHR ming) *n.* growing only enough food to meet the needs of the farmer's family, p. 419

Sun Belt (sun belt) *n.* the area of the United States stretching from the southern Atlantic Coast to the coast of California, known for its warm weather, p. 260

A totem pole in Alaska

T

tariff (TAR if) *n.* a tax charged on imported goods, p. 208

technology (tek NAHL uh jee) *n.* a way of putting knowledge to practical use, p. 76

temperature (TEM pur uh chur) *n.* the hotness or coldness of the air or some other substance, p. 40

tenement (TEN uh munt) *n.* an apartment house that is crowded and poorly built, p. 187

Tenochtitlán (teh nawch tee TLAHN) *n.* the capital of the Aztec Empire, located on the site of present-day Mexico City, p. 370

terrorist (TEHR ur ist) *n.* a person who uses violence and fear to achieve goals, p. 192

textile (TEKS tyl) *n.* cloth, p. 183

Topa Inca (TOH puh ING kuh) *n.* an emperor of the Incas, who expanded their empire, p. 374

tornado (tawr NAY doh) *n.* a storm in the form of a swirling funnel of wind, moving as fast as 200 miles (320 kilometers) per hour, p. 47

totem pole (TOHT um pohl) *n.* a tall, carved wooden pole containing symbols, found among Native Americans of the Pacific Northwest, p. 305

treaty (TREE tee) *n.* an agreement in writing made between two or more countries, p. 84

tributary (TRIB yoo tehr ee) *n.* a river or stream that flows into a larger river, p. 152

tropical cyclone (TRAHP ih kul SY klohn) *n.* an intense wind and rain storm that forms over oceans in the tropics, p. 47

tundra (TUN druh) *n.* an area of cold climate and low-lying vegetation, p. 51

U

urban (UR bun) *adj.* located in cities and nearby towns, p. 71

urbanization (ur ban ih ZAY shun) *n.* the movement of people to cities, p. 70

V

vegetation (vej uh TAY shun) *n.* plants that grow in a region, p. 50

vertical climate (VUR tih kul KLY mut) *n.* the overall weather patterns of a region, as influenced by elevation; the higher the elevation, the colder the climate, p. 54

W

weather (WETH ur) *n.* the condition of the air and sky from day to day, p. 40

weathering (WETH ur ing) *n.* a process that breaks rocks down into tiny pieces, p. 39

West Indies (west IN deez) *n.* the Caribbean islands, p. 410

Index

The *m, g,* or *p* following some page numbers refers to maps (*m*), charts, tables, graphs, timelines or diagrams (*g*), or pictures (*p*).

Blue indicates Teacher's Edition entries.

A

abolitionists, 185, 562
Aborigines, 108*p*
absolute location, M1, 12, 562
absolute monarchy, 82, 562
Acadia, 194, 314, 556
acculturation, 104, 106, 562
acid rain, 204, 204*m*, 204*p*, 562
Acoma Pueblo, New Mexico, 176, 176*p*
Ada, Alma Flor, 362–365
Addams, Jane, 188
adobe, 176, 176*p*
aerial photographs, 17, 562
Afghanistan, 191*g*, 192, 199, 542*m*
Africa, M10*m*, M11*m*, 3*m*, 5*m*, 7*m*, 531*m*, 533*m*, 540*m*, 541*m*, 556
  developing nations, 77
  independence, 388
  population, 63*m*, 66
  slave trade, 68, 178, 384
  urbanization, 71
African Americans
  civil rights of, 191
  Jim Crow laws and, 186
  literature of, 225, 225*p*
  migration of, 256, 256*g*
  music of, 225–226, 225*p*
  rights of, 182
  slavery and, 392
  soldiers, 185*p*
agribusiness, 164, 562
Agricultural Revolution, 94
agriculture, M16, 562
  in Canada, 286–289
  in the Caribbean, 458
  colonization, 125
  cultural change and, 106
  cultural development, 94, 94*p*
  cultural landscape, 93, 93*p*, 565
  defined, 562
  developed nations, 76
  developing nations, 77
  early farming and industrialization, 61*m*
  economic activity, 122, 122*p*
  effects on environment, 128, 129
  irrigation, 121, 121*p*
  land use, 121
  population distribution, 61, 61*m*
  population growth, 65
  renewable resources, 116
  in the South, 257, 257*p*
  subsistence farmers, M16, 77, 377, 419, 490*p*, 573
  in the United States, 236–247
  See also farming
air circulation, 43*g*
air pollution, 132, 204, 204*m*, 204*p*
air pressure,
  tornadoes, 47
air temperature, 40
Alabama, 141*m*, 235*m*, 537*m*
  data about, 236
  farming in, 257
  land use in, 256*m*
  mining in, 258
  in Sun Belt, 260*m*
Alaska, 4*p*, 148, 148*p*, 149, 158, 181*m*, 271, 530*m*, 536*m*
  data about, 141*m*, 235*m*, 236
  glaciers in, 150
  land bridge to, 175
  natural resources of, 165, 166
  purchase of, 188
Albania, 550
Albany, New York, 243
Alberta, 167, 196*m*, 298, 300*m*
  data about, 141*m*, 285*m*, 286
  indigenous people of, 299
  population of, 301
Alexander Island, 35*p*, 545*m*
Algeria, 546
Allende, Isabel, 418

alliances, 562
  nations, 84
  trade, 79
Allied Powers, 189
alluvial soil, 164, 562
ally, 464, 562
Alonso, Vanesa, 467
Altiplano, 489, 491, 503, 504, 562
Alvarado, Elvia, 404
Amazon Basin, 4*m*, 332, 332*m*, 494, 532*m*, 535*m*
Amazon rain forest, 26h, 489, 494, 556, 562
  importance of, 496–497, 496*g*, 497*p*
  medicine and, 112f
  photosynthesis and, 495
  threats to the, 497
Amazon River, 336f, 342, 494, 556, 562
American Indian Movement (AIM), 223, 223*p*
American Revolution. *See* Revolutionary War
Americas, migration to, M14, M14*m*, M15*m*
America's Breadbasket, 145*p*
Amritsar, India, 101*p*
Amsterdam, Netherlands, 72*p*
Anasazi people, 103
Andes Mountains, 336f, 341, 417, 488, 491, 509, 512, 535*m*, 556, 562
Angola, 546
animals, 129
Annapolis, Maryland, 240
Antarctic Circle, 32, 556
Antarctic Peninsula, 4*m*
Antarctica, 530*m*–531*m*, 532–533*m*, 545*m*, 556
  ice floes, 35*p*
  ocean currents, 42
antibiotics, 65
Antigua and Barbuda, 456, 456*p*
Antofagasta, 43, 556
Appalachian Mountains, 4*m*, 39, 149, 556
aquaculture, 313*g*, 315, 562
aqueducts, 376, 562
Arawaks, 411

archaeological dig, 311, 311*p*
Arches National Park, Utah, 26–27*p*
architecture, 419–420, 420*p*
  Incan, 376, 376*p*
  See also housing
Arctic, 31*p*, 120, 545*m*, 556
Arctic Circle, 30*g*, 31*g*, 32, 51, 556
Arctic Ocean, 2*m*, 3*m*, 4*m*, 5*m*, 6*m*, 7*m*, 56, 142*m*, 149, 152, 545*m*
areas of influence, 173*m*
Argentina, 487*m*, 488, 534*m*, 556
  beef industry, 417
  climate of, 345
  culture of, 417
  farming in, 419
  foreign debt of, 394*g*, 395
  gauchos in, 341*p*
  government of, 418, 418*p*, 488
  independence in, 387*m*
  landforms of, 341
  Mothers of Plaza de Mayo, 418, 418*p*
  natural resources in, 355, 355*p*
  vegetation of, 347, 348*m*
  waterways in, 342
arid, 44, 562
arid climates, 44*p*, 51
Aristide, Jean Bertrand, 470, 473, 562
Arizona, 158, 536*m*
  climate in, 272*m*
  data about, 141*m*, 235*m*, 237
  hydroelectricity in, 272*g*
  in Sun Belt, 260*m*
Armenia, 548
Arkansas, 537*m*
  data about, 141*m*, 235*m*, 237
  farming in, 257
  land use in, 256*m*
  in Sun Belt, 260*m*
Armstrong, Louis, 225*p*, 226
art
  Aztec, 403
  Mayan, 428*p*
  of Middle America, 403–404, 403*p*
  of Native Americans, 404
  Pre-Columbian, 403

Articles of Confederation, 179
Aruba, 455*m*
Asantehene, 3*p*
Ashanti people, 3*p*
Asia, 3*m*, 5*m*, 7*m*, 531*m*, 533*m*, 556
  cultural change, 104
  developing nations, 77
  maps of, 542*m*, 543*m*
  population, 63*m*, 66
  religions, 100
  Silk Road, 78
  urbanization, 71
Asian Americans, 276
Assiniboine people, 299
astrolabe, 379*p*
Atacama Desert, 337*m*, 345, 347, 348*m*, 509, 509*p*, 511, 556
Atlanta, Georgia, 239, 259, 556
Atlantic Ocean, 2*m*, 4*m*, 6*m*, 56, 142*m*, 149, 152, 203, 206*g*, 207
  currents, 42
  hurricanes, 47
  slave trade, 68
Atlantic Provinces, 145*m*, 145*p*, 311–315
  economy of, 313, 313*g*, 313*m*
  fishing in, 313*g*, 313*m*, 315
  natural resources of, 313*m*
  profile of, 313, 313*g*, 313*m*
atmosphere, 34*g*, 35, 562
atomic bomb, 190
atomic energy, 118
Atwood, Margaret, 230
Augusta, Maine, 240
aurora borealis, 318, 318*p*
Austin, Texas, 245, 259
Australia, 3*m*, 5*m*, 7*m*, 531*m*, 533*m*, 544*m*, 556
  colonization, 125, 125*p*
  cultural change, 107, 108*p*
  families, 97
  immigrants, 68
Austria-Hungary, 189
automobile industry, 269
  See also cars
Avery Island
  Tabasco industry, 258
Avila, Ramiro, 431

axis, Earth's, 28, 29, 30, 30*p*, 562
Aymara people, 417, 505, 505*p*
Aztecs, 370–372, 370*p*, 371*p*, 372*p*, 374, 375*p*
  art of, 403
  Cortés and, 378*p*, 380–381
  farming and the, 371
  Spain and, 378*p*, 380–381
  See also Native Americans

B

Baffin Bay, 545*m*
Bahamas, 455*m*, 457, 534*m*
bammy, 414
Bahrain, 548
Balboa, Vasco Nuñez de, 444, 444*p*
Bali, 93, 93*p*
bammy, 414
balloons, weather, 46
bananas, 349, 353*m*, 354, 460
Bangladesh, 66*p*, 542*m*, 556
banks, 75
Banks, Dennis, 223, 223*p*
Barbados, 414, 455*m*, 457
barometers, 89, 562
Barton, Clara, 186*p*
baseball, 106, 218*p*, 226, 454*f*, 465, 466
basins, 150, 554
basketball, 226, 226*p*
Basseterre, 460
Batista, Fulgencio, 463, 463*p*
Baton Rouge, Louisiana, 240
bauxite, 353*m*, 354, 355
bay, 554
Bay of Bengal, 5*m*
Bay of Fundy, 314
Beatrix, Queen of the Netherlands, 83*p*
Beaubrun, Bazelais, 471, 471*p*
Beaufort Sea, 4*m*
Bedspread Alley, 255
Behaim Martin, M4
Belgium, 550

Belize, 425*m*, 426, 534*m*
  cultural heritage of, 403
  languages of, 403
  Mayas in, 369
Belize City, 426
Belmopan, Belize, 426
Benin, 546
Bering Sea, 4*m*
Bhutan, 548
bilingual, 197, 562
biodiversity, 128, 129, 562
biomass energy, 118
birthrate, 60, 64–65, 64*g*, 562
Bismarck, North Dakota, 244
bison, 299, 562
Black Sea, 5*m*
Blackfoot people, 299
blizzards, 47, 562
Boiling Lake, 458
Boise, Idaho, 239
Bolívar, Simón, 387–388, 389, 390*p*,
  521, 562
Bolivia, 332*m*, 489, 534*m*, 556
  culture of, 417
  economy of, 352, 352*p*, 394*g*
  independence in, 387*m*
boll weevil, 257, 257*p*
Bonneville Dam, 117*p*
boom, 517, 563
boomtown, 307, 563
borders, 2, 2*p*
  international, 141
Bosnia and Herzegovina, 550
Boston, Massachusetts, 124*m*, 124*p*,
  240, 249*m*, 251, 251*p*, 254, 556
boycott, 179, 563
Brasília, 420, 495, 496*g*, 566, 563
Brazil, 52*p*, 71, 487*m*, 489, 534*m*, 556
  Carnival in, 496, 498
  cities of, 420, 420*p*
  climate of, 345, 494
  culture of, 417, 498, 498*g*
  economy of, 358, 394*g*, 525
  ethnic groups of, 489, 498*g*, 499,
   499*p*
  exports of, 489, 500
  farming in, 499–500

  geography of, 495–498, 495*p*, 496*g*,
   497*p*, 498*g*, 498*m*
  government of, 489
  hydroelectricity in, 333, 333*g*, 333*p*
  immigrants in, 499
  independence in, 387*m*, 389
  indigenous people in, 497, 498
  landforms of, 341
  languages of, 331*m*, 331*p*, 417, 489
  mining in, 497
  Native Americans in, 499, 499*p*
  natural resources in, 353*m*, 354*p*, 355
  population of, 489, 495, 498*m*
  Portugal and, 380
  rain forest in, 335, 335*m*, 335*p*, 486*g*,
   494, 494*p*, 495, 495*p*
  religion in, 489
  revolution, 366h
  rivers in, 342*p*
  slavery in, 384, 489, 498, 499
Brazilian Highlands, 4*m*, 532*m*, 535*m*
bridges, 376
Bridgetown, 457
Britain. *See* England; Great Britain;
  United Kingdom
British Columbia, 144*p*, 168, 196*m*,
  205, 205*p*, 217*p*, 218,
  304–310
  data about, 141*m*, 285*m*, 286
  economy of, 309–310, 309*m*
  gold rush in, 307, 307*p*
  Haida people, 193, 193*p*
  indigenous people in, 305, 305*p*, 307–
   308, 308*p*
  mining in, 306, 306*g*, 306*m*
  natural resources in, 306, 306*g*, 306*m*
  Pacific Rim and, 309–310, 309*m*
  profile of, 306, 306*g*, 306*m*
British Honduras. *See* Belize
British North America Act (1867),
  196, 284h
Brunei, 548
Buddhism, 100, 100*p*
Buenos Aires, Argentina, 417, 417*p*,
  419, 420*p*
buffalo, 299, 562
buildings. *See* architecture
bulletin boards, 526

Burkina Faso, 546
Burma, *See* Myanmar
buttes, 142*p*, 554, 554*p*

C

Cabot, John, 312
cacao, 353*m*, 354
Cajuns, 314
calendars, 369, 370, 370*p*
Calgary, Alberta, 303, 303*p*, 556
California, 53*p*, 133*p*, 149, 158, 216,
  236–237*p*, 536*m*
  admitted to the Union, 184
  climate in, 272*m*
  data about, 141*m*, 235*m*, 237
  forests, 163, 163*p*
  Gold Rush, 161, 224, 273
  hydroelectricity in, 272*g*
  natural resources of, 273, 274
  in Sun Belt, 260*m*
  water resources in, 272*g*
calypso music, 413, 414, 461
Cambodia, 548
campesinos, 402, 430, 441, 563
Canada, 141*m*, 285*m*, 530*m*, 534*m*,
  556
  agriculture in, 286–289
  climates of, 157, 157*g*
  Commonwealth of Nations, 199
  cultural diversity and, 215
  cultural patterns of, 216–219, 217*p*,
   218*p*, 219*p*
  culture of, 230, 230*p*
  economic issues, 76, 206–208, 206*g*
  energy resources, 118
  environmental issues of, 203–205,
   203*p*, 204*m*, 204*p*, 205*p*
  ethnic groups in, 293
  First Nations, 193, 193*p*, 228–229,
   229*p*
  flag of, 162
  France and, 194, 194*p*, 195–196, 294,
   314, 314*m*
  French Canadians in, 228
  geographic features of, 151

government of, 83, 198, 291, 291*g*, 292, 292*g*, 319

Great Britain and, 194, 194*p*, 195–196, 198, 291, 291*g*, 292, 292*g*, 294, 314, 314*m*

immigration to, 197, 214, 216–219, 216*p*, 227, 228*g*, 229–230, 293, 299

imports and exports of, 207

industry in, 286–289

inventions, 167

lakes, 151, 151*p*

landforms of, 149–151

languages of, 99, 197, 286–289

literature of, 230

location of, 149

mining in, 196

music of, 230

NAFTA and, 79, 208, 395, 436

natural resources of, 164*m*, 167–168, 167*p*, 168*p*

parliamentary democracy, 198, 198*p*

peaceful revolution in, 196

physical map, 147*m*

population density, 62*p*, 63

population of, 218, 228, 229, 286–289

railroads in, 308

regions of, 144–145, 144–145*m*, 144*p*, 145*p*

religion in, 218

rivers of, 152–153

Spain and, 314, 314*m*

sports in, 230, 230*p*

standard of living in, 219

territories of, 141*m*

trade, 79, 207–208

United States and, 199, 202–208, 214, 218–219, 218*p*, 230

vegetation zones, 159–162, 159*p*, 160*m*, 161*p*, 162*p*

World War I and, 196

World War II and, 172h

See also North America; individual provinces

Canada Day, 227*p*

Canada's Breadbasket, 302

Canadian National Tower, 293, 293*p*

Canadian Pacific Railway, 195*p*, 308

Canadian Shield, 146f, 151, 167, 291, 532*m*, 535*m*, 556

Canal Zone, 448, 556, 563

canals, 153, 371, 371*p*, 376. *See also* Panama Canal

canopy, rain forest, 50, 52, 494, 563

canyon, 554

Cape Canaveral, Florida, 259

Cape Horn, 337*m*, 508*m*, 509

Cape Town, South Africa, 70*p*

capitalism, 74, 75, 563

capoeira, 499

Caracas, 516, 516*p*, 517, 521, 556, 563

carbon cycle, 115

carbon dioxide, 35, 497

cardinal directions, 10, 11, 563

Carib Indians, 458

Carib people, 411

Caribbean Islands, 455*m*, 530*m*

Carnival in, 413, 413*p*

climate of, 345, 346

cultures of, 410–414, 410*p*, 411*p*, 412*p*, 413–414, 413*p*, 414*p*

ethnic groups of, 411–412, 411*p*, 456–461

exports of, 456–461

farming in, 412

food of, 414, 414*p*

government in, 456–461

immigrants from, 67

immigrants in, 411

landforms of, 340

languages of, 412, 456–461

location of, 339, 339*m*, 484*m*

music of, 413, 414, 461

natural resources of, 353*m*, 354, 354*p*

population of, 456–461

religion in, 412, 456–461

Spain and, 175

See also individual islands

Caribbean Sea, 4*m*, 56, 340, 556

Cariboo Mountains, 307, 556

Carnival, 413, 413*p*, 496, 498, 563

Caroni Swamp, 461

Carrillo, Fermin, 407

cars, 269

air pollution, 132

cultural change and, 105

energy consumption, 119

hybrid, 119, 130, 130*g*, 132

suburbanization and, 70

traffic jams, 130*p*

Carson City, Nevada, 242

Carter, Jimmy, 448

Cartier, Jacques, 294

Cascade Mountains, 150

cash crops, 400f, 419, 466, 563

Castries, 460

Castro, Fidel, 457, 462, 463–464, 464*p*, 465, 467, 563

cataract, 554, 554*p*

Cather, Willa, 264

Catholic Church, 382, 404, 413, 413*p*

caudillos, 389, 563

cells, air circulation, 42*p*

census, 375, 563

Central America, 425*m*, 530*m*, 557

early civilizations of, 367*m*, 368–372, 369*p*, 370*p*, 371*p*, 372*p*

ethnic groups in, 426–429

exports of, 426–429

immigrants from, 67, 68

landforms of, 340

languages of, 403, 426–429

location of, 339, 339*m*, 452*m*

Mayas, 103

natural resources of, 353*m*, 354

population of, 405, 426–429

religion in, 404, 404*p*, 426–429

vegetation of, 348*m*, 349

See also Middle America; individual countries

Central American Common Market, 427

Central Plains, 149, 152

Cerrado, 495

Chad, 546

Chaparro, Julia de Jesus, 478–479

Charleston, West Virginia, 247

Charlottetown, Prince Edward Island, 288

Chavez, Hugo, 521, 522

Cherokee people, 182*m*, 215*m*, 232*m*

Cherrapunji, India, 41*p*

Chesapeake Bay, 258

Cheyenne, Wyoming, 247

Cheyenne people, 215*m*, 232*m*

Chicago, Illinois, 204*m*, 265*g*, 265*m*, 268, 268*p*, 269*m*, 557

Chichén Itzá, 369*p*

Chickasaw, 182*m*

children, families, 96, 97

Childtimes **(Greenfield and Little),** 280–283

Chile, 42, 335, 335*m*, 335*p*, 487*m*, 334*m*, 557

climate of, 345, 509

culture of, 417

data about, 489

economy of, 356, 394*g*, 508, 508*g*

exports, 489, 508, 508*g*, 509, 512

farming in, 419, 511–512, 512*p*

geography of, 509–510, 509*p*, 510*p*

government, 489, 513, 513*p*

human rights in, 513

independence in, 387*m*, 388

landforms of, 489, 509

literature of, 418

Native Americans in, 511

natural resources in, 356

vegetation of, 347, 348*m*

China, 135, 542*m*, 557

economy, 77

emigrants, 67, 68

government, 82

language, 98*p*, 99

population, 6*p*

rice harvest, 58–59*p*, 85*p*

Silk Road, 78

Chinchorro, 347

chinampas, 370, 371, 371*p*

Chinook effect, 157

Chipewyan people, 299

Chippewa people, 232*m*

Choctaw people, 182*m*

Christianity, 98, 100, 101, 382, 404

Chrysler Building, 252, 252*p*

Chukchi people, 216

Churchill, Manitoba, 51

Ciboney, 411

circumnavigate, 509, 563

Cisneros, Sandra, 225*p*

cities

development of culture, 94

growth of, 61

industrialization and, 125

of the Midwest, 268–270, 268*p*, 269*m*, 270*p*

of the Northeast, 248–254

population of, 405*g*, 406

of the South, 259–261, 261*p*

of South America, 419–420, 420*p*

suburbs, 70, 105, 125

urbanization, 67, 70–71, 70*g*

of the West, 274–276, 275*p*, 276*p*

citizenship, 83, 477, 563

citrus fruits, 257

city-states, 80, 81, 563

civil engineering, 128, 131, 563

civil rights, 191, 191*g*, 563

Civil War, 184*m*, 563, 563*p*

causes of, 184

Lincoln and, 185

Reconstruction and, 186

slavery and, 184–186

civil war, 429, 440–441

civilization, 92, 94, 563

early, 367*m*, 368–372, 369*p*, 370*p*, 371*p*, 372*p*, 374

Clark, William, 180, 180*p*, 181, 272

Clayoquot Sound, 205, 205*p*

Clemente, Roberto, 454f

Clermont **(steamboat),** 183*p*

Cleveland, Ohio, 203

climate, M1, 40–55, 150, 157, 343–349, 343*p*, 344*m*, 346*g*, 348*m*, 360, 360*m*, 563

air pollution and, 132

arid and semiarid, 44*p*, 51

of Brazil, 494, 496

of Canada, 143, 143*m*, 157, 157*g*

of Chile, 509

climate change, 132

defined, 40

differences from weather, 40

dry, 43*g*, 50, 51

effect on vegetation, 50–54, 53*m*

factors affecting, 346

graphs, 48–49, 48*g*, 56

land use and, 121

latitude and, 32, 41

of Peru, 502*g*

polar, 43*g*, 50, 51

regions, M44–45, 50

of the South, 255–256

temperate continental, 50, 51

temperate marine, 50, 51

tropical, 50

of United States, 143, 143*m*

vertical, 54

of the West, 272*m*

See also weather

climate maps, M12*m*, 350–351, 350*m*, 351*m*, 360

climate regions, M1, 44–45*m*, 50, 343*p*, 344*m*, 345–349, 346*g*, 348*m*, 351*m*

climate zones, 157–158, 157*g*, 158*p*

clothes, 104

clouds, water cycle, 41

coal, 117, 117*p*, 164*m*, 165, 333, 333*g*

Coast Mountains, 151

Coast Ranges, 150, 557

coffee, 349, 353*m*, 354, 355, 356*g*, 439, 500

cold climates, 41

Cold War, 191, 191*g*, 464, 563

Colombia, 487*m*, 490, 534*m*, 557

culture of, 416

foreign debt of, 394*g*

independence in, 387*m*, 388

literature of, 418

natural resources in, 353*m*, 355

Panama Canal and, 394, 447

volcanoes in, 336f

Colón, 405, 429

colonization, 120, 125, 382–384, 382*m*, 383*g*, 564

Colorado, 271*p*, 536*m*

climate in, 272*m*

data about, 141*m*, 235*m*, 237

natural resources of, 273

in Sun Belt, 260*m*

Colorado River, 44, 152

Columbia Icefield, 151

Columbia, South Carolina, 245

Columbia River, 152

Columbian exchange, 383*g*

Columbus, Christopher, M14, 175, 379, 382*m,* 564
Columbus, Ohio, 244
Comanche people, 215*m,* 232*m*
commercial farmers, 76, 564
commonwealth, 564, 564*p*
Commonwealth of Nations, 199
communications, 450
  cultural change and, 107
  language, 98
communism, 74, 75, 82, 463, 564
communities
  political systems, 80, 82–83
  social structure, 96
commute, 248, 564
compass, M5
compass rose, M8, 16, 20*m,* 21, 564
computers, 275
  cultural change, 106, 107
  finding cures for disease, 90f
  geographic information systems (GIS), 16, 17
  trade, 78, 79
Concord, New Hampshire, 242
Condado, 480
Confederate States of America, 184*m,* 185
conformal maps, 18, 564
Congaree Swamp National Monument, 245*p*
Congo, Democratic Republic of the, 546
Congo, Republic of the, 546
coniferous trees and forests, 50, 51, 52, 53*p,* 54, 162, 564
Connecticut, 537*m*
  data about, 141*m,* 235*m,* 238
conquistadors, 380–381, 564
constitution, 80, 83, 476, 564
Constitution, Canadian, 198
Constitution, U.S., 172h, 179
constitutional monarchy, 83, 564
consumers, 74, 79, 564
container ships, 79
continental climate, 51, 158
Continental Divide, 152, 564
continents, 2–3*m,* 3
  compare, 7

  location of, 86
  origins of, 38
  movement of, 36, 36*g,* 38
Cook, James, 305
Copán, Honduras, 369
copper, 164*m,* 166, 167, 353*m,* 355, 508, 508*g,* 509
copses, 89, 564
coral islands, 340
coral reefs, 460, 461
core, Earth's, 33, 34, 34*g,* 564
corporate farm, 267, 564
Cortés, Hernán, 378*p,* 380–381, 382*m,* 399, 564
Costa, Daniel Monteiro, 499
Costa Rica, 405, 425*m,* 427, 534*m*
  cultural heritage of, 403
cotton, 117, 257, 257*p,* 257, 353*m,* 354
cotton gin, 184
coup, 521, 564
cowboys, 341*p*
Cree people, 299
Creek people, 182*m*
Creoles, 474, 564
criollos, 386, 387, 392–393, 564
critical thinking
  analyze, 32, 47, 54, 56, 79, 132, 134, 186, 219, 232, 297, 310, 315, 324, 360, 365, 389, 482, 500, 524
  analyze cause and effect, 506
  analyze graphic data, 65, 394
  analyze images, 35, 160, 194*p,* 203*p,* 205*p,* 217*p,* 229*p,* 294, 295, 299*p,* 305*p,* 341, 346, 371, 386, 406, 435, 438, 449, 467, 475
  analyze information, 226, 266*g,* 275*g,* 307*p,* 342, 356, 374, 389, 420
  analyze primary sources, 122, 189, 380
  apply information, 22, 24, 56, 110, 119, 170, 349, 524
  bar graphs, 493
  categorize, 24, 84, 119, 125, 132, 247, 289, 360, 414, 429, 461, 493
  compare, 89, 168, 210, 254, 302*p,* 358, 384, 398, 484, 506, 519
  compare and contrast, 39, 44, 54, 71, 79, 84, 86, 108, 110, 125, 134, 170, 228*g,* 232, 247, 278, 289, 322, 324,

  355, 396, 420, 429, 461, 475, 493, 497, 509, 524
  conclude, 218*p,* 273*p,* 372, 398, 422, 504
  contrast, 13, 47, 56, 66, 86, 170, 289, 291*g,* 297, 360, 493
  decision making, 83, 217, 465
  define, 13, 22, 32, 54, 66, 84, 86, 95, 170, 210, 360, 422, 450, 467, 475
  describe, 24, 32, 56, 79, 89, 108, 110, 125, 134, 153, 206*g,* 210, 266*g,* 275*g,* 356, 372, 377, 384, 422, 436, 441, 450, 467, 475, 482, 484, 506, 522, 524
  draw conclusions, 12, 24, 101, 110, 119, 153, 170, 183*p,* 185*p,* 188*p,* 195*p,* 197*p,* 198*p,* 210, 216, 219, 224*g,* 230, 232, 247, 261, 278, 289, 303, 346, 358, 377, 384, 396, 398, 405, 414, 416, 417, 422, 429, 447, 450, 452, 461, 478, 484, 493, 500, 510, 520, 522
  draw inferences, 12, 189*p,* 210, 216, 226, 270, 413, 503
  evaluate, 22, 32, 54, 56, 89
  evaluate information, 360, 365, 384, 436
  explain, 13, 39, 47, 54, 56, 66, 71, 79, 86, 95, 101, 108, 110, 134, 153, 168, 170, 179, 192, 199, 208, 210, 226, 230, 232, 261, 270, 276, 278, 303, 315, 324, 398, 450, 482
  explore main idea, 170, 186, 219, 270
  find main idea, 467, 475, 484
  generalize, 86, 162, 208, 230, 247, 297, 354, 360, 375, 398, 411, 452
  identify, 22, 24, 32, 39, 47, 56, 71, 79, 84, 86, 89, 95, 101, 119, 170, 186, 190, 210, 224*g,* 228*g,* 278, 291*g,* 297, 342, 346, 349, 358, 360, 372, 374, 377, 383, 384, 388, 389, 398, 405, 407, 414, 420, 422, 441, 452, 477, 484, 500, 513, 524
  identify cause, 30, 125, 186, 192, 216, 226, 232, 360, 393, 398, 407, 414, 422, 436, 441, 452, 513, 524
  identify cause and effect, 32, 66, 71, 86, 95, 101, 132, 170, 178, 179, 192, 210, 254, 261, 276, 342, 358, 384, 394, 407, 420, 422, 450, 452, 475, 484, 513
  identify effect, 153, 162, 186, 190, 206*g,* 208, 253, 270, 303, 310, 322, 324, 360, 422, 452, 467, 484, 500, 512, 522, 524

identify frame of reference, 69, 210, 232, 505

identify main idea, 76, 208, 230, 254, 412

identify point of view, 69, 179, 232, 322, 505

infer, 24, 86, 110, 125, 134, 162, 168, 276, 289, 342, 349, 360, 365, 369, 372, 377, 383, 389, 403, 404, 419, 420, 429, 431, 433, 445, 461, 463, 464, 471, 473, 477, 480, 500, 505, 519, 522, 524

interpret, 89

link past and present, 110, 199, 310

list, 24, 39, 54, 79, 84, 86, 108, 110, 119, 132, 134, 168, 186, 192, 199, 219, 230, 261, 278, 303, 310, 315, 322, 324, 482, 484

locate, 153, 162, 278, 324, 379

make a bar graph, 289

make a reasonable judgment, 513

make a timeline, 247

make valid generalizations, 165, 340

name, 179, 210, 278, 342, 349, 398, 484, 500, 513

note, 168, 208, 226

predict, 13, 22, 39, 47, 56, 79, 101, 108, 134, 153, 175p, 219, 232, 270, 276, 278, 315, 324, 357, 406, 407, 441, 467, 482, 506, 524

problem-solving, 118, 195, 439

recall, 13, 14, 21, 22, 24, 30, 32, 37, 39, 47, 49, 54, 56, 61, 66, 68, 70, 71, 79, 86, 89, 92, 94, 101, 108, 110, 113, 122, 124, 125, 132, 134, 139, 153, 156, 162, 170, 179, 192, 199, 219, 232, 254, 261, 270, 276, 278, 297, 303, 310, 315, 322, 324, 342, 349, 358, 360, 365, 377, 384, 389, 396, 398, 407, 414, 420, 422, 436, 441, 450, 452, 467, 484, 513, 522

recognizing bias, 94, 294, 382

respond, 365

sequence, 18, 95, 179, 192, 199, 321, 372, 377, 450, 475, 482, 484, 522

summarize, 162, 168, 179, 199, 208, 261, 276, 278, 297, 315, 324, 360, 412, 441, 452, 524

supporting a position, 131, 295, 474

synthesize, 22, 24, 32, 39, 56, 100, 226, 250, 342, 349, 360, 436, 441, 452, 467, 474, 482, 499

transfer information, 53, 54, 66, 183, 481, 498

using cartographer's tools, 43, 251, 432

using reliable information, 225, 446

Croatia, 538m

***Crown of Columbus* (Erdrich),** 174

crust, Earth's, 33, 34, 34g, 36–37, 36–37p, 565

Cruz, Cecilia, 406

Cry of Dolores, 386

cuatro, 480p

Cuba, 340, 455m, 457, 534m, 557
  baseball and, 465
  dictatorship, 82
  immigrants from, 68, 68p, 462, 462p
  exiles from, 465–467, 466p
  government of, 462, 463–464, 465, 465g, 465m
  independence in, 388, 463
  literature of, 362–365, 362p, 363p, 364p
  natural resources of, 353m, 354
  Spain and, 388
  timeline of, 485

Cuban Missile Crisis, 464

cultural diffusion, 104, 106, 565

cultural diversity, 214–215, 215, 225, 565

cultural exchange, 215–216, 565

cultural landscape, 92, 93, 93p, 565

cultural patterns, 216–219, 217p, 218p, 219p

cultural trait, 92, 565

culture, M1, 1, 90–111, 136, 565
  Aztec, 370
  of Brazil, 498
  cultural change, 104–108
  cultural diffusion, 104, 106, 565
  cultural landscape, 92, 93, 93p, 565
  cultural traits, 92, 565
  defined, 92–93
  development of, 94–95
  environment and, 93
  geography and, 506
  of Guatemala, 439
  land use and, 120–121
  language and, 92, 98–99, 98–99m
  of Middle America, 402–404, 402p, 403p, 404p

migration and, M14–M15
  of Peru, 506
  of Prairie Provinces, 303, 303p
  projects, 136, 526
  of Quebec, 294–297, 296, 296g, 297, 297p
  religions, 100m, 101
  social structure and, 96–97
  of the South, 256, 256g, 256m

culture regions, M1

currents
  air, 42g
  ocean, 43

customs, 218p

Cuyahoga River, 203, 203p, 557

Cuzco, 374, 375, 381, 503, 504, 557, 565

Czech Republic, 550

D

Dakar, Senegal, M10

Dakota people, 299

dams, 165, 274
  civil engineering, 131
  hydroelectric power, 117, 117p
  water supply, 127

Dawson, Canada, 321, 557

day and night, 29

death rates, 60, 64–65, 64g, 565

Death Valley, 150, 158, 160, 557

Deccan Plateau, 5m, 543m

deciduous trees and forests, 50, 51, 52, 162, 565

Declaration of Independence, 179

Defoe, Daniel, 511

deforestation, 121, 128, 129, 129p, 447, 565

degrees, latitude and longitude, 11, 565

Delaware, 537m
  data about, 141m, 235m, 238
  land use in, 256m

Delaware River, 249m, 251

Delhi, M12

Delicate Arch, Utah, 55p

delta, 554, 555p

democracy, 58g, 82, 83, 513

demography, 60, 565

Dene people, 215m, 319

Denmark, 2p, 18, 557

Denver, Colorado, 237, 273

dependency, government, 80, 81, 565

Des Moines, Iowa, 239

descendant, 294, 565

descent, 299, 565

desert scrub, 50, 51, 52, 160–161, 160m, 565

deserts, 52, 565
  air circulation and, 43g
  Sahara, 53p

Detroit, Michigan, 241p, 269, 269m, 557

developed nations, 565
  economies, 74, 75
  land use, 122, 123
  levels of development, 77m
  trade, 78, 79

developing nations, 565
  economies, 74, 76, 77
  levels of development, 77m
  trade, 78, 79

dictatorships, 82, 393, 565

Differentiated Instruction

Advanced Readers, RW1, M, M5, M11, M14, 20, 46, 52, 64, 70, 82, 99, 106, 116, 123, 161, 182, 194, 206, 221, 224, 240, 253, 263, 267, 282, 287, 296, 300, 306, 317, 345, 355, 381, 387, 405, 434, 447, 457, 478, 490, 497, 504, 509, 511

English Language Learners, RW5, M, M8, M12, M17, 21, 36, 46, 70, 106, 117, 123, 145, 150, 161, 190, 196, 207, 229, 246, 252, 259, 266, 292, 301, 307, 314, 335, 347, 381, 395, 419, 440, 473, 478, 489, 496, 511, 520

Gifted and Talented, RW4, M6, M12, 19, 21, 31, 36, 45, 63, 64, 77, 99, 116, 142, 152, 158, 166, 190, 198, 201, 207, 218, 244, 260, 268, 273, 275, 293, 300, 302, 309, 333, 348, 371, 375, 418, 440, 443, 472, 481, 492, 496, 503, 515

Less Proficient Readers, RW1, M5, M8, M14, 15, 31, 45, 52, 62, 63, 77, 103, 117, 150, 158, 166, 198, 218, 237, 267, 268, 273, 287, 296, 302, 305, 316, 320, 354, 364, 387, 405, 409, 418, 428, 433, 447, 457, 464, 481, 489, 504, 510, 519, 521

Special Needs Students, RW1, M3, M6, M11, 15, 20, 42, 49, 62, 73, 103, 127, 142, 155, 159, 191, 196, 201, 204, 229, 252, 263, 266, 275, 301, 309, 314, 331, 351, 357, 391, 395, 409, 419, 428, 433, 443, 448, 464, 469, 473, 497, 510, 515, 519, 521

Dion, Celine, 230

direct democracy, 82, 565

directions
  cardinal, 11
  intermediate, 11

Discovery (space shuttle), 8–9p

discrimination, 191, 565

diseases, 381, 384, 447–448, 497
  migration and, 68
  Native Americans and, 177, 301
  population growth and, 64, 65

distance, 21

distortion, maps, 16, 17, 18–19, 565

District of Columbia, 537m

diversify, 500, 511–512, 512p, 521, 565

diversity, 128, 129, 358, 428, 461, 565

Dom Pedro, 389

Dominica, 411, 458

Dominican Republic, 455m, 458, 534m
  culture of, 412
  natural resources of, 353m, 354

dominion, 196, 565

Dominion of Canada, 291

Dover, Delaware, 239

drilling, 258, 258p

drought, 357p

dry climates, 43g, 50, 51

Dubai, United Arab Emirates, 79p

Durham, Earl of, 195

Dutch colonies, 411, 416, 491, 492

Duvalier, François, 473

Duvalier, Jean-Claude, 473

E

Earth
  atmosphere, 34g, 35
  axis, 28, 29, 30, 30g

core of, 33, 34, 34g

crust of, 33, 34, 34g, 36–37, 36–37g

day and night, 29

distance from sun, 28

forces inside, 36–38, 36–37g, 38m

forces on surface, 39

forces shaping, 33–39

hemispheres, M5, 10, 11g, 11p, 567

mantle, 33, 34, 34g, 36g

maps and globes, M4, M4–M5, 16–22

movements of, M2–M3, M2

orbit of, 28, 30

rotation of, 29

seasons and latitude, 30–32, 30–31g

structure, 34–35, 34g

time zones, 29, 29m

viewed from space, 8–9p, 23p

earthquakes, 33, 37, 37p, 340, 376, 427, 429, 435

east, 11

East Timor, 3p, 542m

Eastern Hemisphere, M5, 11g

Eastern Orthodox Church, 100p

economies and economic systems, 74–79
  of Atlantic Provinces, 313, 313g, 313m
  of Brazil, 525
  of British Columbia, 309–310, 309m
  of Canada, 219
  of Chile, 508, 508g
  climate and, 349
  diversifying, 358, 428, 500, 511–512, 512p, 521
  economic downturns, 192
  foreign debt, 394, 394g, 395–396
  Great Depression, 189, 190g
  of Guatemala, 439
  of Honduras, 428
  international alliances, 84
  kinds of, 74–75
  land use and, 122–123
  levels of economic development, 76–77
  of Mexico, 432g, 432m
  of the Midwest, 265, 265g, 265m
  migration and, 68

natural resources and, 356–358, 356g, 357p, 358p
of Northeast, 250, 250g, 250m
one resource, 356, 357
of Prairie Provinces, 300, 300g, 300m
projects, 136, 526
of Puerto Rico, 459
recession, 266
stages of economic activity, 122–123
standard of living, 219
of the United States, 206–208, 206g, 219
of Venezuela, 518, 518g, 518m, 519–520
world, 357
world trade patterns, 78–79, 78g
economy, 74, 565
ecotourism, 450, 450p, 565
Ecuador, 487m, 490, 490p, 534m
culture of, 417
factories in, 358p
farming in, M16m, M16p, 419p
foreign debt of, 394g
independence in, 387m, 388
editorial pages, RW1
Edmonton, Alberta, 286, 303
education, 251
Egypt, 60p, 540m, 557
El Niño, 343, 343p, 357, 566
El Salvador, 425m, 427, 534m, 557
economy of, 358
languages of, 403
Mayas in, 366h
elections, 83
electricity, 115
hybrid cars, 119, 130, 130g, 132
elevation, M10, M11, 332, 332, 332m, 346, 349, 565
Elizabeth II, Queen of England, 199, 199p
Ellington, Duke, 225p, 226
Ellis Island, New York, 67p, 222, 254, 254p
Emancipation Proclamation, 185
Emerson, Ralph Waldo, 225, 225p
emigration, 406p, 407, 566
from Cuba, 462, 462p

Empire of Gold, 383p
Empire State Building, 252
empires, 80, 81, 566
employment
developed nations, 76
land use and, 131
in Mexico City, 433–434, 436
encomiendas, 384, 566
endangered species, 301
energy, 333, 566
fossil fuels, 117, 118, 119
geothermal, 115, 118, 119p
resources, 115, 117–119, 132, 164m, 165, 167, 333, 333g
engineering, civil, 131
England
colonies of, 382, 411, 416, 426, 457, 458, 460
See also Great Britain; United Kingdom
English language, 98, 99
enslave, 177, 566
entertainment industry, 276, 276p, 310
environment, 13, 112–135, 566
climate and, 343–349
cultural landscape, 92, 93, 93p, 565
culture and, 93
defined, 120
earthquakes and, 340, 376, 427, 429
human-environment interaction, M1, 128–132
importance of the rain forest to, 496–497, 496g, 497p
issues regarding, 203–205, 203p, 204m, 204p, 205p
land use, 120–125
modification of, 131
natural resources, 114–119
photosynthesis and, 495
population growth and, 66
smog and the, 511
See also pollution
equal-area maps, M7, 19, 19p, 566
Equator, M2, M3, M4, M7, 11, 11g, 157, 330, 344m, 346, 557, 566
air circulation and, 43g
global grid, 12g

Mercator projection, 18
ocean currents, 42
seasons, 30g, 31g
equinoxes, 30g, 566
Erdrich, Louise, 174
Ericsson, Leif, 311, 311p
Eritrea, 80p, 540m
erosion, 33, 39, 39p, 566
Eskimos, 159
ethics, 101, 566
Ethiopia, 546
Ethiopian Highlands, 5m, 541m
ethnic groups, 216, 224g, 228, 411–412, 411p, 566
of Argentina, 488
of Bolivia, 489
of Brazil, 489, 498g, 499, 499p
of British Columbia, 304, 304p, 305, 309–310
of Canada, 293
of the Caribbean, 456–461
of Central America, 426–429
of Chile, 489
of Colombia, 490
of Ecuador, 490
of Guatemala, 437, 438, 439, 439g, 439m
of Guyana, 491
of Haiti, 474
of Mexico, 428
of Panama, 446g
of Paraguay, 491
of Peru, 491
of South America, 488–493
of Suriname, 492
of the United States, 236–247, 263g
of Uruguay, 492
of Venezuela, 493
Europe, 3m, 5m, 7m, 135, 531m, 533m, 557
acid rain in, 205
climate, 43
colonization, 125
cultural change, 104
economy, 76
emigration, 67
land use, 121

nation-states, 81
physical map, 539*m*
political map, 538*m*
suburbanization, 70
See also individual countries
European Union, 79, 84
Evans Manufacturing Company, 255
Everglades National Park, 238*p*
exiles, 314, 465–467, 466*p*, 566
exports, 207, 393, 405, 419, 566
  of Argentina, 488
  of Bolivia, 489
  of Brazil, 489
  of the Caribbean, 456–461
  of Central America, 426–429
  of Chile, 489, 508, 508*g*, 509, 512
  of Colombia, 490
  of Ecuador, 490
  of Guyana, 491
  of Mexico, 428, 432*g*, 432*m*
  of Paraguay, 491
  of Peru, 491
  of South America, 488–493
  of Suriname, 492
  of Uruguay, 492
  of Venezuela, 493, 518, 518*g*, 518*m*
expository essays, RW4
extended families, 96, 97, 103*p*, 566

F

factories, 183, 197*p*, 358, 358*p*, 450,
  499–500. *See also* industrialization
Falkland Islands, 337*m*, 487*m*, 534*m*
fall, 31, 31*g*, 32
fallout shelters, 191*p*
families, 96, 96*p*, 97, 97*p*, 103*p*, 566,
  570
farming, 164, 164*m*, 167, 279*g*, 357
  Aztec, 370–371, 371*p*
  in Brazil, 499–500
  in Canada, 216*p*
  in Caribbean Islands, 353*m*, 354, 412
  in Chile, 510, 511–512, 512*p*
  in Ecuador, M16*m*, M16*p*
  in Guatemala, 438, 438*p*

  in Mexico, 431
  in the Midwest, 264–265, 264*p*, 266–
    267, 266*g*
  on the plains, 149
  in Prairie Provinces, 300*g*, 302, 302*p*
  in the South, 257, 257*p*
  in South America, 355, 419
  subsistence, 377, 419, 490*p*, M16
  technology and, 264*p*, 266–267, 300
  in the United States, M16*m*, M16*p*
  in Vietnam, M17*p*
  See also agriculture
faults, 37, 566
favelas, 420, 420*p*, 500
federation, 291, 566
Ferdinand, Prince of Spain, 387, 388
fertilizers, 129
festivals, 90–91*p*, 99
fiber-optic networks, 450
fire, 94, 106
First Nations, 228–229, 229*p*. *See also*
  Native Americans
fishing, 202, 202*p*, 258, 353*m*, 354,
  355, 355*p*, 357
  in Atlantic Provinces, 313*g*, 313*m*, 315
  effect on environment, 129
flags, 162, 234*p*
floating beds, 371, 371*p*
flood plain, 554
flooding, 47, 66, 131, 152, 520*p*, 521,
  521*p*
Florida, 156, 158, 181*m*, 217*p*, 218,
  238*p*, 537*m*, 557
  data about, 141*m*, 235*m*, 238
  farming in, 257
  fishing in, 258
  Hurricane Katrina, 47*p*
  land use in, 256*m*
  Spain and, 175
  in Sun Belt, 260*m*
folk art, 90f
food, 349, 353*m*, 354, 414, 414*p*, 460
  and development of culture, 94
  natural resources, 114
  and population growth, 66
  See also agriculture; farming
Food and Agriculture Organization,
  84

football, 226
foreign aid, 84
foreign debt, 394, 394*g*, 395–396, 566
foreign trade, 207–208
forests and forestry, 160*m*, 162,
  162*p*, 163, 163*p*, 164*m*, 165, 168,
  168*p*, 205, 205*p*, 258
  in Canada, 306, 306*g*, 306*m*, 315
  coniferous, 51, 52, 53*p*, 54
  deciduous, 51, 52
  deforestation, 121, 128, 129, 129*p*,
    447
  effect on environment, 129
  mixed, 52, 53*p*
  population growth and, 66
  rain forest, 50, 52, 52*p*
  See also trees
Fort Garry, 214*p*
forty-niner, 273, 273*p*, 566
fossil fuels, 117, 118, 119, 164*m*, 165,
  166, 204, 566
fossils, 51*p*
Fox, Vicente, 428, 436, 436*p*
France, 104, 538*m*
  areas of influence, 173*m*, 177*m*
  Canada and, 194, 194*p*, 195–196, 294,
    314, 314*m*
  colonization by, 382, 411, 416, 471
  French and Indian War, 178
  Louisiana Territory, 181, 181*m*
  Native Americans and, 177, 177*m*
  Panama Canal and, 446
  revolution in, 386
Francophone, 294–295, 566
Frankfort, Kentucky, 240
Fraser River, 152, 305, 307, 557
Fredericton, New Brunswick, 287
free-market economy, 75
free trade, 567
Free Trade Agreement (FTA), 208
French and Indian War, 178, 194
French Canadians, 194, 197, 228
French Guiana, 416
French language, 99
fresh water, 35
fruit trees, 349
FTA. *See* Free Trade Agreement (FTA)

fuels
fossil, 117, 118, 119, 164*m*, 165, 166, 204
natural resources, 116, 117
See also energy
fugitive, 184, 566
Fugitive Slave Act, 184
Fujimori, Alberto, 395
Fulton, Robert, 183*p*
fur trade, 177, 193, 194, 214*p*, 305

G

Gabon, 540*m*
Gabrielino, 216
Gadsden Purchase, 181*m*
Galápagos Islands, 337*m*, 535*m*
galaxies, 28, 28*p*
games, 368, 413. *See also* sports
gas
atmospheric, 34*g*, 35
natural resources, 116, 117
gasoline engines, 119, 130, 130*g*, 132
Gatún Locks, 449, 449*p*
gauchos, 341*p*, 347, 417, 492*p*, 567
Genoa, Italy, 104, 557
geographic information systems (GIS), 16, 17, 567
geographic signature, M1
geography, 567
of Brazil, 495–498, 495*p*, 496*g*, 497*p*, 498*g*, 498*m*
of British Columbia, 306, 306*g*, 306*m*
of Chile, 509–510, 509*p*, 510*p*
culture and, 506
defined, 10
five themes of, 10–13, 23
fields of, 8e
Guiding Questions, 1, 139, 329
of Latin America, 339*m*
maps and globes, 16–22, 23
of Mexico City, 435, 435*p*
of Panama, 444–448, 446, 446*g*, 446*m*
of Peru, 501, 501*p*, 502, 502*g*, 502*m*, 503–506
physical geography, 25–57
projects, 136, 526

themes of, M1–M2, 10–13, 23
of the West, 272, 272*g*, 272*m*
writing skills, 24
See also physical geography
George, Jean Craighead, 88–89, 89*p*
George Washington Bridge, 234h
Georgia, Republic of, 548
Georgia, (United States), 120, 120*p*, 121, 537*m*, 542*m*, 557
data about, 141*m*, 235*m*, 238
farming in, 257
industry in, 255, 257
land use in, 256*m*
in Sun Belt, 260*m*
textile industry, 259
geothermal energy, 115, 118, 119*p*
Germany, 97, 98, 116*p*, 118, 189, 190, 538*m*, 557
geyser, 274*p*
Ghana, M15, 3*p*, 540*m*
GIS. *See* geographic information systems
Glacier National Park, 274
glaciers, 4*p*, 150, 151, 554, 554*p*, 567
global grid, M5, 12, 12*g*
globes, M4, M4–M5, M6, 16, 567. *See also* maps
GOES (Geostationary Operational Environmental Satellites), 46*p*
gold, 164*m*, 166, 167, 196, 353*m*, 355
in British Columbia, 307, 307*p*
in Yukon Territory, 321
Gold Rush, 161, 224, 273
Gondwanaland, 38*m*
goods, 75, 567
gores, M6, M7
gorges, 376
government, 567
of Argentina, 418, 418*p*, 488
of Bolivia, 489
of Brazil, 489
of Canada, 198, 291, 291*g*, 292, 292*g*, 319
of the Caribbean, 456–461
of Chile, 489, 513, 513*p*
of Colombia, 490
of Cuba, 462, 463–464, 465, 465*g*, 465*m*

development of culture and, 94
of Ecuador, 490
government ownership, 75
of Guyana, 491
of Haiti, 470, 470*p*, 473
Incan, 375
of Mexico, 428
of Northern Territories, 320, 320*g*, 320*m*
oil boom and, 517, 520
of Paraguay, 491
of Peru, 491
projects, 136, 526
of Puerto Rico, 476, 479, 479*g*, 479*m*
in South America, 488–493
of Suriname, 492
types of, 80–81, 82–83
of United States, 292*g*
of Uruguay, 492
of Venezuela, 493, 521, 522, 522*p*
governor-general, 198
Gran Colombia, 387*m*, 389, 493
Grand Banks, 312
Grand Canyon, 44*p*, 219*p*
Grand Coulee Dam, 165
graphs, climate, 48–49, 48*g*, 56
grasslands, 51, 52, 54, 159, 159*p*, 160*m*, 567
Grasslands National Park, 301
Great Basin, 150, 160–161, 160*m*
Great Britain, 539*m*
areas of influence, 173*m*, 177*m*
Canada and, 194, 194*p*, 195–196, 198, 291, 291*g*, 292, 292*g*, 294, 314, 314*m*
colonies of, 177*m*, 178, 178*p*
Commonwealth of Nations, 199
French and Indian War, 178
Native Americans and, 177*m*, 178, 178*p*
parliamentary system of, 198
Revolutionary War, 179, 179*p*
See also England; United Kingdom
Great Depression, 189, 190, 190*g*, 190*p*
Great Lakes, 142*m*, 142*p*, 151, 151*p*, 202, 203, 204*m*, 537*m*, 557, 567
transportation on, 206–207, 206*g*

Great Lakes Fishery Commission, 202

Great Plains, 4*m,* 128, 149, 158, 160, 532*m,* 535*m,* 557

Great Salt Lake, 150

Greece, 93, 100*p,* 538*m,* 557

Green Revolution, 65, 567

Greenfield, Eloise, 280–283

Greenland, 18, 62*m,* 530*m,* 532*m,* 545*m,* 557

Greenwich, England, M5, 12*p,* 557

Grenada, 414*p,* 455*m,* 458

Guam, 188, 544*m*

Guantánamo Bay, 457

Guaraní, 491

Guatemala, 425*m,* 427, 534*m,* 557
civil war in, 424*f,* 440–441
coffee from, 439
culture of, 403, 439
economy of, 439
ethnic groups in, 437, 438, 439, 439*g,* 439*m*
farming in, 438, 438*p*
indigenous people in, 440
land reform in, 438, 438*p*
languages of, 403, 439*m*
Mayas in, 369, 427, 427, 439, 439*g,* 439*m*
Native Americans in, 437, 438, 439, 439*g,* 439*m,* 440
political movements in, 440–441, 440*p*
population of, 453*g*
weather in, 357*p*
women in, 424*p,* 440

Guatemala City, 427

Guinea, 546

Guinea-Bissau, 546

Gulf-Atlantic Coastal Plains, 150

Gulf of Mexico, 142*m,* 149, 152

Gulf Stream, 42, 558

Guyana, 487*m,* 491, 534*m*
culture of, 416
data about, 491
landforms of, 341

Guyana Highlands, 4*m*

H

haciendas, 383, 384, 392, 567

Haida people, 193, 193*p*

hail, 40

Hainan, 50*p*

Haiti, 385, 455*m,* 458, 459, 534*m,* 558
culture of, 412
data about, 474
government of, 470, 470*p,* 473
history of, 472, 472*g,* 472*m*
housing in, 474*p*
human rights in, 473
poverty in, 474–475
refugees, 471, 471*p*
slaves in, 334, 334*p,* 471
United States and, 471, 473

Halifax, Nova Scotia, 287

Harrisburg, Pennsylvania, 244

Hartford, Connecticut, 239

Harvard University, 251

Havana, 457

Hawaii, M1, 33*p,* 37, 37, 37*p,* 74*p,* 149, 158, 181*m,* 188, 271, 536*m*
data about, 141*m,* 235*m,* 239
volcanoes in, 150
in World War II, 190

haze, 204, 567

health, 64, 65, 68

Heat, inside Earth, 36

Helena, Montana, 242

Helsinki, Finland, 56*g*

hemispheres, M5, 10, 11*g,* 11*p,* 567

hemlock, 89, 567

herding, M17*p,* 229, 347

Hernandez, Orlando, 466

Hidalgo, Miguel, 386–387, 386*p*

hieroglyphics, 369, 370, 370, 567

high latitudes, 32, 32*m,* 41, 567

highland vegetation, 52

highlands, 341

highways, 21*m,* 265*g,* 265*m*

hills, 35, 554, 567

Himalayas, 341

Hindi language, M13*m,* M13

Hinduism, 69*m,* 100, 412

Hispanic Americans, 256, 256*g,* 276

Hispaniola, 340, 412, 454*f,* 458, 459, 471, 558

history
of Haiti, 472, 472*g,* 472*m*
interdisciplinary links, 78
projects, 136, 326, 526

Hitler, Adolf, 190

hockey, 230, 230*p*

Hohokam people, 103

Holocaust, 190, 567

Holy See. *See* Vatican City

Homestead Act (1862), 188, 567

Honduras, 425*m,* 428, 534*m*
cultural heritage of, 402*p,* 403
economy of, 428
Mayas in, 369
vegetation of, 348*m,* 349

Hong Kong, China, 45*p*

Honolulu, Hawaii, 74*p,* 239

horses, 215–216, 215*p*

hot climates, 41

House of Commons, 198, 319

housing
cultural change and, 105
in Haiti, 474*p*
in Mexico, 433–436, 433*p,* 434*m,* 435*p*
natural resources, 114
in Peru, 503, 503*p*
and population growth, 66
See also architecture

Houston, Texas, 259

***How the Other Half Lives* (Riis),** 187, 187*p*

Hudson Bay, 142*m,* 194, 298, 298*p*

Hudson River, 253

human-environment interaction, M1, 13, 123, 124, 128–132, 567
economic activity, 122–123
Boston, Massachusetts, 124
land use, 131*p*
landforms as barriers, 5, 5*p*
population density, 72*p*
railroads, 269*m*

human geography, 58–89
economic systems, 74–79
migration, 67–71
political systems, 80–84
population, 60–66

human rights, 473, 513
humid continental climate, 51, 567
humid subtropical climate, 51, 345
Hungary, 550
Huntsville, Alabama, 259, 259*p*
Huron, 215*m*, 232*m*
Hurricane Katrina, 47*p*
hurricanes, 46, 46*p*, 47, 47*p*, 158, 191*g*, 345, 345*p*, 428, 429, 567
Hurston, Zora Neale, 225, 225*p*
hybrid cars, 119, 130, 130*g*, 132
hydroelectricity, 117, 117*p*, 165, 167, 272*g*, 333, 333*m*, 353*m*, 354, 567

ice
  ice caps, 51, 52
  ice floes, 35*p*
  ice packs, 52
  ice sheets, 35
  on mountains, 54
  weathering and erosion, 39
ice age, 175
Iceland, 119*p*, 538*m*
Idaho, 536*m*
  climate in, 272*m*
  data about, 141*m*, 235*m*, 239
  hydroelectricity in, 272*g*
  natural resources of, 273
ideas, cultural change and, 106, 107
Illinois, 537*m*
  data about, 141*m*, 235*m*, 239
illiterate, 464, 567
immigrant, 67, 567
immigration, 67, 67*p*, 213*m*, 220, 407, 411, 568
  to Brazil, 489, 499
  to Canada, 197, 214, 216–219, 216*p*, 227, 228*g*, 229–230, 293
  Ellis Island, 254, 254*p*
  Industrial Revolution and, 183, 188
  to the United States, 216–219, 222–226, 222*p*, 223*p*, 224*g*, 225*p*, 301
immunity, 301, 568
imports, 207, 393, 568

Incas, 373–376, 373*p*, 374, 374*p*, 375*p*, 376*p*
  aqueduct, 376
  in Ecuador, 490*p*
  Machu Picchu, 504, 504*p*
  in Peru, 503, 506, 506*p*
  Pizarro and, 381
indentured servants, 178, 568
India, 558
  agriculture, 13*p*
  climate of, M12*m*
  cultural landscape, 93
  government, 83
  languages of, M13*m*, 99
  migration, 67, 69*m*
  religions, 100, 101*p*
  traditional dress, 90*p*–91*p*, 109*p*
  weather, 40
Indian Ocean, 3*m*, 5*m*, 7*m*, 56
Indian Removal Act (1830), 182, 182*m*
Indiana, 537*m*, 542*m*
  data about, 141*m*, 235*m*, 239
Indianapolis, Indiana, 239
Indians. *See* First Nations; indigenous people; Native Americans
indigenous people, 175, 402, 417, 491, 568
  aurora borealis and, 318
  in Brazil, 497, 498
  in British Columbia, 305, 305*p*, 307–308, 308*p*
  diseases and, 301
  in Guatemala, 440
  in Northern Territories, 319, 319*p*, 320*g*, 320*m*
  of Prairie Provinces, 298, 299, 301
  in rain forest, 497, 498
  of Venezuela, 493
  See also Native Americans
Indonesia, 71, 93, 93*p*, 542*m*, 558
Industrial Revolution, 76, 95, 183, 188, 568
industrialization, 259, 358, 358*p*, 450, 568
  cultural change and, 105
  defined, 120
  developing nations, 77

  early farming and, 61*m*
  economic development and, 76
  land use, 125, 131–132, 131*p*
  urbanization and, 70
industry, 236–247
  in Canada, 286–289
  ownership, 74–75
  in the South, 259–261
informational texts, RW1
Ingstad, Helge, 311
injustice, 404
institutions, 92, 95, 568
Instructional Strategies
  author's craft, 90f, 284h, 486g–486h
  choral reading, T34, 26h, 234g, 366h
  discussion ideas, 58h, 284h
  encouraging active participation, 212f, 424f
  give one, get one, T37
  high-use academic words, T33 *See also* vocabulary strategies
  idea wave, T35
  numbered heads, T36, 486g
  oral cloze, T33, 90f
  paragraph puzzle, 26g
  paragraph shrinking, T34, 112f, 146f
  power notes, 26g
  previewing and prereading, 8e, 146f, 336f
  questions and answers, 486h
  read-cover-recite-check, 26h
  ReQuest (reciprocal questions),T35
  scaffolding, 8f, 234g
  seed discussions, 454f
  set a purpose for reading, T32, T33
  structured silent reading, T34, 58g
  structuring paragraphs, 234h
  summarizing, 112f, 212f, 400f, 454f
  think-write-pair-share, T36
  vocabulary strategies, T33, 8e, 8f, 58g, 58h, 172h, 234h, 366h, 400f, 424f
interaction, M1
interdependence, 79, 568
Interdisciplinary
  history, 78
  language arts, 412, 511
  math, 11, 29, 129, 216, 369

music, 107
science, 51, 150, 301, 314, 345, 345p, 360, 376, 495
technology, 107
time, 191p, 340
world, 268, 466
interest payments, 75
Interior Plains, 149
intermediate directions, 11
international, 84, 568
International Monetary Fund, 395
international organizations, 84
Internet, 107g, 192, 275g
Inti (sun god), 376
Inuit, 40p, 120, 121, 155, 155p, 215m, 229, 288, 319, 319p, 320, 322, 322p
Inuktitut, 322, 568
investment, 75
involuntary migration, 68
Iowa, 537m
data about, 141m, 235m, 239
Iqaluit, Nunavut, 31p, 288, 321p, 322, 558
Iran, 82, 542m, 558
Iraq, 135, 191p, 191g, 192, 199, 542m
Ireland, 68, 538m, 539m
iron ore, 164m, 166, 353m, 355
Iroquois people, 202p, 215m, 232m, 294
irrigation, 94, 121, 121p, 568
Isabella, Queen of Spain, 379
Islam, 69m, 100, 101, 103p
island, 554
Isle of Spice, 458
Israel, 548
isthmus, 340, 554, 568
Isthmus of Panama, 337m, 535m, 558
Itaipú Dam, 333, 333p
Italy, 104, 538m, 558
Iturbide, Agustín de, 387
Ivory Coast (Côte d'Ivoire), 546

J

jackfruit, 50p
Jackson, Mississippi, 241
Jakarta, Indonesia, 71, 558

Jamaica, 340, 455m, 459, 558
farming in, 412
music of, 414
natural resources of, 353m, 354
Jamestown, Virginia, 178, 558
Japan, 5p, 135, 542m, 558
bullet trains, 105p
cultural change, 104, 106
culture, 92p, 93
economy, 76
energy resources, 118
land use, 120, 121
population density, 63
in World War II, 190
jeans, 104
Jefferson, Thomas, 179, 180
Jefferson City, Missouri, 241
Jews, 98, 190. See also Judaism
jíbaros, 479
Jim Crow laws, 186
Johnson, Andrew, 186
Jordan, 39p, 542m
Judaism, 100, 101, 412. See also Jews
Juneau, Alaska, 236

K

Kahlo, Frida, 403p
Kalahari Desert, 5m, 541m
Kamchatka Peninsula, 5m
Kansas, 537m
data about, 141m, 235m, 240
farming in, 267
Kazakhstan, 548
Kennedy, John F., 206, 464
Kentucky, 537m
data about, 141m, 235m, 240
land use in, 256m
mining in, 258
natural resources of, 164m, 166
population density, 249
Kenya, M17p, 114p, 540m
keys, maps, M8, M9, 16, 20m, 21, 57
Khrushchev, Nikita, 464, 464p
Kilimanjaro, M10
Kim Jong Il, 82

King, Martin Luther, Jr., 191
Kings and queens, 82, 83
Kingston, Jamaica, 459
Kingstown, St. Vincent and the Grenadines, 460
Klondike River, 321
Kocour, Ruth, 148
Korea, North, 82, 83, 548
Korea, South, 67, 548
Korean War, 191, 191g
Kremer, Gerhard, M7
Kuwait, 83, 542m
Kyoto, Protocol, 130

L

La Paz, Bolivia, 338, 338p, 489
labor force, 188, 568
Labrador, 196m
Labrador Sea, 4m
lacrosse, 226
ladinos, 438, 439, 439g, 439m, 568
Lake Erie, 151, 203, 203p, 210m, 537m
Lake Huron, 151, 537m
Lake Maracaibo, 342, 517
Lake Michigan, 151, 537m
Lake Ontario, 151, 537m
Lake Superior, 142m, 142p, 151, 206g, 207, 537m
Lake Texcoco, 370
Lake Titicaca, 333, 333p, 342, 415, 415p, 501, 503, 558
Lake Washington, 275
lakes, 35, 44, 151–152, 151p
Lakes Region, 510
land bridge, 175, 568
land reform, 438, 438p, 568
land use, M16–M17, 120–125, 438, 438p
changes in, 125
culture and, 120–121
economics and, 122–123
in Prairie Provinces, 300g
in the South, 256m
See also farming
landforms, M1, 35, 149–151, 149p, 151p, 340–341, 340p, 341p, 568

as barriers, 5, 5p
of Chile, 489, 509
of Latin America, 332, 332m
landmasses, 19, 568
landscape. See environment
landslides, 520p, 521, 521p
language arts, 134, 210, 324, 412, 511
languages, M1, 401m
of Argentina, 488
of Bolivia, 489
of Brazil, 331m, 331p, 417, 489
of Canada, 197, 212f, 286–289
of Caribbean Islands, 412, 456–461
of Central America, 403, 426–429
of Chile, 489
of Colombia, 490
culture and, 92, 98–99, 106
of Ecuador, 490
of El Salvador, 403
English, 98, 99
of First Nations, 228
French, 99, 194, 197
of Guatemala, 403, 427, 439m
of Guyana, 491
of Haiti, 472, 474
Hindi, M13
Incan, 377
of the Inuit, 322, 322p
Latin, 340
of Latin America, 340, 377, 401m, 403, 412, 416, 417, 426–429
major groups of, 98–99m
maps of, M13m
of Mexico, 428
movement and, 331
of Native Americans, 377
of Panama, 403
of Paraguay, 491
of Peru, 491, 502g
of Puerto Rico, 477
of Quebec, 295, 296g
Russian, 99p
shrinking number of, 90f
of South America, 416, 486g, 488–493
Spanglish, 478
Spanish, 99
of Suriname, 492

of Uruguay, 492
of Venezuela, 493
L'Anse aux Meadows, 311, 311p, 558
Lansing, Michigan, 241
Laos, 548
Las Casas, Bartolomé de, 383
Latin America, 330m, 331m, 332m, 334m
climate of, 343–349, 343p, 344m, 346g, 348m
developing nations, 77
foreign debt of, 394, 394g
geographic features of, 339
landforms of, 340–341, 340p, 341p
languages of, 331, 340, 377, 401m, 403, 412, 416, 417, 426–429
location of, 330m, 339, 339m, 360m, 398m, 422m
migration to, M15m
natural resources of, 352–358, 352p, 353m, 354p, 355p, 356g, 357p, 358p
physical geography, 337m
regions of, 339m
United States and, 330
urbanization, 71
waterways in, 342, 342p
See also Middle America; South America
latitude, M4, 11–12, 11p, 157, 568
climate and, 41
defined, 10
global grid, 12, 12g
high, 32, 32m, 41
low, 32, 32m, 41
middle, 32, 32m
seasons and, 30–32, 30–31g
winds and, 43g
zones of, 32m
Laurentian Highlands, 149
lava, 36, 142p, 150
laws, 80, 81, 94
lead, 164m, 166
Lebanon, 549
Legend, maps, 21
Lent, 413, 413p
Lesage, Jean, 295
Lewis, Meriwether, 180, 180p, 181, 272

Liberia, 546
Libya, 82, 540m, 558
lichen, 34, 568
life expectancy, 64, 65, 568
Lima, Peru, 383, 419, 491, 503, 503p, 558
Lincoln, Abraham, 185–186
Lincoln, Nebraska, 242
Line of Demarcation, 380
literacy, 457, 464, 568
literature, 225, 225p
of Canada, 230
of the Caribbean, 400f
Childtimes (Greenfield and Little), 280–283
of Chile, 418
of Colombia, 418
of Cuba, 362–365, 362p, 363p, 364p
My Side of the Mountain (George), 88–89
Surveyor (Ada), 362–365
of Trinidad, 412
Uncle Tom's Cabin (Stowe), 185
Lithuania, 538m
Little, Lessie Jones, 280–283
Little Havana, 463, 466p
Little Rock, Arkansas, 237
living resources, 116
llamas, 334, 334p, 347, 416p
location, M1, 11–12, 330
borders, 2, 2p
Canada, 140m
climate and, 41
hydroelectricity, 333, 333g
United States, 140m
See also place location
locator globe, M8
locks, 153, 568
locomotive, 201p
logging, 205, 205p, 497, 497p
Loihi (volcano), 150
London, England, M9, 22, 22m, 558
Lone Star Republic, 183
longitude, M5, 11–12, 11p, 568
defined, 10
determined at sea, 8e
global grid, 12, 12g

Mercator projection, 18
time zones and, 29
Los Angeles, California, 276, 276*p*, 558
Louisiana, M5, 177*m*, 537*m*
Cajuns in, 314
data about, 141*m*, 235*m*, 240
drilling in, 258
farming in, 257
land use in, 256*m*
music of, 225
natural resources of, 164*m*, 166
in Sun Belt, 260*m*
Louisiana Purchase, 181–182, 181*m*, 569
Louisiana Territory, 181, 181*m*, 272
L'Ouverture, Toussaint, 385, 385*p*, 471, 473, 568
low latitudes, 32, 32*m*, 41, 569
Lower Canada, 194, 195, 291
lowlands, 151, 569. *See also* plains
Loyalists, 194
lumber, 164*m*, 165, 205, 205*p*

M

Macdonald-Cartier Bridge, 290, 290*p*
Machapuchare, Nepal, 54*p*
machines, 76. *See also* industrialization
Machu Picchu, 376, 504, 504*p*
Mackenzie, William, 195
Mackenzie River, 152, 167, 558
Madeira, 46*p*
Madison, Wisconsin, 247
magazines, 107
Magellan, Ferdinand, 507, 507*p*, 509, 510, 569
magma, 33, 36, 36–37*g*, 150, 569
Maine, 30*p*, 537*m*
data about, 141*m*, 235*m*, 240
maize, 369, 569
malaria, 424f, 447–448
Malay Peninsula, 5*m*
Malaysia, 103*p*, 542*m*
Malcolm, Andrew H., 227
Mali, 547

Malthus, Thomas, 58h
Manifest Destiny, 183, 569
Manitoba, Canada, 196*m*, 216*p*, 298, 300*m*
data about, 141*m*, 285*m*, 287
indigenous people of, 299
mantle, Earth's, 33, 34, 34*p*, 36*p*, 569
manufacturing, 120, 123, 569. *See also* industrialization
map key, M8, M9, 568
map skills
analyze, 22, 173*m*, 502, 508
apply information, 455*m*
compare, 63, 249*m*
compare and contrast, 45, 53, 124, 337*m*, 348*m*, 508
contrast, 69, 235*m*
draw conclusions, 177*m*, 184*m*, 204*m*, 215*m*, 260*m*, 269*m*, 285*m*, 309*m*, 314*m*, 344*m*, 353*m*, 367*m*, 508, 518
draw inferences, 77, 100
human-environment interaction, 124, 269*m*, 434*m*
identify, 63, 69, 77, 124, 173*m*, 177*m*, 181*m*, 309*m*, 502, 508
identify effects, 181*m*, 487
infer, 4, 115, 339*m*, 502
interaction, 115, 204*m*
link past and present, 99
list, 184*m*, 215*m*, 249*m*, 269*m*
locate, 173*m*, 204*m*, 213*m*, 260*m*, 285*m*
location, 53, 330*m*, 344*m*, 348*m*, 360*m*, 398*m*, 422*m*, 425*m*, 508, 524*m*
make generalizations, 182*m*
movement, 69, 182*m*, 213*m*, 249*m*, 260*m*, 309*m*, 353*m*, 382*m*, 445*m*
name, 182*m*, 196*m*
natural resources, 164*m*
physical map, 147*m*
place, 99, 100, 177*m*, 196*m*, 337*m*
place location, 210*m*, 232*m*
predict, 213*m*
read a map key, 235*m*, 314*m*
regions, 45, 63, 77, 181*m*, 184*m*, 215*m*, 235*m*, 285*m*, 314*m*, 337*m*, 351*m*, 367*m*, 387*m*, 401*m*
tornadoes, 158*m*, 158*p*

use cartographer's tools, 43, 251
vegetation, 160*m*
maple leaf, 162
maps, 16–22
colors of, 21
conformal, 18
of different scales, M9
distortion, 16, 17, 18–19
equal-area, M7, 19, 19*p*, 566
highway, 21*m*
how to use, M8–M9
keys, M8, M9, 16, 20*m*, 21, 57, 235*m*, 314*m*, 568
latitude and longitude in, 11–12, 11*g*, 12*g*
legend, 21
locator globes, 20*m*
mental maps, 25
Mercator projection, M6, 18, 18*g*
parts of, 21
physical, M11, M339, 20, 20*m*, 136, 332, 332*m*, 532–533*m*, 535*m*, 539*m*, 541*m*, 543*m*, 544*m*, 545*m*
political, M10, 331*m*, 487*m*, 530–531*m*, 534*m*, 536–537*m*, 538*m*, 540*m*, 542*m*
population density, 6–7*m*, 72–73, 73*m*, 86
projections, M6–M7, 16, 18–19, 18*g*, 19*g*
reading, 20–22
Robinson projection, M7, 19, 19*g*
same-shape, M6
scale, 16, 21, 22*m*
scale bars, 20*m*, 21, 573
special purpose, M12*m*, M13*m*
symbols, 21
titles, M8
trimetrogon method, 8f
weather forecasting, 46*p*
See also globes
maquiladoras, 405, 569
Marconi, Guglielmo, 312
Mardi Gras, 144*p*
marine west coast climate, 51, 157, 569
maritime, 315, 569
Maritime Provinces, 315

markets, 74p
Márquez, Gabriel García, 418
Marshall Islands, 544m, 549
Martí, José de San, 388
Martin, Lydia, 466
Martinique, 455m
Maryland, 537m
  data about, 141m, 235m, 240
  fishing in, 258
mass transit, 275, 569
Massachusetts, 537m
  data about, 141m, 235m, 240
  Pilgrims in, 178
Massachusetts Institute of
  Technology, 251
Massif Central, 539m
materials. See resources
math, 86, 110, 216, 232, 369
  interdisciplinary links, 11, 29, 129, 216,
  369
  population bar graphs, 86
  predictions, 110
  writing activities, 86, 110
Mayas, M14, 103, 368–369, 368p, 369p,
  374, 374p, 427, 439, 439g, 439m
  art of, 403, 428p
  civil war and, 440–441
  village of Cerén, 366h
  women, 437, 440
  writing system, 370
  See also Native Americans
Mayflower, 178p
measles, 177
medicine
  Aztec, 372
  population growth and, 65
  from the rain forest, 496, 497
Mediterranean climate, 51, 569
Mediterranean Sea, 5m, 56
Mediterranean vegetation,
  51, 52
megalopolis, 249, 249m, 569
Meining, D. W., 214
Melanesia, 5m, 532m
melting pot, 227, 569
Mendes, Francisco "Chico," 486g
mental maps, 25
Mercator, Gerardus, M7, 18

Mercator projection, M6, M7, 18, 18g
meridians, 10, 12, 569
mesa, 554
mestizos, 383, 392, 417, 504, 511, 569
  in Middle America, 402
  revolts led by, 386
metals, 116
Métis people, 195, 319
Mexican Americans, 191
Mexican Territory, 183
Mexico, 135, 149, 181m, 334, 334p,
  425m, 426, 428, 530m, 534m, 536m,
  558
  art of, 403–404, 403p, 428p
  cities of, 424f
  climate of, 345
  data about, 428
  early civilizations of, 367m, 368–372,
  369p, 370p, 371p, 372p
  economy of, 394g, 395, 432g, 432m
  energy resources, 118
  exports of, 428, 432g, 432m
  farming in, 431
  immigrants, 67
  independence in, 386–387, 386p
  landforms of, 340
  languages of, 403, 428
  location of, 330, 330p, 339, 339m,
  452m
  Mayas in, M14, 103, 369
  NAFTA and, 79, 208, 395, 436
  Native Americans in, 407p, 428
  natural hazards in, 434
  natural resources of, 353m, 354, 357
  population of, 400f 405, 424f, 428,
  430, 434
  religion in, 404, 404p, 423g, 428
  trade, 79
  vegetation of, 348m, 349
  volcanoes in, 332, 332p
  youth, 400f
Mexico City, 334, 334p, 383, 405,
  434m, 558, 569
  employment in, 433–434, 436
  geography of, 435, 435p
  housing in, 433–436, 433p, 434m,
  435p
  pollution in, 435, 435p

Miami, Florida, 42, 43p, 217p, 218,
  260, 463, 466p, 558
Miami Indians, 182m
Michigan, 537m
  data about, 141m, 235m, 241
Micronesia, 5m, 532m
Middle America, 339, 558, 569
  art of, 403–404, 403p
  Aztecs in, 370–372, 370p, 371p, 372p
  cultures of, 402–404, 402p, 403p, 404p
  early civilizations of, 367m, 368–372,
  369p, 370p, 371p, 372p
  natural resources of, 353m, 354
  See also Central America
middle class, 188
Middle East, 121, 121p
middle latitudes, 32, 32m, 569
Midwest (United States), 145m,
  145p, 188, 235m, 264–270, 264p,
  266g, 267p, 268p, 269m, 270p
  cities in, 268–270, 268p, 269m, 270p
  economy of, 265, 265g, 265m
  farming in, 264–265, 264p, 266–267,
  266g
  profile of, 265, 265g, 265m
  railroads in, 268, 269m
migrant workers, 430, 569, 569p
migration, M1, M14–M15, M14m,
  M15m, 67–71, 405, 407, 411, 570
  of African Americans, 256, 256g
  of Native Americans, 174–175, 182m
  to North America, 213m
  in South Asia, 69m
  urbanization, 67, 70–71, 70g
  voluntary, 68
  warfare and, 68
Milky Way Galaxy, 28, 28p, 558
mineral resources, 116, 164m, 165,
  166, 166p, 167, 353m, 354, 489, 570
mines and mining, 258, 273, 273p,
  384, 497, 510
  in Canada, 196, 306, 306g, 306m
Minneapolis-St. Paul, Minnesota,
  270, 558
Minnesota, 207, 537m
  data about, 141m, 235m, 241
Minutemen, 179p
missionaries, 177, 382, 570

Mississippi, 537*m*
data about, 141*m*, 235*m*, 241
farming in, 257
land use in, 256*m*
in Sun Belt, 260*m*
Mississippi River, 146f, 152, 165, 177, 177*m*, 181, 181*m*, 269, 269*m*, 558
Mississippi Valley, 68
Missouri, 152, 537*m*
data about, 141*m*, 235*m*, 241
Missouri River, 152, 165, 180, 559
Mistral, Gabriela, 418
mixed-crop farm, 266, 570
mixed forests, 52, 53*p*
mixed ownership, 75
Mixtec people, 403
Moctezuma, 378, 378*p*, 380–381, 399, 570
Mojave Desert, 12
Moon
map of, 8f
monarchy, 82, 83, 198
money, 75
Mongolia, 549
Montana, 536*m*
climate in, 272*m*
data about, 141*m*, 235*m*, 242, 242*p*
hydroelectricity in, 272*g*
natural resources of, 273, 274
Montenegro, 551
Montevideo, 492
Montgomery, Alabama, 236
Montgomery, Lucy Maud, 230
Montpelier, Vermont, 246
Montreal, Canada, 289*p*, 294, 296*g*, 559
Morocco, 547
mosquitoes, 448, 448*p*
Mother Jones, 188
Mothers of Plaza de Mayo, 418, 418*p*
Mount Everest, 54, 559
Mount Fuji, 5*p*
Mount Kenya, M10
Mount Logan, 151
Mount McKinley, 148, 148*p*
Mount St. Helens, 150
mountain effects, 157–158

mountain pass, 555
mountain sickness, 338
mountains, 35, 88–89*g*, 148*p*, 149, 554, 555*p*, 570
Appalachian, 39
climate and, 41
formation, 36*g*
Rocky, 12, 39
vertical climate zones, 54
water cycle, 41*g*
movement, M1, 13
continents, 7
languages and, 331
mummies, 347
Munduruku Indian, 499
Munro, Alice, 230
music, 107, 225–226, 225*p*, 230, 526
of the Caribbean, 413, 414, 458, 461
of Puerto Rico, 480*p*
Motown, 269
Muslims, 69*m*, 100, 101, 103*p*, 412
***My Side of the Mountain* (George),** 88–89
Myanmar (Burma), 82, 542*m*, 559

N

NAFTA. *See* North American Free Trade Agreement
Naipaul, V. S., 412
narrative essays, RW2
NASA. *See* National Aeronautics and Space Administration
Nashville, Tennessee, 245
Nassau, 457
Natchez, 215*m*
nation-states, 80, 81, 84, 570
National Aeronautics and Space Administration (NASA), 259
national parks, 274, 274*p*
Native Americans, 173*m*, 410
American Indian Movement and, 223, 233*p*
in Andean countries, 417
art of, 403, 404
artifacts, 174*p*
in Bolivia, 352, 352*p*

in Brazil, 499, 499*p*
in Chile, 347, 511
Columbus and, 379, 411
diseases and, 177, 381, 384, 497
in El Salvador, 366h
encomiendas, 384
Europeans and, 215*m*
fishing, 202, 202*p*
France and, 177, 177*m*
French and Indian War, 178
Great Britain and, 177*m*, 178, 178*p*
in Guatemala, 437, 438, 439, 439*g*, 439*m*, 440
horses and, 215–216, 215*p*
housing, 176, 176*p*
Indian Removal Act (1830), 182, 182*m*
lacrosse and, 226
languages of, 99, 377
Lewis and Clark and, 180, 180*p*
literature of, 225
llamas and, 347
in Mexico, 407*p*, 428
migration of, 174–175, 182*m*
number systems and, 216
in Peru, 383, 503–504
population, 223
poverty and, 392
rain forest and, 335, 335*m*, 335*p*
religion of, 404
reservations and, 223
revolts led by, 386
rights of, 182
Spain and, 175, 175*p*, 177, 177*m*
totora reeds and, 415, 415*p*
treaties and, 223
See also First Nations; indigenous people; individual cultures
NATO. *See* North Atlantic Treaty Organization
natural gas, 164*m*, 165, 166, 333, 333*g*, 353*m*, 354
natural resources, 570
in Atlantic Provinces, 313*m*
in British Columbia, 306, 306*g*, 306*m*
in Canada, 167–168, 167*p*, 168*p*
defined, 114–119, 115*m*, 134*m*
economy and, 356–358, 356*g*, 357*p*, 358*p*

in Latin America, 352–358, 352*p*, 353*m*, 354*p*, 355*p*, 356*g*, 357*p*, 358*p*

in the United States, 164–166, 164*m*, 165*p*, 166*p*

in the West, 272–274, 273*p*, 274*p*

navigate, 18, 570

Nebraska, 537*m*

data about, 141*m*, 235*m*, 242

Nepal, 54, 54*p*, 542*m*, 559

Neruda, Pablo, 418

Netherlands, the, 72, 83, 83*p*, 538*m*

land use, 124

Nevada, 160, 536*m*

climate in, 272*m*

data about, 141*m*, 235*m*, 242

natural resources of, 273

in Sun Belt, 260*m*

New Brunswick, 195, 196*m*, 291, 314

data about, 141*m*, 285*m*, 287

New Deal, 189

New England, 82

New Hampshire, 537*m*

data about, 141*m*, 235*m*, 242

New Jersey, 537*m*

data about, 141*m*, 235*m*, 243

population density, 249, 249*m*

New Mexico, 175*p*, 176, 176*p*, 536*m*

climate in, 272*m*

data about, 141*m*, 235*m*, 243

in Sun Belt, 260*m*

New Orleans, M5, 225, 260, 261

New Spain, 383, 384, 434

New York, 153, 537*m*, 559

data about, 141*m*, 235*m*, 243

hydroelectricity in, 272*g*

New York City, 67*p*, 248, 248*p*, 249*m*, 252, 252*p*, 253, 253*p*, 254, 559

population, 253

September 11th attacks, 191*g*, 192, 192*p*, 253

New York Stock Exchange, 75*p*, 253

New Zealand, 7*p*, 122–123*p*, 530*m*, 544*m*, 559

Newfoundland, 167, 194, 195, 196*m*

Newfoundland and Labrador, 312*p*, 313, 313*g*, 313*m*, 315

data about, 141*m*, 285*m*, 287

newspapers, RW1

Niagara Falls, 2*p*, 141*p*, 206, 559

Nicaragua, 403, 425*m*, 429, 534*m*

Niger, 547

Nigeria, 547

night and day, 29

Night of Fire, 385

Nile River, 60*p*, 541*m*

Nile River Valley, 63, 63*m*, 559

nitrogen cycle, 115

nomadic herding, M17*p*, 229, 570

nonrenewable resources, 114, 116, 570

Nootka people, 305

north, 11

North America, 2*m*, 4*m*, 6*m*, 379*m*, 530*m*, 532*m*, 534*m*, 535*m*, 559

colonization, 125

human-environment interaction, 128

migration to, 213*m*

physical maps, 535*m*

political maps, 534*m*

population density, 62*m*

revolution in, 386

satellite image, 17*p*

slave trade, 68

storms, 47

suburbanization, 70

See also Canada; United States

North American Free Trade Agreement (NAFTA), 79, 208, 395, 436, 570

North Atlantic Current, 42, 559

North Atlantic Treaty Organization (NATO), 84

North Carolina, 537*m*

data about, 141*m*, 235*m*, 243

forestry in, 258

land use in, 256*m*

in Sun Belt, 260*m*

textile industry, 259

North China Plain, 5*m*, 543*m*

North Dakota, 537*m*

data about, 141*m*, 235*m*, 244

North Korea, 82, 82*p*, 542*m*, 559

North Pole, M2, M4, M5, M7, 11*p*, 12, 12*g*, 29, 35, 346, 545*m*, 559

North West Mounted Police, 308

Northeast (United States), 235*m*, 248*p*, 249*m*, 251*p*, 253*p*, 254*p*

cities of, 248–254

population density, 249, 249*m*, 250*g*, 250*m*

profile of, 250, 250*g*, 250*m*

Northern Hemisphere, M3, M4, 11*g*, 512

seasons, 30–31, 30–31*g*

northern lights, 318, 318*p*

Northern Territories, 140*p*, 318–322

government in, 319, 320*g*

indigenous people in, 319, 319*p*, 320*g*, 320*m*

population of, 319, 320*g*, 320*m*

Northwest Territories, 196*m*, 319, 320, 320*g*, 320*m*, 321, 559

data about, 141*m*, 285*m*, 287

Norway, 118, 538*m*, 559

Nova Scotia, 195, 196*m*, 284*p*, 291, 314, 315*p*

data about, 141*m*, 285*m*, 287

nuclear energy, 333, 333*g*

nuclear families, 96, 96*p*, 97, 570

nuclear radiation, 191, 191*p*

Nukuj Akpop, 440

number systems, 216, 369

Nunavut, 155, 199, 199*p*, 319, 320, 320*g*, 320*m*, 321*p*, 322, 325, 559

data about, 141*m*, 285*m*, 288

Nunivak Island, 545*m*

O

***O Pioneers!* (Cather),** 264

OAS. *See* Organization of American States (OAS)

oasis, 53*p*, 503, 570, 570*p*

ocean effects, 157

oceans, 35

climate and, 41, 42, 44–45

currents, 42, 570

ocean floor, 36, 37

tidal energy, 118

tropical cyclones, 47

See also individual oceans

Ohio, 537*m*

culture of, 480, 480p
government of, 476, 479, 479g, 479m
independence question, 482, 482p
languages of, 477
music of, 480p
population of, 479m
Spain and, 388
statehood question, 481, 481p
timeline of, 485
United States and, 476–478, 477g, 477p, 479, 479g, 481–482, 481p, 482p
push-pull theory, M15, 68, 571

Q

qanats, 121, 121p
Qatar, 549
Quebec, 145m, 145p, 162p, 167, 168, 194, 196m, 197, 210m, 228, 560
data about, 141m, 285m, 289
French culture in, 294–297, 296, 296g, 297, 297p
history of, 296
language in, 295, 296g
Ontario and, 290
population density, 296m
Quiet Revolution in, 295, 295p
Separatists in, 295, 295p
timeline, 296
Quebec, Battle of, 194, 194p, 212f
Quebec Act, 194
Quebec City, 219p
Quechua, 377, 417, 504, 505, 505p, 506
language, 486
Queen Elizabeth Islands, 545m
Quetzalcoatl, 381, 381p
Quiché Maya, 427, 437
Quiet Revolution, 295, 295p, 571
quipu, 373p, 375, 571

R

radar, 46
radio, 106, 107
radioactivity, atomic energy, 118

railroads, 105p, 183, 188, 188p, 190g, 195p, 393p
in Canada, 308
in the Midwest, 268, 269m
rain, 40, 41, 42m, 158
climate graphs, 48–49, 48g, 56
dry climates, 51
storms, 47
temperate marine climates, 51
tropical climate, 50
tropical cyclones, 47
water cycle, 35, 41g, 115
rain forest, 4p, 50, 52, 52p, 341, 347, 348m, 450, 450p, 460, 572
in Brazil, 335, 335m, 335p, 494, 494p, 495, 495p
deforestation, 129p
importance of, 496–497, 496g, 497p
indigenous people in, 498
medicine from, 496, 497
of Peru, 502
threats to, 497
rain shadow, 161, 572
Raleigh, North Carolina, 243, 243p, 259
rancho, 420
raw materials, 112f, 114, 128, 572
reading skills
analyze author's purpose, RW1
asking questions, 163, 352
cause and effect, 400, 402
clarifying meaning, 8, 172, 366
compare and contrast, 54, 58, 60, 234, 248, 486, 494, 507
context clues, 26, 28, 30, 32, 33, 35, 39, 40, 50, 52, 284, 290, 304, 311, 318, 424, 430, 437, 444
contrast signal words, 80
distinguish between facts and opinions, RW1
evaluate credibility, RW1
identify contrasts, 67, 264, 501
identify evidence, RW1
identify main ideas, 87, 112, 114, 128, 135, 212, 214, 227, 454, 462, 476
identify supporting details, 120, 222, 470
informational texts, RW1
interpret nonliteral meanings, 298

make comparisons, 74, 271, 516
paraphrasing, 16, 22, 187, 378, 382
predicting, 156, 343
prereading strategies, 42
previewing, 163, 338, 343, 352
reading ahead, 10, 180, 202, 373, 392
reading process, 146, 336
recognizing multiple causes, 410
recognizing words that signal sequence, 104
rereading, 10, 174, 202, 392
setting a purpose, 148, 151, 338
signal words, 80, 255
summarize, 193, 385
understanding effects, 415
understanding sequence, 90, 92, 96
See also writing skills
recession, 266, 572
Reconstruction, 186, 190g, 572
recycling, 116, 132, 132p
Red Cross, 186p
Red River Basin, 181m
Redonda, 456
redwood forests, 163, 163p
referendum, 295, 572
reforms, 295, 395
refugees, 471, 572
reggae music, 414, 458, 526
regime, 395, 572
Regina, Saskatchewan, 289, 299
regions, M1, 12, 330, 572
Atlantic Provinces, 311–315
British Columbia, 304–310
of Canada, 140, 140m, 144–145, 144–145m, 144p, 145p
Midwest, 264–270
Northeast, 248–254
Northern Territories, 318–322
Ontario and Quebec, 290–297
Prairie Provinces, 298–303
South, 255–261
of United States, 140, 140m, 144–145, 144–145m, 144p, 145p, 235m
West, 271–276
relative location, M1, 12, 572
relief, M11
religion, 95, 98, 100m, 101, 110m
in Argentina, 488

Aztec, 370
in Bolivia, 489
in Brazil, 489
in Canada, 218, 263g
in Caribbean Islands, 412, 456–461
in Central America, 404, 404p, 426–429
in Chile, 489
in Colombia, 490
in daily life, 98
in Ecuador, 490
in Guyana, 491
Incan, 376
Mayan, 369, 369p
in Mexico, 404, 404p, 423g, 428
missionaries and, 177
Native American, 404
in Paraguay, 491
in Peru, 491
in South America, 488–493
in Suriname, 492
in United States, 218, 263g
in Uruguay, 492
in Venezuela, 493
renewable resources, 114, 115–116, 118, 132, 572
representative democracy, 83, 572
research papers, RW4–RW5
reservations, 223, 572
reserves, 228, 572
reservoirs, 131
resources
industry and, 131
living, 116
natural, 114–119, 115m, 134m
nonrenewable, 114, 116
recycling, 116
renewable, 114, 115–116, 118, 132
responsible development, 274, 572
Revere, Paul, 251
revolution, 28, 385–386, 572
Revolutionary War, 179, 179p, 214, 251, 572
Rhode Island, 537m
data about, 141m, 235m, 244
rice, M17p, 58–59p, 76p, 85p, 93p, 120, 121, 257
Richmond, Virginia, 246

ridges, underwater, 37g
Riel, Louis, 195
Riis, Jacob, 187, 187p, 188
Ring of Fire, 33, 37, 560
Rio de Janeiro, Brazil, 331m, 331p, 392p, 495, 500, 500p, 560, 572
Río de la Plata, 336f, 342
river mouth, 555
River Platte, 492
Rivera, Diego, 404, 403p, 428p
rivers, 35, 152, 152p, 342, 342p
erosion, 39
water energy, 118
water supply, 127
roads, 131, 376
***Robinson Crusoe* (Defoe),** 511
Robinson projection, M7, 19, 19g
rocks
Earth's crust, 34, 34g
magma, 36, 36–37g
plant fossils, 51p
weathering and erosion, 39, 39p
Rocky Mountains, 4m, 12, 39, 149, 152, 181, 181m, 203, 271p, 532m, 535m, 545m, 560, 573
Rome, Italy, 81
Romero y Galdamez, Oscar Arnulfo, 404
Roosevelt, Franklin D., 189, 190
Roosevelt, Theodore, 394, 447
Roseau, Dominica, 458
rotation, M2, 28, 29, 43g, 573
Rotterdam, the Netherlands, 131p, 560
rural areas, 67, 71, 573
Russia, 3p, 135, 188, 538m, 542m, 560
Russian language, 99p
Ruth, Babe, 226
Rwanda, 547

S

Sacajawea, 180, 180p
Sacramento, California, 237
Sahara, 5m, 53p, 541m, 560
Sahel, 5m, 541m
Saint-Domingue, 385

Saint George's, 458
St. Jean-Baptiste, 297
St. John's, Newfoundland, 287, 456, 456p
St. Kitts and Nevis, 460
St. Lawrence Lowlands, 151, 167
St. Lawrence River, 151, 153, 167, 177, 194, 206, 560
St. Lawrence Seaway, 206–207, 206g, 210m, 560
St. Louis, Missouri, 45, 269, 269m, 560
St. Lucia, 455m, 460
St. Paul, Minnesota, 241, 270
St. Vincent and the Grenadines, 455m, 460
Salamon, Lazarus, 222
Salem, Oregon, 244
Salt Lake City, 161, 246
salt water, 35
same-shape maps, M6
Samoa, 544, 549
Samuels, Dorothy, 412
San Andreas Fault, 36p
San Francisco, California, 45, 560
San Geronimo Fortress, 480p
San Jose, California, 275, 560
San José, Costa Rica, 405, 427
San Juan, 459, 480, 480p, 560
San Martín, José de, 573
San Salvador, 427, 457
sanitation, 65, 66, 573
Santa Fe, New Mexico, 242, 243
Santiago, Chile, 489, 510, 511, 560
Santiago, Esmeralda, 478, 478p
Santo Domingo, 458
São Paulo, Brazil, 71, 71p, 335, 335m, 417, 417p, 560
Sao Tomé and Príncipe, 540m
Saskatchewan, 196m, 298, 300m
data about, 141m, 285m, 289
farming in, 302, 302p
Grasslands National Park, 301
indigenous people of, 299
satellite image, 17, 573
satellites, 8–9p, 17, 17p, 46, 46p
Saudi Arabia, 77, 78, 82, 101, 118, 135, 542m, 560

Sault Sainte Marie, 202
Saulteaux people, 298, 299
savanna, 50, 52, 495, 573
scale bar, M8, 20*m*, 21, 573
scale, maps, 16, 21, 22*m*
schools, 66
science, 345, 345*p*, 360, 376, 452, 495
  aurora borealis, 318, 318*p*
  Bay of Fundy, 314
  interdisciplinary links, 51, 150, 301, 314, 345, 345*p*, 360, 376, 495
  prairies, 301
  volcanoes, 150
  writing skills, 56, 278
  See also technology
Sears Tower, 268
seas, 35
seasons, 30–32, 30–31*g*
Seattle, Washington, 275, 560
Sechelt Indians, 308
Segovia Aqueduct, 376
segregation, 185, 186, 191, 573
Selkirk, Alexander, 511
selva, 502*g*, 503
semiarid climate, 44*p*, 51, 573
Seminole people, 182*m*
Senate, Canadian, 198
Senegal, 547
Separatists, 295, 573
September 11th attacks, 191*g*, 192, 192*p*, 253
Serbia, 551
services, 123, 131, 573
Seven Years' War, 194, 194*p*
Shawnee people, 182*m*
sheep, 122, 122*p*
shipbuilding, 315
shipping, 445, 445*p*, 449, 449*p*
  on the Great Lakes, 151
  on the Mackenzie River, 152–153
  on the Mississippi River, 152
  trade, 79*p*
shopping malls, 131
Siberia, 5*m*, 175, 542*m*
sierra, 502, 503, 573
Sierra Leone, 135, 540*m*
Sierra Nevada, 150, 560

sign language, 98*p*
Sikhism, 100, 101*p*
Silicon Valley, 275
Silk Road, 78
silver, 167
Singapore, 549
Sioux people, 299
Sisi, 499*p*
ska music, 414
skyscrapers, 234*g*, 252, 252*p*, 253, 268, 293, 293*p*
Slave Coast, M15
slave trade, 68
slavery, 178, 384, 385, 392, 392*p*
  African Americans and, 392
  in Brazil, 489, 498, 499
  in the Caribbean, 456
  Civil War and, 184–186
  Emancipation Proclamation, 185
  Haiti and, 334, 334*p*, 471
  in Suriname, 492
sleet, 40
slums, 187, 187*p*, 573
smallpox, 177
smog, 435, 435*p*, 511
smuggling, 497
snow, 40, 41, 47
soccer, 499*p*
social classes, 96, 97, 383, 573
Social Security, 189
social structure, 96, 573
Social Studies Skills
  analyzing climate maps, 350–351, 350*m*, 351*m*, 360, 360*p*
  analyzing graphic data, 65, 394
  analyzing primary sources, 122, 189, 380
  comparing and contrasting, 44, 468–469, 468*p*, 469*p*, 484
  decision making, 83, 217, 465
  distinguishing fact and opinion, 107, 274, 408–409, 409*p*, 422
  drawing inferences, 442–443, 442*p*, 443*p*, 452
  drawing inferences and conclusions, 12, 216
  identifying cause and effect, 30, 178

  identifying frame of reference, 69, 154–155, 170, 505
  identifying main ideas, 76, 412
  interpreting diagrams, 200–201, 200*p*, 201*p*, 210
  making predictions, 110, 126–127, 134, 406
  making timelines, 390–391, 390*p*, 398
  making valid generalizations, 102–103, 110, 165, 340
  problem solving, 118, 195, 439
  recognizing bias, 94, 294, 382
  sequencing, 18, 321
  supporting a position, 131, 295, 474
  synthesizing information, 100, 250, 514–515, 514*p*, 515*p*, 524
  transferring information from one medium to another, 53, 183, 498
  understanding circle graphs, 262–263, 263*g*, 278
  using cartographer's tools, 43, 251, 432
  using climate graphs, 48–49
  using graphic organizers, 220–221, 232
  using population density maps, 72–73, 86
  using reliable information, 14–15, 24, 225, 446
  using special geography graphs, 56
  writing a summary, 316–317, 324, 412
  writing and, RW2–RW5
society, 96–97, 573
sod, 298, 573
soddies, 298
soil, 39, 66
solar energy, 112*f*, 115, 116*p*, 117, 118, 132
solar system, M2, 26*g*, 28
solstices, 30, 30*g*, 31, 31*g*, 573
Somalia, 547
Sonoran Desert, 345
Soufrière, 460
South (United States), 144*p*, 235*m*, 257*p*, 258*p*, 259*p*, 260*m*, 261*p*
  agriculture in, 257, 257*p*
  cities of, 259–261, 261*p*
  climate of, 255–256
  culture of, 256, 256*g*, 256*m*

land use, 256*m*

profile of, 256, 256*g,* 256*m*

tourism in, 261

transportation in, 260

south, 11

South Africa, 77, 540*m,* 560

South America, 2*m,* 4*m,* 6*m,* 379*m,* 487*m,* 530*m,* 532*m,* 560

cities of, 419–420, 420*p*

climate, 42

colonization, 125

cultural regions of, 416

early civilizations of, 367*m*

ethnic groups of, 488–493

exports of, 488–493

farming in, 400f, 419

geography of, 488

government in, 488–493

independence in, 387–389, 387*m,* 388*p*

landforms of, 341

languages of, 416, 488–493

literature of, 418

location of, 339, 339*m,* 524*m*

Mercator projection, 18

natural resources in, 353*m,* 355

plate movements, 38*m*

political map, 487*m,* 534*m*

population of, 488–493

religions in, 488–493

satellite image, 17*p*

slave trade, 68

women in, 418

See also Latin America

South Asia

migration, 69*m*

population density, 73*m*

See also Asia

South Carolina, 537*m*

data about, 141*m,* 235*m,* 245, 245*p*

land use in, 256*m*

in Sun Belt, 260*m*

textile industry, 259

South Dakota, 537*m*

data about, 141*m,* 235*m,* 245

South Korea, 67, 542*m,* 560

South Pole, M2, M4, M5, M7, 12, 12*g,* 29, 35, 346, 545*m,* 560

Southern Hemisphere, M3, M4, 11*g,* 512, 544*m*

seasons, 31

Southern Ocean, 56

Southwest, U.S., 176, 176*p*

Southwest Asia

population growth, 66

religions, 100

states, 81

water supply, 127

See also Asia

Soviet Union, 191, 464, 467

space shuttle, 8–9*p*

Spain, 538*m*

areas of influence, 173*m,* 175, 177*m*

Aztecs and, 378*p,* 380–381

Canada and, 314, 314*m*

colonization by, 382–384, 416, 458, 476, 490, 493, 511

conquistadors and, 380–381

exploration by, 379–380

Incas and, 377

Louisiana Territory, 181, 181*m*

Native Americans and, 175, 175*p,* 177, 177*m*

revolts against, 386–387, 386*p*

settlers from, 340

Spanglish, 478

Spanish American War, 188, 190*g,* 454f, 463, 476

Spanish language, 99

sports, 218*p,* 226, 226*p,* 230, 230*p,* 413. *See also* games

spring, 30*g,* 31, 32

Springfield, Illinois, 239

squatter, 433, 573

Sri Lanka, 549

Stadacona, 294

standard of living, 219, 573

Standardized Test Prep

analyze a reading selection, 325, 453

analyze graphs and charts, 279*g,* 423

analyze point of view, 399

analyze primary sources, 211

analyzing main ideas, 87, 135

find the main idea, 87, 135, 233, 525

make mental maps, 25, 171, 361

sequence, 485

use map keys, 57

use prior knowledge, 111

stars, 28

states, 80–83, 95, 573

Statue of Liberty, 222*p*

steam engine, 183, 183*p*

steel drums, 414, 461

stock exchange, 75*p*

storms, 17*p,* 47, 158

Stowe, Harriet Beecher, 185

strait, 555

Strait of Magellan, 508*m,* 509, 510, 560

Strauss, Levi, 104

strike, 441, 573

stumptown, 307

subarctic climate, 51, 573

subsistence farming, M16, 77, 377, 419, 490*p,* 573

suburbs, 70, 105, 125

Sudan, 547

Suez Canal, 449

sugar cane, 349, 353*m,* 354, 460, 466

sulphur springs, 460

summer, 30, 30*g,* 32, 51

sun

air circulation and, 43*g*

climate and, 41

day and night, 29

Earth's distance from, 28

renewable resources, 115

seasons, 30–31, 30–31*g*

Sun Belt, 234h, 260–261, 260*m,* 573

Suriname, 416, 487*m,* 492, 534*m*

Surveyor (Ada), 362–365

surveys, mapmaking, 17

suspension bridge, 506, 506*p*

Sweden, 551

Switzerland, 78, 561

Syria, 549

T

Taiwan, 549

Tallahassee, Florida, 239

Tanzania, 64*p,* 540*m*

Taos, New Mexico, 175p, 176, 176p
tariff, 208, 574
taxes, 179
technology, 574
  Aztec farming, 371, 371p
  culture and, 93, 94–95, 105–106, 107
  dams, 165
  economic development and, 76
  energy consumption and, 119
  environmental issues and, 203
  farming and, 264p, 266–267, 300
  hybrid cars, 119, 130, 130g, 132
  hydroelectricity, 165, 167
  Inuits and, 319, 319p
  Panama Canal, 449, 449p
  Pueblo village, 176, 176p
  skyscrapers, 252, 252p
  in the South, 259
  suspension bridge, 506, 506p
  trade, 79
  weather forecasting, 46, 46p
  See also science
telegraph, 312
telephones, 107, 131
television, 106, 107
temperate continental climate, 43g, 50, 51
temperate grasslands, 52
temperate marine climate, 43g, 50, 51
temperate zones, 32
temperature, 40, 574
  climate graphs, 48–49, 48g
  Earth's structure, 34g
  oceans and, 42, 44–45
tenement, 187, 574
Tennessee, 537m
  data about, 141m, 235m, 245
  land use in, 256m
  mining in, 258
  in Sun Belt, 260m
Tenochtitlán, 370, 371, 371p, 380–381, 434, 561, 574
territories, 141m, 184m, 574
terrorists, 192, 574
Texas, 68, 537m, 561
  annexation of, 181m
  data about, 141m, 235m, 245

  drilling in, 258
  farming in, 257
  fishing in, 258
  land use in, 256m
  Mexico and, 183
  natural resources of, 164m, 166
  in Sun Belt, 260m
Texas, Republic of, 181m
textile industry, 183, 184, 259, 574
Thailand, 76p, 100p, 542m
thunderstorms, 47
tidal energy, 118
Tierra del Fuego, 487m, 510, 561
Tigre River, 4p
Tikal, Guatemala, 369
time, 191p, 340
time zones, 29, 29m
timelines, 190–191g, 326, 390–391, 390p
  of Cuba, 485
  of early civilizations, 374, 374p
  of Haiti, 472
  making, 390–391, 398
  of Puerto Rico, 485
  of Quebec, 296
tin, 352, 352p, 353m, 355
Tobago. *See* Trinidad and Tobago
Toco Indians, 416p
Togo, 540m
Tokyo, Japan, 63, 63p, 561
tools, 94, 94p
Topa Inca, 374, 574
Topeka, Kansas, 240
tornadoes, 47, 158m, 158p, 574
Toronto, 156, 157g, 204p, 229, 288, 293, 293p, 561
totem pole, 305, 305p, 574, 574p
totora reeds, 415, 415p, 501, 501p
tourism, 450, 450p
  in the Caribbean, 456, 457, 458, 459, 460
  in Cuba, 467, 467p
  in the South, 261
  in Uruguay, 492
trade, 198–208, 383g
  Aztec, 372
  development of culture and, 94
  exports and imports, 393

  fur, 177, 193, 194, 214p, 305
  NAFTA, 79, 208, 395, 436
  Pacific Rim, 309–310, 309m
  world trade patterns, 78–79, 78g
traditions, 108, 218p
traffic jams, 130p
transportation, 376
  cultural change and, 106, 107
  Great Lakes, 206–207, 206g
  river, 152
  in the South, 260
  See also cars; railroads
treaties, 84, 223, 380, 575
Treaty of Paris (1763), 194
Treaty of Paris (1783), 177m, 179, 181m
Treaty of Tordesillas, 380
Treaty of Versailles (1918), 189
trees, 50, 52, 114, 115, 353m, 355. *See also* forests and forestry
Trenton, New Jersey, 243
tribal rule, 82
Tribuna, 501
tributaries, 152, 342, 555, 575
tribute, 370
Trinidad and Tobago, 455m, 461, 461p, 561
  Carnival in, 413, 413p
  literature of, 412
  natural resources of, 353m, 354
Tropic of Cancer, M2, 30g, 32, 54, 561
Tropic of Capricorn, M3, 31g, 32, 561
tropical climate region, M1
tropical cyclones, 40, 47, 575
tropical rain forest, 347, 348m
tropical storms, 158
tropical wet and dry climate, M12, 345
tropical wet climate, M12, 345
tropics, 32, 32m
  air circulation, 43g
  climate, 41, 50
  rain forest, 50, 52, 52p
  savanna, 52
Truman, Harry S., 190
Tubman, Harriet, 184
tufa, 236–237p

tundra, 50, 51, 51*p*, 52, 54, 159, 159*p*, 160*m*, 503, 575
Tunisia, 547
Turkey, 127, 189, 538*m*, 542*m*
Twain, Shania, 230
Twin Cities, 270
Twin Pitons, 460
Tzoc, Justina, 440

U

Uganda, 547
Ukraine, 552
Uncle Tom's Cabin **(Stowe),** 185
unemployment, 76
Union states (Civil War), 184*m*
United Arab Emirates, 79*p*, 542*m*
United Kingdom, 6*g*, 68, 83, 538*m*. *See also* England; Great Britain
United Nations, 84, 84*g*
United Nations Children's Fund (UNICEF), 84, 58h
United States, 135, 141*m*, 147*m*, 530*m*, 534*m*, 536–537*m*, 561
  agriculture in, 236–247
  Canada and, 199, 202–208, 214, 218–219, 218*p*, 230
  Chile and, 508, 508*g*
  climate of, 158, 158*m*, 158*p*
  Cuba and, 457, 463, 464, 465–467, 466*p*
  cultural change, 104–105, 106
  cultural diversity and, 215
  cultural patterns of, 216–219, 217*p*, 218*p*, 219*p*
  culture of, 225–226, 225*p*, 226*p*
  economic issues, 75, 76, 206–208, 206*g*
  employment, 131
  energy resources, 118
  environmental issues of, 132, 132*p*, 203–205, 203*p*, 204*m*, 204*p*, 205*p*
  ethnic groups in, 236–247
  families, 97
  farming in, M16*m*, M16*p*
  food exports in, 239
  geographic features of, 150
  government, 83
  Haiti and, 471, 473
  immigration to, 67, 67*p*, 68, 216–219, 222–226, 222*p*, 223*p*, 224*g*, 225*p*, 407
  imports and exports, 207
  industry in, 236–247
  international alliances, 84
  irrigation, 121, 121*p*
  lakes, 151–152, 151*p*
  land use, 120
  landforms of, 149–151
  languages, 99
  Latin America and, 330, 394, 394*g*
  life expectancy, 65
  literature of, 225, 225*p*
  location of, 149
  music of, 225–226, 225*p*
  NAFTA and, 395
  Native American treaties and, 223
  natural resources of, 164–166, 164*m*, 165*p*, 166*p*
  oil imports, 517*g*
  Panama Canal and, 394, 446–448
  physical maps, 147*m*
  political maps, 536*m*–537*m*
  population of, 218, 222, 236–247
  Puerto Rico and, 476–478, 477*g*, 477*p*, 479, 479*g*, 481–482, 481*p*, 482*p*
  regions of, 144–145, 144*m*–145*m*, 144*p*, 145*p*, 235*m*
  religion in, 101, 218
  rivers, 152, 152*p*
  sports in, 226, 226*p*
  standard of living in, 219
  states, 80, 81
  suburbanization, 70, 125
  Sun Belt, 260, 260*m*
  trade, 78, 79, 207–208
  trade agreements, 208, 395
  vegetation zones, 159–162, 159*p*, 160*m*, 161*p*, 162*p*
  See also North America; individual states
Upper Canada, 194, 195, 291
Upper Mississippi Valley, 152
uranium, 167
urban, 71, 575
urbanization, 67, 70–71, 70*g*, 405, 405*g*, 406, 409, 419–420, 420*p*, 575

Uros, 501, 503, 506
Uruguay, 487*m*, 492, 492*p*, 534*m*
  climate of, 345
  culture of, 417
  farming in, 419
  foreign debt of, 394*g*
  independence in, 387*m*
  landforms of, 341
  vegetation of, 347, 348*m*
  waterways in, 342
Uruguay River, 342
Utah, 142*p*, 160, 536*m*
  climate in, 272*m*
  data about, 141*m*, 235*m*, 246
  in Sun Belt, 260*m*
Uzbekistan, 550

V

vaccines, 64*p*, 65
valley, 555
Valley of Mexico, 370, 561
Vancouver, British Columbia, 205, 205*p*, 217*p*, 218, 229, 304, 304*p*, 561
Vancouver Island, 305, 307
Vatican City, 81, 81*p*, 561
vegetation, 446*m*, 575
  climate and, 50–54, 347–349, 347*p*, 348*m*, 349*p*
  defined, 50
  regions, 50, 51–53, 53*m*
  vertical climate zones, 54
  See also agriculture
vegetation zones, 159–162, 159*p*, 160*m*, 161*p*, 162*p*
Venezuela, 135, 387, 487*m*, 493, 493*p*, 516, 534*m*
  culture of, 416
  economy of, 358, 498, 498*m*, 518, 518*g*, 518*m*, 519–520
  exports of, 493, 518, 518*g*, 518*m*
  foreign debt of, 394*g*
  government of, 493, 521, 522, 522*p*
  independence in, 387*m*, 388
  landforms of, 341
  natural disasters in, 520, 520*p*, 521*p*
  natural resources of, 353*m*, 355, 357

oil and, 517, 517g, 517p, 518g, 519–520
population of, 423g, 493
tourism in, 486h
waterways in, 342
Vermont, 537m
data about, 141m, 235m, 246
vertical climate zones, 54, 346, 346g, 349, 575
Viaud, Louane, 473
Victoria, British Columbia, 286, 307, 561
Vietnam, 6g, 67, 68, 542m, 561
Vietnam War, 191, 191g
Vikings, 311, 311p
villages, 61p
vineyards, 125p
Vinland, 311
Viracocha, 376
Virginia, 178, 537m
data about, 141m, 235m, 246
fishing in, 258
land use in, 256m
textile industry, 259
Virginia City, Nevada, 234g
volcanoes, 26g, 35, 36, 150, 332, 332p, 336f, 340, 427, 429, 460, 555, 555p
Hawaiian Islands, 33p, 37, 37, 37p
plate boundaries and, 37, 37g
Ring of Fire, 33, 37
voluntary migration, 68
vote, right to, 189

W

wagon trains, 183, 188p
Walcott, Derek, 400f
Waldman, Louis, 254
Wales, 117p
Wall Street, 253
War in Iraq, 191p, 191g
War of 1812, 195
Ware, Otumfuo Opoku, 3p
warfare, migration and, 68
Washington, 536m
climate in, 272m
data about, 141m, 235m, 246

hydroelectricity in, 272g
natural resources of, 165, 273
Washington, D.C., 192, 261, 261p, 561
Washington, George, 179
waste recycling, 132, 132p
water, 35, 164m, 165, 167
bodies of, 142m, 142p
in California, 272, 272g
hydroelectric power, 117, 117p
irrigation, 94, 121, 121p
natural resources, 114, 115
oases, 53p
pollution, 129, 203, 203p
reservoirs, 131
water cycle, 41g, 115
water supply, 35, 65, 66, 127
weathering and erosion, 39
See also lakes; oceans; rain; rivers; seas
Watt, James, 183p
weather, 88–89g, 326, 357, 575
balloons, 46
defined, 40
differences from climate, 40
forecasting, 26g, 46, 46p
storms, 47
See also climate
weathering, 33, 39, 39p, 575
weaving, 377
Weddell Sea, 4m, 545m
West (United States), 144p, 235m, 271–276, 271p, 273p, 274p, 275g, 275p, 276p
boundaries of, 271
cities of, 274–276, 275p, 276p
climate of, 272m
natural resources of, 272–274, 273p, 274p
profile of, 272, 272g, 272m
west, 11
West Indies, 561, 575. See Caribbean Islands
West Virginia, 537m
data about, 141m, 235m, 247
land use in, 256m
mining in, 258
natural resources of, 164m, 166
Western Europe, M8m
Western Hemisphere, 11g, M5

Weyburn, Saskatchewan, 303
wheat, 300, 300g, 300m, 301, 301p, 302, 302p
White House, 126p
Whitehorse, Yukon Territory, 289
Whitener, Catherine Evans, 255, 255p
Whitney, Eli, 184
Wilson, Woodrow, 189
wind, 157, 204m
ocean currents and, 42
patterns, 43g, 346
tornadoes, 47
tropical cyclones, 47
wind energy, 112–113p, 115, 117, 132, 133p
Winnipeg, Manitoba, 157, 287, 303
winter, 31, 31g, 32, 51
Winter Carnival, 297, 297p
Wisconsin, 537m
data about, 141m, 235m, 247, 247p
women
in Brazil, 499p
in the Civil War, 186p
in Guatemala, 424p, 440
Mayan, 437, 440
mountain climbers, 148, 148p
rights of, 182, 191
in South America, 418
voting rights, 189
wood, deforestation and, 129
wool, 122, 122p
workplaces, 74
world, 268, 466
physical maps, 532m–533m
political maps, 530m–531m
population, 6, 6g
World Bank, 395
World Trade Center, 192, 192p, 253
World War I, 189, 189p, 190g, 196
World War II, 190, 191g, 196
writing activities
five themes of geography, 24
language arts, 134
math, 86, 110
science, 56
writing skills, 342, 349, 377, 396
advertisement, 261, 303

compare and contrast, 54, 199, 210, 414, 436, RW4

descriptive, 22, 54, 66, 153, 162, 276, 322, 349, 384

diary entries, 186

editorial, 450

encyclopedia article, 125

essays, RW2, RW3, RW4, 89, 358

ethnic groups, 232

evaluating your writing, RW5

explain a process, RW4

explain cause and effect, RW4

expository essays, RW4

first person, 389

geography, 24, 422

interviewing, 372

journal entry, 101, 119, 132, 226, 310, 436, 482, 513

language arts, 134, 210, 324, 398

letter writing, 79, 139, 270, 467, 500, 506

list, 108

math, 86, 110, 232, 398, 484

narrative essays, RW2

newspaper, 420, 450, 475

paragraphs, 13, 39, 47, 71, 84, 95, 168, 179, 192, 208, 230, 254, 297, 315, 377, 396

passages, 32

persuasive essays, RW3, 358

poetry, 219

point of view, 384, 407, 467, 482

radio, 441

reporting, 441, 475

reports, 278

research papers, RW4–RW5

science, 56, 170, 278, 360, 452, 524

short story, 365, 398

social studies, RW2–RW5

songs, 398

storyboard, 324

television script, 522

See also reading skills

writing systems, 94, 369

Wyoming, 51*p*, 536*m*

climate in, 272*m*

data about, 141*m*, 235*m*, 247

natural resources of, 164*m*, 166, 274*p*

Y

Yanomami, 498, 499

year (Earth's orbit), 28

yellow fever, 447–448

Yellowknife, Northwest Territories, 287

Yellowstone National Park, 274*p*

Yemen, 121*p*, 542*m*

Yosemite National Park, 274

Yucatán Peninsula, 535*m*

Yukon Territory, 151, 196, 196*m*, 210*m*, 319, 320, 320*g*, 320*m*, 561

data about, 141*m*, 285*m*, 289

gold in, 321

Z

zero, concept of, 369

Zimbabwe, 547

zinc, 167

Acknowledgments

Cover Design

Pronk&Associates

Staff Credits

The people who made up *World Studies* team—representing design services, editorial, editorial services, educational technology, marketing, market research, photo research and art development, production services, project office, publishing processes, and rights & permissions—are listed below. Bold type denotes core team members.

Greg Abrom, Ernie Albanese, Rob Aleman, Susan Andariese, **Rachel Avenia-Prol,** Leann Davis Alspaugh, Penny Baker, Barbara Bertell, **Peter Brooks,** Rui Camarinha, John Carle, **Lisa Del Gatto,** Paul Delsignore, Kathy Dempsey, Anne Drowns, Deborah Dukeshire, Marlies Dwyer, **Frederick Fellows,** Paula C. Foye, Lara Fox, Julia Gecha, **Mary Hanisco,** Salena Hastings, Lance Hatch, Kerri Hoar, **Beth Hyslip,** Katharine Ingram, Nancy Jones, John Kingston, Deborah Levheim, Constance J. McCarty, **Kathleen Mercandetti,** Art Mkrtchyan, Ken Myett, **Mark O'Malley,** Jen Paley, Ray Parenteau, **Gabriela Pérez Fiato,** Linda Punskovsky, Kirsten Richert, **Lynn Robbins,** Nancy Rogier, Bruce Rolff, Robin Samper, Mildred Schulte, Siri Schwartzman, **Malti Sharma,** Lisa Smith-Ruvalcaba, Roberta Warshaw, Sarah Yezzi

Additional Credits

Jonathan Ambar, Tom Benfatti, Lisa D. Ferrari, Paul Foster, Florrie Gadson, Phil Gagler, Ella Hanna, Jeffrey LaFountain, Karen Mancinelli, Michael McLaughlin, Lesley Pierson, Debi Taffet

The DK Designs team who contributed to *World Studies* were as follows: Hilary Bird, Samantha Borland, Marian Broderick, Richard Czapnik, Nigel Duffield, Heather Dunleavy, Cynthia Frazer, James A. Hall, Lucy Heaver, Rose Horridge, Paul Jackson, Heather Jones, Ian Midson, Marie Ortu, Marie Osborn, Leyla Ostovar, Ralph Pitchford, Ilana Sallick, Pamela Shiels, Andrew Szudek, Amber Tokeley.

Maps

Maps and globes were created by **DK Cartography.** The team consisted of Tony Chambers, Damien Demaj, Julia Lunn, Ed Merritt, David Roberts, Ann Stephenson, Gail Townsley, and Iorwerth Watkins.

Illustrations

DK images: 31, 34, 36, 41, 43; Kevin Jones Associates: 140; Kenneth Batelman: 291, 320, 383, 469 t; Geosystems: 206; Morgan Cain & Associates: 435; Jill Ort: 221, 263; Jen Paley: 148, 156, 157, 163, 167, 174, 180, 187, 190–191, 193, 202, 214, 222, 224, 227, 228, 248, 250, 255, 256, 264, 265, 266, 271, 272, 275, 279, 290, 292, 296, 298, 300, 304, 306, 311, 313, 318, 320, 338, 343, 352, 356, 368, 373, 374–375, 378, 385, 392, 394, 402, 405, 408, 409, 410, 415, 423, 430, 432, 437, 439, 444, 446, 453, 459 b, 459 t, 462, 465, 468, 469, 470, 472, 476, 477, 479, 485, 489, 494, 496, 498, 501, 502, 507, 508, 514, 515, 516, 517, 518

Photos

Cover

tl, Steve Dunwell/Getty Images, Inc.; **tm,** David Muir/Masterfile Corporation; **tr,** Dann Tardif/Corbis/Magmaphoto; **b,** Karl Kummels/SuperStock, Inc.

Title Page

Karl Kummels/SuperStock, Inc.

Table of Contents

T4–T5 b, Philip Blenkinsop/Dorling Kindersley; **T5 t,** Steve Gorton/Dorling Kindersley; **T6–T7 t,** Royalty-Free/Corbis; **T7 b,** Brenda Tharp/Corbis; **T8 t,** Kevin Fleming/Corbis; **T8 b,** Michio Hoshino/Minden Pictures; **T9 t,** Joe Caveretta/LatinFocus.com; **T9 b,** Allen Prier/Panoramic Images; **T10 t,** Michel Zab/Dorling Kindersley; **T10 b,** Robert Frerck/Odyssey Productions, Inc.; **T11,** Wayne Lynch/DRK Photo; **T13,** Rudi von Briel/PhotoEdit; **T15,** David Zimmerman/Corbis; **T17,** Bob Krist/Corbis; **T18–T19,** Andre Jenny/Visuals Unlimited

Professional Development

T35, Royalty-Free/Corbis; **T36,** PhotoDisc/Getty Images Inc.; **T37** Comstock

Reading and Writing Handbook

RW, Michael Newman/PhotoEdit; **RW1,** Walter Hodges/Getty Images, Inc.; **RW2,** Digital Vision/Getty Images, Inc.; **RW3,** Will Hart/PhotoEdit; **RW5,** Jose Luis Pelaez, Inc./Corbis

MapMaster Skills Handbook

M, James Hall/DK Images; **M1,** Mertin Harvey/Gallo Images/Corbis; **M2–3 m,** NASA; **M2–3,** (globes) Planetary Visions: **M5 br,** Barnabas Kindersley/DK Images; **M6 tr,** Mike Dunning/DK Images; **M10 b,** Bernard and Catherine Desjeux/Corbis; **M11,** Hutchinson Library; **M12 b,** Pa Photos; **M13 r,** Panos Pictures; **M14 l,** Macduff Everton/Corbis; **M14 t,** MSCF/NASA; **M15 b,** Ariadne Van Zandbergen/Lonely Planet Images; **M16 l,** Bill Stormont/Corbis; **M16 b,** Pablo Corral/Corbis; **M17 t,** Stone Les/Sygma/Corbis; **M17 b,** W. Perry Conway/Corbis

Guiding Questions

1, Christine Osborne/World Religions Photo Library

World Overview

2 l, 2 t, DK Images; **3 l,** Daniel Laine/Corbis; **3 tr,** DK Images; **3 br,** Sipa/Rex Features; **4 bl,** Layne Kennedy/Corbis; **4 tr,** DK Images; **5 t,** Royalty Free Images/Corbis; **6 t,** Roger Ressmeyer/Corbis; **7 br,** Amet Jean Pierre/Sygma/Corbis; **7tr,** DK Images

Chapter One

8e l, Royalty-Free/Corbis; **8e r,** PhotoDisc/Getty Images, Inc.; **8f l,** GeoStock/Getty Images, Inc.; **8f ml,** Comstock; **8f mr,** PhotoDisc/Getty Images, Inc.; **8f r,** SW Productions/Getty Images, Inc.; **8–9,** Johnson Space Center/NASA; **10,** Steve Gorton/DK Images; **13,** M. Balan/DK Images; **14,** Will & Deni McIntyre/Corbis; **15 b,** Richard Powers/Corbis; **15 t,** DK Images; **16,** Peter Wilson/DK Images; **17,** MSFC/NASA; **23,** Johnson Space Center/NASA

Chapter Two

26g l, Royalty-Free/Corbis; **26g r,** PhotoDisc/Getty Images, Inc.; **26h l,** GeoStock/GettyImages, Inc.; **26h ml,** Comstock; **26h mr,** PhotoDisc/Getty Images, Inc.; **26h r,** SW Productions/Getty Images, Inc.; **26–27,** George H. Huey/Corbis; **28,** Daniel Pyne/DK Images; **30 bl,** Alan Briere/DK Images; **30–31,** sun, DK Images; globes, Planetary Visions; **31 tr,** Barnabas Kindersley/DK Images; **33,** Brenda Tharp/Corbis; **35,** C. M. Leask/Eye Ubiquitous; **36 bl,** James Balog/Getty Images; **37 tr,** James A. Sugar/Corbis; **39,** Alan Hills/DK Images; **40,** Galen Rowell/Corbis; **41 tr,** Hutchison Library; **43 tr,** Royalty Free Images/Corbis; **44 b,** Demetrio Carrasco/DK Images; **45 bl,** Chris Stowers/DK Images; **46 m,** DK Images; **46 bl,** NASA; **46 tr,** N.H.P.A.; **46 mr,** Lelan Statom, meteorologist; Mark Martin, photojournalist/network operations manager, WTVF-Newschannel 5 Network, Nashville, Tenn.; **47,** Chris Graythen/Getty Images; **48 t,** Michael S. Yamashita/Corbis; **50,** Liu Liqun/Corbis; **51 br,** Terry W. Eggers/Corbis; **51 tr,** Denver Museum of Nature and Science; **52,** Alan Watson/DK Images; **53 t,** Photowood Inc./Corbis; **53 bl,** Neil Lukas; **53 br,** Stephen Hayward/DK Images; **54,** Galen Rowell/Corbis; **55,** George H. Huey/Corbis

Chapter Three

58g l, Royalty-Free/Corbis; **58g r,** PhotoDisc/Getty Images, Inc.; **58h l,** GeoStock/GettyImages, Inc.; **58h ml,** Comstock; **58h mr,** PhotoDisc/Getty Images, Inc.; **58h r,** SW Productions/Getty Images, Inc.; **58–59,** Keren Su/Corbis; **60,** James Strachan/Getty Images; **61 t,** Royalty Free Images/Corbis; **62 bl,** Wolfgang Kaehler/Corbis; **63 br,** Peter Wilson/DK Images; **64 t,** Howard Davies/Corbis; **65 b,** Patricia Aithie/Ffotograff; **66,** Dirk R. Frans/Hutchison Library; **67,** Bettmann Corbis; **68,** Dave King/DK Images; **69 bl,** Bettmann/Corbis; **70 bl,** Hulton-Deutsch Collection/Corbis; **70 br,** Paul Almasy/Corbis; **71,** Stephanie Maze/Corbis; **72,** Bill Ross/Corbis; **74,** Rob

Reichenfeld/DK Images; **75 t,** Corbis; **76,** Philip Blenkinsop/DK Images; **77 b,** Tom Wagner/Corbis; **78 l,** Mark E. Gibson/Corbis; **78 b,** Annebicque Bernard/Sygma/Corbis; **78 r,** Mary Ann McDonald/Corbis; **79,** Peter Blakely/SABA/Corbis; **80,** Patrick Durand/ Sygma/Corbis; **81,** Franz-Marc Frei/Corbis; **82,** Tom Haskell/ Sygma/Corbis; **83 t,** Pa Photos; **83 b,** Ron Sachs/Rex Features; **84,** Joseph Sohm/Chromosohm Inc./Corbis; **85,** Keren Su/Corbis; **88,** Peter Finger/Corbis

Chapter Four

90f l, Royalty-Free/Corbis; **90f r,** PhotoDisc/Getty Images, Inc.; **90–91,** Bryan Colton/Assignments Photographers/Corbis; **92,** Royalty Free Images/Corbis; **93 b,** Dennis Degnan/Corbis; **94 tl,** Geoff Brightling/DK Images; **94 b,** Richard Leeney/DK Images; **94 ml,** Museum of English Rural Life; **95,** Kim Sayer/DK Images; **96,** DK Images; **97,** Rob Lewine/Corbis; **98 t,** Richard T. Nowitz/Corbis; **98 b,** Barnabas Kindersley/DK Images; **99 b,** Demetrio Carrasco/DK Images; **100 t,** Barnabas Kindersley/DK Images; **100 b,** Peter Wilson/DK Images; **101,** B.P.S. Walia/DK Images; **102,** Foodpix/Getty Images; **103 l,** Christine Osborne/World Religions Photo Library; **104,** DK Images; **105 b,** Dallas and John Heaton/Corbis; **105 t,** Royalty Free Images/Corbis; **106,** DK Images; **107 mr,** Tom Wagner/Corbis; **107 tr,** Sony/Newscast; **108,** Penny Tweedy/Panos Pictures; **109,** Bryan Colton/Assignments photographers/Corbis

Chapter Five

112f l, Royalty-Free/Corbis; **112f r,** PhotoDisc/Getty Images, Inc.; **112–113,** M. L. Sinibaldi/Corbis; **114,** Liba Taylor/Corbis; **116 t, 116–117,** Chinch Gryniewitz/Ecoscene/Corbis; **117 t,** Royalty Free Images/Corbis; **118,** Corbis; **119,** Bob Krist/Corbis; **120,** Holt Studios International; **121 t,** Bob Rowan; Progressive Image/Corbis; **121 b,** Hutchison Library; **122 l,** Paul A. Souders/Corbis; **122 r,** DK Images; **123 l,** James L. Amos/Corbis; **123 m, r,** DK Images; **124,** David Noble/Pictures Colour Library; **125,** Oliver Strewe/Getty Images; **126,** Dennis O'Clair/Getty Images; **127,** DK Images; **128,** Paul A. Souders/Corbis; **129 t,** Wayne Lawler; Ecoscene/Corbis; **129 b,** Martin Wyness/Still Pictures; **130 t,** Benjamin Rondel/Corbis; **130 b,** DK Images; **131,** Frans Lemmens/Getty Images; **132,** Syracuse Newspapers/David Lassman/The Image Works/Topfoto; **133,** M. L. Sinibaldi/Corbis

Guiding Questions

139 t, Ohio Historical Society; **139 b,** Bob Winsett/Index Stock Imagery, Inc.

Regional Overview

140, Staffan Widstrand/Corbis; **141,** R. Rainford/Robert Harding Picture Library; **142 t,** Jim Wark/Lonely Planet Images; **142 b,** Charles O'Rear/Corbis; **143,** Bohemian Nomad Picturemakers/Corbis; **144 t,** John Elk III/Lonely Planet Images; **144 bl,** DK Images; **144 br,** Luis/Castaneda/Getty Images, Inc.; **145 t,** Richard T. Nowitz/Corbis; **145 m,** Yann Arthus-Bertrand; **145 b,** Peter Beck/Corbis

Chapter Six

146f l, Royalty-Free/Corbis; **146f r,** PhotoDisc/Getty Images, Inc.; **146–147,** Frank Perkins/Index Stock Imagery, Inc.; **148,** Scott Darsney/Alaska Stock; **149 t,** Andre Jenny/Visuals Unlimited; **149 b,** Discovery Channel School; **150,** Richard A. Cooke/Corbis; **151,** U.S. Geological Survey, Denver; **152–153 t,** Joseph Sohm; ChromoSohm Inc/Corbis; **152 b,** Joe McDonald/Corbis; **154,** Nancy Sheehan/PhotoEdit; **155,** J. Eastcott/Yva Momatiuk/Valan Photos; **156,** Donald Nausbaum/Getty Images, Inc.; **157,** Bob Winsett/Index Stock Imagery, Inc.; **158,** Alan R. Moller/Getty Images, Inc.; **159 t,** Gerry Ellis/Minden Pictures; **159 b,** Norbert Rising/National Geographic Society/Getty Images, Inc.; **161 t,** David A. Northcott/Corbis; **161 b,** Gordon Whitten/Corbis; **162,** Jean du Boisberranger/ Getty Images, Inc.; **163,** Royalty-Free/Corbis; **165 t,** Bruce Forster/Getty Images, Inc.; **165 b,** Randy Brandon/Alaska Stock; **166,** Melvin Grubb/Grubb Photo Service, Inc.; **167,** Jeff Greenberg/Visuals Unlimited; **168,** Vince Streano/Getty Images, Inc.; **169 t,** Joe McDonald/Corbis; **169 b,** David A. Northcott/Corbis.

Chapter Seven

172h l, Royalty-Free/Corbis; **172h r,** PhotoDisc/Getty Images, Inc.; **172–173,** Robert Essel NYC/Corbis; **174 l,** Ohio Historical Society; **174 r,** Ohio Historical Society; **175 t,** Discovery Channel School; **175 b,** Tom Bean/Corbis; **176 t,** Marc Muench/Corbis; **176 m,** DK Images, **176 b,** Michael Freeman/ Corbis; **178 t,** Sarony & Major/Library of Congress; **178 b,** Bettmann/Corbis; **179,** Kevin Fleming/Corbis; **180,** The Granger Collection, NY; **183,** The Granger Collection, NY; **185,** Magma Photo News/Corbis; **185 inset,** Seth Goltzer/William Gladstone/West Point Museum Collections; **186,** Bettmann/ Corbis; **186 inset,** C Squared Studios/Getty Images, Inc.; **187,** Bettmann/Corbis; **188–189 t,** Corbis; **188 b,** Bettmann/Corbis; **189 m,** Library of Congress; **189 b,** Underwood & Underwood/Corbis; **190 t,** Corbis; **190 b,** Bettmann/Corbis; **191 t,** Bettmann/ Corbis; **191 b,** Mirrorpix/Getty Images, Inc.; **192,** Reuters NewMedia Inc./Corbis; **193,** Christie's Images/Corbis; **194,** Library of Congress; **195,** Hulton/Getty Images Inc.; **197 l,** Getty Images, Inc.; **197 r,** Bettmann/ Corbis; **198,** Paul A. Souders/Corbis; **199,** Reuters NewMedia Inc./Corbis; **200 t,** Michael Newman/PhotoEdit; **200 b,** David Young-Wolff/PhotoEdit; **202,** Illustration by ML Kirk of Longfellow's *Hiawatha,* 1910/Mary Evans Picture Library; **203 t,** Mark Gibson/Index Stock Imagery, Inc.; **203 b,** Bettmann/ Corbis; **204,** Didier Dorval/Masterfile Corporation; **205 t,** Weyerhaeuser Company; **205 b,** Joel W. Rogers/Corbis; **206–207,** Nik Wheeler/Nik Wheeler Photography; **208,** AP Photo/Martin Mejia; **209 t,** Ohio Historical Society; **209 b,** Magma Photo News/Corbis.

Chapter Eight

212f l, Royalty-Free/Corbis; **212f r,** PhotoDisc/Getty Images, Inc.; **212–213** Kwame Zikomo/SuperStock Inc.; **214,** H A Strong/Mary Evans Picture Library; **215,** Library of Congress, Washington D.C., USA/Bridgeman Art Library; **216,** Mary Evans Picture Library; **217 l,** Connie Ricca/Danita Delimont; **217 r,** Nik Wheeler/Corbis; **218,** Rudi von Briel/Index Stock Imagery, Inc.; **219 t,** Tom Bean/Getty Images, Inc.; **219 b,** Palmer & Brilliant/Index Stock Imagery, Inc.; **220,** Jim Cummins/Corbis; **221 all,** Courtesy of Don Manning; **222,** Foto World/Getty Images, Inc.; **223,** Rick Smolan/Against All Odds; **224,** AP Photos/Alex Quesada; **225 tl,** Corbis; **225 tm,** Corbis; **225 tr,** AP/Wide World Photos; **225 b,** AP/Wide World Photos; **226,** David Young-Wolff/Getty Images, Inc.; **227,** Garry Black/Masterfile Corporation; **228,** Discovery Channel School; **229,** Dave G. Houser/Dave Houser Photography; **230,** Dennis MacDonald/ PhotoEdit; **231,** Garry Black/Masterfile Corporation.

Chapter Nine

234g l, Royalty-Free/Corbis; **234g r,** PhotoDisc/Getty Images, Inc.; **234h l,** GeoStock/Getty Images, Inc.; **234h ml,** Comstock; **234h mr,** PhotoDisc/Getty Images, Inc.; **234h r,** SW Productions/Getty Images, Inc.; **234–235,** AP/Wide World Photos; **236 t,** Discovery Channel School; **236–237 b,** Panoramic Images; **238,** C. McIntyre/PhotoLink/Getty Images, Inc.; **239,** AP/Wide World Photos/Michael Conroy; **241,** James Blan/Index Stock Imagery, Inc.; **242,** EyeWire Collection/Getty Images, Inc.; **243,** Stephen Alvarez/Aurora Photos; **245,** Mary Steinbacher/PhotoEdit; **246,** Tim McGuire/Corbis; **247,** Richard Hamilton Smith/Corbis; **248,** Wayne Eastep/Getty Images, Inc.; **251 t,** Joe Sohm/The Image Works; **251 b,** Discovery Channel School; **253 t,** David Ball/Corbis; **253 b,** Jeff Greenberg/Index Stock Imagery, Inc.; **254,** Bettmann/Corbis; **255,** Whitfield Murray Historical Society; **255 inset,** C Squared Studios/Getty Images, Inc.; **256 tr,** DK Images; **256 m,** DK Images; **256 bl,** Bettmann/Corbis; **257 t,** George D. Lepp/Corbis; **257 m (both),** George D. Lepp/Corbis; **257 b,** Andy Sacks/Getty Images, Inc.; **258,** Terry Vine/Getty Images, Inc.; **259 l,** Richard T. Nowitz/Corbis; **259 r,** Richard T. Nowitz/Corbis; **260,** Discovery Channel School; **261,** Richard T. Nowitz/Corbis; **262,** Russ Lappa; **264 l,** Anthony Boccaccio/Getty Images, Inc.; **264 r,** Wes McManigal/ Grant Heilman Photography, Inc.; **266–267,** Mark Segal/Panoramic Images; **268** Sandy Felsenthal/Corbis; **269,** Discovery Channel School; **270,** Cleo Photography/PhotoEdit; **271,** Bonnie Kamin/PhotoEdit; **273 t,** Discovery Channel School; **273 b,** Minnesota Historical Society/Corbis; **273 inset,** Color-Pic, Inc.; **274,** Gary Randall/Getty Images, Inc.; **275,** Manrico Mirabelli/Index

Stock Imagery, Inc.; **276 t,** Robert Landau/Corbis; **276 b,** PhotoDisc/Getty Images, Inc.; **277,** Joe Sohm/The Image Works; **281,** Archive Holdings/Getty Images, Inc.; **282,** Ben Shahn/Corbis; **283,** Courtesy of Eloise Greenfield.

Chapter Ten

284h l, Royalty-Free/Corbis; **284h r,** PhotoDisc/Getty Images, Inc.; **284–285,** Dennis Macdonald/Index Stock Imagery, Inc.; **286 t,** Discovery Channel School; **286 b,** J. A. Kraulis/Masterfile Corporation; **287,** Gerry Ellis/Minden Pictures; **288,** Dale Wilson/Masterfile Corporation; **289,** Mark Lightbody/Lonely Planet Images; **290,** Jim Fowler; **291,** Jim Young/Reuters/Corbis; **293 t,** Larry Fisher/Masterfile Corporation; **293 m,** Greg Scott/Masterfile Corporation; **293 b,** Discovery Channel School; **294,** Nik Wheeler/Danita Delimont; **295 t,** Reuters NewMedia Inc./Corbis; **295 b,** Kennon Cooke/Valan Photos; **297,** Scott Gilchrist/Masterfile Corporation; **298,** Norbert Rosing/Getty Images, Inc.; **299 t,** Francis G. Mayer/Corbis; **299 b,** Discovery Channel School; **300–301 b,** Bob Burch/Index Stock Imagery, Inc.; **301 t,** Visuals Unlimited; **302,** George Hunter/Getty Images, Inc.; **303,** Toby Rankin/Masterfile Corporation; **304,** Gunter Marx Stock Photos; **305 l,** Dewitt Jones/Corbis; **305 r,** Harvey Lloyd/Getty Images, Inc.; **307 t,** Alexander Alland Sr./Corbis-Bettmann; **307 b,** Discovery Channel School; **308,** Vince Streano/Corbis; **310,** Barry Rowland/Getty Images, Inc.; **311** Patrick J. Wall/Danita Delimont; **312 t,** Discovery Channel School; **312–313 b,** Michael S. Lewis/Corbis; **315,** Patrick J. Wall/Danita Delimont; **316 t,** Antonio Mo/Getty Images, Inc.; **316 b,** Amos Morgan/Getty Images, Inc.; **317,** Mark Antman/Image Works; **318,** Michio Hoshino/Minden Pictures; **319,** Jim Brandenburg/Minden Pictures; **321 t,** Discovery Channel School; **321 b,** AFP/Corbis/Magma; **322,** Wolfgang Kaehler/Corbis; **323,** Harvey Lloyd/Getty Images, Inc.

Projects

326 t, Bob Winsett/Index Stock Imagery, Inc.; **326 b,** National Archives and Records Administration/Presidential Library

Guiding Questions

329 t, Michel Zab/Dorling Kindersley; **329 b,** Travel Pix/Getty Images, Inc.

Regional Overview

330 l, Linda Whitwam/DK Images; **331 tr,** Art Directors & TRIP; **332 tr,** Charles and Josette Lenars/Corbis; **333 b,** Hubert Stadler/Corbis; **333 tr,** Getty Images; **334 b,** Galen Rowell/Corbis; **334 l,** Nik Wheeler/Corbis; **334 r,** Carol Halebian Photography; **335 t,** Owen Franken/Corbis: **335 br,** T. Bognar/Art Directors & TRIP

Chapter Eleven

336f l, Royalty-Free/Corbis; **336f r,** PhotoDisc/Getty Images, Inc.; **336–337,** Darell Gulin/Getty Images, Inc.; **338,** Jimmy Dorantes/ LatinFocus.com; **339,** Discovery Channel School; **340,** Jeff Hunter/Getty Images, Inc.; **341,** Corbis; **342,** Herve Collart/Corbis; **343,** R. B. Husar/ NASA/SPL/Photo Researchers, Inc.; **345,** Prenas Nicaragua/Corbis Sygma; **346 t,** Bobby Model/Getty Images, Inc.; **346 b,** Ed Simpson/Getty Images, Inc.; **347,** Jonathan Blair/Corbis; **349,** Miguel Reyes/LatinFocus.com; **350,** Richard Haynes; **351,** Warren Morgan/Corbis; **352,** Fenno Jacobs/SuperStock, Inc.; **354 t,** Richard Bickel/Corbis; **354 b,** Jacques Jangoux/Peter Arnold, Inc.; **355 l,** Jonathan Smith; Cordaiy Photo/Corbis; **355 r,** Carlos Goldin/DDB Stock Photo; **356,** Sean Sprague/Stock Boston; **357,** AP/Wide World Photos/Jaime Puebla; **358,** Pablo Corral Vega/Corbis; **359 t,** Corbis; **359 m,** Miguel Reyes/LatinFocus.com; **359 b,** Jacques Jangoux/Peter Arnold, Inc.; **362,** Bryan Knox/Corbis; **363,** EyeWire Collection/Getty Images, Inc.; **364,** David Zimmerman/Corbis; **365,** Courtesy of Alma Flor Ada

Chapter Twelve

366h l, Royalty-Free/Corbis; **366h r,** PhotoDisc/Getty Images, Inc.; **366–367,** Macduff Everton/Corbis; **368-369 b,** Allen Prier/Panoramic Images; **369 t,** Private Collection/Bridgeman Art Library; **370,** Chip and Rosa Maria de la Cueva Peterson; **371 m,** DK Images, **371 t,** Mary Evans Picture Library; **371 b,** South American Pictures; **372,** David Hiser/ PictureQuest; **373,** Werner Forman/Art Resource, New York; **374 t,** Chris Sharp/DDB Stock Photo; **374 b,** Bowers Museum of Cultural Art/Corbis; **375 t,** Charles & Josette Lenars/Corbis; **375 m,** Lee Boltin/Boltin Picture Library; **375 b,** Dorling Kindersley; **376,** Katie Attenborough/Bridgeman Art Library; **377,** Larry Luxner/Luxner News; **378,** Bridgeman Art Library; **379 t,** Sebastian Munster/The New York Public Library/Art Resource, New York; **379 b,** The Granger Collection, New York; **380,** Gianni Dagli Orti/Corbis; **381,** Biblioteca Nacional Madrid, Spain/Bridgeman Art Library; **381 inset l,** Dave King/Dorling Kindersley; **381 inset m,** Michel Zab/Dorling Kindersley; **381 inset r,** Michel Zab/Dorling Kindersley; **381 inset b,** Dorling Kindersley; **383,** Discovery Channel School; **384,** The Granger Collection, New York; **385,** North Wind Picture Archives; **386,** Robert Frerck/Odyssey Productions; **388,** Rudi von Briel/PhotoEdit; **389,** AFP/Corbis; **390 t,** Werner Forman/Art Resource, New York; **390 b,** Bettmann/Corbis; **391,** Richard Haynes; **392,** Bibliothèque Nationale, Paris, France/Bridgeman Art Library; **393,** Underwood & Underwood/Corbis; **394,** Brand X Pictures/Getty Images, Inc.; **395,** AP/Wide World Photos/ Natacha Pisarenko; **396,** D. Donne Bryant/DDB Stock Photo; **397,** Lee Boltin/Boltin Picture Library

Chapter Thirteen

400f l, Royalty-Free/Corbis; **400f r,** PhotoDisc/Getty Images, Inc.; **400–401,** Steve Simonsen/Lonely Planet Images; **402,** Sheryl Bjorkgren/LatinFocus.com; **403 t,** CNAC/MNAM/Dist. Réunion des Musées Nationaux/Art Resource, New York; **403 b,** Philadelphia Museum of Art/Corbis; **404,** AP/Wide World Photos/Victor M. Camacho; **405,** Tibor Bognar/Corbis; **406,** Lonely Planet Images; **407,** Joe Caveretta/LatinFocus.com; **410,** Michael Graham-Stewart/Bridgeman Art Library; **411,** Robert Fried Photography; **412 t,** MC Pherson Colin/Corbis Sygma; **412 b,** Doug Armand/Getty Images, Inc.; **413 t,** Discovery Channel School; **413 b,** Craig Duncan/DDB Stock Photo; **414,** Bob Krist/Corbis; **415,** Alex Irvin Photography; **416,** A. Ramey/Woodfin Camp & Associates; **417,** D. Donne Bryant/DDB Stock Photo; **417 inset,** Larry Luxner/Luxner News; **418,** Pelletier Micheline/Corbis Sygma; **419 t,** Owen Franken/Corbis; **419 b,** Bo Zaunders/Corbis; **420,** Michael Brennan/Corbis; **421 t,** Joe Caveretta/ LatinFocus.com; **421 m,** Robert Fried Photography; **421 b,** Owen Franken/Corbis

Chapter Fourteen

424f l, Royalty-Free/Corbis; **424f r,** PhotoDisc/Getty Images, Inc.; **424–425,** Sandy Ostroff/Index Stock Imagery, Inc.; **426 t,** Discovery Channel School; **426 b,** Frans Lanting/Minden Pictures; **428 t,** National Geographic Image Collection; **428 b,** Ben Blackwell/San Francisco Museum of Modern Art; **430,** Jimmy Dorantes/LatinFocus.com; **431,** Bob Krist/Corbis; **433 l,** Mark Edwards/Peter Arnold, Inc.; **433 r,** National Geographic Image Collection; **434 t,** Discovery Channel School; **434 b,** Keith Dannemiller/Corbis; **436,** Cuartoscuro/Corbis Sygma; **437 t,** Keith Gunnar/Bruce Coleman Inc.; **437 b,** Michel Zab/Dorling Kindersley; **438,** Suzanne Murphy-Larronde; **439,** Discovery Channel School; **440,** AP/Wide World Photos/Jaime Puebla; **441,** Stone/Allstock/Getty Images Inc.; **442,** GoodShoot/SuperStock, Inc.; **443 t,** AP/Wide World Photos/Rodrigo Abd; **443 b,** Wesley Bocxe/Photo Researchers, Inc.; **444,** Jimmy Dorantes/LatinFocus.com; **445,** Alex Farnsworth/The Image Works; **447 t,** Discovery Channel School; **447 m,** Panama Canal Museum; **447 b,** Getty Images, Inc./Hulton Archive Photos; **448 t,** C. W. Brown/Photo Researchers, Inc.; **448 b,** J. Raga/Masterfile Corporation; **449 t,** Corbis; **449 b,** DK Images; **450,** Danny Lehmann/Corbis; **451 t,** Keith Dannemiller/Corbis; **451 m,** Michel Zab/Dorling Kindersley; **451 b,** Alex Farnsworth/The Image Works

Chapter Fifteen

454f l, Royalty-Free/Corbis; **454f r,** PhotoDisc/Getty Images, Inc.; **454–455,** Philip Coblentz/Digital Vision/Getty Images, Inc.; **456 t,** Discovery Channel School; **456 b,** Bob Krist/Corbis; **458,** Reinhard Eisele/Corbis; **459 t,** Jimmy Dorantes/LatinFocus.com; **459 b,** Jimmy Dorantes/LatinFocus.com; **461,** Konrad Wothe/Minden Pictures; **462,** Najlah Feanny/Corbis; **463,** Bettmann/Corbis; **464 l,** AP/Wide World Photos; **464 r,** 2002 Getty Images Inc.; **465,** Discovery Channel School; **466 t,** Peter Muhly/AFP/Corbis; **466 b,** Robert

Holmes/Corbis; **467,** Angelo Cavalli/SuperStock Inc.; **468** Paul Thompson/Eye Ubiquitous/Corbis; **469,** Jan Butchofsky-Houser/Corbis; **470,** AP Wide World Photos; **471 t,** Carol Halebian Photography; **471 b,** Discovery Channel School; **473,** Bettmann/Corbis; **474 t,** Wesley Bocxe/Photo Researchers, Inc.; **474 b,** Philip Gould/Corbis; **475,** Owen Franken/Corbis; **476,** Robert Fried Photography; **477,** Rudy Von Briel/PhotoEdit; **478 t,** Benno Friedman; **478 b,** Tom Bean/Corbis; **479,** Discovery Channel School; **480 t,** Stephanie Maze/Corbis; **480 b,** Robert Frerck/Odyssey Productions Inc.; **481,** AP/Wide World Photos; **482,** Stephanie Maze/Corbis; **483,** Angelo Cavalli/SuperStock Inc.

Chapter Sixteen

486 l, Royalty-Free/Corbis; **486g r,** PhotoDisc/Getty Images, Inc.; **486h l,** GeoStock/Getty Images, Inc.; **486h ml,** Comstock; **486h mr,** PhotoDisc/Getty Images, Inc.; **486h r,** SW Productions/Getty Images, Inc.; **486–487,** Barbara Haynor/Index Stock Imagery, Inc.; **488 t,** Discovery Channel School; **488 b,** Paul A. Souders/Corbis; **490,** Art Wolfe/Getty Images, Inc.; **492,** Carlos Goldin/Focus/DDB Stock Photo; **493,** Ulrike Welsch/PhotoEdit; **494,** Wayne Lynch/DRK Photo; **495,** Fabio Colombini/Animals Animals/Earth Scenes; **496 t,** Discovery Channel School; **496 m,** David Frazier/Image Works; **496 bl,** Larry Luxner/Luxner News; **497,** Domingo Rodrigues/UNEP/Peter Arnold, Inc.; **498 l,** AFP/Vanderlei Almeida/Corbis; **498 r,** Joel W. Rogers/Corbis; **499 t,** Greg Fiume/Corbis; **499 b,** Cynthia Brito/DDB Stock Photo; **500,** PhotoDisc/Getty Images, Inc.; **501,** Roman Soumar/Corbis; **503 t,** Inga Spence/DDB Stock Photo; **503 b,** Alejandro Balaguer/Getty Images, Inc.; **504 t,** Discovery Channel School; **504 b,** Philippe Colombi/Getty Images, Inc.; **505 l,** David Mangurian/Intern-American Development Bank; **505 r,** David Mangurian/Intern-American Development Bank; **506,** Stuart Westmorland/Corbis; **507,** Gebbie & Co./Library of Congress; **509 l,** Joseph Van Os/Getty Images, Inc.; **509 r,** Charles O'Rear/Corbis; **510 t,** Zezmer Amos/Omni-Photo Communications, Inc.; **510 b,** Ludovic Maisant/Corbis; **511,** The Wilmington Library; **512 t,** Discovery Channel School; **512 m,** Jaime Villaseca/Getty Images, Inc.; **512 b,** HIRB/Index Stock Imagery, Inc.; **513,** AP/Wide World Photos/Alistair Grant; **514 lt,** Hubert Stadler/Corbis; **514 lb,** Hubert Stadler/Corbis; **514 rt,** Jeremy Horner/Corbis; **514 rb,** Frank Perkins/Index Stock Imagery, Inc.; **515,** Yann Arthus-Bertrand/Corbis; **516,** Larry Lee/Corbis; **517,** AP/Wide World Photos/Jose Caruci; **519,** Pablo Corral V/Corbis; **520,** Kike Arnal/Corbis; **521 t,** Discovery Channel School; **521 b,** AFP/Corbis; **522 l,** Reuters NewMedia Inc./Corbis; **522 r,** AFP/Corbis; **523,** Greg Fiume/Corbis

Projects

526 t, Travel Pix/Getty Images, Inc.; **526 m,** C Squared Studios/Getty Images, Inc.; **526 b,** Steve Cole/Getty Images, Inc.

Reference

528, Johnson Space Center/NASA

Glossary of Geographic Terms

554 t, A & L Sinibaldi/Getty Images, Inc.; **554 b,** John Beatty/Getty Images, Inc.; **554–555 b,** Spencer Swanger/Tom Stack & Associates; **555 t,** Hans Strand/Getty Images, Inc.; **555 m,** Paul Chesley/Getty Images, Inc.

Glossary

563, Magma Photo News/Corbis; **564,** Robert Fried Photography; **566,** Nik Wheeler/Nik Wheeler Photography; **569,** Jimmy Dorantes/LatinFocus.com; **570,** Photowood, Inc./Corbis; **572,** AP/Wide World Photos/Natacha Pisarenko; **574,** Harvey Lloyd/Getty Images, Inc.